MATERIALS ON EUROPEAN CRIMINAL LAW

# MATERIALS ON EUROPEAN CRIMINAL LAW

*Edited by*

André Klip

2nd edition

intersentia
Cambridge – Antwerp – Portland

Intersentia Ltd
Sheraton House | Castle Park
Cambridge | CB3 0AX | United Kingdom
Tel.: +44 1223 370 170 | Email: mail@intersentia.co.uk

*Distribution for the UK:*
NBN International
Airport Business Centre, 10 Thornbury Road
Plymouth, PL6 7PP
United Kingdom
Tel.: +44 1752 202 301 | Fax: +44 1752 202 331
Email: orders@nbninternational.com

*Distribution for the USA and Canada:*
International Specialized Book Services
920 NE 58th Ave. Suite 300
Portland, OR 97213
USA
Tel.: +1 800 944 6190 (toll free)
Email: info@isbs.com

*Distribution for Austria:*
Neuer Wissenschaftlicher Verlag
Argentinierstraße 42/6
1040 Wien
Austria
Tel.: +43 1 535 61 03 24
Email: office@nwv.at

*Distribution for other countries:*
Intersentia Publishing nv
Groenstraat 31
2640 Mortsel
Belgium
Tel.: +32 3 680 15 50
Email: mail@intersentia.be

Materials on European Criminal Law. 2nd edition
André Klip (ed.)



ISBN 978-1-78068-261-7
D/2014/7849/128
NUR 828

British Library Cataloguing in Publication Data. A catalogue record for this book is available from the British Library.

# PREFACE

European criminal law deals with a multi-layered patchwork of legislation and case law in which European and national courts, European and national legislators, and other authorities and bodies play a role. It is a hybrid system but it also possesses some common notions and values, which justify its classification as a separate field of law.*

Over the years students, academics and practitioners alike struggled to find their way in all these layers of national and European legislation. *Materials on European Criminal Law* is composed to meet these needs. The collection comprises the most important legal instruments in the field of European criminal law and is published in one concise volume.

The first edition of this collection was used widely and received well. However, as it appeared in early 2012, and the European Union continued its impressive pace in adopting new legislation, a revision was necessary. This edition includes legal developments up to 1 July 2014.

There are a few caveats of which the user of this book should be aware. This collection only contains the most important legal instruments on European criminal law. Whilst in the beginning of the compilation of the book the aim was to produce an exhaustive collection of materials with even a remote link to criminal law the idea was abandoned during the preparation of this book. Length and dimension would have negatively affected the usability for the reader. Legal instruments included in this collection have been chosen according to the following criteria: they are or are expected to be the subject of (future) frequent use in practice and must frequently be mentioned in the relevant literature. Legal instruments for which it is uncertain whether they will ever enter into force or do not have an impact on the practice of the criminal justice systems in the Member States have not been included in this collection.

The user will not find any information relating to the entry into force of a legal instrument for individual Member States. It should also be noted that conventions included in this collection may not have entered into force for all Member States. Some are provisionally applied between some Member States only. Furthermore, other legal instruments may not have entered into force yet, for instance, because the

* See André Klip, European Criminal Law. An Integrative Approach, Intersentia Cambridge-Antwerp, 2nd edition 2012, p. 1.

implementation period is still running. The user should therefore always check the applicability for the relevant Member State.

Most texts are reproduced as they were published in the Official Journal. Other texts (especially the consolidated versions) were downloaded from the EUR-Lex website of the European Union. Please note that up to 1 July 2013 only European Union legislation printed in the paper edition of the *Official Journal of the European Union* is deemed authentic. Since then, the electronic version of the Official Journal (e-OJ) is authentic and produces legal effects.

The second edition appears both as a hard copy and in electronic format via Bookshelf. The latter greatly facilitates searches.

I would be most grateful to receive any remarks, suggestions, questions and criticism on the selection, as well as on the applicability of the legal instrument in question.

André Klip
andre.klip@maastrichtuniversity.nl
Maastricht
August 2014

# CONTENTS

# Convention implementing the Schengen Agreement of 14 June 1985 between the Governments of the States of the Benelux Economic Union, the Federal Republic of Germany and the French Republic on the gradual abolition of checks at their common borders, 19 June 1990

**[Consolidated version as published in OJ 2000, L 239/19 and later amendments]**

**[Editor's note: Articles 2–38 and 102–142 omitted]**

**CONVENTION IMPLEMENTING THE SCHENGEN AGREEMENT of 14 June 1985 between the Governments of the States of the Benelux Economic Union, the Federal Republic of Germany and the French Republic on the gradual abolition of checks at their common borders**

The KINGDOM OF BELGIUM, the FEDERAL REPUBLIC OF GERMANY, the FRENCH REPUBLIC, the GRAND DUCHY OF LUXEMBOURG and the KINGDOM OF THE NETHERLANDS, hereinafter referred to as "the Contracting Parties",

TAKING as their basis the Schengen Agreement of 14 June 1985 on the gradual abolition of checks at their common borders,

HAVING DECIDED to fulfil the resolve expressed in that Agreement to abolish checks at their common borders on the movement of persons and facilitate the transport and movement of goods at those borders,

WHEREAS the Treaty establishing the European Communities, supplemented by the Single European Act, provides that the internal market shall comprise an area without internal frontiers,

WHEREAS the aim pursued by the Contracting Parties is in keeping with that objective, without prejudice to the measures to be taken to implement the provisions of the Treaty,

WHEREAS the fulfilment of that resolve requires a series of appropriate measures and close cooperation between the Contracting Parties,

HAVE AGREED AS FOLLOWS:

## TITLE I

## DEFINITIONS

### *Article 1*

For the purposes of this Convention:

internal borders: shall mean the common land borders of the Contracting Parties, their airports for internal flights and their sea ports for regular ferry connections exclusively from or to other ports within the territories of the Contracting Parties and not calling at any ports outside those territories;

external borders: shall mean the Contracting Parties' land and sea borders and their airports and sea ports, provided that they are not internal borders;

internal flight: shall mean any flight exclusively to or from the territories of the Contracting Parties and not landing in the territory of a third State;

third State: shall mean any State other than the Contracting Parties;

alien: shall mean any person other than a national of a Member State of the European Communities;

alien for whom an alert has been issued for the purposes of refusing entry: shall mean an alien for whom an alert has been introduced into the Schengen Information System in accordance with Article 96 with a view to that person being refused entry;

border crossing point: shall mean any crossing point authorised by the competent authorities for crossing external borders;

border check: shall mean a check carried out at a border in response exclusively to an intention to cross that border, regardless of any other consideration;

carrier: shall mean any natural or legal person whose occupation it is to provide passenger transport by air, sea or land;

residence permit: shall mean an authorisation of whatever type issued by a Contracting Party which grants right of residence within its territory. This definition shall not include temporary permission to reside in the territory of a Contracting Party for the purposes of processing an application for asylum or a residence permit;

application for asylum: shall mean any application submitted in writing, orally or otherwise by an alien at an external border or within the territory of a Contracting Party with a view to obtaining recognition as a refugee in accordance with the Geneva Convention relating to the Status of Refugees of 28 July 1951, as amended by the New York Protocol of 31 January 1967, and as such obtaining the right of residence;

asylum seeker: shall mean any alien who has lodged an application for asylum within the meaning of this Convention and in respect of which a final decision has not yet been taken;

processing applications for asylum: shall mean all the procedures for examining and taking a decision on applications for asylum, including measures taken under a final decision thereon, with the exception of the determination of the Contracting Party responsible for processing applications for asylum pursuant to this Convention.

[Articles 2–38 omitted]

# TITLE III

# POLICE AND SECURITY

## CHAPTER 1

## POLICE COOPERATION

### *Article 39*

1. The Contracting Parties undertake to ensure that their police authorities shall, in compliance with national law and within the scope of their powers, assist each other for the purposes of preventing and detecting criminal offences, in so far as national law does not stipulate that the request has to be made and channelled via the judicial authorities and provided that the request or the implementation thereof does not involve the application of measures of constraint by the requested Contracting Party. Where the requested police authorities do not have the power to deal with a request, they shall forward it to the competent authorities.

2. Written information provided by the requested Contracting Party under paragraph 1 may not be used by the requesting Contracting Party as evidence of the offence charged other than with the consent of the competent judicial authorities of the requested Contracting Party.

3. Requests for assistance referred to in paragraph 1 and the replies to such requests may be exchanged between the central bodies responsible in each Contracting Party for international police cooperation. Where the request cannot be made in good time using the above procedure, the police authorities of the requesting Contracting Party may address it directly to the competent authorities of the requested Party, which may reply directly. In such cases, the requesting police authority shall at the earliest opportunity inform the central body responsible for international police cooperation in the requested Contracting Party of its direct request.

4. In border areas, cooperation may be covered by arrangements between the competent Ministers of the Contracting Parties.

5. The provisions of this Article shall not preclude more detailed present or future bilateral agreements between Contracting Parties with a common border. The Contracting Parties shall inform each other of such agreements.

### *Article 40*

1. Officers of one of the Member States who are keeping a person under surveillance in their country as part of a criminal investigation into an extraditable criminal offence because he is suspected of involvement in an extraditable criminal offence or, as a necessary part of a criminal investigation, because there is serious reason to believe that he can assist in identifying or tracing such a person, shall be authorised to continue their surveillance in the territory of another Member State where the latter has authorised cross-border surveillance in response to a request for assistance made in advance with supporting reasons. Conditions may be attached to the authorisation.

On request, the surveillance will be entrusted to officers of the Contracting Party in whose territory this is carried out.

The request for assistance referred to in the first subparagraph must be sent to an authority designated by each of the Contracting Parties and empowered to grant or to pass on the requested authorisation.

2. Where, for particularly urgent reasons, prior authorisation cannot be requested from the other Contracting Party, the officers carrying out the surveillance shall be authorised to continue beyond the border the surveillance of a person presumed to have committed criminal offences listed in paragraph 7, provided that the following conditions are met:

(a) the authority of the Contracting Party designated under paragraph 5, in whose territory the surveillance is to be continued, must be notified immediately, during the surveillance, that the border has been crossed;

(b) a request for assistance submitted in accordance with paragraph 1 and outlining the grounds for crossing the border without prior authorisation shall be submitted immediately.

Surveillance shall cease as soon as the Contracting Party in whose territory it is taking place so requests, following the notification referred to in (a) or the request referred to in (b) or, where authorisation has not been obtained, five hours after the border was crossed.

3. The surveillance referred to in paragraphs 1 and 2 shall be carried out only under the following general conditions:

(a) The officers carrying out the surveillance must comply with the provisions of this Article and with the law of the Contracting Party in whose territory they are operating; they must obey the instructions of the competent local authorities.

(b) Except in the situations outlined in paragraph 2, the officers shall, during the surveillance, carry a document certifying that authorisation has been granted.

(c) The officers carrying out the surveillance must at all times be able to prove that they are acting in an official capacity.

(d) The officers carrying out the surveillance may carry their service weapons during the surveillance save where specifically otherwise decided by the requested Party; their use shall be prohibited save in cases of legitimate self-defence.

(e) Entry into private homes and places not accessible to the public shall be prohibited.

(f) The officers carrying out the surveillance may neither challenge nor arrest the person under surveillance.

(g) All operations shall be the subject of a report to the authorities of the Contracting Party in whose territory they took place; the officers carrying out the surveillance may be required to appear in person.

(h) The authorities of the Contracting Party from which the surveillance officers have come shall, when requested by the authorities of the Contracting Party in whose territory the surveillance took place, assist the enquiry subsequent to the operation in which they took part, including judicial proceedings.

4. The officers referred to in paragraphs 1 and 2 shall be:

- as regards the Kingdom of Belgium: members of the "police judiciaire près les Parquets" (Criminal Police attached to the Public Prosecutor's Office), the "gendarmerie" and the "police communale" (municipal police), as well as customs officers, under the conditions laid down in appropriate bilateral agreements referred to in paragraph 6, with respect to their powers regarding illicit trafficking in narcotic drugs and psychotropic substances, trafficking in arms and explosives, and the illicit transportation of toxic and hazardous waste;

- as regards the Federal Republic of Germany: officers of the "Polizeien des Bundes und der Länder" (Federal Police and Federal State Police), as well as, with respect only to illicit trafficking in narcotic drugs and psychotropic substances and arms trafficking, officers of the "Zollfahndungsdienst" (customs investigation service) in their capacity as auxiliary officers of the Public Prosecutor's Office;

- as regards the French Republic: criminal police officers of the national police and national "gendarmerie", as well as customs officers, under the conditions laid down in appropriate bilateral agreements referred to in paragraph 6, with respect to their powers regarding illicit trafficking in narcotic drugs and psychotropic substances, trafficking in arms and explosives, and the illicit transportation of toxic and hazardous waste;

- as regards the Grand Duchy of Luxembourg: officers of the "gendarmerie" and the police, as well as customs officers, under the conditions laid down in appropriate bilateral agreements referred to in paragraph 6, with respect to their powers regarding illicit trafficking in narcotic drugs and psychotropic substances, trafficking in arms and explosives, and the illicit transportation of toxic and hazardous waste;

- as regards the Kingdom of the Netherlands: officers of the "Rijkspolitie" (national police) and the "Gemeentepolitie" (municipal police), as well as, under the conditions laid down in appropriate bilateral agreements referred to in paragraph 6, with respect to their powers regarding illicit trafficking in narcotic drugs and psychotropic substances, trafficking in arms and explosives and the illicit transportation of toxic and hazardous waste, officers of the tax inspection and investigation authorities responsible for import and excise duties.

5. The authority referred to in paragraphs 1 and 2 shall be:

- as regards the Kingdom of Belgium: the "Commissariat général de la Police judiciaire" (Criminal Investigation Department),

- as regards the Federal Republic of Germany: the "Bundeskriminalamt" (Federal Crime Office),

- as regards the French Republic: the "Direction centrale de la Police judiciaire" (Central Headquarters of the Criminal Police),

- as regards the Grand Duchy of Luxembourg: the "Procureur général d'Etat" (Principal State Prosecutor),

- as regards the Kingdom of the Netherlands: the "Landelijk Officier van Justitie" (National Public Prosecutor) responsible for cross-border surveillance.

6. The Contracting Parties may, at bilateral level, extend the scope of this Article and adopt additional measures in application thereof.

7. The surveillance referred to in paragraph 2 may only be carried out where one of the following criminal offences is involved:

- murder,

- manslaughter,

- a serious offence of a sexual nature,

- arson,

- counterfeiting and forgery of means of payment,

- aggravated burglary and robbery and receiving stolen goods,

- extortion,

- kidnapping and hostage taking,

- trafficking in human beings,

- illicit trafficking in narcotic drugs and psychotropic substances,

- breach of the laws on arms and explosives,

- wilful damage through the use of explosives,

- illicit transportation of toxic and hazardous waste,

- serious fraud;

- smuggling of aliens;

- money laundering;

- illicit trafficking in nuclear and radioactive substances;

- participation in a criminal organisation as referred to in Council Joint Action 98/733/JHA of 21 December 1998 on making it a criminal offence to participate in a criminal organisation in the Member States of the European Union;

- terrorist offences as referred to in Council Framework Decision 2002/475/JHA of 13 June 2002 on combating terrorism.

*Article 41*

1. Officers of one of the Contracting Parties who are pursuing in their country an individual caught in the act of committing or of participating in one of the offences referred to in paragraph 4 shall be authorised to continue pursuit in the territory of another Contracting Party without the latter's prior authorisation where, given the particular urgency of the situation, it is not possible to notify the competent authorities of the other Contracting Party by one of the means provided for in Article 44 prior to entry into that territory or where these authorities are unable to reach the scene in time to take over the pursuit.

The same shall apply where the person being pursued has escaped from provisional custody or while serving a sentence involving deprivation of liberty.

The pursuing officers shall, not later than when they cross the border, contact the competent authorities of the Contracting Party in whose territory the hot pursuit is to take place. The hot pursuit will cease as soon as the Contracting Party in whose territory the pursuit is taking place so requests. At the request of the pursuing officers, the competent local authorities shall challenge the pursued person in order to establish the person's identity or to make an arrest.

2. Hot pursuit shall be carried out in accordance with one of the following procedures, defined by the declaration laid down in paragraph 9:

(a) The pursuing officers shall not have the right to apprehend the pursued person;

(b) If no request to cease the hot pursuit is made and if the competent local authorities are unable to intervene quickly enough, the pursuing officers may detain the person pursued until the officers of the Contracting Party in whose territory the pursuit is taking place, who must be informed immediately, are able to establish the person's identity or make an arrest.

3. Hot pursuit shall be carried out in accordance with paragraphs 1 and 2 and in one of the following ways as defined by the declaration provided for in paragraph 9:

(a) in an area or during a period as from the crossing of the border, to be established in the declaration;

(b) without limit in space or time.

4. In the declaration referred to in paragraph 9, the Contracting Parties shall define the offences referred to in paragraph 1 in accordance with one of the following procedures:

(a) The following criminal offences:

- murder,

- manslaughter,

- rape,

- arson,

- forgery of money,

- aggravated burglary and robbery and receiving stolen goods,

- extortion,

- kidnapping and hostage taking,

- trafficking in human beings,

- illicit trafficking in narcotic drugs and psychotropic substances,

- breach of the laws on arms and explosives,

- wilful damage through the use of explosives,

- illicit transportation of toxic and hazardous waste,

- failure to stop and give particulars after an accident which has resulted in death or serious injury.

(b) Extraditable offences.

5. Hot pursuit shall be carried out only under the following general conditions:

(a) The pursuing officers must comply with the provisions of this Article and with the law of the Contracting Party in whose territory they are operating; they must obey the instructions issued by the competent local authorities.

(b) Pursuit shall be solely over land borders.

(c) Entry into private homes and places not accessible to the public shall be prohibited.

(d) The pursuing officers shall be easily identifiable, either by their uniform, by means of an armband or by accessories fitted to their vehicles; the use of civilian clothes combined with the use of unmarked vehicles without the aforementioned identification is prohibited; the pursuing officers must at all times be able to prove that they are acting in an official capacity.

(e) The pursuing officers may carry their service weapons; their use shall be prohibited save in cases of legitimate self-defence.

(f) Once the pursued person has been apprehended as provided for in paragraph 2(b), for the purpose of being brought before the competent local authorities that person may only be subjected to a security search; handcuffs may be used during the transfer; objects carried by the pursued person may be seized.

(g) After each operation referred to in paragraphs 1, 2 and 3, the pursuing officers shall appear before the competent local authorities of the Contracting Party in whose territory they were operating and shall report on their mission; at the request of those authorities, they shall remain at their disposal until the circumstances surrounding their action have been sufficiently clarified; this condition shall apply even where the hot pursuit has not resulted in the arrest of the person pursued.

(h) The authorities of the Contracting Party from which the pursuing officers have come shall, when requested by the authorities of the Contracting Party in whose territory the hot pursuit took place, assist the enquiry subsequent to the operation in which they took part, including judicial proceedings.

6. A person who, following the action provided for in paragraph 2, has been arrested by the competent local authorities may, whatever that person's nationality, be held for questioning. The relevant rules of national law shall apply mutatis mutandis.

If the person is not a national of the Contracting Party in whose territory the person was arrested, that person shall be released no later than six hours after the arrest was made, not including the hours between midnight and 9.00 a.m., unless the competent local authorities have previously received a request for that person's provisional arrest for the purposes of extradition in any form whatsoever.

7. The officers referred to in the previous paragraphs shall be:

- as regards the Kingdom of Belgium: members of the "police judiciaire près les Parquets" (Criminal Police attached to the Public Prosecutor's Office), the "gendarmerie" and the "police communale" (municipal police), as well as customs officers, under the conditions laid down in appropriate bilateral agreements referred to in paragraph 10, with respect to their powers regarding illicit trafficking in narcotic drugs and psychotropic substances, trafficking in arms and explosives, and the illicit transportation of toxic and hazardous waste;

- as regards the Federal Republic of Germany: officers of the "Polizeien des Bundes und der Länder" (Federal and Federal State Police), as well as, with respect only to illegal trafficking in narcotic drugs and psychotropic substances and arms trafficking, officers of the "Zollfahndungsdienst" (customs investigation service) in their capacity as auxiliary officers of the Public Prosecutor's Office;

- as regards the French Republic: criminal police officers of the national police and national "gendarmerie", as well as customs officers, under the conditions laid down in the appropriate bilateral agreements referred to in paragraph 10, with respect to their powers regarding illicit trafficking in narcotic drugs and psychotropic substances, trafficking in arms and explosives, and the illicit transportation of toxic and hazardous waste;

- as regards the Grand Duchy of Luxembourg: officers of the "gendarmerie" and the police, as well as customs officers, under the conditions laid down in the appropriate bilateral agreements referred to in paragraph 10, with respect to their powers regarding illicit trafficking in narcotic drugs and psychotropic substances, trafficking in arms and explosives, and the illicit transportation of toxic and hazardous waste:

- as regards the Kingdom of the Netherlands: officers of the "Rijkspolitie" (national police) and the "Gemeentepolitie" (municipal police) as well as, under the conditions laid down in the appropriate bilateral agreements referred to in paragraph 10, with respect to their powers regarding the illicit trafficking in narcotic drugs and psychotropic substances, trafficking in arms and explosives and the illicit transportation of toxic and hazardous waste, officers of the tax inspection and investigation authorities responsible for import and excise duties.

8. For the Contracting Parties concerned this Article shall apply without prejudice to Article 27 of the Benelux Treaty concerning Extradition and Mutual Assistance in Criminal Matters of 27 June 1962, as amended by the Protocol of 11 May 1974.

9. At the time of signing this Convention, each Contracting Party shall make a declaration in which it shall define for each of the Contracting Parties with which it has a common border, on the basis of paragraphs 2, 3 and 4, the procedures for carrying out a hot pursuit in its territory.

A Contracting Party may at any time replace its declaration by another declaration provided the latter does not restrict the scope of the former.

Each declaration shall be made after consultation with each of the Contracting Parties concerned and with a view to obtaining equivalent arrangements on both sides of internal borders.

10. The Contracting Parties may, on a bilateral basis, extend the scope of paragraph 1 and adopt additional provisions in implementation of this Article.

### *Article 42*

During the operations referred to in Articles 40 and 41, officers operating in the territory of another Contracting Party shall be regarded as officers of that Party with respect to offences committed against them or by them.

*Article 43*

1. Where, in accordance with Articles 40 and 41 of this Convention, officers of a Contracting Party are operating in the territory of another Contracting Party, the first Contracting Party shall be liable for any damage caused by them during their operations, in accordance with the law of the Contracting Party in whose territory they are operating.

2. The Contracting Party in whose territory the damage referred to in paragraph 1 was caused shall make good such damage under the conditions applicable to damage caused by its own officers.

3. The Contracting Party whose officers have caused damage to any person in the territory of another Contracting Party shall reimburse the latter in full any sums it has paid to the victims or persons entitled on their behalf.

4. Without prejudice to the exercise of its rights vis-à-vis third parties and with the exception of paragraph 3, each Contracting Party shall refrain in the case provided for in paragraph 1 from requesting reimbursement of damages it has sustained from another Contracting Party.

*Article 44*

1. In accordance with the relevant international agreements and account being taken of local circumstances and technical possibilities, the Contracting Parties shall install, in particular in border areas, telephone, radio, and telex lines and other direct links to facilitate police and customs cooperation, in particular for the timely transmission of information for the purposes of cross-border surveillance and hot pursuit.

2. In addition to these short-term measures, they will in particular consider the following options:

(a) exchanging equipment or posting liaison offers provided with appropriate radio equipment;

(b) widening the frequency bands used in border areas;

(c) establishing common links for police and customs services operating in these same areas;

(d) coordinating their programmes for the procurement of communications equipment, with a view to installing standardised and compatible communications systems.

*Article 45*

1. The Contracting Parties undertake to adopt the necessary measures in order to ensure that:

(a) the managers of establishments providing accommodation or their agents see to it that aliens accommodated therein, including nationals of the other Contracting Parties and those of other Member States of the European Communities, with the exception of accompanying spouses or accompanying minors or members of travel groups, personally complete and sign registration forms and confirm their identity by producing a valid identity document;

(b) the completed registration forms will be kept for the competent authorities or forwarded to them where such authorities deem this necessary for the prevention of threats, for criminal investigations or for clarifying the circumstances of missing persons or accident victims, save where national law provides otherwise.

2. Paragraph 1 shall apply mutatis mutandis to persons staying in any commercially rented accommodation, in particular tents, caravans and boats.

*Article 46*

1. In specific cases, each Contracting Party may, in compliance with its national law and without being so requested, send the Contracting Party concerned any information which may be important in helping it combat future crime and prevent offences against or threats to public policy and public security.

2. Information shall be exchanged, without prejudice to the arrangements for cooperation in border areas referred to in Article 39(4), via a central body to be designated. In particularly urgent cases, the exchange of information within the meaning of this Article may take place directly between the police authorities concerned, unless national provisions stipulate otherwise. The central body shall be informed of this as soon as possible.

*Article 47*

1. The Contracting Parties may conclude bilateral agreements providing for the secondment, for a specified or unspecified period, of liaison officers from one Contracting Party to the police authorities of another Contracting Party.

2. The secondment of liaison officers for a specified or unspecified period is intended to further and accelerate cooperation between the Contracting Parties, particularly by providing assistance:

(a) in the form of the exchange of information for the purposes of combating crime by means of both prevention and law enforcement;

(b) in executing requests for mutual police and judicial assistance in criminal matters;

(c) with the tasks carried out by the authorities responsible for external border surveillance.

3. Liaison officers shall have the task of providing advice and assistance. They shall not be empowered to take independent police action. They shall supply information and perform their duties in accordance with the instructions given to them by the seconding Contracting Party and by the Contracting Party to which they are seconded. They shall report regularly to the head of the police department to which they are seconded.

4. (repealed)

## CHAPTER 2

## MUTUAL ASSISTANCE IN CRIMINAL MATTERS

### *Article 48*

1. The provisions of this Chapter are intended to supplement the European Convention on Mutual Assistance in Criminal Matters of 20 April 1959 as well as, in relations between the Contracting Parties which are members of the Benelux Economic Union, Chapter II of the Benelux Treaty concerning Extradition and Mutual Assistance in Criminal Matters of 27 June 1962, as amended by the Protocol of 11 May 1974, and to facilitate the implementation of those Agreements.

2. Paragraph 1 shall not affect the application of the broader provisions of the bilateral agreements in force between the Contracting Parties.

### *Article 49*

Mutual assistance shall also be afforded:

(a) in proceedings brought by the administrative authorities in respect of acts which are punishable under the national law of one of the two Contracting Parties, or of both, by virtue of being infringements of the rules of law, and where the decision may give rise to proceedings before a court having jurisdiction in particular in criminal matters;

(b) in proceedings for claims for damages arising from wrongful prosecution or conviction;

(c) in clemency proceedings;

(d) in civil actions joined to criminal proceedings, as long as the criminal court has not yet taken a final decision in the criminal proceedings;

(e) in the service of judicial documents relating to the enforcement of a sentence or a preventive measure, the imposition of a fine or the payment of costs for proceedings;

(f) in respect of measures relating to the deferral of delivery or suspension of enforcement of a sentence or a preventive measure, to conditional release or to a stay or interruption of enforcement of a sentence or a preventive measure.

*Article 50* (repealed)

*Article 51*

The Contracting Parties may not make the admissibility of letters rogatory for search or seizure dependent on conditions other than the following:

(a) the act giving rise to the letters rogatory is punishable under the law of both Contracting Parties by a penalty involving deprivation of liberty or a detention order of a maximum period of at least six months, or is punishable under the law of one of the two Contracting Parties by an equivalent penalty and under the law of the other Contracting Party by virtue of being an infringement of the rules of law which is being prosecuted by the administrative authorities, and where the decision may give rise to proceedings before a court having jurisdiction in particular in criminal matters;

(b) execution of the letters rogatory is consistent with the law of the requested Contracting Party.

*Article 52*

1. Each Contracting Party may send procedural documents directly by post to persons who are in the territory of another Contracting Party. The Contracting Parties shall send the Executive Committee a list of the documents which may be forwarded in this way.

2. Where there is reason to believe that the addressee does not understand the language in which the document is written, the document - or at least the important passages thereof - must be translated into (one of) the language(s) of the Contracting Party in whose territory the addressee is staying. If the authority forwarding the document knows that the addressee understands only some other language, the document - or at least the important passages thereof - must be translated into that other language.

3. Experts or witnesses who have failed to answer a summons to appear sent to them by post shall not, even if the summons contains a notice of penalty, be subjected to any punishment or measure of constraint, unless subsequently they voluntarily enter into the territory of the requesting Party and are there again duly summoned. Authorities sending a postal summons to appear shall ensure that this does not involve a notice of penalty. This provision shall be without prejudice to Article 34 of the

Benelux Treaty concerning Extradition and Mutual Assistance in Criminal Matters of 27 June 1962, as amended by the Protocol of 11 May 1974.

4. If the act on which the request for assistance is based is punishable under the law of both Contracting Parties by virtue of being an infringement of the rules of law which is being prosecuted by the administrative authorities, and where the decision may give rise to proceedings before a court having jurisdiction in particular in criminal matters, the procedure outlined in paragraph 1 must in principle be used for the forwarding of procedural documents.

5. Notwithstanding paragraph 1, procedural documents may be forwarded via the judicial authorities of the requested Contracting Party where the addressee's address is unknown or where the requesting Contracting Party requires a document to be served in person.

*Article 53*

1. Requests for assistance may be made directly between judicial authorities and returned via the same channels.

2. Paragraph 1 shall not prejudice the possibility of requests being sent and returned between Ministries of Justice or through national central bureaux of the International Criminal Police Organisation.

3. Requests for the temporary transfer or transit of persons who are under provisional arrest, being detained or who are the subject of a penalty involving deprivation of liberty, and the periodic or occasional exchange of information from the judicial records must be effected through the Ministries of Justice.

4. Within the meaning of the European Convention on Mutual Assistance in Criminal Matters of 20 April 1959, where the Federal Republic of Germany is concerned, Ministry of Justice shall mean the Federal Minister of Justice and the Justice Ministers or Senators in the Federal States (Länder).

5. Information laid in connection with proceedings against infringement of the legislation on driving and rest periods, in accordance with Article 21 of the European Convention on Mutual Assistance in Criminal Matters of 20 April 1959 or Article 42 of the Benelux Treaty on Extradition and Mutual Assistance in Criminal Matters of 27 June 1962, as amended by the Protocol of 11 May 1974, may be sent by the judicial authorities of the requesting Contracting Party directly to the judicial authorities of the requested Contracting Party.

# CHAPTER 3

## APPLICATION OF THE NE BIS IN IDEM PRINCIPLE

### *Article 54*

A person whose trial has been finally disposed of in one Contracting Party may not be prosecuted in another Contracting Party for the same acts provided that, if a penalty has been imposed, it has been enforced, is actually in the process of being enforced or can no longer be enforced under the laws of the sentencing Contracting Party.

### *Article 55*

1. A Contracting Party may, when ratifying, accepting or approving this Convention, declare that it is not bound by Article 54 in one or more of the following cases:

(a) where the acts to which the foreign judgment relates took place in whole or in part in its own territory; in the latter case, however, this exception shall not apply if the acts took place in part in the territory of the Contracting Party where the judgment was delivered;

(b) where the acts to which the foreign judgment relates constitute an offence against national security or other equally essential interests of that Contracting Party;

(c) where the acts to which the foreign judgment relates were committed by officials of that Contracting Party in violation of the duties of their office.

2. A Contracting Party which has made a declaration regarding the exception referred to in paragraph 1(b) shall specify the categories of offences to which this exception may apply.

3. A Contracting Party may at any time withdraw a declaration relating to one or more of the exceptions referred to in paragraph 1.

4. The exceptions which were the subject of a declaration under paragraph 1 shall not apply where the Contracting Party concerned has, in connection with the same acts, requested the other Contracting Party to bring the prosecution or has granted extradition of the person concerned.

### *Article 56*

If a further prosecution is brought in a Contracting Party against a person whose trial, in respect of the same acts, has been finally disposed of in another Contracting Party, any period of deprivation of liberty served in the latter Contracting Party arising from those acts shall be deducted from any penalty imposed. To the extent permitted by national law, penalties not involving deprivation of liberty shall also be taken into account.

*Article 57*

1. Where a Contracting Party charges a person with an offence and the competent authorities of that Contracting Party have reason to believe that the charge relates to the same acts as those in respect of which the person's trial has been finally disposed of in another Contracting Party, those authorities shall, if they deem it necessary, request the relevant information from the competent authorities of the Contracting Party in whose territory judgment has already been delivered.

2. The information requested shall be provided as soon as possible and shall be taken into consideration as regards further action to be taken in the proceedings under way.

3. Each Contracting Party shall, when ratifying, accepting or approving this Convention, nominate the authorities authorised to request and receive the information provided for in this Article.

*Article 58*

The above provisions shall not preclude the application of broader national provisions on the ne bis in idem principle with regard to judicial decisions taken abroad.

## CHAPTER 4

## EXTRADITION

Articles 59-66 replaced by Framework Decision 2002/584 on the European Arrest Warrant.

## CHAPTER 5

## TRANSFER OF THE ENFORCEMENT OF CRIMINAL JUDGMENTS

*Article 67*

The following provisions shall apply between the Contracting Parties which are Parties to the Council of Europe Convention on the Transfer of Sentenced Persons of 21 March 1983, for the purposes of supplementing that Convention.

*Article 68*

1. The Contracting Party in whose territory a penalty involving deprivation of liberty or a detention order has been imposed by a judgment which has obtained the force of res judicata in respect of a national of another Contracting Party who, by escaping to the national's own country, has avoided the enforcement of that penalty or detention

order may request the latter Contracting Party, if the escaped person is within its territory, to take over the enforcement of the penalty or detention order.

2. The requested Contracting Party may, at the request of the requesting Contracting Party, prior to the arrival of the documents supporting the request that the enforcement of the penalty or detention order or part thereof remaining to be served be taken over, and prior to the decision on that request, take the sentenced person into police custody or take other measures to ensure that the person remains within the territory of the requested Contracting Party.

### *Article 69*

The transfer of enforcement under Article 68 shall not require the consent of the person on whom the penalty or the detention order has been imposed. The other provisions of the Council of Europe Convention on the Transfer of Sentenced Persons of 21 March 1983 shall apply mutatis mutandis.

## CHAPTER 6

## NARCOTIC DRUGS

### *Article 70*

1. The Contracting Parties shall set up a permanent working party to examine common problems relating to combating crime involving narcotic drugs and to draw up proposals, where necessary, to improve the practical and technical aspects of cooperation between the Contracting Parties. The working party shall submit its proposals to the Executive Committee.

2. The working party referred to in paragraph 1, whose members shall be nominated by the competent national authorities, shall include representatives of the police and customs authorities.

### *Article 71*

1. The Contracting Parties undertake as regards the direct or indirect sale of narcotic drugs and psychotropic substances of whatever type, including cannabis, and the possession of such products and substances for sale or export, to adopt in accordance with the existing United Nations Conventions(1), all necessary measures to prevent and punish the illicit trafficking in narcotic drugs and psychotropic substances.

2. The Contracting Parties undertake to prevent and punish by administrative and penal measures the illegal export of narcotic drugs and psychotropic substances, including cannabis, as well as the sale, supply and handing over of such products and substances, without prejudice to the relevant provisions of Articles 74, 75 and 76.

3. To combat the illegal import of narcotic drugs and psychotropic substances, including cannabis, the Contracting Parties shall step up their checks on the movement of persons, goods and means of transport at their external borders. Such measures shall be drawn up by the working party provided for in Article 70. This working party shall consider, inter alia, transferring some of the police and customs staff released from internal border duty and the use of modern drug-detection methods and sniffer dogs.

4. To ensure compliance with this Article, the Contracting Parties shall specifically carry out surveillance of places known to be used for drug trafficking.

5. The Contracting Parties shall do their utmost to prevent and combat the negative effects arising from the illicit demand for narcotic drugs and psychotropic substances of whatever type, including cannabis. Each Contracting Party shall be responsible for the measures adopted to this end.

*Article 72*

The Contracting Parties shall, in accordance with their constitutions and their national legal systems, ensure that legislation is enacted to enable the seizure and confiscation of the proceeds of the illicit trafficking in narcotic drugs and psychotropic substances.

*Article 73*

1. The Contracting Parties undertake, in accordance with their constitutions and their national legal systems, to adopt measures to allow controlled deliveries to be made in the context of the illicit trafficking in narcotic drugs and psychotropic substances.

2. In each individual case, a decision to allow controlled deliveries will be taken on the basis of prior authorisation from each Contracting Party concerned.

3. Each Contracting Party shall retain responsibility for and control over any operation carried out in its own territory and shall be entitled to intervene.

*Article 74*

As regards the legal trade in narcotic drugs and psychotropic substances, the Contracting Parties agree that the checks arising from obligations under the United Nations Conventions listed in Article 71 and which are carried out at internal borders shall, wherever possible, be transferred to within the country.

*Article 75*

1. As regards the movement of travellers to the territories of the Contracting Parties or their movement within these territories, persons may carry the narcotic drugs and psychotropic substances that are necessary for their medical treatment provided that,

at any check, they produce a certificate issued or authenticated by a competent authority of their State of residence.

2. The Executive Committee shall lay down the form and content of the certificate referred to in paragraph 1 and issued by one of the Contracting Parties, with particular reference to details on the nature and quantity of the products and substances and the duration of the journey.

3. The Contracting Parties shall notify each other of the authorities responsible for the issue and authentication of the certificate referred to in paragraph 2.

### *Article 76*

1. The Contracting Parties shall, where necessary, and in accordance with their medical, ethical and practical usage, adopt appropriate measures for the control of narcotic drugs and psychotropic substances which in the territory of one or more Contracting Parties are subject to more rigorous controls than in their own territory, so as not to jeopardise the effectiveness of such controls.

2. Paragraph 1 shall also apply to substances frequently used in the manufacture of narcotic drugs and psychotropic substances.

3. The Contracting Parties shall notify each other of the measures taken in order to monitor the legal trade of the substances referred to in paragraphs 1 and 2.

4. Problems experienced in this area shall be raised regularly in the Executive Committee.

## CHAPTER 7

## FIREARMS AND AMMUNITION

### *Article 77*

1. The Contracting Parties undertake to adapt their national laws, regulations and administrative provisions relating to the acquisition, possession, trade in and handing over of firearms and ammunition to the provisions of this chapter.

2. This chapter covers the acquisition, possession, trade in and handing over of firearms and ammunition by natural and legal persons; it does not cover the supply of firearms or ammunition to, or their acquisition or possession by, the central and territorial authorities, the armed forces or the police or the manufacture of firearms and ammunition by public undertakings.

*Article 78*

1. For the purposes of this chapter, firearms shall be classified as follows:

(a) prohibited firearms;

(b) firearms subject to authorisation;

(c) firearms subject to declaration.

2. The breach-closing mechanism, the magazine and the barrel of firearms shall be subject mutatis mutandis to the regulations governing the weapon of which they are, or are intended to be, mounted.

3. For the purposes of this Convention, "short firearms" shall mean firearms with a barrel not exceeding 30 cm or whose overall length does not exceed 60 cm; "long firearms" shall mean all other firearms.

*Article 79*

1. The list of prohibited firearms and ammunition shall include the following:

(a) firearms normally used as weapons of war;

(b) automatic firearms, even if they are not weapons of war;

(c) firearms disguised as other objects;

(d) ammunition with penetrating, explosive or incendiary projectiles and the projectiles for such ammunition;

(e) ammunition for pistols and revolvers with dumdum or hollow-pointed projectiles and projectiles for such ammunition.

2. In special cases the competent authorities may grant authorisations for the firearms and ammunition referred to in paragraph 1 if this is not contrary to public policy or public security.

*Article 80*

1. The list of firearms the acquisition and possession of which is subject to authorisation shall include at least the following if they are not prohibited:

(a) semi-automatic or repeating short firearms;

(b) single-shot short firearms with centrefire percussion;

(c) single-shot short firearms with rimfire percussion, with an overall length of less than 28 cm;

(d) semi-automatic long firearms whose magazine and chamber can together hold more than three rounds;

(e) repeating semi-automatic long firearms with smoothbore barrels not exceeding 60 cm in length;

(f) semi-automatic firearms for civilian use which resemble weapons of war with automatic mechanisms.

2. The list of firearms subject to authorisation shall not include:

(a) arms used as warning devices or alarms or to fire non-lethal incapacitants, provided that it is guaranteed by technical means that such arms cannot be converted, using ordinary tools, to fire ammunition with projectiles and provided that the firing of an irritant substance does not cause permanent injury to persons;

(b) semi-automatic long firearms whose magazine and chamber cannot hold more than three rounds without being reloaded, provided that the loading device is non-removable or that it is certain that the firearms cannot be converted, using ordinary tools, into firearms whose magazine and chamber can together hold more than three rounds.

*Article 81*

The list of firearms subject to declaration shall include, if such arms are neither prohibited nor subject to authorisation:

(a) repeating long firearms;

(b) long firearms with single-shot rifled barrel or barrels;

(c) single-shot short firearms with rimfire percussion whose overall length exceeds 28 cm;

(d) the arms listed in Article 80(2)(b).

*Article 82*

The list of arms referred to in Articles 79, 80 and 81 shall not include:

(a) firearms whose model or year of manufacture, save in exceptional cases, predates 1 January 1870, provided that they cannot fire ammunition intended for prohibited arms or arms subject to authorisation;

(b) reproductions of arms listed under (a), provided that they cannot be used to fire metal-case cartridges;

(c) firearms which by technical procedures guaranteed by the stamp of an official body or recognised by such a body have been rendered unfit to fire any kind of ammunition.

*Article 83*

Authorisation to acquire and to possess a firearm listed in Article 80 may be issued only:

(a) if the person concerned is over 18 years of age, with the exception of dispensations for hunting or sporting purposes;

(b) if the person concerned is not unfit, as a result of mental illness or any other mental or physical disability, to acquire or possess a firearm;

(c) if the person concerned has not been convicted of an offence, or if there are no other indications that the person might be a danger to public policy or public security;

(d) if the reasons given by the person concerned for acquiring or possessing firearms can be considered legitimate.

*Article 84*

1. Declarations in respect of the firearms mentioned in Article 81 shall be entered in a register kept by the persons referred to in Article 85.

2. If a firearm is transferred by a person not referred to in Article 85, a declaration of transfer must be made in accordance with procedures to be laid down by each Contracting Party.

3. The declarations referred to in this Article shall contain the details necessary in order to identify the persons and the arms concerned.

*Article 85*

1. The Contracting Parties undertake to impose an authorisation requirement on manufacturers of, and on dealers in, firearms subject to authorisation and to impose a declaration requirement on manufacturers of, and on dealers in, firearms subject to declaration. Authorisation for firearms subject to authorisation shall also cover firearms subject to declaration. The Contracting Parties shall carry out checks on arms manufacturers and arms dealers, thereby guaranteeing effective control.

2. The Contracting Parties undertake to adopt measures to ensure that, as a minimum requirement, all firearms are permanently marked with a serial number enabling identification and that they carry the manufacturer's mark.

3. The Contracting Parties shall require manufacturers and dealers to keep a register of all firearms subject to authorisation or declaration; the register shall enable rapid identification of the type and origin of the firearms and the persons acquiring them.

4. As regards firearms subject to authorisation under Articles 79 and 80, the Contracting Parties undertake to adopt measures to ensure that the serial number and the manufacturer's mark on the firearm are entered in the authorisation issued to its holder.

*Article 86*

1. The Contracting Parties undertake to adopt measures prohibiting legitimate holders of firearms subject to authorisation or declaration from handing such arms over to persons who do not hold either an authorisation to acquire them or a declaration certificate.

2. The Contracting Parties may authorise the temporary handing over of such firearms in accordance with procedures that they shall lay down.

*Article 87*

1. The Contracting Parties shall incorporate in their national law provisions enabling authorisation to be withdrawn from persons who no longer satisfy the conditions for the issue of authorisations under Article 83.

2. The Contracting Parties undertake to adopt appropriate measures, including the seizure of firearms and withdrawal of authorisations, and to lay down appropriate penalties for any infringements of the laws and regulations on firearms. Such penalties may include the confiscation of firearms.

*Article 88*

1. A person who holds an authorisation to acquire a firearm shall not require an authorisation to acquire ammunition for that firearm.

2. The acquisition of ammunition by persons not holding an authorisation to acquire arms shall be subject to the arrangements governing the weapon for which the ammunition is intended. The authorisation may be issued for a single category or for all categories of ammunition.

*Article 89*

The lists of firearms which are prohibited, subject to authorisation or subject to declaration, may be amended or supplemented by the Executive Committee to take account of technical and economic developments and national security.

*Article 90*

The Contracting Parties may adopt more stringent laws and provisions on the acquisition and possession of firearms and ammunition.

*Article 91*

1. The Contracting Parties agree, on the basis of the European Convention on the Control of the Acquisition and Possession of Firearms by Individuals of 28 June 1978, to set up within the framework of their national laws an exchange of information on the acquisition of firearms by persons - whether private individuals or firearms dealers - habitually resident or established in the territory of another Contracting Party. A firearms dealer shall mean any person whose trade or business consists, in whole or in part, in the retailing of firearms.

2. The exchange of information shall concern:

(a) between two Contracting Parties having ratified the Convention referred to in paragraph 1: the firearms listed in Appendix 1(A)(1)(a) to (h) of the said Convention;

(b) between two Contracting Parties at least one of which has not ratified the Convention referred to in paragraph 1: firearms which are subject to authorisation or declaration in each of the Contracting Parties.

3. Information on the acquisition of firearms shall be communicated without delay and shall include the following:

(a) the date of acquisition of the firearm and the identity of the person acquiring it, i.e.:

- in the case of a natural person: surname, forenames, date and place of birth, address and passport or identity card number, date of issue and details of the issuing authority, whether firearms dealer or not,

- in the case of a legal person: the name or business name and registered place of business and the surname, forenames, date and place of birth, address and passport or identity card number of the person authorised to represent the legal person;

(b) the model, manufacturer's number, calibre and other characteristics of the firearm in question and its serial number.

4. Each Contracting Party shall designate the national authority responsible for sending and receiving the information referred to in paragraphs 2 and 3 and shall immediately inform the other Contracting Parties of any change of designated authority.

5. The authority designated by each Contracting Party may forward the information it has received to the competent local police authorities and the authorities responsible for border surveillance, for the purposes of preventing or prosecuting criminal offences and infringements of rules of law.

# TITLE IV

# THE SCHENGEN INFORMATION SYSTEM

## CHAPTER 1

## ESTABLISHMENT OF THE SCHENGEN INFORMATION SYSTEM

### *Article 92*

1. The Contracting Parties shall set up and maintain a joint information system, hereinafter referred to as "the Schengen Information System", consisting of a national section in each of the Contracting Parties and a technical support function. The Schengen Information System shall enable the authorities designated by the Contracting Parties, by means of an automated search procedure, to have access to alerts on persons and property for the purposes of border checks and other police and customs checks carried out within the country in accordance with national law and, in the case of the specific category of alerts referred to in Article 96, for the purposes of issuing visas, residence permits and the administration of legislation on aliens in the context of the application of the provisions of this Convention relating to the movement of persons.

2. Each Contracting Party shall set up and maintain, for its own account and at its own risk, its national section of the Schengen Information System, the data file of which shall be made materially identical to the data files of the national sections of each of the other Contracting Parties by means of the technical support function. To ensure the rapid and effective transmission of data as referred to in paragraph 3, each Contracting Party shall observe, when setting up its national section, the protocols and procedures which the Contracting Parties have jointly established for the technical support function. Each national section's data file shall be available for the purposes of carrying out automated searches in the territory of each of the Contracting Parties. It shall not be possible to search the data files of other Contracting Parties' national sections.

3. The Contracting Parties shall set up and maintain, on a common cost basis and bearing joint liability, the technical support function of the Schengen Information System. The French Republic shall be responsible for the technical support function, which shall be located in Strasbourg. The technical support function shall comprise a

data file which will ensure via on-line transmission that the data files of the national sections contain identical information. The data files of the technical support function shall contain alerts for persons and property in so far as these concern all the Contracting Parties. The data file of the technical support function shall contain no data other than those referred to in this paragraph and in Article 113(2).

4. Member States shall in accordance with national legislation exchange through the authorities designated for that purpose (Sirene) all supplementary information necessary in connection with the entry of alerts and for allowing the appropriate action to be taken in cases where persons in respect of whom, and objects in respect of which, data have been entered in the Schengen Information System, are found as a result of searches made in this System. Such information shall be used only for the purpose for which it was transmitted.

*Article 92A*

1. As from the entry into force of Council Regulation (EC) No 1104/2008 [] and Council Decision 2008/839/JHA [] and relying on the definitions in Article 2 of that Regulation, the technical architecture of the Schengen Information System may be supplemented by:

(a) an additional central system composed of:

- technical support function (Central SIS II), located in France and backup Central SIS II located in Austria, containing the SIS II database and a uniform national interface (NI-SIS),

- a technical connection between the C.SIS and the Central SIS II via the converter allowing the conversion and synchronisation of data between the C.SIS and the Central SIS II;

(b) a national system (N.SIS II), consisting of the national data systems, which communicates with the Central SIS II;

(c) an infrastructure for communication between Central SIS II and the N.SIS II connected to the NI-SIS.

2. The N.SIS II may replace the national section referred to in Article 92 of this Convention, in which case the Member States need not hold a national data file.

3. The central SIS II database shall be available for the purpose of carrying out automated searches in the territory of each Member State.

4. In case any of the Member States replace their national section by N.SIS II, the compulsory functions of the technical support function towards that national section as mentioned in Article 92(2) and (3) become compulsory functions towards Central SIS II, without prejudice to the obligations referred to in Decision 2008/839/JHA and in Articles 5(1), 10(1), (2) and (3) of Regulation (EC) No 1104/2008.

5. Central SIS II shall provide the services necessary for the entry and processing of SIS data, the online update of N.SIS II national copies, the synchronisation of and consistency between N.SIS II national copies and the Central SIS II database and provide operations for initialisation and restoration of N.SIS II national copies.

6. France, responsible for the technical support function, the other Member States and the Commission shall cooperate to ensure that a search in the data files of N.SIS II or in the SIS II database produces a result equivalent to that of a search in the data file of the national sections referred to in Article 92(2).

2. In Article 119 first paragraph, the first sentence shall be replaced by the following:

"The costs of installing and operating the technical support function referred to in Article 92(3), including the cost of lines connecting the national sections of the Schengen Information System to the technical support function, and of activities performed in conjunction with tasks conferred upon France in application of Decision (JHA) 2008/839/JHA and of Regulation (EC) No 1104/2008 shall be borne jointly by the Member States."

3. In Article 119, the second paragraph shall be replaced by the following:

"The costs of installing and operating the national section of the Schengen Information System and of tasks conferred upon national systems under Decision 2008/839/JHA and Regulation (EC) No 1104/2008 shall be borne by each Member State individually."

## CHAPTER 2

## OPERATION AND USE OF THE SCHENGEN INFORMATION SYSTEM

### *Article 93*

The purpose of the Schengen Information System shall be in accordance with this Convention to maintain public policy and public security, including national security, in the territories of the Contracting Parties and to apply the provisions of this Convention relating to the movement of persons in those territories, using information communicated via this system.

### *Article 94*

1. The Schengen Information System shall contain only those categories of data which are supplied by each of the Contracting Parties, as required for the purposes laid down in Articles 95 to 100. The Contracting Party issuing an alert shall determine whether the case is important enough to warrant entry of the alert in the Schengen Information System.

2. The categories of data shall be as follows:

(a) persons for whom an alert has been issued;

(b) objects referred to in Articles 99 and 100.

3. For persons, the information shall be no more than the following:

(a) surname and forenames, any aliases possibly entered separately;

(b) any specific objective physical characteristics not subject to change;

(c) (…);

(d) place and date of birth;

(e) sex;

(f) nationality;

(g) whether the persons concerned are armed, violent or have escaped;

(h) reason for the alert;

(i) action to be taken;

(j) in cases of alerts under Article 95: the type of offence(s);

Other information, in particular the data listed in the first sentence of Article 6 of the Council of Europe Convention for the Protection of Individuals with regard to Automatic Processing of Personal Data of 28 January 1981, shall not be authorised.

4. Where a Contracting Party considers that an alert in accordance with Articles 95, 97 or 99 is incompatible with its national law, its international obligations or essential national interests, it may subsequently add to the alert contained in the data file of the national section of the Schengen Information System a flag to the effect that the action to be taken on the basis of the alert will not be taken in its territory. Consultation must be held in this connection with the other Contracting Parties. If the Contracting Party issuing the alert does not withdraw the alert, it shall continue to apply in full for the other Contracting Parties.

*Article 95*

1. Data on persons wanted for arrest for extradition purposes shall be entered at the request of the judicial authority of the requesting Contracting Party.

2. Before issuing an alert, the Contracting Party shall check whether the arrest is authorised under the national law of the requested Contracting Parties. If the Contracting Party issuing the alert has any doubts, it must consult the other Contracting Parties concerned.

The Contracting Party issuing the alert shall send the requested Contracting Parties by the quickest means possible both the alert and the following essential information relating to the case:

(a) the authority which issued the request for arrest;

(b) whether there is an arrest warrant or other document having the same legal effect, or an enforceable judgment;

(c) the nature and legal classification of the offence;

(d) a description of the circumstances in which the offence was committed, including the time, place and the degree of participation in the offence by the person for whom the alert has been issued;

(e) in so far as is possible, the consequences of the offence.

3. A requested Contracting Party may add to the alert in the data file of its national section of the Schengen Information System a flag prohibiting arrest on the basis of the alert until the flag is deleted. The flag must be deleted no later than 24 hours after the alert has been entered, unless the Contracting Party refuses to make the requested arrest on legal grounds or for special reasons of expediency. In particularly exceptional cases where this is justified by the complex nature of the facts behind the alert, the above time limit may be extended to one week. Without prejudice to a flag or a decision to refuse the arrest, the other Contracting Parties may make the arrest requested in the alert.

4. If, for particularly urgent reasons, a Contracting Party requests an immediate search, the requested Contracting Party shall examine whether it is able to withdraw its flag. The requested Contracting Party shall take the necessary steps to ensure that the action to be taken can be carried out immediately if the alert is validated.

5. If the arrest cannot be made because an investigation has not been completed or because a requested Contracting Party refuses, the latter must regard the alert as being an alert for the purposes of communicating the place of residence of the person concerned.

6. The requested Contracting Parties shall carry out the action as requested in the alert in accordance with extradition Conventions in force and with national law. They shall not be obliged to carry out the action requested where one of their nationals is involved, without prejudice to the possibility of making the arrest in accordance with national law.

### *Article 96*

1. Data on aliens for whom an alert has been issued for the purposes of refusing entry shall be entered on the basis of a national alert resulting from decisions taken by the

competent administrative authorities or courts in accordance with the rules of procedure laid down by national law.

2. Decisions may be based on a threat to public policy or public security or to national security which the presence of an alien in national territory may pose.

This situation may arise in particular in the case of:

(a) an alien who has been convicted of an offence carrying a penalty involving deprivation of liberty of at least one year;

(b) an alien in respect of whom there are serious grounds for believing that he has committed serious criminal offences, including those referred to in Article 71, or in respect of whom there is clear evidence of an intention to commit such offences in the territory of a Contracting Party.

3. Decisions may also be based on the fact that the alien has been subject to measures involving deportation, refusal of entry or removal which have not been rescinded or suspended, including or accompanied by a prohibition on entry or, where applicable, a prohibition on residence, based on a failure to comply with national regulations on the entry or residence of aliens.

### *Article 97*

Data on missing persons or persons who, for their own protection or in order to prevent threats, need temporarily to be placed under police protection at the request of the competent authority or the competent judicial authority of the Party issuing the alert shall be entered, so that the police authorities may communicate their whereabouts to the Party issuing the alert or may move the persons to a safe place in order to prevent them from continuing their journey, if so authorised by national law. This shall apply in particular to minors and persons who must be interned following a decision by a competent authority. The communication of data on a missing person who is of age shall be subject to the person's consent.

### *Article 98*

1. Data on witnesses, persons summoned to appear before the judicial authorities in connection with criminal proceedings in order to account for acts for which they are being prosecuted, or persons who are to be served with a criminal judgment or a summons to report in order to serve a penalty involving deprivation of liberty shall be entered, at the request of the competent judicial authorities, for the purposes of communicating their place of residence or domicile.

2. Information requested shall be communicated to the requesting Party in accordance with national law and the Conventions in force on mutual assistance in criminal matters.

*Article 99*

1. Data on persons or vehicles, boats, aircraft and containers shall be entered in accordance with the national law of the Member State issuing the alert, for the purposes of discreet surveillance or of specific checks in accordance with paragraph 5.

2. Such an alert may be issued for the purposes of prosecuting criminal offences and for the prevention of threats to public security:

(a) where there is clear evidence that the person concerned intends to commit or is committing numerous and extremely serious criminal offences; or

(b) where an overall assessment of the person concerned, in particular on the basis of past criminal offences, gives reason to suppose that that person will also commit extremely serious criminal offences in the future.

3. In addition, the alert may be issued in accordance with national law, at the request of the authorities responsible for national security, where there is clear evidence that the information referred to in paragraph 4 is necessary in order to prevent a serious threat by the person concerned or other serious threats to internal or external national security. The Member State issuing the alert pursuant to this paragraph shall be obliged to inform the other Member States thereof.

4. For the purposes of discreet surveillance, all or some of the following information may be collected and communicated to the authority issuing the alert when border checks or other police and customs checks are carried out within the country:

(a) the fact that the person for whom or the vehicle for which an alert has been issued has been found;

(b) the place, time or reason for the check;

(c) the route and destination of the journey;

(d) persons accompanying the person concerned or occupants of the vehicle;

(e) the vehicle used;

(f) objects carried;

(g) the circumstances under which the person or the vehicle was found.

During the collection of this information steps must be taken not to jeopardise the discreet nature of the surveillance.

5. During the specific checks referred to in paragraph 1, persons, vehicles, boats, aircraft, containers and objects carried may be searched in accordance with national law for the purposes referred to in paragraphs 2 and 3. If the specific check is not authorised under the law of a Contracting Party, it shall automatically be replaced, for that Contracting Party, by discreet surveillance.

6. A requested Contracting Party may add to the alert in the data file of its national section of the Schengen Information System a flag prohibiting, until the flag is deleted, performance of the action to be taken on the basis of the alert for the purposes of discreet surveillance or specific checks. The flag must be deleted no later than 24 hours after the alert has been entered unless the Contracting Party refuses to take the action requested on legal grounds or for special reasons of expediency. Without prejudice to a flag or a refusal, the other Contracting Parties may carry out the action requested in the alert.

### *Article 100*

1. Data on objects sought for the purposes of seizure or use as evidence in criminal proceedings shall be entered in the Schengen Information System.

2. If a search brings to light an alert for an object which has been found, the authority which matched the two items of data shall contact the authority which issued the alert in order to agree on the measures to be taken. For this purpose, personal data may also be communicated in accordance with this Convention. The measures to be taken by the Contracting Party which found the object must be in accordance with its national law.

3. The following categories of readily identifiable objects shall be entered:

(a) motor vehicles with a cylinder capacity exceeding 50 cc, boats and aircraft which have been stolen, misappropriated or lost;

(b) trailers with an unladen weight exceeding 750 kg, caravans, industrial equipment, outboard engines and containers which have been stolen, misappropriated or lost;

(c) firearms which have been stolen, misappropriated or lost;

(d) blank official documents which have been stolen, misappropriated or lost;

(e) issued identity papers such as passports, identity cards, driving licences, residence permits and travel documents which have been stolen, misappropriated, lost or invalidated;

(f) vehicle registration certificates and vehicle number plates which have been stolen, misappropriated, lost or invalidated;

(g) banknotes (registered notes);

(h) securities and means of payment such as cheques, credit cards, bonds, stocks and shares which have been stolen, misappropriated or lost.

*Article 101*

1. Access to data entered in the Schengen Information System and the right to search such data directly shall be reserved exclusively to the authorities responsible for:

(a) border checks;

(b) other police and customs checks carried out within the country, and the coordination of such checks.

However, access to data entered in the SIS and the right to search such data directly may also be exercised by national judicial authorities, inter alia, those responsible for the initiation of public prosecutions in criminal proceedings and judicial inquiries prior to indictment, in the performance of their tasks, as set out in national legislation.

2. In addition, access to data entered in accordance with Article 96 and data concerning documents relating to persons entered in accordance with Article 100(3)(d) and (e) and the right to search such data directly may be exercised by the authorities responsible for issuing visas, the central authorities responsible for examining visa applications and the authorities responsible for issuing residence permits and for the administration of legislation on aliens in the context of the application of the provisions of this Convention relating to the movement of persons. Access to data by these authorities shall be governed by the national law of each Member State.

3. Users may only search data which they require for the performance of their tasks.

4. Each Contracting Party shall send the Executive Committee a list of competent authorities which are authorised to search the data contained in the Schengen Information System directly. That list shall specify, for each authority, which data it may search and for what purposes.

*Article 101A*

1. The European Police Office (Europol) shall within its mandate and at its own expense have the right to have access to, and to search directly, data entered into the Schengen Information System in accordance with Articles 95, 99 and 100.

2. Europol may only search data which it requires for the performance of its tasks.

3. Where a search by Europol reveals the existence of an alert in the Schengen Information System, Europol shall inform, via the channels defined by the Europol Convention, the Member State which issued the alert thereof.

4. Use of information obtained from a search in the Schengen Information System is subject to the consent of the Member State concerned. If the Member State allows the use of such information, the handling thereof shall be governed by the Europol Convention. Europol may only communicate such information to third States and third bodies with the consent of the Member State concerned.

5. Europol may request supplementary information from the Member State concerned in accordance with the provisions set out in the Europol Convention.

6. Europol shall:

(a) record every search made by it, in accordance with the provisions of Article 103;

(b) without prejudice to paragraphs 4 and 5, not connect parts of the Schengen Information System nor transfer the data contained therein to which it has access to any computer system for data collection and processing in operation by or at Europol nor download or otherwise copy any parts of the Schengen Information System;

(c) limit access to data entered into the Schengen Information System to specifically authorised staff of Europol;

(d) adopt and apply the measures provided for in Article 118;

(e) allow the Joint Supervisory Body, set up under Article 24 of the Europol Convention, to review the activities of Europol in the exercise of its right to accede to and to search data entered into the Schengen Information System.

*Article 101B*

1. The national members of Eurojust and their assistants shall have the right to have access to, and search, data entered in accordance with Articles 95 and 98 into the Schengen Information System.

2. The national members of Eurojust and their assistants may only search data which they require for the performance of their tasks.

3. Where a search by a national member of Eurojust reveals the existence of an alert in the Schengen Information System, he or she shall inform the Member State having issued the alert thereof. Any communication of information obtained from such a search may only be communicated to third States and third bodies with the consent of the Member State having issued the alert.

4. Nothing in this Article shall be interpreted as affecting the provisions of the Council Decision setting up Eurojust concerning data protection and the liability for any unauthorised or incorrect processing of such data by the national members of Eurojust or their assistants, or as affecting the powers of the Joint Supervisory Body set up pursuant to Article 23 of that Council Decision.

5. Every search made by a national member of Eurojust or an assistant shall be recorded in accordance with the provisions of Article 103 and every use made by them of data to which they have acceded shall be registered.

6. No parts of the Schengen Information System shall be connected nor shall the data contained therein to which the national members or their assistants have access be

transferred to any computer system for data collection and processing in operation by or at Eurojust nor shall any parts of the Schengen Information System be downloaded.

7. The access to data entered into the Schengen Information System shall be limited to the national members and their assistants and not be extended to Eurojust staff.

8. Measures as provided for in Article 118 shall be adopted and applied

[Articles 102–142 omitted]

# Regulation 2988/95 on the protection of the European Communities financial interests, 18 December 1995

[OJ 1995, C 312/1–4]

23. 12. 95 EN Official Journal of the European Communities No L 312/1

I

*(Acts whose publication is obligatory)*

**COUNCIL REGULATION (EC, EURATOM) No 2988/95**
**of 18 December 1995**
**on the protection of the European Communities financial interests**

THE COUNCIL OF THE EUROPEAN UNION,

Having regard to the Treaty establishing the European Community, and in particular Article 235 thereof,

Having regard to the Treaty establishing the European Atomic Energy Community, and in particular Article 203 thereof,

Having regard to the proposal from the Commission [1],

Having regard to the opinion of the European Parliament [2],

Whereas the general budget of the European Communities is financed by own resources and administered by the Commission within the limit of the appropriations authorized and in accordance with the principle of sound financial management; whereas the Commission works in close cooperation with the Member States to that end;

Whereas more than half of Community expenditure is paid to beneficiaries through the intermediary of the Member States;

Whereas detailed rules governing this decentralized administration and the monitoring of their use are the subject of differing detailed provisions according to the Community policies concerned; whereas acts detrimental to the Communities' financial interests must, however, be countered in all areas;

Whereas the effectiveness of the combating of fraud against the Communities' financial interests calls for a common set of legal rules to be enacted for all areas covered by Community policies;

Whereas irregular conduct, and the administrative measures and penalties relating thereto, are provided for in sectoral rules in accordance with this Regulation;

Whereas the aforementioned conduct includes fraudulent actions as defined in the Convention on the protection of the European Communities' financial interests;

Whereas Community administrative penalties must provide adequate protection for the said interests; whereas it is necessary to define general rules applicable to these penalties;

Whereas Community law has established Community administrative penalties in the framework of the common agricultural policy; whereas such penalties must be established in other fields as well;

Whereas Community measures and penalties laid down in pursuance of the objectives of the common agricultural poilcy form an integral part of the aid systems; whereas they pursue their own ends which do not affect the assessment of the conduct of the economic operators concerned by the competent authorities of the Member States from the point of view of criminal law; whereas their effectiveness must be ensured by the immediate effect of Community rules and by applying in full Community measures as a whole, where the adoption of preventive measures has not made it possible to achieve that objective;

Whereas not only under the general principle of equity and the principle of proportionality but also in the light of the principle of *ne bis in idem*, appropriate provisions must be adopted while respecting the *acquis communautaire* and the provisions laid down in specific Community rules existing at the time of entry into force of this Regulation, to prevent any overlap of Community financial penalties and national criminal penalties imposed on the same persons for the same reasons;

(1) OJ No C 216, 6. 8. 1994, p. 11.
(2) OJ No C 89, 10. 4. 1995, p. 83 and opinion delivered on 30 November 1995 (not yet published in the Official Journal).

No L 312/2 EN Official Journal of the European Communities 23. 12. 95

Whereas, for the purposes of applying this Regulation, criminal proceedings may be regarded as having been completed where the competent national authority and the person concerned come to an arrangement;

Whereas this Regulation will apply without prejudice to the application of the Member States' criminal law;

Whereas Community law imposes on the Commission and the Member States an obligation to check that Community budget resources are used for their intended purpose; whereas there is a need for common rules to supplement existing provisions;

Whereas the Treaties make no provision for the specific powers necessary for the adoption of substantive law of horizontal scope on checks, measures and penalties with a view to ensuring the protection of the Communities' financial interests; whereas recourse should therefore be had to Article 235 of the EC Treaty and to Article 203 of the EAEC Treaty;

Whereas additional general provisions relating to checks and inspections on the spot will be adopted at a later stage,

HAS ADOPTED THIS REGULATION:

## TITLE I

## General principles

### *Article 1*

1. For the purposes of protecting the European Communities' financial interests, general rules are hereby adopted relating to homogenous checks and to administrative measures and penalties concerning irregularities with regard to Community law.

2. 'Irregularity' shall mean any infringement of a provision of Community law resulting from an act or omission by an economic operator, which has, or would have, the effect of prejudicing the general budget of the Communities or budgets managed by them, either by reducing or losing revenue accruing from own resources collected directly on behalf of the Communities, or by an unjustified item of expenditure.

### *Article 2*

1. Administrative checks, measures and penalties shall be introduced in so far as they are necessary to ensure the proper application of Community law. They shall be effective, proportionate and dissuasive so that they provide adequate protection for the Communities' financial interests.

2. No administrative penalty may be imposed unless a Community act prior to the irregularity has made provision for it. In the event of a subsequent amendment of the provisions which impose administrative penalties and are contained in Community rules, the less severe provisions shall apply retroactively.

3. Community law shall determine the nature and scope of the administrative measures and penalties necessary for the correct application of the rules in question, having regard to the nature and seriousness of the irregularity, the advantage granted or received and the degree of responsibility.

4. Subject to the Community law applicable, the procedures for the application of Community checks, measures and penalties shall be governed by the laws of the Member States.

### *Article 3*

1. The limitation period for proceedings shall be four years as from the time when the irregularity referred to in Article 1 (1) was committed. However, the sectoral rules may make provision for a shorter period which may not be less than three years.

In the case of continuous or repeated irregularities, the limitation period shall run from the day on which the irregularity ceases. In the case of multiannual programmes, the limitation period shall in any case run until the programme is definitively terminated.

The limitation period shall be interrupted by any act of the competent authority, notified to the person in question, relating to investigation or legal proceedings concerning the irregularity. The limitation period shall start again following each interrupting act.

However, limitation shall become effective at the latest on the day on which a period equal to twice the limitation period expires without the competent authority having imposed a penalty, except where the administrative procedure has been suspended in accordance with Article 6 (1).

2. The period for implementing the decision establishing the administrative penalty shall be three years. That period shall run from the day on which the decision becomes final.

Instances of interruption and suspension shall be governed by the relevant provisions of national law.

3. Member States shall retain the possibility of applying a period which is longer than that provided for in paragraphs 1 and 2 respectively.

23. 12. 95 EN Official Journal of the European Communities No L 312/3

TITLE II

**Administrative measures and penalties**

*Article 4*

1. As a general rule, any irregularity shall involve withdrawal of the wrongly obtained advantage:

— by an obligation to pay or repay the amounts due or wrongly received,

— by the total or partial loss of the security provided in support of the request for an advantage granted or at the time of the receipt of an advance.

2. Application of the measures referred to in paragraph 1 shall be limited to the withdrawal of the advantage obtained plus, where so provided for, interest which may be determined on a flat-rate basis.

3. Acts which are established to have as their purpose the obtaining of an advantage contrary to the objectives of the Community law applicable in the case by artificially creating the conditions required for obtaining that advantage shall result, as the case shall be, either in failure to obtain the advantage or in its withdrawal.

4. The measures provided for in this Article shall not be regarded as penalties.

*Article 5*

1. Intentional irregularities or those caused by negligence may lead to the following administrative penalties:

(a) payment of an administrative fine;

(b) payment of an amount greater than the amounts wrongly received or evaded, plus interest where appropriate; this additional sum shall be determined in accordance with a percentage to be set in the specific rules, and may not exceed the level strictly necessary to constitute a deterrent;

(c) total or partial removal of an advantage granted by Community rules, even if the operator wrongly benefited from only a part of that advantage;

(d) exclusion from, or withdrawal of, the advantage for a period subsequent to that of the irregularity;

(e) temporary withdrawal of the approval or recognition necessary for participation in a Community aid scheme;

(f) the loss of a security or deposit provided for the purpose of complying with the conditions laid down by rules or the replenishment of the amount of a security wrongly released;

(g) other penalties of a purely economic type, equivalent in nature and scope, provided for in the sectoral rules adopted by the Council in the light of the specific requirements of the sectors concerned and in compliance with the implementing powers conferred on the Commission by the Council.

2. Without prejudice to the provisions laid down in the sectoral rules existing at the time of entry into force of this Regulation, other irregularities may give rise only to those penalties not equivalent to a criminal penalty that are provided for in paragraph 1, provided that such penalties are essential to ensure correct application of the rules.

*Article 6*

1. Without prejudice to the Community administrative measures and penalties adopted on the basis of the sectoral rules existing at the time of entry into force of this Regulation, the imposition of financial penalties such as administrative fines may be suspended by decision of the competent authority if criminal proceedings have been initiated against the person concerned in connection with the same facts. Suspension of the administrative proceedings shall suspend the period of limitation provided for in Article 3.

2. If the criminal proceedings are not continued, the suspended administrative proceedings shall be resumed.

3. When the criminal proceedings are concluded, the suspended administrative proceedings shall be resumed, unless that is precluded by general legal principles.

4. Where the administrative procedure is resumed, the administrative authority shall ensure that a penalty at least equivalent to that prescribed by Community rules is imposed, which may take into account any penalty imposed by the judicial authority on the same person in respect of the same facts.

5. Paragraphs 1 to 4 shall not apply to financial penalties which form an integral part of financial support systems and may be applied independently of any criminal penalties, if and in so far as they are not equivalent to such penalties.

*Article 7*

Community administrative measures and penalties may be applied to the economic operators referred to in Article 1, namely the natural or legal persons and the other entities on which national law confers legal capacity who have committed the irregularity and to those who are under a duty to take responsibility for the irregularity or to ensure that it is not committed.

No L 312/4 EN Official Journal of the European Communities 23. 12. 95

TITLE III

**Checks**

*Article 8*

1. In accordance with their national laws, regulations and administrative provisions, the Member States shall take the measures necessary to ensure the regularity and reality of transactions involving the Communities' financial interests.

2. Measures providing for checks shall be appropriate to the specific nature of each sector and in proportion to the objectives pursued. They shall take account of existing administrative practice and structures in the Member States and shall be determined so as not to entail excessive economic constraints or administrative costs.

The nature and frequency of the checks and inspections on the spot to be carried out by the Member States and the procedure for performing them shall be determined as necessary by sectoral rules in such a way as to ensure uniform and effective application of the relevant rules and in particular to prevent and detect irregularities.

3. The sectoral rules shall include the provisions necessary to ensure equivalent checks through the approximation of procedures and checking methods.

*Article 9*

1. Without prejudice to the checks carried out by the Member States in accordance with their national laws, regulations and administrative provisions and without prejudice to the checks carried out by the Community institutions in accordance with the EC Treaty, and in particular Article 188c thereof, the Commission shall, on its responsibility, have checks carried out on:

(a) the conformity of administrative practices with Community rules;

(b) the existence of the necessary substantiating documents and their concordance with the Communities' revenue and expenditure as referred to in Article 1;

(c) the circumstances in which such financial transactions are carried out and checked.

2. In addition, it may carry out checks and inspections on the spot under the conditions laid down in the sectoral rules.

Before carrying out such checks and inspections, in accordance with the rules in force, the Commission shall inform the Member State concerned accordingly in order to obtain any assistance necessary.

*Article 10*

Additional general provisions relating to checks and inspections on the spot shall be adopted later in accordance with the procedures laid down in Article 235 of the EC Treaty and Article 203 of the EAEC Treaty.

*Article 11*

This Regulation shall enter into force on the third day following its publication in the *Official Journal of the European Communities.*

This Regulation shall be binding in its entirety and directly applicable in all Member States.

Done at Brussels, 18 December 1995.

*For the Council*

*The President*

J. BORRELL FONTELLES

# Joint Action 96/277 concerning a framework for the exchange of liaison magistrates to improve judicial cooperation between the Member States of the European Union, 22 April 1996

[OJ 1996, L 105/1–2]

27. 4. 96 EN Official Journal of the European Communities No L 105/1

*(Acts adopted under Title VI of the Treaty on European Union)*

**JOINT ACTION**

**of 22 April 1996**

**adopted by the Council on the basis of Article K.3 of the Treaty on European Union, concerning a framework for the exchange of liaison magistrates to improve judicial cooperation between the Member States of the European Union**

(96/277/JHA)

THE COUNCIL OF THE EUROPEAN UNION,

Having regard to Article K.3 (2) (b) of the Treaty on European Union,

Having regard to the initiative of the Italian Republic,

Whereas the Member States consider that they have a common interest in adopting measures to improve judicial cooperation, in both criminal and civil matters;

Whereas, to that end, the exchange of magistrates or officials to liaise between the Member States which so wish constitutes a useful and desirable measure;

Whereas the exchange of liaison magistrates of officials could increase the speed and effectiveness of judicial cooperation and at the same time facilitate better mutual understanding between Member States' legal and judicial systems;

Whereas more effective judicial cooperation in criminal matters could also help in effectively combating all forms of transnational crime, particularly organized crime and terrorism as well as fraud affecting the financial interests of the Community;

Whereas this joint action does not affect existing rules of procedure for judicial cooperation or exchanges of information between the Member States and the Commission based on other instruments;

Taking a positive view of the initiatives already undertaken by a number of Member States in sending liaison magistrates or officials to or receiving them from authorities competent for judicial cooperation and current initiatives to establish an effective network of judicial contact points to combat international organized crime;

Having considered the need to define a clear and useful judicial framework for initiatives already under way in order to increase their effectiveness and promote coordination,

HAS ADOPTED THIS JOINT ACTION;

*Article 1*

**Exchange of liaison magistrates**

1. This joint action establishes a framework for the posting or the exchange of magistrates of officials with special expertise in judicial cooperation procedures hereafter, referred to as 'liaison magistrates', as between Member States, on the basis of bilateral or multilateral arrangements.

2. The Member States agree that, the guidelines laid down in this joint action will serve as a reference when they decide to send liaison magistrates to another Member State or to exchange liaison magistrates.

3. The main aim of creating a framework for the exchange of liaison magistrates is to increase the speed and effectiveness of judicial cooperation and to promote the pooling of information on the legal and judicial systems of the Member States and to improve their operation.

*Article 2*

**Functions of liaison magistrates**

1. The tasks of liaison magistrates shall normally include any activity designed to encourage and accelerate all forms of judicial cooperation in criminal and, where appropriate, civil matters, in particular by establishing direct links with the competent departments and judicial authorities of the host State.

No L 105/2 EN Official Journal of the European Communities 27. 4. 96

2. Under arrangements agreed between the home Member State and the host Member State, liaison magistrates' tasks may also include any activity connected with handling the exchange of information and statistics designed to promote mutual understanding of the legal systems and legal data bases of the States concerned and to further relations between the legal professions of each of those States.

*Article 3*

**Exchange of information**

Member States shall keep each other informed within the Council of initiatives already under way and those taken to implement this joint action. The Member States concerned shall forward information on their exchanges of liaison magistrates to the General Secretariat of the Council annually.

*Article 4*

**Final provision**

This joint action shall be published in the Official Journal and shall enter into force on the date of its publication.

Done at Luxembourg, 22 April 1996.

*For the Council*

*The President*

S. AGNELLI

# Joint Action 96/443 concerning action to combat racism and xenophobia, 15 July 1996

[OJ 1996, L 185/5–7]

24. 7. 96 | EN | Official Journal of the European Communities | No L 185/5

*(Acts adopted pursuant to Title VI of the Treaty on European Union)*

## JOINT ACTION

**of 15 July 1996**

**adopted by the Council on the basis of Article K.3 of the Treaty on European Union, concerning action to combat racism and xenophobia**

(96/443/JHA)

THE COUNCIL OF THE EUROPEAN UNION,

Having regard to Article K.3 (2) (b) of the Treaty on European Union,

Having regard to the initiative from the Kingdom of Spain,

Whereas the Member States regard the adoption of rules in connection with action to combat racism and xenophobia as a matter of common interest, in accordance with Article K.1 (7) of the Treaty in particular;

Whereas regard should be had to the conclusions on racism and xenophobia adopted by the European Council in Corfu on 24 and 25 June 1994, in Essen on 9 and 10 December 1994, in Cannes on 26 and 27 June 1995 and in Madrid on 15 and 16 December 1995;

Whereas the Consultative Commission on Racism and Xenophobia, established by the Corfu European Council, adopted recommendations;

Whereas, despite the efforts made over recent years by the Member States, racism and xenophobia offences are still on the increase;

Concerned at the differences between some criminal law systems regarding the punishment of specific types of racist and xenophobic behaviour, which constitute barriers to international judicial cooperation;

Acknowledging that international cooperation by all States, including those which are not affected at domestic level by the problem of racism and xenophobia, is necessary to prevent the perpetrators of such offences from exploiting the fact that racist and xenophobic activities are classified differently in different States by moving from one country to another in order to escape criminal proceedings or avoid serving sentences and thus pursue their activities with impunity;

Emphasizing that the right to freedom of expression implies duties and responsibilities, including respect for the rights of others, as laid down in Article 19 of the United Nations International Covenant on Civil and Political Rights of 19 December 1966;

Determined, in keeping with their common humanitarian tradition, to guarantee that, above all, Articles 10 and 11 of the European Convention for the Protection of Human Rights and Fundamental Freedoms of 4 November 1950 are complied with;

Wishing to build upon the work begun within the framework of Title VI of the Treaty during 1994 concerning the criminal aspects of the fight against racism and xenophobia,

HAS ADOPTED THIS JOINT ACTION:

### TITLE I

A. In the interests of combating racism and xenophobia, each Member State shall undertake, in accordance with the procedure laid down in Title II, to ensure effective judicial cooperation in respect of offences based on the following types of behaviour, and, if necessary for the purposes of that cooperation, either to take steps to see that such behaviour is punishable as a criminal offence or, failing that, and pending the adoption of any necessary provisions, to derogate from the principle of double criminality for such behaviour:

(a) public incitement to discrimination, violence or racial hatred in respect of a group of persons or a member of such a group defined by reference to colour, race, religion or national or ethnic origin;

(b) public condoning, for a racist or xenophobic purpose, of crimes against humanity and human rights violations;

(c) public denial of the crimes defined in Article 6 of the Charter of the International Military Tribunal appended to the London Agreement of 8 April 1945 insofar as it includes behaviour which is contemptuous of, or degrading to, a group of persons defined by reference to colour, race, religion or national or ethnic origin;

(d) public dissemination or distribution of tracts, pictures or other material containing expressions of racism and xenophobia;

(e) participation in the activities of groups, organizations or associations, which involve discrimination, violence, or racial, ethnic or religious hatred.

B. In the case of investigations into, and/or proceedings against, offences based on the types of behaviour listed in paragraph A, each Member State shall, in accordance with Title II, improve judicial cooperation in the following areas and take appropriate measures for:

(a) seizure and confiscation of tracts, pictures or other material containing expressions of racism and xenophobia intended for public dissemination, where such material is offered to the public in the territory of a Member State;

(b) acknowledgement that the types of behaviour listed in paragraph A should not be regarded as political offences justifying refusal to comply with requests for mutual legal assistance;

(c) providing information to another Member State to enable that Member State to initiate, in accordance with its law, legal proceedings or proceedings for confiscation in cases where it appears that tracts, pictures or other material containing expressions of racism and xenophobia are being stored in a Member State for the purposes of distribution or dissemination in another Member State;

(d) the establishment of contact points in the Member States which would be responsible for collecting and exchanging any information which might be useful for investigations and proceedings against offences based on the types of behaviour listed in paragraph A.

C. Nothing in this Joint Action may be interpreted as affecting any obligations which Member States may have under the international instruments listed below. Member States shall implement this Joint Action consistently with such obligations and will refer to the definitions and principles contained in such instruments when so doing:

— the European Convention for the Protection of Human Rights and Fundamental Freedoms of 4 November 1950,

— the Convention relating to the Status of Refugees of 28 July 1951, as amended by the New York Protocol of 31 January 1967,

— the United Nations Convention on Genocide of 9 December 1948,

— the International Convention on the Elimination of All Forms of Racial Discrimination of 7 March 1966,

— the Geneva Conventions of 12 August 1949 and Protocols I and II of 12 December 1977 to those Conventions,

— Resolutions 827(93) and 955(94) of the United Nations Security Council,

— Council Resolution of 23 November 1995 on the protection of witnesses in the fight against international organized crime [1], in cases of criminal proceedings for the types of behaviour listed in paragraph A, if witnesses have been summoned in another Member State.

TITLE II

Each Member State shall bring forward appropriate proposals to implement this Joint Action for consideration by the competent authorities with a view to their adoption.

The Council will assess the fulfilment by Member States of their obligations under this Joint Action, taking into account the declarations annexed to it, by the end of June 1998.

This Joint Action and the annexed declarations, which are approved by the Council and are without prejudice to the application of this Joint Action by Member States other than those whom these declarations concern, will be published in the Official Journal.

Done at Brussels, 15 July 1996.

*For the Council*

*The President*

D. SPRING

---

[1] OJ No C 327, 7. 12. 1995, p. 5.

24. 7. 96 EN Official Journal of the European Communities No L 185/7

*ANNEX*

**DECLARATIONS REFERRED TO IN TITLE II**

1. **Declaration by the Greek delegation re Title I.B (b):**

   'Greece interprets Title I.B (b) in the light of those provisions of its Constitution which prohibit any action being taken against persons facing prosecution on political grounds.'

2. **Declaration by the French delegation re Title I.C, fifth indent:**

   'France points out that Additional Protocol I of 8 June 1977 to the Geneva Conventions of 1949 cannot be invoked against it, in that France has neither ratified nor signed that instrument and that it cannot be taken as a translation of international customary law applicable in armed conflicts.'

3. **Declaration by the United Kingdom delegation re Title I:**

   'The United Kingdom delegation declares that for the purposes of the application of the Joint Action by the United Kingdom, and taking into account the provisions and general principles of United Kingdom criminal law, the United Kingdom will apply Title I, paragraph A, points (a) to (e) and references thereto where the relevant behaviour is threatening, abusive or insulting and is carried out with the intention of stirring up racial hatred or is likely to do so.

   This would include, in accordance with Title I.B and Title II, enabling the relevant United Kingdom authorities in this context to search for and seize tracts, pictures or other material in the UK which is intended for dissemination in another Member State and which is likely to incite racial hatred there.

   If problems arise from the application of this declaration, the UK will consult with the Member State concerned with a view to overcoming the problems raised.'

4. **Declaration by the Danish delegation re Title I:**

   'The Danish delegation declares that for the purposes of the application of the Joint Action by Denmark, and taking into account the provisions and general principles of Danish criminal law, Denmark will apply Title I, paragraph A, points (a) to (e) and references thereto only where the relevant behaviour is threatening, insulting or degrading.'

# Joint Action 96/698 on cooperation between customs authorities and business organizations in combating drug trafficking, 29 November 1996

[OJ 1996, L 322/3–4]

12. 12. 96 EN Official Journal of the European Communities No L 322/3

*(Acts adopted pursuant to Title VI of the Treaty on European Union)*

**JOINT ACTION**

**of 29 November 1996**

**adopted by the Council on the basis of Article K.3 of the Treaty on European Union, on cooperation between customs authorities and business organizations in combating drug trafficking**

(96/698/JHA)

THE COUNCIL OF THE EUROPEAN UNION,

Having regard to the Treaty on European Union and, in particular, Article K.3 (2) (b) thereof,

Having regard to the initiative of Ireland,

Having regard to the report of the Expert Group on Drugs, as approved by the European Council in Madrid in 1995,

Recognizing that facilities and services of legitimate business organizations can be surreptiously used by illegal drug traffickers,

Whereas the highest degree of cooperation is essential between customs authorities and business organizations in combating drug trafficking;

Whereas support for the strengthening of cooperation between customs authorities and business organizations in the fight against drug trafficking was expressed by the Group of Seven (G7) at its summit meetings in London (1991) and Munich (1992);

Whereas UN Economic and Social Council Resolutions 1993/41 of 27 July 1993 and 1995/18 of 24 July 1995 endorsed the use of Memoranda of Understanding as a practical means of obtaining tangible results in drug enforcement, whilst maintaining the momentum of trade facilitation;

Whereas an action plan to develop systematically Memoranda of Understanding in the customs field was adopted by the Council of the World Customs Organization (WCO),

Noting that the Memoranda of Understanding programme initiated by the WCO has been successful worldwide in consolidating cooperation between customs authorities and business organizations;

Further noting that some Member States of the European Union have already embarked on national Memoranda of Understanding programmes with business organizations in relation to both drug trafficking and other customs offences;

Aware that the expansion of these programmes to all Member States and to a greater number of business organizations can bring further enforcement advantages,

HAS ADOPTED THE FOLLOWING JOINT ACTION:

*Article 1*

In order to consolidate the already cooperative relationship between the customs authorities of the Member States and business organizations operating in the European Union in combating drug trafficking, Member States shall establish or further develop Memoranda of Understanding programmes at national level under the guidelines laid down in this joint action and shall invite participation in such programmes.

*Article 2*

Memoranda of Understanding between customs authorities and business organizations may contain, but need not be confined to, provisions in respect of the following:

— the exchange of contact names in customs and in the signatory organization,

- the provision to customs, by the signatory, of advance cargo or passenger data as appropriate,
- access by customs to the signatory's information systems,
- assessment by customs of the signatory's security procedures,
- development and implementation of plans to improve such security,
- checking of newly recruited staff by the signatory,
- provision by customs of training for the signatory's staff.

*Article 3*

Customs authorities shall periodically review the operation of national Memoranda of Understanding programmes and shall also review the implementation of individual Memoranda of Understanding and, in agreement with signatories, adapt them as necessary to ensure maximum effectiveness.

*Article 4*

Member States shall notify the Council Secretariat of the measures they have taken to implement the provisions of this joint action one year after its entry into force and thereafter as requested by the Presidency.

*Article 5*

Member States may at their discretion extend the scope of Memoranda of Understanding established under the programmes referred to in Article 1 to cover other offences for which the customs authorities are competent in addition to drug trafficking.

*Article 6*

This joint action shall be published in the Official Journal.

It shall enter into force on the day of its publication.

Done at Brussels, 29 November 1996.

*For the Council*

*The President*

N. OWEN

# Joint Action 96/750 concerning the approximation of the laws and practices of the Member States of the European Union to combat drug addiction and to prevent and combat illegal drug trafficking, 17 December 1996

**[OJ 1997, L 342/6–8]**

No L 342/6 EN Official Journal of the European Communities 31. 12. 96

## JOINT ACTION

**of 17 December 1996**

**adopted by the Council on the basis of Article K.3 of the Treaty on European Union concerning the approximation of the laws and practices of the Member States of the European Union to combat drug addiction and to prevent and combat illegal drug trafficking**

(96/750/JHA)

THE COUNCIL OF THE EUROPEAN UNION,

Having regard to the Treaty on European Union, and in particular Articles K.1 (4) and K.3 (2) (b) thereof,

Having regard to the French initiative,

Recalling that the Cannes European Council, of 26 and 27 June 1995, approved the work relating to the European action plan to combat drugs (1996 to 1999) and recognized the need for an integrated approach in this area;

Recalling that the Madrid European Council, of 15 and 16 December 1995, approved the report from the group of experts on 'Drugs' and that some of its 66 proposals have already been converted into precise, coordinated operational activities within the European Union, in accordance with the European Council's instructions;

Recalling that the European Council also invited the Italian and Irish Presidencies to prepare, after consultation of the Member States, the Commission, the Europol Drugs Unit and the European Monitoring Centre for Drugs and Drug Addiction, a programme of activities which took account of that report, progress with which would be examined at the Dublin European Council on 13 and 14 December 1996;

Considering that the Florence European Council on 21 and 22 June 1996 stressed the vital importance of reinforced cooperation between Member States to fight against drugs;

Considering that the same European Council restated the importance of speedily completing the study on harmonization of Member States' laws and its impact on reducing consumption of and illicit trafficking in drugs;

Taking note of the report on harmonization of national legislation on drugs as requested by the Madrid and Florence European Councils;

Recalling the priority attached by the Irish Presidency to the fight against drugs, and the initiatives taken further to the instructions of the Madrid and Florence European Councils to give it a specific content, and in particular the Council resolution on sentencing for serious drug trafficking;

Considering that Member States fulfil their obligations under the United Nations Conventions of 1961, 1971 and 1988 and that they will examine ways of making strict compliance with those Conventions more effective, in particular by helping third countries to fulfil their obligations;

Considering that Member States reaffirm their common determination to put an end to illegal drug trafficking in order to protect society from its devastating effects and from the other deep-seated causes of the problem of drug abuse, in particular the illegal demand for drugs and the enormous profits from the illegal trade, and that an approximation of laws and practices designed to render cooperation more effective would be a positive contribution to that objective;

Noting the memorandum 'On a European social model' submitted by France at the Turin European Council on 29 March 1996, advocating harmonization of national legislation on combating drugs;

Considering the dangers inherent in the development of synthetic drugs;

Considering that the report on harmonization drawn up by the Council and the Commission in response to the aforementioned instructions recognizes that synthetic drugs might constitute a priority area for putting the report into practice;

Considering that, in the absence of harmonized legislation, mutually compatible practices would reinforce European cooperation in fighting drug addiction and in preventing and combating illegal drug trafficking;

Considering that a high level of European and international cooperation between police, customs services and judicial authorities would help to increase the efficiency of the fight against drug trafficking;

Considering that the fight against drug trafficking mut be combined with an active policy of prevention, care and rehabilitation of drug addicts;

Noting the Community action programme on the prevention of drug dependence and in particular the fifteen priority actions which it contains;

Considering that the provisions of this joint action are without prejudice to the general principle that a Member State may maintain or step up its national policy in the fight against drugs in its territory;

Without prejudice to the powers of the Community,

HAS ADOPTED THIS JOINT ACTION:

*Article 1*

Member States shall undertake to cooperate fully in the fight against drug addiction and shall endeavour to approximate their laws to make them mutually compatible to the extent necessary to prevent and combat illegal drug trafficking in the Union.

*Article 2*

Member States shall endeavour to make the practices of their police, customs services and judicial authorities more compatible with each other, thus making for closer European cooperation to prevent and comba illegal drug trafficking in the Union.

*Article 3*

Member States shall undertake to combat illicit movements of narcotic drugs and psychotropic substances within the Community, including 'drug tourism'.

*Article 4*

Member States shall ensure that under their legal systems the penalties imposed for serious drug trafficking are among the most severe penalties available for crimes of comparable gravity.

*Article 5*

Member States shall endeavour to draft convergent legislation to the extent necessary to make up legal ground or fill legal vacuums as regards synthetic drugs. In particular they shall promote the establishment of a rapid information system to enable such drugs to be identified as substances liable to be prohibited as soon as they appear anywhere in a Member State.

*Article 6*

Without prejudice to the powers of the Community, Member States shall undertake to adopt the necessary measures to efect a tangible increase in operational cooperation between police, customs services and judicial authorities in combating drug addiction and preventing and combating illegal drug trafficking.

*Article 7*

Member States shall ensure that their obligations under the United Nations Conventions on narcotic drugs and psychotropic substances of 1961, 1971, and 1988 are applied strictly and effectively.

*Article 8*

Member States undertake to take the most appropriate steps to combat the illicit cultivation of plants containing active ingredients with narcotic properties.

*Article 9*

Member States undertake, subject to their constitutional principles and the basic concepts of their legal systems, to make it an offence publicly and intentionally to incite or induce others, by any means, to commit offences of illicit use or production of narcotic drugs. They shall be especially vigilant as regards the use made of on-line data services and in particular the Internet.

*Article 10*

Nothing in this joint action shall prevent a Member State, with due regard for its international commitments, from maintaining or introducing in its territory any additional measure it deems appropriate to fight drug addiction and to prevent and combat illicit drug trafficking.

No L 342/8 EN Official Journal of the European Communities 31. 12. 96

*Article 11*

The Governments of the Member States shall undertake to take all appropriate steps to implement this joint action as soon as it is adopted.

The Presidency shall report to the Council each year on the implementation of this joint action.

*Article 12*

This joint action shall come into force on the day of its adoption.

*Article 13*

This joint action shall be published in the Official Journal.

Done at Brussels, 17 December 1996.

*For the Council*

*The President*

I. YATES

# Joint Action 97/339 with regard to cooperation on law and order and security, 26 May 1997

**[OJ 1997, L 147/1–2]**

5. 6. 97 | EN | Official Journal of the European Communities | No L 147/1

*(Acts adopted pursuant to Title VI of the Treaty on European Union)*

**JOINT ACTION**

**of 26 May 1997**

**adopted by the Council on the basis of Article K.3 of the Treaty on European Union with regard to cooperation on law and order and security**

(97/339/JHA)

THE COUNCIL OF THE EUROPEAN UNION,

Having regard to the Treaty on European Union, and in particular Article K.3 (2) (b) thereof,

Having regard to the initiative from the Kingdom of the Netherlands,

Bearing in mind that, under Article K.1(9), police cooperation is regarded by Member States as a matter of common interest;

Whereas, further to previous initiatives, particularly as regards football hooliganism, efforts should be made to extend and strengthen cooperation on law and order and security;

Whereas more detailed arrangements need to be made for cooperation with regard to events taken in a broad sense, i.e. meetings attended by large numbers of people from more than one Member State, at which policing is primarily aimed at maintaining law and order and security and preventing criminal offences;

Whereas such meetings include sporting events, rock concerts, demonstrations and road-blocking protest campaigns, but related matters such as guarding and protecting people and property may also form part of the cooperation in question;

Whereas, in addition to neighbouring Member States, it is also possible for non-neighbouring Member States and Member States of transit to be involved in that cooperation;

Whereas exchange of information on groups of people that may pose a threat to law and order and security in various Member States as well as secondment of liaison officers and cooperation between central bodies have a part to play in such cooperation;

Whereas this joint action is intended to supplement existing bilateral and multilateral arrangements and is without prejudice to closer cooperation between Member States,

HAS ADOPTED THIS JOINT ACTION:

*Article 1*

1. Member States shall provide Member States concerned with information, upon request or unsolicited, via central bodies, if sizeable groups which may pose a threat to law and order and security are travelling to another Member State in order to participate in events. The information shall be supplied at as early a stage as possible to all Member States concerned, regardless of whether they are neighbours, including Member States of transit.

2. The information shall include the fullest possible details regarding:

(a) the group in question:

— overall composition,

— nature of the group (whether aggressive and whether any chance of disturbances);

(b) routes to be taken and stopping-off points;

(c) means of transport;

(d) any other relevant information;

(e) reliability of the information.

The information to be provided shall be supplied in compliance with national law.

*Article 2*

1. Member States may temporarily post liaison officers to other Member States which so request. Liaison officers shall play an advice and assistance role. They shall

have no powers and be unarmed. They shall provide information and carry out their duties in accordance with instructions from their home Member State and guidelines from the Member State to which they are seconded. The host Member State shall ensure that liaison officers are protected.

2. The competent authorities of the host Member State shall determine the activities to be engaged in by liaison officers. Liaison officers shall be required to follow guidelines from the competent authorities.

*Article 3*

In order to promote cooperation between Member States by way of the competent central bodies, the following arrangements shall be made:

(a) each spring the Presidency shall organize a meeting of heads of central bodies for law and order and security to discuss matters of common interest;

(b) particulars concerning those central bodies shall be updated each spring via the Presidency (see Annex). Central bodies shall notify one another of any intervening changes;

(c) in the interests of better knowledge of one another's organization, heads of central bodies shall encourage the holding of exercises and exchanges and training secondments for their staff.

*Article 4*

This joint action shall be published in the Official Journal.

It shall enter into force on the day following its publication.

Done at Brussels, 26 May 1997.

*For the Council*
*The President*
W. SORGDRAGER

---

*ANNEX*

Central bodies are to supply one another each year, or at more frequent intervals where changes occur, with the following particulars:

Member State:

Name of central body:

Name of authority (e.g. Ministry):

Address:

Phone number(s):

Fax number(s):

E-mail address:

Liaison office:

Names of contacts:

Languages spoken (in addition to national language(s)):

# Convention on the fight against corruption involving officials of the European Communities or officials of Member States of the European Union, 26 May 1997

[OJ 1997, C 195/2–11]

**Convention drawn up on the basis of Article K.3 (2) (c) of the Treaty on European Union on the fight against corruption involving officials of the European Communities or officials of Member States of the European Union**

THE HIGH CONTRACTING PARTIES to this Convention, Member States of the European Union,

REFERRING to the Act of the Council of the European Union of 26 May 1997,

WHEREAS the Member States consider the improvement of judicial cooperation in the fight against corruption to be a matter of common interest, coming under the cooperation provided for in Title VI of the Treaty;

WHEREAS by its Act of 27 September 1996 the Council drew up a Protocol directed in particular at acts of corruption involving national or Community officials and damaging or likely to damage the European Communities' financial interests;

WHEREAS, for the purpose of improving judicial cooperation in criminal matters between Member States, it is necessary to go further than the said Protocol and to draw up a Convention directed at acts of corruption involving officials of the European Communities or officials of the Member States in general;

DESIROUS of ensuring consistent and effective application of this Convention throughout the European Union,

HAVE AGREED ON THE FOLLOWING PROVISIONS:

*Article 1*

**Definitions**

For the purposes of this Convention:

(a) 'official` shall mean any Community or national official, including any national official of another Member State;

(b) 'Community official` shall mean:

- any person who is an official or other contracted employee within the meaning of the Staff Regulations of officials of the European Communities or the Conditions of Employment of other servants of the European Communities,

- any person seconded to the European Communities by the Member States or by any public or private body, who carries out functions equivalent to those performed by European Community officials or other servants.

Members of bodies set up in accordance with the Treaties establishing the European Communities and the staff of such bodies shall be treated as Community officials, inasmuch as the Staff Regulations of officials of the European Communities or the Conditions of Employment of other servants of the European Communities do not apply to them;

(c) 'national official' shall be understood by reference to the definition of 'official' or 'public officer' in the national law of the Member State in which the person in question performs that function for the purposes of application of the criminal law of that Member State.

Nevertheless, in the case of proceedings involving a Member State's official initiated by another Member State, the latter shall not be bound to apply the definition of 'national official' except insofar as that definition is compatible with its national law.

*Article 2*

**Passive corruption**

1. For the purposes of this Convention, the deliberate action of an official, who, directly or through an intermediary, requests or receives advantages of any kind whatsoever, for himself or for a third party, or accepts a promise of such an advantage, to act or refrain from acting in accordance with his duty or in the exercise of his functions in breach of his official duties shall constitute passive corruption.

2. Each Member State shall take the necessary measures to ensure that conduct of the type referred to in paragraph 1 is made a criminal offence.

*Article 3*

**Active corruption**

1. For the purposes of this Convention, the deliberate action of whosoever promises or gives, directly or through an intermediary, an advantage of any kind whatsoever to an official for himself or for a third party for him to act or refrain from acting in accordance with his duty or in the exercise of his functions in breach of his official duties shall constitute active corruption.

2. Each Member State shall take the necessary measures to ensure that conduct of the type referred to in paragraph 1 is made a criminal offence.

*Article 4*

**Assimilation**

1. Each Member State shall take the necessary measures to ensure that in its criminal law the descriptions of the offences referred to in Articles 2 and 3 committed by or against its Government Ministers, elected members of its parliamentary chambers, the members of its highest Courts or the members of its Court of Auditors in the exercise of their functions apply similarly in cases where such offences are committed by or against Members of the Commission of the European Communities, the European Parliament, the Court of Justice and the Court of Auditors of the European Communities respectively in the exercise of their duties.

2. Where a Member State has enacted special legislation concerning acts or omissions for which Government Ministers are responsible by reason of their special political position in that Member State, paragraph 1 may not apply to such legislation, provided that the Member State ensures that Members of the Commission of the European Communities are also covered by the criminal legislation implementing Articles 2 and 3.

3. Paragraphs 1 and 2 shall be without prejudice to the provisions applicable in each Member State concerning criminal proceedings and the determination of the competent court.

4. This Convention shall apply in full accordance with the relevant provisions of the Treaties establishing the European Communities, the Protocol on the Privileges and Immunities of the European Communities, the Statutes of the Court of Justice and the texts adopted for the purpose of their implementation, as regards the withdrawal of immunity.

*Article 5*

**Penalties**

1. Each Member State shall take the necessary measures to ensure that the conduct referred to in Articles 2 and 3, and participating in and instigating the conduct in question, is punishable by effective, proportionate and dissuasive criminal penalties, including, at least in serious cases, penalties involving deprivation of liberty which can give rise to extradition.

2. Paragraph 1 shall be without prejudice to the exercise of disciplinary powers by the competent authorities against national officials or Community officials. In determining the penalty to be imposed, the national criminal courts may, in accordance with the principles of their national law, take into account any disciplinary penalty already imposed on the same person for the same conduct.

*Article 6*

**Criminal liability of heads of businesses**

Each Member State shall take the necessary measures to allow heads of businesses or any persons having power to take decisions or exercise control within a business to be declared criminally liable in accordance with the principles defined by its national law in cases of corruption, as referred to in Article 3, by a person under their authority acting on behalf of the business.

*Article 7*

**Jurisdiction**

1. Each Member State shall take the measures necessary to establish its jurisdiction over the offences it has established in accordance with the obligations arising out of Articles 2, 3 and 4 where:

(a) the offence is committed in whole or in part within its territory;

(b) the offender is one of its nationals or one of its officials;

(c) the offence is committed against one of the persons referred to in Article 1 or a member of one of the European Community institutions referred to in Article 4 (1) who is at the same time one of its nationals;

(d) the offender is a Community official working for a European Community institution or a body set up in accordance with the Treaties establishing the European Communities which has its headquarters in the Member State in question.

2. Each Member State may declare, when giving the notification provided for in Article 13 (2), that it will not apply or will apply only in specific cases or conditions one or more of the jurisdiction rules laid down in paragraph 1 (b), (c) and (d).

*Article 8*

**Extradition and prosecution**

1. Any Member State which, under its law, does not extradite its own nationals shall take the necessary measures to establish its jurisdiction over the offences it has established in accordance with the obligations arising out of Articles 2, 3 and 4, when committed by its own nationals outside its territory.

2. Each Member State shall, when one of its nationals is alleged to have committed in another Member State an offence established in accordance with the obligations arising out of Articles 2, 3 and 4 and it does not extradite that person to that other Member State solely on the ground of his nationality, submit the case to its competent authorities for the purpose of prosecution if appropriate. In order to enable prosecution to take place, the files, information and exhibits relating to the offence shall be transmitted in accordance with the procedures laid down in Article 6 of the European Convention on Extradition of 13 December 1957. The requesting Member State shall be informed of the prosecution initiated and of its outcome.

3. For the purposes of this Article, the term 'national' of a Member State shall be construed in accordance with any declaration made by that State under Article 6 (1) (b) of the European Convention on Extradition and with paragraph 1 (c) of that Article.

*Article 9*

**Cooperation**

1. If any procedure in connection with an offence established in accordance with the obligations arising out of Articles 2, 3 and 4 concerns at least two Member States, those States shall cooperate effectively in the investigation, the prosecution and in carrying out the punishment imposed by means, for example, of mutual legal assistance, extradition, transfer of proceedings or enforcement of sentences passed in another Member State.

2. Where more than one Member State has jurisdiction and has the possibility of viable prosecution of an offence based on the same facts, the Member States involved shall cooperate in deciding which shall prosecute the offender or offenders with a view to centralizing the prosecution in a single Member States where possible.

*Article 10*

**Ne bis in idem**

1. Member States shall apply, in their national criminal laws, the ne bis in idem rule, under which a person whose trial has been finally disposed of in a Member State may not be prosecuted in another Member State in respect of the same facts, provided that if a penalty was imposed, it has been enforced, is actually in the process of being enforced or can no longer be enforced under the laws of the sentencing State.

2. A Member State may, when giving the notification referred to in Article 13 (2), declare that it shall not be bound by paragraph 1 of this Article in one or more of the following cases:

(a) if the facts which were the subject of the judgment rendered abroad took place in its own territory either in whole or in part; in the latter case this exception shall not apply if those facts took place partly in the territory of the Member State where the judgment was rendered;

(b) if the facts which where the subject of the judgment rendered abroad constitute an offence directed against the security or other equally essential interests of that Member State;

(c) if the facts which were the subject of the judgment rendered abroad were committed by an official of that Member State contrary to the duties of his office.

3. If a further prosecution is brought in a Member State against a person whose trial, in respect of the same facts, has been finally disposed of in another Member State, any period of deprivation of liberty served in the latter Member State arising from those facts shall be deducted from any sanction imposed. To the extent permitted by national law, sanctions not involving deprivation of liberty shall also be taken into account insofar as they have been enforced.

4. The exceptions which may be the subject of a declaration under paragraph 2 shall not apply if the Member State concerned in respect of the same facts requested the other Member State to bring the prosecution or granted extradition of the person concerned.

5. Relevant bilateral or multilateral agreements concluded between Member States and relevant declarations shall remain unaffected by this Article.

*Article 11*

**Internal provisions**

No provision in this Convention shall prevent Member States from adopting internal legal provisions which go beyond the obligations deriving from this Convention.

*Article 12*

**Court of Justice**

1. Any dispute between Member States on the interpretation or application of this Convention which it has proved impossible to resolve bilaterally must in an initial stage be examined by the Council in accordance with the procedure set out in Title VI of the Treaty on European Union with a view to reaching a solution. If no solution has been found within six months, the matter may be referred to the Court of Justice of the European Communities by one of the parties to the dispute.

2. Any dispute between one or more Member States and the Commission of the European Communities concerning Article 1, with the exception of point (c), or Articles 2, 3 and 4, insofar as it concerns a question of Community law or the Communities' financial interests, or involves members of officials of Community institutions of bodies set up in accordance with the Treaties establishing the European Communities, which it has proved impossible to settle through negotiation, may be submitted to the Court of Justice by one of the parties to the dispute.

3. Any court in a Member State may ask the Court of Justice to give a preliminary ruling on a matter concerning the interpretation of Articles 1 to 4 and 12 to 16 raised in a case pending before it and involving members or officials of Community institutions or bodies set up in accordance with the Treaties establishing the European Communities, acting in the exercise of their functions, if it considers that a decision on that matter is necessary to enable it to give judgment.

4. The competence of the Court of Justice provided for in paragraph 3 shall be subject to its acceptance by the Member State concerned in a declaration to that effect made at the time of the notification referred to in Article 13 (2) or at any subsequent time.

5. A Member State making a declaration under paragraph 4 may restrict the possibility of asking the Court of Justice to give a preliminary ruling to those of its courts against the decisions of which there is no judicial remedy under national law.

6. The Statute of the Court of Justice of the European Community and its Rules of Procedure shall apply. In accordance with those Statutes, any Member State, or the Commission, whether or not it has made a declaration pursuant to paragraph 4, shall be entitled to submit statements of case or written observations to the Court of Justice in cases which arise under paragraph 3.

*Article 13*

**Entry into force**

1. This Convention shall be subject to adoption by the Member States in accordance with their respective constitutional requirements.

2. Member States shall notify the Secretary-General of the Council of the European Union of the completion of the procedures laid down by their respective constitutional requirements for adopting this Convention.

3. This Convention shall enter into force ninety days after the notification, referred to in paragraph 2, by the last Member State to fulfil that formality.

4. Until the entry into force of this Convention, any Member State may, when giving the notification referred to in paragraph 2 or at any time thereafter, declare that this Convention, with the exception of Article 12 thereof, shall apply to it in its relationships with those Member States which have made the same declaration. This Convention shall become applicable in respect of the Member State that makes such a declaration on the first day of the month following the expiry of a period of ninety days after the date of deposit of its declaration.

5. A Member State that has not made any declaration as referred to in paragraph 4 may apply this Convention with respect to the other contracting Member States on the basis of bilateral agreements.

*Article 14*

**Accession of new Member States**

1. This Convention shall be open to accession by any State that becomes a member of the European Union.

2. The text of this Convention in the language of the acceding State, drawn up by the Council of the European Union, shall be authentic.

3. Instruments of accession shall be deposited with the depositary.

4. This Convention shall enter into force with respect to any State acceding to it ninety days after the date of deposit of its instrument of accession or on the date of entry into force of the Convention if it has not already entered into force at the time of expiry of the said period of ninety days.

5. If this Convention has not yet entered into force when the instrument of accession is deposited, Article 13 (4) shall apply to acceding States.

*Article 15*

**Reservations**

1. No reservation shall be authorized with the exception of those provided for in Articles 7 (2) and 10 (2).

2. Any Member State which has entered a reservation may withdraw it at any time in whole or in part by notifying the depositary. Withdrawal shall take effect on the date on which the depositary receives the notification.

*Article 16*

**Depositary**

1. The Secretary-General of the Council of the European Union shall act as depositary of this Convention.

2. The depositary shall publish in the Official Journal of the European Communities information on the progress of adoptions and accessions, declarations and reservations and any other notification concerning this Convention.

# Joint Action 97/372 for the refining of targeting criteria, selection methods, et., and collection of customs and police information, 9 June 1997

[OJ 1997, L 159/1–2]

17. 6. 97 EN Official Journal of the European Communities No L 159/1

*(Acts adopted pursuant to Title VI of the Treaty on European Union)*

**JOINT ACTION**

**of 9 June 1997**

**adopted by the Council on the basis of Article K.3 of the Treaty on European Union, for the refining of targeting criteria, selection methods, et., and collection of customs and police information**

(97/372/JHA)

THE COUNCIL OF THE EUROPEAN UNION,

Having regard to the Treaty establishing the European Community, and in particular Article K.3 (2) (b) thereof,

Having regard to the importance of further improving the effectiveness of action to combat drug trafficking,

Having regard to the report from the Group of Experts on Drugs, approved at the European Council meeting in Madrid in 1995, which included a proposal to refine targeting criteria, selection methods etc., and collection of customs and police information,

Having regard to the Convention of 26 July 1995 on the use of information technology for customs purposes (CIS-Convention) (1),

Having regard to the Joint Action of the Council of 29 November 1996 on the cooperation between customs authorities and business organizations in combating drug trafficking (2),

Having regard to the mandate of the Council of 29 November 1996 on approved revised arrangements for joint customs surveillance operations,

Having regard to the resolution of the Council of 29 November 1996 on the drawing up of police/customs agreements in the fight against drugs (3),

Whereas targeting criteria for controls, structured methods of selection, etc. and the more integrated use of customs and police information are important instruments for efficient planning of law enforcement measures in combating drug trafficking;

Whereas, in the implementation of customs legislation, the use of targeting criteria and structured selection methods is designed to focus customs controls on situations where there is a high risk of drug smuggling, while at the same time allowing speedy customs clearance of legitimate passenger and freight traffic;

Whereas the use of targeting criteria, structured selection methods, etc., enables customs authorities better to set priorities, in such a way that their resources can be applied to the best possible effect;

Whereas European Union and international institutions like EDU/Europol, the World Customs Organization and Interpol play an important role in the exchange of information;

Whereas customs authorities need to be continually adjusting and reassessing their priorities in response to changing circumstances and new information, given that drug smugglers commonly switch their chosen smuggling routes at short notice to borders where, from advance information or otherwise, customs controls are believed to be less intensive,

(1) OJ No C 316, 27. 11. 1995, p. 33.
(2) OJ No L 322, 12. 12. 1996, p. 3.
(3) OJ No C 375, 12. 12. 1996, p. 1.

HAS ADOPTED THIS JOINT ACTION:

*Article 1*

Member States' customs authorities shall strive to optimise the use of targeting criteria and structured selection methods, and collection of customs and police information regarding the combating of drugs trafficking. To this purpose the authorities shall take the following measures within the existing judicial and practical possibilities provided for in Articles 2 to 8.

*Article 2*

Member States' customs authorities shall make more intensive use of information, available from all business sectors concerned, notably the transport sector.

*Article 3*

Member States' customs authorities shall strengthen the mutual exchange of intelligence and information for the purpose of risk analysis. Pending the operational development of the CIS database, Member States' customs authorities shall make greater use of the CIS electronic mailbox system for the aforementioned exchanging of intelligence data.

*Article 4*

Member States' customs authorities shall make greater use of all available European customs information systems regarding sea-, air-, land traffic and others (e. g. AIR-Info, BALKAN-Info, CARGO-Info, MAR-Info, YACHT-Info).

*Article 5*

Member States' customs authorities shall improve targeting procedures by organizing international joint customs surveillance operations as set out in the revised arrangements on this area approved by the Council of 29 November 1996. Participation in such operations by third countries shall be encouraged, where appropriate.

*Article 6*

Member States' customs, police and other law enforcement authorities shall as far as possible intensify mutual exchanges of available intelligence and information. This shall apply at national, European Union and international level and shall also include European Union and international institutions.

*Article 7*

Member States' law enforcement authorities shall, where appropriate, analyse the intelligence and information available.

*Article 8*

Member States' customs authorities shall draw up guidelines for best practice to encourage greater use of risk analysis techniques.

*Article 9*

This Joint Action shall enter into force on the date of its adoption.

*Article 10*

This Joint Action shall be published in the Official Journal.

Done at Luxembourg, 9 June 1997.

*For the Council*

*The President*

G. ZALM

# Convention on mutual assistance and cooperation between customs administrations, 18 December 1997

**[OJ 1998, C 24/1–22; amendment of the text of Article 31 in OJ 2008, L 9/21–22 as of 13 January 2008]**

**Council Act of 18 December 1997 drawing up, on the basis of Article K.3 of the Treaty on European Union, the Convention on mutual assistance and cooperation between customs administrations**

THE HIGH CONTRACTING PARTIES to this Convention, Member States of the European Union,

REFERRING to the Act of the Council of the European Union of 18 December 1997,

RECALLING the need to strengthen the commitments contained in the Convention on mutual assistance between customs administrations, signed in Rome on 7 September 1967,

CONSIDERING that customs administrations are responsible on the customs territory of the Community and, in particular at its points of entry and exit, for the prevention, investigation and suppression of offences not only against Community rules, but also against national laws, in particular the cases covered by Articles 36 and 223 of the Treaty establishing the European Community,

CONSIDERING that a serious threat to public health, morality and security is constituted by the developing trend towards illicit trafficking of all kinds,

CONSIDERING that particular forms of cooperation involving cross-border actions for the prevention, investigation and prosecution of certain infringements of both the national legislation of the Member States and Community customs regulations should be regulated, and that such cross-border actions must always be carried out in compliance with the principles of legality (conforming with the relevant law applicable in the requested Member State and with the Directives of the competent authorities of that Member State), subsidiarity (such actions to be launched only if it is clear that other less significant actions are not appropriate) and proportionality (the scale and duration of the action to be determined in the light of the seriousness of the presumed infringement),

CONVINCED that it is necessary to reinforce cooperation between customs administrations, by laying down procedures under which customs administrations may act jointly and exchange data concerned with illicit trafficking activities,

BEARING IN MIND that the customs administrations in their day-to-day work have to implement both Community and national provisions, and that there is consequently an obvious need to ensure that the provisions of mutual assistance and cooperation in both sectors evolve as far as possible in parallel,

HAVE AGREED ON THE FOLLOWING PROVISIONS:

# TITLE I GENERAL PROVISIONS

*Article 1*

**Scope**

1. Without prejudice to the competences of the Community, the Member States of the European Union shall provide each other with mutual assistance and shall cooperate with one another through their customs administrations, with a view to:

- preventing and detecting infringements of national customs provisions,

and

- prosecuting and punishing infringements of Community and national customs provisions.

2. Without prejudice to Article 3, this Convention shall not affect the provisions applicable regarding mutual assistance in criminal matters between judicial authorities, more favourable provisions in bi-lateral or multilateral agreements between Member States governing cooperation as provided for in paragraph 1 between the customs authorities or other competent authorities of the Member States, or arrangements in the same field agreed on the basis of uniform legislation or of a special system providing for the reciprocal application of measures of mutual assistance.

*Article 2*

**Powers**

The customs administrations shall apply this Convention with the limits of the powers conferred upon them under national provisions. Nothing in this Convention may be construed as affecting the powers conferred under national provisions upon the customs administrations within the meaning of this Convention.

*Article 3*

**Relationship to mutual assistance provided by the judicial authorities**

1. This Convention covers mutual assistance and cooperation in the framework of criminal investigations concerning infringements of national and Community customs provisions, concerning which the applicant authority has jurisdiction on the basis of the national provisions of the relevant Member State.

2. Where a criminal investigation is carried out by or under the direction of a judicial authority, that authority shall determine whether requests for mutual assistance or cooperation in that connection shall be submitted on the basis of the provisions applicable concerning mutual assistance in criminal matters or on the basis of this Convention.

*Article 4*

**Definitions**

For the purposes of this Convention, the following definitions shall apply:

1. 'national customs provisions': all laws, regulations and administrative provisions of a Member State the application of which comes wholly or partly within the juris-diction of the customs administration of the Member State concerning:

- cross-border traffic in goods subject to bans, restrictions or controls, in particular pursuant to Articles 36 and 223 of the Treaty establishing the European Community,
- non-harmonised excise duties;

2. 'Community customs provisions':

- the body of Community provisions and associated implementing provisions governing the import, export, transit and presence of goods traded between Member States and third countries, and between Member States in the case of goods that do not have Community status within the meaning of Article 9(2) of the Treaty establishing the European Community or goods subject to additional controls or investigations for the purposes of establishing their Community status,
- the body of provisions adopted at Community level under the common agricultural policy and the specific provisions adopted with regard to goods resulting from the processing of agricultural products,
- the body of provisions adopted at Community level for harmonised excise duties and for value-added tax on importation together with the national provisions implementing them;

3. 'infringement': acts in conflict with national or Community customs provisions, including, inter alia:

- participation in, or attempts to commit, such infringements,
- participation in a criminal organization committing such infringements,
- the laundering of money deriving from the infringements referred to in this paragraph;

4. 'mutual assistance': the granting of assistance between customs administrations as provided for in this Convention;

5. 'applicant authority': the competent authority of the Member State which makes a request for assistance;

6. 'requested authority': the competent authority of the Member State to which a request for assistance is made;

7. 'customs administrations': Member States' customs authorities as well as other authorities with jurisdiction for implementing the provisions of this Convention;

8. 'personal data': all information relating to an identified or identifiable natural person; a person is considered to be identifiable if he or she can be directly or indirectly identified, inter alia by means of an identification number or of one or more specific elements which are characteristic of his or her physical, physiological, psychological, economic, cultural or social identity;

9. 'cross-border cooperation': cooperation between customs administrations across the borders of each Member State.

*Article 5*

**Central coordinating units**

1. Member States shall appoint in their customs authorities a central unit (coordinating unit). It shall be responsible for receiving all applications for mutual assistance under this Convention and for coordinating mutual assistance, without prejudice to paragraph 2. The unit shall also be responsible for cooperation with other authorities involved in an assistance measure under this Convention. The coordinating units of the Member States shall maintain the necessary direct contact with each other, particularly in the cases covered by Title IV.

2. The activity of the central coordinating units shall not exclude, particularly in an emergency, direct cooperation between other services of the customs authorities of the Member States. For reasons of efficiency and consistency, the central coordinating units shall be informed of any action involving such direct cooperation.

3. If the customs authority is not, or not completely, competent to process a request, the central coordinating unit shall forward the request to the competent national authority and inform the applicant authority that it has done so.

4. If it is not possible to accede to the request for legal or substantive reasons, the coordinating unit shall return the request to the applicant authority with an explanation as to why the request could not be processed.

*Article 6*

**Liaison officers**

1. Member States may make agreements between themselves on the exchange of liaison officers for limited or unlimited periods, and on mutually-agreed conditions.

2. Liaison officers shall have no powers of intervention in the host country.

3. In order to promote cooperation between Member States' customs administrations, liaison officers may, with the agreement or at the request of the competent authorities of the Member States, have the following duties:

(a) promoting and speeding up the exchange of information between the Member States;

(b) providing assistance in investigations which relate to their own Member State or the Member State they represent;

(c) providing support in dealing with requests for assistance;

(d) advising and assisting the host country in preparing and carrying out cross-border operations;

(e) any other duties which Member States may agree between themselves.

4. Member States may agree bilaterally of multilaterally on the terms of reference and the location of the liaison officers. Liaison officers may also represent the interests of one or more Member States.

*Article 7*

**Obligation to prove identity**

Unless otherwise specified in this Convention, officers of the applicant authority present in another Member State in order to exercise the rights laid down in this Convention shall at all times be able to produce written authority stating their identity and their official functions.

## TITLE II ASSISTANCE ON REQUEST

*Article 8*

**Principles**

1. In order to provide the assistance required under this Title, the requested authority or the competent authority which it has addressed shall proceed as though it were acting on its own account or at the request of another authority in its own Member State. In so doing it shall avail itself of all the legal powers at its disposal within the framework of its national law in order to respond to the request.

2. The requested authority shall extend this assistance to all circumstances of the infringement which have any recognisable bearing on the subject of the request for assistance without this requiring any additional request. In case of doubt, the requested authority shall firstly contact the applicant authority.

*Article 9*

**Form and content of the request for assistance**

1. Requests for assistance shall always be made in writing. Documents necessary for the execution of such requests shall accompany the request.

2. Requests pursuant to paragraph 1 shall include the following information:

(a) the applicant authority making the request;

(b) the measure requested;

(c) the object of, and the reason for, the request;

(d) the laws, rules and other legal provisions involved;

(e) indications as exact and comprehensive as possible on the natural or legal persons being the target of the investigations;

(f) a summary of the relevant facts, except in cases provided for in Article 13.

3. Requests shall be submitted in an official language of the Member State of the requested authority or in a language acceptable to such authority.

4. When required because of the urgency of the situation, oral requests shall be accepted, but must be confirmed in writing as soon as possible.

5. If a request does not meet the formal requirements, the requested authority may ask for it to be corrected or completed; measures necessary to comply with the request may be commenced in the meantime.

6. The requested authority shall agree to apply a particular procedure in response to a request, provided that that procedure is not in conflict with the legal and administrative provisions of the requested Member State.

*Article 10*

**Requests for information**

1. At the request of the applicant authority, the requested authority shall communicate to it all information which may enable it to prevent, detect and prosecute infringements.

2. The information communicated is to be accompanied by reports and other documents, or certified copies or extracts of the same, on which that information is based and which are in the possession of the request authority or which were produced or obtained in order to execute the request for information.

3. By agreement between the applicant authority and the requested authority, officers authorised by the applicant authority may, subject to detailed instructions from the requested authority, obtain information pursuant to paragraph 1 from the offices of the requested Member State. This shall apply to all information derived from the documentation to which the staff of those offices have access. Those officers shall be authorised to take copies of the said documentation.

*Article 11*

**Requests for surveillance**

At the request of the applicant authority, the requested authority shall as far as possible keep a special watch or arrange for a special watch to be kept on persons where there are serious grounds for believing that they have infringed Community or national customs provisions or that they are committing or have carried out preparatory acts with a view to the commission of such infringements. At the request of the applicant authority, the requested authority shall also keep a watch on places, means of transport and goods connected with activities which might be in breach of the abovementioned customs provisions.

*Article 12*

**Requests for enquiries**

1. The requested authority shall at the request of the applicant authority carry out, or arrange to have carried out, appropriate enquiries concerning operations which constitute, or appear to the applicant authority to constitute, infringements.

The requested authority shall communicate the results of such enquiries to the applicant authority. Article 10(2) shall apply mutatis mutandis.

2. By agreement between the applicant authority and the requested authority, officers appointed by the applicant authority may be present at the enquiries referred to in paragraph 1. Enquiries shall at all times be carried out by officers of the requested authority. The applicant authority's officers may not, of their own initiative, assume the powers conferred on officers of the requested authority. They shall, however, have access to the same premises and the same documents as the latter, through their intermediary and for the sole purpose of the enquiry being carried out.

*Article 13*

**Notification**

1. At the request of the applicant authority, the requested authority shall, in accordance with the national rules of the Member State in which it is based, notify the addressee or have it notified of all instruments or decisions which emanate from the competent authorities of the Member State in which the applicant authority is based and concern the application of this Convention.

2. Requests for notification, mentioning the subject of the instrument or decision to be notified, shall be accompanied by a translation in the official language or an official language of the Member State in which the requested authority is based, without prejudice to the latter's right to waive such a translation.

*Article 14*

**Use as evidence**

Findings, certificates, information, documents, certified true copies and other papers obtained in accordance with their national law by officers of the requested authority and transmitted to the applicant authority in the cases of assistance provided for in Articles 10 to 12 may be used as evidence in accordance with national law by the competent bodies of the Member State where the applicant authority is based.

## TITLE III SPONTANEOUS ASSISTANCE

*Article 15*

**Principle**

The competent authorities of each Member State shall, as laid down in Articles 16 and 17, subject to any limitations imposed by national law, provide assistance to the competent authorities of the other Member States without prior request.

*Article 16*

**Surveillance**

Where it serves the prevention, detection and prosecution of infringements in another Member State, each Member State's competent authorities shall:

(a) as far as is possible keep, or have kept, the special watch described in Article 11;

(b) communicate to the competent authorities of the other Member States concerned all information in their possession and, in particular, reports and other documents or certified true copies or extracts thereof, concerning operations which are connected with a planned or committed infringement.

*Article 17*

**Spontaneous information**

The competent authorities of each Member State shall immediately send to the competent authorities of the other Member States concerned all relevant information concerning planned or committed infringements and, in particular, information concerning the goods involved and new ways and means of committing such infringements.

*Article 18*

**Use as evidence**

Surveillance reports and information obtained by officers of one Member State and communicated to another Member State in the course of the spontaneous assistance provided for in Articles 15 to 17 may be used in accordance with national law as evidence by the competent bodies of the Member State receiving the information.

## TITLE IV SPECIAL FORMS OF COOPERATION

*Article 19*

**Principles**

1. Customs administrations shall engage in cross-border cooperation in accordance with this Title. They shall provide each other with the necessary assistance in terms of staff and organisational support. Requests for cooperation shall, as a rule, take the form of requests for assistance in accordance with Article 9. In specific cases referred to in this Title, officers of the applicant authority may engage in activities in the territory of the requested State, with the approval of the requested authority.

Coordination and planning of cross-border operations shall be the responsibility of the central coordinating units in accordance with Article 5.

2. Cross-border cooperation within the meaning of paragraph 1 shall be permitted for the prevention, investigation and prosecution of infringements in cases of:

(a) illicit traffic in drugs and psychotropic substances, weapons, munitions, explosive materials, cultural goods, dangerous and toxic waste, nuclear material or materials or equipment intended for the manufacture of atomic, biological and/or chemical weapons (prohibited goods),

(b) trade in substances listed in Tables I and II of the United Nations Convention against illicit traffic in narcotic drugs and psychotropic substances and intended for the illegal manufacture of drugs (precursor substances);

(c) illegal cross-border commercial trade in taxable goods to evade tax or to obtain unauthorised State payments in connection with the import or export of goods, where the extent of the trade and the related risk to taxes and subsidies is such that the potential financial cost to the budget of the European Com-munities or the Member States is considerable;

(d) any other trade in goods prohibited by Community or national rules.

3. The requested authority shall not be obliged to engage in the specific forms of cooperation referred to in this Title if the type of investigation sought is not permitted or not provided for under the national law of the requested Member State. In this case, the applicant authority shall be entitled to refuse, for the same reason, the corresponding type of cross-border cooperation in the reverse case, where it is requested by an authority of the requested Member State.

4. If necessary under the national law of the Member States, the participating authorities shall apply to their judicial authorities for approval of the planned investigations. Where the competent judicial authorities make their approval subject to certain conditions and requirements, the participating authorities shall ensure that those conditions and requirements are observed in the course of the investigations.

5. Where officers of a Member State engage in activities in the territory of another Member State by virtue of this Title and cause damage by their activities, the Member State in whose territory the damage was caused shall make good the damage, in accordance with its national legislation in the same way as it would have done if the damage had been caused by its own officers. That Member State will be reimbursed in full by the Member State whose officers have caused the damage for the amounts it has paid to the victims or to other entitled persons or institutions.

6. Without prejudice to the exercise of its rights vis-à-vis third parties and notwithstanding the obligation to make good damages according to the second sentence of paragraph 5, each Member State shall refrain, in the case provided for in the first sentence of paragraph 5, from requesting reimbursement of the amount of damages it has sustained from another Member State.

7. Information obtained by officers during cross-border cooperation provided for in Articles 20 to 24 may be used, in accordance with national law and subject to particular conditions laid down by the competent authorities of the State in which the information was obtained, as evidence by the competent bodies of the Member State receiving the information.

8. In the course of the operations referred to in Articles 20 to 24, officers on mission in the territory of another Member State shall be treated in the same way as officers of that State as regards infringements committed against them or by them.

*Article 20*

**Hot pursuit**

1. Officers of the customs administration of one of the Member States pursuing in their country, an individual observed in the act of committing one of the infringements referred to in Article 19(2) which could give rise to extradition, or participating in such an infringement, shall be authorised to continue pursuit in the territory of another Member State without prior authorisation where, given the particular urgency of the situation, it was not possible to notify the competent authorities of the other Member State prior to entry into that territory or where these authorities have been unable to reach the scene in time to take the pursuit.

The pursuing officers shall, not later than when they cross the border, contact the competent authorities of the Member State in whose territory the pursuit is to take place. The pursuit shall cease as soon as the Member State in whose territory the pursuit is taking place so requests. At the request of the pursuing officers, the competent authorities of the said Member State shall challenge the pursued person so as to establish his identity or to arrest him. Member States shall inform the depositary of the pursuing officers to whom this provision applies; the depositary shall inform the other Member States.

2. The pursuit shall be carried out in accordance with the following procedures, defined by the declaration provided for in paragraph 6:

(a) the pursuing officers shall not have the right to apprehend;

(b) however, if no request to cease the pursuit is made and if the competent authorities of the Member State in whose territory the pursuit is taking place are unable to intervene quickly enough, the pursuing officers may apprehend the person pursued until the officers of the said Member State, who must be informed without delay, are able to establish his identity or arrest him.

3. Pursuit shall be carried out in accordance with paragraphs 1 and 2 in one of the following ways as defined by the declaration provided for in paragraph 6:

(a) in an area or during a period, as from the crossing of the border, to be established in the declaration;

(b) without limit in space or time.

4. Pursuit shall be subject to the following general conditions:

(a) the pursuing officers shall comply with the provisions of this Article and with the law of the Member State in whose territory they are operating; they shall obey the instructions of the competent authorities of the said Member State;

(b) when the pursuit takes place on the sea, it shall, where it extends to the high sea or the exclusive economic zone, be carried out in conformity with the international law of the sea as reflected in the United Nations Convention on the Law of the Sea, and, when it takes place in the territory of another Member State, it shall be carried out in accordance with the provisions of this Article;

(c) entry into private homes and places not accessible to the public shall be prohibited;

(d) the pursuing officers shall be easily identifiable, either by their uniform or an armband or by means of accessories fitted to their means of transport; the use of civilian clothes combined with the use of unmarked means of transport without the aforementioned identification is prohibited; the pursuing officers shall at all times be able to prove that they are acting in an official capacity;

(e) the pursuing officers may carry their service weapons, save (i) where the requested Member State has made a general declaration that weapons may never be carried into its territory or (ii) where specifically decided otherwise by the requested Member State. When officers of another Member State are permitted to carry their service weapons, their use shall be prohibited save in cases of legitimate self-defence;

(f) once the pursued person has been apprehended as provided for in paragraph 2(b), for the purpose of bringing him before the competent authorities of the Member State in whose territory the pursuit took place he may be subjected only to a security search; handcuffs may be used during his transfer; objects carried by the pursued person may be seized;

(g) after each operation mentioned in paragraphs 1, 2 and 3, the pursuing officers shall present themselves before the competent authorities of the Member State in whose territory they were operating and shall give an account of their mission; at the request of those authorities, they must remain at their disposal until the circumstances of their action have been adequately elucidated; this condition shall apply even where the pursuit has not resulted in the arrest of the pursued person;

(h) the authorities of the Member State from which the pursuing officers have come shall, when requested by the authorities of the Member State in whose territory the pursuit took place, assist the enquiry subsequent to the operation in which they took part, including legal proceedings.

5. A person who, following the action provided for in paragraph 2, has been arrested by the competent authorities of the Member State in whose territory the pursuit took place may, whatever his nationality, be held for questioning. The relevant rules of national law shall apply mutatis mutandis.
If the person is not a national of the Member State in whose territory he was arrested, he shall be released no later than six hours after his arrest, not including the hours between midnight and 9 a.m., unless the competent authorities of the said Member State have previously received a request for his provisional arrest for the purposes of extradition in any form.

6. On signing this convention, each Member State shall make a declaration in which it shall define, on the basis of paragraphs 2, 3 and 4, the procedures for implementing pursuit in its territory.

A Member State may at any time replace its declaration by another declaration, provided the latter does not restrict the scope of the former.

Each declaration shall be made after consultations with each of the Member States concerned and with a view to obtaining equivalent arrangements in those States.

7. Member States may, on a bilateral basis, extend the scope of paragraph 1 and adopt additional provisions in implementation of this Article.

8. When depositing its instruments of adoption of this Convention, a Member State may declare that it is not bound by this Article or by part thereof. Such declaration may be withdrawn at any time.

*Article 21*

**Cross-border surveillance**

1. Officers of the customs administration of one of the Member States who are keeping under observation in their country persons in respect of whom there are serious grounds for believing that they are involved in one of the infringements referred to in Article 19(2) shall be authorised to continue their observation in the territory of another Member State where the latter has authorised cross-border observation in response to a request for assistance which has previously been submitted. Conditions may be attached to the authorisation.

Member States shall inform the depositary of the officers to whom this provision applies; the depositary shall inform the other Member States.

On request, the observation shall be entrusted to officers of the Member State in whose territory it is carried out.

The request referred to in the first subparagraph shall be sent to an authority designated by each of the Member States empowered to grant the requested authorisation or pass on the request.

Member States shall inform the depositary of the authority designated for this purpose; the depositary shall inform the other Member States.

2. Where, for particularly urgent reasons, prior authorisation of the other Member State cannot be requested, the officers conducting the observation shall be authorised to continue beyond the border the observation of persons in respect of whom there are serious grounds for believing that they are involved in one of the infringements referred to in Article 19(2), provided that the following conditions are met:

(a) the competent authorities of the Member State in whose territory the observation is to be continued shall be notified immediately of the crossing of the border, during the observation;

(b) a request submitted in accordance with paragraph 1 and outlining the grounds for crossing the border without prior authorisation shall be submitted without delay.

Observation shall cease as soon as the Member State in whose territory it is taking place so requests, following the notification referred to in (a) or the request referred to in (b), or where authorisation has not been obtained five hours after the border was crossed.

3. The observation referred to in paragraph 1 and 2 shall be carried out only under the following general conditions:

(a) the officers conducting the observation shall comply with the provisions of this Article and with the law of the Member State in whose territory they are operating; they must obey the instructions of the competent authorities of the said Member State;

(b) except in the situations provided for in paragraph 2, the officers shall, during the observation, carry a document certifying that authorisation has been granted;

(c) the officers conducting the observation shall be able at all times to provide proof that they are acting in an official capacity;

(d) the officers conducting the observation may carry their service weapons during the observation save (i) where the requested Member State has made a general declaration that weapons may never be carried into its territory or (ii) where specifically decided otherwise by the requested Member State. When officers of another Member State are permitted to carry their service weapons, their use shall be prohibited save in cases of legitimate self-defence;

(e) entry into private homes and places not accessible to the public shall be prohibited;

(f) the officers conducting the observation may neither challenge nor arrest the person under observation;

(g) all operations shall be the subject of a report to the authorities of the Member State in whose territory they took place; the officers conducting the observation may be required to appear in person;

(h) the authorities of the Member State from which the observing officers have come shall, when requested by the authorities of the Member State in whose territory the observation took place, assist the enquiry subsequent to the operation in which they took part, including legal proceedings.

4. The Member States may, at bilateral level, extend the scope of this Article and adopt additional measures in implementation thereof.

5. When depositing its instruments of adoption of this Convention, a Member State may declare that it is not bound by this Article or by part thereof. Such declaration may be withdrawn at any time.

*Article 22*

**Controlled delivery**

1. Each Member State shall undertake to ensure that, at the request of another Member State, controlled deliveries may be permitted on its territory in the framework of criminal investigations into extraditable offences.

2. The decision to carry out controlled deliveries shall be taken in each individual case by the competent authorities of the requested Member State, with due regard for the national law of that State.

3. Controlled deliveries shall take place in accordance with the procedures of the requested Member State. Competence to act and to direct operations shall lie with the competent authorities of that Member State.

The requested authority shall take over control of the delivery when the goods cross the border or at an agreed hand-over point in order to avoid any interruption of surveillance. During the rest of the journey it shall ensure that the goods are kept permanently under surveillance in such a way that at any time it has the possibility of arresting the perpetrators and seizing the goods.

4. Consignments the controlled delivery of which is agreed to may, with the consent of the Member States concerned, be intercepted and allowed to continue with the initial contents intact or removed or replaced in whole or in part.

*Article 23*

**Covert investigations**

1. At the request of the applicant authority, the requested authority may authorise officers of the customs administration of the requesting Member State or officers acting on behalf of

such administration operating under cover of a false identity (covert investigators) to operate on the territory of the requested Member State. The applicant authority shall make the request only where it would be extremely difficult to elucidate the facts without recourse to the proposed investigative measures. The officers in question shall be authorised in the course of their activities to collect information and make contact with subjects or other persons associated with them.

2. Covert investigations in the requested Member State shall have a limited duration. The preparation and supervision of the investigations shall take place in close cooperation between the relevant authorities of the requested and applicant Member States.

3. The conditions under which a covert investigation is allowed, as well as the conditions under which it is carried out, shall be determined by the requested authority in accordance with its national law. If, in the course of a covert investigation, information is acquired in relation to an infringement other than that covered by the original request, then the conditions concerning the use to which such information may be put shall also be determined by the requested authority in accordance with its national law.

4. The requested authority shall provide the necessary manpower and technical support. It shall take measures to protect the officers referred to in paragraph 1, while they are active in the requested Member State.

5. When depositing its instruments of adoption of this Convention, a Member State may declare that it is not bound by this Article or part thereof. Such declaration may be withdrawn at any time.

*Article 24*

**Joint special investigation teams**

1. By mutual agreement, the authorities of several Member States may set up a joint special investigation team based in a Member State and comprising officers with the relevant specialisations.

The joint special investigation team shall have the following tasks:

- implementation of difficult and demanding investigations of specific infringements, requiring simultaneous, coordinated action in the Member States concerned,
- coordination of joint activities to prevent and detect particular types of infringement and obtain information on the persons involved, their associates and the methods used.

2. Joint special investigation teams shall operate under the following general conditions:

(a) they shall be set up only for a specific purpose and for a limited period;

(b) an officer from the Member State in which the team's activities take place shall head the team;

(c) the participating officers shall be bound by the law of the Member State in whose territory the team's activities take place;

(d) the Member State in which the team's activities take place shall make the necessary organisational arrangements for the team to operate.

3. Membership of the team shall not bestow on officers any powers of intervention in the territory of another Member State.

## TITLE V DATA PROTECTION

*Article 25*

**Data protection for the exchange of data**

1. When information is exchanged, the customs administrations shall take into account in each specific case the requirements for the protection of personal data. They shall respect the relevant provisions of the Convention of the Council of Europe of 28 January 1981 for the protection of individuals with regard to automatic processing of personal data. In the interest of data protection, a Member State may, in accordance with paragraph 2, impose conditions concerning the processing of personal data by another Member State to which such personal data may be passed.

2. Without prejudice to the provisions of the Convention concerning the use of information technology for customs purposes, the following provisions shall apply to personal data which are communicated pursuant to the application of this Convention:

(a) processing of the personal data by the recipient authority shall be authorised only for the purpose referred to in Article 1(1). That authority may forward them, without prior consent from the Member State supplying them, to its customs administrations, its investigative authorities and its judicial bodies to enable them to prosecute and punish infringements within the meaning of Article 4(3). In all other cases of data transmission, the consent of the Member State which supplied the information is necessary;

(b) the authority of the Member State which communicates data shall ensure that they are accurate and up-to-date. If it emerges that inaccurate data have been communicated or data have been communicated which should not have been communicated or that lawfully communicated data are required at a later stage to be erased in accordance with the law of the communicating Member State, the recipient authority shall be immediately informed thereof. It shall be obliged to correct such data or have them erased. If the recipient authority has reason to believe that communicated data are inaccurate or should be erased, it shall inform the communicating Member State;

(c) in cases where communicated data should, according to the law of the communicating Member State, be erased or amended, the persons concerned must be given the effective right to correct the data;

(d) the forwarding and receipt of exchanged data shall be recorded by the authorities concerned;

(e) if so requested, the communicating and recipient authorities shall inform the person concerned, at that person's request, of the personal data communicated and the use to which they are to be put. There is no obligation to provide the information if it is found, on consideration of the matter, that the importance to the public of the information being withheld outweighs the importance to the person concerned of receiving it. Moreover, the right of the person concerned to receive information about the personal data communicated shall be determined in accordance with the national laws, regulations and procedures of the Member State in whose territory the information is requested. Before any decision is taken on providing information, the communicating authority shall be given the opportunity of stating its position;

(f) Member States shall be liable, in accordance with their own laws, regulations and procedures, for injury caused to a person through the processing of data communicated in the Member State concerned. This shall also be the case where the injury was caused by the communication of inaccurate data or the fact that the communicating authority communicated data in violation of the Convention;

(g) the data communicated shall be kept for a period not exceeding that necessary for the purposes for which they were communicated. The need to keep them shall be examined at the appropriate moment by the Member State concerned;

(h) in any event, the data shall enjoy at least the same protection as is given to similar data in the Member State which received them;

(i) every Member State shall take the appropriate measures to ensure compliance with this Article by the application of effective controls. Every Member State may assign the task of control to the national supervisory authority mentioned in Article 17 of the Convention concerning the use of information technology for customs purposes.

3. For the purposes of this Article, 'the processing of personal data` shall be understood in accordance with the definition in Article 2(b) of Directive 95/46/EC of the European Parliament and of the Council of 24 October 1995 on the protection of individuals with regard to the processing of personal data and on the free movement of such data (1).

## TITLE VI INTERPRETATION OF THE CONVENTION

*Article 26*

**Court of Justice**

1. The Court of Justice of the European Communities shall have jurisdiction to rule on any dispute between Member States regarding the interpretation or the application of this Convention whenever it has proved impossible for the dispute to be settled by the Council within six months of its being referred to the Council by one of its members.

2. The Court of Justice of the European Communities shall have jurisdiction to rule on any dispute between Member States and the Commission concerning the interpretation or application of this Convention which it has proved impossible to settle through negotiation. The dispute may be submitted to the Court of Justice after the expiry of a period of six months from the data on which one of the parties notified the other of the existence of a dispute.

3. The Court of Justice shall have jurisdiction, subject to the conditions laid down in paragraphs 4 to 7, to give preliminary rulings on the interpretation of this Convention.

4. By a declaration made at the time of the signing of this Convention or at any time thereafter, any Member State shall be able to accept the jurisdiction of the Court of Justice of the European Communities to give preliminary rulings on the interpretation of this Convention as specified in either paragraph 5(a) or (b).

5. A Member State which has made a declaration pursuant to paragraph 4 shall specify that either:

(a) any court or tribunal of that State against whose decisions there is no judicial remedy under national law may request the Court of Justice of the European Communities to give a preliminary ruling on a question raised in a case pending before it and concerning the interpretation of this Convention if that court or tribunal considers that a decision on the question is necessary to enable it to give judgement, or

(b) any court or tribunal of that State may request the Court of Justice of the European Communities to give a preliminary ruling on a question raised in a case pending before it and concerning the interpretation of this Convention if that court or tribunal considers that a decision on the question is necessary to enable it to give judgment.

6. The Protocol on the Statute of the Court of Justice of the European Communities and the Rules of Procedure of that Court of Justice shall apply.

7. Any Member State, whether or not it has made a declaration pursuant to paragraph 4, shall be entitled to submit statements of case or written observations to the Court in cases which arise under paragraph 5.

8. The Court of Justice shall not have jurisdiction to check the validity or proportionality of operations carried out by competent law enforcement agencies under this Convention nor to rule on the exercise of responsibilities which devolve upon Member States for maintaining law and order and for safeguarding internal security.

## TITLE VII IMPLEMENTATION AND FINAL PROVISIONS

*Article 27*

### Confidentiality

The customs administrations shall take account, in each specific case of exchange of information, of the requirements of investigation secrecy. To that end, a Member State may impose conditions covering the use of information by another Member State to which that information may be passed.

*Article 28*

### Exemptions from the obligation to provide assistance

1. This Convention shall not oblige the authorities of Member States to provide mutual assistance where such assistance would be likely to harm the public policy or other essential interests of the State concerned, particularly in the field of data protection, or where the scope of the action requested, in particular in the context of the special forms of cooperation provided for in Title IV, is obviously disproportionate to the seriousness of the presumed infringement. In such cases, assistance may be refused in whole or in part or made subject to compliance with certain conditions.

2. Reasons must be given for any refusal to provide assistance.

*Article 29*

### Expenses

1. Member States shall normally waive all claims for reimbursement of costs incurred in the implementation of this Convention, with the exception of expenses for fees paid to experts.

2. If expenses of a substantial and extraordinary nature are, or will be, required to execute the request, the customs administrations involved shall consult to determine the terms and conditions under which a request shall be executed as well as the manner in which the costs shall be borne.

*Article 30*

**Reservations**

1. Save as provided in Article 20(8), Article 21(5) and Article 23(5), this Convention shall not be the subject of any reservations.

2. Member States which have already established agreements between them covering matters regulated in Title IV of this Convention may make reservations pursuant to paragraph 1 only in so far as such reservations do not affect their obligations under such agreements.

3. Accordingly, the obligations arising out of the provisions of the Convention of 19 June 1990 implementing the Schengen Agreement of 14 June 1985 on the gradual abolition of checks at their common borders which provide for closer cooperation shall not be affected by this Convention in the context of relations between the Member States which are bound by those provisions.

*Article 31*

**Territorial application**

1. This Convention shall apply to the territories of the Member States as referred to in Article 3(1) of Council Regulation (EEC) No 2913/92 of 12 October 1992 establishing the Community Customs Code (2), as revised by the Act concerning the conditions of accession of the Republic of Austria, the Republic of Finland and the Kingdom of Sweden and the adjustments to the Treaties on which the European Union is founded (3) and in Regulation (EC) No 82/97 of the European Parliament and of the Council of 19 December 1996 (4), including, for the Federal Republic of Germany, the Island of Heligoland and the territory of Büsingen (within the framework of and pursuant to the Treaty of 23 November 1964 between the Federal Republic of Germany and the Swiss Confederation on the inclusion of the commune of Büsingen am Hochrhein in the customs territory of the Swiss Confederation, or the current version thereof) and, for the Italian Republic, the municipalities of Livigno and Campione d'Italia, and to the territorial waters, the inland maritime waters and the airspace of the territories of the Member States.

2. The Council, acting unanimously by the procedure provided for in Title VI of the Treaty on European Union, may adapt paragraph 1 to any amendment of the provisions of Community law referred to therein.

*Article 32*

**Entry into force**

1. This Convention shall be subject to adoption by the Member States in accordance with their respective constitutional requirements.

2. Member States shall notify the depositary of the completion of the constitutional procedures for the adoption of this Convention.

3. This convention shall enter into force 90 days after the notification referred to in paragraph 2 by the State, Member of the European Union at the time of adoption by the Council of the Act drawing up this Convention, which is last to complete that formality.

4. Until this Convention enters into force, any Member State may, when giving the notification referred to in paragraph 2, or at any other later time, declare that as far as it is concerned this Convention, with the exception of Article 23 thereof, shall apply to its relations with Member States that have made the same declaration. Such declarations shall take effect 90 days after the date of deposit thereof.

5. This Convention shall apply only to requests submitted after the date on which it enters into force or is applied as between the requested Member State and the applicant Member State.

6. On the date of entry into force of this Convention, the Convention on the provision of mutual assistance between customs administrations of 7 September 1967 shall be repealed.

*Article 33*

**Accession**

1. This Convention shall be open to accession by any State that becomes a Member State of the European Union.

2. The text of the Convention in the language of the acceding Member State, as drawn up by the Council of the European Union, shall be authentic.

3. The instruments of accession shall be deposited with the depositary.

4. This Convention shall come into force with respect to any State that accedes to it 90 days after the deposit of its instrument of accession or on the date of entry into force of the Convention if it has not already entered into force upon expiry of the said period of 90 days.

5. Where this Convention has not yet entered into force at the time of the deposit of their instrument of accession, Article 32(4) shall apply to acceding Member States.

*Article 34*

**Amendments**

1. Amendments to this Convention may be proposed by any Member State that is a High Contracting Party. Any proposed amendment shall be sent to the depositary, who shall communicate it to the Council and the Commission.

2. Without prejudice to Article 31(2), the amendments to the Convention shall be adopted by the Council, which shall recommend them to the Member States for adoption in accordance with their respective constitutional requirements.

3. Amendments adopted in accordance with paragraph 2 shall come into force in accordance with Article 32(3).

*Article 35*

**Depositary**

1. The Secretary-General of the Council of the European Union shall act as depositary of this Convention.

2. The depositary shall publish in the Official Journal of the European Com-munities information on the progress of adoptions and accessions, implementation, declarations and reservations, and also any other notification concerning this Convention.

ANNEX

DECLARATIONS TO BE ANNEXED TO THE CONVENTION AND PUBLISHED IN THE OFFICIAL JOURNAL

1. Re Articles 1(1) and 28

With reference to the exceptions to the obligation to provide assistance under Article 28 of the Convention, Italy declares that the execution of mutual assistance requests, on the basis of the Convention, concerning infringements which under Italian law are not infringements of national or community customs provisions, may - for reasons relating to the subdivision of competence among domestic authorities in prevention and prosecution of crimes - harm the public policy or other national essential interests.

2. Re Articles 1(2) and 3(2)

Denmark and Finland declare that they interpret the term 'judicial authorities` or 'judicial authority` in Articles 1(2) and 3(2) of the Convention in the sense of their declarations made pursuant to Article 24 of the European Convention on mutual assistance in criminal matters, signed in Strasbourg on 20 April 1959.

3. Re Article 4(3) second indent

Denmark declares, as far as it is concerned, that Article 4(3), second indent, covers only actions by which a person participates in the commission by a group of people, acting toward a common goal, of one or more of the infringements concerned, including situations where the person concerned does not take part in the actual commission of the offence or offences in question; such participation must be based on knowledge of the purpose and general criminal activities of the group, or on knowledge of the group's intention to commit the offence(s) in question.

4. Re Article 4(3), third indent

Denmark declares, as far as it is concerned, that Article 4(3), third indent, applies only to the predicate offences in respect of which at any time receiving stolen goods is punishable under Danish law, including Section 191a of the Danish criminal Code on receiving stolen drugs and Section 284 of the Criminal Code on receiving goods in connection with smuggling of a particularly aggravated nature.

5. Re Article 6(4)

Denmark, Finland and Sweden declare that the liaison officers referred to in Article 6(4) may also represent the interests of Norway and Iceland or vice versa. The five Nordic countries have since 1982 had an arrangement whereby the stationed liaison officers from one of the countries involved also represent the other Nordic countries. This arrangement was made in order to strengthen the fight against drug trafficking and to limit the economic burden imposed on individual countries by the stationing of the liaison officers. Denmark, Finland and Sweden attach great importance to the continuation of this arrangement, which operates well.

6. Re Article 20(8)

Denmark declares that it accepts the provisions of Article 20, subject to the following conditions:

In case of a hot pursuit exercised by the customs authorities of another Member State at sea or through the air, such pursuit may be extended to Danish territory, including Danish territorial waters and the airspace above Danish territory and territorial waters, only if the competent Danish authorities have received prior notice thereof.

7. Re Article 21(5)

Denmark declares that it accepts the provisions of Article 21, subject to the following conditions:

Cross-border surveillance without prior authorisation may be carried out only in accordance with Article 21(2) and (3) if there are serious grounds for believing that the persons under observation are involved in one of the infringements referred to in Article 19(2) which could give rise to extradition.

8. Re Article 25(2)(i)

Member States undertake to keep each other informed in the Council on measures taken to ensure that the commitments referred to in point (i) are observed.

9. Declaration made pursuant to Article 26(4)

At the time of the signing of this Convention, the following declared that they accepted the jurisdiction of the Court of Justice in accordance with the procedures laid down in Article 26(5):

- Ireland in accordance with the procedures laid down in Article 26(5)(a),
- the Federal Republic of Germany, the Hellenic Republic, the Italian Republic and the Republic of Austria in accordance with the procedures laid down in Article 26(5)(b).

DECLARATION

The Federal Republic of Germany, the Italian Republic and the Republic of Austria, reserve the right to make provision in their national law to the effect that, where a question relating to the interpretation of the Convention on mutual assistance and cooperation between customs administrations is raised in a case pending before a national court or tribunal against whose decision there is no judicial remedy under national law, that court or tribunal will be required to refer the matter to the Court of Justice of the European Communities.

# Joint Action 98/427 on good practice in mutual legal assistance in criminal matters, 29 June 1998

[OJ 1998, L 191/1–3]

7. 7. 98 EN Official Journal of the European Communities L 191/1

*(Acts adopted pursuant to Title VI of the Treaty on European Union)*

## JOINT ACTION

### of 29 June 1998

### adopted by the Council on the basis of Article K.3 of the Treaty on European Union, on good practice in mutual legal assistance in criminal matters

(98/427/JHA)

THE COUNCIL OF THE EUROPEAN UNION,

Having regard to the Treaty on European Union, and in particular Article K.3(2)(b) thereof,

Having regard to the Report from the high-level group on organised crime [1] approved by the European Council held at Amsterdam on 16 and 17 June 1997, and in particular Recommendation No 16 of the Report,

Having regard to the results of the seminar on 'Improving judicial cooperation and protecting human rights' held in Luxembourg on 1 and 2 October 1997,

Taking into account the Joint Action 98/428/JHA of 29 June 1998, adopted by the Council on the basis of Article K.3 of the Treaty on European Union, on the creation of a European Judicial Network [2], and in particular Articles 4 and 5 thereof,

Having regard to the European Convention on Mutual Assistance in Criminal Matters of 20 April 1959, other conventions in force in this area and the proposed Convention on mutual assistance in criminal matters between the Member States,

Whereas it is necessary to make further practical improvements regarding mutual legal assistance between the Member States, particularly for the purpose of combating serious crime,

Having examined the views of the European Parliament [3], following consultation carried out by the Presidency in accordance with Article K.6 of the Treaty,

HAS ADOPTED THE FOLLOWING JOINT ACTION:

*Article 1*

**Statements of good practice**

1. Each Member State shall deposit with the General Secretariat of the Council of the European Union within 12 months of the coming into force of this Joint Action a Statement of good practice in executing requests, including transmission of results, from other Member States and sending requests to other Member States for legal assistance in criminal matters.

2. The General Secretariat of the Council shall translate the Statements referred to in Article 1 into the official languages of the Community and circulate the translations to Member States.

3. The Statements by each Member State referred to in paragraph 1 shall, without prejudice to the provisions of the proposed Convention on mutual assistance in criminal matters between the Member States, and subject to the Declaration annexed to this Joint Action, include undertakings to promote the following practices in accordance with its national law and legal procedures:

(a) where requested to do so by the requesting Member State, to acknowledge all requests and written enquiries concerning the execution of requests unless a substantive reply is sent quickly; the requesting Member State may not require an acknowledgment unless the request is marked 'urgent' by that Member State or, in its view, an acknowledgment is necessary in the light of the circumstnaces of the case;

(b) when acknowledging the requests and enquiries referred to in this paragraph, to provide the requesting authority with the name and contact details, including telephone and fax numbers, of the authority, and if possible the person, responsible for executing the request;

(c) to give priority, as far as it is not contrary to the law of the requested Member State, to requests which have clearly been marked 'urgent' by the requesting authority; and to treat requests, whether or not marked 'urgent', no less favourably than comprable enquiries made in the requested Member State on behalf of that Member State's own authorities;

[1] OJ C 251, 15. 8. 1997, p. 1.
[2] See page 4 of this Official Journal.
[3] Opinion delivered on 3 April 1998 (OJ C 138, 4.5.1998).

(d) where the assistance requested cannot be executed in whole or in part, to give the requesting authorities a written or oral report explaining the difficulty and where possible offering to consider jointly with the requesting authority how the difficulty might be overcome;

(e) where it is foreseeable that the assistance cannot, or cannot fully, be provided within any deadline set by the requesting Member State and that this will impair proceedings in the requesting Member State, promptly to give its authority a written or oral report, and any further reports requested by that authority explaining when the assistance requested is likely to be provided;

(f) to submit requests for assistance as soon as the precise assistance needed is identified and, where a request is marked 'urgent' or a deadline is indicated, to explain the reasons for the urgency or deadline; the Statement shall include an undertaking not to mark as 'urgent' requests which are of minor importance;

(g) to ensure that requests are submitted in compliance with the relevant treaty or other international arrangements;

(h) when submitting requests for assistance, to provide the requested authorities with the name and contact details, including telephone and fax numbers, of the authority and, if possible, the person responsible for issuing the request.

4. Each Member State shall bring its Statement to the attention of its judicial or competent authorities, inviting them to promote measures within their competence as may be necessary with a view to its implementation.

5. Any Statement submitted in accordance with this Article may, without prejudice to paragraph 3, be modified at any time by the Member State which made it by means of a further Statement deposited with the General Secretariat of the Council. Any such further Statement shall be for the purposes of further improving good practice in executing requests for legal assistance in criminal matters.

*Article 2*

**Review of performance**

Without prejudice to the mechanism for evaluating the application and implementation at national level of international undertakings in the fight against organised crime, established in Joint Action 97/827/JHA (1), each Member State shall periodically review compliance with its Statements made in accordance with Article 1. The mechanism for such review shall be for each Member State to determine having regard to its own arrangements for legal assistance in criminal matters.

*Article 3*

**European Judicial Network**

The General Secretariat of the Council shall make the Statements referred to in Article 1(1) available to the European Judicial Network as soon as they are deposited. The Network shall take stock of the Statements in the light of its own competencies and experience, and may make any proposals it considers appropriate with a view to improving legal assistance in criminal matters, including finding common methods for evaluation of performance.

*Article 4*

**Review**

The Council shall review this Joint Action in the light of the results of the operation of the mechanism for evaluating the application and implementation at national level of international undertakings in the fight against organised crime, established in Joint Action 97/827/JHA.

*Article 5*

**Entry into force**

This Joint Action shall enter into force on the day of its publication.

*Article 6*

**Publication**

This Joint Action shall be published in the Official Journal.

Done at Luxembourg, 29 June 1998.

*For the Council*

*The President*

R. COOK

(1) OJ L 344, 15. 12. 1997, p. 7.

*ANNEX*

**DECLARATION BY THE FEDERAL REPUBLIC OF GERMANY**

The Federal Republic of Germany states that the German authorities will issue acknowledgements pursuant to Article 1(3)(a) and (b) of the Joint Action on good practice in mutual legal assistance in criminal matters if they are of the opinion that these are appropriate for expediting the execution of the relevant request or the written enquiry.

# Joint Action 98/699 on money laundering, the identification, tracing, freezing, seizing and confiscation of instrumentalities and the proceeds from crime, 3 December 1998

[OJ 1998, L 333/1–3 amended by OJ 2001, L 182/1–2]

*(Acts adopted pursuant to Title VI of the Treaty on European Union)*

**JOINT ACTION**

**of 3 December 1998**

**adopted by the Council on the basis of Article K.3 of the Treaty on European Union, on money laundering, the identification, tracing, freezing, seizing and confiscation of instrumentalities and the proceeds from crime**

(98/699/JHA)

THE COUNCIL OF THE EUROPEAN UNION,

Having regard to the Treaty on European Union and, in particular, Article K.3(2)(b) thereof,

Having regard to the initiative of the United Kingdom,

Having regard to the action plan of the High Level Group on Organised Crime approved by the Amsterdam European Council on 16 and 17 June 1997, and in particular recommendation 26(b) on strengthening the tracing and seizure of the proceeds from crime,

Having examined the views of the European Parliament following the consultation conducted by the Presidency in accordance with Article K.6 of the Treaty on European Union,

Having regard to the Joint Actions of 5 December 1997 establishing a mechanism for evaluating the application and implementation at national level for international undertakings in the fight against organised crime ([1]), and of 19 March 1998, establishing a programme of exchanges, training and cooperation for persons responsible for action to combat organised crime (Falcone Programme) ([2]),

Considering the commitment of Member States of the principles of the Council of Europe Convention on Laundering, Search, Seizure and Confiscation of the Proceeds from Crime 1990,

Having regard to the proposed Joint Action on making it a criminal offence to participate in a criminal organisation in the Member States of the European Union, and in particular to the offences covered by that Joint Action,

Considering the requirements of Council Directive 91/308/EEC of 10 June 1991 on prevention of the use of the financial system for the purpose of money laundering ([3]), and the 40 recommendations to combat money laundering of the Financial Action Task Force on Money Laundering (FATF) as formulated in 1996, and in particular recommendation 4 thereof,

([1]) OJ L 344, 15. 12. 1997, p. 7.
([2]) OJ L 99, 31. 3. 1998, p. 8.
([3]) OJ L 166, 28. 6. 1991, p. 77.

Having regard to the Joint Action of 17 December 1996 concerning the approximation of the laws and practices of the Member States of the European Union to combat drug addiction and to prevent and combat illegal drug trafficking ([4]),

Mindful of the common objective of improving coordination between law enforcement authorities,

Recalling the Joint Action on the creation of a European Judicial Network, adopted by the Council on 29 June 1998 ([5]),

Whereas the potential for disrupting criminal activity in the field of organised crime, by more effective cooperation between Member States in identifying, tracing, freezing or seizing, and confiscating the assets deriving from crime, is being improved;

Whereas mutually compatible practices are making cooperation at European level more efficient at identifying, tracing, freezing or seizing, and confiscating illegal assets;

Whereas recommendation No 16 of the abovementioned action plan to combat organised crime emphasised the need to accelerate procedures for judicial cooperation in matters relating to organised crime, while considerably reducing delay in transmission and responses to requests;

Considering the Member States' adherence to the 1959 European Convention on Mutual Assistance in Criminal Matters;

In the light of the United Nations Convention against Illicit Traffic in Narcotic Drugs and Psychotropic Substances 1988 and the 1998 United Nations General Assembly Special Session on Drugs;

([4]) OJ L 342, 31. 12. 1996, p. 6.
([5]) OJ L 191, 7. 7. 1998, p. 4.

Recognising the achievement of the 1996 Dublin Seminar on asset confiscation in identifying obstacles to effective cooperation;

On the understanding that the forms of cooperation laid down in this Joint Action are without prejudice to other forms of bilateral or multilateral cooperation,

HAS ADOPTED THIS JOINT ACTION:

*Article 1*

[Repealed]

*Article 2*

1. Within the framework of the functioning of the European Judicial Network, each Member State shall prepare a user-friendly guide, including information about where to obtain advice, setting out the assistance it can provide in identifying, tracing, freezing or seizing and confiscating instrumentalities and the proceeds from crime. The guide shall also include any important restrictions on such assistance and the information which requesting States should supply.

2. The General Secretariat of the Council of the European Union shall be sent the guides referred to in paragraph 1 and shall translate them into the official languages of the institutions of the European Community. The General Secretariat shall distribute the guides to Member States, the European Judicial Network and Europol.

3. Each Member State shall ensure that the guide referred to in paragraph 1 is kept up to date and that any changes are sent to the General Secretariat of the Council for translation and distribution in accordance with paragraph 2.

*Article 3*

[Repealed]

*Article 4*

1. Member States shall encourage direct contact between investigators, investigating magistrates and prosecutors of Member States making appropriate use of available cooperation arrangements, to ensure that requests for assistance through formal channels are not made unnecessarily. When a formal request is necessary, the requesting State shall ensure that it is properly prepared and meets all the requirements of the requested State.

2. Where it is not possible to execute a request for assistance in the manner expected by the requesting State, the requested State shall endeavour to satisfy the request in some alternative way, after appropriate consultation with the requesting State, while fully respecting national legislation and international obligations.

3. Member States shall submit requests for assistance as soon as the precise nature of the assistance required is identified and, where a request is marked 'urgent' or a deadline is indicated, explain the reasons for the urgency or deadline.

*Article 5*

[Repealed]

2. Where, in the course of fulfilling a request for legal assistance in one area of a Member State the need arises to pursue further enquiries in another area of that Member State, the Member State shall, where it is not contrary to its law, take all possible steps to enable the necessary assistance to be rendered without the need for preparation of a further letter of request.

3. Where the execution of a request leads to the need to pursue further enquiries on a related issue, and the requesting State issues a supplementary letter of request, the requested State shall, where it is not contrary to its law, take all possible steps to expedite the execution of such a supplementary request.

*Article 6*

1. Member States shall ensure that arrangements are in place to acquaint their judiciary with best practice in international cooperation in the identification, tracing, freezing or seizing, and confiscation of instrumentalities and the proceeds from crime.

2. Member States shall ensure that appropriate training, reflecting best practice, is provided to all investigators, investigating magistrates, prosecutors and other officials concerned with international cooperation in asset identification, tracing, freezing or seizing and confiscation matters.

3. The Presidency and interested Member States, in cooperation as appropriate with the European Judicial Network and Europol, shall as necessary arrange seminars for officials from Member States and other practitioners involved to promote and develop best practice and to encourage compatibility of procedures.

*Article 7*

The Council shall, before the end of 2000, review this Joint Action in the light of the results of the operation of the Joint Action of 5 December 1997 establishing a mechanism for evaluating the application and implementation at national level of international undertakings in the fight against organised crime.

*Article 8*

1. Subject to paragraph 2, Member States shall take all appropriate steps to implement this Joint Ation as soon as it enters into force, and shall ensure that its contents are brought to the attention of their relevant national and local authorities.

[Repealed]

*Article 9*

This Joint Action shall be published in the Official Journal and shall enter into force on the day of its publication.

Done at Brussels, 3 December 1998.

*For the Council*
*The President*
K. SCHLÖGL

# Convention on Mutual Assistance in Criminal Matters between the Member States of the European Union, 29 May 2000

**[OJ 2000, C 197/3–18+23]**

**[Editor's note: signatures omitted]**

12.7.2000 EN Official Journal of the European Communities C 197/3

*ANNEX*

# CONVENTION

## established by the Council in accordance with Article 34 of the Treaty on European Union, on Mutual Assistance in Criminal Matters between the Member States of the European Union

THE HIGH CONTRACTING PARTIES to this Convention, Member States of the European Union,

REFERRING to the Council Act establishing the Convention on Mutual Assistance in Criminal Matters between the Member States of the European Union,

WISHING to improve judicial cooperation in criminal matters between the Member States of the Union, without prejudice to the rules protecting individual freedom,

POINTING OUT the Member States' common interest in ensuring that mutual assistance between the Member States is provided in a fast and efficient manner compatible with the basic principles of their national law, and in compliance with the individual rights and principles of the European Convention for the Protection of Human Rights and Fundamental Freedoms, signed in Rome on 4 November 1950,

EXPRESSING their confidence in the structure and functioning of their legal systems and in the ability of all Member States to guarantee a fair trial,

RESOLVED to supplement the European Convention on Mutual Assistance in Criminal Matters of 20 April 1959 and other Conventions in force in this area, by a Convention of the European Union,

RECOGNISING that the provisions of those Conventions remain applicable for all matters not covered by this Convention,

CONSIDERING that the Member States attach importance to strengthening judicial cooperation, while continuing to apply the principle of proportionality,

RECALLING that this Convention regulates mutual assistance in criminal matters, based on the principles of the Convention of 20 April 1959,

WHEREAS, however, Article 20 of this Convention covers certain specific situations concerning interception of telecommunications, without having any implications with regard to other such situations outside the scope of the Convention,

WHEREAS the general principles of international law apply in situations which are not covered by this Convention,

RECOGNISING that this Convention does not affect the exercise of the responsibilities incumbent upon Member States with regard do the maintenance of law and order and the safeguarding of internal security, and that it is a matter for each Member State to determine, in accordance with Article 33 of the Treaty on European Union, under which conditions it will maintain law and order and safeguard internal security,

HAVE AGREED ON THE FOLLOWING PROVISIONS:

TITLE I

**GENERAL PROVISIONS**

*Article 1*

**Relationship to other conventions on mutual assistance**

1. The purpose of this Convention is to supplement the provisions and facilitate the application between the Member States of the European Union, of:

(a) the European Convention on Mutual Assistance in Criminal Matters of 20 April 1959, hereinafter referred to as the 'European Mutual Assistance Convention';

(b) the Additional Protocol of 17 March 1978 to the European Mutual Assistance Convention;

(c) the provisions on mutual assistance in criminal matters of the Convention of 19 June 1990 implementing the Schengen Agreement of 14 June 1985 on the gradual abolition of checks at common borders (hereinafter referred to as the 'Schengen Implementation Convention') which are not repealed pursuant to Article 2(2);

(d) Chapter 2 of the Treaty on Extradition and Mutual Assistance in Criminal Matters between the Kingdom of Belgium, the Grand Duchy of Luxembourg and the Kingdom of the Netherlands of 27 June 1962, as amended by the Protocol of 11 May 1974, (hereinafter referred to as the 'Benelux Treaty'), in the context of relations between the Member States of the Benelux Economic Union.

2. This Convention shall not affect the application of more favourable provisions in bilateral or multilateral agreements between Member States or, as provided for in Article 26(4) of the European Mutual Assistance Convention, arrangements in the field of mutual assistance in criminal matters agreed on the basis of uniform legislation or of a special system providing for the reciprocal application of measures of mutual assistance in their respective territories.

*Article 2*

**Provisions relating to the Schengen *acquis***

1. The provisions of Articles 3, 5, 6, 7, 12 and 23 and, to the extent relevant to Article 12, of Articles 15 and 16, to the extent relevant to the Articles referred to, of Article 1 constitute measures amending or building upon the provisions referred to in Annex A to the Agreement concluded by the Council of the European Union and the Republic of Iceland and the Kingdom of Norway concerning the latters' association with the implementation, application and development of the Schengen *acquis* [1].

2. The provisions of Articles 49(a), 52, 53 and 73 of the Schengen Implementation Convention are hereby repealed.

*Article 3*

**Proceedings in connection with which mutual assistance is also to be afforded**

1. Mutual assistance shall also be afforded in proceedings brought by the administrative authorities in respect of acts which are punishable under the national law of the requesting or the requested Member State, or both, by virtue of being infringements of the rules of law, and where the decision may give rise to proceedings before a court having jurisdiction in particular in criminal matters.

2. Mutual assistance shall also be afforded in connection with criminal proceedings and proceedings as referred to in paragraph 1 which relate to offences or infringements for which a legal person may be held liable in the requesting Member State.

[1] OJ L 176, 10.7.1999, p. 36.

*Article 4*

**Formalities and procedures in the execution of requests for mutual assistance**

1. Where mutual assistance is afforded, the requested Member State shall comply with the formalities and procedures expressly indicated by the requesting Member State, unless otherwise provided in this Convention and provided that such formalities and procedures are not contrary to the fundamental principles of law in the requested Member State.

2. The requested Member State shall execute the request for assistance as soon as possible, taking as full account as possible of the procedural deadlines and other deadlines indicated by the requesting Member State. The requesting Member State shall explain the reasons for the deadline.

3. If the request cannot, or cannot fully, be executed in accordance with the requirements set by the requesting Member State, the authorities of the requested Member State shall promptly inform the authorities of the requesting Member State and indicate the conditions under which it might be possible to execute the request. The authorities of the requesting and the requested Member State may subsequently agree on further action to be taken concerning the request, where necessary by making such action subject to the fulfilment of those conditions.

4. If it is foreseeable that the deadline set by the requesting Member State for executing its request cannot be met, and if the reasons referred to in paragraph 2, second sentence, indicate explicitly that any delay will lead to substantial impairment of the proceedings being conducted in the requesting Member State, the authorities of the requested Member State shall promptly indicate the estimated time needed for execution of the request. The authorities of the requesting Member State shall promptly indicate whether the request is to be upheld nonetheless. The authorities of the requesting and requested Member States may subsequently agree on further action to be taken concerning the request.

*Article 5*

**Sending and service of procedural documents**

1. Each Member State shall send procedural documents intended for persons who are in the territory of another Member State to them directly by post.

2. Procedural documents may be sent via the competent authorities of the requested Member State only if:

(a) the address of the person for whom the document is intended is unknown or uncertain; or

(b) the relevant procedural law of the requesting Member State requires proof of service of the document on the addressee, other than proof that can be obtained by post; or

(c) it has not been possible to serve the document by post; or

(d) the requesting Member State has justified reasons for considering that dispatch by post will be ineffective or is inappropriate.

3. Where there is reason to believe that the addressee does not understand the language in which the document is drawn up, the document, or at least the important passages thereof, must be translated into (one of) the language(s) of the Member State in the territory of which the addressee is staying. If the authority by which the procedural document was issued knows that the addressee understands only some other language, the document, or at least the important passages thereof, must be translated into that other language.

4. All procedural documents shall be accompanied by a report stating that the addressee may obtain information from the authority by which the document was issued or from other authorities in that Member State regarding his or her rights and obligations concerning the document. Paragraph 3 shall also apply to that report.

5. This Article shall not affect the application of Articles 8, 9 and 12 of the European Mutual Assistance Convention and Articles 32, 34 and 35 of the Benelux Treaty.

*Article 6*

**Transmission of requests for mutual assistance**

1. Requests for mutual assistance and spontaneous exchanges of information referred to in Article 7 shall be made in writing, or by any means capable of producing a written record under conditions allowing the receiving Member State to establish authenticity. Such requests shall be made directly between judicial authorities with territorial competence for initiating and executing them, and shall be returned through the same channels unless otherwise specified in this Article.

Any information laid by a Member State with a view to proceedings before the courts of another Member State within the meaning of Article 21 of the European Mutual Assistance Convention and Article 42 of the Benelux Treaty may be the subject of direct communications between the competent judicial authorities.

2. Paragraph 1 shall not prejudice the possibility of requests being sent or returned in specific cases:

(a) between a central authority of a Member State and a central authority of another Member State; or

(b) between a judicial authority of one Member State and a central authority of another Member State.

3. Notwithstanding paragraph 1, the United Kingdom and Ireland, respectively, may, when giving the notification provided for in Article 27(2), declare that requests and communications to it, as specified in the declaration, must be sent via its central authority. These Member States may at any time by a further declaration limit the scope of such a declaration for the purpose of giving greater effect to paragraph 1. They shall do so when the provisions on mutual assistance of the Schengen Implementation Convention are put into effect for them.

Any Member State may apply the principle of reciprocity in relation to the declarations referred to above.

4. Any request for mutual assistance may, in case of urgency, be made via the International Criminal Police Organisation (Interpol) or any body competent under provisions adopted pursuant to the Treaty on European Union.

5. Where, in respect of requests pursuant to Articles 12, 13 or 14, the competent authority is a judicial authority or a central authority in one Member State and a police or customs authority in the other Member State, requests may be made and answered directly between these authorities. Paragraph 4 shall apply to these contacts.

6. Where, in respect of requests for mutual assistance in relation to proceedings as envisaged in Article 3(1), the competent authority is a judicial authority or a central authority in one Member State and an administrative authority in the other Member State, requests may be made and answered directly between these authorities.

7. Any Member State may declare, when giving the notification provided for in Article 27(2), that it is not bound by the first sentence of paragraph 5 or by paragraph 6 of this Article, or both or that it will apply those provisions only under certain conditions which it shall specify. Such a declaration may be withdrawn or amended at any time.

8. The following requests or communications shall be made through the central authorities of the Member States:

(a) requests for temporary transfer or transit of persons held in custody as referred to in Article 9 of this Convention, in Article 11 of the European Mutual Assistance Convention and in Article 33 of the Benelux Treaty;

(b) notices of information from judicial records as referred to in Article 22 of the European Mutual Assistance Convention and Article 43 of the Benelux Treaty. However, requests for copies of convictions and measures as referred to in Article 4 of the Additional Protocol to the European Mutual Assistance Convention may be made directly to the competent authorities.

12.7.2000 EN Official Journal of the European Communities C 197/7

*Article 7*

**Spontaneous exchange of information**

1. Within the limits of their national law, the competent authorities of the Member States may exchange information, without a request to that effect, relating to criminal offences and the infringements of rules of law referred to in Article 3(1), the punishment or handling of which falls within the competence of the receiving authority at the time the information is provided.

2. The providing authority may, pursuant to its national law, impose conditions on the use of such information by the receiving authority.

3. The receiving authority shall be bound by those conditions.

TITLE II

**REQUEST FOR CERTAIN SPECIFIC FORMS OF MUTUAL ASSISTANCE**

*Article 8*

**Restitution**

1. At the request of the requesting Member State and without prejudice to the rights of *bona fide* third parties, the requested Member State may place articles obtained by criminal means at the disposal of the requesting State with a view to their return to their rightful owners.

2. In applying Articles 3 and 6 of the European Mutual Assistance Convention and Articles 24(2) and 29 of the Benelux Treaty, the requested Member State may waive the return of articles either before or after handling them over to the requesting Member State if the restitution of such articles to the rightful owner may be facilitated thereby. The rights of *bona fide* third parties shall not be affected.

3. In the event of a waiver before handing over the articles to the requesting Member State, the requested Member State shall exercise no security right or other right of recourse under tax or customs legislation in respect of these articles.

A waiver as referred to in paragraph 2 shall be without prejudice to the right of the requested Member State to collect taxes or duties from the rightful owner.

*Article 9*

**Temporary transfer of persons held in custody for purpose of investigation**

1. Where there is agreement between the competent authorities of the Member States concerned, a Member State which has requested an investigation for which the presence of the person held in custody on its own territory is required may temporarily transfer that person to the territory of the Member State in which the investigation is to take place.

2. The agreement shall cover the arrangements for the temporary transfer of the person and the date by which he or she must be returned to the territory of the requesting Member State.

3. Where consent to the transfer is required from the person concerned, a statement of consent or a copy thereof shall be provided promptly to the requested Member State.

4. The period of custody in the territory of the requested Member State shall be deducted from the period of detention which the person concerned is or will be obliged to undergo in the territory of the requesting Member State.

5. The provisions of Articles 11(2) and (3), 12 and 20 of the European Mutual Assistance Convention shall apply *mutatis mutandis* to this Article.

6. When giving the notification provided for in Article 27(2), each Member State may declare that, before an agreement is reached under paragraph 1 of this Article, the consent referred to in paragraph 3 of this Article will be required or will be required under certain conditions indicated in the declaration.

C 197/8 EN Official Journal of the European Communities 12.7.2000

*Article 10*

**Hearing by videoconference**

1. If a person is in one Member State's territory and has to be heard as a witness or expert by the judicial authorities of another Member State, the latter may, where it is not desirable or possible for the person to be heard to appear in its territory in person, request that the hearing take place by videoconference, as provided for in paragraphs 2 to 8.

2. The requested Member State shall agree to the hearing by videoconference provided that the use of the videoconference is not contrary to fundamental principles of its law and on condition that it has the technical means to carry out the hearing. If the requested Member State has no access to the technical means for videoconferencing, such means may be made available to it by the requesting Member State by mutual agreement.

3. Requests for a hearing by videoconference shall contain, in addition to the information referred to in Article 14 of the European Mutual Assistance Convention and Article 37 of the Benelux Treaty, the reason why it is not desirable or possible for the witness or expert to attend in person, the name of the judicial authority and of the persons who will be conducting the hearing.

4. The judicial authority of the requested Member State shall summon the person concerned to appear in accordance with the forms laid down by its law.

5. With reference to hearing by videoconference, the following rules shall apply:

(a) a judicial authority of the requested Member State shall be present during the hearing, where necessary assisted by an interpreter, and shall also be responsible for ensuring both the identification of the person to be heard and respect for the fundamental principles of the law of the requested Member State. If the judicial authority of the requested Member State is of the view that during the hearing the fundamental principles of the law of the requested Member State are being infringed, it shall immediately take the necessary measures to ensure that the hearing continues in accordance with the said principles;

(b) measures for the protection of the person to be heard shall be agreed, where necessary, between the competent authorities of the requesting and the requested Member States;

(c) the hearing shall be conducted directly by, or under the direction of, the judicial authority of the requesting Member State in accordance with its own laws;

(d) at the request of the requesting Member State or the person to be heard the requested Member State shall ensure that the person to be heard is assisted by an interpreter, if necessary;

(e) the person to be heard may claim the right not to testify which would accrue to him or her under the law of either the requested or the requesting Member State.

6. Without prejudice to any measures agreed for the protection of the persons, the judicial authority of the requested Member State shall on the conclusion of the hearing draw up minutes indicating the date and place of the hearing, the identity of the person heard, the identities and functions of all other persons in the requested Member State participating in the hearing, any oaths taken and the technical conditions under which the hearing took place. The document shall be forwarded by the competent authority of the requested Member State to the competent authority of the requesting Member State.

7. The cost of establishing the video link, costs related to the servicing of the video link in the requested Member State, the remuneration of interpreters provided by it and allowances to witnesses and experts and their travelling expenses in the requested Member State shall be refunded by the requesting Member State to the requested Member State, unless the latter waives the refunding of all or some of these expenses.

8. Each Member State shall take the necessary measures to ensure that, where witnesses or experts are being heard within its territory in accordance with this Article and refuse to testify when under an obligation to testify or do not testify according to the truth, its national law applies in the same way as if the hearing took place in a national procedure.

9. Member States may at their discretion also apply the provisions of this Article, where appropriate and with the agreement of their competent judicial authorities, to hearings by videoconference involving an accused person. In this case, the decision to hold the videoconference, and the manner in which the videoconference shall be carried out, shall be subject to agreement between the Member States concerned, in accordance with their national law and relevant international instruments, including the 1950 European Convention for the Protection of Human Rights and Fundamental Freedoms.

Any Member State may, when giving its notification pursuant to Article 27(2), declare that it will not apply the first subparagraph. Such a declaration may be withdrawn at any time.

Hearings shall only be carried out with the consent of the accused person. Such rules as may prove to be necessary, with a view to the protection of the rights of accused persons, shall be adopted by the Council in a legally binding instrument.

*Article 11*

**Hearing of witnesses and experts by telephone conference**

1. If a person is one Member State's territory and has to be heard as a witness or expert by judicial authorities of another Member State, the latter may, where its national law so provides, request assistance of the former Member State to enable the hearing to take place by telephone conference, as provided for in paragraphs 2 to 5.

2. A hearing may be conducted by telephone conference only if the witness or expert agrees that the hearing take place by that method.

3. The requested Member State shall agree to the hearing by telephone conference where this is not contrary to fundamental principles of its law.

4. A request for a hearing by telephone conference shall contain, in addition to the information referred to in Article 14 of the European Mutual Assistance Convention and Article 37 of the Benelux Treaty, the name of the judicial authority and of the persons who will be conducting the hearing and an indication that the witness or expert is willing to take part in a hearing by telephone conference.

5. The practical arrangements regarding the hearing shall be agreed between the Member States concerned. When agreeing such arrangements, the requested Member State shall undertake to:

(a) notify the witness or expert concerned of the time and the venue of the hearing;

(b) ensure the identification of the witness or expert;

(c) verify that the witness or expert agrees to the hearing by telephone conference.

The requested Member State may make its agreement subject, fully or in part, to the relevant provisions of Article 10(5) and (8). Unless otherwise agreed, the provisions of Article 10(7) shall apply *mutatis mutandis.*

*Article 12*

**Controlled deliveries**

1. Each Member State shall undertake to ensure that, at the request of another Member State, controlled deliveries may be permitted on its territory in the framework of criminal investigations into extraditable offences.

2. The decision to carry out controlled deliveries shall be taken in each individual case by the competent authorities of the requested Member State, with due regard for the national law of that Member State.

3. Controlled deliveries shall take place in accordance with the procedures of the requested Member State. The right to act and to direct and control operations shall lie with the competent authorities of that Member State.

*Article 13*

**Joint investigation teams**

1. By mutual agreement, the competent authorities of two or more Member States may set up a joint investigation team for a specific purpose and a limited period, which may be extended by mutual consent, to carry out criminal investigations in one or more of the Member States setting up the team. The composition of the team shall be set out in the agreement.

C 197/10 | EN | Official Journal of the European Communities | 12.7.2000

A joint investigation team may, in particular, be set up where:

(a) a Member State's investigations into criminal offences require difficult and demanding investigations having links with other Member States;

(b) a number of Member States are conducting investigations into criminal offences in which the circumstances of the case necessitate coordinated, concerted action in the Member States involved.

A request for the setting up of a joint investigation team may be made by any of the Member States concerned. The team shall be set up in one of the Member States in which the investigations are expected to be carried out.

2. In addition to the information referred to in the relevant provisions of Article 14 of the European Mutual Assistance Convention and Article 37 of the Benelux Treaty, requests for the setting up of a joint investigation team shall include proposals for the composition of the team.

3. A joint investigation team shall operate in the territory of the Member States setting up the team under the following general conditions:

(a) the leader of the team shall be a representative of the competent authority participating in criminal investigations from the Member State in which the team operates. The leader of the team shall act within the limits of his or her competence under national law;

(b) the team shall carry out its operations in accordance with the law of the Member State in which it operates. The members of the team shall carry out their tasks under the leadership of the person referred to in subparagraph (a), taking into account the conditions set by their own authorities in the agreement on setting up the team;

(c) the Member State in which the team operates shall make the necessary organisational arrangements for it to do so.

4. In this Article, members of the joint investigation team from Member States other than the Member State in which the team operates are referred to as being 'seconded' to the team.

5. Seconded members of the joint investigation team shall be entitled to be present when investigative measures are taken in the Member State of operation. However, the leader of the team may, for particular reasons, in accordance with the law of the Member State where the team operates, decide otherwise.

6. Seconded members of the joint investigation team may, in accordance with the law of the Member State where the team operates, be entrusted by the leader of the team with the task of taking certain investigative measures where this has been approved by the competent authorities of the Member State of operation and the seconding Member State.

7. Where the joint investigation team needs investigative measures to be taken in one of the Member States setting up the team, members seconded to the team by that Member State may request their own competent authorities to take those measures. Those measures shall be considered in that Member State under the conditions which would apply if they were requested in a national investigation.

8. Where the joint investigation team needs assistance from a Member State other than those which have set up the team, or from a third State, the request for assistance may be made by the competent authorities of the State of operations to the competent authorities of the other State concerned in accordance with the relevant instruments or arrangements.

9. A member of the joint investigation team may, in accordance with his or her national law and within the limits of his or her competence, provide the team with information available in the Member State which has seconded him or her for the purpose of the criminal investigations conducted by the team.

10. Information lawfully obtained by a member or seconded member while part of a joint investigation team which is not otherwise available to the competent authorities of the Member States concerned may be used for the following purposes:

(a) for the purposes for which the team has been set up;

(b) subject to the prior consent of the Member State where the information became available, for detecting, investigation and prosecuting other criminal offences. Such consent may be withheld only in cases where such use would endanger criminal investigations in the Member State concerned or in respect of which that Member State could refuse mutual assistance;

(c) for preventing an immediate and serious threat to public security, and without prejudice to subparagraph (b) if subsequently a criminal investigation is opened;

(d) for other purposes to the extent that this is agreed between Member States setting up the team.

11. This Article shall be without prejudice to any other existing provisions or arrangements on the setting up or operation of joint investigation teams.

12. To the extent that the laws of the Member States concerned or the provisions of any legal instrument applicable between them permit, arrangements may be agreed for persons other than representatives of the competent authorities of the Member States setting up the joint investigation team to take part in the activities of the team. Such persons may, for example, include officials of bodies set up pursuant to the Treaty on European Union. The rights conferred upon the members or seconded members of the team by virtue of this Article shall not apply to these persons unless the agreement expressly states otherwise.

*Article 14*

## Covert investigations

1. The requesting and the requested Member State may agree to assist one another in the conduct of investigations into crime by officers acting under covert or false identity (covert investigations).

2. The decision on the request is taken in each individual case by the competent authorities of the requested Member State with due regard to its national law and procedures. The duration of the covert investigation, the detailed conditions, and the legal status of the officers concerned during covert investigations shall be agreed between the Member States with due regard to their national law and procedures.

3. Covert investigations shall take place in accordance with the national law and procedures of the Member States on the territory of which the covert investigation takes place. The Member States involved shall cooperate to ensure that the covert investigation is prepared and supervised and to make arrangements for the security of the officers acting under covert or false identity.

4. When giving the notification provided for in Article 27(2), any Member State may declare that it is not bound by this Article. Such a declaration may be withdrawn at any time.

*Article 15*

## Criminal liability regarding officials

During the operations referred to in Articles 12, 13 and 14, officials from a Member State other than the Member State of operation shall be regarded as officials of the Member State of operation with respect of offences committed against them or by them.

*Article 16*

## Civil liability regarding officials

1. Where, in accordance with Articles 12, 13 and 14, officials of a Member State are operating in another Member State, the first Member State shall be liable for any damage caused by them during their operations, in accordance with the law of the Member State in whose territory they are operating.

2. The Member State in whose territory the damage referred to in paragraph 1 was caused shall make good such damage under the conditions applicable to damage caused by its own officials.

3. The Member State whose officials have caused damage to any person in the territory of another Member State shall reimburse the latter in full any sums it has paid to the victims or persons entitled on their behalf.

4. Without prejudice to the exercise of its rights vis-à-vis third parties and with the exception of paragraph 3, each Member State shall refrain in the case provided for in paragraph 1 from requesting reimbursement of damages it has sustained from another Member State.

TITLE III

**INTERCEPTION OF TELECOMMUNICATIONS**

*Article 17*

**Authorities competent to order interception of telecommunications**

For the purpose of the application of the provisions of Articles 18, 19 and 20, 'competent authority' shall mean a judicial authority, or, where judicial authorities have no competence in the area covered by those provisions, an equivalent competent authority, specified pursuant to Article 24(1)(e) and acting for the purpose of a criminal investigation.

*Article 18*

**Requests for interception of telecommunications**

1. For the purpose of a criminal investigation, a competent authority in the requesting Member State may, in accordance with the requirements of its national law, make a request to a competent authority in the requested Member State for:

(a) the interception and immediate transmission to the requesting Member State of telecommunications; or

(b) the interception, recording and subsequent transmission to the requesting Member State of the recording of telecommunications.

2. Requests under paragraph 1 may be made in relation to the use of means of telecommunications by the subject of the interception, if this subject is present in:

(a) the requesting Member State and the requesting Member State needs the technical assistance of the requested Member State to intercept his or her communications;

(b) the requesting Member State and his or her communications can be intercepted in that Member State;

(c) a third Member State which has been informed pursuant to Article 20(2)(a) and the requesting Member State needs the technical assistance of the requested Member State to intercept his or her communications.

3. By way of derogation from Article 14 of the European Mutual Assistance Convention and Article 37 of the Benelux Treaty, requests under this Article shall include the following:

(a) an indication of the authority making the request;

(b) confirmation that a lawful interception order or warrant has been issued in connection with a criminal investigation;

(c) information for the purpose of identifying the subject of this interception;

(d) an indication of the criminal conduct under investigation;

(e) the desired duration of the interception; and

(f) if possible, the provision of sufficient technical data, in particular the relevant network connection number, to ensure that the request can be met.

4. In the case of a request pursuant to paragraph 2(b), a request shall also include a summary of the facts. The requested Member State may require any further information to enable it to decide whether the requested measure would be taken by it in a similar national case.

5. The requested Member State shall undertake to comply with requests under paragraph 1(a):

(a) in the case of a request pursuant to paragraph 2(a) and 2(c), on being provided with the information in paragraph 3. The requested Member State may allow the interception to proceed without further formality;

12.7.2000 EN Official Journal of the European Communities C 197/13

(b) in the case of a request pursuant to paragraph 2(b), on being provided with the information in paragraphs 3 and 4 and where the requested measure would be taken by it in a similar national case. The requested Member State may make its consent subject to any conditions which would have to be observed in a similar national case.

6. Where immediate transmission is not possible, the requested Member State shall undertake to comply with requests under paragraph 1(b) on being provided with the information in paragraphs 3 and 4 and where the requested measure would be taken by it in a similar national case. The requested Member State may make its consent subject to any condition which would have to be observed in a similar national case.

7. When giving the notification provided for in Article 27(2), any Member State may declare that it is bound by paragraph 6 only when it is unable to provide immediate transmission. In this case the other Member State may apply the principle of reciprocity.

8. When making a request under paragraph 1(b), the requesting Member State may, where it has a particular reason to do so, also request a transcription of the recording. The requested Member State shall consider such requests in accordance with its national law and procedures.

9. The Member State receiving the information provided under paragraphs 3 and 4 shall keep that information confidential in accordance with its national law.

*Article 19*

**Interceptions of telecommunications on national territory by the use of service providers**

1. Member States shall ensure that systems of telecommunications services operated via a gateway on their territory, which for the lawful interception of the communications of a subject present in another Member State are not directly accessible on the territory of the latter, may be made directly accessible for the lawful interception by that Member State through the intermediary of a designated service provider present on its territory.

2. In the case referred to in paragraph 1, the competent authorities of a Member State shall be entitled, for the purposes of a criminal investigation and in accordance with applicable national law and provided that the subject of the interception is present in that Member State, to carry out the interception through the intermediary of a designated service provider present on its territory without involving the Member State on whose territory the gateway is located.

3. Paragraph 2 shall also apply where the interception is carried out upon a request made pursuant to Article 18(2)(b).

4. Nothing in this Article shall prevent a Member State from making a request to the Member State on whose territory the gateway is located for the lawful interception of telecommunications in accordance with Article 18, in particular where there is no intermediary in the requesting Member State.

*Article 20*

**Interception of telecommunications without the technical assistance of another Member State**

1. Without prejudice to the general principles of international law as well as to the provisions of Article 18(2)(c), the obligations under this Article shall apply to interception orders made or authorised by the competent authority of one Member State in the course of criminal investigations which present the characteristics of being an investigation following the commission of a specific criminal offence, including attempts in so far as they are criminalised under national law, in order to identify and arrest, charge, prosecute or deliver judgment on those responsible.

C 197/14 EN Official Journal of the European Communities 12.7.2000

2. Where for the purpose of a criminal investigation, the interception of telecommunications is authorised by the competent authority of one Member State (the 'intercepting Member State'), and the telecommunication address of the subject specified in the interception order is being used on the territory of another Member State (the 'notified Member State') from which no technical assistance is needed to carry out the interception, the intercepting Member State shall inform the notified Member State of the interception:

(a) prior to the interception in cases where it knows when ordering the interception that the subject is on the territory of the notified Member State;

(b) in other cases, immediately after it becomes aware that the subject of the interception is on the territory of the notified Member State.

3. The information to be notified by the intercepting Member State shall include:

(a) an indication of the authority ordering the interception;

(b) confirmation that a lawful interception order has been issued in connection with a criminal investigation;

(c) information for the purpose of identifying the subject of the interception;

(d) an indication of the criminal conduct under investigation; and

(e) the expected duration of the interception.

4. The following shall apply where a Member State is notified pursuant to paragraphs 2 and 3:

(a) Upon receipt of the information provided under paragraph 3 the competent authority of the notified Member State shall, without delay, and at the latest within 96 hours, reply to the intercepting Member State, with a view to:

   (i) allowing the interception to be carried out or to be continued. The notified Member State may make its consent subject to any conditions which would have to be observed in a similar national case;

   (ii) requiring the interception not to be carried out or to be terminated where the interception would not be permissible pursuant to the national law of the notified Member State, or for the reasons specified in Article 2 of the European Mutual Assistance Convention. Where the notified Member State imposes such a requirement, it shall give reasons for its decision in writing,

   (iii) in cases referred to in point (ii), requiring that any material already intercepted while the subject was on its territory may not be used, or may only be used under conditions which it shall specify. The notified Member State shall inform the intercepting Member State of the reasons justifying the said conditions;

   (iv) requiring a short extension, of up to a maximum period of eight days, to the original 96-hour deadline, to be agreed with the intercepting Member State, in order to carry out internal procedures under its national law. The notified Member State shall communicate, in writing, to the intercepting Member State, the conditions which, pursuant to its national law, justify the requested extension of the deadline.

(b) Until a decision has been taken by the notified Member State pursuant to points (i) or (ii) of subparagraph (a), the intercepting Member State:

   (i) may continue the interception; and

   (ii) may not use the material already intercepted, except:

   — if otherwise agreed between the Member States concerned; or

   — for taking urgent measures to prevent an immediate and serious threat to public security. The notified Member State shall be informed of any such use and the reasons justifying it.

(c) The notified Member State may request a summary of the facts of the case and any further information necessary to enable it to decide whether interception would be authorised in a similar national case. Such a request does not affect the application of subparagraph (b), unless otherwise agreed between the notified Member State and the intercepting Member State.

(d) The Member States shall take the necessary measures to ensure that a reply can be given within the 96-hour period. To this end they shall designate contact points, on duty twenty-four hours a day, and include them in their statements under Article 24(1)(e).

5. The notified Member State shall keep the information provided under paragraph 3 confidential in accordance with its national law.

6. Where the intercepting Member State is of the opinion that the information to be provided under paragraph 3 is of a particularly sensitive nature, it may be transmitted to the competent authority through a specific authority where that has been agreed on a bilateral basis between the Member States concerned.

7. When giving its notification under Article 27(2), or at any time thereafter, any Member State may declare that it will not be necessary to provide it with information on interceptions as envisaged in this Article.

*Article 21*

**Responsibility for charges made by telecommunications operators**

Costs which are incurred by telecommunications operators or service providers in executing requests pursuant to Article 18 shall be borne by the requesting Member State.

*Article 22*

**Bilateral arrangements**

Nothing in this Title shall preclude any bilateral or multilateral arrangements between Member States for the purpose of facilitating the exploitation of present and future technical possibilities regarding the lawful interception of telecommunications.

TITLE IV

*Article 23*

**Personal data protection**

1. Personal data communicated under this Convention may be used by the Member State to which they have been transferred:

(a) for the purpose of proceedings to which this Convention applies;

(b) for other judicial and administrative proceedings directly related to proceedings referred to under point (a);

(c) for preventing an immediate and serious threat to public security;

(d) for any other purpose, only with the prior consent of the communicating Member State, unless the Member State concerned has obtained the consent of the data subject.

2. This Article shall also apply to personal data not communicated but obtained otherwise under this Convention.

3. In the circumstances of the particular case, the communicating Member State may require the Member State to which the personal data have been transferred to give information on the use made of the data.

4. Where conditions on the use of personal data have been imposed pursuant to Articles 7(2), 18(5)(b), 18(6) or 20(4), these conditions shall prevail. Where no such conditions have been imposed, this Article shall apply.

5. The provisions of Article 13(10) shall take precedence over this Article regarding information obtained under Article 13.

6. This Article does not apply to personal data obtained by a Member State under this Convention and originating from that Member State.

7. Luxembourg may, when signing the Convention, declare that where personal data are communicated by Luxembourg under this Convention to another Member State, the following applies:

Luxembourg may, subject to paragraph 1(c), in the circumstances of a particular case require that unless that Member State concerned has obtained the consent of the data subject, the personal data may only be used for the purposes referred to in paragraph 1(a) and (b) with the prior consent of Luxembourg in respect of proceedings for which Luxembourg could have refused or limited the transmission or use of the personal data in accordance with the provisions of this Convention or the instruments referred to in Article 1.

If, in a particular case, Luxembourg refuses to give its consent to a request from a Member State pursuant to the provisions of paragraph 1, it must give reasons for its decision in writing.

## TITLE V

## FINAL PROVISIONS

*Article 24*

### Statements

1. When giving the notification referred to in Article 27(2), each Member State shall make a statement naming the authorities which, in addition to those already indicated in the European Mutual Assistance Convention and the Benelux Treaty, are competent for the application of this Convention and the application between the Member States of the provisions on mutual assistance in criminal matters of the instruments referred to in Article 1(1), including in particular:

(a) the competent administrative authorities within the meaning of Article 3(1), if any;

(b) one or more central authorities for the purposes of applying Article 6 as well as the authorities competent to deal with the requests referred to in Article 6(8);

(c) the police or customs authorities competent for the purpose of Article 6(5), if any;

(d) the administrative authorities competent for the purposes of Article 6(6), if any; and

(e) the authority or authorities competent for the purposes of the application of Articles 18 and 19 and Article 20(1) to (5).

2. Statements made in accordance with paragraph 1 may be amended in whole or in part at any time by the same procedure.

*Article 25*

### Reservations

No reservations may be entered in respect of this Convention, other than those for which it makes express provision.

*Article 26*

### Territorial application

The application of this Convention to Gibraltar will take effect upon extension of the European Mutual Assistance Convention to Gibraltar.

The United Kingdom shall notify in writing the President of the Council when it wishes to apply the Convention to the Channel Islands and the Isle of Man following extension of the European Mutual Assistance Convention to those territories. A decision on this request shall be taken by the Council acting with the unanimity of its members.

12.7.2000 EN Official Journal of the European Communities C 197/17

*Article 27*

**Entry into force**

1. This Convention shall be subject to adoption by the Member States in accordance with their respective constitutional requirements.

2. Member States shall notify the Secretary-General of the Council of the European Union of the completion of the constitutional procedures for the adoption of this Convention.

3. This Convention shall, 90 days after the notification referred to in paragraph 2 by the State, member of the European Union at the time of adoption by the Council of the Act establishing this Convention, which is the eighth to complete this formality, enter into force for the eight Member States concerned.

4. Any notification by a Member State subsequent to the receipt of the eighth notification referred to in paragraph 2 shall have the effect that, 90 days after the subsequent notification, this Convention shall enter into force as between this Member State and those Member States for which the Convention has already entered into force.

5. Before the Convention has entered into force pursuant to paragraph 3, any Member State may, when giving the notification referred to in paragraph 2 or at any time thereafter, declare that it will apply this Convention in its relations with Member States which have made the same declaration. Such declarations shall take effect 90 days after the date of deposit thereof.

6. This Convention shall apply to mutual assistance initiated after the date on which it has entered into force, or is applied pursuant to paragraph 5, between the Member States concerned.

*Article 28*

**Accession of new Member States**

1. This Convention shall be open to accession by any State which becomes a member of the European Union.

2. The text of this Convention in the language of the acceding State, drawn up by the Council of the European Union, shall be authentic.

3. The instruments of accession shall be deposited with the depositary.

4. This Convention shall enter into force with respect to any State which accedes to it 90 days after the deposit of its instrument of accession or on the date of entry into force of this Convention if it has not already entered into force at the time of expiry of the said period of 90 days.

5. Where this Convention is not yet in force at the time of the deposit of their instrument of accession, Article 27(5) shall apply to acceding Member States.

*Article 29*

**Entry into force for Iceland and Norway**

1. Without prejudice to Article 8 of the Agreement concluded by the Council of the European Union and the Republic of Iceland and the Kingdom of Norway concerning the latters' association with the implementation, application and development of the Schengen *acquis* (the 'Association Agreement'), the provisions referred to in Article 2(1) shall enter into force for Iceland and Norway 90 days after the receipt by the Council and the Commission of the information pursuant to Article 8(2) of the Association Agreement upon fulfilment of their constitutional requirements, in their mutual relations with any Member State for which this Convention has already entered into force pursuant to Article 27(3) or (4).

2. Any entry into force of this Convention for a Member State after the date of entry into force of the provisions referred to in Article 2(1) for Iceland and Norway, shall render these provisions also applicable in the mutual relations between that Member State and Iceland and Norway.

3. The provisions referred to in Article 2(1) shall in any event not become binding on Iceland and Norway before the date to be fixed pursuant to Article 15(4) of the Association Agreement.

4. Without prejudice to paragraphs 1, 2 and 3 above, the provisions referred to in Article 2(1) shall enter into force for Iceland and Norway not later than on the date of entry into force of this Convention for the fifteenth State, being a member of the European Union at the time of the adoption by the Council of the Act establishing this Convention.

*Article 30*

**Depositary**

1. The Secretary-General of the Council of the European Union shall act as depositary of this Convention.

2. The depositary shall publish in the *Official Journal of the European Communities* information on the progress of adoptions and accessions, statements and reservations and also any other notification concerning this Convention.

12.7.2000 EN Official Journal of the European Communities C 197/23

**Council Declaration on Article 10(9)**

When considering the adoption of an instrument as referred to in Article 10(9), the Council shall respect Member States' obligations under the European Convention on Human Rights.

**Declaration by the United Kingdom on Article 20**

This Declaration shall form an agreed, integral part of the Convention

In the United Kingdom, Article 20 will apply in respect of interception warrants issued by the Secretary of State to the police service or HM Customs & Excise where, in accordance with national law on the interception of communications, the stated purpose of the warrant is the detection of serious crime. It will also apply to such warrants issued to the Security Service where, in accordance with national law, it is acting in support of an investigation presenting the characteristics described in Article 20(1).

# Decision 2000/375 to combat child pornography on the Internet, 29 May 2000

[OJ 2000, L 138/1–4]

9.6.2000 EN Official Journal of the European Communities L 138/1

*(Acts adopted pursuant to Title VI of the Treaty on European Union)*

**COUNCIL DECISION**

**of 29 May 2000**

**to combat child pornography on the Internet**

(2000/375/JHA)

THE COUNCIL OF THE EUROPEAN UNION,

Having regard to the Treaty establishing the European Community, and in particular Article 34(2)(c) thereof,

Having regard to the opinion of the European Parliament (1),

Having regard to the initiative of the Republic of Austria,

Taking account of the resolutions adopted by the European Parliament on 19 September 1996 on minors who are victims of violence (2), 12 December 1996 on measures to protect minors in the European Union (3), 24 April 1997 on the Commission communication on illegal and harmful content on the Internet (4) and 6 November 1997 on the Commission communication on combating child sex tourism, and the *aide-memoire* on the European Union's contribution to reinforcing the prevention of the sexual abuse and exploitation of children (5),

Bearing in mind the Declaration and Agenda for Action, unanimously accepted by delegates at the World Congress against commercial sexual exploitation of children, held in Stockholm in August 1996, and the conclusions and recommendations of the European follow-up conference to the World Congress, held in Strasbourg in April 1998;

Bearing in mind the European Convention for the Protection of Human Rights and Fundamental Freedoms, adopted in Rome on 4 November 1950, and in particular Articles 2, 3 and 10(2) thereof;

Recalling the European Convention on the Exercise of Children's Rights, adopted in Strasbourg on 25 January 1996, and in particular Articles 1, 6, 7, 8, 9, 10, 11, 12 and 15 thereof;

Having regard to the Universal Declaration of Human Rights, adopted by the UN General Assembly in its Resolution 217 A (III) on 10 December 1948 in Paris, and in particular Articles 2, 3, 7, 25 and 26 thereof;

Recalling Article 34 of the Convention on the Rights of the Child of 20 November 1989;

Bearing in mind Council Joint Action 96/700/JHA of 29 November 1996 establishing an incentive and exchange programme for persons responsible for combating trade in human beings and the sexual exploitation of children (6);

Bearing in mind the Resolution of the Council and of the Representatives of the Governments of the Member States, meeting within the Council, of 17 February 1997 on illegal and harmful content on the Internet (7);

Bearing in mind Joint Action 97/154/JHA of 24 February 1997 adopted by the Council concerning action to combat trafficking in human beings and sexual exploitation of children (8);

Bearing in mind the Council decision of 3 December 1998 supplementing the definition of the form of crime 'traffic in human beings' in the Annex to the Europol Convention (9), and having regard to the Declaration of 3 December 1998 approved by the Council;

(1) Opinion delivered on 11 April 2000 (not yet published in the Official Journal).
(2) OJ C 320, 28.10.1996, p. 190.
(3) OJ C 20, 20.1.1997, p. 170.
(4) OJ C 150, 19.5.1997, p. 38.
(5) OJ C 358, 24.11.1997, p. 37.
(6) OJ L 322, 12.12.1996, p. 7.
(7) OJ C 70, 6.3.1997, p. 1.
(8) OJ L 63, 4.3.1997, p. 2.
(9) OJ C 26, 30.1.1999, p. 21.

Taking into account the recommendation adopted by the Council on 24 September 1998 on the development of the competitiveness of the European audiovisual and information services industry by promoting national frameworks aimed at achieving a comparable and effective level of protection of minors and human dignity [1];

Recalling the action plan adopted by the Council on 28 April 1997 to combat organised crime [2], approved by the Amsterdam European Council in June 1997, and the 10 principles of the G8 regarding high-tech crime of which the Council took note at its meeting on 19 March 1998 as well as the recommendation of the European Council in Vienna on 11 and 12 December 1998 to ensure an effective follow-up to the initiatives for the protection of children at European and international level, especially in the area of child pornography in the Internet;

Taking into account Decision No 276/1999/EC of the European Parliament and of the Council of 25 January 1999 adopting a multiannual Community action plan on promoting safer use of the Internet by combating illegal and harmful content on global networks [3];

Recalling Council common position 1999/364/JHA of 27 May 1999 on negotiations relating to the Draft Convention on Cyber Crime held in the Council of Europe on 27 May 1999 [4];

Whereas the traffic in human beings and the sexual exploitation of children constitute a serious infringement of fundamental human rights and in particular of human dignity;

Aware of the fact that the sexual abuse of children and the production, processing, possession and distribution of child pornography material may constitute an important form of international organised crime, the extent of which within the European Union gives cause for ever-increasing concern;

Convinced that respect for the physical and emotional integrity of children and the protection of victims of sexual exploitation are of fundamental importance and must lie at the heart of the Union's concerns;

Aware of the need for further measures by the Union to promote the safe use of the Internet;

In order to prevent and combat the sexual abuse of children and, in particular, the production, processing, distribution and possession of child pornography material through the Internet,

HAS DECIDED AS FOLLOWS:

*Article 1*

1. Within the framework of Decision No 276/1999/EC of the European Parliament and of the Council and in order to intensify measures to prevent and combat the production, processing, possession and distribution of child pornography material and to promote the effective investigation and prosecution of offences in this area, Member States shall take the necessary measures to encourage Internet users to inform law enforcement authorities, either directly or indirectly, on suspected distribution of child pornography material on the Internet, if they come across such material. Internet users shall be made aware of ways to make contact with law enforcement authorities or entities which have privileged links with law enforcement authorities, to enable such authorities to fulfil their task of preventing and combating child pornography on the Internet.

2. Where necessary, and taking account of the administrative structure of each Member State, measures for the promotion of effective investigation and prosecution of offences in this area may be the setting-up of specialised units within law enforcement authorities with the necessary expertise and resources to be able to deal swiftly with information on suspected production, processing, distribution and possession of child pornography.

(1) OJ L 270, 7.10.1998, p. 48.
(2) OJ C 251, 15.8.1997, p. 1.
(3) OJ L 33, 6.2.1999, p. 1.
(4) OJ L 142, 5.6.1999, p. 1.

3. Member States shall ensure that the law enforcement authorities act swiftly when they have received information on suspected production, processing, possession and distribution of child pornography material. Law enforcement authorities may defer taking action if and as long as tactically necessary, for instance with a view to getting at those behind the criminal operations, or at networks (child pornography rings).

*Article 2*

1. Member States shall ensure the widest and speediest possible cooperation to facilitate an effective investigation and prosecution of offences concerning child pornography on the Internet in accordance with existing arrangements and agreements.

2. To ensure a timely and effective response to these offences, Member States shall communicate already established points of contact, which are set up on a 24-hour basis and consist of knowledgeable personnel, as well as the specialised units which are referred to in Article 1(2) and which can be used for exchange of information and for further contacts between Member States. Points of contact, which Member States have already set up for other duties, may also be used for these purposes. Likewise, existing channels for communication, such as Europol and Interpol shall be used.

3. Member States shall ensure that Europol, within the limits of its mandate, is informed of suspected cases of child pornography.

4. Member States, in appropriate cooperation with Europol, shall examine the possibility of organising regular meetings of competent authorities specialising in combating child pornography on the Internet with a view to promoting general information exchanges, analysis of the situation and the coordination of measures in criminal tactics.

5. Each Member State shall notify the General Secretariat of the Council of its organisational unit or units acting as points of contact pursuant to paragraph 2. The General Secretariat shall inform all other Member States of these points of contact.

*Article 3*

Member States shall engage in constructive dialogue with industry and examine appropriate measures, of a voluntary or a legally binding nature, to eliminate child pornography on the Internet. In particular, Member States shall exchange experiences on the effectiveness of any measures they have taken to eliminate child pornography on the Internet. In this context, they shall examine the following measures, which would place Internet providers under a duty:

(a) to advise the competent entities mentioned in Article 1 (1) or the units mentioned in Article 1(2) of child pornography material of which they have been informed or of which they are aware and which is distributed through them;

(b) to withdraw from circulation child pornography material of which they have been informed or of which they are aware and which is distributed through them unless otherwise specified by the competent authorities;

(c) in accordance with the Council resolution of 17 January 1995 on the lawful interception of telecommunications [1] to retain traffic-related data, where applicable and technically feasible — in particular for criminal prosecution purposes in cases of suspected sexual abuse of children, production, processing and distribution of child pornography — for such time as may be specified under the applicable national law, to allow the data to be made available for inspection by the criminal prosecution authorities in accordance with the applicable rules of procedure;

(d) to set up their own control systems for combating the production, processing, possession and distribution of child pornography material.

*Article 4*

Member States shall regularly verify whether technological developments require, in order to maintain the efficiency of the fight against child pornography on the Internet, changes to criminal procedural law, while respecting the fundamental principles thereof and, where necessary, shall initiate appropriate new legislation to that end.

(1) OJ C 329, 4.11.1996, p. 1.

*Article 5*

Member States shall cooperate, in contact with industry, by sharing their experiences and encouraging, as far as possible, the production of filters and other technical means to prevent the distribution of child pornography material and to make possible the detection thereof.

*Article 6*

1. The Council shall examine the extent to which Member States have fulfilled their obligations pursuant to Joint Action 97/154/JHA and the extent to which the measures proposed in this Decision have proved effective.

2. The examination referred to in paragraph 1 shall be carried out under Joint Action 97/827/JHA adopted by the Council on 5 December 1997 establishing a mechanism for evaluating the application and implementation at national level of international undertakings in the fight against organised crime [1], subject to the following:

(a) evaluation teams shall consist of two experts;

(b) on-the-spot evaluation shall be made so as to avoid cumbersome procedures.

3. The assessment specified in Title IV B of Joint Action 97/154/JHA shall not be carried out. It shall be replaced by the evaluation referred to in paragraph 2 of this Article.

4. On the basis of the information received in the course of the evaluation pursuant to paragraph 2, the Council shall examine any further measure it may wish to take in order to make the combating of child pornography and sexual exploitation of children more effective.

*Article 7*

This Decision shall apply to Gibraltar.

*Article 8*

The measures contained in this Decision shall be implemented by the Member States at the latest on 31 December 2000.

Done at Brussels, 29 May 2000.

*For the Council*

*The President*

A. COSTA

(1) OJ L 344, 15.12.1997, p. 7.

# Decision 2000/642 concerning arrangements for cooperation between financial intelligence units of the Member States in respect of exchanging information, 17 October 2000

[OJ 2000, L 271/4–6]

L 271/4 EN Official Journal of the European Communities 24.10.2000

# COUNCIL DECISION

## of 17 October 2000

## concerning arrangements for cooperation between financial intelligence units of the Member States in respect of exchanging information

(2000/642/JHA)

THE COUNCIL OF THE EUROPEAN UNION,

Having regard to the Treaty on European Union, and in particular Article 34(2)(c) thereof,

Having regard to the initiative of the Republic of Finland,

Having regard to the opinion of the European Parliament,

Whereas:

(1) The action plan to combat organised crime was approved by the Amsterdam European Council on 16 to 17 June 1997 [1]. The action plan recommended, in particular in recommendation 26(e), that there should be an improvement in cooperation between contact points competent to receive suspicious transaction reports pursuant to Council Directive 91/308/EEC of 10 June 1991 on prevention of the use of the financial system for the purpose of money laundering [2].

(2) All Member States have set up financial intelligence units (FIUs) to collect and analyse information received under the provisions of Directive 91/308/EEC with the aim of establishing links between suspicious financial transactions and underlying criminal activity in order to prevent and to combat money laundering.

(3) Improvement of the mechanisms for exchanging information between the FIUs is one of the objectives recognised by the Money Laundering Experts' Group set up within the Multidisciplinary Group on Organised Crime, along with an improvement in the exchange of information between FIUs and the investigating authorities in Member States and in the multidisciplinary organisation of FIUs, to incorporate knowledge of the financial, law enforcement and judicial sectors.

(4) The Council conclusions of March 1995 highlighted the fact that the strengthening of systems for combating money laundering depends on closer cooperation between the different authorities involved in fighting it.

(5) The second Commission report to the European Parliament and the Council on the implementation of Directive 91/308/EEC identifies the difficulties which still appear to prevent the communication and exchange of information between certain units having a different legal status.

(6) It is necessary that close cooperation take place between the relevant authorities of the Member States involved in the fight against money laundering and that provision be made for direct communication between those authorities.

(7) Arrangements have already been successfully adopted by Member States in relation to this matter based mainly on the principles laid down in the model memorandum of understanding proposed by the informal worldwide network of FIUs referred to as 'the Egmont Group'.

(8) Member States must organise the FIUs in such a way as to ensure that information and documents are submitted within a reasonable space of time.

(9) This Decision does not affect any Convention or arrangement regarding mutual assistance in criminal matters between judicial authorities,

HAS ADOPTED THIS DECISION:

*Article 1*

1. Member States shall ensure that FIUs, set up or designated to receive disclosures of financial information for the purpose of combating money laundering shall cooperate to assemble, analyse and investigate relevant information within the FIU on any fact which might be an indication of money laundering in accordance with their national powers.

2. For the purposes of paragraph 1, Member States shall ensure that FIUs exchange, spontaneously or on request and either in accordance with this Decision or in accordance with existing or future memoranda of understanding, any available information that may be relevant to the processing or analysis of information or to investigation by the FIU regarding financial transactions related to money laundering and the natural or legal persons involved.

3. Where a Member State has designated a police authority as its FIU, it may supply information held by that FIU to be exchanged pursuant to this Decision to an authority of the receiving Member State designated for that purpose and being competent in the areas mentioned in paragraph 1.

[1] OJ C 251, 15.8.1997, p. 1.
[2] OJ L 166, 28.6.1991, p. 77.

*Article 2*

1. Member States shall ensure that, for the purposes of this Decision, FIUs shall be a single unit for each Member State and shall correspond to the following definition:

'A central, national unit which, in order to combat money laundering, is responsible for receiving (and to the extent permitted, requesting), analysing and disseminating to the competent authorities, disclosures of financial information which concern suspected proceeds of crime or are required by national legislation or regulation'.

2. In the context of paragraph 1, a Member State may establish a central unit for the purpose of receiving or transmitting information to or from decentralised agencies.

3. Member States shall indicate the unit which is an FIU within the meaning of this Article. They shall notify this information to the General Secretariat of the Council in writing. This notification does not affect the current relations concerning cooperation between the FIUs.

*Article 3*

Member States shall ensure that the performance of the functions of the FIUs under this Decision shall not be affected by their internal status, regardless of whether they are administrative, law enforcement or judicial authorities.

*Article 4*

1. Each request made under this Decision shall be accompanied by a brief statement of the relevant facts known to the requesting FIU. The FIU shall specify in the request how the information sought will be used.

2. When a request is made in accordance with this Decision, the requested FIU shall provide all relevant information, including available financial information and requested law enforcement data, sought in the request, without the need for a formal letter of request under applicable conventions or agreements between Member States.

3. An FIU may refuse to divulge information which could lead to impairment of a criminal investigation being conducted in the requested Member State or, in exceptional circumstances, where divulgation of the information would be clearly disproportionate to the legitimate interests of a natural or legal person or the Member State concerned or would otherwise not be in accordance with fundamental principles of national law. Any such refusal shall be appropriately explained to the FIU requesting the information.

*Article 5*

1. Information or documents obtained under this Decision are intended to be used for the purposes laid down in Article 1(1).

2. When transmitting information or documents pursuant to this Decision, the transmitting FIU may impose restrictions and conditions on the use of information for purposes other than those stipulated in paragraph 1. The receiving FIU shall comply with any such restrictions and conditions.

3. Where a Member State wishes to use transmitted information or documents for criminal investigations or prosecutions for the purposes laid down in Article 1(1), the transmitting Member State may not refuse its consent to such use unless it does so on the basis of restrictions under its national law or conditions referred to in Article 4(3). Any refusal to grant consent shall be appropriately explained.

4. FIUs shall undertake all necessary measures, including security measures, to ensure that information submitted under this Decision is not accessible by any other authorities, agencies or departments.

5. The information submitted will be protected, in conformity with the Council of Europe Convention of 28 January 1981 for the Protection of Individuals with regard to Automatic Processing of Personal Data and taking account of Recommendation No R(87)15 of 15 September 1987 of the Council of Europe Regulating the Use of Personal Data in the Police Sector, by at least the same rules of confidentiality and protection of personal data as those that apply under the national legislation applicable to the requesting FIU.

*Article 6*

1. FIUs may, within the limits of the applicable national law and without a request to that effect, exchange relevant information.

2. Article 5 shall apply in relation to information forwarded under this Article.

*Article 7*

Member States shall provide for, and agree on, appropriate and protected channels of communication between FIUs.

*Article 8*

This Decision shall be implemented without prejudice to the Member States' obligations towards Europol, as they have been laid down in the Europol Convention.

*Article 9*

1. To the extent that the level of cooperation between FIUs, as expressed in memoranda of understanding concluded or to be concluded between authorities of the Member States, is compatible with this Decision or goes further than the provisions thereof, it shall remain unaffected by this Decision. Where the provisions of this Decision go further than the provisions of any memorandum of understanding concluded between the authorities of Member States, this Decision shall supersede such memoranda of understanding two years after this Decision takes effect.

2. The Member States shall ensure that they are able to cooperate fully in accordance with the provisions of this Decision at the latest three years after this Decision takes effect.

3. The Council will assess Member States' compliance with this Decision within four years of the date on which it takes effect, and may decide to continue such assessments on a regular basis.

*Article 10*

This Decision shall apply to Gibraltar. To this effect, notwithstanding Article 2, the United Kingdom may notify to the General Secretariat of the Council an FIU in Gibraltar.

*Article 11*

This Decision shall take effect on 17 October 2000.

Done at Luxembourg, 17 October 2000.

*For the Council*

*The President*

É. GUIGOU

# Charter of Fundamental Rights of the European Union, 7 December 2000

[OJ 2010, C 83/391–403]

30.3.2010 EN Official Journal of the European Union C 83/391

The European Parliament, the Council and the Commission solemnly proclaim the following text as the Charter of Fundamental Rights of the European Union.

## CHARTER OF FUNDAMENTAL RIGHTS OF THE EUROPEAN UNION

*Preamble*

The peoples of Europe, in creating an ever closer union among them, are resolved to share a peaceful future based on common values.

Conscious of its spiritual and moral heritage, the Union is founded on the indivisible, universal values of human dignity, freedom, equality and solidarity; it is based on the principles of democracy and the rule of law. It places the individual at the heart of its activities, by establishing the citizenship of the Union and by creating an area of freedom, security and justice.

The Union contributes to the preservation and to the development of these common values while respecting the diversity of the cultures and traditions of the peoples of Europe as well as the national identities of the Member States and the organisation of their public authorities at national, regional and local levels; it seeks to promote balanced and sustainable development and ensures free movement of persons, services, goods and capital, and the freedom of establishment.

To this end, it is necessary to strengthen the protection of fundamental rights in the light of changes in society, social progress and scientific and technological developments by making those rights more visible in a Charter.

This Charter reaffirms, with due regard for the powers and tasks of the Union and for the principle of subsidiarity, the rights as they result, in particular, from the constitutional traditions and international obligations common to the Member States, the European Convention for the Protection of Human Rights and Fundamental Freedoms, the Social Charters adopted by the Union and by the Council of Europe and the case-law of the Court of Justice of the European Union and of the European Court of Human Rights. In this context the Charter will be interpreted by the courts of the Union and the Member States with due regard to the explanations prepared under the authority of the Praesidium of the Convention which drafted the Charter and updated under the responsibility of the Praesidium of the European Convention.

Enjoyment of these rights entails responsibilities and duties with regard to other persons, to the human community and to future generations.

The Union therefore recognises the rights, freedoms and principles set out hereafter.

C 83/392 EN Official Journal of the European Union 30.3.2010

## TITLE I

## DIGNITY

### *Article 1*

**Human dignity**

Human dignity is inviolable. It must be respected and protected.

### *Article 2*

**Right to life**

1. Everyone has the right to life.

2. No one shall be condemned to the death penalty, or executed.

### *Article 3*

**Right to the integrity of the person**

1. Everyone has the right to respect for his or her physical and mental integrity.

2. In the fields of medicine and biology, the following must be respected in particular:

(a) the free and informed consent of the person concerned, according to the procedures laid down by law;

(b) the prohibition of eugenic practices, in particular those aiming at the selection of persons;

(c) the prohibition on making the human body and its parts as such a source of financial gain;

(d) the prohibition of the reproductive cloning of human beings.

### *Article 4*

**Prohibition of torture and inhuman or degrading treatment or punishment**

No one shall be subjected to torture or to inhuman or degrading treatment or punishment.

### *Article 5*

**Prohibition of slavery and forced labour**

1. No one shall be held in slavery or servitude.

2. No one shall be required to perform forced or compulsory labour.

3. Trafficking in human beings is prohibited.

30.3.2010 EN Official Journal of the European Union C 83/393

# TITLE II

## FREEDOMS

### *Article 6*

**Right to liberty and security**

Everyone has the right to liberty and security of person.

### *Article 7*

**Respect for private and family life**

Everyone has the right to respect for his or her private and family life, home and communications.

### *Article 8*

**Protection of personal data**

1. Everyone has the right to the protection of personal data concerning him or her.

2. Such data must be processed fairly for specified purposes and on the basis of the consent of the person concerned or some other legitimate basis laid down by law. Everyone has the right of access to data which has been collected concerning him or her, and the right to have it rectified.

3. Compliance with these rules shall be subject to control by an independent authority.

### *Article 9*

**Right to marry and right to found a family**

The right to marry and the right to found a family shall be guaranteed in accordance with the national laws governing the exercise of these rights.

### *Article 10*

**Freedom of thought, conscience and religion**

1. Everyone has the right to freedom of thought, conscience and religion. This right includes freedom to change religion or belief and freedom, either alone or in community with others and in public or in private, to manifest religion or belief, in worship, teaching, practice and observance.

2. The right to conscientious objection is recognised, in accordance with the national laws governing the exercise of this right.

*Article 11*

**Freedom of expression and information**

1. Everyone has the right to freedom of expression. This right shall include freedom to hold opinions and to receive and impart information and ideas without interference by public authority and regardless of frontiers.

2. The freedom and pluralism of the media shall be respected.

*Article 12*

**Freedom of assembly and of association**

1. Everyone has the right to freedom of peaceful assembly and to freedom of association at all levels, in particular in political, trade union and civic matters, which implies the right of everyone to form and to join trade unions for the protection of his or her interests.

2. Political parties at Union level contribute to expressing the political will of the citizens of the Union.

*Article 13*

**Freedom of the arts and sciences**

The arts and scientific research shall be free of constraint. Academic freedom shall be respected.

*Article 14*

**Right to education**

1. Everyone has the right to education and to have access to vocational and continuing training.

2. This right includes the possibility to receive free compulsory education.

3. The freedom to found educational establishments with due respect for democratic principles and the right of parents to ensure the education and teaching of their children in conformity with their religious, philosophical and pedagogical convictions shall be respected, in accordance with the national laws governing the exercise of such freedom and right.

*Article 15*

**Freedom to choose an occupation and right to engage in work**

1. Everyone has the right to engage in work and to pursue a freely chosen or accepted occupation.

2. Every citizen of the Union has the freedom to seek employment, to work, to exercise the right of establishment and to provide services in any Member State.

3. Nationals of third countries who are authorised to work in the territories of the Member States are entitled to working conditions equivalent to those of citizens of the Union.

*Article 16*

**Freedom to conduct a business**

The freedom to conduct a business in accordance with Union law and national laws and practices is recognised.

*Article 17*

**Right to property**

1. Everyone has the right to own, use, dispose of and bequeath his or her lawfully acquired possessions. No one may be deprived of his or her possessions, except in the public interest and in the cases and under the conditions provided for by law, subject to fair compensation being paid in good time for their loss. The use of property may be regulated by law in so far as is necessary for the general interest.

2. Intellectual property shall be protected.

*Article 18*

**Right to asylum**

The right to asylum shall be guaranteed with due respect for the rules of the Geneva Convention of 28 July 1951 and the Protocol of 31 January 1967 relating to the status of refugees and in accordance with the Treaty on European Union and the Treaty on the Functioning of the European Union (hereinafter referred to as 'the Treaties').

*Article 19*

**Protection in the event of removal, expulsion or extradition**

1. Collective expulsions are prohibited.

2. No one may be removed, expelled or extradited to a State where there is a serious risk that he or she would be subjected to the death penalty, torture or other inhuman or degrading treatment or punishment.

TITLE III

**EQUALITY**

*Article 20*

**Equality before the law**

Everyone is equal before the law.

*Article 21*

**Non-discrimination**

1. Any discrimination based on any ground such as sex, race, colour, ethnic or social origin, genetic features, language, religion or belief, political or any other opinion, membership of a national minority, property, birth, disability, age or sexual orientation shall be prohibited.

2. Within the scope of application of the Treaties and without prejudice to any of their specific provisions, any discrimination on grounds of nationality shall be prohibited.

*Article 22*

**Cultural, religious and linguistic diversity**

The Union shall respect cultural, religious and linguistic diversity.

*Article 23*

**Equality between women and men**

Equality between women and men must be ensured in all areas, including employment, work and pay.

The principle of equality shall not prevent the maintenance or adoption of measures providing for specific advantages in favour of the under-represented sex.

*Article 24*

**The rights of the child**

1. Children shall have the right to such protection and care as is necessary for their well-being. They may express their views freely. Such views shall be taken into consideration on matters which concern them in accordance with their age and maturity.

2. In all actions relating to children, whether taken by public authorities or private institutions, the child's best interests must be a primary consideration.

3. Every child shall have the right to maintain on a regular basis a personal relationship and direct contact with both his or her parents, unless that is contrary to his or her interests.

*Article 25*

**The rights of the elderly**

The Union recognises and respects the rights of the elderly to lead a life of dignity and independence and to participate in social and cultural life.

*Article 26*

**Integration of persons with disabilities**

The Union recognises and respects the right of persons with disabilities to benefit from measures designed to ensure their independence, social and occupational integration and participation in the life of the community.

## TITLE IV

## SOLIDARITY

*Article 27*

**Workers' right to information and consultation within the undertaking**

Workers or their representatives must, at the appropriate levels, be guaranteed information and consultation in good time in the cases and under the conditions provided for by Union law and national laws and practices.

*Article 28*

**Right of collective bargaining and action**

Workers and employers, or their respective organisations, have, in accordance with Union law and national laws and practices, the right to negotiate and conclude collective agreements at the appropriate levels and, in cases of conflicts of interest, to take collective action to defend their interests, including strike action.

*Article 29*

**Right of access to placement services**

Everyone has the right of access to a free placement service.

*Article 30*

**Protection in the event of unjustified dismissal**

Every worker has the right to protection against unjustified dismissal, in accordance with Union law and national laws and practices.

*Article 31*

**Fair and just working conditions**

1. Every worker has the right to working conditions which respect his or her health, safety and dignity.

2. Every worker has the right to limitation of maximum working hours, to daily and weekly rest periods and to an annual period of paid leave.

*Article 32*

**Prohibition of child labour and protection of young people at work**

The employment of children is prohibited. The minimum age of admission to employment may not be lower than the minimum school-leaving age, without prejudice to such rules as may be more favourable to young people and except for limited derogations.

Young people admitted to work must have working conditions appropriate to their age and be protected against economic exploitation and any work likely to harm their safety, health or physical, mental, moral or social development or to interfere with their education.

*Article 33*

**Family and professional life**

1. The family shall enjoy legal, economic and social protection.

2. To reconcile family and professional life, everyone shall have the right to protection from dismissal for a reason connected with maternity and the right to paid maternity leave and to parental leave following the birth or adoption of a child.

*Article 34*

**Social security and social assistance**

1. The Union recognises and respects the entitlement to social security benefits and social services providing protection in cases such as maternity, illness, industrial accidents, dependency or old age, and in the case of loss of employment, in accordance with the rules laid down by Union law and national laws and practices.

2. Everyone residing and moving legally within the European Union is entitled to social security benefits and social advantages in accordance with Union law and national laws and practices.

3. In order to combat social exclusion and poverty, the Union recognises and respects the right to social and housing assistance so as to ensure a decent existence for all those who lack sufficient resources, in accordance with the rules laid down by Union law and national laws and practices.

*Article 35*

**Health care**

Everyone has the right of access to preventive health care and the right to benefit from medical treatment under the conditions established by national laws and practices. A high level of human health protection shall be ensured in the definition and implementation of all the Union's policies and activities.

*Article 36*

**Access to services of general economic interest**

The Union recognises and respects access to services of general economic interest as provided for in national laws and practices, in accordance with the Treaties, in order to promote the social and territorial cohesion of the Union.

*Article 37*

**Environmental protection**

A high level of environmental protection and the improvement of the quality of the environment must be integrated into the policies of the Union and ensured in accordance with the principle of sustainable development.

*Article 38*

**Consumer protection**

Union policies shall ensure a high level of consumer protection.

TITLE V

**CITIZENS' RIGHTS**

*Article 39*

**Right to vote and to stand as a candidate at elections to the European Parliament**

1. Every citizen of the Union has the right to vote and to stand as a candidate at elections to the European Parliament in the Member State in which he or she resides, under the same conditions as nationals of that State.

2. Members of the European Parliament shall be elected by direct universal suffrage in a free and secret ballot.

*Article 40*

**Right to vote and to stand as a candidate at municipal elections**

Every citizen of the Union has the right to vote and to stand as a candidate at municipal elections in the Member State in which he or she resides under the same conditions as nationals of that State.

*Article 41*

**Right to good administration**

1. Every person has the right to have his or her affairs handled impartially, fairly and within a reasonable time by the institutions, bodies, offices and agencies of the Union.

2. This right includes:

(a) the right of every person to be heard, before any individual measure which would affect him or her adversely is taken;

(b) the right of every person to have access to his or her file, while respecting the legitimate interests of confidentiality and of professional and business secrecy;

(c) the obligation of the administration to give reasons for its decisions.

3. Every person has the right to have the Union make good any damage caused by its institutions or by its servants in the performance of their duties, in accordance with the general principles common to the laws of the Member States.

4. Every person may write to the institutions of the Union in one of the languages of the Treaties and must have an answer in the same language.

*Article 42*

**Right of access to documents**

Any citizen of the Union, and any natural or legal person residing or having its registered office in a Member State, has a right of access to documents of the institutions, bodies, offices and agencies of the Union, whatever their medium.

*Article 43*

**European Ombudsman**

Any citizen of the Union and any natural or legal person residing or having its registered office in a Member State has the right to refer to the European Ombudsman cases of maladministration in the activities of the institutions, bodies, offices or agencies of the Union, with the exception of the Court of Justice of the European Union acting in its judicial role.

*Article 44*

**Right to petition**

Any citizen of the Union and any natural or legal person residing or having its registered office in a Member State has the right to petition the European Parliament.

*Article 45*

**Freedom of movement and of residence**

1. Every citizen of the Union has the right to move and reside freely within the territory of the Member States.

2. Freedom of movement and residence may be granted, in accordance with the Treaties, to nationals of third countries legally resident in the territory of a Member State.

*Article 46*

**Diplomatic and consular protection**

Every citizen of the Union shall, in the territory of a third country in which the Member State of which he or she is a national is not represented, be entitled to protection by the diplomatic or consular authorities of any Member State, on the same conditions as the nationals of that Member State.

TITLE VI

**JUSTICE**

*Article 47*

**Right to an effective remedy and to a fair trial**

Everyone whose rights and freedoms guaranteed by the law of the Union are violated has the right to an effective remedy before a tribunal in compliance with the conditions laid down in this Article.

Everyone is entitled to a fair and public hearing within a reasonable time by an independent and impartial tribunal previously established by law. Everyone shall have the possibility of being advised, defended and represented.

Legal aid shall be made available to those who lack sufficient resources in so far as such aid is necessary to ensure effective access to justice.

*Article 48*

**Presumption of innocence and right of defence**

1. Everyone who has been charged shall be presumed innocent until proved guilty according to law.

2. Respect for the rights of the defence of anyone who has been charged shall be guaranteed.

*Article 49*

**Principles of legality and proportionality of criminal offences and penalties**

1. No one shall be held guilty of any criminal offence on account of any act or omission which did not constitute a criminal offence under national law or international law at the time when it was committed. Nor shall a heavier penalty be imposed than the one that was applicable at the time the criminal offence was committed. If, subsequent to the commission of a criminal offence, the law provides for a lighter penalty, that penalty shall be applicable.

2. This Article shall not prejudice the trial and punishment of any person for any act or omission which, at the time when it was committed, was criminal according to the general principles recognised by the community of nations.

3. The severity of penalties must not be disproportionate to the criminal offence.

C 83/402 EN Official Journal of the European Union 30.3.2010

*Article 50*

**Right not to be tried or punished twice in criminal proceedings for the same criminal offence**

No one shall be liable to be tried or punished again in criminal proceedings for an offence for which he or she has already been finally acquitted or convicted within the Union in accordance with the law.

## TITLE VII

## GENERAL PROVISIONS GOVERNING THE INTERPRETATION AND APPLICATION OF THE CHARTER

*Article 51*

**Field of application**

1. The provisions of this Charter are addressed to the institutions, bodies, offices and agencies of the Union with due regard for the principle of subsidiarity and to the Member States only when they are implementing Union law. They shall therefore respect the rights, observe the principles and promote the application thereof in accordance with their respective powers and respecting the limits of the powers of the Union as conferred on it in the Treaties.

2. The Charter does not extend the field of application of Union law beyond the powers of the Union or establish any new power or task for the Union, or modify powers and tasks as defined in the Treaties.

*Article 52*

**Scope and interpretation of rights and principles**

1. Any limitation on the exercise of the rights and freedoms recognised by this Charter must be provided for by law and respect the essence of those rights and freedoms. Subject to the principle of proportionality, limitations may be made only if they are necessary and genuinely meet objectives of general interest recognised by the Union or the need to protect the rights and freedoms of others.

2. Rights recognised by this Charter for which provision is made in the Treaties shall be exercised under the conditions and within the limits defined by those Treaties.

3. In so far as this Charter contains rights which correspond to rights guaranteed by the Convention for the Protection of Human Rights and Fundamental Freedoms, the meaning and scope of those rights shall be the same as those laid down by the said Convention. This provision shall not prevent Union law providing more extensive protection.

4. In so far as this Charter recognises fundamental rights as they result from the constitutional traditions common to the Member States, those rights shall be interpreted in harmony with those traditions.

30.3.2010 EN Official Journal of the European Union C 83/403

5. The provisions of this Charter which contain principles may be implemented by legislative and executive acts taken by institutions, bodies, offices and agencies of the Union, and by acts of Member States when they are implementing Union law, in the exercise of their respective powers. They shall be judicially cognisable only in the interpretation of such acts and in the ruling on their legality.

6. Full account shall be taken of national laws and practices as specified in this Charter.

7. The explanations drawn up as a way of providing guidance in the interpretation of this Charter shall be given due regard by the courts of the Union and of the Member States.

*Article 53*

**Level of protection**

Nothing in this Charter shall be interpreted as restricting or adversely affecting human rights and fundamental freedoms as recognised, in their respective fields of application, by Union law and international law and by international agreements to which the Union or all the Member States are party, including the European Convention for the Protection of Human Rights and Fundamental Freedoms, and by the Member States' constitutions.

*Article 54*

**Prohibition of abuse of rights**

Nothing in this Charter shall be interpreted as implying any right to engage in any activity or to perform any act aimed at the destruction of any of the rights and freedoms recognised in this Charter or at their limitation to a greater extent than is provided for herein.

o

o o

The above text adapts the wording of the Charter proclaimed on 7 December 2000, and will replace it as from the date of entry into force of the Treaty of Lisbon.

# Framework Decision 2001/413 combating fraud and counterfeiting of non-cash means of payment, 28 May 2001

[OJ 2001, L 149/1–4]

2.6.2001 EN Official Journal of the European Communities L 149/1

*(Acts adopted pursuant to Title VI of the Treaty on European Union)*

**COUNCIL FRAMEWORK DECISION**

**of 28 May 2001**

**combating fraud and counterfeiting of non-cash means of payment**

(2001/413/JHA)

THE COUNCIL OF THE EUROPEAN UNION,

Having regard to the Treaty on European Union, and in particular Article 34(2)(b) thereof,

Having regard to the initiative of the Commission [1],

Having regard to the opinion of the European Parliament [2],

Whereas:

(1) Fraud and counterfeiting of non-cash means of payment often operate on an international scale.

(2) The work developed by various international organisations (i.e. the Council of Europe, the Group of Eight, the OECD, Interpol and the UN) is important but needs to be complemented by action of the European Union.

(3) The Council considers that the seriousness and development of certain forms of fraud regarding non-cash means of payment require comprehensive solutions. Recommendation No 18 of the Action Plan to combat organised crime [3], approved by the Amsterdam European Council on 16 and 17 June 1997, as well as point 46 of the Action Plan of the Council and the Commission on how to implement the provisions of the Treaty of Amsterdam on an area of freedom, security and justice [4], approved by the Vienna European Council on 11 and 12 December 1998, call for an action on this subject.

(4) Since the objectives of this Framework Decision, namely to ensure that fraud and counterfeiting involving all forms of non-cash means of payment are recognised as criminal offences and are subject to effective, proportionate and dissuasive sanctions in all Member States cannot be sufficiently achieved by the Member States in view of the international dimension of those offences and can therefore be better achieved at Union level, the Union may adopt measures, in accordance with the principle of subsidiarity as set out in Article 5 of the Treaty establishing the European Community. In accordance with the principle of proportionality, as set out in that Article, this Framework Decision does not go beyond what is necessary in order to achieve those objectives.

(5) This Framework Decision should assist in the fight against fraud and counterfeiting involving non-cash means of payment together with other instruments already agreed by the Council such as Joint Action 98/428/JHA on the creation of a European Judicial Network [5], Joint Action 98/733/JHA on making it a criminal offence to participate in a criminal organisation in the Member States of the European Union [6], Joint Action 98/699/JHA on money laundering, the identification, tracing, freezing, seizing and confiscation of instrumentalities and the proceeds from crime [7], as well as the Decision of 29 April 1999 extending Europol's mandate to deal with forgery of money and means of payment [8].

(6) The Commission submitted to the Council, on 1 July 1998, the Communication entitled 'A framework for action combating fraud and counterfeit of non-cash means of payment' which advocates a Union Policy covering both preventive and repressive aspects of the problem.

(7) The Communication contains a Draft Joint Action which is one element of that comprehensive approach, and constitutes the starting point for this Framework Decision.

(8) It is necessary that a description of the different forms of behaviour requiring criminalisation in relation to fraud and counterfeiting of non-cash means of payment cover the whole range of activities that together constitute the menace of organised crime in this regard.

(9) It is necessary that these forms of behaviour be classified as criminal offences in all Member States, and that effective, proportionate and dissuasive sanctions be provided for natural and legal persons having committed, or being liable for, such offences.

[1] OJ C 376 E, 28.12.1999, p. 20.
[2] OJ C 121, 24.4.2001, p. 105.
[3] OJ C 251, 15.8.1997, p. 1.
[4] OJ C 19, 23.1.1999, p. 1.
[5] OJ L 191, 7.7.1998, p. 4.
[6] OJ L 351, 29.12.1998, p. 1.
[7] OJ L 333, 9.12.1998, p. 1.
[8] OJ C 149, 28.5.1999, p. 16.

(10) By giving protection by penal law primarily to payment instruments that are provided with a special form of protection against imitation or abuse, the intention is to encourage operators to provide that protection to payment instruments issued by them, and thereby to add an element of prevention to the instrument.

(11) It is necessary that Member States afford each other the widest measure of mutual assistance, and that they consult each other when two or more Member States have jurisdiction over the same offence,

HAS ADOPTED THIS FRAMEWORK DECISION:

*Article 1*

**Definitions**

For the purpose of this Framework Decision:

(a) 'Payment instrument' shall mean a corporeal instrument, other than legal tender (bank notes and coins), enabling, by its specific nature, alone or in conjunction with another (payment) instrument, the holder or user to transfer money or monetary value, as for example credit cards, eurocheque cards, other cards issued by financial institutions, travellers' cheques, eurocheques, other cheques and bills of exchange, which is protected against imitation or fraudulent use, for example through design, coding or signature;

(b) 'Legal person' shall mean any entity having such status under the applicable law, except for States or other public bodies in the exercise of State authority and for public international organisations.

*Article 2*

**Offences related to payment instruments**

Each Member State shall take the necessary measures to ensure that the following conduct is a criminal offence when committed intentionally, at least in respect of credit cards, eurocheque cards, other cards issued by financial institutions, travellers cheques, eurocheques, other cheques and bills of exchange:

(a) theft or other unlawful appropriation of a payment instrument;

(b) counterfeiting or falsification of a payment instrument in order for it to be used fraudulently;

(c) receiving, obtaining, transporting, sale or transfer to another person or possession of a stolen or otherwise unlawfully appropriated, or of a counterfeited or falsified payment instrument in order for it to be used fraudulently;

(d) fraudulent use of a stolen or otherwise unlawfully appropriated, or of a counterfeited or falsified payment instrument;

*Article 3*

**Offences related to computers**

Each Member State shall take the necessary measures to ensure that the following conduct is a criminal offence when committed intentionally:

performing or causing a transfer of money or monetary value and thereby causing an unauthorised loss of property for another person, with the intention of procuring an unauthorised economic benefit for the person committing the offence or for a third party, by:

— without right introducing, altering, deleting or suppressing computer data, in particular identification data, or

— without right interfering with the functioning of a computer programme or system.

*Article 4*

**Offences related to specifically adapted devices**

Each Member State shall take the necessary measures to ensure that the following conduct is established as a criminal offence when committed intentionally:

the fraudulent making, receiving, obtaining, sale or transfer to another person or possession of:

— instruments, articles, computer programmes and any other means peculiarly adapted for the commission of any of the offences described under Article 2(b);

— computer programmes the purpose of which is the commission of any of the offences described under Article 3.

*Article 5*

**Participation, instigation and attempt**

Each Member State shall take the necessary measures to ensure that participating in and instigating the conduct referred to in Articles 2, 3 and 4, or attempting the conduct referred to in Article 2(a), (b) and (d) and Article 3, are punishable.

*Article 6*

**Penalties**

Each Member State shall take the necessary measures to ensure that the conduct referred to in Articles 2 to 5 is punishable by effective, proportionate and dissuasive criminal penalties, including, at least in serious cases, penalties involving deprivation of liberty which can give rise to extradition.

*Article 7*

**Liability of legal persons**

1. Each Member State shall take the necessary measures to ensure that legal persons can be held liable for conduct referred to in Article 2(b), (c) and (d) and Articles 3 and 4 committed for their benefit by any person, acting either individually or as part of an organ of the legal person, who has a leading position within the legal person, based on:

— a power of representation of the legal person, or

— an authority to take decisions on behalf of the legal person, or

— an authority to exercise control within the legal person,

as well as for involvement as accessories or instigators in the commission of such an offence.

2. Apart from the cases provided for in paragraph 1, each Member State shall take the necessary measures to ensure that a legal person can be held liable where the lack of supervision or control by a person referred to in paragraph 1 has made possible the commission referred to in Article 2(b), (c) and (d) and Articles 3 and 4 for the benefit of that legal person by a person under its authority.

3. Liability of a legal person under paragraphs 1 and 2 shall not exclude criminal proceedings against natural persons who are perpetrators, instigators or accessories in the conduct referred to in Article 2(b), (c) and (d) and Articles 3 and 4.

*Article 8*

**Sanctions for legal persons**

1. Each Member State shall take the necessary measures to ensure that a legal person held liable pursuant to Article 7(1) is punishable by effective, proportionate and dissuasive sanctions, which shall include criminal or non-criminal fines and may include other sanctions such as:

(a) exclusion from entitlement to public benefits or aid;

(b) temporary or permanent disqualification from the practice of commercial activities;

(c) placing under judicial supervision;

(d) a judicial winding-up order.

2. Each Member State shall take the necessary measures to ensure that a legal person held liable pursuant to Article 7(2) is punishable by effective, proportionate and dissuasive sanctions or measures.

*Article 9*

**Jurisdiction**

1. Each Member State shall take the necessary measures to establish its jurisdiction with regard to the offences referred to in Articles 2, 3, 4 and 5 where the offence has been committed:

(a) in whole or in part within its territory; or

(b) by one of its nationals, provided that the law of that Member State may require the conduct to be punishable also in the country where it occurred; or

(c) for the benefit of a legal person that has its head office in the territory of that Member State.

2. Subject to of Article 10, any Member State may decide that it will not apply, or that it will apply only in specific cases or circumstances, the jurisdiction rule set out in:

— paragraph 1(b);

— paragraph 1(c).

3. Member States shall inform the General Secretariat of the Council accordingly where they decide to apply paragraph 2, where appropriate with an indication of the specific cases or circumstances in which the decision applies.

*Article 10*

**Extradition and prosecution**

1. (a) Any Member State which, under its law, does not extradite its own nationals shall take the necessary measures to establish its jurisdiction over the offences provided for in Articles 2, 3, 4 and 5 when committed by its own nationals outside its territory.

(b) Each Member State shall, when one of its nationals is alleged to have committed, in another Member State, an offence involving the conduct described in Articles 2, 3, 4 or 5, and it does not extradite that person to that other Member State solely on the ground of his nationality, submit the case to its competent authorities for the purpose of prosecution if appropriate. In order to enable prosecution to take place, the files, information and exhibits relating to the offence shall be forwarded in accordance with the procedures laid down in Article 6(2) of the European Convention on Extradition of 13 December 1957. The requesting Member State shall be informed of the prosecution initiated and of its outcome.

2. For the purpose of this Article, a 'national' of a Member State shall be construed in accordance with any declaration made by that State under Article 6(1)(b) and (c) of the European Convention on Extradition.

*Article 11*

**Cooperation between Member States**

1. In accordance with the applicable conventions, multilateral or bilateral agreements or arrangements, Member States shall afford each other the widest measure of mutual assistance in respect of proceedings relating to the offences provided for in this Framework Decision.

2. Where several Member States have jurisdiction in respect of offences envisaged by this Framework Decision, they shall consult one another with a view to coordinating their action in order to prosecute effectively.

*Article 12*

**Exchange of information**

1. Member States shall designate operational contact points or may use existing operational structures for the exchange of information and for other contacts between Member States for the purposes of applying this Framework Decision.

2. Each Member State shall inform the General Secretariat of the Council and the Commission of its department or departments acting as contact points in accordance with paragraph 1. The General Secretariat shall notify the other Member States of these contact points.

*Article 13*

**Territorial application**

This Framework Decision shall apply to Gibraltar.

*Article 14*

**Implementation**

1. Member States shall bring into force the measures necessary to comply with this Framework Decision by 2 June 2003.

2. By 2 June 2003, Member States shall forward to the General Secretariat of the Council and to the Commission the text of the provisions transposing into their national law the obligations imposed upon them under this Framework Decision. The Council shall, by 2 September 2003, on the basis of a report established on the basis of this information and a written report by the Commission, assess the extent to which Member States have taken the necessary measures in order to comply with this Framework Decision.

*Article 15*

**Entry into force**

This Framework Decision shall enter into force on the date of its publication in the *Official Journal of the European Communities.*

Done at Brussels, 28 May 2001.

*For the Council*

*The President*

T. BODSTRÖM

# Framework Decision 2001/500 on money laundering, the identification, tracing, freezing, seizing and confiscation of instrumentalities and the proceeds of crime, 26 June 2001

**[OJ 2001, L 182/1–2]**

5.7.2001 EN Official Journal of the European Communities L 182/1

*(Acts adopted pursuant to Title VI of the Treaty on European Union)*

**COUNCIL FRAMEWORK DECISION**

**of 26 June 2001**

**on money laundering, the identification, tracing, freezing, seizing and confiscation of instrumentalities and the proceeds of crime**

(2001/500/JHA)

THE COUNCIL OF THE EUROPEAN UNION,

Having regard to the Treaty on European Union, and in particular Article 31(a), (c) and (e) and Article 34(2)(b) thereof,

Having regard to the initiative of the French Republic,

Having regard to the opinion of the European Parliament,

Whereas:

(1) On 3 December 1998 the Council adopted Joint Action 98/699/JHA on money laundering, the identification, tracing, freezing, seizing and confiscation of instrumentalities and the proceeds from crime [1].

(2) Account should be taken of the Presidency conclusions of the European Council meeting in Tampere on 15 and 16 October 1999, and of the Presidency conclusions of the European Council meeting in Vienna on 11 and 12 December 1998.

(3) The European Council, noting that serious forms of crime increasingly have tax and duty aspects, calls on Member States to provide full mutual legal assistance in the investigation and prosecution of this type of crime.

(4) The European Council calls for the approximation of criminal law and procedures on money laundering (in particular, confiscating funds), adding that the scope of criminal activities which constitute principal offences for money laundering should be uniform and sufficiently broad in all Member States.

(5) The European Council in Tampere considered that, with regard to national criminal law, efforts to agree on common definitions, incriminations and sanctions should be focused in the first instance on a limited number of sectors of particular relevance, such as financial crime.

(6) The European Council in Tampere noted that money laundering is at the very heart of organised crime and should be rooted out wherever it occurs. The European Council is determined to ensure that concrete steps are taken to trace, freeze, seize and confiscate the proceeds of crime.

(7) Member States have subscribed to the principles of the 1990 Council of Europe Convention on Laundering, Search, Seizure and Confiscation of the Proceeds from Crime, hereinafter referred to as 'the 1990 Convention',

HAS ADOPTED THIS FRAMEWORK DECISION:

*Article 1*

**Reservations in respect of the 1990 Convention**

In order to enhance action against organised crime, Member States shall take the necessary steps not to make or uphold reservations in respect of the following articles of the 1990 Convention:

(a) Article 2, in so far as the offence is punishable by deprivation of liberty or a detention order for a maximum of more than one year.

However, Member States may uphold reservations on Article 2 of the 1990 Convention in respect of the confiscation of the proceeds from tax offences for the sole purpose of their being able to confiscate such proceeds, both nationally and through international cooperation, under national, Community and international tax-debt recovery legislation;

(b) Article 6, in so far as serious offences are concerned. Such offences shall in any event include offences which are punishable by deprivation of liberty or a detention order for a maximum of more than one year or, as regards those States which have a minimum threshold for offences in their legal system, offences punishable by deprivation of liberty or a detention order for a minimum of more than six months.

[1] OJ L 333, 9.12.1998, p. 1.

L 182/2 EN Official Journal of the European Communities 5.7.2001

*Article 2*

**Penalties**

Each Member State shall take the necessary steps consistent with its system of penalties to ensure that the offences referred to in Article 6(1)(a) and (b) of the 1990 Convention, as they result from the Article 1(b) of this framework Decision, are punishable by deprivation of liberty for a maximum of not less than 4 years.

*Article 3*

**Value confiscation**

Each Member State shall take the necessary steps to ensure that its legislation and procedures on the confiscation of the proceeds of crime also allow, at least in cases where these proceeds cannot be seized, for the confiscation of property the value of which corresponds to such proceeds, both in purely domestic proceedings and in proceedings instituted at the request of another Member State, including requests for the enforcement of foreign confiscation orders. However, Member States may exclude the confiscation of property the value of which corresponds to the proceeds of crime in cases in which that value would be less than EUR 4 000.

The words 'property', 'proceeds' and 'confiscation' shall have the same meaning as in Article 1 of the 1990 Convention.

*Article 4*

**Processing of requests for mutual assistance**

Member States shall take the necessary steps to ensure that all requests from other Member States which relate to asset identification, tracing, freezing or seizing and confiscation are processed with the same priority as is given to such measures in domestic proceedings.

*Article 5*

**Repeal of existing provisions**

Articles 1, 3, 5(1) and 8(2) of Joint Action 98/699/JHA are hereby repealed.

*Article 6*

**Implementation**

1. Member States shall adopt the measures necessary to comply with the provisions of this framework Decision by 31 December 2002.

2. By 1 March 2003, Member States shall forward to the General Secretariat of the Council and to the Commission the text of the provisions transposing into their national law the obligations arising for them from this framework Decision and, where appropriate, the notifications made pursuant to Article 40(2) of the 1990 Convention. On the basis of this information and a written report from the Commission, the Council shall ascertain, by 31 December 2003, to what extent Member States have taken the measures necessary to comply with this framework Decision.

*Article 7*

**Territorial application**

This framework Decision shall apply to Gibraltar as soon as application of the 1990 Convention is extended to Gibraltar.

*Article 8*

**Entry into force**

This framework Decision shall enter into force on the day of its publication in the Official Journal.

Done at Luxembourg, 26 June 2001.

*For the Council*

*The President*

T. ÖSTROS

# Protocol to the Convention on Mutual Assistance in Criminal Matters between the Member States of the European Union, 16 October 2001

**[OJ 2001, C 326/2–5]**

**[Editor's note: signatures omitted]**

C 326/2 EN Official Journal of the European Communities 21.11.2001

*ANNEX*

**PROTOCOL**

**established by the Council in accordance with Article 34 of the Treaty on European Union to the Convention on Mutual Assistance in Criminal Matters between the Member States of the European Union**

THE HIGH CONTRACTING PARTIES to this Protocol, Member States of the European Union,

REFERRING to the Council Act of 16 October 2001 establishing the Protocol to the Convention on Mutual Assistance in Criminal Matters between the Member States of the European Union,

TAKING ACCOUNT of the conclusions adopted at the European Council held in Tampere on 15 and 16 October 1999, and of the need to implement them immediately in order to achieve an area of freedom, security and justice,

BEARING IN MIND the recommendations made by the experts when presenting the mutual evaluation reports based on Council Joint Action 97/827/JHA of 5 December 1997 establishing a mechanism for evaluating the application and implementation at national level of international undertakings in the fight against organised crime ([1]),

CONVINCED of the need for additional measures in the field of mutual assistance in criminal matters for the purpose of the fight against crime, including in particular organised crime, money laundering and financial crime,

HAVE AGREED UPON THE FOLLOWING PROVISIONS, which shall be annexed to, and form an integral part of, the Convention on Mutual Assistance in Criminal Matters between the Member States of the European Union of 29 May 2000 ([2]), hereinafter referred to as the '2000 Mutual Assistance Convention':

*Article 1*

**Request for information on bank accounts**

1. Each Member State shall, under the conditions set out in this Article, take the measures necessary to determine, in answer to a request sent by another Member State, whether a natural or legal person that is the subject of a criminal investigation holds or controls one or more accounts, of whatever nature, in any bank located in its territory and, if so, provide all the details of the identified accounts.

The information shall also, if requested and to the extent that it can be provided within a reasonable time, include accounts for which the person that is the subject of the proceedings has powers of attorney.

2. The obligation set out in this Article shall apply only to the extent that the information is in the possession of the bank keeping the account.

3. The obligation set out in this Article shall apply only if the investigation concerns:

— an offence punishable by a penalty involving deprivation of liberty or a detention order of a maximum period of at least four years in the requesting State and at least two years in the requested State, or

— an offence referred to in Article 2 of the 1995 Convention on the Establishment of a European Police Office (Europol Convention), or in the Annex to that Convention, as amended, or

— to the extent that it may not be covered by the Europol Convention, an offence referred to in the 1995 Convention on the Protection of the European Communities' Financial Interests, the 1996 Protocol thereto, or the 1997 Second Protocol thereto.

4. The authority making the request shall, in the request:

— state why it considers that the requested information is likely to be of substantial value for the purpose of the investigation into the offence,

— state on what grounds it presumes that banks in the requested Member State hold the account and, to the extent available, which banks may be involved,

— include any information available which may facilitate the execution of the request.

5. Member States may make the execution of a request according to this Article dependent on the same conditions as they apply in respect of requests for search and seizure.

6. The Council may decide, pursuant to Article 34(2)(c) of the Treaty of European Union, to extend the scope of paragraph 3.

([1]) OJ L 344, 15.12.1997, p. 7.
([2]) OJ C 197, 12.7.2000, p. 3.

*Article 2*

**Requests for information on banking transactions**

1. On request by the requesting State, the requested State shall provide the particulars of specified bank accounts and of banking operations which have been carried out during a specified period through one or more accounts specified in the request, including the particulars of any sending or recipient account.

2. The obligation set out in this Article shall apply only to the extent that the information is in the possession of the bank holding the account.

3. The requesting Member State shall in its request indicate why it considers the requested information relevant for the purpose of the investigation into the offence.

4. Member States may make the execution of a request according to this Article dependent on the same conditions as they apply in respect of requests for search and seizure.

*Article 3*

**Requests for the monitoring of banking transactions**

1. Each Member State shall undertake to ensure that, at the request of another Member State, it is able to monitor, during a specified period, the banking operations that are being carried out through one or more accounts specified in the request and communicate the results thereof to the requesting Member State.

2. The requesting Member State shall in its request indicate why it considers the requested information relevant for the purpose of the investigation into the offence.

3. The decision to monitor shall be taken in each individual case by the competent authorities of the requested Member State, with due regard for the national law of that Member State.

4. The practical details regarding the monitoring shall be agreed between the competent authorities of the requesting and requested Member States.

*Article 4*

**Confidentiality**

Each Member State shall take the necessary measures to ensure that banks do not disclose to the bank customer concerned or to other third persons that information has been transmitted to the requesting State in accordance with Articles 1, 2 or 3 or that an investigation is being carried out.

*Article 5*

**Obligation to inform**

If the competent authority of the requested Member State in the course of the execution of a request for mutual assistance considers that it may be appropriate to undertake investigations not initially foreseen, or which could not be specified when the request was made, it shall immediately inform the requesting authority accordingly in order to enable it to take further action.

*Article 6*

**Additional requests for mutual assistance**

1. Where the competent authority of the requesting Member State makes a request for mutual assistance which is additional to an earlier request, it shall not be required to provide information already provided in the initial request. The additional request shall contain information necessary for the purpose of identifying the initial request.

2. Where, in accordance with the provisions in force, the competent authority which has made a request for mutual assistance participates in the execution of the request in the requested Member State, it may, without prejudice to Article 6(3) of the 2000 Mutual Assistance Convention, make an additional request directly to the competent authority of the requested Member State while present in that State.

*Article 7*

**Banking secrecy**

A Member State shall not invoke banking secrecy as a reason for refusing any cooperation regarding a request for mutual assistance from another Member State.

*Article 8*

**Fiscal offences**

1. Mutual assistance may not be refused solely on the ground that the request concerns an offence which the requested Member State considers a fiscal offence.

2. If a Member State has made the execution of a request for search and seizure dependent on the condition that the offence giving rise to the request is also punishable under its law, this condition shall be fulfilled, with regard to offences referred to in paragraph 1, if the offence corresponds to an offence of the same nature under its law.

C 326/4 EN Official Journal of the European Communities 21.11.2001

The request may not be refused on the ground that the law of the requested Member State does not impose the same kind of tax or duty or does not contain a tax, duty, customs and exchange regulation of the same kind as the law of the requesting Member State.

3. Article 50 of the Schengen Implementation Convention is hereby repealed.

*Article 9*

**Political offences**

1. For the purposes of mutual legal assistance between Member States, no offence may be regarded by the requested Member State as a political offence, an offence connected with a political offence or an offence inspired by political motives.

2. Each Member State may, when giving the notification referred to in Article 13(2), declare that it will apply paragraph 1 only in relation to:

(a) the offences referred to in Articles 1 and 2 of the European Convention on the Suppression of Terrorism of 27 January 1977; and

(b) offences of conspiracy or association, which correspond to the description of behaviour referred to in Article 3(4) of the Convention of 27 September 1996 relating to extradition between the Member States of the European Union, to commit one or more of the offences referred to in Articles 1 and 2 of the European Convention on the Suppression of Terrorism.

3. Reservations made pursuant to Article 13 of the European Convention on the Suppression of Terrorism shall not apply to mutual legal assistance between Member States.

*Article 10*

**Forwarding refusals to the Council and involvement of Eurojust**

1. If a request is refused on the basis of:

— Article 2(b) of the European Mutual Assistance Convention or Article 22(2)(b) of the Benelux Treaty, or

— Article 51 of the Schengen Implementation Convention or Article 5 of the European Mutual Assistance Convention, or

— Article 1(5) or Article 2(4) of this Protocol,

and the requesting Member State maintains its request, and no solution can be found, the reasoned decision to refuse the request shall be forwarded to the Council for information by the requested Member State, for possible evaluation of the functioning of judicial cooperation between Member States.

2. The competent authorities of the requesting Member State may report to Eurojust, once it has been established, any problem encountered concerning the execution of a request in relation to the provisions referred to in paragraph 1 for a possible practical solution in accordance with the provisions laid down in the instrument establishing Eurojust.

*Article 11*

**Reservations**

No reservations may be entered in respect of this Protocol, other than those provided for in Article 9(2).

*Article 12*

**Territorial application**

The application of this Protocol to Gibraltar will take effect when the 2000 Mutual Assistance Convention has taken effect in Gibraltar, in accordance with Article 26 of that Convention.

*Article 13*

**Entry into force**

1. This Protocol shall be subject to adoption by the Member States in accordance with their respective constitutional requirements.

2. Member States shall notify the Secretary-General of the Council of the European Union of the completion of the constitutional procedures for the adoption of this Protocol.

3. This Protocol shall enter into force in the eight Member States concerned 90 days after the notification referred to in paragraph 2 by the State, member of the European Union at the time of adoption by the Council of the Act establishing this Protocol, which is the eighth to complete that formality. If, however, the 2000 Mutual Assistance Convention has not entered into force on that date, this Protocol shall enter into force on the date on which that Convention enters into force.

4. Any notification by a Member State subsequent to the entry into force of this Protocol under paragraph 3 shall have the effect that, 90 days after such notification, this Protocol shall enter into force as between that Member State and those Member States for which this Protocol has already entered into force.

5. Before the entry into force of this Protocol pursuant to paragraph 3, any Member State may, when giving the notification referred to in paragraph 2 or at any time thereafter, declare that it will apply this Protocol in its relations with Member States which have made the same declaration. Such declarations shall take effect 90 days after the date of deposit thereof.

6. Notwithstanding paragraphs 3 to 5, the entry into force or application of this Protocol shall not take effect in relations between any two Member States before the entry into force or application of the 2000 Mutual Assistance Convention between these Member States.

7. This Protocol shall apply to mutual assistance initiated after the date on which it enters into force, or is applied pursuant to paragraph 5, between the Member States concerned.

*Article 14*

**Acceding States**

1. This Protocol shall be open to accession by any State which becomes a member of the European Union and which accedes to the 2000 Mutual Assistance Convention.

2. The text of this Protocol in the language of the acceding State, drawn up by the Council of the European Union, shall be authentic.

3. The instruments of accession shall be deposited with the depositary.

4. This Protocol shall enter into force with respect to any State which accedes to it 90 days after the deposit of its instrument of accession or on the date of entry into force of this Protocol if it has not already entered into force at the time of expiry of the said period of 90 days.

5. Where this Protocol is not yet in force at the time of the deposit of their instrument of accession, Article 13(5) shall apply to acceding Member States.

6. Notwithstanding paragraphs 4 and 5, the entry into force or application of this Protocol with respect to the acceding State shall not take effect before the entry into force or application of the 2000 Mutual Assistance Convention with respect to that State.

*Article 15*

**Position of Iceland and Norway**

Article 8 shall constitute measures amending or based upon the provisions referred to in Annex A to the Agreement concluded by the Council of the European Union with the Republic of Iceland and the Kingdom of Norway concerning the latters' association with the implementation, application and development of the Schengen *acquis* (1) (hereinafter referred to as the 'Association Agreement').

*Article 16*

**Entry into force for Iceland and Norway**

1. Without prejudice to Article 8 of the Association Agreement, the provision referred to in Article 15 shall enter into force for Iceland and Norway 90 days after the receipt by the Council and the Commission of the information pursuant to Article 8(2) of the Association Agreement upon fulfilment of their constitutional requirements, in their mutual relations with any Member State for which this Protocol has already entered into force pursuant to Article 13(3) or (4).

2. Any entry into force of this Protocol for a Member State after the date of entry into force of the provision referred to in Article 15 for Iceland and Norway, shall render that provision also applicable in the mutual relations between that Member State and Iceland and Norway.

3. The provision referred to in Article 15 shall in any event not become binding on Iceland and Norway before the entry into force of the provisions referred to in Article 2(1) of the 2000 Mutual Assistance Convention with respect to those two States.

4. Without prejudice to paragraphs 1, 2 and 3, the provision referred to in Article 15 shall enter into force for Iceland and Norway not later than on the date of entry into force of this Protocol for the fifteenth State, being a member of the European Union at the time of the adoption by the Council of the Act establishing this Protocol.

*Article 17*

**Depositary**

The Secretary-General of the Council of the European Union shall act as depositary of this Protocol.

The depositary shall publish in the *Official Journal of the European Communities* information on the progress of adoptions and accessions, declarations and also any other notification concerning this Protocol.

(1) OJ L 176, 10.7.1999, p. 36.

# Decision 2002/187 setting up Eurojust with a view to reinforcing the fight against serious crime, 28 February 2002

**[Consolidated version. Original version OJ 2002, L 63/1–13; rectified by OJ 2002, L 196/63 and amended OJ 2003, L 245/44 and OJ 2009, L 138/14–16. Date of entry into force 4 June 2011. Preamble of Decision 2009/425 included, OJ 2009, L 138/14–16]**

**This document is meant purely as a documentation tool and the institutions do not assume any liability for its contents**

►B

**COUNCIL DECISION**

**of 28 February 2002**

**setting up Eurojust with a view to reinforcing the fight against serious crime**

(2002/187/JHA)

(OJ L 63, 6.3.2002, p. 1)

Amended by:

| | | Official Journal | | |
|---|---|---|---|---|
| | | No | page | date |
| ►M1 | Council Decision 2003/659/JHA of 18 June 2003 | L 245 | 44 | 29.9.2003 |
| ►M2 | Council Decision 2009/426/JHA of 16 December 2008 | L 138 | 14 | 4.6.2009 |

▼B

**COUNCIL DECISION**

**of 28 February 2002**

**setting up Eurojust with a view to reinforcing the fight against serious crime**

(2002/187/JHA)

THE COUNCIL OF THE EUROPEAN UNION,

Having regard to the Treaty on European Union, and in particular Articles 31 and 34(2)(c) thereof,

Having regard to the initiative of the Federal Republic of Germany and to that of the Portuguese Republic, the French Republic, the Kingdom of Sweden and the Kingdom of Belgium (1),

Having regard to the opinion of the European Parliament (2),

Whereas:

(1) It is necessary to improve judicial cooperation between the Member States further, in particular in combating forms of serious crime often perpetrated by transnational organisations.

(2) The effective improvement of judicial cooperation between the Member States requires the immediate adoption of structural measures at European Union level to facilitate the optimal coordination of action for investigations and prosecutions covering the territory of more than one Member State with full respect for fundamental rights and freedoms.

(3) In order to reinforce the fight against serious organised crime, the Tampere European Council of 15 and 16 October 1999, in particular in point 46 of its conclusions, decided on the setting up of a unit (Eurojust) composed of prosecutors, magistrates or police officers of equivalent competence.

(4) This Eurojust unit is set up by this Decision as a body of the European Union with legal personality and financed from the general budget of the European Union, except as regards the salaries and emoluments of the national members and assisting persons, which are borne by their Member State of origin.

(5) The objectives of Regulation (EC) No 1073/1999 of the European Parliament and of the Council of 25 May 1999 concerning investigations conducted by the European Anti-Fraud Office (OLAF) (3) are also relevant to Eurojust. The Eurojust College should adopt the necessary implementing measures to achieve those objectives. It should take full account of the sensitive work carried out by Eurojust in the context of investigations and prosecutions. In this connection, OLAF should be denied access to documents, evidence, reports, notes or information, in whatever form, which are held or created in the course of these activities, whether under way or already concluded, and the transmission of such documents, evidence, reports, notes and information to OLAF should be prohibited.

(1) OJ C 206, 19.7.2000, p. 1 and
OJ C 243, 24.8.2000, p. 15.
(2) OJ C 34 E, 7.2.2002, p. 347 and opinion delivered on 29 November 2001 (not yet published in the Official Journal).
(3) OJ L 136, 31.5.1999, p. 1.

▼B

(6) In order to be able to attain its objectives as efficiently as possible, Eurojust should fulfil its tasks either through one or more of its national members or acting as a College.

(7) The competent authorities of the Member States should be able to exchange information with Eurojust in accordance with arrangements which serve and observe the interests of public service.

(8) Eurojust's jurisdiction is without prejudice to the Community's competence to protect its own financial interests and is also without prejudice to existing conventions and agreements, in particular the European Convention on Mutual Assistance in Criminal Matters (Council of Europe) signed in Strasbourg on 20 April 1959, and also the Convention on Mutual Assistance on Criminal Matters between the Member States of the European Union (1) adopted by the Council on 29 May 2000, and the Protocol (2) thereto adopted on 16 October 2001.

(9) In order to achieve its objectives, Eurojust processes personal data by automated means or in structured manual files. Accordingly, the necessary steps should be taken to guarantee a level of data protection which corresponds at least to that which results from the application of the principles of the Convention for the Protection of Individuals with regard to Automatic Processing of Personal Data (Council of Europe) signed in Strasbourg on 28 January 1981, together with subsequent amendments thereto, in particular the Protocol opened for signature on 8 November 2001, once such amendments are in force between the Member States.

(10) In order to help ensure and check that personal data are processed properly by Eurojust, a joint supervisory body should be set up which, given the composition of Eurojust, should consist of a panel of judges or, if the constitutional or national system of a Member State so requires, of persons exercising an equivalent function which gives them sufficient independence. The powers of this joint supervisory body should be without prejudice to the jurisdiction of national courts or to the arrangements for any appeals which may be brought before them.

(11) In order to ensure harmonious coordination of the various activities pursued by the Union and the Community and having regard to Article 29 and Article 36(2) of the Treaty, the Commission should be fully involved in Eurojust's proceedings concerning general questions and questions coming within its competence. Eurojust's rules of procedure should detail the arrangements for the Commission to participate in Eurojust's proceedings in areas within its jurisdiction.

(12) Provisions should be laid down to ensure that Eurojust and the European Police Office (Europol) (3) establish and maintain close cooperation.

(13) Eurojust and the European Judicial Network set up by Joint Action 98/428/JHA (4) should have a privileged relationship. To that end, the secretariat of the Network should be placed within the Eurojust secretariat.

(14) In order to facilitate activities of Eurojust, the Member States should put in place or designate one or more national correspondents.

(15) Insofar as is necessary for the fulfilment of its tasks, it should be possible for Eurojust to initiate cooperation with non-Member

(1) OJ C 197, 12.7.2000, p. 3.
(2) OJ C 326, 26.11.2001, p. 2.
(3) OJ C 316, 27.11.1995, p. 1.
(4) OJ L 191, 7.7.1998, p. 4.

▼B

States and for agreements to be concluded to that effect, primarily with the candidate countries for accession to the Union and other countries with which arrangements have been agreed.

(16) Since the adoption of this Decision means that major new legislative measures must be approved in the Member States, provision should be made for certain transitional provisions.

(17) Point 57 of the Laeken European Council conclusions of 14 and 15 December 2001 provided for Eurojust to be able to begin operations in The Hague, pending overall agreement on the seats of certain agencies.

(18) This Decision respects the fundamental rights and observes the principles recognised by Article 6(2) of the Treaty and reflected in the Charter of Fundamental Rights of the European Union,

HAS DECIDED AS FOLLOWS:

*Article 1*

**Establishment and legal personality**

This Decision establishes a unit, referred to as 'Eurojust', as a body of the Union.

Eurojust shall have legal personality.

▼M2

*Article 2*

**Composition of Eurojust**

1. Eurojust shall have one national member seconded by each Member State in accordance with its legal system, who is a prosecutor, judge or police officer of equivalent competence.

2. Member States shall ensure continuous and effective contribution to the achievement by Eurojust of its objectives under Article 3. To fulfil those objectives:

(a) the national member shall be required to have his regular place of work at the seat of Eurojust;

(b) each national member shall be assisted by one deputy and by another person as an assistant. The deputy and the assistant may have their regular place of work at Eurojust. More deputies or assistants may assist the national member and may, if necessary and with the agreement of the College, have their regular place of work at Eurojust.

3. The national member shall have a position which grants him the powers referred to in this Decision in order to be able to fulfil his tasks.

4. National members, deputies and assistants shall be subject to the national law of their Member State as regards their status.

5. The deputy shall fulfil the criteria provided for in paragraph 1 and be able to act on behalf of or to substitute the national member. An assistant may also act on behalf of or substitute the national member if he fulfils the criteria provided for in paragraph 1.

6. Eurojust shall be linked to a Eurojust national coordination system in accordance with Article 12.

7. Eurojust shall have the possibility of posting liaison magistrates in third States in accordance with this Decision.

8. Eurojust shall, in accordance with this Decision, have a Secretariat headed by an Administrative Director.

▼B

*Article 3*

**Objectives**

1. In the context of investigations and prosecutions, concerning two or more Member States, of criminal behaviour referred to in Article 4 in relation to serious crime, particularly when it is organised, the objectives of Eurojust shall be:

(a) to stimulate and improve the coordination, between the competent authorities of the Member States, of investigations and prosecutions in the Member States, taking into account any request emanating from a competent authority of a Member State and any information provided by any body competent by virtue of provisions adopted within the framework of the Treaties;

(b) to improve cooperation between the competent authorities of the Member States, in particular by facilitating the execution of ►M2 requests for, and decisions on, judicial cooperation, including regarding instruments giving effect to the principle of mutual recognition; ◄

(c) to support otherwise the competent authorities of the Member States in order to render their investigations and prosecutions more effective.

2. In accordance with the rules laid down by this Decision and at the request of a Member State's competent authority, Eurojust may also assist investigations and prosecutions concerning only that Member State and a non-Member State where an agreement establishing cooperation pursuant to ►M2 Article 26a(2) ◄ has been concluded with the said State or where in a specific case there is an essential interest in providing such assistance.

3. In accordance with the rules laid down by this Decision and at the request either of a Member State's competent authority or of the Commission, Eurojust may also assist investigations and prosecutions concerning only that Member State and the Community.

*Article 4*

**Competences**

1. The general competence of Eurojust shall cover:

▼M2

(a) the types of crime and the offences in respect of which Europol is at all times competent to act (1);

__________

▼B

(c) other offences committed together with the types of crime and the offences referred to ►M2 in point (a) ◄.

2. For types of offences other than those referred to in paragraph 1, Eurojust may in addition, in accordance with its objectives, assist in investigations and prosecutions at the request of a competent authority of a Member State.

(1) At the time of adoption of this Decision, the competence of Europol is set out in Article 2(1) of the Convention of 26 July 1995 on the establishment of a European Police Office (Europol Convention) (OJ C 316, 27.11.1995, p. 2), as amended by the 2003 Protocol (OJ C 2, 6.1.2004, p. 1), and in the Annex thereto. However, once the Council Decision establishing the European Police Office (Europol) enters into force, the competence of Eurojust will be as set out in Article 4(1) of that Decision and in the Annex thereto.

▼B

*Article 5*

**Tasks of Eurojust**

1. In order to accomplish its objectives, Eurojust shall fulfil its tasks:

(a) through one or more of the national members concerned in accordance with Article 6, or

(b) as a College in accordance with Article 7:

(i) when so requested by one or more of the national members concerned by a case dealt with by Eurojust, or

(ii) when the case involves investigations or prosecutions which have repercussions at Union level or which might affect Member States other than those directly concerned, or

(iii) when a general question relating to the achievement of its objectives is involved, or

(iv) when otherwise provided for in this Decision.

2. When it fulfils its tasks, Eurojust shall indicate whether it is acting through one or more of the national members within the meaning of Article 6 or as a College within the meaning of Article 7.

▼M2

*Article 5a*

**On-Call Coordination**

1. In order to fulfil its tasks in urgent cases, Eurojust shall put in place an On-Call Coordination (OCC) able to receive and process at all times requests referred to it. The OCC shall be contactable, through a single OCC contact point at Eurojust, on a 24-hour/7-day basis.

2. The OCC shall rely on one representative (OCC representative) per Member State who may be either the national member, his deputy, or an assistant entitled to replace the national member. The OCC representative shall be able to act on a 24-hour/7-day basis.

3. When in urgent cases a request for, or a decision on, judicial cooperation, including regarding instruments giving effect to the principle of mutual recognition, needs to be executed in one or more Member States, the requesting or issuing competent authority may forward it to the OCC. The OCC contact point shall immediately forward it to the OCC representative of the Member State from which the request originates and, if explicitly requested by the transmitting or issuing authority, to the OCC representatives of the Member States on the territory of which the request should be executed. These OCC representatives shall act without delay, in relation to the execution of the request in their Member State, through the exercise of tasks or powers available to them and referred to in Article 6 and Articles 9a to 9f.

▼B

*Article 6*

**Tasks of Eurojust acting through its national members**

►M2 1. ◄ When Eurojust acts through its national members concerned, it:

▼M2

(a) may ask the competent authorities of the Member States concerned, giving its reasons, to:

(i) undertake an investigation or prosecution of specific acts;

▼M2

(ii) accept that one of them may be in a better position to undertake an investigation or to prosecute specific acts;

(iii) coordinate between the competent authorities of the Member States concerned;

(iv) set up a joint investigation team in keeping with the relevant cooperation instruments;

(v) provide it with any information that is necessary for it to carry out its tasks;

(vi) take special investigative measures;

(vii) take any other measure justified for the investigation or prosecution;

▼B

(b) shall ensure that the competent authorities of the Member States concerned inform each other on investigations and prosecutions of which it has been informed;

(c) shall assist the competent authorities of the Member States, at their request, in ensuring the best possible coordination of investigations and prosecutions;

(d) shall give assistance in order to improve cooperation between the competent national authorities;

(e) shall cooperate and consult with the European Judicial Network, including making use of and contributing to the improvement of its documentary database;

(f) shall, in the cases referred to Article 3(2) and (3) and with the agreement of the College, assist investigations and prosecutions concerning the competent authorities of only one Member State.

▼M2

—————

2. The Member States shall ensure that competent national authorities respond without undue delay to requests made under this Article.

▼B

*Article 7*

**Tasks of Eurojust acting as a College**

►M2 1. ◄ When Eurojust acts as a College, it:

(a) may in relation to the types of crime and the offences referred to in Article 4(1) ask the competent authorities of the Member States concerned, giving its reasons:

(i) to undertake an investigation or prosecution of specific acts;

(ii) to accept that one of them may be in a better position to undertake an investigation or to prosecute specific acts;

(iii) to coordinate between the competent authorities of the Member States concerned;

(iv) to set up a joint investigation team in keeping with the relevant cooperation instruments;

(v) to provide it with any information that is necessary for it to carry out its tasks;

(b) shall ensure that the competent authorities of the Member States inform each other of investigations and prosecutions of which it has been informed and which have repercussions at Union level or which might affect Member States other than those directly concerned;

▼B

(c) shall assist the competent authorities of the Member States, at their request, in ensuring the best possible coordination of investigations and prosecutions;

(d) shall give assistance in order to improve cooperation between the competent authorities of the Member States, in particular on the basis of Europol's analysis;

(e) shall cooperate and consult with the European Judicial Network, including making use of and contributing to the improvement of its documentary database;

(f) may assist Europol, in particular by providing it with opinions based on analyses carried out by Europol;

(g) may supply logistical support in the cases referred to in points (a), (c) and (d) above. Such logistical support may include assistance for translation, interpretation and the organisation of coordination meetings.

▼M2

2. Where two or more national members can not agree on how to resolve a case of conflict of jurisdiction as regards the undertaking of investigations or prosecution pursuant to Article 6 and in particular Article 6(1)(c), the College shall be asked to issue a written non-binding opinion on the case, provided the matter could not be resolved through mutual agreement between the competent national authorities concerned. The opinion of the College shall be promptly forwarded to the Member States concerned. This paragraph is without prejudice to paragraph 1(a)(ii).

3. Notwithstanding the provisions contained in any instruments adopted by the European Union regarding judicial cooperation, a competent authority may report to Eurojust recurrent refusals or difficulties concerning the execution of requests for, and decisions on, judicial cooperation, including regarding instruments giving effect to the principle of mutual recognition, and request the College to issue a written non-binding opinion on the matter, provided it could not be resolved through mutual agreement between the competent national authorities or through the involvement of the national members concerned. The opinion of the College shall be promptly forwarded to the Member States concerned.

*Article 8*

**Follow up to requests and opinions of Eurojust**

If the competent authorities of the Member States concerned decide not to comply with a request referred to in Article 6(1)(a) or Article 7(1)(a) or decide not to follow a written opinion referred to in Article 7(2) and (3), they shall inform Eurojust without undue delay of their decision and of the reasons for it. Where it is not possible to give the reasons for refusing to comply with a request because to do so would harm essential national security interests or would jeopardise the safety of individuals, the competent authorities of the Member States may cite operational reasons.

*Article 9*

**National members**

1. The length of a national member's term of office shall be at least four years. The Member State of origin may renew the term of office. The national member shall not be removed before the end of a term without informing the Council before the removal and indicating to it the reason therefor. Where a national member is President or Vice-President of Eurojust, his term of office as a member shall at least be

▼M2

such that he can fulfil his function as President or Vice-President for the full elected term.

2. All information exchanged between Eurojust and Member States shall be directed through the national member.

3. In order to meet Eurojust's objectives, the national member shall have at least equivalent access to, or at least be able to obtain the information contained in, the following types of registers of his Member State as would be available to him in his role as a prosecutor, judge or police officer, whichever is applicable, at national level:

(a) criminal records;

(b) registers of arrested persons;

(c) investigation registers;

(d) DNA registers;

(e) other registers of his Member State where he deems this information necessary for him to be able to fulfil his tasks.

4. A national member may contact the competent authorities of his Member State directly.

*Article 9a*

**Powers of the national member granted to him at national level**

1. When a national member exercises the powers referred to in Articles 9b, 9c and 9d, he does so in his capacity as a competent national authority acting in accordance with national law and subject to the conditions laid down in this Article and Articles 9b to 9e. In the performance of his tasks the national member shall, where appropriate, make it known whenever he is acting in accordance with the powers granted to national members under this Article and Articles 9b, 9c and 9d.

2. Each Member State shall define the nature and extent of the powers it grants its national member as regards judicial cooperation in respect of that Member State. However, each Member State shall grant its national member at least the powers described in Article 9b and, subject to Article 9e, the powers described in Articles 9c and 9d, which would be available to him as a judge, prosecutor or police officer, whichever is applicable, at national level.

3. When appointing its national member and at any other time if appropriate, the Member State shall notify Eurojust and the General Secretariat of the Council of its decision regarding the implementation of paragraph 2 so that the latter can inform the other Member States. The Member States shall undertake to accept and recognise the prerogatives thus granted in so far as they are in conformity with international commitments.

4. Each Member State shall define the right for a national member to act in relation to foreign judicial authorities, in accordance with its international commitments.

*Article 9b*

**Ordinary powers**

1. National members, in their capacity as competent national authorities, shall be entitled to receive, transmit, facilitate, follow up and provide supplementary information in relation to the execution of requests for, and decisions on, judicial cooperation, including regarding instruments giving effect to the principle of mutual recognition. When powers referred to in this paragraph are exercised, the competent national authority shall be informed promptly.

▼M2

2. In case of partial or inadequate execution of a request for judicial cooperation, national members, in their capacity as competent national authorities, shall be entitled to ask the competent national authority of their Member State for supplementary measures in order for the request to be fully executed.

*Article 9c*

**Powers exercised in agreement with a competent national authority**

1. National members may, in their capacity as competent national authorities, in agreement with a competent national authority, or at its request and on a case-by-case basis, exercise the following powers:

(a) issuing and completing requests for, and decisions on, judicial cooperation, including regarding instruments giving effect to the principle of mutual recognition;

(b) executing in their Member State requests for, and decisions on, judicial cooperation, including regarding instruments giving effect to the principle of mutual recognition;

(c) ordering in their Member State investigative measures considered necessary at a coordination meeting organised by Eurojust to provide assistance to competent national authorities concerned by a concrete investigation and to which competent national authorities concerned with the investigation are invited to participate;

(d) authorising and coordinating controlled deliveries in their Member State.

2. Powers referred to in this Article shall, in principle, be exercised by a competent national authority.

*Article 9d*

**Powers exercised in urgent cases**

In their capacity as competent national authorities, national members shall, in urgent cases and in so far as it is not possible for them to identify or to contact the competent national authority in a timely manner, be entitled:

(a) to authorise and to coordinate controlled deliveries in their Member State;

(b) to execute, in relation to their Member State a request for, or a decision on, judicial cooperation, including regarding instruments giving effect to the principle of mutual recognition.

As soon as the competent national authority is identified or contacted, it shall be informed of the exercise of powers referred to in this Article.

*Article 9e*

**Requests from national members where powers cannot be exercised**

1. The national member, in his capacity as a competent national authority, shall be at least competent to submit a proposal to the authority competent for the carrying out of powers referred to in Articles 9c and 9d when granting such powers to the national member is contrary to:

(a) constitutional rules;

or

(b) fundamental aspects of the criminal justice system:

▼M2

(i) regarding the division of powers between the police, prosecutors and judges;

(ii) regarding the functional division of tasks between prosecution authorities;

or

(iii) related to the federal structure of the Member State concerned.

2. Member States shall ensure that, in cases referred to in paragraph 1, the request issued by the national member be handled without undue delay by the competent national authority.

*Article 9f*

**Participation of national members in joint investigation teams**

National members shall be entitled to participate in joint investigation teams, including in their setting up, in accordance with Article 13 of the Convention on Mutual Assistance in Criminal Matters between the Member States of the European Union or Council Framework Decision 2002/465/JHA of 13 June 2002 on joint investigation teams ([1]), concerning their own Member State. However, Member States may make the participation of the national member subject to the agreement of the competent national authority. National members, their deputies or their assistants, shall be invited to participate in any joint investigation team involving their Member State and for which Community funding is provided under the applicable financial instruments. Each Member State shall define whether the national member participates in the joint investigation team as a national competent authority or on behalf of Eurojust.

▼B

*Article 10*

**College**

1. The College shall consist of all the national members. Each national member shall have one vote.

2. ►M2 The Council shall, acting by qualified majority, approve Eurojust's Rules of Procedure on a proposal from the College. The College shall adopt its proposal by a two-thirds majority after consulting the Joint Supervisory Board provided for in Article 23 as regards the provisions on the processing of personal data. ◄ The provisions of the rules of procedure which concern the processing of personal data may be made the subject of separate approval by the Council.

3. When acting ►M2 in accordance with Article 7(1)(a), (2) and (3) ◄, the College shall take its decisions by a two-thirds majority. Other decisions of the College shall be taken in accordance with the rules of procedure.

*Article 11*

**Role of the Commission**

1. The Commission shall be fully associated with the work of Eurojust, in accordance with Article 36(2) of the Treaty. It shall participate in that work in the areas within its competence.

2. As regards work carried out by Eurojust on the coordination of investigations and prosecutions, the Commission may be invited to provide its expertise.

([1]) OJ L 162, 20.6.2002, p. 1.

▼B

3. For the purpose of enhancing cooperation between Eurojust and the Commission, Eurojust may agree on necessary practical arrangements with the Commission.

▼M2

*Article 12*

**Eurojust national coordination system**

1. Each Member State shall designate one or more national correspondents for Eurojust.

2. Each Member State shall, before 4 June 2011, set up a Eurojust national coordination system to ensure coordination of the work carried out by:

(a) the national correspondents for Eurojust;

(b) the national correspondent for Eurojust for terrorism matters;

(c) the national correspondent for the European Judicial Network and up to three other contact points of the European Judicial Network;

(d) national members or contact points of the Network for Joint Investigation Teams and of the networks set up by Council Decision 2002/494/JHA of 13 June 2002 setting up a European network of contact points in respect of persons responsible for genocide, crimes against humanity and war crimes (1), Council Decision 2007/845/JHA of 6 December 2007 concerning cooperation between Asset Recovery Offices of the Member States in the field of tracing and identification of proceeds from, or other property related to, crime (2) and by Council Decision 2008/852/JHA of 24 October 2008 on a contact-point network against corruption (3).

3. The persons referred to in paragraphs 1 and 2 shall maintain their position and status under national law.

4. The national correspondents for Eurojust shall be responsible for the functioning of the Eurojust national coordination system. When several correspondents for Eurojust are designated, one of them shall be responsible for the functioning of the Eurojust national coordination system.

5. The Eurojust national coordination system shall facilitate, within the Member State, the carrying out of the tasks of Eurojust, in particular by:

(a) ensuring that the Case Management System referred to in Article 16 receives information related to the Member State concerned in an efficient and reliable manner;

(b) assisting in determining whether a case should be dealt with with the assistance of Eurojust or of the European Judicial Network;

(c) assisting the national member to identify relevant authorities for the execution of requests for, and decisions on, judicial cooperation, including regarding instruments giving effect to the principle of mutual recognition;

(d) maintaining close relations with the Europol National Unit.

6. In order to meet the objectives referred to in paragraph 5, persons referred to in paragraph 1 and paragraph 2(a), (b) and (c) shall, and persons referred to in paragraph 2(d) may, be connected to the Case Management System in accordance with this Article and Articles 16, 16a, 16b and 18 as well as with the Rules of Procedure of Eurojust. The

(1) OJ L 167, 26.6.2002, p. 1.
(2) OJ L 332, 18.12.2007, p. 103.
(3) OJ L 301, 12.11.2008, p. 38.

▼M2

connection to the Case Management System shall be at the charge of the general budget of the European Union.

7. Nothing in this Article shall be construed to affect direct contacts between competent judicial authorities as provided for in instruments on judicial cooperation, such as Article 6 of the Convention on Mutual Assistance in Criminal Matters between the Member States of the European Union. Relations between the national member and national correspondents shall not preclude direct contacts between the national member and his competent authorities.

*Article 13*

**Exchanges of information with the Member States and between national members**

1. The competent authorities of the Member States shall exchange with Eurojust any information necessary for the performance of its tasks in accordance with Articles 4 and 5 as well as with the rules on data protection set out in this Decision. This shall at least include the information referred to in paragraphs 5, 6 and 7.

2. The transmission of information to Eurojust shall be interpreted as a request for the assistance of Eurojust in the case concerned only if so specified by a competent authority.

3. The national members of Eurojust shall be empowered to exchange any information necessary for the performance of the tasks of Eurojust, without prior authorisation, among themselves or with their Member State's competent authorities. In particular national members shall be promptly informed of a case which concerns them.

4. This Article shall be without prejudice to other obligations regarding the transmission of information to Eurojust, including Council Decision 2005/671/JHA of 20 September 2005 on the exchange of information and cooperation concerning terrorist offences ([1]).

5. Member States shall ensure that national members are informed of the setting up of a joint investigation team, whether it is set up under Article 13 of the Convention on Mutual Assistance in Criminal Matters between the Member States of the European Union or under Framework Decision 2002/465/JHA, and of the results of the work of such teams.

6. Member States shall ensure that their national member is informed without undue delay of any case in which at least three Member States are directly involved and for which requests for or decisions on judicial cooperation, including regarding instruments giving effect to the principle of mutual recognition, have been transmitted to at least two Member States and

(a) the offence involved is punishable in the requesting or issuing Member State by a custodial sentence or a detention order for a maximum period of at least five or six years, to be decided by the Member State concerned, and is included in the following list:

   (i) trafficking in human beings;

   (ii) sexual exploitation of children and child pornography;

   (iii) drug trafficking;

   (iv) trafficking in firearms, their parts and components and ammunition;

   (v) corruption;

   (vi) fraud affecting the financial interests of the European Communities;

([1]) OJ L 253, 29.9.2005, p. 22.

▼M2

(vii) counterfeiting of the euro;

(viii) money laundering;

(ix) attacks against information systems;

or

(b) there are factual indications that a criminal organisation is involved;

or

(c) there are indications that the case may have a serious cross-border dimension or repercussions at European Union level or that it might affect Member States other than those directly involved.

7. Member States shall ensure that their national member is informed of:

(a) cases where conflicts of jurisdiction have arisen or are likely to arise;

(b) controlled deliveries affecting at least three States, at least two of which are Member States;

(c) repeated difficulties or refusals regarding the execution of requests for, and decisions on, judicial cooperation, including regarding instruments giving effect to the principle of mutual recognition.

8. National authorities shall not be obliged in a particular case to supply information if this would mean:

(a) harming essential national security interests; or

(b) jeopardising the safety of individuals.

9. This Article shall be without prejudice to conditions set in bilateral or multilateral agreements or arrangements between Member States and third countries including any conditions set by third countries concerning the use of information once supplied.

10. Information transmitted to Eurojust pursuant to paragraphs 5, 6 and 7 shall at least include, where available, the types of information contained in the list provided for in the Annex.

11. Information referred to in this Article shall be transmitted to Eurojust in a structured way.

12. By 4 June 2014 ([20]), the Commission shall establish, on the basis of information transmitted by Eurojust, a report on the implementation of this Article, accompanied by any proposal it may deem appropriate, including with a view to considering an amendment of paragraphs 5, 6 and 7 and the Annex.

*Article 13a*

**Information provided by Eurojust to competent national authorities**

1. Eurojust shall provide competent national authorities with information and feedback on the results of the processing of information, including the existence of links with cases already stored in the Case Management System.

2. Furthermore, where a competent national authority requests Eurojust to provide it with information, Eurojust shall transmit it in the timeframe requested by that authority.

▼B

*Article 14*

**Processing of personal data**

1. Insofar as it is necessary to achieve its objectives, Eurojust may, within the framework of its competence and in order to carry out its tasks, process personal data, by automated means or in structured manual files.

2. Eurojust shall take the necessary measures to guarantee a level of protection for personal data at least equivalent to that resulting from the application of the principles of the Council of Europe Convention of 28 January 1981 and subsequent amendments thereto where they are in force in the Member States.

3. Personal data processed by Eurojust shall be adequate, relevant and not excessive in relation to the purpose of the processing, and, taking into account the information provided by the competent authorities of the Member States or other partners ►M2 in accordance with Articles 13, 26 and 26a ◄, accurate and up-to-date. Personal data processed by Eurojust shall be processed fairly and lawfully.

▼M2

————

▼B

*Article 15*

**Restrictions on the processing of personal data**

1. When processing data in accordance with Article 14(1), Eurojust may process only the following personal data on persons who, under the national legislation of the Member States concerned, ►M2 are suspected of having committed or having taken part in a criminal offence in respect of which Eurojust is competent or who have been convicted of such an offence ◄:

(a) surname, maiden name, given names and any alias or assumed names;

(b) date and place of birth;

(c) nationality;

(d) sex;

(e) place of residence, profession and whereabouts of the person concerned;

(f) social security numbers, driving licences, identification documents and passport data;

(g) information concerning legal persons if it includes information relating to identified or identifiable individuals who are the subject of a judicial investigation or prosecution;

(h) bank accounts and accounts with other financial institutions;

(i) description and nature of the alleged offences, the date on which they were committed, the criminal category of the offences and the progress of the investigations;

(j) the facts pointing to an international extension of the case;

(k) details relating to alleged membership of a criminal organisation;

▼M2

(l) telephone numbers, e-mail addresses and data referred to in Article 2(2)(a) of Directive 2006/24/EC of the European Parliament and of the Council of 15 March 2006 on the retention of data generated or processed in connection with the provision of

▼M2

publicly available electronic communications services or of public communications networks (1);

(m) vehicle registration data;

(n) DNA profiles established from the non-coding part of DNA, photographs and fingerprints.

▼B

2. When processing data in accordance with Article 14(1), Eurojust may process only the following personal data on persons who, under the national legislation of the Member States concerned, are regarded as witnesses or victims in a criminal investigation or prosecution regarding one or more of the types of crime and the offences defined in Article 4:

(a) surname, maiden name, given names and any alias or assumed names;

(b) date and place of birth;

(c) nationality;

(d) sex;

(e) place of residence, profession and whereabouts of the person concerned;

(f) the description and nature of the offences involving them, the date on which they were committed, the criminal category of the offences and the progress of the investigations.

3. However, in exceptional cases, Eurojust may also, for a limited period of time, process other personal data relating to the circumstances of an offence where they are immediately relevant to and included in ongoing investigations which Eurojust is helping to coordinate, provided that the processing of such specific data is in accordance with Articles 14 and 21.

The Data Protection Officer referred to in Article 17 shall be informed immediately of recourse to this paragraph.

Where such other data refer to witnesses or victims within the meaning of paragraph 2, the decision to process them shall be taken jointly by at least two national members.

4. Personal data, processed by automated or other means, revealing racial or ethnic origin, political opinions, religious or philosophical beliefs, trade union membership, and data concerning health or sex life may be processed by Eurojust only when such data are necessary for the national investigations concerned as well as for coordination within Eurojust.

The Data Protection Officer shall be informed immediately of recourse to this paragraph.

Such data may not be processed in the index referred to in Article 16(1).

Where such other data refer to witnesses or victims within the meaning of paragraph 2, the decision to process them shall be taken by the College.

▼M2

*Article 16*

**Case Management System, index and temporary work files**

1. In accordance with this Decision, Eurojust shall establish a Case Management System composed of temporary work files and of an index which contain personal and non-personal data.

2. The Case Management System shall be intended to:

(1) OJ L 105, 13.4.2006, p. 54.

▼M2

(a) support the management and coordination of investigations and prosecutions for which Eurojust is providing assistance, in particular by the cross-referencing of information;

(b) facilitate access to information on ongoing investigations and prosecutions;

(c) facilitate the monitoring of lawfulness and compliance with the provisions of this Decision concerning the processing of personal data.

3. The Case Management System, in so far as this is in conformity with rules on data protection contained in this Decision, may be linked to the secure telecommunications connection referred to in Article 9 of Council Decision 2008/976/JHA of 16 December 2008 on the European Judicial Network (1).

4. The index shall contain references to temporary work files processed within the framework of Eurojust and may contain no personal data other than those referred to in Article 15(1)(a) to (i), (k) and (m) and in Article 15(2).

5. In the performance of their duties in accordance with this Decision, the national members of Eurojust may process data on the individual cases on which they are working in a temporary work file. They shall allow the Data Protection Officer to have access to the work file. The Data Protection Officer shall be informed by the national member concerned of the opening of each new temporary work file that contains personal data.

6. For the processing of case related personal data, Eurojust may not establish any automated data file other than the Case Management System.

*Article 16a*

**Functioning of temporary work files and the index**

1. A temporary work file shall be opened by the national member concerned for every case with respect to which information is transmitted to him in so far as this transmission is in accordance with this Decision or with instruments referred to in Article 13(4). The national member shall be responsible for the management of the temporary work files which he has opened.

2. The national member who has opened a temporary work file shall decide, on a case-by-case basis, whether to keep the temporary work file restricted or to give access to it or to parts of it, where necessary to enable Eurojust to carry out its tasks, to other national members or to authorised Eurojust staff.

3. The national member who has opened a temporary work file shall decide which information related to this temporary work file shall be introduced in the index.

*Article 16b*

**Access to the Case Management System at national level**

1. Persons referred to in Article 12(2) in so far as they are connected to the Case Management System in accordance with Article 12(6) may only have access to:

(a) the index, unless the national member who has decided to introduce the data in the index expressly denied such access;

(1) OJ L 348, 24.12.2008, p. 130.

▼M2

(b) temporary work files opened or managed by the national member of their Member State;

(c) temporary work files opened or managed by national members of other Member States and to which the national member of their Member States has received access unless the national member who opened or manages the temporary work file expressly denied such access.

2. The national member shall, within the limitations provided for in paragraph 1, decide on the extent of access to the temporary work files which is granted in his Member State to persons referred to in Article 12(2) in so far as they are connected to the Case Management System in accordance with Article 12(6).

3. Each Member State shall decide, after consultation with its national member, on the extent of access to the index which is granted in that Member State to persons referred to in Article 12(2) in so far as they are connected to the Case Management System in accordance with Article 12(6). Member States shall notify Eurojust and the General Secretariat of the Council of their decision regarding the implementation of this paragraph so that the latter can inform the other Member States.

However, persons referred to in Article 12(2), in so far as they are connected to the Case Management System in accordance with Article 12(6), shall at least have access to the index to the extent necessary to access the temporary work files to which they have been granted access ın accordance with paragraph 2 of this Article.

4. By 4 June 2013, Eurojust shall report to the Council and the Commission on the implementation of paragraph 3. Each Member State shall consider, on the basis of that report, the opportunity to review the extent of access provided in accordance with paragraph 3.

▼B

*Article 17*

**Data Protection Officer**

1. Eurojust shall have a specially appointed Data Protection Officer, who shall be a member of the staff. Within that framework, he shall be under the direct authority of the College. In the performance of the duties referred to in this Article, he shall ►M2 act independently ◄.

2. The Data Protection Officer shall in particular have the following tasks:

(a) ensuring, in an independent manner, lawfulness and compliance with the provisions of this Decision concerning the processing of personal data;

(b) ensuring that a written record of the transmission and receipt, for the purposes of Article 19(3) in particular, of personal data is kept in accordance with the provisions to be laid down in the rules of procedure, under the security conditions laid down in Article 22;

(c) ensuring that data subjects are informed of their rights under this Decision at their request.

3. In the performance of his tasks, ►M2 the Data Protection Officer ◄ shall have access to all the data processed by Eurojust and to all Eurojust premises.

4. When he finds that in his view processing has not complied with this Decision, ►M2 the Data Protection Officer ◄ shall:

(a) inform the College, which shall acknowledge receipt of the information;

▼B

(b) refer the matter to the joint supervisory body if the College has not resolved the non-compliance of the processing within a reasonable time.

▼M2

*Article 18*

**Authorised access to personal data**

Only national members, their deputies and their assistants referred to in Article 2(2), persons referred to in Article 12(2) in so far as they are connected to the Case Management System in accordance with Article 12(6) and authorised Eurojust staff may, for the purpose of achieving Eurojust's objectives and within the limits provided for in Articles 16, 16a and 16b, have access to personal data processed by Eurojust.

▼B

*Article 19*

**Right of access to personal data**

1. Every individual shall be entitled to have access to personal data concerning him processed by Eurojust under the conditions laid down in this Article.

2. Any individual wishing to exercise his right to have access to data concerning him which are stored at Eurojust, or to have them checked in accordance with Article 20, may make a request to that effect free of charge in the Member State of his choice, to the authority appointed for that purpose in that Member State, and that authority shall refer it to Eurojust without delay.

3. The right of any individual to have access to personal data concerning him or to have them checked shall be exercised in accordance with the laws and procedures of the Member State in which the individual has made his request. If, however, Eurojust can ascertain which authority in a State transmitted the data in question, that authority may require that the right of access be exercised in accordance with the rules of the law of that Member State.

4. Access to personal data shall be denied if:

(a) such access may jeopardise one of Eurojust's activities;

(b) such access may jeopardise any national investigation ►M2 ———— ◄;

(c) such access may jeopardise the rights and freedoms of third parties.

5. The decision to grant this right of access shall take due account of the status, with regard to the data stored by Eurojust, of those individuals submitting the request.

6. The national members concerned by the request shall deal with it and reach a decision on Eurojust's behalf. The request shall be dealt with in full within three months of receipt. Where the members are not in agreement, they shall refer the matter to the College, which shall take its decision on the request by a two-thirds majority.

7. If access is denied or if no personal data concerning the applicant are processed by Eurojust, the latter shall notify the applicant that it has carried out checks, without giving any information which could reveal whether or not the applicant is known.

8. If the applicant is not satisfied with the reply given to his request, he may appeal against that decision before the joint supervisory body. The joint supervisory body shall examine whether or not the decision taken by Eurojust is in conformity with this Decision.

▼B

9. The competent law enforcement authorities of the Member States shall be consulted by Eurojust before a decision is taken. They shall subsequently be notified of its contents through the national members concerned.

*Article 20*

**Correction and deletion of personal data**

1. In accordance with Article 19(3), every individual shall be entitled to ask Eurojust to correct, block or delete data concerning him if they are incorrect or incomplete or if their input or storage contravenes this Decision.

2. Eurojust shall notify the applicant if it corrects, blocks or deletes the data concerning him. If the applicant is not satisfied with Eurojust's reply, he may refer the matter to the Joint Supervisory Body within thirty days of receiving Eurojust's decision.

3. At the request of a Member State's competent authorities, national member or national correspondent, if any, and under their responsibility, Eurojust shall, in accordance with its rules of procedure, correct or delete personal data being processed by Eurojust which were transmitted or entered by that Member State, its national member or its national correspondent. The Member States' competent authorities and Eurojust, including the national member or national correspondent, if any, shall in this context ensure that the principles laid down in Article 14(2) and (3) and in Article 15(4) are complied with.

4. If it emerges that personal data processed by Eurojust are incorrect or incomplete or that their input or storage contravenes the provisions of this Decision, Eurojust shall block, correct or delete such data.

5. In the cases referred to in paragraphs 3 and 4, all the suppliers and addressees of such data shall be notified immediately. In accordance with the rules applicable to them, the addressees, shall then correct, block or delete those data in their own systems.

*Article 21*

**Time limits for the storage of personal data**

1. Personal data processed by Eurojust shall be stored by Eurojust for only as long as is necessary for the achievement of its objectives.

2. The personal data referred to in Article 14(1) which have been processed by Eurojust may not be stored beyond ►M2 the first applicable date among the following dates ◄:

(a) the date on which prosecution is barred under the statute of limitations of all the Member States concerned by the investigation and prosecutions;

▼M2

(aa) the date on which the person was acquitted and the decision became final;

(b) three years after the date on which the judicial decision of the last of the Member States concerned by the investigation or prosecutions became final;

▼B

(c) the date on which Eurojust and the Member States concerned mutually established or agreed that it was no longer necessary for Eurojust to coordinate the investigation and prosecutions ►M2 , unless there is an obligation to provide Eurojust with this information in accordance with Article 13(6) and (7) or with instruments referred to in Article 13(4); ◄

▼M2

(d) three years after the date on which data were transmitted in accordance with Article 13(6) and (7) or with the instruments referred to in Article 13(4).

▼B

3. (a) Observance of the storage periods referred to ►M2 in paragraph 2(a), (b), (c) and (d) ◄ shall be reviewed constantly by appropriate automated processing. Nevertheless, a review of the need to store the data shall be carried out every three years after they were entered.

(b) When one of the storage deadlines referred to ►M2 in paragraph 2(a), (b), (c) and (d) ◄ has expired, Eurojust shall review the need to store the data longer in order to enable it to achieve its objectives and it may decide by way of derogation to store those data until the following review. ►M2 However, once prosecution is statute barred in all Member States concerned as referred to in paragraph 2(a), data may only be stored if they are necessary in order for Eurojust to provide assistance in accordance with this Decision. ◄

(c) Where data has been stored by way of derogation pursuant to point (b) a review of the need to store those data shall take place every three years.

4. Where a file exists containing non-automated and unstructured data, once the deadline for storage of the last item of automated data from the file has elapsed all the documents in the file shall be returned to the authority which supplied them and any copies shall be destroyed.

5. Where Eurojust has coordinated an investigation or prosecutions, the national members concerned shall inform Eurojust and the other Member States concerned of all the judicial decisions relating to the case which have become final in order, *inter alia*, that paragraph 2(b) may be applied.

*Article 22*

**Data security**

1. Eurojust and, insofar as it is concerned by data transmitted from Eurojust, each Member State, shall, as regards the processing of personal data within the framework of this Decision, protect personal data against accidental or unlawful destruction, accidental loss or unauthorised disclosure, alteration and access or any other unauthorised form of processing.

2. The rules of procedure shall contain the technical measures and the organisational arrangements needed to implement this Decision with regard to data security and in particular measures designed to:

(a) deny unauthorised persons access to data processing equipment used for processing personal data;

(b) prevent the unauthorised reading, copying, modification or removal of data media;

(c) prevent the unauthorised input of data and the unauthorised inspection, modification or deletion of stored personal data;

(d) prevent the use of automated data processing systems by unauthorised persons using data communication equipment;

(e) ensure that persons authorised to use an automated data processing system only have access to the data covered by their access authorisation;

(f) ensure that it is possible to verify and establish to which bodies personal data are transmitted when data are communicated;

▼B

(g) ensure that it is subsequently possible to verify and establish which personal data have been input into automated data processing systems and when and by whom the data were input;

(h) prevent unauthorised reading, copying, modification or deletion of personal data during transfers of personal data or during transportation of data media.

*Article 23*

**Joint Supervisory Body**

1. An independent joint supervisory body shall be established to monitor collectively the Eurojust activities referred to ►M2 in Articles 14 to 22, 26, 26a and 27 ◄ in order to ensure that the processing of personal data is carried out in accordance with this Decision. In order to fulfil these tasks, the Joint Supervisory Body shall be entitled to have full access to all files where such personal data are processed. Eurojust shall provide the Joint Supervisory Body with all information from such files that it requests and shall assist that body in its tasks by every other means.

▼M2

The Joint Supervisory Body shall meet at least once in each half year. It shall also meet within the three months following the lodging of an appeal referred to in Article 19(8) or within three months following the date when a case was referred to it in accordance with Article 20(2). The Joint Supervisory Body may also be convened by its chairman when at least two Member States so request.

▼B

In order to set up the Joint Supervisory Body, each Member State, acting in accordance with its legal system, shall appoint a judge who is not a member of Eurojust, or, if its constitutional or national system so requires a person holding an office giving him sufficient independence, for inclusion on the list of judges who may sit on the Joint Supervisory Body as members or ad hoc judges. No such appointment shall be for less than ►M2 three years ◄. Revocation of the appointment shall be governed by the principles for removal applicable under the national law of the Member State of origin. Appointment and removal shall be communicated to both the Council General Secretariat and Eurojust.

2. The Joint Supervisory Body shall be composed of three permanent members and, as provided for in paragraph 4, ad hoc judges.

▼M2

3. A judge appointed by a Member State shall become a permanent member after being elected by the plenary meeting of the persons appointed by the Member States in accordance with paragraph 1, and shall remain a permanent member for three years. Elections shall be held yearly for one permanent member of the Joint Supervisory Body by means of secret ballot. The Joint Supervisory Body shall be chaired by the member who is in his third year of mandate after elections. Permanent members may be re-elected. Appointees wishing to be elected shall present their candidacy in writing to the Secretariat of the Joint Supervisory Body 10 days before the meeting in which the election is to take place.

▼B

4. One or more ad hoc judges shall also have seats, but only for the duration of the examination of an appeal concerning personal data from the Member State which has appointed them.

▼M2

4a. The Joint Supervisory Body shall adopt in its rules of procedure measures necessary to implement paragraphs 3 and 4.

▼B

5. The composition of the Joint Supervisory Body shall remain the same for the duration of an appeals procedure even if the permanent members have reached the end of their term of office pursuant to paragraph 3.

6. Each member and ad hoc judge shall be entitled to one vote. In the event of a tied vote, the chairman shall have the casting vote.

7. The Joint Supervisory Body shall examine appeals submitted to it in accordance with Article 19(8) and Article 20(2) and carry out controls in accordance with paragraph 1, first subparagraph, of this Article. If the Joint Supervisory Body considers that a decision taken by Eurojust or the processing of data by it is not compatible with this Decision, the matter shall be referred to Eurojust, which shall accept the decision of the Joint Supervisory Body.

8. Decisions of the Joint Supervisory Body shall be final and binding on Eurojust.

9. The persons appointed by the Member States in accordance with paragraph 1, third subparagraph, presided over by the chairman of the Joint Supervisory Body, shall adopt internal rules of procedure which, for the purpose of the examination of appeals, lay down objective criteria for the appointment of the Body's members.

10. Secretariat costs shall be borne by the Eurojust budget. The secretariat of the Joint Supervisory Body shall enjoy independence in the discharge of its function within the Eurojust secretariat. ►M2 The Secretariat of the Joint Supervisory Body may rely upon the expertise of the secretariat established by Decision 2000/641/JHA [1]. ◄

11. The members of the Joint Supervisory Body shall be subject to the obligation of confidentiality laid down in Article 25.

12. The Joint Supervisory Body shall submit an annual report to the Council.

*Article 24*

**Liability for unauthorised or incorrect processing of data**

1. Eurojust shall be liable, in accordance with the national law of the Member State where its headquarters are situated, for any damage caused to an individual which results from unauthorised or incorrect processing of data carried out by it.

2. Complaints against Eurojust pursuant to the liability referred to in paragraph 1 shall be heard by the courts of the Member State where its headquarters are situated.

3. Each Member State shall be liable, in accordance with its national law, for any damage caused to an individual which results from unauthorised or incorrect processing carried out by it of data which were communicated to Eurojust.

[1] Council Decision 2000/641/JHA of 17 October 2000 establishing a secretariat for the joint supervisory data-protection bodies set up by the Convention on the Establishment of a European Police Office (Europol Convention), the Convention on the Use of Information Technology for Customs Purposes and the Convention implementing the Schengen Agreement on the gradual abolition of checks at the common borders (Schengen Convention) (OJ L 271, 24.10.2000, p. 1).

▼B

*Article 25*

**Confidentiality**

▼M2

1. The national members, their deputies and their assistants referred to in Article 2(2), Eurojust staff, national correspondents and the Data Protection Officer shall be bound by an obligation of confidentiality, without prejudice to Article 2(4).

▼B

2. The obligation of confidentiality shall apply to all persons and to all bodies called upon to work with Eurojust.

3. The obligation of confidentiality shall also apply after leaving office or employment or after the termination of the activities of the persons referred to in paragraphs 1 and 2.

4. Without prejudice to ►M2 Article 2(4) ◄, the obligation of confidentiality shall apply to all information received by Eurojust.

▼M2

*Article 25a*

**Cooperation with the European Judicial Network and other networks of the European Union involved in cooperation in criminal matters**

1. Eurojust and the European Judicial Network shall maintain privileged relations with each other, based on consultation and complementarity, especially between the national member, the European Judicial Network contact points of the same Member State and the national correspondents for Eurojust and the European Judicial Network. In order to ensure efficient cooperation, the following measures shall be taken:

(a) national members shall, on a case by case basis, inform the European Judicial Network contact points of all cases which they consider the Network to be in a better position to deal with;

(b) the Secretariat of the European Judicial Network shall form part of the staff of Eurojust. It shall function as a separate unit. It may draw on the administrative resources of Eurojust which are necessary for the performance of the European Judicial Network's tasks, including for covering the costs of the plenary meetings of the Network. Where plenary meetings are held at the premises of the Council in Brussels, the costs may only cover travel expenses and costs for interpretation. Where plenary meetings are held in the Member State holding the Presidency of the Council, the costs may only cover part of the overall costs of the meeting;

(c) European Judicial Network contact points may be invited on a case-by-case basis to attend Eurojust meetings.

2. Without prejudice to Article 4(1), the Secretariat of the Network for Joint Investigation Teams and of the network set up by Decision 2002/494/JHA shall form part of the staff of Eurojust. These secretariats shall function as separate units. They may draw on the administrative resources of Eurojust which are necessary for the performance of their tasks. Coordination between the secretariats shall be ensured by Eurojust.

This paragraph shall apply to the secretariat of any new network set up by a decision of the Council where that decision provides that the secretariat shall be provided by Eurojust.

3. The network set up by Decision 2008/852/JHA may request that Eurojust provide a secretariat to the network. If such request is made, paragraph 2 shall apply.

▼M2

*Article 26*

**Relations with Community or Union related institutions, bodies and agencies**

1. In so far as is relevant for the performance of its tasks, Eurojust may establish and maintain cooperative relations with the institutions, bodies and agencies set up by, or on the basis of, the Treaties establishing the European Communities or the Treaty on European Union. Eurojust shall establish and maintain cooperative relations with at least:

(a) Europol;

(b) OLAF;

(c) the European Agency for the Management of Operational Cooperation at the External Borders of the Member States of the European Union (Frontex);

(d) the Council, in particular its Joint Situation Centre.

Eurojust shall also establish and maintain cooperative relations with the European Judicial Training Network.

2. Eurojust may conclude agreements or working arrangements with the entities referred to in paragraph 1. Such agreements or working arrangements may, in particular, concern the exchange of information, including personal data, and the secondment of liaison officers to Eurojust. Such agreements or working arrangements may only be concluded after consultation by Eurojust with the Joint Supervisory Body concerning the provisions on data protection and after the approval by the Council, acting by qualified majority. Eurojust shall inform the Council of any plans it has for entering into any such negotiations and the Council may draw any conclusions it deems appropriate.

3. Prior to the entry into force of an agreement or arrangement as referred to in paragraph 2, Eurojust may directly receive and use information, including personal data, from the entities referred to in paragraph 1, in so far as this is necessary for the legitimate performance of its tasks, and it may directly transmit information, including personal data, to such entities, in so far as this is necessary for the legitimate performance of the recipient's tasks and in accordance with the rules on data protection provided in this Decision.

4. OLAF may contribute to Eurojust's work to coordinate investigations and prosecution procedures regarding the protection of the financial interests of the European Communities, either on the initiative of Eurojust or at the request of OLAF where the competent national authorities concerned do not oppose such participation.

5. For purposes of the receipt and transmission of information between Eurojust and OLAF, and without prejudice to Article 9, Member States shall ensure that the national members of Eurojust shall be regarded as competent authorities of the Member States solely for the purposes of Regulation (EC) No 1073/1999 and Council Regulation (Euratom) No 1074/1999 of 25 May 1999 concerning investigations conducted by the European Anti-Fraud Office (OLAF) [1]. The exchange of information between OLAF and national members shall be without prejudice to the information which must be given to other competent authorities under those Regulations.

---

(1) OJ L 136, 31.5.1999, p. 8.

▼M2

*Article 26a*

**Relations with third States and organisations**

1. In so far as is required for the performance of its tasks, Eurojust may establish and maintain cooperative relations with the following entities:

(a) third States;

(b) organisations such as:

(i) international organisations and their subordinate bodies governed by public law;

(ii) other bodies governed by public law which are based on an agreement between two or more States; and

(iii) the International Criminal Police Organisation (Interpol).

2. Eurojust may conclude agreements with the entities referred to in paragraph 1. Such agreements may, in particular, concern the exchange of information, including personal data, and the secondment of liaison officers or liaison magistrates to Eurojust. Such agreements may only be concluded after consultation by Eurojust with the Joint Supervisory Body concerning the provisions on data protection and after the approval by the Council, acting by qualified majority. Eurojust shall inform the Council of any plans it has for entering into any such negotiations and the Council may draw any conclusions it deems appropriate.

3. Agreements referred to in paragraph 2 containing provisions on the exchange of personal data may only be concluded if the entity concerned is subject to the Council of Europe Convention of 28 January 1981 or after an assessment confirming the existence of an adequate level of data protection ensured by that entity.

4 Agreements referred to in paragraph 2 shall include provisions on the monitoring of their implementation, including implementation of the rules on data protection.

5. Prior to the entry into force of the agreements referred to in paragraph 2, Eurojust may directly receive information, including personal data in so far as this is necessary for the legitimate performance of its tasks.

6. Prior to the entry into force of the agreements referred to in paragraph 2, Eurojust may under the conditions laid down in Article 27(1), directly transmit information, except for personal data, to these entities, in so far as this is necessary for the legitimate performance of the recipient's tasks.

7. Eurojust may, under the conditions laid down in Article 27(1), transmit personal data to the entities referred to in paragraph 1, where:

(a) this is necessary in individual cases for the purposes of preventing or combating criminal offences for which Eurojust is competent; and

(b) Eurojust has concluded an agreement as referred to in paragraph 2 with the entity concerned which has entered into force and which permits the transmission of such data.

8. Any subsequent failure, or substantial likelihood of failure, on the part of the entities referred to in paragraph 1 to meet the conditions referred to in paragraph 3, shall immediately be communicated by Eurojust to the Joint Supervisory Body and the Member States concerned. The Joint Supervisory Body may prevent the further exchange of personal data with the relevant entities until it is satisfied that adequate remedies have been provided.

▼M2

9. However, even if the conditions referred to in paragraph 7 are not fulfilled, a national member may, acting in his capacity as a competent national authority and in conformity with the provisions of his own national law, by way of exception and with the sole aim of taking urgent measures to counter imminent serious danger threatening a person or public security, carry out an exchange of information involving personal data. The national member shall be responsible for the legality of authorising the communication. The national member shall keep a record of communications of data and of the grounds for such communications. The communication of data shall be authorised only if the recipient gives an undertaking that the data will be used only for the purpose for which they were communicated.

*Article 27*

**Transmission of data**

1. Before Eurojust exchanges any information with the entities referred to in Article 26a, the national member of the Member State which submitted the information shall give his consent to the transfer of that information. In appropriate cases the national member shall consult the competent authorities of the Member States.

2. Eurojust shall be responsible for the legality of the transmission of data. Eurojust shall keep a record of all transmissions of data under Articles 26 and 26a and of the grounds for such transmissions. Data shall only be transmitted if the recipient gives an undertaking that the data will be used only for the purpose for which they were transmitted.

*Article 27a*

**Liaison magistrates posted to third States**

1. For the purpose of facilitating judicial cooperation with third States in cases in which Eurojust is providing assistance in accordance with this Decision, the College may post liaison magistrates to a third State, subject to an agreement as referred to in Article 26a with that third State. Before negotiations are entered into with a third State, the Council, acting by qualified majority, shall give its approval. Eurojust shall inform the Council of any plans it has for entering into any such negotiations and the Council may draw any conclusions it deems appropriate.

2. The liaison magistrate referred to in paragraph 1 is required to have experience of working with Eurojust and adequate knowledge of judicial cooperation and how Eurojust operates. The posting of a liaison magistrate on behalf of Eurojust shall be subject to the prior consent of the magistrate and of his Member State.

3. Where the liaison magistrate posted by Eurojust is selected among national members, deputies or assistants:

(i) he shall be replaced in his function as a national member, deputy or assistant, by the Member State;

(ii) he ceases to be entitled to exercise the powers granted to him in accordance with Articles 9a to 9e.

4. Without prejudice to Article 110 of the Staff Regulations of Officials of the European Communities laid down by Regulation (EEC, Euratom, ECSC) No 259/68 [1], the College shall draw up rules on the posting of liaison magistrates and adopt the necessary implementing arrangements in this respect in consultation with the Commission.

5. The activities of liaison magistrates posted by Eurojust shall be the subject of supervision by the Joint Supervisory Body. The liaison

(1) OJ L 56, 4.3.1968, p. 1.

▼M2

magistrates shall report to the College, which shall inform the European Parliament and the Council in the annual report and in an appropriate manner of their activities. The liaison magistrates shall inform national members and national competent authorities of all cases concerning their Member State.

6. Competent authorities of the Member States and liaison magistrates referred to in paragraph 1 may contact each other directly. In such cases, the liaison magistrate shall inform the national member concerned of such contacts.

7. The liaison magistrates referred to in paragraph 1 shall be connected to the Case Management System.

*Article 27b*

**Requests for judicial cooperation to and from third States**

1. Eurojust may, with the agreement of the Member States concerned, coordinate the execution of requests for judicial cooperation issued by a third State where these requests are part of the same investigation and require execution in at least two Member States. Requests referred to in this paragraph may also be transmitted to Eurojust by a competent national authority.

2. In case of urgency and in accordance with Article 5a, the OCC may receive and process requests referred to in paragraph 1 of this Article and issued by a third State which has concluded a cooperation agreement with Eurojust.

3. Without prejudice to Article 3(2), where requests for judicial cooperation, which relate to the same investigation and require execution in a third State, are made, Eurojust may also, with the agreement of the Member States concerned, facilitate judicial cooperation with that third State.

4. Requests referred to in paragraphs 1, 2 and 3 may be transmitted through Eurojust if it is in conformity with the instruments applicable to the relationship between that third State and the European Union or the Member States concerned.

*Article 27c*

**Liability other than liability for unauthorised or incorrect processing of data**

1. Eurojust's contractual liability shall be governed by the law applicable to the contract in question.

2. In the case of non-contractual liability, Eurojust shall, independently of any liability under Article 24, make good any damage caused through the fault of the College or the staff of Eurojust in the performance of their duties in so far as it may be imputed to them and regardless of the different procedures for claiming damages which exist under the law of the Member States.

3. Paragraph 2 shall also apply to damage caused through the fault of a national member, a deputy or an assistant in the performance of his duties. However, when he is acting on the basis of the powers granted to him pursuant to Articles 9a to 9e, his Member State of origin shall reimburse Eurojust the sums which Eurojust has paid to make good such damage.

4. The injured party shall have the right to demand that Eurojust refrain from taking, or cease, any action.

5. The national courts of the Member States competent to deal with disputes involving Eurojust's liability as referred to in this Article shall

▼M2

be determined by reference to Council Regulation (EC) No 44/2001 of 22 December 2000 on jurisdiction and the recognition and enforcement of judgments in civil and commercial matters (1).

▼B

*Article 28*

**Organisation and operation**

1. The College shall be responsible for the organisation and operation of Eurojust.

2. The College shall elect a President from among the national members and may, if it considers it necessary, elect at most two Vice-Presidents. The result of the election shall be submitted to the Council ►M2 acting by qualified majority, ◄for its approval.

3. The President shall exercise his duties on behalf of the College and under its authority, direct its work and monitor the daily management ensured by the Administrative Director. The rules of procedure shall specify the cases in which his decisions or actions shall require prior authorisation or a report to the College.

4. The term of office of the President shall be three years. He may be re-elected once. The term of office of any Vice-President(s) shall be governed by the rules of procedure.

5. Eurojust shall be assisted by a secretariat headed by an Administrative Director.

6. Eurojust shall exercise over its staff the powers devolved to the Appointing Authority. The College shall adopt appropriate rules for the implementation of this paragraph in accordance with the rules of procedure.

*Article 29*

**Administrative Director**

1. The Administrative Director of Eurojust shall be appointed ►M2 by two-thirds majority ◄ by the College. The College shall set up a selection board which, following a call for applications, shall establish a list of candidates from among whom the College shall choose the Administrative Director. ►M2 The Commission shall be entitled to participate in the selection process and to sit on the selection board. ◄

2. The term of office of the Administrative Director shall be five years. ►M2 It may be extended once without a need for a call for applications, provided that the College so decides by a three-fourths majority and appoints the Administrative Director with the same majority. ◄

3. The Administrative Director shall be subject to the rules and regulations applicable to officials and other servants of the European Communities.

4. The Administrative Director shall work under the authority of the College and its President, acting in accordance with Article 28(3). He may be removed from office by the College by a two-thirds majority.

5. The Administrative Director shall be responsible, under the supervision of the President, for the day-to-day administration of Eurojust and for staff management. ►M2 To that end, he shall be responsible for establishing and implementing, in cooperation with the College, an effective monitoring and evaluation procedure relating to the

(1) OJ L 12, 16.1.2001, p. 1.

▼B

performance of Eurojust's administration in terms of achieving its objectives. The Administrative Director shall report regularly to the College on the results of that monitoring. ◄

*Article 30*

**Staff**

1. Eurojust staff shall be subject to the rules and regulations applicable to the officials and other servants of the European Communities, particularly as regards their recruitment and status.

2. Eurojust staff shall consist of staff recruited according to the rules and regulations referred to in paragraph 1, taking into account all the criteria referred to in Article 27 of the Staff Regulations of Officials of the European Communities laid down by Regulation (EEC, Euratom, ECSC) No 259/68 (1), including their geographical distribution. They shall have the status of permanent staff, temporary staff or local staff. At the request of the Administrative Director, and in agreement with the President on behalf of the College, Community officials may be seconded to Eurojust by the Community institutions as temporary staff. Member States may second national experts to Eurojust ►M2 who may also assist the national member ◄. ►M2 The College shall adopt the necessary implementing arrangements for seconded national experts. ◄

3. Under the authority of the College, the staff shall carry out its tasks bearing in mind the objectives and mandate of Eurojust, without seeking or accepting instructions from any government, authority, organisation or person extraneous to Eurojust ►M2 without prejudice to Article 25a(1)(c) and (2) ◄.

*Article 31*

**Assistance with interpreting and translation**

1. The official linguistic arrangements of the Union shall apply to Eurojust proceedings.

2. The annual report to the Council, referred to in the second subparagraph of Article 32(1), shall be drawn up in the official languages of the Union institutions.

*Article 32*

**►M2 Informing the European Parliament, the Council and the Commission ◄**

1. The President, on behalf of the College, shall report to the Council in writing every year on the activities and management, including budgetary management, of Eurojust.

To that end, the College shall prepare an annual report on the activities of Eurojust and on any criminal policy problems within the Union highlighted as a result of Eurojust's activities. In that report, Eurojust may also make proposals for the improvement of judicial cooperation in criminal matters.

The President shall also submit any report or any other information on the operation of Eurojust which may be required of him by the Council.

2. Each year the Presidency of the Council shall forward a report to the European Parliament on the work carried out by Eurojust and on the activities of the Joint Supervisory Body.

(1) OJ L 56, 4.3.1968. Regulation as last amended by Regulation (EC, ECSC, Euratom) No 2581/2001 (OJ L 345, 29.12.2001, p. 1).

▼M2

3. The Commission or the Council may seek Eurojust's opinion on all draft instruments prepared under Title VI of the Treaty.

*Article 33*

**Finance**

1. The salaries and emoluments of the national members, deputies and assistants referred to in Article 2(2) shall be borne by their Member State of origin.

2. Where national members, deputies and assistants act within the framework of Eurojust's tasks, the relevant expenditure related to these activities shall be regarded as operational expenditure within the meaning of Article 41(3) of the Treaty.

▼B

*Article 34*

**Budget**

1. Forecasts shall be made of all Eurojust revenue and expenditure for each financial year, which shall be the same as the calendar year. Revenue and expenditure shall be entered in the budget, which shall include the establishment plan which shall be submitted to the budget authority competent for the general budget of the European Union. The establishment plan shall consist of posts of a permanent or temporary nature and a reference to national experts seconded, and shall state the number, grade and category of the staff employed by Eurojust for the financial year in question.

2. Revenue and expenditure shall be balanced in the Eurojust budget.

3. Without prejudice to other resources, Eurojust revenue may include a subsidy entered in the general budget of the European Union.

4. Eurojust expenditure shall include *inter alia* expenditure relating to interpreters and translators, expenditure on security, administrative and infrastructure expenditure, operational and rental costs, travel expenses of members of Eurojust and its staff and costs arising from contracts with third parties.

▼M1

*Article 35*

**Drawing up of the budget**

1. Each year the College, on the basis of a draft drawn up by the Administrative Director, shall produce an estimate of revenue and expenditure for Eurojust for the following financial year. This estimate, which shall include a draft establishment plan, shall be forwarded by the College to the Commission by ►M2 10 February ◄ at the latest. ►M2 The European Judicial Network and networks referred to in Article 25a(2) shall be informed on the parts related to the activities of their secretariats in due time before the forwarding of the estimate to the Commission. ◄

2. On the basis of the estimate, the Commission shall propose in the preliminary draft general budget of the European Union the amount of the annual subsidy as well as the posts of a permanent or temporary nature and submit this proposal to the budgetary authority in accordance with Article 272 of the Treaty.

3. The budgetary authority shall authorise the appropriations for the subsidy to Eurojust and determine the posts of a permanent or temporary nature within the framework of the Staff Regulations of officials and other Servants of the European Communities.

▼M1

4. Before the beginning of the financial year, the College of Eurojust shall adopt the budget, including the establishment plan referred to in Article 34(1), third sentence, on the basis of the annual subsidy and posts authorised by the budgetary authority in accordance with paragraph 3 of this Article, adjusting it to the various contributions granted to Eurojust and the funds from other sources.

*Article 36*

**Implementation of the budget and discharge**

1. The Administrative Director shall, as authorising officer, implement the Eurojust budget. He shall report to the College on the implementation of the budget.

2. ►M2 By 1 March at the latest following each financial year, the accounting officer of Eurojust shall communicate the provisional accounts to the Commission's accounting officer and the Court of Auditors together with a report on the budgetary and financial management for that financial year. ◄ The Commission's accounting officer shall consolidate the provisional accounts of the institutions and decentralised bodies in accordance with Article 128 of the general Financial Regulation.

▼M2

3. Eurojust shall send the report on the budgetary and financial management for the financial year to the European Parliament and the Council by 31 March of the following year.

▼M1

4. On receipt of the Court of Auditors' observations on Eurojust's provisional accounts, pursuant to Article 129 of the general Financial Regulation, the Administrative Director shall draw up Eurojust's final accounts under his own responsibility and submit them to the College of Eurojust for an opinion.

5. The College of Eurojust shall deliver an opinion on Eurojust's final accounts.

6. The Administrative Director shall, by 1 July at the latest following each financial year, forward the final accounts to the European Parliament, the Council, the Commission and the Court of Auditors, together with the College of Eurojust's opinion.

7. The final accounts shall be published.

8. The Administrative Director shall send the Court of Auditors a reply to its observations by 30 September at the latest. He shall also send this reply to the College of Eurojust.

9. The Administrative Director, acting under the authority of the College of Eurojust and its President, shall submit to the European Parliament at the latter's request any information required for the smooth application of the discharge procedure for the financial year in question, as laid down in Article 146(3) of the general Financial Regulation.

10. The European Parliament, on a recommendation from the Council acting by a qualified majority, shall, before ►M2 15 May ◄ of year N + 2, give a discharge to the Administrative Director in respect of the implementation of the budget for year N.

*Article 37*

**Financial regulation applicable to the budget**

1. The financial rules applicable to Eurojust's budget shall be adopted unanimously by the College after the Commission has been consulted.

▼M1

They may not depart from Commission Regulation (EC, Euratom) No 2343/2002 of 19 November 2002 on the framework Financial Regulation for the bodies referred to in Article 185 of Council Regulation (EC, Euratom) No 1605/2002 on the Financial Regulation applicable to the general budget of the European Communities (1) unless specifically required for Eurojust's operation and with the Commission's prior consent.

▼B

*Article 38*

**Audit**

▼M1

1. The responsibility for putting in place internal control systems and procedures suitable for carrying out his tasks shall lie with the authorising officer.

▼B

2. The College shall appoint an internal auditor who shall be responsible in particular for providing, in accordance with the relevant international standards, an assurance regarding the proper functioning of the systems and procedures for implementing the budget. The internal auditor may not be either the authorising officer or the accountant. The College may ask the Commission's internal auditor to carry out these duties.

3. The auditor shall report his findings and recommendations to Eurojust and submit a copy of the report to the Commission. Eurojust shall, in the light of the auditor's reports, take the necessary measures in response to these recommendations.

4. The rules laid down by Regulation (EC) No 1073/1999 shall apply to Eurojust. The College shall adopt the necessary implementing measures.

*Article 39*

**Access to documents**

On the basis of a proposal by the Administrative Director, the College shall adopt rules for access to Eurojust documents, taking account of the principles and limits stated in Regulation (EC) No 1049/2001 of the European Parliament and of the Council of 30 May 2001 regarding public access to European Parliament, Council and Commission documents (2).

▼M2

*Article 39a*

**EU classified information**

Eurojust shall apply the security principles and minimum standards set out in Council Decision 2001/264/EC of 19 March 2001 adopting the Council's security regulations (3) in the management of EU classified information.

(1) OJ L 357, 31.12.2002, p. 72 with Corrigendum in OJ L 2, 7.1.2003, p. 39.
(2) OJ L 145, 31.5.2001, p. 43.
(3) OJ L 101, 11.4.2001, p. 1.

▼B

*Article 40*

**Territorial application**

This Decision shall apply to Gibraltar, which shall be represented by the national member for the United Kingdom.

▼M2

*Article 41*

**Reporting**

1. Member States shall notify Eurojust and the General Secretariat of the Council of the designation of national members, deputies, assistants as well as persons referred to in Article 12(1) and (2) and of any change to this designation. The General Secretariat of the Council shall keep an updated list of these persons and shall make their names and contact details available to all Member States and to the Commission.

2. The definitive appointment of a national member can not take effect before the day on which the General Secretariat of the Council receives the official notifications referred to in paragraph 1 and Article 9a(3).

*Article 41a*

**Evaluation**

1. Before 4 June 2014 and every five years thereafter, the College shall commission an independent external evaluation of the implementation of this Decision as well as of the activities carried out by Eurojust.

2. Each evaluation shall assess the impact of this Decision, Eurojust's performance in terms of achieving the objectives referred to in this Decision as well as the effectiveness and efficiency of Eurojust. The College shall issue specific terms of reference in consultation with the Commission.

3. The evaluation report shall include the evaluation findings and recommendations. This report shall be forwarded to the European Parliament, the Council and the Commission and shall be made public.

▼B

*Article 42*

**Transposition**

If necessary the Member States shall bring their national law into conformity with this Decision at the earliest opportunity and in any case no later than 6 September 2003.

*Article 43*

**Entry into force**

This Decision shall enter into force on the day of its publication in the *Official Journal of the European Communities* without prejudice to Article 41. On that date the Provisional Judicial Cooperation Unit shall cease to exist.

▼**M2**

*ANNEX*

**List referred to in Article 13(10) setting out the minimum types of information to be transmitted, where available, to Eurojust pursuant to Article 13(5), (6) and (7)**

1. For situations referred to in Article 13(5):

   (a) participating Member States;

   (b) type of offences concerned;

   (c) date of the agreement setting up the team;

   (d) planned duration of the team, including modification of this duration;

   (e) details of the leader of the team for each participating Member State;

   (f) short summary of the results of the joint investigation teams.

2. For situations referred to in Article 13(6):

   (a) data which identify the person, group or entity that is the object of a criminal investigation or prosecution;

   (b) Member States concerned;

   (c) the offence concerned and its circumstances;

   (d) data related to the requests for, or decisions on, judicial cooperation including regarding instruments giving effect to the principle of mutual recognition, which are issued, including:

      (i) date of the request;

      (ii) requesting or issuing authority;

      (iii) requested or executing authority;

      (iv) type of request (measures requested);

      (v) whether or not the request has been executed, and if not on what grounds.

3. For situations referred to in Article 13(7)(a):

   (a) Member States and competent authorities concerned;

   (b) data which identify the person, group or entity that is the object of a criminal investigation or prosecution;

   (c) the offence concerned and its circumstances.

4. For situations referred to in Article 13(7)(b):

   (a) Member States and competent authorities concerned;

   (b) data which identify the person, group or entity that is the object of a criminal investigation or prosecution;

   (c) type of delivery;

   (d) type of offence in connection with which the controlled delivery is carried out.

5. For situations referred to in Article 13(7)(c):

   (a) requesting or issuing State;

   (b) requested or executing State;

   (c) description of the difficulties.

L 138/14 EN Official Journal of the European Union 4.6.2009

III

*(Acts adopted under the EU Treaty)*

# ACTS ADOPTED UNDER TITLE VI OF THE EU TREATY

## COUNCIL DECISION 2009/426/JHA

### of 16 December 2008

### on the strengthening of Eurojust and amending Decision 2002/187/JHA setting up Eurojust with a view to reinforcing the fight against serious crime

THE COUNCIL OF THE EUROPEAN UNION,

Having regard to the Treaty on European Union, and in particular Articles 31(2) and 34(2)(c) thereof,

Having regard to the initiative of the Kingdom of Belgium, the Czech Republic, the Republic of Estonia, the Kingdom of Spain, the French Republic, the Italian Republic, the Grand Duchy of Luxembourg, the Kingdom of the Netherlands, the Republic of Austria, the Republic of Poland, the Portuguese Republic, the Republic of Slovenia, the Slovak Republic and the Kingdom of Sweden,

Having regard to the Opinion of the European Parliament [1],

Whereas:

(1) Eurojust was set up by Council Decision 2002/187/JHA [2] as a body of the European Union with legal personality to stimulate and to improve coordination and cooperation between competent judicial authorities of the Member States.

(2) On the basis of an assessment of the experience gained by Eurojust, a further enhancement of its operational effectiveness is needed by taking account of that experience.

(3) The time has come to ensure that Eurojust becomes more operational and that the status of national members is approximated.

(4) In order to ensure continuous and effective contribution from the Member States to the achievement by Eurojust of its objectives, the national member should be required to have his regular place of work at the seat of Eurojust.

(5) It is necessary to define a common basis of powers which every national member should have in his capacity as a competent national authority acting in accordance with national law. Some of these powers should be granted to the national member for urgent cases where it is not possible for him to identify or to contact the competent national authority in a timely manner. It is understood that these powers will not have to be exercised in so far as it is possible to identify and to contact the competent authority.

(6) This Decision does not affect the manner in which the Member States organise their internal judicial system or administrative procedures for the designation of the national member and the setting up of the internal working of the national desks at Eurojust.

(7) The setting up of an On-Call Coordination (OCC) within Eurojust is necessary to make Eurojust available around the clock and to enable it to intervene in urgent cases. It should be the responsibility of each Member State to ensure that their representatives in the OCC are able to act on a 24-hour/7-day basis.

(8) Member States should ensure that competent national authorities respond without undue delay to requests made under this Decision, even if competent national authorities refuse to comply with requests made by the national member.

(9) The role of the College should be enhanced in cases of conflict of jurisdiction and in cases of recurrent refusals or difficulties concerning the execution of requests for, and decisions on, judicial cooperation, including regarding instruments giving effect to the principle of mutual recognition.

(1) Opinion delivered on 2 September 2008 (not yet published in the Official Journal).
(2) OJ L 63, 6.3.2002, p. 1.

(10) Eurojust national coordination systems should be set up in the Member States to coordinate the work carried out by the national correspondents for Eurojust, the national correspondent for Eurojust for terrorism matters, the national correspondent for the European Judicial Network and up to three other contact points of the European Judicial Network, as well as representatives in the Networks for Joint Investigation Teams, War Crimes, Asset Recovery and Corruption.

(11) The Eurojust national coordination system should ensure that the Case Management System receives information related to the Member State concerned in an efficient and reliable manner. However, the Eurojust national coordination system should not have to be responsible for actually transmitting information to Eurojust. Member States should decide on the best channel to be used for the transmission of information to Eurojust.

(12) In order to enable the Eurojust national coordination system to fulfil its tasks, a connection to the Case Management System should be ensured. The connection to the Case Management System should be made taking due account of national information technology systems. Access to the Case Management System at national level should be based on the central role played by the national member who is responsible for the opening and management of temporary work files.

(13) Council Framework Decision 2008/977/JHA of 27 November 2008 on the protection of personal data processed in the framework of police and judicial cooperation in criminal matters [1] is applicable to the processing by the Member States of the personal data transferred between the Member States and Eurojust. The relevant set of data protection provisions of Decision 2002/187/JHA will not be affected by Framework Decision 2008/977/JHA and contains specific provisions on the protection of personal data regulating these matters in more detail because of the particular nature, functions and competences of Eurojust.

(14) Eurojust should be authorised to process certain personal data on persons who, under the national legislation of the Member States concerned, are suspected of having committed or having taken part in a criminal offence in respect of which Eurojust is competent, or who have been convicted of such an offence. The list of such personal data should include telephone numbers, e-mail addresses, vehicle registration data, DNA profiles established from the non-coding part of DNA, photographs and fingerprints. The list should also include traffic data and location data and the related data necessary to identify the subscriber or user of a publicly available electronic communications service; this should not include data revealing the content of the communication. It is not intended that Eurojust carry out an automated comparison of DNA profiles or fingerprints.

(15) Eurojust should be given the opportunity to extend the deadlines for storage of personal data in order to achieve its objectives. Such decisions should be taken following careful consideration of particular needs. Any extension of deadlines for processing personal data, where prosecution is statute barred in all Member States concerned, should be decided only where there is a specific need to provide assistance under this Decision.

(16) The Rules on the Joint Supervisory Body should facilitate its functioning.

(17) With a view to increasing the operational effectiveness of Eurojust, transmission of information to Eurojust should be improved by providing clear and limited obligations for national authorities.

(18) Eurojust should implement priorities set by the Council, in particular those set on the basis of the Organised Crime Threat Assessment (OCTA), as referred to in the Hague Programme [2].

(19) Eurojust is to maintain privileged relations with the European Judicial Network based on consultation and complementarity. This Decision should help clarify the respective roles of Eurojust and the European Judicial Network and their mutual relations, while maintaining the specificity of the European Judicial Network.

(20) Nothing in this Decision should be construed to affect the autonomy of the secretariats of the networks mentioned in this Decision when they discharge their function as Eurojust staff in accordance with the Staff Regulations of Officials of the European Communities laid down by Regulation (EEC, Euratom, ECSC) No 259/68 of the Council [3].

(21) It is also necessary to strengthen Eurojust's capacity to work with external partners, such as third States, the European Police Office (Europol), the European Anti-Fraud Office (OLAF), the Council's Joint Situation Centre and the European Agency for the Management of Operational Cooperation at the External Borders of the Member States of the European Union (Frontex).

[1] OJ L 350, 30.12.2008, p. 60.

[2] OJ C 53, 3.3.2005, p. 1.

[3] OJ L 56, 4.3.1968, p. 1.

L 138/16 EN Official Journal of the European Union 4.6.2009

(22) Provision should be made for Eurojust to post liaison magistrates to third States in order to achieve objectives similar to those assigned to liaison magistrates seconded by the Member States on the basis of Council Joint Action 96/277/JHA of 22 April 1996 concerning a framework for the exchange of liaison magistrates to improve judicial cooperation between the Member States of the European Union (1).

(23) This Decision allows the principle of public access to official documents to be taken into account,

HAS DECIDED AS FOLLOWS:

*Article 1*

[Editor's Note: all amendments have been incorporated in the consolidated version reproduced above]

(1) OJ L 105, 27.4.1996, p. 1.

# Framework Decision 2002/465 on joint investigation teams, 13 June 2002

[OJ 2002, L 162/1–3]

20.6.2002 EN Official Journal of the European Communities L 162/1

*(Acts adopted pursuant to Title VI of the Treaty on European Union)*

**COUNCIL FRAMEWORK DECISION**
**of 13 June 2002**
**on joint investigation teams**

(2002/465/JHA)

THE COUNCIL OF THE EUROPEAN UNION,

Having regard to the Treaty on the European Union, and in particular Article 34(2)(b) thereof,

Having regard to the initiative of the Kingdom of Belgium, the French Republic, the Kingdom of Spain and the United Kingdom ([1]),

Having regard to the opinion of the European Parliament ([2]),

Whereas:

(1) One of the Union's objectives is to provide citizens with a high level of safety within an area of freedom, security and justice and this objective is to be achieved by preventing and combating crime through closer cooperation between police forces, customs authorities and other competent authorities in the Member States, while respecting the principles of human rights and fundamental freedoms and the rule of law on which the Union is founded and which are common to the Member States.

(2) The European Council held in Tampere on 15 and 16 October 1999 called for joint investigation teams as foreseen in the Treaty to be set up without delay, as a first step, to combat trafficking in drugs and human beings as well as terrorism.

(3) Provision has been made in Article 13 of the Convention established by the Council in accordance with Article 34 of the Treaty on European Union on Mutual Assistance in Criminal Matters between the Member States of the European Union ([3]) for the establishment and operation of joint investigation teams.

(4) The Council urges that all measures be taken to ensure that this Convention is ratified as soon as possible, and in any event in the course of 2002.

(5) The Council recognises that it is important to respond quickly to the European Council's call for the setting up of joint investigative teams without delay.

(6) The Council considers that for the purpose of combating international crime as effectively as possible, it is appropriate that at this stage a specific legally binding instrument on joint investigation teams should be adopted at the level of the Union which should apply to joint investigations into trafficking in drugs and human beings as well as terrorism.

(7) The Council considers that such teams should be set up, as a matter of priority, to combat offences committed by terrorists.

(8) The Member States that set up a team should decide on its composition, purpose and duration.

(9) The Member States setting up a team should have the possibility to decide, where possible and in accordance with applicable law, to let persons not representing the competent authorities of Member States take part in the activities of the team, and that such persons may include representatives of, for example, Europol, the Commission (OLAF) or representatives of authorities of non Member States, and in particular representatives of law enforcement authorities of the United States. In such cases the agreement setting up the team should specify issues relating to possible liability for such representatives.

(10) A joint investigating team should operate in the territory of a Member State in conformity with the law applicable to that Member State.

(11) This Framework Decision should be without prejudice to any other existing provisions or arrangements on the setting up or operation of joint investigation teams,

HAS ADOPTED THIS FRAMEWORK DECISION:

*Article 1*

**Joint investigation teams**

1. By mutual agreement, the competent authorities of two or more Member States may set up a joint investigation team for a specific purpose and a limited period, which may be extended by mutual consent, to carry out criminal investigations in one or more of the Member States setting up the team. The composition of the team shall be set out in the agreement.

([1]) OJ C 295, 20.10.2001, p. 9.
([2]) Opinion delivered on 13 November 2001 (not yet published in the Official Journal).
([3]) OJ C 197, 12.7.2000, p. 1.

A joint investigation team may, in particular, be set up where:

(a) a Member State's investigations into criminal offences require difficult and demanding investigations having links with other Member States;

(b) a number of Member States are conducting investigations into criminal offences in which the circumstances of the case necessitate coordinated, concerted action in the Member States involved.

A request for the setting up of a joint investigation team may be made by any of the Member States concerned. The team shall be set up in one of the Member States in which the investigations are expected to be carried out.

2. In addition to the information referred to in the relevant provisions of Article 14 of the European Convention on Mutual Assistance in Criminal Matters and Article 37 of the Benelux Treaty of 27 June 1962, as amended by the Protocol of 11 May 1974, requests for the setting up of a joint investigation team shall include proposals for the composition of the team.

3. A joint investigation team shall operate in the territory of the Member States setting up the team under the following general conditions:

(a) The leader of the team shall be a representative of the competent authority participating in criminal investigations from the Member State in which the team operates. The leader of the team shall act within the limits of his or her competence under national law.

(b) The team shall carry out its operations in accordance with the law of the Member State in which it operates. The members of the team shall carry out their tasks under the leadership of the person referred to in subparagraph (a), taking into account the conditions set by their own authorities in the agreement on setting up the team.

(c) The Member State in which the team operates shall make the necessary organisational arrangements for it to do so.

4. In this Framework Decision, members of the joint investigation team from Member States other than the Member State in which the team operates are referred to as being 'seconded' to the team.

5. Seconded members of the joint investigation team shall be entitled to be present when investigative measures are taken in the Member State of operation. However, the leader of the team may, for particular reasons, in accordance with the law of the Member State where the team operates, decide otherwise.

6. Seconded members of the joint investigation team may, in accordance with the law of the Member State where the team operates, be entrusted by the leader of the team with the task of taking certain investigative measures where this has been approved by the competent authorities of the Member State of operation and the seconding Member State.

7. Where the joint investigation team needs investigative measures to be taken in one of the Member States setting up the team, members seconded to the team by that Member State may request their own competent authorities to take those measures. Those measures shall be considered in that Member State under the conditions which would apply if they were requested in a national investigation.

8. Where the joint investigation team needs assistance from a Member State other than those which have set up the team, or from a third State, the request for assistance may be made by the competent authorities of the State of operations to the competent authorities of the other State concerned in accordance with the relevant instruments or arrangements.

9. A member of the joint investigation team may, in accordance with his or her national law and within the limits of his or her competence, provide the team with information available in the Member State which has seconded him or her for the purpose of the criminal investigations conducted by the team.

10. Information lawfully obtained by a member or seconded member while part of a joint investigation team which is not otherwise available to the competent authorities of the Member States concerned may be used for the following purposes:

(a) for the purposes for which the team has been set up;

(b) subject to the prior consent of the Member State where the information became available, for detecting, investigating and prosecuting other criminal offences. Such consent may be withheld only in cases where such use would endanger criminal investigations in the Member State concerned or in respect of which that Member State could refuse mutual assistance;

(c) for preventing an immediate and serious threat to public security, and without prejudice to subparagraph (b) if subsequently a criminal investigation is opened;

(d) for other purposes to the extent that this is agreed between Member States setting up the team.

11. This Framework Decision shall be without prejudice to any other existing provisions or arrangements on the setting up or operation of joint investigation teams.

12. To the extent that the laws of the Member States concerned or the provisions of any legal instrument applicable between them permit, arrangements may be agreed for persons other than representatives of the competent authorities of the Member States setting up the joint investigation team to take part in the activities of the team. Such persons may, for example, include officials of bodies set up pursuant to the Treaty. The rights conferred upon the members or seconded members of the team by virtue of this Framework Decision shall not apply to these persons unless the agreement expressly states otherwise.

*Article 2*

**Criminal liability regarding officials**

During the operations referred to in Article 1, officials from a Member State other than the Member State of operation shall be regarded as officials of the Member State of operation with respect to offences committed against them or by them.

*Article 3*

**Civil liability regarding officials**

1. Where, in accordance with Article 1, officials of a Member State are operating in another Member State, the first Member State shall be liable for any damage caused by them during their operations, in accordance with the law of the Member State in whose territory they are operating.

2. The Member State in whose territory the damage referred to in paragraph 1 was caused shall make good such damage under the conditions applicable to damage caused by its own officials.

3. The Member State whose officials have caused damage to any person in the territory of another Member State shall reimburse the latter in full any sums it has paid to the victims or persons entitled on their behalf.

4. Without prejudice to the exercise of its rights vis-à-vis third parties and with the exception of paragraph 3, each Member State shall refrain, in the case provided for in paragraph 1, from requesting reimbursement of damages it has sustained from another Member State.

*Article 4*

**Implementation**

1. Member States shall take the necessary measures to comply with the provisions of this Framework Decision by 1 January 2003.

2. Member States shall transmit to the General Secretariat of the Council and the Commission the text of any provisions transposing into their national law the obligations imposed on them under this Framework Decision. On the basis of this and other information, the Commission shall, by 1 July 2004, submit a report to the Council on the operation of this Framework Decision. The Council shall assess the extent to which the Member States have complied with this Framework Decision.

*Article 5*

**Entry into force**

This Framework Decision shall enter into force on the date of its publication in the Official Journal. It shall cease to have effect when the Convention on Mutual Assistance in Criminal Matters between Member States of the European Union has entered into force in all Member States.

Done at Luxembourg, 13 June 2002.

*For the Council*

*The President*

M. RAJOY BREY

# Framework Decision 2002/475 on combating terrorism, 13 June 2002

**[Consolidated version. Original version OJ 2002, L 164/3–7 amended by OJ 2008, L 330/21–23 as of 9 December 2010]**

►B

**COUNCIL FRAMEWORK DECISION**

**of 13 June 2002**

**on combating terrorism**

(2002/475/JHA)

(OJ L 164, 22.6.2002, p. 3)

Amended by:

| | | Official Journal | | |
|---|---|---|---|---|
| | | No | page | date |
| ►M1 | Council Framework Decision 2008/919/JHA of 28 November 2008 | L 330 | 21 | 9.12.2008 |

▼B

**COUNCIL FRAMEWORK DECISION**

**of 13 June 2002**

**on combating terrorism**

(2002/475/JHA)

THE COUNCIL OF THE EUROPEAN UNION,

Having regard to the Treaty establishing the European Union, and in particular Article 29, Article 31(e) and Article 34(2)(b) thereof,

Having regard to the proposal from the Commission ([1]),

Having regard to the opinion of the European Parliament ([2]),

Whereas:

(1) The European Union is founded on the universal values of human dignity, liberty, equality and solidarity, respect for human rights and fundamental freedoms. It is based on the principle of democracy and the principle of the rule of law, principles which are common to the Member States.

(2) Terrorism constitutes one of the most serious violations of those principles. The La Gomera Declaration adopted at the informal Council meeting on 14 October 1995 affirmed that terrorism constitutes a threat to democracy, to the free exercise of human rights and to economic and social development.

(3) All or some Member States are party to a number of conventions relating to terrorism. The Council of Europe Convention of 27 January 1977 on the Suppression of Terrorism does not regard terrorist offences as political offences or as offences connected with political offences or as offences inspired by political motives. The United Nations has adopted the Convention for the suppression of terrorist bombings of 15 December 1997 and the Convention for the suppression of financing terrorism of 9 December 1999. A draft global Convention against terrorism is currently being negotiated within the United Nations.

(4) At European Union level, on 3 December 1998 the Council adopted the Action Plan of the Council and the Commission on how best to implement the provisions of the Treaty of Amsterdam on an area of freedom, security and justice ([3]). Account should also be taken of the Council Conclusions of 20 September 2001 and of the Extraordinary European Council plan of action to combat terrorism of 21 September 2001. Terrorism was referred to in the conclusions of the Tampere European Council of 15 and 16 October 1999, and of the Santa María da Feira European Council of 19 and 20 June 2000. It was also mentioned in the Commission communication to the Council and the European Parliament on the biannual update of the scoreboard to review progress on the creation of an area of 'freedom, security and justice' in the European Union (second half of 2000). Furthermore, on 5 September 2001 the European Parliament adopted a recommendation on the role of the European Union in combating terrorism. It should, moreover, be recalled that on 30 July 1996 twenty-five measures to fight against terrorism were advocated by the leading industrialised countries (G7) and Russia meeting in Paris.

(5) The European Union has adopted numerous specific measures having an impact on terrorism and organised crime, such as the Council Decision of 3 December 1998 instructing Europol to deal

([1]) OJ C 332 E, 27.11.2001, p. 300.
([2]) Opinion delivered on 6 February 2002 (not yet published in the Official Journal).
([3]) OJ C 19, 23.1.1999, p. 1.

▼B

with crimes committed or likely to be committed in the course of terrorist activities against life, limb, personal freedom or property [1]; Council Joint Action 96/610/JHA of 15 October 1996 concerning the creation and maintenance of a Directory of specialised counter-terrorist competences, skills and expertise to facilitate counter-terrorism cooperation between the Member States of the European Union [2]; Council Joint Action 98/428/JHA of 29 June 1998 on the creation of a European Judicial Network [3], with responsibilities in terrorist offences, in particular Article 2; Council Joint Action 98/733/JHA of 21 December 1998 on making it a criminal offence to participate in a criminal organisation in the Member States of the European Union [4]; and the Council Recommendation of 9 December 1999 on cooperation in combating the financing of terrorist groups [5].

(6) The definition of terrorist offences should be approximated in all Member States, including those offences relating to terrorist groups. Furthermore, penalties and sanctions should be provided for natural and legal persons having committed or being liable for such offences, which reflect the seriousness of such offences.

(7) Jurisdictional rules should be established to ensure that the terrorist offence may be effectively prosecuted.

(8) Victims of terrorist offences are vulnerable, and therefore specific measures are necessary with regard to them.

(9) Given that the objectives of the proposed action cannot be sufficiently achieved by the Member States unilaterally, and can therefore, because of the need for reciprocity, be better achieved at the level of the Union, the Union may adopt measures, in accordance with the principle of subsidiarity. In accordance with the principle of proportionality, this Framework Decision does not go beyond what is necessary in order to achieve those objectives.

(10) This Framework Decision respects fundamental rights as guaranteed by the European Convention for the Protection of Human Rights and Fundamental Freedoms and as they emerge from the constitutional traditions common to the Member States as principles of Community law. The Union observes the principles recognised by Article 6(2) of the Treaty on European Union and reflected in the Charter of Fundamental Rights of the European Union, notably Chapter VI thereof. Nothing in this Framework Decision may be interpreted as being intended to reduce or restrict fundamental rights or freedoms such as the right to strike, freedom of assembly, of association or of expression, including the right of everyone to form and to join trade unions with others for the protection of his or her interests and the related right to demonstrate.

(11) Actions by armed forces during periods of armed conflict, which are governed by international humanitarian law within the meaning of these terms under that law, and, inasmuch as they are governed by other rules of international law, actions by the armed forces of a State in the exercise of their official duties are not governed by this Framework Decision,

HAS ADOPTED THIS FRAMEWORK DECISION:

(1) OJ C 26, 30.1.1999, p. 22.
(2) OJ L 273, 25.10.1996, p. 1.
(3) OJ L 191, 7.7.1998, p. 4.
(4) OJ L 351, 29.12.1998, p. 1.
(5) OJ C 373, 23.12.1999, p. 1.

▼B

*Article 1*

**Terrorist offences and fundamental rights and principles**

1. Each Member State shall take the necessary measures to ensure that the intentional acts referred to below in points (a) to (i), as defined as offences under national law, which, given their nature or context, may seriously damage a country or an international organisation where committed with the aim of:

— seriously intimidating a population, or

— unduly compelling a Government or international organisation to perform or abstain from performing any act, or

— seriously destabilising or destroying the fundamental political, constitutional, economic or social structures of a country or an international organisation,

shall be deemed to be terrorist offences:

(a) attacks upon a person's life which may cause death;

(b) attacks upon the physical integrity of a person;

(c) kidnapping or hostage taking;

(d) causing extensive destruction to a Government or public facility, a transport system, an infrastructure facility, including an information system, a fixed platform located on the continental shelf, a public place or private property likely to endanger human life or result in major economic loss;

(e) seizure of aircraft, ships or other means of public or goods transport;

(f) manufacture, possession, acquisition, transport, supply or use of weapons, explosives or of nuclear, biological or chemical weapons, as well as research into, and development of, biological and chemical weapons;

(g) release of dangerous substances, or causing fires, floods or explosions the effect of which is to endanger human life;

(h) interfering with or disrupting the supply of water, power or any other fundamental natural resource the effect of which is to endanger human life;

(i) threatening to commit any of the acts listed in (a) to (h).

2. This Framework Decision shall not have the effect of altering the obligation to respect fundamental rights and fundamental legal principles as enshrined in Article 6 of the Treaty on European Union.

*Article 2*

**Offences relating to a terrorist group**

1. For the purposes of this Framework Decision, 'terrorist group' shall mean: a structured group of more than two persons, established over a period of time and acting in concert to commit terrorist offences. 'Structured group' shall mean a group that is not randomly formed for the immediate commission of an offence and that does not need to have formally defined roles for its members, continuity of its membership or a developed structure.

2. Each Member State shall take the necessary measures to ensure that the following intentional acts are punishable:

(a) directing a terrorist group;

(b) participating in the activities of a terrorist group, including by supplying information or material resources, or by funding its

▼B

activities in any way, with knowledge of the fact that such participation will contribute to the criminal activities of the terrorist group.

▼M1

*Article 3*

**Offences linked to terrorist activities**

1. For the purposes of this Framework Decision:

(a) 'public provocation to commit a terrorist offence' shall mean the distribution, or otherwise making available, of a message to the public, with the intent to incite the commission of one of the offences listed in Article 1(1)(a) to (h), where such conduct, whether or not directly advocating terrorist offences, causes a danger that one or more such offences may be committed;

(b) 'recruitment for terrorism' shall mean soliciting another person to commit one of the offences listed in Article 1(1)(a) to (h), or in Article 2(2);

(c) 'training for terrorism' shall mean providing instruction in the making or use of explosives, firearms or other weapons or noxious or hazardous substances, or in other specific methods or techniques, for the purpose of committing one of the offences listed in Article 1(1)(a) to (h), knowing that the skills provided are intended to be used for this purpose.

2. Each Member State shall take the necessary measures to ensure that offences linked to terrorist activities include the following intentional acts:

(a) public provocation to commit a terrorist offence;

(b) recruitment for terrorism;

(c) training for terrorism;

(d) aggravated theft with a view to committing one of the offences listed in Article 1(1);

(e) extortion with a view to the perpetration of one of the offences listed in Article 1(1);

(f) drawing up false administrative documents with a view to committing one of the offences listed in Article 1(1)(a) to (h) and Article 2(2)(b).

3. For an act as set out in paragraph 2 to be punishable, it shall not be necessary that a terrorist offence be actually committed.

*Article 4*

**Aiding or abetting, inciting and attempting**

1. Each Member State shall take the necessary measures to ensure that aiding or abetting an offence referred to in Article 1(1), Articles 2 or 3 is made punishable.

2. Each Member State shall take the necessary measures to ensure that inciting an offence referred to in Article 1(1), Article 2 or Article 3(2)(d) to (f) is made punishable.

3. Each Member State shall take the necessary measures to ensure that attempting to commit an offence referred to in Article 1(1) and Article 3(2)(d) to (f), with the exception of possession as provided for in Article 1(1)(f) and the offence referred to in Article 1(1)(i), is made punishable.

4. Each Member State may decide to take the necessary measures to ensure that attempting to commit an offence referred to in Article 3(2)(b) and (c) is made punishable.

▼B

*Article 5*

**Penalties**

1. Each Member State shall take the necessary measures to ensure that the offences referred to in Articles 1 to 4 are punishable by effective, proportionate and dissuasive criminal penalties, which may entail extradition.

2. Each Member State shall take the necessary measures to ensure that the terrorist offences referred to in Article 1(1) and offences referred to in Article 4, inasmuch as they relate to terrorist offences, are punishable by custodial sentences heavier than those imposable under national law for such offences in the absence of the special intent required pursuant to Article 1(1), save where the sentences imposable are already the maximum possible sentences under national law.

3. Each Member State shall take the necessary measures to ensure that offences listed in Article 2 are punishable by custodial sentences, with a maximum sentence of not less than fifteen years for the offence referred to in Article 2(2)(a), and for the offences listed in Article 2(2)(b) a maximum sentence of not less than eight years. In so far as the offence referred to in Article 2(2)(a) refers only to the act in Article 1(1)(i), the maximum sentence shall not be less than eight years.

*Article 6*

**Particular circumstances**

Each Member State may take the necessary measures to ensure that the penalties referred to in Article 5 may be reduced if the offender:

(a) renounces terrorist activity, and

(b) provides the administrative or judicial authorities with information which they would not otherwise have been able to obtain, helping them to:

(i) prevent or mitigate the effects of the offence;

(ii) identify or bring to justice the other offenders;

(iii) find evidence; or

(iv) prevent further offences referred to in Articles 1 to 4.

*Article 7*

**Liability of legal persons**

1. Each Member State shall take the necessary measures to ensure that legal persons can be held liable for any of the offences referred to in Articles 1 to 4 committed for their benefit by any person, acting either individually or as part of an organ of the legal person, who has a leading position within the legal person, based on one of the following:

(a) a power of representation of the legal person;

(b) an authority to take decisions on behalf of the legal person;

(c) an authority to exercise control within the legal person.

2. Apart from the cases provided for in paragraph 1, each Member State shall take the necessary measures to ensure that legal persons can be held liable where the lack of supervision or control by a person referred to in paragraph 1 has made possible the commission of any of the offences referred to in Articles 1 to 4 for the benefit of that legal person by a person under its authority.

▼B

3. Liability of legal persons under paragraphs 1 and 2 shall not exclude criminal proceedings against natural persons who are perpetrators, instigators or accessories in any of the offences referred to in Articles 1 to 4.

*Article 8*

**Penalties for legal persons**

Each Member State shall take the necessary measures to ensure that a legal person held liable pursuant to Article 7 is punishable by effective, proportionate and dissuasive penalties, which shall include criminal or non-criminal fines and may include other penalties, such as:

(a) exclusion from entitlement to public benefits or aid;

(b) temporary or permanent disqualification from the practice of commercial activities;

(c) placing under judicial supervision;

(d) a judicial winding-up order;

(e) temporary or permanent closure of establishments which have been used for committing the offence.

*Article 9*

**Jurisdiction and prosecution**

1. Each Member State shall take the necessary measures to establish its jurisdiction over the offences referred to in Articles 1 to 4 where:

(a) the offence is committed in whole or in part in its territory. Each Member State may extend its jurisdiction if the offence is committed in the territory of a Member State;

(b) the offence is committed on board a vessel flying its flag or an aircraft registered there;

(c) the offender is one of its nationals or residents;

(d) the offence is committed for the benefit of a legal person established in its territory;

(e) the offence is committed against the institutions or people of the Member State in question or against an institution of the European Union or a body set up in accordance with the Treaty establishing the European Community or the Treaty on European Union and based in that Member State.

2. When an offence falls within the jurisdiction of more than one Member State and when any of the States concerned can validly prosecute on the basis of the same facts, the Member States concerned shall cooperate in order to decide which of them will prosecute the offenders with the aim, if possible, of centralising proceedings in a single Member State. To this end, the Member States may have recourse to any body or mechanism established within the European Union in order to facilitate cooperation between their judicial authorities and the coordination of their action. Sequential account shall be taken of the following factors:

— the Member State shall be that in the territory of which the acts were committed,

— the Member State shall be that of which the perpetrator is a national or resident,

— the Member State shall be the Member State of origin of the victims,

▼B

— the Member State shall be that in the territory of which the perpetrator was found.

3. Each Member State shall take the necessary measures also to establish its jurisdiction over the offences referred to in Articles 1 to 4 in cases where it refuses to hand over or extradite a person suspected or convicted of such an offence to another Member State or to a third country.

4. Each Member State shall ensure that its jurisdiction covers cases in which any of the offences referred to in Articles 2 and 4 has been committed in whole or in part within its territory, wherever the terrorist group is based or pursues its criminal activities.

5. This Article shall not exclude the exercise of jurisdiction in criminal matters as laid down by a Member State in accordance with its national legislation.

*Article 10*

**Protection of, and assistance to, victims**

1. Member States shall ensure that investigations into, or prosecution of, offences covered by this Framework Decision are not dependent on a report or accusation made by a person subjected to the offence, at least if the acts were committed on the territory of the Member State.

2. In addition to the measures laid down in the Council Framework Decision 2001/220/JHA of 15 March 2001 on the standing of victims in criminal proceedings ([1]), each Member State shall, if necessary, take all measures possible to ensure appropriate assistance for victims' families.

*Article 11*

**Implementation and reports**

1. Member States shall take the necessary measures to comply with this Framework Decision by 31 December 2002.

2. By 31 December 2002, Member States shall forward to the General Secretariat of the Council and to the Commission the text of the provisions transposing into their national law the obligations imposed on them under this Framework Decision. On the basis of a report drawn up from that information and a report from the Commission, the Council shall assess, by 31 December 2003, whether Member States have taken the necessary measures to comply with this Framework Decision.

3. The Commission report shall specify, in particular, transposition into the criminal law of the Member States of the obligation referred to in Article 5(2).

*Article 12*

**Territorial application**

This Framework Decision shall apply to Gibraltar.

*Article 13*

**Entry into force**

This Framework Decision shall enter into force on the day of its publication in the Official Journal.

([1]) OJ L 82, 22.3.2001, p. 1.

# Framework Decision 2002/584 on the European arrest warrant and the surrender procedures between Member States, 13 June 2002

**[Consolidated version. Original version OJ 2002, L 190/1–18 rectified by OJ 2003, L 43/47 and amended as of 28 March 2011 by OJ 2009, L81/24–36]**

►B

**COUNCIL FRAMEWORK DECISION**

**of 13 June 2002**

**on the European arrest warrant and the surrender procedures between Member States**

(2002/584/JHA)

(OJ L 190, 18.7.2002, p. 1)

Amended by:

| | | Official Journal | | |
|---|---|---|---|---|
| | | No | page | date |
| ►M1 | Council Framework Decision 2009/299/JHA of 26 February 2009 | L 81 | 24 | 27.3.2009 |

▼B

**COUNCIL FRAMEWORK DECISION**

**of 13 June 2002**

**on the European arrest warrant and the surrender procedures between Member States**

(2002/584/JHA)

THE COUNCIL OF THE EUROPEAN UNION,

Having regard to the Treaty on European Union, and in particular Article 31(a) and (b) and Article 34(2)(b) thereof,

Having regard to the proposal from the Commission [1],

Having regard to the opinion of the European Parliament [2],

Whereas:

(1) According to the Conclusions of the Tampere European Council of 15 and 16 October 1999, and in particular point 35 thereof, the formal extradition procedure should be abolished among the Member States in respect of persons who are fleeing from justice after having been finally sentenced and extradition procedures should be speeded up in respect of persons suspected of having committed an offence.

(2) The programme of measures to implement the principle of mutual recognition of criminal decisions envisaged in point 37 of the Tampere European Council Conclusions and adopted by the Council on 30 November 2000 [3], addresses the matter of mutual enforcement of arrest warrants.

(3) All or some Member States are parties to a number of conventions in the field of extradition, including the European Convention on extradition of 13 December 1957 and the European Convention on the suppression of terrorism of 27 January 1977. The Nordic States have extradition laws with identical wording.

(4) In addition, the following three Conventions dealing in whole or in part with extradition have been agreed upon among Member States and form part of the Union *acquis*: the Convention of 19 June 1990 implementing the Schengen Agreement of 14 June 1985 on the gradual abolition of checks at their common borders [4] (regarding relations between the Member States which are parties to that Convention), the Convention of 10 March 1995 on simplified extradition procedure between the Member States of the European Union [5] and the Convention of 27 September 1996 relating to extradition between the Member States of the European Union [6].

(5) The objective set for the Union to become an area of freedom, security and justice leads to abolishing extradition between Member States and replacing it by a system of surrender between judicial authorities. Further, the introduction of a new simplified system of surrender of sentenced or suspected persons for the purposes of execution or prosecution of criminal sentences makes it possible to remove the complexity and potential for delay inherent in the present extradition procedures. Traditional cooperation relations which have prevailed up till now between Member States should be replaced by a system of free movement

---

(1) OJ C 332 E, 27.11.2001, p. 305.
(2) Opinion delivered on 9 January 2002 (not yet published in the Official Journal).
(3) OJ C 12 E, 15.1.2001, p. 10.
(4) OJ L 239, 22.9.2000, p. 19.
(5) OJ C 78, 30.3.1995, p. 2.
(6) OJ C 313, 13.10.1996, p. 12.

▼B

of judicial decisions in criminal matters, covering both pre-sentence and final decisions, within an area of freedom, security and justice.

(6) The European arrest warrant provided for in this Framework Decision is the first concrete measure in the field of criminal law implementing the principle of mutual recognition which the European Council referred to as the 'cornerstone' of judicial cooperation.

(7) Since the aim of replacing the system of multilateral extradition built upon the European Convention on Extradition of 13 December 1957 cannot be sufficiently achieved by the Member States acting unilaterally and can therefore, by reason of its scale and effects, be better achieved at Union level, the Council may adopt measures in accordance with the principle of subsidiarity as referred to in Article 2 of the Treaty on European Union and Article 5 of the Treaty establishing the European Community. In accordance with the principle of proportionality, as set out in the latter Article, this Framework Decision does not go beyond what is necessary in order to achieve that objective.

(8) Decisions on the execution of the European arrest warrant must be subject to sufficient controls, which means that a judicial authority of the Member State where the requested person has been arrested will have to take the decision on his or her surrender.

(9) The role of central authorities in the execution of a European arrest warrant must be limited to practical and administrative assistance.

(10) The mechanism of the European arrest warrant is based on a high level of confidence between Member States. Its implementation may be suspended only in the event of a serious and persistent breach by one of the Member States of the principles set out in Article 6(1) of the Treaty on European Union, determined by the Council pursuant to Article 7(1) of the said Treaty with the consequences set out in Article 7(2) thereof.

(11) In relations between Member States, the European arrest warrant should replace all the previous instruments concerning extradition, including the provisions of Title III of the Convention implementing the Schengen Agreement which concern extradition.

(12) This Framework Decision respects fundamental rights and observes the principles recognised by Article 6 of the Treaty on European Union and reflected in the Charter of Fundamental Rights of the European Union ([1]), in particular Chapter VI thereof. Nothing in this Framework Decision may be interpreted as prohibiting refusal to surrender a person for whom a European arrest warrant has been issued when there are reasons to believe, on the basis of objective elements, that the said arrest warrant has been issued for the purpose of prosecuting or punishing a person on the grounds of his or her sex, race, religion, ethnic origin, nationality, language, political opinions or sexual orientation, or that that person's position may be prejudiced for any of these reasons.

This Framework Decision does not prevent a Member State from applying its constitutional rules relating to due process, freedom of association, freedom of the press and freedom of expression in other media.

(13) No person should be removed, expelled or extradited to a State where there is a serious risk that he or she would be subjected to

([1]) OJ C 364, 18.12.2000, p. 1.

▼B

the death penalty, torture or other inhuman or degrading treatment or punishment.

(14) Since all Member States have ratified the Council of Europe Convention of 28 January 1981 for the protection of individuals with regard to automatic processing of personal data, the personal data processed in the context of the implementation of this Framework Decision should be protected in accordance with the principles of the said Convention,

HAS ADOPTED THIS FRAMEWORK DECISION:

## CHAPTER 1

## GENERAL PRINCIPLES

### *Article 1*

### Definition of the European arrest warrant and obligation to execute it

1. The European arrest warrant is a judicial decision issued by a Member State with a view to the arrest and surrender by another Member State of a requested person, for the purposes of conducting a criminal prosecution or executing a custodial sentence or detention order.

2. Member States shall execute any European arrest warrant on the basis of the principle of mutual recognition and in accordance with the provisions of this Framework Decision.

3. This Framework Decision shall not have the effect of modifying the obligation to respect fundamental rights and fundamental legal principles as enshrined in Article 6 of the Treaty on European Union.

### *Article 2*

### Scope of the European arrest warrant

1. A European arrest warrant may be issued for acts punishable by the law of the issuing Member State by a custodial sentence or a detention order for a maximum period of at least 12 months or, where a sentence has been passed or a detention order has been made, for sentences of at least four months.

2. The following offences, if they are punishable in the issuing Member State by a custodial sentence or a detention order for a maximum period of at least three years and as they are defined by the law of the issuing Member State, shall, under the terms of this Framework Decision and without verification of the double criminality of the act, give rise to surrender pursuant to a European arrest warrant:

— participation in a criminal organisation,

— terrorism,

— trafficking in human beings,

— sexual exploitation of children and child pornography,

— illicit trafficking in narcotic drugs and psychotropic substances,

— illicit trafficking in weapons, munitions and explosives,

— corruption,

— fraud, including that affecting the financial interests of the European Communities within the meaning of the Convention of 26 July 1995 on the protection of the European Communities' financial interests,

— laundering of the proceeds of crime,

▼B

— counterfeiting currency, including of the euro,

— computer-related crime,

— environmental crime, including illicit trafficking in endangered animal species and in endangered plant species and varieties,

— facilitation of unauthorised entry and residence,

— murder, grievous bodily injury,

— illicit trade in human organs and tissue,

— kidnapping, illegal restraint and hostage-taking,

— racism and xenophobia,

— organised or armed robbery,

— illicit trafficking in cultural goods, including antiques and works of art,

— swindling,

— racketeering and extortion,

— counterfeiting and piracy of products,

— forgery of administrative documents and trafficking therein,

— forgery of means of payment,

— illicit trafficking in hormonal substances and other growth promoters,

— illicit trafficking in nuclear or radioactive materials,

— trafficking in stolen vehicles,

— rape,

— arson,

— crimes within the jurisdiction of the International Criminal Court,

— unlawful seizure of aircraft/ships,

— sabotage.

3. The Council may decide at any time, acting unanimously after consultation of the European Parliament under the conditions laid down in Article 39(1) of the Treaty on European Union (TEU), to add other categories of offence to the list contained in paragraph 2. The Council shall examine, in the light of the report submitted by the Commission pursuant to Article 34(3), whether the list should be extended or amended.

4. For offences other than those covered by paragraph 2, surrender may be subject to the condition that the acts for which the European arrest warrant has been issued constitute an offence under the law of the executing Member State, whatever the constituent elements or however it is described.

*Article 3*

**Grounds for mandatory non-execution of the European arrest warrant**

The judicial authority of the Member State of execution (hereinafter 'executing judicial authority') shall refuse to execute the European arrest warrant in the following cases:

1. if the offence on which the arrest warrant is based is covered by amnesty in the executing Member State, where that State had jurisdiction to prosecute the offence under its own criminal law;

▼B

2. if the executing judicial authority is informed that the requested person has been finally judged by a Member State in respect of the same acts provided that, where there has been sentence, the sentence has been served or is currently being served or may no longer be executed under the law of the sentencing Member State;

3. if the person who is the subject of the European arrest warrant may not, owing to his age, be held criminally responsible for the acts on which the arrest warrant is based under the law of the executing State.

*Article 4*

**Grounds for optional non-execution of the European arrest warrant**

The executing judicial authority may refuse to execute the European arrest warrant:

1. if, in one of the cases referred to in Article 2(4), the act on which the European arrest warrant is based does not constitute an offence under the law of the executing Member State; however, in relation to taxes or duties, customs and exchange, execution of the European arrest warrant shall not be refused on the ground that the law of the executing Member State does not impose the same kind of tax or duty or does not contain the same type of rules as regards taxes, duties and customs and exchange regulations as the law of the issuing Member State;

2. where the person who is the subject of the European arrest warrant is being prosecuted in the executing Member State for the same act as that on which the European arrest warrant is based;

3. where the judicial authorities of the executing Member State have decided either not to prosecute for the offence on which the European arrest warrant is based or to halt proceedings, or where a final judgment has been passed upon the requested person in a Member State, in respect of the same acts, which prevents further proceedings;

4. where the criminal prosecution or punishment of the requested person is statute-barred according to the law of the executing Member State and the acts fall within the jurisdiction of that Member State under its own criminal law;

5. if the executing judicial authority is informed that the requested person has been finally judged by a third State in respect of the same acts provided that, where there has been sentence, the sentence has been served or is currently being served or may no longer be executed under the law of the sentencing country;

6. if the European arrest warrant has been issued for the purposes of execution of a custodial sentence or detention order, where the requested person is staying in, or is a national or a resident of the executing Member State and that State undertakes to execute the sentence or detention order in accordance with its domestic law;

7. where the European arrest warrant relates to offences which:

   (a) are regarded by the law of the executing Member State as having been committed in whole or in part in the territory of the executing Member State or in a place treated as such; or

   (b) have been committed outside the territory of the issuing Member State and the law of the executing Member State does not allow prosecution for the same offences when committed outside its territory.

▼M1

*Article 4a*

**Decisions rendered following a trial at which the person did not appear in person**

1. The executing judicial authority may also refuse to execute the European arrest warrant issued for the purpose of executing a custodial sentence or a detention order if the person did not appear in person at the trial resulting in the decision, unless the European arrest warrant states that the person, in accordance with further procedural requirements defined in the national law of the issuing Member State:

(a) in due time:

(i) either was summoned in person and thereby informed of the scheduled date and place of the trial which resulted in the decision, or by other means actually received official information of the scheduled date and place of that trial in such a manner that it was unequivocally established that he or she was aware of the scheduled trial;

and

(ii) was informed that a decision may be handed down if he or she does not appear for the trial;

or

(b) being aware of the scheduled trial, had given a mandate to a legal counsellor, who was either appointed by the person concerned or by the State, to defend him or her at the trial, and was indeed defended by that counsellor at the trial;

or

(c) after being served with the decision and being expressly informed about the right to a retrial, or an appeal, in which the person has the right to participate and which allows the merits of the case, including fresh evidence, to be re-examined, and which may lead to the original decision being reversed:

(i) expressly stated that he or she does not contest the decision;

or

(ii) did not request a retrial or appeal within the applicable time frame;

or

(d) was not personally served with the decision but:

(i) will be personally served with it without delay after the surrender and will be expressly informed of his or her right to a retrial, or an appeal, in which the person has the right to participate and which allows the merits of the case, including fresh evidence, to be re-examined, and which may lead to the original decision being reversed;

and

(ii) will be informed of the time frame within which he or she has to request such a retrial or appeal, as mentioned in the relevant European arrest warrant.

2. In case the European arrest warrant is issued for the purpose of executing a custodial sentence or detention order under the conditions of paragraph 1(d) and the person concerned has not previously received any official information about the existence of the criminal proceedings against him or her, he or she may, when being informed about the content of the European arrest warrant, request to receive a copy of the judgment before being surrendered. Immediately after having been informed about the request, the issuing authority shall provide the copy of the judgment via the executing authority to the person sought. The request of the person

▼M1

sought shall neither delay the surrender procedure nor delay the decision to execute the European arrest warrant. The provision of the judgment to the person concerned is for information purposes only; it shall neither be regarded as a formal service of the judgment nor actuate any time limits applicable for requesting a retrial or appeal.

3. In case a person is surrendered under the conditions of paragraph (1)(d) and he or she has requested a retrial or appeal, the detention of that person awaiting such retrial or appeal shall, until these proceedings are finalised, be reviewed in accordance with the law of the issuing Member State, either on a regular basis or upon request of the person concerned. Such a review shall in particular include the possibility of suspension or interruption of the detention. The retrial or appeal shall begin within due time after the surrender.

▼B

*Article 5*

**Guarantees to be given by the issuing Member State in particular cases**

The execution of the European arrest warrant by the executing judicial authority may, by the law of the executing Member State, be subject to the following conditions:

▼M1

————

▼B

2. if the offence on the basis of which the European arrest warrant has been issued is punishable by custodial life sentence or life-time detention order, the execution of the said arrest warrant may be subject to the condition that the issuing Member State has provisions in its legal system for a review of the penalty or measure imposed, on request or at the latest after 20 years, or for the application of measures of clemency to which the person is entitled to apply for under the law or practice of the issuing Member State, aiming at a non-execution of such penalty or measure;

3. where a person who is the subject of a European arrest warrant for the purposes of prosecution is a national or resident of the executing Member State, surrender may be subject to the condition that the person, after being heard, is returned to the executing Member State in order to serve there the custodial sentence or detention order passed against him in the issuing Member State.

*Article 6*

**Determination of the competent judicial authorities**

1. The issuing judicial authority shall be the judicial authority of the issuing Member State which is competent to issue a European arrest warrant by virtue of the law of that State.

2. The executing judicial authority shall be the judicial authority of the executing Member State which is competent to execute the European arrest warrant by virtue of the law of that State.

3. Each Member State shall inform the General Secretariat of the Council of the competent judicial authority under its law.

*Article 7*

**Recourse to the central authority**

1. Each Member State may designate a central authority or, when its legal system so provides, more than one central authority to assist the competent judicial authorities.

▼B

2. A Member State may, if it is necessary as a result of the organisation of its internal judicial system, make its central authority(ies) responsible for the administrative transmission and reception of European arrest warrants as well as for all other official correspondence relating thereto.

Member State wishing to make use of the possibilities referred to in this Article shall communicate to the General Secretariat of the Council information relating to the designated central authority or central authorities. These indications shall be binding upon all the authorities of the issuing Member State.

*Article 8*

**Content and form of the European arrest warrant**

1. The European arrest warrant shall contain the following information set out in accordance with the form contained in the Annex:

(a) the identity and nationality of the requested person;

(b) the name, address, telephone and fax numbers and e-mail address of the issuing judicial authority;

(c) evidence of an enforceable judgment, an arrest warrant or any other enforceable judicial decision having the same effect, coming within the scope of Articles 1 and 2;

(d) the nature and legal classification of the offence, particularly in respect of Article 2;

(e) a description of the circumstances in which the offence was committed, including the time, place and degree of participation in the offence by the requested person;

(f) the penalty imposed, if there is a final judgment, or the prescribed scale of penalties for the offence under the law of the issuing Member State;

(g) if possible, other consequences of the offence.

2. The European arrest warrant must be translated into the official language or one of the official languages of the executing Member State. Any Member State may, when this Framework Decision is adopted or at a later date, state in a declaration deposited with the General Secretariat of the Council that it will accept a translation in one or more other official languages of the Institutions of the European Communities.

CHAPTER 2

**SURRENDER PROCEDURE**

*Article 9*

**Transmission of a European arrest warrant**

1. When the location of the requested person is known, the issuing judicial authority may transmit the European arrest warrant directly to the executing judicial authority.

2. The issuing judicial authority may, in any event, decide to issue an alert for the requested person in the Schengen Information System (SIS).

3. Such an alert shall be effected in accordance with the provisions of Article 95 of the Convention of 19 June 1990 implementing the Schengen Agreement of 14 June 1985 on the gradual abolition of controls at common borders. An alert in the Schengen Information

▼B

System shall be equivalent to a European arrest warrant accompanied by the information set out in Article 8(1).

For a transitional period, until the SIS is capable of transmitting all the information described in Article 8, the alert shall be equivalent to a European arrest warrant pending the receipt of the original in due and proper form by the executing judicial authority.

*Article 10*

**Detailed procedures for transmitting a European arrest warrant**

1. If the issuing judicial authority does not know the competent executing judicial authority, it shall make the requisite enquiries, including through the contact points of the European Judicial Network [1], in order to obtain that information from the executing Member State.

2. If the issuing judicial authority so wishes, transmission may be effected via the secure telecommunications system of the European Judicial Network.

3. If it is not possible to call on the services of the SIS, the issuing judicial authority may call on Interpol to transmit a European arrest warrant.

4. The issuing judicial authority may forward the European arrest warrant by any secure means capable of producing written records under conditions allowing the executing Member State to establish its authenticity.

5. All difficulties concerning the transmission or the authenticity of any document needed for the execution of the European arrest warrant shall be dealt with by direct contacts between the judicial authorities involved, or, where appropriate, with the involvement of the central authorities of the Member States.

6. If the authority which receives a European arrest warrant is not competent to act upon it, it shall automatically forward the European arrest warrant to the competent authority in its Member State and shall inform the issuing judicial authority accordingly.

*Article 11*

**Rights of a requested person**

1. When a requested person is arrested, the executing competent judicial authority shall, in accordance with its national law, inform that person of the European arrest warrant and of its contents, and also of the possibility of consenting to surrender to the issuing judicial authority.

2. A requested person who is arrested for the purpose of the execution of a European arrest warrant shall have a right to be assisted by a legal counsel and by an interpreter in accordance with the national law of the executing Member State.

*Article 12*

**Keeping the person in detention**

When a person is arrested on the basis of a European arrest warrant, the executing judicial authority shall take a decision on whether the requested person should remain in detention, in accordance with the law of the executing Member State. The person may be released provisionally at any time in conformity with the domestic law of the

(1) Council Joint Action 98/428/JHA of 29 June 1998 on the creation of a European Judicial Network (OJ L 191, 7.7.1998, p. 4).

▼B

executing Member State, provided that the competent authority of the said Member State takes all the measures it deems necessary to prevent the person absconding.

*Article 13*

**Consent to surrender**

1. If the arrested person indicates that he or she consents to surrender, that consent and, if appropriate, express renunciation of entitlement to the 'speciality rule', referred to in Article 27(2), shall be given before the executing judicial authority, in accordance with the domestic law of the executing Member State.

2. Each Member State shall adopt the measures necessary to ensure that consent and, where appropriate, renunciation, as referred to in paragraph 1, are established in such a way as to show that the person concerned has expressed them voluntarily and in full awareness of the consequences. To that end, the requested person shall have the right to legal counsel.

3. The consent and, where appropriate, renunciation, as referred to in paragraph 1, shall be formally recorded in accordance with the procedure laid down by the domestic law of the executing Member State.

4. In principle, consent may not be revoked. Each Member State may provide that consent and, if appropriate, renunciation may be revoked, in accordance with the rules applicable under its domestic law. In this case, the period between the date of consent and that of its revocation shall not be taken into consideration in establishing the time limits laid down in Article 17. A Member State which wishes to have recourse to this possibility shall inform the General Secretariat of the Council accordingly when this Framework Decision is adopted and shall specify the procedures whereby revocation of consent shall be possible and any amendment to them.

*Article 14*

**Hearing of the requested person**

Where the arrested person does not consent to his or her surrender as referred to in Article 13, he or she shall be entitled to be heard by the executing judicial authority, in accordance with the law of the executing Member State.

*Article 15*

**Surrender decision**

1. The executing judicial authority shall decide, within the time-limits and under the conditions defined in this Framework Decision, whether the person is to be surrendered.

2. If the executing judicial authority finds the information communicated by the issuing Member State to be insufficient to allow it to decide on surrender, it shall request that the necessary supplementary information, in particular with respect to Articles 3 to 5 and Article 8, be furnished as a matter of urgency and may fix a time limit for the receipt thereof, taking into account the need to observe the time limits set in Article 17.

3. The issuing judicial authority may at any time forward any additional useful information to the executing judicial authority.

*Article 16*

**Decision in the event of multiple requests**

1. If two or more Member States have issued European arrest warrants for the same person, the decision on which of the European arrest warrants shall be executed shall be taken by the executing judicial

▼B

authority with due consideration of all the circumstances and especially the relative seriousness and place of the offences, the respective dates of the European arrest warrants and whether the warrant has been issued for the purposes of prosecution or for execution of a custodial sentence or detention order.

2. The executing judicial authority may seek the advice of Eurojust ([1]) when making the choice referred to in paragraph 1.

3. In the event of a conflict between a European arrest warrant and a request for extradition presented by a third country, the decision on whether the European arrest warrant or the extradition request takes precedence shall be taken by the competent authority of the executing Member State with due consideration of all the circumstances, in particular those referred to in paragraph 1 and those mentioned in the applicable convention.

4. This Article shall be without prejudice to Member States' obligations under the Statute of the International Criminal Court.

*Article 17*

**Time limits and procedures for the decision to execute the European arrest warrant**

1. A European arrest warrant shall be dealt with and executed as a matter of urgency.

2. In cases where the requested person consents to his surrender, the final decision on the execution of the European arrest warrant should be taken within a period of 10 days after consent has been given.

3. In other cases, the final decision on the execution of the European arrest warrant should be taken within a period of 60 days after the arrest of the requested person.

4. Where in specific cases the European arrest warrant cannot be executed within the time limits laid down in paragraphs 2 or 3, the executing judicial authority shall immediately inform the issuing judicial authority thereof, giving the reasons for the delay. In such case, the time limits may be extended by a further 30 days.

5. As long as the executing judicial authority has not taken a final decision on the European arrest warrant, it shall ensure that the material conditions necessary for effective surrender of the person remain fulfilled.

6. Reasons must be given for any refusal to execute a European arrest warrant.

7. Where in exceptional circumstances a Member State cannot observe the time limits provided for in this Article, it shall inform Eurojust, giving the reasons for the delay. In addition, a Member State which has experienced repeated delays on the part of another Member State in the execution of European arrest warrants shall inform the Council with a view to evaluating the implementation of this Framework Decision at Member State level.

*Article 18*

**Situation pending the decision**

1. Where the European arrest warrant has been issued for the purpose of conducting a criminal prosecution, the executing judicial authority must:

(a) either agree that the requested person should be heard according to Article 19;

([1]) Council Decision 2002/187/JHA of 28 February 2002 setting up Eurojust with a view to reinforcing the fight against serious crime (OJ L 63, 6.3.2002, p. 1).

▼B

(b) or agree to the temporary transfer of the requested person.

2. The conditions and the duration of the temporary transfer shall be determined by mutual agreement between the issuing and executing judicial authorities.

3. In the case of temporary transfer, the person must be able to return to the executing Member State to attend hearings concerning him or her as part of the surrender procedure.

*Article 19*

**Hearing the person pending the decision**

1. The requested person shall be heard by a judicial authority, assisted by another person designated in accordance with the law of the Member State of the requesting court.

2. The requested person shall be heard in accordance with the law of the executing Member State and with the conditions determined by mutual agreement between the issuing and executing judicial authorities.

3. The competent executing judicial authority may assign another judicial authority of its Member State to take part in the hearing of the requested person in order to ensure the proper application of this Article and of the conditions laid down.

*Article 20*

**Privileges and immunities**

1. Where the requested person enjoys a privilege or immunity regarding jurisdiction or execution in the executing Member State, the time limits referred to in Article 17 shall not start running unless, and counting from the day when, the executing judicial authority is informed of the fact that the privilege or immunity has been waived.

The executing Member State shall ensure that the material conditions necessary for effective surrender are fulfilled when the person no longer enjoys such privilege or immunity.

2. Where power to waive the privilege or immunity lies with an authority of the executing Member State, the executing judicial authority shall request it to exercise that power forthwith. Where power to waive the privilege or immunity lies with an authority of another State or international organisation, it shall be for the issuing judicial authority to request it to exercise that power.

*Article 21*

**Competing international obligations**

This Framework Decision shall not prejudice the obligations of the executing Member State where the requested person has been extradited to that Member State from a third State and where that person is protected by provisions of the arrangement under which he or she was extradited concerning speciality. The executing Member State shall take all necessary measures for requesting forthwith the consent of the State from which the requested person was extradited so that he or she can be surrendered to the Member State which issued the European arrest warrant. The time limits referred to in Article 17 shall not start running until the day on which these speciality rules cease to apply. Pending the decision of the State from which the requested person was extradited, the executing Member State will ensure that the material conditions necessary for effective surrender remain fulfilled.

▼B

*Article 22*

**Notification of the decision**

The executing judicial authority shall notify the issuing judicial authority immediately of the decision on the action to be taken on the European arrest warrant.

*Article 23*

**Time limits for surrender of the person**

1. The person requested shall be surrendered as soon as possible on a date agreed between the authorities concerned.

2. He or she shall be surrendered no later than 10 days after the final decision on the execution of the European arrest warrant.

3. If the surrender of the requested person within the period laid down in paragraph 2 is prevented by circumstances beyond the control of any of the Member States, the executing and issuing judicial authorities shall immediately contact each other and agree on a new surrender date. In that event, the surrender shall take place within 10 days of the new date thus agreed.

4. The surrender may exceptionally be temporarily postponed for serious humanitarian reasons, for example if there are substantial grounds for believing that it would manifestly endanger the requested person's life or health. The execution of the European arrest warrant shall take place as soon as these grounds have ceased to exist. The executing judicial authority shall immediately inform the issuing judicial authority and agree on a new surrender date. In that event, the surrender shall take place within 10 days of the new date thus agreed.

5. Upon expiry of the time limits referred to in paragraphs 2 to 4, if the person is still being held in custody he shall be released.

*Article 24*

**Postponed or conditional surrender**

1. The executing judicial authority may, after deciding to execute the European arrest warrant, postpone the surrender of the requested person so that he or she may be prosecuted in the executing Member State or, if he or she has already been sentenced, so that he or she may serve, in its territory, a sentence passed for an act other than that referred to in the European arrest warrant.

2. Instead of postponing the surrender, the executing judicial authority may temporarily surrender the requested person to the issuing Member State under conditions to be determined by mutual agreement between the executing and the issuing judicial authorities. The agreement shall be made in writing and the conditions shall be binding on all the authorities in the issuing Member State.

*Article 25*

**Transit**

1. Each Member State shall, except when it avails itself of the possibility of refusal when the transit of a national or a resident is requested for the purpose of the execution of a custodial sentence or detention order, permit the transit through its territory of a requested person who is being surrendered provided that it has been given information on:

(a) the identity and nationality of the person subject to the European arrest warrant;

(b) the existence of a European arrest warrant;

▼B

(c) the nature and legal classification of the offence;

(d) the description of the circumstances of the offence, including the date and place.

Where a person who is the subject of a European arrest warrant for the purposes of prosecution is a national or resident of the Member State of transit, transit may be subject to the condition that the person, after being heard, is returned to the transit Member State to serve the custodial sentence or detention order passed against him in the issuing Member State.

2. Each Member State shall designate an authority responsible for receiving transit requests and the necessary documents, as well as any other official correspondence relating to transit requests. Member States shall communicate this designation to the General Secretariat of the Council.

3. The transit request and the information set out in paragraph 1 may be addressed to the authority designated pursuant to paragraph 2 by any means capable of producing a written record. The Member State of transit shall notify its decision by the same procedure.

4. This Framework Decision does not apply in the case of transport by air without a scheduled stopover. However, if an unscheduled landing occurs, the issuing Member State shall provide the authority designated pursuant to paragraph 2 with the information provided for in paragraph 1.

5. Where a transit concerns a person who is to be extradited from a third State to a Member State this Article will apply *mutatis mutandis*. In particular the expression 'European arrest warrant' shall be deemed to be replaced by 'extradition request'.

## CHAPTER 3

## EFFECTS OF THE SURRENDER

### *Article 26*

### Deduction of the period of detention served in the executing Member State

1. The issuing Member State shall deduct all periods of detention arising from the execution of a European arrest warrant from the total period of detention to be served in the issuing Member State as a result of a custodial sentence or detention order being passed.

2. To that end, all information concerning the duration of the detention of the requested person on the basis of the European arrest warrant shall be transmitted by the executing judicial authority or the central authority designated under Article 7 to the issuing judicial authority at the time of the surrender.

### *Article 27*

### Possible prosecution for other offences

1. Each Member State may notify the General Secretariat of the Council that, in its relations with other Member States that have given the same notification, consent is presumed to have been given for the prosecution, sentencing or detention with a view to the carrying out of a custodial sentence or detention order for an offence committed prior to his or her surrender, other than that for which he or she was surrendered, unless in a particular case the executing judicial authority states otherwise in its decision on surrender.

▼B

2. Except in the cases referred to in paragraphs 1 and 3, a person surrendered may not be prosecuted, sentenced or otherwise deprived of his or her liberty for an offence committed prior to his or her surrender other than that for which he or she was surrendered.

3. Paragraph 2 does not apply in the following cases:

(a) when the person having had an opportunity to leave the territory of the Member State to which he or she has been surrendered has not done so within 45 days of his or her final discharge, or has returned to that territory after leaving it;

(b) the offence is not punishable by a custodial sentence or detention order;

(c) the criminal proceedings do not give rise to the application of a measure restricting personal liberty;

(d) when the person could be liable to a penalty or a measure not involving the deprivation of liberty, in particular a financial penalty or a measure in lieu thereof, even if the penalty or measure may give rise to a restriction of his or her personal liberty;

(e) when the person consented to be surrendered, where appropriate at the same time as he or she renounced the speciality rule, in accordance with Article 13;

(f) when the person, after his/her surrender, has expressly renounced entitlement to the speciality rule with regard to specific offences preceding his/her surrender. Renunciation shall be given before the competent judicial authorities of the issuing Member State and shall be recorded in accordance with that State's domestic law. The renunciation shall be drawn up in such a way as to make clear that the person has given it voluntarily and in full awareness of the consequences. To that end, the person shall have the right to legal counsel;

(g) where the executing judicial authority which surrendered the person gives its consent in accordance with paragraph 4.

4. A request for consent shall be submitted to the executing judicial authority, accompanied by the information mentioned in Article 8(1) and a translation as referred to in Article 8(2). Consent shall be given when the offence for which it is requested is itself subject to surrender in accordance with the provisions of this Framework Decision. Consent shall be refused on the grounds referred to in Article 3 and otherwise may be refused only on the grounds referred to in Article 4. The decision shall be taken no later than 30 days after receipt of the request.

For the situations mentioned in Article 5 the issuing Member State must give the guarantees provided for therein.

*Article 28*

**Surrender or subsequent extradition**

1. Each Member State may notify the General Secretariat of the Council that, in its relations with other Member States which have given the same notification, the consent for the surrender of a person to a Member State other than the executing Member State pursuant to a European arrest warrant issued for an offence committed prior to his or her surrender is presumed to have been given, unless in a particular case the executing judicial authority states otherwise in its decision on surrender.

2. In any case, a person who has been surrendered to the issuing Member State pursuant to a European arrest warrant may, without the consent of the executing Member State, be surrendered to a Member State other than the executing Member State pursuant to a European

▼B

arrest warrant issued for any offence committed prior to his or her surrender in the following cases:

(a) where the requested person, having had an opportunity to leave the territory of the Member State to which he or she has been surrendered, has not done so within 45 days of his final discharge, or has returned to that territory after leaving it;

(b) where the requested person consents to be surrendered to a Member State other than the executing Member State pursuant to a European arrest warrant. Consent shall be given before the competent judicial authorities of the issuing Member State and shall be recorded in accordance with that State's national law. It shall be drawn up in such a way as to make clear that the person concerned has given it voluntarily and in full awareness of the consequences. To that end, the requested person shall have the right to legal counsel;

(c) where the requested person is not subject to the speciality rule, in accordance with Article 27(3)(a), (e), (f) and (g).

3. The executing judicial authority consents to the surrender to another Member State according to the following rules:

(a) the request for consent shall be submitted in accordance with Article 9, accompanied by the information mentioned in Article 8 (1) and a translation as stated in Article 8(2);

(b) consent shall be given when the offence for which it is requested is itself subject to surrender in accordance with the provisions of this Framework Decision;

(c) the decision shall be taken no later than 30 days after receipt of the request;

(d) consent shall be refused on the grounds referred to in Article 3 and otherwise may be refused only on the grounds referred to in Article 4.

For the situations referred to in Article 5, the issuing Member State must give the guarantees provided for therein.

4. Notwithstanding paragraph 1, a person who has been surrendered pursuant to a European arrest warrant shall not be extradited to a third State without the consent of the competent authority of the Member State which surrendered the person. Such consent shall be given in accordance with the Conventions by which that Member State is bound, as well as with its domestic law.

*Article 29*

**Handing over of property**

1. At the request of the issuing judicial authority or on its own initiative, the executing judicial authority shall, in accordance with its national law, seize and hand over property which:

(a) may be required as evidence, or

(b) has been acquired by the requested person as a result of the offence.

2. The property referred to in paragraph 1 shall be handed over even if the European arrest warrant cannot be carried out owing to the death or escape of the requested person.

3. If the property referred to in paragraph 1 is liable to seizure or confiscation in the territory of the executing Member State, the latter may, if the property is needed in connection with pending criminal proceedings, temporarily retain it or hand it over to the issuing Member State, on condition that it is returned.

4. Any rights which the executing Member State or third parties may have acquired in the property referred to in paragraph 1 shall be

▼B

preserved. Where such rights exist, the issuing Member State shall return the property without charge to the executing Member State as soon as the criminal proceedings have been terminated.

*Article 30*

**Expenses**

1. Expenses incurred in the territory of the executing Member State for the execution of a European arrest warrant shall be borne by that Member State.

2. All other expenses shall be borne by the issuing Member State.

CHAPTER 4

**GENERAL AND FINAL PROVISIONS**

*Article 31*

**Relation to other legal instruments**

1. Without prejudice to their application in relations between Member States and third States, this Framework Decision shall, from 1 January 2004, replace the corresponding provisions of the following conventions applicable in the field of extradition in relations between the Member States:

(a) the European Convention on Extradition of 13 December 1957, its additional protocol of 15 October 1975, its second additional protocol of 17 March 1978, and the European Convention on the suppression of terrorism of 27 January 1977 as far as extradition is concerned;

(b) the Agreement between the 12 Member States of the European Communities on the simplification and modernisation of methods of transmitting extradition requests of 26 May 1989;

(c) the Convention of 10 March 1995 on simplified extradition procedure between the Member States of the European Union;

(d) the Convention of 27 September 1996 relating to extradition between the Member States of the European Union;

(e) Title III, Chapter 4 of the Convention of 19 June 1990 implementing the Schengen Agreement of 14 June 1985 on the gradual abolition of checks at common borders.

2. Member States may continue to apply bilateral or multilateral agreements or arrangements in force when this Framework Decision is adopted in so far as such agreements or arrangements allow the objectives of this Framework Decision to be extended or enlarged and help to simplify or facilitate further the procedures for surrender of persons who are the subject of European arrest warrants.

Member States may conclude bilateral or multilateral agreements or arrangements after this Framework Decision has come into force in so far as such agreements or arrangements allow the prescriptions of this Framework Decision to be extended or enlarged and help to simplify or facilitate further the procedures for surrender of persons who are the subject of European arrest warrants, in particular by fixing time limits shorter than those fixed in Article 17, by extending the list of offences laid down in Article 2(2), by further limiting the grounds for refusal set out in Articles 3 and 4, or by lowering the threshold provided for in Article 2(1) or (2).

The agreements and arrangements referred to in the second subparagraph may in no case affect relations with Member States which are not parties to them.

▼B

Member States shall, within three months from the entry into force of this Framework Decision, notify the Council and the Commission of the existing agreements and arrangements referred to in the first subparagraph which they wish to continue applying.

Member States shall also notify the Council and the Commission of any new agreement or arrangement as referred to in the second subparagraph, within three months of signing it.

3. Where the conventions or agreements referred to in paragraph 1 apply to the territories of Member States or to territories for whose external relations a Member State is responsible to which this Framework Decision does not apply, these instruments shall continue to govern the relations existing between those territories and the other Members States.

*Article 32*

**Transitional provision**

1. Extradition requests received before 1 January 2004 will continue to be governed by existing instruments relating to extradition. Requests received after that date will be governed by the rules adopted by Member States pursuant to this Framework Decision. However, any Member State may, at the time of the adoption of this Framework Decision by the Council, make a statement indicating that as executing Member State it will continue to deal with requests relating to acts committed before a date which it specifies in accordance with the extradition system applicable before 1 January 2004. The date in question may not be later than 7 August 2002. The said statement will be published in the *Official Journal of the European Communities*. It may be withdrawn at any time.

*Article 33*

**Provisions concerning Austria and Gibraltar**

1. As long as Austria has not modified Article 12(1) of the 'Auslieferungs- und Rechtshilfegesetz' and, at the latest, until 31 December 2008, it may allow its executing judicial authorities to refuse the enforcement of a European arrest warrant if the requested person is an Austrian citizen and if the act for which the European arrest warrant has been issued is not punishable under Austrian law.

2. This Framework Decision shall apply to Gibraltar.

*Article 34*

**Implementation**

1. Member States shall take the necessary measures to comply with the provisions of this Framework Decision by 31 December 2003.

2. Member States shall transmit to the General Secretariat of the Council and to the Commission the text of the provisions transposing into their national law the obligations imposed on them under this Framework Decision. When doing so, each Member State may indicate that it will apply immediately this Framework Decision in its relations with those Member States which have given the same notification.

The General Secretariat of the Council shall communicate to the Member States and to the Commission the information received pursuant to Article 7(2), Article 8(2), Article 13(4) and Article 25(2). It shall also have the information published in the *Official Journal of the European Communities*.

▼B

3. On the basis of the information communicated by the General Secretariat of the Council, the Commission shall, by 31 December 2004 at the latest, submit a report to the European Parliament and to the Council on the operation of this Framework Decision, accompanied, where necessary, by legislative proposals.

4. The Council shall in the second half of 2003 conduct a review, in particular of the practical application, of the provisions of this Framework Decision by the Member States as well as the functioning of the Schengen Information System.

*Article 35*

**Entry into force**

This Framework Decision shall enter into force on the twentieth day following that of its publication in the *Official Journal of the European Communities*.

▼B

*ANNEX*

**EUROPEAN ARREST WARRANT** (1)

This warrant has been issued by a competent judicial authority. I request that the person mentioned below be arrested and surrendered for the purposes of conducting a criminal prosecution or executing a custodial sentence or detention order.

(1) This warrant must be written in, or translated into, one of the official languages of the executing Member State, when that State is known, or any other language accepted by that State.

▼B

(a) Information regarding the identity of the requested person: ....................................

Name: ..........................................................................

Forename(s): ....................................................................

Maiden name, where applicable: ..................................................

Aliases, where applicable: ......................................................

Sex: ............................................................................

Nationality: ....................................................................

Date of birth: ..................................................................

Place of birth: .................................................................

Residence and/or known address: ...............................................

Language(s) which the requested person understands (if known): ..............................

..................................................................................

Distinctive marks/description of the requested person: ......................................

..................................................................................

Photo and fingerprints of the requested person, if they are available and can be transmitted, or contact details of the person to be contacted in order to obtain such information or a DNA profile (where this evidence can be supplied but has not been included)

(b) Decision on which the warrant is based:

1. Arrest warrant or judicial decision having the same effect: ....................................

Type: ..........................................................................

2. Enforceable judgement: .......................................................

..................................................................................

Reference: ......................................................................

▼B

(c) Indications on the length of the sentence:

1. Maximum length of the custodial sentence or detention order which may be imposed for the offence(s):

...

...

2. Length of the custodial sentence or detention order imposed:

...

Remaining sentence to be served: ...

...

...

►(1) (d) Indicate if the person appeared in person at the trial resulting in the decision:

1. ☐ Yes, the person appeared in person at the trial resulting in the decision.

2. ☐ No, the person did not appear in person at the trial resulting in the decision.

3. If you have ticked the box under point 2, please confirm the existence of one of the following:

☐ 3.1a. the person was summoned in person on … (day/month/year) and thereby informed of the scheduled date and place of the trial which resulted in the decision and was informed that a decision may be handed down if he or she does not appear for the trial;

OR

☐ 3.1b. the person was not summoned in person but by other means actually received official information of the scheduled date and place of the trial which resulted in the decision, in such a manner that it was unequivocally established that he or she was aware of the scheduled trial, and was informed that a decision may be handed down if he or she does not appear for the trial;

OR

☐ 3.2. being aware of the scheduled trial, the person had given a mandate to a legal counsellor, who was either appointed by the person concerned or by the State, to defend him or her at the trial, and was indeed defended by that counsellor at the trial;

OR

☐ 3.3. the person was served with the decision on … (day/month/year) and was expressly informed about the right to a retrial or appeal, in which he or she has the right to participate and which allows the merits of the case, including fresh evidence, to be re-examined, and which may lead to the original decision being reversed, and

☐ the person expressly stated that he or she does not contest this decision,

OR

☐ the person did not request a retrial or appeal within the applicable time frame;

OR

☐ 3.4. the person was not personally served with the decision, but

— the person will be personally served with this decision without delay after the surrender, and

— when served with the decision, the person will be expressly informed of his or her right to a retrial or appeal, in which he or she has the right to participate and which allows the merits of the case, including fresh evidence, to be re-examined, and which may lead to the original decision being reversed, and

— the person will be informed of the time frame within which he or she has to request a retrial or appeal, which will be … days.

4. If you have ticked the box under points 3.1b, 3.2 or 3.3 above, please provide information about how the relevant condition has been met:

...

... ◄

►(1) M1

▼B

(e) Offences:

This warrant relates to in total: .............................. offences.

Description of the circumstances in which the offence(s) was (were) committed, including the time, place and degree of participation in the offence(s) by the requested person:

...........................................................................

...........................................................................

...........................................................................

Nature and legal classification of the offence(s) and the applicable statutory provision/code:

...........................................................................

...........................................................................

...........................................................................

...........................................................................

...........................................................................

I. If applicable, tick one or more of the following offences punishable in the issuing Member State by a custodial sentence or detention order of a maximum of at least 3 years as defined by the laws of the issuing Member State:

☐ participation in a criminal organisation;
☐ terrorism;
☐ trafficking in human beings;
☐ sexual exploitation of children and child pornography;
☐ illicit trafficking in narcotic drugs and psychotropic substances;
☐ illicit trafficking in weapons, munitions and explosives;
☐ corruption;
☐ fraud, including that affecting the financial interests of the European Communities within the meaning of the Convention of 26 July 1995 on the protection of European Communities' financial interests;
☐ laundering of the proceeds of crime;
☐ counterfeiting of currency, including the euro;
☐ computer-related crime;
☐ environmental crime, including illicit trafficking in endangered animal species and in endangered plant species and varieties;
☐ facilitation of unauthorised entry and residence;
☐ murder, grievous bodily injury;
☐ illicit trade in human organs and tissue;
☐ kidnapping, illegal restraint and hostage-taking;
☐ racism and xenophobia;
☐ organised or armed robbery;
☐ illicit trafficking in cultural goods, including antiques and works of art;
☐ swindling;
☐ racketeering and extortion;
☐ counterfeiting and piracy of products;
☐ forgery of administrative documents and trafficking therein;
☐ forgery of means of payment;
☐ illicit trafficking in hormonal substances and other growth promoters;
☐ illicit trafficking in nuclear or radioactive materials;
☐ trafficking in stolen vehicles;
☐ rape;
☐ arson;
☐ crimes within the jurisdiction of the International Criminal Court;
☐ unlawful seizure of aircraft/ships;
☐ sabotage.

II. Full descriptions of offence(s) not covered by section I above:

...........................................................................

...........................................................................

▼B

(f) Other circumstances relevant to the case (optional information):

*(NB: This could cover remarks on extraterritoriality, interruption of periods of time limitation and other consequences of the offence)*

.....................................................................................

.....................................................................................

(g) This warrant pertains also to the seizure and handing over of property which may be required as evidence:

This warrant pertains also to the seizure and handing over of property acquired by the requested person as a result of the offence:

Description of the property (and location) (if known):

.....................................................................................

.....................................................................................

.....................................................................................

(h) The offence(s) on the basis of which this warrant has been issued is(are) punishable by/has(have) led to a custodial life sentence or lifetime detention order:

— the legal system of the issuing Member State allows for a review of the penalty or measure imposed — on request or at least after 20 years — aiming at a non-execution of such penalty or measure,

and/or

— the legal system of the issuing Member State allows for the application of measures of clemency to which the person is entitled under the law or practice of the issuing Member State, aiming at non-execution of such penalty or measure.

(i) The judicial authority which issued the warrant:

Official name:

Name of its representative [1]: .......................................................

.....................................................................................

Post held (title/grade): .............................................................

.....................................................................................

File reference: .......................................................................

Address: .............................................................................

.....................................................................................

Tel: (country code) (area/city code) (...) ...........................................

Fax: (country code) (area/city code) (...) ...........................................

E-mail: ..............................................................................

Contact details of the person to contact to make necessary practical arrangements for the surrender: ....

.....................................................................................

[1] In the different language versions a reference to the 'holder' of the judicial authority will be included.

▼B

Where a central authority has been made responsible for the transmission and administrative reception of European arrest warrants:

Name of the central authority:

..........................................................................................

Contact person, if applicable (title/grade and name):

..........................................................................................

Address: ..........................................................................................

..........................................................................................

Tel: (country code) (area/city code) (...) ..........................................................

Fax: (country code) (area/city code) (...) ..........................................................

E-mail: ..........................................................................................

Signature of the issuing judicial authority and/or its representative:

..........................................................................................

Name: ..........................................................................................

Post held (title/grade): ..........................................................................

Date: ..........................................................................................

Official stamp (if available)

18.7.2002 EN Official Journal of the European Communities L 190/19

**Statements made by certain Member States on the adoption of the Framework Decision**

Statements provided for in Article 32

Statement by France:

Pursuant to Article 32 of the framework decision on the European arrest warrant and the surrender procedures between Member States, France states that as executing Member State it will continue to deal with requests relating to acts committed before 1 November 1993, the date of entry into force of the Treaty on European Union signed in Maastricht on 7 February 1992, in accordance with the extradition system applicable before 1 January 2004.

Statement by Italy:

Italy will continue to deal in accordance with the extradition rules in force with all requests relating to acts committed before the date of entry into force of the framework decision on the European arrest warrant, as provided for in Article 32 thereof.

Statement by Austria:

Pursuant to Article 32 of the framework decision on the European arrest warrant and the surrender procedures between Member States, Austria states that as executing Member State it will continue to deal with requests relating to punishable acts committed before the date of entry into force of the framework decision in accordance with the extradition system applicable before that date.

Statements provided for in Article 13(4)

Statement by Belgium:

The consent of the person concerned to his or her surrender may be revoked until the time of surrender.

Statement by Denmark:

Consent to surrender and express renunciation of entitlement to the speciality rule may be revoked in accordance with the relevant rules applicable at any time under Danish law.

Statement by Ireland:

In Ireland, consent to surrender and, where appropriate, express renunciation of the entitlement to the 'specialty' rule referred to in Article 27(2) may be revoked. Consent may be revoked in accordance with domestic law until surrender has been executed.

Statement by Finland:

In Finland, consent to surrender and, where appropriate, express renunciation of entitlement to the 'speciality rule' referred to in Article 27(2) may be revoked. Consent may be revoked in accordance with domestic law until surrender has been executed.

Statement by Sweden:

Consent or renunciation within the meaning of Article 13(1) may be revoked by the party whose surrender has been requested. Revocation must take place before the decision on surrender is executed.

# Directive 2002/90 defining the facilitation of unauthorised entry, transit and residence, 28 November 2002

**[OJ 2002, L 328/17–18]**

5.12.2002 EN Official Journal of the European Communities L 328/17

**COUNCIL DIRECTIVE 2002/90/EC**

**of 28 November 2002**

**defining the facilitation of unauthorised entry, transit and residence**

THE COUNCIL OF THE EUROPEAN UNION,

Having regard to the Treaty establishing the European Community, and in particular Article 61(a) and Article 63(3)(b) thereof,

Having regard to the initiative of the French Republic (1),

Having regard to the opinion of the European Parliament (2),

Whereas:

(1) One of the objectives of the European Union is the gradual creation of an area of freedom, security and justice, which means, *inter alia*, that illegal immigration must be combated.

(2) Consequently, measures should be taken to combat the aiding of illegal immigration both in connection with unauthorised crossing of the border in the strict sense and for the purpose of sustaining networks which exploit human beings.

(3) To that end it is essential to approximate existing legal provisions, in particular, on the one hand, the precise definition of the infringement in question and the cases of exemption, which is the subject of this Directive and, on the other hand, minimum rules for penalties, liability of legal persons and jurisdiction, which is the subject of Council framework Decision 2002/946/JHA of 28 November 2002 on the strengthening of the penal framework to prevent the facilitation of unauthorised entry, transit and residence (3).

(4) The purpose of this Directive is to provide a definition of the facilitation of illegal immigration and consequently to render more effective the implementation of framework Decision 2002/946/JHA in order to prevent that offence.

(5) This Directive supplements other instruments adopted in order to combat illegal immigration, illegal employment, trafficking in human beings and the sexual exploitation of children.

(6) As regards Iceland and Norway, this Directive constitutes a development of provisions of the Schengen *acquis* within the meaning of the Agreement concluded by the Council of the European Union and the Republic of Iceland and the Kingdom of Norway concerning the association of those two States with the implementation, application and development of the Schengen *acquis* (4), which fall within the area referred to in Article 1(E) of Council Decision 1999/437/EC of 17 May 1999 on certain arrangements for the application of that Agreement (5).

(7) The United Kingdom and Ireland are taking part in the adoption and application of this Directive in accordance with the relevant provisions of the Treaties.

(8) In accordance with Articles 1 and 2 of the Protocol on the position of Denmark annexed to the Treaty on European Union and to the Treaty establishing the European Community, Denmark is not taking part in the adoption of this Directive and is not bound by it or subject to its application. Given that this Directive builds upon the Schengen *acquis* under the provisions of Title IV of Part Three of the Treaty establishing the European Community, Denmark shall, in accordance with Article 5 of the said Protocol, decide within a period of six months after the Council has adopted this Directive whether it will implement it in its national law,

HAS ADOPTED THIS DIRECTIVE:

*Article 1*

**General infringement**

1. Each Member State shall adopt appropriate sanctions on:

(a) any person who intentionally assists a person who is not a national of a Member State to enter, or transit across, the territory of a Member State in breach of the laws of the State concerned on the entry or transit of aliens;

(b) any person who, for financial gain, intentionally assists a person who is not a national of a Member State to reside within the territory of a Member State in breach of the laws of the State concerned on the residence of aliens.

2. Any Member State may decide not to impose sanctions with regard to the behaviour defined in paragraph 1(a) by applying its national law and practice for cases where the aim of the behaviour is to provide humanitarian assistance to the person concerned.

*Article 2*

**Instigation, participation and attempt**

Each Member State shall take the measures necessary to ensure that the sanctions referred to in Article 1 are also applicable to any person who:

(a) is the instigator of,

(b) is an accomplice in, or

(c) attempts to commit

an infringement as referred to in Article 1(1)(a) or (b).

(1) OJ C 253, 4.9.2000, p. 1.
(2) OJ C 276, 1.10.2001, p. 244.
(3) See page 1 of this Official Journal.
(4) OJ L 176, 10.7.1999, p. 36.
(5) OJ L 176, 10.7.1999, p. 31.

*Article 3*

**Sanctions**

Each Member State shall take the measures necessary to ensure that the infringements referred to in Articles 1 and 2 are subject to effective, proportionate and dissuasive sanctions.

*Article 4*

**Implementation**

1. Member States shall bring into force the laws, regulations and administrative provisions necessary to comply with this Directive before 5 December 2004. They shall forthwith inform the Commission thereof.

When Member States adopt these measures, they shall contain a reference to this Directive or shall be accompanied by such reference on the occasion of their official publication. The methods of making such a reference shall be laid down by the Member States.

2. Member States shall communicate to the Commission the text of the main provisions of their national law which they adopt in the field covered by this Directive, together with a table showing how the provisions of this Directive correspond to the national provisions adopted. The Commission shall inform the other Member States thereof.

*Article 5*

**Repeal**

Article 27(1) of the 1990 Schengen Convention shall be repealed as from 5 December 2004. Where a Member State implements this Directive pursuant to Article 4(1) in advance of that date, the said provision shall cease to apply to that Member State from the date of implementation.

*Article 6*

**Entry into force**

This Directive shall enter into force on the day of its publication in the *Official Journal of the European Communities.*

*Article 7*

**Addressees**

This Directive is addressed to the Member States in accordance with the Treaty establishing the European Community.

Done at Brussels, 28 November 2002.

*For the Council*

*The President*

B. HAARDER

# Framework Decision 2002/946 on the strengthening of the penal framework to prevent the facilitation of unauthorised entry, transit and residence, 28 November 2002

**[OJ 2002, L 328/1–3]**

Only European Union legislation printed in the paper edition of the *Official Journal of the European Union* is deemed authentic.

5.12.2002 EN Official Journal of the European Communities L 328/1

*(Acts adopted pursuant to Title VI of the Treaty on European Union)*

**COUNCIL FRAMEWORK DECISION**

**of 28 November 2002**

**on the strengthening of the penal framework to prevent the facilitation of unauthorised entry, transit and residence**

(2002/946/JHA)

THE COUNCIL OF THE EUROPEAN UNION,

Having regard to the Treaty establishing the European Union, and in particular Article 29, Article 31(e) and Article 34(2)(b) thereof,

Having regard to the initiative of the French Republic (1),

Having regard to the opinion of the European Parliament (2),

Whereas:

(1) One of the objectives of the European Union is to provide citizens with a high level of safety within an area of freedom, security and justice by developing common action among the Member States in the fields of police and judicial cooperation in criminal matters.

(2) In this framework, measures should be taken to combat the aiding of illegal immigration both in connection with unauthorised crossing of the border in the strict sense and for the purpose of sustaining networks which exploit human beings.

(3) To that end it is essential to approximate existing legal provisions, in particular, on the one hand, the precise definition of the infringement in question and the cases of exemption, which is the subject of Council Directive 2002/90/EC of 28 November 2002 defining the facilitation of unauthorised entry, transit and residence (3) and, on the other hand, minimum rules for penalties, liability of legal persons and jurisdiction, which is the subject of this framework Decision.

(4) It is likewise essential not to confine possible actions to natural persons only but to provide for measures relating to the liability of legal persons.

(1) OJ C 253, 4.9.2000, p. 6.
(2) OJ C 276, 1.10.2001, p. 244.
(3) See page 17 of this Official Journal.

(5) This framework Decision supplements other instruments adopted in order to combat illegal immigration, illegal employment, trafficking in human beings and the sexual exploitation of children.

(6) As regards Iceland and Norway, this framework Decision constitutes a development of provisions of the Schengen *acquis* within the meaning of the Agreement concluded by the Council of the European Union and the Republic of Iceland and the Kingdom of Norway concerning the association of those two States with the implementation, application and development of the Schengen *acquis* (4), which fall within the area referred to in Article 1(E) of Council Decision 1999/437/EC of 17 May 1999 on certain arrangements for the application of that Agreement (5).

(7) The United Kingdom is taking part in this framework Decision in accordance with Article 5 of the Protocol integrating the Schengen *acquis* into the framework of the European Union annexed to the Treaty on European Union and to the Treaty establishing the European Community, and Article 8(2) of Council Decision 2000/365/EC of 29 May 2000 concerning the request of the United Kingdom of Great Britain and Northern Ireland to take part in some of the provisions of the Schengen *acquis* (6).

(8) Ireland is taking part in this framework Decision in accordance with Article 5 of the Protocol integrating the Schengen *acquis* into the framework of the European Union annexed to the Treaty on European Union and to the Treaty establishing the European Community, and Article 6(2) of Council Decision 2002/192/EC of 28 February 2002 concerning Ireland's request to take part in some of the provisions of the Schengen *acquis* (7),

(4) OJ L 176, 10.7.1999, p. 36.
(5) OJ L 176, 10.7.1999, p. 31.
(6) OJ L 131, 1.6.2000, p. 43.
(7) OJ L 64, 7.3.2002, p. 20.

L 328/2 EN Official Journal of the European Communities 5.12.2002

HAS ADOPTED THIS FRAMEWORK DECISION:

*Article 1*

**Penalties**

1. Each Member State shall take the measures necessary to ensure that the infringements defined in Articles 1 and 2 of Directive 2002/90/EC are punishable by effective, proportionate and dissuasive criminal penalties which may entail extradition.

2. Where appropriate, the criminal penalties covered in paragraph 1 may be accompanied by the following measures:

— confiscation of the means of transport used to commit the offence,

— a prohibition on practising directly or through an intermediary the occupational activity in the exercise of which the offence was committed,

— deportation.

3. Each Member State shall take the measures necessary to ensure that, when committed for financial gain, the infringements defined in Article 1(1)(a) and, to the extent relevant, Article 2(a) of Directive 2002/90/EC are punishable by custodial sentences with a maximum sentence of not less than eight years where they are committed in any of the following circumstances:

— the offence was committed as an activity of a criminal organisation as defined in Joint Action 98/733/JHA [1],

— the offence was committed while endangering the lives of the persons who are the subject of the offence.

4. If imperative to preserve the coherence of the national penalty system, the actions defined in paragraph 3 shall be punishable by custodial sentences with a maximum sentence of not less than six years, provided that it is among the most severe maximum sentences available for crimes of comparable gravity.

*Article 2*

**Liability of legal persons**

1. Each Member State shall take the measures necessary to ensure that legal persons can be held liable for the infringements referred to in Article 1(1) and which are committed for their benefit by any person, acting either individually or as part of an organ of the legal person, who has a leading position within the legal person, based on:

— a power of representation of the legal person,

— an authority to take decisions on behalf of the legal person, or

— an authority to exercise control within the legal person.

2. Apart from the cases already provided for in paragraph 1, each Member State shall take the necessary measures to ensure that a legal person can be held liable where the lack of supervision or control by a person referred to in paragraph 1 has made possible the commission of the infringements referred to in Article 1(1) for the benefit of that legal person by a person under its authority.

3. Liability of a legal person under paragraphs 1 and 2 shall not exclude criminal proceedings against natural persons who are perpetrators or instigators of or accessories in the offences referred to in paragraph 1.

*Article 3*

**Sanctions for legal persons**

1. Each Member State shall take the measures necessary to ensure that a legal person held liable pursuant to Article 2(1) is punishable by effective, proportionate and dissuasive sanctions, which shall include criminal or non-criminal fines and may include other sanctions such as:

(a) exclusion from entitlement to public benefits or aid;

(b) temporary or permanent disqualification from the practice of commercial activities;

(c) placing under judicial supervision;

(d) a judicial winding-up order.

2. Each Member State shall take the measures necessary to ensure that a legal person held liable pursuant to Article 2(2) is punishable by effective, proportionate and dissuasive sanctions or measures.

*Article 4*

**Jurisdiction**

1. Each Member State shall take the measures necessary to establish its jurisdiction with regard to the infringements referred to in Article 1(1) and committed

(a) in whole or in part within its territory;

(b) by one of its nationals, or

(c) for the benefit of a legal person established in the territory of that Member State.

2. Subject to the provisions of Article 5, any Member State may decide that it will not apply, or that it will apply only in specific cases or circumstances, the jurisdiction rule set out in:

— paragraph 1(b),

— paragraph 1(c).

[1] OJ L 351, 29.12.1998, p. 1.

3. Each Member State shall inform the Secretary-General of the Council in writing if it decides to apply paragraph 2, where appropriate with an indication of the specific circumstances or conditions in which its decision applies.

*Article 5*

**Extradition and prosecution**

1. (a) Any Member State which, under its law, does not extradite its own nationals shall take the necessary measures to establish its jurisdiction over the infringements referred to in Article 1(1) when such infringements are committed by its own nationals outside its territory.

(b) Each Member State shall, when one of its nationals is alleged to have committed in another Member State the infringements referred to in Article 1(1) and it does not extradite that person to that other Member State solely on the ground of his nationality, submit the case to its competent authorities for the purpose of prosecution, if appropriate. In order to enable prosecution to take place, the files, information and exhibits relating to the offence shall be transmitted in accordance with the procedures laid down in Article 6(2) of the European Convention on Extradition of 13 December 1957. The requesting Member State shall be informed of the prosecution initiated and of its outcome.

2. For the purpose of this Article, a 'national' of a Member State shall be construed in accordance with any declaration made by that State under Article 6(1)(b) and (c) of the European Convention on Extradition, where appropriate as amended by any declarations made with respect to the Convention relating to extradition between the Member States of the European Union [1].

*Article 6*

**International law on refugees**

This framework Decision shall apply without prejudice to the protection afforded refugees and asylum seekers in accordance with international law on refugees or other international instruments relating to human rights, in particular Member States' compliance with their international obligations pursuant to Articles 31 and 33 of the 1951 Convention relating to the status of refugees, as amended by the Protocol of New York of 1967.

*Article 7*

**Communication of information between the Member States**

1. If a Member State is informed of infringements referred to in Article 1(1) which are in breach of the law on the entry and residence of aliens of another Member State, it shall inform the latter accordingly.

2. Any Member State which requests another Member State to prosecute, on the grounds of a breach of its own laws on the entry and residence of aliens, infringements referred to in Article 1(1) must specify, by means of an official report or a certificate from the competent authorities, the provisions of its law which have been breached.

*Article 8*

**Territorial application**

This framework Decision shall apply to Gibraltar.

*Article 9*

**Implementation**

1. Member States shall adopt the measures necessary to comply with the provisions of this framework Decision before 5 December 2004.

2. By the same date, Member States shall transmit to the General Secretariat of the Council and to the Commission the text of the provisions transposing into their national law the obligations imposed on them by this framework Decision. On the basis of a report established using this information by the Commission, the Council shall, before 5 June 2005, assess the extent to which Member States have complied with the provisions of this framework Decision.

*Article 10*

**Repeal**

The provisions of Article 27(2) and (3) of the 1990 Schengen Convention shall be repealed as from 5 December 2004. Where a Member State implements this framework Decision pursuant to Article 9(1) in advance of that date, the said provisions shall cease to apply to that Member State from the date of implementation.

*Article 11*

**Entry into force**

This framework Decision shall enter into force on the day of its publication in the Official Journal.

Done at Brussels, 28 November 2002.

*For the Council*

*The President*

B. HAARDER

---

[1] OJ C 313, 23.10.1996, p. 12.

# Directive 2003/6 on insider dealing and market manipulation (market abuse), 28 January 2003

**[Consolidated version. Original version OJ 2003, L 96/16 amended by OJ 2008, L 42/81 and OJ 2010, L 331/220]**

►B **DIRECTIVE 2003/6/EC OF THE EUROPEAN PARLIAMENT AND OF THE COUNCIL**

**of 28 January 2003**

**on insider dealing and market manipulation (market abuse)**

(OJ L 96, 12.4.2003, p. 16)

Amended by:

| | | Official Journal | | |
|---|---|---|---|---|
| | | No | page | date |
| ►M1 | Directive 2008/26/EC of the European Parliament and of the Council of 11 March 2008 | L 81 | 42 | 20.3.2008 |
| ►M2 | Directive 2010/78/EU of the European Parliament and of the Council of 24 November 2010 | L 331 | 120 | 15.12.2010 |

▼B

**DIRECTIVE 2003/6/EC OF THE EUROPEAN PARLIAMENT AND OF THE COUNCIL**

**of 28 January 2003**

**on insider dealing and market manipulation (market abuse)**

THE EUROPEAN PARLIAMENT AND THE COUNCIL OF THE EUROPEAN UNION,

Having regard to the Treaty establishing the European Community, and in particular Article 95 thereof,

Having regard to the proposal from the Commission ([1]),

Having regard to the opinion of the European Economic and Social Committee ([2]),

Having regard to the opinion of the European Central Bank ([3]),

Acting in accordance with the procedure laid down in Article 251 ([4]),

Whereas:

(1) A genuine Single Market for financial services is crucial for economic growth and job creation in the Community.

(2) An integrated and efficient financial market requires market integrity. The smooth functioning of securities markets and public confidence in markets are prerequisites for economic growth and wealth. Market abuse harms the integrity of financial markets and public confidence in securities and derivatives.

(3) The Commission Communication of 11 May 1999 entitled 'Implementing the framework for financial markets: action plan' identifies a series of actions that are needed in order to complete the single market for financial services. The Lisbon European Council of April 2000 called for the implementation of that action plan by 2005. The action plan stresses the need to draw up a Directive against market manipulation.

([1]) OJ C 240 E, 28.8.2001, p. 265.
([2]) OJ C 80, 3.4.2002, p. 61.
([3]) OJ C 24, 26.1.2002, p. 8.
([4]) Opinion of the European Parliament of 14 March 2002 (not yet published in the Official Journal), Council Common Position of 19 July 2002 (OJ C 228 E, 25.9.2002, p. 19) and Decision of the European Parliament of 24 October 2002 (not yet published in the Official Journal).

▼B

(4) At its meeting on 17 July 2000, the Council set up the Committee of Wise Men on the Regulation of European Securities Markets. In its final report, the Committee of Wise Men proposed the introduction of new legislative techniques based on a four-level approach, namely framework principles, implementing measures, cooperation and enforcement. Level 1, the Directive, should confine itself to broad general 'framework' principles while Level 2 should contain technical implementing measures to be adopted by the Commission with the assistance of a committee.

(5) The Resolution adopted by the Stockholm European Council of March 2001 endorsed the final report of the Committee of Wise Men and the proposed four-level approach to make the regulatory process for Community securities legislation more efficient and transparent.

(6) The Resolution of the European Parliament of 5 February 2002 on the implementation of financial services legislation also endorsed the Committee of Wise Men's report, on the basis of the solemn declaration made before Parliament the same day by the Commission and the letter of 2 October 2001 addressed by the Internal Market Commissioner to the chairman of Parliament's Committee on Economic and Monetary Affairs with regard to the safeguards for the European Parliament's role in this process.

(7) The measures necessary for the implementation of this Directive should be adopted in accordance with Council Decision 1999/468/EC of 28 June 1999 laying down the procedures for the exercise of implementing powers conferred on the Commission ([1]).

(8) According to the Stockholm European Council, Level 2 implementing measures should be used more frequently, to ensure that technical provisions can be kept up to date with market and supervisory developments, and deadlines should be set for all stages of Level 2 work.

(9) The European Parliament should be given a period of three months from the first transmission of draft implementing measures to allow it to examine them and to give its opinion. However, in urgent and duly justified cases, this period may be shortened. If, within that period, a resolution is passed by the European Parliament, the Commission should re-examine the draft measures.

(10) New financial and technical developments enhance the incentives, means and opportunities for market abuse: through new products, new technologies, increasing cross-border activities and the Internet.

(11) The existing Community legal framework to protect market integrity is incomplete. Legal requirements vary from one Member State to another, leaving economic actors often uncertain over concepts, definitions and enforcement. In some Member States there is no legislation addressing the issues of price manipulation and the dissemination of misleading information.

([1]) OJ L 184, 17.7.1999, p. 23.

▼B

(12) Market abuse consists of insider dealing and market manipulation. The objective of legislation against insider dealing is the same as that of legislation against market manipulation: to ensure the integrity of Community financial markets and to enhance investor confidence in those markets. It is therefore advisable to adopt combined rules to combat both insider dealing and market manipulation. A single Directive will ensure throughout the Community the same framework for allocation of responsibilities, enforcement and cooperation.

(13) Given the changes in financial markets and in Community legislation since the adoption of Council Directive 89/592/EEC of 13 November 1989 coordinating regulations on insider dealing [1], that Directive should now be replaced, to ensure consistency with legislation against market manipulation. A new Directive is also needed to avoid loopholes in Community legislation which could be used for wrongful conduct and which would undermine public confidence and therefore prejudice the smooth functioning of the markets.

(14) This Directive meets the concerns expressed by the Member States following the terrorist attacks on 11 September 2001 as regards the fight against financing terrorist activities.

(15) Insider dealing and market manipulation prevent full and proper market transparency, which is a prerequisite for trading for all economic actors in integrated financial markets.

(16) Inside information is any information of a precise nature which has not been made public, relating, directly or indirectly, to one or more issuers of financial instruments or to one or more financial instruments. Information which could have a significant effect on the evolution and forming of the prices of a regulated market as such could be considered as information which indirectly relates to one or more issuers of financial instruments or to one or more related derivative financial instruments.

(17) As regards insider dealing, account should be taken of cases where inside information originates not from a profession or function but from criminal activities, the preparation or execution of which could have a significant effect on the prices of one or more financial instruments or on price formation in the regulated market as such.

[1] OJ L 334, 18.11.1989, p. 30.

▼B

(18) Use of inside information can consist in the acquisition or disposal of financial instruments by a person who knows, or ought to have known, that the information possessed is inside information. In this respect, the competent authorities should consider what a normal and reasonable person would know or should have known in the circumstances. Moreover, the mere fact that market-makers, bodies authorised to act as counterparties, or persons authorised to execute orders on behalf of third parties with inside information confine themselves, in the first two cases, to pursuing their legitimate business of buying or selling financial instruments or, in the last case, to carrying out an order dutifully, should not in itself be deemed to constitute use of such inside information.

(19) Member States should tackle the practice known as 'front running', including 'front running' in commodity derivatives, where it constitutes market abuse under the definitions contained in this Directive.

(20) A person who enters into transactions or issues orders to trade which are constitutive of market manipulation may be able to establish that his reasons for entering into such transactions or issuing orders to trade were legitimate and that the transactions and orders to trade were in conformity with accepted practice on the regulated market concerned. A sanction could still be imposed if the competent authority established that there was another, illegitimate, reason behind these transactions or orders to trade.

(21) The competent authority may issue guidance on matters covered by this Directive, e.g. definition of inside information in relation to derivatives on commodities or implementation of the definition of accepted market practices relating to the definition of market manipulation. This guidance should be in conformity with the provisions of the Directive and the implementing measures adopted in accordance with the comitology procedure.

(22) Member States should be able to choose the most appropriate way to regulate persons producing or disseminating research concerning financial instruments or issuers of financial instruments or persons producing or disseminating other information recommending or suggesting investment strategy, including appropriate mechanisms for self-regulation, which should be notified to the Commission.

(23) Posting of inside information by issuers on their internet sites should be in accordance with the rules on transfer of personal data to third countries as laid down in Directive 95/46/EC of the European Parliament and of the Council of 24 October 1995 on the protection of individuals with regard to the processing of personal data and on the movement of such data [1].

(1) OJ L 281, 23.11.1995, p. 31.

▼B

(24) Prompt and fair disclosure of information to the public enhances market integrity, whereas selective disclosure by issuers can lead to a loss of investor confidence in the integrity of financial markets. Professional economic actors should contribute to market integrity by various means. Such measures could include, for instance, the creation of 'grey lists', the application of 'window trading' to sensitive categories of personnel, the application of internal codes of conduct and the establishment of 'Chinese walls'. Such preventive measures may contribute to combating market abuse only if they are enforced with determination and are dutifully controlled. Adequate enforcement control would imply for instance the designation of compliance officers within the bodies concerned and periodic checks conducted by independent auditors.

(25) Modern communication methods make it possible for financial market professionals and private investors to have more equal access to financial information, but also increase the risk of the spread of false or misleading information.

(26) Greater transparency of transactions conducted by persons discharging managerial responsibilities within issuers and, where applicable, persons closely associated with them, constitutes a preventive measure against market abuse. The publication of those transactions on at least an individual basis can also be a highly valuable source of information to investors.

(27) Market operators should contribute to the prevention of market abuse and adopt structural provisions aimed at preventing and detecting market manipulation practices. Such provisions may include requirements concerning transparency of transactions concluded, total disclosure of price-regularisation agreements, a fair system of order pairing, introduction of an effective atypical-order detection scheme, sufficiently robust financial instrument reference price-fixing schemes and clarity of rules on the suspension of transactions.

(28) This Directive should be interpreted, and implemented by Member States, in a manner consistent with the requirements for effective regulation in order to protect the interests of holders of transferable securities carrying voting rights in a company (or which may carry such rights as a consequence of the exercise of rights or conversion) when the company is subject to a public take-over bid or other proposed change of control. In particular, this Directive does not in any way prevent a Member State from putting or having in place such measures as it sees fit for these purposes.

(29) Having access to inside information relating to another company and using it in the context of a public take-over bid for the purpose of gaining control of that company or proposing a merger with that company should not in itself be deemed to constitute insider dealing.

▼B

(30) Since the acquisition or disposal of financial instruments necessarily involves a prior decision to acquire or dispose taken by the person who undertakes one or other of these operations, the carrying out of this acquisition or disposal should not be deemed in itself to constitute the use of inside information.

(31) Research and estimates developed from publicly available data should not be regarded as inside information and, therefore, any transaction carried out on the basis of such research or estimates should not be deemed in itself to constitute insider dealing within the meaning of this Directive.

(32) Member States and the European System of Central Banks, national central banks or any other officially designated body, or any person acting on their behalf, should not be restricted in carrying out monetary, exchange-rate or public debt management policy.

(33) Stabilisation of financial instruments or trading in own shares in buy-back programmes can be legitimate, in certain circumstances, for economic reasons and should not, therefore, in themselves be regarded as market abuse. Common standards should be developed to provide practical guidance.

(34) The widening scope of financial markets, the rapid change and the range of new products and developments require a wide application of this Directive to financial instruments and techniques involved, in order to guarantee the integrity of Community financial markets.

(35) Establishing a level playing field in Community financial markets requires wide geographical application of the provisions covered by this Directive. As regards derivative instruments not admitted to trading but falling within the scope of this Directive, each Member State should be competent to sanction actions carried out on its territory or abroad which concern underlying financial instruments admitted to trading on a regulated market situated or operating within its territory or for which a request for admission to trading on such a regulated market has been made. Each Member State should also be competent to sanction actions carried out on its territory which concern underlying financial instruments admitted to trading on a regulated market in a Member State or for which a request for admission to trading on such a market has been made.

(36) A variety of competent authorities in Member States, having different responsibilities, may create confusion among economic actors. A single competent authority should be designated in each Member State to assume at least final responsibility for supervising compliance with the provisions adopted pursuant to this Directive, as well as international collaboration. Such an authority should be of an administrative nature guaranteeing its independence of economic actors and avoiding conflicts of interest. In accordance with national law, Member States should ensure appropriate financing of the competent authority. That authority should have adequate arrangements for consultation concerning possible changes in national legislation such as a consultative committee composed of representatives of issuers, financial services providers and consumers, so as to be fully informed of their views and concerns.

▼B

(37) A common minimum set of effective tools and powers for the competent authority of each Member State will guarantee supervisory effectiveness. Market undertakings and all economic actors should also contribute at their level to market integrity. In this sense, the designation of a single competent authority for market abuse does not exclude collaboration links or delegation under the responsibility of the competent authority, between that authority and market undertakings with a view to guaranteeing efficient supervision of compliance with the provisions adopted pursuant to this Directive.

(38) In order to ensure that a Community framework against market abuse is sufficient, any infringement of the prohibitions or requirements laid down pursuant to this Directive will have to be promptly detected and sanctioned. To this end, sanctions should be sufficiently dissuasive and proportionate to the gravity of the infringement and to the gains realised and should be consistently applied.

(39) Member States should remain alert, in determining the administrative measures and sanctions, to the need to ensure a degree of uniformity of regulation from one Member State to another.

(40) Increasing cross-border activities require improved cooperation and a comprehensive set of provisions for the exchange of information between national competent authorities. The organisation of supervision and of investigatory powers in each Member State should not hinder cooperation between the competent national authorities.

(41) Since the objective of the proposed action, namely to prevent market abuse in the form of insider dealing and market manipulation, cannot be sufficiently achieved by the Member States and can therefore, by reason of the scale and effects of the measures, be better achieved at Community level, the Community may adopt measures, in accordance with the principle of subsidiarity as set out in Article 5 of the Treaty. In accordance with the principle of proportionality, as set out in that Article, this Directive does not go beyond what is necessary in order to achieve that objective.

(42) Technical guidance and implementing measures for the rules laid down in this Directive may from time to time be necessary to take account of new developments on financial markets. The Commission should accordingly be empowered to adopt implementing measures, provided that these do not modify the essential elements of this Directive and the Commission acts according to the principles set out in this Directive, after consulting the European Securities Committee established by Commission Decision 2001/528/EC [1].

(43) In exercising its implementing powers in accordance with this Directive, the Commission should respect the following principles:

— the need to ensure confidence in financial markets among investors by promoting high standards of transparency in financial markets,

---

[1] OJ L 191, 13.7.2001, p. 45.

▼B

— the need to provide investors with a wide range of competing investments and a level of disclosure and protection tailored to their circumstances,

— the need to ensure that independent regulatory authorities enforce the rules consistently, especially as regards the fight against economic crime,

— the need for high levels of transparency and consultation with all market participants and with the European Parliament and the Council,

— the need to encourage innovation in financial markets if they are to be dynamic and efficient,

— the need to ensure market integrity by close and reactive monitoring of financial innovation,

— the importance of reducing the cost of, and increasing access to, capital,

— the balance of costs and benefits to market participants on a long-term basis (including small and medium-sized businesses and small investors) in any implementing measures,

— the need to foster the international competitiveness of EU financial markets without prejudice to a much-needed extension of international cooperation,

— the need to achieve a level playing field for all market participants by establishing EU-wide regulations every time it is appropriate,

— the need to respect differences in national markets where these do not unduly impinge on the coherence of the single market,

— the need to ensure coherence with other Community legislation in this area, as imbalances in information and a lack of transparency may jeopardise the operation of the markets and above all harm consumers and small investors.

(44) This Directive respects the fundamental rights and observes the principles recognised in particular by the Charter of Fundamental Rights of the European Union and in particular by Article 11 thereof and Article 10 of the European Convention on Human Rights. In this regard, this Directive does not in any way prevent Member States from applying their constitutional rules relating to freedom of the press and freedom of expression in the media,

HAVE ADOPTED THIS DIRECTIVE:

*Article 1*

For the purposes of this Directive:

1. 'Inside information' shall mean information of a precise nature which has not been made public, relating, directly or indirectly, to one or more issuers of financial instruments or to one or more financial instruments and which, if it were made public, would be likely to have a significant effect on the prices of those financial instruments or on the price of related derivative financial instruments.

▼B

In relation to derivatives on commodities, 'inside information' shall mean information of a precise nature which has not been made public, relating, directly or indirectly, to one or more such derivatives and which users of markets on which such derivatives are traded would expect to receive in accordance with accepted market practices on those markets.

For persons charged with the execution of orders concerning financial instruments, 'inside information' shall also mean information conveyed by a client and related to the client's pending orders, which is of a precise nature, which relates directly or indirectly to one or more issuers of financial instruments or to one or more financial instruments, and which, if it were made public, would be likely to have a significant effect on the prices of those financial instruments or on the price of related derivative financial instruments.

2. 'Market manipulation' shall mean:

(a) transactions or orders to trade:

— which give, or are likely to give, false or misleading signals as to the supply of, demand for or price of financial instruments, or

— which secure, by a person, or persons acting in collaboration, the price of one or several financial instruments at an abnormal or artificial level,

unless the person who entered into the transactions or issued the orders to trade establishes that his reasons for so doing are legitimate and that these transactions or orders to trade conform to accepted market practices on the regulated market concerned;

(b) transactions or orders to trade which employ fictitious devices or any other form of deception or contrivance;

(c) dissemination of information through the media, including the Internet, or by any other means, which gives, or is likely to give, false or misleading signals as to financial instruments, including the dissemination of rumours and false or misleading news, where the person who made the dissemination knew, or ought to have known, that the information was false or misleading. In respect of journalists when they act in their professional capacity such dissemination of information is to be assessed, without prejudice to Article 11, taking into account the rules governing their profession, unless those persons derive, directly or indirectly, an advantage or profits from the dissemination of the information in question.

In particular, the following instances are derived from the core definition given in points (a), (b) and (c) above:

— conduct by a person, or persons acting in collaboration, to secure a dominant position over the supply of or demand for a financial instrument which has the effect of fixing, directly or indirectly, purchase or sale prices or creating other unfair trading conditions,

▼B

— the buying or selling of financial instruments at the close of the market with the effect of misleading investors acting on the basis of closing prices,

— taking advantage of occasional or regular access to the traditional or electronic media by voicing an opinion about a financial instrument (or indirectly about its issuer) while having previously taken positions on that financial instrument and profiting subsequently from the impact of the opinions voiced on the price of that instrument, without having simultaneously disclosed that conflict of interest to the public in a proper and effective way.

The definitions of market manipulation shall be adapted so as to ensure that new patterns of activity that in practice constitute market manipulation can be included.

3. 'Financial instrument' shall mean:

— transferable securities as defined in Council Directive 93/22/EEC of 10 May 1993 on investment services in the securities field [1],

— units in collective investment undertakings,

— money-market instruments,

— financial-futures contracts, including equivalent cash-settled instruments,

— forward interest-rate agreements,

— interest-rate, currency and equity swaps,

— options to acquire or dispose of any instrument falling into these categories, including equivalent cash-settled instruments. This category includes in particular options on currency and on interest rates,

— derivatives on commodities,

— any other instrument admitted to trading on a regulated market in a Member State or for which a request for admission to trading on such a market has been made.

4. 'Regulated market' shall mean a market as defined by Article 1(13) of Directive 93/22/EEC.

▼M1

5. 'Accepted market practices' shall mean practices that are reasonably expected in one or more financial markets and are accepted by the competent authority in accordance with guidelines adopted by the Commission in accordance with the regulatory procedure with scrutiny laid down in Article 17(2a).

[1] OJ L 141, 11.6.1993, p. 27. Directive as last amended by European Parliament and Council Directive 2000/64/EC (OJ L 290, 17.11.2000, p. 27).

▼M2

The European Supervisory Authority (European Securities and Markets Authority) (hereinafter 'ESMA'), established by Regulation (EU) No 1095/2010 of the European Parliament and of the Council ([1]) may develop draft implementing technical standards to ensure uniform conditions of application of the acts adopted by the Commission in accordance with this Article in relation to accepted market practices.

Power is conferred on the Commission to adopt the implementing technical standards referred to in the second subparagraph in accordance with Article 15 of Regulation (EU) No 1095/2010.

▼B

6. 'Person' shall mean any natural or legal person.

7. 'Competent authority' shall mean the competent authority designated in accordance with Article 11.

In order to take account of developments on financial markets and to ensure uniform application of this Directive in the Community, the Commission, ►M1 ———— ◄ shall adopt implementing measures concerning points 1, 2 and 3 of this Article. ►M1 Those measures, designed to amend non-essential elements of this Directive by supplementing it, shall be adopted in accordance with the regulatory procedure with scrutiny referred to in Article 17(2a). ◄

*Article 2*

1. Member States shall prohibit any person referred to in the second subparagraph who possesses inside information from using that information by acquiring or disposing of, or by trying to acquire or dispose of, for his own account or for the account of a third party, either directly or indirectly, financial instruments to which that information relates.

The first subparagraph shall apply to any person who possesses that information:

(a) by virtue of his membership of the administrative, management or supervisory bodies of the issuer; or

(b) by virtue of his holding in the capital of the issuer; or

(c) by virtue of his having access to the information through the exercise of his employment, profession or duties; or

(d) by virtue of his criminal activities.

2. Where the person referred to in paragraph 1 is a legal person, the prohibition laid down in that paragraph shall also apply to the natural persons who take part in the decision to carry out the transaction for the account of the legal person concerned.

3. This Article shall not apply to transactions conducted in the discharge of an obligation that has become due to acquire or dispose of financial instruments where that obligation results from an agreement concluded before the person concerned possessed inside information.

---

([1]) OJ L 331, 15.12.2010, p. 84.

▼B

*Article 3*

Member States shall prohibit any person subject to the prohibition laid down in Article 2 from:

(a) disclosing inside information to any other person unless such disclosure is made in the normal course of the exercise of his employment, profession or duties;

(b) recommending or inducing another person, on the basis of inside information, to acquire or dispose of financial instruments to which that information relates.

*Article 4*

Member States shall ensure that Articles 2 and 3 also apply to any person, other than the persons referred to in those Articles, who possesses inside information while that person knows, or ought to have known, that it is inside information.

*Article 5*

Member States shall prohibit any person from engaging in market manipulation.

*Article 6*

1. Member States shall ensure that issuers of financial instruments inform the public as soon as possible of inside information which directly concerns the said issuers.

Without prejudice to any measures taken to comply with the provisions of the first subparagraph, Member States shall ensure that issuers, for an appropriate period, post on their Internet sites all inside information that they are required to disclose publicly.

2. An issuer may under his own responsibility delay the public disclosure of inside information, as referred to in paragraph 1, such as not to prejudice his legitimate interests provided that such omission would not be likely to mislead the public and provided that the issuer is able to ensure the confidentiality of that information. Member States may require that an issuer shall without delay inform the competent authority of the decision to delay the public disclosure of inside information.

3. Member States shall require that, whenever an issuer, or a person acting on his behalf or for his account, discloses any inside information to any third party in the normal exercise of his employment, profession or duties, as referred to in Article 3(a), he must make complete and effective public disclosure of that information, simultaneously in the case of an intentional disclosure and promptly in the case of a non-intentional disclosure.

The provisions of the first subparagraph shall not apply if the person receiving the information owes a duty of confidentiality, regardless of whether such duty is based on a law, on regulations, on articles of association or on a contract.

Member States shall require that issuers, or persons acting on their behalf or for their account, draw up a list of those persons working for them, under a contract of employment or otherwise, who have access to inside information. Issuers and persons acting on their behalf or for their account shall regularly update this list and transmit it to the competent authority whenever the latter requests it.

▼B

4. Persons discharging managerial responsibilities within an issuer of financial instruments and, where applicable, persons closely associated with them, shall, at least, notify to the competent authority the existence of transactions conducted on their own account relating to shares of the said issuer, or to derivatives or other financial instruments linked to them. Member States shall ensure that public access to information concerning such transactions, on at least an individual basis, is readily available as soon as possible.

5. Member States shall ensure that there is appropriate regulation in place to ensure that persons who produce or disseminate research concerning financial instruments or issuers of financial instruments and persons who produce or disseminate other information recommending or suggesting investment strategy, intended for distribution channels or for the public, take reasonable care to ensure that such information is fairly presented and disclose their interests or indicate conflicts of interest concerning the financial instruments to which that information relates. Details of such regulation shall be notified to the Commission.

6. Member States shall ensure that market operators adopt structural provisions aimed at preventing and detecting market manipulation practices.

7. With a view to ensuring compliance with paragraphs 1 to 5, the competent authority may take all necessary measures to ensure that the public is correctly informed.

8. Public institutions disseminating statistics liable to have a significant effect on financial markets shall disseminate them in a fair and transparent way.

9. Member States shall require that any person professionally arranging transactions in financial instruments who reasonably suspects that a transaction might constitute insider dealing or market manipulation shall notify the competent authority without delay.

10. In order to take account of technical developments on financial markets and to ensure uniform application of this Directive, the Commission shall adopt, ►M1 ——— ◄ implementing measures concerning:

— the technical modalities for appropriate public disclosure of inside information as referred to in paragraphs 1 and 3,

— the technical modalities for delaying the public disclosure of inside information as referred to in paragraph 2,

— the technical modalities designed to favour a common approach in the implementation of the second sentence of paragraph 2,

— the conditions under which issuers, or entities acting on their behalf, are to draw up a list of those persons working for them and having access to inside information, as referred to in paragraph 3, together with the conditions under which such lists are to be updated,

— the categories of persons who are subject to a duty of disclosure as referred to in paragraph 4 and the characteristics of a transaction, including its size, which trigger that duty, and the technical arrangements for disclosure to the competent authority,

▼B

— technical arrangements, for the various categories of person referred to in paragraph 5, for fair presentation of research and other information recommending investment strategy and for disclosure of particular interests or conflicts of interest as referred to in paragraph 5. Such arrangements shall take into account the rules, including self-regulation, governing the profession of journalist,

— technical arrangements governing notification to the competent authority by the persons referred to in paragraph 9.

▼M1

Those measures, designed to amend non-essential elements of this Directive by supplementing it, shall be adopted in accordance with the regulatory procedure with scrutiny referred to in Article 17(2a).

▼M2

11. ESMA may develop draft implementing technical standards to ensure uniform conditions of application of the acts adopted by the Commission in accordance with the sixth indent of the first subparagraph of paragraph 10.

Power is conferred on the Commission to adopt the implementing technical standards referred to in the first subparagraph in accordance with Article 15 of Regulation (EU) No 1095/2010.

▼B

*Article 7*

This Directive shall not apply to transactions carried out in pursuit of monetary, exchange-rate or public debt-management policy by a Member State, by the European System of Central Banks, by a national central bank or by any other officially designated body, or by any person acting on their behalf. Member States may extend this exemption to their federated States or similar local authorities in respect of the management of their public debt.

*Article 8*

►M2 1. ◄ The prohibitions provided for in this Directive shall not apply to trading in own shares in 'buy-back' programmes or to the stabilisation of a financial instrument provided such trading is carried out in accordance with implementing measures ►M1 ———— ◄. ►M1 Those measures, designed to amend non-essential elements of this Directive by supplementing it, shall be adopted in accordance with the regulatory procedure with scrutiny referred to in Article 17(2a). ◄

▼M2

2. ESMA may develop draft implementing technical standards to ensure uniform conditions of application of acts adopted by the Commission in accordance with paragraph 1.

Power is conferred on the Commission to adopt the implementing technical standards referred to in the first subparagraph in accordance with Article 15 of Regulation (EU) No 1095/2010.

▼B

*Article 9*

This Directive shall apply to any financial instrument admitted to trading on a regulated market in at least one Member State, or for which a request for admission to trading on such a market has been made, irrespective of whether or not the transaction itself actually takes place on that market.

Articles 2, 3 and 4 shall also apply to any financial instrument not admitted to trading on a regulated market in a Member State, but whose value depends on a financial instrument as referred to in paragraph 1.

Article 6(1) to (3) shall not apply to issuers who have not requested or approved admission of their financial instruments to trading on a regulated market in a Member State.

*Article 10*

Each Member State shall apply the prohibitions and requirements provided for in this Directive to:

(a) actions carried out on its territory or abroad concerning financial instruments that are admitted to trading on a regulated market situated or operating within its territory or for which a request for admission to trading on such market has been made;

(b) actions carried out on its territory concerning financial instruments that are admitted to trading on a regulated market in a Member State or for which a request for admission to trading on such market has been made.

*Article 11*

Without prejudice to the competences of the judicial authorities, each Member State shall designate a single administrative authority competent to ensure that the provisions adopted pursuant to this Directive are applied.

Member States shall establish effective consultative arrangements and procedures with market participants concerning possible changes in national legislation. These arrangements may include consultative committees within each competent authority, the membership of which should reflect as far as possible the diversity of market participants, be they issuers, providers of financial services or consumers.

*Article 12*

1. The competent authority shall be given all supervisory and investigatory powers that are necessary for the exercise of its functions. It shall exercise such powers:

(a) directly; or

(b) in collaboration with other authorities or with the market undertakings; or

(c) under its responsibility by delegation to such authorities or to the market undertakings; or

(d) by application to the competent judicial authorities.

▼B

2. Without prejudice to Article 6(7), the powers referred to in paragraph 1 of this Article shall be exercised in conformity with national law and shall include at least the right to:

(a) have access to any document in any form whatsoever, and to receive a copy of it;

(b) demand information from any person, including those who are successively involved in the transmission of orders or conduct of the operations concerned, as well as their principals, and if necessary, to summon and hear any such person;

(c) carry out on-site inspections;

(d) require existing telephone and existing data traffic records;

(e) require the cessation of any practice that is contrary to the provisions adopted in the implementation of this Directive;

(f) suspend trading of the financial instruments concerned;

(g) request the freezing and/or sequestration of assets;

(h) request temporary prohibition of professional activity.

3. This Article shall be without prejudice to national legal provisions on professional secrecy.

*Article 13*

The obligation of professional secrecy shall apply to all persons who work or who have worked for the competent authority or for any authority or market undertaking to whom the competent authority has delegated its powers, including auditors and experts instructed by the competent authority. Information covered by professional secrecy may not be disclosed to any other person or authority except by virtue of provisions laid down by law.

*Article 14*

1. Without prejudice to the right of Member States to impose criminal sanctions, Member States shall ensure, in conformity with their national law, that the appropriate administrative measures can be taken or administrative sanctions be imposed against the persons responsible where the provisions adopted in the implementation of this Directive have not been complied with. Member States shall ensure that these measures are effective, proportionate and dissuasive.

2. In accordance with the procedure laid down in Article 17(2), the Commission shall, for information, draw up a list of the administrative measures and sanctions referred to in paragraph 1.

3. Member States shall determine the sanctions to be applied for failure to cooperate in an investigation covered by Article 12.

4. Member States shall provide that the competent authority may disclose to the public every measure or sanction that will be imposed for infringement of the provisions adopted in the implementation of this Directive, unless such disclosure would seriously jeopardise the financial markets or cause disproportionate damage to the parties involved.

▼M2

5. Member States shall provide ESMA annually with aggregated information regarding all administrative measures and sanctions imposed in accordance with paragraphs 1 and 2.

Where the competent authority has disclosed an administrative measure or a sanction to the public, it shall contemporaneously report that fact to ESMA.

Where a published sanction relates to an investment firm authorised in accordance with Directive 2004/39/EC, ESMA shall add a reference to the published sanction in the register of investment firms established under Article 5(3) of Directive 2004/39/EC.

▼B

*Article 15*

Member States shall ensure that an appeal may be brought before a court against the decisions taken by the competent authority.

▼M2

*Article 15a*

1. The competent authorities shall cooperate with ESMA for the purposes of this Directive, in accordance with Regulation (EU) No 1095/2010.

2. The competent authorities shall, without delay, provide ESMA with all information necessary to carry out its duties, in accordance with Article 35 of Regulation (EU) No 1095/2010.

▼B

*Article 16*

1. Competent authorities shall cooperate with each other whenever necessary for the purpose of carrying out their duties, making use of their powers whether set out in this Directive or in national law. Competent authorities shall render assistance to competent authorities of other Member States. In particular, they shall exchange information and cooperate in investigation activities.

2. Competent authorities shall, on request, immediately supply any information required for the purpose referred to in paragraph 1. Where necessary, the competent authorities receiving any such request shall immediately take the necessary measures in order to gather the required information. If the requested competent authority is not able to supply the required information immediately, it shall notify the requesting competent authority of the reasons. Information thus supplied shall be covered by the obligation of professional secrecy to which the persons employed or formerly employed by the competent authorities receiving the information are subject.

The competent authorities may refuse to act on a request for information where:

— communication might adversely affect the sovereignty, security or public policy of the Member State addressed,

— judicial proceedings have already been initiated in respect of the same actions and against the same persons before the authorities of the Member State addressed, or

— where a final judgment has already been delivered in relation to such persons for the same actions in the Member State addressed.

▼B

In any such case, they shall notify the requesting competent authority accordingly, providing as detailed information as possible on those proceedings or the judgment.

▼M2

Without prejudice to Article 258 of the Treaty on the Functioning of the European Union (TFEU), a competent authority whose request for information is not acted upon within a reasonable time or whose request for information is rejected may refer that rejection or absence of action within a reasonable timeframe to ESMA. In the situations referred to in the first sentence, ESMA may act in accordance with Article 19 of Regulation (EU) No 1095/2010, without prejudice to the possibilities for refusing to act on a request for information provided for in the second subparagraph of this paragraph and to the possibility of ESMA acting in accordance with Article 17 of Regulation (EU) No 1095/2010.

▼B

Without prejudice to the obligations to which they are subject in judicial proceedings under criminal law, the competent authorities which receive information pursuant to paragraph 1 may use it only for the exercise of their functions within the scope of this Directive and in the context of administrative or judicial proceedings specifically related to the exercise of those functions. However, where the competent authority communicating information consents thereto, the authority receiving the information may use it for other purposes or forward it to other States' competent authorities.

3. Where a competent authority is convinced that acts contrary to the provisions of this Directive are being, or have been, carried out on the territory of another Member State or that acts are affecting financial instruments traded on a regulated market situated in another Member State, it shall give notice of that fact in as specific a manner as possible to the competent authority of the other Member State. The competent authority of the other Member State shall take appropriate action. It shall inform the notifying competent authority of the outcome and, so far as possible, of significant interim developments. This paragraph shall not prejudice the competences of the competent authority that has forwarded the information. The competent authorities of the various Member States that are competent for the purposes of Article 10 shall consult each other on the proposed follow-up to their action.

4. A competent authority of one Member State may request that an investigation be carried out by the competent authority of another Member State, on the latter's territory.

It may further request that members of its own personnel be allowed to accompany the personnel of the competent authority of that other Member State during the course of the investigation.

The investigation shall, however, be subject throughout to the overall control of the Member State on whose territory it is conducted.

The competent authorities may refuse to act on a request for an investigation to be conducted as provided for in the first subparagraph, or on a request for its personnel to be accompanied by personnel of the competent authority of another Member State as provided for in the second subparagraph, where such an investigation might adversely affect the sovereignty, security or public policy of the State addressed, or where judicial proceedings have already been initiated in respect of the same actions and against the same persons before the authorities of the State addressed or where a final judgment has already been delivered in relation to such persons for the same actions in the State addressed. In such case, they shall notify the requesting competent authority accordingly, providing information, as detailed as possible, on those proceedings or judgment.

▼M2

Without prejudice to Article 258 TFEU, a competent authority whose application to open an inquiry or whose request for authorisation for its officials to accompany those of the other Member State's competent authority is not acted upon within a reasonable time or is rejected may refer that rejection or absence of action within a reasonable timeframe to ESMA. In the situations referred to in the first sentence, ESMA may act in accordance with Article 19 of Regulation (EU) No 1095/2010, without prejudice to the possibilities for refusing to act on a request for information provided in the fourth subparagraph of this paragraph and to the possibility of ESMA acting in accordance with Article 17 of Regulation (EU) No 1095/2010.

5. In order to ensure uniform conditions of application of paragraphs 2 and 4, ESMA may develop draft implementing technical standards on the procedures and forms for exchange of information and for cross-border inspections as referred to in this Article.

Power is conferred on the Commission to adopt the implementing technical standards referred to in the first subparagraph in accordance with Article 15 of Regulation (EU) No 1095/2010.

▼B

*Article 17*

1. The Commission shall be assisted by the European Securities Committee instituted by Decision 2001/528/EC (hereinafter referred to as the 'Committee').

2. Where reference is made to this paragraph, Articles 5 and 7 of Decision 1999/468/EC shall apply, having regard to the provisions of Article 8 thereof, provided that the implementing measures adopted according to this procedure do not modify the essential provisions of this Directive.

The period laid down in Article 5(6) of Decision 1999/468/EC shall be set at three months.

▼M1

2a. Where reference is made to this paragraph, Article 5a(1) to (4) and Article 7 of Decision 1999/468/EC shall apply, having regard to the provisions of Article 8 thereof.

3. By 31 December 2010, and, thereafter, at least every three years, the Commission shall review the provisions concerning its implementing powers and present a report to the European Parliament and to the Council on the functioning of those powers. The report shall examine, in particular, the need for the Commission to propose amendments to this Directive in order to ensure the appropriate scope of the implementing powers conferred on the Commission. The conclusion as to whether or not amendment is necessary shall be accompanied by a detailed statement of reasons. If necessary, the report shall be accompanied by a legislative proposal to amend the provisions conferring implementing powers on the Commission.

▼M2

*Article 17a*

By 1 December 2011 the Commission shall review Articles 1, 6, 8, 14, and 16 and present any appropriate legislative proposals in order to allow the full application of the delegated acts under Article 290 TFEU and implementing acts under Article 291 TFEU in respect of this Directive. Without prejudice to implementing measures already adopted, the powers conferred on the Commission in Article 17 to adopt implementing measures that remain after the entry into force of the Lisbon Treaty shall cease to apply on 1 December 2012.

▼B

*Article 18*

Member States shall bring into force the laws, regulations and administrative provisions necessary to comply with this Directive not later than 12 October 2004. They shall forthwith inform the Commission thereof.

When Member States adopt those measures, they shall contain a reference to this Directive or be accompanied by such a reference on the occasion of their official publication. Member States shall determine how such reference is to be made.

*Article 19*

Article 11 shall not prejudge the possibility for a Member State to make separate legal and administrative arrangements for overseas European territories for whose external relations that Member State is responsible.

*Article 20*

Directive 89/592/EEC and Article 68(1) and Article 81(1) of Directive 2001/34/EC of the European Parliament and of the Council of 28 May 2001 on the admission of securities to official stock exchange listing and on information to be published on those securities [1] shall be repealed with effect from the date of entry into force of this Directive.

*Article 21*

This Directive shall enter into force on the day of its publication in the *Official Journal of the European Union.*

*Article 22*

This Directive is addressed to the Member States.

(1) OJ L 184, 6.7.2001, p. 1.

# Decision 2003/170 on the common use of liaison officers posted abroad by the law enforcement agencies of the Member States, 27 February 2003

**[Consolidated version. Original version OJ 2003, L 67/27–30 amended by OJ 2006, L 219/31–32]**

►B

**COUNCIL DECISION 2003/170/JHA**

**of 27 February 2003**

**on the common use of liaison officers posted abroad by the law enforcement agencies of the Member States**

(OJ L 67, 12.3.2003, p. 27)

Amended by:

| | | Official Journal | | |
|---|---|---|---|---|
| | | No | page | date |
| ►M1 | Council Decision 2006/560/JHA of 24 July 2006 | L 219 | 31 | 10.8.2006 |

▼B

**COUNCIL DECISION 2003/170/JHA**

**of 27 February 2003**

**on the common use of liaison officers posted abroad by the law enforcement agencies of the Member States**

THE COUNCIL OF THE EUROPEAN UNION,

Having regard to the Treaty on European Union, and in particular Article 30(1)(a), (b) and (c), Article 30(2)(c) and Article 34(2)(c) thereof,

Having regard to the initiative of the Kingdom of Denmark (1),

Having regard to the opinion of the European Parliament (2),

Whereas:

(1) At its meeting of 3 December 1998 the Council of Justice and Home Affairs Ministers adopted the Action Plan of the Council and the Commission on how best to implement the provisions of the Treaty of Amsterdam on an area of freedom, security and justice (3), measure 48 of which states that, within five years of the Treaty's entering into force, action should be taken to promote cooperation and joint initiatives in training, the exchange of liaison officers, secondment, the use of equipment and forensic research.

(2) At its meeting in Vienna on 11 and 12 December 1998 the European Council endorsed, in its conclusion 83, the Council and Commission Action Plan on how best to implement the provisions of the Treaty of Amsterdam on an area of freedom, security and justice, and in its conclusion 89 it called for a strengthening of action against organised crime in the light of the new possibilities opened up by the Treaty.

(3) At its meeting in Tampere on 15 and 16 October 1999 the European Council invited the Council and the Commission, in close cooperation with the European Parliament, to promote the full and immediate implementation of the Treaty of Amsterdam, on the basis of the Action Plan adopted on 3 December 1998 by the Council of Home Affairs Ministers and endorsed at the meeting of the European Council in Vienna on 11 and 12 December 1998 and of the political guidelines and concrete objectives involving a deepening of police cooperation for the purpose of combating cross-border crime which were agreed in Tampere.

(4) At its meeting in Helsinki on 10 and 11 December 1999, the European Council urged the European Union to intensify its efforts at the international level by stepping up cooperation with third countries in reducing the demand for and supply of drugs, and on justice and home affairs. The European Council also noted that there would be a need for combined efforts by all the relevant authorities, with a particular role for Europol.

(5) At its meeting in Laeken on 14 and 15 December 2001 the European Council confirmed, in its conclusion 37, the guidelines and objectives defined at Tampere and also noted that there was a

(1) OJ C 176, 24.7.2002, p. 8.
(2) Opinion of the European Parliament of 20 November 2002 (not yet published in the Official Journal).
(3) OJ C 19, 23.1.1999, p. 1.

▼B

need for new impetus and guidelines to make good delays in some areas.

(6) On 14 October 1996 the Council adopted Joint Action 96/602/JHA providing for a common framework for the initiatives of the Member States concerning liaison officers (1).

(7) In the light of experience in applying the Joint Action and in the light of the provisions of the Treaty of Amsterdam on combating cross-border crime, cooperation amongst Member States on the tasks assigned to, and the posting of liaison officers to third countries and international organisations needs to be strengthened and developed.

(8) Insofar as is relevant for performing the tasks defined in the Europol Convention (2), Europol will establish and maintain cooperative relations with third countries and international organisations.

(9) Europol has established and will continue to establish and maintain cooperative relations with a wide range of third countries and international organisations.

(10) Europol needs to be given the necessary support and means to function effectively as the focal point of European police cooperation. The European Council has stressed that Europol plays a central role in cooperation between the authorities of the Member States in investigating cross-border crime by supporting the prevention, analysis and investigation of crime at Union level.

(11) Europol needs to be given the opportunity to make use to some extent of Member States' liaison officers in third countries, so as to strengthen Europol's operative support function in relation to national police authorities.

(12) Member States recognise that extensive cooperation is already taking place between liaison officers posted by Member States in view of their national needs to third countries and international organisations. However, there is a need to strengthen some aspects of cooperation between those liaison officers, to make the best possible use of Member States' resources.

(13) Cooperation between Member States in this area needs to be strengthened so as to facilitate the exchange of information with a view to combating serious cross-border crime.

(14) Member States attach particular weight to cooperation in combating cross-border crime, as they believe that strengthening cooperation regarding the exchange of information will enhance the national authorities' capabilities to combat crime effectively. Member States believe that Europol should play a central role in this.

(15) The aim of this Decision is to regulate questions relating to the fight against serious cross-border crime.

(16) The provisions in the Convention implementing the Schengen Agreement of 14 June 1985 between the Governments of the States of the Benelux Economic Union, the Federal Republic of Germany and the French Republic on the gradual abolition of checks at their common borders (3) (hereinafter 'Convention implementing the Schengen Agreement') which relates to the common use of liaison officers should be developed further, with a view to strengthening cooperation between Member States in the fight against cross-border crime.

(1) OJ L 268, 19.10.1996, p. 2.
(2) OJ C 316, 27.11.1995, p. 2.
(3) OJ L 239, 22.9.2000, p. 19.

▼B

(17) As regards Iceland and Norway, this Decision constitutes, with the exception of Article 8, a development of provisions of the Schengen *acquis* within the meaning of the Agreement concluded by the Council of the European Union and the Republic of Iceland and the Kingdom of Norway concerning the latters' association with the implementation, application and development of the Schengen *acquis* ([1]), which fall within the area referred to in Article 1(H) of Council Decision 1999/437/EC ([2]) on certain arrangements for the application of that Agreement.

(18) The United Kingdom is taking part in this Decision in accordance with Article 5 of the Protocol integrating the Schengen *acquis* into the European Union annexed to the Treaty on European Union and to the Treaty establishing the European Community, and Article 8(2) of Council Decision 2000/365/EC of 29 May 2000 concerning the request of the United Kingdom of Great Britain and Northern Ireland to take part in some of the provisions of the Schengen *acquis* ([3]).

(19) Ireland is taking part in this Decision in accordance with Article 5 of the Protocol integrating the Schengen *acquis* into the European Union annexed to the Treaty on European Union and to the Treaty establishing the European Community, and Article 6(2) of Council Decision 2002/192/EC of 28 February 2002 concerning Ireland's request to take part in some of the provisions of the Schengen *acquis* ([4]).

(20) Council Joint Action 96/602/JHA and the provision of Article 47(4) of the Convention implementing the Schengen Agreement should accordingly be repealed,

HAS DECIDED AS FOLLOWS:

*Article 1*

**Definition**

1. In this Decision, 'liaison officer' means a representative of one of the Member States, posted abroad by a law enforcement agency to one or more third countries or to international organisations to establish and maintain contacts with the authorities in those countries or organisations with a view to contributing to preventing or investigating criminal offences.

▼M1

In this Decision, 'Europol liaison officer' means a Europol employee, posted abroad to one or more third countries or to international organisations to enhance the cooperation between the authorities in those countries or organisations and Europol in order to support the Member States, in particular the liaison officers posted abroad by the law enforcement agencies of the Member States, in combating of serious forms of international crime, in particular through the exchange of information.

▼B

2. This Decision is without prejudice to Member States' liaison officers' tasks within the framework of their responsibilities and in compliance with national law, national needs, and any more favourable agreements concluded with the host State or the international organisation.

([1]) OJ L 176, 10.7.1999, p. 36.
([2]) OJ L 176, 10.7.1999, p. 31.
([3]) OJ L 131, 1.6.2000, p. 43.
([4]) OJ L 64, 7.3.2002, p. 20.

▼M1

This Decision shall be without prejudice to Europol's and Europol liaison officers' tasks within the framework of the Europol Convention, the arrangements made for the implementation thereof, and cooperation agreements concluded between Europol and the third country or international organisation concerned.

▼B

*Article 2*

**Tasks of liaison officers**

1. Each Member State shall ensure that its liaison officers establish and maintain direct contacts with competent authorities in the host State or the international organisation, with a view to facilitating and expediting the collection and exchange of information.

2. Each Member State's liaison officer shall also contribute to the collection and exchange of information which may be used to combat serious cross-border crime, including information providing a readier knowledge of the legal systems and operational methods available in the States or international organisations concerned.

3. Liaison officers shall carry out their tasks within the framework of their responsibilities and in compliance with the provisions, including those on the protection of personal data, laid down in their national laws and in any agreements concluded with host States or international organisations.

*Article 3*

**Notification of the posting of liaison officers**

1. Member States shall inform one another of their intentions as regards the secondment of liaison officers to third States and international organisations and the General Secretariat of the Council of the European Union (the General Secretariat) each year of the posting of liaison officers, including their duties and any cooperative agreements between the Member States on the posting of liaison officers.

▼M1

2. The General Secretariat shall draw up an annual summary to be sent to Member States, the Commission and to Europol concerning Member States' postings of liaison officers, including their duties and any cooperative agreements between the Member States on the posting of liaison officers. This summary shall list the Member States who, with the agreement of other Member States through coordination in the Council structures, have been given responsibility for the coordination of EU cooperation in a particular country or region, as referred to in Article 4(1). Details of Europol liaison officers posted to third countries or international organisations shall also be included.

▼B

*Article 4*

**Liaison officer networks in third countries**

1. Member States shall ensure that Member States' liaison officers posted to the same third country or international organisation meet regularly or when necessary to exchange relevant information. The Member State holding the Presidency of the Council of the European Union shall ensure that its liaison officers take the initiative to hold such meetings. If the Member State holding the Presidency is not represented in the third country or international organisation concerned, then the representative of the incoming or next incoming Presidency shall take the initiative to hold the meeting. The Commission and Europol shall,

▼B

where appropriate, be invited to such meetings. ►M1 Such meetings may also be held, following consultation with the Member State holding the Presidency, at the initiative of any other Member State and especially of those Member States that have been given responsibility for the coordination of the EU cooperation in a particular country or region. ◄

2. Member States shall ensure that its liaison officers posted to the same third country or international organisation provide one another with assistance in contacts with the authorities of the host State. Where relevant, Member States may agree that their liaison officers shall share tasks among themselves.

3. Member States may bilaterally or multilaterally agree that liaison officers who are posted to a third country or international organisation by a Member State shall also look after the interests of one or more other Member States.

*Article 5*

**Cooperation between Member States regarding the exchange of information via liaison officers in third countries**

1. Member States shall ensure that their liaison officers in third countries and international organisations shall, in accordance with national law and relevant international instruments and subject to compliance with applicable provisions governing the protection of personal data, provide its respective national authorities with information relating to serious criminal threats to other Member States not represented by their own liaison officers in the third country or international organisation concerned. National authorities shall assess, in accordance with national law and according to the seriousness of the threat, whether the Member States concerned should be informed.

2. Member States' liaison officers in third countries or international organisations may, in accordance with national law and relevant international instruments and subject to compliance with applicable provisions governing the protection of personal data, provide information relating to serious criminal threats to other Member States directly to the liaison officers of the Member State in question, if that Member State is represented in the third country or international organisation concerned.

3. In accordance with national law and relevant international instruments, Member States which do not have liaison officers in a third country or international organisation may make a request to another Member State which does have liaison officers in the third country or international organisation concerned, with a view to the exchange of relevant information.

4. Member States shall deal with any request as described in paragraph 3 in accordance with their respective national law and relevant international instruments, and shall state as speedily as possible whether such a request may be met.

5. Member States may consent to information being exchanged directly between liaison officers in third countries and international organisations and the authorities of other Member States, subject to compliance with applicable provisions governing the protection of personal data.

▼B

6. The performance of the tasks described in paragraph 1 and 2 must not hinder liaison officers in the performance of their original duties.

*Article 6*

**Joint seminars for liaison officers**

1. To enhance cooperation between liaison officers in one or more third countries and international organisations, where there are specific needs for knowledge of and intervention in the third countries and international organisations concerned, Member States may hold joint seminars on crime trends and on the most effective methods of combating cross-border crime taking due account of the EU *acquis*. The Commission and Europol shall be invited to such seminars.

2. Participation in the seminars described in paragraph 1 must not hinder liaison officers in the performance of their original duties.

*Article 7*

**Competent national authorities**

1. Member States shall designate contact points within their competent authorities to facilitate the tasks referred to in this Decision and ensure that the national contact points are able to carry out their duties efficiently and speedily.

2. Member States shall inform the General Secretariat in writing of its contact points within their competent authorities and of any subsequent changes pursuant to this Decision. The General Secretariat shall publish the information in the *Official Journal of the European Union*.

3. This Decision applies without prejudice to existing national provisions, particularly as regards the division of competence between the various authorities and services in the Member States concerned.

*Article 8*

**Europol**

1. Member States shall facilitate, in accordance with national law and the Europol Convention, the processing of requests made by Europol to obtain information from Member States' liaison officers in third countries or international organisations where Europol is not represented. Europol's requests shall be addressed to the Member States' National Units, which, in accordance with national law and the Europol Convention, shall take a decision on the request. Information from Member States' liaison officers in third countries or international organisations shall be transmitted to Europol in accordance with national law and the Europol Convention.

2. When establishing the duties of their liaison officers, Member States shall where appropriate pay attention to the tasks, which under the Europol Convention are to be carried out by Europol. ►M1 Member States shall also ensure that the information contributed in accordance with Article 2(2) shall be exchanged with Europol in accordance with the Europol Convention. ◄

▼M1

3. In accordance with the national law and the Europol Convention, Member States may make a request to Europol to use Europol liaison officers seconded to third countries or international organisations, with a view to the exchange of relevant information in compliance with the cooperation agreements concluded between Europol and the third country or organisation concerned. Requests shall be addressed to Europol via the Member States' national units in accordance with the Europol Convention.

4. Europol shall ensure that its liaison officers seconded to third countries and international organisations provide it with information relating to serious threats of criminal offences to Member States for those criminal offences for which Europol is competent under the Europol Convention. Such information shall be communicated to the competent authorities of the Member States concerned via the national units in accordance with the Europol Convention.

▼B

*Article 9*

**Application to Gibraltar**

This Decision shall apply to Gibraltar.

*Article 10*

**Evaluation**

The Council shall evaluate the implementation of this Decision within two years of its adoption.

*Article 11*

**Repeal**

1. Joint Action 96/602/JHA is hereby repealed.

2. The provision of Article 47(4) of the Convention implementing the Schengen Agreement is hereby repealed.

*Article 12*

**Entry into force**

This Decision shall enter into force 14 days after its publication in the *Official Journal of the European Union*.

# Decision 2003/335 on the investigation and prosecution of genocide, crimes against humanity and war crimes, 8 May 2003

[OJ 2003, L 118/12–14]

L 118/12 EN Official Journal of the European Union 14.5.2003

*(Acts adopted pursuant to Title VI of the Treaty on European Union)*

**COUNCIL DECISION 2003/335/JHA**

**of 8 May 2003**

**on the investigation and prosecution of genocide, crimes against humanity and war crimes**

THE COUNCIL OF THE EUROPEAN UNION,

Having regard to the Treaty on European Union, and in particular Articles 30, 31 and 34(2)(c) thereof,

Having regard to the initiative of the Kingdom of Denmark ([1]),

Having regard to the opinion of the European Parliament ([2]),

Whereas:

(1) The International Criminal Tribunals for the former Yugoslavia and for Rwanda have since 1995 been investigating, prosecuting and bringing to justice violations of international law in connection with war, genocide and crimes against humanity.

(2) The Rome Statute of the International Criminal Court of 17 July 1998, which has been ratified by all Member States of the European Union, affirms that the most serious crimes of concern to the international community as a whole, in particular genocide, crimes against humanity and war crimes, must not go unpunished and that their effective prosecution must be ensured by taking measures at national level and by enhancing international cooperation.

(3) The Rome Statute recalls that it is the duty of every State to exercise its criminal jurisdiction over those responsible for such international crimes.

(4) The Rome Statute emphasises that the International Criminal Court established under it is to be complementary to national criminal jurisdictions. Effective investigation and, as appropriate, prosecution of genocide, crimes against humanity and war crimes should be ensured without interference with the jurisdiction of the International Criminal Court.

(5) The investigation and prosecution of, and exchange of information on, genocide, crimes against humanity and war crimes is to remain the responsibility of national authorities, except as affected by international law.

([1]) OJ C 223, 19.9.2002, p. 19.
([2]) Opinion of 17 December 2002 (not yet published in the Official Journal).

(6) Member States are being confronted on a regular basis with persons who were involved in such crimes and who are trying to enter and reside in the European Union.

(7) The competent authorities of the Member States are to ensure that, where they receive information that a person who has applied for a residence permit is suspected of having committed or participated in the commission of genocide, crimes against humanity or war crimes, the relevant acts may be investigated, and, where justified, prosecuted in accordance with national law.

(8) The relevant national law enforcement and immigration authorities, although having separate tasks and responsibilities, should cooperate very closely in order to enable effective investigation and prosecution of such crimes by the competent authorities that have jurisdiction at national level.

(9) Member States should ensure that law enforcement authorities and immigration authorities have the appropriate resources and structures to enable their effective cooperation and the effective investigation and, as appropriate, prosecution of genocide, crimes against humanity and war crimes.

(10) The successful outcome of effective investigation and prosecution of such crimes also requires close cooperation at transnational level between authorities of the States Parties to the Rome Statute, including the Member States.

(11) On 13 June 2002, the Council adopted Decision 2002/494/JHA setting up a European network of contact points in respect of persons responsible for genocide, crimes against humanity and war crimes ([3]). Member States should ensure that full use is made of the contact points to facilitate cooperation between the competent international authorities.

([3]) OJ L 167, 26.6.2002, p. 1.

14.5.2003 EN Official Journal of the European Union L 118/13

(12) In Council Common Position 2001/443/CFSP of 11 June 2001 on the International Criminal Court ([1]), the Member States declared that the crimes within the jurisdiction of the International Criminal Court are of concern for all Member States, which are determined to cooperate for the prevention of those crimes and for putting an end to the impunity of the perpetrators thereof,

HAS DECIDED AS FOLLOWS:

*Article 1*

**Objective**

The aim of this Decision is to increase cooperation between national units in order to maximise the ability of law enforcement authorities in different Member States to cooperate effectively in the field of investigation and prosecution of persons who have committed or participated in the commission of genocide, crimes against humanity or war crimes as defined in Articles 6, 7 and 8 of the Rome Statute of the International Criminal Court of 17 July 1998.

*Article 2*

**Information to law enforcement authorities**

1. The Member States shall take the necessary measures in order for the law enforcement authorities to be informed when facts are established which give rise to a suspicion that an applicant for a residence permit has committed crimes as referred to in Article 1 which may lead to prosecution in a Member State or in international criminal courts.

2. Member States shall take the necessary measures to ensure that the relevant national law enforcement and immigration authorities are able to exchange the information, which they require in order to carry out their tasks effectively.

*Article 3*

**Investigation and prosecution**

1. Member States shall assist one another in investigating and prosecuting the crimes referred to in Article 1 in accordance with relevant international agreements and national law.

2. Where, in connection with the processing of an application for a residence permit, the immigration authorities become aware of facts which give rise to a suspicion that the applicant has participated in crimes referred to in Article 1, and where it emerges that the applicant has previously sought permission to reside in another Member State, the law enforcement authorities may apply to the competent law enforcement authorities in the latter Member State with a view to obtaining relevant information, including information from the immigration authorities.

3. Insofar as the law enforcement authorities in a Member State become aware that a person suspected of crimes as referred to in Article 1 is in another Member State, they shall inform the competent authorities in the latter Member State of their suspicions and the basis thereof. Such information shall be provided in accordance with relevant international agreements and national law.

*Article 4*

**Structures**

Member States shall consider the need to set up or designate specialist units within the competent law enforcement authorities with particular responsibility for investigating and, as appropriate, prosecuting the crimes in question.

*Article 5*

**Coordination and periodic meetings**

1. Member States shall coordinate ongoing efforts to investigate and prosecute persons suspected of having committed or participated in the commission of genocide, crimes against humanity or war crimes.

2. At the Presidency's initiative, the contact points designated under Article 1 of Decision 2002/494/JHA, shall meet at regular intervals with a view to exchanging information about experiences, practices and methods. These meetings may take place in conjunction with meetings within the European Judicial Network and, depending on the circumstances, representatives from the International Criminal Tribunals for the former Yugoslavia and for Rwanda, the International Criminal Court and other international bodies may also be invited to take part in such meetings.

*Article 6*

**Compliance with data protection legislation**

Any kind of exchange of information or other kind of processing of personal data under this Decision shall take place in full compliance with the requirements flowing from the applicable international and domestic data protection legislation.

*Article 7*

**Implementation**

Member States shall take the necessary measures to comply with this Decision by 8 May 2005.

([1]) OJ L 155, 12.6.2001, p. 19.

*Article 8*

**Territorial application**

This Decision shall apply to Gibraltar.

*Article 9*

**Taking effect**

This Decision shall take effect on the day of its publication in the *Official Journal of the European Union*.

Done at Brussels, 8 May 2003.

*For the Council*

*The President*

M. CHRISOCHOÏDIS

# Agreement on extradition between the European Union and the United States of America, 25 June 2003

**[OJ 2003, L 181/ 27–31+33]**

**[Editor's note: signatures omitted]**

19.7.2003 EN Official Journal of the European Union L 181/27

**AGREEMENT**

**on extradition between the European Union and the United States of America**

THE EUROPEAN UNION AND THE UNITED STATES OF AMERICA,

DESIRING further to facilitate cooperation between the European Union Member States and the United States of America,

DESIRING to combat crime in a more effective way as a means of protecting their respective democratic societies and common values,

HAVING DUE REGARD for rights of individuals and the rule of law,

MINDFUL of the guarantees under their respective legal systems which provide for the right to a fair trial to an extradited person, including the right to adjudication by an impartial tribunal established pursuant to law,

DESIRING to conclude an Agreement relating to the extradition of offenders,

HAVE AGREED AS FOLLOWS:

*Article 1*

**Object and Purpose**

The Contracting Parties undertake, in accordance with the provisions of this Agreement, to provide for enhancements to cooperation in the context of applicable extradition relations between the Member States and the United States of America governing extradition of offenders.

*Article 2*

**Definitions**

1. 'Contracting Parties' shall mean the European Union and the United States of America.

2. 'Member State' shall mean a Member State of the European Union.

3. 'Ministry of Justice' shall, for the United States of America, mean the United States Department of Justice; and for a Member State, its Ministry of Justice, except that with respect to a Member State in which functions described in Articles 3, 5, 6, 8 or 12 are carried out by its Prosecutor General, that body may be designated to carry out such function in lieu of the Ministry of Justice in accordance with Article 19, unless the United States and the Member State concerned agree to designate another body.

*Article 3*

**Scope of application of this Agreement in relation to bilateral extradition treaties with Member States**

1. The European Union, pursuant to the Treaty on European Union, and the United States of America shall ensure that the provisions of this Agreement are applied in relation to bilateral extradition treaties between the Member States and the United States of America, in force at the time of the entry into force of this Agreement, under the following terms:

(a) Article 4 shall be applied in place of bilateral treaty provisions that authorise extradition exclusively with respect to a list of specified criminal offences;

(b) Article 5 shall be applied in place of bilateral treaty provisions governing transmission, certification, authentication or legalisation of an extradition request and supporting documents transmitted by the requesting State;

(c) Article 6 shall be applied in the absence of bilateral treaty provisions authorising direct transmission of provisional arrest requests between the United States Department of Justice and the Ministry of Justice of the Member State concerned;

(d) Article 7 shall be applied in addition to bilateral treaty provisions governing transmission of extradition requests;

(e) Article 8 shall be applied in the absence of bilateral treaty provisions governing the submission of supplementary information; where bilateral treaty provisions do not specify the channel to be used, paragraph 2 of that Article shall also be applied;

(f) Article 9 shall be applied in the absence of bilateral treaty provisions authorising temporary surrender of persons being proceeded against or serving a sentence in the requested State;

(g) Article 10 shall be applied, except as otherwise specified therein, in place of, or in the absence of, bilateral treaty provisions pertaining to decision on several requests for extradition of the same person;

(h) Article 11 shall be applied in the absence of bilateral treaty provisions authorising waiver of extradition or simplified extradition procedures;

(i) Article 12 shall be applied in the absence of bilateral treaty provisions governing transit; where bilateral treaty provisions do not specify the procedure governing unscheduled landing of aircraft, paragraph 3 of that Article shall also be applied;

(j) Article 13 may be applied by the requested State in place of, or in the absence of, bilateral treaty provisions governing capital punishment;

(k) Article 14 shall be applied in the absence of bilateral treaty provisions governing treatment of sensitive information in a request.

2. (a) The European Union, pursuant to the Treaty on European Union, shall ensure that each Member State acknowledges, in a written instrument between such Member State and the United States of America, the application, in the manner set forth in this Article, of its bilateral extradition treaty in force with the United States of America.

(b) The European Union, pursuant to the Treaty on European Union, shall ensure that new Member States acceding to the European Union after the entry into force of this Agreement and having bilateral extradition treaties with the United States of America, take the measures referred to in subparagraph (a).

(c) The Contracting Parties shall endeavour to complete the process described in subparagraph (b) prior to the scheduled accession of a new Member State, or as soon as possible thereafter. The European Union shall notify the United States of America of the date of accession of new Member States.

3. If the process described in paragraph 2(b) is not completed by the date of accession, the provisions of this Agreement shall apply in the relations between that new Member State and the United States of America as from the date on which they have notified each other and the European Union of the completion of their internal procedures for that purpose.

*Article 4*

**Extraditable offences**

1. An offence shall be an extraditable offence if it is punishable under the laws of the requesting and requested States by deprivation of liberty for a maximum period of more than one year or by a more severe penalty. An offence shall also be an extraditable offence if it consists of an attempt or conspiracy to commit, or participation in the commission of, an extraditable offence. Where the request is for enforcement of the sentence of a person convicted of an extraditable offence, the deprivation of liberty remaining to be served must be at least four months.

2. If extradition is granted for an extraditable offence, it shall also be granted for any other offence specified in the request if the latter offence is punishable by one year's deprivation of liberty or less, provided that all other requirements for extradition are met.

3. For the purposes of this Article, an offence shall be considered an extraditable offence:

(a) regardless of whether the laws in the requesting and requested States place the offence within the same category of offences or describe the offence by the same terminology;

(b) regardless of whether the offence is one for which United States federal law requires the showing of such matters as interstate transportation, or use of the mails or of other facilities affecting interstate or foreign commerce, such matters being merely for the purpose of establishing jurisdiction in a United States federal court; and

(c) in criminal cases relating to taxes, customs duties, currency control and the import or export of commodities, regardless of whether the laws of the requesting and requested States provide for the same kinds of taxes, customs duties, or controls on currency or on the import or export of the same kinds of commodities.

4. If the offence has been committed outside the territory of the requesting State, extradition shall be granted, subject to the other applicable requirements for extradition, if the laws of the requested State provide for the punishment of an offence committed outside its territory in similar circumstances. If the laws of the requested State do not provide for the punishment of an offence committed outside its territory in similar circumstances, the executive authority of the requested State, at its discretion, may grant extradition provided that all other applicable requirements for extradition are met.

*Article 5*

**Transmission and authentication of documents**

1. Requests for extradition and supporting documents shall be transmitted through the diplomatic channel, which shall include transmission as provided for in Article 7.

2. Documents that bear the certificate or seal of the Ministry of Justice, or Ministry or Department responsible for foreign affairs, of the requesting State shall be admissible in extradition proceedings in the requested State without further certification, authentication, or other legalisation.

*Article 6*

**Transmission of requests for provisional arrest**

Requests for provisional arrest may be made directly between the Ministries of Justice of the requesting and requested States, as an alternative to the diplomatic channel. The facilities of the International Criminal Police Organisation (Interpol) may also be used to transmit such a request.

*Article 7*

**Transmission of documents following provisional arrest**

1. If the person whose extradition is sought is held under provisional arrest by the requested State, the requesting State may satisfy its obligation to transmit its request for extradition and supporting documents through the diplomatic channel pursuant to Article 5(1), by submitting the request and documents to the Embassy of the requested State located in the requesting State. In that case, the date of receipt of such request by the Embassy shall be considered to be the date of receipt by the requested State for purposes of applying the time limit that must be met under the applicable extradition treaty to enable the person's continued detention.

2. Where a Member State on the date of signature of this Agreement, due to the established jurisprudence of its domestic legal system applicable at such date, cannot apply the measures referred to in paragraph 1, this Article shall not apply to it, until such time as that Member State and the United States of America, by exchange of diplomatic note, agree otherwise.

*Article 8*

**Supplemental information**

1. The requested State may require the requesting State to furnish additional information within such reasonable length of time as it specifies, if it considers that the information furnished in support of the request for extradition is not sufficient to fulfil the requirements of the applicable extradition treaty.

2. Such supplementary information may be requested and furnished directly between the Ministries of Justice of the States concerned.

*Article 9*

**Temporary surrender**

1. If a request for extradition is granted in the case of a person who is being proceeded against or is serving a sentence in the requested State, the requested State may temporarily surrender the person sought to the requesting State for the purpose of prosecution.

2. The person so surrendered shall be kept in custody in the requesting State and shall be returned to the requested State at the conclusion of the proceedings against that person, in accordance with the conditions to be determined by mutual agreement of the requesting and requested States. The time spent in custody in the territory of the requesting State pending prosecution in that State may be deducted from the time remaining to be served in the requested State.

*Article 10*

**Requests for extradition or surrender made by several States**

1. If the requested State receives requests from the requesting State and from any other State or States for the extradition of the same person, either for the same offence or for different offences, the executive authority of the requested State shall determine to which State, if any, it will surrender the person.

2. If a requested Member State receives an extradition request from the United States of America and a request for surrender pursuant to the European arrest warrant for the same person, either for the same offence or for different offences, the competent authority of the requested Member State shall determine to which State, if any, it will surrender the person. For this purpose, the competent authority shall be the requested Member State's executive authority if, under the bilateral extradition treaty in force between the United States and the Member State, decisions on competing requests are made by that authority; if not so provided in the bilateral extradition treaty, the competent authority shall be designated by the Member State concerned pursuant to Article 19.

3. In making its decision under paragraphs 1 and 2, the requested State shall consider all of the relevant factors, including, but not limited to, factors already set forth in the applicable extradition treaty, and, where not already so set forth, the following:

(a) whether the requests were made pursuant to a treaty;

(b) the places where each of the offences was committed;

(c) the respective interests of the requesting States;

(d) the seriousness of the offences;

(e) the nationality of the victim;

(f) the possibility of any subsequent extradition between the requesting States; and

(g) the chronological order in which the requests were received from the requesting States.

*Article 11*

**Simplified extradition procedures**

If the person sought consents to be surrendered to the requesting State, the requested State may, in accordance with the principles and procedures provided for under its legal system, surrender the person as expeditiously as possible without further proceedings. The consent of the person sought may include agreement to waiver of protection of the rule of specialty.

*Article 12*

**Transit**

1. A Member State may authorise transportation through its territory of a person surrendered to the United States of America by a third State, or by the United States of America to a third State. The United States of America may authorise transportation through its territory of a person surrendered to a Member State by a third State, or by a Member State to a third State.

2. A request for transit shall be made through the diplomatic channel or directly between the United States Department of Justice and the Ministry of Justice of the Member State concerned. The facilities of Interpol may also be used to transmit such a request. The request shall contain a description of the person being transported and a brief statement of the facts of the case. A person in transit shall be detained in custody during the period of transit.

3. Authorisation is not required when air transportation is used and no landing is scheduled on the territory of the transit State. If an unscheduled landing does occur, the State in which the unscheduled landing occurs may require a request for transit pursuant to paragraph 2. All measures necessary to prevent the person from absconding shall be taken until transit is effected, as long as the request for transit is received within 96 hours of the unscheduled landing.

*Article 13*

**Capital punishment**

Where the offence for which extradition is sought is punishable by death under the laws in the requesting State and not punishable by death under the laws in the requested State, the requested State may grant extradition on the condition that the death penalty shall not be imposed on the person sought, or if for procedural reasons such condition cannot be complied with by the requesting State, on condition that the death penalty if imposed shall not be carried out. If the requesting State accepts extradition subject to conditions pursuant to this Article, it shall comply with the conditions. If the requesting State does not accept the conditions, the request for extradition may be denied.

19.7.2003 EN Official Journal of the European Union L 181/31

*Article 14*

**Sensitive information in a request**

Where the requesting State contemplates the submission of particularly sensitive information in support of its request for extradition, it may consult the requested State to determine the extent to which the information can be protected by the requested State. If the requested State cannot protect the information in the manner sought by the requesting State, the requesting State shall determine whether the information shall nonetheless be submitted.

*Article 15*

**Consultations**

The Contracting Parties shall, as appropriate, consult to enable the most effective use to be made of this Agreement, including to facilitate the resolution of any dispute regarding the interpretation or application of this Agreement.

*Article 16*

**Temporal application**

1. This Agreement shall apply to offences committed before as well as after it enters into force.

2. This Agreement shall apply to requests for extradition made after its entry into force. Nevertheless, Articles 4 and 9 shall apply to requests pending in a requested State at the time this Agreement enters into force.

*Article 17*

**Non-derogation**

1. This Agreement is without prejudice to the invocation by the requested State of grounds for refusal relating to a matter not governed by this Agreement that is available pursuant to a bilateral extradition treaty in force between a Member State and the United States of America.

2. Where the constitutional principles of, or final judicial decisions binding upon, the requested State may pose an impediment to fulfilment of its obligation to extradite, and resolution of the matter is not provided for in this Agreement or the applicable bilateral treaty, consultations shall take place between the requested and requesting States.

*Article 18*

**Future bilateral extradition treaties with Member States**

This Agreement shall not preclude the conclusion, after its entry into force, of bilateral Agreements between a Member State and the United States of America consistent with this Agreement.

*Article 19*

**Designation and notification**

The European Union shall notify the United States of America of any designation pursuant to Article 2(3) and Article 10(2), prior to the exchange of written instruments described in Article 3(2) between the Member States and the United States of America.

*Article 20*

**Territorial application**

1. This Agreement shall apply:

(a) to the United States of America;

(b) in relation to the European Union to:

- Member States,
- territories for whose external relations a Member State has responsibility, or countries that are not Member States for whom a Member State has other duties with respect to external relations, where agreed upon by exchange of diplomatic note between the Contracting Parties, duly confirmed by the relevant Member State.

2. The application of this Agreement to any territory or country in respect of which extension has been made in accordance with subparagraph (b) of paragraph 1 may be terminated by either Contracting Party giving six months' written notice to the other Contracting Party through the diplomatic channel, where duly confirmed between the relevant Member State and the United States of America.

*Article 21*

**Review**

The Contracting Parties agree to carry out a common review of this Agreement as necessary, and in any event no later than five years after its entry into force. The review shall address in particular the practical implementation of the Agreement and may also include issues such as the consequences of further development of the European Union relating to the subject matter of this Agreement, including Article 10.

*Article 22*

**Entry into force and termination**

1. This Agreement shall enter into force on the first day following the third month after the date on which the Contracting Parties have exchanged instruments indicating that they have completed their internal procedures for this purpose. These instruments shall also indicate that the steps specified in Article 3(2) have been completed.

2. Either Contracting Party may terminate this Agreement at any time by giving written notice to the other Party, and such termination shall be effective six months after the date of such notice.

19.7.2003 EN Official Journal of the European Union L 181/33

**Explanatory Note on the Agreement on Extradition between the European Union and the United States of America**

This Explanatory Note reflects understandings regarding the application of certain provisions of the Agreement on Extradition between the European Union and the United States of America (hereinafter 'the Agreement') agreed between the Contracting Parties.

*On Article 10*

Article 10 is not intended to affect the obligations of States Parties to the Rome Statute of the International Criminal Court, nor to affect the rights of the United States of America as a non-Party with regard to the International Criminal Court.

*On Article 18*

Article 18 provides that the Agreement shall not preclude the conclusion, after its entry into force, of bilateral agreements on extradition between a Member State and the United States of America consistent with the Agreement.

Should any measures set forth in the Agreement create an operational difficulty for either one or more Member States or the United States of America, such difficulty should in the first place be resolved, if possible, through consultations between the Member State or Member States concerned and the United States of America, or, if appropriate, through the consultation procedures set out in this Agreement. Where it is not possible to address such operational difficulty through consultations alone, it would be consistent with the Agreement for future bilateral agreements between the Member State or Member States and the United States of America to provide an operationally feasible alternative mechanism that would satisfy the objectives of the specific provision with respect to which the difficulty has arisen.

# Agreement on mutual legal assistance between the European Union and the United States of America, 25 June 2003

**[OJ 2003, L 181/34–39, 41, 42]**

**[Editor's note: signatures omitted]**

L 181/34 EN Official Journal of the European Union 19.7.2003

## AGREEMENT

### on mutual legal assistance between the European Union and the United States of America

THE EUROPEAN UNION AND THE UNITED STATES OF AMERICA,

DESIRING further to facilitate cooperation between the European Union Member States and the United States of America,

DESIRING to combat crime in a more effective way as a means of protecting their respective democratic societies and common values,

HAVING DUE REGARD for rights of individuals and the rule of law,

MINDFUL of the guarantees under their respective legal systems which provide an accused person with the right to a fair trial, including the right to adjudication by an impartial tribunal established pursuant to law,

DESIRING to conclude an Agreement relating to mutual legal assistance in criminal matters,

HAVE AGREED AS FOLLOWS:

*Article 1*

**Object and purpose**

The Contracting Parties undertake, in accordance with the provisions of this Agreement, to provide for enhancements to cooperation and mutual legal assistance.

*Article 2*

**Definitions**

1. 'Contracting Parties' shall mean the European Union and the United States of America.

2. 'Member State' shall mean a Member State of the European Union.

*Article 3*

**Scope of application of this Agreement in relation to bilateral mutual legal assistance treaties with Member States and in the absence thereof**

1. The European Union, pursuant to the Treaty on European Union, and the United States of America shall ensure that the provisions of this Agreement are applied in relation to bilateral mutual legal assistance treaties between the Member States and the United States of America, in force at the time of the entry into force of this Agreement, under the following terms:

(a) Article 4 shall be applied to provide for identification of financial accounts and transactions in addition to any authority already provided under bilateral treaty provisions;

(b) Article 5 shall be applied to authorise the formation and activities of joint investigative teams in addition to any authority already provided under bilateral treaty provisions;

(c) Article 6 shall be applied to authorise the taking of testimony of a person located in the requested State by use of video transmission technology between the requesting and requested States in addition to any authority already provided under bilateral treaty provisions;

(d) Article 7 shall be applied to provide for the use of expedited means of communication in addition to any authority already provided under bilateral treaty provisions;

(e) Article 8 shall be applied to authorise the providing of mutual legal assistance to the administrative authorities concerned, in addition to any authority already provided under bilateral treaty provisions;

(f) subject to Article 9(4) and (5), Article 9 shall be applied in place of, or in the absence of bilateral treaty provisions governing limitations on use of information or evidence provided to the requesting State, and governing the conditioning or refusal of assistance on data protection grounds;

(g) Article 10 shall be applied in the absence of bilateral treaty provisions pertaining to the circumstances under which a requesting State may seek the confidentiality of its request.

2. (a) The European Union, pursuant to the Treaty on European Union, shall ensure that each Member State acknowledges, in a written instrument between such Member State and the United States of America, the application, in the manner set forth in this Article, of its bilateral mutual legal assistance treaty in force with the United States of America.

(b) The European Union, pursuant to the Treaty on European Union, shall ensure that new Member States acceding to the European Union after the entry into force of this Agreement, and having bilateral mutual legal assistance treaties with the United States of America, take the measures referred to in subparagraph (a).

(c) The Contracting Parties shall endeavour to complete the process described in subparagraph (b) prior to the scheduled accession of a new Member State, or as soon as possible thereafter. The European Union shall notify the United States of America of the date of accession of new Member States.

3. (a) The European Union, pursuant to the Treaty on European Union, and the United States of America shall also ensure that the provisions of this Agreement are applied in the absence of a bilateral mutual legal assistance treaty in force between a Member State and the United States of America.

(b) The European Union, pursuant to the Treaty on European Union, shall ensure that such Member State acknowledges, in a written instrument between such Member State and the United States of America, the application of the provisions of this Agreement.

(c) The European Union, pursuant to the Treaty on European Union, shall ensure that new Member States acceding to the European Union after the entry into force of this Agreement, which do not have bilateral mutual legal assistance treaties with the United States of America, take the measures referred to in subparagraph (b).

L 181/36 EN Official Journal of the European Union 19.7.2003

4. If the process described in paragraph 2(b) and 3(c) is not completed by the date of accession, the provisions of this Agreement shall apply in the relations between the United States of America and that new Member State as from the date on which they have notified each other and the European Union of the completion of their internal procedures for that purpose.

5. The Contracting Parties agree that this Agreement is intended solely for mutual legal assistance between the States concerned. The provisions of this Agreement shall not give rise to a right on the part of any private person to obtain, suppress, or exclude any evidence, or to impede the execution of a request, nor expand or limit rights otherwise available under domestic law.

*Article 4*

**Identification of bank information**

1. (a) Upon request of the requesting State, the requested State shall, in accordance with the terms of this Article, promptly ascertain if the banks located in its territory possess information on whether an identified natural or legal person suspected of or charged with a criminal offence is the holder of a bank account or accounts. The requested State shall promptly communicate the results of its enquiries to the requesting State.

(b) The actions described in subparagraph (a) may also be taken for the purpose of identifying:

(i) information regarding natural or legal persons convicted of or otherwise involved in a criminal offence;

(ii) information in the possession of non-bank financial institutions; or

(iii) financial transactions unrelated to accounts.

2. A request for information described in paragraph 1 shall include:

(a) the identity of the natural or legal person relevant to locating such accounts or transactions; and

(b) sufficient information to enable the competent authority of the requested State to:

(i) reasonably suspect that the natural or legal person concerned has engaged in a criminal offence and that banks or non-bank financial institutions in the territory of the requested State may have the information requested; and

(ii) conclude that the information sought relates to the criminal investigation or proceeding;

(c) to the extent possible, information concerning which bank or non-bank financial institution may be involved, and other information the availability of which may aid in reducing the breadth of the enquiry.

3. Requests for assistance under this Article shall be transmitted between:

(a) central authorities responsible for mutual legal assistance in Member States, or national authorities of Member States responsible for investigation or prosecution of criminal offences as designated pursuant to Article 15(2); and

(b) national authorities of the United States responsible for investigation or prosecution of criminal offences, as designated pursuant to Article 15(2).

The Contracting Parties may, following the entry into force of this Agreement, agree by Exchange of Diplomatic Note to modify the channels through which requests under this Article are made.

4. (a) Subject to subparagraph (b), a State may, pursuant to Article 15, limit its obligation to provide assistance under this Article to:

(i) offences punishable under the laws of both the requested and requesting States;

(ii) offences punishable by a penalty involving deprivation of liberty or a detention order of a maximum period of at least four years in the requesting State and at least two years in the requested State; or

(iii) designated serious offences punishable under the laws of both the requested and requesting States.

(b) A State which limits its obligation pursuant to subparagraph (a)(ii) or (iii) shall, at a minimum, enable identification of accounts associated with terrorist activity and the laundering of proceeds generated from a comprehensive range of serious criminal activities, punishable under the laws of both the requesting and requested States.

5. Assistance may not be refused under this Article on grounds of bank secrecy.

6. The requested State shall respond to a request for production of the records concerning the accounts or transactions identified pursuant to this Article, in accordance with the provisions of the applicable mutual legal assistance treaty in force between the States concerned, or in the absence thereof, in accordance with the requirements of its domestic law.

7. The Contracting Parties shall take measures to avoid the imposition of extraordinary burdens on requested States through application of this Article. Where extraordinary burdens on a requested State nonetheless result, including on banks or by operation of the channels of communications foreseen in this Article, the Contracting Parties shall immediately consult with a view to facilitating the application of this Article, including the taking of such measures as may be required to reduce pending and future burdens.

*Article 5*

**Joint investigative teams**

1. The Contracting Parties shall, to the extent they have not already done so, take such measures as may be necessary to enable joint investigative teams to be established and operated in the respective territories of each Member State and the United States of America for the purpose of facilitating criminal investigations or prosecutions involving one or more Member States and the United States of America where deemed appropriate by the Member State concerned and the United States of America.

2. The procedures under which the team is to operate, such as its composition, duration, location, organisation, functions, purpose, and terms of participation of team members of a State in investigative activities taking place in another State's territory shall be as agreed between the competent authorities responsible for the investigation or prosecution of criminal offences, as determined by the respective States concerned.

3. The competent authorities determined by the respective States concerned shall communicate directly for the purposes of the establishment and operation of such team except that where the exceptional complexity, broad scope, or other circumstances involved are deemed to require more central coordination as to some or all aspects, the States may agree upon other appropriate channels of communications to that end.

4. Where the joint investigative team needs investigative measures to be taken in one of the States setting up the team, a member of the team of that State may request its own competent authorities to take those measures without the other States having to submit a request for mutual legal assistance. The required legal standard for obtaining the measure in that State shall be the standard applicable to its domestic investigative activities.

*Article 6*

**Video conferencing**

1. The Contracting Parties shall take such measures as may be necessary to enable the use of video transmission technology between each Member State and the United States of America for taking testimony in a proceeding for which mutual legal assistance is available of a witness or expert located in a requested State, to the extent such assistance is not currently available. To the extent not specifically set forth in this Article, the modalities governing such procedure shall be as provided under the applicable mutual legal assistance treaty in force between the States concerned, or the law of the requested State, as applicable.

2. Unless otherwise agreed by the requesting and requested States, the requesting State shall bear the costs associated with establishing and servicing the video transmission. Other costs arising in the course of providing assistance (including costs associated with travel of participants in the requested State) shall be borne in accordance with the applicable provisions of the mutual legal assistance treaty in force between the States concerned, or where there is no such treaty, as agreed upon by the requesting and requested States.

3. The requesting and requested States may consult in order to facilitate resolution of legal, technical or logistical issues that may arise in the execution of the request.

4. Without prejudice to any jurisdiction under the law of the requesting State, making an intentionally false statement or other misconduct of the witness or expert during the course of the video conference shall be punishable in the requested State in the same manner as if it had been committed in the course of its domestic proceedings.

5. This Article is without prejudice to the use of other means for obtaining of testimony in the requested State available under applicable treaty or law.

6. This Article is without prejudice to application of provisions of bilateral mutual legal assistance agreements between Member States and the United States of America that require or permit the use of video conferencing technology for purposes other than those described in paragraph 1, including for purposes of identification of persons or objects, or taking of investigative statements. Where not already provided for under applicable treaty or law, a State may permit the use of video conferencing technology in such instances.

*Article 7*

**Expedited transmission of requests**

Requests for mutual legal assistance, and communications related thereto, may be made by expedited means of communications, including fax or e-mail, with formal confirmation to follow where required by the requested State. The requested State may respond to the request by any such expedited means of communication.

*Article 8*

**Mutual legal assistance to administrative authorities**

1. Mutual legal assistance shall also be afforded to a national administrative authority, investigating conduct with a view to a criminal prosecution of the conduct, or referral of the conduct to criminal investigation or prosecution authorities, pursuant to its specific administrative or regulatory authority to undertake such investigation. Mutual legal assistance may also be afforded to other administrative authorities under such circumstances. Assistance shall not be available for matters in which the administrative authority anticipates that no prosecution or referral, as applicable, will take place.

2. (a) Requests for assistance under this Article shall be transmitted between the central authorities designated pursuant to the bilateral mutual legal assistance treaty in force between the States concerned, or between such other authorities as may be agreed by the central authorities.

   (b) In the absence of a treaty, requests shall be transmitted between the United States Department of Justice and the Ministry of Justice or, pursuant to Article 15(1), comparable Ministry of the Member State concerned responsible for transmission of mutual legal assistance requests, or between such other authorities as may be agreed by the Department of Justice and such Ministry.

3. The Contracting Parties shall take measures to avoid the imposition of extraordinary burdens on requested States through application of this Article. Where extraordinary burdens on a requested State nonetheless result, the Contracting Parties shall immediately consult with a view to facilitating the application of this Article, including the taking of such measures as may be required to reduce pending and future burdens.

*Article 9*

**Limitations on use to protect personal and other data**

1. The requesting State may use any evidence or information obtained from the requested State:

(a) for the purpose of its criminal investigations and proceedings;

(b) for preventing an immediate and serious threat to its public security;

(c) in its non-criminal judicial or administrative proceedings directly related to investigations or proceedings:

   (i) set forth in subparagraph (a); or

   (ii) for which mutual legal assistance was rendered under Article 8;

(d) for any other purpose, if the information or evidence has been made public within the framework of proceedings for which they were transmitted, or in any of the situations described in subparagraphs (a), (b) and (c); and

(e) for any other purpose, only with the prior consent of the requested State.

2. (a) This Article shall not prejudice the ability of the requested State to impose additional conditions in a particular case where the particular request for assistance could not be complied with in the absence of such conditions. Where additional conditions have been imposed in accordance with this subparagraph, the requested State may require the requesting State to give information on the use made of the evidence or information.

   (b) Generic restrictions with respect to the legal standards of the requesting State for processing personal data may not be imposed by the requested State as a condition under subparagraph (a) to providing evidence or information.

3. Where, following disclosure to the requesting State, the requested State becomes aware of circumstances that may cause it to seek an additional condition in a particular case, the requested State may consult with the requesting State to determine the extent to which the evidence and information can be protected.

4. A requested State may apply the use limitation provision of the applicable bilateral mutual legal assistance treaty in lieu of this Article, where doing so will result in less restriction on the use of information and evidence than provided for in this Article.

5. Where a bilateral mutual legal assistance treaty in force between a Member State and the United States of America on the date of signature of this Agreement, permits limitation of the obligation to provide assistance with respect to certain tax offences, the Member State concerned may indicate, in its exchange of written instruments with the United States of America described in Article 3(2), that, with respect to such offences, it will continue to apply the use limitation provision of that treaty.

*Article 10*

**Requesting State's request for confidentiality**

The requested State shall use its best efforts to keep confidential a request and its contents if such confidentiality is requested by the requesting State. If the request cannot be executed without breaching the requested confidentiality, the central authority of the requested State shall so inform the requesting State, which shall then determine whether the request should nevertheless be executed.

*Article 11*

**Consultations**

The Contracting Parties shall, as appropriate, consult to enable the most effective use to be made of this Agreement, including to facilitate the resolution of any dispute regarding the interpretation or application of this Agreement.

*Article 12*

**Temporal application**

1. This Agreement shall apply to offences committed before as well as after it enters into force.

2. This Agreement shall apply to requests for mutual legal assistance made after its entry into force. Nevertheless, Articles 6 and 7 shall apply to requests pending in a requested State at the time this Agreement enters into force.

*Article 13*

**Non-derogation**

Subject to Article 4(5) and Article 9(2)(b), this Agreement is without prejudice to the invocation by the requested State of grounds for refusal of assistance available pursuant to a bilateral mutual legal assistance treaty, or, in the absence of a treaty, its applicable legal principles, including where execution of the request would prejudice its sovereignty, security, ordre public or other essential interests.

*Article 14*

**Future bilateral mutual legal assistance treaties with Member States**

This Agreement shall not preclude the conclusion, after its entry into force, of bilateral Agreements between a Member State and the United States of America consistent with this Agreement.

*Article 15*

**Designations and notifications**

1. Where a Ministry other than the Ministry of Justice has been designated under Article 8(2)(b), the European Union shall notify the United States of America of such designation prior to the exchange of written instruments described in Article 3(3) between the Member States and the United States of America.

2. The Contracting Parties, on the basis of consultations between them on which national authorities responsible for the investigation and prosecution of offences to designate pursuant to Article 4(3), shall notify each other of the national authorities so designated prior to the exchange of written instruments described in Article 3(2) and (3) between the Member States and the United States of America. The European Union shall, for Member States having no mutual legal assistance treaty with the United States of America, notify the United States of America prior to such exchange of the identity of the central authorities under Article 4(3).

3. The Contracting Parties shall notify each other of any limitations invoked under Article 4(4) prior to the exchange of written instruments described in Article 3(2) and (3) between the Member States and the United States of America.

*Article 16*

**Territorial application**

1. This Agreement shall apply:

(a) to the United States of America;

(b) in relation to the European Union, to:

— Member States,

— territories for whose external relations a Member State has responsibility, or countries that are not Member States for whom a Member State has other duties with respect to external relations, where agreed upon by exchange of diplomatic note between the Contracting Parties, duly confirmed by the relevant Member State.

2. The application of this Agreement to any territory or country in respect of which extension has been made in accordance with subparagraph (b) of paragraph 1 may be terminated by either Contracting Party giving six months' written notice to the other Contracting Party through the diplomatic channel, where duly confirmed between the relevant Member State and the United States of America.

*Article 17*

**Review**

The Contracting Parties agree to carry out a common review of this Agreement no later than five years after its entry into force. The review shall address in particular the practical implementation of the Agreement and may also include issues such as the consequences of further development of the European Union relating to the subject matter of this Agreement.

*Article 18*

**Entry into force and termination**

1. This Agreement shall enter into force on the first day following the third month after the date on which the Contracting Parties have exchanged instruments indicating that they have completed their internal procedures for this purpose. These instruments shall also indicate that the steps specified in Article 3(2) and (3) have been completed.

2. Either Contracting Party may terminate this Agreement at any time by giving written notice to the other Party, and such termination shall be effective six months after the date of such notice.

**Explanatory Note on the Agreement on Mutual Legal Assistance between the European Union and the United States of America**

This note reflects understandings regarding the application of certain provisions of the Agreement on Mutual Legal Assistance between the European Union and the United States of America (hereinafter 'the Agreement') agreed between the Contracting Parties.

*On Article 8*

With respect to the mutual legal assistance to administrative authorities under Article 8(1), the first sentence of Article 8(1) imposes an obligation to afford mutual legal assistance to requesting United States of America federal administrative authorities and to requesting national administrative authorities of Member States. Under the second sentence of that paragraph mutual legal assistance may also be made available to other, that is non-federal or local, administrative authorities. This provision however, is available at the discretion of the requested State.

The Contracting Parties agree that under the first sentence of Article 8(1) mutual legal assistance will be made available to a requesting administrative authority that is, at the time of making the request, conducting investigations or proceedings in contemplation of criminal prosecution or referral of the investigated conduct to the competent prosecuting authorities, within the terms of its statutory mandate, as further described immediately below. The fact that, at the time of making the request referral for criminal prosecution is being contemplated does not exclude that, other sanctions than criminal ones may be pursued by that authority. Thus, mutual legal assistance obtained under Article 8(1) may lead the requesting administrative authority to the conclusion that pursuance of criminal proceedings or criminal referral would not be appropriate. These possible consequences do not affect the obligation upon the Contracting Parties to provide assistance under this Article.

However, the requesting administrative authority may not use Article 8(1) to request assistance where criminal prosecution or referral is not being contemplated, or for matters in which the conduct under investigation is not subject to criminal sanction or referral under the laws of the requesting State.

The European Union recalls that the subject matter of the Agreement for its part falls under the provisions on police and judicial cooperation in criminal matters set out in Title VI of the Treaty on European Union and that the Agreement has been concluded within the scope of these provisions.

*On Article 9*

Article 9(2)(b) is meant to ensure that refusal of assistance on data protection grounds may be invoked only in exceptional cases. Such a situation could arise if, upon balancing the important interests involved in the particular case (on the one hand, public interests, including the sound administration of justice and, on the other hand, privacy interests), furnishing the specific data sought by the requesting State would raise difficulties so fundamental as to be considered by the requested State to fall within the essential interests grounds for refusal. A broad, categorical, or systematic application of data protection principles by the requested State to refuse cooperation is therefore precluded. Thus, the fact the requesting and requested States have different systems of protecting the privacy of data (such as that the requesting State does not have the equivalent of a specialised data protection authority) or have different means of protecting personal data (such as that the requesting State uses means other than the process of deletion to protect the privacy or the accuracy of the personal data received by law enforcement authorities), may as such not be imposed as additional conditions under Article 9(2a).

*On Article 14*

Article 14 provides that the Agreement shall not preclude the conclusion, after its entry into force, of bilateral agreements on mutual legal assistance between a Member State and the United States of America consistent with the Agreement.

Should any measures set forth in the Agreement create an operational difficulty for the United States of America and one or more Member States, such difficulty should in the first place be resolved, if possible, through consultations between the Member State or Member States concerned and the United States of America, or, if appropriate, through the consultation procedures set out in the Agreement. Where it is not possible to address such operational difficulty through consultations alone, it would be consistent with the Agreement for future bilateral agreements between a Member State and the United States of America to provide an operationally feasible alternative mechanism that would satisfy the objectives of the specific provision with respect to which the difficulty has arisen.

# Framework Decision 2003/568 on combating corruption in the private sector, 22 July 2003

[OJ 2003, L 192/54–56]

L 192/54 EN Official Journal of the European Union 31.7.2003

*(Acts adopted pursuant to Title VI of the Treaty on European Union)*

**COUNCIL FRAMEWORK DECISION 2003/568/JHA**

**of 22 July 2003**

**on combating corruption in the private sector**

THE COUNCIL OF THE EUROPEAN UNION,

Having regard to the Treaty on European Union, and in particular Article 29, Article 31(1)(e) and Article 34(2)(b) thereof,

Having regard to the initiative of the Kingdom of Denmark ([1]),

Having regard to the opinion of the European Parliament ([2]),

Whereas:

(1) Along with globalisation, recent years have brought an increase in cross-border trade in goods and services. Any corruption in the private sector within a Member State is thus not just a domestic problem but also a transnational problem, most effectively tackled by means of a European Union joint action.

(2) On 27 September 1996 the Council adopted the Act drawing up a Protocol to the Convention on the Protection of the European Communities' Financial Interests ([3]). The Protocol, which entered into force on 17 October 2002, contains definitions of and harmonised penalties for offences of corruption.

(3) On 26 May 1997 the Council approved a Convention on the fight against corruption involving officials of the European Communities or officials of Member States of the European Union ([4]).

(4) On 22 December 1998, the Council also adopted Joint Action 98/742/JHA on corruption in the private sector ([5]). In connection with the adoption of that Joint Action, the Council issued a statement to the effect that it agreed that the Joint Action represents the first step at European Union level towards combating such corruption, and that additional measures will be implemented at a later stage in the light of the outcome of the assessment which is to take place pursuant to Article 8(2) of the Joint Action. A report on Member States' transposition of that Joint Action into national law is not yet available.

(5) On 13 June 2002 the Council adopted Framework Decision 2002/584/JHA on the European arrest warrant and the surrender procedures between the Member States ([6]), in which corruption is included in the list of offences falling within the scope of the European arrest warrant, in respect of which prior verification of double criminality is not required.

(6) Under Article 29 of the Treaty on European Union, it is the Union's objective to provide citizens with a high level of safety within an area of freedom, security and justice, an objective to be achieved by preventing and combating crime, organised or otherwise, including corruption.

(7) According to point 48 of the conclusions of the European Council meeting in Tampere on 15 and 16 October 1999, corruption is an area of particular relevance in establishing minimum rules on what constitutes a criminal offence in Member States and the penalties applicable.

(8) An OECD Convention on Combating Bribery of Foreign Public Officials in International Business Transactions was approved at a negotiating conference on 21 November 1997, and the Council of Europe has also approved a Criminal Law Convention on Corruption, which opened for signature on 27 January 1999. That Convention is accompanied by an Agreement establishing the Group of States against Corruption (GRECO). Negotiations have also been opened for a UN Convention on combating corruption.

(9) Member States attach particular importance to combating corruption in both the public and the private sector, in the belief that in both those sectors it poses a threat to a law-abiding society as well as distorting competition in relation to the purchase of goods or commercial services and impeding sound economic development. In that context the Member States which have not yet ratified the European Union Convention of 26 May 1997 and the Council of Europe Convention of 27 January 1999 will consider how to do so as soon as possible.

([1]) OJ C 184, 2.8.2002, p. 5.
([2]) Opinion of 22 November 2002 (not yet published in the Official Journal).
([3]) OJ C 313, 23.10.1996, p. 1.
([4]) OJ C 195, 25.6.1997, p. 2.
([5]) OJ L 358, 31.12.1998, p. 2.
([6]) OJ L 190, 18.7.2002, p. 1.

31.7.2003 EN Official Journal of the European Union L 192/55

(10) The aim of this Framework Decision is in particular to ensure that both active and passive corruption in the private sector are criminal offences in all Member States, that legal persons may also be held responsible for such offences, and that these offences incur effective, proportionate and dissuasive penalties,

HAS ADOPTED THIS FRAMEWORK DECISION:

*Article 1*

**Definitions**

For the purposes of this Framework Decision:

— 'legal person' means any entity having such status under the applicable national law, except for States or other public bodies acting in the exercise of State authority and for public international organisations,

— 'breach of duty' shall be understood in accordance with national law. The concept of breach of duty in national law should cover as a minimum any disloyal behaviour constituting a breach of a statutory duty, or, as the case may be, a breach of professional regulations or instructions, which apply within the business of a person who in any capacity directs or works for a private sector entity.

*Article 2*

**Active and passive corruption in the private sector**

1. Member States shall take the necessary measures to ensure that the following intentional conduct constitutes a criminal offence, when it is carried out in the course of business activities:

(a) promising, offering or giving, directly or through an intermediary, to a person who in any capacity directs or works for a private-sector entity an undue advantage of any kind, for that person or for a third party, in order that that person should perform or refrain from performing any act, in breach of that person's duties;

(b) directly or through an intermediary, requesting or receiving an undue advantage of any kind, or accepting the promise of such an advantage, for oneself or for a third party, while in any capacity directing or working for a private-sector entity, in order to perform or refrain from performing any act, in breach of one's duties.

2. Paragraph 1 applies to business activities within profit and non-profit entities.

3. A Member State may declare that it will limit the scope of paragraph 1 to such conduct which involves, or could involve, a distortion of competition in relation to the purchase of goods or commercial services.

4. Declarations referred to in paragraph 3 shall be communicated to the Council at the time of the adoption of this Framework Decision and shall be valid for five years as from 22 July 2005.

5. The Council shall review this Article in due time before 22 July 2010 with a view to considering whether it shall be possible to renew declarations made under paragraph 3.

*Article 3*

**Instigation, aiding and abetting**

Member States shall take the necessary measures to ensure that instigating, aiding and abetting the conduct referred to in Article 2 constitute criminal offences.

*Article 4*

**Penalties and other sanctions**

1. Each Member State shall take the necessary measures to ensure that the conduct referred to in Articles 2 and 3 is punishable by effective, proportionate and dissuasive criminal penalties.

2. Each Member State shall take the necessary measures to ensure that the conduct referred to in Article 2 is punishable by a penalty of a maximum of at least one to three years of imprisonment.

3. Each Member State shall take the necessary measures in accordance with its constitutional rules and principles to ensure that where a natural person in relation to a certain business activity has been convicted of the conduct referred to in Article 2, that person may, where appropriate, at least in cases where he or she had a leading position in a company within the business concerned, be temporarily prohibited from carrying on this particular or comparable business activity in a similar position or capacity, if the facts established give reason to believe there to be a clear risk of abuse of position or of office by active or passive corruption.

*Article 5*

**Liability of legal persons**

1. Each Member State shall take the necessary measures to ensure that legal persons can be held liable for offences referred to in Articles 2 and 3 committed for their benefit by any person, acting either individually or as part of an organ of the legal person, who has a leading position within the legal person, based on:

(a) a power of representation of the legal person;

(b) an authority to take decisions on behalf of the legal person; or

(c) an authority to exercise control within the legal person.

L 192/56 EN Official Journal of the European Union 31.7.2003

2. Apart from the cases provided for in paragraph 1, each Member State shall take the necessary measures to ensure that a legal person can be held liable where the lack of supervision or control by a person referred to in paragraph 1 has made possible the commission of an offence of the type referred to in Articles 2 and 3 for the benefit of that legal person by a person under its authority.

3. Liability of a legal person under paragraphs 1 and 2 shall not exclude criminal proceedings against natural persons who are involved as perpetrators, instigators or accessories in an offence of the type referred to in Articles 2 and 3.

*Article 6*

**Penalties for legal persons**

1. Each Member State shall take the necessary measures to ensure that a legal person held liable pursuant to Article 5(1) is punishable by effective, proportionate and dissuasive penalties, which shall include criminal or non-criminal fines and may include other penalties such as:

(a) exclusion from entitlement to public benefits or aid;

(b) temporary or permanent disqualification from the practice of commercial activities;

(c) placing under judicial supervision; or

(d) a judicial winding-up order.

2. Each Member State shall take the necessary measures to ensure that a legal person held liable pursuant to Article 5(2) is punishable by penalties or measures which are effective, proportionate and dissuasive.

*Article 7*

**Jurisdiction**

1. Each Member State shall take the necessary measures to establish its jurisdiction with regard to the offences referred to in Articles 2 and 3, where the offence has been committed:

(a) in whole or in part within its territory;

(b) by one of its nationals; or

(c) for the benefit of a legal person that has its head office in the territory of that Member State.

2. Any Member State may decide that it will not apply the jurisdiction rules in paragraph 1(b) and (c), or will apply them only in specific cases or circumstances, where the offence has been committed outside its territory.

3. Any Member State which, under its domestic law, does not as yet surrender its own nationals shall take the necessary measures to establish its jurisdiction with regard to the offences referred to in Articles 2 and 3, when committed by its own nationals outside its territory.

4. Member States which decide to apply paragraph 2 shall inform the General Secretariat of the Council and the Commission accordingly, where appropriate with an indication of the specific cases or circumstances in which the decision applies.

*Article 8*

**Repeal**

Joint Action 98/742/JHA shall be repealed.

*Article 9*

**Implementation**

1. Member States shall take the necessary measures to comply with the provisions of this Framework Decision before 22 July 2005.

2. By the same date, Member States shall transmit to the General Secretariat of the Council and the Commission the text of the provisions transposing into their national law the obligations imposed on them under this Framework Decision. On the basis of a report established using this information and a written report from the Commission, the Council shall before 22 October 2005 assess the extent to which Member States have complied with the provisions of this Framework Decision.

*Article 10*

**Territorial application**

This Framework Decision shall apply to Gibraltar.

*Article 11*

**Entry into force**

This Framework Decision shall enter into force on the day of its publication in the *Official Journal of the European Union*.

Done at Brussels, 22 July 2003.

*For the Council*

*The President*

G. ALEMANNO

# Framework Decision 2003/577 on the execution in the European Union of orders freezing property or evidence, 22 July 2003

**[Consolidated version. Original version OJ 2003, L 196/45–55 corrected by OJ 2006, L 374/20]**

►B

# COUNCIL FRAMEWORK DECISION 2003/577/JHA

**of 22 July 2003**

**on the execution in the European Union of orders freezing property or evidence**

(OJ L 196, 2.8.2003, p. 45)

Corrected by:

►C1 Corrigendum, OJ L 374, 27.12.2006, p. 20 (2003/577/JHA)

▼B

**COUNCIL FRAMEWORK DECISION 2003/577/JHA**

**of 22 July 2003**

**on the execution in the European Union of orders freezing property or evidence**

THE COUNCIL OF THE EUROPEAN UNION,

Having regard to the Treaty on European Union, and in particular Article 31(a) and Article 34(2)(b) thereof,

Having regard to the initiative by the Republic of France, the Kingdom of Sweden and the Kingdom of Belgium [1],

Having regard to the opinion of the European Parliament [2],

Whereas:

(1) The European Council, meeting in Tampere on 15 and 16 October 1999, endorsed the principle of mutual recognition, which should become the cornerstone of judicial cooperation in both civil and criminal matters within the Union.

(2) The principle of mutual recognition should also apply to pre-trial orders, in particular to those which would enable competent judicial authorities quickly to secure evidence and to seize property which are easily movable.

(3) On 29 November 2000 the Council, in accordance with the Tampere conclusions, adopted a programme of measures to implement the principle of mutual recognition in criminal matters, giving first priority (measures 6 and 7) to the adoption of an instrument applying the principle of mutual recognition to the freezing of evidence and property.

(4) Cooperation between Member States, based on the principle of mutual recognition and immediate execution of judicial decisions, presupposes confidence that the decisions to be recognised and enforced will always be taken in compliance with the principles of legality, subsidiarity and proportionality.

(5) Rights granted to the parties or bona fide interested third parties should be preserved.

(6) This Framework Decision respects the fundamental rights and observes the principles recognised by Article 6 of the Treaty and reflected by the Charter of Fundamental Rights of the European Union, notably Chapter VI thereof. Nothing in this Framework Decision may be interpreted as prohibiting refusal to freeze property for which a freezing order has been issued when there are reasons to believe, on the basis of objective elements, that the freezing order is issued for the purpose of prosecuting or punishing a person on account of his or her sex, race, religion, ethnic origin, nationality, language, political opinions or sexual orientation, or that that person's position may be prejudiced for any of these reasons.

This Framework Decision does not prevent any Member State from applying its constitutional rules relating to due process, freedom of association, freedom of the press and freedom of expression in other media,

(1) OJ C 75, 7.3.2001, p. 3.
(2) Opinion delivered on 11 June 2002 (not yet published in the Official Journal).

▼B

HAS ADOPTED THIS FRAMEWORK DECISION:

## TITLE I SCOPE

*Article 1*

**Objective**

The purpose of the Framework Decision is to establish the rules under which a Member State shall recognise and execute in its territory a freezing order issued by a judicial authority of another Member State in the framework of criminal proceedings. It shall not have the effect of amending the obligation to respect the fundamental rights and fundamental legal principles as enshrined in Article 6 of the Treaty.

*Article 2*

**Definitions**

For the purposes of this Framework Decision:

(a) 'issuing State' shall mean the Member State in which a judicial authority, as defined in the national law of the issuing State, has made, validated or in any way confirmed a freezing order in the framework of criminal proceedings;

(b) 'executing State' shall mean the Member State in whose territory the property or evidence is located;

▼C1

(c) 'freezing order' shall mean any measure taken by a competent judicial authority in the issuing State in order provisionally to prevent the destruction, transformation, moving, transfer or disposal of property that could be subject to confiscation or evidence;

▼B

(d) 'property' includes property of any description, whether corporeal or incorporeal, movable or immovable, and legal documents and instruments evidencing title to or interest in such property, which the competent judicial authority in the issuing State considers:

— is the proceeds of an offence referred to in Article 3, or equivalent to either the full value or part of the value of such proceeds, or

— constitutes the instrumentalities or the objects of such an offence;

(e) 'evidence' shall mean objects, documents or data which could be produced as evidence in criminal proceedings concerning an offence referred to in Article 3.

*Article 3*

**Offences**

1. This Framework Decision applies to freezing orders issued for purposes of:

(a) securing evidence, or

(b) subsequent confiscation of property.

2. The following offences, as they are defined by the law of the issuing State, and if they are punishable in the issuing State by a

▼B

custodial sentence of a maximum period of at least three years shall not be subject to verification of the double criminality of the act:

— participation in a criminal organisation,

— terrorism,

— trafficking in human beings,

— sexual exploitation of children and child pornography,

— illicit trafficking in narcotic drugs and psychotropic substances,

— illicit trafficking in weapons, munitions and explosives,

— corruption,

— fraud, including that affecting the financial interests of the European Communities within the meaning of the Convention of 26 July 1995 on the Protection of the European Communities' Financial Interests,

— laundering of the proceeds of crime,

— counterfeiting currency, including of the euro,

— computer-related crime,

— environmental crime, including illicit trafficking in endangered animal species and in endangered plant species and varieties,

— facilitation of unauthorised entry and residence,

— murder, grievous bodily injury,

— illicit trade in human organs and tissue,

— kidnapping, illegal restraint and hostage-taking,

— racism and xenophobia,

— organised or armed robbery,

— illicit trafficking in cultural goods, including antiques and works of art,

— swindling,

— racketeering and extortion,

— counterfeiting and piracy of products,

— forgery of administrative documents and trafficking therein,

— forgery of means of payment,

— illicit trafficking in hormonal substances and other growth promoters,

— illicit trafficking in nuclear or radioactive materials,

— trafficking in stolen vehicles,

— rape,

— arson,

— crimes within the jurisdiction of the International Criminal Tribunal,

— unlawful seizure of aircraft/ships,

— sabotage.

3. The Council may decide, at any time, acting unanimously after consultation of the European Parliament under the conditions laid down in Article 39(1) of the Treaty, to add other categories of offence to the list contained in paragraph 2. The Council shall examine, in the light of the report submitted by the Commission pursuant to Article 14 of this Framework Decision, whether the list should be extended or amended.

▼B

4. For cases not covered by paragraph 2, the executing State may subject the recognition and enforcement of a freezing order made for purposes referred to in paragraph 1(a) to the condition that the acts for which the order was issued constitute an offence under the laws of that State, whatever the constituent elements or however described under the law of the issuing State.

For cases not covered by paragraph 2, the executing State may subject the recognition and enforcement of a freezing order made for purposes referred to in paragraph 1(b) to the condition that the acts for which the order was issued constitute an offence which, under the laws of that State, allows for such freezing, whatever the constituent elements or however described under the law of the issuing State.

## TITLE II PROCEDURE FOR EXECUTING FREEZING ORDERS

*Article 4*

**Transmission of freezing orders**

1. A freezing order within the meaning of this Framework Decision, together with the certificate provided for in Article 9, shall be transmitted by the judicial authority which issued it directly to the competent judicial authority for execution by any means capable of producing a written record under conditions allowing the executing State to establish authenticity.

2. The United Kingdom and Ireland, respectively, may, before the date referred to in Article 14(1), state in a declaration that the freezing order together with the certificate must be sent via a central authority or authorities specified by it in the declaration. Any such declaration may be modified by a further declaration or withdrawn any time. Any declaration or withdrawal shall be deposited with the General Secretariat of the Council and notified to the Commission. These Member States may at any time by a further declaration limit the scope of such a declaration for the purpose of giving greater effect to paragraph 1. They shall do so when the provisions on mutual assistance of the Convention implementing the Schengen Agreement are put into effect for them.

3. If the competent judicial authority for execution is unknown, the judicial authority in the issuing State shall make all necessary inquiries, including via the contact points of the European Judicial Network ([1]), in order to obtain the information from the executing State.

4. When the judicial authority in the executing State which receives a freezing order has no jurisdiction to recognise it and take the necessary measures for its execution, it shall, *ex officio*, transmit the freezing order to the competent judicial authority for execution and shall so inform the judicial authority in the issuing State which issued it.

*Article 5*

**Recognition and immediate execution**

1. The competent judicial authorities of the executing State shall recognise a freezing order, transmitted in accordance with Article 4, without any further formality being required and shall forthwith take the necessary measures for its immediate execution in the same way as for a freezing order made by an authority of the executing State, unless that authority decides to invoke one of the grounds for non-recognition

([1]) Council Joint Action 98/428/JHA of 29 June 1998 on the Creation of the European Judicial Network (OJ L 191, 7.7.1998, p. 4).

▼B

or non-execution provided for in Article 7 or one of the grounds for postponement provided for in Article 8.

Whenever it is necessary to ensure that the evidence taken is valid and provided that such formalities and procedures are not contrary to the fundamental principles of law in the executing State, the judicial authority of the executing State shall also observe the formalities and procedures expressly indicated by the competent judicial authority of the issuing State in the execution of the freezing order.

A report on the execution of the freezing order shall be made forthwith to the competent authority in the issuing State by any means capable of producing a written record.

2. Any additional coercive measures rendered necessary by the freezing order shall be taken in accordance with the applicable procedural rules of the executing State.

3. The competent judicial authorities of the executing State shall decide and communicate the decision on a freezing order as soon as possible and, whenever practicable, within 24 hours of receipt of the freezing order.

*Article 6*

**Duration of the freezing**

1. The property shall remain frozen in the executing State until that State has responded definitively to any request made under Article 10(1) (a) or (b).

2. However, after consulting the issuing State, the executing State may in accordance with its national law and practices lay down appropriate conditions in the light of the circumstances of the case in order to limit the period for which the property will be frozen. If, in accordance with those conditions, it envisages lifting the measure, it shall inform the issuing State, which shall be given the opportunity to submit its comments.

3. The judicial authorities of the issuing State shall forthwith notify the judicial authorities of the executing State that the freezing order has been lifted. In these circumstances it shall be the responsibility of the executing State to lift the measure as soon as possible.

*Article 7*

**Grounds for non-recognition or non-execution**

1. The competent judicial authorities of the executing State may refuse to recognise or execute the freezing order only if:

(a) the certificate provided for in Article 9 is not produced, is incomplete or manifestly does not correspond to the freezing order;

(b) there is an immunity or privilege under the law of the executing State which makes it impossible to execute the freezing order;

(c) it is instantly clear from the information provided in the certificate that rendering judicial assistance pursuant to Article 10 for the offence in respect of which the freezing order has been made, would infringe the *ne bis in idem* principle;

(d) if, in one of the cases referred to in Article 3(4), the act on which the freezing order is based does not constitute an offence under the law of the executing State; however, in relation to taxes or duties, customs and exchange, execution of the freezing order may not be refused on the ground that the law of the executing State does not impose the same kind of tax or duty or does not contain a tax, duty,

▼B

customs and exchange regulation of the same kind as the law of the issuing State.

2. In case of paragraph 1(a), the competent judicial authority may:

(a) specify a deadline for its presentation, completion or correction; or

(b) accept an equivalent document; or

(c) exempt the issuing judicial authority from the requirement if it considers that the information provided is sufficient.

3. Any decision to refuse recognition or execution shall be taken and notified forthwith to the competent judicial authorities of the issuing State by any means capable of producing a written record.

4. In case it is in practice impossible to execute the freezing order for the reason that the property or evidence have disappeared, have been destroyed, cannot be found in the location indicated in the certificate or the location of the property or evidence has not been indicated in a sufficiently precise manner, even after consultation with the issuing State, the competent judicial authorities of the issuing State shall likewise be notified forthwith.

*Article 8*

**Grounds for postponement of execution**

1. The competent judicial authority of the executing State may postpone the execution of a freezing order transmitted in accordance with Article 4:

(a) where its execution might damage an ongoing criminal investigation, until such time as it deems reasonable;

(b) where the property or evidence concerned have already been subjected to a freezing order in criminal proceedings, and until that freezing order is lifted;

(c) where, in the case of an order freezing property in criminal proceedings with a view to its subsequent confiscation, that property is already subject to an order made in the course of other proceedings in the executing State and until that order is lifted. However, this point shall only apply where such an order would have priority over subsequent national freezing orders in criminal proceedings under national law.

2. A report on the postponement of the execution of the freezing order, including the grounds for the postponement and, if possible, the expected duration of the postponement, shall be made forthwith to the competent authority in the issuing State by any means capable of producing a written record.

3. As soon as the ground for postponement has ceased to exist, the competent judicial authority of the executing State shall forthwith take the necessary measures for the execution of the freezing order and inform the competent authority in the issuing State thereof by any means capable of producing a written record.

4. The competent judicial authority of the executing State shall inform the competent authority of the issuing State about any other restraint measure to which the property concerned may be subjected.

*Article 9*

**Certificate**

1. The certificate, the standard form for which is given in the Annex, shall be signed, and its contents certified as accurate, by the competent judicial authority in the issuing State that ordered the measure.

▼B

2. The certificate must be translated into the official language or one of the official languages of the executing State.

3. Any Member State may, either when this Framework Decision is adopted or at a later date, state in a declaration deposited with the General Secretariat of the Council that it will accept a translation in one or more other official languages of the institutions of the European Communities.

*Article 10*

**Subsequent treatment of the frozen property**

1. The transmission referred to in Article 4:

(a) shall be accompanied by a request for the evidence to be transferred to the issuing State;

or

(b) shall be accompanied by a request for confiscation requiring either enforcement of a confiscation order that has been issued in the issuing State or confiscation in the executing State and subsequent enforcement of any such order;

or

(c) shall contain an instruction in the certificate that the property shall remain in the executing State pending a request referred to in (a) or (b). The issuing State shall indicate in the certificate the (estimated) date for submission of this request. Article 6(2) shall apply.

2. Requests referred to in paragraph 1(a) and (b) shall be submitted by the issuing State and processed by the executing State in accordance with the rules applicable to mutual assistance in criminal matters and the rules applicable to international cooperation relating to confiscation.

3. However, by way of derogation from the rules on mutual assistance referred to in paragraph 2, the executing State may not refuse requests referred to under paragraph 1(a) on grounds of absence of double criminality, where the requests concern the offences referred to in Article 3(2) and those offences are punishable in the issuing State by a prison sentence of at least three years.

*Article 11*

**Legal remedies**

1. Member States shall put in place the necessary arrangements to ensure that any interested party, including bona fide third parties, have legal remedies without suspensive effect against a freezing order executed pursuant to Article 5, in order to preserve their legitimate interests; the action shall be brought before a court in the issuing State or in the executing State in accordance with the national law of each.

2. The substantive reasons for issuing the freezing order can be challenged only in an action brought before a court in the issuing State.

3. If the action is brought in the executing State, the judicial authority of the issuing State shall be informed thereof and of the grounds of the action, so that it can submit the arguments that it deems necessary. It shall be informed of the outcome of the action.

4. The issuing and executing States shall take the necessary measures to facilitate the exercise of the right to bring an action mentioned in paragraph 1, in particular by providing adequate information to interested parties.

▼B

5. The issuing State shall ensure that any time limits for bringing an action mentioned in paragraph 1 are applied in a way that guarantees the possibility of an effective legal remedy for the interested parties.

*Article 12*

**Reimbursement**

1. Without prejudice to Article 11(2), where the executing State under its law is responsible for injury caused to one of the parties mentioned in Article 11 by the execution of a freezing order transmitted to it pursuant to Article 4, the issuing State shall reimburse to the executing State any sums paid in damages by virtue of that responsibility to the said party except if, and to the extent that, the injury or any part of it is exclusively due to the conduct of the executing State.

2. Paragraph 1 is without prejudice to the national law of the Member States on claims by natural or legal persons for compensation of damage.

## TITLE III FINAL PROVISIONS

*Article 13*

**Territorial application**

This Framework Decision shall apply to Gibraltar.

*Article 14*

**Implementation**

1. Member States shall take the necessary measures to comply with the provisions of this Framework Decision before 2 August 2005.

2. By the same date Member States shall transmit to the General Secretariat of the Council and to the Commission the text of the provisions transposing into their national law the obligations imposed on them under this Framework Decision. On the basis of a report established using this information and a written report by the Commission, the Council shall, before 2 August 2006, assess the extent to which Member States have complied with the provisions of this Framework Decision.

3. The General Secretariat of the Council shall notify Member States and the Commission of the declarations made pursuant to Article 9(3).

*Article 15*

**Entry into force**

This Framework Decision shall enter into force on the day of its publication in the *Official Journal of the European Union.*

▼B

*ANNEX*

**CERTIFICATE PROVIDED FOR IN ARTICLE 9**

(a) The judicial authority which issued the freezing order:

Official name: ..........................................................................................................

..........................................................................................................

Name of its representative: ..........................................................................................................

Post held (title/grade): ..........................................................................................................

File reference: ..........................................................................................................

Address: ..........................................................................................................

..........................................................................................................

Tel: (country code) (area/city code) (...) ..........................................................................................................

Fax: (country code) (area/city code) (...) ..........................................................................................................

E-mail: ..........................................................................................................

Languages in which it is possible to communicate with the issuing judicial authority ..........................................

..........................................................................................................

Contact details (including languages in which it is possible to communicate with the person(s)) of the person(s) to contact if additional information on the execution of the order is necessary or to make necessary practical arrangements for the transfer of evidence (if applicable): ..........................................................................................................

..........................................................................................................

..........................................................................................................

(b) The authority competent for the enforcement of the freezing order in the issuing State

Official name: ..........................................................................................................

..........................................................................................................

Name of its representative: ..........................................................................................................

Post held (title/grade): ..........................................................................................................

File reference: ..........................................................................................................

Address: ..........................................................................................................

..........................................................................................................

Tel: (country code) (area/city code) (...) ..........................................................................................................

Fax: (country code) (area/city code) (...) ..........................................................................................................

E-mail: ..........................................................................................................

Languages in which it is possible to communicate with the authority competent for the enforcement ..........................................

..........................................................................................................

Contact details (including languages in which it is possible to communicate with the person(s)) of the person(s) to contact if additional information on the execution of the order is necessary or to make necessary practical arrangements for the transfer of evidence (if applicable): ..........................................................................................................

..........................................................................................................

▼B

(c) In the case where points (a) and (b) have been filled, this point must be filled in order to indicate which/or both of these two authorities must be contacted: ..............................................................................

□ Authority mentioned under point (a)

□ Authority mentioned under point (b)

(d) Where a central authority has been made responsible for the transmission and administrative reception of freezing orders (only applicable for Ireland and the United Kingdom):

Name of the central authority: ..............................................................................

..............................................................................

Contact person, if applicable (title/grade and name): ..............................................................................

..............................................................................

Address: ..............................................................................

..............................................................................

File reference ..............................................................................

Tel: (country code) (area/city code) ..............................................................................

Fax: (country code) (area/city code) ..............................................................................

E-mail: ..............................................................................

(e) The freezing order:

1. Date and if applicable reference number

2. State the purpose of the order

2.1. Subsequent confiscation

2.2. Securing evidence

3. Description of formalities and procedures to be observed when executing a freezing order concerning evidence (if applicable)

(f) Information regarding the property or evidence in the executing State covered by the freezing order:

Description of the property or evidence and location:

1. (a) Precise description of the property and, where applicable, the maximum amount for which recovery is sought (if such maximum amount is indicated in the order concerning the value of proceeds)

(b) Precise description of the evidence

2. Exact location of the property or evidence (if not known, the last known location)

3. Party having custody of the property or evidence or known beneficial owner of the property or evidence, if different from the person suspected of the offence or convicted (if applicable under the national law of the issuing State)

..............................................................................

..............................................................................

▼B

(g) Information regarding the identity of the (1) natural or (2) legal person(s), suspected of the offence or convicted (if applicable under the national law of the issuing State) or/and the person(s) to whom the freezing order relates (if available):

1. Natural persons

Name: ..................................................

Forename(s): ..................................................

Maiden name, where applicable: ..................................................

Aliases, where applicable: ..................................................

Sex: ..................................................

Nationality: ..................................................

Date of birth: ..................................................

Place of birth: ..................................................

Residence and/or known address; if not known state the last known address: ..................................................

..................................................

Language(s) which the person understands (if known): ..................................................

..................................................

2. Legal persons

Name: ..................................................

Form of legal person: ..................................................

Registration number: ..................................................

Registered seat: ..................................................

..................................................

(h) Action to be taken by the executing State after executing the freezing order

Confiscation

1.1. The property is to be kept in the executing State for the purpose of subsequent confiscation of the property

1.1.1. Find enclosed request regarding enforcement of a confiscation order issued in the issuing State on ............. (date)

1.1.2. Find enclosed request regarding confiscation in the executing State and subsequent enforcement of that order

1.1.3. Estimated date for submission of a request referred to in 1.1.1 or 1.1.2. ..........................................

or

Securing of evidence

2.1. The property is to be transferred to the issuing State to serve as evidence

2.1.1. Find enclosed a request for the transfer

or

2.2. The property is to be kept in the executing State for the purpose of subsequent use as evidence in the issuing State

2.2.2. Estimated date for submission of a request referred to in 2.1.1. ..................................................

▼B

(i) Offences:

Description of the relevant grounds for the freezing order and a summary of facts as known to the judicial authority issuing the freezing order and certificate:

……………………………………………………………………………………………………

……………………………………………………………………………………………………

……………………………………………………………………………………………………

Nature and legal classification of the offence(s) and the applicable statutory provision/code on basis of which the freezing order was made:

……………………………………………………………………………………………………

……………………………………………………………………………………………………

……………………………………………………………………………………………………

……………………………………………………………………………………………………

1. If applicable, tick one or more of the following offences to which the offence(s) identified above relate(s), if the offence(s) are punishable in the issuing State by a custodial sentence of a maximum of at least three years:
   - ☐ participation in a criminal organisation;
   - ☐ terrorism;
   - ☐ trafficking in human beings;
   - ☐ sexual exploitation of children and child pornography;
   - ☐ illicit trafficking in narcotic drugs and psychotropic substances;
   - ☐ illicit trafficking in weapons, munitions and explosives;
   - ☐ corruption;
   - ☐ fraud, including that affecting the financial interests of the European Communities within the meaning of the Convention of 26 July 1995 on the Protection of the European Communities' Financial Interests;
   - ☐ laundering of the proceeds of crime;
   - ☐ counterfeiting currency, including of the euro;
   - ☐ computer-related crime;
   - ☐ environmental crime, including illicit trafficking in endangered animal species and in endangered plant species and varieties;
   - ☐ facilitation of unauthorised entry and residence;
   - ☐ murder, grievous bodily injury;
   - ☐ illicit trade in human organs and tissue;
   - ☐ kidnapping, illegal restraint and hostage-taking;
   - ☐ racism and xenophobia;
   - ☐ organised or armed robbery;
   - ☐ illicit trafficking in cultural goods, including antiques and works of art;
   - ☐ swindling;
   - ☐ racketeering and extortion;
   - ☐ counterfeiting and piracy of products;
   - ☐ forgery of administrative documents and trafficking therein;
   - ☐ forgery of means of payment;
   - ☐ illicit trafficking in hormonal substances and other growth promoters;
   - ☐ illicit trafficking in nuclear or radioactive materials;
   - ☐ trafficking in stolen vehicles;
   - ☐ rape;
   - ☐ arson;
   - ☐ crimes within the jurisdiction of the International Criminal Court;
   - ☐ unlawful seizure of aircraft/ships;
   - ☐ sabotage.

2. Full descriptions of offence(s) not covered by section 1 above:

   ……………………………………………………………………………………………………

   ……………………………………………………………………………………………………

   ……………………………………………………………………………………………………

▼B

(j) Legal remedies against the freezing order for interested parties, including bona fide third parties, available in the issuing State:

Description of the legal remedies available including necessary steps to take

Court before which the action may be taken

Information as to those for whom the action is available

Time limit for submission of the action

Authority in the issuing State who can supply further information on procedures for submitting appeals in the issuing State and on whether legal assistance and translation is available:

Name

Contact person (if applicable): ……………………………………………………

Address: ……………………………………………………

Tel: (country code) (area/city code) ……………………………………………………

Fax: (country code) (area/city code) ……………………………………………………

E-mail: ……………………………………………………

(k) Other circumstances relevant to the case (optional information): ……………………………………………………

……………………………………………………

……………………………………………………

(l) The text of the freezing order is attached to the certificate.

Signature of the issuing judicial authority and/or its representative certifying the content of the certificate as accurate:

……………………………………………………

Name: ……………………………………………………

Post held (title/grade): ……………………………………………………

Date: ……………………………………………………

Official stamp (if available)

# Directive 2004/38 on the right of citizens of the Union and their family members to move and reside freely within the territory of the Member States, 29 April 2004

**[OJ 2004, L 158/77–88, 113–119]**

**[Editor's note: articles 3–26 omitted]**

30.4.2004 EN Official Journal of the European Union L 158/ 77

**DIRECTIVE 2004/38/EC OF THE EUROPEAN PARLIAMENT AND OF THE COUNCIL**
**of 29 April 2004**

on the right of citizens of the Union and their family members
to move and reside freely within the territory of the Member States
amending Regulation (EEC) No 1612/68 and repealing Directives 64/221/EEC,
68/360/EEC, 72/194/EEC, 73/148/EEC, 75/34/EEC, 75/35/EEC,
90/364/EEC, 90/365/EEC and 93/96/EEC

(Text with EEA relevance)

THE EUROPEAN PARLIAMENT AND THE COUNCIL OF THE EUROPEAN UNION,

Having regard to the Treaty establishing the European Community, and in particular Articles 12, 18, 40, 44 and 52 thereof,

Having regard to the proposal from the Commission [1],

Having regard to the Opinion of the European Economic and Social Committee [2],

Having regard to the Opinion of the Committee of the Regions [3],

Acting in accordance with the procedure laid down in Article 251 of the Treaty [4],

---

1 OJ C 270 E, 25.9.2001, p. 150.
2 OJ C 149, 21.6.2002, p. 46.
3 OJ C 192, 12.8.2002, p. 17.
4 Opinion of the European Parliament of 11 February 2003 (OJ C 43 E, 19.2.2004, p. 42), Council Common Position of 5 December 2003 (OJ C 54 E, 2.3.2004, p. 12) and Position of the European Parliament of 10 March 2004 (not yet published in the Official Journal).

30.4.2004 EN Official Journal of the European Union L 158/ 78

Whereas:

(1) Citizenship of the Union confers on every citizen of the Union a primary and individual right to move and reside freely within the territory of the Member States, subject to the limitations and conditions laid down in the Treaty and to the measures adopted to give it effect.

(2) The free movement of persons constitutes one of the fundamental freedoms of the internal market, which comprises an area without internal frontiers, in which freedom is ensured in accordance with the provisions of the Treaty.

(3) Union citizenship should be the fundamental status of nationals of the Member States when they exercise their right of free movement and residence. It is therefore necessary to codify and review the existing Community instruments dealing separately with workers, self-employed persons, as well as students and other inactive persons in order to simplify and strengthen the right of free movement and residence of all Union citizens.

(4) With a view to remedying this sector-by-sector, piecemeal approach to the right of free movement and residence and facilitating the exercise of this right, there needs to be a single legislative act to amend Council Regulation (EEC) No 1612/68 of 15 October 1968 on freedom of movement for workers within the Community [1], and to repeal the following acts: Council Directive 68/360/EEC of 15 October 1968 on the abolition of restrictions on movement and residence within the Community for workers of Member States and their families [2], Council Directive 73/148/EEC of 21 May 1973 on the abolition of restrictions on movement and residence within the Community for nationals of Member States with regard to establishment and the provision of services [3], Council Directive 90/364/EEC of 28 June 1990 on the right of residence [4], Council Directive 90/365/EEC of 28 June 1990 on the right of residence for employees and self-employed persons who have ceased their occupational activity [5] and Council Directive 93/96/EEC of 29 October 1993 on the right of residence for students [6].

(5) The right of all Union citizens to move and reside freely within the territory of the Member States should, if it is to be exercised under objective conditions of freedom and dignity, be also granted to their family members, irrespective of nationality. For the purposes of this Directive, the definition of "family member" should also include the registered partner if the legislation of the host Member State treats registered partnership as equivalent to marriage.

1 OJ L 257, 19.10.1968, p. 2. Regulation as last amended by Regulation (EEC) No 2434/92 (OJ L 245, 26.8.1992, p. 1).
2 OJ L 257, 19.10.1968, p. 13. Directive as last amended by the 2003 Act of Accession.
3 OJ L 172, 28.6.1973, p. 14.
4 OJ L 180, 13.7.1990, p. 26.
5 OJ L 180, 13.7.1990, p. 28.
6 OJ L 317, 18.12.1993, p. 59.

(6) In order to maintain the unity of the family in a broader sense and without prejudice to the prohibition of discrimination on grounds of nationality, the situation of those persons who are not included in the definition of family members under this Directive, and who therefore do not enjoy an automatic right of entry and residence in the host Member State, should be examined by the host Member State on the basis of its own national legislation, in order to decide whether entry and residence could be granted to such persons, taking into consideration their relationship with the Union citizen or any other circumstances, such as their financial or physical dependence on the Union citizen.

(7) The formalities connected with the free movement of Union citizens within the territory of Member States should be clearly defined, without prejudice to the provisions applicable to national border controls.

(8) With a view to facilitating the free movement of family members who are not nationals of a Member State, those who have already obtained a residence card should be exempted from the requirement to obtain an entry visa within the meaning of Council Regulation (EC) No 539/2001 of 15 March 2001 listing the third countries whose nationals must be in possession of visas when crossing the external borders and those whose nationals are exempt from that requirement [1] or, where appropriate, of the applicable national legislation.

(9) Union citizens should have the right of residence in the host Member State for a period not exceeding three months without being subject to any conditions or any formalities other than the requirement to hold a valid identity card or passport, without prejudice to a more favourable treatment applicable to job-seekers as recognised by the case-law of the Court of Justice.

1 OJ L 81, 21.3.2001, p. 1. Regulation as last amended by Regulation (EC) No 453/2003 (OJ L 69, 13.3.2003, p. 10).

30.4.2004 EN Official Journal of the European Union L 158/ 81

(10) Persons exercising their right of residence should not, however, become an unreasonable burden on the social assistance system of the host Member State during an initial period of residence. Therefore, the right of residence for Union citizens and their family members for periods in excess of three months should be subject to conditions.

(11) The fundamental and personal right of residence in another Member State is conferred directly on Union citizens by the Treaty and is not dependent upon their having fulfilled administrative procedures.

(12) For periods of residence of longer than three months, Member States should have the possibility to require Union citizens to register with the competent authorities in the place of residence, attested by a registration certificate issued to that effect.

(13) The residence card requirement should be restricted to family members of Union citizens who are not nationals of a Member State for periods of residence of longer than three months.

(14) The supporting documents required by the competent authorities for the issuing of a registration certificate or of a residence card should be comprehensively specified in order to avoid divergent administrative practices or interpretations constituting an undue obstacle to the exercise of the right of residence by Union citizens and their family members.

30.4.2004 EN Official Journal of the European Union L 158/ 82

(15) Family members should be legally safeguarded in the event of the death of the Union citizen, divorce, annulment of marriage or termination of a registered partnership. With due regard for family life and human dignity, and in certain conditions to guard against abuse, measures should therefore be taken to ensure that in such circumstances family members already residing within the territory of the host Member State retain their right of residence exclusively on a personal basis.

(16) As long as the beneficiaries of the right of residence do not become an unreasonable burden on the social assistance system of the host Member State they should not be expelled. Therefore, an expulsion measure should not be the automatic consequence of recourse to the social assistance system. The host Member State should examine whether it is a case of temporary difficulties and take into account the duration of residence, the personal circumstances and the amount of aid granted in order to consider whether the beneficiary has become an unreasonable burden on its social assistance system and to proceed to his expulsion. In no case should an expulsion measure be adopted against workers, self-employed persons or job-seekers as defined by the Court of Justice save on grounds of public policy or public security.

(17) Enjoyment of permanent residence by Union citizens who have chosen to settle long term in the host Member State would strengthen the feeling of Union citizenship and is a key element in promoting social cohesion, which is one of the fundamental objectives of the Union. A right of permanent residence should therefore be laid down for all Union citizens and their family members who have resided in the host Member State in compliance with the conditions laid down in this Directive during a continuous period of five years without becoming subject to an expulsion measure.

30.4.2004 EN Official Journal of the European Union L 158/ 83

(18) In order to be a genuine vehicle for integration into the society of the host Member State in which the Union citizen resides, the right of permanent residence, once obtained, should not be subject to any conditions.

(19) Certain advantages specific to Union citizens who are workers or self-employed persons and to their family members, which may allow these persons to acquire a right of permanent residence before they have resided five years in the host Member State, should be maintained, as these constitute acquired rights, conferred by Commission Regulation (EEC) No 1251/70 of 29 June 1970 on the right of workers to remain in the territory of a Member State after having been employed in that State [1] and Council Directive 75/34/EEC of 17 December 1974 concerning the right of nationals of a Member State to remain in the territory of another Member State after having pursued therein an activity in a self-employed capacity [2].

(20) In accordance with the prohibition of discrimination on grounds of nationality, all Union citizens and their family members residing in a Member State on the basis of this Directive should enjoy, in that Member State, equal treatment with nationals in areas covered by the Treaty, subject to such specific provisions as are expressly provided for in the Treaty and secondary law.

1 OJ L 142, 30.6.1970, p. 24.
2 OJ L 14, 20.1.1975, p. 10.

(21) However, it should be left to the host Member State to decide whether it will grant social assistance during the first three months of residence, or for a longer period in the case of job-seekers, to Union citizens other than those who are workers or self-employed persons or who retain that status or their family members, or maintenance assistance for studies, including vocational training, prior to acquisition of the right of permanent residence, to these same persons.

(22) The Treaty allows restrictions to be placed on the right of free movement and residence on grounds of public policy, public security or public health. In order to ensure a tighter definition of the circumstances and procedural safeguards subject to which Union citizens and their family members may be denied leave to enter or may be expelled, this Directive should replace Council Directive 64/221/EEC of 25 February 1964 on the coordination of special measures concerning the movement and residence of foreign nationals, which are justified on grounds of public policy, public security or public health [1].

(23) Expulsion of Union citizens and their family members on grounds of public policy or public security is a measure that can seriously harm persons who, having availed themselves of the rights and freedoms conferred on them by the Treaty, have become genuinely integrated into the host Member State. The scope for such measures should therefore be limited in accordance with the principle of proportionality to take account of the degree of integration of the persons concerned, the length of their residence in the host Member State, their age, state of health, family and economic situation and the links with their country of origin.

1 OJ 56, 4.4.1964, p. 850. Directive as last amended by Directive 75/35/EEC (OJ 14, 20.1.1975, p. 14).

(24) Accordingly, the greater the degree of integration of Union citizens and their family members in the host Member State, the greater the degree of protection against expulsion should be. Only in exceptional circumstances, where there are imperative grounds of public security, should an expulsion measure be taken against Union citizens who have resided for many years in the territory of the host Member State, in particular when they were born and have resided there throughout their life. In addition, such exceptional circumstances should also apply to an expulsion measure taken against minors, in order to protect their links with their family, in accordance with the United Nations Convention on the Rights of the Child, of 20 November 1989.

(25) Procedural safeguards should also be specified in detail in order to ensure a high level of protection of the rights of Union citizens and their family members in the event of their being denied leave to enter or reside in another Member State, as well as to uphold the principle that any action taken by the authorities must be properly justified.

(26) In all events, judicial redress procedures should be available to Union citizens and their family members who have been refused leave to enter or reside in another Member State.

(27) In line with the case-law of the Court of Justice prohibiting Member States from issuing orders excluding for life persons covered by this Directive from their territory, the right of Union citizens and their family members who have been excluded from the territory of a Member State to submit a fresh application after a reasonable period, and in any event after a three year period from enforcement of the final exclusion order, should be confirmed.

30.4.2004 EN Official Journal of the European Union L 158/ 86

(28) To guard against abuse of rights or fraud, notably marriages of convenience or any other form of relationships contracted for the sole purpose of enjoying the right of free movement and residence, Member States should have the possibility to adopt the necessary measures.

(29) This Directive should not affect more favourable national provisions.

(30) With a view to examining how further to facilitate the exercise of the right of free movement and residence, a report should be prepared by the Commission in order to evaluate the opportunity to present any necessary proposals to this effect, notably on the extension of the period of residence with no conditions.

(31) This Directive respects the fundamental rights and freedoms and observes the principles recognised in particular by the Charter of Fundamental Rights of the European Union. In accordance with the prohibition of discrimination contained in the Charter, Member States should implement this Directive without discrimination between the beneficiaries of this Directive on grounds such as sex, race, colour, ethnic or social origin, genetic characteristics, language, religion or beliefs, political or other opinion, membership of an ethnic minority, property, birth, disability, age or sexual orientation,

HAVE ADOPTED THIS DIRECTIVE:

30.4.2004 EN Official Journal of the European Union L 158/ 87

## CHAPTER I

## General provisions

### Article 1
### Subject

This Directive lays down:

(a) the conditions governing the exercise of the right of free movement and residence within the territory of the Member States by Union citizens and their family members;

(b) the right of permanent residence in the territory of the Member States for Union citizens and their family members;

(c) the limits placed on the rights set out in (a) and (b) on grounds of public policy, public security or public health.

### Article 2
### Definitions

For the purposes of this Directive:

1) "Union citizen" means any person having the nationality of a Member State;

30.4.2004 EN Official Journal of the European Union L 158/ 88

2) "Family member" means:

(a) the spouse;

(b) the partner with whom the Union citizen has contracted a registered partnership, on the basis of the legislation of a Member State, if the legislation of the host Member State treats registered partnerships as equivalent to marriage and in accordance with the conditions laid down in the relevant legislation of the host Member State;

(c) the direct descendants who are under the age of 21 or are dependants and those of the spouse or partner as defined in point (b);

(d) the dependent direct relatives in the ascending line and those of the spouse or partner as defined in point (b);

3) "Host Member State" means the Member State to which a Union citizen moves in order to exercise his/her right of free movement and residence.

(...)

30.4.2004 EN Official Journal of the European Union L 158/ 113

CHAPTER VI

Restrictions on the right of entry and the right of residence on grounds of public policy, public security or public health

Article 27

General principles

1. Subject to the provisions of this Chapter, Member States may restrict the freedom of movement and residence of Union citizens and their family members, irrespective of nationality, on grounds of public policy, public security or public health. These grounds shall not be invoked to serve economic ends.

2. Measures taken on grounds of public policy or public security shall comply with the principle of proportionality and shall be based exclusively on the personal conduct of the individual concerned. Previous criminal convictions shall not in themselves constitute grounds for taking such measures.

The personal conduct of the individual concerned must represent a genuine, present and sufficiently serious threat affecting one of the fundamental interests of society. Justifications that are isolated from the particulars of the case or that rely on considerations of general prevention shall not be accepted.

3. In order to ascertain whether the person concerned represents a danger for public policy or public security, when issuing the registration certificate or, in the absence of a registration system, not later than three months from the date of arrival of the person concerned on its territory or from the date of reporting his/her presence within the territory, as provided for in Article 5(5), or when issuing the residence card, the host Member State may, should it consider this essential, request the Member State of origin and, if need be, other Member States to provide information concerning any previous police record the person concerned may have. Such enquiries shall not be made as a matter of routine. The Member State consulted shall give its reply within two months.

4. The Member State which issued the passport or identity card shall allow the holder of the document who has been expelled on grounds of public policy, public security, or public health from another Member State to re-enter its territory without any formality even if the document is no longer valid or the nationality of the holder is in dispute.

30.4.2004 EN Official Journal of the European Union L 158/ 115

Article 28

Protection against expulsion

1. Before taking an expulsion decision on grounds of public policy or public security, the host Member State shall take account of considerations such as how long the individual concerned has resided on its territory, his/her age, state of health, family and economic situation, social and cultural integration into the host Member State and the extent of his/her links with the country of origin.

2. The host Member State may not take an expulsion decision against Union citizens or their family members, irrespective of nationality, who have the right of permanent residence on its territory, except on serious grounds of public policy or public security.

3. An expulsion decision may not be taken against Union citizens, except if the decision is based on imperative grounds of public security, as defined by Member States, if they:

(a) have resided in the host Member State for the previous ten years; or

(b) are a minor, except if the expulsion is necessary for the best interests of the child, as provided for in the United Nations Convention on the Rights of the Child of 20 November 1989.

30.4.2004 EN Official Journal of the European Union L 158/ 116

Article 29

Public health

1. The only diseases justifying measures restricting freedom of movement shall be the diseases with epidemic potential as defined by the relevant instruments of the World Health Organisation and other infectious diseases or contagious parasitic diseases if they are the subject of protection provisions applying to nationals of the host Member State.

2. Diseases occurring after a three-month period from the date of arrival shall not constitute grounds for expulsion from the territory.

3. Where there are serious indications that it is necessary, Member States may, within three months of the date of arrival, require persons entitled to the right of residence to undergo, free of charge, a medical examination to certify that they are not suffering from any of the conditions referred to in paragraph 1. Such medical examinations may not be required as a matter of routine.

Article 30

Notification of decisions

1. The persons concerned shall be notified in writing of any decision taken under Article 27(1), in such a way that they are able to comprehend its content and the implications for them.

2. The persons concerned shall be informed, precisely and in full, of the public policy, public security or public health grounds on which the decision taken in their case is based, unless this is contrary to the interests of State security.

30.4.2004 EN Official Journal of the European Union L 158/ 117

3. The notification shall specify the court or administrative authority with which the person concerned may lodge an appeal, the time limit for the appeal and, where applicable, the time allowed for the person to leave the territory of the Member State. Save in duly substantiated cases of urgency, the time allowed to leave the territory shall be not less than one month from the date of notification.

### Article 31

### Procedural safeguards

1. The persons concerned shall have access to judicial and, where appropriate, administrative redress procedures in the host Member State to appeal against or seek review of any decision taken against them on the grounds of public policy, public security or public health.

2. Where the application for appeal against or judicial review of the expulsion decision is accompanied by an application for an interim order to suspend enforcement of that decision, actual removal from the territory may not take place until such time as the decision on the interim order has been taken, except:

– where the expulsion decision is based on a previous judicial decision; or

– where the persons concerned have had previous access to judicial review; or

– where the expulsion decision is based on imperative grounds of public security under Article 28(3).

3. The redress procedures shall allow for an examination of the legality of the decision, as well as of the facts and circumstances on which the proposed measure is based. They shall ensure that the decision is not disproportionate, particularly in view of the requirements laid down in Article 28.

4. Member States may exclude the individual concerned from their territory pending the redress procedure, but they may not prevent the individual from submitting his/her defence in person, except when his/her appearance may cause serious troubles to public policy or public security or when the appeal or judicial review concerns a denial of entry to the territory.

Article 32

Duration of exclusion orders

1. Persons excluded on grounds of public policy or public security may submit an application for lifting of the exclusion order after a reasonable period, depending on the circumstances, and in any event after three years from enforcement of the final exclusion order which has been validly adopted in accordance with Community law, by putting forward arguments to establish that there has been a material change in the circumstances which justified the decision ordering their exclusion.

The Member State concerned shall reach a decision on this application within six months of its submission.

2. The persons referred to in paragraph 1 shall have no right of entry to the territory of the Member State concerned while their application is being considered.

### Article 33

### Expulsion as a penalty or legal consequence

1. Expulsion orders may not be issued by the host Member State as a penalty or legal consequence of a custodial penalty, unless they conform to the requirements of Articles 27, 28 and 29.

2. If an expulsion order, as provided for in paragraph 1, is enforced more than two years after it was issued, the Member State shall check that the individual concerned is currently and genuinely a threat to public policy or public security and shall assess whether there has been any material change in the circumstances since the expulsion order was issued.

# Directive 2004/80 relating to compensation to crime victims, 29 April 2004

[OJ 2004, L 261/15–18]

6.8.2004 EN Official Journal of the European Union L 261/15

**COUNCIL DIRECTIVE 2004/80/EC**

**of 29 April 2004**

**relating to compensation to crime victims**

THE COUNCIL OF THE EUROPEAN UNION,

Having regard to the Treaty establishing the European Community, and in particular Article 308 thereof,

Having regard to the proposal from the Commission [1],

Having regard to the opinion of the European Parliament [2],

Having regard to the opinion of the European Economic and Social Committee [3],

Whereas:

(1) One of the objectives of the European Community is to abolish, as between Member States, obstacles to the free movement of persons and services.

(2) The Court of Justice held in the Cowan [4] Case that, when Community law guarantees to a natural person the freedom to go to another Member State, the protection of that person from harm in the Member State in question, on the same basis as that of nationals and persons residing there, is a corollary of that freedom of movement. Measures to facilitate compensation to victims of crimes should form part of the realisation of this objective.

(3) At its meeting in Tampere on 15 and 16 October 1999, the European Council called for the drawing-up of minimum standards on the protection of the victims of crime, in particular on crime victims' access to justice and their rights to compensation for damages, including legal costs.

(4) The Brussels European Council, meeting on 25 and 26 March 2004, in the Declaration on Combating Terrorism, called for the adoption of this Directive before 1 May 2004.

(5) On 15 March 2001 the Council adopted Framework Decision 2001/220/JHA on the standing of victims in criminal proceedings. [5] This Decision, based on Title VI of the Treaty on the European Union, allows crime victims to claim compensation from the offender in the course of criminal proceedings.

(6) Crime victims in the European Union should be entitled to fair and appropriate compensation for the injuries they have suffered, regardless of where in the European Community the crime was committed

(7) This Directive sets up a system of cooperation to facilitate access to compensation to victims of crimes in cross-border situations, which should operate on the basis of Member States' schemes on compensation to victims of violent intentional crime, committed in their respective territories. Therefore, a compensation mechanism should be in place in all Member States.

(8) Most Member States have already established such compensation schemes, some of them in fulfilment of their obligations under the European Convention of 24 November 1983 on the compensation of victims of violent crimes.

(9) Since the measures contained in this Directive are necessary in order to attain objectives of the Community and the Treaty provides for no powers other than those in Article 308 thereof for the adoption of this Directive, that Article should be applied.

(10) Crime victims will often not be able to obtain compensation from the offender, since the offender may lack the necessary means to satisfy a judgment on damages or because the offender cannot be identified or prosecuted.

(11) A system of cooperation between the authorities of the Member States should be introduced to facilitate access to compensation in cases where the crime was committed in a Member State other than that of the victim's residence.

(12) This system should ensure that crime victims could always turn to an authority in their Member State of residence and should ease any practical and linguistic difficulties that occur in a cross-border situation.

(13) The system should include the provisions necessary for allowing the crime victim to find the information needed to make the application and for allowing for efficient cooperation between the authorities involved.

(14) This Directive respects the fundamental rights and observes the principles reaffirmed in particular by the Charter of Fundamental Rights of the European Union as general principles of Community law.

[1] OJ C 45 E, 25.2.2003, p. 69.
[2] Opinion delivered on 23 October 2003 (not yet published in the Official Journal).
[3] OJ C 95, 23.4.2003, p. 40.
[4] Case 186/87, European Court reports 1989, p. 195.
[5] OJ L 82, 22.3.2001, p. 1.

(15) Since the objective of facilitating access to compensation to victims of crimes of cross-border situations cannot be sufficiently achieved by the Member States because of the cross-border elements and can therefore, by reason of the scale or effects of the action, be better achieved at Community level, the Community may adopt measures, in accordance with the principle of subsidiarity as set out in Article 5 of the Treaty. In accordance with the principle of proportionality, as set out in that Article, this Directive does not go beyond what is necessary in order to achieve that objective.

(16) The measures necessary for the implementation of the Directive should be adopted in accordance with Council Decision 1999/468/EC of 28 June 1999 laying down the procedures for the exercise of implementing powers conferred on the Commission [1],

HAS ADOPTED THIS DIRECTIVE:

CHAPTER I

## ACCESS TO COMPENSATION IN CROSS-BORDER SITUATIONS

*Article 1*

### Right to submit an application in the Member State of residence

Member States shall ensure that where a violent intentional crime has been committed in a Member State other than the Member State where the applicant for compensation is habitually resident, the applicant shall have the right to submit the application to an authority or any other body in the latter Member State.

*Article 2*

### Responsibility for paying compensation

Compensation shall be paid by the competent authority of the Member State on whose territory the crime was committed.

*Article 3*

### Responsible authorities and administrative procedures

1. Member States shall establish or designate one or several authorities or any other bodies, hereinafter referred to as 'assisting authority or authorities', to be responsible for applying Article 1.

2. Member States shall establish or designate one or several authorities or any other bodies to be responsible for deciding upon applications for compensation, hereinafter referred to as 'deciding authority or authorities'.

3. Member States shall endeavour to keep to a minimum the administrative formalities required of an applicant for compensation.

*Article 4*

### Information to potential applicants

Member States shall ensure that potential applicants for compensation have access to essential information on the possibilities to apply for compensation, by any means Member States deem appropriate.

*Article 5*

### Assistance to the applicant

1. The assisting authority shall provide the applicant with the information referred to in Article 4 and the required application forms, on the basis of the manual drawn up in accordance with Article 13(2).

2. The assisting authority shall, upon the request of the applicant, provide him or her with general guidance and information on how the application should be completed and what supporting documentation may be required.

3. The assisting authority shall not make any assessment of the application.

*Article 6*

### Transmission of applications

1. The assisting authority shall transmit the application and any supporting documentation as quickly as possible to the deciding authority.

2. The assisting authority shall transmit the application using the standard form referred to in Article 14.

3. The language of the application and any supporting documentation shall be determined in accordance with Article 11(1).

*Article 7*

### Receipt of applications

Upon receipt of an application transmitted in accordance with Article 6, the deciding authority shall send the following information as soon as possible to the assisting authority and to the applicant:

(a) the contact person or the department responsible for handling the matter;

(b) an acknowledgement of receipt of the application;

(c) if possible, an indication of the approximate time by which a decision on the application will be made.

[1] OJ L 184, 17.7.1999, p. 23.

*Article 8*

**Requests for supplementary information**

The assisting authority shall if necessary provide general guidance to the applicant in meeting any request for supplementary information from the deciding authority.

It shall upon the request of the applicant subsequently transmit it as soon as possible directly to the deciding authority, enclosing, where appropriate, a list of any supporting documentation transmitted.

*Article 9*

**Hearing of the applicant**

1. If the deciding authority decides, in accordance with the law of its Member State, to hear the applicant or any other person such as a witness or an expert, it may contact the assisting authority for the purpose of arranging for:

(a) the person(s) to be heard directly by the deciding authority, in accordance with the law of its Member State, through the use in particular of telephone- or video-conferencing; or

(b) the person(s) to be heard by the assisting authority, in accordance with the law of its Member State, which will subsequently transmit a report of the hearing to the deciding authority.

2. The direct hearing in accordance with paragraph 1(a) may only take place in cooperation with the assisting authority and on a voluntary basis without the possibility of coercive measures being imposed by the deciding authority.

*Article 10*

**Communication of the decision**

The deciding authority shall send the decision on the application for compensation, by using the standard form referred to in Article 14, to the applicant and to the assisting authority, as soon as possible, in accordance with national law, after the decision has been taken.

*Article 11*

**Other provisions**

1. Information transmitted between the authorities pursuant to Articles 6 to 10 shall be expressed in:

(a) the official languages or one of the languages of the Member State of the authority to which the information is sent, which corresponds to one of the languages of the Community institutions; or

(b) another language of the Community institutions that that Member State has indicated it can accept;

with the exception of:

(i) the full text of decisions taken by the deciding authority, where the use of languages shall be governed by the law of its Member State;

(ii) reports drawn up following a hearing in accordance with Article 9(1)(b), where the use of languages shall be determined by the assisting authority, subject to the requirement that it corresponds to one of the languages of the Community institutions.

2. Services rendered by the assisting authority in accordance with Articles 1 to 10 shall not give rise to a claim for any reimbursement of charges or costs from the applicant or from the deciding authority.

3. Application forms and any other documentation transmitted in accordance with Articles 6 to 10 shall be exempted from authentication or any equivalent formality.

CHAPTER II

**NATIONAL SCHEMES ON COMPENSATION**

*Article 12*

1. The rules on access to compensation in cross-border situations drawn up by this Directive shall operate on the basis of Member States' schemes on compensation to victims of violent intentional crime committed in their respective territories.

2. All Member States shall ensure that their national rules provide for the existence of a scheme on compensation to victims of violent intentional crimes committed in their respective territories, which guarantees fair and appropriate compensation to victims.

CHAPTER III

**IMPLEMENTING PROVISIONS**

*Article 13*

**Information to be sent to the Commission and the manual**

1. Member States shall, no later than 1 July 2005, send to the Commission details of:

(a) the list of authorities established or designated in accordance with Articles 3(1) and 3(2), including, where appropriate, information on the special and territorial jurisdiction of these authorities;

(b) the language(s) referred to in Article 11(1)(a) which the authorities can accept for the purpose of applying Articles 6 to 10 and the official language or languages other than its own which is or are acceptable to it for the transmission of applications in accordance with Article 11(1)(b).

(c) the information established in accordance with Article 4;

(d) the application forms for compensation;

Member States shall inform the Commission of any subsequent changes to this information.

2. The Commission shall, in cooperation with the Member States establish and publish on the internet a manual containing the information provided by the Member States pursuant to paragraph 1. The Commission shall be responsible for arranging the necessary translations of the manual.

*Article 14*

**Standard form for transmission of applications and decisions**

Standard forms shall be established, at the latest by 31 October 2005, for the transmission of applications and decisions in accordance with the procedure referred to in Article 15(2).

*Article 15*

**Committee**

1. The Commission shall be assisted by a Committee.

2. Where reference is made to this paragraph, Articles 3 and 7 of Decision 1999/468/EC shall apply.

3. The Committee shall adopt its Rules of Procedure.

*Article 16*

**Central contact points**

Member States shall appoint a central contact point for the purposes of:

(a) assisting with the implementation of Article 13(2);

(b) furthering close cooperation and exchange of information between the assisting and deciding authorities in the Member States; and

(c) giving assistance and seeking solutions to any difficulties that may occur in the application of Articles 1 to 10.

The contact points shall meet regularly.

*Article 17*

**More favourable provisions**

This Directive shall not prevent Member States, in so far as such provisions are compatible with this Directive, from:

(a) introducing or maintaining more favourable provisions for the benefit of victims of crime or any other persons affected by crime;

(b) introducing or retaining provisions for the purpose of compensating victims of crime committed outside their territory, or any other person affected by such a crime, subject to any conditions that Member States may specify for that purpose.

*Article 18*

**Implementation**

1. Member States shall bring into force the laws, regulations and administrative provisions necessary to comply with this Directive by 1 January 2006 at the latest, with the exception of Article 12(2), in which case the date of compliance shall be 1 July 2005. They shall forthwith inform the Commission thereof.

2. Member States may provide that the measures necessary to comply with this Directive shall apply only to applicants whose injuries result from crimes committed after 30 June 2005.

3. When Member States adopt these measures, they shall contain a reference to this Directive or be accompanied by such a reference on the occasion of their official publication. The methods of making such reference shall be laid down by the Member States.

4. Member States shall communicate to the Commission the text of the main provisions of domestic law, which they adopt in the field governed by this Directive.

*Article 19*

**Review**

No later than by 1 January 2009, the Commission shall present to the European Parliament, the Council and the European Economic and Social Committee a report on the application of this Directive.

*Article 20*

**Entry into force**

This Directive shall enter into force on the twentieth day following that of its publication in the *Official Journal of the European Union*.

*Article 21*

**Addressees**

This Directive is addressed to the Member States.

Done at Luxembourg, 29 April 2004.

*For the Council*

*The President*

M. McDOWELL

# Framework Decision 2004/757 laying down minimum provisions on the constituent elements of criminal acts and penalties in the field of illicit drug trafficking, 25 October 2004

[OJ 2004, L 335/8–11]

L 335/8 EN Official Journal of the European Union 11.11.2004

*(Acts adopted under Title VI of the Treaty on European Union)*

## COUNCIL FRAMEWORK DECISION 2004/757/JHA

### of 25 october 2004

### laying down minimum provisions on the constituent elements of criminal acts and penalties in the field of illicit drug trafficking

THE COUNCIL OF THE EUROPEAN UNION,

Having regard to the Treaty on European Union, and in particular Article 31(e) and Article 34(2)(b) thereof,

Having regard to the proposal from the Commission [1],

Having regard to the opinion of the European Parliament [2],

Whereas:

(1) Illicit drug trafficking poses a threat to health, safety and the quality of life of citizens of the European Union, and to the legal economy, stability and security of the Member States.

(2) The need for legislative action to tackle illicit drug trafficking has been recognised in particular in the Action Plan of the Council and the Commission on how best to implement the provisions of the Amsterdam Treaty on an area of freedom, security and justice [3], adopted by the Justice and Home Affairs Council in Vienna on 3 December 1998, the conclusions of the Tampere European Council of 15 and 16 October 1999, in particular point 48 thereof, the European Union's Drugs Strategy (2000-2004) endorsed by the Helsinki European Council from 10 to 12 December 1999 and the European Union's Action Plan on Drugs (2000-2004) endorsed by the European Council in Santa Maria da Feira on 19 and 20 June 2000.

(3) It is necessary to adopt minimum rules relating to the constituent elements of the offences of illicit trafficking in drugs and precursors which will allow a common approach at European Union level to the fight against such trafficking.

(4) By virtue of the principle of subsidiarity, European Union action should focus on the most serious types of drug offence. The exclusion of certain types of behaviour as regards personal consumption from the scope of this Framework Decision does not constitute a Council guideline on how Member States should deal with these other cases in their national legislation.

(5) Penalties provided for by the Member States should be effective, proportionate and dissuasive, and include custodial sentences. To determine the level of penalties, factual elements such as the quantities and the type of drugs trafficked, and whether the offence was committed within the framework of a criminal organisation, should be taken into account.

(6) Member States should be allowed to make provision for reducing the penalties when the offender has supplied the competent authorities with valuable information.

(7) It is necessary to take measures to enable the confiscation of the proceeds of the offences referred to in this Framework Decision.

(8) Measures should be taken to ensure that legal persons can be held liable for the criminal offences referred to by this Framework Decision which are committed for their benefit.

(9) The effectiveness of the efforts made to tackle illicit drug trafficking depends essentially on the harmonisation of the national measures implementing this Framework Decision,

[1] OJ C 304 E, 30.10.2001, p. 172.
[2] Opinion of 9 March 2004 (not yet published in the Official Journal).
[3] OJ C 19, 23.1.1999, p. 1.

11.11.2004 EN Official Journal of the European Union L 335/9

HAS DECIDED AS FOLLOWS:

*Article 1*

**Definitions**

For the purposes of this Framework Decision:

1. 'drugs': shall mean any of the substances covered by the following United Nations Conventions:

   (a) the 1961 Single Convention on Narcotic Drugs (as amended by the 1972 Protocol);

   (b) the 1971 Vienna Convention on Psychotropic Substances. It shall also include the substances subject to controls under Joint Action 97/396/JHA of 16 June 1997 concerning the information exchange risk assessment and the control of new synthetic drugs [1];

2. 'precursors': shall mean any substance scheduled in the Community legislation giving effect to the obligations deriving from Article 12 of the United Nations Convention against Illicit Traffic in Narcotic Drugs and Psychotropic Substances of 20 December 1988;

3. 'legal person': shall mean any legal entity having such status under the applicable national law, except for States or other public bodies acting in the exercise of their sovereign rights and for public international organisations.

*Article 2*

**Crimes linked to trafficking in drugs and precursors**

1. Each Member State shall take the necessary measures to ensure that the following intentional conduct when committed without right is punishable:

(a) the production, manufacture, extraction, preparation, offering, offering for sale, distribution, sale, delivery on any terms whatsoever, brokerage, dispatch, dispatch in transit, transport, importation or exportation of drugs;

(b) the cultivation of opium poppy, coca bush or cannabis plant;

(c) the possession or purchase of drugs with a view to conducting one of the activities listed in (a);

(d) the manufacture, transport or distribution of precursors, knowing that they are to be used in or for the illicit production or manufacture of drugs.

2. The conduct described in paragraph 1 shall not be included in the scope of this Framework Decision when it is committed by its perpetrators exclusively for their own personal consumption as defined by national law.

*Article 3*

**Incitement, aiding and abetting and attempt**

1. Each Member State shall take the necessary measures to make incitement to commit, aiding and abetting or attempting one of the offences referred to in Article 2 a criminal offence.

2. A Member State may exempt from criminal liability the attempt to offer or prepare drugs referred to in Article 2(1)(a) and the attempt to possess drugs referred to in Article 2(1)(c).

*Article 4*

**Penalties**

1. Each Member State shall take the measures necessary to ensure that the offences defined in Articles 2 and 3 are punishable by effective, proportionate and dissuasive criminal penalties.

Each Member State shall take the necessary measures to ensure that the offences referred to in Article 2 are punishable by criminal penalties of a maximum of at least between one and three years of imprisonment.

2. Each Member State shall take the necessary measures to ensure that the offences referred to in Article 2(1)(a), (b) and (c) are punishable by criminal penalties of a maximum of at least between 5 and 10 years of imprisonment in each of the following circumstances:

(a) the offence involves large quantities of drugs;

(b) the offence either involves those drugs which cause the most harm to health, or has resulted in significant damage to the health of a number of persons.

[1] OJ L 167, 25.6.1997, p. 1.

3. Each Member State shall take the necessary measures to ensure that the offences referred to in paragraph 2 are punishable by criminal penalties of a maximum of at least 10 years of deprivation of liberty, where the offence was committed within the framework of a criminal organisation as defined in Joint Action 98/733/JHA of 21 December 1998 on making it a criminal offence to participate in a criminal organisation in the Member States of the European Union ([1]).

4. Each Member State shall take the necessary measures to ensure that the offences referred to in Article 2(1)(d) are punishable by criminal penalties of a maximum of at least between 5 and 10 years of deprivation of liberty, where the offence was committed within the framework of a criminal organisation as defined in Joint Action 98/733/JHA and the precursors are intended to be used in or for the production or manufacture of drugs under the circumstances referred to in paragraphs 2(a) or (b).

5. Without prejudice to the rights of victims and of other bona fide third parties, each Member State shall take the necessary measures to enable the confiscation of substances which are the object of offences referred to in Articles 2 and 3, instrumentalities used or intended to be used for these offences and proceeds from these offences or the confiscation of property the value of which corresponds to that of such proceeds, substances or instrumentalities.

The terms 'confiscation', 'instrumentalities', 'proceeds' and 'property' shall have the same meaning as in Article 1 of the 1990 Council of Europe Convention on Laundering, Search, Seizure and Confiscation of the Proceeds from Crime.

*Article 5*

**Particular circumstances**

Notwithstanding Article 4, each Member State may take the necessary measures to ensure that the penalties referred to in Article 4 may be reduced if the offender:

(a) renounces criminal activity relating to trafficking in drugs and precursors, and

(b) provides the administrative or judicial authorities with information which they would not otherwise have been able to obtain, helping them to:

(i) prevent or mitigate the effects of the offence,

(ii) identify or bring to justice the other offenders,

(iii) find evidence, or

(iv) prevent further offences referred to in Articles 2 and 3.

*Article 6*

**Liability of legal persons**

1. Each Member State shall take the necessary measures to ensure that legal persons can be held liable for any of the criminal offences referred to in Articles 2 and 3 committed for their benefit by any person, acting either individually or as a member of an organ of the legal person in question, who has a leading position within the legal person, based on one of the following:

(a) a power of representation of the legal person;

(b) an authority to take decisions on behalf of the legal person;

(c) an authority to exercise control within the legal person.

2. Apart from the cases provided for in paragraph 1, each Member State shall take the necessary measures to ensure that legal persons can be held liable where the lack of supervision or control by a person referred to in paragraph 1 has made possible the commission of any of the offences referred to in Articles 2 and 3 for the benefit of that legal person by a person under its authority.

3. Liability of legal persons under paragraphs 1 and 2 shall not exclude criminal proceedings against natural persons who are perpetrators, instigators or accessories in any of the offences referred to in Articles 2 and 3.

*Article 7*

**Sanctions for legal persons**

1. Member States shall take the necessary measures to ensure that a legal person held liable pursuant to Article 6(1) is punishable by effective, proportionate and dissuasive sanctions, which shall include criminal or non-criminal fines and may include other sanctions, such as:

(a) exclusion from entitlement to tax relief or other benefits or public aid;

(b) temporary or permanent disqualification from the pursuit of commercial activities;

(c) placing under judicial supervision;

([1]) OJ L 351, 29.12.1998, p. 1.

(d) a judicial winding-up order;

(e) temporary or permanent closure of establishments used for committing the offence;

(f) in accordance with Article 4(5), the confiscation of substances which are the object of offences referred to in Articles 2 and 3, instrumentalities used or intended to be used for these offences and proceeds from these offences or the confiscation of property the value of which corresponds to that of such proceeds, substances or instrumentalities.

2. Each Member State shall take the necessary measures to ensure that a legal person held liable pursuant to Article 6(2) is punishable by effective, proportionate and dissuasive sanctions or measures.

*Article 8*

**Jurisdiction and prosecution**

1. Each Member State shall take the necessary measures to establish its jurisdiction over the offences referred to in Articles 2 and 3 where:

(a) the offence is committed in whole or in part within its territory;

(b) the offender is one of its nationals; or

(c) the offence is committed for the benefit of a legal person established in the territory of that Member State.

2. A Member State may decide that it will not apply, or that it will apply only in specific cases or circumstances, the jurisdiction rules set out in paragraphs 1(b) and 1(c) where the offence is committed outside its territory.

3. A Member State which, under its laws, does not extradite its own nationals shall take the necessary measures to establish its jurisdiction over and to prosecute, where appropriate, an offence referred to in Articles 2 and 3 when it is committed by one of its own nationals outside its territory.

4. Member States shall inform the General Secretariat of the Council and the Commission when they decide to apply paragraph 2, where appropriate with an indication of the specific cases or circumstances in which the decision applies.

*Article 9*

**Implementation and reports**

1. Member States shall take the necessary measures to comply with the provisions of this Framework Decision by 12 May 2006.

2. By the deadline referred to in paragraph 1, Member States shall transmit to the General Secretariat of the Council and to the Commission the text of the provisions transposing into their national law the obligations imposed on them under this Framework Decision. The Commission shall, by 12 May 2009, submit a report to the European Parliament and to the Council on the functioning of the implementation of the Framework Decision, including its effects on judicial cooperation in the field of illicit drug trafficking. Following this report, the Council shall assess, at the latest within six months after submission of the report, whether Member States have taken the necessary measures to comply with this Framework Decision.

*Article 10*

**Territorial application**

This Framework Decision shall apply to Gibraltar.

*Article 11*

**Entry into force**

This Framework Decision shall enter into force on the day following its publication in the *Official Journal of the European Union*.

Done at Luxembourg, 25 October 2004.

*For the Council*

*The President*

R. VERDONK

# Cooperation agreement between the European Community and its Member States, of the one part, and the Swiss Confederation, of the other part, to combat fraud and any other illegal activity to the detriment of their financial interests, 26 October 2004

**[OJ 2009, L 46/8–18, 26, 34–35]**

**[Editor's note: signatures omitted]**

L 46/8 EN Official Journal of the European Union 17.2.2009

**COOPERATION AGREEMENT**

**between the European Community and its Member States, of the one part, and the Swiss Confederation, of the other part, to combat fraud and any other illegal activity to the detriment of their financial interests**

THE EUROPEAN COMMUNITY,

THE KINGDOM OF BELGIUM,

THE CZECH REPUBLIC,

THE KINGDOM OF DENMARK,

THE FEDERAL REPUBLIC OF GERMANY,

THE REPUBLIC OF ESTONIA,

THE HELLENIC REPUBLIC,

THE KINGDOM OF SPAIN,

THE FRENCH REPUBLIC,

IRELAND,

THE ITALIAN REPUBLIC,

THE REPUBLIC OF CYPRUS,

THE REPUBLIC OF LATVIA,

THE REPUBLIC OF LITHUANIA,

THE GRAND DUCHY OF LUXEMBOURG,

THE REPUBLIC OF HUNGARY,

THE REPUBLIC OF MALTA,

THE KINGDOM OF THE NETHERLANDS,

THE REPUBLIC OF AUSTRIA,

THE REPUBLIC OF POLAND,

THE PORTUGUESE REPUBLIC,

THE REPUBLIC OF SLOVENIA,

THE SLOVAK REPUBLIC,

THE REPUBLIC OF FINLAND,

THE KINGDOM OF SWEDEN,

THE UNITED KINGDOM OF GREAT BRITAIN AND NORTHERN IRELAND,

of the one part, and

THE SWISS CONFEDERATION,

of the other part,

hereinafter referred to as the 'Contracting Parties',

CONSIDERING the close relations between the European Community and its Member States, of the one part, and the Swiss Confederation, of the other part,

DESIRING to be effective in combating fraud and any other illegal activity to the detriment of the Contracting Parties' financial interests,

TAKING ACCOUNT of the need to step up administrative assistance in these areas,

CONVINCED that mutual legal assistance, extending to searches and seizures, must be afforded, including in all cases of smuggling and evasion in the field of indirect taxation, in particular value added tax and customs and excise duties,

RECOGNISING the importance of combating money laundering,

HAVE DECIDED TO CONCLUDE THIS AGREEMENT:

TITLE I

**GENERAL PROVISIONS**

*Article 1*

**Objective**

The objective of this Agreement is to extend administrative and mutual legal assistance in criminal matters between the European Community and its Member States, of the one part, and the Swiss Confederation, of the other part, so as to combat the illegal activities to which Article 2 applies.

*Article 2*

**Scope**

1. This Agreement is applicable to:

(a) the administrative and criminal prevention, detection, investigation, prosecution and repression of fraud and any other illegal activity to the detriment of the Contracting Parties' respective financial interests concerning:

— trade in goods contrary to customs and agricultural legislation,

— trade contrary to tax legislation applicable to value added tax, special taxes on consumption and excise duties,

— the charging or retention of funds — including their use for purposes other than those for which they were initially granted — from the budget of the Contracting Parties or budgets managed by them or on their behalf, such as grants and refunds,

— procedures for the award of contracts by the Contracting Parties,

(b) the seizure and recovery of amounts due or wrongly received as a result of the illegal activities referred to in point (a).

2. Cooperation within the meaning of Titles II (Administrative assistance) and III (Mutual legal assistance) may not be withheld on the sole ground that the request relates to an offence treated as a tax offence in the requested Contracting Party or that the legislation of the requested Contracting Party does not provide for the same type of levy or expenditure or does not contain the same type of rules or the same legal characterisation of the facts as the legislation of the requesting Contracting Party.

3. The scope of this Agreement includes the laundering of the proceeds of the activities covered by the Agreement provided that the activities which constitute the precursor offence are punishable under the law of the two Contracting Parties by a penalty involving deprivation of liberty or a detention order of a maximum period of more than six months.

4. Direct taxes are excluded from the scope of this Agreement.

*Article 3*

**Minor cases**

1. The authority of the requested Contracting Party may refuse a request for cooperation where the alleged amount of duty underpaid or evaded does not exceed EUR 25 000 or where the presumed value of the goods exported or imported without authorisation does not exceed EUR 100 000, unless, given the circumstances or identity of the suspect, the case is deemed to be extremely serious by the requesting Contracting Party.

2. The authority of the requested Contracting Party shall inform the authority of the requesting Contracting Party without delay of its reasons for refusing the request for cooperation.

*Article 4*

**Ordre public**

Cooperation may be refused if the requested Contracting Party considers that execution of the request is likely to prejudice the sovereignty, security, *ordre public* or other essential interests of the requested Contracting Party.

*Article 5*

**Transmission of information and evidence**

1. Information and evidence transmitted or received under this Agreement, whatever its form, shall be subject to professional confidentiality and shall enjoy the protection enjoyed by comparable information conferred by the domestic law of the Contracting Party receiving it and by the corresponding provisions applicable to the Community institutions.

In particular, such information and evidence may not be divulged to persons other than those who, in the Community institutions, the Member States or the Swiss Confederation, are required by their functions to be acquainted with it, nor used by them for purposes that are not within the scope of this Agreement.

2. The information and evidence obtained by the requesting Contracting Party under this Agreement may be transmitted to any Contracting Party if this Contracting Party is conducting an investigation in respect of which cooperation is not excluded or if there are clear indications that this Contracting Party could usefully conduct such an investigation. No such transmission may serve any purpose other than those of this Agreement.

3. The transmission of information and evidence obtained pursuant to this Agreement by a Contracting Party to another Contracting Party or to more than one Contracting Party may not be open to appeal in the Contracting Party initially requested.

4. Any Contracting Party to which information or evidence is transmitted in conformity with paragraph 2 shall respect such limits as are put by the requested Contracting Party on the use of the information by the requesting Contracting Party of the first transmission.

5. The transmission of information and evidence obtained under this Agreement by a Contracting Party to a third State shall be subject to authorisation from the Contracting Party from which the information or evidence originated.

*Article 6*

**Confidentiality**

The requesting Contracting Party may ask the requested Contracting Party to ensure that the request and the content thereof remain confidential, except in so far as this is incompatible with the execution of the request. If the requested Contracting Party cannot comply with confidentiality requirements, it shall inform the authority of the requesting Contracting Party in advance.

TITLE II

**ADMINISTRATIVE ASSISTANCE**

CHAPTER 1

***General provisions***

*Article 7*

**Relationship with other agreements**

This Title shall not affect the provisions applicable to mutual legal assistance in criminal matters or more extensive obligations in the field of administrative assistance or more favourable provisions of bilateral or multilateral cooperation arrangements between the Contracting Parties, in particular the Additional Protocol on mutual administrative assistance in customs matters of 9 June 1997.

*Article 8*

**Scope**

1. The Contracting Parties shall provide each other with mutual assistance to combat illegal activities to which this Agreement applies, in particular in preventing and detecting operations and other acts of commission and omission contrary to the relevant legislation and in conducting investigations relating thereto.

2. The assistance provided for by this Title shall apply to all competent administrative authorities in the Contracting Parties acting in the exercise of administrative investigation powers or criminal prosecution powers, including cases where these authorities exercise powers at the request of the judicial authorities.

Where a criminal investigation is carried out by or under the direction of a judicial authority, that authority shall determine whether requests for mutual assistance or cooperation in that connection shall be submitted on the basis of the provisions applicable concerning mutual legal assistance in criminal matters or on the basis of this Title.

*Article 9*

**Powers**

1. The authorities of the Contracting Parties shall apply this Title with the limits of the powers conferred upon them under national provisions. Nothing in this Title may be construed as affecting the powers conferred under national provisions upon the authorities of the Contracting Parties within the meaning of this Title.

They shall proceed as though they were acting on their own account or at the request of another authority of the same Contracting Party. In so doing they shall avail themselves of all the legal powers at their disposal within the framework of their national law to respond to the request.

2. Requests addressed to non-competent authorities shall be forwarded without delay to the competent authority.

*Article 10*

**Proportionality**

The authority of the requested Contracting Party may refuse a request for cooperation where it is clear that:

(a) the number and the nature of the requests for information made by the requesting Contracting Party within a specific period impose a disproportionate administrative burden on that requested authority;

(b) the authority of the requesting Contracting Party has not exhausted the usual sources of information which it could have used in the circumstances to obtain the information requested without running the risk of jeopardising the achievement of the desired end.

*Article 11*

**Central units**

1. Each Contracting Party shall designate one or more central unit empowered to process requests for administrative assistance under this Title.

These units shall call on all competent administrative authorities for the execution of the assistance requested.

2. The central units shall communicate directly with each other.

3. The activities of the central units shall not exclude, especially in an emergency, direct cooperation between the other authorities in the Contracting Parties having power to act in matters to which this Agreement applies. The central units shall be informed of any action involving such direct cooperation.

4. The Contracting Parties, when making the notification provided for by Article 44(2), shall announce which are the authorities regarded as the central units for the purposes of this Article.

*CHAPTER 2*

***Assistance on request***

*Article 12*

**Requests for information**

1. At the request of the authority of the requesting Contracting Party, the authority of the requested Contracting Party shall communicate to it, within the limits of the scope of this Agreement, all information which may enable it or other authorities of the same Contracting Party to prevent, detect and prosecute the illegal activities to which the Agreement applies or needed to recover a claim. The authority of the requested Contracting Party shall undertake all requisite administrative inquiries needed to gather such information.

2. The information communicated is to be accompanied by reports and other documents, or certified copies of or extracts of the same, on which the information notified is based and which are in the possession of the authorities of the requested Contracting Party or which were produced or obtained in order to execute the request for information.

3. By agreement between the authority of the requesting Contracting Party and the authority of the requested Contracting Party, officers authorised by the authority of the requesting Contracting Party may, subject to detailed instructions from the authority of the requested Party, have access in the offices of the authorities of the requested Contracting Party to documents and information pursuant to paragraph 1 held by the authorities of the requested Contracting Party which refer to specific illegal activities falling within the scope of this Agreement. Those officers shall be authorised to take copies of the said documentation.

*Article 13*

**Requests for surveillance**

At the request of the authority of the requesting Contracting Party, the authority of the requested Contracting Party shall as far as possible exercise surveillance over trade in goods in breach of the legislation referred to in Article 2. Such surveillance may relate to a person suspected on reasonable grounds of having participated or of participating in the commission of such illegal activities or having carried out preparatory acts with a view to the commission of such illegal activities, as well as to the premises, means of transport and goods connected with such activities.

*Article 14*

**Notification and transmission by post**

1. At the request of the authority of the requesting Contracting Party, the authority of the requested Contracting Party shall, in accordance with the national rules of the requested Contracting Party, notify the addressee or have it notified, of all instruments or decisions emanating from the competent authorities of the requesting Contracting Party which are within the scope of this Agreement.

2. Requests for notification, mentioning the subject of the instrument or decision to be notified, shall be accompanied by a translation in an official language of the requested Contracting Party or in a language acceptable to that Contracting Party.

3. The Contracting Parties may post acts of notification and requests for information and documents direct to the operators concerned by the third and fourth indents of Article 2(1)(a) residing in the other Contracting Party's territory.

Such persons may respond thereto and provide the relevant documents and information in the form provided for by the rules and arrangements under which the funds were granted.

*Article 15*

**Requests for enquiries**

1. The requested Contracting Party shall at the request of the requesting Contracting Party carry out or arrange to have carried out appropriate enquiries concerning operations or forms of conduct that constitute illegal activities to which this Agreement applies or which prompt the authority of the requesting Contracting Party to suspect on reasonable grounds that such illegal activities have been committed.

2. The requested Contracting Party shall avail themselves of all investigation means at its disposal within the framework of their national law as though it were acting on its own account or at the request of another internal authority, including the involvement or authorisation of the judicial authorities where required.

This provision shall be without prejudice to the duty of economic operators to cooperate under Article 17.

The authority of the requested Contracting Party shall communicate the results of such investigations to the authority of the requesting Contracting Party. Article 12(2) shall apply *mutatis mutandis*.

3. The authority of the requested Contracting Party shall extend assistance to all circumstances, objects and persons apparently linked to the object of the request for assistance, without any need for a supplementary request. In cases of doubt, the authority of the requested Contracting Party shall first contact the authority of the requesting Contracting Party.

*Article 16*

**Presence of authorised staff from the authority of the requesting Contracting Party**

1. By agreement between the authority of the requesting Contracting Party and the authority of the requested Contracting Party, officers appointed by the authority of the requesting Contracting Party may be present at the enquiries referred to in the previous Article. Their presence shall not require the consent of the person or economic operator being investigated.

2. Officers of the authority of the requested Contracting Party shall at all times carry out the enquiries. Officers of the authority of the requesting Contracting Party may not, of their own initiative, exercise the powers conferred on officers of the authority of the requested Contracting Party.

They shall, however, have access to the same premises and the same documents as the latter, through them and for the sole purposes of the enquiry being carried out.

3. Conditions may be attached to the authorisation.

4. The information brought to the knowledge of the authority of the requesting Contracting Party may not be used as evidence until the transmission of the documents relating to execution has been authorised.

*Article 17*

**Duty to cooperate**

Economic operators shall be required to cooperate with the execution of the request for administrative assistance by giving access to their premises, means of transport and documentation and providing all relevant information.

*Article 18*

**Form and content of requests for assistance**

1. Requests for assistance shall be made in writing. Documents necessary for the execution of such requests shall accompany the requests.

In cases of urgency, oral requests shall be accepted, but must be confirmed in writing as soon as possible.

2. Requests shall be accompanied by the following information:

(a) the requesting authority;

(b) the measure requested;

(c) the object and the grounds for the request;

(d) the laws, rules and other legal provisions involved;

(e) indications as exact and comprehensive as possible of the natural or legal persons being the target of the investigations;

(f) a summary of the relevant facts and of the enquiries already carried out, except in cases provided for in Article 14.

3. Requests shall be submitted in an official language of the requested Contracting Party or in a language that is acceptable to that Contracting Party.

4. Incorrect or incomplete requests may be corrected or completed. The measures necessary to comply with the request shall be commenced in the meantime.

*Article 19*

**Use of information**

1. The information obtained shall be used exclusively for the purposes of this Agreement. Where a Contracting Party asks to use such information for other purposes, it shall request the prior written agreement of the supplying authority. Such use shall then be subject to any restrictions laid down by that authority.

2. Paragraph 1 shall not preclude the use of the information in judicial or administrative proceedings for failure to comply with the legislation to which the request for administrative assistance applies if the same forms of assistance were to be available for these proceedings. The competent authority of the Contracting Party which supplied the information shall be advised without delay of such use.

3. The Contracting Parties may, in their records of evidence, reports and testimonies and in proceedings and charges brought before the courts, use as evidence the information obtained and the documents consulted in accordance with this Agreement.

CHAPTER 3

***Spontaneous assistance***

*Article 20*

**Spontaneous assistance**

1. The forms of cooperation established by the foregoing Chapter may be given without the prior request of another Contracting Party.

2. The authority of the Contracting Party transmitting the information may, in accordance with its domestic law, attach conditions to the use of the information by the authority of the recipient Contracting Party.

3. All the authorities of the Contracting Parties shall be bound by such conditions.

CHAPTER 4

***Special forms of cooperation***

*Article 21*

**Joint operations**

1. On imports, exports and transit of goods, where the extent of the trade and the related risk to taxes and subsidies is such that the potential financial loss to the budget of the Contracting Parties is considerable, those Parties may agree to conduct joint cross-border operations for the prevention and prosecution of illegal activities to which this Agreement applies.

2. The coordination and planning of such cross-border operations shall be the responsibility of the central unit or of an office designated by it.

*Article 22*

**Joint special investigation teams**

1. By mutual agreement, the authorities of several Contracting Parties may set up a joint special investigation team based in a Contracting Party.

2. The joint team shall conduct difficult investigations requiring the mobilisation of substantial resources and shall coordinate joint actions.

3. Membership of the team shall not bestow on representatives of the participating Contracting Parties' authorities any powers of intervention in the territory of the Contracting Party in which the investigations are conducted,

*Article 23*

**Liaison officers**

1. The competent authorities of the Contracting Parties may decide on the secondment, for limited or unlimited periods, of liaison officers of a Contracting Party to the competent services of another Contracting Party in order to provide mutual support in the execution of administrative assistance.

2. Liaison officers shall have the task of providing advice and assistance. They shall have no independent power to act in the territory of the host Contracting Party. With the agreement or at the request of the competent authorities of the Contracting Parties, they may:

(a) promote and speed up the exchange of information;

(b) provide assistance in investigations;

(c) provide support in dealing with requests for assistance;

(d) advise and assist the host Contracting Party in preparing and carrying out cross-border operations;

(e) perform any other duties on which the Contracting Parties may agree between themselves.

3. The competent authorities of the Contracting Parties shall settle the details by agreement.

4. Liaison officers may represent the interests of one or more Contracting Parties.

*CHAPTER 5*

***Recovery***

*Article 24*

**Recovery**

1. At the request of the requesting Contracting Party, the requested Contracting Party shall proceed to the recovery of claims to which this Agreement applies as if they were its own claims.

2. The request for recovery of a claim shall be accompanied by an official copy or a certified copy of the document permitting execution, issued by the requesting Contracting Party and, where appropriate, the original or a certified copy of other documents needed for recovery.

3. The requested Contracting Party shall take precautionary measures to ensure recovery of a claim.

4. The authority of the Contracting Party requested shall transfer to the authority of the requesting Contracting Party the amount of the claim that it has recovered. In agreement with the requesting Contracting Party, it may deduct a percentage corresponding to the administrative costs it has incurred.

5. Notwithstanding paragraph 1, claims to be recovered shall not necessarily enjoy the same priority status as comparable claims arising in the requested Contracting Party.

TITLE III

**MUTUAL LEGAL ASSISTANCE**

*Article 25*

**Relationship with other Agreements**

1. The provisions of this Title are intended to supplement the European Convention on Mutual Assistance in Criminal Matters of 20 April 1959, and the Convention on Laundering, Search, Seizure and Confiscation of the Proceeds from Crime of 8 November 1990, and to facilitate their implementation between the Contracting Parties.

2. More favourable provisions of bilateral or multilateral Agreements between the Contracting Parties are not affected.

*Article 26*

**Procedures in which mutual legal assistance shall also be afforded**

1. Mutual legal assistance shall also be afforded:

(a) in proceedings brought by the administrative authorities in respect of acts which are punishable under the national law of one of the two Contracting Parties, or of both, by virtue of being infringements of the rules of law, and where the decision may give rise to proceedings before a court having jurisdiction in particular in criminal matters;

(b) in civil actions joined to criminal proceedings, as long as the criminal court has not yet taken a final decision in the criminal proceedings;

(c) for offences or infringements for which a legal person of the requesting Contracting Party may be liable.

2. Assistance shall also be given for the purposes of investigations and proceedings for the seizure and confiscation of the instruments and products of these illegal activities.

*Article 27*

**Transmission of requests**

1. Requests under this Title shall be presented by the authority of the requesting Contracting Party either via a relevant central authority of the requested Contracting Party, or direct to the Contracting Party's authority which is empowered to execute the requesting Contracting Party's request. The authority of the requesting Contracting Party and, where appropriate, the authority of the Contracting Party requested shall send a copy of the request to its central authority for information.

2. All documents relating to requests or the execution thereof may be sent by the same channels. They, or at least a copy, must be sent directly to the authority of the requesting Contracting Party.

3. If the authority of the Contracting Party receiving a request has no power to authorise assistance, it shall forthwith forward it to the competent authority.

4. Defective or incomplete requests shall be applied if they contain the information needed to satisfy them, without prejudice to subsequent regularisation by the authority of the requesting Contracting Party. The authority of the Contracting Party requested shall inform the authority of the requesting Contracting Party of the defects and allow it time to regularise them.

The authority of the Contracting Party requested shall without delay send the authority of the requesting Contracting Party all other indications that may help it to complete its request or extend it to include other measures.

5. The Contracting Parties, when making the notification provided for by Article 44(2), shall announce which are the competent central authorities for the purposes of this Article.

*Article 28*

**Service by post**

1. As a rule the Contracting Parties shall, in proceedings for illegal activities covered by this Agreement, send procedural documents intended for persons who are in the territory of the other Contracting Party directly by post.

2. If the authority of the Contracting Party that issued the documents knows or has reason to believe that the addressee understands only some other language, the documents, or at least the most important passages thereof, shall be accompanied by a translation into that other language.

3. The authority of the serving Contracting Party shall advise the addressee that no measure of restraint or punishment may be enforced directly by that authority in the territory of the other Contracting Party.

4. All procedural documents shall be accompanied by a report indicating that the addressee may obtain information from the authority identified in the report regarding his or her rights and obligations concerning the documents.

*Article 29*

**Provisional measures**

1. Within the limits of its domestic law and its respective powers and at the request of the authority of the requesting Contracting Party, the competent authority of the requested Contracting Party shall order the necessary provisional measures for the purpose of maintaining an existing situation, protecting endangered legal interests or preserving evidence, if the request for mutual assistance does not appear manifestly inadmissible.

2. Preventive freezing and seizure of instrumentalities and proceeds of offences shall be ordered in cases where assistance is requested. If the proceeds of an offence no longer exist in whole or in part, the same measures shall be ordered in relation to assets located within the territory of the requested Contracting Party corresponding in value to the proceeds in question.

*Article 30*

**Presence of the authorities of the requesting Contracting Party**

1. The requested Contracting Party shall, at the request of the requesting Contracting Party, authorise the representatives of the latter Party's authorities to attend the execution of the request for mutual legal assistance. Their presence shall not require the consent of the person concerned by the measure.

Conditions may be attached to the authorisation.

2. The persons present shall have access to the same premises and the same documents as the representatives of the requested Contracting Party, through them and for the sole purposes of execution of the request for mutual legal assistance. In particular they may be authorised to put or propose questions and suggest measures of investigation.

3. Their presence shall not result in facts being divulged to persons other than those authorised by virtue of the preceding paragraphs in breach of judicial confidentiality or the rights of the person concerned. The information brought to the knowledge of the authority of the requesting Contracting Party may not be used as evidence until the decision on transmission of the documents relating to execution has acquired the force of *res judicata*.

*Article 31*

**Searches and seizures**

1. The Contracting Parties may not make the admissibility of letters rogatory for search or seizure dependent on conditions other than the following:

(a) the act giving rise to the letters rogatory is punishable under the law of both Contracting Parties by a penalty involving deprivation of liberty or a detention order of a maximum period of at least six months, or is punishable under the law of one of the two Contracting Parties by an equivalent penalty and under the law of the other Contracting Party by virtue of being an infringement of the rules of law which is being prosecuted by the administrative authorities, and where the decision may give rise to proceedings before a court having jurisdiction in particular in criminal matters;

(b) execution of the letters rogatory is consistent with the law of the requested Contracting Party.

2. Letters rogatory for purposes of search and seizure for laundering offences within the scope of this Agreement shall also be admissible provided that the activities making up the precursor offence are punishable under the law of the two Contracting Parties by a penalty involving deprivation of liberty or a detention order of a maximum period of more than six months.

*Article 32*

**Requests for banking and financial information**

1. Where the conditions of Article 31 are met, the requested Contracting Party shall execute requests for assistance in obtaining and transmitting banking and financial information, including:

(a) the identification of, and information concerning, bank accounts opened at banks established in its territory and where persons under investigation are the account holders, authorised signatories or in effective control;

(b) the identification of, and all information concerning, banking transactions and operations conducted from, to or via one or more bank accounts or by specified persons during a specified period.

2. To the extent authorised by virtue of its law governing criminal proceedings for similar domestic cases, the requested Contracting Party may order surveillance of banking operations conducted from, to or via one or more bank accounts or by specified persons during a specified period, and transmission of the results to the requesting Contracting Party. The decision to monitor transactions and transmit the results shall be taken in each individual case by the competent authorities of the requested Contracting Party and shall comply with that Contracting Party's national law. The practical details regarding the monitoring shall be determined by agreement between the competent authorities of the requesting and requested Contracting Parties.

3. Each Contracting Party shall take the necessary measures to ensure the financial institutions do not disclose to the customer concerned or to other third persons that measures are being executed at the request of the requesting Contracting Party or that an investigation is under way, for such time as is necessary to avoid compromising the results.

4. The authority of the Contracting Party issuing the request shall:

(a) state why it considers that the requested information is likely to be of substantial value for the purpose of the investigation into the offence;

(b) state on what grounds it presumes that banks in the requested Contracting Party hold the account and, to the extent available, which banks may be involved;

(c) include all information available which may facilitate the execution of the request.

5. A Contracting Party shall not invoke banking secrecy as grounds for rejecting all cooperation on a request for mutual assistance from another Contracting Party.

*Article 33*

**Controlled deliveries**

1. The competent authority in the requested Contracting Party shall undertake to ensure that, at the request of the authority of the requesting Contracting Party, controlled deliveries may be permitted in its territory within the framework of criminal investigations into extraditable offences.

2. The decision to carry out controlled deliveries shall be taken in each individual case by the competent authorities of the requested Contracting Party, with due regard for its national law.

3. Controlled deliveries shall take place in accordance with the procedures provided for in the law of the requested Contracting Party. The right to act and to direct and control operations shall lie with the competent authorities of that Contracting Party.

*Article 34*

**Handing-over for confiscation or return**

1. At the request of the requesting Contracting Party, all objects, documents, funds or other items of value that have been seized on a precautionary basis may be handed over for confiscation or for return to the rightful owner.

2. The requested Contracting Party may not refuse to return funds on the sole ground that they correspond to a tax or customs debt.

3. Rights asserted by a third party in good faith shall remain reserved.

*Article 35*

**Speeding up assistance**

1. The authority of the requested Contracting Party shall execute the request for mutual legal assistance as soon as possible, taking as full account as possible of the procedural deadlines and other deadlines indicated by the authority of the requesting Contracting Party. The requesting Contracting Party shall explain the reasons for the deadline.

2. If the request cannot, or cannot fully, be executed in accordance with the requirements set by the authority of the requesting Contracting Party, the authority of the requested Contracting Party shall promptly inform the authority of the requesting Contracting Party and indicate the conditions under which it might be possible to execute the request. The authorities of the requesting and the requested Contracting Parties may subsequently agree on further action to be taken concerning the request, where necessary by making such action subject to the fulfilment of those conditions.

If it is foreseeable that the deadline set by the authority of the requesting Contracting Party for executing its request cannot be met and if the reasons referred to in the second sentence of paragraph 1, indicate explicitly that any delay will lead to substantial impairment of the proceedings being conducted by that authority, the authority of the requested Contracting Party shall promptly indicate the estimated time needed for execution of the request. The authority of the requesting Contracting Party shall promptly indicate whether the request is to be upheld nonetheless. The authorities of the requesting and requested Contracting Parties may subsequently agree on further action to be taken concerning the request.

*Article 36*

**Use of information and evidence**

Information and evidence transmitted in the course of the assistance procedure may be used for the following purposes in addition to the purposes of the assistance procedure for which it was supplied:

(a) in criminal proceedings in the requesting Contracting Party against other persons who participated in the commission of the offence for which assistance was given;

(b) where the infringements on which the request is based constitute another offence for which assistance ought also to be given;

(c) in proceedings for the confiscation of the instrumentalities and proceeds of offences for which assistance ought to be given and in proceedings for damages in respect of infringements for which assistance had been given.

*Article 37*

**Spontaneous transmission**

1. Within the limits of their national law and their powers, the judicial authorities of a Contracting Party may spontaneously transmit information or evidence to the judicial authorities of another Contracting Party, when they consider that such information or evidence might assist the receiving Contracting Party's authority in initiating or carrying out investigations or proceedings, or might lead to a request for mutual legal assistance by the receiving authority.

2. The authority of the Contracting Party transmitting the information may, pursuant to its national law, impose conditions on the use of such information by the authority of the receiving Contracting Party.

3. All the authorities of the Contracting Parties shall be bound by such conditions.

*Article 38*

**Procedures in the requested Contracting Party**

The request for assistance shall be without prejudice to such rights as the requesting Contracting Party may enjoy as a result of its status as *partie civile* in domestic judicial criminal proceedings commenced before the authorities of the requested Contracting Party.

TITLE IV

**FINAL PROVISIONS**

*Article 39*

**Joint Committee**

1. A Joint Committee shall be established, consisting of representatives of the Contracting Parties, and shall be responsible for the sound application of this Agreement. To that end, it shall make recommendations and take decisions in the cases provided for by the Agreement. It shall act by mutual agreement.

2. The Joint Committee shall adopt its Rules of Procedure, which shall include provisions governing the convening of meetings, the designation of the Chair and the determination of his or her functions.

3. The Joint Committee shall meet as required but no less than once every year. Any Contracting Party may request that a meeting be convened.

4. The Joint Committee may decide to establish working parties or expert groups to assist it in the performance of its tasks.

*Article 40*

**Dispute settlement**

1. Each Contracting Party may submit to the Joint Committee a dispute relating to the interpretation or application of this Agreement, in particular if it considers that another Contracting Party is failing repeatedly to take action on requests for cooperation made to it.

2. The Joint Committee shall endeavour to settle the dispute as quickly as possible. The Joint Committee shall be supplied with all relevant items of information to assist its detailed examination of the situation with a view to identifying a satisfactory solution. To that end, the Joint Committee shall examine all possibilities of preserving the sound operation of this Agreement.

*Article 41*

**Reciprocity**

1. The authority of the requested Contracting Party may refuse a request for cooperation where the requesting Contracting Party fails repeatedly to take action on a request for cooperation in similar cases.

2. Before a request for cooperation is refused on the grounds of reciprocity, the Joint Committee shall be informed to give it the opportunity to state its opinion on the matter.

*Article 42*

**Revision**

If a Contracting Party wishes this Agreement to be revised, it shall lay a proposal before the Joint Committee, which shall make recommendations, notably for the commencement of negotiations.

*Article 43*

**Territorial scope**

This Agreement shall apply, on the one hand, to the territory of the Swiss Confederation and, on the other hand, to the territories in which the Treaty establishing the European Community is applied and under the conditions laid down in that Treaty.

*Article 44*

**Entry into force**

1. This Agreement shall be concluded for an indefinite period.

2. It shall be ratified or approved by the Contracting Parties in accordance with their respective procedures. It shall enter into force on the first day of the second month after the last notification of instruments of ratification or approval.

3. Until the entry into force of this Agreement, each Contracting Party may, at the time of the notification referred to in paragraph 2 or at any other subsequent time, declare that it shall consider itself bound by the Agreement in its relations with any other Contracting Party having made the same declaration. These declarations shall take effect 90 days after the date of receipt of the notification.

*Article 45*

**Denunciation**

The European Community or the Swiss Confederation may denounce this Agreement by notifying the other Contracting Party of its decision. The denunciation shall take effect six months after the date of receipt of the notification of the denunciation.

*Article 46*

**Application over time**

The provisions of this Agreement shall be applicable to requests concerning illegal activities committed at least six months after it was signed.

*Article 47*

**Extension of the Agreement to the new Member States of the European Union**

1. Any State which becomes a Member State of the European Union may, by written notification to the Contracting Parties, become a Contracting Party to this Agreement.

2. The text of the Agreement in the language of the new acceding Member State as established by the Council of the European Union shall be authenticated by an Exchange of Letters between the European Community and the Swiss Confederation. It shall be considered to be authentic within the meaning of Article 48.

3. This Agreement shall enter into force in relation to any new Member State of the European Union which accedes to it 90 days after the receipt of its instrument of accession, or on the date of entry into force of this Agreement if it was not yet in force when that 90-day period expired.

4. If this Agreement is not yet in force when the new acceding State notifies its instrument of accession, Article 44(3) shall apply.

*Article 48*

**Languages**

1. This Agreement is drawn up in duplicate in the Czech, Danish, Dutch, English, Estonian, Finnish, French, German, Greek, Hungarian, Italian, Latvian, Lithuanian, Polish, Portuguese, Slovak, Slovenian, Spanish and Swedish languages, each of these texts being equally authentic.

2. The Maltese language version of this Agreement shall be authenticated by the Contracting Parties on the basis of an Exchange of Letters. It shall also be authentic, in the same way as for the languages referred to in paragraph 1.

IN WITNESS WHEREOF, the undersigned Plenipotentiaries have hereunto set their hands.

L 46/26 EN Official Journal of the European Union 17.2.2009

## FINAL ACT

The plenipotentiaries of

THE KINGDOM OF BELGIUM,

THE CZECH REPUBLIC,

THE KINGDOM OF DENMARK,

THE FEDERAL REPUBLIC OF GERMANY,

THE REPUBLIC OF ESTONIA,

THE HELLENIC REPUBLIC,

THE KINGDOM OF SPAIN,

THE FRENCH REPUBLIC,

IRELAND,

THE ITALIAN REPUBLIC,

THE REPUBLIC OF CYPRUS,

THE REPUBLIC OF LATVIA,

THE REPUBLIC OF LITHUANIA,

THE GRAND DUCHY OF LUXEMBOURG,

THE REPUBLIC OF HUNGARY,

THE REPUBLIC OF MALTA,

THE KINGDOM OF THE NETHERLANDS,

THE REPUBLIC OF AUSTRIA,

THE REPUBLIC OF POLAND,

THE PORTUGUESE REPUBLIC,

THE REPUBLIC OF SLOVENIA,

THE SLOVAK REPUBLIC,

THE REPUBLIC OF FINLAND,

THE KINGDOM OF SWEDEN,

THE UNITED KINGDOM OF GREAT BRITAIN AND NORTHERN IRELAND,

THE EUROPEAN COMMUNITY,

of the one part, and of

THE SWISS CONFEDERATION,

of the other part,

meeting on 26 October 2004 for the signature of the Cooperation Agreement between the European Community and its Member States, of the one part, and the Swiss Confederation, of the other part, to combat fraud and any other illegal activity to the detriment of their financial interests, have adopted the joint declarations listed below and attached to this Final Act:

1. Joint declaration on money laundering;

2. Joint declaration on cooperation by the Swiss Confederation with Eurojust and, if possible, with the European Judicial Network.

The plenipotentiaries of the European Union and of its Member States and the plenipotentiaries of the Swiss Confederation have furthermore adopted the Agreed Minute of the negotiations attached to this Final Act. The Agreed Minute is binding.

L 46/34 EN Official Journal of the European Union 17.2.2009

JOINT DECLARATION ON MONEY LAUNDERING

The Contracting Parties hereby agree that Article 2(3) of the Agreement on cooperation in combating money laundering shall include as precursor offences those which constitute tax fraud or professional smuggling under Swiss law. Information received in response to a request concerning laundering may be used in proceedings for laundering, save in proceedings against Swiss persons if all the acts relevant to the offence were committed in Switzerland only.

JOINT DECLARATION ON COOPERATION BY THE SWISS CONFEDERATION WITH EUROJUST AND, IF POSSIBLE, WITH THE EUROPEAN JUDICIAL NETWORK

The Contracting Parties take note of the Swiss Confederation's wish to study the possibility of cooperating in the work of Eurojust and, if possible, the European Judicial Network.

17.2.2009 EN Official Journal of the European Union L 46/35

AGREED MINUTE OF THE NEGOTIATIONS ON THE COOPERATION AGREEMENT BETWEEN THE EUROPEAN COMMUNITY AND ITS MEMBER STATES, OF THE ONE PART, AND THE SWISS CONFEDERATION, OF THE OTHER PART, TO COMBAT FRAUD AND ANY OTHER ILLEGAL ACTIVITY TO THE DETRIMENT OF THEIR FINANCIAL INTERESTS

The Contracting Parties have agreed as follows:

Ad Article 2(1)(a)

The expression 'fraud and any other illegal activity' extends to smuggling, corruption and laundering of the proceeds of the activities covered by this Agreement, subject to Article 2(3).

The expression 'trade in goods contrary to customs and agricultural legislation' is to be understood independently of the passage (departure, destination or transit) or otherwise of the goods through the territory of the other Contracting Party.

The expression 'trade contrary to tax legislation applicable to value added tax, special taxes on consumption and excise duties' is to be understood independently of the passage (departure, destination or transit) or otherwise of the goods or services through the territory of the other Contracting Party.

Ad Article 15(2)

The term 'investigation means' includes the questioning of persons, the searching of premises and means of transport, the copying of documents, the requesting of information and the seizure of objects, documents and items of value.

Ad second subparagraph of Article 16(2)

This subparagraph also means that those present may in particular be authorised to put questions and propose measures of investigation.

Ad Article 25(2)

The concept of multilateral Agreements between the Contracting Parties includes in particular, as of its entry into force, the Agreement between the European Union, the European Community and the Swiss Confederation concerning the latter's association with the implementation, application and development of the Schengen *acquis*.

Ad Article 35(1)

'Request for mutual legal assistance' also means the transmission of information and evidence to the authority of the requesting Contracting Party.

Ad Article 43

The European Commission will, at the latest at the date of signature of this Agreement, send an indicative list of the territories to which this Agreement applies.

# Framework Decision 2005/212 on confiscation of crime-related proceeds, instrumentalities and property, 24 February 2005

[OJ 2005, L 68/49–51]

15.3.2005 EN Official Journal of the European Union L 68/49

**COUNCIL FRAMEWORK DECISION 2005/212/JHA**

**of 24 February 2005**

**on Confiscation of Crime-Related Proceeds, Instrumentalities and Property**

THE COUNCIL OF THE EUROPEAN UNION,

Having regard to the Treaty on European Union, and in particular Articles 29, 31(1)(c) and 34(2)(b) thereof,

Having regard to the initiative of the Kingdom of Denmark (1),

Having regard to the opinion of the European Parliament,

Whereas:

(1) The main motive for cross-border organised crime is financial gain. In order to be effective, therefore, any attempt to prevent and combat such crime must focus on tracing, freezing, seizing and confiscating the proceeds from crime. However, this is made difficult, *inter alia*, as a result of differences between Member States' legislation in this area.

(2) In the conclusions of the Vienna European Council of December 1998, the European Council called for a strengthening of EU efforts to combat international organised crime in accordance with an action plan on how best to implement the provisions of the Treaty of Amsterdam in an area of freedom, security and justice (2).

(3) Pursuant to paragraph 50(b) of the Vienna Action Plan, within five years of the entry into force of the Treaty of Amsterdam, national provisions governing seizures and confiscation of the proceeds from crime must be improved and approximated where necessary, taking account of the rights of third parties in bona fide.

(4) Paragraph 51 of the conclusions of the Tampere European Council of 15 and 16 October 1999 stresses that money laundering is at the very heart of organised crime, and should be rooted out wherever it occurs and that the European Council is determined to ensure that concrete steps are taken to trace, freeze, seize and confiscate the proceeds from crime. The European Council also calls, in paragraph 55, for the approximation of criminal law and procedures on money laundering (e.g. tracing, freezing and confiscating funds).

(5) Pursuant to Recommendation 19 in the 2000 action plan entitled 'The prevention and control of organised crime: a European Union strategy for the beginning of the new millennium', which was approved by the Council on 27 March 2000 (3), an examination should be made of the possible need for an instrument which, taking into account best practice in the Member States and with due respect for fundamental legal principles, introduces the possibility of mitigating, under criminal, civil or fiscal law, as appropriate, the onus of proof regarding the source of assets held by a person convicted of an offence related to organised crime.

(6) Pursuant to Article 12, on confiscation and seizure, of the UN Convention of 12 December 2000 against Transnational Organised Crime, States Parties may consider the possibility of requiring that an offender demonstrate the lawful origin of alleged proceeds of crime or other property liable to confiscation, to the extent that such a requirement is consistent with the principles of their domestic law and with the nature of judicial proceedings.

(7) All Member States have ratified the Council of Europe Convention of 8 November 1990 on Laundering, Search, Seizure and Confiscation of the Proceeds from Crime. Some Member States have submitted declarations with regard to Article 2 of the Convention concerning confiscation so as to be obliged to confiscate proceeds only from a number of specified offences.

(8) The Council Framework Decision 2001/500/JHA (4) lays down provisions on money laundering, the identification, tracing, freezing, seizing and confiscation of instrumentalities and the proceeds from crime. Under that Framework Decision, Member States are also obliged not to make or uphold reservations in respect of the provisions of the Council of Europe Convention concerning confiscation, insofar as the offence is punishable by deprivation of liberty or a detention order for a maximum of more than one year.

(9) The existing instruments in this area have not to a sufficient extent achieved effective cross-border co-operation with regard to confiscation as there are still a number of Member States which are unable to confiscate the proceeds from all offences punishable by deprivation of liberty for more than one year.

(1) OJ C 184, 2.8.2002, p. 3.
(2) OJ C 19, 23.1.1999, p. 1.
(3) OJ C 124, 3.5.2000, p. 1.
(4) OJ L 182, 5.7.2001, p. 1.

(10) The aim of this Framework Decision is to ensure that all Member States have effective rules governing the confiscation of proceeds from crime, *inter alia*, in relation to the onus of proof regarding the source of assets held by a person convicted of an offence related to organised crime. This Decision is linked to a Danish draft Framework Decision on the mutual recognition within the European Union of decisions concerning the confiscation of proceeds from crime and asset-sharing, which is being submitted at the same time.

(11) This Framework Decision does not prevent a Member State from applying its fundamental principles relating to due process, in particular the presumption of innocence, property rights, freedom of association, freedom of the press and freedom of expression in other media,

HAS ADOPTED THIS FRAMEWORK DECISION:

*Article 1*

**Definitions**

For the purposes of this Framework Decision:

— 'proceeds' means any economic advantage from criminal offences. It may consist of any form of property as defined in the following indent,

'property' includes property of any description, whether corporeal or incorporeal, movable or immovable, and legal documents or instruments evidencing title to or interest in such property,

— 'instrumentalities' means any property used or intended to be used, in any manner, wholly or in part, to commit a criminal offence or criminal offences,

— 'confiscation' means a penalty or measure, ordered by a court following proceedings in relation to a criminal offence or criminal offences, resulting in the final deprivation of property,

— 'legal person' means any entity having such status under the applicable national law, except for States or other public bodies in the exercise of State authority and for public international organisations.

*Article 2*

**Confiscation**

1. Each Member State shall take the necessary measures to enable it to confiscate, either wholly or in part, instrumentalities and proceeds from criminal offences punishable by deprivation of liberty for more than one year, or property the value of which corresponds to such proceeds.

2. In relation to tax offences, Member States may use procedures other than criminal procedures to deprive the perpetrator of the proceeds of the offence.

*Article 3*

**Extended powers of confiscation**

1. Each Member State shall as a minimum adopt the necessary measures to enable it, under the circumstances referred to in paragraph 2, to confiscate, either wholly or in part, property belonging to a person convicted of an offence

(a) committed within the framework of a criminal organisation as defined in Joint Action 98/733/JHA of 21 December 1998 on making it a criminal offence to participate in a criminal organisation in the Member States of the European Union [1], when the offence is covered by:

— Council Framework Decision 2000/383/JHA of 29 May 2000 on increasing protection by criminal penalties and other sanctions against counterfeiting in connection with the introduction of the euro [2],

— Council Framework Decision 2001/500/JHA of 26 June 2001 on money laundering, the identification, tracing, freezing, seizing and confiscation of instrumentalities and the proceeds of crime [3],

— Council Framework Decision 2002/629/JHA of 19 July 2002 on combating trafficking in human beings [4],

— Council Framework Decision 2002/946/JHA of 28 November 2002 on the strengthening of the penal framework to prevent the facilitation of unauthorised entry, transit and residence [5],

— Council Framework Decision 2004/68/JHA of 22 December 2003 on combating the sexual exploitation of children and child pornography [6],

(1) OJ L 351, 29.12.1998, p. 1.
(2) OJ L 140, 14.6.2000, p. 1.
(3) OJ L 182, 5.7.2001, p. 1.
(4) OJ L 203, 1.8.2002, p. 1.
(5) OJ L 328, 5.12.2002, p. 1.
(6) OJ L 13, 20.1.2004, p. 44.

— Council Framework Decision 2004/757/JHA of 25 October 2004 laying down minimum provisions on the constituent elements of criminal acts and penalties in the field of illicit drug trafficking (1),

(b) which is covered by the Council Framework Decision 2002/475/JHA of 13 June 2002 on combating terrorism (2),

provided that the offence according to the Framework Decisions referred to above

— regarding offences other than money laundering are punishable with criminal penalties of a maximum of at least between 5 and 10 years of imprisonment,

— regarding money laundering, are punishable with criminal penalties of a maximum of at least 4 years of imprisonment,

and the offence is of such a nature that it can generate financial gain.

2. Each Member State shall take the necessary measures to enable confiscation under this Article at least:

(a) where a national court based on specific facts is fully convinced that the property in question has been derived from criminal activities of the convicted person during a period prior to conviction for the offence referred to in paragraph 1 which is deemed reasonable by the court in the circumstances of the particular case, or, alternatively,

(b) where a national court based on specific facts is fully convinced that the property in question has been derived from similar criminal activities of the convicted person during a period prior to conviction for the offence referred to in paragraph 1 which is deemed reasonable by the court in the circumstances of the particular case, or, alternatively,

(c) where it is established that the value of the property is disproportionate to the lawful income of the convicted person and a national court based on specific facts is fully convinced that the property in question has been derived from the criminal activity of that convicted person.

3. Each Member State may also consider adopting the necessary measures to enable it to confiscate, in accordance with the conditions set out in paragraphs 1 and 2, either wholly or in part, property acquired by the closest relations of the person concerned and property transferred to a legal person in respect of which the person concerned — acting either alone or in conjunction with his closest relations — has a controlling influence. The same shall apply if the person concerned receives a significant part of the legal person's income.

4. Member States may use procedures other than criminal procedures to deprive the perpetrator of the property in question.

*Article 4*

**Legal remedies**

Each Member State shall take the necessary measures to ensure that interested parties affected by measures under Articles 2 and 3 have effective legal remedies in order to preserve their rights.

*Article 5*

**Safeguards**

This Framework Decision shall not have the effect of altering the obligation to respect fundamental rights and fundamental principles, including in particular the presumption of innocence, as enshrined in Article 6 of the Treaty on European Union.

*Article 6*

**Implementation**

1. Member States shall adopt the necessary measures to comply with this Framework Decision by 15 March 2007.

2. Member States shall transmit to the General Secretariat of the Council and to the Commission, by 15 March 2007, the text of the provisions transposing into their national law the obligations imposed on them under this Framework Decision. In accordance with a report established on the basis of this information and a written report from the Commission, the Council shall assess, by 15 June 2007, the extent to which Member States have taken the necessary measures in order to comply with this Framework Decision.

*Article 7*

**Entry into force**

This Framework Decision shall enter into force on the day of its publication in the *Official Journal of the European Union.*

Done at Brussels, 24 February 2005.

*For the Council*

*The President*

N. SCHMIT

(1) OJ L 335, 11.11.2004, p. 8.
(2) OJ L 164, 22.6.2002, p. 3.

# Framework Decision 2005/214 on the application of the principle of mutual recognition to financial penalties, 24 February 2005

**[Consolidated version. Original version OJ 2005, L 76/16–30 amended as of 28 March 2011 by OJ 2009, L 81/24–36]**

►B

**COUNCIL FRAMEWORK DECISION 2005/214/JHA**

**of 24 February 2005**

**on the application of the principle of mutual recognition to financial penalties**

(OJ L 76, 22.3.2005, p. 16)

Amended by:

| | | Official Journal | | |
|---|---|---|---|---|
| | | No | page | date |
| ►M1 | Council Framework Decision 2009/299/JHA of 26 February 2009 | L 81 | 24 | 27.3.2009 |

▼B

**COUNCIL FRAMEWORK DECISION 2005/214/JHA**

**of 24 February 2005**

**on the application of the principle of mutual recognition to financial penalties**

THE COUNCIL OF THE EUROPEAN UNION,

Having regard to the Treaty on European Union, and in particular Articles 31(a) and 34(2)(b) thereof,

Having regard to the initiative of the United Kingdom of Great Britain and Northern Ireland, the French Republic and the Kingdom of Sweden ([1]),

Having regard to the opinion of the European Parliament ([2]),

Whereas:

(1) The European Council meeting in Tampere on 15 and 16 October 1999 endorsed the principle of mutual recognition, which should become the cornerstone of judicial cooperation in both civil and criminal matters within the Union.

(2) The principle of mutual recognition should apply to financial penalties imposed by judicial or administrative authorities for the purpose of facilitating the enforcement of such penalties in a Member State other than the State in which the penalties are imposed.

(3) On 29 November 2000 the Council, in accordance with the Tampere conclusions, adopted a programme of measures to implement the principle of mutual recognition of decisions in criminal matters ([3]), giving priority to the adoption of an instrument applying the principle of mutual recognition to financial penalties (measure 18).

(4) This Framework Decision should also cover financial penalties imposed in respect of road traffic offences.

(5) This Framework Decision respects fundamental rights and observes the principles recognised by Article 6 of the Treaty and reflected by the Charter of Fundamental Rights of the European Union ([4]), in particular Chapter VI thereof. Nothing in this Framework Decision may be interpreted as prohibiting refusal to execute a decision when there are reasons to believe, on the basis of objective elements, that the financial penalty has the purpose of punishing a person on the grounds of his or her sex, race, religion, ethnic origin, nationality, language, political opinions or sexual orientation, or that that person's position may be prejudiced for any of these reasons.

(6) This Framework Decision does not prevent a Member State from applying its constitutional rules relating to due process, freedom of association, freedom of the press and freedom of expression in other media,

HAS ADOPTED THIS FRAMEWORK DECISION:

([1]) OJ C 278, 2.10.2001, p. 4.
([2]) OJ C 271 E, 7.11.2002, p. 423.
([3]) OJ C 12, 15.1.2001, p. 10.
([4]) OJ C 364, 18.12.2000, p. 1.

▼B

*Article 1*

**Definitions**

For the purposes of this Framework Decision:

(a) 'decision' shall mean a final decision requiring a financial penalty to be paid by a natural or legal person where the decision was made by:

(i) a court of the issuing State in respect of a criminal offence under the law of the issuing State;

(ii) an authority of the issuing State other than a court in respect of a criminal offence under the law of the issuing State, provided that the person concerned has had an opportunity to have the case tried by a court having jurisdiction in particular in criminal matters;

(iii) an authority of the issuing State other than a court in respect of acts which are punishable under the national law of the issuing State by virtue of being infringements of the rules of law, provided that the person concerned has had an opportunity to have the case tried by a court having jurisdiction in particular in criminal matters;

(iv) a court having jurisdiction in particular in criminal matters, where the decision was made regarding a decision as referred to in point (iii);

(b) 'financial penalty' shall mean the obligation to pay:

(i) a sum of money on conviction of an offence imposed in a decision;

(ii) compensation imposed in the same decision for the benefit of victims, where the victim may not be a civil party to the proceedings and the court is acting in the exercise of its criminal jurisdiction;

(iii) a sum of money in respect of the costs of court or administrative proceedings leading to the decision;

(iv) a sum of money to a public fund or a victim support organisation, imposed in the same decision.

A financial penalty shall not include:

— orders for the confiscation of instrumentalities or proceeds of crime,

— orders that have a civil nature and arise out of a claim for damages and restitution and which are enforceable in accordance with Council Regulation (EC) No 44/2001 of 22 December 2000 on jurisdiction and the recognition and enforcement of judgments in civil and commercial matters [1];

(c) 'issuing State' shall mean the Member State in which a decision within the meaning of this Framework Decision was delivered;

(d) 'executing State' shall mean the Member State to which a decision has been transmitted for the purpose of enforcement.

*Article 2*

**Determination of the competent authorities**

1. Each Member State shall inform the General Secretariat of the Council which authority or authorities, under its national law, are

[1] OJ L 12, 16.1.2001, p. 1. Regulation as last amended by Commission Regulation (EC) No 2245/2004 (OJ L 381, 28.12.2004, p. 10).

▼B

competent according to this Framework Decision, when that Member State is the issuing State or the executing State.

2. Notwithstanding Article 4, each Member State may designate, if it is necessary as a result of the organisation of its internal system, one or more central authorities responsible for the administrative transmission and reception of the decisions and to assist the competent authorities.

3. The General Secretariat of the Council shall make the information received available to all Member States and the Commission.

*Article 3*

**Fundamental rights**

This Framework Decision shall not have the effect of amending the obligation to respect fundamental rights and fundamental legal principles as enshrined in Article 6 of the Treaty.

*Article 4*

**Transmission of decisions and recourse to the central authority**

1. A decision, together with a certificate as provided for in this Article, may be transmitted to the competent authorities of a Member State in which the natural or legal person against whom a decision has been passed has property or income, is normally resident or, in the case of a legal person, has its registered seat.

2. The certificate, the standard form for which is given in the Annex, must be signed, and its contents certified as accurate, by the competent authority in the issuing State.

3. The decision or a certified copy of it, together with the certificate, shall be transmitted by the competent authority in the issuing State directly to the competent authority in the executing State by any means which leaves a written record under conditions allowing the executing State to establish its authenticity. The original of the decision, or a certified copy of it, and the original of the certificate, shall be sent to the executing State if it so requires. All official communications shall also be made directly between the said competent authorities.

4. The issuing State shall only transmit a decision to one executing State at any one time.

5. If the competent authority in the executing State is not known to the competent authority in the issuing State, the latter shall make all necessary inquiries, including via the contact points of the European Judicial Network [1] in order to obtain the information from the executing State.

6. When an authority in the executing State which receives a decision has no jurisdiction to recognise it and take the necessary measures for its execution, it shall, *ex officio*, transmit the decision to the competent authority and shall inform the competent authority in the issuing State accordingly.

7. The United Kingdom and Ireland, respectively, may state in a declaration that the decision together with the certificate must be sent via its central authority or authorities specified by it in the declaration. These Member States may at any time by a further declaration limit the scope of such a declaration for the purpose of giving greater effect to paragraph 3. They shall do so when the provisions on mutual assistance of the Schengen Implementation Convention are put into effect for

(1) Council Joint Action 98/428/JHA of 29 June 1998 on the creation of a European Judicial Network (OJ L 191, 7.7.1998, p. 4).

▼B

them. Any declaration shall be deposited with the General Secretariat of the Council and notified to the Commission.

*Article 5*

**Scope**

1. The following offences, if they are punishable in the issuing State and as they are defined by the law of the issuing State, shall, under the terms of this Framework Decision and without verification of the double criminality of the act, give rise to recognition and enforcement of decisions:

— participation in a criminal organisation,

— terrorism,

— trafficking in human beings,

— sexual exploitation of children and child pornography,

— illicit trafficking in narcotic drugs and psychotropic substances,

— illicit trafficking in weapons, munitions and explosives,

— corruption,

— fraud, including that affecting the financial interests of the European Communities within the meaning of the Convention of 26 July 1995 on the protection of the European Communities' financial interests,

— laundering of the proceeds of crime,

— counterfeiting currency, including of the euro,

— computer-related crime,

— environmental crime, including illicit trafficking in endangered animal species and in endangered plant species and varieties,

— facilitation of unauthorised entry and residence,

— murder, grievous bodily injury,

— illicit trade in human organs and tissue,

— kidnapping, illegal restraint and hostage-taking,

— racism and xenophobia,

— organised or armed robbery,

— illicit trafficking in cultural goods, including antiques and works of art,

— swindling,

— racketeering and extortion,

— counterfeiting and piracy of products,

— forgery of administrative documents and trafficking therein,

— forgery of means of payment,

— illicit trafficking in hormonal substances and other growth promoters,

— illicit trafficking in nuclear or radioactive materials,

— trafficking in stolen vehicles,

— rape,

— arson,

— crimes within the jurisdiction of the International Criminal Court,

▼B

— unlawful seizure of aircraft/ships,

— sabotage,

— conduct which infringes road traffic regulations, including breaches of regulations pertaining to driving hours and rest periods and regulations on hazardous goods,

— smuggling of goods,

— infringements of intellectual property rights,

— threats and acts of violence against persons, including violence during sport events,

— criminal damage,

— theft,

— offences established by the issuing State and serving the purpose of implementing obligations arising from instruments adopted under the EC Treaty or under Title VI of the EU Treaty.

2. The Council may decide to add other categories of offences to the lists in paragraph 1 at any time, acting unanimously after consultation of the European Parliament under the conditions laid down in Article 39(1) of the EU Treaty.

The Council shall consider, in the light of the report submitted to it pursuant to Article 20(5), whether the list should be extended or amended. The Council shall consider the issue further at a later stage on the basis of a report on the practical application of the Framework Decision established by the Commission within 5 years after the date mentioned in Article 20(1).

3. For offences other than those covered by paragraph 1, the executing State may make the recognition and execution of a decision subject to the condition that the decision is related to conduct which would constitute an offence under the law of the executing State, whatever the constituent elements or however it is described.

*Article 6*

**Recognition and execution of decisions**

The competent authorities in the executing State shall recognise a decision which has been transmitted in accordance with Article 4 without any further formality being required and shall forthwith take all the necessary measures for its execution, unless the competent authority decides to invoke one of the grounds for non-recognition or non-execution provided for in Article 7.

*Article 7*

**Grounds for non-recognition and non-execution**

1. The competent authorities in the executing State may refuse to recognise and execute the decision if the certificate provided for in Article 4 is not produced, is incomplete or manifestly does not correspond to the decision.

2. The competent authority in the executing State may also refuse to recognise and execute the decision if it is established that:

(a) decision against the sentenced person in respect of the same acts has been delivered in the executing State or in any State other than the issuing or the executing State, and, in the latter case, that decision has been executed;

(b) in one of the cases referred to in Article 5(3), the decision relates to acts which would not constitute an offence under the law of the executing State;

▼B

(c) the execution of the decision is statute-barred according to the law of the executing State and the decision relates to acts which fall within the jurisdiction of that State under its own law.

(d) the decision relates to acts which:

(i) are regarded by the law of the executing State as having been committed in whole or in part in the territory of the executing State or in a place treated as such, or

(ii) have been committed outside the territory of the issuing State and the law of the executing State does not allow prosecution for the same offences when committed outside its territory;

(e) there is immunity under the law of the executing State, which makes it impossible to execute the decision;

(f) the decision has been imposed on a natural person who under the law of the executing State due to his or her age could not yet have been held criminally liable for the acts in respect of which the decision was passed;

▼M1

(g) according to the certificate provided for in Article 4, the person concerned, in case of a written procedure, was not, in accordance with the law of the issuing State, informed personally or via a representative, competent according to national law, of his/her right to contest the case and of the time limits for such a legal remedy;

▼B

(h) the financial penalty is below EUR 70 or the equivalent to that amount;

▼M1

(i) according to the certificate provided for in Article 4, the person did not appear in person at the trial resulting in the decision, unless the certificate states that the person, in accordance with further procedural requirements defined in the national law of the issuing State:

(i) in due time:

— either was summoned in person and thereby informed of the scheduled date and place of the trial which resulted in the decision, or by other means actually received official information of the scheduled date and place of that trial in such a manner that it was unequivocally established that he or she was aware of the scheduled trial,

and

— was informed that a decision may be handed down if he or she does not appear for the trial;

or

(ii) being aware of the scheduled trial, had given a mandate to a legal counsellor, who was either appointed by the person concerned or by the State, to defend him or her at the trial, and was indeed defended by that counsellor at the trial;

or

(iii) after being served with the decision and being expressly informed of the right to a retrial, or an appeal, in which he or she has the right to participate and which allows the merits of the case, including fresh evidence, to be re-examined, and which may lead to the original decision being reversed:

— expressly stated that he or she does not contest the decision,

▼M1

or

— did not request a retrial or appeal within the applicable time frame;

(j) according to the certificate provided for in Article 4, the person did not appear in person, unless the certificate states that the person, having been expressly informed about the proceedings and the possibility to appear in person in a trial, expressly waived his or her right to an oral hearing and has expressly indicated that he or she does not contest the case.

3. In the cases referred to in paragraphs 1 and 2(c), (g), (i) and (j), before deciding not to recognise and to execute a decision, either totally or in part, the competent authority in the executing State shall consult the competent authority in the issuing State, by any appropriate means, and shall, where appropriate, ask it to supply any necessary information without delay.

▼B

*Article 8*

**Determination of the amount to be paid**

1. Where it is established that the decision is related to acts which were not carried out within the territory of the issuing State, the executing State may decide to reduce the amount of the penalty enforced to the maximum amount provided for acts of the same kind under the national law of the executing State, when the acts fall within the jurisdiction of that State.

2. The competent authority of the executing State shall, if necessary, convert the penalty into the currency of the executing State at the rate of exchange obtaining at the time when the penalty was imposed.

*Article 9*

**Law governing enforcement**

1. Without prejudice to paragraph 3 of this Article, and to Article 10, the enforcement of the decision shall be governed by the law of the executing State in the same way as a financial penalty of the executing State. The authorities of the executing State alone shall be competent to decide on the procedures for enforcement and to determine all the measures relating thereto, including the grounds for termination of enforcement.

2. In the case where the sentenced person is able to furnish proof of a payment, totally or in part, in any State, the competent authority of the executing State shall consult the competent authority of the Issuing State in the way provided for in Article 7(3). Any part of the penalty recovered in whatever manner in any State shall be deducted in full from the amount, which is to be enforced in the executing State.

3. A financial penalty imposed on a legal person shall be enforced even if the executing State does not recognise the principle of criminal liability of legal persons.

*Article 10*

**Imprisonment or other alternative sanction by way of substitution for non-recovery of the financial penalty**

Where it is not possible to enforce a decision, either totally or in part, alternative sanctions, including custodial sanctions, may be applied by the executing State if its laws so provide in such cases and the issuing State has allowed for the application of such alternative sanctions in the certificate referred to in Article 4. The severity of the alternative

▼B

sanction shall be determined in accordance with the law of the executing State, but shall not exceed any maximum level stated in the certificate transmitted by the issuing State.

*Article 11*

**Amnesty, pardon, review of sentence**

1. Amnesty and pardon may be granted by the issuing State and also by the executing State.

2. Without prejudice to the Article 10, only the issuing State may determine any application for review of the decision.

*Article 12*

**Termination of enforcement**

1. The competent authority of the issuing State shall forthwith inform the competent authority of the executing State of any decision or measure as a result of which the decision ceases to be enforceable or is withdrawn from the executing State for any other reason.

2. The executing State shall terminate enforcement of the decision as soon as it is informed by the competent authority of the issuing State of that decision or measure.

*Article 13*

**Accrual of monies obtained from enforcement of decisions**

Monies obtained from the enforcement of decisions shall accrue to the executing State unless otherwise agreed between the issuing and the executing State, in particular in the cases referred to in Article 1(b)(ii).

*Article 14*

**Information from the executing State**

The competent authority of the executing State shall without delay inform the competent authority of the issuing State by any means which leaves a written record:

(a) of the transmission of the decision to the competent authority, according to Article 4(6);

(b) of any decision not to recognise and execute a decision, according to Articles 7 or 20(3), together with the reasons for the decision;

(c) of the total or partial non-execution of the decision for the reasons referred to in Article 8, Article 9(1) and (2), and Article 11(1);

(d) of the execution of the decision as soon as the execution has been completed;

(e) of the application of alternative sanction, according to Article 10.

*Article 15*

**Consequences of transmission of a decision**

1. Subject to paragraph 2, the issuing State may not proceed with the execution of a decision transmitted pursuant to Article 4.

2. The right of execution of the decision shall revert to the issuing State:

(a) upon it being informed by the executing State of the total or partial non-execution or the non-recognition or the non-enforcement of the decision in the case of Article 7, with the exception of

▼B

Article 7(2)(a), in the case of Article 11(1), and in the case of Article 20(3); or

(b) when the executing State has been informed by the issuing State that the decision has been withdrawn from the executing State pursuant to Article 12.

3. If, after transmission of a decision in accordance with Article 4, an authority of the issuing State receives any sum of money which the sentenced person has paid voluntarily in respect of the decision, that authority shall inform the competent authority in the executing State without delay. Article 9(2) shall apply.

*Article 16*

**Languages**

1. The certificate, the standard form for which is given in the Annex, must be translated into the official language or one of the official languages of the executing State. Any Member State may, either when this Framework Decision is adopted or at a later date, state in a declaration deposited with the General Secretariat of the Council that it will accept a translation in one or more other official languages of the Institutions of the Union.

2. The execution of the decision may be suspended for the time necessary to obtain its translation at the expense of the executing State.

*Article 17*

**Costs**

Member States shall not claim from each other the refund of costs resulting from application of this Framework Decision.

*Article 18*

**Relationship with other agreements and arrangements**

This Framework Decision shall not preclude the application of bilateral or multilateral agreements or arrangements between Member States in so far as such agreements or arrangements allow the prescriptions of this Framework Decision to be exceeded and help to simplify or facilitate further the procedures for the enforcement of financial penalties.

*Article 19*

**Territorial application**

This Framework Decision shall apply to Gibraltar.

*Article 20*

**Implementation**

1. Member States shall take the necessary measures to comply with the provisions of this Framework Decision by 22 March 2007.

2. Each Member State may for a period of up to five years from the date of entry into force of this Framework Decision limit its application to:

(a) decisions mentioned in Article 1 (a)(i) and (iv); and/or

(b) with regard to legal persons, decisions related to conduct for which a European instrument provides for the application of the principle of liability of legal persons.

▼B

Any Member State that wants to make use of this paragraph, shall notify a declaration to that effect to the Secretary General of the Council upon the adoption of this Framework Decision. The declaration shall be published in the *Official Journal of the European Union*.

3. Each Member State may, where the certificate referred to in Article 4 gives rise to an issue that fundamental rights or fundamental legal principles as enshrined in Article 6 of the Treaty may have been infringed, oppose the recognition and the execution of decisions. The procedure referred to in Article 7(3) shall apply.

4. Any Member State may apply the principle of reciprocity in relation to any Member State making use of paragraph 2.

5. Member States shall transmit to the General Secretariat of the Council and to the Commission the text of the provisions transposing into their national law the obligations imposed on them under this Framework Decision. On the basis of a report established on the basis of this information by the Commission, the Council shall, no later than 22 March 2008, assess the extent to which Member States have complied with this Framework Decision.

6. The General Secretariat of the Council shall notify the Member States and the Commission of the declarations made pursuant to Articles 4(7) and 16.

7. Without prejudice to Article 35(7) of the Treaty, a Member State which has experienced repeated difficulties or lack of activity by another Member State in the mutual recognition and execution of decisions, which have not been solved through bilateral consultations, may inform the Council with a view to evaluating the implementation of this Framework Decision at Member State level.

8. Any Member State which during a calendar year has applied paragraph 3, shall in the beginning of the following calendar year inform the Council and the Commission of cases in which the grounds referred to in that provision for non-recognition or non-execution of a decision have been applied.

9. Within seven years after the entry into force of this Framework Decision, the Commission shall establish a report on the basis of the information received, accompanied by any initiatives it may deem appropriate. The Council shall on the basis of the report review this Article with a view to considering whether paragraph 3 shall be retained or replaced by a more specific provision.

*Article 21*

**Entry into force**

This Framework Decision shall enter into force on the day of its publication in the *Official Journal of the European Union*.

▼B

*ANNEX*

## CERTIFICATE

**referred to in Article 4 of Council Framework Decision 2005/214/JHA on the application of the principle of mutual recognition to financial penalties**

(a)

* Issuing State: ..................................................
* Executing State: ..............................................

(b) The authority which issued the decision imposing the financial penalty:

Official name: .....................................................

Address: ...........................................................

......................................................................

File reference (...) .................................................

Tel. No: (country code) (area/city code) ...........................

Fax No (country code) (area/city code) .............................

E-mail (when available) ...........................................

Languages in which it is possible to communicate with the issuing authority ...........................................................

......................................................................

Contact details for person(s) to contact to obtain additional information for the purpose of the enforcement of the decision or, where applicable, for the purpose of the transfer to the issuing State of monies obtained from the enforcement (name, title/grade, tel. No., fax No., and, when available, E-mail) ..................................................

......................................................................

......................................................................

▼B

(c) The authority competent for the enforcement of the decision imposing the financial penalty in the issuing State (if the authority is different from the authority under point (b)):

Official name: ..................................................

..................................................................

Address: .........................................................

..................................................................

Tel. No: (country code) (area/city code) ............................

Fax No (country code) (area/city code) .............................

E-mail (when available) ............................................

Languages in which it is possible to communicate with the authority competent for the enforcement .....................................

..................................................................

Contact details for person(s) to contact to obtain additional information for the purpose of the enforcement of the decision or, where applicable, for the purpose of the transfer to the issuing State of monies obtained from the enforcement (name, title/grade, tel. No., fax No., and, when available, E-mail): .................................................

..................................................................

..................................................................

(d) Where a central authority has been made responsible for the administrative transmission of decisions imposing financial penalties in the issuing State:

Name of the central authority: .....................................

..................................................................

Contact person, if applicable (title/grade and name): ...............

..................................................................

Address: .........................................................

..................................................................

File reference ...................................................

Tel. No: (country code) (area/city code) ............................

Fax No: (country code) (area/city code) .............................

E-mail (when available): ...........................................

▼B

(e) The authority or authorities which may be contacted (in the case where point (c) and/or (d) has been filled):

☐ Authority mentioned under point (b)

Can be contacted for questions concerning: ....................

☐ Authority mentioned under point (c)

Can be contacted for questions concerning: ....................

☐ Authority mentioned under point (d)

Can be contacted for questions concerning: ....................

(f) Information regarding the natural or legal person on which the financial penalty has been imposed:

1. In case of a natural person

Name: ..........................................................

Forename(s): ...................................................

Maiden name, where applicable: ..................................

Aliases, where applicable: ......................................

Sex: ...........................................................

Nationality: ....................................................

Identity number or social security number (when available): ........

Date of birth: .................................................

Place of birth: ................................................

Last known address: ............................................

..................................................................

Language(s) which the person understands (if known): .............

..................................................................

(a) If the decision is transmitted to the executing State because the person against whom the decision has been passed is normally resident, add the following information:

Normal residence in the executing State: ......................

..................................................................

..................................................................

(b) If the decision is transmitted to the executing State because the person against whom the decision has been passed has property in the executing State, add the following information:

Description of the property of the person: ......................

Location of the property of the person: .........................

(c) If the decision is transmitted to the executing State because the person against whom the decision has been passed has income in the executing State, add the following information:

Description of the source(s) of income of the person: ..........

Location of the source(s) of income of the person: .............

▼B

2. In case of a legal person:

Name: ............................................................

Form of legal person: ...............................................

Registration number (if available) ([1]): ...............................

Registered seat (if available) ([1]): ....................................

Address of the legal person:

(a) If the decision is transmitted to the executing State because the legal person against whom the decision has been passed has property in the executing State, add the following information:

Description of the property of the legal person: ...............

Location of the property of the legal person: ..................

..............................................................

(b) If the decision is transmitted to the executing State because the legal person against whom the decision has been passed has income in the executing State, add the following information:

Description of the source(s) of income of the legal person: .....

Location of the source(s) of income of the legal person: ........

..............................................................

(g) The decision imposing a financial penalty:

1. The nature of the decision imposing the financial penalty (tick the relevant box):

☐ (i) Decision of a court of the issuing State in respect of a criminal offence under the law of the issuing State

☐ (ii) Decision of an authority of the issuing State other than a court in respect of a criminal offence under the law of the issuing State. It is confirmed that the person concerned has had an opportunity to have the case tried by a court having jurisdiction in particular in criminal matters.

☐ (iii) Decision of an authority of the issuing State other than a court in respect of acts which are punishable under the national law of the issuing State by virtue of being infringements of the rules of law. It is confirmed that the person concerned has had an opportunity to have the case tried by a court having jurisdiction in particular in criminal matters.

☐ (iv) Decision of a court having jurisdiction in particular in criminal matters regarding a decision as referred to in point iii.

The decision was made on (date) .............................

The decision became final on (date) ...........................

Reference number of the decision (if available): ...............

The financial penalty constitutes an obligation to pay (tick the relevant box(es) and indicate the amount(s) with indication of currency):

☐ (i) A sum of money on conviction of an offence imposed in a decision.

Amount: ............................................

([1]) Where a decision is transmitted to the executing State because the legal person against whom the decision has been passed has its registered seat in that State, Registration number and Registered seat must be completed.

▼B

☐ (ii) Compensation imposed in the same decision for the benefit of victims, where the victim may not be a civil party to the proceedings and the court is acting in its exercise of its criminal jurisdiction.

Amount: ............................................

☐ (iii) A sum of money in respect of the costs of court or administrative proceedings leading to the decision.

Amount: ............................................

☐ (iv) A sum of money to a public fund or a victim support organisation, imposed in the same decision.

Amount: ............................................

The total amount of the financial penalty with indication of currency: ....................................................

.................................................................

2. A summary of facts and a description of the circumstances in which the offence(s) has(have) been committed, including time and place: ....................................................

.................................................................

.................................................................

.................................................................

.................................................................

.................................................................

Nature and legal classification of the offence(s) and the applicable statutory provision/code on basis of which the decision was made: ...........................................

.................................................................

.................................................................

.................................................................

3. To the extent that the offence(s) identified under point 2 above constitute(s) one or more of the following offences, confirm that by ticking the relevant box(es):

☐ participation in a criminal organisation;

☐ terrorism;

☐ trafficking in human beings;

☐ sexual exploitation of children and child pornography;

☐ illicit trafficking in narcotic drugs and psychotropic substances;

☐ illicit trafficking in weapons, munitions and explosives;

☐ corruption;

☐ fraud, including that affecting the financial interests of the European Communities within the meaning of the Convention of 26 July 1995 on the protection of the European Communities' financial interests;

☐ laundering of the proceeds of crime;

☐ counterfeiting currency, including of the euro;

☐ computer-related crime;

☐ environmental crime, including illicit trafficking in endangered animal species and in endangered plant species and varieties;

☐ facilitation of unauthorised entry and residence;

▼B

- ☐ murder, grievous bodily injury;
- ☐ illicit trade in human organs and tissue;
- ☐ kidnapping, illegal restraint and hostage-taking;
- ☐ racism and xenophobia;
- ☐ organised or armed robbery;
- ☐ illicit trafficking in cultural goods, including antiques and works of art;
- ☐ swindling;
- ☐ racketeering and extortion;
- ☐ counterfeiting and piracy of products;
- ☐ forgery of administrative documents and trafficking therein;
- ☐ forgery of means of payment;
- ☐ illicit trafficking in hormonal substances and other growth promoters;
- ☐ illicit trafficking in nuclear or radioactive materials;
- ☐ trafficking in stolen vehicles;
- ☐ rape;
- ☐ arson;
- ☐ crimes within the jurisdiction of the International Criminal Court;
- ☐ unlawful seizure of aircraft/ships;
- ☐ sabotage;
- ☐ conduct which infringes road traffic regulations, including breaches of regulations pertaining to driving hours and rest periods and regulations on hazardous goods;
- ☐ smuggling of goods;
- ☐ infringements of intellectual property rights;
- ☐ threats and acts of violence against persons, including violence during sport events;
- ☐ criminal damage;
- ☐ theft;
- ☐ offences established by the issuing State and serving the purpose of implementing obligations arising from instruments adopted under the EC Treaty or under Title VI of the EU Treaty.

  If this box is ticked, indicate the exact provisions of the instrument adopted on the basis of the EC Treaty or the EU Treaty that the offence relates to: ……………………

  ……………………………………………………

  ……………………………………………………

4. To the extent that the offence(s) identified under point 2 above are not covered by point 3, give a full description of the offence(s) concerned: ……………………………………………

……………………………………………………

……………………………………………………

……………………………………………………

▼B

(h) Status of the decision imposing the financial penalty

1. Confirm that (tick the boxes):

☐ (a) the decision is a final decision

☐ (b) to the knowledge of the authority issuing the Certificate, a decision against the same person in respect of the same acts has not been delivered in the executing State and that no such decision delivered in any State other than the issuing State or the executing State has been executed.

2. Indicate if the case been subject to a written procedure:

☐ (a) No, it has not.

☐ (b) Yes, it has. It is confirmed that the person concerned was, in accordance with the law of the issuing State, informed personally or via a representative competent according to national law of his right to contest the case and of time limits of such a legal remedy

▼M1

3. Indicate if the person concerned appeared in person at the trial resulting in the decision:

1. ☐ Yes, the person appeared in person at the trial resulting in the decision.

2. ☐ No, the person did not appear in person at the trial resulting in the decision.

3. If you have ticked the box under point 2, please confirm the existence of one of the following:

☐ 3.1a. the person was summoned in person on … (day/month/year) and thereby informed of the scheduled date and place of the trial which resulted in the decision and was informed that a decision may be handed down if he or she does not appear for the trial;

OR

☐ 3.1b. the person was not summoned in person but by other means actually received official information of the scheduled date and place of the trial which resulted in the decision, in such a manner that it was unequivocally established that he or she was aware of the scheduled trial, and was informed that a decision may be handed down if he or she does not appear for the trial;

OR

☐ 3.2. being aware of the scheduled trial, the person had given a mandate to a legal counsellor, who was either appointed by the person concerned or by the State, to defend him or her at the trial, and was indeed defended by that counsellor at the trial;

OR

☐ 3.3. the person was served with the decision on … (day/month/year) and was expressly informed about the right to a retrial or appeal, in which he or she has the right to participate and which allows the merits of the case, including fresh evidence, to be re-examined, and which may lead to the original decision being reversed, and

☐ the person expressly stated that he or she does not contest this decision,

OR

☐ the person did not request a retrial or appeal within the applicable time frame;

▼M1

OR

☐ 3.4. the person, having been expressly informed about the proceedings and the possibility to appear in person in a trial, expressly waived his or her right to an oral hearing and has expressly indicated that he or she does not contest the case.

4. If you have ticked the box under points 3.1b, 3.2, 3.3 or 3.4 above, please provide information about how the relevant condition has been met:

..........................................................

..........................................................

▼B

4. Partial payment of the penalty

If any part of the penalty has already been paid to the issuing State, or, to the knowledge of the authority issuing the Certificate, to any other State, indicate the amount which has been paid:

..............................................................

(i) Alternative sanctions, including custodial sanctions

1. State whether the issuing State allows for the application by the executing State of alternative sanctions in case it is not possible to enforce the decision imposing a penalty, either totally or in part:

☐ yes

☐ no

2. If yes, state which sanctions may be applied (nature of the sanctions, maximum level of the sanctions):

☐ Custody. Maximum period: ...............................

☐ Community service (or equivalent). Maximum period ......

☐ Other sanctions. Description: ..............................

..........................................................

(j) Other circumstances relevant to the case (optional information):

..................................................................

..................................................................

(k) The text of the decision imposing the financial penalty is attached to the certificate.

Signature of the authority issuing the certificate and/or its representative certifying the content of the certificate as accurate: ................

..................................................................

Name: ...........................................................

Post held (title/grade): .............................................

Date: ............................................................

Official stamp (if available)

# Directive 2005/35 on ship-source pollution and on the introduction of penalties for infringements, 7 September 2005

**[Consolidated version. Original version OJ 2005, L 255/11–21 amended by OJ 2009, L 280/52–55]**

**►B ►M1 DIRECTIVE 2005/35/EC OF THE EUROPEAN PARLIAMENT AND OF THE COUNCIL**

**of 7 September 2005**

**on ship-source pollution and on the introduction of penalties, including criminal penalties, for pollution offences ◄**

**►C2 (Text with EEA relevance) ◄**

(OJ L 255, 30.9.2005, p. 11)

Amended by:

| | | Official Journal | | |
|---|---|---|---|---|
| | | No | page | date |
| ►M1 | Directive 2009/123/EC of the European Parliament and of the Council of 21 October 2009 | L 280 | 52 | 27.10.2009 |

Corrected by:

►C1 Corrigendum, OJ L 33, 4.2.2006, p. 87 (2005/35/EC)

►C2 Corrigendum, OJ L 105, 13.4.2006, p. 65 (2005/35/EC)

▼B

**►M1 DIRECTIVE 2005/35/EC OF THE EUROPEAN PARLIAMENT AND OF THE COUNCIL**

**of 7 September 2005**

**on ship-source pollution and on the introduction of penalties, including criminal penalties, for pollution offences ◄**

**►C2 (Text with EEA relevance) ◄**

THE EUROPEAN PARLIAMENT AND THE COUNCIL OF THE EUROPEAN UNION,

Having regard to the Treaty establishing the European Community, and in particular Article 80(2) thereof,

Having regard to the proposal from the Commission,

Having regard to the opinion of the European Economic and Social Committee (1),

After consulting the Committee of the Regions,

Acting in accordance with the procedure laid down in Article 251 of the Treaty (2),

Whereas:

(1) The Community's maritime safety policy is aimed at a high level of safety and environmental protection and is based on the understanding that all parties involved in the transport of goods by sea have a responsibility for ensuring that ships used in Community waters comply with applicable rules and standards.

(2) The material standards in all Member States for discharges of polluting substances from ships are based upon the Marpol 73/78 Convention; however these rules are being ignored on a daily basis by a very large number of ships sailing in Community waters, without corrective action being taken.

(3) The implementation of Marpol 73/78 shows discrepancies among Member States and there is thus a need to harmonise its implementation at Community level; in particular the practices of Member States relating to the imposition of penalties for discharges of polluting substances from ships differ significantly.

(4) Measures of a dissuasive nature form an integral part of the Community's maritime safety policy, as they ensure a link between the responsibility of each of the parties involved in the transport of polluting goods by sea and their exposure to penalties; in order to achieve effective protection of the environment there is therefore a need for effective, dissuasive and proportionate penalties.

(5) To that end it is essential to approximate, by way of the proper legal instruments, existing legal provisions, in particular on the precise definition of the infringement in question, the cases of exemption and minimum rules for penalties, and on liability and jurisdiction.

(6) This Directive is supplemented by detailed rules on criminal offences and penalties as well as other provisions set out in Council Framework Decision 2005/667/JHA of 12 July 2005 to

(1) OJ C 220, 16.9.2003, p. 72.

(2) Opinion of the European Parliament of 13 January 2004 (OJ C 92 E, 16.4.2004, p. 77), Council Common Position of 7 October 2004 (OJ C 25 E, 1.2.2005, p. 29), Position of the European Parliament of 23 February 2005 (not yet published in the Official Journal) and Council Decision of 12 July 2005.

▼B

strengthen the criminal law framework for the enforcement of the law against ship-source pollution ([1]).

(7) Neither the international regime for the civil liability and compensation of oil pollution nor that relating to pollution by other hazardous or noxious substances provides sufficient dissuasive effects to discourage the parties involved in the transport of hazardous cargoes by sea from engaging in substandard practices; the required dissuasive effects can only be achieved through the introduction of penalties applying to any person who causes or contributes to marine pollution; penalties should be applicable not only to the shipowner or the master of the ship, but also the owner of the cargo, the classification society or any other person involved.

(8) Ship-source discharges of polluting substances should be regarded as infringements if committed with intent, recklessly or by serious negligence. These infringements are regarded as criminal offences by, and in the circumstances provided for in, Framework Decision 2005/667/JHA supplementing this Directive.

(9) Penalties for discharges of polluting substances from ships are not related to the civil liability of the parties concerned and are thus not subject to any rules relating to the limitation or channelling of civil liabilities, nor do they limit the efficient compensation of victims of pollution incidents.

(10) There is a need for further effective cooperation among Member States to ensure that discharges of polluting substances from ships are detected in time and that the offenders are identified. For this reason, the European Maritime Safety Agency set up by Regulation (EC) No 1406/2002 of the European Parliament and of the Council of 27 June 2002 ([2]) has a key role to play in working with the Member States in developing technical solutions and providing technical assistance relating to the implementation of this Directive and in assisting the Commission in the performance of any task assigned to it for the effective implementation of this Directive.

(11) In order better to prevent and combat marine pollution, synergies should be created between enforcement authorities such as national coastguard services. In this context, the Commission should undertake a feasibility study on a European coastguard dedicated to pollution prevention and response, making clear the costs and benefits. This study should, if appropriate, be followed by a proposal on a European coastguard.

(12) Where there is clear, objective evidence of a discharge causing major damage or a threat of major damage, Member States should submit the matter to their competent authorities with a view to instituting proceedings in accordance with Article 220 of the 1982 United Nations Convention on the Law of the Sea.

(13) The enforcement of Directive 2000/59/EC of the European Parliament and of the Council of 27 November 2000 on port reception facilities for ship-generated waste and cargo residues ([3]) is, together with this Directive, a key instrument in the set of measures to prevent ship-source pollution.

(14) The measures necessary for the implementation of this Directive should be adopted in accordance with Council Decision 1999/468/EC of 28 June 1999 laying down the procedures for

---

([1]) See page 164 of this Official Journal.
([2]) OJ L 208, 5.8.2002, p. 1. Regulation as last amended by Regulation (EC) No 724/2004 (OJ L 129, 29.4.2004, p. 1).
([3]) OJ L 332, 28.12.2000, p. 81. Directive as amended by Directive 2002/84/EC (OJ L 324, 29.11.2002, p. 53).

▼B

the exercise of implementing powers conferred on the Commission ([1]).

(15) Since the objectives of this Directive, namely the incorporation of the international ship-source pollution standards into Community law and the establishment of penalties — criminal or administrative — for violation of them in order to ensure a high level of safety and environmental protection in maritime transport, cannot be sufficiently achieved by the Member States and can therefore be better achieved at Community level, the Community may adopt measures, in accordance with the principle of subsidiarity as set out in Article 5 of the Treaty. In accordance with the principle of proportionality, as set out in that Article, this Directive does not go beyond what is necessary in order to achieve those objectives.

(16) This Directive fully respects the Charter of fundamental rights of the European Union; any person suspected of having committed an infringement must be guaranteed a fair and impartial hearing and the penalties must be proportional,

HAVE ADOPTED THIS DIRECTIVE:

*Article 1*

**Purpose**

▼M1

1. The purpose of this Directive is to incorporate international standards for ship-source pollution into Community law and to ensure that persons responsible for discharges of polluting substances are subject to adequate penalties, including criminal penalties, in order to improve maritime safety and to enhance protection of the marine environment from pollution by ships.

▼B

2. This Directive does not prevent Member States from taking more stringent measures against ship-source pollution in conformity with international law.

*Article 2*

**Definitions**

For the purpose of this Directive:

1. 'Marpol 73/78' shall mean the International Convention for the Prevention of Pollution from Ships, 1973 and its 1978 Protocol, in its up-to-date version;

2. 'polluting substances' shall mean substances covered by Annexes I (oil) and II (noxious liquid substances in bulk) to Marpol 73/78;

3. 'discharge' shall mean any release howsoever caused from a ship, as referred to in Article 2 of Marpol 73/78;

4. 'ship' shall mean a seagoing vessel, irrespective of its flag, of any type whatsoever operating in the marine environment and shall include hydrofoil boats, air-cushion vehicles, submersibles and floating craft;

▼M1

5. 'Legal person' shall mean any legal entity in possession of such status under applicable national law, other than States themselves or public bodies in the exercise of State authority or public international organisations.

([1]) OJ L 184, 17.7.1999, p. 23.

▼B

*Article 3*

**Scope**

1. This Directive shall apply, in accordance with international law, to discharges of polluting substances in:

(a) the internal waters, including ports, of a Member State, in so far as the Marpol regime is applicable;

(b) the territorial sea of a Member State;

(c) straits used for international navigation subject to the regime of transit passage, as laid down in Part III, section 2, of the 1982 United Nations Convention on the Law of the Sea, to the extent that a Member State exercises jurisdiction over such straits;

(d) the exclusive economic zone or equivalent zone of a Member State, established in accordance with international law; and

(e) the high seas.

2. This Directive shall apply to discharges of polluting substances from any ship, irrespective of its flag, with the exception of any warship, naval auxiliary or other ship owned or operated by a State and used, for the time being, only on government non-commercial service.

▼M1

*Article 4*

**Infringements**

1. Member States shall ensure that ship-source discharges of polluting substances, including minor cases of such discharges, into any of the areas referred to in Article 3(1) are regarded as infringements if committed with intent, recklessly or with serious negligence.

2. Each Member State shall take the necessary measures to ensure that any natural or legal person having committed an infringement within the meaning of paragraph 1 can be held liable therefor.

*Article 5*

**Exceptions**

1. A discharge of polluting substances into any of the areas referred to in Article 3(1) shall not be regarded as an infringement, if it satisfies the conditions set out in Annex I, Regulations 15, 34, 4,1 or 4,3 or in Annex II, Regulations 13, 3.1.1 or 3.1.3 of Marpol 73/78.

2. A discharge of polluting substances into the areas referred to in Article 3(1)(c), (d) and (e) shall not be regarded as an infringement for the owner, the master or the crew, if it satisfies the conditions set out in Annex I, Regulation 4,2 or in Annex II, Regulation 3.1.2 of Marpol 73/78.

*Article 5a*

**Criminal offences**

1. Member States shall ensure that infringements within the meaning of Articles 4 and 5 are regarded as criminal offences.

2. Paragraph 1 shall not apply to minor cases, where the act committed does not cause deterioration in the quality of water.

3. Repeated minor cases that do not individually but in conjunction result in deterioration in the quality of water shall be regarded as a criminal offence, if committed with intent, recklessly or with serious negligence.

▼M1

*Article 5b*

**Inciting, aiding and abetting**

Member States shall ensure that any act of inciting, or aiding and abetting an offence committed with intent and referred to in Article 5a(1) and (3), is punishable as a criminal offence.

▼B

*Article 6*

**Enforcement measures with respect to ships within a port of a Member State**

1. If irregularities or information give rise to a suspicion that a ship which is voluntarily within a port or at an off-shore terminal of a Member State has been engaged in or is engaging in a discharge of polluting substances into any of the areas referred to in Article 3(1), that Member State shall ensure that an appropriate inspection, taking into account the relevant guidelines adopted by the International Maritime Organisation (IMO), is undertaken in accordance with its national law.

2. In so far as the inspection referred to in paragraph 1 reveals facts that could indicate an infringement within the meaning of Article 4, the competent authorities of that Member State and of the flag State shall be informed.

*Article 7*

**Enforcement measures by coastal States with respect to ships in transit**

1. If the suspected discharge of polluting substances takes place in the areas referred to in Article 3(1)(b), (c), (d) or (e) and the ship which is suspected of the discharge does not call at a port of the Member State holding the information relating to the suspected discharge, the following shall apply:

(a) If the next port of call of the ship is in another Member State, the Member States concerned shall cooperate closely in the inspection referred to in Article 6(1) and in deciding on the appropriate measures in respect of any such discharge;

(b) If the next port of call of the ship is a port of a State outside the Community, the Member State shall take the necessary measures to ensure that the next port of call of the ship is informed about the suspected discharge and shall request the State of the next port of call to take the appropriate measures in respect of any such discharge.

2. Where there is clear, objective evidence that a ship navigating in the areas referred to in Article 3(1)(b) or (d) has, in the area referred to in Article 3(1)(d), committed an infringement resulting in a discharge causing major damage or a threat of major damage to the coastline or related interests of the Member State concerned, or to any resources of the areas referred to in Article 3(1)(b) or (d), that State shall, subject to Part XII, Section 7 of the 1982 United Nations Convention on the Law of the Sea and provided that the evidence so warrants, submit the matter to its competent authorities with a view to instituting proceedings, including detention of the ship, in accordance with its national law.

3. In any event, the authorities of the flag State shall be informed.

▼M1

*Article 8*

**Penalties**

Each Member State shall take the necessary measures to ensure that infringements within the meaning of Articles 4 and 5 are punishable by effective, proportionate and dissuasive penalties.

*Article 8a*

**Penalties against natural persons**

Each Member State shall take the necessary measures to ensure that the offences referred to in Article 5a(1), and (3) and Article 5b are punishable by effective, proportionate and dissuasive criminal penalties.

*Article 8b*

**Liability of legal persons**

1. Each Member State shall take the necessary measures to ensure that legal persons can be held liable for the criminal offences referred to in Article 5a(1) and (3) and Article 5b, committed for their benefit by any natural person acting either individually or as part of an organ of the legal person, and who has a leading position within the structure of the legal person, based on:

(a) a power of representation of the legal person;

(b) authority to take decisions on behalf of the legal person; or

(c) authority to exercise control within the legal person.

2. Each Member State shall also ensure that a legal person can be held liable where lack of supervision or control by a natural person referred to in paragraph 1 has made the commission of a criminal offence referred to in Article 5a(1) and (3) and Article 5b possible for the benefit of that legal person by a natural person under its authority.

3. The liability of a legal person under paragraphs 1 and 2 shall not exclude criminal proceedings against natural persons involved as perpetrators, inciters or accessories in the criminal offences referred to in Article 5a(1) and (3) and Article 5b.

*Article 8c*

**Penalties against legal persons**

Each Member State shall take the necessary measures to ensure that a legal person held liable pursuant to Article 8b is punishable by effective, proportionate and dissuasive penalties.

▼B

*Article 9*

**Compliance with international law**

Member States shall apply the provisions of this Directive without any discrimination in form or in fact against foreign ships and in accordance with applicable international law, including Section 7 of Part XII of the 1982 United Nations Convention on the Law of the Sea, and they shall promptly notify the flag State of the vessel and any other State concerned of measures taken in accordance with this Directive.

▼B

*Article 10*

**Accompanying measures**

1. For the purposes of this Directive, Member States and the Commission shall cooperate, where appropriate, in close collaboration with the European Maritime Safety Agency and taking account of the action programme to respond to accidental or deliberate marine pollution set up by Decision No 2850/2000/EC ([1]) and if appropriate, of the implementation of Directive 2000/59/EC in order to:

(a) develop the necessary information systems required for the effective implementation of this Directive;

(b) establish common practices and guidelines on the basis of those existing at international level, in particular for:

— the monitoring and early identification of ships discharging polluting substances in violation of this Directive, including, where appropriate, on-board monitoring equipment,

— reliable methods of tracing polluting substances in the sea to a particular ship, and

— the effective enforcement of this Directive.

2. In accordance with its tasks as defined in Regulation (EC) No 1406/2002, the European Maritime Safety Agency shall:

(a) work with the Member States in developing technical solutions and providing technical assistance in relation to the implementation of this Directive, in actions such as tracing discharges by satellite monitoring and surveillance;

(b) assist the Commission in the implementation of this Directive, including, if appropriate, by means of visits to the Member States, in accordance with Article 3 of Regulation (EC) No 1406/2002.

*Article 11*

**Feasibility Study**

The Commission shall, before the end of 2006, submit to the European Parliament and the Council a feasibility study on a European coastguard dedicated to pollution prevention and response, making clear the costs and benefits.

*Article 12*

**Reporting**

Every three years, Member States shall transmit a report to the Commission on the application of this Directive by the competent authorities. On the basis of these reports, the Commission shall submit a Community report to the European Parliament and the Council. In this report, the Commission shall assess, *inter alia*, the desirability of revising or extending the scope of this Directive. It shall also describe the evolution of relevant case-law in the Member States and shall consider the possibility of creating a public database containing such relevant case-law.

([1]) Decision No 2850/2000/EC of the European Parliament and of the Council of 20 December 2000 setting up a Community framework for cooperation in the field of accidental or deliberate marine pollution (OJ L 332, 28.12.2000, p. 1). Decision as amended by Decision No 787/2004/EC (OJ L 138, 30.4.2004, p. 12).

▼B

*Article 13*

**Committee procedure**

1. The Commission shall be assisted by the Committee on Safe Seas and the Prevention of Pollution from Ships (COSS), established by Article 3 of Regulation (EC) No 2099/2002 of the European Parliament and of the Council, of 5 November 2002 [1].

2. Where reference is made to this Article, Articles 5 and 7 of Decision 1999/468/EC shall apply, having regard to the provisions of Article 8 thereof.

The period laid down in Article 5(6) of Decision 1999/468/EC shall be set at one month.

*Article 14*

**Provision of information**

The Commission shall regularly inform the Committee set up by Article 4 of Decision No 2850/2000/EC of any proposed measures or other relevant activities concerning the response to marine pollution.

*Article 15*

**Amendment procedure**

In accordance with Article 5 of Regulation (EC) No 2099/2002 and following the procedure referred to in Article 13 of this Directive, the COSS may exclude amendments to Marpol 73/78 from the scope of this Directive.

*Article 16*

**Implementation**

▼C1

Member States shall bring into force the laws, regulations and administrative provisions necessary to comply with this Directive by 1 April 2007 and forthwith inform the Commission thereof.

▼B

When Member States adopt those provisions, they shall contain a reference to this Directive or be accompanied by such a reference on the occasion of their official publication. Member States shall determine how such reference is to be made.

*Article 17*

**Entry into force**

This Directive shall enter into force on the day following its publication in the *Official Journal of the European Union.*

*Article 18*

**Addressees**

This Directive is addressed to the Member States.

---

[1] OJ L 324, 29.11.2002, p. 1. Regulation as amended by Commission Regulation (EC) No 415/2004 (OJ L 68, 6.3.2004, p. 10).

▼B

*ANNEX*

**Summary, for reference purposes, of the Marpol 73/78 discharge regulations relating to discharges of oil and noxious liquid substances, as referred to in Article 2.2**

**Part I: Oil (Marpol 73/78, Annex I)**

For the purposes of Marpol 73/78 Annex I, 'oil' means petroleum in any form including crude oil, fuel oil, sludge, oil refuse and refined products (other than petrochemicals which are subject to the provisions of Marpol 73/78 Annex II) and 'oily mixture' means a mixture with any oil content.

Excerpts of the relevant provisions of Marpol 73/78 Annex I:

Regulation 9: Control of discharge of oil

1. Subject to the provisions of Regulations 10 and 11 of this Annex and paragraph 2 of this Regulation, any discharge into the sea of oil or oily mixtures from ships to which this Annex applies shall be prohibited except when all the following conditions are satisfied:

   (a) for an oil tanker, except as provided for in subparagraph (b) of this paragraph:

      (i) the tanker is not within a special area;

      (ii) the tanker is more than 50 nautical miles from the nearest land;

      (iii) the tanker is proceeding en route;

      (iv) the instantaneous rate of discharge of oil content does not exceed 30 litres per nautical mile;

      (v) the total quantity of oil discharged into the sea does not exceed for existing tankers 1/15000 of the total quantity of the particular cargo of which the residue formed a part, and for new tankers 1/30000 of the total quantity of the particular cargo of which the residue formed a part; and

      (vi) the tanker has in operation an oil discharge monitoring and control system and a slop tank arrangement as required by Regulation 15 of this Annex.

   (b) from a ship of 400 tons gross tonnage and above other than an oil tanker and from machinery space bilges excluding cargo pump-room bilges of an oil tanker unless mixed with oil cargo residue:

      (i) the ship is not within a special area;

      (ii) the ship is proceeding en route;

      (iii) the oil content of the effluent without dilution does not exceed 15 parts per million; and

      (iv) the ship has in operation (monitoring, control and filtering equipment) as required by regulation 16 of this Annex.

2. In the case of a ship of less than 400 tons gross tonnage other than an oil tanker whilst outside the special area, the (flag State) Administration shall ensure that it is equipped as far as practicable and reasonable with installations to ensure the storage of oil residues on board and their discharge to reception facilities or into the sea in compliance with the requirements of paragraph (1) (b) of this Regulation.

3. […].

4. The provisions of paragraph 1 of this Regulation shall not apply to the discharge of clean or segregated ballast or unprocessed oily mixtures which without dilution have an oil content not exceeding 15 parts per million and which do not originate from cargo pump-room bilges and are not mixed with oil cargo residues.

5. No discharge into the sea shall contain chemicals or other substances in quantities or concentrations which are hazardous to the marine environment or chemicals or other substances introduced for the purpose of circumventing the conditions of discharge specified in this regulation.

▼B

6. The oil residues which cannot be discharged into the sea in compliance with paragraphs 1, 2 and 4 of this Regulation shall be retained on board or discharged to reception facilities.

7. […].

Regulation 10: Methods for the prevention of oil pollution from ships while operating in special areas

1. For the purpose of this Annex, the special areas are the Mediterranean Sea area, the Baltic Sea area, the Black Sea area, the Red Sea area, the 'Gulfs area', the Gulf of Aden area, the Antarctic area and the North-West European waters, (as further defined and specified).

2. Subject to the provisions of regulation 11 of this Annex:

   (a) Any discharge into the sea of oil or oily mixture from any oil tanker and any ship of 400 tons gross tonnage and above other than an oil tanker shall be prohibited while in a special area. […];

   (b) […] Any discharge into the sea of oil or oily mixture from a ship of less than 400 tons gross tonnage, other than an oil tanker, shall be prohibited while in a special area, except when the oil content of the effluent without dilution does not exceed 15 parts per million.

3. (a) The provisions of paragraph 2 of this Regulation shall not apply to the discharge of clean or segregated ballast.

   (b) The provisions of subparagraph (2)(a) of this regulation shall not apply to the discharge of processed bilge water from machinery spaces, provided that all of the following conditions are satisfied:

      (i) the bilge water does not originate from cargo pump-room bilges;

      (ii) the bilge water is not mixed with oil cargo residues;

      (iii) the ship is proceeding en route;

      (iv) the oil content of the effluent without dilution does not exceed 15 parts per million;

      (v) the ship has in operation oil filtering equipment complying with Regulation 16(5) of this Annex; and

      (vi) the filtering system is equipped with a stopping device which will ensure that the discharge is automatically stopped when the oil content of the effluent exceeds 15 parts per million.

4. (a) No discharge into the sea shall contain chemicals or other substances in quantities or concentrations which are hazardous to the marine environment or chemicals or other substances introduced for the purpose of circumventing the conditions of discharge specified in this regulation.

   (b) The oil residues which cannot be discharged into the sea in compliance with paragraph 2 or 3 of this Regulation shall be retained on board or discharged to reception facilities.

5. Nothing in this Regulation shall prohibit a ship on a voyage only part of which is in a special area from discharging outside the special area in accordance with Regulation 9 of this Annex.

6. […].

7. […].

8. […].

Regulation 11: Exceptions

Regulations 9 and 10 of this Annex shall not apply to:

(a) the discharge into the sea of oil or oily mixture necessary for the purpose of securing the safety of a ship or saving life at sea; or

(b) the discharge into the sea of oil or oily mixture resulting from damage to a ship or its equipment:

   (i) provided that all reasonable precautions have been taken after the occurrence of the damage or discovery of the discharge for the purpose of preventing or minimising the discharge; and

▼B

(ii) except if the owner or the master acted either with intent to cause damage, or recklessly and with knowledge that damage would probably result; or

(c) the discharge into the sea of substances containing oil, approved by the (flag State) administration, when being used for the purpose of combating specific pollution incidents in order to minimise the damage from pollution. Any such discharge shall be subject to the approval of any Government in whose jurisdiction it is contemplated the discharge will occur.

**Part II: Noxious liquid substances (Marpol 73/78 Annex II)**

Excerpts of the relevant provisions of Marpol 73/78 Annex II:

Regulation 3: Categorisation and listing of noxious liquid substances

1. For the purpose of the Regulations of this Annex, noxious liquid substances shall be divided into four categories as follows:

   (a) Category A: noxious liquid substances which if discharged into the sea from tank cleaning or deballasting operations would present a major hazard to either marine resources or human health or cause serious harm to amenities or other legitimate uses of the sea and therefore justify the application of stringent anti-pollution measures;

   (b) Category B: noxious liquid substances which if discharged into the sea from tank cleaning or deballasting operations would present a hazard to either marine resources or human health or cause harm to amenities or other legitimate uses of the sea and therefore justify the application of special anti-pollution measures;

   (c) Category C: noxious liquid substances which if discharged into the sea from tank cleaning or deballasting operations would present a minor hazard to either marine resources or human health or cause minor harm to amenities or other legitimate uses of the sea and therefore require special operational conditions;

   (d) Category D: noxious liquid substances which if discharged into the sea from tank cleaning or deballasting operations would present a recognisable hazard to either marine resources or human health or cause minimal harm to amenities or other legitimate uses of the sea and therefore require some attention in operational conditions.

2. [...].

3. […].

4. […].

(Further guidelines on the categorisation of substances, including a list of categorised substances are given in Regulation 3(2) to (4) and Regulation 4 and the Appendices to Marpol 73/78 Annex II)

Regulation 5: Discharge of noxious liquid substances

Category A, B and C substances outside special areas and Category D substances in all areas

Subject to the provisions of […] Regulation 6 of this Annex,

1. The discharge into the sea of substances in Category A as defined in Regulation 3(1)(a) of this Annex or of those provisionally assessed as such or ballast water, tank washings, or other residues or mixtures containing such substances shall be prohibited. If tanks containing such substances or mixtures are to be washed, the resulting residues shall be discharged to a reception facility until the concentration of the substance in the effluent to such facility is at or below 0,1 % by weight and until the tank is empty, with the exception of phosphorus, yellow or white, for which the residual concentration shall be 0,01 % by weight. Any water subsequently added to the tank may be discharged into the sea when all the following conditions are satisfied:

   (a) the ship is proceeding en route at a speed of at least 7 knots in the case of self-propelled ships or at least 4 knots in the case of ships which are not self-propelled;

   (b) the discharge is made below the waterline, taking into account the location of the seawater intakes; and

   (c) the discharge is made at a distance of not less than 12 nautical miles from the nearest land in a depth of water of not less than 25 m.

▼B

2. The discharge into the sea of substances in Category B as defined in Regulation 3(1)(b) of this Annex or of those provisionally assessed as such, or ballast water, tank washings, or other residues or mixtures containing such substances shall be prohibited except when all the following conditions are satisfied:

   (a) the ship is proceeding en route at a speed of at least 7 knots in the case of self-propelled ships or at least 4 knots in the case of ships which are not self-propelled;

   (b) the procedures and arrangements for discharge are approved by the (flag State) administration. Such procedures and arrangements shall be based upon standards developed by the (IMO) and shall ensure that the concentration and rate of discharge of the effluent is such that the concentration of the substance in the wake astern of the ship does not exceed 1 part per million;

   (c) the maximum quantity of cargo discharged from each tank and its associated piping system does not exceed the maximum quantity approved in accordance with the procedures referred to in subparagraph (b) of this paragraph, which shall in no case exceed the greater of 1 $m^3$ or 1/3000 of the tank capacity in $m^3$;

   (d) the discharge is made below the waterline, taking into account the location of the seawater intakes; and

   (e) the discharge is made at a distance of not less than 12 nautical miles from the nearest land and in a depth of water of not less than 25 m.

3. The discharge into the sea of substances in Category C as defined in Regulation 3(1)(c) of this Annex or of those provisionally assessed as such, or ballast water, tank washings, or other residues or mixtures containing such substances shall be prohibited except when all the following conditions are satisfied:

   (a) the ship is proceeding en route at a speed of at least 7 knots in the case of self-propelled ships or at least 4 knots in the case of ships which are not self-propelled;

   (b) the procedures and arrangements for discharge are approved by the (flag State) administration. Such procedures and arrangements shall be based upon standards developed by the (IMO) and shall ensure that the concentration and rate of discharge of the effluent is such that the concentration of the substance in the wake astern of the ship does not exceed 10 parts per million;

   (c) the maximum quantity of cargo discharged from each tank and its associated piping system does not exceed the maximum quantity approved in accordance with the procedures referred to in subparagraph (b) of this paragraph, which shall in no case exceed the greater of 3 $m^3$ or 1/1000 of the tank capacity in $m^3$;

   (d) the discharge is made below the waterline, taking into account the location of the seawater intakes; and

   (e) the discharge is made at a distance of not less than 12 nautical miles from the nearest land and in a depth of water of not less than 25 m.

4. The discharge into the sea of substances in Category D as defined in Regulation 3(1)(d) of this Annex, or of those provisionally assessed as such, or ballast water, tank washings, or other residues or mixtures containing such substances shall be prohibited except when all the following conditions are satisfied:

   (a) the ship is proceeding en route at a speed of at least 7 knots in the case of self-propelled ships or at least 4 knots in the case of ships which are not self-propelled;

   (b) such mixtures are of a concentration not greater than one part of the substance in ten parts of water; and

   (c) the discharge is made at a distance of not less than 12 nautical miles from the nearest land.

5. Ventilation procedures approved by the (flag State) administration may be used to remove cargo residues from a tank. Such procedures shall be based upon standards developed by the (IMO). Any water subsequently introduced into the tank shall be regarded as clean and shall not be subject to paragraphs 1, 2, 3 or 4 of this Regulation.

▼B

6. The discharge into the sea of substances which have not been categorised, provisionally assessed, or evaluated as referred to in Regulation 4(1) of this Annex, or of ballast water, tank washings, or other residues or mixtures containing such substances shall be prohibited.

Category A, B and C substances within special areas (as defined in Marpol 73/78 Annex II, Regulation 1, including the Baltic Sea)

Subject to the provisions of [...] Regulation 6 of this Annex,

7. The discharge into the sea of substances in Category A as defined in Regulation 3(1)(a) of this Annex or of those provisionally assessed as such, or ballast water, tank washings, or other residues or mixtures containing such substances shall be prohibited. If tanks containing such substances or mixtures are to be washed, the resulting residues shall be discharged to a reception facility which the States bordering the special area shall provide in accordance with Regulation 7 of this Annex, until the concentration of the substance in the effluent to such facility is at or below 0,05 % by weight and until the tank is empty, with the exception of phosphorus, yellow or white, for which the residual concentration shall be 0,005 % by weight. Any water subsequently added to the tank may be discharged into the sea when all the following conditions are satisfied:

   (a) the ship is proceeding en route at a speed of at least 7 knots in the case of self-propelled ships or at least 4 knots in the case of ships which are not self-propelled;

   (b) the discharge is made below the waterline, taking into account the location of the seawater intakes; and

   (c) the discharge is made at a distance of not less than 12 nautical miles from the nearest land and in a depth of water of not less than 25 m.

8. The discharge into the sea of substances in Category B as defined in Regulation (3)(1)(b) of this Annex or of those provisionally assessed as such, or ballast water, tank washings, or other residues or mixtures containing such substances shall be prohibited except when all the following conditions are satisfied:

   (a) the tank has been prewashed in accordance with the procedure approved by the (flag State) Administration and based on standards developed by the (IMO) and the resulting tank washings have been discharged to a reception facility;

   (b) the ship is proceeding en route at a speed of at least 7 knots in the case of self-propelled ships or at least 4 knots in the case of ships which are not self-propelled;

   (c) the procedures and arrangements for discharge and washings are approved by the (flag State) Administration. Such procedures and arrangements shall be based upon standards developed by the (IMO) and shall ensure that the concentration and rate of discharge of the effluent is such that the concentration of the substance in the wake astern of the ship does not exceed 1 part per million;

   (d) the discharge is made below the waterline, taking into account the location of the seawater intakes; and

   (e) the discharge is made at a distance of not less than 12 nautical miles from the nearest land and in a depth of water of not less than 25 m.

9. The discharge into the sea of substances in Category C as defined in Regulation 3(1)(c) of this Annex or of those provisionally assessed as such, or ballast water, tank washings, or other residues or mixtures containing such substances shall be prohibited except when all the following conditions are satisfied:

   (a) the ship is proceeding en route at a speed of at least 7 knots in the case of self-propelled ships or at least 4 knots in the case of ships which are not self-propelled;

   (b) the procedures and arrangements for discharge are approved by the (flag State) administration. Such procedures and arrangements shall be based upon standards developed by the (IMO) and shall ensure that the concentration and rate of discharge of the effluent is such that the concentration of the substance in the wake astern of the ship does not exceed 1 part per million;

▼B

(c) the maximum quantity of cargo discharged from each tank and its associated piping system does not exceed the maximum quantity approved in accordance with the procedures referred to in subparagraph (b) of this paragraph which shall in no case exceed the greater of 1 $m^3$ or 1/3000 of the tank capacity in $m^3$;

(d) the discharge is made below the waterline, taking into account the location of the seawater intakes; and

(e) the discharge is made at a distance of not less than 12 nautical miles from the nearest land and in a depth of water of not less than 25 m.

10. Ventilation procedures approved by the (flag State) administration may be used to remove cargo residues from a tank. Such procedures shall be based upon standards developed by the (IMO). Any water subsequently introduced into the tank shall be regarded as clean and shall not be subject to paragraphs 7, 8 or 9 of this Regulation.

11. The discharge into the sea of substances which have not been categorised, provisionally assessed or evaluated as referred to in Regulation 4(1) of this Annex, or of ballast water, tank washings, or other residues or mixtures containing such substances shall be prohibited.

12. Nothing in this regulation shall prohibit a ship from retaining on board the residues from a Category B or C cargo and discharging such residues into the sea outside a special area in accordance with paragraphs 2 or 3 of this Regulation, respectively.

Regulation 6: Exceptions

Regulation 5 of this Annex shall not apply to:

(a) the discharge into the sea of noxious liquid substances or mixtures containing such substances necessary for the purpose of securing the safety of a ship or saving life at sea; or

(b) the discharge into the sea of noxious liquid substances or mixtures containing such substances resulting from damage to a ship or its equipment:

(i) provided that all reasonable precautions have been taken after the occurrence of the damage or discovery of the discharge for the purpose of preventing or minimising the discharge; and

(ii) except if the owner or the master acted either with intent to cause damage, or recklessly and with knowledge that damage would probably result; or

(c) the discharge into the sea of noxious liquid substances or mixtures containing such substances, approved by the (flag State) administration, when being used for the purpose of combating specific pollution incidents in order to minimise the damage from pollution. Any such discharge shall be subject to the approval of any government in whose jurisdiction it is contemplated the discharge will occur.

# Decision 2005/671 on the exchange of information and cooperation concerning terrorist offences, 20 September 2005

[OJ 2005, L 253/22–24]

L 253/22 EN Official Journal of the European Union 29.9.2005

*(Acts adopted under Title VI of the Treaty on European Union)*

**COUNCIL DECISION 2005/671/JHA**

**of 20 September 2005**

**on the exchange of information and cooperation concerning terrorist offences**

THE COUNCIL OF THE EUROPEAN UNION,

Having regard to the Treaty on European Union, and in particular Articles 29, 30(1), 31 and 34(2)(c) thereof,

Having regard to the proposal from the Commission,

Having regard to the Opinion of the European Parliament [1],

Whereas:

(1) At its extraordinary meeting on 21 September 2001, the European Council stated that terrorism was a real challenge to the world and to Europe and that the fight against terrorism would be a priority objective of the European Union.

(2) On 19 October 2001 the European Council stated that it was determined to combat terrorism in every form throughout the world and that it would continue its efforts to strengthen the coalition of the international community to combat terrorism in every shape and form, for example by increased cooperation between the operational services responsible for combating terrorism: Europol, Eurojust, the intelligence services, police forces and judicial authorities.

(3) It is essential in the fight against terrorism for the relevant services to have the fullest and most up-to-date information possible in their respective fields. The Member States' specialised national services, the judicial authorities and relevant bodies of the European Union such as Europol and Eurojust absolutely need information if they are to perform their tasks.

(4) Council Decision 2003/48/JHA of 19 December 2002 on the implementation of specific measures for police and judicial cooperation to combat terrorism in accordance with Article 4 of Common Position 2001/931/CFSP [2] is a major step forward. The persistence of the terrorist threat and the complexity of the phenomenon raise the need for ever greater exchanges of information. The scope of information exchanges must be extended to all stages of criminal proceedings, including convictions, and to all persons, groups or entities investigated, prosecuted or convicted for terrorist offences.

(5) Since the objectives of this decision cannot be sufficiently achieved by the Member States acting alone and can therefore, given the need for reciprocity, be better achieved at Community level, the Community may adopt measures, act in accordance with the principle of subsidiarity as set out in Article 5 of the Treaty. In accordance with the principle of proportionality, as set out in that Article, this Decision does not go beyond what is necessary to achieve those objectives.

(6) In the execution of the exchange of information, this Decision is without prejudice to essential national security interests, and it should not jeopardise the safety of individuals or the success of a current investigation or specific intelligence activities in the field of State security.

(7) This Decision respects the fundamental rights and observes the principles recognised in particular by the Charter of Fundamental Rights of the European Union,

HAS DECIDED AS FOLLOWS:

*Article 1*

**Definitions**

For the purposes of this Decision, the following definitions shall apply:

(a) 'terrorist offences': the offences specified in Articles 1, 2 and 3 of Council Framework Decision 2002/475/JHA of 13 June 2002 on combating terrorism [3];

[1] Opinion given on 7 June 2005 (not yet published in the Official Journal).

[2] OJ L 16, 22.1.2003, p. 68.

[3] OJ L 164, 22.6.2002, p. 3.

29.9.2005 EN Official Journal of the European Union L 253/23

(b) 'Europol Convention': the Convention of 26 July 1995 on the establishment of a European Police Office ([1]);

(c) 'Eurojust Decision': Council Decision 2002/187/JHA of 28 February 2002 setting up Eurojust with a view to reinforcing the fight against serious crime ([2]);

(d) 'group or entity': 'terrorist groups' within the meaning of Article 2 of Council Framework Decision 2002/475/JHA and the groups and entities listed in the Annex to Council Common Position 2001/931/CFSP of 27 December 2001 on the application of specific measures to combat terrorism ([3]).

*Article 2*

**Provision of information concerning terrorist offences to Eurojust, Europol and the Member States**

1. Each Member State shall designate a specialised service within its police services or other law enforcement authorities, which, in accordance with national law, will have access to and collect all relevant information concerning and resulting from criminal investigations conducted by its law enforcement authorities with respect to terrorist offences and send it to Europol in accordance with paragraphs 3 and 4.

2. Each Member State shall designate one, or where its legal system so provides more than one authority, as Eurojust national correspondent for terrorism matters or an appropriate judicial or other competent authority which, in accordance with national law, shall have access to and can collect all relevant information concerning prosecutions and convictions for terrorist offences and send it to Eurojust in accordance with paragraph 5.

3. Each Member State shall take the necessary measures to ensure that at least the information referred to in paragraph 4 concerning criminal investigations and the information referred to in paragraph 5 concerning prosecutions and convictions for terrorist offences which affect or may affect two or more Member States, gathered by the relevant authority, is transmitted to:

(a) Europol, in accordance with national law and with the provisions of the Europol Convention, for processing; and

(b) Eurojust, in accordance with national law and where the provisions of the Eurojust Decision so allow.

4. The information to be transmitted in accordance with paragraph 3 to Europol shall be the following:

(a) data which identify the person, group or entity;

(b) acts under investigation and their specific circumstances;

(c) the offence concerned;

(d) links with other relevant cases;

(e) the use of communication technologies;

(f) the threat posed by the possession of weapons of mass destruction.

5. The information to be transmitted in accordance with paragraph 3 to Eurojust shall be the following:

(a) data which identify the person, group or entity that is the object of a criminal investigation or prosecution;

(b) the offence concerned and its specific circumstances;

(c) information about final convictions for terrorist offences and the specific circumstances surrounding those offences;

(d) links with other relevant cases;

(e) requests for judicial assistance, including letters rogatory, addressed to or by another Member State and the response.

6. Each Member State shall take the necessary measures to ensure that any relevant information included in documents, files, items of information, objects or other means of evidence, seized or confiscated in the course of criminal investigations or criminal proceedings in connection with terrorist offences can be made accessible as soon as possible, taking account of the need not to jeopardise current investigations, to the authorities of other interested Member States in accordance with national law and relevant international legal instruments where investigations are being carried out or might be initiated or where prosecutions are in progress in connection with terrorist offences.

*Article 3*

**Joint investigation teams**

In appropriate cases Member States shall take the necessary measures to set up joint investigation teams to conduct criminal investigations into terrorist offences.

([1]) OJ C 316, 27.11.1995, p. 2. Convention as last amended by the Protocol of 27.11.2003 (OJ C 2, 6.1.2004, p. 3).
([2]) OJ L 63, 6.3.2002, p. 1. Decision as amended by Council Decision 2003/659/JHA (OJ L 245, 29.9.2003, p. 44).
([3]) OJ L 344, 28.12.2001, p. 93. Common Position as last amended by Common Position 2005/220/CFSP (OJ L 69, 16.3.2005, p. 59).

*Article 4*

**Requests for judicial assistance and enforcement of judgments**

Each Member State shall take the necessary measures to ensure that requests from other Member States for mutual legal assistance and recognition and enforcement of judgments in connection with terrorist offences are dealt with as a matter of urgency and are given priority.

*Article 5*

**Repeal of existing provisions**

Decision 2003/48/JHA is hereby repealed.

*Article 6*

**Implementation**

Member States shall take the necessary measures to comply with the provisions of this Decision at the latest by 30 June 2006.

*Article 7*

**Territorial Application**

This Decision shall apply to Gibraltar.

*Article 8*

**Entry into force**

This Decision shall take effect on the day following its publication in the *Official Journal of the European Union*.

Done at Brussels, 20 September 2005.

*For the Council*
*The President*
M. BECKETT

# Directive 2005/60 on the prevention of the use of the financial system for the purpose of money laundering and terrorist financing, 26 October 2005

**[OJ 2005, L 309/15–32]**

**[Editor's note: Annex correlation table omitted]**

Only European Union legislation printed in the paper edition of the *Official Journal of the European Union* is deemed authentic.

25.11.2005 EN Official Journal of the European Union L 309/15

# DIRECTIVE 2005/60/EC OF THE EUROPEAN PARLIAMENT AND OF THE COUNCIL

## of 26 October 2005

## on the prevention of the use of the financial system for the purpose of money laundering and terrorist financing

**(Text with EEA relevance)**

THE EUROPEAN PARLIAMENT AND THE COUNCIL OF THE EUROPEAN UNION,

Having regard to the Treaty establishing the European Community, and in particular Article 47(2), first and third sentences, and Article 95 thereof,

Having regard to the proposal from the Commission,

Having regard to the opinion of the European Economic and Social Committee ([1]),

Having regard to the opinion of the European Central Bank ([2]),

Acting in accordance with the procedure laid down in Article 251 of the Treaty ([3]),

Whereas:

(1) Massive flows of dirty money can damage the stability and reputation of the financial sector and threaten the single market, and terrorism shakes the very foundations of our society. In addition to the criminal law approach, a preventive effort via the financial system can produce results.

(2) The soundness, integrity and stability of credit and financial institutions and confidence in the financial system as a whole could be seriously jeopardised by the efforts of criminals and their associates either to disguise the origin of criminal proceeds or to channel lawful or unlawful money for terrorist purposes. In order to avoid Member States' adopting measures to protect their financial systems which could be inconsistent with the functioning of the internal market and with the prescriptions of the rule of law and Community public policy, Community action in this area is necessary.

(3) In order to facilitate their criminal activities, money launderers and terrorist financers could try to take advantage of the freedom of capital movements and the freedom to supply financial services which the integrated financial area entails, if certain coordinating measures are not adopted at Community level.

(4) In order to respond to these concerns in the field of money laundering, Council Directive 91/308/EEC of 10 June 1991 on prevention of the use of the financial system for the purpose of money laundering ([4]) was adopted. It required Member States to prohibit money laundering and to oblige the financial sector, comprising credit institutions and a wide range of other financial institutions, to identify their customers, keep appropriate records, establish internal procedures to train staff and guard against money laundering and to report any indications of money laundering to the competent authorities.

(5) Money laundering and terrorist financing are frequently carried out in an international context. Measures adopted solely at national or even Community level, without taking account of international coordination and cooperation, would have very limited effects. The measures adopted by the Community in this field should therefore be consistent with other action undertaken in other international fora. The Community action should continue to take particular account of the Recommendations of the Financial Action Task Force (hereinafter referred to as the FATF), which constitutes the foremost international body active in the fight against money laundering and terrorist financing. Since the FATF Recommendations were substantially revised and expanded in 2003, this Directive should be in line with that new international standard.

(6) The General Agreement on Trade in Services (GATS) allows Members to adopt measures necessary to protect public morals and prevent fraud and adopt measures for prudential reasons, including for ensuring the stability and integrity of the financial system.

(7) Although initially limited to drugs offences, there has been a trend in recent years towards a much wider definition of money laundering based on a broader range of predicate offences. A wider range of predicate offences facilitates the reporting of suspicious transactions and international cooperation in this area. Therefore, the definition of serious crime should be brought into line with the definition of serious crime in Council Framework Decision 2001/500/JHA of 26 June 2001 on money laundering, the identification, tracing, freezing, seizing and confiscation of instrumentalities and the proceeds of crime ([5]).

([1]) Opinion delivered on 11 May 2005 (not yet published in the Official Journal).
([2]) OJ C 40, 17.2.2005, p. 9.
([3]) Opinion of the European Parliament of 26 May 2005 (not yet published in the Official Journal) and Council Decision of 19 September 2005.
([4]) OJ L 166, 28.6.1991, p. 77. Directive as amended by Directive 2001/97/EC of the European Parliament and of the Council (OJ L 344, 28.12.2001, p. 76).
([5]) OJ L 182, 5.7.2001, p. 1.

(8) Furthermore, the misuse of the financial system to channel criminal or even clean money to terrorist purposes poses a clear risk to the integrity, proper functioning, reputation and stability of the financial system. Accordingly, the preventive measures of this Directive should cover not only the manipulation of money derived from crime but also the collection of money or property for terrorist purposes.

(9) Directive 91/308/EEC, though imposing a customer identification obligation, contained relatively little detail on the relevant procedures. In view of the crucial importance of this aspect of the prevention of money laundering and terrorist financing, it is appropriate, in accordance with the new international standards, to introduce more specific and detailed provisions relating to the identification of the customer and of any beneficial owner and the verification of their identity. To that end a precise definition of 'beneficial owner' is essential. Where the individual beneficiaries of a legal entity or arrangement such as a foundation or trust are yet to be determined, and it is therefore impossible to identify an individual as the beneficial owner, it would suffice to identify the class of persons intended to be the beneficiaries of the foundation or trust. This requirement should not include the identification of the individuals within that class of persons.

(10) The institutions and persons covered by this Directive should, in conformity with this Directive, identify and verify the identity of the beneficial owner. To fulfil this requirement, it should be left to those institutions and persons whether they make use of public records of beneficial owners, ask their clients for relevant data or obtain the information otherwise, taking into account the fact that the extent of such customer due diligence measures relates to the risk of money laundering and terrorist financing, which depends on the type of customer, business relationship, product or transaction.

(11) Credit agreements in which the credit account serves exclusively to settle the loan and the repayment of the loan is effected from an account which was opened in the name of the customer with a credit institution covered by this Directive pursuant to Article 8(1)(a) to (c) should generally be considered as an example of types of less risky transactions.

(12) To the extent that the providers of the property of a legal entity or arrangement have significant control over the use of the property they should be identified as a beneficial owner.

(13) Trust relationships are widely used in commercial products as an internationally recognised feature of the comprehensively supervised wholesale financial markets. An obligation to identify the beneficial owner does not arise from the fact alone that there is a trust relationship in this particular case.

(14) This Directive should also apply to those activities of the institutions and persons covered hereunder which are performed on the Internet.

(15) As the tightening of controls in the financial sector has prompted money launderers and terrorist financers to seek alternative methods for concealing the origin of the proceeds of crime and as such channels can be used for terrorist financing, the anti-money laundering and anti-terrorist financing obligations should cover life insurance intermediaries and trust and company service providers.

(16) Entities already falling under the legal responsibility of an insurance undertaking, and therefore falling within the scope of this Directive, should not be included within the category of insurance intermediary.

(17) Acting as a company director or secretary does not of itself make someone a trust and company service provider. For that reason, the definition covers only those persons that act as a company director or secretary for a third party and by way of business.

(18) The use of large cash payments has repeatedly proven to be very vulnerable to money laundering and terrorist financing. Therefore, in those Member States that allow cash payments above the established threshold, all natural or legal persons trading in goods by way of business should be covered by this Directive when accepting such cash payments. Dealers in high-value goods, such as precious stones or metals, or works of art, and auctioneers are in any event covered by this Directive to the extent that payments to them are made in cash in an amount of EUR 15 000 or more. To ensure effective monitoring of compliance with this Directive by that potentially wide group of institutions and persons, Member States may focus their monitoring activities in particular on those natural and legal persons trading in goods that are exposed to a relatively high risk of money laundering or terrorist financing, in accordance with the principle of risk-based supervision. In view of the different situations in the various Member States, Member States may decide to adopt stricter provisions, in order to properly address the risk involved with large cash payments.

25.11.2005 EN Official Journal of the European Union L 309/17

(19) Directive 91/308/EEC brought notaries and other independent legal professionals within the scope of the Community anti-money laundering regime; this coverage should be maintained unchanged in this Directive; these legal professionals, as defined by the Member States, are subject to the provisions of this Directive when participating in financial or corporate transactions, including providing tax advice, where there is the greatest risk of the services of those legal professionals being misused for the purpose of laundering the proceeds of criminal activity or for the purpose of terrorist financing.

(20) Where independent members of professions providing legal advice which are legally recognised and controlled, such as lawyers, are ascertaining the legal position of a client or representing a client in legal proceedings, it would not be appropriate under this Directive to put those legal professionals in respect of these activities under an obligation to report suspicions of money laundering or terrorist financing. There must be exemptions from any obligation to report information obtained either before, during or after judicial proceedings, or in the course of ascertaining the legal position for a client. Thus, legal advice shall remain subject to the obligation of professional secrecy unless the legal counsellor is taking part in money laundering or terrorist financing, the legal advice is provided for money laundering or terrorist financing purposes or the lawyer knows that the client is seeking legal advice for money laundering or terrorist financing purposes.

(21) Directly comparable services need to be treated in the same manner when provided by any of the professionals covered by this Directive. In order to ensure the respect of the rights laid down in the European Convention for the Protection of Human Rights and Fundamental Freedoms and the Treaty on European Union, in the case of auditors, external accountants and tax advisors, who, in some Member States, may defend or represent a client in the context of judicial proceedings or ascertain a client's legal position, the information they obtain in the performance of those tasks should not be subject to the reporting obligations in accordance with this Directive.

(22) It should be recognised that the risk of money laundering and terrorist financing is not the same in every case. In line with a risk-based approach, the principle should be introduced into Community legislation that simplified customer due diligence is allowed in appropriate cases.

(23) The derogation concerning the identification of beneficial owners of pooled accounts held by notaries or other independent legal professionals should be without prejudice to the obligations that those notaries or other independent legal professionals have pursuant to this Directive. Those obligations include the need for such notaries or other independent legal professionals themselves to identify the beneficial owners of the pooled accounts held by them.

(24) Equally, Community legislation should recognise that certain situations present a greater risk of money laundering or terrorist financing. Although the identity and business profile of all customers should be established, there are cases where particularly rigorous customer identification and verification procedures are required.

(25) This is particularly true of business relationships with individuals holding, or having held, important public positions, particularly those from countries where corruption is widespread. Such relationships may expose the financial sector in particular to significant reputational and/or legal risks. The international effort to combat corruption also justifies the need to pay special attention to such cases and to apply the complete normal customer due diligence measures in respect of domestic politically exposed persons or enhanced customer due diligence measures in respect of politically exposed persons residing in another Member State or in a third country.

(26) Obtaining approval from senior management for establishing business relationships should not imply obtaining approval from the board of directors but from the immediate higher level of the hierarchy of the person seeking such approval.

(27) In order to avoid repeated customer identification procedures, leading to delays and inefficiency in business, it is appropriate, subject to suitable safeguards, to allow customers to be introduced whose identification has been carried out elsewhere. Where an institution or person covered by this Directive relies on a third party, the ultimate responsibility for the customer due diligence procedure remains with the institution or person to whom the customer is introduced. The third party, or introducer, also retains his own responsibility for all the requirements in this Directive, including the requirement to report suspicious transactions and maintain records, to the extent that he has a relationship with the customer that is covered by this Directive.

(28) In the case of agency or outsourcing relationships on a contractual basis between institutions or persons covered by this Directive and external natural or legal persons not covered hereby, any anti-money laundering and anti-terrorist financing obligations for those agents or outsourcing service providers as part of the institutions or persons covered by this Directive, may only arise from contract and not from this Directive. The responsibility for complying with this Directive should remain with the institution or person covered hereby.

(29) Suspicious transactions should be reported to the financial intelligence unit (FIU), which serves as a national centre for receiving, analysing and disseminating to the competent authorities suspicious transaction reports and other information regarding potential money laundering or terrorist financing. This should not compel Member States to change their existing reporting systems where the reporting is done through a public prosecutor or other law enforcement authorities, as long as the information is forwarded promptly and unfiltered to FIUs, allowing them to conduct their business properly, including international cooperation with other FIUs.

(30) By way of derogation from the general prohibition on executing suspicious transactions, the institutions and persons covered by this Directive may execute suspicious transactions before informing the competent authorities, where refraining from the execution thereof is impossible or likely to frustrate efforts to pursue the beneficiaries of a suspected money laundering or terrorist financing operation. This, however, should be without prejudice to the international obligations accepted by the Member States to freeze without delay funds or other assets of terrorists, terrorist organisations or those who finance terrorism, in accordance with the relevant United Nations Security Council resolutions.

(31) Where a Member State decides to make use of the exemptions provided for in Article 23(2), it may allow or require the self-regulatory body representing the persons referred to therein not to transmit to the FIU any information obtained from those persons in the circumstances referred to in that Article.

(32) There has been a number of cases of employees who report their suspicions of money laundering being subjected to threats or hostile action. Although this Directive cannot interfere with Member States' judicial procedures, this is a crucial issue for the effectiveness of the anti-money laundering and anti-terrorist financing system. Member States should be aware of this problem and should do whatever they can to protect employees from such threats or hostile action.

(33) Disclosure of information as referred to in Article 28 should be in accordance with the rules on transfer of personal data to third countries as laid down in Directive 95/46/EC of the European Parliament and of the Council of 24 October 1995 on the protection of individuals with regard to the processing of personal data and on the free movement of such data ([1]). Moreover, Article 28 cannot interfere with national data protection and professional secrecy legislation.

(34) Persons who merely convert paper documents into electronic data and are acting under a contract with a credit institution or a financial institution do not fall within the scope of this Directive, nor does any natural or legal person that provides credit or financial institutions solely with a message or other support systems for transmitting funds or with clearing and settlement systems.

(35) Money laundering and terrorist financing are international problems and the effort to combat them should be global. Where Community credit and financial institutions have branches and subsidiaries located in third countries where the legislation in this area is deficient, they should, in order to avoid the application of very different standards within an institution or group of institutions, apply the Community standard or notify the competent authorities of the home Member State if this application is impossible.

(36) It is important that credit and financial institutions should be able to respond rapidly to requests for information on whether they maintain business relationships with named persons. For the purpose of identifying such business relationships in order to be able to provide that information quickly, credit and financial institutions should have effective systems in place which are commensurate with the size and nature of their business. In particular it would be appropriate for credit institutions and larger financial institutions to have electronic systems at their disposal. This provision is of particular importance in the context of procedures leading to measures such as the freezing or seizing of assets (including terrorist assets), pursuant to applicable national or Community legislation with a view to combating terrorism.

([1]) OJ L 281, 23.11.1995, p. 31. Directive as amended by Regulation (EC) No 1882/2003 (OJ L 284, 31.10.2003, p. 1).

(37) This Directive establishes detailed rules for customer due diligence, including enhanced customer due diligence for high-risk customers or business relationships, such as appropriate procedures to determine whether a person is a politically exposed person, and certain additional, more detailed requirements, such as the existence of compliance management procedures and policies. All these requirements are to be met by each of the institutions and persons covered by this Directive, while Member States are expected to tailor the detailed implementation of those provisions to the particularities of the various professions and to the differences in scale and size of the institutions and persons covered by this Directive.

(38) In order to ensure that the institutions and others subject to Community legislation in this field remain committed, feedback should, where practicable, be made available to them on the usefulness and follow-up of the reports they present. To make this possible, and to be able to review the effectiveness of their systems to combat money laundering and terrorist financing Member States should keep and improve the relevant statistics.

(39) When registering or licensing a currency exchange office, a trust and company service provider or a casino nationally, competent authorities should ensure that the persons who effectively direct or will direct the business of such entities and the beneficial owners of such entities are fit and proper persons. The criteria for determining whether or not a person is fit and proper should be established in conformity with national law. As a minimum, such criteria should reflect the need to protect such entities from being misused by their managers or beneficial owners for criminal purposes.

(40) Taking into account the international character of money laundering and terrorist financing, coordination and cooperation between FIUs as referred to in Council Decision 2000/642/JHA of 17 October 2000 concerning arrangements for cooperation between financial intelligence units of the Member States in respect of exchanging information (1), including the establishment of an EU FIU-net, should be encouraged to the greatest possible extent. To that end, the Commission should lend such assistance as may be needed to facilitate such coordination, including financial assistance.

(41) The importance of combating money laundering and terrorist financing should lead Member States to lay down effective, proportionate and dissuasive penalties in national law for failure to respect the national provisions adopted pursuant to this Directive. Provision should be made for penalties in respect of natural and legal persons. Since legal persons are often involved in complex money laundering or terrorist financing operations, sanctions should also be adjusted in line with the activity carried on by legal persons.

(42) Natural persons exercising any of the activities referred to in Article 2(1)(3)(a) and (b) within the structure of a legal person, but on an independent basis, should be independently responsible for compliance with the provisions of this Directive, with the exception of Article 35.

(43) Clarification of the technical aspects of the rules laid down in this Directive may be necessary to ensure an effective and sufficiently consistent implementation of this Directive, taking into account the different financial instruments, professions and risks in the different Member States and the technical developments in the fight against money laundering and terrorist financing. The Commission should accordingly be empowered to adopt implementing measures, such as certain criteria for identifying low and high risk situations in which simplified due diligence could suffice or enhanced due diligence would be appropriate, provided that they do not modify the essential elements of this Directive and provided that the Commission acts in accordance with the principles set out herein, after consulting the Committee on the Prevention of Money Laundering and Terrorist Financing.

(44) The measures necessary for the implementation of this Directive should be adopted in accordance with Council Decision 1999/468/EC of 28 June 1999 laying down the procedures for the exercise of implementing powers conferred on the Commission (2). To that end a new Committee on the Prevention of Money Laundering and Terrorist Financing, replacing the Money Laundering Contact Committee set up by Directive 91/308/EEC, should be established.

(45) In view of the very substantial amendments that would need to be made to Directive 91/308/EEC, it should be repealed for reasons of clarity.

(46) Since the objective of this Directive, namely the prevention of the use of the financial system for the purpose of money laundering and terrorist financing, cannot be sufficiently achieved by the Member States and can therefore, by reason of the scale and effects of the action, be better achieved at Community level, the Community may adopt measures, in accordance with the principle of subsidiarity as set out in Article 5 of the Treaty. In accordance with the principle of proportionality, as set out in that Article, this Directive does not go beyond what is necessary in order to achieve that objective.

(1) OJ L 271, 24.10.2000, p. 4.

(2) OJ L 184, 17.7.1999, p. 23.

L 309/20 EN Official Journal of the European Union 25.11.2005

(47) In exercising its implementing powers in accordance with this Directive, the Commission should respect the following principles: the need for high levels of transparency and consultation with institutions and persons covered by this Directive and with the European Parliament and the Council; the need to ensure that competent authorities will be able to ensure compliance with the rules consistently; the balance of costs and benefits to institutions and persons covered by this Directive on a long-term basis in any implementing measures; the need to respect the necessary flexibility in the application of the implementing measures in accordance with a risk-sensitive approach; the need to ensure coherence with other Community legislation in this area; the need to protect the Community, its Member States and their citizens from the consequences of money laundering and terrorist financing.

(48) This Directive respects the fundamental rights and observes the principles recognised in particular by the Charter of Fundamental Rights of the European Union. Nothing in this Directive should be interpreted or implemented in a manner that is inconsistent with the European Convention on Human Rights,

HAVE ADOPTED THIS DIRECTIVE:

CHAPTER I

## SUBJECT MATTER, SCOPE AND DEFINITIONS

*Article 1*

1. Member States shall ensure that money laundering and terrorist financing are prohibited.

2. For the purposes of this Directive, the following conduct, when committed intentionally, shall be regarded as money laundering:

(a) the conversion or transfer of property, knowing that such property is derived from criminal activity or from an act of participation in such activity, for the purpose of concealing or disguising the illicit origin of the property or of assisting any person who is involved in the commission of such activity to evade the legal consequences of his action;

(b) the concealment or disguise of the true nature, source, location, disposition, movement, rights with respect to, or ownership of property, knowing that such property is derived from criminal activity or from an act of participation in such activity;

(c) the acquisition, possession or use of property, knowing, at the time of receipt, that such property was derived from criminal activity or from an act of participation in such activity;

(d) participation in, association to commit, attempts to commit and aiding, abetting, facilitating and counselling the commission of any of the actions mentioned in the foregoing points.

3. Money laundering shall be regarded as such even where the activities which generated the property to be laundered were carried out in the territory of another Member State or in that of a third country.

4. For the purposes of this Directive, 'terrorist financing' means the provision or collection of funds, by any means, directly or indirectly, with the intention that they should be used or in the knowledge that they are to be used, in full or in part, in order to carry out any of the offences within the meaning of Articles 1 to 4 of Council Framework Decision 2002/475/JHA of 13 June 2002 on combating terrorism [1].

5. Knowledge, intent or purpose required as an element of the activities mentioned in paragraphs 2 and 4 may be inferred from objective factual circumstances.

*Article 2*

1. This Directive shall apply to:

(1) credit institutions;

(2) financial institutions;

(3) the following legal or natural persons acting in the exercise of their professional activities:

(a) auditors, external accountants and tax advisors;

(b) notaries and other independent legal professionals, when they participate, whether by acting on behalf of and for their client in any financial or real estate transaction, or by assisting in the planning or execution of transactions for their client concerning the:

(i) buying and selling of real property or business entities;

(ii) managing of client money, securities or other assets;

[1] OJ L 164, 22.6.2002, p. 3.

(iii) opening or management of bank, savings or securities accounts;

(iv) organisation of contributions necessary for the creation, operation or management of companies;

(v) creation, operation or management of trusts, companies or similar structures;

(c) trust or company service providers not already covered under points (a) or (b);

(d) real estate agents;

(e) other natural or legal persons trading in goods, only to the extent that payments are made in cash in an amount of EUR 15 000 or more, whether the transaction is executed in a single operation or in several operations which appear to be linked;

(f) casinos.

2. Member States may decide that legal and natural persons who engage in a financial activity on an occasional or very limited basis and where there is little risk of money laundering or terrorist financing occurring do not fall within the scope of Article 3(1) or (2).

*Article 3*

For the purposes of this Directive the following definitions shall apply:

(1) 'credit institution' means a credit institution, as defined in the first subparagraph of Article 1(1) of Directive 2000/12/EC of the European Parliament and of the Council of 20 March 2000 relating to the taking up and pursuit of the business of credit institutions ([1]), including branches within the meaning of Article 1(3) of that Directive located in the Community of credit institutions having their head offices inside or outside the Community;

(2) 'financial institution' means:

(a) an undertaking other than a credit institution which carries out one or more of the operations included in points 2 to 12 and 14 of Annex I to Directive 2000/12/EC, including the activities of currency exchange offices (bureaux de change) and of money transmission or remittance offices;

(b) an insurance company duly authorised in accordance with Directive 2002/83/EC of the European Parliament and of the Council of 5 November 2002 concerning life assurance ([2]), insofar as it carries out activities covered by that Directive;

(c) an investment firm as defined in point 1 of Article 4(1) of Directive 2004/39/EC of the European Parliament and of the Council of 21 April 2004 on markets in financial instruments ([3]);

(d) a collective investment undertaking marketing its units or shares;

(e) an insurance intermediary as defined in Article 2(5) of Directive 2002/92/EC of the European Parliament and of the Council of 9 December 2002 on insurance mediation ([4]), with the exception of intermediaries as mentioned in Article 2(7) of that Directive, when they act in respect of life insurance and other investment related services;

(f) branches, when located in the Community, of financial institutions as referred to in points (a) to (e), whose head offices are inside or outside the Community;

(3) 'property' means assets of every kind, whether corporeal or incorporeal, movable or immovable, tangible or intangible, and legal documents or instruments in any form including electronic or digital, evidencing title to or an interest in such assets;

(4) 'criminal activity' means any kind of criminal involvement in the commission of a serious crime;

(5) 'serious crimes' means, at least:

(a) acts as defined in Articles 1 to 4 of Framework Decision 2002/475/JHA;

(b) any of the offences defined in Article 3(1)(a) of the 1988 United Nations Convention against Illicit Traffic in Narcotic Drugs and Psychotropic Substances;

(c) the activities of criminal organisations as defined in Article 1 of Council Joint Action 98/733/JHA of 21 December 1998 on making it a criminal offence to participate in a criminal organisation in the Member States of the European Union ([5]);

(d) fraud, at least serious, as defined in Article 1(1) and Article 2 of the Convention on the Protection of the European Communities' Financial Interests ([6]);

(e) corruption;

(f) all offences which are punishable by deprivation of liberty or a detention order for a maximum of more than one year or, as regards those States which have a minimum threshold for offences in their legal system, all offences punishable by deprivation of liberty or a detention order for a minimum of more than six months;

([1]) OJ L 126, 26.5.2000, p. 1. Directive as last amended by Directive 2005/1/EC (OJ L 79, 24.3.2005, p. 9).
([2]) OJ L 345, 19.12.2002, p. 1. Directive as last amended by Directive 2005/1/EC.
([3]) OJ L 145, 30.4.2004, p. 1.
([4]) OJ L 9, 15.1.2003, p. 3.
([5]) OJ L 351, 29.12.1998, p. 1.
([6]) OJ C 316, 27.11.1995, p. 49.

(6) 'beneficial owner' means the natural person(s) who ultimately owns or controls the customer and/or the natural person on whose behalf a transaction or activity is being conducted. The beneficial owner shall at least include:

(a) in the case of corporate entities:

(i) the natural person(s) who ultimately owns or controls a legal entity through direct or indirect ownership or control over a sufficient percentage of the shares or voting rights in that legal entity, including through bearer share holdings, other than a company listed on a regulated market that is subject to disclosure requirements consistent with Community legislation or subject to equivalent international standards; a percentage of 25 % plus one share shall be deemed sufficient to meet this criterion;

(ii) the natural person(s) who otherwise exercises control over the management of a legal entity:

(b) in the case of legal entities, such as foundations, and legal arrangements, such as trusts, which administer and distribute funds:

(i) where the future beneficiaries have already been determined, the natural person(s) who is the beneficiary of 25 % or more of the property of a legal arrangement or entity;

(ii) where the individuals that benefit from the legal arrangement or entity have yet to be determined, the class of persons in whose main interest the legal arrangement or entity is set up or operates;

(iii) the natural person(s) who exercises control over 25 % or more of the property of a legal arrangement or entity;

(7) 'trust and company service providers' means any natural or legal person which by way of business provides any of the following services to third parties:

(a) forming companies or other legal persons;

(b) acting as or arranging for another person to act as a director or secretary of a company, a partner of a partnership, or a similar position in relation to other legal persons;

(c) providing a registered office, business address, correspondence or administrative address and other related services for a company, a partnership or any other legal person or arrangement;

(d) acting as or arranging for another person to act as a trustee of an express trust or a similar legal arrangement;

(e) acting as or arranging for another person to act as a nominee shareholder for another person other than a company listed on a regulated market that is subject to disclosure requirements in conformity with Community legislation or subject to equivalent international standards;

(8) 'politically exposed persons' means natural persons who are or have been entrusted with prominent public functions and immediate family members, or persons known to be close associates, of such persons;

(9) 'business relationship' means a business, professional or commercial relationship which is connected with the professional activities of the institutions and persons covered by this Directive and which is expected, at the time when the contact is established, to have an element of duration;

(10) 'shell bank' means a credit institution, or an institution engaged in equivalent activities, incorporated in a jurisdiction in which it has no physical presence, involving meaningful mind and management, and which is unaffiliated with a regulated financial group.

*Article 4*

1. Member States shall ensure that the provisions of this Directive are extended in whole or in part to professions and to categories of undertakings, other than the institutions and persons referred to in Article 2(1), which engage in activities which are particularly likely to be used for money laundering or terrorist financing purposes.

2. Where a Member State decides to extend the provisions of this Directive to professions and to categories of undertakings other than those referred to in Article 2(1), it shall inform the Commission thereof.

*Article 5*

The Member States may adopt or retain in force stricter provisions in the field covered by this Directive to prevent money laundering and terrorist financing.

CHAPTER II

**CUSTOMER DUE DILIGENCE**

*SECTION 1*

***General provisions***

*Article 6*

Member States shall prohibit their credit and financial institutions from keeping anonymous accounts or anonymous passbooks. By way of derogation from Article 9(6), Member States shall in all cases require that the owners and beneficiaries of existing anonymous accounts or anonymous passbooks be made the subject of customer due diligence measures as soon as possible and in any event before such accounts or passbooks are used in any way.

*Article 7*

The institutions and persons covered by this Directive shall apply customer due diligence measures in the following cases:

(a) when establishing a business relationship;

(b) when carrying out occasional transactions amounting to EUR 15 000 or more, whether the transaction is carried out in a single operation or in several operations which appear to be linked;

(c) when there is a suspicion of money laundering or terrorist financing, regardless of any derogation, exemption or threshold;

(d) when there are doubts about the veracity or adequacy of previously obtained customer identification data.

*Article 8*

1. Customer due diligence measures shall comprise:

(a) identifying the customer and verifying the customer's identity on the basis of documents, data or information obtained from a reliable and independent source;

(b) identifying, where applicable, the beneficial owner and taking risk-based and adequate measures to verify his identity so that the institution or person covered by this Directive is satisfied that it knows who the beneficial owner is, including, as regards legal persons, trusts and similar legal arrangements, taking risk-based and adequate measures to understand the ownership and control structure of the customer;

(c) obtaining information on the purpose and intended nature of the business relationship;

(d) conducting ongoing monitoring of the business relationship including scrutiny of transactions undertaken throughout the course of that relationship to ensure that the transactions being conducted are consistent with the institution's or person's knowledge of the customer, the business and risk profile, including, where necessary, the source of funds and ensuring that the documents, data or information held are kept up-to-date.

2. The institutions and persons covered by this Directive shall apply each of the customer due diligence requirements set out in paragraph 1, but may determine the extent of such measures on a risk-sensitive basis depending on the type of customer, business relationship, product or transaction. The institutions and persons covered by this Directive shall be able to demonstrate to the competent authorities mentioned in Article 37, including self-regulatory bodies, that the extent of the measures is appropriate in view of the risks of money laundering and terrorist financing.

*Article 9*

1. Member States shall require that the verification of the identity of the customer and the beneficial owner takes place before the establishment of a business relationship or the carrying-out of the transaction.

2. By way of derogation from paragraph 1, Member States may allow the verification of the identity of the customer and the beneficial owner to be completed during the establishment of a business relationship if this is necessary not to interrupt the normal conduct of business and where there is little risk of money laundering or terrorist financing occurring. In such situations these procedures shall be completed as soon as practicable after the initial contact.

3. By way of derogation from paragraphs 1 and 2, Member States may, in relation to life insurance business, allow the verification of the identity of the beneficiary under the policy to take place after the business relationship has been established. In that case, verification shall take place at or before the time of payout or at or before the time the beneficiary intends to exercise rights vested under the policy.

4. By way of derogation from paragraphs 1 and 2, Member States may allow the opening of a bank account provided that there are adequate safeguards in place to ensure that transactions are not carried out by the customer or on its behalf until full compliance with the aforementioned provisions is obtained.

5. Member States shall require that, where the institution or person concerned is unable to comply with points (a), (b) and (c) of Article 8(1), it may not carry out a transaction through a bank account, establish a business relationship or carry out the transaction, or shall terminate the business relationship, and shall consider making a report to the financial intelligence unit (FIU) in accordance with Article 22 in relation to the customer.

Member States shall not be obliged to apply the previous subparagraph in situations when notaries, independent legal professionals, auditors, external accountants and tax advisors are in the course of ascertaining the legal position for their client or performing their task of defending or representing that client in, or concerning judicial proceedings, including advice on instituting or avoiding proceedings.

6. Member States shall require that institutions and persons covered by this Directive apply the customer due diligence procedures not only to all new customers but also at appropriate times to existing customers on a risk-sensitive basis.

*Article 10*

1. Member States shall require that all casino customers be identified and their identity verified if they purchase or exchange gambling chips with a value of EUR 2 000 or more.

2. Casinos subject to State supervision shall be deemed in any event to have satisfied the customer due diligence requirements if they register, identify and verify the identity of their customers immediately on or before entry, regardless of the amount of gambling chips purchased.

SECTION 2

***Simplified customer due diligence***

*Article 11*

1. By way of derogation from Articles 7(a), (b) and (d), 8 and 9(1), the institutions and persons covered by this Directive shall not be subject to the requirements provided for in those Articles where the customer is a credit or financial institution covered by this Directive, or a credit or financial institution situated in a third country which imposes requirements equivalent to those laid down in this Directive and supervised for compliance with those requirements.

2. By way of derogation from Articles 7(a), (b) and (d), 8 and 9(1) Member States may allow the institutions and persons covered by this Directive not to apply customer due diligence in respect of:

(a) listed companies whose securities are admitted to trading on a regulated market within the meaning of Directive 2004/39/EC in one or more Member States and listed companies from third countries which are subject to disclosure requirements consistent with Community legislation;

(b) beneficial owners of pooled accounts held by notaries and other independent legal professionals from the Member States, or from third countries provided that they are subject to requirements to combat money laundering or terrorist financing consistent with international standards and are supervised for compliance with those requirements and provided that the information on the identity of the beneficial owner is available, on request, to the institutions that act as depository institutions for the pooled accounts;

(c) domestic public authorities,

or in respect of any other customer representing a low risk of money laundering or terrorist financing which meets the technical criteria established in accordance with Article 40(1)(b).

3. In the cases mentioned in paragraphs 1 and 2, institutions and persons covered by this Directive shall in any case gather sufficient information to establish if the customer qualifies for an exemption as mentioned in these paragraphs.

4. The Member States shall inform each other and the Commission of cases where they consider that a third country meets the conditions laid down in paragraphs 1 or 2 or in other situations which meet the technical criteria established in accordance with Article 40(1)(b)

5. By way of derogation from Articles 7(a), (b) and (d), 8 and 9(1), Member States may allow the institutions and persons covered by this Directive not to apply customer due diligence in respect of:

(a) life insurance policies where the annual premium is no more than EUR 1 000 or the single premium is no more than EUR 2 500;

(b) insurance policies for pension schemes if there is no surrender clause and the policy cannot be used as collateral;

(c) a pension, superannuation or similar scheme that provides retirement benefits to employees, where contributions are made by way of deduction from wages and the scheme rules do not permit the assignment of a member's interest under the scheme;

(d) electronic money, as defined in Article 1(3)(b) of Directive 2000/46/EC of the European Parliament and of the Council of 18 September 2000 on the taking up, pursuit of and prudential supervision of the business of electronic money institutions [1], where, if the device cannot be recharged, the maximum amount stored in the device is no more than EUR 150, or where, if the device can be recharged, a limit of EUR 2 500 is imposed on the total amount transacted in a calendar year, except when an amount of EUR 1 000 or more is redeemed in that same calendar year by the bearer as referred to in Article 3 of Directive 2000/46/EC,

or in respect of any other product or transaction representing a low risk of money laundering or terrorist financing which meets the technical criteria established in accordance with Article 40(1)(b).

*Article 12*

Where the Commission adopts a decision pursuant to Article 40(4), the Member States shall prohibit the institutions and persons covered by this Directive from applying simplified due diligence to credit and financial institutions or listed companies from the third country concerned or other entities following from situations which meet the technical criteria established in accordance with Article 40(1)(b).

*SECTION 3*

***Enhanced customer due diligence***

*Article 13*

1. Member States shall require the institutions and persons covered by this Directive to apply, on a risk-sensitive basis, enhanced customer due diligence measures, in addition to the measures referred to in Articles 7, 8 and 9(6), in situations which by their nature can present a higher risk of money laundering or terrorist financing, and at least in the situations set out in paragraphs 2, 3, 4 and in other situations representing a high risk of money laundering or terrorist financing which meet the technical criteria established in accordance with Article 40(1)(c).

2. Where the customer has not been physically present for identification purposes, Member States shall require those institutions and persons to take specific and adequate measures to compensate for the higher risk, for example by applying one or more of the following measures:

(a) ensuring that the customer's identity is established by additional documents, data or information;

(b) supplementary measures to verify or certify the documents supplied, or requiring confirmatory certification by a credit or financial institution covered by this Directive;

(c) ensuring that the first payment of the operations is carried out through an account opened in the customer's name with a credit institution.

3. In respect of cross-frontier correspondent banking relationships with respondent institutions from third countries, Member States shall require their credit institutions to:

(a) gather sufficient information about a respondent institution to understand fully the nature of the respondent's business and to determine from publicly available information the reputation of the institution and the quality of supervision;

(b) assess the respondent institution's anti-money laundering and anti-terrorist financing controls;

(c) obtain approval from senior management before establishing new correspondent banking relationships;

(d) document the respective responsibilities of each institution;

(e) with respect to payable-through accounts, be satisfied that the respondent credit institution has verified the identity of and performed ongoing due diligence on the customers having direct access to accounts of the correspondent and that it is able to provide relevant customer due diligence data to the correspondent institution, upon request.

4. In respect of transactions or business relationships with politically exposed persons residing in another Member State or in a third country, Member States shall require those institutions and persons covered by this Directive to:

(a) have appropriate risk-based procedures to determine whether the customer is a politically exposed person;

(b) have senior management approval for establishing business relationships with such customers;

(c) take adequate measures to establish the source of wealth and source of funds that are involved in the business relationship or transaction;

(d) conduct enhanced ongoing monitoring of the business relationship.

[1] OJ L 275, 27.10.2000, p. 39.

5. Member States shall prohibit credit institutions from entering into or continuing a correspondent banking relationship with a shell bank and shall require that credit institutions take appropriate measures to ensure that they do not engage in or continue correspondent banking relationships with a bank that is known to permit its accounts to be used by a shell bank.

6. Member States shall ensure that the institutions and persons covered by this Directive pay special attention to any money laundering or terrorist financing threat that may arise from products or transactions that might favour anonymity, and take measures, if needed, to prevent their use for money laundering or terrorist financing purposes.

*SECTION 4*

***Performance by third parties***

*Article 14*

Member States may permit the institutions and persons covered by this Directive to rely on third parties to meet the requirements laid down in Article 8(1)(a) to (c). However, the ultimate responsibility for meeting those requirements shall remain with the institution or person covered by this Directive which relies on the third party.

*Article 15*

1. Where a Member State permits credit and financial institutions referred to in Article 2(1)(1) or (2) situated in its territory to be relied on as a third party domestically, that Member State shall in any case permit institutions and persons referred to in Article 2(1) situated in its territory to recognise and accept, in accordance with the provisions laid down in Article 14, the outcome of the customer due diligence requirements laid down in Article 8(1)(a) to (c), carried out in accordance with this Directive by an institution referred to in Article 2(1)(1) or (2) in another Member State, with the exception of currency exchange offices and money transmission or remittance offices, and meeting the requirements laid down in Articles 16 and 18, even if the documents or data on which these requirements have been based are different to those required in the Member State to which the customer is being referred.

2. Where a Member State permits currency exchange offices and money transmission or remittance offices referred to in Article 3(2)(a) situated in its territory to be relied on as a third party domestically, that Member State shall in any case permit them to recognise and accept, in accordance with Article 14, the outcome of the customer due diligence requirements laid down in Article 8(1)(a) to (c), carried out in accordance with this Directive by the same category of institution in another Member State and meeting the requirements laid down in Articles 16 and 18, even if the documents or data on which these requirements have been based are different to those required in the Member State to which the customer is being referred.

3. Where a Member State permits persons referred to in Article 2(1)(3)(a) to (c) situated in its territory to be relied on as a third party domestically, that Member State shall in any case permit them to recognise and accept, in accordance with Article 14, the outcome of the customer due diligence requirements laid down in Article 8(1)(a) to (c), carried out in accordance with this Directive by a person referred to in Article 2(1)(3)(a) to (c) in another Member State and meeting the requirements laid down in Articles 16 and 18, even if the documents or data on which these requirements have been based are different to those required in the Member State to which the customer is being referred.

*Article 16*

1. For the purposes of this Section, 'third parties' shall mean institutions and persons who are listed in Article 2, or equivalent institutions and persons situated in a third country, who meet the following requirements:

(a) they are subject to mandatory professional registration, recognised by law;

(b) they apply customer due diligence requirements and record keeping requirements as laid down or equivalent to those laid down in this Directive and their compliance with the requirements of this Directive is supervised in accordance with Section 2 of Chapter V, or they are situated in a third country which imposes equivalent requirements to those laid down in this Directive.

2. Member States shall inform each other and the Commission of cases where they consider that a third country meets the conditions laid down in paragraph 1(b).

*Article 17*

Where the Commission adopts a decision pursuant to Article 40(4), Member States shall prohibit the institutions and persons covered by this Directive from relying on third parties from the third country concerned to meet the requirements laid down in Article 8(1)(a) to (c).

*Article 18*

1. Third parties shall make information requested in accordance with the requirements laid down in Article 8(1)(a) to (c) immediately available to the institution or person covered by this Directive to which the customer is being referred.

2. Relevant copies of identification and verification data and other relevant documentation on the identity of the customer or the beneficial owner shall immediately be forwarded, on request, by the third party to the institution or person covered by this Directive to which the customer is being referred.

*Article 19*

This Section shall not apply to outsourcing or agency relationships where, on the basis of a contractual arrangement, the outsourcing service provider or agent is to be regarded as part of the institution or person covered by this Directive.

CHAPTER III

**REPORTING OBLIGATIONS**

*SECTION 1*

***General provisions***

*Article 20*

Member States shall require that the institutions and persons covered by this Directive pay special attention to any activity which they regard as particularly likely, by its nature, to be related to money laundering or terrorist financing and in particular complex or unusually large transactions and all unusual patterns of transactions which have no apparent economic or visible lawful purpose.

*Article 21*

1. Each Member State shall establish a FIU in order effectively to combat money laundering and terrorist financing.

2. That FIU shall be established as a central national unit. It shall be responsible for receiving (and to the extent permitted, requesting), analysing and disseminating to the competent authorities, disclosures of information which concern potential money laundering, potential terrorist financing or are required by national legislation or regulation. It shall be provided with adequate resources in order to fulfil its tasks.

3. Member States shall ensure that the FIU has access, directly or indirectly, on a timely basis, to the financial, administrative and law enforcement information that it requires to properly fulfil its tasks.

*Article 22*

1. Member States shall require the institutions and persons covered by this Directive, and where applicable their directors and employees, to cooperate fully:

(a) by promptly informing the FIU, on their own initiative, where the institution or person covered by this Directive knows, suspects or has reasonable grounds to suspect that money laundering or terrorist financing is being or has been committed or attempted;

(b) by promptly furnishing the FIU, at its request, with all necessary information, in accordance with the procedures established by the applicable legislation.

2. The information referred to in paragraph 1 shall be forwarded to the FIU of the Member State in whose territory the institution or person forwarding the information is situated. The person or persons designated in accordance with the procedures provided for in Article 34 shall normally forward the information.

*Article 23*

1. By way of derogation from Article 22(1), Member States may, in the case of the persons referred to in Article 2(1)(3)(a) and (b), designate an appropriate self-regulatory body of the profession concerned as the authority to be informed in the first instance in place of the FIU. Without prejudice to paragraph 2, the designated self-regulatory body shall in such cases forward the information to the FIU promptly and unfiltered.

2. Member States shall not be obliged to apply the obligations laid down in Article 22(1) to notaries, independent legal professionals, auditors, external accountants and tax advisors with regard to information they receive from or obtain on one of their clients, in the course of ascertaining the legal position for their client or performing their task of defending or representing that client in, or concerning judicial proceedings, including advice on instituting or avoiding proceedings, whether such information is received or obtained before, during or after such proceedings.

*Article 24*

1. Member States shall require the institutions and persons covered by this Directive to refrain from carrying out transactions which they know or suspect to be related to money laundering or terrorist financing until they have completed the necessary action in accordance with Article 22(1)(a). In conformity with the legislation of the Member States, instructions may be given not to carry out the transaction.

2. Where such a transaction is suspected of giving rise to money laundering or terrorist financing and where to refrain in such manner is impossible or is likely to frustrate efforts to pursue the beneficiaries of a suspected money laundering or terrorist financing operation, the institutions and persons concerned shall inform the FIU immediately afterwards.

*Article 25*

1. Member States shall ensure that if, in the course of inspections carried out in the institutions and persons covered by this Directive by the competent authorities referred to in Article 37, or in any other way, those authorities discover facts that could be related to money laundering or terrorist financing, they shall promptly inform the FIU.

2. Member States shall ensure that supervisory bodies empowered by law or regulation to oversee the stock, foreign exchange and financial derivatives markets inform the FIU if they discover facts that could be related to money laundering or terrorist financing.

*Article 26*

The disclosure in good faith as foreseen in Articles 22(1) and 23 by an institution or person covered by this Directive or by an employee or director of such an institution or person of the information referred to in Articles 22 and 23 shall not constitute a breach of any restriction on disclosure of information imposed by contract or by any legislative, regulatory or administrative provision, and shall not involve the institution or person or its directors or employees in liability of any kind.

*Article 27*

Member States shall take all appropriate measures in order to protect employees of the institutions or persons covered by this Directive who report suspicions of money laundering or terrorist financing either internally or to the FIU from being exposed to threats or hostile action.

SECTION 2

***Prohibition of disclosure***

*Article 28*

1. The institutions and persons covered by this Directive and their directors and employees shall not disclose to the customer concerned or to other third persons the fact that information has been transmitted in accordance with Articles 22 and 23 or that a money laundering or terrorist financing investigation is being or may be carried out.

2. The prohibition laid down in paragraph 1 shall not include disclosure to the competent authorities referred to in Article 37, including the self-regulatory bodies, or disclosure for law enforcement purposes.

3. The prohibition laid down in paragraph 1 shall not prevent disclosure between institutions from Member States, or from third countries provided that they meet the conditions laid down in Article 11(1), belonging to the same group as defined by Article 2(12) of Directive 2002/87/EC of the European Parliament and of the Council of 16 December 2002 on the supplementary supervision of credit institutions, insurance undertakings and investment firms in a financial conglomerate ([1]).

4. The prohibition laid down in paragraph 1 shall not prevent disclosure between persons referred to in Article 2(1)(3)(a) and (b) from Member States, or from third countries which impose requirements equivalent to those laid down in this Directive, who perform their professional activities, whether as employees or not, within the same legal person or a network. For the purposes of this Article, a 'network' means the larger structure to which the person belongs and which shares common ownership, management or compliance control.

5. For institutions or persons referred to in Article 2(1)(1), (2) and (3)(a) and (b) in cases related to the same customer and the same transaction involving two or more institutions or persons, the prohibition laid down in paragraph 1 shall not prevent disclosure between the relevant institutions or persons provided that they are situated in a Member State, or in a third country which imposes requirements equivalent to those laid down in this Directive, and that they are from the same professional category and are subject to equivalent obligations as regards professional secrecy and personal data protection. The information exchanged shall be used exclusively for the purposes of the prevention of money laundering and terrorist financing.

6. Where the persons referred to in Article 2(1)(3)(a) and (b) seek to dissuade a client from engaging in illegal activity, this shall not constitute a disclosure within the meaning of the paragraph 1.

7. The Member States shall inform each other and the Commission of cases where they consider that a third country meets the conditions laid down in paragraphs 3, 4 or 5.

*Article 29*

Where the Commission adopts a decision pursuant to Article 40(4), the Member States shall prohibit the disclosure between institutions and persons covered by this Directive and institutions and persons from the third country concerned.

([1]) OJ L 35, 11.2.2003, p. 1.

CHAPTER IV

**RECORD KEEPING AND STATISTICAL DATA**

*Article 30*

Member States shall require the institutions and persons covered by this Directive to keep the following documents and information for use in any investigation into, or analysis of, possible money laundering or terrorist financing by the FIU or by other competent authorities in accordance with national law:

(a) in the case of the customer due diligence, a copy or the references of the evidence required, for a period of at least five years after the business relationship with their customer has ended;

(b) in the case of business relationships and transactions, the supporting evidence and records, consisting of the original documents or copies admissible in court proceedings under the applicable national legislation for a period of at least five years following the carrying-out of the transactions or the end of the business relationship.

*Article 31*

1. Member States shall require the credit and financial institutions covered by this Directive to apply, where applicable, in their branches and majority-owned subsidiaries located in third countries measures at least equivalent to those laid down in this Directive with regard to customer due diligence and record keeping.

Where the legislation of the third country does not permit application of such equivalent measures, the Member States shall require the credit and financial institutions concerned to inform the competent authorities of the relevant home Member State accordingly.

2. Member States and the Commission shall inform each other of cases where the legislation of the third country does not permit application of the measures required under the first subparagraph of paragraph 1 and coordinated action could be taken to pursue a solution.

3. Member States shall require that, where the legislation of the third country does not permit application of the measures required under the first subparagraph of paragraph 1, credit or financial institutions take additional measures to effectively handle the risk of money laundering or terrorist financing.

*Article 32*

Member States shall require that their credit and financial institutions have systems in place that enable them to respond fully and rapidly to enquiries from the FIU, or from other authorities, in accordance with their national law, as to whether they maintain or have maintained during the previous five years a business relationship with specified natural or legal persons and on the nature of that relationship.

*Article 33*

1. Member States shall ensure that they are able to review the effectiveness of their systems to combat money laundering or terrorist financing by maintaining comprehensive statistics on matters relevant to the effectiveness of such systems.

2. Such statistics shall as a minimum cover the number of suspicious transaction reports made to the FIU, the follow-up given to these reports and indicate on an annual basis the number of cases investigated, the number of persons prosecuted, the number of persons convicted for money laundering or terrorist financing offences and how much property has been frozen, seized or confiscated.

3. Member States shall ensure that a consolidated review of these statistical reports is published.

CHAPTER V

**ENFORCEMENT MEASURES**

*SECTION 1*

***Internal procedures, training and feedback***

*Article 34*

1. Member States shall require that the institutions and persons covered by this Directive establish adequate and appropriate policies and procedures of customer due diligence, reporting, record keeping, internal control, risk assessment, risk management, compliance management and communication in order to forestall and prevent operations related to money laundering or terrorist financing.

2. Member States shall require that credit and financial institutions covered by this Directive communicate relevant policies and procedures where applicable to branches and majority-owned subsidiaries in third countries.

*Article 35*

1. Member States shall require that the institutions and persons covered by this Directive take appropriate measures so that their relevant employees are aware of the provisions in force on the basis of this Directive.

These measures shall include participation of their relevant employees in special ongoing training programmes to help them recognise operations which may be related to money laundering or terrorist financing and to instruct them as to how to proceed in such cases.

Where a natural person falling within any of the categories listed in Article 2(1)(3) performs his professional activities as an employee of a legal person, the obligations in this Section shall apply to that legal person rather than to the natural person.

2. Member States shall ensure that the institutions and persons covered by this Directive have access to up-to-date information on the practices of money launderers and terrorist financers and on indications leading to the recognition of suspicious transactions.

3. Member States shall ensure that, wherever practicable, timely feedback on the effectiveness of and follow-up to reports of suspected money laundering or terrorist financing is provided.

*SECTION 2*

***Supervision***

*Article 36*

1. Member States shall provide that currency exchange offices and trust and company service providers shall be licensed or registered and casinos be licensed in order to operate their business legally. Without prejudice to future Community legislation, Member States shall provide that money transmission or remittance offices shall be licensed or registered in order to operate their business legally.

2. Member States shall require competent authorities to refuse licensing or registration of the entities referred to in paragraph 1 if they are not satisfied that the persons who effectively direct or will direct the business of such entities or the beneficial owners of such entities are fit and proper persons.

*Article 37*

1. Member States shall require the competent authorities at least to effectively monitor and to take the necessary measures with a view to ensuring compliance with the requirements of this Directive by all the institutions and persons covered by this Directive.

2. Member States shall ensure that the competent authorities have adequate powers, including the power to compel the production of any information that is relevant to monitoring compliance and perform checks, and have adequate resources to perform their functions.

3. In the case of credit and financial institutions and casinos, competent authorities shall have enhanced supervisory powers, notably the possibility to conduct on-site inspections.

4. In the case of the natural and legal persons referred to in Article 2(1)(3)(a) to (e), Member States may allow the functions referred to in paragraph 1 to be performed on a risk-sensitive basis.

5. In the case of the persons referred to in Article 2(1)(3)(a) and (b), Member States may allow the functions referred to in paragraph 1 to be performed by self-regulatory bodies, provided that they comply with paragraph 2.

*SECTION 3*

***Cooperation***

*Article 38*

The Commission shall lend such assistance as may be needed to facilitate coordination, including the exchange of information between FIUs within the Community.

*SECTION 4*

***Penalties***

*Article 39*

1. Member States shall ensure that natural and legal persons covered by this Directive can be held liable for infringements of the national provisions adopted pursuant to this Directive. The penalties must be effective, proportionate and dissuasive.

2. Without prejudice to the right of Member States to impose criminal penalties, Member States shall ensure, in conformity with their national law, that the appropriate administrative measures can be taken or administrative sanctions can be imposed against credit and financial institutions for infringements of the national provisions adopted pursuant to this Directive. Member States shall ensure that these measures or sanctions are effective, proportionate and dissuasive.

3. In the case of legal persons, Member States shall ensure that at least they can be held liable for infringements referred to in paragraph 1 which are committed for their benefit by any person, acting either individually or as part of an organ of the legal person, who has a leading position within the legal person, based on:

(a) a power of representation of the legal person;

(b) an authority to take decisions on behalf of the legal person, or

(c) an authority to exercise control within the legal person.

4. In addition to the cases already provided for in paragraph 3, Member States shall ensure that legal persons can be held liable where the lack of supervision or control by a person referred to in paragraph 3 has made possible the commission of the infringements referred to in paragraph 1 for the benefit of a legal person by a person under its authority.

CHAPTER VI

**IMPLEMENTING MEASURES**

*Article 40*

1. In order to take account of technical developments in the fight against money laundering or terrorist financing and to ensure uniform implementation of this Directive, the Commission may, in accordance with the procedure referred to in Article 41(2), adopt the following implementing measures:

(a) clarification of the technical aspects of the definitions in Article 3(2)(a) and (d), (6), (7), (8), (9) and (10);

(b) establishment of technical criteria for assessing whether situations represent a low risk of money laundering or terrorist financing as referred to in Article 11(2) and (5);

(c) establishment of technical criteria for assessing whether situations represent a high risk of money laundering or terrorist financing as referred to in Article 13;

(d) establishment of technical criteria for assessing whether, in accordance with Article 2(2), it is justified not to apply this Directive to certain legal or natural persons carrying out a financial activity on an occasional or very limited basis.

2. In any event, the Commission shall adopt the first implementing measures to give effect to paragraphs 1(b) and 1(d) by 15 June 2006.

3. The Commission shall, in accordance with the procedure referred to in Article 41(2), adapt the amounts referred to in Articles 2(1)(3)(e), 7(b), 10(1) and 11(5)(a) and (d) taking into account Community legislation, economic developments and changes in international standards.

4. Where the Commission finds that a third country does not meet the conditions laid down in Article 11(1) or (2), Article 28(3), (4) or (5), or in the measures established in accordance with paragraph 1(b) of this Article or in Article 16(1)(b), or that the legislation of that third country does not permit application of the measures required under the first subparagraph of Article 31(1), it shall adopt a decision so stating in accordance with the procedure referred to in Article 41(2).

*Article 41*

1. The Commission shall be assisted by a Committee on the Prevention of Money Laundering and Terrorist Financing, hereinafter 'the Committee'.

2. Where reference is made to this paragraph, Articles 5 and 7 of Decision 1999/468/EC shall apply, having regard to the provisions of Article 8 thereof and provided that the implementing measures adopted in accordance with this procedure do not modify the essential provisions of this Directive.

The period laid down in Article 5(6) of Decision 1999/468/EC shall be set at three months.

3. The Committee shall adopt its Rules of Procedure.

4. Without prejudice to the implementing measures already adopted, the implementation of the provisions of this Directive concerning the adoption of technical rules and decisions in accordance with the procedure referred to in paragraph 2 shall be suspended four years after the entry into force of this Directive. On a proposal from the Commission, the European Parliament and the Council may renew the provisions concerned in accordance with the procedure laid down in Article 251 of the Treaty and, to that end, shall review them prior to the expiry of the four-year period.

CHAPTER VII

**FINAL PROVISIONS**

*Article 42*

By 15 December 2009, and at least at three-yearly intervals thereafter, the Commission shall draw up a report on the implementation of this Directive and submit it to the European Parliament and the Council. For the first such report, the Commission shall include a specific examination of the treatment of lawyers and other independent legal professionals.

*Article 43*

By 15 December 2010, the Commission shall present a report to the European Parliament and to the Council on the threshold percentages in Article 3(6), paying particular attention to the possible expediency and consequences of a reduction of the percentage in points (a)(i), (b)(i) and (b)(iii) of Article 3(6) from 25 % to 20 %. On the basis of the report the Commission may submit a proposal for amendments to this Directive.

*Article 44*

Directive 91/308/EEC is hereby repealed.

References made to the repealed Directive shall be construed as being made to this Directive and should be read in accordance with the correlation table set out in the Annex.

*Article 45*

1. Member States shall bring into force the laws, regulations and administrative provisions necessary to comply with this Directive by 15 December 2007. They shall forthwith communicate to the Commission the text of those provisions together with a table showing how the provisions of this Directive correspond to the national provisions adopted.

When Member States adopt those measures, they shall contain a reference to this Directive or be accompanied by such a reference on the occasion of their official publication. The methods of making such reference shall be laid down by Member States.

2. Member States shall communicate to the Commission the text of the main provisions of national law which they adopt in the field covered by this Directive.

*Article 46*

This Directive shall enter into force on the 20th day after its publication in the *Official Journal of the European Union*.

*Article 47*

This Directive is addressed to the Member States.

Done at Strasbourg, 26 October 2005.

| *For the European Parliament* | *For the Council* |
|---|---|
| *The President* | *The President* |
| J. BORRELL FONTELLES | D. ALEXANDER |

# Directive 2006/24 on the retention of data generated or processed in connection with the provision of publicly available electronic communications services or of public communications networks and amending Directive 2002/58/EC, 15 March 2006

[OJ 2006, L 105/54–63]

L 105/54 EN Official Journal of the European Union 13.4.2006

**DIRECTIVE 2006/24/EC OF THE EUROPEAN PARLIAMENT AND OF THE COUNCIL**

**of 15 March 2006**

**on the retention of data generated or processed in connection with the provision of publicly available electronic communications services or of public communications networks and amending Directive 2002/58/EC**

THE EUROPEAN PARLIAMENT AND THE COUNCIL OF THE EUROPEAN UNION,

Having regard to the Treaty establishing the European Community, and in particular Article 95 thereof,

Having regard to the proposal from the Commission,

Having regard to the Opinion of the European Economic and Social Committee ([1]),

Acting in accordance with the procedure laid down in Article 251 of the Treaty ([2]),

Whereas:

(1) Directive 95/46/EC of the European Parliament and of the Council of 24 October 1995 on the protection of individuals with regard to the processing of personal data and on the free movement of such data ([3]) requires Member States to protect the rights and freedoms of natural persons with regard to the processing of personal data, and in particular their right to privacy, in order to ensure the free flow of personal data in the Community.

(2) Directive 2002/58/EC of the European Parliament and of the Council of 12 July 2002 concerning the processing of personal data and the protection of privacy in the electronic communications sector (Directive on privacy and electronic communications) ([4]) translates the principles set out in Directive 95/46/EC into specific rules for the electronic communications sector.

(3) Articles 5, 6 and 9 of Directive 2002/58/EC lay down the rules applicable to the processing by network and service providers of traffic and location data generated by using electronic communications services. Such data must be erased or made anonymous when no longer needed for the purpose of the transmission of a communication, except for the data necessary for billing or interconnection payments. Subject to consent, certain data may also be processed for marketing purposes and the provision of value-added services.

(4) Article 15(1) of Directive 2002/58/EC sets out the conditions under which Member States may restrict the scope of the rights and obligations provided for in Article 5, Article 6, Article 8(1), (2), (3) and (4), and Article 9 of that Directive. Any such restrictions must be necessary, appropriate and proportionate within a democratic society for specific public order purposes, i.e. to safeguard national security (i.e. State security), defence, public security or the prevention, investigation, detection and prosecution of criminal offences or of unauthorised use of the electronic communications systems.

(5) Several Member States have adopted legislation providing for the retention of data by service providers for the prevention, investigation, detection, and prosecution of criminal offences. Those national provisions vary considerably.

(6) The legal and technical differences between national provisions concerning the retention of data for the purpose of prevention, investigation, detection and prosecution of criminal offences present obstacles to the internal market for electronic communications, since service providers are faced with different requirements regarding the types of traffic and location data to be retained and the conditions and periods of retention.

(7) The Conclusions of the Justice and Home Affairs Council of 19 December 2002 underline that, because of the significant growth in the possibilities afforded by electronic communications, data relating to the use of electronic communications are particularly important and therefore a valuable tool in the prevention, investigation, detection and prosecution of criminal offences, in particular organised crime.

(8) The Declaration on Combating Terrorism adopted by the European Council on 25 March 2004 instructed the Council to examine measures for establishing rules on the retention of communications traffic data by service providers.

([1]) Opinion delivered on 19 January 2006 (not yet published in the Official Journal).

([2]) Opinion of the European Parliament of 14 December 2005 (not yet published in the Official Journal) and Council Decision of 21 February 2006.

([3]) OJ L 281, 23.11.1995, p. 31. Directive as amended by Regulation (EC) No 1882/2003 (OJ L 284, 31.10.2003, p. 1).

([4]) OJ L 201, 31.7.2002, p. 37.

13.4.2006 EN Official Journal of the European Union L 105/55

(9) Under Article 8 of the European Convention for the Protection of Human Rights and Fundamental Freedoms (ECHR), everyone has the right to respect for his private life and his correspondence. Public authorities may interfere with the exercise of that right only in accordance with the law and where necessary in a democratic society, *inter alia*, in the interests of national security or public safety, for the prevention of disorder or crime, or for the protection of the rights and freedoms of others. Because retention of data has proved to be such a necessary and effective investigative tool for law enforcement in several Member States, and in particular concerning serious matters such as organised crime and terrorism, it is necessary to ensure that retained data are made available to law enforcement authorities for a certain period, subject to the conditions provided for in this Directive. The adoption of an instrument on data retention that complies with the requirements of Article 8 of the ECHR is therefore a necessary measure.

(10) On 13 July 2005, the Council reaffirmed in its declaration condemning the terrorist attacks on London the need to adopt common measures on the retention of telecommunications data as soon as possible.

(11) Given the importance of traffic and location data for the investigation, detection, and prosecution of criminal offences, as demonstrated by research and the practical experience of several Member States, there is a need to ensure at European level that data that are generated or processed, in the course of the supply of communications services, by providers of publicly available electronic communications services or of a public communications network are retained for a certain period, subject to the conditions provided for in this Directive.

(12) Article 15(1) of Directive 2002/58/EC continues to apply to data, including data relating to unsuccessful call attempts, the retention of which is not specifically required under this Directive and which therefore fall outside the scope thereof, and to retention for purposes, including judicial purposes, other than those covered by this Directive.

(13) This Directive relates only to data generated or processed as a consequence of a communication or a communication service and does not relate to data that are the content of the information communicated. Data should be retained in such a way as to avoid their being retained more than once. Data generated or processed when supplying the communications services concerned refers to data which are accessible. In particular, as regards the retention of data relating to Internet e-mail and Internet telephony, the obligation to retain data may apply only in respect of data from the providers' or the network providers' own services.

(14) Technologies relating to electronic communications are changing rapidly and the legitimate requirements of the competent authorities may evolve. In order to obtain advice and encourage the sharing of experience of best practice in these matters, the Commission intends to establish a group composed of Member States' law enforcement authorities, associations of the electronic communications industry, representatives of the European Parliament and data protection authorities, including the European Data Protection Supervisor.

(15) Directive 95/46/EC and Directive 2002/58/EC are fully applicable to the data retained in accordance with this Directive. Article 30(1)(c) of Directive 95/46/EC requires the consultation of the Working Party on the Protection of Individuals with regard to the Processing of Personal Data established under Article 29 of that Directive.

(16) The obligations incumbent on service providers concerning measures to ensure data quality, which derive from Article 6 of Directive 95/46/EC, and their obligations concerning measures to ensure confidentiality and security of processing of data, which derive from Articles 16 and 17 of that Directive, apply in full to data being retained within the meaning of this Directive.

(17) It is essential that Member States adopt legislative measures to ensure that data retained under this Directive are provided to the competent national authorities only in accordance with national legislation in full respect of the fundamental rights of the persons concerned.

(18) In this context, Article 24 of Directive 95/46/EC imposes an obligation on Member States to lay down sanctions for infringements of the provisions adopted pursuant to that Directive. Article 15(2) of Directive 2002/58/EC imposes the same requirement in relation to national provisions adopted pursuant to Directive 2002/58/EC. Council Framework Decision 2005/222/JHA of 24 February 2005 on attacks against information systems [1] provides that the intentional illegal access to information systems, including to data retained therein, is to be made punishable as a criminal offence.

(19) The right of any person who has suffered damage as a result of an unlawful processing operation or of any act incompatible with national provisions adopted pursuant to Directive 95/46/EC to receive compensation, which derives from Article 23 of that Directive, applies also in relation to the unlawful processing of any personal data pursuant to this Directive.

(1) OJ L 69, 16.3.2005, p. 67.

(20) The 2001 Council of Europe Convention on Cybercrime and the 1981 Council of Europe Convention for the Protection of Individuals with Regard to Automatic Processing of Personal Data also cover data being retained within the meaning of this Directive.

(21) Since the objectives of this Directive, namely to harmonise the obligations on providers to retain certain data and to ensure that those data are available for the purpose of the investigation, detection and prosecution of serious crime, as defined by each Member State in its national law, cannot be sufficiently achieved by the Member States and can therefore, by reason of the scale and effects of this Directive, be better achieved at Community level, the Community may adopt measures, in accordance with the principle of subsidiarity as set out in Article 5 of the Treaty. In accordance with the principle of proportionality, as set out in that Article, this Directive does not go beyond what is necessary in order to achieve those objectives.

(22) This Directive respects the fundamental rights and observes the principles recognised, in particular, by the Charter of Fundamental Rights of the European Union. In particular, this Directive, together with Directive 2002/58/EC, seeks to ensure full compliance with citizens' fundamental rights to respect for private life and communications and to the protection of their personal data, as enshrined in Articles 7 and 8 of the Charter.

(23) Given that the obligations on providers of electronic communications services should be proportionate, this Directive requires that they retain only such data as are generated or processed in the process of supplying their communications services. To the extent that such data are not generated or processed by those providers, there is no obligation to retain them. This Directive is not intended to harmonise the technology for retaining data, the choice of which is a matter to be resolved at national level.

(24) In accordance with paragraph 34 of the Interinstitutional agreement on better law-making ([1]), Member States are encouraged to draw up, for themselves and in the interests of the Community, their own tables illustrating, as far as possible, the correlation between this Directive and the transposition measures, and to make them public.

(25) This Directive is without prejudice to the power of Member States to adopt legislative measures concerning the right of access to, and use of, data by national authorities, as designated by them. Issues of access to data retained pursuant to this Directive by national authorities for such activities as are referred to in the first indent of Article 3(2) of Directive 95/46/EC fall outside the scope of Community law. However, they may be subject to national law or action pursuant to Title VI of the Treaty on European Union. Such laws or action must fully respect fundamental rights as they result from the common constitutional traditions of the Member States and as guaranteed by the ECHR. Under Article 8 of the ECHR, as interpreted by the European Court of Human Rights, interference by public authorities with privacy rights must meet the requirements of necessity and proportionality and must therefore serve specified, explicit and legitimate purposes and be exercised in a manner that is adequate, relevant and not excessive in relation to the purpose of the interference,

HAVE ADOPTED THIS DIRECTIVE:

*Article 1*

**Subject matter and scope**

1. This Directive aims to harmonise Member States' provisions concerning the obligations of the providers of publicly available electronic communications services or of public communications networks with respect to the retention of certain data which are generated or processed by them, in order to ensure that the data are available for the purpose of the investigation, detection and prosecution of serious crime, as defined by each Member State in its national law.

2. This Directive shall apply to traffic and location data on both legal entities and natural persons and to the related data necessary to identify the subscriber or registered user. It shall not apply to the content of electronic communications, including information consulted using an electronic communications network.

*Article 2*

**Definitions**

1. For the purpose of this Directive, the definitions in Directive 95/46/EC, in Directive 2002/21/EC of the European Parliament and of the Council of 7 March 2002 on a common regulatory framework for electronic communications networks and services (Framework Directive) ([2]), and in Directive 2002/58/EC shall apply.

2. For the purpose of this Directive:

(a) 'data' means traffic data and location data and the related data necessary to identify the subscriber or user;

([1]) OJ C 321, 31.12.2003, p. 1.

([2]) OJ L 108, 24.4.2002, p. 33.

(b) 'user' means any legal entity or natural person using a publicly available electronic communications service, for private or business purposes, without necessarily having subscribed to that service;

(c) 'telephone service' means calls (including voice, voicemail and conference and data calls), supplementary services (including call forwarding and call transfer) and messaging and multi-media services (including short message services, enhanced media services and multi-media services);

(d) 'user ID' means a unique identifier allocated to persons when they subscribe to or register with an Internet access service or Internet communications service;

(e) 'cell ID' means the identity of the cell from which a mobile telephony call originated or in which it terminated;

(f) 'unsuccessful call attempt' means a communication where a telephone call has been successfully connected but not answered or there has been a network management intervention.

*Article 3*

**Obligation to retain data**

1. By way of derogation from Articles 5, 6 and 9 of Directive 2002/58/EC, Member States shall adopt measures to ensure that the data specified in Article 5 of this Directive are retained in accordance with the provisions thereof, to the extent that those data are generated or processed by providers of publicly available electronic communications services or of a public communications network within their jurisdiction in the process of supplying the communications services concerned.

2. The obligation to retain data provided for in paragraph 1 shall include the retention of the data specified in Article 5 relating to unsuccessful call attempts where those data are generated or processed, and stored (as regards telephony data) or logged (as regards Internet data), by providers of publicly available electronic communications services or of a public communications network within the jurisdiction of the Member State concerned in the process of supplying the communication services concerned. This Directive shall not require data relating to unconnected calls to be retained.

*Article 4*

**Access to data**

Member States shall adopt measures to ensure that data retained in accordance with this Directive are provided only to the competent national authorities in specific cases and in accordance with national law. The procedures to be followed and the conditions to be fulfilled in order to gain access to retained data in accordance with necessity and proportionality requirements shall be defined by each Member State in its national law, subject to the relevant provisions of European Union law or public international law, and in particular the ECHR as interpreted by the European Court of Human Rights.

*Article 5*

**Categories of data to be retained**

1. Member States shall ensure that the following categories of data are retained under this Directive:

(a) data necessary to trace and identify the source of a communication:

(1) concerning fixed network telephony and mobile telephony:

(i) the calling telephone number;

(ii) the name and address of the subscriber or registered user;

(2) concerning Internet access, Internet e-mail and Internet telephony:

(i) the user ID(s) allocated;

(ii) the user ID and telephone number allocated to any communication entering the public telephone network;

(iii) the name and address of the subscriber or registered user to whom an Internet Protocol (IP) address, user ID or telephone number was allocated at the time of the communication;

(b) data necessary to identify the destination of a communication:

(1) concerning fixed network telephony and mobile telephony:

(i) the number(s) dialled (the telephone number(s) called), and, in cases involving supplementary services such as call forwarding or call transfer, the number or numbers to which the call is routed;

(ii) the name(s) and address(es) of the subscriber(s) or registered user(s);

(2) concerning Internet e-mail and Internet telephony:

(i) the user ID or telephone number of the intended recipient(s) of an Internet telephony call;

(ii) the name(s) and address(es) of the subscriber(s) or registered user(s) and user ID of the intended recipient of the communication;

(c) data necessary to identify the date, time and duration of a communication:

(1) concerning fixed network telephony and mobile telephony, the date and time of the start and end of the communication;

(2) concerning Internet access, Internet e-mail and Internet telephony:

(i) the date and time of the log-in and log-off of the Internet access service, based on a certain time zone, together with the IP address, whether dynamic or static, allocated by the Internet access service provider to a communication, and the user ID of the subscriber or registered user;

(ii) the date and time of the log-in and log-off of the Internet e-mail service or Internet telephony service, based on a certain time zone;

(d) data necessary to identify the type of communication:

(1) concerning fixed network telephony and mobile telephony: the telephone service used;

(2) concerning Internet e-mail and Internet telephony: the Internet service used;

(e) data necessary to identify users' communication equipment or what purports to be their equipment:

(1) concerning fixed network telephony, the calling and called telephone numbers;

(2) concerning mobile telephony:

(i) the calling and called telephone numbers;

(ii) the International Mobile Subscriber Identity (IMSI) of the calling party;

(iii) the International Mobile Equipment Identity (IMEI) of the calling party;

(iv) the IMSI of the called party;

(v) the IMEI of the called party;

(vi) in the case of pre-paid anonymous services, the date and time of the initial activation of the service and the location label (Cell ID) from which the service was activated;

(3) concerning Internet access, Internet e-mail and Internet telephony:

(i) the calling telephone number for dial-up access;

(ii) the digital subscriber line (DSL) or other end point of the originator of the communication;

(f) data necessary to identify the location of mobile communication equipment:

(1) the location label (Cell ID) at the start of the communication;

(2) data identifying the geographic location of cells by reference to their location labels (Cell ID) during the period for which communications data are retained.

2. No data revealing the content of the communication may be retained pursuant to this Directive.

*Article 6*

**Periods of retention**

Member States shall ensure that the categories of data specified in Article 5 are retained for periods of not less than six months and not more than two years from the date of the communication.

*Article 7*

**Data protection and data security**

Without prejudice to the provisions adopted pursuant to Directive 95/46/EC and Directive 2002/58/EC, each Member State shall ensure that providers of publicly available electronic communications services or of a public communications network respect, as a minimum, the following data security principles with respect to data retained in accordance with this Directive:

(a) the retained data shall be of the same quality and subject to the same security and protection as those data on the network;

(b) the data shall be subject to appropriate technical and organisational measures to protect the data against accidental or unlawful destruction, accidental loss or alteration, or unauthorised or unlawful storage, processing, access or disclosure;

(c) the data shall be subject to appropriate technical and organisational measures to ensure that they can be accessed by specially authorised personnel only;

and

(d) the data, except those that have been accessed and preserved, shall be destroyed at the end of the period of retention.

*Article 8*

**Storage requirements for retained data**

Member States shall ensure that the data specified in Article 5 are retained in accordance with this Directive in such a way that the data retained and any other necessary information relating to such data can be transmitted upon request to the competent authorities without undue delay.

*Article 9*

**Supervisory authority**

1. Each Member State shall designate one or more public authorities to be responsible for monitoring the application within its territory of the provisions adopted by the Member States pursuant to Article 7 regarding the security of the stored data. Those authorities may be the same authorities as those referred to in Article 28 of Directive 95/46/EC.

2. The authorities referred to in paragraph 1 shall act with complete independence in carrying out the monitoring referred to in that paragraph.

*Article 10*

**Statistics**

1. Member States shall ensure that the Commission is provided on a yearly basis with statistics on the retention of data generated or processed in connection with the provision of publicly available electronic communications services or a public communications network. Such statistics shall include:

— the cases in which information was provided to the competent authorities in accordance with applicable national law,

— the time elapsed between the date on which the data were retained and the date on which the competent authority requested the transmission of the data,

— the cases where requests for data could not be met.

2. Such statistics shall not contain personal data.

*Article 11*

**Amendment of Directive 2002/58/EC**

The following paragraph shall be inserted in Article 15 of Directive 2002/58/EC:

'1a. Paragraph 1 shall not apply to data specifically required by Directive 2006/24/EC of the European Parliament and of the Council of 15 March 2006 on the retention of data generated or processed in connection with the provision of publicly available electronic communications services or of public communications networks (*) to be retained for the purposes referred to in Article 1(1) of that Directive.

(*) OJ L 105, 13.4.2006, p. 54.'

*Aricle 12*

**Future measures**

1. A Member State facing particular circumstances that warrant an extension for a limited period of the maximum retention period referred to in Article 6 may take the necessary measures. That Member State shall immediately notify the Commission and inform the other Member States of the measures taken under this Article and shall state the grounds for introducing them.

2. The Commission shall, within a period of six months after the notification referred to in paragraph 1, approve or reject the national measures concerned, after having examined whether they are a means of arbitrary discrimination or a disguised restriction of trade between Member States and whether they constitute an obstacle to the functioning of the internal market. In the absence of a decision by the Commission within that period the national measures shall be deemed to have been approved.

3. Where, pursuant to paragraph 2, the national measures of a Member State derogating from the provisions of this Directive are approved, the Commission may consider whether to propose an amendment to this Directive.

*Article 13*

**Remedies, liability and penalties**

1. Each Member State shall take the necessary measures to ensure that the national measures implementing Chapter III of Directive 95/46/EC providing for judicial remedies, liability and sanctions are fully implemented with respect to the processing of data under this Directive.

2. Each Member State shall, in particular, take the necessary measures to ensure that any intentional access to, or transfer of, data retained in accordance with this Directive that is not permitted under national law adopted pursuant to this Directive is punishable by penalties, including administrative or criminal penalties, that are effective, proportionate and dissuasive.

*Article 14*

**Evaluation**

1. No later than 15 September 2010, the Commission shall submit to the European Parliament and the Council an evaluation of the application of this Directive and its impact on economic operators and consumers, taking into account further developments in electronic communications technology and the statistics provided to the Commission pursuant to Article 10 with a view to determining whether it is necessary to amend the provisions of this Directive, in particular with regard to the list of data in Article 5 and the periods of retention provided for in Article 6. The results of the evaluation shall be made public.

2. To that end, the Commission shall examine all observations communicated to it by the Member States or by the Working Party established under Article 29 of Directive 95/46/EC.

*Article 15*

**Transposition**

1. Member States shall bring into force the laws, regulations and administrative provisions necessary to comply with this Directive by no later than 15 September 2007. They shall forthwith inform the Commission thereof. When Member States adopt those measures, they shall contain a reference to this Directive or shall be accompanied by such reference on the occasion of their official publication. The methods of making such reference shall be laid down by Member States.

2. Member States shall communicate to the Commission the text of the main provisions of national law which they adopt in the field covered by this Directive.

3. Until 15 March 2009, each Member State may postpone application of this Directive to the retention of communications data relating to Internet Access, Internet telephony and Internet e-mail. Any Member State that intends to make use of this paragraph shall, upon adoption of this Directive, notify the Council and the Commission to that effect by way of a declaration. The declaration shall be published in the *Official Journal of the European Union*.

*Article 16*

**Entry into force**

This Directive shall enter into force on the twentieth day following that of its publication in the *Official Journal of the European Union*.

*Article 17*

**Addressees**

This Directive is addressed to the Member States.

Done at Strasbourg, 15 March 2006.

| *For the European Parliament* | *For the Council* |
|---|---|
| *The President* | *The President* |
| J. BORRELL FONTELLES | H. WINKLER |

13.4.2006 EN Official Journal of the European Union L 105/61

**Declaration by the Netherlands**

**pursuant to Article 15(3) of Directive 2006/24/EC**

Regarding the Directive of the European Parliament and of the Council on the retention of data processed in connection with the provision of publicly available electronic communications services and amending Directive 2002/58/EC, the Netherlands will be making use of the option of postponing application of the Directive to the retention of communications data relating to Internet access, Internet telephony and Internet e-mail, for a period not exceeding 18 months following the date of entry into force of the Directive.

**Declaration by Austria**

**pursuant to Article 15(3) of Directive 2006/24/EC**

Austria declares that it will be postponing application of this Directive to the retention of communications data relating to Internet access, Internet telephony and Internet e-mail, for a period of 18 months following the date specified in Article 15(1).

**Declaration by Estonia**

**pursuant to Article 15(3) of Directive 2006/24/EC**

In accordance with Article 15(3) of the Directive of the European Parliament and of the Council on the retention of data generated or processed in connection with the provision of publicly available electronic communications services or of public communications networks and amending Directive 2002/58/EC, Estonia hereby states its intention to make use of use that paragraph and to postpone application of the Directive to retention of communications data relating to Internet access, Internet telephony and Internet e-mail until 36 months after the date of adoption of the Directive.

**Declaration by the United Kingdom**

**pursuant to Article 15(3) of Directive 2006/24/EC**

The United Kingdom declares in accordance with Article 15(3) of the Directive on the retention of data generated or processed in connection with the provision of publicly available electronic communications services or of public communications networks and amending Directive 2002/58/EC that it will postpone application of that Directive to the retention of communications data relating to Internet access, Internet telephony and Internet e-mail.

**Declaration by the Republic of Cyprus**

**pursuant to Article 15(3) of Directive 2006/24/EC**

The Republic of Cyprus declares that it is postponing application of the Directive in respect of the retention of communications data relating to Internet access, Internet telephony and Internet e-mail until the date fixed in Article 15(3).

**Declaration by the Hellenic Republic**

**pursuant to Article 15(3) of Directive 2006/24/EC**

Greece declares that, pursuant to Article 15(3), it will postpone application of this Directive in respect of the retention of communications data relating to Internet access, Internet telephony and Internet e-mail until 18 months after expiry of the period provided for in Article 15(1).

**Declaration by the Grand Duchy of Luxembourg**

**pursuant to Article 15(3) of Directive 2006/24/EC**

Pursuant to Article 15(3) of the Directive of the European Parliament and of the Council on the retention of data generated or processed in connection with the provision of publicly available electronic communications services or of public communications networks and amending Directive 2002/58/EC, the Government of the Grand Duchy of Luxembourg declares that it intends to make use of Article 15(3) of the Directive in order to have the option of postponing application of the Directive to the retention of communications data relating to Internet access, Internet telephony and Internet e-mail.

**Declaration by Slovenia**

**pursuant to Article 15(3) of Directive 2006/24/EC**

Slovenia is joining the group of Member States which have made a declaration under Article 15(3) of the Directive of the European Parliament and the Council on the retention of data generated or processed in connection with the provision of publicly available electronic communications services or of public communications networks, for the 18 months postponement of the application of the Directive to the retention of communication data relating to Internet, Internet telephony and Internet e-mail.

**Declaration by Sweden**

**pursuant to Article 15(3) of Directive 2006/24/EC**

Pursuant to Article 15(3), Sweden wishes to have the option of postponing application of this Directive to the retention of communications data relating to Internet access, Internet telephony and Internet e-mail.

**Declaration by the Republic of Lithuania**

**pursuant to Article 15(3) of Directive 2006/24/EC**

Pursuant to Article 15(3) of the draft Directive of the European Parliament and of the Council on the retention of data generated or processed in connection with the provision of publicly available electronic communications services or public communications networks and amending Directive 2002/58/EC (hereafter the 'Directive'), the Republic of Lithuania declares that once the Directive has been adopted it will postpone the application thereof to the retention of communications data relating to Internet access, Internet telephony and Internet e-mail for the period provided for in Article 15(3).

**Declaration by the Republic of Latvia**

**pursuant to Article 15(3) of Directive 2006/24/EC**

Latvia states in accordance with Article 15(3) of Directive 2006/24/EC of 15 March 2006 on the retention of data generated or processed in connection with the provision of publicly available electronic communications services or of public communications networks and amending Directive 2002/58/EC that it is postponing application of the Directive to the retention of communications data relating to Internet access, Internet telephony and Internet e-mail until 15 March 2009.

**Declaration by the Czech Republic**

**pursuant to Article 15(3) of Directive 2006/24/EC**

Pursuant to Article 15(3), the Czech Republic hereby declares that it is postponing application of this Directive to the retention of communications data relating to Internet access, Internet telephony and Internet e-mail until 36 months after the date of adoption thereof.

**Declaration by Belgium**

**pursuant to Article 15(3) of Directive 2006/24/EC**

Belgium declares that, taking up the option available under Article 15(3), it will postpone application of this Directive, for a period of 36 months after its adoption, to the retention of communications data relating to Internet access, Internet telephony and Internet e-mail.

**Declaration by the Republic of Poland**

**pursuant to Article 15(3) of Directive 2006/24/EC**

Poland hereby declares that it intends to make use of the option provided for under Article 15(3) of the Directive of the European Parliament and of the Council on the retention of data processed in connection with the provision of publicly available electronic communications services and amending Directive 2002/58/EC and postpone application of the Directive to the retention of communications data relating to Internet access, Internet telephony and Internet e-mail for a period of 18 months following the date specified in Article 15(1).

**Declaration by Finland**

**pursuant to Article 15(3) of Directive 2006/24/EC**

Finland declares in accordance with Article 15(3) of the Directive on the retention of data generated or processed in connection with the provision of publicly available electronic communications services or of public communications networks and amending Directive 2002/58/EC that it will postpone application of that Directive to the retention of communications data relating to Internet access, Internet telephony and Internet e-mail.

**Declaration by Germany**

**pursuant to Article 15(3) of Directive 2006/24/EC**

Germany reserves the right to postpone application of this Directive to the retention of communications data relating to Internet access, Internet telephony and Internet e-mail for a period of 18 months following the date specified in the first sentence of Article 15(1).

# Framework Decision 2006/783 on the application of the principle of mutual recognition to confiscation orders, 6 October 2006

**[Consolidated version. Orignal version OJ 2006, L 328/59–78 amended as of 28 March 2011 by OJ 2009, L 81/24–36]**

2006F0783 — EN — 28.03.2009 — 001.001 — 1



►B

**COUNCIL FRAMEWORK DECISION 2006/783/JHA**

**of 6 October 2006**

**on the application of the principle of mutual recognition to confiscation orders**

(OJ L 328, 24.11.2006, p. 59)

Amended by:

| | | Official Journal | | |
|---|---|---|---|---|
| | | No | page | date |
| ►M1 | Council Framework Decision 2009/299/JHA of 26 February 2009 | L 81 | 24 | 27.3.2009 |

▼B

**COUNCIL FRAMEWORK DECISION 2006/783/JHA**

**of 6 October 2006**

**on the application of the principle of mutual recognition to confiscation orders**

THE COUNCIL OF THE EUROPEAN UNION,

Having regard to the Treaty on European Union, and in particular Articles 31(1)(a) and 34(2)(b) thereof,

Having regard to the initiative of the Kingdom of Denmark ([1]),

Having regard to the opinion of the European Parliament ([2]),

Whereas:

(1) The European Council, meeting in Tampere on 15 and 16 October 1999, stressed that the principle of mutual recognition should become the cornerstone of judicial cooperation in both civil and criminal matters within the Union.

(2) According to paragraph 51 of the conclusions of the Tampere European Council, money laundering is at the very heart of organised crime, and should be rooted out wherever it occurs; the European Council is determined to ensure that concrete steps are taken to trace, freeze, seize and confiscate the proceeds of crime. In that connection, in paragraph 55 of the conclusions, the European Council calls for the approximation of criminal law and procedures on money laundering (e.g. tracing, freezing and confiscating funds).

(3) All Member States have ratified the Council of Europe Convention of 8 November 1990 on Laundering, Search, Seizure and Confiscation of the Proceeds from Crime (the 1990 Convention). The Convention obliges signatories to recognise and enforce a confiscation order made by another party, or to submit a request to its competent authorities for the purpose of obtaining an order of confiscation and, if such order is granted, enforce it. The Parties may refuse requests for confiscation *inter alia* if the offence to which the request relates would not be an offence under the law of the requested Party, or if under the law of the requested Party confiscation is not provided for in respect of the type of offence to which the request relates.

(4) On 30 November 2000 the Council adopted a programme of measures to implement the principle of mutual recognition of decisions in criminal matters, giving first priority (measures 6 and 7) to the adoption of an instrument applying the principle of mutual recognition to the freezing of evidence and property. Moreover, pursuant to paragraph 3.3 of the programme, the aim is to improve, in accordance with the principle of mutual recognition, execution in one Member State of a confiscation order issued in another Member State, *inter alia* for the purpose of restitution to a victim of a criminal offence, taking into account the existence of the 1990 Convention. With a view to achieving this aim, this Framework Decision, within its field of application, reduces the grounds for refusal of enforcement and suppresses, among Member States, any system of conversion of the confiscation order into a national one.

(5) Council Framework Decision 2001/500/JHA ([3]) lays down provisions on money laundering, the identification, tracing, freezing, seizing and confiscation of instrumentalities and the proceeds from crime. Under that Framework Decision, Member

([1]) OJ C 184, 2.8.2002, p. 8.
([2]) Opinion delivered on 20 November 2002 (OJ C 25 E, 29.1.2004, p. 205).
([3]) OJ L 182, 5.7.2001, p. 1.

▼B

States are also obliged not to make or uphold reservations in respect of Article 2 of the 1990 Convention, in so far as the offence is punishable by deprivation of liberty or a detention order for a maximum of more than one year.

(6) Finally, on 22 July 2003 the Council adopted Framework Decision 2003/577/JHA on the execution in the European Union of orders freezing property or evidence [1].

(7) The main motive for organised crime is financial gain. In order to be effective, therefore, any attempt to prevent and combat such crime must focus on tracing, freezing, seizing and confiscating the proceeds from crime. It is not enough merely to ensure mutual recognition within the European Union of temporary legal measures such as freezing and seizure; effective control of economic crime also requires the mutual recognition of orders to confiscate the proceeds from crime.

(8) The purpose of this Framework Decision is to facilitate cooperation between Member States as regards the mutual recognition and execution of orders to confiscate property so as to oblige a Member State to recognise and execute in its territory confiscation orders issued by a court competent in criminal matters of another Member State. This Framework Decision is linked to Council Framework Decision 2005/212/JHA of 24 February 2005 on Confiscation of Crime-Related Proceeds, Instrumentalities and Property [2]. The purpose of that Framework Decision is to ensure that all Member States have effective rules governing the confiscation of proceeds from crime, *inter alia* in relation to the onus of proof regarding the source of assets held by a person convicted of an offence related to organised crime.

(9) Cooperation between Member States, based on the principle of mutual recognition and immediate execution of judicial decisions, presupposes confidence that the decisions to be recognised and executed will always be taken in compliance with the principles of legality, subsidiarity and proportionality. It also presupposes that the rights granted to the parties or bona fide interested third parties will be preserved. In this context, due consideration should be given to preventing successful dishonest claims by legal or natural persons.

(10) The proper practical operation of this Framework Decision presupposes close liaison between the competent national authorities involved, in particular in cases of simultaneous execution of a confiscation order in more than one Member State.

(11) The terms 'proceeds' and 'instrumentalities' used in this Framework Decision are sufficiently broadly defined to include objects of offences whenever necessary.

(12) Where there are doubts with regard to the location of property which is the subject of a confiscation order, Member States should use all available means in order to identify the correct location of that property, including the use of all available information systems.

(13) This Framework Decision respects fundamental rights and observes the principles recognised by Article 6 of the Treaty on European Union and reflected by the Charter of Fundamental Rights of the European Union, in particular Chapter VI thereof. Nothing in this Framework Decision may be interpreted as prohibiting refusal to confiscate property for which a confiscation order has been issued when objective grounds exist for believing that the confiscation order was issued for the purpose

[1] OJ L 196, 2.8.2003, p. 45.
[2] OJ L 68, 15.3.2005, p. 49.

▼B

of prosecuting or punishing a person on account of his or her sex, race, religion, ethnic origin, nationality, language, political opinion or sexual orientation, or that that person's position may be prejudiced for any of these reasons.

(14) This Framework Decision does not prevent any Member State from applying its constitutional rules relating to due process, freedom of association, freedom of the press and freedom of expression in other media.

(15) This Framework Decision does not address the restitution of property to its rightful owner.

(16) This Framework Decision does not prejudice the end to which the Member States apply the amounts obtained as a consequence of its application.

(17) This Framework Decision does not affect the exercise of the responsibilities incumbent upon Member States with regard to the maintenance of law and order and the safeguarding of internal security in accordance with Article 33 of the Treaty on European Union,

HAS ADOPTED THIS FRAMEWORK DECISION:

*Article 1*

**Objective**

1. The purpose of this Framework Decision is to establish the rules under which a Member State shall recognise and execute in its territory a confiscation order issued by a court competent in criminal matters of another Member State.

2. This Framework Decision shall not have the effect of modifying the obligation to respect fundamental rights and fundamental legal principles as enshrined in Article 6 of the Treaty on European Union, and any obligations incumbent on judicial authorities in this respect shall remain unaffected.

*Article 2*

**Definitions**

For the purpose of this Framework Decision,

(a) 'issuing State' shall mean the Member State in which a court has issued a confiscation order within the framework of criminal proceedings;

(b) 'executing State' shall mean the Member State to which a confiscation order has been transmitted for the purpose of execution;

(c) 'confiscation order' shall mean a final penalty or measure imposed by a court following proceedings in relation to a criminal offence or offences, resulting in the definitive deprivation of property;

(d) 'property' shall mean property of any description, whether corporeal or incorporeal, movable or immovable, and legal documents and instruments evidencing title to or interest in such property, which the court in the issuing State has decided:

(i) is the proceeds of an offence, or equivalent to either the full value or part of the value of such proceeds,

or

(ii) constitutes the instrumentalities of such an offence,

or

▼B

(iii) is liable to confiscation resulting from the application in the issuing State of any of the extended powers of confiscation specified in Article 3(1) and (2) of Framework Decision 2005/212/JHA,

or

(iv) is liable to confiscation under any other provisions relating to extended powers of confiscation under the law of the issuing State;

(e) 'proceeds' shall mean any economic advantage derived from criminal offences. It may consist of any form of property;

(f) 'instrumentalities' shall mean any property used or intended to be used, in any manner, wholly or in part, to commit a criminal offence or criminal offences;

(g) 'cultural objects forming part of the national cultural heritage' shall be defined in accordance with Article 1(1) of Council Directive 93/7/EEC of 15 March 1993 on the return of cultural objects unlawfully removed from the territory of a Member State [1];

(h) where the criminal proceedings leading to a confiscation order involve a predicate offence as well as money laundering, a 'criminal offence' mentioned in Article 8(2)(f) shall mean a predicate offence.

*Article 3*

**Determination of the competent authorities**

1. Each Member State shall inform the General Secretariat of the Council which authority or authorities, under its law, are competent according to this Framework Decision when that Member State is:

— the issuing State,

or

— the executing State.

2. Notwithstanding Articles 4(1) and (2), each Member State may designate, if it is necessary as a result of the organisation of its internal system, one or more central authorities responsible for the administrative transmission and reception of the confiscation orders and to assist the competent authorities.

3. The General Secretariat of the Council shall make the information received available to all Member States and the Commission.

*Article 4*

**Transmission of confiscation orders**

1. A confiscation order, together with the certificate provided for in paragraph 2, the standard form for which is given in the Annex, may, in the case of a confiscation order concerning an amount of money, be transmitted to the competent authority of a Member State in which the competent authority of the issuing State has reasonable grounds to believe that the natural or legal person against whom the confiscation order has been issued has property or income.

In the case of a confiscation order concerning specific items of property, the confiscation order and the certificate may be transmitted to the competent authority of a Member State in which the competent

(1) OJ L 74, 27.3.1993, p. 74. Directive as last amended by Directive 2001/38/EC of the European Parliament and of the Council (OJ L 187, 10.7.2001, p. 43).

▼B

authority of the issuing State has reasonable grounds to believe that property covered by the confiscation order is located.

If there are no reasonable grounds which would allow the issuing State to determine the Member State to which the confiscation order may be transmitted, the confiscation order may be transmitted to the competent authority of the Member State where the natural or legal person against whom the confiscation order has been issued is normally resident or has its registered seat respectively.

2. The confiscation order or a certified copy thereof, together with the certificate, shall be transmitted by the competent authority of the issuing State directly to the authority of the executing State which is competent to execute it, by any means capable of producing a written record, under conditions allowing the executing State to establish authenticity. The original of the confiscation order, or a certified copy thereof, and the original of the certificate shall be transmitted to the executing State if it so requires. All official communications shall be made directly between the said competent authorities.

3. The certificate, shall be signed, and its contents certified as accurate, by the competent authority of the issuing State.

4. If the authority competent to execute the confiscation order is not known to the competent authority of the issuing State, the latter shall make all necessary enquiries, including via the contact points of the European judicial network, in order to obtain information from the executing State.

5. Where the authority of the executing State which receives a confiscation order has no jurisdiction to recognise it and take the necessary measures for its execution, it shall, *ex officio*, transmit the order to the authority competent to execute it, and shall inform the competent authority of the issuing State accordingly.

*Article 5*

**Transmission of a confiscation order to one or more executing States**

1. Subject to paragraphs 2 and 3, a confiscation order may only be transmitted pursuant to Article 4 to one executing State at any one time.

2. A confiscation order concerning specific items of property may be transmitted to more than one executing State at the same time in cases where:

— the competent authority of the issuing State has reasonable grounds to believe that different items of property covered by the confiscation order are located in different executing States,

— the confiscation of a specific item of property covered by the confiscation order involves action in more than one executing State,

or

— the competent authority of the issuing State has reasonable grounds to believe that a specific item of property covered by the confiscation order is located in one of two or more specified executing States.

3. A confiscation order concerning an amount of money may be transmitted to more than one executing State at the same time, where the competent authority of the issuing State deems there is a specific need to do so, for example where:

— the property concerned has not been frozen under Council Framework Decision 2003/577/JHA of,

or

▼B

— the value of the property which may be confiscated in the issuing State and any one executing State is not likely to be sufficient for the execution of the full amount covered by the confiscation order.

*Article 6*

**Offences**

1. If the acts giving rise to the confiscation order constitute one or more of the following offences, as defined by the law of the issuing State, and are punishable in the issuing State by a custodial sentence of a maximum of at least three years, the confiscation order shall give rise to execution without verification of the double criminality of the acts:

— participation in a criminal organisation,

— terrorism,

— trafficking in human beings,

— sexual exploitation of children and child pornography,

— illicit trafficking in narcotic drugs and psychotropic substances,

— illicit trafficking in weapons, munitions and explosives,

— corruption,

— fraud, including that affecting the financial interests of the European Communities within the meaning of the Convention of 26 July 1995 on the protection of the European Communities' financial interests,

— laundering of the proceeds of crime,

— counterfeiting currency, including of the euro,

— computer-related crime,

— environmental crime, including illicit trafficking in endangered animal species and in endangered plant species and varieties,

— facilitation of unauthorised entry and residence,

— murder, grievous bodily injury,

— illicit trade in human organs and tissue,

— kidnapping, illegal restraint and hostage-taking,

— racism and xenophobia,

— organised or armed robbery,

— illicit trafficking in cultural goods, including antiques and works of art,

— swindling,

— racketeering and extortion,

— counterfeiting and piracy of products,

— forgery of administrative documents and trafficking therein,

— forgery of means of payment,

— illicit trafficking in hormonal substances and other growth promoters,

— illicit trafficking in nuclear or radioactive materials,

— trafficking in stolen vehicles,

— rape,

— arson,

— crimes within the jurisdiction of the International Criminal Court,

▼B

— unlawful seizure of aircraft/ships,

— sabotage.

2. The Council may decide to add other categories of offences to the list contained in paragraph 1 at any time, acting unanimously after consultation of the European Parliament under the conditions laid down in Article 39(1) of the TEU. The Council shall consider, in the light of the report submitted by the Commission pursuant to Article 22, whether the list should be extended or amended.

3. For offences other than those covered by paragraph 1, the executing State may make the recognition and execution of a confiscation order subject to the condition that the acts giving rise to the confiscation order constitute an offence which permits confiscation under the law of the executing State, whatever its constituent elements or however it is described under the law of the issuing State.

*Article 7*

**Recognition and execution**

1. The competent authorities in the executing State shall without further formality recognise a confiscation order which has been transmitted in accordance with Articles 4 and 5, and shall forthwith take all the necessary measures for its execution, unless the competent authorities decide to invoke one of the grounds for non-recognition or non-execution provided for in Article 8, or one of the grounds for postponement of execution provided for in Article 10.

2. If a request for confiscation concerns a specific item of property, the competent authorities of the issuing and the executing States may, if provided for under the law of those States, agree that confiscation in the executing State may take the form of a requirement to pay a sum of money corresponding to the value of the property.

3. If a confiscation order concerns an amount of money, the competent authorities of the executing State shall, if payment is not obtained, execute the confiscation order in accordance with paragraph 1 on any item of property available for that purpose.

4. If a confiscation order concerns an amount of money, the competent authorities of the executing State shall, if necessary, convert the amount to be confiscated into the currency of the executing State at the rate of exchange obtaining at the time when the confiscation order was issued.

5. Each Member State may state in a declaration deposited with the General Secretariat of the Council that its competent authorities will not recognise and execute confiscation orders under circumstances where confiscation of the property was ordered under the extended powers of confiscation referred to in Article 2(d)(iv). Any such declaration may be withdrawn at any time.

*Article 8*

**Reasons for non-recognition or non-execution**

1. The competent authority of the executing State may refuse to recognise and execute the confiscation order if the certificate provided for in Article 4 is not produced, is incomplete, or manifestly does not correspond to the order.

2. The competent judicial authority of the executing State, as defined in the law of that State, may also refuse to recognise and execute the confiscation order if it is established that:

(a) execution of the confiscation order would be contrary to the principle of ne bis in idem;

▼B

(b) in one of the cases referred to in Article 6(3), the confiscation order relates to acts which do not constitute an offence which permits confiscation under the law of the executing State; however, in relation to taxes, duties, customs duties and exchange activities, execution of a confiscation order may not be refused on the ground that the law of the executing State does not impose the same kind of tax or duty or does not contain the same types of rules concerning taxes, duties, customs duties and exchange activities as the law of the issuing State;

(c) there is immunity or privilege under the law of the executing State which would prevent the execution of a domestic confiscation order on the property concerned;

(d) the rights of any interested party, including bona fide third parties, under the law of the executing State make it impossible to execute the confiscation order, including where this is a consequence of the application of legal remedies in accordance with Article 9;

▼M1

(e) according to the certificate provided for in Article 4(2), the person did not appear in person at the trial resulting in the confiscation order, unless the certificate states that the person, in accordance with further procedural requirements defined in the national law of the issuing State:

(i) in due time:

— either was summoned in person and thereby informed of the scheduled date and place of the trial which resulted in the confiscation order, or by other means actually received official information of the scheduled date and place of that trial in such a manner that it was unequivocally established that he or she was aware of the scheduled trial,

and

— was informed that such a confiscation order may be handed down if he or she does not appear for the trial;

or

(ii) being aware of the scheduled trial, had given a mandate to a legal counsellor, who was either appointed by the person concerned or by the State, to defend him or her at the trial, and was indeed defended by that counsellor at the trial;

or

(iii) after being served with the confiscation order and being expressly informed of the right to a retrial, or an appeal, in which the person has the right to participate and which allows the merits of the case, including fresh evidence, to be re-examined, and which may lead to the original decision being reversed:

— expressly stated that he or she does not contest the confiscation order,

or

— did not request a retrial or appeal within the applicable time frame.

▼B

(f) the confiscation order is based on criminal proceedings in respect of criminal offences which:

— under the law of the executing State, are regarded as having been committed wholly or partly within its territory, or in a place equivalent to its territory,

or

▼B

— were committed outside the territory of the issuing State, and the law of the executing State does not permit legal proceedings to be taken in respect of such offences where they are committed outside that State's territory;

(g) the confiscation order, in the view of that authority, was issued in circumstances where confiscation of the property was ordered under the extended powers of confiscation referred to in Article 2(d)(iv);

(h) the execution of a confiscation order is barred by statutory time limitations in the executing State, provided that the acts fall within the jurisdiction of that State under its own criminal law.

3. If it appears to the competent authority of the executing State that:

— the confiscation order was issued in circumstances where confiscation of the property was ordered under the extended powers of confiscation referred to in Article 2(d)(iii),

and

— the confiscation order falls outside the scope of the option adopted by the executing State under Article 3(2) of Framework Decision 2005/212/JHA,

it shall execute the confiscation order at least to the extent provided for in similar domestic cases under national law.

4. The competent authorities of the executing State shall give specific consideration to consulting, by any appropriate means, the competent authorities of the issuing State before deciding not to recognise and execute a confiscation order pursuant to paragraph 2, or to limit the execution thereof pursuant to paragraph 3. Consultation is obligatory where the decision is likely to be based on:

— paragraph 1,

— paragraph 2(a), (e), (f) or (g),

— paragraph 2(d) and information is not being provided under Article 9(3),

or

— paragraph 3.

5. Where it is impossible to execute the confiscation order for the reason that the property to be confiscated has already been confiscated, has disappeared, has been destroyed, cannot be found in the location indicated in the certificate or the location of the property has not been indicated in a sufficiently precise manner, even after consultation with the issuing State, the competent authority of the issuing State shall be notified forthwith.

*Article 9*

**Legal remedies in the executing State against recognition and execution**

1. Each Member State shall put in place the necessary arrangements to ensure that any interested party, including bona fide third parties, has legal remedies against the recognition and execution of a confiscation order pursuant to Article 7, in order to preserve his or her rights. The action shall be brought before a court in the executing State in accordance with the law of that State. The action may have suspensive effect under the law of the executing State.

2. The substantial reasons for issuing the confiscation order cannot be challenged before a court in the executing State.

3. If action is brought before a court in the executing State, the competent authority of the issuing State shall be informed thereof.

▼B

*Article 10*

**Postponement of execution**

1. The competent authority of the executing State may postpone the execution of a confiscation order transmitted in accordance with Articles 4 and 5:

(a) if, in the case of a confiscation order concerning an amount of money, it considers that there is a risk that the total value derived from its execution may exceed the amount specified in the confiscation order because of simultaneous execution of the confiscation order in more than one Member State;

(b) in the cases of legal remedies referred to in Article 9;

(c) where the execution of the confiscation order might damage an ongoing criminal investigation or proceedings, until such time as it deems reasonable;

(d) where it is considered necessary to have the confiscation order or parts thereof translated at the expense of the executing State, for the time necessary to obtain its translation,

or

(e) where the property is already the subject of confiscation proceedings in the executing State.

2. The competent authority of the executing State shall, for the duration of postponement, take all the measures it would take in a similar domestic case to prevent the property from no longer being available for the purpose of execution of the confiscation order.

3. In the case of postponement pursuant to paragraph 1(a), the competent authority of the executing State shall inform the competent authority of the issuing State thereof immediately by any means capable of producing a written record, and the competent authority of the issuing State shall comply with the obligations referred to in Article 14(3).

4. In the cases referred to in paragraph 1(b), (c), (d) and (e), a report on the postponement, including the grounds for the postponement and, if possible, the expected duration of the postponement, shall be made forthwith by the competent authority of the executing State to the competent authority of the issuing State by any means capable of producing a written record.

As soon as the ground for postponement has ceased to exist, the competent authority of the executing State shall forthwith take the necessary measures for the execution of the confiscation order and inform the competent authority of the issuing State thereof by any means capable of producing a written record.

*Article 11*

**Multiple confiscation orders**

If the competent authorities of the executing State are processing:

— two or more confiscation orders concerning an amount of money, which have been issued against the same natural or legal person, and the person concerned does not have sufficient means in the executing State to enable all the orders to be executed,

or

— two or more confiscation orders concerning the same specific item of property,

the decision on which of the confiscation orders is or are to be executed shall be taken by the competent authority of the executing State

▼B

according to the law of the executing State, with due consideration of all the circumstances, which may include the involvement of frozen assets, the relative seriousness and the place of the offence, the dates of the respective orders and the dates of transmission of the respective orders.

*Article 12*

**Law governing execution**

1. Without prejudice to paragraph 3, the execution of the confiscation order shall be governed by the law of the executing State and its authorities alone shall be competent to decide on the procedures for execution and to determine all the measures relating thereto.

2. In the case where the person concerned is able to furnish proof of confiscation, totally or in part, in any State, the competent authority of the executing State shall consult the competent authority of the issuing State by any appropriate means. Any part of the amount, in the case of confiscation of proceeds, that is recovered pursuant to the confiscation order in any State other than the executing State shall be deducted in full from the amount to be confiscated in the executing State.

3. A confiscation order issued against a legal person shall be executed even if the executing State does not recognise the principle of criminal liability of legal persons.

4. The executing State may not impose measures as an alternative to the confiscation order, including custodial sanctions or any other measure limiting a person's freedom, as a result of a transmission pursuant to Articles 4 and 5, unless the issuing State has given its consent.

*Article 13*

**Amnesty, pardon, review of confiscation order**

1. Amnesty and pardon may be granted by the issuing State and also by the executing State.

2. Only the issuing State may determine any application for review of the confiscation order.

*Article 14*

**Consequences of transmission of confiscation orders**

1. The transmission of a confiscation order to one or more executing States in accordance with Articles 4 and 5 does not restrict the right of the issuing State to execute the confiscation order itself.

2. In the case of transmission of a confiscation order concerning an amount of money to one or more executing States, the total value derived from its execution may not exceed the maximum amount specified in the confiscation order.

3. The competent authority of the issuing State shall immediately inform the competent authority of any executing State concerned by any means capable of producing a written record:

(a) if it considers that there is a risk that execution beyond the maximum amount may occur, for example on the basis of information notified to it by an executing State pursuant to Article 10(3). In the event of the application of Article 10(1)(a), the competent authority of the issuing State shall as soon as possible inform the competent authority of the executing State whether the risk referred to has ceased to exist;

▼B

(b) if all or a part of the confiscation order has been executed in the issuing State or in another executing State. The amount for which the confiscation order has not yet been executed shall be specified;

(c) if, after transmission of a confiscation order in accordance with Articles 4 and 5, an authority of the issuing State receives any sum of money which the person concerned has paid voluntarily in respect of the confiscation order. Article 12(2) shall apply.

*Article 15*

**Termination of execution**

The competent authority of the issuing State shall forthwith inform the competent authority of the executing State by any means capable of reducing a written record of any decision or measure as a result of which the order ceases to be enforceable or shall be withdrawn from the executing State for any other reason. The executing State shall terminate execution of the order as soon as it is informed by the competent authority of the issuing State of that decision or measure.

*Article 16*

**Disposal of confiscated property**

1. Money which has been obtained from the execution of the confiscation order shall be disposed of by the executing State as follows:

(a) if the amount obtained from the execution of the confiscation order is below EUR 10 000, or the equivalent to that amount, the amount shall accrue to the executing State;

(b) in all other cases, 50 % of the amount which has been obtained from the execution of the confiscation order shall be transferred by the executing State to the issuing State.

2. Property other than money, which has been obtained from the execution of the confiscation order, shall be disposed of in one of the following ways, to be decided by the executing State:

(a) the property may be sold. In that case, the proceeds of the sale shall be disposed of in accordance with paragraph 1;

(b) the property may be transferred to the issuing State. If the confiscation order covers an amount of money, the property may only be transferred to the issuing State when that State has given its consent;

(c) when it is not possible to apply (a) or (b), the property may be disposed of in another way in accordance with the law of the executing State.

3. Notwithstanding paragraph 2, the executing State shall not be required to sell or return specific items covered by the confiscation order which constitute cultural objects forming part of the national heritage of that State.

4. Paragraphs 1, 2 and 3 apply unless otherwise agreed between the issuing State and the executing State.

*Article 17*

**Information on the result of the execution**

The competent authority of the executing State shall without delay inform the competent authority of the issuing State by any means capable of producing a written record:

(a) of the transmission of the confiscation order to the competent authority, according to Article 4(5);

▼B

(b) of any decision not to recognise the confiscation order, together with the reasons for the decision;

(c) of the total or partial non-execution of the order for the reasons referred to in Article 11, Article 12(1) and (2) or Article 13(1);

(d) as soon as the execution of the order has been completed;

(e) of the application of alternative measures, according to Article 12(4).

*Article 18*

**Reimbursement**

1. Without prejudice to Article 9(2), where the executing State under its law is responsible for injury caused to one of the interested parties mentioned in Article 9 by the execution of a confiscation order transmitted to it pursuant to Articles 4 and 5, the issuing State shall reimburse to the executing State any sums paid in damages by virtue of that responsibility to the said party except if, and to the extent that, the injury or any part of it is exclusively due to the conduct of the executing State.

2. Paragraph 1 is without prejudice to the law of the Member States on claims by natural or legal persons for compensation of damage.

*Article 19*

**Languages**

1. The certificate shall be translated into the official language or one of the official languages of the executing State.

2. Any Member State may, when this Framework Decision is adopted or at a later date, state in a declaration deposited with the General Secretariat of the Council that it will accept a translation in one or more other official languages of the Institutions of the European Communities.

*Article 20*

**Costs**

1. Without prejudice to Article 16, Member States may not claim from each other the refund of costs resulting from application of this Framework Decision.

2. Where the executing State has had costs which it considers large or exceptional, it may propose to the issuing State that the costs be shared. The issuing State shall take into account any such proposal on the basis of detailed specifications given by the executing State.

*Article 21*

**Relationship with other agreements and arrangements**

This Framework Decision shall not affect the application of bilateral or multilateral agreements or arrangements between Member States in so far as such agreements or arrangements help to further simplify or facilitate the procedures for the execution of confiscation orders.

*Article 22*

**Implementation**

1. Member States shall take the necessary measures to comply with this Framework Decision by 24 November 2008.

▼B

2. Member States shall communicate to the General Secretariat of the Council and to the Commission the text of the provisions transposing into their national law the obligations resulting from this Framework Decision. On the basis of a report established on the basis of this information by the Commission, the Council shall, by 24 November 2009, assess the extent to which Member States have taken the necessary measures to comply with this Framework Decision.

3. The General Secretariat of the Council shall notify the Member States and the Commission of the declarations made pursuant to Articles 7(5) and 19(2).

4. A Member State which has experienced repeated difficulties or lack of activity by another Member State in the mutual recognition and execution of confiscation orders, which have not been resolved through bilateral consultations, may inform the Council with a view to evaluating the implementation of this Framework Decision at Member State level.

5. The Member States, acting as executing States, shall inform the Council and the Commission, at the beginning of the calendar year, of the number of cases in which Article 17(b) has been applied and a summary of reasons for this.

By 24 November 2013, the Commission shall establish a report on the basis of the information received, accompanied by any initiatives it may deem appropriate.

*Article 23*

**Entry into force**

This Framework Decision shall enter into force on the day of its publication in the *Official Journal of the European Union*.

▼B

*ANNEX*

**CERTIFICATE**

**referred to in Article 4 of Council Framework Decision 2006/783/JHA on the application of the principle of mutual recognition to confiscation orders**

(a) Issuing and executing States:

Issuing State: ..............................

Executing State: ..............................

(b) Court which issued the confiscation order:

Official name: ..............................

Address: ..............................

..............................

File reference: ..............................

Tel. (country code) (area/city code): ..............................

Fax (country code) (area/city code): ..............................

E mail (when available): ..............................

Languages in which it is possible to communicate with the Court: ..............................

..............................

Contact details for person(s) to contact in order to obtain additional information for the purpose of the execution of the confiscation order, or, where applicable, for the purpose of coordination of the execution of a confiscation order transmitted to two or more executing States, or for the purpose of the transfer to the issuing State of monies or properties obtained from the execution (name, title/grade, tel., fax, and, when available, e mail):

..............................

..............................

..............................

▼B

(c) Authority competent for the execution of the confiscation order in the issuing State (if the authority is different from the Court under point (b)):

Official name: ...........................................................................................................

...........................................................................................................

Address: ...........................................................................................................

...........................................................................................................

Tel. (country code) (area/city code): ...........................................................................................................

Fax (country code) (area/city code): ...........................................................................................................

E mail (when available): ...........................................................................................................

...........................................................................................................

Languages in which it is possible to communicate with the authority competent for the execution: ...........................................................................................................

...........................................................................................................

...........................................................................................................

Contact details for person(s) to contact in order to obtain additional information for the purpose of the execution of the confiscation order or, where applicable, for the purpose of coordination of the execution of a confiscation order transmitted to two or more executing States, or for the purpose of the transfer to the issuing State of monies or properties obtained from the execution, (name, title/grade, tel., fax, and, when available, e mail): ...........................................................................................................

...........................................................................................................

...........................................................................................................

(d) Where a central authority has been made responsible for the administrative transmission and reception of confiscation orders in the issuing State:

Name of the central authority: ...........................................................................................................

...........................................................................................................

...........................................................................................................

Contact person, if applicable (title/grade and name): ...........................................................................................................

...........................................................................................................

Address: ...........................................................................................................

...........................................................................................................

File reference: ...........................................................................................................

Tel. (country code) (area/city code): ...........................................................................................................

Fax (country code) (area/city code): ...........................................................................................................

E mail (when available): ...........................................................................................................

▼B

(e) Authority or authorities which may be contacted (if point (c) and/or (d) has(have) been completed):

☐ Authority mentioned under point (b)

Can be contacted for questions concerning: ...............................................

☐ Authority mentioned under point (c)

Can be contacted for questions concerning: ...............................................

☐ Authority mentioned under point (d)

Can be contacted for questions concerning: ...............................................

(f) Where the confiscation order is a follow up to a freezing order transmitted to the executing State pursuant to Council Framework Decision 2003/577/JHA of 22 July 2003 on the execution in the European Union of orders freezing property or evidence ([1]), provide relevant information to identify the freezing order (the dates of issue and transmission of the freezing order, the authority to which it was transmitted, reference number, if available): ...............................................

...............................................

...............................................

(g) Where the confiscation order has been transmitted to more than one executing State, provide the following information:

1. The confiscation order has been transmitted to the following other executing State(s) (country and authority): ...............................................

...............................................

...............................................

2. The confiscation order has been transmitted to more than one executing State for the following reason (tick the relevant box):

2.1. Where the confiscation order concerns one or more specific items of property:

☐ Different specific items of property covered by the confiscation order are believed to be located in different executing States.

☐ The confiscation of a specific item of property involves action in more than one executing State.

☐ A specific item of property covered by the confiscation order is believed to be located in one of two or more specified executing States.

2.2. Where the confiscation order concerns an amount of money:

☐ The property concerned has not been frozen under Framework Decision 2003/577/JHA of 22 July 2003 on the execution in the European Union of orders freezing property or evidence.

☐ The value of the property which may be confiscated in the issuing State and any one executing State is not likely to be sufficient for the execution of the full amount covered by the confiscation order.

☐ Other reason(s) (to be specified): ...............................................

...............................................

...............................................

([1]) OJ L 196, 2.8.2003, p. 45.

▼B

(h) Information regarding the natural or legal person against whom the confiscation order has been issued:

1. **In the case of a natural person:**

Name: ..........

Forename(s): ..........

Maiden name, (where applicable): ..........

Aliases, (where applicable): ..........

Sex: ..........

Nationality: ..........

Identity number or social security number (when possible): ..........

Date of birth: ..........

Place of birth: ..........

Last known address: ..........

..........

Language(s) which the person understands (if known): ..........

..........

1.1. If the confiscation order concerns an amount of money:

The confiscation order is transmitted to the executing State because (tick the relevant box):

☐ (a) the issuing State has reasonable grounds to believe that the person against whom the confiscation order has been issued has property or income in the executing State. Add the following information:

Grounds for believing that the person has property/income: ..........

..........

Description of the property of the person/source of income: ..........

..........

Location of the property of the person/source of income (if not known, the last known location): ..........

..........

☐ (b) there are no reasonable grounds, as referred to under (a), which would allow the issuing State to determine the Member State to which the confiscation order may be sent, but the person against whom the confiscation order has been issued is normally resident in the executing State. Add the following information:

Normal residence in the executing State: ..........

..........

..........

▼B

1.2. If the confiscation order concerns specific item(s) of property:

The confiscation order is transmitted to the executing State because (tick the relevant box):

☐ (a) the specific item(s) of property is(are) located in the executing State. (See point (i))

☐ (b) the issuing State has reasonable grounds to believe that all or part of the specific item(s) of property covered by the confiscation order is (are) located in the executing State. Add the following information:

Grounds for believing that the specific item(s) of property is located in the executing State: ....................................

........................................................................................................................................................

☐ (c) there are no reasonable grounds, as referred to in (b), which would allow the issuing State to determine the Member State to which the confiscation order may be transmitted, but the person against whom the confiscation order has been issued is normally resident in the executing State. Add the following information:

Normal residence in the executing State: ....................................................................................................

........................................................................................................................................................

........................................................................................................................................................

2. **In the case of a legal person:**

Name: ........................................................................................................................................................

Form of legal person: ....................................................................................................................................

Registration number (if available) (1): ..........................................................................................................

Registered seat (if available) (1): ................................................................................................................

Address of the legal person: .........................................................................................................................

2.1. If the confiscation order concerns an amount of money:

The confiscation order is transmitted to the executing State because (tick the relevant box):

☐ (a) the issuing State has reasonable grounds to believe that the legal person against whom the confiscation order has been issued has property or income in the executing State. Add the following information:

Grounds for believing that the person has property/income: .....................................................................

........................................................................................................................................................

Description of the property of the person/source of income: ......................................................................

........................................................................................................................................................

Location of the property of the person/source of income (if not known, the last known location): ..............................

........................................................................................................................................................

(1) Where a confiscation order is transmitted to the executing State because the legal person against whom the confiscation order has been issued has its registered seat in that State, Registration number and Registered seat must be completed.

▼B

☐ (b) there are no reasonable grounds, as referred to in (a), which would allow the issuing State to determine the Member State to which the confiscation order may be sent but the legal person against whom the confiscation order has been issued has its registered seat in the executing State. Add the following information:

Registered Seat in the executing State: ..........................................................................................................

..........................................................................................................

..........................................................................................................

2.2. If the confiscation order concerns specific item(s) of property:

The confiscation order is transmitted to the executing State because (tick the relevant box):

☐ (a) the specific item(s) of property is (are) located in the executing State. (See point (i)).

☐ (b) the issuing State has reasonable grounds to believe that all or part of the specific item(s) of property covered by the confiscation order is (are) located in the executing State. Add the following information:

Grounds for believing that the specific item(s) of property is (are) located in the executing State: ............................

..........................................................................................................

..........................................................................................................

☐ (c) there are no reasonable grounds, as referred to in (b), which would allow the issuing State to determine the Member State to which the confiscation order may be transmitted but the legal person against whom the confiscation order has been issued has its registered seat in the executing State. Add the following information:

Registered seat in the executing State: ..........................................................................................................

..........................................................................................................

..........................................................................................................

(i) The confiscation order

The confiscation order was issued on (date): ..........................................................................................................

..........................................................................................................

The confiscation order became final on (date): ..........................................................................................................

Reference number of the confiscation order (if available): ..........................................................................................................

▼B

1. Information on the nature of the confiscation order

1.1. Indicate (by ticking in the relevant box(es)) if the confiscation order concerns:

☐ an amount of money

The amount for execution in the executing State with indication of currency (in figures and words): ..........................................

..........................................................................................................................................................

The total amount covered by the confiscation order with indication of currency (in figures and words): ....................................

..........................................................................................................................................................

☐ specific item(s) of property

Description of the specific item(s) of property: ..........................................................................................................

..........................................................................................................................................................

Location of the specific item(s) of property (if not known, the last known location): ...................................................

..........................................................................................................................................................

..........................................................................................................................................................

Where the confiscation of the specific item(s) of property involves action in more than one executing State, description of the action to be taken: ..........................................................................................................................................

..........................................................................................................................................................

1.2. The Court has decided that the property (tick the relevant box(es)):

☐ (i) is the proceeds of an offence, or is equivalent to either the full value or part of the value of such proceeds,

☐ (ii) constitutes the instrumentalities of such an offence,

☐ (iii) is liable to confiscation resulting from the application in the issuing State of extended powers of confiscation as specified in (a), (b) and (c). The basis for the decision is that the Court, based on specific facts, is fully convinced that the property in question has been derived from:

☐ (a) criminal activities of the convicted person during a period prior to conviction for the offence concerned which is deemed to be reasonable by the Court in the circumstances of the particular case,

☐ (b) similar criminal activities of the convicted person during a period prior to conviction for the offence concerned which is deemed to be reasonable by the Court in the circumstances of the particular case, or

☐ (c) the criminal activity of the convicted person, and it has been established that the value of the property is disproportionate to the lawful income of that person.

▼B

☐ (iv) is liable to confiscation under any other provision relating to extended powers of confiscation under the law of the issuing State.

If two or more categories of confiscation are involved, provide details on which property is confiscated in relation to which category: ................................................................

................................................................

2. Information on the offence(s) resulting in the confiscation order

2.1. A summary of facts and a description of the circumstances in which the offence(s) resulting in the confiscation order has(have) been committed, including time and place:

................................................................

................................................................

................................................................

................................................................

................................................................

2.2. Nature and legal classification of the offence(s) resulting in the confiscation order and the applicable statutory provision/code on basis of which the decision was made:

................................................................

................................................................

................................................................

................................................................

................................................................

................................................................

2.3. If applicable, indicate one or more of the following offences to which the offence(s) identified under point 2.2 relate(s), if the offence(s) are punishable in the issuing State by a custodial sentence of a maximum of at least 3 years (tick the relevant box(es)):

☐ participation in a criminal organisation;

☐ terrorism;

☐ trafficking in human beings;

☐ sexual exploitation of children and child pornography;

☐ illicit trafficking in narcotic drugs and psychotropic substances;

☐ illicit trafficking in weapons, munitions and explosives;

☐ corruption;

☐ fraud, including that affecting the financial interests of the European Communities within the meaning of the Convention of 26 July 1995 on the protection of the European Communities' financial interests;

▼B

- ☐ laundering of the proceeds of crime;
- ☐ counterfeiting currency, including of the euro;
- ☐ computer related crime;
- ☐ environmental crime, including illicit trafficking in endangered animal species and in endangered plant species and varieties;
- ☐ facilitation of unauthorised entry and residence;
- ☐ murder, grievous bodily injury;
- ☐ illicit trade in human organs and tissue;
- ☐ kidnapping, illegal restraint and hostage taking;
- ☐ racism and xenophobia;
- ☐ organised or armed robbery;
- ☐ illicit trafficking in cultural goods, including antiques and works of art;
- ☐ swindling;
- ☐ racketeering and extortion;
- ☐ counterfeiting and piracy of products;
- ☐ forgery of administrative documents and trafficking therein;
- ☐ forgery of means of payment;
- ☐ illicit trafficking in hormonal substances and other growth promoters;
- ☐ illicit trafficking in nuclear or radioactive materials;
- ☐ trafficking in stolen vehicles;
- ☐ rape;
- ☐ arson;
- ☐ crimes within the jurisdiction of the International Criminal Court;
- ☐ unlawful seizure of aircraft/ships;
- ☐ sabotage.

▼B

2.4. To the extent that the offence(s) resulting in the confiscation order identified under point 2.2 is (are) not covered by point 2.3, give a full description of the offence(s) concerned (this should cover the actual criminal activity involved as opposed for instance to legal classifications): ..........................................................................

..........................................................................

..........................................................................

..........................................................................

..........................................................................

..........................................................................

..........................................................................

(j) Proceedings resulting in the confiscation order

Indicate the following concerning the proceedings resulting in the confiscation order (tick the relevant box(es)):

☐ (a) The person concerned appeared personally in the proceedings.

☐ (b) The person concerned did not appear personally in the proceedings, but was represented by a legal counsellor.

☐ (c) The person concerned did not appear in the proceedings and was not represented by a legal counsellor. It is confirmed that:

☐ the person was informed personally, or via a representative competent according to national law, of the proceedings in accordance with the law of the issuing State, or

☐ the person has indicated that he or she does not contest the confiscation order.

(k) Conversion and transfer of property

1. If the confiscation order concerns a specific item of property, state whether the issuing State allows for the confiscation in the executing State to take the form of a requirement to pay a sum of money corresponding to the value of the property.

☐ yes

☐ no

2. If the confiscation order concerns an amount of money, state whether property, other than money obtained from the execution of the confiscation order, may be transferred to the issuing State:

☐ yes

☐ no

►(1) M1

▼B

(l) Alternative measures, including custodial sanctions

1. State whether the issuing State allows for the application by the executing State of alternative measures where it is not possible to execute the confiscation order, either totally or in part:

☐ yes

☐ no

2. If yes, state which sanctions may be applied (nature and maximum level of the sanctions):

☐ Custody ( maximum period): ..........

☐ Community service (or equivalent) ( maximum period): ..........

☐ Other sanctions (description): ..........

..........

(m) Other circumstances relevant to the case (optional information): ..........

..........

..........

(n) The confiscation order is attached to the certificate.

Signature of the authority issuing the certificate and/or its representative certifying the content of the certificate as accurate: ..........

..........

Name: ..........

Post held (title/grade): ..........

Date: ..........

Official stamp (if available):

# Framework Decision 2006/960 on simplifying the exchange of information and intelligence between law enforcement authorities of the Member States of the European Union, 18 December 2006

**[Consolidated version. Original version OJ 2006, L 386/89–100 rectified by OJ 2007, L 75/26]**

►B

**COUNCIL FRAMEWORK DECISION 2006/960/JHA**

**of 18 December 2006**

**on simplifying the exchange of information and intelligence between law enforcement authorities of the Member States of the European Union**

(OJ L 386, 29.12.2006, p. 89)

Corrected by:

►C1 Corrigendum, OJ L 75, 15.3.2007, p. 26 (2006/960/JHA)

▼B

**COUNCIL FRAMEWORK DECISION 2006/960/JHA**

**of 18 December 2006**

**on simplifying the exchange of information and intelligence between law enforcement authorities of the Member States of the European Union**

THE COUNCIL OF THE EUROPEAN UNION,

Having regard to the Treaty on European Union, and in particular Articles 30(1)(a) and (b) and 34(2)(b) thereof,

Having regard to the initiative of the Kingdom of Sweden,

Having regard to the opinion of the European Parliament,

Whereas:

(1) One of the core objectives of the European Union is to provide its citizens with a high level of security within an area of freedom, security and justice.

(2) That objective is to be achieved by preventing and combating crime through closer cooperation between law enforcement authorities in the Member States, while respecting the principles and rules relating to human rights, fundamental freedoms and the rule of law on which the Union is founded and which are common to the Member States.

(3) Exchange of information and intelligence on crime and criminal activities is the basis for law enforcement cooperation in the Union serving the overall objective of improving the safety of the Union's citizens.

(4) The timely access to accurate and up to date information and intelligence is a crucial element for the possibility of law enforcement authorities to successfully detect, prevent and investigate crime or criminal activity, in particular within an area where internal border controls have been abolished. As the activities of criminals are carried out clandestinely, they need to be controlled, and information relating to them needs to be exchanged particularly expeditiously.

(5) It is important that the possibilities for law enforcement authorities to obtain information and intelligence concerning serious crime and terrorist acts from other Member States be viewed horizontally and not in terms of differences with regard to type of crime or division of competencies between law enforcement or judicial authorities.

(6) Currently, effective and expeditious exchange of information and intelligence between law enforcement authorities is seriously hampered by formal procedures, administrative structures and legal obstacles laid down in Member States' legislation; such a state of affairs is unacceptable to the citizens of the European Union and it therefore calls for greater security and more efficient law enforcement while protecting human rights.

(7) It is necessary for law enforcement authorities to be able to request and obtain information and intelligence from other Member States at different stages of investigation, from the phase of gathering criminal intelligence to the phase of criminal investigation. The Member State's systems are different in that respect, but this Framework Decision does not purport to change these systems. However, it seeks, as regards certain types of information and intelligence, to ensure that certain information

▼B

vital for law enforcement authorities is exchanged expeditiously within the Union.

(8) The absence of a common legal framework for the effective and expeditious exchange of information and intelligence between the law enforcement authorities of the Member States is a deficiency that will have to be remedied; the Council of the European Union therefore deems it necessary to adopt a legally binding instrument on simplifying the exchange of information and intelligence. This Framework Decision should not affect existing or future instruments which allow the objectives of this Framework Decision to be extended or which facilitate the procedures for exchanging information and intelligence, such as the Convention of 18 December 1997 drawn up on the basis of Article K.3 of the Treaty on European Union on Mutual Assistance and Cooperation between Customs Administrations ([1]).

(9) As regards the exchange of information, this Framework Decision is without prejudice to essential national security interests, the jeopardizing of the success of a current investigation or the safety of individuals, or specific intelligence activities in the field of State security.

(10) It is important to promote the exchange of information as widely as possible, in particular in relation to offences linked directly or indirectly to organised crime and terrorism, and in a way which does not detract from the required level of cooperation between Member States under existing arrangements.

(11) The common interest of Member States in fighting crime of a cross-border nature must strike the appropriate balance between fast and efficient law enforcement cooperation and agreed principles and rules on data protection, fundamental freedoms, human rights and individual liberties.

(12) In the Declaration on combating terrorism as adopted by the European Council at its meeting on 25 March 2004, the European Council instructed the Council to examine measures for simplifying the exchange of information and intelligence between law enforcement authorities of the Member States.

(13) As regards Iceland and Norway, this Framework Decision constitutes a development of the provisions of the Schengen acquis which fall within the area referred to in Article 1 of Council Decision 1999/437/EC of 17 May 1999 on certain arrangements for the application of the Agreement concluded by the Council of the European Union and the Republic of Iceland and the Kingdom of Norway concerning the association of those two States with the implementation, application and development of the Schengen acquis ([2]). The procedures set out in that Agreement have been followed in respect of this Framework Decision.

(14) As regards Switzerland, this Framework Decision constitutes a development of provisions of the Schengen acquis within the meaning of the Agreement signed between the European Union, the European Community and the Swiss Confederation concerning the association of the Swiss Confederation with the implementation, application and development of the Schengen acquis, which fall within the area referred to in Article 1(H) of Decision 1999/437/EC read in conjunction with Article 4(1) of Decision 2004/860/EC ([3]) on the signing on behalf of the European Community and on the provisional application of certain provisions of that Agreement, and with Article 4(1)

([1]) OJ C 24, 23.1.1998, p. 2.
([2]) OJ L 176, 10.7.1999, p. 31.
([3]) OJ L 370, 17.12.2004, p. 78.

▼B

of Decision 2004/849/EC (1) on the signing on behalf of the European Union, and on the provisional application of certain provisions of that Agreement,

HAS ADOPTED THIS FRAMEWORK DECISION:

TITLE I

## SCOPE AND DEFINITIONS

*Article 1*

### Objective and scope

1. The purpose of this Framework Decision is to establish the rules under which Member States' law enforcement authorities may exchange existing information and intelligence effectively and expeditiously for the purpose of conducting criminal investigations or criminal intelligence operations.

2. This Framework Decision shall be without prejudice to bilateral or multilateral agreements or arrangements between Member States and third countries and to instruments of the European Union on mutual legal assistance or mutual recognition of decisions regarding criminal matters, including any conditions set by third countries concerning the use of information once supplied.

3. This Framework Decision covers all information and/or intelligence as defined in Article 2(d). It does not impose any obligation on the part of the Member States to gather and store information and intelligence for the purpose of providing it to the competent law enforcement authorities of other Member States.

4. This Framework Decision does not impose any obligation on the part of the Member States to provide information and intelligence to be used as evidence before a judicial authority nor does it give any right to use such information or intelligence for that purpose. Where a Member State has obtained information or intelligence in accordance with this Framework Decision, and wishes to use it as evidence before a judicial authority, it has to obtain consent of the Member State that provided the information or intelligence, where necessary under the national law of the Member State that provided the information or intelligence, through the use of instruments regarding judicial cooperation in force between the Member States. Such consent is not required where the requested Member State has already given its consent for the use of information or intelligence as evidence at the time of transmittal of the information or intelligence.

5. This Framework Decision does not impose any obligation to obtain any information or intelligence by means of coercive measures, defined in accordance with national law, in the Member State receiving the request for information or intelligence.

6. Member States shall, where permitted by and in accordance with their national law, provide information or intelligence previously obtained by means of coercive measures.

7. This Framework Decision shall not have the effect of modifying the obligation to respect fundamental rights and fundamental legal principles as enshrined in Article 6 of the Treaty on European Union and any obligations incumbent on law enforcement authorities in this respect shall remain unaffected.

(1) OJ L 368, 15.12.2004, p. 26.

▼B

*Article 2*

**Definitions**

For the purposes of this Framework Decision:

(a) 'competent law enforcement authority': a national police, customs or other authority that is authorised by national law to detect, prevent and investigate offences or criminal activities and to exercise authority and take coercive measures in the context of such activities. Agencies or units dealing especially with national security issues are not covered by the concept of competent law enforcement authority. Every Member State shall, by 18 December 2007, state in a declaration deposited with the General Secretariat of the Council which authorities are covered by the concept of 'competent law enforcement authority'. Such a declaration may be modified at any time.

(b) 'criminal investigation': a procedural stage within which measures are taken by competent law enforcement or judicial authorities, including public prosecutors, with a view to establishing and identifying facts, suspects and circumstances regarding one or several identified concrete criminal acts;

(c) 'criminal intelligence operation': a procedural stage, not yet having reached the stage of a criminal investigation, within which a competent law enforcement authority is entitled by national law to collect, process and analyse information about crime or criminal activities with a view to establishing whether concrete criminal acts have been committed or may be committed in the future;

(d) 'information and/or intelligence':

(i) any type of information or data which is held by law enforcement authorities;

and

(ii) any type of information or data which is held by public authorities or by private entities and which is available to law enforcement authorities without the taking of coercive measures, in accordance with Article 1(5).

(e) 'offences referred to in Article 2(2) of the Framework Decision 2002/584/JHA on the European arrest warrant [1]' (hereinafter referred to as 'offences referred to in Article 2(2) of the Framework Decision 2002/584/JHA'): offences under national law which correspond to or are equivalent to those referred to in that provision.

TITLE II

## EXCHANGE OF INFORMATION AND INTELLIGENCE

*Article 3*

**Provision of information and intelligence**

1. Member States shall ensure that information and intelligence can be provided to the competent law enforcement authorities of other Member States in accordance with this Framework Decision.

2. Information and intelligence shall be provided at the request of a competent law enforcement authority, acting in accordance with the powers conferred upon it by national law, conducting a criminal investigation or a criminal intelligence operation.

(1) OJ L 190, 18.7.2002, p. 1.

▼B

3. Member States shall ensure that conditions not stricter than those applicable at national level for providing and requesting information and intelligence are applied for providing information and intelligence to competent law enforcement authorities of other Member States. In particular, a Member State shall not subject the exchange, by its competent law enforcement authority with a competent law enforcement authority of another Member State, of information or intelligence which in an internal procedure may be accessed by the requested competent law enforcement authority without a judicial agreement or authorisation, to such an agreement or authorisation.

4. Where the information or intelligence sought may, under the national law of the requested Member State, be accessed by the requested competent law enforcement authority only pursuant to an agreement or authorisation of a judicial authority, the requested competent law enforcement authority shall be obliged to ask the competent judicial authority for an agreement or authorisation to access and exchange the information sought. The competent judicial authority of the requested Member State shall apply the same rules for its decision, without prejudice to Article 10(1) and (2), as in a purely internal case.

5. Where the information or intelligence sought has been obtained from another Member State or from a third country and is subject to the rule of speciality, its transmission to the competent law enforcement authority of another Member State may only take place with the consent of the Member State or third country that provided the information or intelligence.

*Article 4*

**Time limits for provision of information and intelligence**

1. Member States shall ensure that they have procedures in place so that they can respond within at most eight hours to urgent requests for information and intelligence regarding offences referred to in Article 2 (2) of Framework Decision 2002/584/JHA, when the requested information or intelligence is held in a database directly accessible by a law enforcement authority.

2. If the requested competent law enforcement authority is unable to respond within eight hours, it shall provide reasons for that on the form set out in Annex A. Where the provision of the information or intelligence requested within the period of eight hours would put a disproportionate burden on the requested law enforcement authority, it may postpone the provision of the information or intelligence. In that case the requested law enforcement authority shall immediately inform the requesting law enforcement authority of this postponement and shall provide the requested information or intelligence as soon as possible, but not later than within three days. The use made of the provisions under this paragraph shall be reviewed by 19 December 2009.

3. Member States shall ensure that for non-urgent cases, requests for information and intelligence regarding offences referred to in Article 2 (2) of Framework Decision 2002/584/JHA should be responded to within one week if the requested information or intelligence is held in a database directly accessible by a law enforcement authority. If the requested competent law enforcement authority is unable to respond within one week, it shall provide reasons for that on the form set out in Annex A.

4. In all other cases, Member States shall ensure that the information sought is communicated to the requesting competent law enforcement authority within 14 days. If the requested competent law enforcement authority is unable to respond within 14 days, it shall provide reasons for that on the form set out in Annex A.

▼B

*Article 5*

**Requests for information and intelligence**

1. Information and intelligence may be requested for the purpose of detection, prevention or investigation of an offence where there are factual reasons to believe that relevant information and intelligence is available in another Member State. The request shall set out those factual reasons and explain the purpose for which the information and intelligence is sought and the connection between the purpose and the person who is the subject of the information and intelligence.

2. The requesting competent law enforcement authority shall refrain from requesting more information or intelligence or setting narrower time frames than necessary for the purpose of the request.

3. Requests for information or intelligence shall contain at least the information set out in Annex B.

*Article 6*

**Communication channels and language**

1. Exchange of information and intelligence under this Framework Decision may take place via any existing channels for international law enforcement cooperation. The language used for the request and the exchange of information shall be the one applicable for the channel used. Member States shall, when making their declarations in accordance with Article 2(a), also provide the General Secretariat of the Council with details of the contacts to which requests may be sent in cases of urgency. These details may be modified at any time. The General Secretariat of the Council shall communicate to the Member States and the Commission the declarations received.

2. Information or intelligence shall also be exchanged with Europol in accordance with the Convention based on Article K.3 of the Treaty on European Union, on the establishment of a European Police Office (Europol Convention) (1) and with Eurojust in accordance with the Council Decision 2002/187/JHA of 28 February 2002 setting up Eurojust with a view to reinforcing the fight against serious crime (2), insofar as the exchange refers to an offence or criminal activity within their mandate.

*Article 7*

**Spontaneous exchange of information and intelligence**

1. Without prejudice to Article 10, the competent law enforcement authorities shall, without any prior request being necessary, provide to the competent law enforcement authorities of other Member States concerned information and intelligence in cases where there are factual reasons to believe that the information and intelligence could assist in the detection, prevention or investigation of offences referred to in Article 2(2) of Framework Decision 2002/584/JHA. The modalities of such spontaneous exchange shall be regulated by the national law of the Member States providing the information.

2. The provision of information and intelligence shall be limited to what is deemed relevant and necessary for the successful detection, prevention or investigation of the crime or criminal activity in question.

(1) OJ C 316, 27.11.1995, p. 2. Convention as last amended by the Protocol drawn up on the basis of Article 43(1) of the Europol Convention (OJ C 2, 6.1.2004, p. 3).

(2) OJ L 63, 6.3.2002, p. 1. Decision as last amended by Decision 2003/659/JHA (OJ L 245, 29.9.2003, p. 44).

▼B

*Article 8*

**Data protection**

1. Each Member State shall ensure that the established rules on data protection provided for when using the communication channels referred to in Article 6(1) are applied also within the procedure on exchange of information and intelligence provided for by this Framework Decision.

2. The use of information and intelligence which has been exchanged directly or bilaterally under this Framework Decision shall be subject to the national data protection provisions of the receiving Member State, where the information and intelligence shall be subject to the same data protection rules as if they had been gathered in the receiving Member State. The personal data processed in the context of the implementation of this Framework Decision shall be protected in accordance with the Council of Europe Convention of 28 January 1981 for the Protection of Individuals with regard to Automatic Processing of Personal Data, and, for those Member States which have ratified it, the Additional Protocol of 8 November 2001 to that Convention, regarding Supervisory Authorities and Transborder Data Flows. The principles of Recommendation No. R(87) 15 of the Council of Europe Regulating the Use of Personal Data in the Police Sector should also be taken into account when law enforcement authorities handle personal data obtained under this Framework Decision.

3. Information and intelligence provided under this Framework Decision may be used by the competent law enforcement authorities of the Member State to which it has been provided solely for the purposes for which it has been supplied in accordance with this Framework Decision or for preventing an immediate and serious threat to public security; processing for other purposes shall be permitted solely with the prior authorisation of the communicating Member State and subject to the national law of the receiving Member State. The authorisation may be granted insofar as the national law of the communicating Member State permits.

4. When providing information and intelligence in accordance with this Framework Decision, the providing competent law enforcement authority may pursuant to its national law impose conditions on the use of the information and intelligence by the receiving competent law enforcement authority. Conditions may also be imposed on reporting the result of the criminal investigation or criminal intelligence operation within which the exchange of information and intelligence has taken place. The receiving competent law enforcement authority shall be bound by such conditions, except in the specific case where national law lays down that the restrictions on use be waived for judicial authorities, legislative bodies or any other independent body set up under the law and made responsible for supervising the competent law enforcement authorities. In such cases, the information and intelligence may only be used after prior consultation with the communicating Member State whose interests and opinions must be taken into account as far as possible. The receiving Member State may, in specific cases, be requested by the communicating Member State to give information about the use and further processing of the transmitted information and intelligence.

*Article 9*

**Confidentiality**

The competent law enforcement authorities shall take due account, in each specific case of exchange of information or intelligence, of the requirements of investigation secrecy. To that end the competent law enforcement authorities shall, in accordance with their national law,

▼B

guarantee the confidentiality of all provided information and intelligence determined as confidential.

*Article 10*

**Reasons to withhold information or intelligence**

1. Without prejudice to Article 3(3), a competent law enforcement authority may refuse to provide information or intelligence only if there are factual reasons to assume that the provision of the information or intelligence would:

(a) harm essential national security interests of the requested Member State;

or

(b) jeopardise the success of a current investigation or a criminal intelligence operation or the safety of individuals;

or

(c) clearly be disproportionate or irrelevant with regard to the purposes for which it has been requested.

2. Where the request pertains to an offence punishable by a term of imprisonment of one year or less under the law of the requested Member State, the competent law enforcement authority may refuse to provide the requested information or intelligence.

3. The competent law enforcement authority shall refuse to provide information or intelligence if the competent judicial authority has not authorised the access and exchange of the information requested pursuant to Article 3(4).

TITLE III

**FINAL PROVISIONS**

*Article 11*

**Implementation**

1. Member States shall take the necessary measures ►C1 to comply with the provisions of this Framework Decision before 19 December 2008. ◄

2. Member States shall transmit to the General Secretariat of the Council and to the Commission the text of the provisions transposing into their national laws the obligations imposed on them under this Framework Decision. On the basis of this and other information provided by the Member States on request, ►C1 the Commission shall, before 19 December 2010, submit a report to the Council ◄ on the operation of this Framework Decision. ►C1 The Council shall before 19 December 2011 assess ◄ the extent to which Member States have complied with the provisions of this Framework Decision.

▼B

*Article 12*

**Relation to other instruments**

1. The provisions of Article 39(1), (2) and (3) and of Article 46 of the Convention Implementing the Schengen Agreement ([1]), in as far as they relate to exchange of information and intelligence for the purpose of conducting criminal investigations or criminal intelligence operations as provided for by this Framework Decision, shall be replaced by the provisions of this Framework Decision.

2. The Decision of the Schengen Executive Committee of 16 December 1998 on cross-border police cooperation in the area of crime prevention and detection (SCH/Com-ex (98) 51 rev 3) ([2]) and the Decision of the Schengen Executive Committee of 28 April 1999 on the improvement of police cooperation in preventing and detecting criminal offences (SCH/Com-ex (99) 18) ([3]) are hereby repealed.

3. Member States may continue to apply bilateral or multilateral agreements or arrangements in force when this Framework Decision is adopted in so far as such agreements or arrangements allow the objectives of this Framework Decision to be extended and help to simplify or facilitate further the procedures for exchanging information and intelligence falling within the scope of this Framework Decision.

4. Member States may conclude or bring into force bilateral or multilateral agreements or arrangements after this Framework Decision has come into force in so far as such agreements or arrangements allow the objectives of this Framework Decision to be extended and help to simplify or facilitate further the procedures for exchanging information and intelligence falling within the scope of this Framework Decision.

5. The agreements and arrangements referred to in paragraphs 3 and 4 may in no case affect relations with Member States which are not parties to them.

6. ►C1 Member States shall no later than 19 December 2007, notify the Council and the Commission ◄ of the existing agreements and arrangements referred to in paragraph 3 which they wish to continue applying.

7. Member States shall also notify the Council and the Commission of any new agreement or arrangement as referred to in paragraph 4, within three months of their signature or, for those instruments which had already been signed before the adoption of this Framework Decision, their entry into force.

*Article 13*

**Entry into force**

This Framework Decision shall enter into force on the day following its publication in the *Official Journal of the European Union*.

([1]) OJ L 239, 22.9.2000, p. 19. Convention as last amended by Regulation (EC) No 1160/2005 of the European Parliament and of the Council (OJ L 191, 22.7.2005, p. 18).
([2]) OJ L 239, 22.9.2000, p. 407.
([3]) OJ L 239, 22.9.2000, p. 421.

▼B

*ANNEX A*

**INFORMATION EXCHANGE UNDER COUNCIL FRAMEWORK DECISION 2006/960/JHA FORM TO BE USED BY THE REQUESTED MEMBER STATE IN CASE OF TRANSMISSION/DELAY/REFUSAL OF INFORMATION**

This form shall be used to transmit the requested information and/or intelligence, to inform the requesting authority of the impossibility of meeting the normal deadline, of the necessity of submitting the request to a judicial authority for an authorisation, or of the refusal to transmit the information.

This form may be used more than once during the procedure (e.g. if the request has first to be submitted to a judicial authority and it later transpires that the execution of the request has to be refused).

| | |
|---|---|
| **Requested authority (name, address, telephone, fax, e-mail, Member State)** | |
| **Details of the handling agent (optional):** | |
| **Reference number of this answer** | |
| **Date and reference number of previous answer** | |
| | |
| **Answering to the following requesting authority** | |
| **Date and time of the request** | |
| **Reference number of the request** | |

| **Normal time limit under Article 4 of Framework Decision 2006/960/JHA** | | |
|---|---|---|
| The offence falls under Article 2(2) of Framework Decision 2002/584/JHA<br>and<br>the requested information or intelligence is held in a database directly accessible by a law enforcement authority in the requested Member State | Urgency requested | → ❑ 8 hours |
| | Urgency not requested | → ❑ 1 week |
| Other cases | | → ❑ 14 days |

| **Information transmitted under Framework Decision 2006/960/JHA: information and intelligence provided** |
|---|
| 1. Use of transmitted information or intelligence<br>❑ may be used solely for the purposes for which it has been supplied or for preventing an immediate and serious threat to public security;<br>❑ is authorised also for other purposes, subject to the following conditions (optional): |
| 2. Reliability of the source<br>❑ Reliable<br>❑ Mostly reliable<br>❑ Not reliable<br>❑ Cannot be assessed |
| 3. Accuracy of the information or intelligence<br>❑ Certain<br>❑ Established by the source<br>❑ Hearsay-confirmed<br>❑ Hearsay- not confirmed |

▼B

4. The result of the criminal investigation or criminal intelligence operation within which the exchange of information has taken place has to be reported to the transmitting authority

❑ No
❑ Yes

5. In case of spontaneous exchange, reasons for believing that the information or intelligence could assist in the detection, prevention or investigation of offences referred to in Article 2(2) of Framework Decision 2002/584/JHA:

**DELAY – It is not possible to respond within the applicable time limit under Article 4 of Framework Decision 2006/960/JHA**

The information or intelligence cannot be provided within the given time-limit for the following reasons:

It is likely to be given within:

❑ 1 day ❑ 2 days ❑ 3 days
❑ .... weeks
❑ 1 month

❑ The authorisation of a judicial authority has been requested.
The procedure leading up to the granting/refusal of the authorisation is expected to last ... weeks

**REFUSAL** — The information or intelligence:
❑ could not be provided and requested at national level; or
❑ cannot be provided, for one or more of the following reasons:

A — Reason related to judicial control which prevents the transmission or requires the use of mutual legal assistance

❑ the competent judicial authority has not authorised the access and exchange of the information or intelligence

❑ the requested information or intelligence has previously been obtained by means of coercive measures and its provision is not permitted under the national law

❑ the information or intelligence is not held

- by law enforcement authorities; or
- by public authorities or by private entities in a way which makes it available to law enforcement authorities without the taking of coercive measures

❑ B — The provision of the requested information or intelligence would harm essential national security interests or would jeopardise the success of a current investigation or a criminal intelligence operation or the safety of individuals or would clearly be disproportionate or irrelevant with regard to the purposes for which it has been requested.

If case A or B is used, provide, if deemed necessary, additional information or reasons for refusal (optional):

❑ D — The requested authority decides to refuse execution because the request pertains, under the law of the requested Member State, to the following offence (nature of the offence and its legal qualification to be specified) ........................ which is punishable by one year or less of imprisonment

❑ E — The requested information or intelligence is not available

❑ F — The requested information or intelligence has been obtained from another Member State or from a third country and is subject to the rule of speciality and that Member State or third country has not given its consent to the transmission of the information or intelligence.

▼B

*ANNEX B*

**INFORMATION EXCHANGE UNDER COUNCIL FRAMEWORK DECISION 2006/960/JHA REQUEST FORM FOR INFORMATION AND INTELLIGENCE TO BE USED BY THE REQUESTING MEMBER STATE**

This form shall be used when requesting information and intelligence under Framework Decision 2006/960/JHA

I — Administrative information

| | |
|---|---|
| **Requesting authority (name, address, telephone, fax, e-mail, Member State):** | |
| **Details of the handling agent (optional):** | |
| **To the following Member State:** | |
| **Date and time of this request:** | |
| **Reference number of this request:** | |

| | | | | |
|---|---|---|---|---|
| **Previous requests** | | | | |
| ❑ This is the first request on this case | | | | |
| ❑ This request follows previous requests in the same case | | | | |
| Previous request(s) | | | Answer(s) | |
| | Date | Reference number (in the requesting Member State) | Date | Reference number (in the requested Member State) |
| 1. | | | | |
| 2. | | | | |
| 3. | | | | |
| 4. | | | | |

| | |
|---|---|
| **If the request is sent to more than one authority in the requested Member State, please specify each of the channels used:** | |
| ❑ ENU/Europol Liaison Officer | ❑ For information<br>❑ For execution |
| ❑ Interpol NCB | ❑ For information<br>❑ For execution |
| ❑ Sirene | ❑ For information<br>❑ For execution |
| ❑ Liaison Officer | ❑ For information<br>❑ For execution |
| ❑ Other (please specify): | ❑ For information<br>❑ For execution |
| **If the same request is sent to other Member States, please specify the other Member States and the channel used (optional)** | |
| | |

▼B

II — Time limits

Reminder: time limits under Article 4 of Framework Decision 2006/960/JHA

A — The offence falls under Article 2(2) of Framework Decision 2002/584/JHA

and

the requested information or intelligence is held in a database directly accessible by a law enforcement authority

→ The request is urgent → Time limit: 8 hours with possibility to postpone

→ The request is not urgent → Time limit: 1 week

B — Other cases: time limit: 14 days

| |
|---|
| ❑ **Urgency IS requested** |
| ❑ **Urgency is NOT requested** |
| Grounds for urgency (e.g.: suspects are being held in custody, the case has to go to court before a specific date): |
| **Information or intelligence requested** |
| |

| |
|---|
| **Type of crime(s) or criminal activity(ies) being investigated** |
| Description of the circumstances in which the offence(s) was (were) committed, including the time, place and degree of participation in the offence(s) by the person who is the subject of the request for information or intelligence: |

▼B

**Nature of the offence(s)**

A — Application of Article 4(1) or 4(3) of the Framework Decision 2006/960/JHA

❑ A.1. The offence is punishable by a maximum term of imprisonment of at least three years in the requesting Member State
AND
A.2. The offence is one (or more) of the following:

- ❑ Participation in a criminal organisation
- ❑ Terrorism
- ❑ Trafficking in human beings
- ❑ Sexual exploitation of children and child pornography
- ❑ Illicit trafficking in narcotic drugs and psychotropic substances
- ❑ Illicit trafficking in weapons, munitions and explosives
- ❑ Corruption
- ❑ Fraud, including that affecting the financial interests of the European Communities within the meaning of the Convention of 26 July 1995 on the protection of the European Communities' financial interests
- ❑ Organised or armed robbery
- ❑ Illicit trafficking in cultural goods, including antiques and works of art
- ❑ Swindling
- ❑ Racketeering and extortion
- ❑ Counterfeiting and piracy of products
- ❑ Forgery of administrative documents and trafficking therein
- ❑ Forgery of means of payment
- ❑ Illicit trafficking in hormonal substances and other growth promoters
- ❑ Laundering of the proceeds of crime
- ❑ Counterfeiting of currency, including the euro
- ❑ Computer-related crime
- ❑ Environmental crime, including illicit trafficking in endangered animal species and in endangered plant species and varieties
- ❑ Facilitation of unauthorised entry and residence
- ❑ Murder, grievous bodily injury
- ❑ Illicit trade in human organs and tissue
- ❑ Kidnapping, illegal restraint and hostage-taking
- ❑ Racism and xenophobia
- ❑ Illicit trafficking in nuclear or radioactive materials
- ❑ Trafficking in stolen vehicles
- ❑ Rape
- ❑ Arson
- ❑ Crimes within the jurisdiction of the International Criminal Court
- ❑ Unlawful seizure of aircraft/ships
- ❑ Sabotage

→ The offence therefore falls under Article 2(2) of Framework Decision 2002/584/JHA→ Article 4(1) (urgent cases) and 4(3) (non urgent cases) of Framework Decision 2006/960/JHA are therefore applicable as regards time limits for responding to this request

Or

❑ B — The offence(s) is(are) not covered under A.
In this case, description of the offence(s):

**Purpose for which the information or intelligence is requested**

**Connection between the purpose for which the information or intelligence is requested and the person who is the subject of the information or intelligence**

**Identity(ies) (as far as known) of the person(s) being the main subject(s) of the criminal investigation or criminal intelligence operation underlying the request for information or intelligence**

**Reasons for believing that the information or intelligence is in the requested Member State**

**Restrictions on the use of information contained in this request for purposes other than those for which it has been supplied or for preventing an immediate and serious threat to public security**

❑ use granted
❑ use granted, but do not mention the information provider
❑ do not use without authorisation of the information provider
❑ do not use

# Articles 82–89 of the Consolidated Version of the Treaty on the Functioning of the European Union, 13 December 2007

[OJ 2012, C 326/79–84]

**ARTICLES 82-89 OF THE CONSOLIDATED VERSION OF THE TREATY ON THE FUNCTIONING OF THE EUROPEAN UNION**

CHAPTER 4

JUDICIAL COOPERATION IN CRIMINAL MATTERS

*Article 82*

*(ex Article 31 TEU)*

1. Judicial cooperation in criminal matters in the Union shall be based on the principle of mutual recognition of judgments and judicial decisions and shall include the approximation of the laws and regulations of the Member States in the areas referred to in paragraph 2 and in Article 83.

The European Parliament and the Council, acting in accordance with the ordinary legislative procedure, shall adopt measures to:

(a) lay down rules and procedures for ensuring recognition throughout the Union of all forms of judgments and judicial decisions;

(b) prevent and settle conflicts of jurisdiction between Member States;

(c) support the training of the judiciary and judicial staff;

(d) facilitate cooperation between judicial or equivalent authorities of the Member States in relation to proceedings in criminal matters and the enforcement of decisions.

2. To the extent necessary to facilitate mutual recognition of judgments and judicial decisions and police and judicial cooperation in criminal matters having a cross-border dimension, the European Parliament and the Council may, by means of directives adopted in accordance with the ordinary legislative procedure, establish minimum rules. Such rules shall take into account the differences between the legal traditions and systems of the Member States.

They shall concern:

(a) mutual admissibility of evidence between Member States;

(b) the rights of individuals in criminal procedure;

(c) the rights of victims of crime;

(d) any other specific aspects of criminal procedure which the Council has identified in advance by a decision; for the adoption of such a decision, the Council shall act unanimously after obtaining the consent of the European Parliament.

Adoption of the minimum rules referred to in this paragraph shall not prevent Member States from maintaining or introducing a higher level of protection for individuals.

3. Where a member of the Council considers that a draft directive as referred to in paragraph 2 would affect fundamental aspects of its criminal justice system, it may request that the draft directive be referred to the European Council. In that case, the ordinary legislative procedure shall be suspended. After discussion, and in case of a consensus, the European Council shall, within four months of this suspension, refer the draft back to the Council, which shall terminate the suspension of the ordinary legislative procedure.

Within the same timeframe, in case of disagreement, and if at least nine Member States wish to establish enhanced cooperation on the basis of the draft directive concerned, they shall notify the European Parliament, the Council and the Commission accordingly. In such a case, the authorisation to proceed with enhanced cooperation referred to in Article 20(2) of the Treaty on European Union and Article 329(1) of this Treaty shall be deemed to be granted and the provisions on enhanced cooperation shall apply.

*Article 83*

*(ex Article 31 TEU)*

1. The European Parliament and the Council may, by means of directives adopted in accordance with the ordinary legislative procedure, establish minimum rules concerning the definition of criminal offences and sanctions in the areas of particularly serious crime with a cross-border dimension resulting from the nature or impact of such offences or from a special need to combat them on a common basis.

These areas of crime are the following: terrorism, trafficking in human beings and sexual exploitation of women and children, illicit drug trafficking, illicit arms trafficking, money laundering, corruption, counterfeiting of means of payment, computer crime and organised crime.

On the basis of developments in crime, the Council may adopt a decision identifying other areas of crime that meet the criteria specified in this paragraph. It shall act unanimously after obtaining the consent of the European Parliament.

2. If the approximation of criminal laws and regulations of the Member States proves essential to ensure the effective implementation of a Union policy in an area which has been subject to harmonisation measures, directives may establish minimum rules with regard to the definition of criminal offences and sanctions in the area concerned. Such directives shall be adopted by the same ordinary or special legislative procedure as was followed for the adoption of the harmonisation measures in question, without prejudice to Article 76.

3. Where a member of the Council considers that a draft directive as referred to in paragraph 1 or 2 would affect fundamental aspects of its criminal justice system, it may request that the draft directive be referred to the European Council. In that case, the ordinary legislative procedure shall be suspended. After discussion, and in case of a consensus, the European Council shall, within four months of this suspension, refer the draft back to the Council, which shall terminate the suspension of the ordinary legislative procedure.

Within the same timeframe, in case of disagreement, and if at least nine Member States wish to establish enhanced cooperation on the basis of the draft directive concerned, they shall notify the European Parliament, the Council and the Commission accordingly. In such a case, the authorisation to proceed with enhanced cooperation referred to in Article 20(2) of the Treaty on European Union and Article 329(1) of this Treaty shall be deemed to be granted and the provisions on enhanced cooperation shall apply.

*Article 84*

The European Parliament and the Council, acting in accordance with the ordinary legislative procedure, may establish measures to promote and support the action of Member States in the field of crime prevention, excluding any harmonisation of the laws and regulations of the Member States.

*Article 85*

*(ex Article 31 TEU)*

1. Eurojust's mission shall be to support and strengthen coordination and cooperation between national investigating and prosecuting authorities in relation to serious crime affecting two or more Member States or requiring a prosecution on common bases, on the basis of operations conducted and information supplied by the Member States' authorities and by Europol.

In this context, the European Parliament and the Council, by means of regulations adopted in accordance with the ordinary legislative procedure, shall determine Eurojust's structure, operation, field of action and tasks. These tasks may include:

(a) the initiation of criminal investigations, as well as proposing the initiation of prosecutions conducted by competent national authorities, particularly those relating to offences against the financial interests of the Union;

(b) the coordination of investigations and prosecutions referred to in point (a);

(c) the strengthening of judicial cooperation, including by resolution of conflicts of jurisdiction and by close cooperation with the European Judicial Network.

These regulations shall also determine arrangements for involving the European Parliament and national Parliaments in the evaluation of Eurojust's activities.

2. In the prosecutions referred to in paragraph 1, and without prejudice to Article 86, formal acts of judicial procedure shall be carried out by the competent national officials.

*Article 86*

1. In order to combat crimes affecting the financial interests of the Union, the Council, by means of regulations adopted in accordance with a special legislative procedure, may establish a European Public Prosecutor's Office from Eurojust. The Council shall act unanimously after obtaining the consent of the European Parliament.

In the absence of unanimity in the Council, a group of at least nine Member States may request that the draft regulation be referred to the European Council. In that case, the procedure in the Council shall be suspended. After discussion, and in case of a consensus, the European Council shall, within four months of this suspension, refer the draft back to the Council for adoption.

Within the same timeframe, in case of disagreement, and if at least nine Member States wish to establish enhanced cooperation on the basis of the draft regulation concerned, they shall notify the European Parliament, the Council and the Commission accordingly. In such a case, the authorisation to proceed with enhanced cooperation referred to in Article 20(2) of the Treaty on European Union and Article 329(1) of this Treaty shall be deemed to be granted and the provisions on enhanced cooperation shall apply.

2. The European Public Prosecutor's Office shall be responsible for investigating, prosecuting and bringing to judgment, where appropriate in liaison with Europol, the perpetrators of, and accomplices in, offences against the Union's financial interests, as determined by the regulation provided for in paragraph 1. It shall exercise the functions of prosecutor in the competent courts of the Member States in relation to such offences.

3. The regulations referred to in paragraph 1 shall determine the general rules applicable to the European Public Prosecutor's Office, the conditions governing the performance of its functions, the rules of procedure applicable to its activities, as well as those governing the admissibility of evidence, and the rules applicable to the judicial review of procedural measures taken by it in the performance of its functions.

4. The European Council may, at the same time or subsequently, adopt a decision amending paragraph 1 in order to extend the powers of the European Public Prosecutor's Office to include serious crime having a cross-border dimension and amending accordingly paragraph 2 as regards the perpetrators of, and accomplices in, serious crimes affecting more than one Member State. The European Council shall act unanimously after obtaining the consent of the European Parliament and after consulting the Commission.

## CHAPTER 5

## POLICE COOPERATION

### *Article 87*

*(ex Article 30 TEU)*

1. The Union shall establish police cooperation involving all the Member States' competent authorities, including police, customs and other specialised law enforcement services in relation to the prevention, detection and investigation of criminal offences.

2. For the purposes of paragraph 1, the European Parliament and the Council, acting in accordance with the ordinary legislative procedure, may establish measures concerning:

(a) the collection, storage, processing, analysis and exchange of relevant information;

(b) support for the training of staff, and cooperation on the exchange of staff, on equipment and on research into crime-detection;

(c) common investigative techniques in relation to the detection of serious forms of organised crime.

3. The Council, acting in accordance with a special legislative procedure, may establish measures concerning operational cooperation between the authorities referred to in this Article. The Council shall act unanimously after consulting the European Parliament.

In case of the absence of unanimity in the Council, a group of at least nine Member States may request that the draft measures be referred to the European Council. In that case, the procedure in the Council shall be suspended. After discussion, and in case of a consensus, the European Council shall, within four months of this suspension, refer the draft back to the Council for adoption.

Within the same timeframe, in case of disagreement, and if at least nine Member States wish to establish enhanced cooperation on the basis of the draft measures concerned, they shall notify the European Parliament, the Council and the Commission accordingly. In such a case, the authorisation to proceed with enhanced cooperation referred to in Article 20(2) of the Treaty on European Union and Article 329(1) of this Treaty shall be deemed to be granted and the provisions on enhanced cooperation shall apply.

The specific procedure provided for in the second and third subparagraphs shall not apply to acts which constitute a development of the Schengen acquis.

### *Article 88*

*(ex Article 30 TEU)*

1. Europol's mission shall be to support and strengthen action by the Member States' police authorities and other law enforcement services and their mutual cooperation in preventing and combating serious crime affecting two or more Member States, terrorism and forms of crime which affect a common interest covered by a Union policy.

2. The European Parliament and the Council, by means of regulations adopted in accordance with the ordinary legislative procedure, shall determine Europol's structure, operation, field of action and tasks. These tasks may include:

(a) the collection, storage, processing, analysis and exchange of information, in particular that forwarded by the authorities of the Member States or third countries or bodies;

(b) the coordination, organisation and implementation of investigative and operational action carried out jointly with the Member States' competent authorities or in the context of joint investigative teams, where appropriate in liaison with Eurojust.

These regulations shall also lay down the procedures for scrutiny of Europol's activities by the European Parliament, together with national Parliaments.

3. Any operational action by Europol must be carried out in liaison and in agreement with the authorities of the Member State or States whose territory is concerned. The application of coercive measures shall be the exclusive responsibility of the competent national authorities.

*Article 89*

*(ex Article 32 TEU)*

The Council, acting in accordance with a special legislative procedure, shall lay down the conditions and limitations under which the competent authorities of the Member States referred to in Articles 82 and 87 may operate in the territory of another Member State in liaison and in agreement with the authorities of that State. The Council shall act unanimously after consulting the European Parliament.

# Decision 2008/615 on the stepping up of cross-border cooperation, particularly in combating terrorism and cross-border crime, 23 June 2008

[OJ 2008, L 210/1–11]

6.8.2008 EN Official Journal of the European Union L 210/1

III

*(Acts adopted under the EU Treaty)*

# ACTS ADOPTED UNDER TITLE VI OF THE EU TREATY

## COUNCIL DECISION 2008/615/JHA

**of 23 June 2008**

**on the stepping up of cross-border cooperation, particularly in combating terrorism and cross-border crime**

THE COUNCIL OF THE EUROPEAN UNION,

Having regard to the Treaty on European Union, and in particular Article 30(1)(a) and (b), Article 31(1)(a), Article 32 and Article 34(2)(c) thereof,

Having regard to the initiative of the Kingdom of Belgium, the Republic of Bulgaria, the Federal Republic of Germany, the Kingdom of Spain, the French Republic, the Grand Duchy of Luxembourg, the Kingdom of the Netherlands, the Republic of Austria, the Republic of Slovenia, the Slovak Republic, the Italian Republic, the Republic of Finland, the Portuguese Republic, Romania and the Kingdom of Sweden,

Having regard to the Opinion of the European Parliament [1],

Whereas:

(1) Following the entry into force of the Treaty between the Kingdom of Belgium, the Federal Republic of Germany, the Kingdom of Spain, the French Republic, the Grand Duchy of Luxembourg, the Kingdom of the Netherlands and the Republic of Austria on the stepping up of cross-border cooperation, particularly in combating terrorism, cross-border crime and illegal migration hereinafter (Prüm Treaty), this initiative is submitted, in consultation with the European Commission, in compliance with the provisions of the Treaty on European Union, with the aim of incorporating the substance of the provisions of the Prüm Treaty into the legal framework of the European Union.

(2) The conclusions of the European Council meeting in Tampere in October 1999 confirmed the need for improved exchange of information between the competent authorities of the Member States for the purpose of detecting and investigating offences.

(3) In the Hague Programme for strengthening freedom, security and justice in the European Union of November 2004, the European Council set forth its conviction that for that purpose an innovative approach to the cross-border exchange of law enforcement information was needed.

(4) The European Council accordingly stated that the exchange of such information should comply with the conditions applying to the principle of availability. This means that a law enforcement officer in one Member State of the Union who needs information in order to carry out his duties can obtain it from another Member State and that the law enforcement authorities in the Member State that holds this information will make it available for the declared purpose, taking account of the needs of investigations pending in that Member State.

(5) The European Council set 1 January 2008 as the deadline for achieving this objective in the Hague Programme.

(6) Council Framework Decision 2006/960/JHA of 18 December 2006 on simplifying the exchange of information and intelligence between law enforcement authorities of the Member States of the European Union [2] already lays down rules whereby the Member States' law enforcement authorities may exchange existing information and intelligence expeditiously and effectively for the purpose of carrying out criminal investigations or criminal intelligence operations.

(7) The Hague Programme for strengthening freedom, security and justice states also that full use should be made of new technology and that there should also be reciprocal access to national databases, while stipulating that new centralised European databases should be created only on the basis of studies that have shown their added value.

---

[1] Opinion of 10 June 2007 (not yet published in the Official Journal).

[2] OJ L 386, 29.12.2006, p. 89.

(8) For effective international cooperation it is of fundamental importance that precise information can be exchanged swiftly and efficiently. The aim is to introduce procedures for promoting fast, efficient and inexpensive means of data exchange. For the joint use of data these procedures should be subject to accountability and incorporate appropriate guarantees as to the accuracy and security of the data during transmission and storage as well as procedures for recording data exchange and restrictions on the use of information exchanged.

(9) These requirements are satisfied by the Prüm Treaty. In order to meet the substantive requirements of the Hague Programme for all Member States within the time-scale set by it, the substance of the essential parts of the Prüm Treaty should become applicable to all Member States.

(10) This Decision therefore contains provisions which are based on the main provisions of the Prüm Treaty and are designed to improve the exchange of information, whereby Member States grant one another access rights to their automated DNA analysis files, automated dactyloscopic identification systems and vehicle registration data. In the case of data from national DNA analysis files and automated dactyloscopic identification systems, a hit/no hit system should enable the searching Member State, in a second step, to request specific related personal data from the Member State administering the file and, where necessary, to request further information through mutual assistance procedures, including those adopted pursuant to Framework Decision 2006/960/JHA.

(11) This would considerably speed up existing procedures enabling Member States to find out whether any other Member State, and if so, which, has the information it needs.

(12) Cross-border data comparison should open up a new dimension in crime fighting. The information obtained by comparing data should open up new investigative approaches for Member States and thus play a crucial role in assisting Member States' law enforcement and judicial authorities.

(13) The rules are based on networking Member States' national databases.

(14) Subject to certain conditions, Member States should be able to supply personal and non-personal data in order to improve the exchange of information with a view to preventing criminal offences and maintaining public order and security in connection with major events with a cross-border dimension.

(15) In the implementation of Article 12, Member States may decide to give priority to combating serious crime bearing in mind the limited technical capacities available for transmitting data.

(16) In addition to improving the exchange of information, there is a need to regulate other forms of closer cooperation between police authorities, in particular by means of joint security operations (e.g. joint patrols).

(17) Closer police and judicial cooperation in criminal matters must go hand in hand with respect for fundamental rights, in particular the right to respect for privacy and to protection of personal data, to be guaranteed by special data protection arrangements, which should be tailored to the specific nature of different forms of data exchange. Such data protection provisions should take particular account of the specific nature of cross-border online access to databases. Since, with online access, it is not possible for the Member State administering the file to make any prior checks, a system ensuring post hoc monitoring should be in place.

(18) The hit/no hit system provides for a structure of comparing anonymous profiles, where additional personal data is exchanged only after a hit, the supply and receipt of which is governed by national law, including the legal assistance rules. This set-up guarantees an adequate system of data protection, it being understood that the supply of personal data to another Member State requires an adequate level of data protection on the part of the receiving Member States.

(19) Aware of the comprehensive exchange of information and data resulting from closer police and judicial cooperation, this Decision seeks to warrant an appropriate level of data protection. It observes the level of protection designed for the processing of personal data in the Council of Europe Convention of 28 January 1981 for the Protection of Individuals with regard to Automatic Processing of Personal Data, the Additional Protocol of 8 November 2001 to the Convention and the principles of Recommendation No R (87) 15 of the Council of Europe Regulating the Use of Personal Data in the Police Sector.

(20) The data protection provisions contained in this Decision also include data protection principles which were necessary due to the lack of a Framework Decision on data protection in the Third Pillar. This Framework Decision should be applied to the entire area of police and judicial cooperation in criminal matters under the condition that its level of data protection is not lower than the protection laid down in the Council of Europe Convention for the Protection of Individuals with regard to automatic Processing of Personal Data of 28 January 1981 and its additional Protocol of 8 November 2001 and takes account of Recommendation No R (87) 15 of 17 September 1987 of the Committee of Ministers to Member States regulating the use of personal data in the police sector, also where data are not processed automatically.

(21) Since the objectives of this Decision, in particular the improvement of information exchange in the European Union, cannot be sufficiently achieved by the Member States in isolation owing to the cross-border nature of crime fighting and security issues so that the Member States are obliged to rely on one another in these matters, and can therefore be better achieved at European Union level, the Council may adopt measures in accordance with the principle of subsidiarity as set out in Article 5 of the Treaty establishing the European Community, to which Article 2 of the Treaty on European Union refers. In accordance with the principle of proportionality pursuant to Article 5 of the EC Treaty, this Decision does not go beyond what is necessary to achieve those objectives.

(22) This Decision respects the fundamental rights and observes the principles set out in particular in the Charter of Fundamental Rights of the European Union,

HAS DECIDED AS FOLLOWS:

CHAPTER 1

## GENERAL ASPECTS

*Article 1*

### Aim and scope

By means of this Decision, the Member States intend to step up cross-border cooperation in matters covered by Title VI of the Treaty, particularly the exchange of information between authorities responsible for the prevention and investigation of criminal offences. To this end, this Decision contains rules in the following areas:

(a) provisions on the conditions and procedure for the automated transfer of DNA profiles, dactyloscopic data and certain national vehicle registration data (Chapter 2);

(b) provisions on the conditions for the supply of data in connection with major events with a cross-border dimension (Chapter 3);

(c) provisions on the conditions for the supply of information in order to prevent terrorist offences (Chapter 4);

(d) provisions on the conditions and procedure for stepping up cross-border police cooperation through various measures (Chapter 5).

CHAPTER 2

## ONLINE ACCESS AND FOLLOW-UP REQUESTS

*SECTION 1*

### *DNA profiles*

*Article 2*

### Establishment of national DNA analysis files

1. Member States shall open and keep national DNA analysis files for the investigation of criminal offences. Processing of data kept in those files, under this Decision, shall be carried out in accordance with this Decision, in compliance with the national law applicable to the processing.

2. For the purpose of implementing this Decision, the Member States shall ensure the availability of reference data from their national DNA analysis files as referred to in the first sentence of paragraph 1. Reference data shall only include DNA profiles established from the non-coding part of DNA and a reference number. Reference data shall not contain any data from which the data subject can be directly identified. Reference data which is not attributed to any individual (unidentified DNA profiles) shall be recognisable as such.

3. Each Member State shall inform the General Secretariat of the Council of the national DNA analysis files to which Articles 2 to 6 apply and the conditions for automated searching as referred to in Article 3(1) in accordance with Article 36.

*Article 3*

### Automated searching of DNA profiles

1. For the investigation of criminal offences, Member States shall allow other Member States' national contact points as referred to in Article 6, access to the reference data in their DNA analysis files, with the power to conduct automated searches by comparing DNA profiles. Searches may be conducted only in individual cases and in compliance with the requesting Member State's national law.

2. Should an automated search show that a DNA profile supplied matches DNA profiles entered in the receiving Member State's searched file, the national contact point of the searching Member State shall receive in an automated way the reference data with which a match has been found. If no match can be found, automated notification of this shall be given.

*Article 4*

**Automated comparison of DNA profiles**

1. For the investigation of criminal offences, the Member States shall, by mutual consent, via their national contact points, compare the DNA profiles of their unidentified DNA profiles with all DNA profiles from other national DNA analysis files' reference data. Profiles shall be supplied and compared in automated form. Unidentified DNA profiles shall be supplied for comparison only where provided for under the requesting Member State's national law.

2. Should a Member State, as a result of the comparison referred to in paragraph 1, find that any DNA profiles supplied match any of those in its DNA analysis files, it shall, without delay, supply the other Member State's national contact point with the reference data with which a match has been found.

*Article 5*

**Supply of further personal data and other information**

Should the procedures referred to in Articles 3 and 4 show a match between DNA profiles, the supply of further available personal data and other information relating to the reference data shall be governed by the national law, including the legal assistance rules, of the requested Member State.

*Article 6*

**National contact point and implementing measures**

1. For the purposes of the supply of data as referred to in Articles 3 and 4, each Member State shall designate a national contact point. The powers of the national contact points shall be governed by the applicable national law.

2. Details of technical arrangements for the procedures set out in Articles 3 and 4 shall be laid down in the implementing measures as referred to in Article 33.

*Article 7*

**Collection of cellular material and supply of DNA profiles**

Where, in ongoing investigations or criminal proceedings, there is no DNA profile available for a particular individual present within a requested Member State's territory, the requested Member State shall provide legal assistance by collecting and examining cellular material from that individual and by supplying the DNA profile obtained, if:

(a) the requesting Member State specifies the purpose for which this is required;

(b) the requesting Member State produces an investigation warrant or statement issued by the competent authority, as required under that Member State's law, showing that the requirements for collecting and examining cellular material would be fulfilled if the individual concerned were present within the requesting Member State's territory; and

(c) under the requested Member State's law, the requirements for collecting and examining cellular material and for supplying the DNA profile obtained are fulfilled.

*SECTION 2*

***Dactyloscopic data***

*Article 8*

**Dactyloscopic data**

For the purpose of implementing this Decision, Member States shall ensure the availability of reference data from the file for the national automated fingerprint identification systems established for the prevention and investigation of criminal offences. Reference data shall only include dactyloscopic data and a reference number. Reference data shall not contain any data from which the data subject can be directly identified. Reference data which is not attributed to any individual (unidentified dactyloscopic data) must be recognisable as such.

*Article 9*

**Automated searching of dactyloscopic data**

1. For the prevention and investigation of criminal offences, Member States shall allow other Member States' national contact points, as referred to in Article 11, access to the reference data in the automated fingerprint identification systems which they have established for that purpose, with the power to conduct automated searches by comparing dactyloscopic data. Searches may be conducted only in individual cases and in compliance with the requesting Member State's national law.

2. The confirmation of a match of dactyloscopic data with reference data held by the Member State administering the file shall be carried out by the national contact point of the requesting Member State by means of the automated supply of the reference data required for a clear match.

*Article 10*

**Supply of further personal data and other information**

Should the procedure referred to in Article 9 show a match between dactyloscopic data, the supply of further available personal data and other information relating to the reference data shall be governed by the national law, including the legal assistance rules, of the requested Member State.

*Article 11*

**National contact point and implementing measures**

1. For the purposes of the supply of data as referred to in Article 9, each Member State shall designate a national contact point. The powers of the national contact points shall be governed by the applicable national law.

2. Details of technical arrangements for the procedure set out in Article 9 shall be laid down in the implementing measures as referred to in Article 33.

*SECTION 3*

***Vehicle registration data***

*Article 12*

**Automated searching of vehicle registration data**

1. For the prevention and investigation of criminal offences and in dealing with other offences coming within the jurisdiction of the courts or the public prosecution service in the searching Member State, as well as in maintaining public security, Member States shall allow other Member States' national contact points, as referred to in paragraph 2, access to the following national vehicle registration data, with the power to conduct automated searches in individual cases:

(a) data relating to owners or operators; and

(b) data relating to vehicles.

Searches may be conducted only with a full chassis number or a full registration number. Searches may be conducted only in compliance with the searching Member State's national law.

2. For the purposes of the supply of data as referred to in paragraph 1, each Member State shall designate a national contact point for incoming requests. The powers of the national contact points shall be governed by the applicable national law. Details of technical arrangements for the procedure shall be laid down in the implementing measures as referred to in Article 33.

CHAPTER 3

**MAJOR EVENTS**

*Article 13*

**Supply of non-personal data**

For the prevention of criminal offences and in maintaining public order and security for major events with a cross-border dimension, in particular for sporting events or European Council meetings, Member States shall, both upon request and of their own accord, in compliance with the supplying Member State's national law, supply one another with any non-personal data required for those purposes.

*Article 14*

**Supply of personal data**

1. For the prevention of criminal offences and in maintaining public order and security for major events with a cross-border dimension, in particular for sporting events or European Council meetings, Member States shall, both upon request and of their own accord, supply one another with personal data if any final convictions or other circumstances give reason to believe that the data subjects will commit criminal offences at the events or pose a threat to public order and security, in so far as the supply of such data is permitted under the supplying Member State's national law.

2. Personal data may be processed only for the purposes laid down in paragraph 1 and for the specified events for which they were supplied. The data supplied must be deleted without delay once the purposes referred to in paragraph 1 have been achieved or can no longer be achieved. The data supplied must in any event be deleted after not more than a year.

*Article 15*

**National contact point**

For the purposes of the supply of data as referred to in Articles 13 and 14, each Member State shall designate a national contact point. The powers of the national contact points shall be governed by the applicable national law.

CHAPTER 4

**MEASURES TO PREVENT TERRORIST OFFENCES**

*Article 16*

**Supply of information in order to prevent terrorist offences**

1. For the prevention of terrorist offences, Member States may, in compliance with national law, in individual cases, even without being requested to do so, supply other Member States' national contact points, as referred to in paragraph 3, with the personal data and information specified in paragraph 2, in so far as is necessary because particular circumstances give reason to believe that the data subjects will commit criminal offences as referred to in Articles 1 to 3 of Council Framework Decision 2002/475/JHA of 13 June 2002 on combating terrorism (1).

(1) OJ L 164, 22.6.2002, p. 3.

2. The data to be supplied shall comprise surname, first names, date and place of birth and a description of the circumstances giving rise to the belief referred to in paragraph 1.

3. Each Member State shall designate a national contact point for exchange of information with other Member States' national contact points. The powers of the national contact points shall be governed by the applicable national law.

4. The supplying Member State may, in compliance with national law, impose conditions on the use made of such data and information by the receiving Member State. The receiving Member State shall be bound by any such conditions.

CHAPTER 5

## OTHER FORMS OF COOPERATION

*Article 17*

### Joint operations

1. In order to step up police cooperation, the competent authorities designated by the Member States may, in maintaining public order and security and preventing criminal offences, introduce joint patrols and other joint operations in which designated officers or other officials (officers) from other Member States participate in operations within a Member State's territory.

2. Each Member State may, as a host Member State, in compliance with its own national law, and with the seconding Member State's consent, confer executive powers on the seconding Member States' officers involved in joint operations or, in so far as the host Member State's law permits, allow the seconding Member States' officers to exercise their executive powers in accordance with the seconding Member State's law. Such executive powers may be exercised only under the guidance and, as a rule, in the presence of officers from the host Member State. The seconding Member States' officers shall be subject to the host Member State's national law. The host Member State shall assume responsibility for their actions.

3. Seconding Member States' officers involved in joint operations shall be subject to the instructions given by the host Member State's competent authority.

4. Member States shall submit declarations as referred to in Article 36 in which they lay down the practical aspects of cooperation.

*Article 18*

### Assistance in connection with mass gatherings disasters and serious accidents

Member States' competent authorities shall provide one another with mutual assistance, in compliance with national law, in connection with mass gatherings and similar major events, disasters and serious accidents, by seeking to prevent criminal offences and maintain public order and security by:

(a) notifying one another as promptly as possible of such situations with a cross-border impact and exchanging any relevant information;

(b) taking and coordinating the necessary policing measures within their territory in situations with a cross-border impact;

(c) as far as possible, dispatching officers, specialists and advisers and supplying equipment, at the request of the Member State within whose territory the situation has arisen.

*Article 19*

### Use of arms, ammunition and equipment

1. Officers from a seconding Member State who are involved in a joint operation within another Member State's territory pursuant to Article 17 or 18 may wear their own national uniforms there. They may carry such arms, ammunition and equipment as they are allowed to under the seconding Member State's national law. The host Member State may prohibit the carrying of particular arms, ammunition or equipment by a seconding Member State's officers.

2. Member States shall submit declarations as referred to in Article 36 in which they list the arms, ammunition and equipment that may be used only in legitimate self-defence or in the defence of others. The host Member State's officer in actual charge of the operation may in individual cases, in compliance with national law, give permission for arms, ammunition and equipment to be used for purposes going beyond those specified in the first sentence. The use of arms, ammunition and equipment shall be governed by the host Member State's law. The competent authorities shall inform one another of the arms, ammunition and equipment permitted and of the conditions for their use.

3. If officers from a Member State make use of vehicles in action under this Decision within another Member State's territory, they shall be subject to the same road traffic regulations as the host Member State's officers, including as regards right of way and any special privileges.

4. Member States shall submit declarations as referred to in Article 36 in which they lay down the practical aspects of the use of arms, ammunition and equipment.

6.8.2008 EN Official Journal of the European Union L 210/7

*Article 20*

**Protection and assistance**

Member States shall be required to provide other Member States' officers crossing borders with the same protection and assistance in the course of those officers' duties as for their own officers.

*Article 21*

**General rules on civil liability**

1. Where officials of a Member State are operating in another Member State pursuant to Article 17, their Member State shall be liable for any damage caused by them during their operations, in accordance with the law of the Member State in whose territory they are operating.

2. The Member State in whose territory the damage referred to in paragraph 1 was caused shall make good such damage under the conditions applicable to damage caused by its own officials.

3. In the case provided for in paragraph 1, the Member State whose officials have caused damage to any person in the territory of another Member State shall reimburse the latter in full any sums it has paid to the victims or persons entitled on their behalf.

4. Where officials of a Member State are operating in another Member State pursuant to Article 18, the latter Member State shall be liable in accordance with its national law for any damage caused by them during their operations.

5. Where the damage referred to in paragraph 4 results from gross negligence or wilful misconduct, the host Member State may approach the seconding Member State in order to have any sums it has paid to the victims or persons entitled on their behalf reimbursed by the latter.

6. Without prejudice to the exercise of its rights vis-à-vis third parties and with the exception of paragraph 3, each Member State shall refrain, in the case provided for in paragraph 1, from requesting reimbursement of damages it has sustained from another Member State.

*Article 22*

**Criminal liability**

Officers operating within another Member State's territory under this Decision, shall be treated in the same way as officers of the host Member State with regard to any criminal offences that might be committed by, or against them, save as otherwise provided in another agreement which is binding on the Member States concerned.

*Article 23*

**Employment relationship**

Officers operating within another Member State's territory, under this Decision, shall remain subject to the employment law provisions applicable in their own Member State, particularly as regards disciplinary rules.

CHAPTER 6

**GENERAL PROVISIONS ON DATA PROTECTION**

*Article 24*

**Definitions and scope**

1. For the purposes of this Decision:

(a) 'processing of personal data' shall mean any operation or set of operations which is performed upon personal data, whether or not by automatic means, such as collection, recording, organisation, storage, adaptation or alteration, sorting, retrieval, consultation, use, disclosure by supply, dissemination or otherwise making available, alignment, combination, blocking, erasure or destruction of data. Processing within the meaning of this Decision shall also include notification of whether or not a hit exists;

(b) 'automated search procedure' shall mean direct access to the automated files of another body where the response to the search procedure is fully automated;

(c) 'referencing' shall mean the marking of stored personal data without the aim of limiting their processing in future;

(d) 'blocking' shall mean the marking of stored personal data with the aim of limiting their processing in future.

2. The following provisions shall apply to data which are or have been supplied pursuant to this Decision, save as otherwise provided in the preceding Chapters.

*Article 25*

**Level of data protection**

1. As regards the processing of personal data which are or have been supplied pursuant to this Decision, each Member State shall guarantee a level of protection of personal data in its national law at least equal to that resulting from the Council of Europe Convention for the Protection of Individuals with regard to Automatic Processing of Personal Data of 28 January 1981 and its Additional Protocol of 8 November 2001 and in doing so, shall take account of Recommendation No R (87) 15 of 17 September 1987 of the Committee of Ministers of the Council of Europe to the Member States regulating the use of personal data in the police sector, also where data are not processed automatically.

2. The supply of personal data provided for under this Decision may not take place until the provisions of this Chapter have been implemented in the national law of the territories of the Member States involved in such supply. The Council shall unanimously decide whether this condition has been met.

3. Paragraph 2 shall not apply to those Member States where the supply of personal data as provided for in this Decision has already started pursuant to the Treaty of 27 May 2005 between the Kingdom of Belgium, the Federal Republic of Germany, the Kingdom of Spain, the French Republic, the Grand Duchy of Luxembourg, the Kingdom of the Netherlands and the Republic of Austria on the stepping up of cross-border cooperation, particularly in combating terrorism, cross-border crime and illegal migration (Prüm Treaty).

*Article 26*

**Purpose**

1. Processing of personal data by the receiving Member State shall be permitted solely for the purposes for which the data have been supplied in accordance with this Decision. Processing for other purposes shall be permitted solely with the prior authorisation of the Member State administering the file and subject only to the national law of the receiving Member State. Such authorisation may be granted provided that processing for such other purposes is permitted under the national law of the Member State administering the file.

2. Processing of data supplied pursuant to Articles 3, 4 and 9 by the searching or comparing Member State shall be permitted solely in order to:

(a) establish whether the compared DNA profiles or dactyloscopic data match;

(b) prepare and submit a police or judicial request for legal assistance in compliance with national law if those data match;

(c) record within the meaning of Article 30.

The Member State administering the file may process the data supplied to it in accordance with Articles 3, 4 and 9 solely where this is necessary for the purposes of comparison, providing automated replies to searches or recording pursuant to Article 30. The supplied data shall be deleted immediately following data comparison or automated replies to searches unless further processing is necessary for the purposes mentioned under points (b) and (c) of the first subparagraph.

3. Data supplied in accordance with Article 12 may be used by the Member State administering the file solely where this is necessary for the purpose of providing automated replies to search procedures or recording as specified in Article 30. The data supplied shall be deleted immediately following automated replies to searches unless further processing is necessary for recording pursuant to Article 30. The searching Member State may use data received in a reply solely for the procedure for which the search was made.

*Article 27*

**Competent authorities**

Personal data supplied may be processed only by the authorities, bodies and courts with responsibility for a task in furtherance of the aims mentioned in Article 26. In particular, data may be supplied to other entities only with the prior authorisation of the supplying Member State and in compliance with the law of the receiving Member State.

*Article 28*

**Accuracy, current relevance and storage time of data**

1. The Member States shall ensure the accuracy and current relevance of personal data. Should it transpire *ex officio* or from a notification by the data subject, that incorrect data or data which should not have been supplied have been supplied, this shall be notified without delay to the receiving Member State or Member States. The Member State or Member States concerned shall be obliged to correct or delete the data. Moreover, personal data supplied shall be corrected if they are found to be incorrect. If the receiving body has reason to believe that the supplied data are incorrect or should be deleted the supplying body shall be informed forthwith.

2. Data, the accuracy of which the data subject contests and the accuracy or inaccuracy of which cannot be established shall, in accordance with the national law of the Member States, be marked with a flag at the request of the data subject. If a flag exists, this may be removed subject to the national law of the Member States and only with the permission of the data subject or based on a decision of the competent court or independent data protection authority

3. Personal data supplied which should not have been supplied or received shall be deleted. Data which are lawfully supplied and received shall be deleted:

(a) if they are not or no longer necessary for the purpose for which they were supplied; if personal data have been supplied without request, the receiving body shall immediately check if they are necessary for the purposes for which they were supplied;

(b) following the expiry of the maximum period for keeping data laid down in the national law of the supplying Member State where the supplying body informed the receiving body of that maximum period at the time of supplying the data.

Where there is reason to believe that deletion would prejudice the interests of the data subject, the data shall be blocked instead of being deleted in compliance with national law. Blocked data may be supplied or used solely for the purpose which prevented their deletion.

*Article 29*

**Technical and organisational measures to ensure data protection and data security**

1. The supplying and receiving bodies shall take steps to ensure that personal data is effectively protected against accidental or unauthorised destruction, accidental loss, unauthorised access, unauthorised or accidental alteration and unauthorised disclosure.

2. The features of the technical specification of the automated search procedure are regulated in the implementing measures as referred to in Article 33 which guarantee that:

(a) state-of-the-art technical measures are taken to ensure data protection and data security, in particular data confidentiality and integrity;

(b) encryption and authorisation procedures recognised by the competent authorities are used when having recourse to generally accessible networks; and

(c) the admissibility of searches in accordance with Article 30(2), (4) and (5) can be checked.

*Article 30*

**Logging and recording: special rules governing automated and non-automated supply**

1. Each Member State shall guarantee that every non-automated supply and every non-automated receipt of personal data by the body administering the file and by the searching body is logged in order to verify the admissibility of the supply. Logging shall contain the following information:

(a) the reason for the supply;

(b) the data supplied;

(c) the date of the supply; and

(d) the name or reference code of the searching body and of the body administering the file.

2. The following shall apply to automated searches for data based on Articles 3, 9 and 12 and to automated comparison pursuant to Article 4:

(a) only specially authorised officers of the national contact points may carry out automated searches or comparisons. The list of officers authorised to carry out automated searches or comparisons shall be made available upon request to the supervisory authorities referred to in paragraph 5 and to the other Member States;

(b) each Member State shall ensure that each supply and receipt of personal data by the body administering the file and the searching body is recorded, including notification of whether or not a hit exists. Recording shall include the following information:

(i) the data supplied;

(ii) the date and exact time of the supply; and

(iii) the name or reference code of the searching body and of the body administering the file.

The searching body shall also record the reason for the search or supply as well as an identifier for the official who carried out the search and the official who ordered the search or supply.

3. The recording body shall immediately communicate the recorded data upon request to the competent data protection authorities of the relevant Member State at the latest within four weeks following receipt of the request. Recorded data may be used solely for the following purposes:

(a) monitoring data protection;

(b) ensuring data security.

4. The recorded data shall be protected with suitable measures against inappropriate use and other forms of improper use and shall be kept for two years. After the conservation period the recorded data shall be deleted immediately.

5. Responsibility for legal checks on the supply or receipt of personal data lies with the independent data protection authorities or, as appropriate, the judicial authorities of the respective Member States. Anyone can request these authorities to check the lawfulness of the processing of data in respect of their person in compliance with national law. Independently of such requests, these authorities and the bodies responsible for recording shall carry out random checks on the lawfulness of supply, based on the files involved.

The results of such checks shall be kept for inspection for 18 months by the independent data protection authorities. After this period, they shall be immediately deleted. Each data protection authority may be requested by the independent data protection authority of another Member State to exercise its powers in accordance with national law. The independent data protection authorities of the Member States shall perform the inspection tasks necessary for mutual cooperation, in particular by exchanging relevant information.

*Article 31*

**Data subjects' rights to information and damages**

1. At the request of the data subject under national law, information shall be supplied in compliance with national law to the data subject upon production of proof of his identity, without unreasonable expense, in general comprehensible terms and without unacceptable delays, on the data processed in respect of his person, the origin of the data, the recipient or groups of recipients, the intended purpose of the processing and, where required by national law, the legal basis for the processing. Moreover, the data subject shall be entitled to have inaccurate data corrected and unlawfully processed data deleted. The Member States shall also ensure that, in the event of violation of his rights in relation to data protection, the data subject shall be able to lodge an effective complaint to an independent court or a tribunal within the meaning of Article 6(1) of the European Convention on Human Rights or an independent supervisory authority within the meaning of Article 28 of Directive 95/46/EC of the European Parliament and of the Council of 24 October 1995 on the protection of individuals with regard to the processing of personal data and on the free movement of such data ([1]) and that he is given the possibility to claim for damages or to seek another form of legal compensation. The detailed rules for the procedure to assert these rights and the reasons for limiting the right of access shall be governed by the relevant national legal provisions of the Member State where the data subject asserts his rights.

2. Where a body of one Member State has supplied personal data under this Decision, the receiving body of the other Member State cannot use the inaccuracy of the data supplied as grounds to evade its liability vis-à-vis the injured party under national law. If damages are awarded against the receiving body because of its use of inaccurate transfer data, the body which supplied the data shall refund the amount paid in damages to the receiving body in full.

*Article 32*

**Information requested by the Member States**

The receiving Member State shall inform the supplying Member State on request of the processing of supplied data and the result obtained.

CHAPTER 7

**IMPLEMENTING AND FINAL PROVISIONS**

*Article 33*

**Implementing measures**

The Council, acting by a qualified majority and after Consulting the European Parliament, shall adopt measures necessary to implement this Decision at the level of the Union.

([1]) OJ L 281, 23.11.1995, p. 31. Directive as amended by Regulation (EC) No 1882/2003 (OJ L 284, 31.10.2003, p. 1).

*Article 34*

**Costs**

Each Member State shall bear the operational costs incurred by its own authorities in connection with the application of this Decision. In special cases, the Member States concerned may agree on different arrangements.

*Article 35*

**Relationship with other instruments**

1. For the Member States concerned, the relevant provisions of this Decision shall be applied instead of the corresponding provisions contained in the Prüm Treaty. Any other provision of the Prüm Treaty shall remain applicable between the contracting parties of the Prüm Treaty.

2. Without prejudice to their commitments under other acts adopted pursuant to Title VI of the Treaty:

(a) Member States may continue to apply bilateral or multilateral agreements or arrangements on cross-border cooperation which are in force on the date this Decision is adopted in so far as such agreements or arrangements are not incompatible with the objectives of this Decision;

(b) Member States may conclude or bring into force bilateral or multilateral agreements or arrangements on cross-border cooperation after this Decision has entered into force in so far as such agreements or arrangements provide for the objectives of this Decision to be extended or enlarged.

3. The agreements and arrangements referred to in paragraphs 1 and 2 may not affect relations with Member States which are not parties thereto.

4. Within four weeks of this Decision taking effect Member States shall inform the Council and the Commission of existing agreements or arrangements within the meaning of paragraph 2(a) which they wish to continue to apply.

5. Member States shall also inform the Council and the Commission of all new agreements or arrangements within the meaning of paragraph 2(b) within three months of their signing or, in the case of instruments which were signed before adoption of this Decision, within three months of their entry into force.

6. Nothing in this Decision shall affect bilateral or multilateral agreements or arrangements between Member States and third States.

7. This Decision shall be without prejudice to existing agreements on legal assistance or mutual recognition of court decisions.

6.8.2008 EN Official Journal of the European Union L 210/11

*Article 36*

**Implementation and declarations**

1. Member States shall take the necessary measures to comply with the provisions of this Decision within one year of this Decision taking effect, with the exception of the provisions of Chapter 2 with respect to which the necessary measures shall be taken within three years of this Decision and the Council Decision on the implementation of this Decision taking effect.

2. Member States shall inform the General Secretariat of the Council and the Commission that they have implemented the obligations imposed on them under this Decision and submit the declarations foreseen by this Decision. When doing so, each Member State may indicate that it will apply immediately this Decision in its relations with those Member States which have given the same notification.

3. Declarations submitted in accordance with paragraph 2 may be amended at any time by means of a declaration submitted to the General Secretariat of the Council. The General Secretariat of the Council shall forward any declarations received to the Member States and the Commission.

4. On the basis of this and other information made available by Member States on request, the Commission shall submit a report to the Council by 28 July 2012 on the implementation of this Decision accompanied by such proposals as it deems appropriate for any further development.

*Article 37*

**Application**

This Decision shall take effect 20 days following its publication in the *Official Journal of the European Union.*

Done at Luxembourg, 23 June 2008.

*For the Council*

*The President*

I. JARC

# Decision 2008/616 on the implementation of Decision 2008/615 on the stepping up of cross-border cooperation, particularly in combating terrorism and cross-border crime, 23 June 2008

**[OJ 2008, L 210/12–17]**

**[Editor's note: annex omitted]**

L 210/12 EN Official Journal of the European Union 6.8.2008

**COUNCIL DECISION 2008/616/JHA**

**of 23 June 2008**

**on the implementation of Decision 2008/615/JHA on the stepping up of cross-border cooperation, particularly in combating terrorism and cross-border crime**

THE COUNCIL OF THE EUROPEAN UNION,

Having regard to Article 33 of Council Decision 2008/615/JHA [1],

Having regard to the initiative of the Federal Republic of Germany,

Having regard to the opinion of the European Parliament [2],

Whereas:

(1) On 23 June 2008 the Council adopted Decision 2008/615/JHA on the stepping up of cross-border cooperation, particularly in combating terrorism and cross-border crime.

(2) By means of Decision 2008/615/JHA, the basic elements of the Treaty of 27 May 2005 between the Kingdom of Belgium, the Federal Republic of Germany, the Kingdom of Spain, the French Republic, the Grand Duchy of Luxembourg, the Kingdom of the Netherlands and the Republic of Austria on the stepping up of cross-border cooperation, particularly in combating terrorism, cross-border crime and illegal migration (hereinafter the Prüm Treaty), were transposed into the legal framework of the European Union.

(3) Article 33 of Decision 2008/615/JHA provides that the Council is to adopt the measures necessary to implement Decision 2008/615/JHA at the level of the Union in accordance with the procedure laid down in the second sentence of Article 34(2)(c) of the Treaty on European Union. These measures are to be based on the Implementing Agreement of 5 December 2006 concerning the administrative and technical implementation and application of the Prüm Treaty.

(4) This Decision establishes those common normative provisions which are indispensable for administrative and technical implementation of the forms of cooperation set out in Decision 2008/615/JHA. The Annex to this Decision contains implementing provisions of a technical nature. In addition, a separate Manual, containing exclusively factual information to be provided by the Member States, will be drawn up and kept up to date by the General Secretariat of the Council.

(5) Having regard to technical capabilities, routine searches of new DNA profiles will in principle be carried out by means of single searches, and appropriate solutions for this will be found at the technical level,

HAS DECIDED AS FOLLOWS:

CHAPTER I

**GENERAL**

*Article 1*

**Aim**

The aim of this Decision is to lay down the necessary administrative and technical provisions for the implementation of Decision 2008/615/JHA, in particular as regards the automated exchange of DNA data, dactyloscopic data and vehicle registration data, as set out in Chapter 2 of that Decision, and other forms of cooperation, as set out in Chapter 5 of that Decision.

*Article 2*

**Definitions**

For the purposes of this Decision:

(a) 'search' and 'comparison', as referred to in Articles 3, 4 and 9 of Decision 2008/615/JHA, mean the procedures by which it is established whether there is a match between, respectively, DNA data or dactyloscopic data which have been communicated by one Member State and DNA data or dactyloscopic data stored in the databases of one, several, or all of the Member States;

(b) 'automated searching', as referred to in Article 12 of Decision 2008/615/JHA, means an online access procedure for consulting the databases of one, several, or all of the Member States;

(c) 'DNA profile' means a letter or number code which represents a set of identification characteristics of the non-coding part of an analysed human DNA sample, i.e. the particular molecular structure at the various DNA locations (loci);

(d) 'non-coding part of DNA' means chromosome regions not genetically expressed, i.e. not known to provide for any functional properties of an organism;

(1) See page 1 of this Official Journal.
(2) Opinion of 21 April 2008 (not yet published in the Official Journal).

(e) 'DNA reference data' mean DNA profile and reference number;

(f) 'reference DNA profile' means the DNA profile of an identified person;

(g) 'unidentified DNA profile' means the DNA profile obtained from traces collected during the investigation of criminal offences and belonging to a person not yet identified;

(h) 'note' means a Member State's marking on a DNA profile in its national database indicating that there has already been a match for that DNA profile on another Member State's search or comparison;

(i) 'dactyloscopic data' mean fingerprint images, images of fingerprint latents, palm prints, palm print latents and templates of such images (coded minutiae), when they are stored and dealt with in an automated database;

(j) 'vehicle registration data' mean the data-set as specified in Chapter 3 of the Annex to this Decision;

(k) 'individual case', as referred to in Article 3(1), second sentence, Article 9(1), second sentence and Article 12(1) of Decision 2008/615/JHA, means a single investigation or prosecution file. If such a file contains more than one DNA profile, or one piece of dactyloscopic data or vehicle registration data, they may be transmitted together as one request.

CHAPTER 2

## COMMON PROVISIONS FOR DATA EXCHANGE

*Article 3*

### Technical specifications

Member States shall observe common technical specifications in connection with all requests and answers related to searches and comparisons of DNA profiles, dactyloscopic data and vehicle registration data. These technical specifications are laid down in the Annex to this Decision.

*Article 4*

### Communications network

The electronic exchange of DNA data, dactyloscopic data and vehicle registration data between Member States shall take place using the Trans European Services for Telematics between Administrations (TESTA II) communications network and further developments thereof.

*Article 5*

### Availability of automated data exchange

Member States shall take all necessary measures to ensure that automated searching or comparison of DNA data, dactyloscopic data and vehicle registration data is possible 24 hours a day and seven days a week. In the event of a technical fault, the Member States' national contact points shall immediately inform each other and shall agree on temporary alternative information exchange arrangements in accordance with the legal provisions applicable. Automated data exchange shall be re-established as quickly as possible.

*Article 6*

### Reference numbers for DNA data and dactyloscopic data

The reference numbers referred to in Article 2 and Article 8 of Decision 2008/615/JHA shall consist of a combination of the following:

(a) a code allowing the Member States, in the case of a match, to retrieve personal data and other information in their databases in order to supply it to one, several or all of the Member States in accordance with Article 5 or Article 10 of Decision 2008/615/JHA;

(b) a code to indicate the national origin of the DNA profile or dactyloscopic data; and

(c) with respect to DNA data, a code to indicate the type of DNA profile.

CHAPTER 3

## DNA DATA

*Article 7*

### Principles of DNA data exchange

1. Member States shall use existing standards for DNA data exchange, such as the European Standard Set (ESS) or the Interpol Standard Set of Loci (ISSOL).

2. The transmission procedure, in the case of automated searching and comparison of DNA profiles, shall take place within a decentralised structure.

3. Appropriate measures shall be taken to ensure confidentiality and integrity for data being sent to other Member States, including their encryption.

4. Member States shall take the necessary measures to guarantee the integrity of the DNA profiles made available or sent for comparison to the other Member States and to ensure that these measures comply with international standards such as ISO 17025.

5. Member States shall use Member State codes in accordance with the ISO 3166-1 alpha-2 standard.

*Article 8*

**Rules for requests and answers in connection with DNA data**

1. A request for an automated search or comparison, as referred to in Articles 3 or 4 of Decision 2008/615/JHA, shall include only the following information:

(a) the Member State code of the requesting Member State;

(b) the date, time and indication number of the request;

(c) DNA profiles and their reference numbers;

(d) the types of DNA profiles transmitted (unidentified DNA profiles or reference DNA profiles); and

(e) information required for controlling the database systems and quality control for the automatic search processes.

2. The answer (matching report) to the request referred to in paragraph 1 shall contain only the following information:

(a) an indication as to whether there were one or more matches (hits) or no matches (no hits);

(b) the date, time and indication number of the request;

(c) the date, time and indication number of the answer;

(d) the Member State codes of the requesting and requested Member States;

(e) the reference numbers of the requesting and requested Member States;

(f) the type of DNA profiles transmitted (unidentified DNA profiles or reference DNA profiles);

(g) the requested and matching DNA profiles; and

(h) information required for controlling the database systems and quality control for the automatic search processes.

3. Automated notification of a match shall only be provided if the automated search or comparison has resulted in a match of a minimum number of loci. This minimum is set out in Chapter 1 of the Annex to this Decision.

4. The Member States shall ensure that requests comply with declarations issued pursuant to Article 2(3) of Decision 2008/615/JHA. These declarations shall be reproduced in the Manual referred to in Article 18(2) of this Decision.

*Article 9*

**Transmission procedure for automated searching of unidentified DNA profiles in accordance with Article 3 of Decision 2008/615/JHA**

1. If, in a search with an unidentified DNA profile, no match has been found in the national database or a match has been found with an unidentified DNA profile, the unidentified DNA profile may then be transmitted to all other Member States' databases and if, in a search with this unidentified DNA profile, matches are found with reference DNA profiles and/or unidentified DNA profiles in other Member States' databases, these matches shall be automatically communicated and the DNA reference data transmitted to the requesting Member State; if no matches can be found in other Member States' databases, this shall be automatically communicated to the requesting Member State.

2. If, in a search with an unidentified DNA profile, a match is found in other Member States' databases, each Member State concerned may insert a note to this effect in its national database.

*Article 10*

**Transmission procedure for automated search of reference DNA profiles in accordance with Article 3 of Decision 2008/615/JHA**

If, in a search with a reference DNA profile, no match has been found in the national database with a reference DNA profile or a match has been found with an unidentified DNA profile, this reference DNA profile may then be transmitted to all other Member States' databases and if, in a search with this reference DNA profile, matches are found with reference DNA profiles and/or unidentified DNA profiles in other Member States' databases, these matches shall be automatically communicated and the DNA reference data transmitted to the requesting Member State; if no matches can be found in other Member States' databases, it shall be automatically communicated to the requesting Member State.

*Article 11*

**Transmission procedure for automated comparison of unidentified DNA profiles in accordance with Article 4 of Decision 2008/615/JHA**

1. If, in a comparison with unidentified DNA profiles, matches are found in other Member States' databases with reference DNA profiles and/or unidentified DNA profiles, these matches shall be automatically communicated and the DNA reference data transmitted to the requesting Member State.

2. If, in a comparison with unidentified DNA profiles, matches are found in other Member States' databases with unidentified DNA profiles or reference DNA profiles, each Member State concerned may insert a note to this effect in its national database.

CHAPTER 4

**DACTYLOSCOPIC DATA**

*Article 12*

**Principles for the exchange of dactyloscopic data**

1. The digitalisation of dactyloscopic data and their transmission to the other Member States shall be carried out in accordance with the uniform data format specified in Chapter 2 of the Annex to this Decision.

2. Each Member State shall ensure that the dactyloscopic data it transmits are of sufficient quality for a comparison by the automated fingerprint identification systems (AFIS).

3. The transmission procedure for the exchange of dactyloscopic data shall take place within a decentralised structure.

4. Appropriate measures shall be taken to ensure the confidentiality and integrity of dactyloscopic data being sent to other Member States, including their encryption.

5. The Member States shall use Member State codes in accordance with the ISO 3166-1 alpha-2 standard.

*Article 13*

**Search capacities for dactyloscopic data**

1. Each Member State shall ensure that its search requests do not exceed the search capacities specified by the requested Member State. Member States shall submit declarations as referred to in Article 18(2) to the General Secretariat of the Council in which they lay down their maximum search capacities per day for dactyloscopic data of identified persons and for dactyloscopic data of persons not yet identified.

2. The maximum numbers of candidates accepted for verification per transmission are set out in Chapter 2 of the Annex to this Decision.

*Article 14*

**Rules for requests and answers in connection with dactyloscopic data**

1. The requested Member State shall check the quality of the transmitted dactyloscopic data without delay by a fully automated procedure. Should the data be unsuitable for an automated comparison, the requested Member State shall inform the requesting Member State without delay.

2. The requested Member State shall conduct searches in the order in which requests are received. Requests shall be processed within 24 hours by a fully automated procedure. The requesting Member State may, if its national law so prescribes, ask for accelerated processing of its requests and the requested Member State shall conduct these searches without delay. If deadlines cannot be met for reasons of *force majeure*, the comparison shall be carried out without delay as soon as the impediments have been removed.

CHAPTER 5

**VEHICLE REGISTRATION DATA**

*Article 15*

**Principles of automated searching of vehicle registration data**

1. For automated searching of vehicle registration data Member States shall use a version of the European Vehicle and Driving Licence Information System (Eucaris) software application especially designed for the purposes of Article 12 of Decision 2008/615/JHA, and amended versions of this software.

2. Automated searching of vehicle registration data shall take place within a decentralised structure.

3. The information exchanged via the Eucaris system shall be transmitted in encrypted form.

4. The data elements of the vehicle registration data to be exchanged are specified in Chapter 3 of the Annex to this Decision.

5. In the implementation of Article 12 of Decision 2008/615/JHA, Member States may give priority to searches related to combating serious crime.

*Article 16*

**Costs**

Each Member State shall bear the costs arising from the administration, use and maintenance of the Eucaris software application referred to in Article 15(1).

CHAPTER 6

**POLICE COOPERATION**

*Article 17*

**Joint patrols and other joint operations**

1. In accordance with Chapter 5 of Decision 2008/615/JHA, and in particular with the declarations submitted pursuant to Articles 17(4), 19(2), and 19(4) of that Decision, each Member State shall designate one or more contact points in order to allow

other Member States to address competent authorities and each Member State may specify its procedures for setting up joint patrols and other joint operations, its procedures for initiatives from other Member States with regard to those operations, as well as other practical aspects, and operational modalities in relation to those operations.

2. The General Secretariat of the Council shall compile and keep up to date a list of the contact points and shall inform the competent authorities about any change to that list.

3. The competent authorities of each Member State may take the initiative to set up a joint operation. Before the start of a specific operation, the competent authorities referred to in paragraph 2 shall make written or verbal arrangements that may cover details such as:

(a) the competent authorities of the Member States for the operation;

(b) the specific purpose of the operation;

(c) the host Member State where the operation is to take place;

(d) the geographical area of the host Member State where the operation is to take place;

(e) the period covered by the operation;

(f) the specific assistance to be provided by the seconding Member State(s) to the host Member State, including officers or other officials, material and financial elements;

(g) the officers participating in the operation;

(h) the officer in charge of the operation;

(i) the powers that the officers and other officials of the seconding Member State(s) may exercise in the host Member State during the operation;

(j) the particular arms, ammunition and equipment that the seconding officers may use during the operation in accordance with Decision 2008/615/JHA;

(k) the logistic modalities as regards transport, accommodation and security;

(l) the allocation of the costs of the joint operation if it differs from that provided in the first sentence of Article 34 of Decision 2008/615/JHA;

(m) any other possible elements required.

4. The declarations, procedures and designations provided for in this Article shall be reproduced in the Manual referred to in Article 18(2).

## CHAPTER 7

## FINAL PROVISIONS

*Article 18*

### Annex and Manual

1. Further details concerning the technical and administrative implementation of Decision 2008/615/JHA are set out in the Annex to this Decision.

2. A Manual shall be prepared and kept up to date by the General Secretariat of the Council, comprising exclusively factual information provided by the Member States through declarations made pursuant to Decision 2008/615/JHA or this Decision or through notifications made to the General Secretariat of the Council. The Manual shall be in the form of a Council Document.

*Article 19*

### Independent data protection authorities

Member States shall, in accordance with Article 18(2) of this Decision, inform the General Secretariat of the Council of the independent data protection authorities or the judicial authorities as referred to in Article 30(5) of Decision 2008/615/JHA.

*Article 20*

### Preparation of decisions as referred to in Article 25(2) of Decision 2008/615/JHA

1. The Council shall take a decision as referred to in Article 25(2) of Decision 2008/615/JHA on the basis of an evaluation report which shall be based on a questionnaire.

2. With respect to the automated data exchange in accordance with Chapter 2 of Decision 2008/615/JHA, the evaluation report shall also be based on an evaluation visit and a pilot run that shall be carried out when the Member State concerned has informed the General Secretariat in accordance with the first sentence of Article 36(2) of Decision 2008/615/JHA.

3. Further details of the procedure are set out in Chapter 4 of the Annex to this Decision.

*Article 21*

### Evaluation of the data exchange

1. An evaluation of the administrative, technical and financial application of the data exchange pursuant to Chapter 2 of Decision 2008/615/JHA, and in particular the use of the mechanism of Article 15(5), shall be carried out on a regular basis. The evaluation shall relate to those Member States already applying Decision 2008/615/JHA at the time of the evaluation and shall be carried out with respect to the data categories for

which data exchange has started among the Member States concerned. The evaluation shall be based on reports of the respective Member States.

2. Further details of the procedure are set out in Chapter 4 of the Annex to this Decision.

*Article 22*

**Relationship with the Implementing Agreement of the Prüm Treaty**

For the Member States bound by the Prüm Treaty, the relevant provisions of this Decision and the Annex hereto once fully implemented shall apply instead of the corresponding provisions contained in the Implementing Agreement of the Prüm Treaty. Any other provisions of the Implementing Agreement shall remain applicable between the contracting parties of the Prüm Treaty.

*Article 23*

**Implementation**

Member States shall take the necessary measures to comply with the provisions of this Decision within the periods referred to in Article 36(1) of Decision 2008/615/JHA.

*Article 24*

**Application**

This Decision shall take effect 20 days following its publication in the *Official Journal of the European Union*.

Done at Luxembourg, 23 June 2008.

*For the Council*

*The President*

I. JARC

# Decision 2008/617 on the improvement of cooperation between the special intervention units of the Member States of the European Union in crisis situations, 23 June 2008

[OJ 2008, L 210/73–75]

6.8.2008 EN Official Journal of the European Union L 210/73

**COUNCIL DECISION 2008/617/JHA**

**of 23 June 2008**

**on the improvement of cooperation between the special intervention units of the Member States of the European Union in crisis situations**

THE COUNCIL OF THE EUROPEAN UNION,

Having regard to the Treaty on European Union, and in particular Articles 30, 32 and 34(2)(c) thereof,

Having regard to the initiative of the Republic of Austria ([1]),

Having regard to the opinion of the European Parliament ([2]),

Whereas:

(1) Article 29 of the Treaty states that the Union's objective is to provide citizens with a high level of safety within an area of freedom, security and justice by developing common action among the Member States in the fields of police and judicial cooperation in criminal matters.

(2) In their Declaration on Solidarity against Terrorism of 25 March 2004, the Heads of State and Government of the Member States of the European Union declared their firm intention that the Member States mobilise all the instruments at their disposal to assist a Member State or an acceding State in its territory at the request of its political authorities in the event of a terrorist attack.

(3) Following the attacks of 11 September 2001, the special intervention units of all law enforcement authorities of the Member States have already initiated cooperation activities under the aegis of the Police Chiefs Task Force. Since 2001, their *network, called 'Atlas'*, has conducted various seminars, studies, exchanges of materials, and joint exercises.

(4) No single Member State has all the means, resources and expertise at its disposal to deal effectively with all possible kinds of specific or large-scale crisis situations requiring special intervention. It is therefore of crucial importance that each Member State be able to request the assistance of another Member State.

(5) Council Decision 2008/615/JHA of 23 June 2008 on the stepping up of cross-border cooperation, particularly in combating terrorism and cross-border crime ([3]) (Prüm Decision), and in particular Article 18 thereof, regulates forms of police assistance between Member States in connection with mass gatherings and similar major events, disasters and serious accidents. This Decision does not cover mass gatherings, natural disasters or serious accidents within the meaning of Article 18 of the Prüm Decision but complements those provisions of the Prüm Decision envisaging forms of police assistance between Member States through special intervention units in other situations, namely in man-made crisis situations presenting a serious direct physical threat to persons, property, infrastructure or institutions, in particular hostage taking, hijacking and similar events.

(6) The availability of this legal framework and of a compilation indicating the competent authorities will allow Member States to react speedily and gain time should such a crisis situation arise. Moreover, with a view to enhancing Member States' ability to prevent and respond to such crisis situations, and in particular terrorist incidents, it is essential for the special intervention units to meet regularly and organise joint trainings, so as to benefit from mutual experiences,

HAS DECIDED AS FOLLOWS:

*Article 1*

**Subject matter**

This Decision lays down general rules and conditions to allow for special intervention units of one Member State to provide assistance and/or operate on the territory of another Member State (hereinafter referred to as the requesting Member State) in cases where they have been invited by the requesting Member State and have agreed to do so in order to deal with a crisis situation. The practical details and implementing arrangements complementing this Decision shall be agreed directly between the requesting Member State and the requested Member State.

*Article 2*

**Definitions**

For the purpose of this Decision:

(a) 'special intervention unit' shall mean any law enforcement unit of a Member State which is specialised in the control of a crisis situation;

([1]) OJ C 321, 29.12.2006, p. 45.

([2]) Opinion of 31 January 2008 (not yet published in the Official Journal).

([3]) See page 1 of this Official Journal.

L 210/74 EN Official Journal of the European Union 6.8.2008

(b) 'crisis situation' shall mean any situation in which the competent authorities of a Member State have reasonable grounds to believe that there is a criminal offence presenting a serious direct physical threat to persons, property, infrastructure or institutions in that Member State, in particular those situations referred to in Article 1(1) of Council Framework Decision 2002/475/JHA of 13 June 2002 on combating terrorism [1];

(c) 'competent authority' shall mean the national authority which may make requests and give authorisations regarding the deployment of the special intervention units.

*Article 3*

**Assistance to another Member State**

1. Through a request via the competent authorities, setting out the nature of the assistance requested as well as the operational necessity therefor, a Member State may ask to be assisted by a special intervention unit of another Member State with a view to dealing with a crisis situation. The competent authority of the requested Member State may accept or refuse such a request or may propose a different kind of assistance.

2. Subject to agreement between the Member States concerned, assistance may consist of providing the requesting Member State with equipment and/or expertise and/or of carrying out actions on the territory of that Member State, using weapons if so required.

3. In the case of actions on the territory of the requesting Member State, officers of the assisting special intervention unit shall be authorised to operate in a supporting capacity on the territory of the requesting Member State and take all necessary measures to provide the requested assistance in so far as they:

(a) operate under the responsibility, authority and direction of the requesting Member State and in accordance with the law of the requesting Member State; and

(b) operate within the limits of their powers under their national law.

*Article 4*

**Civil and criminal liability**

When officers of a Member State operate within another Member State and/or equipment is used under this Decision, the provisions on civil and criminal liability, set out in Articles 21(4) and (5) and 22 of the Prüm Decision shall apply.

[1] OJ L 164, 22.6.2002, p. 3.

*Article 5*

**Meetings and joint training**

The participating Member States shall ensure that their special intervention units hold meetings and organise joint training and exercises, whenever necessary, with a view to exchanging experience, expertise and general, practical and technical information on dealing with a crisis situation. Such meetings, training and exercises may be funded under possibilities offered by the financial programmes of the Union to obtain grants from the budget of the European Union. In this context, the Member State holding the Presidency of the Union shall endeavour to ensure that such meetings, training and exercises take place.

*Article 6*

**Costs**

The requesting Member State shall bear the operational costs incurred by the requested Member State's special intervention units in connection with the application of Article 3, including transport and accommodation costs, unless otherwise agreed between the Member States concerned.

*Article 7*

**Relation to other instruments**

1. Without prejudice to their commitments under other acts adopted pursuant to Title VI of the Treaty, in particular the Prüm Decision:

(a) Member States may continue to apply bilateral or multilateral agreements or arrangements on cross-border cooperation in force on 23 June 2008 in so far as such agreements or arrangements are not incompatible with the objectives of this Decision;

(b) Member States may conclude or bring into force bilateral or multilateral agreements or arrangements on cross-border cooperation after 23 December 2008 in so far as such agreements or arrangements provide for the objectives of this Decision to be extended or enlarged.

2. The agreements and arrangements referred to in paragraph 1 may not affect relations with Member States which are not parties thereto.

3. Member States shall inform the Council and the Commission of the agreements or arrangements referred to in paragraph 1.

6.8.2008 EN Official Journal of the European Union L 210/75

*Article 8*

**Final provisions**

The General Secretariat of the Council shall compile and keep up to date the list of the competent authorities of the Member States which may make requests and give authorisations for providing assistance as referred to in Article 3.

The General Secretariat of the Council shall inform the authorities mentioned in paragraph 1 of any change to the list established pursuant to this Article.

*Article 9*

**Entry into force**

This Decision shall enter into force on 23 December 2008.

Done at Luxembourg, 23 June 2008.

*For the Council*

*The President*

I. JARC

# Decision 2008/633 concerning access for consultation of the Visa Information System (VIS) by designated authorities of Member States and by Europol for the purposes of the prevention, detection and investigation of terrorist offences and of other serious criminal offences, 23 June 2008

[OJ 2008, L 218/129–136]

13.8.2008 EN Official Journal of the European Union L 218/129

III

*(Acts adopted under the EU Treaty)*

## ACTS ADOPTED UNDER TITLE VI OF THE EU TREATY

### COUNCIL DECISION 2008/633/JHA

**of 23 June 2008**

**concerning access for consultation of the Visa Information System (VIS) by designated authorities of Member States and by Europol for the purposes of the prevention, detection and investigation of terrorist offences and of other serious criminal offences**

THE COUNCIL OF THE EUROPEAN UNION,

Having regard to the Treaty on European Union, and in particular Article 30(1)(b) and Article 34(2)(c) thereof,

Having regard to the proposal from the Commission,

Having regard to the Opinion of the European Parliament,

Whereas:

(1) Council Decision 2004/512/EC of 8 June 2004 establishing the Visa Information System (VIS) ([1]) established the VIS as a system for the exchange of visa data between Member States. The establishment of the VIS represents one of the key initiatives within the policies of the European Union aimed at establishing an area of freedom, security and justice. The VIS should have the purpose of improving the implementation of the common visa policy and should also contribute towards internal security and to combating terrorism under clearly defined and monitored circumstances.

(2) During its meeting of 7 March 2005 the Council adopted conclusions stating that 'in order to achieve fully the aim of improving internal security and the fight against terrorism', Member State authorities responsible for internal security should be guaranteed access to the VIS, 'in the course of their duties in relation to the prevention, detection and investigation of criminal offences, including terrorist acts and threats', 'subject to strict compliance with the rules governing the protection of personal data'.

(3) It is essential in the fight against terrorism and other serious crimes for the relevant services to have the fullest and most up-to-date information in their respective fields. The Member States' competent national services need information if they are to perform their tasks. The information contained in the VIS may be necessary for the purposes of preventing and combating terrorism and serious crimes and should therefore be available, subject to the conditions set out in this Decision, for consultation by the designated authorities.

(4) Moreover, the European Council has stated that Europol has a key role with respect to cooperation between Member States' authorities in the field of cross-border crime investigation in supporting Union-wide crime prevention, analyses and investigation. Consequently, Europol should also have access to VIS data within the framework of its tasks and in accordance with the Convention of 26 July 1995 on the Establishment of a European Police Office ([2]).

(5) This Decision complements Regulation (EC) No 767/2008 of the European Parliament and of the Council of 9 July 2008 concerning the Visa Information System (VIS) and the exchange of data between Member States on 7 stay-visas (VIS Regulation) ([3]) insofar as it provides for a legal base under Title VI of the Treaty on European Union authorising access to the VIS for designated authorities and for Europol.

([1]) OJ L 213, 15.6.2004, p. 5.

([2]) OJ C 316, 27.11.1995, p. 2. Convention as last amended by the Protocol amending that Convention (OJ C 2, 6.1.2004, p. 3).

([3]) See page 60 of this Official Journal.

(6) It is necessary to designate the competent Member States' authorities as well as the central access points through which access is done and to keep a list of the operating units within the designated authorities that are authorised to access the VIS for the specific purposes of the prevention, detection and investigation of terrorist offences and other serious criminal offences as referred to in Council Framework Decision 2002/584/JHA of 13 June 2002 on the European arrest warrant and the surrender procedures between Member States ([1]). It is essential to ensure that the duly empowered staff with a right to access the VIS is limited to those who 'have a need to know' and possess appropriate knowledge about data security and data protection rules.

(7) Requests for access to the VIS should be made by the operating units within the designated authorities to the central access points. These central access points should then process the requests for access to the VIS following a verification whether all conditions for access are fulfilled. In an exceptional case of urgency the central access points should process the request immediately and only do the verification afterwards.

(8) For the purposes of protection of personal data, and in particular to exclude routine access, the processing of VIS data should only be on a case-by-case basis. Such a specific case exists in particular when the access for consultation is connected to a specific event or to a danger associated with serious crime, or to (a) specific person(s) in respect of whom there are serious grounds for believing that the person(s) will commit or has (have) committed terrorist offences or other serious criminal offences or that the person(s) has (have) a relevant connection with such (a) person(s). The designated authorities and Europol should thus only search data contained in the VIS when they have reasonable grounds to believe that such a search will provide information that will substantially assist them in preventing, detecting or investigating serious crime.

(9) Once the proposed Framework Decision on the protection of personal data processed in the framework of police and judicial cooperation in criminal matters has entered into force it should apply to the personal data which are processed pursuant to this Decision. However, until the rules set out in that Framework Decision are applicable and in order to supplement them, adequate provisions have to be provided for to ensure the necessary data protection. Each Member State should ensure an adequate data protection level in its national law which at least corresponds to that resulting from the Council of Europe Convention of 28 January 1981 for the Protection of Individuals with regard to Automatic Processing of Personal Data and the corresponding case law pursuant to Article 8 of the Convention for the Protection of Human Rights and Fundamental Freedoms and, for those Member States which have ratified it, the Additional Protocol of 8 November 2001 to that Convention, and should take into account Recommendation No R (87) 15 of 17 September 1987 of the Committee of Ministers of the Council of Europe Regulating the Use of Personal Data in the Police Sector.

(10) The effective monitoring of the application of this Decision should be evaluated at regular intervals.

(11) Since the objectives of this Decision, namely the creation of obligations and conditions for access for consultation of VIS data by Member States' designated authorities and by Europol, cannot be sufficiently achieved by the Member States and can, therefore, by reason of the scale and effects of the action, be better achieved at the level of the European Union, the Council may adopt measures in accordance with the principle of subsidiarity, referred to in Article 2 of the Treaty on European Union and defined in Article 5 of the Treaty establishing the European Community. In accordance with the principle of proportionality, as set out in that Article, this Decision does not go beyond what is necessary in order to achieve those objectives.

(12) In accordance with Article 47 of the Treaty on European Union, this Decision does not affect the competences of the European Community, in particular as exercised in Regulation (EC) No 767/2008 and in Directive 95/46/EC of the European Parliament and of the Council of 24 October 1995 on the protection of individuals with regard to the processing of personal data and on the free movement of such data ([2]).

(13) This Decision constitutes a development of provisions of the Schengen *acquis* in which the United Kingdom does not take part in accordance with Council Decision 2000/365/EC of 29 May 2000 concerning the request of the United Kingdom of Great Britain and Northern Ireland to take part in some of the provisions of the Schengen *acquis* ([3]). The United Kingdom is therefore not taking part in its adoption and is not bound by it or subject to its application.

(14) This Decision constitutes a development of provisions of the Schengen *acquis* in which Ireland does not take part in accordance with Council Decision 2002/192/EC of 28 February 2002 concerning Ireland's request to take part in some of the provisions of the Schengen *acquis* ([4]). Ireland is therefore not taking part in its adoption and is not bound by it or subject to its application.

([1]) OJ L 190, 18.7.2002, p. 1.

([2]) OJ L 281, 23.11.1995, p. 31. Directive as amended by Regulation (EC) No 1882/2003 (OJ L 284, 31.10.2003, p. 1).

([3]) OJ L 131, 1.6.2000, p. 43.

([4]) OJ L 64, 7.3.2002, p. 20.

13.8.2008 EN Official Journal of the European Union L 218/131

(15) However, in accordance with Council Framework Decision 2006/960/JHA of 18 December 2006 on simplifying the exchange of information and intelligence between law enforcement authorities of the Member States of the European Union ([1]), information contained in the VIS can be provided to the United Kingdom and Ireland by the competent authorities of the Member States whose designated authorities have access to the VIS pursuant to this Decision. Information held in the national visa registers of the United Kingdom and Ireland can be provided to the competent law enforcement authorities of the other Member States. Any form of direct access for central authorities of the United Kingdom and Ireland to the VIS would, under the present state of their participation in the Schengen *acquis*, require an agreement between the Community and those Member States, possibly to be supplemented by other rules specifying the conditions and procedures for such access.

(16) As regards Iceland and Norway, this Decision constitutes, with the exception of Article 7, a development of provisions of the Schengen *acquis* within the meaning of the Agreement concluded by the Council of the European Union and the Republic of Iceland and the Kingdom of Norway concerning the association of those two States with the implementation, application and development of the Schengen *acquis* ([2]) which fall within the area referred to in Article 1, point B of Council Decision 1999/437/EC ([3]) on certain arrangements for the application of that Agreement.

(17) As regards Switzerland, this Decision constitutes, with the exception of Article 7, a development of the provisions of the Schengen *acquis* within the meaning of the Agreement signed by the European Union, the European Community and the Swiss Confederation concerning the association of the Swiss Confederation with the implementation, application and development of the Schengen *acquis* which fall within the area referred to in Article 1, point B of Decision 1999/437/EC read in conjunction with Article 4(1) of Council Decision 2004/849/EC ([4]).

(18) This Decision, save Article 6, constitutes an act building on the Schengen *acquis* or otherwise related to it within the meaning of Article 3(2) of the 2003 Act of Accession and Article 4(2) of the 2005 Act of Accession.

(19) This Decision respects the fundamental rights and observes the principles reflected in particular in the Charter of Fundamental Rights of the European Union,

([1]) OJ L 386, 18.12.2006, p. 89.
([2]) OJ L 176, 10.7.1999, p. 36.
([3]) OJ L 176, 10.7.1999, p. 31.
([4]) Decision 2004/849/EC of 25 October 2004 on the signing, on behalf of the European Union, and on the provisional application of certain provisions of the Agreement between the European Union, the European Community and the Swiss Confederation concerning the Swiss Confederation's association with the implementation, application and development of the Schengen *acquis* (OJ L 368, 15.12.2004, p. 26).

HAS DECIDED AS FOLLOWS:

*Article 1*

**Subject matter and scope**

This Decision lays down the conditions under which Member States' designated authorities and the European Police Office (Europol) may obtain access for consultation of the Visa Information System (VIS) for the purposes of the prevention, detection and investigation of terrorist offences and of other serious criminal offences.

*Article 2*

**Definitions**

1. For the purposes of this Decision, the following definitions shall apply:

(a) 'Visa Information System (VIS)' means the Visa Information System as established by Decision 2004/512/EC;

(b) 'Europol' means the European Police Office as established by the Convention of 26 July 1995 on the Establishment of a European Police Office (the Europol Convention);

(c) 'terrorist offences' means the offences under national law which correspond or are equivalent to the offences in Articles 1 to 4 of Council Framework Decision 2002/475/JHA of 13 June 2002 on combating terrorism ([5]);

(d) 'serious criminal offences' means the forms of crime which correspond or are equivalent to those referred to in Article 2(2) of Framework Decision 2002/584/JHA;

(e) 'designated authorities' means authorities which are responsible for the prevention, detection or investigation of terrorist offences or of other serious criminal offences and designated by the Member States pursuant to Article 3.

2. The definitions in Regulation (EC) No 767/2008 shall also apply.

*Article 3*

**Designated authorities and central access points**

1. Member States shall designate the authorities referred to in Article 2(1)(e) which are authorised to access VIS data pursuant to this Decision.

2. Every Member State shall keep a list of the designated authorities. By 2 December 2008 every Member State shall notify in a declaration to the Commission and the General Secretariat of the Council their designated authorities and may at any time amend or replace its declaration by another declaration.

([5]) OJ L 164, 22.6.2002, p. 3.

3. Every Member State shall designate the central access point(s) through which the access is done. Member States may designate more than one central access point to reflect their organisational and administrative structure in fulfilment of their constitutional or legal requirements. By 2 December 2008 every Member State shall notify in a declaration to the Commission and the General Secretariat of the Council their central access point(s) and may at any time amend or replace its declaration by another declaration.

4. The Commission shall publish the declarations referred to in paragraphs 2 and 3 in the *Official Journal of the European Union*.

5. At national level, each Member State shall keep a list of the operating units within the designated authorities that are authorised to access the VIS through the central access point(s).

6. Only duly empowered staff of the operational units as well as the central access point(s) shall be authorised to access the VIS in accordance with Article 4.

*Article 4*

**Procedure for access to the VIS**

1. Where the conditions of Article 5 are fulfilled the operating units referred to in Article 3(5) shall submit a reasoned written or electronic request to the central access points referred to in Article 3(3) to access the VIS. Upon receipt of a request for access the central access point(s) shall verify whether the conditions for access referred to in Article 5 are fulfilled. If all conditions for access are fulfilled, the duly authorised staff of the central access point(s) shall process the requests. The VIS data accessed shall be transmitted to the operating units referred to in Article 3(5) in such a way as not to compromise the security of the data.

2. In an exceptional case of urgency, the central access point(s) may receive written, electronic or oral requests. In such cases, the central access point(s) shall process the request immediately and only verify *ex-post* whether all the conditions of Article 5 are fulfilled, including whether an exceptional case of urgency existed. The *ex-post* verification shall take place without undue delay after the processing of the request.

*Article 5*

**Conditions for access to VIS data by designated authorities of Member States**

1. Access to the VIS for consultation by designated authorities shall take place within the scope of their powers and if the following conditions are met:

(a) access for consultation must be necessary for the purpose of the prevention, detection or investigation of terrorist offences or other serious criminal offences;

(b) access for consultation must be necessary in a specific case;

(c) there are reasonable grounds to consider that consultation of VIS data will substantially contribute to the prevention, detection or investigation of any of the criminal offences in question.

2. Consultation of the VIS shall be limited to searching with any of the following VIS data in the application file:

(a) surname, surname at birth (former surname(s)); first name(s); sex; date, place and country of birth;

(b) current nationality and nationality at birth;

(c) type and number of the travel document, the authority which issued it and the date of issue and of expiry;

(d) main destination and duration of the intended stay;

(e) purpose of travel;

(f) intended date of arrival and departure;

(g) intended border of first entry or transit route;

(h) residence;

(i) fingerprints;

(j) type of visa and the number of the visa sticker;

(k) details of the person issuing an invitation and/or liable to pay the applicant's subsistence costs during the stay.

3. Consultation of the VIS shall, in the event of a hit, give access to all of the data listed in paragraph 2 as well as to:

(a) any other data taken from the application form;

(b) photographs;

(c) the data entered in respect of any visa issued, refused, annulled, revoked or extended.

*Article 6*

**Conditions for access to VIS data by designated authorities of a Member State in respect of which Regulation (EC) No 767/2008 has not yet been put into effect**

1. Access to the VIS for consultation by designated authorities of a Member State in respect of which Regulation (EC) No 767/2008 has not yet been put into effect shall take place within the scope of their powers and

(a) subject to the same conditions as referred to in Article 5(1); and

(b) by a duly motivated written or electronic request to a designated authority of a Member State to which Regulation (EC) No 767/2008 applies; that authority shall then request the national central access point(s) to consult the VIS.

2. A Member State in respect of which Regulation (EC) No 767/2008 has not yet been put into effect shall make its visa information available to Member States to which Regulation (EC) No 767/2008 applies, on the basis of a duly reasoned written or electronic request, subject to compliance with the conditions laid down in Article 5(1).

3. Article 8(1) and (3) to (6), Article 9(1), Article 10(1) and (3), Article 12, Article 13(1) and (3) shall apply accordingly.

*Article 7*

**Conditions for access to VIS data by Europol**

1. Access to the VIS for consultation by Europol shall take place within the limits of its mandate and:

(a) when necessary for the performance of its tasks pursuant to Article 3(1), point 2 of the Europol Convention and for the purposes of a specific analysis as referred to in Article 10 of the Europol Convention; or

(b) when necessary for the performance of its tasks pursuant to Article 3(1), point 2 of the Europol Convention and for an analysis of a general nature and of a strategic type, as referred to in Article 10 of the Europol Convention, provided that VIS data is rendered anonymous by Europol prior to such processing and retained in a form in which identification of the data subjects is no longer possible.

2. Article 5(2) and (3) shall apply accordingly.

3. Europol shall designate a specialised unit for the purpose of this Decision with duly empowered Europol officials to act as the central access point to access the VIS for consultation.

4. Processing of information obtained by Europol from access to the VIS shall be subject to the consent of the Member State which has entered that data in the VIS. Such consent shall be obtained via the Europol national unit of that Member State.

*Article 8*

**Protection of personal data**

1. The processing of personal data consulted under this Decision shall be subject to the following rules and to the national law of the consulting Member State. With regard to the processing of personal data consulted under this Decision, each Member State shall ensure an adequate data protection level in its national law which at least corresponds to that resulting from the Council of Europe Convention of 28 January 1981 for the Protection of Individuals with regard to Automatic Processing of Personal Data and, for those Member States which have ratified it, the Additional Protocol of 8 November 2001 to that Convention, and shall take into account Recommendation No R (87)15 of 17 September 1987 of the Committee of Ministers of the Council of Europe Regulating the Use of Personal Data in the Police Sector.

2. The processing of personal data by Europol pursuant to this Decision shall be in accordance with the Europol Convention and the rules adopted in implementation thereof and supervised by the independent joint supervisory body established by Article 24 of the Convention.

3. Personal data obtained pursuant to this Decision from the VIS shall only be processed for the purposes of the prevention, detection, investigation and prosecution of terrorist offences or other serious criminal offences.

4. Personal data obtained pursuant to this Decision from the VIS shall not be transferred or made available to a third country or to an international organisation. However, in an exceptional case of urgency such data may be transferred or made available to a third country or an international organisation, exclusively for the purposes of the prevention and detection of terrorist offences and of other serious criminal offences and under the conditions set out in Article 5(1) of this Decision, subject to the consent of the Member State having entered the data into the VIS and in accordance with the national law of the Member State transferring the data or making them available. In accordance with national law, Member States shall ensure that records are kept of such transfers and make them available to national data protection authorities on request. The transfer of data by the Member State that entered the data in the VIS according to Regulation (EC) No 767/2008 shall be subject to the national law of that Member State.

5. The competent body or bodies which, in accordance with national law, are charged with the supervision of the processing of personal data by the authorities designated under this Decision shall monitor the lawfulness of the processing of personal data pursuant to this Decision. The Member States shall ensure that these bodies have sufficient resources to fulfil the tasks entrusted to them under this Decision.

6. The bodies referred to in paragraph 5 shall ensure that at least every four years an audit of the processing of personal data pursuant to this Decision is carried out, where applicable according to international auditing standards.

7. Member States and Europol shall allow the competent body or bodies referred to in paragraphs 2 and 5 to obtain the necessary information to enable them to carry out their tasks in accordance with this Article.

8. Before being authorised to process data stored in the VIS, the staff of the authorities having a right to access the VIS shall receive appropriate training about data security and data protection rules and shall be informed of any relevant criminal offences and penalties.

*Article 9*

**Data security**

1. The Member State responsible shall ensure the security of the data during transmission to the designated authorities and when received by them.

2. Each Member State shall adopt the necessary security measures with respect to data to be retrieved from the VIS pursuant to this Decision and to be subsequently stored, in particular in order to:

(a) physically protect data, including by making contingency plans for the protection of critical infrastructure;

(b) deny unauthorised persons access to national installations in which the Member State stores data (checks at entrance to the installation);

(c) prevent the unauthorised reading, copying, modification or removal of data media (data media control);

(d) prevent the unauthorised inspection, modification or deletion of stored personal data (storage control);

(e) prevent the unauthorised processing of data from the VIS (control of data processing);

(f) ensure that persons authorised to access the VIS have access only to the data covered by their access authorisation, by means of individual and unique user identities and confidential access modes only (data access control);

(g) ensure that all authorities with a right of access to the VIS create profiles describing the functions and responsibilities of persons who are authorised to access and search the data and make these profiles available to the national supervisory authorities referred to in Article 8(5) without delay upon their request (personnel profiles);

(h) ensure that it is possible to verify and establish to which bodies personal data may be transmitted using data communication equipment (communication control);

(i) ensure that it is possible to verify and establish what data has been retrieved from the VIS, when, by whom and for what purpose (control of data recording);

(j) prevent the unauthorised reading and copying of personal data during their transmission from the VIS, in particular by means of appropriate encryption techniques (transport control);

(k) monitor the effectiveness of the security measures referred to in this paragraph and take the necessary organisational measures related to internal monitoring to ensure compliance with this Decision (self-auditing).

*Article 10*

**Liability**

1. Any person who, or Member State which, has suffered damage as a result of an unlawful processing operation or any act incompatible with this Decision shall be entitled to receive compensation from the Member State which is responsible for the damage suffered. That Member State shall be exempted from its liability, in whole or in part, if it proves that it is not responsible for the event giving rise to the damage.

2. If any failure of a Member State to comply with its obligations under this Decision causes damage to the VIS, that Member State shall be held liable for such damage, unless and insofar as another Member State failed to take reasonable measures to prevent the damage from occurring or to minimise its impact.

3. Claims for compensation against a Member State for the damage referred to in paragraphs 1 and 2 shall be governed by the provisions of national law of the defendant Member State.

*Article 11*

**Self-monitoring**

Member States shall ensure that each authority entitled to access VIS data takes the measures necessary to comply with this Decision and cooperates, where necessary, with the national body or bodies referred to in Article 8(5).

*Article 12*

**Penalties**

Member States shall take the necessary measures to ensure that any use of VIS data contrary to the provisions of this Decision is punishable by penalties, including administrative and/or criminal penalties, that are effective, proportionate and dissuasive.

*Article 13*

**Keeping of VIS data in national files**

1. Data retrieved from the VIS may be kept in national files only when necessary in an individual case in accordance with the purposes set out in this Decision and in accordance with the relevant legal provisions including those concerning data protection and for no longer than necessary in the individual case.

2. Paragraph 1 shall not prejudice the provisions of national law of a Member State concerning the entry by its designated authorities in their national files of data which that Member State entered in the VIS according to Regulation (EC) No 767/2008.

3. Any use of data which does not comply with paragraphs 1 and 2 shall be considered a misuse under the national law of each Member State.

*Article 14*

**Right of access, correction and deletion**

1. The right of persons to have access to data relating to them obtained from the VIS pursuant to this Decision shall be exercised in accordance with the law of the Member State in which they invoke that right.

2. If national law so provides, the national supervisory authority shall decide whether information is to be communicated and by what procedures.

3. A Member State other than that which has entered the data into the VIS according to Regulation (EC) No 767/2008 may communicate information concerning such data only if it first gives the Member State entering the data an opportunity to state its position.

4. Information shall not be communicated to the data subject if this is indispensable for the performance of a lawful task in connection with the data or for the protection of the rights and freedoms of third parties.

5. Any person has the right to have factually inaccurate data relating to him corrected or unlawfully stored data relating to him deleted. If the designated authorities receive such a request or if they have any other evidence to suggest that data processed in the VIS is inaccurate they shall immediately inform the visa authority of the Member State which has entered the data in the VIS, which shall check the data concerned and, if necessary, correct or delete it immediately, pursuant to Article 24 of Regulation (EC) No 767/2008.

6. The individual concerned shall be informed as soon as possible and in any event not later than 60 days from the date on which he applies for access or sooner if national law so provides.

7. The individual concerned shall be informed about the follow-up given to the exercise of his rights of correction and deletion as soon as possible and in any event not later than three months from the date on which he applies for correction or deletion or sooner if national law so provides.

8. In each Member State any person shall have the right to bring an action or a complaint before the competent authorities or courts of that Member State which refused the right of access to or the right of correction or deletion of data relating to him, provided for in this Article.

*Article 15*

**Costs**

Each Member State and Europol shall set up and maintain, at their expense, the technical infrastructure necessary to implement this Decision, and be responsible for bearing the costs resulting from access to the VIS for the purposes of this Decision.

*Article 16*

**Keeping of records**

1. Each Member State and Europol shall ensure that all data processing operations resulting from access to the VIS for consultation pursuant to this Decision are recorded for the purposes of checking whether the search is admissible or not, for the purpose of monitoring the lawfulness of data processing, for self-monitoring, ensuring the proper functioning of the system, data integrity and security.

Those records shall show:

(a) the exact purpose of the access for consultation referred to in Article 5(1)(a), including the form of terrorist offence or other serious criminal offence concerned, and for Europol, the exact purpose of the access for consultation referred to in Article 7(1);

(b) the respective national file reference;

(c) the date and exact time of access;

(d) where applicable that use has been made of the procedure referred to in Article 4(2);

(e) the data used for consultation;

(f) the type of data consulted;

(g) according to national rules or the rules of the Europol Convention the identifying mark of the official who carried out the search and of the official who ordered the search or supply.

2. Records containing personal data shall be used only for the data protection monitoring of the legality of data processing as well as to ensure data security. Only records containing data of a non-personal nature may be used for the monitoring and evaluation referred to in Article 17.

3. These records shall be protected by appropriate measures against unauthorised access and abuse and deleted after a period of one year after the retention period referred to in Article 23(1) of Regulation (EC) No 767/2008 has expired, unless they are required for monitoring procedures referred to in paragraph 2 of this Article which have already begun.

*Article 17*

**Monitoring and evaluation**

1. The Management Authority referred to in Regulation (EC) No 767/2008 shall ensure that systems are in place to monitor the functioning of the VIS pursuant to this Decision against objectives, in terms of output, cost-effectiveness, security and quality of service.

2. For the purpose of technical maintenance, the Management Authority shall have access to the necessary information relating to the processing operations performed in the VIS.

3. Two years after the VIS is brought into operation and every two years thereafter, the Management Authority shall submit a report to the European Parliament, the Council and the Commission on the technical functioning of the VIS pursuant to this Decision. That report shall include information on the performance of the VIS against quantitative indicators predefined by the Commission, and in particular on the need and use made of Article 4(2).

4. Three years after the VIS is brought into operation and every four years thereafter, the Commission shall produce an overall evaluation of the VIS pursuant to this Decision. This evaluation shall include an examination of the results achieved against objectives and an assessment of the continuing validity of the underlying rationale behind this Decision, the application of this Decision in respect of the VIS, the security of the VIS and any implications for future operations. The Commission shall transmit the evaluation reports to the European Parliament and the Council.

5. The Member States and Europol shall provide to the Management Authority and the Commission the information necessary to draft the reports referred to in paragraph 3 and 4. This information shall not jeopardise working methods nor include information that reveals sources, staff members or investigations of the designated authorities.

6. The Management Authority shall provide the Commission with the information necessary to produce the overall evaluations referred to in paragraph 4.

7. During the transitional period before the Management Authority takes up its responsibilities, the Commission shall be responsible for producing and submitting the reports referred to in paragraph 3.

*Article 18*

**Entry into force and date of application**

1. This Decision shall enter into force on the 20th day following its publication in the *Official Journal of the European Union*.

2. This Decision shall take effect from a date to be determined by the Council once the Commission has informed the Council that Regulation (EC) No 767/2008 has entered into force and is fully applicable.

The General Secretariat of the Council shall publish that date in the *Official Journal of the European Union*.

Done at Luxembourg, 23 June 2008.

*For the Council*

*The President*

I. JARC

# Framework Decision 2008/675 on taking account of convictions in the Member States of the European Union in the course of new criminal proceedings, 24 July 2008

[OJ 2008, L 220/32–34]

L 220/32 EN Official Journal of the European Union 15.8.2008

III

*(Acts adopted under the EU Treaty)*

# ACTS ADOPTED UNDER TITLE VI OF THE EU TREATY

## COUNCIL FRAMEWORK DECISION 2008/675/JHA

**of 24 July 2008**

**on taking account of convictions in the Member States of the European Union in the course of new criminal proceedings**

THE COUNCIL OF THE EUROPEAN UNION,

Having regard to the Treaty on European Union, and in particular Articles 31 and 34(2)(b) thereof,

Having regard to the proposal from the Commission,

Having regard to the Opinion of the European Parliament [1],

Whereas:

(1) The European Union has set itself the objective of maintaining and developing an area of freedom, security and justice. This objective requires that it be possible for information on convictions handed down in the Member States to be taken into account outside the convicting Member State, both in order to prevent new offences and in the course of new criminal proceedings.

(2) On 29 November 2000 the Council, in accordance with the conclusions of the Tampere European Council, adopted the programme of measures to implement the principle of mutual recognition of decisions in criminal matters [2], which provides for the 'adoption of one or more instruments establishing the principle that a court in one Member State must be able to take account of final criminal judgments rendered by the courts in other Member States for the purposes of assessing the offender's criminal record and establishing whether he has reoffended, and in order to determine the type of sentence applicable and the arrangements for enforcing it'.

(3) The purpose of this Framework Decision is to establish a minimum obligation for Member States to take into account convictions handed down in other Member States. Thus this Framework Decision should not prevent Member States from taking into account, in accordance with their law and when they have information available, for example, final decisions of administrative authorities whose decisions can be appealed against in the criminal courts establishing guilt of a criminal offence or an act punishable under national law by virtue of being an infringement of the rules of law.

(4) Some Member States attach effects to convictions handed down in other Member States, whereas others take account only of convictions handed down by their own courts.

(5) The principle that the Member States should attach to a conviction handed down in other Member States effects equivalent to those attached to a conviction handed down by their own courts in accordance with national law should be affirmed, whether those effects be regarded by national law as matters of fact or of procedural or substantive law. However, this Framework Decision does not seek to harmonise the consequences attached by the different national legislations to the existence of previous convictions, and the obligation to take into account previous convictions handed down in other Member States exists only to the extent that previous national convictions are taken into account under national law.

(6) In contrast to other instruments, this Framework Decision does not aim at the execution in one Member State of judicial decisions taken in other Member States, but rather aims at enabling consequences to be attached to a previous conviction handed down in one Member State in the course of new criminal proceedings in another Member State to the extent that such consequences are attached to previous national convictions under the law of that other Member State.

(1) Opinion of 27 September 2006 (not yet published in the Official Journal).
(2) OJ C 12, 15.1.2001, p. 10.

Therefore this Framework Decision contains no obligation to take into account such previous convictions, for example, in cases where the information obtained under applicable instruments is not sufficient, where a national conviction would not have been possible regarding the act for which the previous conviction had been imposed or where the previously imposed sanction is unknown to the national legal system.

(7) The effects of a conviction handed down in another Member State should be equivalent to the effects of a national decision at the pre-trial stage of criminal proceedings, at the trial stage and at the time of execution of the sentence.

(8) Where, in the course of criminal proceedings in a Member State, information is available on a previous conviction in another Member State, it should as far as possible be avoided that the person concerned is treated less favourably than if the previous conviction had been a national conviction.

(9) Article 3(5) should be interpreted, *inter alia*, in line with recital 8, in such a manner that if the national court in the new criminal proceedings, when taking into account a previously imposed sentence handed down in another Member State, is of the opinion that imposing a certain level of sentence within the limits of national law would be disproportionately harsh on the offender, considering his or her circumstances, and if the purpose of the punishment can be achieved by a lower sentence, it may reduce the level of sentence accordingly, if doing so would have been possible in purely domestic cases.

(10) This Framework Decision is to replace the provisions of Article 56 of the European Convention of 28 May 1970 on the International Validity of Criminal Judgments, concerning the taking into consideration of criminal judgments, as between the Member States parties to that Convention.

(11) This Framework Decision respects the principle of subsidiarity provided for by Article 2 of the Treaty on European Union and Article 5 of the Treaty establishing the European Community in so far as it aims to approximate the laws and regulations of the Member States, which cannot be done adequately by the Member States acting unilaterally and requires concerted action in the European Union. In accordance with the principle of proportionality, as set out in Article 5 of the Treaty establishing the European Community, this Framework Decision does not go beyond what is necessary in order to achieve that objective.

(12) This Framework Decision respects the fundamental rights and observes the principles recognised by Article 6 of the Treaty on European Union and reflected in the Charter of Fundamental Rights of the European Union.

(13) This Framework Decision respects the variety of domestic solutions and procedures required for taking into account a previous conviction handed down in another Member State. The exclusion of a possibility to review a previous conviction should not prevent a Member State from issuing a decision, if necessary, in order to attach the equivalent legal effects to such previous conviction. However, the procedures involved in issuing such a decision should not, in view of the time and procedures or formalities required, render it impossible to attach equivalent effects to a previous conviction handed down in another Member State.

(14) Interference with a judgment or its execution covers, *inter alia*, situations where, according to the national law of the second Member State, the sanction imposed in a previous judgment is to be absorbed by or included in another sanction, which is then to be effectively executed, to the extent that the first sentence has not already been executed or its execution has not been transferred to the second Member State,

HAS ADOPTED THIS FRAMEWORK DECISION:

*Article 1*

**Subject matter**

1. The purpose of this Framework Decision is to determine the conditions under which, in the course of criminal proceedings in a Member State against a person, previous convictions handed down against the same person for different facts in other Member States, are taken into account.

2. This Framework Decision shall not have the effect of amending the obligation to respect the fundamental rights and fundamental legal principles as enshrined in Article 6 of the Treaty.

*Article 2*

**Definitions**

For the purposes of this Framework Decision 'conviction' means any final decision of a criminal court establishing guilt of a criminal offence.

L 220/34 EN Official Journal of the European Union 15.8.2008

*Article 3*

**Taking into account, in the course of new criminal proceedings, a conviction handed down in another Member State**

1. Each Member State shall ensure that in the course of criminal proceedings against a person, previous convictions handed down against the same person for different facts in other Member States, in respect of which information has been obtained under applicable instruments on mutual legal assistance or on the exchange of information extracted from criminal records, are taken into account to the extent previous national convictions are taken into account, and that equivalent legal effects are attached to them as to previous national convictions, in accordance with national law.

2. Paragraph 1 shall apply at the pre-trial stage, at the trial stage itself and at the time of execution of the conviction, in particular with regard to the applicable rules of procedure, including those relating to provisional detention, the definition of the offence, the type and level of the sentence, and the rules governing the execution of the decision.

3. The taking into account of previous convictions handed down in other Member States, as provided for in paragraph 1, shall not have the effect of interfering with, revoking or reviewing previous convictions or any decision relating to their execution by the Member State conducting the new proceedings.

4. In accordance with paragraph 3, paragraph 1 shall not apply to the extent that, had the previous conviction been a national conviction of the Member State conducting the new proceedings, the taking into account of the previous conviction would, according to the national law of that Member State, have had the effect of interfering with, revoking or reviewing the previous conviction or any decision relating to its execution.

5. If the offence for which the new proceedings being conducted was committed before the previous conviction had been handed down or fully executed, paragraphs 1 and 2 shall not have the effect of requiring Member States to apply their national rules on imposing sentences, where the application of those rules to foreign convictions would limit the judge in imposing a sentence in the new proceedings.

However, the Member States shall ensure that in such cases their courts can otherwise take into account previous convictions handed down in other Member States.

*Article 4*

**Relation to other legal instruments**

This Framework Decision shall replace Article 56 of the European Convention of 28 May 1970 on the International Validity of Criminal Judgments as between the Member States parties to that Convention, without prejudice to the application of that Article in relations between the Member States and third countries.

*Article 5*

**Implementation**

1. Member States shall take the necessary measures to comply with the provisions of this Framework Decision by 15 August 2010.

2. Member States shall communicate to the General Secretariat of the Council and to the Commission the text of the provisions transposing into their national law the obligations imposed on them under this Framework Decision.

3. On the basis of that information the Commission shall, by 15 August 2011, present a report to the European Parliament and the Council on the application of this Framework Decision, accompanied if necessary by legislative proposals.

*Article 6*

**Entry into force**

This Framework Decision shall enter into force on the day of its publication in the *Official Journal of the European Union*.

Done at Brussels, 24 July 2008.

*For the Council*

*The President*

B. HORTEFEUX

# Framework Decision 2008/841 on the fight against organised crime, 24 October 2008

[OJ 2008, L 300/42–45]

L 300/42 EN Official Journal of the European Union 11.11.2008

III

*(Acts adopted under the EU Treaty)*

# ACTS ADOPTED UNDER TITLE V OF THE EU TREATY

## COUNCIL FRAMEWORK DECISION 2008/841/JHA

**of 24 October 2008**

**on the fight against organised crime**

THE COUNCIL OF THE EUROPEAN UNION,

Having regard to the Treaty on European Union, and in particular Articles 29, 31(1)(e) and 34(2)(b) thereof,

Having regard to the proposal of the Commission,

Having regard to the opinion of the European Parliament ([1]),

Whereas:

(1) The objective of the Hague Programme is to improve the common capability of the Union and the Member States for the purpose, among others, of combating transnational organised crime. This objective is to be pursued by, in particular, the approximation of legislation. Closer cooperation between the Member States of the European Union is needed in order to counter the dangers and proliferation of criminal organisations and to respond effectively to citizens' expectations and Member States' own requirements. In this respect point 14 of the conclusions of the Brussels European Council of 4 and 5 November 2004 states that the citizens of Europe expect the European Union, while guaranteeing respect for fundamental freedoms and rights, to take a more effective, combined approach to cross-border problems such as organised crime.

(2) In its Communication of 29 March 2004 on measures to be taken to combat terrorism and other forms of serious crime, the Commission considered that the facilities available for combating organised crime in the EU needed to be strengthened and stated that it would draw up a Framework Decision to replace Joint Action 98/733/JHA of 21 December 1998 on making it a criminal offence to participate in a criminal organisation in the Member States of the European Union ([2]).

(3) Point 3.3.2 of the Hague Programme states that the approximation of substantive criminal law serves the purpose of facilitating mutual recognition of judgments and judicial decisions and police and judicial cooperation in criminal matters and concerns areas of particularly serious crime with cross-border dimensions and that priority should be given to areas of crime that are specifically mentioned in the Treaties. The definition of offences relating to participation in a criminal organisation should therefore be approximated in the Member States. Thus, this Framework Decision should encompass crimes which are typically committed in a criminal organisation. It should provide, moreover, for the imposition of penalties corresponding to the seriousness of those offences, on natural and legal persons who committed them or are responsible for their commission.

(4) The obligations arising by virtue of Article 2(a) should be without prejudice to Member States' freedom to classify other groups of persons as criminal organisations, for example, groups whose purpose is not financial or other material gain.

(5) The obligations arising by virtue of Article 2(a) should be without prejudice to the Member States' freedom to interpret the term 'criminal activities' as implying the carrying out of material acts.

(6) The European Union should build on the important work done by international organisations, in particular the United Nations Convention Against Transnational Organised Crime (the 'Palermo Convention'), which was concluded, on behalf of the European Community, by Council Decision 2004/579/EC ([3]).

([1]) Opinion delivered following non-compulsory consultation (not yet published in the Official Journal).

([2]) OJ L 351, 29.12.1998, p. 1.

([3]) OJ L 261, 6.8.2004, p. 69.

11.11.2008 EN Official Journal of the European Union L 300/43

(7) Since the objectives of this Framework Decision cannot be sufficiently achieved by the Member States, and can therefore, by reason of the scale of the action, be better achieved at Union level, the Union may adopt measures, in accordance with the principle of subsidiarity as set out in Article 5 of the Treaty establishing European Community, as applied by the second paragraph of Article 2 of the Treaty on European Union. In accordance with the principle of proportionality this Framework Decision does not go beyond what is necessary to achieve those objectives.

(8) This Framework Decision respects the fundamental rights and principles recognised by the Charter of Fundamental Rights of the European Union, and in particular Articles 6 and 49 thereof. Nothing in this Framework Decision is intended to reduce or restrict national rules relating to fundamental rights or freedoms such as due process, the right to strike, freedom of assembly, of association, of the press or of expression, including the right of everyone to form and to join trade unions with others for the protection of his or her interests and the related right to demonstrate.

(9) Joint Action 98/733/JHA should therefore be repealed,

HAS ADOPTED THIS FRAMEWORK DECISION:

*Article 1*

**Definitions**

For the purposes of this Framework Decision:

1. 'criminal organisation' means a structured association, established over a period of time, of more than two persons acting in concert with a view to committing offences which are punishable by deprivation of liberty or a detention order of a maximum of at least four years or a more serious penalty, to obtain, directly or indirectly, a financial or other material benefit;

2. 'structured association' means an association that is not randomly formed for the immediate commission of an offence, nor does it need to have formally defined roles for its members, continuity of its membership, or a developed structure.

*Article 2*

**Offences relating to participation in a criminal organisation**

Each Member State shall take the necessary measures to ensure that one or both of the following types of conduct related to a criminal organisation are regarded as offences:

(a) conduct by any person who, with intent and with knowledge of either the aim and general activity of the criminal organisation or its intention to commit the offences in question, actively takes part in the organisation's criminal activities, including the provision of information or material means, the recruitment of new members and all forms of financing of its activities, knowing that such participation will contribute to the achievement of the organisation's criminal activities;

(b) conduct by any person consisting in an agreement with one or more persons that an activity should be pursued, which if carried out, would amount to the commission of offences referred to in Article 1, even if that person does not take part in the actual execution of the activity.

*Article 3*

**Penalties**

1. Each Member State shall take the necessary measures to ensure that:

(a) the offence referred to in Article 2(a) is punishable by a maximum term of imprisonment of at least between two and five years; or

(b) the offence referred to in Article 2(b) is punishable by the same maximum term of imprisonment as the offence at which the agreement is aimed, or by a maximum term of imprisonment of at least between two and five years.

2. Each Member State shall take the necessary measures to ensure that the fact that offences referred to in Article 2, as determined by this Member State, have been committed within the framework of a criminal organisation, may be regarded as an aggravating circumstance.

*Article 4*

**Special circumstances**

Each Member State may take the necessary measures to ensure that the penalties referred to in Article 3 may be reduced or that the offender may be exempted from penalties if he, for example:

(a) renounces criminal activity; and

(b) provides the administrative or judicial authorities with information which they would not otherwise have been able to obtain, helping them to:

(i) prevent, end or mitigate the effects of the offence;

(ii) identify or bring to justice the other offenders;

(iii) find evidence;

L 300/44 EN Official Journal of the European Union 11.11.2008

(iv) deprive the criminal organisation of illicit resources or of the proceeds of its criminal activities; or

(v) prevent further offences referred to in Article 2 from being committed.

*Article 5*

**Liability of legal persons**

1. Each Member State shall take the necessary measures to ensure that legal persons may be held liable for any of the offences referred to in Article 2 committed for their benefit by any person, acting either individually or as part of an organ of the legal person, and having a leading position within the legal person, based on one of the following:

(a) a power of representation of the legal person;

(b) an authority to take decisions on behalf of the legal person; or

(c) an authority to exercise control within the legal person.

2. Member States shall also take the necessary measures to ensure that legal persons may be held liable where the lack of supervision or control by a person referred to in paragraph 1 has made possible the commission, by a person under its authority, of any of the offences referred to in Article 2 for the benefit of that legal person.

3. Liability of legal persons under paragraphs 1 and 2 shall be without prejudice to criminal proceedings against natural persons who are perpetrators of, or accessories to, any of the offences referred to in Article 2.

4. For the purpose of this Framework Decision 'legal person' shall mean any entity having legal personality under the applicable law, except for States or public bodies in the exercise of State authority and for public international organisations.

*Article 6*

**Penalties for legal persons**

1. Each Member State shall take the necessary measures to ensure that a legal person held liable pursuant to Article 5(1) is punishable by effective, proportionate and dissuasive penalties, which shall include criminal or non-criminal fines and may include other penalties, for example:

(a) exclusion from entitlement to public benefits or aid;

(b) temporary or permanent disqualification from the practice of commercial activities;

(c) placing under judicial supervision;

(d) judicial winding-up;

(e) temporary or permanent closure of establishments which have been used for committing the offence.

2. Each Member State shall take the necessary measures to ensure that a legal person held liable pursuant to Article 5(2) is punishable by penalties or measures which are effective, proportionate and dissuasive.

*Article 7*

**Jurisdiction and coordination of prosecution**

1. Each Member State shall ensure that its jurisdiction covers at least the cases in which the offences referred to in Article 2 were committed:

(a) in whole or in part within its territory, wherever the criminal organisation is based or pursues its criminal activities;

(b) by one of its nationals; or

(c) for the benefit of a legal person established in the territory of that Member State.

A Member State may decide that it will not apply, or that it will apply only in specific cases or circumstances, the jurisdiction rules set out in (b) and (c) where the offences referred to in Article 2 are committed outside its territory.

2. When an offence referred to in Article 2 falls within the jurisdiction of more than one Member State and when any one of the States concerned can validly prosecute on the basis of the same facts, the Member States concerned shall cooperate in order to decide which of them will prosecute the offenders, with the aim, if possible, of centralising proceedings in a single Member State. To this end, Member States may have recourse to Eurojust or any other body or mechanism established within the European Union in order to facilitate cooperation between their judicial authorities and the coordination of their action. Special account shall be taken of the following factors:

(a) the Member State in the territory of which the acts were committed;

(b) the Member State of which the perpetrator is a national or resident;

(c) the Member State of the origin of the victims;

(d) the Member State in the territory of which the perpetrator was found.

3. A Member State which, under its law, does not as yet extradite or surrender its own nationals shall take the necessary measures to establish its jurisdiction over and, where appropriate, to prosecute the offence referred to in Article 2, when committed by one of its nationals outside its territory.

4. This Article shall not exclude the exercise of jurisdiction in criminal matters as laid down by a Member State in accordance with its national legislation.

*Article 8*

**Absence of requirement of a report or accusation by victims**

Member States shall ensure that investigations into, or prosecution of, offences referred to in Article 2 are not dependent on a report or accusation made by a person subjected to the offence, at least as regards acts committed in the territory of the Member State.

*Article 9*

**Repeal of existing provisions**

Joint Action 98/733/JHA is hereby repealed.

References to participation in a criminal organisation within the meaning of Joint Action 98/733/JHA in measures adopted pursuant to Title VI of the Treaty on European Union and the Treaty establishing the European Community shall be construed as references to participation in a criminal organisation within the meaning of this Framework Decision.

*Article 10*

**Implementation and reports**

1. Member States shall take the necessary measures to comply with the provisions of this Framework Decision before 11 May 2010.

2. The Member States shall transmit to the General Secretariat of the Council and to the Commission, before 11 May 2010, the text of the provisions transposing into their national law the obligations imposed on them under this Framework Decision. On the basis of a report established using this information and a written report transmitted by the Commission, the Council shall, before 11 November 2012, assess the extent to which Member States have complied with the provisions of this Framework Decision.

*Article 11*

**Territorial application**

This Framework Decision shall apply to Gibraltar.

*Article 12*

**Entry into force**

This Framework Decision shall enter into force on the day of its publication in the *Official Journal of the European Union.*

Done at Luxembourg, 24 October 2008.

*For the Council*

*The President*

M. ALLIOT-MARIE

# Joint Action 2008/851 on a European Union military operation to contribute to the deterrence, prevention and repression of acts of piracy and armed robbery off the Somali coast, 10 November 2008

**[Consolidated version. Original version OJ 2008, L 301/33-37 corrected by OJ 2009, L 253/18 and amended by OJ 2009, L 322/27, OJ 2010, L 210/33, OJ 2010, L 327/49 and OJ 2012, L 89/69–71]**

►B

# COUNCIL JOINT ACTION 2008/851/CFSP

**of 10 November 2008**

**on a European Union military operation to contribute to the deterrence, prevention and repression of acts of piracy and armed robbery off the Somali coast**

(OJ L 301, 12.11.2008, p. 33)

Amended by:

| | | Official Journal | | |
|---|---|---|---|---|
| | | No | page | date |
| ►M1 | Council Decision 2009/907/CFSP of 8 December 2009 | L 322 | 27 | 9.12.2009 |
| ►M2 | Council Decision 2010/437/CFSP of 30 July 2010 | L 210 | 33 | 11.8.2010 |
| ►M3 | Council Decision 2010/766/CFSP of 7 December 2010 | L 327 | 49 | 11.12.2010 |
| ►M4 | Council Decision 2012/174/CFSP of 23 March 2012 | L 89 | 69 | 27.3.2012 |

Corrected by:

►C1 Corrigendum, OJ L 253, 25.9.2009, p. 18 (2008/851/CFSP)

▼B

**COUNCIL JOINT ACTION 2008/851/CFSP**

**of 10 November 2008**

**on a European Union military operation to contribute to the deterrence, prevention and repression of acts of piracy and armed robbery off the Somali coast**

THE COUNCIL OF THE EUROPEAN UNION,

Having regard to the Treaty on European Union, and in particular Article 14, the third subparagraph of Article 25 and Article 28(3) thereof,

Whereas:

(1) In its Resolution 1814 (2008) on the situation in Somalia, adopted on 15 May 2008, the United Nations Security Council (UNSC) has called on States and regional organisations, in close coordination with one another, to take action to protect shipping involved in the transport and delivery of humanitarian aid to Somalia and in activities authorised by the United Nations.

(2) In its Resolution 1816 (2008) on the situation in Somalia, adopted on 2 June 2008, the UNSC expressed its concern at the threat that acts of piracy and armed robbery against vessels pose to the delivery of humanitarian aid to Somalia, the safety of commercial maritime routes and international navigation. The UNSC encouraged, in particular, States interested in the use of commercial maritime routes off the coast of Somalia to increase and coordinate their efforts, in cooperation with the Transitional Federal Government of Somalia (TFG), to deter acts of piracy and armed robbery at sea. It authorised, for a period of six months from the date of the resolution, States cooperating with the TFG, of which advance notification had been given by the TFG to the UN Secretary-General, to enter the territorial waters of Somalia and to use, in a manner consistent with relevant international law, all necessary means to repress acts of piracy and armed robbery at sea.

(3) In its Resolution 1838 (2008) on the situation in Somalia, adopted on 7 October 2008, the UNSC commended the ongoing planning process towards a possible European Union (EU) naval operation, as well as other international or national initiatives taken with a view to implementing Resolutions 1814 (2008) and 1816 (2008), and urged States that have the capacity to do so, to cooperate with the TFG in the fight against piracy and armed robbery at sea in conformity with the provisions of Resolution 1816 (2008). The UNSC also urged States and regional organisations, in conformity with the provisions of Resolution 1814 (2008), to continue to take action to protect the World Food Programme (WFP) maritime convoys, which is vital to bring humanitarian assistance to the affected populations in Somalia.

▼B

(4) In its conclusions of 26 May 2008, the Council expressed its concern at the upsurge of piracy attacks off the Somali coast, which affect humanitarian efforts and international maritime traffic in the region and contribute to continued violations of the UN arms embargo. The Council also commended the sequenced initiatives of some Member States to provide protection to WFP vessels. It stressed the need for wider participation by the international community in these escorts in order to secure the delivery of humanitarian aid to the Somali population.

(5) On 5 August 2008, the Council approved a crisis management concept for action by the EU to help implement UNSC Resolution 1816 (2008) and for peace and international security in the region.

(6) On 15 September 2008, the Council reaffirmed its serious concern at the acts of piracy and armed robbery off the Somali coast, deploring, in particular, their recent resurgence. As regards the EU's contribution to the implementation of UNSC Resolution 1816 (2008) on combating piracy off the Somali coast and to the protection, under Resolutions 1814 (2008) and 1816 (2008), of vessels chartered by the WFP and bound for Somalia, the Council decided to establish a coordination cell in Brussels with the task of supporting the surveillance and protection activities carried out by some Member States off the Somali coast. On the same day, it approved, on the one hand, a plan for the implementation of this military coordination action (EU NAVCO) and, on the other, a strategic military option for a possible EU naval operation for which those Member States wishing to cooperate with the TFG under Resolution 1816 (2008) would make available military resources for the deterrence and repression of acts of piracy and armed robbery off the Somali coast.

(7) On 19 September 2008, the Council adopted Joint Action 2008/749/CFSP on the European Union military coordination action in support of UN Security Council Resolution 1816 (2008) (EU NAVCO) ([1]).

(8) On the launch of the Atalanta military operation, the tasks of the military coordination cell will be exercised under this Joint Action. The coordination cell should then be closed.

(9) The Political and Security Committee (PSC) should exercise political control over the EU military operation in order to help deter acts of piracy off the Somali coast, provide it with strategic direction and take the relevant decisions in accordance with third subparagraph of Article 25 of the Treaty.

([1]) OJ L 252, 20.9.2008, p. 39.

▼B

(10) Under Article 28(3) of the Treaty, the operational expenditure, arising from this Joint Action, which has military or defence implications, should be borne by the Member States in accordance with Council Decision 2007/384/CFSP of 14 May 2007 establishing a mechanism to administer the financing of the common costs of European Union operations having military or defence implications (Athena) [1] (hereinafter referred to as 'Athena').

(11) Article 14(1) of the Treaty calls for Joint Actions to lay down the means to be made available to the European Union. The financial reference amount, for a twelve-month period, for the common costs of the EU military operation constitutes the best current estimate and is without prejudice to the final figures to be included in a budget to be approved in accordance with the rules laid down in the decision regarding Athena.

(12) By letter dated 30 October 2008, the EU made an offer to the TFG, pursuant to point 7 of Resolution 1816 (2008), which contains proposals for States other than Somalia to exercise jurisdiction over persons captured in Somali territorial waters who have committed, or are suspected of having committed, acts of piracy or armed robbery.

(13) In accordance with Article 6 of the Protocol on the position of Denmark annexed to the Treaty on European Union and to the Treaty establishing the European Community, Denmark does not participate in the elaboration and implementation of decisions and actions of the European Union which have defence implications. Denmark does not participate in the implementation of this Joint Action and therefore does not participate in the financing of the operation,

HAS ADOPTED THIS JOINT ACTION:

▼M4

*Article 1*

**Mission**

1. The European Union (EU) shall conduct a military operation in support of Resolutions 1814 (2008), 1816 (2008), 1838 (2008), 1846 (2008) and 1851 (2008) of the United Nations Security Council (UNSC), in a manner consistent with action permitted with respect to piracy under Article 100 et seq. of the United Nations Convention on the Law of the Sea signed in Montego Bay on 10 December 1982 (hereinafter referred to as 'the United Nations Convention on the Law of the Sea') and by means, in particular, of commitments made with third States ('Atalanta') in order to contribute to:

— the protection of vessels of the WFP delivering food aid to displaced persons in Somalia, in accordance with the mandate laid down in UNSC Resolution 1814 (2008), and

[1] OJ L 152, 13.6.2007, p. 14.

▼M4

— the protection of vulnerable vessels cruising off the Somali coast, and the deterrence, prevention and repression of acts of piracy and armed robbery off the Somali coast, in accordance with the mandate laid down in UNSC Resolutions 1846 (2008) and 1851 (2008).

2. The area of operations of the forces deployed to that end shall consist of the Somali coastal territory and internal waters, and the maritime areas off the coasts of Somalia and neighbouring countries within the region of the Indian Ocean, in accordance with the political objective of an EU maritime operation, as defined in the crisis management concept approved by the Council on 5 August 2008.

3. In addition, Atalanta shall contribute to the monitoring of fishing activities off the coast of Somalia.

▼B

*Article 2*

**Mandate**

►C1 Under the conditions set by applicable international law, in particular the United Nations Convention on the Law of the Sea, and by UNSC Resolutions 1814 (2008), 1816 (2008) and 1838 (2008), Atalanta shall, as far as available capabilities allow: ◄

▼M4

(a) provide protection to vessels chartered by the WFP, including by means of the presence on board those vessels of armed units of Atalanta, including when sailing in Somalia's territorial and internal waters;

▼B

(b) provide protection, based on a case-by-case evaluation of needs, to merchant vessels cruising in the areas where it is deployed;

▼M4

(c) keep watch over areas off the Somali coast, including Somalia's territorial and internal waters, in which there are dangers to maritime activities, in particular to maritime traffic;

▼B

(d) take the necessary measures, including the use of force, to deter, prevent and intervene in order to bring to an end acts of piracy and armed robbery which may be committed in the areas where it is present;

▼M3

(e) in view of prosecutions potentially being brought by the relevant States under the conditions in Article 12, arrest, detain and transfer persons suspected of intending, as referred to in Articles 101 and 103 of the United Nations Convention on the Law of the Sea, to commit, committing or having committed acts of piracy or armed robbery in the areas where it is present and seize the vessels of the pirates or armed robbers or the vessels caught following an act of piracy or an armed robbery and which are in the hands of the pirates or armed robbers, as well as the property on board;

▼M4

(f) liaise with organisations and entities, as well as States, working in the region to combat acts of piracy and armed robbery off the Somali coast, in particular the 'Combined Task Force 151' maritime force which operates within the framework of 'Operation Enduring Freedom';

▼M1

(g) once sufficient progress has been made ashore in the area of maritime capacity-building, including security measures for the exchange of information, assist Somali authorities by making available data relating to fishing activities compiled in the course of the operation;

▼M3

(h) collect, in accordance with applicable law, data concerning persons referred to in point (e) related to characteristics likely to assist in their identification, including fingerprints;

(i) for the purpose of circulating the data via INTERPOL's channels and checking it against INTERPOL's databases, transmit to the National Central Bureau ('NCB') of the International Criminal Police Organisation – INTERPOL located in the Member State where the Operational Headquarters is stationed, in accordance with arrangements to be concluded between the EU Operation Commander and the Head of the NCB, the following data:

— personal data concerning persons referred to in point (e) related to characteristics likely to assist in their identification, including fingerprints, as well as the following particulars, with the exclusion of other personal data: surname, maiden name, given names and any alias or assumed name; date and place of birth, nationality, sex; place of residence, profession and whereabouts; driving licenses, identification documents and passport data. This personal data shall not be stored by Atalanta after its transmission to INTERPOL,

— data related to the equipment used by such persons.

▼B

*Article 3*

**Appointment of the EU Operation Commander**

Rear admiral Phillip Jones is hereby appointed EU Operation Commander.

*Article 4*

**Designation of the EU Operational Headquarters**

The EU Operational Headquarters shall be located at Northwood, United Kingdom.

▼B

*Article 5*

**Planning and launch of the operation**

The Decision to launch the EU military operation shall be adopted by the Council following approval of the Operation Plan and the Rules of Engagement and in the light of the notification by the TFG to the Secretary-General of the United Nations of the offer of cooperation made by the EU pursuant to point 7 of UNSC Resolution 1816 (2008).

*Article 6*

**Political control and strategic direction**

▼M2

1. Under the responsibility of the Council and of the High Representative of the Union for Foreign Affairs and Security Policy (hereinafter referred to as the 'HR'), the Political and Security Committee (hereinafter referred to as the 'PSC') shall exercise the political control and strategic direction of the EU military operation. The Council hereby authorises the PSC to take the relevant decisions in accordance with Article 38 of the Treaty. This authorisation shall include the powers to amend the planning documents, including the Operation Plan, the Chain of Command and the Rules of Engagement. It shall also include the powers to take decisions on the appointment of the EU Operation Commander and/or EU Force Commander. The powers of decision with respect to the objectives and termination of the EU military operation shall remain vested in the Council, assisted by the HR.

▼B

2. The PSC shall report to the Council at regular intervals.

3. The PSC shall receive reports from the chairman of the EU Military Committee (EUMC) regarding the conduct of the EU military operation, at regular intervals. The PSC may invite the EU Operation Commander and/or EU Force Commander to its meetings, as appropriate.

*Article 7*

**Military direction**

1. The EUMC shall monitor the proper execution of the EU military operation conducted under the responsibility of the EU Operation Commander.

2. The EUMC shall receive reports from the EU Operation Commander at regular intervals. It may invite the EU Operation Commander and/or EU Force Commander to its meetings as appropriate.

3. The chairman of the EUMC shall act as the primary point of contact with the EU Operation Commander.

▼M2

*Article 8*

**Coherence of EU response**

The HR, the EU Operation Commander and the EU Force Commander shall closely coordinate their respective activities regarding the implementation of this Joint Action.

▼B

*Article 9*

**Relations with the United Nations, neighbouring countries and other actors**

▼M2

1. The HR shall act as the primary point of contact with the United Nations, the Somali authorities, the authorities of neighbouring countries, and other relevant actors. Within the context of his contact with the African Union, the HR shall be assisted by the EU Special Representative (EUSR) to the African Union.

▼B

2. At operational level, the EU Operation Commander shall act as the contact point with, in particular, ship-owners' organisations, as well as with the relevant departments of the UN General Secretariat and the WFP.

*Article 10*

**Participation by third States**

1. Without prejudice to the decision-making autonomy of the EU or to the single institutional framework, and in accordance with the relevant guidelines of the European Council, third States may be invited to participate in the operation.

2. The Council hereby authorises the PSC to invite third States to offer contributions and to take the relevant decisions on acceptance of the proposed contributions, upon the recommendation of the EU Operation Commander and the EUMC.

▼M2

3. Detailed modalities for the participation by third States shall be the subject of agreements concluded in accordance with the procedure laid down in Article 37 of the Treaty. Where the EU and a third State have concluded an agreement establishing a framework for the latter's participation in EU crisis management operations, the provisions of such an agreement shall apply in the context of this operation.

▼B

4. Third States making significant military contributions to the EU military operation shall have the same rights and obligations in terms of day-to-day management of the operation as Member States taking part in the operation.

5. The Council hereby authorises the PSC to take relevant decisions on the setting-up of a Committee of Contributors, should third States provide significant military contributions.

▼B

6. The conditions for the transfer to a State participating in the operation of persons arrested and detained, with a view to the exercise of jurisdiction of that State, shall be established when the participation agreements referred to in paragraph 3 are concluded or implemented.

▼M2

*Article 11*

**Status of EU-led forces**

The status of the EU-led forces and their personnel, including the privileges, immunities and further guarantees necessary for the fulfilment and smooth functioning of their mission, who:

— are stationed on the land territory of third States,

— operate in the territorial or internal waters of third States,

shall be agreed in accordance with the procedure laid down in Article 37 of the Treaty.

▼M4

*Article 12*

**Transfer of persons arrested and detained with a view to their prosecution**

1. On the basis of Somalia's acceptance of the exercise of jurisdiction by Member States or by third States, on the one hand, and Article 105 of the United Nations Convention on the Law of the Sea, on the other hand, persons suspected of intending, as referred to in Articles 101 and 103 of the United Nations Convention of the Law of the Sea, to commit, committing or having committed acts of piracy or armed robbery in Somalia's territorial or internal waters or on the high seas, who are arrested and detained, with a view to their prosecution, and property used to carry out such acts, shall be transferred:

— to the competent authorities of the Member State or of the third State participating in the operation, of which the vessel which took them captive flies the flag, or

— if that State cannot, or does not wish to, exercise its jurisdiction, to a Member State or any third State which wishes to exercise its jurisdiction over the aforementioned persons and property.

2. Persons suspected of intending, as referred to in Articles 101 and 103 of the United Nations Convention of the Law of the Sea, to commit, committing or having committed acts of piracy or armed robbery who are arrested and detained, with a view to their prosecution, by Atalanta in the territorial waters, the internal waters or the archipelagic waters of other States in the region in agreement with these States, and property used to carry out such acts, may be transferred to the competent authorities of the State concerned, or, with the consent of the State concerned, to the competent authorities of another State.

▼M4

3. No persons referred to in paragraphs 1 and 2 may be transferred to a third State unless the conditions for the transfer have been agreed with that third State in a manner consistent with relevant international law, notably international law on human rights, in order to guarantee in particular that no one shall be subjected to the death penalty, to torture or to any cruel, inhuman or degrading treatment.

▼B

*Article 13*

**Relations with the flag States of protected vessels**

The conditions governing the presence on board merchant ships, particularly those chartered by the WFP, of units belonging to Atalanta, including privileges, immunities and other guarantees relating to the proper conduct of the operation, shall be agreed with the flag States of those vessels.

*Article 14*

**Financial arrangements**

1. The common costs of the EU military operation shall be administered by Athena.

2. The financial reference amount for the common costs of the EU military operation shall be EUR 8 300 000. The percentage of the reference amount referred to in Article 33(3) of Athena shall be 30 %.

▼M4

3. The financial reference amount for the common costs of the EU military operation for the period from 13 December 2012 until 12 December 2014 shall be EUR 14 900 000. The percentage of the reference amount referred to in Article 25(1) of Council Decision 2011/871/CFSP shall be 0 %.

▼M2

*Article 15*

**Release of information to the United Nations and other third parties**

1. The HR is hereby authorised to release to the United Nations and to other third parties associated with this Joint Action, classified EU information and documents generated for the purposes of the EU military operation up to the level of classification appropriate for each of them and in accordance with the Council's security regulations (1).

2. The HR is hereby authorised to release to the United Nations and to other third parties associated with this Joint Action, unclassified EU documents relating to Council deliberations on the operation which are covered by the obligation of professional secrecy pursuant to Article 6(1) of the Council's Rules of Procedure (2).

(1) Council Decision 2001/264/EC of 19 March 2001 adopting the Council's security regulations (OJ L 101, 11.4.2001, p. 1).
(2) Council Decision 2009/937/EU of 1 December 2009 adopting the Council's Rules of Procedure (OJ L 325, 11.12.2009, p. 35).

▼M3

3. The HR is hereby authorised to release to the United States-led Coalition Maritime Force ('CMF'), through its Headquarters, as well as to third States not participating in CMF and to international organisations, which are present in the area of the EU military operation, classified EU information and documents generated for the purposes of the EU military operation at the level RESTREINT UE, on the basis of reciprocity, where such release at theatre level is necessary for operational reasons, in accordance with the Council's security regulations and subject to arrangements between the HR and the competent authorities of the third parties referred to above.

▼B

*Article 16*

**Entry into force and termination**

1. This Joint Action shall enter into force on the date of its adoption.

2. Joint Action 2008/749/CFSP shall be repealed as from the date of closure of the coordination cell put in place by that Joint Action. It shall be closed on the launch date of the operation referred to in Article 6 of this Joint Action.

▼M4

3. The EU military operation shall terminate on 12 December 2014.

▼B

4. This Joint Action shall be repealed following the withdrawal of the EU force, in accordance with the plans approved for the termination of the EU military operation, and without prejudice to the relevant provisions of Athena.

*Article 17*

**Publication**

1. This Joint Action shall be published in the *Official Journal of the European Union*.

2. The PSC's decisions on the appointment of an EU Operation Commander and/or EU Force Commander, as well as the PSC's decisions on the acceptance of contributions from third States and the setting-up of a Committee of Contributors shall likewise be published in the *Official Journal of the European Union*.

# Directive 2008/99 on the protection of the environment through criminal law, 19 November 2008

[OJ 2008, L 328/28–37]

L 328/28 EN Official Journal of the European Union 6.12.2008

# DIRECTIVES

## DIRECTIVE 2008/99/EC OF THE EUROPEAN PARLIAMENT AND OF THE COUNCIL

**of 19 November 2008**

**on the protection of the environment through criminal law**

**(Text with EEA relevance)**

THE EUROPEAN PARLIAMENT AND THE COUNCIL OF THE EUROPEAN UNION,

Having regard to the Treaty establishing the European Community, and in particular Article 175(1) thereof,

Having regard to the proposal from the Commission,

Having regard to the opinion of the European Economic and Social Committee ([1]),

After consulting the Committee of the Regions,

Acting in accordance with the procedure laid down in Article 251 of the Treaty ([2]),

Whereas:

(1) According to Article 174(2) of the Treaty, Community policy on the environment must aim at a high level of protection.

(2) The Community is concerned at the rise in environmental offences and at their effects, which are increasingly extending beyond the borders of the States in which the offences are committed. Such offences pose a threat to the environment and therefore call for an appropriate response.

(3) Experience has shown that the existing systems of penalties have not been sufficient to achieve complete compliance with the laws for the protection of the environment. Such compliance can and should be strengthened by the availability of criminal penalties, which demonstrate a social disapproval of a qualitatively different nature compared to administrative penalties or a compensation mechanism under civil law.

(4) Common rules on criminal offences make it possible to use effective methods of investigation and assistance within and between Member States.

(5) In order to achieve effective protection of the environment, there is a particular need for more dissuasive penalties for environmentally harmful activities, which typically cause or are likely to cause substantial damage to the air, including the stratosphere, to soil, water, animals or plants, including to the conservation of species.

(6) Failure to comply with a legal duty to act can have the same effect as active behaviour and should therefore also be subject to corresponding penalties.

(7) Therefore, such conduct should be considered a criminal offence throughout the Community when committed intentionally or with serious negligence.

(8) The legislation listed in the Annexes to this Directive contains provisions which should be subject to criminal law measures in order to ensure that the rules on environmental protection are fully effective.

(9) The obligations under this Directive only relate to the provisions of the legislation listed in the Annexes to this Directive which entail an obligation for Member States, when implementing that legislation, to provide for prohibitive measures.

(10) This Directive obliges Member States to provide for criminal penalties in their national legislation in respect of serious infringements of provisions of Community law on the protection of the environment. This Directive creates no obligations regarding the application of such penalties, or any other available system of law enforcement, in individual cases.

([1]) OJ C 10, 15.1.2008, p. 47.
([2]) Opinion of the European Parliament of 21 May 2008 (not yet published in the Official Journal) and Council Decision of 24 October 2008.

(11) This Directive is without prejudice to other systems of liability for environmental damage under Community law or national law.

(12) As this Directive provides for minimum rules, Member States are free to adopt or maintain more stringent measures regarding the effective criminal law protection of the environment. Such measures must be compatible with the Treaty.

(13) Member States should provide information to the Commission on the implementation of this Directive, in order to enable it to evaluate the effect of this Directive.

(14) Since the objective of this Directive, namely to ensure a more effective protection of the environment, cannot be sufficiently achieved by the Member States and can therefore, by reason of the scale and effects of this Directive, be better achieved at Community level, the Community may adopt measures, in accordance with the principle of subsidiarity as set out in Article 5 of the Treaty. In accordance with the principle of proportionality, as set out in that Article, this Directive does not go beyond what is necessary in order to achieve that objective.

(15) Whenever subsequent legislation on environmental matters is adopted, it should specify where appropriate that this Directive will apply. Where necessary, Article 3 should be amended.

(16) This Directive respects the fundamental rights and observes the principles as recognised in particular by the Charter of Fundamental Rights of the European Union,

HAVE ADOPTED THIS DIRECTIVE:

*Article 1*

**Subject matter**

This Directive establishes measures relating to criminal law in order to protect the environment more effectively.

*Article 2*

**Definitions**

For the purpose of this Directive:

(a) 'unlawful' means infringing:

(i) the legislation adopted pursuant to the EC Treaty and listed in Annex A; or

(ii) with regard to activities covered by the Euratom Treaty, the legislation adopted pursuant to the Euratom Treaty and listed in Annex B; or

(iii) a law, an administrative regulation of a Member State or a decision taken by a competent authority of a Member State that gives effect to the Community legislation referred to in (i) or (ii);

(b) 'protected wild fauna and flora species' are:

(i) for the purposes of Article 3(f), those listed in:

— Annex IV to Council Directive 92/43/EEC of 21 May 1992 on the conservation of natural habitats and of wild fauna and flora [1],

— Annex I to, and referred to in Article 4(2) of, Council Directive 79/409/EEC of 2 April 1979 on the conservation of wild birds [2];

(ii) for the purposes of Article 3(g), those listed in Annex A or B to Council Regulation (EC) No 338/97 of 9 December 1996 on the protection of species of wild fauna and flora by regulating trade therein [3];

(c) 'habitat within a protected site' means any habitat of species for which an area is classified as a special protection area pursuant to Article 4(1) or (2) of Directive 79/409/EEC, or any natural habitat or a habitat of species for which a site is designated as a special area of conservation pursuant to Article 4(4) of Directive 92/43/EEC;

(d) 'legal person' means any legal entity having such status under the applicable national law, except for States or public bodies exercising State authority and for public international organisations.

*Article 3*

**Offences**

Member States shall ensure that the following conduct constitutes a criminal offence, when unlawful and committed intentionally or with at least serious negligence:

(a) the discharge, emission or introduction of a quantity of materials or ionising radiation into air, soil or water, which causes or is likely to cause death or serious injury to any person or substantial damage to the quality of air, the quality of soil or the quality of water, or to animals or plants;

[1] OJ L 206, 22.7.1992, p. 7.
[2] OJ L 103, 25.4.1979, p. 1.
[3] OJ L 61, 3.3.1997, p. 1.

(b) the collection, transport, recovery or disposal of waste, including the supervision of such operations and the after-care of disposal sites, and including action taken as a dealer or a broker (waste management), which causes or is likely to cause death or serious injury to any person or substantial damage to the quality of air, the quality of soil or the quality of water, or to animals or plants;

(c) the shipment of waste, where this activity falls within the scope of Article 2(35) of Regulation (EC) No 1013/2006 of the European Parliament and of the Council of 14 June 2006 on shipments of waste [1] and is undertaken in a non-negligible quantity, whether executed in a single shipment or in several shipments which appear to be linked;

(d) the operation of a plant in which a dangerous activity is carried out or in which dangerous substances or preparations are stored or used and which, outside the plant, causes or is likely to cause death or serious injury to any person or substantial damage to the quality of air, the quality of soil or the quality of water, or to animals or plants;

(e) the production, processing, handling, use, holding, storage, transport, import, export or disposal of nuclear materials or other hazardous radioactive substances which causes or is likely to cause death or serious injury to any person or substantial damage to the quality of air, the quality of soil or the quality of water, or to animals or plants;

(f) the killing, destruction, possession or taking of specimens of protected wild fauna or flora species, except for cases where the conduct concerns a negligible quantity of such specimens and has a negligible impact on the conservation status of the species;

(g) trading in specimens of protected wild fauna or flora species or parts or derivatives thereof, except for cases where the conduct concerns a negligible quantity of such specimens and has a negligible impact on the conservation status of the species;

(h) any conduct which causes the significant deterioration of a habitat within a protected site;

(i) the production, importation, exportation, placing on the market or use of ozone-depleting substances.

[1] OJ L 190, 12.7.2006, p. 1.

*Article 4*

**Inciting, aiding and abetting**

Member States shall ensure that inciting, aiding and abetting the intentional conduct referred to in Article 3 is punishable as a criminal offence.

*Article 5*

**Penalties**

Member States shall take the necessary measures to ensure that the offences referred to in Articles 3 and 4 are punishable by effective, proportionate and dissuasive criminal penalties.

*Article 6*

**Liability of legal persons**

1. Member States shall ensure that legal persons can be held liable for offences referred to in Articles 3 and 4 where such offences have been committed for their benefit by any person who has a leading position within the legal person, acting either individually or as part of an organ of the legal person, based on:

(a) a power of representation of the legal person;

(b) an authority to take decisions on behalf of the legal person; or

(c) an authority to exercise control within the legal person.

2. Member States shall also ensure that legal persons can be held liable where the lack of supervision or control, by a person referred to in paragraph 1, has made possible the commission of an offence referred to in Articles 3 and 4 for the benefit of the legal person by a person under its authority.

3. Liability of legal persons under paragraphs 1 and 2 shall not exclude criminal proceedings against natural persons who are perpetrators, inciters or accessories in the offences referred to in Articles 3 and 4.

*Article 7*

**Penalties for legal persons**

Member States shall take the necessary measures to ensure that legal persons held liable pursuant to Article 6 are punishable by effective, proportionate and dissuasive penalties.

*Article 8*

**Transposition**

1. Member States shall bring into force the laws, regulations and administrative provisions necessary to comply with this Directive before 26 December 2010.

When Member States adopt these measures, they shall contain a reference to this Directive or be accompanied by such a reference on the occasion of their official publication. Member States shall determine how such reference is to be made.

2. Member States shall communicate to the Commission the text of the main provisions of national law which they adopt in the field covered by this Directive and a table indicating the correlation between those provisions and this Directive.

*Article 9*

**Entry into force**

This Directive shall enter into force on the 20th day following its publication in the *Official Journal of the European Union*.

*Article 10*

**Addressees**

This Directive is addressed to the Member States.

Done at Strasbourg, 19 November 2008.

| | |
|---|---|
| *For the European Parliament* | *For the Council* |
| *The President* | *The President* |
| H.-G. PÖTTERING | J.-P. JOUYET |

*ANNEX A*

**List of Community legislation adopted pursuant to the EC Treaty, the infringement of which constitutes unlawful conduct pursuant to Article 2(a)(i) of this Directive**

— Council Directive 70/220/EEC of 20 March 1970 on the approximation of the laws of the Member States on measures to be taken against air pollution by emissions from motor vehicles (1),

— Council Directive 72/306/EEC of 2 August 1972 on the approximation of the laws of the Member States relating to the measures to be taken against the emission of pollutants from diesel engines for use in vehicles (2),

— Council Directive 75/439/EEC of 16 June 1975 on the disposal of waste oils (3),

— Council Directive 76/160/EEC of 8 December 1975 concerning the quality of bathing water (4),

— Council Directive 76/769/EEC of 27 July 1976 on the approximation of the laws, regulations and administrative provisions of the Member States relating to restrictions on the marketing and use of certain dangerous substances and preparations (5),

— Council Directive 77/537/EEC of 28 June 1977 on the approximation of the laws of the Member States relating to the measures to be taken against the emission of pollutants from diesel engines for use in wheeled agricultural or forestry tractors (6),

— Council Directive 78/176/EEC of 20 February 1978 on waste from the titanium dioxide industry (7),

— Council Directive 79/117/EEC of 21 December 1978 prohibiting the placing on the market and use of plant protection products containing certain active substances (8),

— Council Directive 79/409/EEC of 2 April 1979 on the conservation of wild birds (9),

— Council Directive 82/176/EEC of 22 March 1982 on limit values and quality objectives for mercury discharges by the chlor-alkali electrolysis industry (10),

— Council Directive 83/513/EEC of 26 September 1983 on limit values and quality objectives for cadmium discharges (11),

— Council Directive 84/156/EEC of 8 March 1984 on limit values and quality objectives for mercury discharges by sectors other than the chlor-alkali electrolysis industry (12),

— Council Directive 84/360/EEC of 28 June 1984 on the combating of air pollution from industrial plants (13),

— Council Directive 84/491/EEC of 9 October 1984 on limit values and quality objectives for discharges of hexachlorocyclohexane (14),

(1) OJ L 76, 6.4.1970, p. 1.
(2) OJ L 190, 20.8.1972, p. 1.
(3) OJ L 194, 25.7.1975, p. 23.
(4) OJ L 31, 5.2.1976, p. 1.
(5) OJ L 262, 27.9.1976, p. 201.
(6) OJ L 220, 29.8.1977, p. 38.
(7) OJ L 54, 25.2.1978, p. 19.
(8) OJ L 33, 8.2.1979, p. 36.
(9) OJ L 103, 25.4.1979, p. 1.
(10) OJ L 81, 27.3.1982, p. 29.
(11) OJ L 291, 24.10.1983, p. 1.
(12) OJ L 74, 17.3.1984, p. 49.
(13) OJ L 188, 16.7.1984, p. 20.
(14) OJ L 274, 17.10.1984, p. 11.

— Council Directive 85/203/EEC of 7 March 1985 on air quality standards for nitrogen dioxide (1),

— Council Directive 86/278/EEC of 12 June 1986 on the protection of the environment, and in particular of the soil, when sewage sludge is used in agriculture (2),

— Council Directive 86/280/EEC of 12 June 1986 on limit values and quality objectives for discharges of certain dangerous substances included in List I of the Annex to Directive 76/464/EEC (3),

— Council Directive 87/217/EEC of 19 March 1987 on the prevention and reduction of environmental pollution by asbestos (4),

— Council Directive 90/219/EEC of 23 April 1990 on the contained use of genetically modified micro-organisms (5),

— Council Directive 91/271/EEC of 21 May 1991 concerning urban waste-water treatment (6),

— Council Directive 91/414/EEC of 15 July 1991 concerning the placing of plant protection products on the market (7),

— Council Directive 91/676/EEC of 12 December 1991 concerning the protection of waters against pollution caused by nitrates from agricultural sources (8),

— Council Directive 91/689/EEC of 12 December 1991 on hazardous waste (9),

— Council Directive 92/43/EEC of 21 May 1992 on the conservation of natural habitats and of wild fauna and flora (10),

— Council Directive 92/112/EEC of 15 December 1992 on procedures for harmonising the programmes for the reduction and eventual elimination of pollution caused by waste from the titanium dioxide industry (11),

— Directive 94/25/EC of the European Parliament and of the Council of 16 June 1994 on the approximation of the laws, regulations and administrative provisions of the Member States relating to recreational craft: the provisions amended by Directive 2003/44/EC (12),

— European Parliament and Council Directive 94/62/EC of 20 December 1994 on packaging and packaging waste (13),

— European Parliament and Council Directive 94/63/EC of 20 December 1994 on the control of volatile organic compound (VOC) emissions resulting from the storage of petrol and its distribution from terminals to service stations (14),

— Council Directive 96/49/EC of 23 July 1996 on the approximation of the laws of the Member States with regard to the transport of dangerous goods by rail (15),

(1) OJ L 87, 27.3.1985, p. 1.
(2) OJ L 181, 4.7.1986, p. 6.
(3) OJ L 181, 4.7.1986, p. 16.
(4) OJ L 85, 28.3.1987, p. 40.
(5) OJ L 117, 8.5.1990, p. 1.
(6) OJ L 135, 30.5.1991, p. 40.
(7) OJ L 230, 19.8.1991, p. 1.
(8) OJ L 375, 31.12.1991, p. 1.
(9) OJ L 377, 31.12.1991, p. 20.
(10) OJ L 206, 22.7.1992, p. 7.
(11) OJ L 409, 31.12.1992, p. 11.
(12) OJ L 214, 26.8.2003, p. 18.
(13) OJ L 365, 31.12.1994, p. 10.
(14) OJ L 365, 31.12.1994, p. 24.
(15) OJ L 235, 17.9.1996, p. 25.

— Council Directive 96/59/EC of 16 September 1996 on the disposal of polychlorinated biphenyls and polychlorinated terphenyls (PCB/PCT) (1),

— Council Directive 96/62/EC of 27 September 1996 on ambient air quality assessment and management (2),

— Council Directive 96/82/EC of 9 December 1996 on the control of major-accident hazards involving dangerous substances (3),

— Directive 97/68/EC of the European Parliament and of the Council of 16 December 1997 on the approximation of the laws of the Member States relating to measures against the emission of gaseous and particulate pollutants from internal combustion engines to be installed in non-road mobile machinery (4),

— Council Regulation (EC) No 338/97 of 9 December 1996 on the protection of species of wild fauna and flora by regulating trade therein (5),

— Directive 98/8/EC of the European Parliament and of the Council of 16 February 1998 concerning the placing of biocidal products on the market (6),

— Directive 98/70/EC of the European Parliament and of the Council of 13 October 1998 relating to the quality of petrol and diesel fuels (7),

— Council Directive 98/83/EC of 3 November 1998 on the quality of water intended for human consumption (8),

— Council Directive 1999/13/EC of 11 March 1999 on the limitation of emissions of volatile organic compounds due to the use of organic solvents in certain activities and installations (9),

— Council Directive 1999/30/EC of 22 April 1999 relating to limit values for sulphur dioxide, nitrogen dioxide and oxides of nitrogen, particulate matter and lead in ambient air (10),

— Council Directive 1999/31/EC of 26 April 1999 on the landfill of waste (11),

— Council Directive 1999/32/EC of 26 April 1999 relating to a reduction in the sulphur content of certain liquid fuels (12),

— Directive 2000/53/EC of the European Parliament and of the Council of 18 September 2000 on end of life vehicles (13),

— Directive 2000/60/EC of the European Parliament and of the Council of 23 October 2000 establishing a framework for Community action in the field of water policy (14),

— Directive 2000/69/EC of the European Parliament and of the Council of 16 November 2000 relating to limit values for benzene and carbon monoxide in ambient air (15),

(1) OJ L 243, 24.9.1996, p. 31.
(2) OJ L 296, 21.11.1996, p. 55.
(3) OJ L 10, 14.1.1997, p. 13.
(4) OJ L 59, 27.2.1998, p. 1.
(5) OJ L 61, 3.3.1997, p. 1.
(6) OJ L 123, 24.4.1998, p. 1.
(7) OJ L 350, 28.12.1998, p. 58.
(8) OJ L 330, 5.12.1998, p. 32.
(9) OJ L 85, 29.3.1999, p. 1.
(10) OJ L 163, 29.6.1999, p. 41.
(11) OJ L 182, 16.7.1999, p. 1.
(12) OJ L 121, 11.5.1999, p. 13.
(13) OJ L 269, 21.10.2000, p. 34.
(14) OJ L 327, 22.12.2000, p. 1.
(15) OJ L 313, 13.12.2000, p. 12.

— Directive 2000/76/EC of the European Parliament and of the Council of 4 December 2000 on the incineration of waste [1],

— Regulation (EC) No 2037/2000 of the European Parliament and of the Council of 29 June 2000 on substances that deplete the ozone layer [2],

— Directive 2001/18/EC of the European Parliament and of the Council of 12 March 2001 on the deliberate release into the environment of genetically modified organisms [3],

— Directive 2001/80/EC of the European Parliament and of the Council of 23 October 2001 on the limitation of emissions of certain pollutants into the air from large combustion plants [4],

— Directive 2002/3/EC of the European Parliament and of the Council of 12 February 2002 relating to ozone in ambient air [5],

— Directive 2002/95/EC of the European Parliament and of the Council of 27 January 2003 on the restriction of the use of certain hazardous substances in electrical and electronic equipment [6],

— Directive 2002/96/EC of the European Parliament and of the Council of 27 January 2003 on waste electrical and electronic equipment (WEEE) [7],

— Directive 2004/107/EC of the European Parliament and of the Council of 15 December 2004 relating to arsenic, cadmium, mercury, nickel and polycyclic aromatic hydrocarbons in ambient air [8],

— Regulation (EC) No 648/2004 of the European Parliament and of the Council of 31 March 2004 on detergents [9],

— Regulation (EC) No 850/2004 of the European Parliament and of the Council of 29 April 2004 on persistent organic pollutants [10],

— Directive 2005/55/EC of the European Parliament and of the Council of 28 September 2005 on the approximation of the laws of the Member States relating to the measures to be taken against the emission of gaseous and particulate pollutants from compression-ignition engines for use in vehicles, and the emission of gaseous pollutants from positive-ignition engines fuelled with natural gas or liquefied petroleum gas for use in vehicles [11],

— Commission Directive 2005/78/EC of 14 November 2005 implementing Directive 2005/55/EC of the European Parliament and of the Council on the approximation of the laws of the Member States relating to the measures to be taken against the emission of gaseous and particulate pollutants from compression-ignition engines for use in vehicles, and the emission of gaseous pollutants from positive ignition engines fuelled with natural gas or liquefied petroleum gas for use in vehicles and amending Annexes I, II, III, IV and VI thereto [12],

— Directive 2006/7/EC of the European Parliament and of the Council of 15 February 2006 concerning the management of bathing water quality [13],

— Directive 2006/11/EC of the European Parliament and of the Council of 15 February 2006 on pollution caused by certain dangerous substances discharged into the aquatic environment of the Community [14],

— Directive 2006/12/EC of the European Parliament and of the Council of 5 April 2006 on waste [15],

(1) OJ L 332, 28.12.2000, p. 91.
(2) OJ L 244, 29.9.2000, p. 1.
(3) OJ L 106, 17.4.2001, p. 1.
(4) OJ L 309, 27.11.2001, p. 1.
(5) OJ L 67, 9.3.2002, p. 14.
(6) OJ L 37, 13.2.2003, p. 19.
(7) OJ L 37, 13.2.2003, p. 24.
(8) OJ L 23, 26.1.2005, p. 3.
(9) OJ L 104, 8.4.2004, p. 1.
(10) OJ L 158, 30.4.2004, p. 7.
(11) OJ L 275, 20.10.2005, p. 1.
(12) OJ L 313, 29.11.2005, p. 1.
(13) OJ L 64, 4.3.2006, p. 37.
(14) OJ L 64, 4.3.2006, p. 52.
(15) OJ L 114, 27.4.2006, p. 9.

— Directive 2006/21/EC of the European Parliament and of the Council of 15 March 2006 on the management of waste from extractive industries (1),

— Directive 2006/40/EC of the European Parliament and of the Council of 17 May 2006 relating to emissions from air conditioning systems in motor vehicles (2),

— Directive 2006/44/EC of the European Parliament and of the Council of 6 September 2006 on the quality of fresh waters needing protection or improvement in order to support fish life (3),

— Directive 2006/66/EC of the European Parliament and of the Council of 6 September 2006 on batteries and accumulators and waste batteries and accumulators (4),

— Directive 2006/118/EC of the European Parliament and of the Council of 12 December 2006 on the protection of groundwater against pollution and deterioration (5),

— Regulation (EC) No 842/2006 of the European Parliament and of the Council of 17 May 2006 on certain fluorinated greenhouse gases (6),

— Regulation (EC) No 1013/2006 of the European Parliament and of the Council of 14 June 2006 on shipments of waste (7),

— Regulation (EC) No 715/2007 of the European Parliament and of the Council of 20 June 2007 on type approval of motor vehicles with respect to emissions from light passenger and commercial vehicles (Euro 5 and Euro 6) and on access to vehicle repair and maintenance information (8),

— Commission Regulation (EC) No 1418/2007 of 29 November 2007 concerning the export for recovery of certain waste listed in Annex III or IIIA to Regulation (EC) No 1013/2006 of the European Parliament and of the Council to certain countries to which the OECD Decision on the control of transboundary movements of wastes does not apply (9),

— Directive 2008/1/EC of the European Parliament and of the Council of 15 January 2008 concerning integrated pollution prevention and control (10).

(1) OJ L 102, 11.4.2006, p. 15.
(2) OJ L 161, 14.6.2006, p. 12.
(3) OJ L 264, 25.9.2006, p. 20.
(4) OJ L 266, 26.9.2006, p. 1.
(5) OJ L 372, 27.12.2006, p. 19.
(6) OJ L 161, 14.6.2006, p. 1.
(7) OJ L 190, 12.7.2006, p. 1.
(8) OJ L 171, 29.6.2007, p. 1.
(9) OJ L 316, 4.12.2007, p. 6.
(10) OJ L 24, 29.1.2008, p. 8.

6.12.2008 EN Official Journal of the European Union L 328/37

*ANNEX B*

**List of Community Legislation adopted pursuant to the Euratom Treaty, the infringement of which constitutes unlawful conduct pursuant to Article 2(a)(ii) of this Directive**

— Council Directive 96/29/Euratom of 13 May 1996 laying down basic safety standards for the protection of the health of workers and the general public against the dangers arising from ionising radiation (1);

— Council Directive 2003/122/Euratom of 22 December 2003 on the control of high-activity sealed radioactive sources and orphan sources (2);

— Council Directive 2006/117/Euratom of 20 November 2006 on the supervision and control of shipments of radioactive waste and spent fuel (3).

(1) OJ L 159, 29.6.1996, p. 1.
(2) OJ L 346, 31.12.2003, p. 57.
(3) OJ L 337, 5.12.2006, p. 21.

# Framework Decision 2008/909 on the application of the principle of mutual recognition to judgments in criminal matters imposing custodial sentences or measures involving deprivation of liberty for the purpose of their enforcement in the European Union, 27 November 2008

**[Consolidated version. Original version OJ 2008, L 327/27–46 amended as of 28 March 2011 by OJ 2009, L 81/24–36]**

►B

**COUNCIL FRAMEWORK DECISION 2008/909/JHA**

**of 27 November 2008**

**on the application of the principle of mutual recognition to judgments in criminal matters imposing custodial sentences or measures involving deprivation of liberty for the purpose of their enforcement in the European Union**

(OJ L 327, 5.12.2008, p. 27)

Amended by:

| | | Official Journal | | |
|---|---|---|---|---|
| | | No | page | date |
| ►M1 | Council Framework Decision 2009/299/JHA of 26 February 2009 | L 81 | 24 | 27.3.2009 |

 

▼B

**COUNCIL FRAMEWORK DECISION 2008/909/JHA**

**of 27 November 2008**

**on the application of the principle of mutual recognition to judgments in criminal matters imposing custodial sentences or measures involving deprivation of liberty for the purpose of their enforcement in the European Union**

THE COUNCIL OF THE EUROPEAN UNION,

Having regard to the Treaty on European Union, and in particular Articles 31(1)(a) and 34(2)(b) thereof,

Having regard to the initiative of the Republic of Austria, the Republic of Finland and the Kingdom of Sweden,

Having regard to the opinion of the European Parliament,

Whereas:

(1) The European Council meeting in Tampere on 15 and 16 October 1999 endorsed the principle of mutual recognition, which should become the cornerstone of judicial cooperation in both civil and criminal matters within the Union.

(2) On 29 November 2000 the Council, in accordance with the Tampere conclusions, adopted a programme of measures to implement the principle of mutual recognition of decisions in criminal matters ([1]), in which it called for an assessment of the need for modern mechanisms for the mutual recognition of final sentences involving deprivation of liberty (Measure 14) and for extended application of the principle of the transfer of sentenced persons to cover persons resident in a Member State (Measure 16).

(3) The Hague Programme on strengthening freedom, security and justice in the European Union ([2]) requires Member States to complete the programme of measures, in particular in the field of enforcing final custodial sentences.

(4) All the Member States have ratified the Council of Europe Convention on the Transfer of Sentenced Persons of 21 March 1983. Under that Convention, sentenced persons may be transferred to serve the remainder of their sentence only to their State of nationality and only with their consent and that of the States involved. The Additional Protocol to that Convention of 18 December 1997, which allows transfer without the person's consent, subject to certain conditions, has not been ratified by all the Member States. Neither instrument imposes any basic duty to take charge of sentenced persons for enforcement of a sentence or order.

(5) Procedural rights in criminal proceedings are a crucial element for ensuring mutual confidence among the Member States in judicial cooperation. Relations between the Member States, which are characterised by special mutual confidence in other Member States' legal systems, enable recognition by the executing State of decisions taken by the issuing State's authorities. Therefore, a further development of the cooperation provided for in the Council of Europe instruments concerning the enforcement of criminal judgments should be envisaged, in particular where citizens of the Union were the subject of a criminal judgment and were sentenced to a custodial sentence or a measure involving deprivation of liberty in another Member State. Notwithstanding the need to provide the sentenced person with adequate safeguards, his or her involvement in the proceedings

([1]) OJ C 12, 15.1.2001, p. 10.
([2]) OJ C 53, 3.3.2005, p. 1.

▼B

should no longer be dominant by requiring in all cases his or her consent to the forwarding of a judgment to another Member State for the purpose of its recognition and enforcement of the sentence imposed.

(6) This Framework Decision should be implemented and applied in a manner which allows general principles of equality, fairness and reasonableness to be respected.

(7) Article 4(1)(c) contains a discretionary provision which enables the judgment and the certificate to be forwarded, for example, to the Member State of nationality of the sentenced person, in cases other than those provided for in paragraphs 1(a) and (b) or to the Member State in which the sentenced person lives and has been legally residing continuously for at least five years and will retain a permanent right of residence there.

(8) In cases referred to in Article 4(1)(c) the forwarding of the judgment and the certificate to the executing State is subject to consultations between the competent authorities of the issuing and the executing States, and the consent of the competent authority of the executing State. The competent authorities should take into account such elements as, for example, duration of the residence or other links to the executing State. In cases where the sentenced person could be transferred to a Member State and to a third country under national law or international instruments, the competent authorities of the issuing and executing States should, in consultations, consider whether enforcement in the executing State would enhance the aim of social rehabilitation better than enforcement in the third country.

(9) Enforcement of the sentence in the executing State should enhance the possibility of social rehabilitation of the sentenced person. In the context of satisfying itself that the enforcement of the sentence by the executing State will serve the purpose of facilitating the social rehabilitation of the sentenced person, the competent authority of the issuing State should take into account such elements as, for example, the person's attachment to the executing State, whether he or she considers it the place of family, linguistic, cultural, social or economic and other links to the executing State.

(10) The opinion of the sentenced person referred to in Article 6(3) may be useful mainly in applying Article 4(4). The words 'in particular' are intended to cover also cases where the opinion of the sentenced person would include information which might be of relevance in relation to the grounds for non-recognition and non-enforcement. Provisions of Articles 4(4) and 6(3) do not constitute a ground for refusal on social rehabilitation.

(11) Poland needs more time than the other Member States to face the practical and material consequences of transfer of Polish citizens convicted in other Member States, especially in the light of an increased mobility of Polish citizens within the Union. For that reason, a temporary derogation of limited scope for a maximum period of five years should be foreseen.

(12) This Framework Decision should also, *mutatis mutandis*, apply to the enforcement of sentences in the cases under Articles 4(6) and 5(3) of Council Framework Decision 2002/584/JHA of 13 June 2002 on the European Arrest Warrant and the surrender procedures between Member States ([1]). This means, *inter alia*, that, without prejudice to that Framework Decision, the executing State could verify the existence of grounds for non-recognition and non-enforcement as provided in Article 9 of this Framework Decision, including the checking of double criminality to the extent that the executing State makes a declaration

([1]) OJ L 190, 18.7.2002, p. 1.

▼B

under Article 7(4) of this Framework Decision, as a condition for recognising and enforcing the judgment with a view to considering whether to surrender the person or to enforce the sentence in cases pursuant to Article 4(6) of Framework Decision 2002/584/JHA.

(13) This Framework Decision respects fundamental rights and observes the principles recognised by Article 6 of the Treaty on European Union and reflected by the Charter of Fundamental Rights of the European Union, in particular Chapter VI thereof. Nothing in this Framework Decision should be interpreted as prohibiting refusal to execute a decision when there are objective reasons to believe that the sentence was imposed for the purpose of punishing a person on the grounds of his or her sex, race, religion, ethnic origin, nationality, language, political opinions or sexual orientation, or that that person's position may be prejudiced on any one of those grounds.

(14) This Framework Decision should not prevent any Member State from applying its constitutional rules relating to due process, freedom of association, freedom of the press and freedom of expression in other media.

(15) This Framework Decision should be applied in accordance with the right of citizens of the Union to move and reside freely within the territory of the Member States conferred by Article 18 of the Treaty establishing European Community.

(16) This Framework Decision should be applied in accordance with applicable Community legislation, including in particular Council Directive 2003/86/EC ([1]), Council Directive 2003/109/EC ([2]) and Directive 2004/38/EC of the European Parliament and of the Council ([3]).

(17) Where in this Framework Decision reference is made to the State in which the sentenced person 'lives', this indicates the place to which that person is attached based on habitual residence and on elements such as family, social or professional ties.

(18) When applying Article 5(1), it should be possible to transmit a judgment or a certified copy thereof and a certificate to the competent authority in the executing State by any means which leaves a written record, for example e-mail and fax, under conditions allowing the executing State to establish authenticity.

(19) In cases referred to in Article 9(1)(k), the executing State should consider the possibility of adapting the sentence in accordance with this Framework Decision before it refuses to recognise and enforce the sentence involving a measure other than a custodial sentence.

(20) The ground for refusal provided for in Article 9(1)(k) may be applied also in cases where the person has not been found guilty of a criminal offence although the competent authority applied the measure involving the deprivation of liberty other than a custodial sentence as a consequence of a criminal offence.

(21) The ground for refusal relating to territoriality should be applied only in exceptional cases and with a view to cooperating to the greatest extent possible under the provisions of this Framework Decision, while taking into account its purpose. Any decision to apply this ground for refusal, should be based on a case-by-case analysis and consultations between the competent authorities of the issuing and executing States.

([1]) OJ L 251, 3.10.2003, p. 12.
([2]) OJ L 16, 23.1.2004, p. 44.
([3]) OJ L 158, 30.4.2004, p. 77.

▼B

(22) The time limit referred to in Article 12(2) should be implemented by the Member States in such a way that as a general rule, the final decision, including an appeal procedure is completed within a period of 90 days.

(23) Article 18(1) states that, subject to the exceptions listed in paragraph 2, the specialty rule applies only where the person has been transferred to the executing State. It should therefore not be applicable where the person has not been transferred to the executing State, for example where the person has fled to the executing State,

HAS ADOPTED THIS FRAMEWORK DECISION:

CHAPTER I

**GENERAL PROVISIONS**

*Article 1*

**Definitions**

For the purposes of this Framework Decision:

(a) 'judgment' shall mean a final decision or order of a court of the issuing State imposing a sentence on a natural person;

(b) 'sentence' shall mean any custodial sentence or any measure involving deprivation of liberty imposed for a limited or unlimited period of time on account of a criminal offence on the basis of criminal proceedings;

(c) 'issuing State' shall mean the Member State in which a judgment is delivered;

(d) 'executing State' shall mean the Member State to which a judgment is forwarded for the purpose of its recognition and enforcement.

*Article 2*

**Determination of the competent authorities**

1. Each Member State shall inform the General Secretariat of the Council which authority or authorities, under its national law, are competent in accordance with this Framework Decision, when that Member State is the issuing State or the executing State.

2. The General Secretariat of the Council shall make the information received available to all Member States and the Commission.

*Article 3*

**Purpose and scope**

1. The purpose of this Framework Decision is to establish the rules under which a Member State, with a view to facilitating the social rehabilitation of the sentenced person, is to recognise a judgment and enforce the sentence.

2. This Framework Decision shall apply where the sentenced person is in the issuing State or in the executing State.

3. This Framework Decision shall apply only to the recognition of judgments and the enforcement of sentences within the meaning of this Framework Decision. The fact that, in addition to the sentence, a fine and/or a confiscation order has been imposed, which has not yet been paid, recovered or enforced, shall not prevent a judgment from being forwarded. The recognition and enforcement of such fines and confis-

▼B

cation orders in another Member State shall be based on the instruments applicable between the Member States, in particular Council Framework Decision 2005/214/JHA of 24 February 2005 on the application of the principle of mutual recognition to financial penalties (1) and Council Framework Decision 2006/783/JHA of 6 October 2006 on the application of the principle of mutual recognition to confiscation orders (2).

4. This Framework Decision shall not have the effect of modifying the obligation to respect fundamental rights and fundamental legal principles as enshrined in Article 6 of the Treaty on European Union.

CHAPTER II

## RECOGNITION OF JUDGMENTS AND ENFORCEMENT OF SENTENCES

*Article 4*

### Criteria for forwarding a judgment and a certificate to another Member State

1. Provided that the sentenced person is in the issuing State or in the executing State, and provided that this person has given his or her consent where required under Article 6, a judgment, together with the certificate for which the standard form is given in Annex I, may be forwarded to one of the following Member States:

(a) the Member State of nationality of the sentenced person in which he or she lives; or

(b) the Member State of nationality, to which, while not being the Member State where he or she lives, the sentenced person will be deported, once he or she is released from the enforcement of the sentence on the basis of an expulsion or deportation order included in the judgment or in a judicial or administrative decision or any other measure taken consequential to the judgment; or

(c) any Member State other than a Member State referred to in (a) or (b), the competent authority of which consents to the forwarding of the judgment and the certificate to that Member State.

2. The forwarding of the judgment and the certificate may take place where the competent authority of the issuing State, where appropriate after consultations between the competent authorities of the issuing and the executing States, is satisfied that the enforcement of the sentence by the executing State would serve the purpose of facilitating the social rehabilitation of the sentenced person.

3. Before forwarding the judgment and the certificate, the competent authority of the issuing State may consult, by any appropriate means, the competent authority of the executing State. Consultation shall be obligatory in the cases referred to in paragraph 1(c). In such cases the competent authority of the executing State shall promptly inform the issuing State of its decision whether or not to consent to the forwarding of the judgment.

4. During such consultation, the competent authority of the executing State may present the competent authority of the issuing State with a reasoned opinion, that enforcement of the sentence in the executing State would not serve the purpose of facilitating the social rehabilitation and successful reintegration of the sentenced person into society.

Where there has been no consultation, such an opinion may be presented without delay after the transmission of the judgment and the certificate. The competent authority of the issuing State shall

(1) OJ L 76, 22.3.2005, p. 16.
(2) OJ L 328, 24.11.2006, p. 59.

▼B

consider such opinion and decide whether to withdraw the certificate or not.

5. The executing State may, on its own initiative, request the issuing State to forward the judgment together with the certificate. The sentenced person may also request the competent authorities of the issuing State or of the executing State to initiate a procedure for forwarding the judgment and the certificate under this Framework Decision. Requests made under this paragraph shall not create an obligation of the issuing State to forward the judgment together with the certificate.

6. In implementing this Framework Decision, Member States shall adopt measures, in particular taking into account the purpose of facilitating social rehabilitation of the sentenced person, constituting the basis on which their competent authorities have to take their decisions whether or not to consent to the forwarding of the judgment and the certificate in cases pursuant to paragraph 1(c).

7. Each Member State may, either on adoption of this Framework Decision or later, notify the General Secretariat of the Council that, in its relations with other Member States that have given the same notification, its prior consent under paragraph 1(c) is not required for the forwarding of the judgment and the certificate:

(a) if the sentenced person lives in and has been legally residing continuously for at least five years in the executing State and will retain a permanent right of residence in that State, and/or

(b) if the sentenced person is a national of the executing State in cases other than those provided for in paragraph 1(a) and (b).

In cases referred to in point (a), permanent right of residence shall mean that the person concerned:

— has a right of permanent residence in the respective Member State in accordance with the national law implementing Community legislation adopted on the basis of Article 18, 40, 44 and 52 of the Treaty establishing the European Community, or

— possesses a valid residence permit, as a permanent or long-term resident, for the respective Member State, in accordance with the national law implementing Community legislation adopted on the basis of Article 63 of the Treaty establishing the European Community, as regards Member States to which such Community legislation is applicable, or in accordance with national law, as regards Member States to which it is not.

*Article 5*

**Forwarding of the judgment and the certificate**

1. The judgment or a certified copy of it, together with the certificate, shall be forwarded, by the competent authority of the issuing State directly to the competent authority of the executing State by any means which leaves a written record under conditions allowing the executing State to establish its authenticity. The original of the judgment, or a certified copy of it, and the original of the certificate, shall be sent to the executing State if it so requires. All official communications shall also be made directly between the said competent authorities.

2. The certificate, shall be signed, and its content certified as accurate, by the competent authority of the issuing State.

3. The issuing State shall forward the judgment together with the certificate to only one executing State at any one time.

4. If the competent authority of the executing State is not known to the competent authority of the issuing State, the latter shall make all

▼B

necessary inquiries, including via the Contact points of the European Judicial Network set up by Council Joint Action 98/428/JHA ([1]), in order to obtain the information from the executing State.

5. When an authority of the executing State which receives a judgment together with a certificate has no competence to recognise it and take the necessary measures for its enforcement, it shall, *ex officio*, forward the judgment together with the certificate to the competent authority of the executing State and inform the competent authority of the issuing State accordingly.

*Article 6*

**Opinion and notification of the sentenced person**

1. Without prejudice to paragraph 2, a judgment together with a certificate may be forwarded to the executing State for the purpose of its recognition and enforcement of the sentence only with the consent of the sentenced person in accordance with the law of the issuing State.

2. The consent of the sentenced person shall not be required where the judgment together with the certificate is forwarded:

(a) to the Member State of nationality in which the sentenced person lives;

(b) to the Member State to which the sentenced person will be deported once he or she is released from the enforcement of the sentence on the basis of an expulsion or deportation order included in the judgment or in a judicial or administrative decision or any other measure consequential to the judgment;

(c) to the Member State to which the sentenced person has fled or otherwise returned in view of the criminal proceedings pending against him or her in the issuing State or following the conviction in that issuing State.

3. In all cases where the sentenced person is still in the issuing State, he or she shall be given an opportunity to state his or her opinion orally or in writing. Where the issuing State considers it necessary in view of the sentenced person's age or his or her physical or mental condition, that opportunity shall be given to his or her legal representative.

The opinion of the sentenced person shall be taken into account when deciding the issue of forwarding the judgement together with the certificate. Where the person has availed him or her self of the opportunity provided in this paragraph, the opinion of the sentenced person shall be forwarded to the executing State, in particular with a view to Article 4 (4). If the sentenced person stated his or her opinion orally, the issuing State shall ensure that the written record of such statement is available to executing State.

4. The competent authority of the issuing State shall inform the sentenced person, in a language which he or she understands, that it has decided to forward the judgment together with the certificate by using the standard form of the notification set out in Annex II. When the sentenced person is in the executing State at the time of that decision, that form shall be transmitted to the executing State which shall inform the sentenced person accordingly.

5. Paragraph 2(a) shall not apply to Poland as an issuing State and as an executing State in cases where the judgement was issued before the lapse of five years from 5 December 2011. Poland may at any time notify the General Secretariat of the Council that it will no longer avail itself of this derogation.

([1]) OJ L 191, 7.7.1998, p. 4.

▼B

*Article 7*

**Double criminality**

1. The following offences, if they are punishable in the issuing State by a custodial sentence or a measure involving deprivation of liberty for a maximum period of at least three years, and as they are defined by the law of the issuing State, shall, under the terms of this Framework Decision and without verification of the double criminality of the act, give rise to recognition of the judgment and enforcement of the sentence imposed:

— participation in a criminal organisation,

— terrorism,

— trafficking in human beings,

— sexual exploitation of children and child pornography,

— illicit trafficking in narcotic drugs and psychotropic substances,

— illicit trafficking in weapons, munitions and explosives,

— corruption,

— fraud, including that affecting the financial interests of the European Communities within the meaning of the Convention of 26 July 1995 on the protection of the European Communities' financial interests (1),

— laundering of the proceeds of crime,

— counterfeiting currency, including of the euro,

— computer-related crime,

— environmental crime, including illicit trafficking in endangered animal species and in endangered plant species and varieties,

— facilitation of unauthorised entry and residence,

— murder, grievous bodily injury,

— illicit trade in human organs and tissue,

— kidnapping, illegal restraint and hostage-taking,

— racism and xenophobia,

— organised or armed robbery,

— illicit trafficking in cultural goods, including antiques and works of art,

— swindling,

— racketeering and extortion,

— counterfeiting and piracy of products,

— forgery of administrative documents and trafficking therein,

— forgery of means of payment,

— illicit trafficking in hormonal substances and other growth promoters,

— illicit trafficking in nuclear or radioactive materials,

— trafficking in stolen vehicles,

— rape,

— arson,

— crimes within the jurisdiction of the International Criminal Court,

(1) OJ C 316, 27.11.1995, p. 49.

▼B

— unlawful seizure of aircraft/ships,

— sabotage.

2. The Council may decide to add other categories of offences to the list provided for in paragraph 1 at any time, acting unanimously after consultation of the European Parliament under the conditions laid down in Article 39(1) of the Treaty on European Union. The Council shall examine, in the light of the report submitted to it pursuant to Article 29 (5) of this Framework Decision, whether the list should be extended or amended.

3. For offences other than those covered by paragraph 1, the executing State may make the recognition of the judgment and enforcement of the sentence subject to the condition that it relates to acts which also constitute an offence under the law of the executing State, whatever its constituent elements or however it is described.

4. Each Member State may, on adoption of this Framework Decision or later, by a declaration notified to the General Secretariat of the Council declare that it will not apply paragraph 1. Any such declaration may be withdrawn at any time. Such declarations or withdrawals of declarations shall be published in the *Official Journal of the European Union*.

*Article 8*

**Recognition of the judgment and enforcement of the sentence**

1. The competent authority of the executing State shall recognise a judgment which has been forwarded in accordance with Article 4 and following the procedure under Article 5, and shall forthwith take all the necessary measures for the enforcement of the sentence, unless it decides to invoke one of the grounds for non-recognition and non-enforcement provided for in Article 9.

2. Where the sentence is incompatible with the law of the executing State in terms of its duration, the competent authority of the executing State may decide to adapt the sentence only where that sentence exceeds the maximum penalty provided for similar offences under its national law. The adapted sentence shall not be less than the maximum penalty provided for similar offences under the law of the executing State.

3. Where the sentence is incompatible with the law of the executing State in terms of its nature, the competent authority of the executing State may adapt it to the punishment or measure provided for under its own law for similar offences. Such a punishment or measure shall correspond as closely as possible to the sentence imposed in the issuing State and therefore the sentence shall not be converted into a pecuniary punishment.

4. The adapted sentence shall not aggravate the sentence passed in the issuing State in terms of its nature or duration.

*Article 9*

**Grounds for non-recognition and non-enforcement**

1. The competent authority of the executing State may refuse to recognise the judgment and enforce the sentence, if:

(a) the certificate referred to in Article 4 is incomplete or manifestly does not correspond to the judgment and has not been completed or corrected within a reasonable deadline set by the competent authority of the executing State;

(b) the criteria set forth in Article 4(1) are not met;

(c) enforcement of the sentence would be contrary to the principle of *ne bis in idem*;

▼B

(d) in a case referred to in Article 7(3) and, where the executing State has made a declaration under Article 7(4), in a case referred to in Article 7(1), the judgment relates to acts which would not constitute an offence under the law of the executing State. However, in relation to taxes or duties, customs and exchange, execution of a judgment may not be refused on the ground that the law of the executing State does not impose the same kind of tax or duty or does not contain the same type of rules as regards taxes, duties and customs and exchange regulations as the law of the issuing State;

(e) the enforcement of the sentence is statute-barred according to the law of the executing State;

(f) there is immunity under the law of the executing State, which makes it impossible to enforce the sentence;

(g) the sentence has been imposed on a person who, under the law of the executing State, owing to his or her age, could not have been held criminally liable for the acts in respect of which the judgment was issued;

(h) at the time the judgment was received by the competent authority of the executing State, less than six months of the sentence remain to be served;

▼M1

(i) according to the certificate provided for in Article 4, the person did not appear in person at the trial resulting in the decision, unless the certificate states that the person, in accordance with further procedural requirements defined in the national law of the issuing State:

(i) in due time:

— either was summoned in person and thereby informed of the scheduled date and place of the trial which resulted in the decision, or by other means actually received official information of the scheduled date and place of that trial in such a manner that it was unequivocally established that he or she was aware of the scheduled trial,

and

— was informed that a decision may be handed down if he or she does not appear for the trial;

or

(ii) being aware of the scheduled trial had given a mandate to a legal counsellor, who was either appointed by the person concerned or by the State, to defend him or her at the trial, and was indeed defended by that counsellor at the trial;

or

(iii) after being served with the decision and being expressly informed of the right to a retrial, or an appeal, in which the person has the right to participate and which allows the merits of the case, including fresh evidence, to be re-examined, and which may lead to the original decision being reversed:

— expressly stated that he or she does not contest the decision,

or

— did not request a retrial or appeal within the applicable time frame;

▼B

(j) the executing State, before a decision is taken in accordance with Article 12(1), makes a request, in accordance with Article 18(3), and the issuing State does not consent, in accordance with

▼B

Article 18(2)(g), to the person concerned being prosecuted, sentenced or otherwise deprived of his or her liberty in the executing State for an offence committed prior to the transfer other than that for which the person was transferred;

(k) the sentence imposed includes a measure of psychiatric or health care or another measure involving deprivation of liberty, which, notwithstanding Article 8(3), cannot be executed by the executing State in accordance with its legal or health care system;

(l) the judgment relates to criminal offences which under the law of the executing State are regarded as having been committed wholly or for a major or essential part within its territory, or in a place equivalent to its territory.

2. Any decision under paragraph 1(l) in relation to offences committed partly within the territory of the executing State, or in a place equivalent to its territory, shall be taken by the competent authority of the executing State in exceptional circumstances and on a case-by-case basis, having regard to the specific circumstances of the case, and in particular to whether a major or essential part of the conduct in question has taken place in the issuing State.

3. In the cases referred to in paragraph 1(a), (b), (c), (i), (k) and (l), before deciding not to recognise the judgment and enforce the sentence, the competent authority of the executing State shall consult the competent authority of the issuing State, by any appropriate means, and shall, where appropriate, ask it to supply any necessary additional information without delay.

*Article 10*

**Partial recognition and enforcement**

1. If the competent authority of the executing State could consider recognition of the judgment and enforcement of the sentence in part, it may, before deciding to refuse recognition of the judgment and enforcement of the sentence in whole, consult the competent authority of the issuing State with a view to finding an agreement, as provided for in paragraph 2.

2. The competent authorities of the issuing and the executing States may agree, on a case-by-case basis, to the partial recognition and enforcement of a sentence in accordance with the conditions set out by them, provided such recognition and enforcement does not result in the aggravation of the duration of the sentence. In the absence of such agreement, the certificate shall be withdrawn.

*Article 11*

**Postponement of recognition of the judgment**

The recognition of the judgment may be postponed in the executing State where the certificate referred to in Article 4 is incomplete or manifestly does not correspond to the judgment, until such reasonable deadline set by the executing State for the certificate to be completed or corrected.

*Article 12*

**Decision on the enforcement of the sentence and time limits**

1. The competent authority in the executing State shall decide as quickly as possible whether to recognise the judgment and enforce the sentence and shall inform the issuing State thereof, including of any decision to adapt the sentence in accordance with Article 8(2) and (3).

▼B

2. Unless a ground for postponement exists under Article 11 or Article 23(3), the final decision on the recognition of the judgment and the enforcement of the sentence shall be taken within a period of 90 days of receipt of the judgment and the certificate.

3. When in exceptional cases it is not practicable for the competent authority of the executing State to comply with the period provided for in paragraph 2, it shall without delay inform the competent authority of the issuing State by any means, giving the reasons for the delay and the estimated time needed for the final decision to be taken.

*Article 13*

**Withdrawal of the certificate**

As long as the enforcement of the sentence in the executing State has not begun, the issuing State may withdraw the certificate from that State, giving reasons for doing so. Upon withdrawal of the certificate, the executing State shall no longer enforce the sentence.

*Article 14*

**Provisional arrest**

Where the sentenced person is in the executing State, the executing State may, at the request of the issuing State, before the arrival of the judgment and the certificate, or before the decision to recognise the judgment and enforce the sentence, arrest the sentenced person, or take any other measure to ensure that the sentenced person remains in its territory, pending a decision to recognise the judgment and enforce the sentence. The duration of the sentence shall not be aggravated as a result of any period spent in custody by reason of this provision.

*Article 15*

**Transfer of sentenced persons**

1. If the sentenced person is in the issuing State, he or she shall be transferred to the executing State at a time agreed between the competent authorities of the issuing and the executing States, and no later than 30 days after the final decision of the executing State on the recognition of the judgment and enforcement of the sentence has been taken.

2. If the transfer of the sentenced person within the period laid down in paragraph 1 is prevented by unforeseen circumstances, the competent authorities of the issuing and executing States shall immediately contact each other. Transfer shall take place as soon as these circumstances cease to exist. The competent authority of the issuing State shall immediately inform the competent authority of the executing State and agree on a new transfer date. In that event, transfer shall take place within 10 days of the new date thus agreed.

*Article 16*

**Transit**

1. Each Member State shall, in accordance with its law, permit the transit through its territory of a sentenced person who is being transferred to the executing State, provided that a copy of the certificate referred to in Article 4 has been forwarded to it by the issuing State together with the transit request. The transit request and the certificate may be transmitted by any means capable of producing a written record. Upon request of the Member State to permit transit, the issuing State shall provide a translation of the certificate into one of the languages, to be indicated in the request, which the Member State requested to permit transit accepts.

▼B

2. When receiving a request to permit transit, the Member State requested to permit transit shall inform the issuing State if it cannot guarantee that the sentenced person will not be prosecuted, or, except as provided in paragraph 1, detained or otherwise subjected to any restriction of his or her liberty in its territory for any offence committed or sentence imposed before his or her departure from the territory of the issuing State. In such a case, the issuing State may withdraw its request.

3. The Member State requested to permit transit shall notify its decision, which shall be taken on a priority basis and not later than one week after having received the request, by the same procedure. Such a decision may be postponed until the translation has been transmitted to the Member State requested to permit transit, where such translation is required under paragraph 1.

4. The Member State requested to permit transit may hold the sentenced person in custody only for such time as transit through its territory requires.

5. A transit request shall not be required in the case of transport by air without a scheduled stopover. However, if an unscheduled landing occurs, the issuing State shall provide the information provided for in paragraph 1 within 72 hours.

*Article 17*

**Law governing enforcement**

1. The enforcement of a sentence shall be governed by the law of the executing State. The authorities of the executing State alone shall, subject to paragraphs 2 and 3, be competent to decide on the procedures for enforcement and to determine all the measures relating thereto, including the grounds for early or conditional release.

2. The competent authority of the executing State shall deduct the full period of deprivation of liberty already served in connection with the sentence in respect of which the judgment was issued from the total duration of the deprivation of liberty to be served.

3. The competent authority of the executing State shall, upon request, inform the competent authority of the issuing State of the applicable provisions on possible early or conditional release. The issuing State may agree to the application of such provisions or it may withdraw the certificate.

4. Member States may provide that any decision on early or conditional release may take account of those provisions of national law, indicated by the issuing State, under which the person is entitled to early or conditional release at a specified point in time.

*Article 18*

**Specialty**

1. A person transferred to the executing State pursuant to this Framework Decision shall not, subject to paragraph 2, be prosecuted, sentenced or otherwise deprived of his or her liberty for an offence committed before his or her transfer other than that for which he or she was transferred.

2. Paragraph 1 shall not apply in the following cases:

(a) when the person having had an opportunity to leave the territory of the executing State has not done so within 45 days of his or her final discharge, or has returned to that territory after leaving it;

(b) when the offence is not punishable by a custodial sentence or detention order;

▼B

(c) when the criminal proceedings do not give rise to the application of a measure restricting personal liberty;

(d) when the sentenced person could be liable to a penalty or a measure not involving deprivation of liberty, in particular a financial penalty or a measure *in lieu* thereof, even if the penalty or measure *in lieu* may give rise to a restriction of his or her personal liberty;

(e) when the sentenced person consented to the transfer;

(f) when the sentenced person, after his or her transfer, has expressly renounced entitlement to the specialty rule with regard to specific offences preceding his or her transfer. Renunciation shall be given before the competent judicial authorities of the executing State and shall be recorded in accordance with that State's national law. The renunciation shall be drawn up in such a way as to make clear that the person has given it voluntarily and in full awareness of the consequences. To that end, the person shall have the right to legal counsel;

(g) for cases other than those mentioned under points (a) to (f), where the issuing State gives its consent in accordance with paragraph 3.

3. A request for consent shall be submitted to the competent authority of the issuing State, accompanied by the information mentioned in Article 8(1) of Framework Decision 2002/584/JHA and a translation as referred to in Article 8(2) thereof. Consent shall be given where there is an obligation to surrender the person under that Framework Decision. The decision shall be taken no later than 30 days after receipt of the request. For the situations mentioned in Article 5 of that Framework Decision, the executing State shall give the guarantees provided for therein.

*Article 19*

**Amnesty, pardon, review of judgment**

1. An amnesty or pardon may be granted by the issuing State and also by the executing State.

2. Only the issuing State may decide on applications for review of the judgment imposing the sentence to be enforced under this Framework Decision.

*Article 20*

**Information from the issuing State**

1. The competent authority of the issuing State shall forthwith inform the competent authority of the executing State of any decision or measure as a result of which the sentence ceases to be enforceable immediately or within a certain period of time.

2. The competent authority of the executing State shall terminate enforcement of the sentence as soon as it is informed by the competent authority of the issuing State of the decision or measure referred to in paragraph 1.

*Article 21*

**Information to be given by the executing State**

The competent authority of the executing State shall without delay inform the competent authority of the issuing State by any means which leaves a written record:

(a) of the forwarding of the judgment and the certificate to the competent authority responsible for its execution in accordance with Article 5(5);

▼B

(b) of the fact that it is in practice impossible to enforce the sentence because after transmission of the judgment and the certificate to the executing State, the sentenced person cannot be found in the territory of the executing State, in which case there shall be no obligation on the executing State to enforce the sentence;

(c) of the final decision to recognise the judgment and enforce the sentence together with the date of the decision;

(d) of any decision not to recognise the judgment and enforce the sentence in accordance with Article 9, together with the reasons for the decision;

(e) of any decision to adapt the sentence in accordance with Article 8 (2) or (3), together with the reasons for the decision;

(f) of any decision not to enforce the sentence for the reasons referred to in Article 19(1) together with the reasons for the decision;

(g) of the beginning and the end of the period of conditional release, where so indicated in the certificate by the issuing State;

(h) of the sentenced person's escape from custody;

(i) of the enforcement of the sentence as soon as it has been completed.

*Article 22*

**Consequences of the transfer of the sentenced person**

1. Subject to paragraph 2, the issuing State shall not proceed with the enforcement of the sentence once its enforcement in the executing State has begun.

2. The right to enforce the sentence shall revert to the issuing State upon its being informed by the executing State of the partial non-enforcement of the sentence pursuant to Article 21(h).

*Article 23*

**Languages**

1. The certificate shall be translated into the official language or one of the official languages of the executing State. Any Member State may, on adoption of this Framework Decision or later, state in a declaration deposited with the General Secretariat of the Council that it will accept a translation in one or more other official languages of the Institutions of the European Union.

2. Subject to paragraph 3, no translation of the judgment shall be required.

3. Any Member State may, on adoption of this Framework Decision or later, in a declaration deposited with the General Secretariat of the Council state that it, as an executing State, may without delay after receiving the judgment and the certificate, request, in cases where it finds the content of the certificate insufficient to decide on the enforcement of the sentence, that the judgment or essential parts of it be accompanied by a translation into the official language or one of the official languages of the executing State or into one or more other official languages of the Institutions of the European Union. Such a request shall be made, after consultation, where necessary, to indicate the essential parts of the judgments to be translated, between the competent authorities of the issuing and the executing States.

The decision on recognition of the judgment and enforcement of the sentence may be postponed until the translation has been transmitted by the issuing State to the executing State or, where the executing State decides to translate the judgment at its own expenses, until the translation has been obtained.

▼B

*Article 24*

**Costs**

Costs resulting from the application of this Framework Decision shall be borne by the executing State, except for the costs of the transfer of the sentenced person to the executing State and those arising exclusively in the sovereign territory of the issuing State.

*Article 25*

**Enforcement of sentences following a European arrest warrant**

Without prejudice to Framework Decision 2002/584/JHA, provisions of this Framework Decision shall apply, *mutatis mutandis* to the extent they are compatible with provisions under that Framework Decision, to enforcement of sentences in cases where a Member State undertakes to enforce the sentence in cases pursuant to Article 4(6) of that Framework Decision, or where, acting under Article 5(3) of that Framework Decision, it has imposed the condition that the person has to be returned to serve the sentence in the Member State concerned, so as to avoid impunity of the person concerned.

CHAPTER III

**FINAL PROVISIONS**

*Article 26*

**Relationship with other agreements and arrangements**

1. Without prejudice to their application between Member States and third States and their transitional application according to Article 28, this Framework Decision shall, from 5 December 2011, replace the corresponding provisions of the following conventions applicable in relations between the Member States:

— The European Convention on the transfer of sentenced persons of 21 March 1983 and the Additional Protocol thereto of 18 December 1997;

— The European Convention on the International Validity of Criminal Judgements of 28 May 1970;

— Title III, Chapter 5, of the Convention of 19 June 1990 implementing the Schengen Convention of 14 June 1985 on the gradual abolition of checks at common borders;

— The Convention between the Member States of the European Communities on the Enforcement of Foreign Criminal Sentences of 13 November 1991.

2. Member States may continue to apply bilateral or multilateral agreements or arrangements in force after 27 November 2008, in so far as they allow the objectives of this Framework Decision to be extended or enlarged and help to simplify or facilitate further the procedures for the enforcement of sentences.

3. Member States may conclude bilateral or multilateral agreements or arrangements after 5 December 2008 in so far as such agreements or arrangements allow the provisions of this Framework Decision to be extended or enlarged and help to simplify or facilitate further the procedures for the enforcement of sentences.

4. Member States shall by 5 March 2009, notify the Council and the Commission of the existing agreements and arrangements referred to in paragraph 2 which they wish to continue applying. Member States shall also notify the Council and the Commission of any new agreement or

▼B

arrangement as referred to in paragraph 3, within three months of signing it.

*Article 27*

**Territorial application**

This Framework Decision shall apply to Gibraltar.

*Article 28*

**Transitional provision**

1. Requests received before 5 December 2011 shall continue to be governed in accordance with the existing legal instruments on the transfer of sentenced persons. Requests received after that date shall be governed by the rules adopted by Member States pursuant to this Framework Decision.

2. However, any Member State may, on the adoption of this Framework Decision, make a declaration indicating that, in cases where the final judgment has been issued before the date it specifies, it will as an issuing and an executing State, continue to apply the existing legal instruments on the transfer of sentenced persons applicable before 5 December 2011. If such a declaration is made, those instruments shall apply in such cases in relation to all other Member States irrespective of whether or not they have made the same declaration. The date in question may not be later than 5 December 2011. The said declaration shall be published in the *Official Journal of the European Union*. It may be withdrawn at any time.

*Article 29*

**Implementation**

1. Member States shall take the necessary measures to comply with the provisions of this Framework Decision by 5 December 2011.

2. Member States shall transmit to the General Secretariat of the Council and to the Commission the text of the provisions transposing into their national law the obligations imposed on them under this Framework Decision. On the basis of a report established using this information by the Commission, the Council shall, no later than 5 December 2012, assess the extent to which Member States have complied with the provisions of this Framework Decision.

3. The General Secretariat of the Council shall notify the Member States and the Commission of the notifications or declarations made pursuant to Article 4(7) and Article 23(1) or (3).

4. Without prejudice to Article 35(7) of the Treaty on European Union, a Member State which has experienced repeated difficulties in the application of Article 25 of this Framework Decision, which have not been solved through bilateral consultations, shall inform the Council and the Commission of its difficulties. The Commission shall, on the basis of this information and any other information available to it, establish a report, accompanied by any initiatives it may deem appropriate, with a view to resolving these difficulties.

5. By 5 December 2013, the Commission shall establish a report on the basis of the information received, accompanied by any initiatives it may deem appropriate. The Council shall on the basis of any report from the Commission and any initiative, review, in particular Article 25, with a view to considering whether it is to be replaced by more specific provisions.

▼B

*Article 30*

**Entry into force**

This Framework Decision shall enter into force on the day of its publication in the *Official Journal of the European Union*.

▼B

*ANNEX I*

**CERTIFICATE**

**referred to in Article 4 of Council Framework Decision 2008/909/JHA of 27 November 2008 on the application of the principle of mutual recognition to judgments in criminal matters imposing custodial sentences or measures involving deprivation of liberty for the purpose of their enforcement in the European Union** (1)

(a) * Issuing State: ..........

* Executing State: ..........

(b) The court which delivered the judgment imposing the sentence that became final:

Official name: ..........

The judgment was delivered on (give date: dd-mm-yyyy): ..........

The judgment became final on (give date: dd-mm-yyyy): ..........

Reference number of the judgment (if available): ..........

(c) Information related to the authority that may be contacted for any question related to the certificate:

1. Type of authority: Please tick the relevant box:

☐ Central authority ..........

☐ Court ..........

☐ Other authority ..........

2. Contact details of the authority indicated under point (c) 1:

Official name: ..........

..........

Address: ..........

..........

Tel.: (country code) (area/city code) ..........

Fax: (country code) (area/city code) ..........

E-mail address (if available): ..........

3. Languages in which it is possible to communicate with the authority:

4. Contact details of person(s) to be contacted to obtain additional information for the purposes of enforcement of the judgment or agreement on the transfer procedures (name, title/grade, telephone No, fax, e-mail address), if different from 2: ..........

..........

..........

(1) This certificate must be written in, or translated into, one of the official languages of the executing Member State or any other language accepted by that State.

▼B

(d) Information regarding the person on whom the sentence has been imposed:

Name: ...............................................................................................

Forename(s): ...............................................................................................

Maiden name, where applicable: ...............................................................................................

Aliases, where applicable: ...............................................................................................

Sex: ...............................................................................................

Nationality: ...............................................................................................

Identity number or social security number (if available): ...............................................................................................

Date of birth: ...............................................................................................

Place of birth: ...............................................................................................

Last known addresses/residences: ...............................................................................................

Language(s) which the person understands (if known): ...............................................................................................

...............................................................................................

The sentenced person is:

☐ in the issuing State and is to be transferred to the executing State.

☐ in the executing State and enforcement is to take place in that State.

Additional information to be provided, if available and if appropriate:

1. Photo and fingerprints of the person, and/or contact details of the person to be contacted in order to obtain such information:

   ...............................................................................................

2. Type and reference number of the sentenced person's identity card or passport:

   ...............................................................................................

3. Type and reference number of the sentenced person's residence permit:

   ...............................................................................................

4. Other relevant information about the sentenced person's family, social or professional ties to the executing State:

   ...............................................................................................

   ...............................................................................................

(e) Request for provisional arrest by the issuing State (where the sentenced person is in the executing State):

☐ The issuing State requests the executing State to arrest the sentenced person, or to take any other measure to ensure that the sentenced person remains in its territory, pending a decision to recognise and enforce the sentence.

☐ The issuing State has already requested the executing State to arrest the sentenced person, or to take any other measure to ensure that the sentenced person remains in its territory, pending a decision to recognise and enforce the sentence. Please provide the name of the authority in the executing State that has taken the decision on the request to arrest the person (If applicable and available):

...............................................................................................

...............................................................................................

...............................................................................................

▼B

(f) Relation to any earlier European Arrest Warrant (EAW):

☐ An EAW has been issued for the purpose of the execution of a custodial sentence or detention order and the executing Member State undertakes to execute the sentence or detention order (Article 4(6) of the EAW Framework Decision).

Date of issue of the EAW and, if available, reference number:

..............................................................................................................................................................

Name of the authority that issued the EAW: ..............................................................................................

Date of decision to undertake execution and, if available, reference number:

..............................................................................................................................................................

Name of the authority that issued the decision to undertake execution of the sentence:

..............................................................................................................................................................

☐ An EAW has been issued for the purpose of prosecution of a person who is a national or resident of the executing State and the executing State has surrendered the person under the condition that the person is to be returned to the executing State in order to serve there the custodial sentence or detention order passed against him or her in the issuing Member State (Article 5(3) of the EAW Framework Decision).

Date of the decision to surrender the person: ..............................................................................................

Name of the authority that issued the decision to surrender: ..........................................................................

Reference number of the decision, if available: ...........................................................................................

Date of the surrender of the person, if available: .........................................................................................

(g) Reasons for forwarding the judgment and the certificate (if you have filled in Box (f), there is no need to fill in this box):

The judgment and the certificate are forwarded to the executing State because the issuing authority is satisfied that the enforcement of the sentence by the executing State would serve the purpose of facilitating the social rehabilitation of the sentenced person and:

☐ (a) The executing State is the State of nationality of the sentenced person in which he or she lives.

☐ (b) The executing State is the State of nationality of the sentenced person, to which the sentenced person will be deported, once he or she is released from the enforcement of the sentence on the basis of an expulsion or deportation order included in the judgment or in a judicial or administrative decision or any other measure taken consequential to the judgment. If the expulsion or deportation order is not included in the judgment, please provide the name of the authority that issued the order, the date of issue, and, if available, the reference number: ..............................................................................................................................

☐ (c) The executing State is a State, other than a State referred to in (a) or (b), the competent authority of which consents to the forwarding of the judgment and the certificate to that State.

☐ (d) The executing State has given a notification under Article 4(7) of the Framework Decision, and:

☐ it is confirmed that, to the knowledge of the competent authority of the issuing State, the sentenced person lives and has been legally residing continuously for at least five years in the executing State and will retain a permanent right of residence in that state, or

☐ it is confirmed that the sentenced person is a national of the executing State.

▼B

(h) Judgment imposing the sentence:

1. The judgment covers ...................... offences in total.

Summary of facts and a description of the circumstances in which the offence(s) was (were) committed, including time and place; and the nature of the involvement of the sentenced person:

..........................................................................................................................................

..........................................................................................................................................

..........................................................................................................................................

..........................................................................................................................................

Nature and legal classification of the offence(s) and the applicable statutory provisions on the basis of which the judgment was made:

..........................................................................................................................................

..........................................................................................................................................

..........................................................................................................................................

2. To the extent that the offence(s) identified under point (h) 1 constitute(s) one or more of the following offences, as defined in the law of the issuing State, which are punishable in the issuing State by a custodial sentence or detention order of a maximum of at least three years, please confirm by ticking the relevant box(es)):

☐ participation in a criminal organisation;

☐ terrorism;

☐ trafficking in human beings;

☐ sexual exploitation of children and child pornography;

☐ illicit trafficking in narcotic drugs and psychotropic substances;

☐ illicit trafficking in weapons, munitions and explosives;

☐ corruption;

☐ fraud, including that affecting the financial interests of the European Communities within the meaning of the Convention of 26 July 1995 on the protection of the European Communities' financial interests;

☐ laundering of the proceeds of crime;

☐ counterfeiting currency, including of the euro;

☐ computer-related crime;

☐ environmental crime, including illicit trafficking in endangered animal species and in endangered plant species and varieties;

☐ facilitation of unauthorised entry and residence;

☐ murder, grievous bodily injury;

☐ illicit trade in human organs and tissue;

☐ kidnapping, illegal restraint and hostage-taking;

☐ racism and xenophobia;

☐ organised or armed robbery;

☐ illicit trafficking in cultural goods, including antiques and works of art;

☐ swindling;

☐ racketeering and extortion;

☐ counterfeiting and piracy of products;

☐ forgery of administrative documents and trafficking therein;

☐ forgery of means of payment;

☐ illicit trafficking in hormonal substances and other growth promoters;

☐ illicit trafficking in nuclear or radioactive materials;

☐ trafficking in stolen vehicles;

☐ rape;

☐ arson;

☐ crimes within the jurisdiction of the International Criminal Court;

☐ unlawful seizure of aircraft/ships;

☐ sabotage.

3. To the extent that the offence(s) identified under point 1 is (are) not covered by point 2 or if the judgment and the certificate is forwarded to the Member State, which has declared that it will verify the double criminality (Article 7(4) of the Framework Decision), please give a full description of the offence(s) concerned:

..........................................................................................................................................

..........................................................................................................................................

..........................................................................................................................................

▼B

(i) Status of the judgment imposing the sentence:

►(1) 1. Indicate if the person appeared in person at the trial resulting in the decision:

1. ☐ Yes, the person appeared in person at the trial resulting in the decision.

2. ☐ No, the person did not appear in person at the trial resulting in the decision.

3. If you have ticked the box under point 2, please confirm the existence of one of the following:

☐ 3.1a. the person was summoned in person on … (day/month/year) and thereby informed of the scheduled date and place of the trial which resulted in the decision and was informed that a decision may be handed down if he or she does not appear for the trial;

OR

☐ 3.1b. the person was not summoned in person but by other means actually received official information of the scheduled date and place of the trial which resulted in the decision, in such a manner that it was unequivocally established that he or she was aware of the scheduled trial, and was informed that a decision may be handed down if he or she does not appear for the trial;

OR

☐ 3.2. being aware of the scheduled trial the person had given a mandate to a legal counsellor, who was either appointed by the person concerned or by the State, to defend him or her at the trial, and was indeed defended by that counsellor at the trial;

OR

☐ 3.3. the person was served with the decision on … (day/month/year) and was expressly informed about the right to a retrial or appeal, in which he or she has the right to participate and which allows the merits of the case, including fresh evidence, to be re-examined, and which may lead to the original decision being reversed, and

☐ the person expressly stated that he or she does not contest this decision,

OR

☐ the person did not request a retrial or appeal within the applicable time frame.

4. If you have ticked the box under points 3.1b, 3.2 or 3.3 above, please provide information about how the relevant condition has been met:

……………………………………………………………………………………………

……………………………………………………………………………………………◄

2. Details of the length of the sentence:

2.1. Total length of the sentence (in days): ……………………………………………

2.2. The full period of deprivation of liberty already served in connection with the sentence in respect of which the judgment was issued (in days):

……………… as per (…) (give date on which calculation was made: dd-mm-yyyy): ………………

2.3. Number of days to be deducted from total length of the sentence for reasons other than the one referred to under 2.2 (e.g.amnesties, pardons or clemencies, etc. already granted with respect to the sentence): .. as per (give date on which calculation was made: dd-mm-yyyy): ...

2.4. Sentence expiry date in the issuing State:

☐ Not applicable, because the person is currently not in custody

☐ The person is currently in custody and the sentence, under the law of the issuing State, would be fully served by (give date: dd-mm-yyyy) ([1]): ……………………………………

3. Type of sentence:

☐ custodial sentence

☐ measure involving deprivation of liberty (please specify):

……………………………………………………………………………………………

(j) Information related to early or conditional release:

1. Under the law of the issuing State the sentenced person is entitled to early or conditional release, having served:

☐ half the sentence

☐ two-thirds of the sentence

☐ another portion of the sentence (please indicate):

2. The competent authority of the issuing State requests to be informed of:

☐ The applicable provisions of the law of the executing State on early or conditional release of the sentenced person;

☐ The beginning and the end of the period of early or conditional release.

([1]) Please insert here the date by which the sentence would be fully served (not taking into account the possibilities of any form of early and/or conditional release) if the person were to stay in the issuing State.

►(1) M1

▼B

(k) Opinion of the sentenced person:

1. ☐ The sentenced person could not be heard because he/she is already in the executing State.

2. ☐ The sentenced person is in the issuing State and:

a. ☐ has requested the forwarding of the judgment and the certificate

☐ consented to the forwarding of the judgment and the certificate

☐ did not consent to the forwarding of the judgment and the certificate (state reasons given by the sentenced person):

.......................................................................................................................................

.......................................................................................................................................

b. ☐ Opinion of the sentenced person is attached.

☐ Opinion of the sentenced person was forwarded to the executing State on (give date: dd-mm-yyyy):

.......................................................................................................................................

(l) Other circumstances relevant to the case (optional information):

.......................................................................................................................................

.......................................................................................................................................

(m) Final information:

The text of the judgment(s) is (are) attached to the certificate [1].

Signature of the authority issuing the certificate and/or its representative certifying the content of the certificate as accurate

.......................................................................................................................................

Name: .......................................................................................................................................

Post held (title/grade): .......................................................................................................................................

Date: .......................................................................................................................................

Official stamp (if available) .......................................................................................................................................

(1) The competent authority of the issuing State must attach all judgments related to the case which are necessary to have all the information on the final sentence to be enforced. Any available translation of the judgment(s) may also be attached.

▼B

*ANNEX II*

**NOTIFICATION OF THE SENTENCED PERSON**

You are hereby notified of the decision of ............ (competent authority of the issuing State) to forward the judgment of ....... (competent court of the issuing State) dated .................... (date of judgment) ................... (reference number; if available) to ................ (executing State) for the purpose of its recognition and enforcement of the sentence imposed therein in accordance with the national law implementing Council Framework Decision 2008/909/JHA of 27 November 2008 on the application of the principle of mutual recognition of judgments in criminal matters imposing custodial sentences or measures involving deprivation of liberty for the purpose of their enforcement in the European Union.

The enforcement of the sentence will be governed by the law of ......... (executing State). The authorities of that State will be competent to decide on the procedures for enforcement and to determine all the measures relating thereto, including the grounds for early or conditional release.

The competent authority of .................. (executing State) has to deduct the full period of deprivation of liberty already served in connection with the sentence from the total duration of deprivation of liberty to be served. An adaptation of the sentence by the competent authority of ..................... (executing State) may take place only if it is incompatible with the law of that State in terms of its duration or nature. The adapted sentence must not aggravate the sentence passed in .............................................. (issuing State) by its nature or duration.

9.10.2009 EN Official Journal of the European Union L 265/41

III

*(Acts adopted under the EU Treaty)*

# ACTS ADOPTED UNDER TITLE VI OF THE EU TREATY

## DECLARATION BY THE NETHERLANDS CONCERNING ARTICLE 28 OF THE FRAMEWORK DECISION

In accordance with Article 28(2), the Netherlands hereby declares that, in cases where the final judgment has been issued within 3 years following the date on which the Framework Decision enters into force, the Netherlands will, as an issuing and an executing State, continue to apply the legal instruments on the transfer of sentenced persons applicable prior to this Framework Decision.

1.6.2011 EN Official Journal of the European Union L 146/21

IV

*(Acts adopted before 1 December 2009 under the EC Treaty, the EU Treaty and the Euratom Treaty)*

**Declaration by the Republic of Poland on Council Framework Decision 2008/909/JHA of 27 November 2008 on the application of the principle of mutual recognition to judgments in criminal matters imposing custodial sentences or measures involving deprivation of liberty for the purpose of their enforcement in the European Union**

In accordance with Article 28(2), the Republic of Poland hereby declares that, in cases where the final judgment is issued within 3 years following the date of entry into force, the Republic of Poland will, as an issuing and an executing State, continue to apply the legal instruments on the transfer of sentenced persons applicable prior to entry into force of the Framework Decision.

# Framework Decision 2008/947 on the application of the principle of mutual recognition to judgments and probation decisions with a view to the supervision of probation measures and alternative sanctions, 27 November 2008

**[Consolidated version. Original version OJ 2008, L 337/102–122 amended as of 28 March 2011 by OJ 2009, L 81/24–36]**

►B

**COUNCIL FRAMEWORK DECISION 2008/947/JHA**

**of 27 November 2008**

**on the application of the principle of mutual recognition to judgments and probation decisions with a view to the supervision of probation measures and alternative sanctions**

(OJ L 337, 16.12.2008, p. 102)

Amended by:

| | | Official Journal | | |
|---|---|---|---|---|
| | | No | page | date |
| ►M1 | Council Framework Decision 2009/299/JHA of 26 February 2009 | L 81 | 24 | 27.3.2009 |

▼B

**COUNCIL FRAMEWORK DECISION 2008/947/JHA**

**of 27 November 2008**

**on the application of the principle of mutual recognition to judgments and probation decisions with a view to the supervision of probation measures and alternative sanctions**

THE COUNCIL OF THE EUROPEAN UNION,

Having regard to the Treaty on European Union, and in particular Article 31(1)(a) and (c) and Article 34(2)(b) thereof,

Having regard to the initiative of the Federal Republic of Germany and of the French Republic ([1]),

Having regard to the Opinion of the European Parliament ([2]),

Whereas:

(1) The European Union has set itself the objective of developing an area of freedom, security and justice. This presupposes that there is an understanding of freedom, security and justice on the part of the Member States which is identical in its essential elements and based on the principles of freedom, democracy, respect for human rights and fundamental freedoms, as well as the rule of law.

(2) The aim of police and judicial cooperation in the European Union is to provide a high degree of security for all citizens. One of the cornerstones for this is the principle of mutual recognition of judicial decisions, established in the conclusions of the European Council meeting in Tampere on 15 and 16 October 1999 and reaffirmed in the Hague Programme of 4 and 5 November 2004 for strengthening freedom, security and justice in the European Union ([3]). In the programme of measures of 29 November 2000 adopted for the purpose of implementing the principle of mutual recognition of decisions in criminal matters, the Council pronounced itself in favour of cooperation in the area of suspended sentences and parole.

(3) Council Framework Decision 2008/909/JHA of 27 November 2008 on the application of the principle of mutual recognition to judgments in criminal matters imposing custodial sentences or measures involving deprivation of liberty for the purpose of their enforcement in the European Union ([4]) concerns the mutual recognition and enforcement of custodial sentences or measures involving deprivation of liberty. Further common rules are required, in particular where a non-custodial sentence involving the supervision of probation measures or alternative sanctions has been imposed in respect of a person who does not have his lawful and ordinary residence in the State of conviction.

(4) The Council of Europe Convention of 30 November 1964 on the Supervision of Conditionally Sentenced or Conditionally Released Offenders has been ratified by only 12 Member States, with, in some cases, numerous reservations. The present Framework Decision provides for a more effective instrument because it is based on the principle of mutual recognition and all Member States participate.

(5) This Framework Decision respects fundamental rights and adheres to the principles recognised in Article 6 of the Treaty on European Union, which are also expressed in the Charter of Fundamental Rights of the European Union, especially in Chapter VI thereof. No provision of this Framework Decision should be

([1]) OJ C 147, 30.6.2007, p. 1.
([2]) Opinion of 25 October 2007 (not yet published in the Official Journal).
([3]) OJ C 53, 3.3.2005, p. 1.
([4]) OJ L 327, 5.12.2008, p. 27.

▼B

interpreted as prohibiting refusal to recognise a judgment and/or supervise a probation measure or alternative sanction if there are objective reasons to believe that the probation measure or alternative sanction was imposed to punish a person because of his or her sex, race, religion, ethnic origin, nationality, language, political opinions or sexual orientation or that this person might be disadvantaged for one of these reasons.

(6) This Framework Decision should not prevent any Member State from applying its constitutional rules relating to entitlement to due process, freedom of association, freedom of the press, freedom of expression in other media and freedom of religion.

(7) The provisions of this Framework Decision should be applied in conformity with the right of the Union's citizens to move and reside freely within the territory of the Member States, pursuant to Article 18 of the Treaty establishing the European Community.

(8) The aim of mutual recognition and supervision of suspended sentences, conditional sentences, alternative sanctions and decisions on conditional release is to enhance the prospects of the sentenced person's being reintegrated into society, by enabling that person to preserve family, linguistic, cultural and other ties, but also to improve monitoring of compliance with probation measures and alternative sanctions, with a view to preventing recidivism, thus paying due regard to the protection of victims and the general public.

(9) There are several types of probation measures and alternative sanctions which are common among the Member States and which all Member States are in principle willing to supervise. The supervision of these types of measures and sanctions should be obligatory, subject to certain exceptions provided for in this Framework Decision. Member States may declare that, in addition, they are willing to supervise other types of probation measures and/or other types of alternative sanctions.

(10) The probation measures and alternative sanctions that are, in principle, obligatory to supervise include, *inter alia*, orders relating to behaviour (such as an obligation to stop the consumption of alcohol), residence (such as an obligation to change residence for reasons of domestic violence), education and training (such as an obligation to follow a 'safe-driving course'), leisure activities (such as an obligation to cease playing or attending a certain sport) and limitations on or modalities of carrying out a professional activity (such as an obligation to seek a professional activity in a different working environment; this obligation does not include the supervision of compliance with any professional disqualifications imposed on the person as part of the sanction).

(11) Where appropriate, electronic monitoring could be used with a view to supervising probation measures or alternative sanctions, in accordance with national law and procedures.

(12) The Member State where the person concerned is sentenced may forward a judgment and, where applicable, a probation decision to the Member State where the sentenced person is lawfully and ordinarily resident with a view to the recognition thereof and to the supervision of probation measures or alternative sanctions contained therein.

(13) The decision on whether to forward the judgment and, where applicable, the probation decision to another Member State should be taken in each individual case by the competent authority of the issuing Member State, taking into account, *inter alia*, the declarations made in accordance with Articles 5(4), 10(4) and 14(3).

▼B

(14) The judgment and, where applicable, the probation decision may also be forwarded to a Member State other than that where the sentenced person is residing, if the competent authority of that executing State, taking account of any conditions set out in the relevant declaration made by that State in accordance with this Framework Decision, consents to such forwarding. In particular, consent may be given, with a view to social rehabilitation, where the sentenced person, without losing his/her right of residence, intends to move to another Member State because he/she is granted an employment contract, if he/she is a family member of a lawful and ordinary resident person of that Member State, or if he/she intends to follow a study or training in that Member State, in accordance with Community law.

(15) Member States should apply their own national law and procedures for the recognition of a judgment and, where applicable, a probation decision. In the case of a conditional sentence or alternative sanction where the judgment does not contain a custodial sentence or measure involving deprivation of liberty to be enforced in case of non-compliance with the obligations or instructions concerned, this could imply that having made the relevant declaration in accordance with this Framework Decision, Member States, when deciding to recognise, agree to supervise the probation measures or alternative sanctions concerned and to assume no other responsibility than just for taking the subsequent decisions consisting of the modification of obligations or instructions contained in the probation measure or alternative sanction, or modification of the duration of the probation period. Consequently, the recognition has, in such cases, no further effect than to enable the executing State to take those types of subsequent decisions.

(16) A Member State may refuse to recognise a judgment and, where applicable, a probation decision, if the judgment concerned was issued against a person who has not been found guilty, such as in the case of a mentally ill person, and the judgment or, where applicable, the probation decision provides for medical/-therapeutic treatment which the executing State cannot supervise in respect of such persons under its national law.

(17) The ground for refusal relating to territoriality should be applied only in exceptional cases and with a view to cooperating to the greatest extent possible under the provisions of this Framework Decision, while taking into account of the objectives thereof. Any decision to apply this ground for refusal should be based on a case-by-case analysis and on consultations between the competent authorities of the issuing and executing States.

(18) If the probation measures or alternative sanctions include community service, then the executing State should be entitled to refuse to recognise the judgment and, where applicable, the probation decision if the community service would normally be completed in less than six months.

(19) The form of the certificate is drafted in such a way so that essential elements of the judgment and, where applicable, of the probation decision are comprised in the certificate, which should be translated into the official language or one of the official languages of the executing State. The certificate should assist the competent authorities in the executing State in taking decisions under this Framework Decision, including decisions on recognition and assumption of responsibility for supervision of probation measures and alternative sanctions, decisions on adaptation of probation measures and alternative sanctions, and subsequent decisions in case, notably, of non-compliance with a probation measure or alternative sanction.

▼B

(20) In view of the principle of mutual recognition, on which this Framework Decision is based, issuing and executing Member States should promote direct contact between their competent authorities in the application of this Framework Decision.

(21) All Member States should ensure that sentenced persons, in respect of whom decisions under this Framework Decision are taken, are subject to a set of legal rights and remedies in accordance with their national law, regardless of whether the competent authorities designated to take decisions under this Framework Decision are of a judicial or a non-judicial nature.

(22) All subsequent decisions relating to a suspended sentence, a conditional sentence or an alternative sanction which result in the imposition of a custodial sentence or measure involving deprivation of liberty should be taken by a judicial authority.

(23) Since all Member States have ratified the Council of Europe Convention of 28 January 1981 for the Protection of Individuals with regard to Automatic Processing of Personal Data, personal data processed when implementing this Framework Decision should be protected in accordance with the principles laid down in that Convention.

(24) Since the objectives of this Framework Decision, namely facilitating the social rehabilitation of sentenced persons, improving the protection of victims and of the general public, and facilitating the application of suitable probation measures and alternative sanctions in case of offenders who do not live in the State of conviction, cannot be sufficiently achieved by the Member States themselves in view of the cross-border nature of the situations involved and can therefore, by reason of the scale of the action, be better achieved at Union level, the Union may adopt measures, in accordance with the principle of subsidiarity as defined in Article 5 of the Treaty establishing the European Community as applied by the second paragraph of Article 2 of the Treaty on European Union. In accordance with the principle of proportionality, as set out in Article 5 of the Treaty establishing the European Community, this Framework Decision does not go beyond what is necessary in order to achieve those objectives,

HAS ADOPTED THIS FRAMEWORK DECISION:

*Article 1*

**Objectives and scope**

1. This Framework Decision aims at facilitating the social rehabilitation of sentenced persons, improving the protection of victims and of the general public, and facilitating the application of suitable probation measures and alternative sanctions, in case of offenders who do not live in the State of conviction. With a view to achieving these objectives, this Framework Decision lays down rules according to which a Member State, other than the Member State in which the person concerned has been sentenced, recognises judgments and, where applicable, probation decisions and supervises probation measures imposed on the basis of a judgment, or alternative sanctions contained in such a judgment, and takes all other decisions relating to that judgment, unless otherwise provided for in this Framework Decision.

2. This Framework Decision shall apply only to:

(a) the recognition of judgments and, where applicable, probation decisions;

(b) the transfer of responsibility for the supervision of probation measures and alternative sanctions;

▼B

(c) all other decisions related to those under (a) and (b);

as described and provided for in this Framework Decision.

3. This Framework Decision shall not apply to:

(a) the execution of judgments in criminal matters imposing custodial sentences or measures involving deprivation of liberty which fall within the scope of Framework Decision 2008/909/JHA;

(b) recognition and execution of financial penalties and confiscation orders which fall within the scope of Council Framework Decision 2005/214/JHA of 24 February 2005 on the application of the principle of mutual recognition to financial penalties ([1]) and Council Framework Decision 2006/783/JHA of 6 October 2006 on the application of the principle of mutual recognition to confiscation orders ([2]).

4. This Framework Decision shall not have the effect of modifying the obligation to respect fundamental rights and fundamental legal principles as enshrined in Article 6 of the Treaty on European Union.

*Article 2*

**Definitions**

For the purposes of this Framework Decision:

1. 'judgment' shall mean a final decision or order of a court of the issuing State, establishing that a natural person has committed a criminal offence and imposing:

   (a) a custodial sentence or measure involving deprivation of liberty, if a conditional release has been granted on the basis of that judgment or by a subsequent probation decision;

   (b) a suspended sentence;

   (c) a conditional sentence;

   (d) an alternative sanction;

2. 'suspended sentence' shall mean a custodial sentence or measure involving deprivation of liberty, the execution of which is conditionally suspended, wholly or in part, when the sentence is passed by imposing one or more probation measures. Such probation measures may be included in the judgment itself or determined in a separate probation decision taken by a competent authority;

3. 'conditional sentence' shall mean a judgment in which the imposition of a sentence has been conditionally deferred by imposing one or more probation measures or in which one or more probation measures are imposed instead of a custodial sentence or measure involving deprivation of liberty. Such probation measures may be included in the judgment itself or determined in a separate probation decision taken by a competent authority;

4. 'alternative sanction' shall mean a sanction, other than a custodial sentence, a measure involving deprivation of liberty or a financial penalty, imposing an obligation or instruction;

5. 'probation decision' shall mean a judgment or a final decision of a competent authority of the issuing State taken on the basis of such judgment:

   (a) granting a conditional release; or

   (b) imposing probation measures;

([1]) OJ L 76, 22.3.2005, p. 16.
([2]) OJ L 328, 24.11.2006, p. 59.

▼B

6. 'conditional release' shall mean a final decision of a competent authority or stemming from the national law on the early release of a sentenced person after part of the custodial sentence or measure involving deprivation of liberty has been served by imposing one or more probation measures;

7. 'probation measures' shall mean obligations and instructions imposed by a competent authority on a natural person, in accordance with the national law of the issuing State, in connection with a suspended sentence, a conditional sentence or a conditional release;

8. 'issuing State' shall mean the Member State in which a judgment is delivered;

9. 'executing State' shall mean the Member State in which the probation measures and alternative sanctions are supervised following a decision in accordance with Article 8.

*Article 3*

**Designation of competent authorities**

1. Each Member State shall inform the General Secretariat of the Council which authority or authorities, under its national law, are competent to act according to this Framework Decision in the situation where that Member State is the issuing State or the executing State.

2. Member States may designate non-judicial authorities as the competent authorities for taking decisions under this Framework Decision, provided that such authorities have competence for taking decisions of a similar nature under their national law and procedures.

3. If a decision under Article 14(1)(b) or (c) is taken by a competent authority other than a court, the Member States shall ensure that, upon request of the person concerned, such decision may be reviewed by a court or by another independent court-like body.

4. The General Secretariat of the Council shall make the information received available to all Member States and to the Commission.

*Article 4*

**Types of probation measures and alternative sanctions**

1. This Framework Decision shall apply to the following probation measures or alternative sanctions:

(a) an obligation for the sentenced person to inform a specific authority of any change of residence or working place;

(b) an obligation not to enter certain localities, places or defined areas in the issuing or executing State;

(c) an obligation containing limitations on leaving the territory of the executing State;

(d) instructions relating to behaviour, residence, education and training, leisure activities, or containing limitations on or modalities of carrying out a professional activity;

(e) an obligation to report at specified times to a specific authority;

(f) an obligation to avoid contact with specific persons;

(g) an obligation to avoid contact with specific objects, which have been used or are likely to be used by the sentenced person with a view to committing a criminal offence;

▼B

(h) an obligation to compensate financially for the prejudice caused by the offence and/or an obligation to provide proof of compliance with such an obligation;

(i) an obligation to carry out community service;

(j) an obligation to cooperate with a probation officer or with a representative of a social service having responsibilities in respect of sentenced persons;

(k) an obligation to undergo therapeutic treatment or treatment for addiction.

2. Each Member State shall notify the General Secretariat of the Council, when implementing this Framework Decision, which probation measures and alternative sanctions, apart from those referred to in paragraph 1, it is prepared to supervise. The General Secretariat of the Council shall make the information received available to all Member States and to the Commission.

*Article 5*

**Criteria for forwarding a judgment and, where applicable, a probation decision**

1. The competent authority of the issuing State may forward a judgment and, where applicable, a probation decision to the competent authority of the Member State in which the sentenced person is lawfully and ordinarily residing, in cases where the sentenced person has returned or wants to return to that State.

2. The competent authority of the issuing State may, upon request of the sentenced person, forward the judgment and, where applicable, the probation decision to a competent authority of a Member State other than the Member State in which the sentenced person is lawfully and ordinarily residing, on condition that this latter authority has consented to such forwarding.

3. When implementing this Framework Decision, Member States shall determine under which conditions their competent authorities may consent to the forwarding of a judgment and, where applicable, a probation decision under paragraph 2.

4. Each Member State shall make a declaration to the General Secretariat of the Council of the determination made under paragraph 3. Member States may modify such a declaration at any time. The General Secretariat shall make the information received available to all Member States and to the Commission.

*Article 6*

**Procedure for forwarding a judgment and, where applicable, a probation decision**

1. When, in application of Article 5(1) or (2), the competent authority of the issuing State forwards a judgment and, where applicable, a probation decision to another Member State, it shall ensure that it is accompanied by a certificate, the standard form for which is set out in Annex I.

2. The judgment and, where applicable, the probation decision, together with the certificate referred to in paragraph 1, shall be forwarded by the competent authority of the issuing State directly to the competent authority of the executing State by any means which leaves a written record under conditions allowing the executing State to establish their authenticity. The original of the judgment and, where applicable, the probation decision, or certified copies thereof, as well as the original of the certificate, shall be sent to the competent authority of

▼B

the executing State if it so requires. All official communications shall also be made directly between the said competent authorities.

3. The certificate referred to in paragraph 1 shall be signed and its content certified as accurate by the competent authority of the issuing State.

4. Apart from the measures and sanctions referred to in Article 4(1), the certificate referred to in paragraph 1 of this Article shall include only such measures or sanctions as notified by the executing State in accordance with Article 4(2).

5. The competent authority of the issuing State shall forward the judgment and, where applicable, the probation decision, together with the certificate referred to in paragraph 1 only to one executing State at any one time.

6. If the competent authority of the executing State is not known to the competent authority of the issuing State, the latter shall make all necessary inquiries, including via the contact points of the European Judicial Network created by Council Joint Action 98/428/JHA ([1]), in order to obtain the information from the executing State.

7. When an authority of the executing State which receives a judgment and, where applicable, a probation decision, together with the certificate referred to in paragraph 1, has no competence to recognise it and take the ensuing necessary measures for the supervision of the probation measure or alternative sanction, it shall, *ex officio*, forward it to the competent authority and shall without delay inform the competent authority of the issuing State accordingly by any means which leaves a written record.

*Article 7*

**Consequences for the issuing State**

1. Once the competent authority of the executing State has recognised the judgment and, where applicable, the probation decision forwarded to it and has informed the competent authority of the issuing State of such recognition, the issuing State shall no longer have competence in relation to the supervision of the probation measures or alternative sanctions imposed, nor to take subsequent measures referred to in Article 14(1).

2. The competence referred to in paragraph 1 shall revert to the issuing State:

(a) as soon as its competent authority has notified withdrawal of the certificate referred to in Article 6(1), pursuant to Article 9(4), to the competent authority of the executing State;

(b) in cases referred to in Article 14(3) in combination with 14(5); and

(c) in cases referred to in Article 20.

*Article 8*

**Decision of the executing State**

1. The competent authority of the executing State shall recognise the judgment and, where applicable, the probation decision forwarded in accordance with Article 5 and following the procedure laid down in Article 6 and shall without delay take all necessary measures for the supervision of the probation measures or alternative sanctions, unless it decides to invoke one of the grounds for refusing recognition and supervision referred to in Article 11.

([1]) OJ L 191, 7.7.1998, p. 4.

▼B

2. The competent authority of the executing State may postpone the decision on recognition of the judgment and, where applicable, the probation decision in the situation where the certificate referred to in Article 6(1) is incomplete or obviously does not correspond to the judgment or, where applicable, the probation decision, until such reasonable deadline set for the certificate to be completed or corrected.

*Article 9*

**Adaptation of the probation measures or alternative sanctions**

1. If the nature or duration of the relevant probation measure or alternative sanction, or the duration of the probation period, are incompatible with the law of the executing State, the competent authority of that State may adapt them in line with the nature and duration of the probation measures and alternative sanctions, or duration of the probation period, which apply, under the law of the executing State, to equivalent offences. The adapted probation measure, alternative sanction or duration of the probation period shall correspond as far as possible to that imposed in the issuing State.

2. Where the probation measure, the alternative sanction or the probation period has been adapted because its duration exceeds the maximum duration provided for under the law of the executing State, the duration of the adapted probation measure, alternative sanction or probation period shall not be below the maximum duration provided for equivalent offences under the law of the executing State.

3. The adapted probation measure, alternative sanction or probation period shall not be more severe or longer than the probation measure, alternative sanction or probation period which was originally imposed.

4. Following receipt of the information referred to in Articles 16(2) or 18(5), the competent authority of the issuing State may decide to withdraw the certificate referred to in Article 6(1) provided that supervision in the executing State has not yet begun. In such cases, the decision shall be taken and communicated as soon as possible and within ten days of the receipt of the information.

*Article 10*

**Double criminality**

1. The following offences, if they are punishable in the issuing State by a custodial sentence or a measure involving deprivation of liberty for a maximum period of at least three years, and as they are defined by the law of the issuing State, shall, under the terms of this Framework Decision and without verification of the double criminality of the act, give rise to recognition of the judgment and, where applicable, the probation decision and to supervision of probation measures and alternative sanctions:

— participation in a criminal organisation,

— terrorism,

— trafficking in human beings,

— sexual exploitation of children and child pornography,

— illicit trafficking in narcotic drugs and psychotropic substances,

— illicit trafficking in weapons, munitions and explosives,

— corruption,

▼B

— fraud, including that affecting the financial interests of the European Communities within the meaning of the Convention of 26 July 1995 on the protection of the European Communities' financial interests (1),

— laundering of the proceeds of crime,

— counterfeiting currency, including of the euro,

— computer-related crime,

— environmental crime, including illicit trafficking in endangered animal species and in endangered plant species and varieties,

— facilitation of unauthorised entry and residence,

— murder, grievous bodily injury,

— illicit trade in human organs and tissue,

— kidnapping, illegal restraint and hostage-taking,

— racism and xenophobia,

— organised or armed robbery,

— illicit trafficking in cultural goods, including antiques and works of art,

— swindling,

— racketeering and extortion,

— counterfeiting and piracy of products,

— forgery of administrative documents and trafficking therein,

— forgery of means of payment,

— illicit trafficking in hormonal substances and other growth promoters,

— illicit trafficking in nuclear or radioactive materials,

— trafficking in stolen vehicles,

— rape,

— arson,

— crimes within the jurisdiction of the International Criminal Court,

— unlawful seizure of aircraft/ships,

— sabotage.

2. The Council may decide to add other categories of offences to the list provided for in paragraph 1 of this Article at any time, acting unanimously after consultation of the European Parliament under the conditions laid down in Article 39(1) of the Treaty on European Union. The Council shall examine, in the light of the report submitted to it pursuant to Article 26(1) of this Framework Decision, whether the list should be extended or amended.

3. For offences other than those covered by paragraph 1, the executing State may make the recognition of the judgment and, where applicable, the probation decision and the supervision of probation measures and of alternative sanctions subject to the condition that the judgment relates to acts which also constitute an offence under the law of the executing State, whatever its constituent elements or however it is described.

4. Each Member State may, on the adoption of this Framework Decision or later, by a declaration notified to the General Secretariat of the Council, declare that it will not apply paragraph 1. Any such

(1) OJ C 316, 27.11.1995, p. 49.

▼B

declaration may be withdrawn at any time. Such declarations or withdrawals of declarations shall be published in the *Official Journal of the European Union.*

*Article 11*

**Grounds for refusing recognition and supervision**

1. The competent authority of the executing State may refuse to recognise the judgment or, where applicable, the probation decision and to assume responsibility for supervising probation measures or alternative sanctions if:

(a) the certificate referred to in Article 6(1) is incomplete or manifestly does not correspond to the judgment or to the probation decision and has not been completed or corrected within a reasonable period set by the competent authority of the executing State;

(b) the criteria set forth in Articles 5(1), 5(2) or 6(4) are not met;

(c) recognition of the judgment and assumption of responsibility for supervising probation measures or alternative sanctions would be contrary to the principle of *ne bis in idem*;

(d) in a case referred to in Article 10(3) and, where the executing State has made a declaration under Article 10(4), in a case referred to in Article 10(1), the judgment relates to acts which would not constitute an offence under the law of the executing State. However, in relation to taxes or duties, customs and exchange, execution of the judgment or, where applicable, the probation decision may not be refused on the grounds that the law of the executing State does not impose the same kind of tax or duty or does not contain the same type of rules as regards taxes or duties, customs and exchange regulations as the law of the issuing State;

(e) the enforcement of the sentence is statute-barred according to the law of the executing State and relates to an act which falls within its competence according to that law;

(f) there is immunity under the law of the executing State, which makes it impossible to supervise probation measures or alternative sanctions;

(g) under the law of the executing State, the sentenced person cannot, owing to his or her age, be held criminally liable for the acts in respect of which the judgment was issued;

▼M1

(h) according to the certificate provided for in Article 6, the person did not appear in person at the trial resulting in the decision, unless the certificate states that the person, in accordance with further procedural requirements defined in the national law of the issuing State:

(i) in due time:

— either was summoned in person and thereby informed of the scheduled date and place of the trial which resulted in the decision, or by other means actually received official information of the scheduled date and place of that trial in such a manner that it was unequivocally established that he or she was aware of the scheduled trial,

and

— was informed that a decision may be handed down if he or she does not appear for the trial;

or

(ii) being aware of the scheduled trial had given a mandate to a legal counsellor, who was either appointed by the person

▼M1

concerned or by the State, to defend him or her at the trial, and was indeed defended by that counsellor at the trial;

or

(iii) after being served with the decision and being expressly informed about the right to a retrial, or an appeal, in which the person has the right to participate and which allows the merits of the case, including fresh evidence, to be re-examined, and which may lead to the original decision being reversed:

— expressly stated that he or she does not contest the decision,

or

— did not request a retrial or appeal within the applicable time frame;

▼B

(i) the judgment or, where applicable, the probation decision provides for medical/therapeutic treatment which, notwithstanding Article 9, the executing State is unable to supervise in view of its legal or health-care system;

(j) the probation measure or alternative sanction is of less than six months' duration; or

(k) the judgment relates to criminal offences which under the law of the executing State are regarded as having been committed wholly or for a major or essential part within its territory, or in a place equivalent to its territory.

2. Any decision under paragraph 1(k) in relation to offences committed partly within the territory of the executing State, or in a place equivalent to its territory, shall be taken by the competent authority of the executing State only in exceptional circumstances and on a case-by case basis, having regard to the specific circumstances of the case, and in particular to whether a major or essential part of the conduct in question has taken place in the issuing State.

3. In the cases referred to in paragraph 1(a), (b), (c), (h), (i), (j) and (k), before deciding not to recognise the judgment or, where applicable, the probation decision and to assume responsibility for supervising probation measures and alternative sanctions, the competent authority of the executing State shall communicate, by appropriate means, with the competent authority of the issuing State and shall, as necessary, ask it to supply all additional information required without delay.

4. Where the competent authority of the executing State has decided to invoke a ground for refusal referred to in paragraph 1 of this Article, in particular the grounds referred to under paragraph 1(d) or (k), it may nevertheless, in agreement with the competent authority of the issuing State, decide to supervise the probation measures or alternative sanctions that are imposed in the judgment and, where applicable, the probation decision forwarded to it, without assuming the responsibility for taking any of the decisions referred to in Article 14(1)(a), (b) and (c).

*Article 12*

**Time limit**

1. The competent authority of the executing State shall decide as soon as possible, and within 60 days of receipt of the judgment and, where applicable, the probation decision, together with the certificate referred to in Article 6(1), whether or not to recognise the judgment and, where applicable, the probation decision and assume responsibility for supervising the probation measures or alternative sanctions. It shall

▼B

immediately inform the competent authority of the issuing State, by any means which leaves a written record, of its decision.

2. When in exceptional circumstances it is not possible for the competent authority of the executing State to comply with the time limit provided for in paragraph 1, it shall immediately inform the competent authority of the issuing State by any means, giving the reasons for the delay and indicating the estimated time needed for the final decision to be taken.

*Article 13*

**Governing law**

1. The supervision and application of probation measures and alternative sanctions shall be governed by the law of the executing State.

2. The competent authority of the executing State may supervise an obligation as referred to in Article 4(1)(h) by requiring the sentenced person to provide proof of compliance with an obligation to compensate for the prejudice caused by the offence.

*Article 14*

**Jurisdiction to take all subsequent decisions and governing law**

1. The competent authority of the executing State shall have jurisdiction to take all subsequent decisions relating to a suspended sentence, conditional release, conditional sentence and alternative sanction, in particular in case of non-compliance with a probation measure or alternative sanction or if the sentenced person commits a new criminal offence.

Such subsequent decisions include notably:

(a) the modification of obligations or instructions contained in the probation measure or alternative sanction, or the modification of the duration of the probation period;

(b) the revocation of the suspension of the execution of the judgment or the revocation of the decision on conditional release; and

(c) the imposition of a custodial sentence or measure involving deprivation of liberty in case of an alternative sanction or conditional sentence.

2. The law of the executing State shall apply to decisions taken pursuant to paragraph 1 and to all subsequent consequences of the judgment including, where applicable, the enforcement and, if necessary, the adaptation of the custodial sentence or measure involving deprivation of liberty.

3. Each Member State may, at the time of adoption of this Framework Decision or at a later stage, declare that as an executing State it will refuse to assume the responsibility provided for in paragraph 1(b) and (c) in cases or categories of cases to be specified by that Member State, in particular:

(a) in cases relating to an alternative sanction, where the judgment does not contain a custodial sentence or measure involving deprivation of liberty to be enforced in case of non-compliance with the obligations or instructions concerned;

(b) in cases relating to a conditional sentence;

(c) in cases where the judgment relates to acts which do not constitute an offence under the law of the executing State, whatever its constituent elements or however it is described.

4. When a Member State makes use of any of the possibilities referred to in paragraph 3, the competent authority of the executing

▼B

State shall transfer jurisdiction back to the competent authority of the issuing State in case of non-compliance with a probation measure or alternative sanction if the competent authority of the executing State is of the view that a subsequent decision as referred to in paragraph 1(b) or (c) needs to be taken.

5. In the cases referred to in paragraph 3 of this Article, the obligation to recognise the judgment and, where applicable, the probation decision, as well as the obligation to take without delay all necessary measures for the supervision of the probation measures or alternative sanctions, as referred to in Article 8(1), shall not be affected.

6. Declarations as mentioned in paragraph 3 shall be made by notification to the General Secretariat of the Council. Any such declaration may be withdrawn at any time. The declarations and withdrawals mentioned in this Article shall be published in the *Official Journal of the European Union*.

*Article 15*

**Consultations between competent authorities**

Where and whenever it is felt appropriate, competent authorities of the issuing State and of the executing State may consult each other with a view to facilitating the smooth and efficient application of this Framework Decision.

*Article 16*

**Obligations of the authorities involved where the executing State has jurisdiction for subsequent decisions**

1. The competent authority of the executing State shall without delay inform the competent authority of the issuing State, by any means which leaves a written record, of all decisions on the:

(a) modification of the probation measure or alternative sanction;

(b) revocation of the suspension of the execution of the judgment or revocation of the decision on conditional release;

(c) enforcement of a custodial sentence or measure involving deprivation of liberty, because of non-compliance with a probation measure or alternative sanction;

(d) lapsing of the probation measure or alternative sanction.

2. If so requested by the competent authority of the issuing State, the competent authority of the executing State shall inform it of the maximum duration of deprivation of liberty that is foreseen in the national law of the executing State for the offence which gave rise to the judgment and that could be imposed on the sentenced person in case of breach of the probation measure or alternative sanction. This information shall be provided immediately after reception of the judgment and, where applicable, the probation decision, together with the certificate referred to in Article 6(1).

3. The competent authority of the issuing State shall immediately inform the competent authority of the executing State, by any means which leaves a written record, of any circumstances or findings which, in its opinion, could entail one or more of the decisions referred to in paragraph 1(a), (b) or (c) being taken.

▼B

*Article 17*

**Obligations of the authorities involved where the issuing State has jurisdiction for subsequent decisions**

1. If the competent authority of the issuing State has jurisdiction for the subsequent decisions mentioned in Article 14(1) pursuant to the application of Article 14(3), the competent authority of the executing State shall immediately notify it of:

(a) any finding which is likely to result in revocation of the suspension of the execution of the judgment or revocation of the decision on conditional release;

(b) any finding which is likely to result in the imposition of a custodial sentence or measure involving deprivation of liberty;

(c) all further facts and circumstances which the competent authority of the issuing State requests to be provided and which are essential in order to allow it to take subsequent decisions in accordance with its national law.

2. When a Member State has made use of the possibility referred to in Article 11(4), the competent authority of that State shall inform the competent authority of the issuing State in case of non-compliance by the sentenced person with a probation measure or alternative sanction.

3. Notice of the findings mentioned in paragraph 1(a) and (b) and in paragraph 2 shall be given using the standard form set out in Annex II. Notice of the facts and circumstances mentioned in paragraph 1(c) shall be given by any means which leaves a written record, including, where possible, through the form set out in Annex II.

4. If, under the national law of the issuing State, the sentenced person must be given a judicial hearing before a decision is taken on the imposition of a sentence, this requirement may be met by following *mutatis mutandis* the procedure contained in instruments of international or European Union law that provide the possibility of using video links for hearing persons.

5. The competent authority of the issuing State shall without delay inform the competent authority of the executing State of all decisions on:

(a) the revocation of the suspension of the execution of the judgment or the revocation of the decision on conditional release;

(b) the enforcement of the custodial sentence or measure involving deprivation of liberty, where such measure is contained in the judgment;

(c) the imposition of a custodial sentence or measure involving deprivation of liberty, where such measure is not contained in the judgment;

(d) the lapsing of the probation measure or alternative sanction.

*Article 18*

**Information from the executing State in all cases**

The competent authority of the executing State shall without delay inform the competent authority of the issuing State, by any means which leaves a written record of:

1. the transmission of the judgment and, where applicable, the probation decision, together with the certificate referred to in Article 6(1) to the competent authority responsible for its recognition and for taking the ensuing measures for the supervision of the probation measures or alternative sanctions in accordance with Article 6(7);

▼B

2. the fact that it is in practice impossible to supervise the probation measures or alternative sanctions for the reason that, after transmission of the judgment and, where applicable, the probation decision, together with the certificate referred to in Article 6(1) to the executing State, the sentenced person cannot be found in the territory of the executing State, in which case the executing State shall be under no obligation to supervise the probation measures or alternative sanctions;

3. the final decision to recognise the judgment and, where applicable, the probation decision and to assume responsibility for supervising the probation measures or alternative sanctions;

4. any decision not to recognise the judgment and, where applicable, the probation decision and to assume responsibility for supervising the probation measures or alternative sanctions in accordance with Article 11, together with the reasons for the decision;

5. any decision to adapt the probation measures or alternative sanctions in accordance with Article 9, together with the reasons for the decision;

6. any decision on amnesty or pardon which leads to not supervising the probation measures or alternative sanctions for the reasons referred to in Article 19(1), together, where applicable, with the reasons for the decision.

*Article 19*

**Amnesty, pardon, review of judgment**

1. An amnesty or pardon may be granted by the issuing State and also by the executing State.

2. Only the issuing State may decide on applications for review of the judgment which forms the basis for the probation measures or alternative sanctions to be supervised under this Framework Decision.

*Article 20*

**End of jurisdiction of the executing State**

1. If the sentenced person absconds or no longer has a lawful and ordinary residence in the executing State, the competent authority of the executing State may transfer the jurisdiction in respect of the supervision of the probation measures or alternative sanctions and in respect of all further decisions relating to the judgment back to the competent authority of the issuing State.

2. If new criminal proceedings against the person concerned are taking place in the issuing State, the competent authority of the issuing State may request the competent authority of the executing State to transfer jurisdiction in respect of the supervision of the probation measures or alternative sanctions and in respect of all further decisions relating to the judgment back to the competent authority of the issuing State. In such a case, the competent authority of the executing State may transfer jurisdiction back to the competent authority of the issuing State.

3. When, in application of this Article, jurisdiction is transferred back to the issuing State, the competent authority of that State shall resume jurisdiction. For the further supervision of the probation measures or alternative sanctions, the competent authority of the issuing State shall take account of the duration and degree of compliance with the probation measures or alternative sanctions in the executing State, as well as of any decisions taken by the executing State in accordance with Article 16(1).

▼B

*Article 21*

**Languages**

The certificate referred to in Article 6(1) shall be translated into the official language or one of the official languages of the executing State. Any Member State may, on adoption of this Framework Decision or later, state in a declaration deposited with the General Secretariat of the Council that it will accept a translation in one or more other official languages of the institutions of the European Union.

*Article 22*

**Costs**

Costs resulting from the application of this Framework Decision shall be borne by the executing State, except for costs arising exclusively within the territory of the issuing State.

*Article 23*

**Relationship with other agreements and arrangements**

1. This Framework Decision shall, in relations between the Member States, from 6 December 2011, replace the corresponding provisions of the Council of Europe Convention of 30 November 1964 on the Supervision of Conditionally Sentenced or Conditionally Released Offenders.

2. Member States may continue to apply bilateral or multilateral agreements or arrangements in force after 6 December 2008, in so far as they allow the objectives of this Framework Decision to be extended or enlarged and help to simplify or facilitate further the procedures for the supervision of probation measures and alternative sanctions.

3. Member States may conclude bilateral or multilateral agreements or arrangements after 6 December 2008, in so far as such agreements or arrangements allow the provisions of this Framework Decision to be extended or enlarged and help to simplify or facilitate further the procedures for the supervision of probation measures and alternative sanctions.

4. Member States shall, by 6 March 2009, notify the Council and the Commission of the existing agreements and arrangements referred to in paragraph 2 which they wish to continue applying. Member States shall also notify the Council and the Commission of any new agreement or arrangement as referred to in paragraph 3, within three months of signing it.

*Article 24*

**Territorial application**

This Framework Decision shall apply to Gibraltar.

*Article 25*

**Implementation**

1. Member States shall take the necessary measures to comply with the provisions of this Framework Decision by 6 December 2011.

2. Member States shall transmit to the General Secretariat of the Council and to the Commission the text of the provisions transposing into their national law the obligations imposed on them under this Framework Decision.

▼B

*Article 26*

**Review**

1. By 6 December 2014, the Commission shall draw up a report on the basis of the information received from Member States under Article 25(2).

2. On the basis of this report, the Council shall assess:

(a) the extent to which the Member States have taken the necessary measures in order to comply with this Framework Decision; and

(b) the application of this Framework Decision.

3. The report shall be accompanied, if necessary, by legislative proposals.

*Article 27*

**Entry into force**

This Framework Decision shall enter into force on the day of its publication in the *Official Journal of the European Union*.

▼B

*ANNEX I*

**CERTIFICATE**

**referred to in Article 6 of Council Framework Decision 2008/947/JHA of 27 November 2008 on the application of the principle of mutual recognition to judgments and probation decisions with a view to the supervision of probation measures and alternative sanctions** (1)

(a) Issuing State:

Executing State:

(b) Court which issued the judgment imposing a suspended sentence, conditional sentence or alternative sanction

Official name:

Please indicate whether any additional information concerning the judgment is to be obtained from:

☐ the court specified above

☐ the central authority; if you ticked this box, please provide the official name of this central authority:

☐ another competent authority; if you ticked this box, please provide the official name of this authority:

Contact details of the court/central authority/other competent authority

Address:

Tel. (country code) (area/city code)

Fax (country code) (area/city code)

Details of the person(s) to be contacted

Surname:

Forename(s):

Position (title/grade):

Tel. (country code) (area/city code)

Fax (country code) (area/city code)

E-mail (if any):

Languages that may be used for communication:

(c) Authority which issued the probation decision (where applicable)

Official name:

Please indicate whether any additional information concerning the probation decision is to be obtained from:

☐ the authority specified above

☐ the central authority; if you ticked this box, please provide the official name of this central authority if this information has not yet been provided under point (b):

☐ another competent authority; if you ticked this box, please provide the official name of this authority:

Contact details of the authority, the central authority or other competent authority, if this information has not yet been provided under point (b)

Address:

Tel. (country code) (area/city code)

Fax (country code) (area/city code)

Details of the person(s) to be contacted

Surname:

Forename(s):

Position (title/grade):

Tel. (country code) (area/city code)

Fax (country code) (area/city code)

E-mail (if any):

Languages that may be used for communication:

(1) This certificate must be written in, or translated into, the official language or one of the official languages of the executing Member State, or any other official language of the institutions of the European Union that is accepted by that State.

▼B

(d) Competent authority for supervision of the probation measures or alternative sanctions

Authority which has competence in the issuing State for supervising the probation measures or alternative sanctions:

☐ the court/authority referred to in point (b)

☐ the authority referred to in point (c)

☐ another authority (please provide its official name):

Please indicate which authority is to be contacted if any additional information is to be obtained for the purposes of supervising the probation measures or alternative sanctions:

☐ the authority specified above

☐ the central authority; if you ticked this box, please provide the official name of this central authority if this information has not yet been provided under point (b) or (c):

Contact details of the authority, or of the central authority if this information has not yet been provided under point (b) or (c)

Address:

Tel. (country code) (area/city code)

Fax (country code) (area/city code)

Details of the person(s) to be contacted

Surname:

Forename(s):

Position (title/grade):

Tel. (country code) (area/city code)

Fax (country code) (area/city code)

E-mail (if any):

Languages that may be used for communication:

(e) Information regarding the natural person in respect of whom the judgment and, where applicable, the probation decision has been issued

Surname:

Forename(s):

Maiden name, where applicable:

Aliases, where applicable:

Sex:

Nationality:

Identity number or social security number (if any):

Date of birth:

Place of birth:

Last known addresses/residences (if any):

— in the issuing State:

— in the executing State:

— elsewhere:

Language(s) understood (if known):

If available, please provide the following information:

— Type and number of the identity document(s) of the sentenced person (ID card, passport):

— Type and number of the residence permit of the sentenced person in the executing State:

▼B

(f) Information regarding the Member State to which the judgment and, where applicable, the probation decision, together with the certificate are being forwarded

The judgment and, where applicable, the probation decision, together with the certificate are being forwarded to the executing State indicated in point (a) for the following reason:

☐ the sentenced person has his/her lawful and ordinary residence in the executing State and has returned or wants to return to that State

☐ the sentenced person has moved or intends to move to the executing State for the following reason(s) (please tick the relevant box):

- ☐ the sentenced person has been granted an employment contract in the executing State;
- ☐ the sentenced person is a family member of a lawful and ordinary resident person of the executing State;
- ☐ the sentenced person intends to follow a study or training in the executing State;
- ☐ other reason (please specify):

(g) Indications regarding the judgment and, where applicable, the probation decision

The judgment was issued on (date: DD-MM-YYYY):

Where applicable, the probation decision was issued on (date: DD-MM-YYYY):

The judgment became final on (date: DD-MM-YYYY):

Where applicable, the probation decision became final on (date: DD-MM-YYYY):

The execution of the judgment started on (if different from the date on which the judgment became final) (date: DD-MM-YYYY):

Where applicable, the execution of the probation decision started on (if different from the date on which the probation decision became final) (date: DD-MM-YYYY):

File reference of the judgment (if available):

Where applicable, file reference of the probation decision (if available):

1. The judgment covers in total: .................... offences.

   Summary of the facts and description of the circumstances in which the offence(s) was (were) committed, including the time and place, and the nature of the involvement of the sentenced person:

   Nature and legal classification of the offence(s) and applicable statutory provisions on the basis of which the judgment was issued:

2. If the offence(s) referred to in point 1 constitute(s) one or more of the following offences, as defined in the law of the issuing State which are punishable in the issuing State by a custodial sentence or measure involving deprivation of liberty of a maximum of at least three years, please confirm by ticking the relevant box(es):

   ☐ participation in a criminal organisation

   ☐ terrorism

   ☐ trafficking in human beings

   ☐ sexual exploitation of children and child pornography

   ☐ illicit trafficking in narcotic drugs and psychotropic substances

   ☐ illicit trafficking in weapons, munitions and explosives

   ☐ corruption

   ☐ fraud, including that affecting the financial interests of the European Communities within the meaning of the Convention of 26 July 1995 on the protection of the European Communities' financial interests

   ☐ laundering of the proceeds of crime

   ☐ counterfeiting of currency, including of the euro

   ☐ computer-related crime

   ☐ environmental crime, including illicit trafficking in endangered animal species and in endangered plant species and varieties

▼B

☐ facilitation of unauthorised entry and residence
☐ murder, grievous bodily injury
☐ illicit trade in human organs and tissue
☐ kidnapping, illegal restraint and hostage-taking
☐ racism and xenophobia
☐ organised or armed robbery
☐ illicit trafficking in cultural goods, including antiques and works of art
☐ swindling
☐ racketeering and extortion
☐ counterfeiting and piracy of products
☐ forgery of administrative documents and trafficking therein
☐ forgery of means of payment
☐ illicit trafficking in hormonal substances and other growth promoters
☐ illicit trafficking in nuclear or radioactive materials
☐ trafficking in stolen vehicles
☐ rape
☐ arson
☐ crimes within the jurisdiction of the International Criminal Court
☐ unlawful seizure of aircraft/ships
☐ sabotage

3. To the extent that the offence(s) identified under point 1 is (are) not covered by point 2 or if the judgment and, where applicable, the probation decision, as well as the certificate are forwarded to a Member State, which has declared that it will verify the double criminality (Article 10(4) of the Framework Decision), please give a full description of the offence(s) concerned:

►[(1)] (h) Indicate if the person appeared in person at the trial resulting in the decision:

1. ☐ Yes, the person appeared in person at the trial resulting in the decision.
2. ☐ No, the person did not appear in person at the trial resulting in the decision.
3. If you have ticked the box under point 2, please confirm the existence of one of the following:

☐ 3.1a. the person was summoned in person on … (day/month/year) and thereby informed of the scheduled date and place of the trial which resulted in the decision and was informed that a decision may be handed down if he or she does not appear for the trial;

OR

☐ 3.1b. the person was not summoned in person but by other means actually received official information of the scheduled date and place of the trial which resulted in the decision, in such a manner that it was unequivocally established that he or she was aware of the scheduled trial, and was informed that a decision may be handed down if he or she does not appear for the trial;

OR

☐ 3.2. being aware of the scheduled trial the person had given a mandate to a legal counsellor, who was either appointed by the person concerned or by the State, to defend him or her at the trial, and was indeed defended by that counsellor at the trial;

OR

☐ 3.3. the person was served with the decision on … (day/month/year) and was expressly informed about the right to a retrial or appeal, in which he or she has the right to participate and which allows the merits of the case, including fresh evidence, to be re-examined, and which may lead to the original decision being reversed, and

☐ the person expressly stated that he or she does not contest this decision,

OR

☐ the person did not request a retrial or appeal within the applicable time frame.

4. If you have ticked the box under points 3.1b, 3.2 or 3.3 above, please provide information about how the relevant condition has been met:

……………………………………………………………………………………………………

……………………………………………………………………………………………………◄

►(1) M1

▼B

(i) Indications regarding the nature of the sentence imposed by the judgment or, where applicable, the probation decision

1. This certificate is related to a:

☐ suspended sentence (= custodial sentence or measure involving deprivation of liberty, the execution of which is conditionally suspended, wholly or in part, when the sentence is passed)

☐ conditional sentence:

☐ the imposition of a sentence has been conditionally deferred by imposing one or more probation measures

☐ one or more probation measures have been imposed instead of a custodial sentence or measure involving deprivation of liberty

☐ alternative sanction:

☐ the judgment contains a custodial sentence or measure involving deprivation of liberty to be enforced in case of non-compliance with the obligation(s) or instruction(s) concerned

☐ the judgment does not contain a custodial sentence or measure involving deprivation of liberty to be enforced in case of non-compliance with the obligation(s) or instruction(s) concerned

☐ conditional release (= early release of a sentenced person after part of the custodial sentence or measure involving deprivation of liberty has been served)

2. Additional information

2.1. The sentenced person was in pre-trial detention during the following period:

2.2. The person was serving a custodial sentence or measure involving deprivation of liberty during the following period (to be filled in only in case of conditional release):

2.3. In case of a suspended sentence

— duration of the custodial period imposed that was conditionally suspended:

— duration of the period of suspension:

2.4. If known, length of deprivation of liberty to be served upon

— revocation of suspension of the execution of the judgment;

— revocation of the decision on conditional release; or

— breach of the alternative sanction (if the judgment contains a custodial sentence or measure involving deprivation of liberty to be enforced in case of such a breach):

▼B

(j) Indications regarding the duration and nature of the probation measure(s) or alternative sanction(s)

1. Total duration of the supervision of the probation measure(s) or alternative sanction(s):

2. Where applicable, duration of each individual obligation imposed as part of the probation measure(s) or alternative sanction(s):

3. Duration of the total probation period (if different from the duration indicated under point 1:

4. Nature of the probation measure(s) or alternative sanction(s) (it is possible to tick multiple boxes):

☐ an obligation for the sentenced person to inform a specific authority of any change of residence or working place

☐ an obligation not to enter certain localities, places or defined areas in the issuing or executing State

☐ an obligation containing limitations on leaving the territory of the executing State

☐ instructions relating to behaviour, residence, education and training, leisure activities, or containing limitations on or modalities of carrying out a professional activity

☐ an obligation to report at specified times to a specific authority

☐ an obligation to avoid contact with specific persons

☐ an obligation to avoid contact with specific objects, which have been used or are likely to be used by the sentenced person with a view to committing a criminal offence

☐ an obligation to compensate financially for the prejudice caused by the offence and/or an obligation to provide proof of compliance with such an obligation

☐ an obligation to carry out community service

☐ an obligation to cooperate with a probation officer or with a representative of a social service having responsibilities in respect of sentenced persons

☐ an obligation to undergo therapeutic treatment or treatment for addiction

☐ other measures that the executing State is prepared to supervise in accordance with a notification under Article 4(2) of the Framework Decision

5. Please provide a detailed description of the probation measure(s) or alternative sanction(s) indicated under 4:

6. Please tick the following box if relevant probation reports are available:

☐ If you ticked this box, please indicate in which language(s) these reports are drawn up ([1]):

(k) Other circumstances relevant to the case, including relevant information on previous convictions or specific reasons for the imposition of the probation measure(s) or alternative sanction(s) (optional information):

The text of the judgment and, where applicable, the probation decision is attached to the certificate.

Signature of the authority issuing the certificate and/or of its representative to confirm the accuracy of the content of the certificate:

Name:

Position (title/grade):

Date:

File reference (if any):

(Where appropriate) Official stamp:

([1]) The issuing State is not obliged to provide translations of these reports.

▼**B**

*ANNEX II*

**FORM**

**referred to in Article 17 of Council Framework Decision 2008/947/JHA of 27 November 2008 on the application of the principle of mutual recognition to judgments and probation decisions with a view to the supervision of probation measures and alternative sanctions**

REPORT OF A BREACH OF A PROBATION MEASURE OR ALTERNATIVE SANCTION, OR OF ANY OTHER FINDINGS

(a) Details of the identity of the person subject to supervision:

Surname:

Forename(s):

Maiden name, where applicable:

Aliases, where applicable:

Sex:

Nationality:

Identity number or social security number (if any):

Date of birth:

Place of birth:

Address:

Language(s) understood (if known):

(b) Details of the judgment and, where applicable, the probation decision concerning the suspended sentence, conditional sentence, alternative sanction or conditional release:

Judgment issued on:
File reference (if any):

Where applicable, probation decision issued on:
File reference (if any):

Court which issued the judgment
Official name:
Address:

Where applicable, authority which issued the probation decision
Official name:
Address:

Certificate issued on:
Authority which issued the certificate:
File reference (if any):

(c) Details of the authority responsible for supervising the probation measure(s) or alternative sanction(s):

Official name of the authority:

Name of the person to be contacted:

Position (title/grade):

Address:

Tel. (country code) (area code)

Fax (country code) (area code)

E-mail:

▼B

(d) Probation measure(s) or alternative sanction(s):

The person referred to in (a) is in breach of the following obligation(s) or instruction(s):

☐ an obligation for the sentenced person to inform a specific authority of any change of residence or working place

☐ an obligation not to enter certain localities, places or defined areas in the issuing or executing State

☐ an obligation containing limitations on leaving the territory of the executing State

☐ instructions relating to behaviour, residence, education and training, leisure activities, or containing limitations on or modalities of carrying out a professional activity

☐ an obligation to report at specified times to a specific authority

☐ an obligation to avoid contact with specific persons

☐ an obligation to avoid contact with specific objects, which have been used or are likely to be used by the sentenced person with a view to committing a criminal offence

☐ an obligation to compensate financially for the prejudice caused by the offence and/or an obligation to provide proof of compliance with such an obligation

☐ an obligation to carry out community service

☐ an obligation to cooperate with a probation officer or with a representative of a social service having responsibilities in respect of sentenced persons

☐ an obligation to undergo therapeutic treatment or treatment for addiction

☐ other measures:

(e) Description of the breach(es) (place, date and specific circumstances):

(f) Other findings (if any)

Description of the findings:

(g) Details of the person to be contacted if additional information is to be obtained concerning the breach:

Surname:

Forename(s):

Address:

Tel. (country code) (area/city code)

Fax (country code) (area/city code)

E-mail (if any):

Signature of the authority issuing the form and/or its representative, to confirm that the contents of the form are correct:

Name:

Position (title/grade):

Date:

Official stamp (where applicable):

# Framework Decision 2008/977 on the protection of personal data processed in the framework of police and judicial cooperation in criminal matters, 27 November 2008

[OJ 2008, L 350/60–71]

L 350/60 EN Official Journal of the European Union 30.12.2008

III

*(Acts adopted under the EU Treaty)*

# ACTS ADOPTED UNDER TITLE VI OF THE EU TREATY

## COUNCIL FRAMEWORK DECISION 2008/977/JHA

**of 27 November 2008**

**on the protection of personal data processed in the framework of police and judicial cooperation in criminal matters**

THE COUNCIL OF THE EUROPEAN UNION,

Having regard to the Treaty on European Union, and in particular Articles 30, 31 and 34(2)(b) thereof,

Having regard to the proposal from the Commission,

Having regard to the opinion of the European Parliament [1],

Whereas:

(1) The European Union has set itself the objective of maintaining and developing the Union as an area of freedom, security and justice in which a high level of safety is to be provided by common action among the Member States in the fields of police and judicial cooperation in criminal matters.

(2) Common action in the field of police cooperation under Article 30(1)(b) of the Treaty on European Union and common action on judicial cooperation in criminal matters under Article 31(1)(a) of the Treaty on European Union imply a need to process the relevant information which should be subject to appropriate provisions on the protection of personal data.

(3) Legislation falling within the scope of Title VI of the Treaty on European Union should foster police and judicial cooperation in criminal matters with regard to its efficiency as well as its legitimacy and compliance with fundamental rights, in particular the right to privacy and to the protection of personal data. Common standards regarding the processing and protection of personal data processed for the purpose of preventing and combating crime contribute to the achieving of both aims.

(4) The Hague Programme on strengthening freedom, security and justice in the European Union, adopted by the European Council on 4 November 2004, stressed the need for an innovative approach to the cross-border exchange of law-enforcement information under the strict observation of key conditions in the area of data protection and invited the Commission to submit proposals in this regard by the end of 2005 at the latest. This was reflected in the Council and Commission Action Plan implementing the Hague Programme on strengthening freedom, security and justice in the European Union [2].

(5) The exchange of personal data within the framework of police and judicial cooperation in criminal matters, notably under the principle of availability of information as laid down in the Hague Programme, should be supported by clear rules enhancing mutual trust between the competent authorities and ensuring that the relevant information is protected in a way that excludes any discrimination in respect of such cooperation between the Member States while fully respecting fundamental rights of individuals. Existing instruments at the European level do not suffice; Directive 95/46/EC of the European Parliament and of the Council of 24 October 1995 on the protection of individuals with regard to the processing of personal data and on the free movement of such data [3] does not apply to the processing of personal data in the course of an activity which falls outside the scope of Community law, such as those provided for by Title VI of the Treaty on European Union, nor, in any case, to processing operations concerning public security, defence, state security or the activities of the State in areas of criminal law.

[1] OJ C 125 E, 22.5.2008, p. 154.

[2] OJ C 198, 12.8.2005, p. 1.

[3] OJ L 281, 23.11.1995, p. 31.

(6) This Framework Decision applies only to data gathered or processed by competent authorities for the purpose of the prevention, investigation, detection or prosecution of criminal offences or the execution of criminal penalties. This Framework Decision should leave it to Member States to determine more precisely at national level which other purposes are to be considered as incompatible with the purpose for which the personal data were originally collected. In general, further processing for historical, statistical or scientific purposes should not be considered as incompatible with the original purpose of the processing.

(7) The scope of this Framework Decision is limited to the processing of personal data transmitted or made available between Member States. No conclusions should be inferred from this limitation regarding the competence of the Union to adopt acts relating to the collection and processing of personal data at national level or the expediency for the Union to do so in the future.

(8) In order to facilitate data exchanges within the Union, Member States intend to ensure that the standard of data protection achieved in national data processing matches that provided for in this Framework Decision. With regard to national data processing, this Framework Decision does not preclude Member States from providing safeguards for the protection of personal data higher than those established in this Framework Decision.

(9) This Framework Decision should not apply to personal data which a Member State has obtained within the scope of this Framework Decision and which originated in that Member State.

(10) The approximation of Member States' laws should not result in any lessening of the data protection they afford but should, on the contrary, seek to ensure a high level of protection within the Union.

(11) It is necessary to specify the objectives of data protection within the framework of police and judicial activities and to lay down rules concerning the lawfulness of processing of personal data in order to ensure that any information that might be exchanged has been processed lawfully and in accordance with fundamental principles relating to data quality. At the same time the legitimate activities of the police, customs, judicial and other competent authorities should not be jeopardised in any way.

(12) The principle of accuracy of data is to be applied taking account of the nature and purpose of the processing concerned. For example, in particular in judicial proceedings data are based on the subjective perception of individuals and in some cases are totally unverifiable. Consequently, the requirement of accuracy cannot appertain to the accuracy of a statement but merely to the fact that a specific statement has been made.

(13) Archiving in a separate data set should be permissible only if the data are no longer required and used for the prevention, investigation, detection or prosecution of criminal offences or the execution of criminal penalties. Archiving in a separate data set should also be permissible if the archived data are stored in a database with other data in such a way that they can no longer be used for the prevention, investigation, detection or prosecution of criminal offences or the execution of criminal penalties. The appropriateness of the archiving period should depend on the purposes of archiving and the legitimate interests of the data subjects. In the case of archiving for historical purposes a very long period may be envisaged.

(14) Data may also be erased by destroying the data medium.

(15) As regards inaccurate, incomplete or no longer up-to-date data transmitted or made available to another Member State and further processed by quasi-judicial authorities, meaning authorities with powers to make legally binding decisions, its rectification, erasure or blocking should be carried out in accordance with national law.

(16) Ensuring a high level of protection of the personal data of individuals requires common provisions to determine the lawfulness and the quality of data processed by competent authorities in other Member States.

(17) It is appropriate to lay down at the European level the conditions under which competent authorities of the Member States should be allowed to transmit and make available personal data received from other Member States to authorities and private parties in Member States. In many cases the transmission of personal data by the judiciary, police or customs to private parties is necessary to prosecute crime or to prevent an immediate and serious threat to public security or to prevent serious harm to the rights of individuals, for example, by issuing alerts concerning forgeries of securities to banks and credit institutions, or, in the area of vehicle crime, by communicating personal data to insurance companies in order to prevent illicit trafficking in stolen motor vehicles or to improve the conditions for the recovery of stolen motor vehicles from abroad. This is not tantamount to the transfer of police or judicial tasks to private parties.

(18) The rules in this Framework Decision regarding the transmission of personal data by the judiciary, police or customs to private parties do not apply to the disclosure of data to private parties (such as defence lawyers and victims) in the context of criminal proceedings.

(19) The further processing of personal data received from, or made available by, the competent authority of another Member State, in particular the further transmission of or making available such data, should be subject to common rules at European level.

(20) Where personal data may be further processed after the Member State from which the data were obtained has given its consent, each Member State should be able to determine the modalities of such consent, including, for example, by means of a general consent for categories of information or categories of further processing.

(21) Where personal data may be further processed for administrative proceedings, these proceedings also include activities by regulatory and supervisory bodies.

(22) The legitimate activities of the police, customs, judicial and other competent authorities may require that data are sent to authorities in third States or international bodies that have obligations for the prevention, investigation, detection or prosecution of criminal offences or the execution of criminal penalties.

(23) Where personal data are transferred from a Member State to third States or international bodies, these data should, in principle, benefit from an adequate level of protection.

(24) Where personal data are transferred from a Member State to third States or international bodies, such transfer should, in principle, take place only after the Member State from which the data were obtained has given its consent to the transfer. Each Member State should be able to determine the modalities of such consent, including, for example, by means of a general consent for categories of information or for specified third States.

(25) The interests of efficient law enforcement cooperation require that where the nature of a threat to the public security of a Member State or a third State is so immediate as to render it impossible to obtain prior consent in good time, the competent authority should be able to transfer the relevant personal data to the third State concerned without such prior consent. The same could apply where other essential interests of a Member State of equal importance are at stake, for example where the critical infrastructure of a Member State could be the subject of an immediate and serious threat or where a Member State's financial system could be seriously disrupted.

(26) It may be necessary to inform data subjects regarding the processing of their data, in particular where there has been particularly serious encroachment on their rights as a result of secret data collection measures, in order to ensure that data subjects can have effective legal protection.

(27) Member States should ensure that the data subject is informed that the personal data could be or are being collected, processed or transmitted to another Member State for the purpose of prevention, investigation, detection, and prosecution of criminal offences or the execution of criminal penalties. The modalities of the right of the data subject to be informed and the exceptions thereto should be determined by national law. This may take a general form, for example, through the law or through the publication of a list of the processing operations.

(28) In order to ensure the protection of personal data without jeopardising the interests of criminal investigations, it is necessary to define the rights of the data subject.

(29) Some Member States have provided for the right of access of the data subject in criminal matters through a system where the national supervisory authority, in place of the data subject, has access to all the personal data related to the data subject without any restriction and may also rectify, erase or update inaccurate data. In such a case of indirect access, the national law of those Member States may provide that the national supervisory authority will inform the data subject only that all the necessary verifications have taken place. However, those Member States also provide for possibilities of direct access for the data subject in specific cases, such as access to judicial records, in order to obtain copies of own criminal records or of documents relating to own hearings by the police services.

(30) It is appropriate to establish common rules on confidentiality and security of processing, on liability and penalties for unlawful use by competent authorities and on judicial remedies available to the data subject. It is, however, for each Member State to determine the nature of its tort rules and of the penalties applicable to violations of domestic data protection provisions.

(31) This Framework Decision allows the principle of public access to official documents to be taken into account when implementing the principles set out in this Framework Decision.

(32) When necessary to protect personal data in relation to processing which by scale or by type holds specific risks for fundamental rights and freedoms, for example processing by means of new technologies, mechanisms or procedures, it is appropriate to ensure that the competent national supervisory authorities are consulted prior to the establishment of filing systems aimed at the processing of these data.

(33) The establishment in Member States of supervisory authorities, exercising their functions with complete independence, is an essential component of the protection of personal data processed within the framework of police and judicial cooperation between the Member States.

(34) The supervisory authorities already established in Member States under Directive 95/46/EC should also be able to assume responsibility for the tasks to be performed by the national supervisory authorities to be established under this Framework Decision.

(35) Such supervisory authorities should have the necessary means to perform their duties, including powers of investigation and intervention, particularly in cases of complaints from individuals, or powers to engage in legal proceedings. These supervisory authorities should help to ensure transparency of processing in the Member States within whose jurisdiction they fall. However, their powers should not interfere with specific rules set out for criminal proceedings or the independence of the judiciary.

(36) Article 47 of the Treaty on European Union stipulates that nothing in it is to affect the Treaties establishing the European Communities or the subsequent Treaties and Acts modifying or supplementing them. Accordingly, this Framework Decision does not affect the protection of personal data under Community law, in particular as provided for in Directive 95/46/EC, in Regulation (EC) No 45/2001 of the European Parliament and of the Council of 18 December 2000 on the protection of individuals with regard to the processing of personal data by the Community institutions and bodies and on the free movement of such data ([1]) and in Directive 2002/58/EC of the European Parliament and of the Council of 12 July 2002 concerning the processing of personal data and the protection of privacy in the electronic communications sector (Directive on privacy and electronic communications) ([2]).

(37) This Framework Decision is without prejudice to the rules pertaining to illicit access to data laid down in Council Framework Decision 2005/222/JHA of 24 February 2005 on attacks against information systems ([3]).

([1]) OJ L 8, 12.1.2001, p. 1.
([2]) OJ L 201, 31.7.2002, p. 37.
([3]) OJ L 69, 16.3.2005, p. 67.

(38) This Framework Decision is without prejudice to existing obligations and commitments incumbent upon Member States or upon the Union by virtue of bilateral and/or multilateral agreements with third States. Future agreements should comply with the rules on exchanges with third States.

(39) Several acts, adopted on the basis of Title VI of the Treaty on European Union, contain specific provisions on the protection of personal data exchanged or otherwise processed pursuant to those acts. In some cases these provisions constitute a complete and coherent set of rules covering all relevant aspects of data protection (principles of data quality, rules on data security, regulation of the rights and safeguards of data subjects, organisation of supervision and liability) and they regulate these matters in more detail than this Framework Decision. The relevant set of data protection provisions of those acts, in particular those governing the functioning of Europol, Eurojust, the Schengen Information System (SIS) and the Customs Information System (CIS), as well as those introducing direct access for the authorities of Member States to certain data systems of other Member States, should not be affected by this Framework Decision. The same applies in respect of the data protection provisions governing the automated transfer between Member States of DNA profiles, dactyloscopic data and national vehicle registration data pursuant to the Council Decision 2008/615/JHA of 23 June 2008 on the stepping up of cross-border cooperation, particularly in combating terrorism and cross-border crime ([4]).

(40) In other cases the provisions on data protection in acts, adopted on the basis of Title VI of the Treaty on European Union, are more limited in scope. They often set specific conditions for the Member State receiving information containing personal data from other Member States as to the purposes for which it can use those data, but refer for other aspects of data protection to the Council of Europe Convention for the Protection of Individuals with regard to Automatic Processing of Personal Data of 28 January 1981 or to national law. To the extent that the provisions of those acts imposing conditions on receiving Member States as to the use or further transfer of personal data are more restrictive than those contained in the corresponding provisions of this Framework Decision, the former provisions should remain unaffected. However, for all other aspects the rules set out in this Framework Decision should be applied.

(41) This Framework Decision does not affect the Council of Europe Convention for the Protection of Individuals with regard to Automatic Processing of Personal Data, the Additional Protocol to that Convention of 8 November 2001 or the Council of Europe conventions on judicial cooperation in criminal matters.

([4]) OJ L 210, 6.8.2008, p. 1.

(42) Since the objective of this Framework Decision, namely the determination of common rules for the protection of personal data processed in the framework of police and judicial cooperation in criminal matters, cannot be sufficiently achieved by the Member States, and can therefore, by reason of the scale and effects of the action, be better achieved at the Union level, the Union may adopt measures in accordance with the principle of subsidiarity as set out in Article 5 of the Treaty establishing the European Community and referred to in Article 2 of the Treaty on European Union. In accordance with the principle of proportionality as set out in Article 5 of the Treaty establishing the European Community, this Framework Decision does not go beyond what is necessary to achieve that objective.

(43) The United Kingdom is taking part in this Framework Decision, in accordance with Article 5 of the Protocol integrating the Schengen *acquis* into the framework of the European Union annexed to the Treaty on European Union and to the Treaty establishing the European Community, and Article 8(2) of Council Decision 2000/365/EC of 29 May 2000 concerning the request of the United Kingdom of Great Britain and Northern Ireland to take part in some of the provisions of the Schengen *acquis* ([1]).

(44) Ireland is taking part in this Framework Decision in accordance with Article 5 of the Protocol integrating the Schengen *acquis* into the framework of the European Union annexed to the Treaty on European Union and to the Treaty establishing the European Community, and Article 6(2) of Council Decision 2002/192/EC of 28 February 2002 concerning Ireland's request to take part in some of the provisions of the Schengen *acquis* ([2]).

(45) As regards Iceland and Norway, this Framework Decision constitutes a development of provisions of the Schengen *acquis* within the meaning of the Agreement concluded by the Council of the European Union and the Republic of Iceland and the Kingdom of Norway concerning the latter's association with the implementation, application and development of the Schengen *acquis* ([3]), which fall within the area referred to in Article 1, points H and I of Council Decision 1999/437/EC ([4]) on certain arrangements for the application of that Agreement.

(46) As regards Switzerland, this Framework Decision constitutes a development of the provisions of the Schengen *acquis* within the meaning of the Agreement between the European Union, the European Community and the Swiss Confederation on the Swiss Confederation's association with the implementation, application and development of the Schengen *acquis* ([5]), which fall within the area referred to in Article 1, point H and I of Decision 1999/437/EC read in conjunction with Article 3 of Council Decision 2008/149/JHA ([6]) on the conclusion of that Agreement on behalf of the European Union.

(47) As regards Liechtenstein, this Framework Decision constitutes a development of the provisions of the Schengen *acquis* within the meaning of the Protocol signed between the European Union, the European Community, the Swiss Confederation and the Principality of Liechtenstein on the accession of the Principality of Liechtenstein to the Agreement between the European Union, the European Community and the Swiss Confederation on the Swiss Confederation's association with the implementation, application and development of the Schengen *acquis*, which fall within the area referred to in Article 1, point H and I of Decision 1999/437/EC read in conjunction with Article 3 of Council Decision 2008/262/JHA ([7]) on the signature of that Protocol on behalf of the European Union.

(48) This Framework Decision respects the fundamental rights and observes the principles recognised in particular by the Charter of Fundamental Rights of the European Union ([8]). This Framework Decision seeks to ensure full respect for the rights to privacy and the protection of personal data reflected in Articles 7 and 8 of the Charter,

HAS ADOPTED THIS FRAMEWORK DECISION:

*Article 1*

**Purpose and scope**

1. The purpose of this Framework Decision is to ensure a high level of protection of the fundamental rights and freedoms of natural persons, and in particular their right to privacy, with respect to the processing of personal data in the framework of police and judicial cooperation in criminal matters, provided for by Title VI of the Treaty on European Union, while guaranteeing a high level of public safety.

2. In accordance with this Framework Decision, Member States shall protect the fundamental rights and freedoms of natural persons, and in particular their right to privacy when, for the purpose of the prevention, investigation, detection or prosecution of criminal offences or the execution of criminal penalties, personal data:

(a) are or have been transmitted or made available between Member States;

([1]) OJ L 131, 1.6.2000, p. 43.
([2]) OJ L 64, 7.3.2002, p. 20.
([3]) OJ L 176, 10.7.1999, p. 36.
([4]) OJ L 176, 10.7.1999, p. 31.
([5]) OJ L 53, 27.2.2008, p. 52.
([6]) OJ L 53, 27.2.2008, p. 50.
([7]) OJ L 83, 26.3.2008, p. 5.
([8]) OJ C 303, 14.12.2007, p. 1.

30.12.2008 EN Official Journal of the European Union L 350/65

(b) are or have been transmitted or made available by Member States to authorities or to information systems established on the basis of Title VI of the Treaty on European Union; or

(c) are or have been transmitted or made available to the competent authorities of the Member States by authorities or information systems established on the basis of the Treaty on European Union or the Treaty establishing the European Community.

3. This Framework Decision shall apply to the processing of personal data wholly or partly by automatic means, and to the processing otherwise than by automatic means, of personal data which form part of a filing system or are intended to form part of a filing system.

4. This Framework Decision is without prejudice to essential national security interests and specific intelligence activities in the field of national security.

5. This Framework Decision shall not preclude Member States from providing, for the protection of personal data collected or processed at national level, higher safeguards than those established in this Framework Decision.

*Article 2*

**Definitions**

For the purposes of this Framework Decision:

(a) 'personal data' mean any information relating to an identified or identifiable natural person ('data subject'); an identifiable person is one who can be identified, directly or indirectly, in particular by reference to an identification number or to one or more factors specific to his physical, physiological, mental, economic, cultural or social identity;

(b) 'processing of personal data' and 'processing' mean any operation or set of operations which is performed upon personal data, whether or not by automatic means, such as collection, recording, organisation, storage, adaptation or alteration, retrieval, consultation, use, disclosure by transmission, dissemination or otherwise making available, alignment or combination, blocking, erasure or destruction;

(c) 'blocking' means the marking of stored personal data with the aim of limiting their processing in future;

(d) 'personal data filing system' and 'filing system' mean any structured set of personal data which are accessible according to specific criteria, whether centralised, decentralised or dispersed on a functional or geographical basis;

(e) 'processor' means any body which processes personal data on behalf of the controller;

(f) 'recipient' means any body to which data are disclosed;

(g) 'the data subject's consent' means any freely given specific and informed indication of his wishes by which the data subject signifies his agreement to personal data relating to him being processed;

(h) 'competent authorities' mean agencies or bodies established by legal acts adopted by the Council pursuant to Title VI of the Treaty on European Union, as well as police, customs, judicial and other competent authorities of the Member States that are authorised by national law to process personal data within the scope of this Framework Decision;

(i) 'controller' means the natural or legal person, public authority, agency or any other body which alone or jointly with others determines the purposes and means of the processing of personal data;

(j) 'referencing' means the marking of stored personal data without the aim of limiting their processing in future;

(k) 'to make anonymous' means to modify personal data in such a way that details of personal or material circumstances can no longer or only with disproportionate investment of time, cost and labour be attributed to an identified or identifiable natural person.

*Article 3*

**Principles of lawfulness, proportionality and purpose**

1. Personal data may be collected by the competent authorities only for specified, explicit and legitimate purposes in the framework of their tasks and may be processed only for the same purpose for which data were collected. Processing of the data shall be lawful and adequate, relevant and not excessive in relation to the purposes for which they are collected.

2. Further processing for another purpose shall be permitted in so far as:

(a) it is not incompatible with the purposes for which the data were collected;

(b) the competent authorities are authorised to process such data for such other purpose in accordance with the applicable legal provisions; and

(c) processing is necessary and proportionate to that other purpose.

The competent authorities may also further process the transmitted personal data for historical, statistical or scientific purposes, provided that Member States provide appropriate safeguards, such as making the data anonymous.

*Article 4*

**Rectification, erasure and blocking**

1. Personal data shall be rectified if inaccurate and, where this is possible and necessary, completed or updated.

2. Personal data shall be erased or made anonymous when they are no longer required for the purposes for which they were lawfully collected or are lawfully further processed. Archiving of those data in a separate data set for an appropriate period in accordance with national law shall not be affected by this provision.

3. Personal data shall be blocked instead of erased if there are reasonable grounds to believe that erasure could affect the legitimate interests of the data subject. Blocked data shall be processed only for the purpose which prevented their erasure.

4. When the personal data are contained in a judicial decision or record related to the issuance of a judicial decision, the rectification, erasure or blocking shall be carried out in accordance with national rules on judicial proceedings.

*Article 5*

**Establishment of time limits for erasure and review**

Appropriate time limits shall be established for the erasure of personal data or for a periodic review of the need for the storage of the data. Procedural measures shall ensure that these time limits are observed.

*Article 6*

**Processing of special categories of data**

The processing of personal data revealing racial or ethnic origin, political opinions, religious or philosophical beliefs or trade-union membership and the processing of data concerning health or sex life shall be permitted only when this is strictly necessary and when the national law provides adequate safeguards.

*Article 7*

**Automated individual decisions**

A decision which produces an adverse legal effect for the data subject or significantly affects him and which is based solely on automated processing of data intended to evaluate certain personal aspects relating to the data subject shall be permitted only if authorised by a law which also lays down measures to safeguard the data subject's legitimate interests.

*Article 8*

**Verification of quality of data that are transmitted or made available**

1. The competent authorities shall take all reasonable steps to provide that personal data which are inaccurate, incomplete or no longer up to date are not transmitted or made available. To that end, the competent authorities shall, as far as practicable, verify the quality of personal data before they are transmitted or made available. As far as possible, in all transmissions of data, available information shall be added which enables the receiving Member State to assess the degree of accuracy, completeness, up-to-dateness and reliability. If personal data were transmitted without request the receiving authority shall verify without delay whether these data are necessary for the purpose for which they were transmitted.

2. If it emerges that incorrect data have been transmitted or data have been unlawfully transmitted, the recipient must be notified without delay. The data must be rectified, erased, or blocked without delay in accordance with Article 4.

*Article 9*

**Time limits**

1. Upon transmission or making available of the data, the transmitting authority may in line with the national law and in accordance with Articles 4 and 5, indicate the time limits for the retention of data, upon the expiry of which the recipient must erase or block the data or review whether or not they are still needed. This obligation shall not apply if, at the time of the expiry of these time limits, the data are required for a current investigation, prosecution of criminal offences or enforcement of criminal penalties.

2. Where the transmitting authority has not indicated a time limit in accordance with paragraph 1, the time limits referred to in Articles 4 and 5 for the retention of data provided for under the national law of the receiving Member State shall apply.

*Article 10*

**Logging and documentation**

1. All transmissions of personal data are to be logged or documented for the purposes of verification of the lawfulness of the data processing, self-monitoring and ensuring proper data integrity and security.

2. Logs or documentation prepared under paragraph 1 shall be communicated on request to the competent supervisory authority for the control of data protection. The competent supervisory authority shall use this information only for the control of data protection and for ensuring proper data processing as well as data integrity and security.

*Article 11*

**Processing of personal data received from or made available by another Member State**

Personal data received from or made available by the competent authority of another Member State may, in accordance with the requirements of Article 3(2), be further processed only for the following purposes other than those for which they were transmitted or made available:

(a) the prevention, investigation, detection or prosecution of criminal offences or the execution of criminal penalties other than those for which they were transmitted or made available;

(b) other judicial and administrative proceedings directly related to the prevention, investigation, detection or prosecution of criminal offences or the execution of criminal penalties;

(c) the prevention of an immediate and serious threat to public security; or

(d) any other purpose only with the prior consent of the transmitting Member State or with the consent of the data subject, given in accordance with national law.

The competent authorities may also further process the transmitted personal data for historical, statistical or scientific purposes, provided that Member States provide appropriate safeguards, such as, for example, making the data anonymous.

*Article 12*

**Compliance with national processing restrictions**

1. Where, under the law of the transmitting Member State, specific processing restrictions apply in specific circumstances to data exchanges between competent authorities within that Member State, the transmitting authority shall inform the recipient of such restrictions. The recipient shall ensure that these processing restrictions are met.

2. When applying paragraph 1, Member States shall not apply restrictions regarding data transmissions to other Member States or to agencies or bodies established pursuant to Title VI of the Treaty on European Union other than those applicable to similar national data transmissions.

*Article 13*

**Transfer to competent authorities in third States or to international bodies**

1. Member States shall provide that personal data transmitted or made available by the competent authority of another Member State may be transferred to third States or international bodies, only if:

(a) it is necessary for the prevention, investigation, detection or prosecution of criminal offences or the execution of criminal penalties;

(b) the receiving authority in the third State or receiving international body is responsible for the prevention, investigation, detection or prosecution of criminal offences or the execution of criminal penalties;

(c) the Member State from which the data were obtained has given its consent to transfer in compliance with its national law; and

(d) the third State or international body concerned ensures an adequate level of protection for the intended data processing.

2. Transfer without prior consent in accordance with paragraph 1(c) shall be permitted only if transfer of the data is essential for the prevention of an immediate and serious threat to public security of a Member State or a third State or to essential interests of a Member State and the prior consent cannot be obtained in good time. The authority responsible for giving consent shall be informed without delay.

3. By way of derogation from paragraph 1(d), personal data may be transferred if:

(a) the national law of the Member State transferring the data so provides because of:

(i) legitimate specific interests of the data subject; or

(ii) legitimate prevailing interests, especially important public interests; or

(b) the third State or receiving international body provides safeguards which are deemed adequate by the Member State concerned according to its national law.

4. The adequacy of the level of protection referred to in paragraph 1(d) shall be assessed in the light of all the circumstances surrounding a data transfer operation or a set of data transfer operations. Particular consideration shall be given to the nature of the data, the purpose and duration of the proposed processing operation or operations, the State of origin and the State or international body of final destination of the data, the rules of law, both general and sectoral, in force in the third State or international body in question and the professional rules and security measures which apply.

*Article 14*

**Transmission to private parties in Member States**

1. Member States shall provide that personal data received from or made available by the competent authority of another Member State may be transmitted to private parties only if:

(a) the competent authority of the Member State from which the data were obtained has consented to transmission in compliance with its national law;

(b) no legitimate specific interests of the data subject prevent transmission; and

(c) in particular cases transfer is essential for the competent authority transmitting the data to a private party for:

(i) the performance of a task lawfully assigned to it;

(ii) the prevention, investigation, detection or prosecution of criminal offences or the execution of criminal penalties;

(iii) the prevention of an immediate and serious threat to public security; or

(iv) the prevention of serious harm to the rights of individuals.

2. The competent authority transmitting the data to a private party shall inform the latter of the purposes for which the data may exclusively be used.

*Article 15*

**Information on request of the competent authority**

The recipient shall, on request, inform the competent authority which transmitted or made available the personal data about their processing.

*Article 16*

**Information for the data subject**

1. Member States shall ensure that the data subject is informed regarding the collection or processing of personal data by their competent authorities, in accordance with national law.

2. When personal data have been transmitted or made available between Member States, each Member State may, in accordance with the provisions of its national law referred to in paragraph 1, ask that the other Member State does not inform the data subject. In such case the latter Member State shall not inform the data subject without the prior consent of the other Member State.

*Article 17*

**Right of access**

1. Every data subject shall have the right to obtain, following requests made at reasonable intervals, without constraint and without excessive delay or expense:

(a) at least a confirmation from the controller or from the national supervisory authority as to whether or not data relating to him have been transmitted or made available and information on the recipients or categories of recipients to whom the data have been disclosed and communication of the data undergoing processing; or

(b) at least a confirmation from the national supervisory authority that all necessary verifications have taken place.

2. The Member States may adopt legislative measures restricting access to information pursuant to paragraph 1(a), where such a restriction, with due regard for the legitimate interests of the person concerned, constitutes a necessary and proportional measure:

(a) to avoid obstructing official or legal inquiries, investigations or procedures;

(b) to avoid prejudicing the prevention, detection, investigation and prosecution of criminal offences or for the execution of criminal penalties;

(c) to protect public security;

(d) to protect national security;

(e) to protect the data subject or the rights and freedoms of others.

3. Any refusal or restriction of access shall be set out in writing to the data subject. At the same time, the factual or legal reasons on which the decision is based shall also be communicated to him. The latter communication may be omitted where a reason under paragraph 2(a) to (e) exists. In all of these cases the data subject shall be advised that he may appeal to the competent national supervisory authority, a judicial authority or to a court.

*Article 18*

**Right to rectification, erasure or blocking**

1. The data subject shall have the right to expect the controller to fulfil its duties in accordance with Articles 4, 8 and 9 concerning the rectification, erasure or blocking of personal data which arise from this Framework Decision. Member States shall lay down whether the data subject may assert this right directly against the controller or through the intermediary of the competent national supervisory authority. If the controller refuses rectification, erasure or blocking, the refusal must be communicated in writing to the data subject who must be informed of the possibilities provided for in national law for lodging a complaint or seeking judicial remedy. Upon examination of the complaint or judicial remedy, the data subject shall be informed whether the controller acted properly or not. Member States may also provide that the data subject shall be informed by the competent national supervisory authority that a review has taken place.

30.12.2008 EN Official Journal of the European Union L 350/69

2. If the accuracy of an item of personal data is contested by the data subject and its accuracy or inaccuracy cannot be ascertained, referencing of that item of data may take place.

*Article 19*

**Right to compensation**

1. Any person who has suffered damage as a result of an unlawful processing operation or of any act incompatible with the national provisions adopted pursuant to this Framework Decision shall be entitled to receive compensation for the damage suffered from the controller or other authority competent under national law.

2. Where a competent authority of a Member State has transmitted personal data, the recipient cannot, in the context of its liability vis-à-vis the injured party in accordance with national law, cite in its defence that the data transmitted were inaccurate. If the recipient pays compensation for damage caused by the use of incorrectly transmitted data, the transmitting competent authority shall refund to the recipient the amount paid in damages, taking into account any fault that may lie with the recipient.

*Article 20*

**Judicial remedies**

Without prejudice to any administrative remedy for which provision may be made prior to referral to the judicial authority, the data subject shall have the right to a judicial remedy for any breach of the rights guaranteed to him by the applicable national law.

*Article 21*

**Confidentiality of processing**

1. Any person who has access to personal data which fall within the scope of this Framework Decision may process such data only if that person is a member of, or acts on instructions of, the competent authority, unless he is required to do so by law.

2. Persons working for a competent authority of a Member State shall be bound by all the data protection rules which apply to the competent authority in question.

*Article 22*

**Security of processing**

1. Member States shall provide that the competent authorities must implement appropriate technical and organisational measures to protect personal data against accidental or unlawful destruction or accidental loss, alteration, unauthorised disclosure or access, in particular where the processing involves the transmission over a network or the making available by granting direct automated access, and against all other unlawful forms of processing, taking into account in particular the risks represented by the processing and the nature of the data to be protected. Having regard to the state of the art and the cost of their implementation, such measures shall ensure a level of security appropriate to the risks represented by the processing and the nature of the data to be protected.

2. In respect of automated data processing each Member State shall implement measures designed to:

(a) deny unauthorised persons access to data-processing equipment used for processing personal data (equipment access control);

(b) prevent the unauthorised reading, copying, modification or removal of data media (data media control);

(c) prevent the unauthorised input of data and the unauthorised inspection, modification or deletion of stored personal data (storage control);

(d) prevent the use of automated data-processing systems by unauthorised persons using data communication equipment (user control);

(e) ensure that persons authorised to use an automated data-processing system only have access to the data covered by their access authorisation (data access control);

(f) ensure that it is possible to verify and establish to which bodies personal data have been or may be transmitted or made available using data communication equipment (communication control);

(g) ensure that it is subsequently possible to verify and establish which personal data have been input into automated data-processing systems and when and by whom the data were input (input control);

(h) prevent the unauthorised reading, copying, modification or deletion of personal data during transfers of personal data or during transportation of data media (transport control);

(i) ensure that installed systems may, in case of interruption, be restored (recovery);

(j) ensure that the functions of the system perform, that the appearance of faults in the functions is reported (reliability) and that stored data cannot be corrupted by means of a malfunctioning of the system (integrity).

3. Member States shall provide that processors may be designated only if they guarantee that they observe the requisite technical and organisational measures under paragraph 1 and comply with the instructions under Article 21. The competent authority shall monitor the processor in those respects.

4. Personal data may be processed by a processor only on the basis of a legal act or a written contract.

*Article 23*

**Prior consultation**

Member States shall ensure that the competent national supervisory authorities are consulted prior to the processing of personal data which will form part of a new filing system to be created where:

(a) special categories of data referred to in Article 6 are to be processed; or

(b) the type of processing, in particular using new technologies, mechanism or procedures, holds otherwise specific risks for the fundamental rights and freedoms, and in particular the privacy, of the data subject.

*Article 24*

**Penalties**

Member States shall adopt suitable measures to ensure the full implementation of the provisions of this Framework Decision and shall in particular lay down effective, proportionate and dissuasive penalties to be imposed in case of infringements of the provisions adopted pursuant to this Framework Decision.

*Article 25*

**National supervisory authorities**

1. Each Member State shall provide that one or more public authorities are responsible for advising and monitoring the application within its territory of the provisions adopted by the Member States pursuant to this Framework Decision. These authorities shall act with complete independence in exercising the functions entrusted to them.

2. Each authority shall in particular be endowed with:

(a) investigative powers, such as powers of access to data forming the subject matter of processing operations and powers to collect all the information necessary for the performance of its supervisory duties;

(b) effective powers of intervention, such as, for example, that of delivering opinions before processing operations are carried out, and ensuring appropriate publication of such opinions, of ordering the blocking, erasure or destruction of data, of imposing a temporary or definitive ban on processing, of warning or admonishing the controller, or that of referring the matter to national parliaments or other political institutions;

(c) the power to engage in legal proceedings where the national provisions adopted pursuant to this Framework Decision have been infringed or to bring this infringement to the attention of the judicial authorities. Decisions by the supervisory authority which give rise to complaints may be appealed against through the courts.

3. Each supervisory authority shall hear claims lodged by any person concerning the protection of his rights and freedoms in regard to the processing of personal data. The person concerned shall be informed of the outcome of the claim.

4. Member States shall provide that the members and staff of the supervisory authority are bound by the data protection provisions applicable to the competent authority in question and, even after their employment has ended, are to be subject to a duty of professional secrecy with regard to confidential information to which they have access.

*Article 26*

**Relationship to agreements with third States**

This Framework Decision is without prejudice to any obligations and commitments incumbent upon Member States or upon the Union by virtue of bilateral and/or multilateral agreements with third States existing at the time of adoption of this Framework Decision.

In the application of these agreements, the transfer to a third State of personal data obtained from another Member State, shall be carried out while respecting Article 13(1)(c) or (2), as appropriate.

*Article 27*

**Evaluation**

1. Member States shall report to the Commission by 27 November 2013 on the national measures they have taken to ensure full compliance with this Framework Decision, and particularly with regard to those provisions that already have to be complied with when data is collected. The Commission shall examine in particular the implications of those provisions for the scope of this Framework Decision as laid down in Article 1(2).

2. The Commission shall report to the European Parliament and the Council within one year on the outcome of the evaluation referred to in paragraph 1, and shall accompany its report with any appropriate proposals for amendments to this Framework Decision.

*Article 28*

**Relationship to previously adopted acts of the Union**

Where in acts, adopted under Title VI of the Treaty on European Union prior to the date of entry into force of this Framework Decision and regulating the exchange of personal data between Member States or the access of designated authorities of Member States to information systems established pursuant to the Treaty establishing the European Community, specific conditions have been introduced as to the use of such data by the receiving Member State, these conditions shall take precedence over the provisions of this Framework Decision on the use of data received from or made available by another Member State.

*Article 29*

**Implementation**

1. Member States shall take the necessary measures to comply with the provisions of this Framework Decision before 27 November 2010.

2. By the same date Member States shall transmit to the General Secretariat of the Council and to the Commission the text of the provisions transposing into their national law the obligations imposed on them under this Framework Decision, as well as information on the supervisory authorities referred to in Article 25. On the basis of a report established using this information by the Commission, the Council shall, before 27 November 2011, assess the extent to which Member States have complied with the provisions of this Framework Decision.

*Article 30*

**Entry into force**

This Framework Decision shall enter into force on the 20th day following its publication in the *Official Journal of the European Union*.

Done at Brussels, 27 November 2008.

*For the Council*

*The President*

M. ALLIOT-MARIE

# Framework Decision 2008/913 on combating certain forms and expressions of racism and xenophobia by means of criminal law, 28 November 2008

**[OJ 2008, L 325/55–58]**

6.12.2008 EN Official Journal of the European Union L 328/55

III

*(Acts adopted under the EU Treaty)*

## ACTS ADOPTED UNDER TITLE VI OF THE EU TREATY

### COUNCIL FRAMEWORK DECISION 2008/913/JHA

**of 28 November 2008**

**on combating certain forms and expressions of racism and xenophobia by means of criminal law**

THE COUNCIL OF THE EUROPEAN UNION,

Having regard to the Treaty on European Union, and in particular Articles 29, 31 and 34(2)(b) thereof,

Having regard to the proposal from the Commission,

Having regard to the Opinion of the European Parliament ([1]),

Whereas:

(1) Racism and xenophobia are direct violations of the principles of liberty, democracy, respect for human rights and fundamental freedoms and the rule of law, principles upon which the European Union is founded and which are common to the Member States.

(2) The Action Plan of the Council and the Commission on how best to implement the provisions of the Treaty of Amsterdam on an area of freedom, security and justice ([2]), the Conclusions of the Tampere European Council of 15 and 16 October 1999, the Resolution of the European Parliament of 20 September 2000 on the European Union's position at the World Conference Against Racism and the current situation in the Union ([3]) and the Communication from the Commission to the Council and the European Parliament on the biannual update of the Scoreboard to review progress on the creation of an area of 'freedom, security and justice' in the European Union (second half of 2000) call for action in this field. In the Hague Programme of 4 and 5 November 2004, the Council recalls its firm commitment to oppose any form of racism, anti-Semitism and xenophobia as already expressed by the European Council in December 2003.

(3) Council Joint Action 96/443/JHA of 15 July 1996 concerning action to combat racism and xenophobia ([4]) should be followed by further legislative action addressing the need for further approximation of law and regulations of Member States and for overcoming obstacles for efficient judicial cooperation which are mainly based on the divergence of legal approaches in the Member States.

(4) According to the evaluation of Joint Action 96/443/JHA and work carried out in other international fora, such as the Council of Europe, some difficulties have still been experienced regarding judicial cooperation and therefore there is a need for further approximation of Member States' criminal laws in order to ensure the effective implementation of comprehensive and clear legislation to combat racism and xenophobia.

(5) Racism and xenophobia constitute a threat against groups of persons which are the target of such behaviour. It is necessary to define a common criminal-law approach in the European Union to this phenomenon in order to ensure that the same behaviour constitutes an offence in all Member States and that effective, proportionate and dissuasive penalties are provided for natural and legal persons having committed or being liable for such offences.

(6) Member States acknowledge that combating racism and xenophobia requires various kinds of measures in a comprehensive framework and may not be limited to criminal matters. This Framework Decision is limited to combating particularly serious forms of racism and xenophobia by means of criminal law. Since the Member States' cultural and legal traditions are, to some extent, different, particularly in this field, full harmonisation of criminal laws is currently not possible.

([1]) Opinion of 29 November 2007 (not yet published in the Official Journal).
([2]) OJ C 19, 23.1.1999, p. 1.
([3]) OJ C 146, 17.5.2001, p. 110.
([4]) OJ L 185, 24.7.1996, p. 5.

(7) In this Framework Decision 'descent' should be understood as referring mainly to persons or groups of persons who descend from persons who could be identified by certain characteristics (such as race or colour), but not necessarily all of these characteristics still exist. In spite of that, because of their descent, such persons or groups of persons may be subject to hatred or violence.

(8) 'Religion' should be understood as broadly referring to persons defined by reference to their religious convictions or beliefs.

(9) 'Hatred' should be understood as referring to hatred based on race, colour, religion, descent or national or ethnic origin.

(10) This Framework Decision does not prevent a Member State from adopting provisions in national law which extend Article 1(1)(c) and (d) to crimes directed against a group of persons defined by other criteria than race, colour, religion, descent or national or ethnic origin, such as social status or political convictions.

(11) It should be ensured that investigations and prosecutions of offences involving racism and xenophobia are not dependent on reports or accusations made by victims, who are often particularly vulnerable and reluctant to initiate legal proceedings.

(12) Approximation of criminal law should lead to combating racist and xenophobic offences more effectively, by promoting a full and effective judicial cooperation between Member States. The difficulties which may exist in this field should be taken into account by the Council when reviewing this Framework Decision with a view to considering whether further steps in this area are necessary.

(13) Since the objective of this Framework Decision, namely ensuring that racist and xenophobic offences are sanctioned in all Member States by at least a minimum level of effective, proportionate and dissuasive criminal penalties, cannot be sufficiently achieved by the Member States individually, since such rules have to be common and compatible and since this objective can therefore be better achieved at the level of the European Union, the Union may adopt measures, in accordance with the principle of subsidiarity as referred to in Article 2 of the Treaty on European Union and as set out in Article 5 of the Treaty establishing the European Community. In accordance with the principle of proportionality, as set out in the latter Article, this Framework Decision does not go beyond what is necessary in order to achieve that objective.

(14) This Framework Decision respects the fundamental rights and observes the principles recognised by Article 6 of the Treaty on European Union and by the European Convention for the Protection of Human Rights and Fundamental Freedoms, in particular Articles 10 and 11 thereof, and reflected in the Charter of Fundamental Rights of the European Union, and notably Chapters II and VI thereof.

(15) Considerations relating to freedom of association and freedom of expression, in particular freedom of the press and freedom of expression in other media have led in many Member States to procedural guarantees and to special rules in national law as to the determination or limitation of liability.

(16) Joint Action 96/443/JHA should be repealed since, with the entry into force of the Treaty of Amsterdam, Council Directive 2000/43/EC of 29 June 2000 implementing the principle of equal treatment between persons irrespective of racial or ethnic origin [1] and this Framework Decision, it becomes obsolete,

HAS ADOPTED THIS FRAMEWORK DECISION:

*Article 1*

**Offences concerning racism and xenophobia**

1. Each Member State shall take the measures necessary to ensure that the following intentional conduct is punishable:

(a) publicly inciting to violence or hatred directed against a group of persons or a member of such a group defined by reference to race, colour, religion, descent or national or ethnic origin;

(b) the commission of an act referred to in point (a) by public dissemination or distribution of tracts, pictures or other material;

(c) publicly condoning, denying or grossly trivialising crimes of genocide, crimes against humanity and war crimes as defined in Articles 6, 7 and 8 of the Statute of the International Criminal Court, directed against a group of persons or a member of such a group defined by reference to race, colour, religion, descent or national or ethnic origin when the conduct is carried out in a manner likely to incite to violence or hatred against such a group or a member of such a group;

(d) publicly condoning, denying or grossly trivialising the crimes defined in Article 6 of the Charter of the International Military Tribunal appended to the London Agreement of 8 August 1945, directed against a group of persons or a member of such a group defined by reference to race, colour, religion, descent or national or ethnic origin when the conduct is carried out in a manner likely to incite to violence or hatred against such a group or a member of such a group.

[1] OJ L 180, 19.7.2000, p. 22.

6.12.2008 EN Official Journal of the European Union L 328/57

2. For the purpose of paragraph 1, Member States may choose to punish only conduct which is either carried out in a manner likely to disturb public order or which is threatening, abusive or insulting.

3. For the purpose of paragraph 1, the reference to religion is intended to cover, at least, conduct which is a pretext for directing acts against a group of persons or a member of such a group defined by reference to race, colour, descent, or national or ethnic origin.

4. Any Member State may, on adoption of this Framework Decision or later, make a statement that it will make punishable the act of denying or grossly trivialising the crimes referred to in paragraph 1(c) and/or (d) only if the crimes referred to in these paragraphs have been established by a final decision of a national court of this Member State and/or an international court, or by a final decision of an international court only.

*Article 2*

**Instigation, aiding and abetting**

1. Each Member State shall take the measures necessary to ensure that instigating the conduct referred to in Article 1(1)(c) and (d) is punishable.

2. Each Member State shall take the measures necessary to ensure that aiding and abetting in the commission of the conduct referred to in Article 1 is punishable.

*Article 3*

**Criminal penalties**

1. Each Member State shall take the necessary measures to ensure that the conduct referred to in Articles 1 and 2 is punishable by effective, proportionate and dissuasive criminal penalties.

2. Each Member State shall take the necessary measures to ensure that the conduct referred to in Article 1 is punishable by criminal penalties of a maximum of at least between 1 and 3 years of imprisonment.

*Article 4*

**Racist and xenophobic motivation**

For offences other than those referred to in Articles 1 and 2, Member States shall take the necessary measures to ensure that racist and xenophobic motivation is considered an aggravating circumstance, or, alternatively that such motivation may be taken into consideration by the courts in the determination of the penalties.

*Article 5*

**Liability of legal persons**

1. Each Member State shall take the necessary measures to ensure that a legal person can be held liable for the conduct referred to in Articles 1 and 2, committed for its benefit by any person, acting either individually or as part of an organ of the legal person, who has a leading position within the legal person, based on:

(a) a power of representation of the legal person;

(b) an authority to take decisions on behalf of the legal person; or

(c) an authority to exercise control within the legal person.

2. Apart from the cases provided for in paragraph 1 of this Article, each Member State shall take the necessary measures to ensure that a legal person can be held liable where the lack of supervision or control by a person referred to in paragraph 1 of this Article has made possible the commission of the conduct referred to in Articles 1 and 2 for the benefit of that legal person by a person under its authority.

3. Liability of a legal person under paragraphs 1 and 2 of this Article shall not exclude criminal proceedings against natural persons who are perpetrators or accessories in the conduct referred to in Articles 1 and 2.

4. 'Legal person' means any entity having such status under the applicable national law, with the exception of States or other public bodies in the exercise of State authority and public international organisations.

*Article 6*

**Penalties for legal persons**

1. Each Member State shall take the necessary measures to ensure that a legal person held liable pursuant to Article 5(1) is punishable by effective, proportionate and dissuasive penalties, which shall include criminal or non-criminal fines and may include other penalties, such as:

(a) exclusion from entitlement to public benefits or aid;

(b) temporary or permanent disqualification from the practice of commercial activities;

(c) placing under judicial supervision;

(d) a judicial winding-up order.

2. Member States shall take the necessary measures to ensure that a legal person held liable pursuant to Article 5(2) is punishable by effective, proportionate and dissuasive penalties or measures.

*Article 7*

**Constitutional rules and fundamental principles**

1. This Framework Decision shall not have the effect of modifying the obligation to respect fundamental rights and fundamental legal principles, including freedom of expression and association, as enshrined in Article 6 of the Treaty on European Union.

L 328/58 EN Official Journal of the European Union 6.12.2008

2. This Framework Decision shall not have the effect of requiring Member States to take measures in contradiction to fundamental principles relating to freedom of association and freedom of expression, in particular freedom of the press and the freedom of expression in other media as they result from constitutional traditions or rules governing the rights and responsibilities of, and the procedural guarantees for, the press or other media where these rules relate to the determination or limitation of liability.

*Article 8*

**Initiation of investigation or prosecution**

Each Member State shall take the necessary measures to ensure that investigations into or prosecution of the conduct referred to in Articles 1 and 2 shall not be dependent on a report or an accusation made by a victim of the conduct, at least in the most serious cases where the conduct has been committed in its territory.

*Article 9*

**Jurisdiction**

1. Each Member State shall take the necessary measures to establish its jurisdiction with regard to the conduct referred to in Articles 1 and 2 where the conduct has been committed:

(a) in whole or in part within its territory;

(b) by one of its nationals; or

(c) for the benefit of a legal person that has its head office in the territory of that Member State.

2. When establishing jurisdiction in accordance with paragraph 1(a), each Member State shall take the necessary measures to ensure that its jurisdiction extends to cases where the conduct is committed through an information system and:

(a) the offender commits the conduct when physically present in its territory, whether or not the conduct involves material hosted on an information system in its territory;

(b) the conduct involves material hosted on an information system in its territory, whether or not the offender commits the conduct when physically present in its territory.

3. A Member State may decide not to apply, or to apply only in specific cases or circumstances, the jurisdiction rule set out in paragraphs 1(b) and (c).

*Article 10*

**Implementation and review**

1. Member States shall take the necessary measures to comply with the provisions of this Framework Decision by 28 November 2010.

2. By the same date Member States shall transmit to the General Secretariat of the Council and to the Commission the text of the provisions transposing into their national law the obligations imposed on them under this Framework Decision. On the basis of a report established using this information by the Council and a written report from the Commission, the Council shall, by 28 November 2013, assess the extent to which Member States have complied with the provisions of this Framework Decision.

3. Before 28 November 2013, the Council shall review this Framework Decision. For the preparation of this review, the Council shall ask Member States whether they have experienced difficulties in judicial cooperation with regard to the conduct under Article 1(1). In addition, the Council may request Eurojust to submit a report, on whether differences between national legislations have resulted in any problems regarding judicial cooperation between the Member States in this area.

*Article 11*

**Repeal of Joint Action 96/443/JHA**

Joint Action 96/443/JHA is hereby repealed.

*Article 12*

**Territorial application**

This Framework Decision shall apply to Gibraltar.

*Article 13*

**Entry into force**

This Framework Decision shall enter into force on the day of its publication in the *Official Journal of the European Union*.

Done at Brussels, 28 November 2008.

*For the Council*

*The President*

M. ALLIOT-MARIE

# Decision 2008/976 on the European Judicial Network, 16 December 2008

[OJ 2008, L 348/130–134]

L 348/130 EN Official Journal of the European Union 24.12.2008

III

*(Acts adopted under the EU Treaty)*

# ACTS ADOPTED UNDER TITLE VI OF THE EU TREATY

## COUNCIL DECISION 2008/976/JHA
## of 16 December 2008
## on the European Judicial Network

THE COUNCIL OF THE EUROPEAN UNION,

Having regard to the Treaty on European Union, and in particular Articles 31 and 34(2)(c) thereof,

Having regard to the initiative of the Kingdom of Belgium, the Czech Republic, the Republic of Estonia, the Kingdom of Spain, the French Republic, the Italian Republic, the Grand Duchy of Luxembourg, the Kingdom of the Netherlands, the Republic of Austria, the Republic of Poland, the Portuguese Republic, the Republic of Slovenia, the Slovak Republic and the Kingdom of Sweden,

Having regard to the opinion of the European Parliament (1),

Whereas:

(1) By Joint Action 98/428/JHA (2), the Council set up the European Judicial Network which has demonstrated its usefulness in the facilitation of judicial cooperation in criminal matters.

(2) In accordance with Article 6 of the Convention on Mutual Assistance in Criminal Matters between the Member States of the European Union (3), mutual legal assistance takes place through direct contacts between competent judicial authorities. This decentralisation of mutual legal assistance is now widely implemented.

(3) The principle of mutual recognition of judicial decisions in criminal matters is being implemented gradually. It not only confirms the principle of direct contacts between competent judicial authorities, it also accelerates the procedures and makes them entirely judicial.

(4) The impact of these changes on judicial cooperation was further increased by the enlargement of the European Union in 2004 and 2007. Because of this evolution, the European Judicial Network is even more necessary than at the time of its creation and should therefore be strengthened.

(5) By Decision 2002/187/JHA (4), the Council set up Eurojust to improve coordination and cooperation between competent authorities of the Member States. Decision 2002/187/JHA provides that Eurojust is to maintain privileged relations with the European Judicial Network based on consultation and complementarity.

(6) Five years of coexistence of Eurojust and the European Judicial Network have demonstrated both the need to maintain the two structures and the need to clarify their relationship.

(7) Nothing in this Decision should be construed to affect the independence that contact points may have under national law.

(8) It is necessary to strengthen judicial cooperation between the Member States and to allow contact points of the European Judicial Network and Eurojust for this purpose to communicate, whenever needed, directly and more efficiently through a secure telecommunications connection.

(9) Joint Action 98/428/JHA should therefore be repealed and replaced by this Decision,

(1) Opinion delivered on 2 September 2008 (not yet published in the Official Journal).
(2) OJ L 191, 7.7.1998, p. 4.
(3) OJ C 197, 12.7.2000, p. 3.
(4) OJ L 63, 6.3.2002, p. 1.

24.12.2008 EN Official Journal of the European Union L 348/131

HAS DECIDED AS FOLLOWS:

*Article 1*

**Creation**

The network of judicial contact points set up between the Member States under Joint Action 98/428/JHA, hereinafter referred to as the 'European Judicial Network', shall continue to operate in accordance with the provisions of this Decision.

*Article 2*

**Composition**

1. The European Judicial Network shall be made up, taking into account the constitutional rules, legal traditions and internal structure of each Member State, of the central authorities responsible for international judicial cooperation and the judicial or other competent authorities with specific responsibilities within the context of international cooperation.

2. One or more contact points of each Member State shall be established in accordance with its internal rules and internal division of responsibilities, care being taken to ensure effective coverage of the whole of its territory.

3. Each Member State shall appoint, among the contact points, a national correspondent for the European Judicial Network.

4. Each Member State shall appoint a tool correspondent for the European Judicial Network.

5. Each Member State shall ensure that its contact points have functions in relation to judicial cooperation in criminal matters and adequate knowledge of a language of the European Union other than its own national language, bearing in mind the need to be able to communicate with the contact points in the other Member States.

6. Where the liaison magistrates referred to in Council Joint Action 96/277/JHA of 22 April 1996 concerning a framework for the exchange of liaison magistrates to improve judicial co-operation between the Member States of the European Union ([1]) have been appointed in a Member State and have duties analogous to those assigned by Article 4 of this Decision to the contact points, they shall be linked to the European Judicial Network and to the secure telecommunications connection pursuant to Article 9 of this Decision by the Member State appointing the liaison magistrate in each case, in accordance with the procedures to be laid down by that Member State.

7. The Commission shall designate a contact point for those areas falling within its sphere of competence.

8. The European Judicial Network shall have a Secretariat which shall be responsible for the administration of the Network.

*Article 3*

**Manner of operation of the Network**

The European Judicial Network shall operate in particular in the following three ways:

(a) it shall facilitate the establishment of appropriate contacts between the contact points in the various Member States in order to carry out the functions laid down in Article 4;

(b) it shall organise periodic meetings of the Member States representatives in accordance with the procedures laid down in Articles 5 and 6;

(c) it shall constantly provide a certain amount of up-to-date background information, in particular by means of an appropriate telecommunications network, under the procedures laid down in Articles 7, 8 and 9.

*Article 4*

**Functions of contact points**

1. The contact points shall be active intermediaries with the task of facilitating judicial cooperation between Member States, particularly in actions to combat forms of serious crime. They shall be available to enable local judicial authorities and other competent authorities in their own Member State, contact points in the other Member States and local judicial and other competent authorities in the other Member States to establish the most appropriate direct contacts.

They may if necessary travel to meet other Member States contact points, on the basis of an agreement between the administrations concerned.

2. The contact points shall provide the local judicial authorities in their own Member State, the contact points in the other Member States and the local judicial authorities in the other Member States with the legal and practical information necessary to enable them to prepare an effective request for judicial cooperation or to improve judicial cooperation in general.

3. At their respective level the contact points shall be involved in and promote the organisation of training sessions on judicial cooperation for the benefit of the competent authorities of their Member State, where appropriate in cooperation with the European Judicial Training Network.

([1]) OJ L 105, 27.4.1996, p. 1.

4. The national correspondent, in addition to his tasks as a contact point referred to in paragraphs 1 to 3, shall in particular:

(a) be responsible, in his Member State, for issues related to the internal functioning of the Network, including the coordination of requests for information and replies issued by the competent national authorities;

(b) be the main person responsible for the contacts with the Secretariat of the European Judicial Network including the participation in the meetings referred to in Article 6;

(c) where requested, give an opinion concerning the appointment of new contact points.

5. The European Judicial Network tool correspondent, who may also be a contact point referred to in paragraphs 1 to 4, shall ensure that the information related to his Member State and referred to in Article 7 is provided and updated in accordance with Article 8.

*Article 5*

**Purposes and venues of the plenary meetings of contact points**

1. The purposes of the plenary meetings of the European Judicial Network, to which at least three contact points per Member State shall be invited, shall be as follows:

(a) to allow the contact points to get to know each other and exchange experience, particularly concerning the operation of the Network;

(b) to provide a forum for discussion of practical and legal problems encountered by the Member States in the context of judicial cooperation, in particular with regard to the implementation of measures adopted by the European Union.

2. The relevant experience acquired within the European Judicial Network shall be passed on to the Council and the Commission to serve as a basis for discussion of possible legislative changes and practical improvements in the area of international judicial cooperation.

3. Meetings referred to in paragraph 1 shall be organised regularly and at least three times a year. Once a year, the meeting may be held on the premises of the Council in Brussels or on the premises of Eurojust in The Hague. Two contact points per Member States shall be invited to meetings organised on the premises of the Council and at Eurojust.

Other meetings may be held in the Member States, to enable the contact points of all the Member States to meet authorities of the host Member State other than its contact points and visit specific bodies in that Member State with responsibilities in the context of international judicial cooperation or of combating certain forms of serious crime. The contact points participate in these meetings at their own expense.

*Article 6*

**Meetings of the correspondents**

1. The European Judicial Network national correspondents shall meet on an *ad hoc* basis, at least once a year and as its members deem appropriate, at the invitation of the national correspondent of the Member State which holds the Presidency of the Council, which shall also take account of the Member States wishes for the correspondents to meet. During these meetings, administrative matters related to the Network shall in particular be discussed.

2. The European Judicial Network tool correspondents shall meet on an *ad hoc* basis, at least once a year and as its members deem appropriate, at the invitation of the tool correspondent of the Member State which holds the Presidency of the Council. The meetings shall deal with the issues referred to in Article 4(5).

*Article 7*

**Content of the information disseminated within the European Judicial Network**

The Secretariat of the European Judicial Network shall make the following information available to contact points and competent judicial authorities:

(a) full details of the contact points in each Member State with, where necessary, an explanation of their responsibilities at national level;

(b) an information technology tool allowing the requesting or issuing authority of a Member State to identify the competent authority in another Member State to receive and execute its request for, and decisions on, judicial cooperation, including regarding instruments giving effect to the principle of mutual recognition;

(c) concise legal and practical information concerning the judicial and procedural systems in the Member States;

(d) the texts of the relevant legal instruments and, for conventions currently in force, the texts of declarations and reservations.

*Article 8*

**Updating of information**

1. The information distributed within the European Judicial Network shall be constantly updated.

2. It shall be each Member State's individual responsibility to check the accuracy of the data contained in the system and to inform the Secretariat of the European Judicial Network as soon as data on one of the four points referred to in Article 7 need to be amended.

*Article 9*

**Telecommunication tools**

1. The Secretariat of the European Judicial Network shall ensure that the information provided under Article 7 is made available on a website which is constantly updated.

2. The secure telecommunications connection shall be set up for the operational work of the contact points of the European Judicial Network. The setting up of the secure telecommunications connection shall be at the charge of the general budget of the European Union.

The setting up of the secure telecommunications connection shall make possible the flow of data and of requests for judicial cooperation between Member States.

3. The secure telecommunications connection referred to in paragraph 2 may also be used for their operational work by the national correspondents for Eurojust, national correspondents for Eurojust for terrorist matters, the national members of Eurojust and liaison magistrates appointed by Eurojust. It may be linked to the Case Management System of Eurojust referred to in Article 16 of Decision 2002/187/JHA.

4. Nothing in this Article shall be construed to affect direct contacts between competent judicial authorities as provided for in instruments on judicial cooperation, such as Article 6 of the Convention on Mutual Assistance in Criminal Matters between the Member States of the European Union.

*Article 10*

**Relationship between the European Judicial Network and Eurojust**

The European Judicial Network and Eurojust shall maintain privileged relations with each other, based on consultation and complementarity, especially between the contact points of a Member State, the Eurojust national member of the same Member State and the national correspondents for the European Judicial Network and Eurojust. In order to ensure efficient cooperation, the following measures shall be taken:

(a) the European Judicial Network shall make available to Eurojust the centralised information indicated in Article 7 and the secure telecommunications connection set up under Article 9;

(b) the contact points of the European Judicial Network shall, on a case-by-case basis, inform their own national member of all cases which they deem Eurojust to be in a better position to deal with;

(c) the national members of Eurojust may attend meetings of the European Judicial Network at the invitation of the latter.

*Article 11*

**Budget**

In order for the European Judicial Network to be able to carry out its tasks, the budget of Eurojust shall contain a part related to the activities of the Secretariat of the European Judicial Network.

*Article 12*

**Territorial application**

The United Kingdom shall notify in writing the President of the Council when it wishes to apply this Decision to the Channel Islands and the Isle of Man. A decision on that request shall be taken by the Council.

*Article 13*

**Assessment of the operation of the European Judicial Network**

1. Every second year from 24 December 2008, the European Judicial Network shall report to the European Parliament, the Council and the Commission on its activities and management.

2. The European Judicial Network may, in the report referred to in paragraph 1, also indicate any criminal policy problems within the European Union highlighted as a result of the European Judicial Network's activities and it may also make proposals for the improvement of judicial cooperation in criminal matters.

3. The European Judicial Network may also submit any report or any other information on its operation which may be requested by the Council.

4. The Council shall, every four years from 24 December 2008, carry out an assessment of the operation of the European Judicial Network on the basis of a report drawn up by the Commission in cooperation with the European Judicial Network.

*Article 14*

**Repeal of Joint Action 98/428/JHA**

Joint Action 98/428/JHA is hereby repealed.

L 348/134 EN Official Journal of the European Union 24.12.2008

*Article 15*

**Taking of effect**

This Decision shall take effect on the day of its publication in the *Official Journal of the European Union*.

Done at Brussels, 16 December 2008.

*For the Council*
*The President*
R. BACHELOT-NARQUIN

# Framework Decision 2008/978 on the European evidence warrant for the purpose of obtaining objects, documents and data for use in proceedings in criminal matters, 18 December 2008

[OJ 2008, L 350/72–92]

L 350/72 EN Official Journal of the European Union 30.12.2008

## COUNCIL FRAMEWORK DECISION 2008/978/JHA

### of 18 December 2008

### on the European evidence warrant for the purpose of obtaining objects, documents and data for use in proceedings in criminal matters

THE COUNCIL OF THE EUROPEAN UNION,

Having regard to the Treaty on European Union, and in particular Article 31 and Article 34(2)(b) thereof,

Having regard to the proposal of the Commission,

Having regard to the opinion of the European Parliament [1],

Whereas:

(1) The European Union has set itself the objective of maintaining and developing an area of freedom, security and justice. According to the Conclusions of the Tampere European Council of 15 and 16 October 1999, and in particular point 33 thereof, the principle of mutual recognition should become the cornerstone of judicial cooperation in both civil and criminal matters within the Union.

(2) On 29 November 2000 the Council, in accordance with the Tampere Conclusions, adopted a programme of measures to implement the principle of mutual recognition in criminal matters [2]. This Framework Decision is necessary to complete measures 5 and 6 of that programme, which deal with the mutual recognition of orders to obtain evidence.

(3) Point 3.3.1 of the Hague Programme [3], included in the Conclusions of the European Council of 4 and 5 November 2004, emphasises the importance of the completion of the comprehensive programme of measures to implement the principle of mutual recognition in criminal matters and highlights the introduction of the European evidence warrant (EEW) as a matter of priority.

(4) Council Framework Decision 2002/584/JHA of 13 June 2002 on the European arrest warrant and the surrender procedures between Member States [4] was the first concrete measure in the field of criminal law implementing the principle of mutual recognition.

(5) Council Framework Decision 2003/577/JHA of 22 July 2003 on the execution in the European Union of orders freezing property and evidence [5] addresses the need for immediate mutual recognition of orders to prevent the destruction, transformation, moving, transfer or disposal of evidence. However, this deals only with part of the spectrum of judicial cooperation in criminal matters with respect to evidence, and subsequent transfer of the evidence is left to mutual assistance procedures.

(6) It is therefore necessary further to improve judicial cooperation by applying the principle of mutual recognition to a judicial decision, in the form of an EEW, for the purpose of obtaining objects, documents and data for use in proceedings in criminal matters.

(7) The EEW may be used to obtain any objects, documents and data for use in proceedings in criminal matters for which it may be issued. This may include for example objects, documents or data from a third party, from a search of premises including the private premises of the suspect, historical data on the use of any services including financial transactions, historical records of statements, interviews and hearings, and other records, including the results of special investigative techniques.

(8) The principle of mutual recognition is based on a high level of confidence between Member States. In order to promote this confidence, this Framework Decision should contain important safeguards to protect fundamental rights. The EEW should therefore be issued only by judges, courts, investigating magistrates, public prosecutors and certain other judicial authorities as defined by Member States in accordance with this Framework Decision.

(9) This Framework Decision is adopted under Article 31 of the Treaty and therefore concerns judicial cooperation within the context of that provision, aiming to assist the collection of evidence for proceedings as defined in Article 5 of this Framework Decision. Although authorities other than judges, courts, investigating magistrates and public prosecutors may have a role in the collection of such evidence in accordance with Article 2(c)(ii), this Framework Decision does not cover police, customs, border and administrative cooperation which are regulated by other provisions of the Treaties.

[1] OJ C 103 E, 29.4.2004, p. 452.
[2] OJ C 12, 15.1.2001, p. 10.
[3] OJ C 53, 3.3.2005, p. 1.
[4] OJ L 190, 18.7.2002, p. 1.
[5] OJ L 196, 2.8.2003, p. 45.

30.12.2008 EN Official Journal of the European Union L 350/73

(10) The definition of the term 'search or seizure' should not be invoked for the application of any other instrument applicable between Member States, in particular the Council of Europe Convention on Mutual Assistance in Criminal Matters of 20 April 1959, and the instruments which supplement it.

(11) An EEW should be issued only where obtaining the objects, documents or data sought is necessary and proportionate for the purpose of the criminal or other proceedings concerned. In addition, an EEW should be issued only where the object, documents or data concerned could be obtained under the national law of the issuing State in a comparable case. The responsibility for ensuring compliance with these conditions should lie with the issuing authority. The grounds for non-recognition or non-execution should therefore not cover these matters.

(12) The executing authority should use the least intrusive means to obtain the objects, documents or data sought.

(13) The executing authority should be obliged to execute the EEW for electronic data not located in the executing State only to the extent possible under its law.

(14) It should be possible, if the national law of the issuing State so provides in transposing Article 12, for the issuing authority to ask the executing authority to follow specified formalities and procedures in respect of legal or administrative processes which might assist in making the evidence sought admissible in the issuing State, for example the official stamping of a document, the presence of a representative from the issuing State, or the recording of times and dates to create a chain of evidence. Such formalities and procedures should not encompass coercive measures.

(15) The execution of an EEW should, to the widest extent possible, and without prejudice to fundamental guarantees under national law, be carried out in accordance with the formalities and procedures expressly indicated by the issuing State.

(16) To ensure the effectiveness of judicial cooperation in criminal matters, the possibility of refusing to recognise or execute the EEW, as well as the grounds for postponing its execution, should be limited. In particular, refusal to execute the EEW on the grounds that the act on which it is based does not constitute an offence under the national law of the executing State (dual criminality) should not be possible for certain categories of offences.

(17) It should be possible to refuse an EEW where its recognition or execution in the executing State would involve breaching an immunity or privilege in that State. There is no common definition of what constitutes an immunity or privilege in the European Union and the precise definition of these terms is therefore left to national law, which may include protections which apply to medical and legal professions, but should not be interpreted in a way which would run counter to the obligation to abolish certain grounds for refusal in Article 7 of the Council Act of 16 October 2001 establishing, in accordance with Article 34 of the Treaty on European Union, the Protocol to the Convention on Mutual Assistance in Criminal Matters between the Member States of the European Union ([1]).

(18) It should be possible to refuse to recognise or execute an EEW to the extent that execution would harm essential national security interests, jeopardise the source of the information or involve the use of classified information relating to specific intelligence activities. However, it is accepted that such ground for non-recognition or non-execution would be applied only where, and to the extent that, the objects, documents or data would not be used for those reasons as evidence in a similar domestic case.

(19) The specific provisions in Article 13(3) in relation to Article 13(1)(f)(i) do not prejudice how and the extent to which the other grounds for refusal in Article 13(1) are implemented.

(20) Time limits are necessary to ensure quick, effective and consistent cooperation on obtaining objects, documents or data for use in proceedings in criminal matters throughout the European Union.

(21) Each Member State has in its law legal remedies available against the substantive reasons underlying decisions for obtaining evidence, including whether the decision is necessary and proportionate, although those remedies may differ between Member States and may apply at different stages of proceedings.

(22) It is necessary to establish a mechanism to assess the effectiveness of this Framework Decision.

([1]) OJ C 326, 21.11.2001, p. 1.

(23) Since the objective of this Framework Decision, namely to replace the system of mutual assistance in criminal matters for obtaining objects, documents or data between Member States cannot be sufficiently achieved by the Member States acting unilaterally and can therefore, by reason of its scale and effects, be better achieved at Union level, the Council may adopt measures in accordance with the principle of subsidiarity as referred to in Article 2 of the Treaty on European Union and set out in Article 5 of the Treaty establishing the European Community. In accordance with the principle of proportionality, as set out in the latter Article, this Framework Decision does not go beyond what is necessary in order to achieve that objective.

(24) The personal data processed in the context of the implementation of this Framework Decision will be protected in accordance with the relevant instruments including the principles of the Council of Europe Convention of 28 January 1981 for the protection of individuals with regard to the automatic processing of personal data, as well as by the additional protection afforded by this Framework Decision in line with Article 23 of the Convention on Mutual Assistance in Criminal Matters between the Member States of the European Union of 29 May 2000 [1].

(25) The EEW should coexist with existing mutual assistance procedures, but such coexistence should be considered transitional until, in accordance with the Hague Programme, the types of evidence-gathering excluded from the scope of this Framework Decision are also the subject of a mutual recognition instrument, the adoption of which would provide a complete mutual recognition regime to replace mutual assistance procedures.

(26) Member States are encouraged to draw up, for themselves and in the interest of the European Union, tables which as far as possible show the correlation between the provisions of this Framework Decision and the national implementation measures and to communicate this to the Commission together with the text of the national law implementing this Framework Decision.

(27) This Framework Decision respects the fundamental rights and observes the principles recognised by Article 6 of the Treaty on European Union and reflected by the Charter of Fundamental Rights of the European Union, notably Chapter VI thereof. Nothing in this Framework Decision may be interpreted as prohibiting refusal to execute an EEW when there are reasons to believe, on the basis of objective elements, that the EEW has been issued for the purpose of prosecuting or punishing a person on account of his or her sex, racial or ethnic origin, religion, sexual orientation, nationality, language or political opinions, or that the person's position may be prejudiced for any of these reasons.

(28) This Framework Decision does not prevent any Member State from applying its constitutional rules relating to due process, freedom of association, freedom of the press and freedom of expression in other media.

(29) This Framework Decision does not affect the exercise of the responsibilities incumbent upon Member States with regard to the maintenance of law and order and the safeguarding of internal security in accordance with Article 33 of the Treaty,

HAS ADOPTED THIS FRAMEWORK DECISION:

TITLE I

**THE EUROPEAN EVIDENCE WARRANT (EEW)**

*Article 1*

**Definition of the EEW and obligation to execute it**

1. The EEW shall be a judicial decision issued by a competent authority of a Member State with a view to obtaining objects, documents and data from another Member State for use in proceedings referred to in Article 5.

2. Member States shall execute any EEW on the basis of the principle of mutual recognition and in accordance with the provisions of this Framework Decision.

3. This Framework Decision shall not have the effect of modifying the obligation to respect fundamental rights and fundamental legal principles as enshrined in Article 6 of the Treaty, and any obligations incumbent on judicial authorities in this respect shall remain unaffected.

*Article 2*

**Definitions**

For the purposes of this Framework Decision:

(a) 'issuing State' shall mean the Member State in which the EEW has been issued;

(b) 'executing State' shall mean the Member State in whose territory the objects, documents or data are located or, in the case of electronic data, directly accessible under the law of the executing State;

(c) 'issuing authority' shall mean:

(i) a judge, a court, an investigating magistrate, a public prosecutor; or

[1] OJ C 197, 12.7.2000, p. 1.

(ii) any other judicial authority as defined by the issuing State and, in the specific case, acting in its capacity as an investigating authority in criminal proceedings with competence to order the obtaining of evidence in cross-border cases in accordance with national law;

(d) 'executing authority' shall mean an authority having competence under the national law which implements this Framework Decision to recognise or execute an EEW in accordance with this Framework Decision;

(e) 'search or seizure' shall include any measures under criminal procedure as a result of which a legal or natural person is required, under legal compulsion, to provide or participate in providing objects, documents or data and which, if not complied with, may be enforceable without the consent of such a person or it may result in a sanction.

*Article 3*

**Designation of competent authorities**

1. Each Member State shall inform the General Secretariat of the Council which authority or authorities, under its national law, are competent pursuant to Article 2(c) and (d) when that Member State is the issuing State or the executing State.

2. Member States wishing to make use of the possibility to designate a central authority or authorities in accordance with Article 8(2) shall communicate to the General Secretariat of the Council information relating to the designated central authority(ies). These indications shall be binding upon the authorities of the issuing State.

3. The General Secretariat of the Council shall make the information received available to all Member States and the Commission.

*Article 4*

**Scope of the EEW**

1. Without prejudice to paragraph 2 of this Article, the EEW may be issued under the conditions referred to in Article 7 with a view to obtaining in the executing State objects, documents or data needed in the issuing State for the purpose of proceedings referred to in Article 5. The EEW shall cover the objects, documents and data specified therein.

2. The EEW shall not be issued for the purpose of requiring the executing authority to:

(a) conduct interviews, take statements or initiate other types of hearings involving suspects, witnesses, experts or any other party;

(b) carry out bodily examinations or obtain bodily material or biometric data directly from the body of any person, including DNA samples or fingerprints;

(c) obtain information in real time such as through the interception of communications, covert surveillance or monitoring of bank accounts;

(d) conduct analysis of existing objects, documents or data; and

(e) obtain communications data retained by providers of a publicly available electronic communications service or a public communications network.

3. Exchange of information on criminal convictions extracted from the criminal record shall be carried out in accordance with Council Decision 2005/876/JHA of 21 November 2005 on the exchange of information extracted from the criminal record (1) and other relevant instruments.

4. The EEW may be issued with a view to obtaining objects, documents or data falling within paragraph 2, where the objects, documents or data are already in the possession of the executing authority before the EEW is issued.

5. Notwithstanding paragraph 1, the EEW shall, if so indicated by the issuing authority, also cover any other object, document or data, which the executing authority discovers during the execution of the EEW and without further enquiries considers to be relevant to the proceedings for the purpose of which the EEW was issued.

6. Notwithstanding paragraph 2, the EEW may, if requested by the issuing authority, also cover taking statements from persons present during the execution of the EEW and directly related to the subject of the EEW. The relevant rules of the executing State applicable to national cases shall also be applicable in respect of the taking of such statements.

*Article 5*

**Type of proceedings for which the EEW may be issued**

The EEW may be issued:

(a) with respect to criminal proceedings brought by, or to be brought before, a judicial authority in respect of a criminal offence under the national law of the issuing State;

(1) OJ L 322, 9.12.2005, p. 33.

(b) in proceedings brought by administrative authorities in respect of acts which are punishable under the national law of the issuing State by virtue of being infringements of the rules of law, and where the decision may give rise to proceedings before a court having jurisdiction in particular in criminal matters;

(c) in proceedings brought by judicial authorities in respect of acts which are punishable under the national law of the issuing State by virtue of being infringements of the rules of law, and where the decision may give rise to further proceedings before a court having jurisdiction in particular in criminal matters; and

(d) in connection with proceedings referred to in points (a), (b) and (c) which relate to offences or infringements for which a legal person may be held liable or punished in the issuing State.

*Article 6*

**Content and form of the EEW**

1. The EEW set out in the form provided for in the Annex shall be completed, signed, and its contents certified as accurate, by the issuing authority.

2. The EEW shall be written in, or translated by the issuing State into, the official language or one of the official languages of the executing State.

Any Member State may, when this Framework Decision is adopted or at a later date, state in a declaration deposited with the General Secretariat of the Council that it will accept EEWs or a translation of an EEW in one or more other official languages of the institutions of the Union.

TITLE II

**PROCEDURES AND SAFEGUARDS FOR THE ISSUING STATE**

*Article 7*

**Conditions for issuing the EEW**

Each Member State shall take the necessary measures to ensure that the EEW is issued only when the issuing authority is satisfied that the following conditions have been met:

(a) obtaining the objects, documents or data sought is necessary and proportionate for the purpose of proceedings referred to in Article 5;

(b) the objects, documents or data can be obtained under the law of the issuing State in a comparable case if they were available on the territory of the issuing State, even though different procedural measures might be used.

These conditions shall be assessed only in the issuing State in each case.

*Article 8*

**Transmission of the EEW**

1. The EEW may be transmitted to the competent authority of a Member State in which the competent authority of the issuing State has reasonable grounds to believe that relevant objects, documents or data are located or, in the case of electronic data, directly accessible under the law of the executing State. It shall be transmitted without delay from the issuing authority to the executing authority by any means capable of producing a written record under conditions allowing the executing State to establish authenticity. All further official communications shall be made directly between the issuing authority and the executing authority.

2. Each Member State may designate a central authority or, when its legal system so provides, more than one central authority to assist the competent authorities. A Member State may, if necessary as a result of the organisation of its internal judicial system, make its central authority(ies) responsible for the administrative transmission and reception of the EEW as well as for other official correspondence relating thereto.

3. If the issuing authority so wishes, transmission may be effected via the secure telecommunications system of the European Judicial Network.

4. If the executing authority is unknown, the issuing authority shall make all necessary inquiries, including via the European Judicial Network contact points, in order to obtain the information from the executing State.

5. When the authority in the executing State which receives the EEW has no jurisdiction to recognise it and to take the necessary measures for its execution, it shall, *ex officio*, transmit the EEW to the executing authority and so inform the issuing authority.

6. All difficulties concerning the transmission or the authenticity of any document needed for the execution of the EEW shall be dealt with by direct contacts between the issuing and executing authorities involved, or, where appropriate, with the involvement of the central authorities of the Member States.

*Article 9*

**EEW related to an earlier EEW or a freezing order**

1. Where the issuing authority issues an EEW which supplements an earlier EEW or which is a follow-up to a freezing order transmitted under Framework Decision 2003/577/JHA, it shall indicate this fact in the EEW in accordance with the form provided for in the Annex.

2. Where, in accordance with the provisions in force, the issuing authority participates in the execution of the EEW in the executing State, it may without prejudice to declarations made under Article 3(2) address an EEW which supplements the earlier EEW directly to the competent executing authority while present in that State.

*Article 10*

**Conditions for the use of personal data**

1. Personal data obtained under this Framework Decision may be used by the issuing State for the purpose of:

(a) proceedings for which the EEW may be issued;

(b) other judicial and administrative proceedings directly related to the proceedings referred to under point (a);

(c) preventing an immediate and serious threat to public security.

For any purpose other than those set out in points (a), (b) and (c), personal data obtained under this Framework Decision may be used only with the prior consent of the executing State, unless the issuing State has obtained the consent of the data subject.

2. In the circumstances of the particular case, the executing State may require the Member State to which the personal data have been transferred to give information on the use made of the data.

3. This Article shall not apply to personal data obtained by a Member State under this Framework Decision and originating from that Member State.

TITLE III

**PROCEDURES AND SAFEGUARDS FOR THE EXECUTING STATE**

*Article 11*

**Recognition and execution**

1. The executing authority shall recognise an EEW, transmitted in accordance with Article 8, without any further formality being required and shall forthwith take the necessary measures for its execution in the same way as an authority of the executing State would obtain the objects, documents or data, unless that authority decides to invoke one of the grounds for non-recognition or non-execution provided for in Article 13 or one of the grounds for postponement provided for in Article 16.

2. The executing State shall be responsible for choosing the measures which under its national law will ensure the provision of the objects, documents or data sought by an EEW and for deciding whether it is necessary to use coercive measures to provide that assistance. Any measures rendered necessary by the EEW shall be taken in accordance with the applicable procedural rules of the executing State.

3. Each Member State shall ensure:

(i) that any measures which would be available in a similar domestic case in the executing State are also available for the purpose of the execution of the EEW;

and

(ii) that measures, including search or seizure, are available for the purpose of the execution of the EEW where it is related to any of the offences as set out in Article 14(2).

4. If the issuing authority is not a judge, a court, an investigating magistrate or a public prosecutor and the EEW has not been validated by one of those authorities in the issuing State, the executing authority may, in the specific case, decide that no search or seizure may be carried out for the purpose of the execution of the EEW. Before so deciding, the executing authority shall consult the competent authority of the issuing State.

5. A Member State may, at the time of adoption of this Framework Decision, make a declaration or subsequent notification to the General Secretariat of the Council requiring such validation in all cases where the issuing authority is not a judge, a court, an investigating magistrate or a public prosecutor and where the measures necessary to execute the EEW would have to be ordered or supervised by a judge, a court, an investigating magistrate or a public prosecutor under the law of the executing State in a similar domestic case.

*Article 12*

**Formalities to be followed in the executing State**

The executing authority shall comply with the formalities and procedures expressly indicated by the issuing authority unless otherwise provided in this Framework Decision and provided that such formalities and procedures are not contrary to the fundamental principles of law of the executing State. This Article shall not create an obligation to take coercive measures.

*Article 13*

**Grounds for non-recognition or non-execution**

1. Recognition or execution of the EEW may be refused in the executing State:

(a) if its execution would infringe the *ne bis in idem* principle;

(b) if, in cases referred to in Article 14(3), the EEW relates to acts which would not constitute an offence under the law of the executing State;

(c) if it is not possible to execute the EEW by any of the measures available to the executing authority in the specific case in accordance with Article 11(3);

(d) if there is an immunity or privilege under the law of the executing State which makes it impossible to execute the EEW;

(e) if, in one of the cases referred to in Article 11(4) or (5), the EEW has not been validated;

(f) if the EEW relates to criminal offences which:

(i) under the law of the executing State are regarded as having been committed wholly or for a major or essential part within its territory, or in a place equivalent to its territory; or

(ii) were committed outside the territory of the issuing State, and the law of the executing State does not permit legal proceedings to be taken in respect of such offences where they are committed outside that State's territory;

(g) if, in a specific case, its execution would harm essential national security interests, jeopardise the source of the information or involve the use of classified information relating to specific intelligence activities; or

(h) if the form provided for in the Annex is incomplete or manifestly incorrect and has not been completed or corrected within a reasonable deadline set by the executing authority.

2. The decision to refuse the execution or recognition of the EEW pursuant to paragraph 1 shall be taken by a judge, court, investigating magistrate or public prosecutor in the executing State. Where the EEW has been issued by a judicial authority referred to in Article 2(c)(ii), and the EEW has not been validated by a judge, court, investigating magistrate or public prosecutor in the issuing State, the decision may also be taken by any other judicial authority competent under the law of the executing State if provided for under that law.

3. Any decision under paragraph 1(f)(i) in relation to offences committed partly within the territory of the executing State, or in a place equivalent to its territory, shall be taken by the competent authorities referred to in paragraph 2 in exceptional circumstances and on a case-by-case basis, having regard to the specific circumstances of the case, and in particular to whether a major or essential part of the conduct in question has taken place in the issuing State, whether the EEW relates to an act which is not a criminal offence under the law of the executing State and whether it would be necessary to carry out a search and seizure for the execution of the EEW.

4. Where a competent authority considers using the ground for refusal under paragraph 1(f)(i), it shall consult Eurojust before taking the decision.

Where a competent authority is not in agreement with Eurojust's opinion, Member States shall ensure that it give the reasons for its decision and that the Council be informed.

5. In cases referred to in paragraph 1(a), (g) and (h), before deciding not to recognise or not to execute an EEW, either totally or in part, the competent authority in the executing State shall consult the competent authority in the issuing State, by any appropriate means, and shall, where appropriate, ask it to supply any necessary information without delay.

*Article 14*

**Double criminality**

1. The recognition or execution of the EEW shall not be subject to verification of double criminality unless it is necessary to carry out a search or seizure.

2. If it is necessary to carry out a search or seizure for the execution of the EEW, the following offences, if they are punishable in the issuing State by a custodial sentence or a detention order for a maximum period of at least three years and as they are defined by the law of that State, shall not be subject to verification of double criminality under any circumstances:

— participation in a criminal organisation,

— terrorism,

— trafficking in human beings,

— sexual exploitation of children and child pornography,

— illicit trafficking in narcotic drugs and psychotropic substances,

— illicit trafficking in weapons, munitions and explosives,

— corruption,

— fraud, including that affecting the financial interests of the European Communities within the meaning of the Convention of 26 July 1995 on the protection of the European Communities' financial interests (1),

— laundering of the proceeds of crime,

— counterfeiting currency, including of the euro,

— computer-related crime,

— environmental crime, including illicit trafficking in endangered animal species and in endangered plant species and varieties,

— facilitation of unauthorised entry and residence,

— murder, grievous bodily injury,

— illicit trade in human organs and tissue,

— kidnapping, illegal restraint and hostage-taking,

— racism and xenophobia,

— organised or armed robbery,

— illicit trafficking in cultural goods, including antiques and works of art,

— swindling,

— racketeering and extortion,

— counterfeiting and piracy of products,

— forgery of administrative documents and trafficking therein,

— forgery of means of payment,

— illicit trafficking in hormonal substances and other growth promoters,

— illicit trafficking in nuclear or radioactive materials,

— trafficking in stolen vehicles,

— rape,

— arson,

— crimes within the jurisdiction of the International Criminal Court,

— unlawful seizure of aircraft/ships,

— sabotage.

3. If the EEW is not related to any of the offences set out in paragraph 2 and its execution would require a search or seizure, recognition or execution of the EEW may be subject to the condition of double criminality.

In relation to offences in connection with taxes or duties, customs and exchange, recognition or execution may not be opposed on the ground that the law of the executing State does not impose the same kind of tax or duty or does not contain a tax, duty, customs and exchange regulation of the same kind as the law of the issuing State.

4. The condition of double criminality set out in paragraph 3 shall be further examined by the Council by 19 January 2014 in the light of any information transmitted to the Council.

5. The Council may decide, acting unanimously, after consultation of the European Parliament under the conditions laid down in Article 39(1) of the Treaty, to add other categories of offences to the list contained in paragraph 2.

*Article 15*

**Deadlines for recognition, execution and transfer**

1. Each Member State shall take the necessary measures to ensure compliance with the deadlines provided for in this Article. Where the issuing authority has indicated in the EEW that, due to procedural deadlines or other particularly urgent circumstances, a shorter deadline is necessary, the executing authority shall take as full account as possible of this requirement.

2. Any decision to refuse recognition or execution shall be taken as soon as possible and, without prejudice to paragraph 4, no later than 30 days after the receipt of the EEW by the competent executing authority.

3. Unless either grounds for postponement under Article 16 exist or the executing authority has the objects, documents or data sought already in its possession, the executing authority shall take possession of the objects, documents or data without delay and, without prejudice to paragraph 4, no later than 60 days after the receipt of the EEW by the competent executing authority.

(1) OJ C 316, 27.11.1995, p. 49.

4. When it is not practicable in a specific case for the competent executing authority to meet the deadline set out in paragraphs 2 or 3 respectively, it shall without delay inform the competent authority of the issuing State by any means, giving the reasons for the delay and the estimated time needed for the action to be taken.

5. Unless a legal remedy is pending in accordance with Article 18 or grounds for postponement under Article 16 exist, the executing State shall without undue delay transfer the objects, documents or data obtained under the EEW to the issuing State.

6. When transferring the objects, documents or data obtained, the executing authority shall indicate whether it requires them to be returned to the executing State as soon as they are no longer required by the issuing State.

*Article 16*

**Grounds for postponement of recognition or execution**

1. The recognition of the EEW may be postponed in the executing State where:

(a) the form provided for in the Annex is incomplete or manifestly incorrect, until such time as the form has been completed or corrected; or

(b) in one of the cases referred to in Article 11(4) or (5), the EEW has not been validated, until such time as the validation has been given.

2. The execution of the EEW may be postponed in the executing State where:

(a) its execution might prejudice an ongoing criminal investigation or prosecution, until such time as the executing State deems reasonable; or

(b) the objects, documents or data concerned are already being used in other proceedings until such time as they are no longer required for this purpose.

3. The decision to postpone recognition or execution of the EEW pursuant to paragraphs 1 or 2 shall be taken by a judge, court, investigating magistrate or public prosecutor in the executing State. Where the EEW has been issued by a judicial authority referred to in Article 2(c)(ii), and the EEW has not been validated by a judge, court, investigating magistrate or public prosecutor in the issuing State, the decision may also be taken by any other judicial authority competent under the law of the executing State if provided for under that law.

4. As soon as the ground for postponement has ceased to exist, the executing authority shall forthwith take the necessary measures for the execution of the EEW and inform the relevant competent authority in the issuing State thereof by any means capable of producing a written record.

*Article 17*

**Obligation to inform**

The executing authority shall inform the issuing authority:

1. immediately by any means:

(a) if the executing authority, in the course of the execution of the EEW, considers without further enquiries that it may be appropriate to undertake investigative measures not initially foreseen, or which could not be specified when the EEW was issued, in order to enable the issuing authority to take further action in the specific case;

(b) if the competent authority of the executing State establishes that the EEW was not executed in a manner consistent with the law of the executing State;

(c) if the executing authority establishes that, in the specific case, it cannot comply with formalities and procedures expressly indicated by the issuing authority in accordance with Article 12.

Upon request by the issuing authority, the information shall be confirmed without delay by any means capable of producing a written record;

2. without delay by any means capable of producing a written record:

(a) of the transmission of the EEW to the competent authority responsible for its execution, in accordance with Article 8(5);

(b) of any decision taken in accordance with Article 15(2) to refuse recognition or execution of the EEW, together with the reasons for the decision;

(c) of the postponement of the execution or recognition of the EEW, the underlying reasons and, if possible, the expected duration of the postponement;

(d) of the impossibility to execute the EEW because the objects, documents or data have disappeared, been destroyed or cannot be found in the location indicated in the EEW or because the location of the objects, documents or data has not been indicated in a sufficiently precise manner, even after consultation with the competent authority of the issuing State.

*Article 18*

**Legal remedies**

1. Member States shall put in place the necessary arrangements to ensure that any interested party, including bona fide third parties, have legal remedies against the recognition and execution of an EEW pursuant to Article 11, in order to preserve their legitimate interests. Member States may limit the legal remedies provided for in this paragraph to cases in which the EEW is executed using coercive measures. The action shall be brought before a court in the executing State in accordance with the law of that State.

2. The substantive reasons for issuing the EEW, including whether the conditions established in Article 7 have been met, may be challenged only in an action brought before a court in the issuing State. The issuing State shall ensure the applicability of legal remedies which are available in a comparable domestic case.

3. Member States shall ensure that any time limits for bringing an action mentioned in paragraphs 1 and 2 are applied in a way that guarantees the possibility of an effective legal remedy for interested parties.

4. If the action is brought in the executing State, the judicial authority of the issuing State shall be informed thereof and of the grounds of the action, so that it can submit the arguments that it deems necessary. It shall be informed of the outcome of the action.

5. The issuing and executing authorities shall take the necessary measures to facilitate the exercise of the right to bring actions mentioned in paragraphs 1 and 2, in particular by providing interested parties with relevant and adequate information.

6. The executing State may suspend the transfer of objects, documents and data pending the outcome of a legal remedy.

*Article 19*

**Reimbursement**

1. Without prejudice to Article 18(2), where the executing State under its law is responsible for injury caused to one of the parties mentioned in Article 18 by the execution of an EEW transmitted to it pursuant to Article 8, the issuing State shall reimburse to the executing State any sums paid in damages by virtue of that responsibility to the said party except if, and to the extent that, the injury or any part of it is due to the conduct of the executing State.

2. Paragraph 1 shall be without prejudice to the national law of the Member States on claims by natural or legal persons for compensation of damage.

TITLE IV

**FINAL PROVISIONS**

*Article 20*

**Monitoring the effectiveness of this Framework Decision**

1. A Member State which has experienced repeated problems which it had not been possible to solve by consultation on the part of another Member State in the execution of EEWs shall inform the Council in order to assist in its evaluation of the implementation of this Framework Decision at Member State level.

2. The Council shall conduct a review, in particular, of the practical application of the provisions of this Framework Decision by Member States.

*Article 21*

**Relation to other legal instruments**

1. Subject to paragraph 2 and without prejudice to the application of existing legal instruments in relations between Member States and third countries, this Framework Decision shall coexist with existing legal instruments in relations between the Member States in so far as these instruments concern mutual assistance requests for evidence falling within the scope of this Framework Decision.

2. Without prejudice to paragraphs 3 and 4, issuing authorities shall rely on the EEW when all of the objects, documents or data required from the executing State fall within the scope of this Framework Decision.

3. Issuing authorities may use mutual legal assistance to obtain objects, documents or data falling within the scope of this Framework Decision if they form part of a wider request for assistance or if the issuing authority considers in the specific case that this would facilitate cooperation with the executing State.

4. Member States may conclude bilateral or multilateral agreements or arrangements after this Framework Decision has come into force in so far as such agreements or arrangements allow the objectives of this Framework Decision to be extended or enlarged and help to simplify or facilitate further the procedures for obtaining evidence falling within the scope of this Framework Decision.

5. The agreements and arrangements referred to in paragraph 4 may in no case affect relations with Member States which are not parties to them.

6. Member States shall notify the Council and the Commission of any new agreement or arrangement referred to in paragraph 4, within three months of signing it.

*Article 22*

**Transitional arrangements**

Mutual assistance requests received before 19 January 2011 shall continue to be governed by existing instruments relating to mutual assistance in criminal matters.

*Article 23*

**Implementation**

1. Member States shall take the necessary measures to comply with the provisions of this Framework Decision by 19 January 2011.

2. By 19 January 2011, Member States shall transmit to the General Secretariat of the Council and to the Commission the text of the provisions transposing into their national law the obligations imposed on them under this Framework Decision.

3. Any Member State that intends to transpose the ground for refusal set out in Article 13(1)(f) into its national law shall notify the Secretary-General of the Council thereof upon adoption of this Framework Decision by making a declaration.

4. Germany may by a declaration reserve its right to make the execution of an EEW subject to verification of double criminality in cases referred to in Article 14(2) relating to terrorism, computer-related crime, racism and xenophobia, sabotage, racketeering and extortion or swindling if it is necessary to carry out a search or seizure for the execution of the EEW, except where the issuing authority has declared that the offence concerned under the law of the issuing State falls within the scope of criteria indicated in the declaration.

Should Germany wish to make use of this paragraph, it shall notify a declaration to that effect to the Secretary-General of the Council upon the adoption of this Framework Decision. The declaration shall be published in the *Official Journal of the European Union*.

5. The Commission shall, by 19 January 2012, submit a report to the European Parliament and to the Council, assessing the extent to which the Member States have taken the necessary measures in order to comply with this Framework Decision, accompanied, if necessary, by legislative proposals.

6. The General Secretariat of the Council shall notify Member States, the Commission and Eurojust of the declarations made pursuant to Articles 6 and 11 and to this Article.

*Article 24*

**Review**

1. Each Member State shall each year before 1 May inform the Council and the Commission of any difficulties encountered by it during the previous calendar year concerning the execution of EEWs in relation to Article 13(1).

2. At the beginning of every calendar year, Germany shall inform the Council and the Commission of the number of cases in which the ground for non-recognition or non-execution referred to in Article 23(4) was applied in the previous year.

3. No later than 19 January 2014, the Commission shall establish a report on the basis of the information received in accordance with paragraphs 1 and 2, accompanied by any initiatives it may deem appropriate. On the basis of the report the Council shall review this Framework Decision with a view to considering whether the following provisions should be repealed or modified:

— Article 13(1) and (3), and

— Article 23(4).

*Article 25*

**Entry into force**

This Framework Decision shall enter into force on the 20th day following its publication in the *Official Journal of the European Union*.

Done at Brussels, 18 December 2008.

*For the Council*
*The President*
M. BARNIER

*ANNEX*

**EUROPEAN EVIDENCE WARRANT (EEW)** (1)

This EEW has been issued by a competent judicial authority. I request that the objects, documents or data specified below be obtained and transferred.

**(A)**

Issuing State: ..........

Executing State: ..........

**(B)**

The judicial authority is satisfied that:

(i) ☐ obtaining the objects, documents or data sought by this EEW is necessary and proportionate for the purpose of the proceedings specified below;

(ii) ☐ it would be possible to obtain these objects, documents or data under the law of the issuing State in a comparable domestic case if they were available on the territory of the issuing State, even though different procedural measures might be used.

**(C) THE JUDICIAL AUTHORITY WHICH ISSUED THE EEW**

Official name:

..........

Name of its representative:

..........

Post held (title/grade):

..........

Tick the type of judicial authority which issued the warrant:

☐ (a) judge or court

☐ (b) investigating magistrate

☐ (c) public prosecutor

☐ (d) any other judicial authority as defined by the issuing State and, in the specific case, acting in their capacity as an investigating authority in criminal proceedings with competence to order the obtaining of evidence in cross-border cases in accordance with national law

☐ This EEW has been validated by a judge or court, investigating magistrate or a public prosecutor (see Sections D and O).

File reference:

..........

Address:

..........

..........

Tel. No: (country code) (area/city code)

..........

Fax No: (country code) (area/city code)

..........

E-mail: ..........

Languages in which it is possible to communicate with the issuing authority: ..........

Contact details of the person(s) to contact if additional information on the execution of this EEW is necessary or to make necessary practical arrangements for the transfer of objects, documents or data (if applicable):

..........

(1) This EEW must be written in, or translated into, one of the official languages of the executing State or any other language accepted by that State.

**(D) THE JUDICIAL AUTHORITY VALIDATING THE EEW (WHERE APPLICABLE)**

If point (d) in Section C has been ticked and this EEW is validated, tick the type of judicial authority which has validated this EEW:

☐ (a) judge or court

☐ (b) investigating magistrate

☐ (c) public prosecutor

Official name of the validating authority:

.......................................................................................................................

Name of its representative:

.......................................................................................................................

Post held (title/grade):

.......................................................................................................................

File reference:

.......................................................................................................................

Address:

.......................................................................................................................

.......................................................................................................................

Tel. No: (country code) (area/city code) ..........................................................................

Fax No: (country code) (area/city code) ..........................................................................

E-mail: ..............................................................................................................

**(E) WHERE A CENTRAL AUTHORITY HAS BEEN MADE RESPONSIBLE FOR THE ADMINISTRATIVE TRANSMISSION AND RECEPTION OF EEWS AND, IF APPLICABLE, FOR OTHER OFFICIAL CORRESPONDENCE RELATING THERETO**

Name of the central authority: ..........................................................................

.......................................................................................................................

Contact person, if applicable (title/grade and name): ......................................................

.......................................................................................................................

Address: ..............................................................................................................

.......................................................................................................................

File reference: ......................................................................................................

Tel. No: (country code) (area/city code) ..........................................................................

Fax No: (country code) (area/city code) ..........................................................................

E-mail: ..............................................................................................................

**(F) THE AUTHORITY OR AUTHORITIES WHICH MAY BE CONTACTED (IN THE CASE WHERE SECTION D AND/OR E HAVE BEEN COMPLETED)**

☐ Authority under Section C

Can be contacted for questions concerning ..........................................................

☐ Authority under Section D

Can be contacted for questions concerning ..........................................................

☐ Authority under Section E

Can be contacted for questions concerning ..........................................................

**(G) RELATION TO POSSIBLE EARLIER EEW OR FREEZING ORDER**

If applicable, indicate if this EEW supplements an earlier EEW or is a follow-up to a freezing order and, if so, provide information relevant to identify the earlier EEW or freezing order (the date of issue of such EEW or order, the authority to which it was transmitted and, if available, the date of transmission of the EEW or order and reference numbers given by the issuing and executing authorities).

..........................................................................................

..........................................................................................

..........................................................................................

..........................................................................................

**(H) TYPE OF PROCEEDINGS FOR WHICH THE EEW WAS ISSUED**

Tick the type of proceedings for which the EEW was issued:

☐ (a) with respect to criminal proceedings brought by, or to be brought before, a judicial authority in respect of a criminal offence under the national law of the issuing State; or

☐ (b) proceedings brought by administrative authorities in respect of acts which are punishable under the national law of the issuing State by virtue of being infringements of the rules of law, and where the decision may give rise to proceedings before a court having jurisdiction in particular in criminal matters; or

☐ (c) proceedings brought by judicial authorities in respect of acts which are punishable under the national law of the issuing State by virtue of being infringements of the rules of law, and where the decision may give rise to further proceedings before a court having jurisdiction in particular in criminal matters.

**(I) REASON FOR ISSUING THE EEW**

**1. Summary of facts and description of circumstances in which the offence(s) underlying the EEW has (have) been committed, including time and place, as known to the issuing authority:**

..........................................................................................

..........................................................................................

..........................................................................................

..........................................................................................

Nature and legal classification of the offence(s) resulting in the EEW and the applicable statutory provision/code:

..........................................................................................

..........................................................................................

..........................................................................................

..........................................................................................

..........................................................................................

**2. If applicable, tick one or more of the following offences punishable in the issuing State by a custodial sentence or a detention order of a maximum of at least three years as defined by the laws of the issuing State:**

☐ participation in a criminal organisation;

☐ terrorism (1);

☐ trafficking in human beings;

☐ sexual exploitation of children and child pornography;

☐ illicit trafficking in narcotic drugs and psychotropic substances;

☐ illicit trafficking in weapons, munitions and explosives;

☐ corruption;

☐ fraud, including that affecting the financial interests of the European Communities within the meaning of the Convention of 26 July 1995 on the protection of the European Communities' financial interests;

☐ laundering of the proceeds of crime;

☐ counterfeiting currency, including of the euro;

☐ computer-related crime (1);

☐ environmental crime, including illicit trafficking in endangered animal species and in endangered plant species and varieties;

☐ facilitation of unauthorised entry and residence;

☐ murder, grievous bodily injury;

☐ illicit trade in human organs and tissue;

☐ kidnapping, illegal restraint and hostage-taking;

☐ racism and xenophobia (1);

☐ organised or armed robbery;

☐ illicit trafficking in cultural goods, including antiques and works of art;

☐ swindling (1);

☐ racketeering and extortion (1);

☐ counterfeiting and piracy of products;

☐ forgery of administrative documents and trafficking therein;

☐ forgery of means of payment;

☐ illicit trafficking in hormonal substances and other growth promoters;

☐ illicit trafficking in nuclear or radioactive materials;

☐ trafficking in stolen vehicles;

☐ rape;

☐ arson;

☐ crimes within the jurisdiction of the International Criminal Court;

☐ unlawful seizure of aircraft/ships;

☐ sabotage (1);

(1) Where the EEW is addressed to Germany, and according to the declaration made by Germany in accordance with Article 23(4) of the Council Framework Decision 2008/978/JHA of 18 December 2008 on the European Evidence Warrant for the purpose of obtaining objects, documents and data for use in proceedings in criminal matters, the issuing authority may additionally complete Box No 1 to confirm that the offence(s) fall(s) within the scope of criteria indicated by Germany for this type of offence.

**3. Full descriptions of the offence(s) not covered by point 2 for which the EEW was issued:**

......................................................................................................................................

......................................................................................................................................

......................................................................................................................................

......................................................................................................................................

......................................................................................................................................

**(J) IDENTITY OF THE PERSONS CONCERNED**

Information regarding the identity of the (i) natural or (ii) legal person(s) against whom the proceedings are/may be taking place:

(i) In the case of natural person(s)

Name: ......................................................................................................................................

Forename(s): ......................................................................................................................................

Maiden name, if applicable: ......................................................................................................................................

Aliases, if applicable: ......................................................................................................................................

Sex: ......................................................................................................................................

Nationality: ......................................................................................................................................

Identity number or social security number (when possible): ......................................................................................................................................

Date of birth: ......................................................................................................................................

Place of birth: ......................................................................................................................................

Residence and/or known address; if address not known, state the last known address:

......................................................................................................................................

Language(s) which the person understands (if known): ......................................................................................................................................

(ii) In the case of legal person(s)

Name: ......................................................................................................................................

Form of legal person: ......................................................................................................................................

Shortened name, commonly used name or trading name, if applicable:

......................................................................................................................................

Registered seat (if available): ......................................................................................................................................

Registration number (if available): ......................................................................................................................................

Address of the legal person:

......................................................................................................................................

**(K) OBJECTS, DOCUMENTS OR DATA SOUGHT BY THE EEW**

**1. Description of what is sought by the EEW (tick and complete the appropriate boxes):**

☐ Objects (further details below):

......................................................................................................................................

......................................................................................................................................

......................................................................................................................................

......................................................................................................................................

☐ Documents (further details below):

......................................................................................................................................

......................................................................................................................................

......................................................................................................................................

......................................................................................................................................

☐ Data (further details below):

................................................................................................................

................................................................................................................

................................................................................................................

................................................................................................................

**2. Location of objects, documents or data (if not known, the last known location):** ..............................

................................................................................................................

................................................................................................................

................................................................................................................

**3. If other than the person referred to in Section J (i) or (ii), information regarding the identity of the (i) natural or (ii) legal person(s) believed to hold the objects, documents or data:**

(i) In the case of natural person(s):

Name: ..........................................................................................................

Forename(s): ...................................................................................................

Maiden name, if applicable: .....................................................................................

Aliases, if applicable: .........................................................................................

Sex: ...........................................................................................................

Nationality: ...................................................................................................

Identity number or social security number (when possible): ......................................................

Date of birth: .................................................................................................

Place of birth: ................................................................................................

Residence and/or known address; if address not known, state the last known address:

................................................................................................................

Language(s) which the person understands (if known):

................................................................................................................

(ii) In the case of legal person(s):

Name: ..........................................................................................................

Form of legal person: ..........................................................................................

Shortened name, commonly used name or trading name, if applicable:

................................................................................................................

Registered seat (if available): ................................................................................

Registration number (if available): ............................................................................

Address of the legal person:

................................................................................................................

Other address(es) where business is conducted:

................................................................................................................

**(L) EXECUTION OF THE EEW**

**1. Deadlines for execution of the EEW are laid down in Council Framework Decision 2008/978/JHA ([1]). However, if the request is particularly urgent, please indicate any earlier deadline and the reason for this by ticking the relevant box:**

Earlier deadline: .................................................... (dd/mm/yyyy)

Reasons:

[ ] procedural deadlines

[ ] other particularly urgent circumstances (please specify): ....................................................

**2. Tick and complete, if applicable**

☐ It is requested that the executing authority comply with the following formalities and procedures ([2])

....................................................

....................................................

....................................................

....................................................

☐ The EEW also covers any object, document or data which the executing authority discovers during the execution of this EEW and without further enquiries considers to be relevant to the proceedings for the purpose of which this EEW was issued.

☐ It is requested that the executing authority take statements from persons present during the execution of this EEW and directly related to the subject of this EEW.

**(M) LEGAL REMEDIES**

**1. Description of the legal remedies for interested parties, including bona fide third parties, available in the issuing State, including necessary steps to take:**

....................................................

....................................................

....................................................

....................................................

**2. Court before which the action may be taken:**

....................................................

....................................................

**3. Information as to those for whom the action is available:**

....................................................

....................................................

**4. Time limit for submission of the action:**

....................................................

....................................................

**5. Authority in the issuing State which can supply further information on procedures for seeking legal remedies in the issuing State and on whether legal assistance and interpretation and translation is available:**

Name: ....................................................

Contact person (if applicable): ....................................................

Address: ....................................................

Tel. No: (country code) (area/city code) ....................................................

Fax No: (country code) (area/city code) ....................................................

E-mail: ....................................................

([1]) OJ L 350, 30.12.2008, p. 72.

([2]) It is assumed that the executing authority will comply with the formalities and procedures indicated by the issuing authority unless they are contrary to the fundamental principles of the law of the executing State. However, this does not create any obligation to take coercive measures.

**(N) FINAL PROVISIONS AND SIGNATURE**

**1. Optional information to be given only in relation to Germany:**

☐ It is declared that the offence(s) concerned under the law of the issuing State fall(s) within the scope of criteria indicated by Germany in the declaration (1) made in accordance with Article 23(4) of Framework Decision 2008/978/JHA.

**2. Other information relevant to the case, if any:**

..............................................................................................................................

..............................................................................................................................

**3. Requested means of transfer of the objects, documents or data:**

☐ by e-mail

☐ by fax

☐ in the original by post

☐ by other means (please specify):

..............................................................................................................................

**4. Signature of the issuing authority and/or its representative certifying the content of the EEW as accurate:**

..............................................................................................................................

Name: ..............................................................................................................................

Post held (title/grade): ..............................................................................................................................

Date: ..............................................................................................................................

Official stamp (if available):

**(O) IF SECTION (D) IS COMPLETED, SIGNATURE AND DETAILS OF THE VALIDATING AUTHORITY**

..............................................................................................................................

Name: ..............................................................................................................................

Post held (title/grade):

..............................................................................................................................

Date:

..............................................................................................................................

Official stamp (if available):

(1) OJ L 350, 30.12.2008, p. 72.

**DECLARATION OF THE FEDERAL REPUBLIC OF GERMANY**

Where the execution of a European Evidence Warrant under Council Framework Decision 2008/978/JHA of 18 December 2008 on the European Evidence Warrant for the purpose of obtaining objects, documents and data for use in proceedings in criminal matters ([1]) requires search or seizure, the Federal Republic of Germany reserves the right under Article 23(4) of that Framework Decision to make execution subject to verification of double criminality in the case of the offences relating to terrorism, computer-related crime, racism and xenophobia, sabotage, racketeering and extortion and swindling listed in Article 14(2) of that Framework Decision, unless the issuing authority has stated that the offence in question meets the following criteria under the law of the issuing State:

**Terrorism:**

— An act which constitutes an offence within the meaning of and as defined in the International Convention for the Suppression of Acts of Nuclear Terrorism of 13 April 2005, the International Convention for the Suppression of the Financing of Terrorism of 9 December 1999 or within the meaning of one of the treaties listed in the annex thereto, or

— an act to be criminalised under the Council Framework Decision 2002/475/JHA of 13 June 2002 on combating terrorism ([2]), or

— an act to be prohibited under United Nations Security Council Resolution 1624 (2005) of 14 September 2005.

**Computer-related crime:**

Offences as defined in the Council Framework Decision 2005/222/JHA of 24 February 2005 on attacks against information systems ([3]), or in Title 1 of Section I of the European Convention on Cybercrime of 23 November 2001.

**Racism and xenophobia:**

Offences as defined in the Council Joint Action 96/443/JHA of 15 July 1996 concerning action to combat racism and xenophobia ([4]).

**Sabotage:**

Acts unlawfully and intentionally causing large-scale damage to a government facility, another public facility, a public transport system or other infrastructure which entails or is likely to entail considerable economic loss.

**Racketeering and extortion:**

Demanding by threats, use of force or by any other form of intimidation goods, promises, revenues or the signing of any document containing or resulting in an obligation, alienation or discharge.

**Swindling:**

Using false names or claiming a false position or using fraudulent means to abuse people's trust or good faith with the aim of appropriating something belonging to another person.

---

([1]) OJ L 350, 30.12.2008, p. 72.
([2]) OJ L 164, 22.6.2002, p. 3.
([3]) OJ L 69, 16.3.2005, p. 67.
([4]) OJ L 185, 24.7.1996, p. 5.

# Agreement between the European Community and the Government of the People's Republic of China on drug precursors and substances frequently used in the illicit manufacture of narcotic drugs or psychotropic substances, 30 January 2009

**[OJ 2009, L 56/8–11, 14]**

**[Editor's note: signatures omitted]**

L 56/8 EN Official Journal of the European Union 28.2.2009

# AGREEMENT

## between the European Community and the Government of the People's Republic of China on drug precursors and substances frequently used in the illicit manufacture of narcotic drugs or psychotropic substances

THE EUROPEAN COMMUNITY,

hereinafter referred to as 'the Community',

on the one part, and

THE GOVERNMENT OF THE PEOPLE'S REPUBLIC OF CHINA,

hereinafter referred to as 'the Chinese Government',

on the other part,

hereinafter referred to as the 'the Parties',

WITHIN THE FRAMEWORK of the United Nations Convention of 1988 against Illicit Traffic in Narcotic Drugs and Psychotropic Substances, signed on 20 December 1988 in Vienna, hereinafter referred to as the '1988 Convention' and in accordance with legal provision in force in the People's Republic of China and in the Member States of the Community;

DETERMINED to prevent and to combat the illicit manufacture of narcotic drugs and psychotropic substances by preventing the diversion of drug precursors and substances frequently used for such purposes (hereinafter referred to as drug precursors);

ACKNOWLEDGING Article 12 of the 1988 Convention;

CONVINCED that international trade may be used for the diversion of drug precursors, and that it is necessary to conclude and implement agreements between the regions concerned, establishing wide cooperation and, in particular linking export and import controls;

RECOGNISING that drug precursors are also mainly and widely used for legitimate purposes and that international trade must not be hindered by excessive monitoring procedures;

HAVE DECIDED to conclude an Agreement on the prevention of diversion of drug precursors and substances frequently used in the illicit manufacture of narcotic drugs or psychotropic substances,

HAVE AGREED AS FOLLOWS:

*Article 1*

**Scope of the Agreement**

1. This Agreement sets out measures to strengthen administrative cooperation between the Parties to prevent the diversion of drug precursors and substances frequently used in the illicit manufacture of narcotic drugs and psychotropic substances, without prejudice to the normal activities of trade and the due recognition of the legitimate interests of industry.

2. For this purpose, the Parties shall assist each other, as set out in this Agreement, in particular by:

— monitoring the trade between them in the drug precursors referred to in paragraph 3, with the aim of preventing their diversion to illicit purposes,

— providing mutual administrative assistance ensuring that their respective drug precursors trade control legislation is correctly applied.

3. Without prejudice to possible amendments which might be made pursuant to Article 10, this Agreement applies to the substances listed in the Annexes to this Agreement.

*Article 2*

**Trade monitoring**

1. The Parties shall consult and inform each other on their own initiative whenever they have reasonable grounds to believe that drug precursors may be diverted to the illicit manufacture of narcotic drugs or psychotropic substances, in particular when an import or export shipment occurs in unusual quantities or under unusual circumstances.

2. With regard to the drug precursors listed in Annex A to this Agreement, the competent authority of the exporting Party shall forward a pre-export notification to the competent authority of the importing Party. The reply in writing by the importing Party shall be provided within 15 working days after the receipt of the message from the exporting Party. The absence of a reply within this period shall be considered equivalent to a non-objection to sending the shipment. An objection shall be notified in writing to the exporting Party within this period, giving the reasons for refusal.

3. With regard to the drug precursors listed in Annex B to this Agreement, the competent authority of the exporting Party shall determine whether to conduct international checks according to its domestic legislation.

4. The Parties undertake to reply in writing as soon as possible, in respect of any information provided or measure requested under this Article.

*Article 3*

**Suspension of shipment**

1. Without prejudice to any possible implementation of technical enforcement measures, shipments shall be suspended if, in the opinion of either Party, there are reasonable grounds to believe that drug precursors may be diverted to the illicit manufacture of narcotic drugs or psychotropic substances, or where, in the cases described in Article 2(2), the importing Party requests in writing the suspension, and where appropriate, provides documents of evidence and ensuring measures to be taken within five working days.

2. The Parties shall cooperate in supplying each other with any information relating to suspected diversion operations if based upon a request for mutual administrative assistance.

*Article 4*

**Mutual administrative assistance**

1. The Parties shall provide each other upon request for mutual administrative assistance with any information to prevent the diversion of drug precursors to the illicit manufacture of narcotic drugs or psychotropic substances and shall investigate cases of suspected diversion. Where necessary they shall adopt appropriate precautionary measures to prevent diversion.

2. Any request for information or precautionary measures shall be complied with in time.

3. Requests for administrative assistance shall be executed in accordance with the legal or regulatory provisions of the requested Party.

4. Duly authorised officials of a Party may, with the agreement of the other Party and subject to the conditions laid down by the latter, be present at the inquiries carried out in the territory of the other Party.

5. The Parties shall assist each other to facilitate the provision of evidence if based upon a request for mutual administrative assistance.

6. Administrative assistance provided under this Article shall not prejudice the rules governing mutual assistance in criminal matters, nor shall it apply to information obtained under powers exercised at the request of a judicial authority, except where communication of such information is authorised by that authority.

7. One Party may, on a case-by-case basis and through consultation, provide, on request by the other Party, information in respect of substances which are frequently used in the illicit manufacture of narcotic drugs or psychotropic substances but which are not included in the scope of this Agreement.

*Article 5*

**Information exchange and confidentiality**

1. Any information communicated in whatsoever form pursuant to this Agreement shall be of a confidential or restricted nature, depending on the rules applicable in each of the Parties and shall be covered by the obligation of official secrecy.

2. Personal data may be exchanged only where the Party which may receive it undertakes to protect such data in at least an equivalent way to the one applicable to that particular case in the Party that may supply it. To this end, Parties communicate each other information on their applicable rules, including legal provisions in force in the Member States of the Community.

3. Information obtained under this Agreement shall be used solely for the purposes of this Agreement. Where one of the Parties wishes to use such information for other purposes, it shall obtain the prior written consent of the authority which provided the information. Such use shall then be subject to any restrictions laid down by that authority.

4. The use in proceedings instituted for failure to comply with legislation on drug precursors referred to in Article 3, of information obtained under this Agreement, is considered to be solely for the purposes of this Agreement. Therefore, the Parties may in proceedings use as evidence information obtained and documents consulted in accordance with the provisions of this Agreement. The use of evidence is subject to the prior permission of the competent authority which supplied that information or gave access to those documents.

*Article 6*

**Exceptions to the obligation to provide assistance**

1. Assistance may be refused or may be subject to the satisfaction of certain conditions or requirements, in cases where a Party is of the opinion that assistance under this Agreement would:

(a) be likely to prejudice the sovereignty of the People's Republic of China or that of a Member State of the Community which has been requested to provide assistance under this Agreement; or

(b) be likely to prejudice public policy, security or other essential interests, in particular in the cases referred to under Article 5(2); or

(c) violate an industrial, commercial or professional secret.

2. Assistance may be postponed by the requested authority on the ground that it will interfere with an ongoing investigation, prosecution or proceeding. In such a case, the requested authority shall consult with the applicant authority to determine if assistance can be given subject to such terms or conditions as the requested authority may require.

3. Where the applicant authority seeks assistance which it would itself be unable to provide if so requested, it shall draw attention to that fact in its request. It shall then be for the requested authority to decide how to respond to such a request.

4. For the cases referred to in this Article, the decision of the requested authority and the reasons therefore must be communicated to the applicant authority as promptly as possible.

*Article 7*

**Technical and scientific cooperation**

The Parties shall cooperate in the identification of new diversion methods as well as appropriate countermeasures, including technical cooperation and in particular, training and exchange programmes for the officials concerned, to strengthen administrative and enforcement structures in this field and to promote cooperation with trade and industry.

*Article 8*

**Implementation measures**

1. The Chinese side, the European Commission and each Member State of the Community shall appoint respectively a competent authority to coordinate the implementation of this Agreement. These authorities shall communicate directly with one another for the purposes of this Agreement.

2. The Parties shall consult each other and subsequently keep each other informed of the detailed rules of implementation which are adopted in accordance with the provisions of this Agreement.

*Article 9*

**Joint Follow-Up Group**

1. A Joint Follow-Up Group is hereby established, hereinafter referred to as 'the Joint Follow-Up Group', in which the Parties shall be represented.

2. The Joint Follow-Up Group shall act by mutual agreement.

3. If necessary, the Joint Follow-Up Group shall meet, with the date, place and programme being fixed by mutual agreement.

Extraordinary meetings of the Joint Follow-Up Group may be convened by mutual agreement of the Parties.

*Article 10*

**Role of the Joint Follow-Up Group**

1. The Joint Follow-Up Group shall administer this Agreement and ensure its proper implementation. For this purpose:

— it shall be informed by the Parties of their experience in applying this Agreement,

— in cases provided for in paragraph 2, it shall take decisions,

— it shall study and develop technical cooperation measures,

— it shall study and develop other possible forms of cooperation.

2. The Joint Follow-Up Group may adopt by mutual consent decisions to amend Annexes A and B. Such decisions shall be implemented by the Parties in accordance with their own legislation.

3. The Joint Follow-Up Group may recommend to the Parties:

(a) other amendments to this Agreement;

(b) measures required for the application of this Agreement.

*Article 11*

**Other obligations imposed under other agreements**

1. Taking into account the respective competencies of the Community and its Member States, the provisions of this Agreement shall:

— not affect the obligations of the Parties under any other international agreement or convention,

— not affect the communication between the competent services of the European Commission and the relevant services of the Member States of the Community of any information obtained under this Agreement which could be of interest to the Community.

2. Notwithstanding the provisions of paragraph 1, the provisions of this Agreement shall take precedence over the provisions of any bilateral agreement on drug precursors and other substances frequently used in the illicit manufacture of narcotic drugs and psychotropic substances which have been or may be concluded between individual Member States and the People's Republic of China insofar as the provisions of the latter are incompatible with those of this Agreement.

3. In respect of questions relating to the applicability of this Agreement, the Parties shall consult each other to resolve the matter in the framework of the Joint Follow-Up Group.

4. The Parties shall also notify each other of any measures on controlled substances taken with other countries.

*Article 12*

**Entry into force**

Each Party shall give written notification that it has completed its internal legal procedures for the entry into force of this Agreement to the other Party. This Agreement shall enter into force 60 days from the date on which the last written notification is received.

*Article 13*

**Duration and denunciation**

1. This Agreement shall be concluded for five years and, unless a Party notifies in writing the other Party of its intention to terminate the Agreement at least six months before the expiration of that period, it will be tacitly renewable for successive periods of five years.

2. This Agreement may be amended by mutual consent of the Parties.

Done in duplicate in the Bulgarian, Czech, Danish, Dutch, Estonian, English, Finnish, French, German, Greek, Hungarian, Italian, Latvian, Lithuanian, Maltese, Polish, Portuguese, Romanian, Slovak, Slovenian, Spanish, Swedish and Chinese languages, all these texts being equally authentic. In case there is any divergence of interpretation of this Agreement, the English and the Chinese texts shall be determinative.

# Framework Decision 2009/299 amending Framework Decisions 2002/584, 2005/214, 2006/783, 2008/909 and 2008/947, thereby enhancing the procedural rights of persons and fostering the application of the principle of mutual recognition to decisions rendered in the absence of the person concerned at the trial, 26 February 2009

**[OJ 2009, L 81/24-36]**

**[Editor's note: The amendments of this Framework Decision to other Framework Decisions have been inserted in the respective Framework decisions already. The inclusion of the integral text of Framework Decision 2009/299 allows the user access to its background and context.]**

L 81/24 EN Official Journal of the European Union 27.3.2009

III

*(Acts adopted under the EU Treaty)*

# ACTS ADOPTED UNDER TITLE VI OF THE EU TREATY

## COUNCIL FRAMEWORK DECISION 2009/299/JHA

**of 26 February 2009**

**amending Framework Decisions 2002/584/JHA, 2005/214/JHA, 2006/783/JHA, 2008/909/JHA and 2008/947/JHA, thereby enhancing the procedural rights of persons and fostering the application of the principle of mutual recognition to decisions rendered in the absence of the person concerned at the trial**

THE COUNCIL OF THE EUROPEAN UNION,

Having regard to the Treaty on European Union, and in particular Article 31(1)(a) and Article 34(2)(b) thereof,

Having regard to the initiative of the Republic of Slovenia, the French Republic, the Czech Republic, the Kingdom of Sweden, the Slovak Republic, the United Kingdom of Great Britain and Northern Ireland and the Federal Republic of Germany [1],

Having regard to the opinion of the European Parliament,

Whereas:

(1) The right of an accused person to appear in person at the trial is included in the right to a fair trial provided for in Article 6 of the Convention for the Protection of Human Rights and Fundamental Freedoms, as interpreted by the European Court of Human Rights. The Court has also declared that the right of the accused person to appear in person at the trial is not absolute and that under certain conditions the accused person may, of his or her own free will, expressly or tacitly but unequivocally, waive that right.

(2) The various Framework Decisions implementing the principle of mutual recognition of final judicial decisions do not deal consistently with the issue of decisions rendered following a trial at which the person concerned did not appear in person. This diversity could complicate the work of the practitioner and hamper judicial cooperation.

(3) Solutions provided by these Framework Decisions are not satisfactory as regards cases where the person could not be informed of the proceedings. Framework Decisions 2005/214/JHA on the application of the principle of mutual recognition to financial penalties [2], 2006/783/JHA on the application of the principle of mutual recognition to confiscation orders [3], 2008/909/JHA on the application of the principle of mutual recognition to judgments in criminal matters imposing custodial sentences or measures involving deprivation of liberty for the purpose of their enforcement in the European Union [4] and 2008/947/JHA on the application of the principle of mutual recognition to judgments and probation decisions with a view to the supervision of probation measures and alternative sanctions [5] allow the executing authority to refuse the execution of such judgments. Framework Decision 2002/584/JHA on the European arrest warrant and the surrender procedures between Member States [6] allows the executing authority to require the issuing authority to give an assurance deemed adequate to guarantee the person who is the subject of the European arrest warrant that he or she will have an opportunity to apply for a retrial of the case in the issuing Member State and to be present when the judgment is given. The adequacy of such an assurance is a matter to be decided by the executing authority, and it is therefore difficult to know exactly when execution may be refused.

[1] OJ C 52, 26.2.2008, p. 1.

[2] Framework Decision of 24 February 2005 (OJ L 76, 22.3.2005, p. 16).
[3] Framework Decision of 6 October 2006 (OJ L 328, 24.11.2006, p. 59).
[4] Framework Decision of 27 November 2008 (OJ L 327, 5.12.2008, p. 27).
[5] Framework Decision of 27 November 2008 (OJ L 337, 16.12.2008, p. 102).
[6] Framework Decision of 13 June 2002 (OJ L 190, 18.7.2002, p. 1).

27.3.2009 EN Official Journal of the European Union L 81/25

(4) It is therefore necessary to provide clear and common grounds for non-recognition of decisions rendered following a trial at which the person concerned did not appear in person. This Framework Decision is aimed at refining the definition of such common grounds allowing the executing authority to execute the decision despite the absence of the person at the trial, while fully respecting the person's right of defence. This Framework Decision is not designed to regulate the forms and methods, including procedural requirements, that are used to achieve the results specified in this Framework Decision, which are a matter for the national laws of the Member States.

(5) Such changes require amendment of the existing Framework Decisions implementing the principle of mutual recognition of final judicial decisions. The new provisions should also serve as a basis for future instruments in this field.

(6) The provisions of this Framework Decision amending other Framework Decisions set conditions under which the recognition and execution of a decision rendered following a trial at which the person concerned did not appear in person should not be refused. These are alternative conditions; when one of the conditions is satisfied, the issuing authority, by completing the corresponding section of the European arrest warrant or of the relevant certificate under the other Framework Decisions, gives the assurance that the requirements have been or will be met, which should be sufficient for the purpose of the execution of the decision on the basis of the principle of mutual recognition.

(7) The recognition and execution of a decision rendered following a trial at which the person concerned did not appear in person should not be refused if either he or she was summoned in person and thereby informed of the scheduled date and place of the trial which resulted in the decision, or if he or she actually received, by other means, official information of the scheduled date and place of that trial in such a manner that it was unequivocally established that he or she was aware of the scheduled trial. In this context, it is understood that the person should have received such information 'in due time', meaning sufficiently in time to allow him or her to participate in the trial and to effectively exercise his or her right of defence.

(8) The right to a fair trial of an accused person is guaranteed by the Convention for the Protection of Human Rights and Fundamental Freedoms, as interpreted by the European Court of Human Rights. This right includes the right of the person concerned to appear in person at the trial. In order to exercise this right, the person concerned needs to be aware of the scheduled trial. Under this Framework Decision, the person's awareness of the trial should be ensured by each Member State in accordance with its national law, it being understood that this must comply with the requirements of that Convention. In accordance with the case law of the European Court of Human Rights, when considering whether the way in which the information is provided is sufficient to ensure the person's awareness of the trial, particular attention could, where appropriate, also be paid to the diligence exercised by the person concerned in order to receive information addressed to him or her.

(9) The scheduled date of a trial may for practical reasons initially be expressed as several possible dates within a short period of time.

(10) The recognition and execution of a decision rendered following a trial at which the person concerned did not appear in person should not be refused where the person concerned, being aware of the scheduled trial, was defended at the trial by a legal counsellor to whom he or she had given a mandate to do so, ensuring that legal assistance is practical and effective. In this context, it should not matter whether the legal counsellor was chosen, appointed and paid by the person concerned, or whether this legal counsellor was appointed and paid by the State, it being understood that the person concerned should deliberately have chosen to be represented by a legal counsellor instead of appearing in person at the trial. The appointment of the legal counsellor and related issues are a matter of national law.

(11) Common solutions concerning grounds for non-recognition in the relevant existing Framework Decisions should take into account the diversity of situations with regard to the right of the person concerned to a retrial or an appeal. Such a retrial, or appeal, is aimed at guaranteeing the rights of the defence and is characterised by the following elements: the person concerned has the right to be present, the merits of the case, including fresh evidence are re-examined, and the proceedings can lead to the original decision being reversed.

(12) The right to a retrial or appeal should be guaranteed when the decision has already been served as well as, in the case of the European arrest warrant, when it had not yet been served, but will be served without delay after the surrender. The latter case refers to a situation where the authorities failed in their attempt to contact the person, in particular because he or she sought to evade justice.

(13) In case a European arrest warrant is issued for the purpose of executing a custodial sentence or detention order and the person concerned has not previously received any official information about the existence of the criminal proceedings against him or her, nor has been served with the judgment, this person should, following a request in the executing Member State, receive a copy of the judgment for information purposes only. The issuing and executing judicial authorities should, where appropriate, consult each other on the need and existing possibilities to provide the person concerned with a translation of the judgment, or of essential parts thereof, in a language that the person understands. Such provision of the judgment should neither delay the surrender procedure nor delay the decision to execute the European arrest warrant.

(14) This Framework Decision is limited to refining the definition of grounds for non-recognition in instruments implementing the principle of mutual recognition. Therefore, provisions such as those relating to the right to a retrial have a scope which is limited to the definition of these grounds for non-recognition. They are not designed to harmonise national legislation. This Framework Decision is without prejudice to future instruments of the European Union designed to approximate the laws of the Member States in the field of criminal law.

(15) The grounds for non-recognition are optional. However, the discretion of Member States for transposing these grounds into national law is particularly governed by the right to a fair trial, while taking into account the overall objective of this Framework Decision to enhance the procedural rights of persons and to facilitate judicial cooperation in criminal matters,

HAS ADOPTED THIS FRAMEWORK DECISION:

*Article 1*

**Objectives and scope**

1. The objectives of this Framework Decision are to enhance the procedural rights of persons subject to criminal proceedings, to facilitate judicial cooperation in criminal matters and, in particular, to improve mutual recognition of judicial decisions between Member States.

2. This Framework Decision shall not have the effect of modifying the obligation to respect fundamental rights and fundamental legal principles as enshrined in Article 6 of the Treaty, including the right of defence of persons subject to criminal proceedings, and any obligations incumbent upon judicial authorities in this respect shall remain unaffected.

3. This Framework Decision establishes common rules for the recognition and/or execution of judicial decisions in one Member State (the executing Member State) issued by another Member State (the issuing Member State) following proceedings at which the person concerned was not present, pursuant to the provisions of Article 5(1) of Framework Decision 2002/584/JHA, of Article 7(2)(g) of Framework Decision 2005/214/JHA, of Article 8(2)(e) of Framework Decision 2006/783/JHA, of Article 9(1)(i) of Framework Decision 2008/909/JHA and of Article 11(1)(h) of Framework Decision 2008/947/JHA.

*Article 2*

**Amendments to Framework Decision 2002/584/JHA**

Framework Decision 2002/584/JHA is hereby amended as follows:

1. the following Article shall be inserted:

'*Article 4a*

**Decisions rendered following a trial at which the person did not appear in person**

1. The executing judicial authority may also refuse to execute the European arrest warrant issued for the purpose of executing a custodial sentence or a detention order if the person did not appear in person at the trial resulting in the decision, unless the European arrest warrant states that the person, in accordance with further procedural requirements defined in the national law of the issuing Member State:

(a) in due time:

(i) either was summoned in person and thereby informed of the scheduled date and place of the trial which resulted in the decision, or by other means actually received official information of the scheduled date and place of that trial in such a manner that it was unequivocally established that he or she was aware of the scheduled trial;

and

(ii) was informed that a decision may be handed down if he or she does not appear for the trial;

or

(b) being aware of the scheduled trial, had given a mandate to a legal counsellor, who was either appointed by the person concerned or by the State, to defend him or her at the trial, and was indeed defended by that counsellor at the trial;

or

(c) after being served with the decision and being expressly informed about the right to a retrial, or an appeal, in which the person has the right to participate and which allows the merits of the case, including fresh evidence, to be re-examined, and which may lead to the original decision being reversed:

(i) expressly stated that he or she does not contest the decision;

or

(ii) did not request a retrial or appeal within the applicable time frame;

or

(d) was not personally served with the decision but:

(i) will be personally served with it without delay after the surrender and will be expressly informed of his or her right to a retrial, or an appeal, in which the person has the right to participate and which allows the merits of the case, including fresh evidence, to be re-examined, and which may lead to the original decision being reversed;

and

(ii) will be informed of the time frame within which he or she has to request such a retrial or appeal, as mentioned in the relevant European arrest warrant.

2. In case the European arrest warrant is issued for the purpose of executing a custodial sentence or detention order under the conditions of paragraph 1(d) and the person concerned has not previously received any official information about the existence of the criminal proceedings against him or her, he or she may, when being informed about the content of the European arrest warrant, request to receive a copy of the judgment before being surrendered. Immediately after having been informed about the request, the issuing authority shall provide the copy of the judgment via the executing authority to the person sought. The request of the person sought shall neither delay the surrender procedure nor delay the decision to execute the European arrest warrant. The provision of the judgment to the person concerned is for information purposes only; it shall neither be regarded as a formal service of the judgment nor actuate any time limits applicable for requesting a retrial or appeal.

3. In case a person is surrendered under the conditions of paragraph (1)(d) and he or she has requested a retrial or appeal, the detention of that person awaiting such retrial or appeal shall, until these proceedings are finalised, be reviewed in accordance with the law of the issuing Member State, either on a regular basis or upon request of the person concerned. Such a review shall in particular include the possibility of suspension or interruption of the detention. The retrial or appeal shall begin within due time after the surrender.';

2. in Article 5, paragraph 1 shall be deleted;

3. in the Annex (EUROPEAN ARREST WARRANT), point (d) shall be replaced by the following:

'(d) Indicate if the person appeared in person at the trial resulting in the decision:

1. ☐ Yes, the person appeared in person at the trial resulting in the decision.

2. ☐ No, the person did not appear in person at the trial resulting in the decision.

3. If you have ticked the box under point 2, please confirm the existence of one of the following:

☐ 3.1a. the person was summoned in person on … (day/month/year) and thereby informed of the scheduled date and place of the trial which resulted in the decision and was informed that a decision may be handed down if he or she does not appear for the trial;

OR

☐ 3.1b. the person was not summoned in person but by other means actually received official information of the scheduled date and place of the trial which resulted in the decision, in such a manner that it was unequivocally established that he or she was aware of the scheduled trial, and was informed that a decision may be handed down if he or she does not appear for the trial;

OR

☐ 3.2. being aware of the scheduled trial, the person had given a mandate to a legal counsellor, who was either appointed by the person concerned or by the State, to defend him or her at the trial, and was indeed defended by that counsellor at the trial;

OR

☐ 3.3. the person was served with the decision on … (day/month/year) and was expressly informed about the right to a retrial or appeal, in which he or she has the right to participate and which allows the merits of the case, including fresh evidence, to be re-examined, and which may lead to the original decision being reversed, and

☐ the person expressly stated that he or she does not contest this decision,

OR

☐ the person did not request a retrial or appeal within the applicable time frame;

OR

☐ 3.4. the person was not personally served with the decision, but

— the person will be personally served with this decision without delay after the surrender, and

— when served with the decision, the person will be expressly informed of his or her right to a retrial or appeal, in which he or she has the right to participate and which allows the merits of the case, including fresh evidence, to be re-examined, and which may lead to the original decision being reversed, and

— the person will be informed of the time frame within which he or she has to request a retrial or appeal, which will be … days.

4. If you have ticked the box under points 3.1b, 3.2 or 3.3 above, please provide information about how the relevant condition has been met:

..............................................................................................................................................................

..............................................................................................................................................................,

*Article 3*

**Amendments to Framework Decision 2005/214/JHA**

Framework Decision 2005/214/JHA is hereby amended as follows:

1. Article 7(2) is hereby amended as follows:

(a) point (g) shall be replaced by the following:

'(g) according to the certificate provided for in Article 4, the person concerned, in case of a written procedure, was not, in accordance with the law of the issuing State, informed personally or via a representative, competent according to national law, of his/her right to contest the case and of the time limits for such a legal remedy';

(b) the following points shall be added:

'(i) according to the certificate provided for in Article 4, the person did not appear in person at the trial resulting in the decision, unless the certificate states that the person, in accordance with further procedural requirements defined in the national law of the issuing State:

(i) in due time:

— either was summoned in person and thereby informed of the scheduled date and place of the trial which resulted in the decision, or by other means actually received official information of the scheduled date and place of that trial in such a manner that it was unequivocally established that he or she was aware of the scheduled trial,

and

— was informed that a decision may be handed down if he or she does not appear for the trial;

or

(ii) being aware of the scheduled trial, had given a mandate to a legal counsellor, who was either appointed by the person concerned or by the State, to defend him or her at the trial, and was indeed defended by that counsellor at the trial;

or

(iii) after being served with the decision and being expressly informed of the right to a retrial, or an appeal, in which he or she has the right to participate and which allows the merits of the case, including fresh evidence, to be re-examined, and which may lead to the original decision being reversed:

— expressly stated that he or she does not contest the decision,

or

— did not request a retrial or appeal within the applicable time frame;

(j) according to the certificate provided for in Article 4, the person did not appear in person, unless the certificate states that the person, having been expressly informed about the proceedings and the possibility to appear in person in a trial, expressly waived his or her right to an oral hearing and has expressly indicated that he or she does not contest the case.';

2. Article 7(3) shall be replaced by the following:

'3. In the cases referred to in paragraphs 1 and 2(c), (g), (i) and (j), before deciding not to recognise and to execute a decision, either totally or in part, the competent authority in the executing State shall consult the competent authority in the issuing State, by any appropriate means, and shall, where appropriate, ask it to supply any necessary information without delay.';

3. in point (h) of the Annex (CERTIFICATE), point 3 is replaced by the following:

'3. Indicate if the person concerned appeared in person at the trial resulting in the decision:

1. ☐ Yes, the person appeared in person at the trial resulting in the decision.

2. ☐ No, the person did not appear in person at the trial resulting in the decision.

3. If you have ticked the box under point 2, please confirm the existence of one of the following:

☐ 3.1a. the person was summoned in person on … (day/month/year) and thereby informed of the scheduled date and place of the trial which resulted in the decision and was informed that a decision may be handed down if he or she does not appear for the trial;

OR

☐ 3.1b. the person was not summoned in person but by other means actually received official information of the scheduled date and place of the trial which resulted in the decision, in such a manner that it was unequivocally established that he or she was aware of the scheduled trial, and was informed that a decision may be handed down if he or she does not appear for the trial;

OR

☐ 3.2. being aware of the scheduled trial, the person had given a mandate to a legal counsellor, who was either appointed by the person concerned or by the State, to defend him or her at the trial, and was indeed defended by that counsellor at the trial;

OR

☐ 3.3. the person was served with the decision on … (day/month/year) and was expressly informed about the right to a retrial or appeal, in which he or she has the right to participate and which allows the merits of the case, including fresh evidence, to be re-examined, and which may lead to the original decision being reversed, and

☐ the person expressly stated that he or she does not contest this decision,

OR

☐ the person did not request a retrial or appeal within the applicable time frame;

OR

☐ 3.4. the person, having been expressly informed about the proceedings and the possibility to appear in person in a trial, expressly waived his or her right to an oral hearing and has expressly indicated that he or she does not contest the case.

4. If you have ticked the box under points 3.1b, 3.2, 3.3 or 3.4 above, please provide information about how the relevant condition has been met:

……………………………………………………………………………………………………

……………………………………………………………………………………………………'

*Article 4*

**Amendments to Framework Decision 2006/783/JHA**

Framework Decision 2006/783/JHA is hereby amended as follows:

1. in Article 8(2), point (e) shall be replaced by the following:

'(e) according to the certificate provided for in Article 4(2), the person did not appear in person at the trial resulting in the confiscation order, unless the certificate states that the person, in accordance with further procedural requirements defined in the national law of the issuing State:

(i) in due time:

— either was summoned in person and thereby informed of the scheduled date and place of the trial which resulted in the confiscation order, or by other means actually received official information of the scheduled date and place of that trial in such a manner that it was unequivocally established that he or she was aware of the scheduled trial, and

— was informed that such a confiscation order may be handed down if he or she does not appear for the trial;

or

(ii) being aware of the scheduled trial, had given a mandate to a legal counsellor, who was either appointed by the person concerned or by the State, to defend him or her at the trial, and was indeed defended by that counsellor at the trial;

or

(iii) after being served with the confiscation order and being expressly informed of the right to a retrial, or an appeal, in which the person has the right to participate and which allows the merits of the case, including fresh evidence, to be re-examined, and which may lead to the original decision being reversed:

— expressly stated that he or she does not contest the confiscation order,

or

— did not request a retrial or appeal within the applicable time frame.';

2. in the Annex (CERTIFICATE), point (j) shall be replaced by the following:

'(j) Proceedings resulting in the confiscation order

Indicate if the person appeared in person at the trial resulting in the confiscation order:

1. ☐ Yes, the person appeared in person at the trial resulting in the confiscation order.

2. ☐ No, the person did not appear in person at the trial resulting in the confiscation order.

3. If you have ticked the box under point 2, please confirm the existence of one of the following:

☐ 3.1a. the person was summoned in person on … (day/month/year) and thereby informed of the scheduled date and place of the trial which resulted in the confiscation order and was informed that a decision may be handed down if he or she does not appear for the trial;

OR

☐ 3.1b. the person was not summoned in person but by other means actually received official information of the scheduled date and place of the trial which resulted in the confiscation order, in such a manner that it was unequivocally established that he or she was aware of the scheduled trial, and was informed that a decision may be handed down if he or she does not appear for the trial;

OR

☐ 3.2. being aware of the scheduled trial, the person had given a mandate to a legal counsellor, who was either appointed by the person concerned or by the State, to defend him or her at the trial, and was indeed defended by that counsellor at the trial;

OR

☐ 3.3. the person was served with the confiscation order on … (day/month/year) and was expressly informed about the right to a retrial or appeal, in which he or she has the right to participate and which allows the merits of the case, including fresh evidence, to be re-examined, and which may lead to the original decision being reversed, and

☐ the person expressly stated that he or she does not contest the decision,

OR

☐ the person did not request a retrial or appeal within the applicable time frame.

4. If you have ticked the box under points 3.1b, 3.2, 3.3 or 3.4 above, please provide information about how the relevant condition has been met:

...........................................................................................................................................

...........................................................................................................................................'

*Article 5*

**Amendments to Framework Decision 2008/909/JHA**

Framework Decision 2008/909/JHA is hereby amended as follows:

1. in Article 9(1), point (i) shall be replaced by the following:

'(i) according to the certificate provided for in Article 4, the person did not appear in person at the trial resulting in the decision, unless the certificate states that the person, in accordance with further procedural requirements defined in the national law of the issuing State:

(i) in due time:

— either was summoned in person and thereby informed of the scheduled date and place of the trial which resulted in the decision, or by other means actually received official information of the scheduled date and place of that trial in such a manner that it was unequivocally established that he or she was aware of the scheduled trial,

and

— was informed that a decision may be handed down if he or she does not appear for the trial;

or

(ii) being aware of the scheduled trial had given a mandate to a legal counsellor, who was either appointed by the person concerned or by the State, to defend him or her at the trial, and was indeed defended by that counsellor at the trial;

or

(iii) after being served with the decision and being expressly informed of the right to a retrial, or an appeal, in which the person has the right to participate and which allows the merits of the case, including fresh evidence, to be re-examined, and which may lead to the original decision being reversed:

— expressly stated that he or she does not contest the decision,

or

— did not request a retrial or appeal within the applicable time frame.';

2. in point (i) of Annex I (CERTIFICATE), point 1 shall be replaced by the following:

'1. Indicate if the person appeared in person at the trial resulting in the decision:

1. ☐ Yes, the person appeared in person at the trial resulting in the decision.

2. ☐ No, the person did not appear in person at the trial resulting in the decision.

3. If you have ticked the box under point 2, please confirm the existence of one of the following:

☐ 3.1a. the person was summoned in person on … (day/month/year) and thereby informed of the scheduled date and place of the trial which resulted in the decision and was informed that a decision may be handed down if he or she does not appear for the trial;

OR

☐ 3.1b. the person was not summoned in person but by other means actually received official information of the scheduled date and place of the trial which resulted in the decision, in such a manner that it was unequivocally established that he or she was aware of the scheduled trial, and was informed that a decision may be handed down if he or she does not appear for the trial;

OR

☐ 3.2. being aware of the scheduled trial the person had given a mandate to a legal counsellor, who was either appointed by the person concerned or by the State, to defend him or her at the trial, and was indeed defended by that counsellor at the trial;

OR

☐ 3.3. the person was served with the decision on … (day/month/year) and was expressly informed about the right to a retrial or appeal, in which he or she has the right to participate and which allows the merits of the case, including fresh evidence, to be re-examined, and which may lead to the original decision being reversed, and

☐ the person expressly stated that he or she does not contest this decision,

OR

☐ the person did not request a retrial or appeal within the applicable time frame.

4. If you have ticked the box under points 3.1b, 3.2 or 3.3 above, please provide information about how the relevant condition has been met:

……………………………………………………………………………………………

……………………………………………………………………………………………',

L 81/34 EN Official Journal of the European Union 27.3.2009

*Article 6*

**Amendments to Framework Decision 2008/947/JHA**

Framework Decision 2008/947/JHA is hereby amended as follows:

1. in Article 11(1), point (h) shall be replaced by the following:

'(h) according to the certificate provided for in Article 6, the person did not appear in person at the trial resulting in the decision, unless the certificate states that the person, in accordance with further procedural requirements defined in the national law of the issuing State:

(i) in due time:

— either was summoned in person and thereby informed of the scheduled date and place of the trial which resulted in the decision, or by other means actually received official information of the scheduled date and place of that trial in such a manner that it was unequivocally established that he or she was aware of the scheduled trial,

and

— was informed that a decision may be handed down if he or she does not appear for the trial;

or

(ii) being aware of the scheduled trial had given a mandate to a legal counsellor, who was either appointed by the person concerned or by the State, to defend him or her at the trial, and was indeed defended by that counsellor at the trial;

or

(iii) after being served with the decision and being expressly informed about the right to a retrial, or an appeal, in which the person has the right to participate and which allows the merits of the case, including fresh evidence, to be re-examined, and which may lead to the original decision being reversed:

— expressly stated that he or she does not contest the decision,

or

— did not request a retrial or appeal within the applicable time frame.';

2. in Annex I (CERTIFICATE), point (h) shall be replaced by the following:

'(h) Indicate if the person appeared in person at the trial resulting in the decision:

1. ☐ Yes, the person appeared in person at the trial resulting in the decision.

2. ☐ No, the person did not appear in person at the trial resulting in the decision.

3. If you have ticked the box under point 2, please confirm the existence of one of the following:

☐ 3.1a. the person was summoned in person on … (day/month/year) and thereby informed of the scheduled date and place of the trial which resulted in the decision and was informed that a decision may be handed down if he or she does not appear for the trial;

OR

☐ 3.1b. the person was not summoned in person but by other means actually received official information of the scheduled date and place of the trial which resulted in the decision, in such a manner that it was unequivocally established that he or she was aware of the scheduled trial, and was informed that a decision may be handed down if he or she does not appear for the trial;

OR

☐ 3.2. being aware of the scheduled trial the person had given a mandate to a legal counsellor, who was either appointed by the person concerned or by the State, to defend him or her at the trial, and was indeed defended by that counsellor at the trial;

OR

☐ 3.3. the person was served with the decision on … (day/month/year) and was expressly informed about the right to a retrial or appeal, in which he or she has the right to participate and which allows the merits of the case, including fresh evidence, to be re-examined, and which may lead to the original decision being reversed, and

☐ the person expressly stated that he or she does not contest this decision,

OR

☐ the person did not request a retrial or appeal within the applicable time frame.

4. If you have ticked the box under points 3.1b, 3.2 or 3.3 above, please provide information about how the relevant condition has been met:

…………………………………………………………………………………………………………

…………………………………………………………………………………………………………,

*Article 7*

**Territorial application**

This Framework Decision shall apply to Gibraltar.

*Article 8*

**Implementation and transitional provisions**

1. Member States shall take the necessary measures to comply with the provisions of this Framework Decision by 28 March 2011.

2. This Framework Decision shall apply as from the date mentioned in paragraph 1 to the recognition and enforcement of decisions rendered in the absence of the person concerned at the trial.

3. If a Member State has declared, on the adoption of this Framework Decision, to have serious reasons to assume that it will not be able to comply with the provisions of this Framework Decision by the date referred to in paragraph 1, this Framework Decision shall apply as from 1 January 2014 at the latest to the recognition and enforcement of decisions, rendered in the absence of the person concerned at the trial which are issued by the competent authorities of that Member State. Any other Member State may require that the Member State having made such a declaration shall apply the relevant provisions of the Framework Decisions referred to in Articles 2, 3, 4, 5 and 6 in the versions in which they were adopted originally to the recognition and enforcement of decisions, rendered in the absence of the person concerned at the trial, which were issued by such other Member State.

4. Until the dates mentioned in paragraphs 1 and 3, the relevant provisions of the Framework Decisions referred to in Articles 2, 3, 4, 5 and 6 shall continue to apply in the versions in which they were adopted originally.

5. A declaration made in accordance with paragraph 3 shall be published in the *Official Journal of the European Union*. It may be withdrawn at any time.

6. Member States shall transmit to the General Secretariat of the Council and to the Commission the text of the provisions transposing into their national law the obligations imposed on them under this Framework Decision.

*Article 9*

**Review**

1. By 28 March 2014, the Commission shall draw up a report on the basis of the information received from the Member States pursuant to Article 8(6).

2. On the basis of the report referred to in paragraph 1, the Council shall assess:

(a) the extent to which Member States have taken the necessary measures in order to comply with this Framework Decision; and

(b) the application of this Framework Decision.

3. The report referred to in paragraph 1 shall be accompanied, where necessary, by legislative proposals.

*Article 10*

**Entry into force**

This Framework Decision shall enter into force on the day following its publication in the *Official Journal of the European Union*.

Done at Brussels, 26 February 2009.

*For the Council*

*The President*

I. LANGER

L 97/26 EN Official Journal of the European Union 16.4.2009

III

*(Acts adopted under the EU Treaty)*

# ACTS ADOPTED UNDER TITLE VI OF THE EU TREATY

**Declaration for the purposes of Article 8(3) of Council Framework Decision 2009/299/JHA of 26 February 2009 amending Framework Decisions 2002/584/JHA, 2005/214/JHA, 2006/783/JHA, 2008/909/JHA and 2008/947/JHA, thereby enhancing the procedural rights of persons and fostering the application of the principle of mutual recognition to decisions rendered in the absence of the person concerned at the trial**

'Italy hereby declares that it wishes to avail itself of the opportunity offered by Article 8(3) of Framework Decision 2009/299/JHA (1). As a consequence, the Framework Decision shall apply from 1 January 2014 at the latest to the recognition and enforcement of decisions, rendered in the absence of the person concerned at the trial, which are issued by Italian competent authorities.'

(1) OJ L 81, 27.3.2009, p. 24.

# Framework Decision 2009/315 on the organisation and content of the exchange of information extracted from the criminal record between Member States, 26 February 2009

[OJ 2009, L 93/23–32]

7.4.2009 EN Official Journal of the European Union L 93/23

# ACTS ADOPTED UNDER TITLE VI OF THE EU TREATY

## COUNCIL FRAMEWORK DECISION 2009/315/JHA

### of 26 February 2009

### on the organisation and content of the exchange of information extracted from the criminal record between Member States

THE COUNCIL OF THE EUROPEAN UNION,

Having regard to the Treaty on European Union, and in particular Articles 31 and 34(2)(b) thereof,

Having regard to the proposal from the Commission and the initiative of the Kingdom of Belgium,

Having regard to the opinion of the European Parliament (1),

Whereas:

(1) The European Union has set itself the objective of providing citizens with a high level of safety within the area of freedom, security and justice. This objective presupposes the exchange between the competent authorities of the Member States of information extracted from criminal records.

(2) On 29 November 2000 the Council, in accordance with the conclusions of the Tampere European Council of 15 and 16 October 1999, adopted a programme of measures to implement the principle of mutual recognition of decisions in criminal matters (2). This Framework Decision contributes to achieving the goals provided for by measure 3 of the programme, which calls for the establishment of a standard form like that drawn up for the Schengen bodies, translated into all the official languages of the Union, for criminal records requests.

(3) The Final Report on the first evaluation exercise on mutual legal assistance in criminal matters (3) called on the Member States to simplify the procedures for transferring documents between States, using, if necessary, standard forms to facilitate mutual legal assistance.

(1) Opinion delivered on 17 June 2008 (not yet published in the Official Journal).
(2) OJ C 12, 15.1.2001, p. 10.
(3) OJ C 216, 1.8.2001, p. 14.

(4) The need to improve the quality of information exchanged on convictions was prioritised in the European Council Declaration on Combating Terrorism of 25 and 26 March 2004 and was reiterated in the Hague Programme (4), adopted by the European Council on 4 and 5 November 2004, which called for greater exchange of information from national conviction and disqualification registers. These objectives are reflected in the Action Plan jointly adopted by the Council and the Commission on 2 and 3 June 2005 with a view to carrying out the Hague Programme.

(5) With a view to improving the exchange of information between Member States on criminal records, projects developed with the aim to achieve this objective are welcomed, including the existing project for the interconnection of national criminal registers. The experience gathered from these activities has encouraged the Member States to further enhance their efforts and showed the importance to continue streamlining the mutual exchange of information on convictions between the Member States.

(6) This Framework Decision is a response to the wishes expressed by the Council on 14 April 2005, following the publication of the White Paper on exchanges of information on convictions and the effect of such convictions in the European Union and the subsequent general discussion thereof. Its main aim is to improve the exchange of information on convictions and, where imposed and entered in the criminal records of the convicting Member State, on disqualifications arising from criminal conviction of citizens of the Union.

(7) The application of the mechanisms established by this Framework Decision only to the transmission of information extracted from criminal records concerning natural persons should be without prejudice to a possible future broadening of the scope of application of such mechanisms to the exchange of information concerning legal persons.

(4) OJ C 53, 3.3.2005, p. 1.

(8) Information on convictions handed down in other Member States is currently governed by Articles 13 and 22 of the European Convention on Mutual Assistance in Criminal Matters of 20 April 1959. These provisions are not, however, sufficient to meet the present requirements of judicial cooperation in an area such as the European Union.

(9) As between the Member States, this Framework Decision should replace Article 22 of the European Convention on Mutual Assistance in Criminal Matters. In addition to the obligations of a convicting Member State to transmit information to the Member States of the person's nationality concerning convictions handed down against their nationals which this Framework Decision incorporates and further defines, an obligation on the Member States of the person's nationality to store information so transmitted is also introduced, in order to ensure that they are able to reply fully to requests for information from other Member States.

(10) This Framework Decision should be without prejudice to the possibility of judicial authorities' directly requesting and transmitting information from criminal records pursuant to Article 13 in conjunction with Article 15(3), of the European Convention on Mutual Assistance in Criminal Matters and without prejudice to Article 6(1) of the Convention on Mutual Assistance in Criminal Matters between the Member States of the European Union, established by Council Act of 29 May 2000 (1).

(11) Improving the circulation of information on convictions is of little benefit if Member States are not able to take transmitted information into account. On 24 July 2008, Council adopted Framework Decision 2008/675/JHA on taking account of convictions in the Member States of the European Union in the course of new criminal proceedings (2).

(12) The main objective of the initiative of the Kingdom of Belgium is attained by this Framework Decision to the extent that the central authority of every Member State should request and include all information provided from the criminal records of the Member State of the person's nationality in its extract from criminal records when it replies to a request from the person concerned. Awareness of the existence of the conviction as well as, where imposed and entered in the criminal record, of a disqualification arising from it, is a prerequisite for giving them effect in accordance with the national law of the Member State in which the person intends to perform professional activity related to supervision of children. The mechanism established by this Framework Decision aims at inter alia ensuring that a person convicted of a sexual offence against children should no longer, where the criminal record of that person in the convicting Member State contains such conviction and, if imposed and entered in the criminal record, a disqualification arising from it, be able to conceal this conviction or disqualification with a view to performing professional activity related to supervision of children in another Member State.

(13) This Framework Decision establishes rules on the protection of personal data transmitted between the Member States as a result of its implementation. Existing general rules on the protection of personal data processed in the framework of police and judicial cooperation in criminal matters are complemented by the rules established in this Framework Decision. Furthermore, the Council of Europe Convention of 28 January 1981 for the Protection of Individuals with regard to Automatic Processing of Personal Data applies to the personal data handled on the basis of this Framework Decision. This Framework Decision also incorporates the provisions of Council Decision 2005/876/JHA of 21 November 2005 on the exchange of information extracted from the criminal record (3) which limit the use the requesting Member State can make of information asked for. This Framework Decision supplements such provisions with specific rules applying where the Member State of the person's nationality forwards information on convictions transmitted to it by the convicting Member State.

(14) This Framework Decision does not modify obligations and practices established in relation to third States under the European Convention on Mutual Assistance in Criminal Matters, in so far as that instrument remains applicable.

(15) Under Council of Europe Recommendation No R (84) 10 on criminal records and rehabilitation of convicted persons, the main aim of establishment of criminal records is to inform the authorities responsible for the criminal justice system of the background of a person subject to legal proceedings with a view to adapting the decision to be taken to the individual situation. Since all other use of criminal records that might compromise the chances of social rehabilitation of the convicted person must be as limited as possible, the use of information transmitted under this Framework Decision for purposes other than that of criminal proceedings can be limited in accordance with the national law of the requested Member State and the requesting Member State.

(1) OJ C 197, 12.7.2000, p. 3.
(2) OJ L 220, 15.8.2008, p. 32.
(3) OJ L 322, 9.12.2005, p. 33.

(16) The aim of the provisions of this Framework Decision concerning the transmission of information to the Member State of the person's nationality for the purpose of its storage and retransmission is not to harmonise national systems of criminal records of the Member States. This Framework Decision does not oblige the convicting Member State to change its internal system of criminal records as regards the use of information for domestic purposes.

(17) Improving the circulation of information on convictions is of little benefit if such information cannot be understood by the Member State receiving it. Mutual understanding may be enhanced by the creation of a 'standardised European format' allowing information to be exchanged in a uniform, electronic and easily machine-translatable way. Information on convictions sent by the convicting Member State should be transmitted in the official language or one of the official languages of that Member State. Measures should be taken by Council to set up the information exchange system introduced by this Framework Decision.

(18) This Framework Decision respects the fundamental rights and observes the principles recognised by Article 6 of the Treaty on European Union and reflected by the Charter of Fundamental Rights of the European Union.

(19) This Framework Decision respects the principle of subsidiarity referred to in Article 2 of the Treaty on European Union and set out in Article 5 of the Treaty establishing the European Community since the improvement of systems for the transmission of information on convictions between Member States cannot be carried out adequately by the Member States unilaterally and requires coordinated action in the European Union. In accordance with the principle of proportionality, as set out in the Article 5 of the Treaty establishing the European Community, this Framework Decision does not go beyond what is necessary in order to achieve that objective,

HAS ADOPTED THIS FRAMEWORK DECISION:

*Article 1*

**Objective**

The purpose of this Framework Decision is:

(a) to define the ways in which a Member State where a conviction is handed down against a national of another Member State (the 'convicting Member State') transmits the information on such a conviction to the Member State of the convicted person's nationality (the 'Member State of the person's nationality');

(b) to define storage obligations for the Member State of the person's nationality and to specify the methods to be followed when replying to a request for information extracted from criminal records;

(c) to lay down the framework for a computerised system of exchange of information on convictions between Member States to be built and developed on the basis of this Framework Decision and the subsequent decision referred to in Article 11(4).

*Article 2*

**Definitions**

For the purposes of this Framework Decision:

(a) 'conviction' means any final decision of a criminal court against a natural person in respect of a criminal offence, to the extent these decisions are entered in the criminal record of the convicting Member State;

(b) 'criminal proceedings' means the pre-trial stage, the trial stage itself and the execution of the conviction;

(c) 'criminal record' means the national register or registers recording convictions in accordance with national law.

*Article 3*

**Central authority**

1. For the purposes of this Framework Decision, each Member State shall designate a central authority. However, for the transmission of information under Article 4 and for replies under Article 7 to requests referred to in Article 6, Member States may designate one or more central authorities.

2. Each Member State shall inform the General Secretariat of the Council and the Commission of the central authority or authorities designated in accordance with paragraph 1. The General Secretariat of the Council shall notify the Member States and Eurojust of this information.

*Article 4*

**Obligations of the convicting Member State**

1. Each Member State shall take the necessary measures to ensure that all convictions handed down within its territory are accompanied, when provided to its criminal record, by information on the nationality or nationalities of the convicted person if he is a national of another Member State.

2. The central authority of the convicting Member State shall, as soon as possible, inform the central authorities of the other Member States of any convictions handed down within its territory against the nationals of such other Member States, as entered in the criminal record.

If it is known that the convicted person is a national of several Member States, the relevant information shall be transmitted to each of these Member States, even if the convicted person is a national of the Member State within whose territory he was convicted.

3. Information on subsequent alteration or deletion of information contained in the criminal record shall be immediately transmitted by the central authority of the convicting Member State to the central authority of the Member State of the person's nationality.

4. Any Member State which has provided information under paragraphs 2 and 3 shall communicate to the central authority of the Member State of the person's nationality, on the latter's request in individual cases, a copy of the convictions and subsequent measures as well as any other information relevant thereto in order to enable it to consider whether they necessitate any measure at national level.

*Article 5*

**Obligations of the Member State of the person's nationality**

1. The central authority of the Member State of the person's nationality shall store all information in accordance with Article 11(1) and (2) transmitted under Article 4(2) and (3), for the purpose of retransmission in accordance with Article 7.

2. Any alteration or deletion of information transmitted in accordance with Article 4(3) shall entail identical alteration or deletion by the Member State of the person's nationality regarding information stored in accordance with paragraph 1 of this Article for the purpose of retransmission in accordance with Article 7.

3. For the purpose of retransmission in accordance with Article 7 the Member State of the person's nationality may only use information which has been updated in accordance with paragraph 2 of this Article.

*Article 6*

**Request for information on convictions**

1. When information from the criminal record of a Member State is requested for the purposes of criminal proceedings against a person or for any purposes other than that of criminal proceedings, the central authority of that Member State may, in accordance with its national law, submit a request to the central authority of another Member State for information and related data to be extracted from the criminal record.

2. When a person asks for information on his own criminal record, the central authority of the Member State in which the request is made may, in accordance with its national law, submit a request to the central authority of another Member State for information and related data to be extracted from the criminal record, provided the person concerned is or was a resident or a national of the requesting or requested Member State.

3. Once the time limit set out in Article 11(7) has elapsed, whenever a person asks the central authority of a Member State other than the Member State of the person's nationality for information on his own criminal record, the central authority of the Member State in which the request is made shall submit a request to the central authority of the Member State of the person's nationality for information and related data to be extracted from the criminal record in order to be able to include such information and related data in the extract to be provided to the person concerned.

4. All requests from the central authority of a Member State for information extracted from the criminal record shall be submitted using the form set out in the Annex.

*Article 7*

**Reply to a request for information on convictions**

1. When information extracted from the criminal record is requested under Article 6 from the central authority of the Member State of the person's nationality for the purposes of criminal proceedings, that central authority shall transmit to the central authority of the requesting Member State information on:

(a) convictions handed down in the Member State of the person's nationality and entered in the criminal record;

(b) any convictions handed down in other Member States which were transmitted to it after 27 April 2012, in application of Article 4, and stored in accordance with Article 5(1) and (2);

(c) any convictions handed down in other Member States which were transmitted to it by 27 April 2012, and entered in the criminal record;

(d) any convictions handed down in third countries and subsequently transmitted to it and entered in the criminal record.

2. When information extracted from the criminal record is requested under Article 6 from the central authority of the Member State of the person's nationality for any purposes other than that of criminal proceedings, that central authority shall in respect of convictions handed down in the Member State of the person's nationality and of convictions handed down in third countries, which have been subsequently transmitted to it and entered in its criminal record, reply in accordance with its national law.

In respect of information on convictions handed down in another Member State, which have been transmitted to the Member State of the person's nationality, the central authority of the latter Member State shall in accordance with its national law transmit to the requesting Member State the information which has been stored in accordance with Article 5 (1) and (2) as well as the information which has been transmitted to that central authority by 27 April 2012, and has been entered in its criminal record.

When transmitting the information in accordance with Article 4, the central authority of the convicting Member State may inform the central authority of the Member State of the person's nationality that the information on convictions handed down in the former Member State and transmitted to the latter central authority may not be retransmitted for any purposes other than that of criminal proceedings. In this case, the central authority of the Member State of the person's nationality shall, in respect of such convictions, inform the requesting Member State which other Member State had transmitted such information so as to enable the requesting Member State to submit a request directly to the convicting Member State in order to receive information on these convictions.

3. When information extracted from the criminal record is requested from the central authority of the Member State of the person's nationality by a third country, the Member State of the person's nationality may reply in respect of convictions transmitted by another Member State only within the limitations applicable to the transmission of information to other Member States in accordance with paragraphs 1 and 2.

4. When information extracted from the criminal record is requested under Article 6 from the central authority of a Member State other than the Member State of the person's nationality, the requested Member State shall transmit information on convictions handed down in the requested Member State and on convictions handed down against third country nationals and against stateless persons contained in its criminal record to the same extent as provided for in Article 13 of the European Convention on Mutual Assistance in Criminal Matters.

5. The reply shall be made using the form set out in the Annex. It shall be accompanied by a list of convictions, as provided for by national law.

*Article 8*

**Deadlines for replies**

1. Replies to the requests referred to in Article 6(1) shall be transmitted by the central authority of the requested Member State to the central authority of the requesting Member State immediately and in any event within a period not exceeding ten working days from the date the request was received, as provided for by its national law, rules or practice, using the form set out in the Annex.

When the requested Member State requires further information to identify the person involved in the request, it shall immediately consult the requesting Member State with a view to providing a reply within ten working days from the date the additional information is received.

2. Replies to the request referred to in Article 6(2) shall be transmitted within twenty working days from the date the request was received.

*Article 9*

**Conditions for the use of personal data**

1. Personal data provided under Article 7(1) and (4) for the purposes of criminal proceedings may be used by the requesting Member State only for the purposes of the criminal proceedings for which it was requested, as specified in the form set out in the Annex.

2. Personal data provided under Article 7(2) and (4) for any purposes other than that of criminal proceedings may be used by the requesting Member State in accordance with its national law only for the purposes for which it was requested and within the limits specified by the requested Member State in the form set out in the Annex.

3. Notwithstanding paragraphs 1 and 2, personal data provided under Article 7(1), (2) and (4) may be used by the requesting Member State for preventing an immediate and serious threat to public security.

4. Member States shall take the necessary measures to ensure that personal data received from another Member State under Article 4, if transmitted to a third country in accordance with Article 7(3), is subject to the same usage limitations as those applicable in a requesting Member State in accordance with paragraph 2 of this Article. Member States shall specify that personal data, if transmitted to a third country for the purposes of a criminal proceeding, may be further used by that third country only for the purposes of criminal proceedings.

5. This Article does not apply to personal data obtained by a Member State under this Framework Decision and originating from that Member State.

*Article 10*

**Languages**

When submitting a request referred to in Article 6(1), the requesting Member State shall transmit to the requested Member State the form set out in the Annex in the official language or one of the official languages of the latter Member State.

The requested Member State shall reply either in one of its official languages or in any other language accepted by both Member States.

Any Member State may, at the time of the adoption of this Framework Decision or at a later date, indicate, in a statement to the General Secretariat of the Council, which are the official languages of the institutions of the European Union that it accepts. The General Secretariat of the Council shall notify the Member States of this information.

*Article 11*

**Format and other ways of organising and facilitating exchanges of information on convictions**

1. When transmitting information in accordance with Article 4(2) and (3), the central authority of the convicting Member State shall transmit the following information:

(a) information that shall always be transmitted, unless, in individual cases, such information is not known to the central authority (obligatory information):

(i) information on the convicted person (full name, date of birth, place of birth (town and State), gender, nationality and – if applicable – previous name(s));

(ii) information on the nature of the conviction (date of conviction, name of the court, date on which the decision became final);

(iii) information on the offence giving rise to the conviction (date of the offence underlying the conviction and name or legal classification of the offence as well as reference to the applicable legal provisions); and

(iv) information on the contents of the conviction (notably the sentence as well as any supplementary penalties, security measures and subsequent decisions modifying the enforcement of the sentence);

(b) information that shall be transmitted if entered in the criminal record (optional information):

(i) the convicted person's parents' names;

(ii) the reference number of the conviction;

(iii) the place of the offence; and

(iv) disqualifications arising from the conviction;

(c) information that shall be transmitted, if available to the central authority (additional information):

(i) the convicted person's identity number, or the type and number of the person's identification document;

(ii) fingerprints, which have been taken from that person; and

(iii) if applicable, pseudonym and/or alias name(s).

In addition, the central authority may transmit any other information concerning convictions entered in the criminal record.

2. The central authority of the Member State of the person's nationality shall store all information of the types listed in points (a) and (b) of paragraph 1, which it has received in accordance with Article 5(1) for the purpose of retransmission in accordance with Article 7. For the same purpose it may store the information of the types listed in point (c) of the first subparagraph and in the second subparagraph of paragraph 1.

3. Until the time limit set out in paragraph 7 has elapsed, central authorities of Member States which have not carried out the notification referred to in paragraph 6 shall transmit all information in accordance with Article 4, requests in accordance with Article 6, replies in accordance with Article 7 and other relevant information by any means capable of producing a written record under conditions allowing the central authority of the receiving Member State to establish the authenticity thereof.

7.4.2009 EN Official Journal of the European Union L 93/29

Once the time limit set out in paragraph 7 of this Article has elapsed, central authorities of Member States shall transmit such information electronically using a standardised format.

4. The format referred to in paragraph 3 and any other means of organising and facilitating exchanges of information on convictions between central authorities of Member States shall be set up by the Council in accordance with the relevant procedures of the Treaty on the European Union by 27 April 2012.

Other such means include:

(a) defining all means by which understanding and automatically translating transmitted information may be facilitated;

(b) defining the means by which information may be exchanged electronically, particularly as regards the technical specification to be used and, if need be, any applicable exchange procedures;

(c) possible alterations to the form set out in the Annex.

5. If the mode of transmission referred to in paragraphs 3 and 4 is not available, the first subparagraph of paragraph 3 shall remain applicable for the entire period of such unavailability.

6. Each Member State shall carry out the necessary technical alterations to be able to use the standardised format and electronically transmit it to other Member States. It shall notify the Council of the date from which it will be able to carry out such transmissions.

7. Member States shall carry out the technical alterations referred to in paragraph 6 within three years from the date of adoption of the format and the means by which information on convictions may be exchanged electronically.

*Article 12*

**Relationship to other legal instruments**

1. In relations between the Member States, this Framework Decision supplements the provisions of Article 13 of the European Convention on Mutual Assistance in Criminal Matters, its additional Protocols of 17 March 1978 and 8 November 2001, the Convention on Mutual Assistance in Criminal Matters between the Member States of the European Union and its Protocol of 16 October 2001 [1].

2. For the purposes of this Framework Decision, Member States shall waive the right to rely among themselves on their reservations to Article 13 of the European Convention on Mutual Assistance in Criminal Matters.

3. Without prejudice to their application in relations between Member States and third States, this Framework Decision replaces in relations between Member States which have taken the necessary measures to comply with this Framework Decision and ultimately with effect from 27 April 2012 the provisions of Article 22 of the European Convention on Mutual Assistance in Criminal Matters, as supplemented by Article 4 of said Convention's additional Protocol of 17 March 1978.

4. Decision 2005/876/JHA is hereby repealed.

5. This Framework Decision shall not affect the application of more favourable provisions in bilateral or multilateral agreements between Member States.

*Article 13*

**Implementation**

1. Member States shall take the necessary measures to comply with the provisions of this Framework Decision by 27 April 2012.

2. Member States shall transmit to the General Secretariat of the Council and to the Commission the text of the provisions transposing into their national law the obligations imposed on them under this Framework Decision.

3. On the basis of that information the Commission shall, by 27 April 2015, present a report to the European Parliament and the Council on the application of this Framework Decision, accompanied if necessary by legislative proposals.

*Article 14*

**Entry into force**

This Framework Decision shall enter into force on the 20th day following its publication in the *Official Journal of the European Union*.

Done at Brussels, 26 February 2009.

*For the Council*

*The President*

I. LANGER

(1) OJ C 326, 21.11.2001, p. 1.

*ANNEX*

**Form referred to in Articles 6, 7, 8, 9 and 10 of the Council Framework Decision 2009/315/JHA on the organisation and content of the exchange of information extracted from the criminal record between Member States**

**Request for information extracted from the criminal record**

**Members States are to consult the Manual of Procedures for assistance in filling in this form correctly**

(a) Information on the requesting Member State:

Member State:

Central authority(ies):

Contact person:

Telephone (with STD code):

Fax (with STD code):

E-mail address:

Correspondence address:

File reference, if known:

(b) Information on the identity of the person concerned by the request (*):

Full name (forenames and all surnames)

Previous names:

Pseudonym and/or alias, if any:

Gender: M ☐ F ☐

Nationality:

Date of birth (in figures: dd/mm/yyyy):

Place of birth (town and State):

Father's name:

Mother's name:

Residence or known address:

Person's identity number or type and number of the person's identification document:

Fingerprints:

Other available identification information:

(*) To facilitate the identification of the person as much information as possible is to be provided.

(c) Purpose of the request:

*Please tick the appropriate box*

(1) ☐ criminal proceedings (please identify the authority before which the proceedings are pending and, if available, the case reference number) ..............................

..............................

(2) ☐ request outside the context of criminal proceedings (please identify the authority before which the proceedings are pending and, if available, the case reference number, while ticking the relevant box):

(i) ☐ from a judicial authority ..............................

..............................

(ii) ☐ from a competent administrative authority ..............................

..............................

(iii) ☐ from the person concerned for information on own criminal record ..............................

..............................

Purpose for which the information is requested:

Requesting authority:

☐ the person concerned does not consent for this information to be divulged (if the person concerned was asked for its consent in accordance with the law of the requesting Member State).

Contact person for any further information needed:

Name:

Telephone:

E-mail address:

Other information (e.g. urgency of the request):

**Reply to the request**

Information relating to the person concerned

*Please tick the appropriate box*

The undersigned authority confirms that:

☐ there is no information on convictions in the criminal record of the person concerned

☐ there is information on convictions entered in the criminal record of the person concerned; a list of convictions is attached

☐ there is other information entered in the criminal record of the person concerned; such information is attached (optional)

☐ there is information on convictions entered in the criminal record of the person concerned but the convicting Member State intimated that the information about these convictions may not be retransmitted for any purposes other than that of criminal proceedings. The request for more information may be sent directly to .................. (please indicate the convicting Member State)

☐ in accordance with the national law of the requested Member State, requests made for any purposes other than that of criminal proceedings may not be dealt with.

| |
|---|
| Contact person for any further information needed:<br>Name:<br>Telephone:<br>E-mail address:<br>Other information (limitations of use of the data concerning requests outside the context of criminal proceedings):<br>Please indicate the number of pages attached to the reply form: |
| Done at<br>on<br>Signature and official stamp (if appropriate):<br>Name and position/organisation: |

If appropriate, please attach a list of convictions and send the complete package to the requesting Member State. It is not necessary to translate the form or the list into the language of the requesting Member State.

# Exchange of Letters between the European Union and the Government of Kenya on the conditions and modalities for the transfer of persons suspected of having committed acts of piracy and detained by the European Union-led naval force (EUNAVFOR), and seized property in the possession of EUNAVFOR, from EUNAVFOR to Kenya and for their treatment after such transfer, 6 March 2009

**[OJ 2009, L 79/49–59]**

25.3.2009 EN Official Journal of the European Union L 79/49

**Exchange of Letters between the European Union and the Government of Kenya on the conditions and modalities for the transfer of persons suspected of having committed acts of piracy and detained by the European Union-led naval force (EUNAVFOR), and seized property in the possession of EUNAVFOR, from EUNAVFOR to Kenya and for their treatment after such transfer**

A. *Letter from the European Union*

Nairobi, 6th March 2009, 10.15 a.m.

Sir,

With reference to my letter dated 14 November 2008 and your letter dated 5 December 2008, I have the honour to confirm the intention of the European Union to conclude with the Government of Kenya an Exchange of Letters with a view to defining the conditions and modalities for the transfer of persons suspected of having committed acts of piracy on the high seas and detained by the European Union-led naval force (EUNAVFOR), and seized property in the possession of EUNAVFOR, from EUNAVFOR to Kenya, and for their treatment after such transfer.

This exchange of letters is concluded in the framework of the EU Council Joint Action 2008/851/CFSP of 10 November 2008 on a European Union military operation to contribute to the deterrence, prevention and repression of acts of piracy and armed robbery off the coast of Somalia (operation 'Atalanta').

Furthermore, this exchange of letters does not affect the participant's rights and obligations under international agreements and other instruments establishing international courts and tribunals, and relevant domestic laws and is concluded in full respect of:

— United Nations Security Council Resolutions (UNSCR) 1814 (2008), 1838 (2008), 1846 (2008), 1851 (2008) and successor UNSCRs,

— the 1982 United Nations Convention on the Law of the Sea (UNCLOS), in particular Articles 100 to 107,

— International Human Rights Law, including the 1966 International Covenant on Civil and political Rights, and the 1984 Convention against Torture and Other Cruel, Inhuman or Degrading Treatment or Punishment.

Accordingly, I have the honour to propose, as set out in the Annex to this letter, such provisions defining the conditions and modalities for the transfer of persons suspected of having committed acts of piracy and detained by EUNAVFOR, and seized property in the possession of EUNAVFOR, from EUNAVFOR to Kenya, and for their treatment after such transfer.

I would be grateful if you could confirm, on behalf of the Government of Kenya, your acceptance of those provisions.

This Instrument will be applied provisionally from the date on which it is signed and will enter into force when each of the participants has completed its own internal procedures. This Instrument will continue to have effect until six months after either participant has given the other signatory written notification of a decision to terminate the instrument. This Instrument may be varied by mutual arrangement between the signatories. Termination of this instrument will not affect any benefits or obligations arising out of the application of this Instrument before such termination, including the benefits to any transferred persons as long as they are held in custody or are prosecuted by Kenya.

After the termination of the Operation, as defined in the Annex to this letter, all benefits of EUNAVFOR, as defined in that Annex, under this Instrument may be exercised by any person or entity designated by the State exercising the Presidency of the Council of the EU. A designated person or entity may, inter alia, be a diplomatic agent or consular official of that State accredited to Kenya. After the termination of the Operation, all notifications that were to be made to EUNAVFOR under this Instrument will be made to the State exercising the Presidency of the Council of the EU.

Please accept, Sir, the assurance of my highest consideration.

*For the European Union*

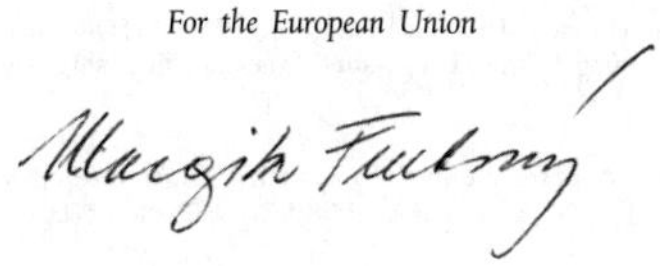

25.3.2009 EN Official Journal of the European Union L 79/51

*ANNEX*

**PROVISIONS ON THE CONDITIONS OF TRANSFER OF SUSPECTED PIRATES AND SEIZED PROPERTY FROM THE EU-LED NAVAL FORCE TO THE REPUBLIC OF KENYA**

1. Definitions

For the purposes of this Exchange of Letters:

(a) 'European Union-led naval force (EUNAVFOR)' means EU military headquarters and national contingents contributing to the EU operation 'Atalanta', their ships, aircrafts and assets;

(b) 'operation' means the preparation, establishment, execution and support of the military mission established by EU Council Joint Action 2008/851/CFSP and/or its successors;

(c) 'EU Operation Commander' means the commander of the operation;

(d) 'EU Force Commander' means the EU commander in the area of operations as defined within Article 1(2) of EU Council Joint Action 2008/851/CFSP;

(e) 'national contingents' means units and ships belonging to the Member States of the European Union and to other States participating in the operation;

(f) 'sending State' means a State providing a national contingent for EUNAVFOR.

(g) 'piracy' means piracy as defined in Article 101 of UNCLOS;

(h) 'transferred person' means any person suspected of intending to commit, committing, or having committed, acts of piracy transferred by EUNAVFOR to Kenya under this Exchange of Letters.

2. General principles

(a) Kenya will accept, upon the request of EUNAVFOR, the transfer of persons detained by EUNAVFOR in connection with piracy and associated seized property by EUNAVFOR and will submit such persons and property to its competent authorities for the purpose of investigation and prosecution.

(b) EUNAVFOR will, when acting under this Exchange of Letters, transfer persons or property only to competent Kenyan law enforcement authorities.

(c) The signatories confirm that they will treat persons transferred under this Exchange of Letters, both prior to and following transfer, humanely and in accordance with international human rights obligations, including the prohibition against torture and cruel, inhumane and degrading treatment or punishment, the prohibition of arbitrary detention and in accordance with the requirement to have a fair trial.

3. Treatment, prosecution and trial of transferred persons

(a) Any transferred person will be treated humanely and will not be subjected to torture or cruel, inhuman or degrading treatment or punishment, will receive adequate accommodation and nourishment, access to medical treatment and will be able to carry out religious observance.

(b) Any transferred person will be brought promptly before a judge or other officer authorised by law to exercise judicial power, who will decide without delay on the lawfulness of his detention and will order his release if the detention is not lawful.

(c) Any transferred person will be entitled to trial within a reasonable time or to release.

(d) In the determination of any criminal charge against him, any transferred person will be entitled to a fair and public hearing by a competent, independent and impartial tribunal established by law.

(e) Any transferred person charged with a criminal offence will be presumed innocent until proved guilty according to law.

(f) In the determination of any criminal charge against him, every transferred person will be entitled to the following minimum guarantees, in full equality:

(1) to be informed promptly and in detail in a language which he understands of the nature and cause of the charge against him;

(2) to have adequate time and facilities for the preparation of his defence and to communicate with counsel of his own choice;

(3) to be tried without undue delay;

(4) to be tried in his presence, and to defend himself in person or through legal assistance of his own choice; to be informed, if he does not have legal assistance, of this right; and to have legal assistance assigned to him, in any case where the interests of justice so require, and without payment by him in any such case if he does not have sufficient means to pay for it;

(5) to examine, or have examined, all evidence against him, including affidavits of witnesses who conducted the arrest, and to obtain the attendance and examination of witnesses on his behalf under the same conditions as witnesses against him;

(6) to have the free assistance of an interpreter if he cannot understand or speak the language used in court;

(7) not to be compelled to testify against himself or to confess guilt.

(g) Any transferred person convicted of a crime will be permitted to have the right to his conviction and sentence reviewed by or appealed to a higher tribunal in accordance with the law of Kenya.

(h) Kenya will not transfer any transferred person to any other State for the purposes of investigation or prosecution without prior written consent from EUNAVFOR.

4. Death penalty

No transferred person will be liable to suffer the death sentence. Kenya will, in accordance with the applicable laws, take steps to ensure that any death sentence is commuted to a sentence of imprisonment.

5. Records and notifications

(a) Any transfer will be the subject of an appropriate document signed by a representative of EUNAVFOR and a representative of the competent Kenyan law enforcement authorities.

(b) EUNAVFOR will provide detention records to Kenya with regard to any transferred person. These records will include, so far as possible, the physical condition of the transferred person while in detention, the time of transfer to Kenyan authorities, the reason for his detention, the time and place of the commencement of his detention, and any decisions taken with regard to his detention.

(c) Kenya will be responsible for keeping an accurate account of all transferred persons, including, but not limited to, keeping records of any seized property, the person's physical condition, the location of their places of detention, any charges against him and any significant decisions taken in the course of his prosecution and trial.

(d) These records will be available to representatives of the EU and EUNAVFOR upon request in writing to the Kenyan Ministry of Foreign Affairs.

(e) In addition, Kenya will notify EUNAVFOR of the place of detention of any person transferred under this Exchange of Letters, any deterioration of his physical condition and of any allegations of alleged improper treatment. Representatives of the EU and EUNAVFOR will have access to any persons transferred under this Exchange of Letters as long as such persons are in custody and will be entitled to question them.

(f) National and international humanitarian agencies will, at their request, be allowed to visit persons transferred under this Exchange of Letters.

(g) For the purposes of ensuring that EUNAVFOR is able to provide timely assistance to Kenya with attendance of witnesses from EUNAVFOR and the provision of relevant evidence, Kenya will notify EUNAVFOR of its intention to initiate criminal trial proceedings against any transferred person and the timetable for provision of evidence, and the hearing of evidence.

6. EUNAVFOR Assistance

(a) EUNAVFOR, within its means and capabilities, will provide all assistance to Kenya with a view to the investigation and prosecution of transferred persons.

(b) In particular, EUNAVFOR will:

(1) hand over detention records drawn up pursuant to paragraph 5(b) of this Exchange of Letters;

(2) process any evidence in accordance with the requirements of the Kenyan competent authorities as agreed in the implementing arrangements described in paragraph 9;

(3) endeavour to produce statements of witness or affidavits by EUNAVFOR personnel involved in any incident in relation to which persons have been transferred under this Exchange of Letters;

(4) hand over all relevant seized property in the possession of EUNAVFOR.

7. Relationship to other rights of transferred persons.

Nothing in this Exchange of Letters is intended to derogate, or may be construed as derogating, from any rights that a transferred person may have under applicable domestic or international law.

8. Liaison and disputes

(a) All issues arising in connection with the application of these provisions will be examined jointly by Kenyan and EU competent authorities.

(b) Failing any prior settlement, disputes concerning the interpretation or application of these provisions will be settled exclusively by diplomatic means between Kenyan and EU representatives.

9. Implementing arrangements

(a) For the purposes of the application of these provisions, operational, administrative and technical matters may be the subject of implementing arrangements to be approved between competent Kenyan authorities on the one hand and the competent EU authorities, as well as the competent authorities of the sending States, on the other hand.

(b) Implementing arrangements may cover, inter alia:

(1) the identification of competent law enforcement authorities of Kenya to whom EUNAVFOR may transfer persons;

(2) the detention facilities where transferred persons will be held;

(3) the handling of documents, including those related to the gathering of evidence, which will be handed over to the competent law enforcement authorities of Kenya upon transfer of a person;

(4) points of contact for notifications;

(5) forms to be used for transfers;

(6) provision of technical support, expertise, training and other assistance upon request of Kenya in order to achieve the objectives of this Exchange of Letters.

B. *Letter from the Republic of Kenya*

Nairobi, 6th March 2009, 10·15a.m

Sir,

I have the honour to acknowledge receipt of your letter dated 6th March 2009 and its Annex regarding the conditions and modalities for the transfer of persons suspected of having committed acts of piracy on the high seas and detained by the European Union-led naval force (EUNAVFOR), and seized property in the possession of EUNAVFOR, from EUNAVFOR to Kenya, and for their treatment after such transfer, which reads as follows:

'With reference to my letter dated 14 November 2008 and your letter dated 5 December 2008, I have the honour to confirm the intention of the European Union to conclude with the Government of Kenya an Exchange of Letters with a view to defining the conditions and modalities for the transfer of persons suspected of having committed acts of piracy on the high seas and detained by the European Union-led naval force (EUNAVFOR), and seized property in the possession of EUNAVFOR, from EUNAVFOR to Kenya, and for their treatment after such transfer.

This exchange of letters is concluded in the framework of the EU Council Joint Action 2008/851/CFSP of 10 November 2008 on a European Union military operation to contribute to the deterrence, prevention and repression of acts of piracy and armed robbery off the coast of Somalia (operation "Atalanta").

Furthermore, this exchange of letters does not affect the participant's rights and obligations under international agreements and other instruments establishing international courts and tribunals, and relevant domestic laws and is concluded in full respect of:

— United Nations Security Council Resolutions (UNSCR) 1814 (2008), 1838 (2008), 1846 (2008), 1851 (2008) and successor UNSCRs,

— the 1982 United Nations Convention on the Law of the Sea (UNCLOS), in particular Articles 100 to 107,

— International Human Rights Law, including the 1966 International Covenant on Civil and political Rights, and the 1984 Convention against Torture and Other Cruel, Inhuman or Degrading Treatment or Punishment.

Accordingly, I have the honour to propose, as set out in the Annex to this letter, such provisions defining the conditions and modalities for the transfer of persons suspected of having committed acts of piracy and detained by EUNAVFOR, and seized property in the possession of EUNAVFOR, from EUNAVFOR to Kenya, and for their treatment after such transfer.

I would be grateful if you could confirm, on behalf of the Government of Kenya, your acceptance of those provisions.

This Instrument will be applied provisionally from the date on which it is signed and will enter into force when each of the participants has completed its own internal procedures. This Instrument will continue to have effect until six months after either participant has given the other signatory written notification of a decision to terminate the instrument. This Instrument may be varied by mutual arrangement between the signatories. Termination of this instrument will not affect any benefits or obligations arising out of the application of this Instrument before such termination, including the benefits to any transferred persons as long as they are held in custody or are prosecuted by Kenya.

After the termination of the Operation, as defined in the Annex to this letter, all benefits of EUNAVFOR, as defined in that Annex, under this Instrument may be exercised by any person or entity designated by the State exercising the Presidency of the Council of the EU. A designated person or entity may, inter alia, be a diplomatic agent or consular official of that State accredited to Kenya. After the termination of the Operation, all notifications that were to be made to EUNAVFOR under this Instrument will be made to the State exercising the Presidency of the Council of the EU.

---

L 79/56 EN Official Journal of the European Union 25.3.2009

*ANNEX*

**PROVISIONS ON THE CONDITIONS OF TRANSFER OF SUSPECTED PIRATES AND SEIZED PROPERTY FROM THE EU-LED NAVAL FORCE TO THE REPUBLIC OF KENYA**

1. Definitions

For the purposes of this Exchange of Letters:

(a) "European Union-led naval force (EUNAVFOR)" means EU military headquarters and national contingents contributing to the EU operation "Atalanta", their ships, aircrafts and assets;

(b) "Operation" means the preparation, establishment, execution and support of the military mission established by EU Council Joint Action 2008/851/CFSP and/or its successors;

(c) "EU Operation Commander" means the commander of the operation;

(d) "EU Force Commander" means the EU commander in the area of operations as defined within Article 1(2) of EU Council Joint Action 2008/851/CFSP;

(e) "national contingents" means units and ships belonging to the Member States of the European Union and to other States participating in the operation;

(f) "sending State" means a State providing a national contingent for EUNAVFOR.

(g) "Piracy" means piracy as defined in Article 101 of UNCLOS;

(h) "Transferred person" means any person suspected of intending to commit, committing, or having committed, acts of piracy transferred by EUNAVFOR to Kenya under this Exchange of Letters.

2. General principles

(a) Kenya will accept, upon the request of EUNAVFOR, the transfer of persons detained by EUNAVFOR in connection with piracy and associated seized property by EUNAVFOR and will submit such persons and property to its competent authorities for the purpose of investigation and prosecution.

(b) EUNAVFOR will, when acting under this Exchange of Letters, transfer persons or property only to competent Kenyan law enforcement authorities.

(c) The signatories confirm that they will treat persons transferred under this Exchange of Letters, both prior to and following transfer, humanely and in accordance with international human rights obligations, including the prohibition against torture and cruel, inhumane and degrading treatment or punishment, the prohibition of arbitrary detention and in accordance with the requirement to have a fair trial.

3. Treatment, prosecution and trial of transferred persons

(a) Any transferred person will be treated humanely and will not be subjected to torture or cruel, inhuman or degrading treatment or punishment, will receive adequate accommodation and nourishment, access to medical treatment and will be able to carry out religious observance.

(b) Any transferred person will be brought promptly before a judge or other officer authorised by law to exercise judicial power, who will decide without delay on the lawfulness of his detention and will order his release if the detention is not lawful.

(c) Any transferred person will be entitled to trial within a reasonable time or to release.

(d) In the determination of any criminal charge against him, any transferred person will be entitled to a fair and public hearing by a competent, independent and impartial tribunal established by law.

(e) Any transferred person charged with a criminal offence will be presumed innocent until proved guilty according to law.

(f) In the determination of any criminal charge against him, every transferred person will be entitled to the following minimum guarantees, in full equality:

(1) to be informed promptly and in detail in a language which he understands of the nature and cause of the charge against him;

(2) to have adequate time and facilities for the preparation of his defence and to communicate with counsel of his own choice;

(3) to be tried without undue delay;

(4) to be tried in his presence, and to defend himself in person or through legal assistance of his own choice; to be informed, if he does not have legal assistance, of this right; and to have legal assistance assigned to him, in any case where the interests of justice so require, and without payment by him in any such case if he does not have sufficient means to pay for it;

(5) to examine, or have examined, all evidence against him, including affidavits of witnesses who conducted the arrest, and to obtain the attendance and examination of witnesses on his behalf under the same conditions as witnesses against him;

(6) to have the free assistance of an interpreter if he cannot understand or speak the language used in court;

(7) not to be compelled to testify against himself or to confess guilt.

(g) Any transferred person convicted of a crime will be permitted to have the right to his conviction and sentence reviewed by or appealed to a higher tribunal in accordance with the law of Kenya.

(h) Kenya will not transfer any transferred person to any other State for the purposes of investigation or prosecution without prior written consent from EUNAVFOR.

4. Death penalty

No transferred person will be liable to suffer the death sentence. Kenya will, in accordance with the applicable laws, take steps to ensure that any death sentence is commuted to a sentence of imprisonment.

5. Records and notifications

(a) Any transfer will be the subject of an appropriate document signed by a representative of EUNAVFOR and a representative of the competent Kenyan law enforcement authorities.

(b) EUNAVFOR will provide detention records to Kenya with regard to any transferred person. These records will include, so far as possible, the physical condition of the transferred person while in detention, the time of transfer to Kenyan authorities, the reason for his detention, the time and place of the commencement of his detention, and any decisions taken with regard to his detention.

(c) Kenya will be responsible for keeping an accurate account of all transferred persons, including, but not limited to, keeping records of any seized property, the persons physical condition, the location of their places of detention, any charges against him and any significant decisions taken in the course of his prosecution and trial.

(d) These records will be available to representatives of the EU and EUNAVFOR upon request in writing to the Kenyan Ministry of Foreign Affairs.

(e) In addition, Kenya will notify EUNAVFOR of the place of detention of any person transferred under this Exchange of Letters, any deterioration of his physical condition and of any allegations of alleged improper treatment. Representatives of the EU and EUNAVFOR will have access to any persons transferred under this Exchange of Letters as long as such persons are in custody and will be entitled to question them.

(f) National and international humanitarian agencies will, at their request, be allowed to visit persons transferred under this Exchange of Letters.

(g) For the purposes of ensuring that EUNAVFOR is able to provide timely assistance to Kenya with attendance of witnesses from EUNAVFOR and the provision of relevant evidence, Kenya will notify EUNAVFOR of its intention to initiate criminal trial proceedings against any transferred person and the timetable for provision of evidence, and the hearing of evidence.

6. EUNAVFOR Assistance

(a) EUNAVFOR, within its means and capabilities, will provide all assistance to Kenya with a view to the investigation and prosecution of transferred persons.

(b) In particular, EUNAVFOR will:

(1) hand over detention records drawn up pursuant to paragraph 5(b) of this Exchange of Letters;

(2) process any evidence in accordance with the requirements of the Kenyan competent authorities as agreed in the implementing arrangements described in paragraph 9;

(3) endeavour to produce statements of witness or affidavits by EUNAVFOR personnel involved in any incident in relation to which persons have been transferred under this Exchange of Letters;

(4) hand over all relevant seized property in the possession of EUNAVFOR.

7. Relationship to other rights of transferred persons.

Nothing in this Exchange of Letters is intended to derogate, or may be construed as derogating, from any rights that a transferred person may have under applicable domestic or international law.

8. Liaison and disputes

(a) All issues arising in connection with the application of these provisions will be examined jointly by Kenyan and EU competent authorities.

(b) Failing any prior settlement, disputes concerning the interpretation or application of these provisions will be settled exclusively by diplomatic means between Kenyan and EU representatives.

9. Implementing arrangements

(a) For the purposes of the application of these provisions, operational, administrative and technical matters may be the subject of implementing arrangements to be approved between competent Kenyan authorities on the one hand and the competent EU authorities, as well as the competent authorities of the sending States on the other hand.

(b) Implementing arrangements may cover, inter alia:

(1) the identification of competent law enforcement authorities of Kenya to whom EUNAVFOR may transfer persons;

(2) the detention facilities where transferred persons will be held;

(3) the handling of documents, including those related to the gathering of evidence, which will be handed over to the competent law enforcement authorities of Kenya upon transfer of a person;

(4) points of contact for notifications;

(5) forms to be used for transfers;

(6) provision of technical support, expertise, training and other assistance upon request of Kenya in order to achieve the objectives of this Exchange of Letters.'

I have the honour to confirm, on behalf of the Government of the Republic of Kenya, that the content of your letter and of its Annex are acceptable to the Government of the Republic of Kenya. As set out in your letter, this instrument will enter into force provisionally from the date of signature of this letter and will enter into force when each of the signatories has completed its own internal procedures.

Please accept, Sir, the assurance of my highest consideration.

*For the Government of the Republic of Kenya*

# Decision 2009/316 on the establishment of the European Criminal Records Information System (ECRIS) in application of Article 11 of Framework Decision 2009/315, 6 April 2009

[OJ 2009, L 93/33–48]

7.4.2009 EN Official Journal of the European Union L 93/33

**COUNCIL DECISION 2009/316/JHA**

**of 6 April 2009**

**on the establishment of the European Criminal Records Information System (ECRIS) in application of Article 11 of Framework Decision 2009/315/JHA**

THE COUNCIL OF THE EUROPEAN UNION,

Having regard to the Treaty on European Union, and in particular Articles 31 and 34(2)(c) thereof,

Having regard to the Council Framework Decision 2009/315/JHA of 26 February 2009 on the organisation and content of the exchange of information extracted from the criminal record between Member States [1], and in particular Article 11(4) thereof,

Having regard to the proposal from the Commission,

Having regard to the opinion of the European Parliament [2],

Whereas:

(1) Article 29 of the Treaty on European Union states that the Union's objective is to provide citizens with a high level of safety in the area of freedom, security and justice. This objective presupposes the systematic exchange between the competent authorities of the Member States of information extracted from criminal records in a way that would guarantee its common understanding and the efficiency of such exchange.

(2) Information on convictions handed down against Member States' nationals by other Member States does not circulate efficiently on the current basis of the European Convention on Mutual Assistance in Criminal Matters of 20 April 1959. Therefore, there is a need for more efficient and accessible procedures of exchange of such information at European Union level.

(3) The need to improve the exchange of information on convictions was prioritised in the European Council Declaration on Combating Terrorism of 25 and 26 March 2004 and was subsequently reiterated in the Hague Programme [3] and in the Action Plan [4] on its implementation. Furthermore, the computerised interconnection of criminal records at European Union level was recognised as a political priority by the European Council in its Conclusions of 21 and 22 June 2007.

(4) The computerised interconnection of criminal records is part of the E-Justice project, which was acknowledged as a priority by the European Council several times in 2007.

(5) A pilot project is currently being developed with a view to interconnecting criminal records. Its achievements constitute a valuable basis for further work on computerised exchange of information at the European Union level.

(6) This Decision aims to implement Framework Decision 2009/315/JHA in order to build and develop a computerised system of exchange of information on convictions between Member States. Such a system should be capable of communicating information on convictions in a form which is easily understandable. Therefore, a standardised format allowing information to be exchanged in a uniform, electronic and easily computer-translatable way as well as any other means of organising and facilitating electronic exchanges of information on convictions between central authorities of Member States should be set up.

(7) This Decision is based on the principles established by Framework Decision 2009/315/JHA and applies and supplements those principles from a technical standpoint.

(8) The categories of data to be entered into the system, the purposes for which the data is to be entered, the criteria for its entry, the authorities permitted to access the data, and some specific rules on protection of personal data are defined in the Framework Decision 2009/315/JHA.

(9) Neither this Decision nor Framework Decision 2009/315/JHA establishes any obligation to exchange information about non-criminal rulings.

(10) Since the objective of this Decision is not to harmonise national systems of criminal records there is no obligation for a convicting Member State to change its internal system of criminal records as regards the use of information for domestic purposes.

[1] See page 23 of this Official Journal.
[2] Opinion delivered on 9 October 2008 (not yet published in the Official Journal).
[3] OJ C 53, 3.3.2005, p. 1.
[4] OJ C 198, 12.8.2005, p. 1.

(11) The European Criminal Records System (ECRIS) is a decentralised information technology system. The criminal records data should be stored solely in databases operated by Member States, and there should be no direct online access to criminal records databases of other Member States. Member States should bear the responsibility for the operation of national criminal records databases and for the efficient exchanges of information between themselves. The common communication infrastructure of ECRIS should be initially the Trans European Services for Telematics between Administrations (S-TESTA) network. All expenditure concerning the common communication infrastructure should be covered by the general budget of the European Union.

(12) The reference tables of categories of offences and categories of penalties and measures provided for in this Decision should facilitate the automatic translation and should enable the mutual understanding of the information transmitted by using a system of codes. The content of the tables is the result of the analysis of the needs of all 27 Member States. That analysis took into account the pilot project categorisation and the results of the clustering exercise of various national offences and penalties and measures. Moreover, in case of the table of offences, it also took into consideration the existing harmonised common definitions on the European and international level as well as the Eurojust and Europol data models.

(13) In order to ensure the mutual understanding and transparency of the common categorisation, each Member State should submit the list of national offences and penalties and measures falling in each category referred to in the respective table. Member States may provide a description of offences and penalties and measures and, given the usefulness of such description, they should be encouraged to do so. Such information should be made accessible to Member States.

(14) The reference tables of categories of offences and categories of penalties and measures provided for in this Decision are not designed to set up legal equivalences between offences and penalties and measures existing at national level. They are a tool aimed at helping the recipient to gain better understanding of the fact(s) and type of penalty(ies) or measure(s) contained in the information transmitted. The accuracy of the codes mentioned cannot be fully guaranteed by the Member State supplying the information and it should not preclude the competent authorities in the receiving Member State from interpreting the information.

(15) The reference tables of categories of offences and categories of penalties and measures should be revised and updated in accordance with the procedure for the adoption of implementing measures for decisions provided for in the Treaty on European Union.

(16) Members States and the Commission should inform and consult one another within the Council in accordance with the modalities set out in the Treaty on European Union, with a view to drawing up a non-binding manual for practitioners which should address the procedures governing the exchange of information, in particular modalities of identification of offenders, common understanding of the categories of offences and penalties and measures, and explanation of problematic national offences and penalties and measures, and ensuring the coordination necessary for the development and operation of ECRIS.

(17) In order to accelerate the development of ECRIS, the Commission should adopt a number of technical measures to assist Member States in preparing the technical infrastructure for interconnecting their criminal records databases. The Commission may provide reference implementation software, namely appropriate software enabling Member States to make this interconnection, which they may choose to apply instead of their own interconnection software implementing a common set of protocols enabling the exchange of information between criminal records databases.

(18) Council Framework Decision 2008/977/JHA of 27 November 2008 on the protection of personal data processed in the framework of police and judicial cooperation in criminal matters [1] should apply in the context of computerised exchange of information extracted from criminal records of Member States, providing for an adequate level of data protection when information is exchanged between Member States, whilst allowing for Member States to require higher standards of protection to national data processing.

(19) Since the objective of this Decision, namely the development of a computerised system for the exchange of information on convictions between Member States, cannot be adequately achieved by the Member States unilaterally, and can therefore, by reason of the necessity for coordinated action in the European Union, be better achieved at the level of the European Union, the Council may adopt measures, in accordance with the principle of subsidiarity referred to in Article 2 of the Treaty on European Union and set out in Article 5 of the Treaty establishing the European Community. In accordance with the principle of proportionality, as set out in the Article 5 of the Treaty establishing the European Community, this Decision does not go beyond what is necessary in order to achieve that objective.

(20) This Decision respects fundamental rights and observes the principles recognised in particular by Article 6 of the Treaty on European Union and reflected by the Charter of Fundamental Rights of the European Union,

(1) OJ L 350, 30.12.2008, p. 60.

HAS DECIDED AS FOLLOWS:

*Article 1*

**Subject matter**

This Decision establishes the European Criminal Records Information System (ECRIS).

This Decision also establishes the elements of a standardised format for the electronic exchange of information extracted from criminal records between the Member States, in particular as regards information on the offence giving rise to the conviction and information on the content of the conviction, as well as other general and technical implementation means related to organising and facilitating the exchange of information.

*Article 2*

**Definitions**

For the purposes of this Decision, the definitions laid down in Framework Decision 2009/315/JHA shall apply.

*Article 3*

**European Criminal Records Information System (ECRIS)**

1. ECRIS is a decentralised information technology system based on the criminal records databases in each Member State. It is composed of the following elements:

(a) an interconnection software built in compliance with a common set of protocols enabling the exchange of information between Member States' criminal records databases;

(b) a common communication infrastructure that provides an encrypted network.

2. This Decision is not aimed at establishing any centralised criminal records database. All criminal records data shall be stored solely in databases operated by the Member States.

3. Central authorities of the Member States referred to in Article 3 of Framework Decision 2009/315/JHA shall not have direct online access to criminal records databases of other Member States. The best available techniques identified together by Member States with the support of the Commission shall be employed to ensure the confidentiality and integrity of criminal records information transmitted to other Member States.

4. The interconnection software and databases storing, sending and receiving information extracted from criminal records shall operate under the responsibility of the Member State concerned.

5. The common communication infrastructure shall be the S-TESTA communications network. Any further developments thereof or any alternative secure network shall ensure that the common communication infrastructure in place continues to meet the conditions set out in paragraph 6.

6. The common communication infrastructure shall be operated under the responsibility of the Commission, and shall fulfil the security requirements and thoroughly respond to the needs of ECRIS.

7. In order to ensure the efficient operation of ECRIS, the Commission shall provide general support and technical assistance, including the collection and drawing up of statistics referred to in Article 6(2)(b)(i) and the reference implementation software.

8. Notwithstanding the possibility of using the European Union financial programmes in accordance with the applicable rules, each Member State shall bear its own costs arising from the implementation, administration, use and maintenance of its criminal records database and the interconnection software referred to in paragraph 1.

The Commission shall bear the costs arising from the implementation, administration, use, maintenance and future developments of the common communication infrastructure of ECRIS, as well as the implementation and future developments of the reference implementation software.

*Article 4*

**Format of transmission of information**

1. When transmitting information in accordance with Article 4(2) and (3) and Article 7 of Framework Decision 2009/315/JHA relating to the name or legal classification of the offence and to the applicable legal provisions, Member States shall refer to the corresponding code for each of the offences referred to in the transmission, as provided for in the table of offences in Annex A. By way of exception, where the offence does not correspond to any specific sub-category, the 'open category' code of the relevant or closest category of offences or, in the absence of the latter, an 'other offences' code, shall be used for that particular offence.

Member States may also provide available information relating to the level of completion and the level of participation in the offence and, where applicable, to the existence of total or partial exemption from criminal responsibility or to recidivism.

2. When transmitting information in accordance with Article 4(2) and (3) and Article 7 of Framework Decision 2009/315/JHA relating to the contents of the conviction, notably the sentence as well as any supplementary penalties, security measures and subsequent decisions modifying the enforcement of the sentence, Member States shall refer to the corresponding code for each of the penalties and measures referred to in the transmission, as provided for in the table of penalties and measures in Annex B. By way of exception, where the penalty or measure does not correspond to any specific sub-category, the 'open category' code of the relevant or closest category of penalties and measures or, in the absence of the latter, an 'other penalties and measures' code, shall be used for that particular penalty or measure.

Member States shall also provide, where applicable, available information relating to the nature and/or conditions of execution of the penalty or measure imposed as provided for in the parameters of Annex B. The parameter 'non-criminal ruling' shall be indicated only in cases where information on such a ruling is provided on a voluntary basis by the Member State of nationality of the person concerned, when replying to a request for information on convictions.

*Article 5*

**Information on national offences and penalties and measures**

1. The following information shall be provided by the Member States to the General Secretariat of the Council, with a view in particular to drawing up the non-binding manual for practitioners referred to in Article 6(2)(a):

(a) the list of national offences in each of the categories referred to in the table of offences in Annex A. The list shall include the name or legal classification of the offence and reference to the applicable legal provisions. It may also include a short description of the constitutive elements of the offence;

(b) the list of types of sentences, possible supplementary penalties and security measures and possible subsequent decisions modifying the enforcement of the sentence as defined in national law, in each of the categories referred to in the table of penalties and measures in Annex B. It may also include a short description of the specific penalty or measure.

2. The lists and descriptions referred to in paragraph 1 shall be regularly updated by Member States. Updated information shall be sent to the General Secretariat of the Council.

3. The General Secretariat of the Council shall communicate to the Member States and to the Commission the information received pursuant to this Article.

*Article 6*

**Implementing measures**

1. The Council, acting by a qualified majority and after consulting the European Parliament, shall adopt any modifications of Annexes A and B as may be necessary.

2. The representatives of the relevant departments of the administrations of the Member States and the Commission shall inform and consult one another within the Council with a view to:

(a) drawing up a non-binding manual for practitioners setting out the procedure for the exchange of information through ECRIS, addressing in particular the modalities of identification of offenders, as well as recording the common understanding of the categories of offences and penalties and measures listed respectively in Annexes A and B;

(b) coordinating their action for the development and operation of ECRIS, concerning in particular:

(i) the establishment of logging systems and procedures making it possible to monitor the functioning of ECRIS and the establishment of non-personal statistics relating to the exchange through ECRIS of information extracted from criminal records;

(ii) the adoption of technical specifications of the exchange, including security requirements, in particular the common set of protocols;

(iii) the establishment of procedures verifying the conformity of the national software applications with the technical specifications.

*Article 7*

**Report**

The Commission services shall regularly publish a report concerning the exchange, through ECRIS, of information extracted from the criminal record based in particular on the statistics referred to in Article 6(2)(b)(i). This report shall be published for the first time one year after submitting the report referred to in Article 13(3) of Framework Decision 2009/315/JHA.

*Article 8*

**Implementation and time limits**

1. Member States shall take the necessary measures to comply with the provisions of this Decision by 7 April 2012.

2. Member States shall use the format specified in Article 4 and comply with the means of organising and facilitating exchanges of information laid down in this Decision from the date notified in accordance with Article 11(6) of Framework Decision 2009/315/JHA.

*Article 9*

**Taking of effect**

This Decision shall take effect on the day of its publication in the *Official Journal of the European Union*.

Done at Luxembourg, 6 April 2009.

*For the Council*
*The President*
J. POSPÍŠIL

L 93/38 EN Official Journal of the European Union 7.4.2009

*ANNEX A*

**Common table of offences categories referred to in Article 4**

| **Parameters** | | |
|---|---|---|
| Level of completion: | Completed act | C |
| | Attempt or preparation | A |
| | Non-transmitted element | Ø |
| Level of participation: | Perpetrator | M |
| | Aider and abettor or instigator/organiser, conspirator | H |
| | Non-transmitted element | Ø |
| Exemption from criminal responsibility: | Insanity or diminished responsibility | S |
| **Recidivism** | | R |

| Code | Categories and sub-categories of offences |
|---|---|
| 0100 00<br>open category | **Crimes within the jurisdiction of the International Criminal Court** |
| 0101 00 | Genocide |
| 0102 00 | Crimes against humanity |
| 0103 00 | War crimes |
| 0200 00<br>open category | **Participation in a criminal organisation** |
| 0201 00 | Directing a criminal organisation |
| 0202 00 | Knowingly taking part in the criminal activities of a criminal organisation |
| 0203 00 | Knowingly taking part in the non-criminal activities of a criminal organisation |
| 0300 00<br>open category | **Terrorism** |
| 0301 00 | Directing a terrorist group |
| 0302 00 | Knowingly participating in the activities of a terrorist group |
| 0303 00 | Financing of terrorism |
| 0304 00 | Public provocation to commit a terrorist offence |
| 0305 00 | Recruitment or training for terrorism |
| 0400 00<br>open category | **Trafficking in human beings** |

| Code | Categories and sub-categories of offences |
|---|---|
| 0401 00 | Trafficking in human beings for the purposes of labour or services exploitation |
| 0402 00 | Trafficking in human beings for the purposes of the exploitation of the prostitution of others or other forms of sexual exploitation |
| 0403 00 | Trafficking in human beings for the purposes of organ or human tissue removal |
| 0404 00 | Trafficking in human beings for the purpose of slavery, practices similar to slavery or servitude |
| 0405 00 | Trafficking in human beings for the purposes of labour or services exploitation of a minor |
| 0406 00 | Trafficking in human beings for the purposes of the exploitation of the prostitution of minors or other forms of their sexual exploitation |
| 0407 00 | Trafficking in human beings for the purposes of organ or human tissue removal of a minor |
| 0408 00 | Trafficking in human beings for the purpose of slavery, practices similar to slavery or servitude of a minor |
| 0500 00<br>open category | **Illicit trafficking** (1) **and other offences related to weapons, firearms, their parts and components, ammunition and explosives** |
| 0501 00 | Illicit manufacturing of weapons, firearms, their parts and components, ammunition and explosives |
| 0502 00 | Illicit trafficking of weapons, firearms, their parts and components ammunition and explosives at national level (2) |
| 0503 00 | Illicit exportation or importation of weapons, firearms, their parts and components, ammunition and explosives |
| 0504 00 | Unauthorised possession or use of weapons, firearms, their parts and components, ammunition and explosives |
| 0600 00<br>open category | **Environmental crime** |
| 0601 00 | Destroying or damaging protected fauna and flora species |
| 0602 00 | Unlawful discharges of polluting substances or ionising radiation into air, soil or water |
| 0603 00 | Offences related to waste, including hazardous waste |
| 0604 00 | Offences related to illicit trafficking (1) in protected fauna and flora species or parts thereof |
| 0605 00 | Unintentional environmental offences |
| 0700 00<br>open category | **Offences related to drugs or precursors, and other offences against public health** |
| 0701 00 | Offences related to illicit trafficking (3) in narcotic drugs, psychotropic substances and precursors not exclusively for own personal consumption |
| 0702 00 | Illicit consumption of drugs and their acquisition, possession, manufacture or production exclusively for own personal consumption |

| Code | Categories and sub-categories of offences |
|---|---|
| 0703 00 | Aiding or inciting others to use narcotic drugs or psychotropic substances illicitly |
| 0704 00 | Manufacture or production of narcotic drugs not exclusively for personal consumption |
| 0800 00<br>open category | **Crimes against the person** |
| 0801 00 | Intentional killing |
| 0802 00 | Aggravated cases of intentional killing (4) |
| 0803 00 | Unintentional killing |
| 0804 00 | Intentional killing of a new-born by his/her mother |
| 0805 00 | Illegal abortion |
| 0806 00 | Illegal euthanasia |
| 0807 00 | Offences related to committing suicide |
| 0808 00 | Violence causing death |
| 0809 00 | Causing grievous bodily injury, disfigurement or permanent disability |
| 0810 00 | Unintentionally causing grievous bodily injury, disfigurement or permanent disability |
| 0811 00 | Causing minor bodily injury |
| 0812 00 | Unintentionally causing minor bodily injury |
| 0813 00 | Exposing to danger of loss of life or grievous bodily injury |
| 0814 00 | Torture |
| 0815 00 | Failure to offer aid or assistance |
| 0816 00 | Offences related to organ or tissue removal without authorisation or consent |
| 0817 00 | Offences related to illicit trafficking (3) in human organs and tissue |
| 0818 00 | Domestic violence or threat |
| 0900 00<br>open category | **Offences against personal liberty, dignity and other protected interests, including racism and xenophobia** |
| 0901 00 | Kidnapping, kidnapping for ransom, illegal restraint |
| 0902 00 | Unlawful arrest or deprivation of liberty by public authority |
| 0903 00 | Hostage-taking |
| 0904 00 | Unlawful seizure of an aircraft or ship |
| 0905 00 | Insults, slander, defamation, contempt |

| Code | Categories and sub-categories of offences |
|---|---|
| 0906 00 | Threats |
| 0907 00 | Duress, pressure, stalking, harassment or aggression of a psychological or emotional nature |
| 0908 00 | Extortion |
| 0909 00 | Aggravated extortion |
| 0910 00 | Illegal entry into private property |
| 0911 00 | Invasion of privacy other than illegal entry into private property |
| 0912 00 | Offences against protection of personal data |
| 0913 00 | Illegal interception of data or communication |
| 0914 00 | Discrimination on grounds of gender, race, sexual orientation, religion or ethnic origin |
| 0915 00 | Public incitement to racial discrimination |
| 0916 00 | Public incitement to racial hatred |
| 0917 00 | Blackmail |
| 1000 00<br>open category | **Sexual offences** |
| 1001 00 | Rape |
| 1002 00 | Aggravated rape (5) other than rape of a minor |
| 1003 00 | Sexual assault |
| 1004 00 | Procuring for prostitution or sexual act |
| 1005 00 | Indecent exposure |
| 1006 00 | Sexual harassment |
| 1007 00 | Soliciting by a prostitute |
| 1008 00 | Sexual exploitation of children |
| 1009 00 | Offences related to child pornography or indecent images of minors |
| 1010 00 | Rape of a minor |
| 1011 00 | Sexual assault of a minor |
| 1100 00<br>open category | **Offences against family law** |
| 1101 00 | Illicit sexual relations between close family members |
| 1102 00 | Polygamy |

L 93/42 EN Official Journal of the European Union 7.4.2009

| Code | Categories and sub-categories of offences |
|---|---|
| 1103 00 | Evading the alimony or maintenance obligation |
| 1104 00 | Neglect or desertion of a minor or a disabled person |
| 1105 00 | Failure to comply with an order to produce a minor or removal of a minor |
| 1200 00<br>open category | **Offences against the State, public order, course of justice or public officials** |
| 1201 00 | Espionage |
| 1202 00 | High treason |
| 1203 00 | Offences related to elections and referendum |
| 1204 00 | Attempt against life or health of the Head of State |
| 1205 00 | Insult of the State, Nation or State symbols |
| 1206 00 | Insult or resistance to a representative of public authority |
| 1207 00 | Extortion, duress, pressure towards a representative of public authority |
| 1208 00 | Assault or threat on a representative of public authority |
| 1209 00 | Public order offences, breach of the public peace |
| 1210 00 | Violence during sports events |
| 1211 00 | Theft of public or administrative documents |
| 1212 00 | Obstructing or perverting the course of justice, making false allegations in the course of criminal or judicial proceedings, perjury |
| 1213 00 | Unlawful impersonation of a person or an authority |
| 1214 00 | Escape from lawful custody |
| 1300 00<br>open category | **Offences against public property or public interests** |
| 1301 00 | Public, social security or family benefit fraud |
| 1302 00 | Fraud affecting European benefits or allowances |
| 1303 00 | Offences related to illegal gambling |
| 1304 00 | Obstructing of public tender procedures |
| 1305 00 | Active or passive corruption of a civil servant, a person holding public office or public authority |
| 1306 00 | Embezzlement, misappropriation or other diversion of property by a public official |
| 1307 00 | Abuse of a function by a public official |

| Code | Categories and sub-categories of offences |
|---|---|
| 1400 00<br>open category | **Tax and customs offences** |
| 1401 00 | Tax offences |
| 1402 00 | Customs offences |
| 1500 00<br>open category | **Economic and trade related offences** |
| 1501 00 | Bankruptcy or fraudulent insolvency |
| 1502 00 | Breach of accounting regulation, embezzlement, concealment of assets or unlawful increase in a company's liabilities |
| 1503 00 | Violation of competition rules |
| 1504 00 | Laundering of proceeds from crime |
| 1505 00 | Active or passive corruption in the private sector |
| 1506 00 | Revealing a secret or breaching an obligation of secrecy |
| 1507 00 | 'Insider trading' |
| 1600 00<br>open category | **Offences against property or causing damage to goods** |
| 1601 00 | Unlawful appropriation |
| 1602 00 | Unlawful appropriation or diversion of energy |
| 1603 00 | Fraud, including swindling |
| 1604 00 | Dealing in stolen goods |
| 1605 00 | Illicit trafficking (6) in cultural goods, including antiques and works of art |
| 1606 00 | Intentional damage or destruction of property |
| 1607 00 | Unintentional damage or destruction of property |
| 1608 00 | Sabotage |
| 1609 00 | Offences against industrial or intellectual property |
| 1610 00 | Arson |
| 1611 00 | Arson causing death or injury to persons |
| 1612 00 | Forest arson |
| 1700 00<br>open category | **Theft offences** |

| Code | Categories and sub-categories of offences |
|---|---|
| 1701 00 | Theft |
| 1702 00 | Theft after unlawful entry into property |
| 1703 00 | Theft, using violence or weapons, or using threat of violence or weapons against person |
| 1704 00 | Forms of aggravated theft which do not involve use of violence or weapons, or use of threat of violence or weapons, against persons. |
| 1800 00<br>open category | **Offences against information systems and other computer-related crime** |
| 1801 00 | Illegal access to information systems |
| 1802 00 | Illegal system interference |
| 1803 00 | Illegal data interference |
| 1804 00 | Production, possession, dissemination of or trafficking in computer devices or data enabling commitment of computer-related offences |
| 1900 00<br>open category | **Forgery of means of payment** |
| 1901 00 | Counterfeiting or forging currency, including the euro |
| 1902 00 | Counterfeiting of non-cash means of payment |
| 1903 00 | Counterfeiting or forging public fiduciary documents |
| 1904 00 | Putting into circulation/using counterfeited or forged currency, non-cash means of payment or public fiduciary documents |
| 1905 00 | Possession of a device for the counterfeiting or forgery of currency or public fiduciary documents |
| 2000 00<br>open category | **Falsification of documents** |
| 2001 00 | Falsification of a public or administrative document by a private individual |
| 2002 00 | Falsification of a document by a civil servant or a public authority |
| 2003 00 | Supply or acquisition of a forged public or administrative document; supply or acquisition of a forged document by a civil servant or a public authority |
| 2004 00 | Using forged public or administrative documents |
| 2005 00 | Possession of a device for the falsification of public or administrative documents |
| 2006 00 | Forgery of private documents by a private individual |
| 2100 00<br>open category | **Offences against traffic regulations** |
| 2101 00 | Dangerous driving |
| 2102 00 | Driving under the influence of alcohol or narcotic drugs |

| Code | Categories and sub-categories of offences |
|---|---|
| 2103 00 | Driving without a licence or while disqualified |
| 2104 00 | Failure to stop after a road accident |
| 2105 00 | Avoiding a road check |
| 2106 00 | Offences related to road transport |
| 2200 00<br>open category | **Offences against labour law** |
| 2201 00 | Unlawful employment |
| 2202 00 | Offences relating to remuneration, including social security contributions |
| 2203 00 | Offences relating to working conditions, health and safety at work |
| 2204 00 | Offences relating to access to or exercise of a professional activity |
| 2205 00 | Offences relating to working hours and rest time |
| 2300 00<br>open category | **Offences against migration law** |
| 2301 00 | Unauthorised entry or residence |
| 2302 00 | Facilitation of unauthorised entry and residence |
| 2400 00<br>open category | **Offences against military obligations** |
| 2500 00<br>open category | **Offences related to hormonal substances and other growth promoters** |
| 2501 00 | Illicit importation, exportation or supply of hormonal substances and other grown promoters |
| 2600 00<br>open category | **Offences related to nuclear materials or other hazardous radioactive substances** |
| 2601 00 | Illicit importation, exportation, supply or acquisition of nuclear or radioactive materials |
| 2700 00<br>open category | **Other offences** |
| 2701 00 | Other intentional offences |
| 2702 00 | Other unintentional offences |

(1) Unless otherwise specified in this category, 'trafficking' means import, export, acquisition, sale, delivery, movement or transfer.
(2) For the purpose of this sub-category trafficking includes acquisition, sale, delivery, movement or transfer.
(3) For the purpose of this sub-category trafficking includes import, export, acquisition, sale, delivery, movement or transfer.
(4) For example: particularly grave circumstances.
(5) For example rape with particular cruelty.
(6) Trafficking includes import, export, acquisition, sale, delivery, movement or transfer.

*ANNEX B*

**Common table of penalties and measures categories referred to in Article 4**

| Code | Categories and sub-categories of offences |
|---|---|
| 1000<br>open category | **Deprivation of freedom** |
| 1001 | Imprisonment |
| 1002 | Life imprisonment |
| 2000<br>open category | **Restriction of personal freedom** |
| 2001 | Prohibition from frequenting some places |
| 2002 | Restriction to travel abroad |
| 2003 | Prohibition to stay in some places |
| 2004 | Prohibition from entry to a mass event |
| 2005 | Prohibition to enter in contact with certain persons through whatever means |
| 2006 | Placement under electronic surveillance (1) |
| 2007 | Obligation to report at specified times to a specific authority |
| 2008 | Obligation to stay/reside in a certain place |
| 2009 | Obligation to be at the place of residence on the set time |
| 2010 | Obligation to comply with the probation measures ordered by the court, including the obligation to remain under supervision |
| 3000<br>open category | **Prohibition of a specific right or capacity** |
| 3001 | Disqualification from function |
| 3002 | Loss/suspension of capacity to hold or to be appointed to public office |
| 3003 | Loss/suspension of the right to vote or to be elected |
| 3004 | Incapacity to contract with public administration |
| 3005 | Ineligibility to obtain public subsidies |
| 3006 | Cancellation of the driving licence (2) |
| 3007 | Suspension of driving licence |
| 3008 | Prohibition to drive certain vehicles |
| 3009 | Loss/suspension of the parental authority |
| 3010 | Loss/suspension of right to be an expert in court proceedings/witness under oath/juror |
| 3011 | Loss/suspension of right to be a legal guardian (3) |
| 3012 | Loss/suspension of right of decoration or title |
| 3013 | Prohibition to exercise professional, commercial or social activity |
| 3014 | Prohibition from working or activity with minors |
| 3015 | Obligation to close an establishment |
| 3016 | Prohibition to hold or to carry weapons |
| 3017 | Withdrawal of a hunting/fishing license |

| Code | Categories and sub-categories of offences |
|---|---|
| 3018 | Prohibition to issue cheques or to use payment/credit cards |
| 3019 | Prohibition to keep animals |
| 3020 | Prohibition to possess or use certain items other than weapons |
| 3021 | Prohibition to play certain games/sports |
| 4000<br>open category | **Prohibition or expulsion from territory** |
| 4001 | Prohibition from national territory |
| 4002 | Expulsion from national territory |
| 5000<br>open category | **Personal obligation** |
| 5001 | Submission to medical treatment or other forms of therapy |
| 5002 | Submission to a social-educational programme |
| 5003 | Obligation to be under the care/control of the family |
| 5004 | Educational measures |
| 5005 | Socio-judicial probation |
| 5006 | Obligation of training/working |
| 5007 | Obligation to provide judicial authorities with specific information |
| 5008 | Obligation to publish the judgment |
| 5009 | Obligation to compensate for the prejudice caused by the offence |
| 6000<br>open category | **Penalty on personal property** |
| 6001 | Confiscation |
| 6002 | Demolition |
| 6003 | Restoration |
| 7000<br>open category | **Placing in an institution** |
| 7001 | Placing in a psychiatric institution |
| 7002 | Placing in a detoxification institution |
| 7003 | Placing in an educational institution |
| 8000<br>open category | **Financial penalty** |
| 8001 | Fine |
| 8002 | Day-fine [4] |
| 8003 | Fine for the benefit of a special recipient [5] |
| 9000<br>open category | **Working penalty** |
| 9001 | Community service or work |
| 9002 | Community service or work accompanied with other restrictive measures |

| Code | Categories and sub-categories of offences |
|---|---|
| 10000<br>open category | **Military penalty** |
| 10001 | Loss of military rank (6) |
| 10002 | Expulsion from professional military service |
| 10003 | Military imprisonment |
| 11000<br>open category | **Exemption/deferment of sentence/penalty, warning** |
| 12000<br>open category | **Other penalties and measures** |

(1) Fixed or mobile placement.
(2) Reapplication in order to obtain a new driving licence is necessary.
(3) Legal guardian for a person who is legally incompetent or for a minor.
(4) Fine expressed in daily units.
(5) E.g.: for an institution, association, foundation or a victim.
(6) Military demotion.

| Parameters (to be specified where applicable) | |
|---|---|
| ø | Penalty |
| m | Measure |
| a | Suspended penalty/measure |
| b | Partially suspended penalty/measure |
| c | Suspended penalty/measure with probation/supervision |
| d | Partially suspended penalty/measure with probation/supervision |
| e | Conversion of penalty/measure |
| f | Alternative penalty/measure imposed as principal penalty |
| g | Alternative penalty/measure imposed initially in case of non-respect of the principal penalty |
| h | Revocation of suspended penalty/measure |
| i | Subsequent formation of an overall penalty |
| j | Interruption of enforcement/postponement of the penalty/measure (1) |
| k | Remission of the penalty |
| l | Remission of the suspended penalty |
| n | End of penalty |
| o | Pardon |
| p | Amnesty |
| q | Release on parole (liberation of a person before end of the sentence under certain conditions) |
| r | Rehabilitation (with or without the deletion of penalty from criminal records) |
| s | Penalty or measure specific to minors |
| t | Non-criminal ruling (2) |

(1) Does not lead to avoidance of enforcement of penalty.
(2) This parameter will be indicated only when such information is provided in reply to the request received by the Member State of nationality of the person concerned.

# Decision 2009/371 establishing the European Police Office (Europol), 6 April 2009

**[OJ 2009, L 121/37–66]**

15.5.2009 EN Official Journal of the European Union L 121/37

III

*(Acts adopted under the EU Treaty)*

# ACTS ADOPTED UNDER TITLE VI OF THE EU TREATY

## COUNCIL DECISION
## of 6 April 2009
## establishing the European Police Office (Europol)

(2009/371/JHA)

THE COUNCIL OF THE EUROPEAN UNION,

Having regard to the Treaty on European Union, and in particular Article 30(1)(b), Article 30(2) and Article 34(2)(c) thereof,

Having regard to the proposal from the Commission,

Having regard to the opinion of the European Parliament [1],

Whereas:

(1) The establishment of a European Police Office (Europol) was agreed in the Treaty on European Union of 7 February 1992, and regulated in the Convention based on Article K.3 of the Treaty on European Union, on the establishment of a European Police Office (Europol Convention) [2].

(2) The Europol Convention has been the subject of a number of amendments enshrined in three protocols which have entered into force after a lengthy process of ratification. Consequently, replacing the Convention by a Decision will ease further amendments as necessary.

(3) Simplification and improvement of Europol's legal framework can be partially achieved by the establishment of Europol as an entity of the Union, funded from the general budget of the European Union, due to the subsequent application of the general rules and procedures.

(4) Recent legal instruments setting up similar Union entities in the areas covered by Title VI of the Treaty on European Union (Council Decision 2002/187/JHA of 28 February 2002 setting up Eurojust with a view to reinforcing the fight against serious crime [3] and Decision 2005/681/JHA of 20 September 2005 establishing the European Police College (CEPOL) [4] have taken the form of Council Decisions, since such Decisions are more easily adaptable to changing circumstances and emerging political priorities.

(5) Establishing Europol as an entity of the Union, funded from the general budget of the European Union, will enhance the role of the European Parliament in the control of Europol through the involvement of the European Parliament in the adoption of that budget, including the establishment plan, and the discharge procedure.

(6) Making Europol subject to the general rules and procedures applicable to similar Union entities will ensure administrative simplification, which will allow Europol to devote more of its resources to its core tasks.

(7) Further simplification and improvement of Europol's functioning can be achieved through measures aimed at widening the possibilities for Europol's assisting and supporting the competent law enforcement authorities of the Member States, without providing for executive powers for Europol staff.

(8) One such improvement is to ensure that Europol can assist the competent authorities of the Member States in combating specific forms of serious crime, without the current limitation that there must be factual indications that an organised criminal structure is involved.

(9) The establishment of joint investigation teams should be encouraged and it is important that Europol staff should be able to participate in them. To ensure that such participation is possible in every Member State, it should be guaranteed that Europol staff do not benefit from the application of immunities while they are participating in a support capacity in joint investigation teams. That will be possible after the adoption of a Regulation to that effect on the basis of Article 16 of the Protocol on the Privileges and Immunities of the European Communities.

(10) Europol national units should have direct access to all data in the Europol Information System to avoid unnecessary procedures.

[1] Opinion of 17 January 2008 (not yet published in the Official Journal).
[2] OJ C 316, 27.11.1995, p. 1.
[3] OJ L 63, 6.3.2002, p. 1.
[4] OJ L 256, 1.10.2005, p. 63.

(11) In order to achieve its objectives, Europol processes personal data by automated means or in structured manual files. Accordingly, the necessary steps should be taken to guarantee a level of data protection which corresponds at least to that which results from the application of the principles of the Council of Europe Convention for the Protection of Individuals with regard to Automatic Processing of Personal Data, signed in Strasbourg on 28 January 1981, together with subsequent amendments thereto, once such amendments are in force between the Member States.

(12) A Council Framework Decision on the protection of personal data processed in the framework of police and judicial cooperation in criminal matters will be applicable to the transfer of personal data by Member States to Europol. The relevant set of data-protection provisions in this Decision will not be affected by that Framework Decision and this Decision should contain specific provisions on the protection of personal data regulating these matters in greater detail because of the particular nature, functions and competences of Europol.

(13) There is a need for a Data Protection Officer who should be responsible for ensuring, in an independent manner, the lawfulness of data processing and compliance with the provisions of this Decision concerning the processing of personal data, including the processing of personal data on Europol staff which are protected by Article 24 of Regulation (EC) No 45/2001 of the European Parliament and of the Council of 18 December 2000 on the protection of individuals with regard to the processing of personal data by the Community institutions and bodies and on the free movement of such data [1].

(14) Europol's existing possibilities for the creation and management of information processing systems in support of its tasks should be widened. Such additional information processing systems should be established and maintained in accordance with the general principles of data protection enshrined in the Council of Europe Convention for the Protection of Individuals with regard to Automatic Processing of Personal Data of 28 January 1981 and in Recommendation No R (87) 15 of the Committee of Ministers of the Council of Europe of 17 September 1987, by means of a Management Board decision approved by the Council.

(15) This Decision allows the principle of public access to official documents to be taken into account.

(16) For the purpose of fulfilling its mission, Europol should cooperate with European institutions, bodies, offices and agencies, including Eurojust, ensuring an adequate level of data protection.

(17) Europol should be able to conclude agreements and working arrangements with Union or Community institutions, bodies, offices and agencies in order to increase mutual effectiveness in combating serious forms of crime which come within the respective competence of both parties and to avoid the duplication of work.

(18) Europol's possibilities for cooperation with third States and organisations should be rationalised in order to ensure consistency with the general policy of the Union in that respect and new provisions on the manner in which such cooperation should take place in future should be laid down.

(19) The governance of Europol should be improved through simplified procedures, more general descriptions of the tasks of the Management Board and the establishment of a common rule that all decisions should be taken by a majority of two thirds.

(20) It is also desirable to provide for enhanced control over Europol by the European Parliament in order to ensure that Europol remains a fully accountable and transparent organisation, due account being taken of the need to safeguard the confidentiality of operational information.

(21) Judicial control over Europol will be exercised in accordance with Article 35 of the Treaty on European Union.

(22) In order to enable Europol to continue to fulfil its tasks to the best of its abilities, carefully designed transitional measures should be laid down.

(23) Since the objective of this Decision, namely the establishment of an entity responsible for law-enforcement cooperation at Union level, cannot be sufficiently achieved by the Member States and can, therefore, by reason of the scale and effects of the action, be better achieved at Union level, the Union may adopt measures, in accordance with the principle of subsidiarity, as set out in Article 5 of the Treaty establishing the European Community and referred to in Article 2 of the Treaty on European Union. In accordance with the principle of proportionality, as set out in Article 5 of the Treaty establishing the European Community, this Decision does not go beyond what is necessary in order to achieve that objective.

[1] OJ L 8, 12.1.2001, p. 1.

(24) This Decision respects the fundamental rights and observes the principles recognised in particular by the Charter of Fundamental Rights of the European Union,

HAS DECIDED AS FOLLOWS:

CHAPTER I

**ESTABLISHMENT AND TASKS**

*Article 1*

**Establishment**

1. This Decision replaces the provisions of the Convention based on Article K.3 of the Treaty on European Union, on the establishment of a European Police Office (Europol Convention).

Europol shall have its seat in The Hague, the Netherlands.

2. Europol, as referred to in this Decision, shall be regarded as the legal successor of Europol, as established by the Europol Convention.

3. Europol shall liaise with a single national unit in each Member State, to be established or designated in accordance with Article 8.

*Article 2*

**Legal capacity**

1. Europol shall have legal personality.

2. In each Member State Europol shall enjoy the most extensive legal and contractual capacity accorded to legal persons under that Member State's law. Europol may, in particular, acquire and dispose of movable and immovable property and may be a party to legal proceedings.

3. Europol shall be empowered to conclude a Headquarters Agreement with the Kingdom of the Netherlands.

*Article 3*

**Objective**

The objective of Europol shall be to support and strengthen action by the competent authorities of the Member States and their mutual cooperation in preventing and combating organised crime, terrorism and other forms of serious crime affecting two or more Member States.

For the purposes of this Decision, 'competent authorities' shall mean all public bodies existing in the Member States which are responsible under national law for preventing and combating criminal offences.

*Article 4*

**Competence**

1. Europol's competence shall cover organised crime, terrorism and other forms of serious crime as listed in the Annex affecting two or more Member States in such a way as to require a common approach by the Member States owing to the scale, significance and consequences of the offences.

2. On a recommendation by the Management Board, the Council shall lay down its priorities for Europol, taking particular account of strategic analyses and threat assessments prepared by Europol.

3. Europol's competence shall also cover related criminal offences. The following offences shall be regarded as related criminal offences:

(a) criminal offences committed in order to procure the means of perpetrating acts in respect of which Europol is competent;

(b) criminal offences committed in order to facilitate or carry out acts in respect of which Europol is competent;

(c) criminal offences committed to ensure the impunity of acts in respect of which Europol is competent.

*Article 5*

**Tasks**

1. Europol shall have the following principal tasks:

(a) to collect, store, process, analyse and exchange information and intelligence;

(b) to notify the competent authorities of the Member States without delay via the national unit referred to in Article 8 of information concerning them and of any connections identified between criminal offences;

(c) to aid investigations in the Member States, in particular by forwarding all relevant information to the national units;

(d) to ask the competent authorities of the Member States concerned to initiate, conduct or coordinate investigations and to suggest the setting up of joint investigation teams in specific cases;

(e) to provide intelligence and analytical support to Member States in connection with major international events;

(f) to prepare threat assessments, strategic analyses and general situation reports relating to its objective, including organised crime threat assessments.

2. The tasks referred to in paragraph 1 shall include providing support to Member States in their tasks of gathering and analysing information from the Internet in order to assist in the identification of criminal activities facilitated by or committed using the Internet.

3. Europol shall have the following additional tasks:

(a) to develop specialist knowledge of the investigative procedures of the competent authorities of the Member States and to provide advice on investigations;

(b) to provide strategic intelligence to assist and promote the efficient and effective use of the resources available at national and Union level for operational activities and the support of such activities.

4. Additionally, in the context of its objective under Article 3, Europol may, in accordance with the staffing and budgetary resources at its disposal and within the limits set by the Management Board, assist Member States through support, advice and research in the following areas:

(a) the training of members of their competent authorities, where appropriate in cooperation with the European Police College;

(b) the organisation and equipment of those authorities by facilitating the provision of technical support between the Member States;

(c) crime prevention methods;

(d) technical and forensic methods and analysis, and investigative procedures.

5. Europol shall also act as the Central Office for combating euro counterfeiting in accordance with Council Decision 2005/511/JHA of 12 July 2005 on protecting the euro against counterfeiting, by designating Europol as the Central Office for combating euro counterfeiting [1]. Europol may also encourage the coordination of measures carried out in order to fight euro counterfeiting by the competent authorities of the Member States or in the context of joint investigation teams, where appropriate in liaison with Union entities and third States' bodies. Upon request, Europol may financially support investigations of euro counterfeiting.

(1) OJ L 185, 16.7.2005, p. 35.

*Article 6*

**Participation in joint investigation teams**

1. Europol staff may participate in supporting capacity in joint investigation teams, including such teams set up in accordance with Article 1 of Council Framework Decision 2002/465/JHA of 13 June 2002 on joint investigation teams [2], in accordance with Article 13 of the Convention of 29 May 2000 on mutual assistance in criminal matters between the Member States of the European Union [3], or in accordance with Article 24 of the Convention of 18 December 1997 on mutual assistance and cooperation between customs administrations [4], in so far as those teams are investigating criminal offences in respect of which Europol is competent under Article 4 of this Decision.

Europol staff may, within the limits provided for by the law of the Member States in which a joint investigation team is operating and in accordance with the arrangement referred to in paragraph 2, assist in all activities and exchange information with all members of the joint investigation team, in accordance with paragraph 4. They shall not, however, take part in the taking of any coercive measures.

2. The administrative implementation of participation by Europol staff in a joint investigation team shall be laid down in an arrangement between the Director and the competent authorities of the Member States participating in the joint investigation team, with the involvement of the national units. The rules governing such arrangements shall be determined by the Management Board.

3. The rules referred to in paragraph 2 shall specify the conditions under which Europol staff are placed at the disposal of the joint investigation team.

4. In accordance with the arrangement referred to in paragraph 2, Europol staff may liaise directly with members of a joint investigation team and provide members and seconded members of the joint investigation team, in accordance with this Decision, with information from any of the components of the information processing systems referred to in Article 10. In the event of such direct liaison, Europol shall at the same time inform the national units of the Member States represented in the team as well as those of the Member States which provided the information thereof.

(2) OJ L 162, 20.6.2002, p. 1.
(3) OJ C 197, 12.7.2000, p. 3.
(4) OJ C 24, 23.1.1998, p. 2.

5. Information obtained by a Europol staff member while part of a joint investigation team may, with the consent and under the responsibility of the Member State which provided the information, be included in any of the components of the information processing systems referred to in Article 10 under the conditions laid down in this Decision.

6. During the operations of a joint investigation team, Europol staff shall, with respect to offences committed against or by them, be subject to the national law of the Member State of operation applicable to persons with comparable functions.

*Article 7*

**Requests by Europol for the initiation of criminal investigations**

1. Member States shall deal with any request by Europol to initiate, conduct or coordinate investigations in specific cases and shall give such requests due consideration. The Member States shall inform Europol whether the investigation requested will be initiated.

2. Before making a request for the initiation of criminal investigations, Europol shall inform Eurojust accordingly.

3. If the competent authorities of the Member State decide not to comply with a request made by Europol, they shall inform Europol of their decision and of the reasons therefor unless they are unable to give their reasons because:

(a) to do so would harm essential national security interests; or

(b) to do so would jeopardise the success of investigations under way or the safety of individuals.

4. Replies to requests by Europol for the initiation, conduct or coordination of investigations in specific cases and information for Europol concerning the results of investigations shall be forwarded through the competent authorities of the Member States in accordance with the rules laid down in this Decision and the relevant national legislation.

*Article 8*

**National units**

1. Each Member State shall establish or designate a national unit responsible for carrying out the tasks set out in this Article. An official shall be appointed in each Member State as the head of the national unit.

2. The national unit shall be the only liaison body between Europol and the competent authorities of the Member States. Member States, however, may allow direct contacts between designated competent authorities and Europol subject to conditions determined by the Member State in question, including prior involvement of the national unit.

The national unit shall at the same time receive from Europol any information exchanged in the course of direct contacts between Europol and designated competent authorities. Relations between the national unit and the competent authorities shall be governed by national law, and in particular, the relevant national constitutional requirements.

3. Member States shall take the measures necessary to ensure that their national units are able to fulfil their tasks and, in particular, have access to relevant national data.

4. The national units shall:

(a) supply Europol on their own initiative with the information and intelligence necessary for it to carry out its tasks;

(b) respond to Europol's requests for information, intelligence and advice;

(c) keep information and intelligence up to date;

(d) evaluate information and intelligence in accordance with national law for the competent authorities and transmit that material to them;

(e) issue requests for advice, information, intelligence and analysis to Europol;

(f) supply Europol with information for storage in its databases;

(g) ensure compliance with the law in every exchange of information between themselves and Europol.

5. Without prejudice to the Member States' discharging the responsibilities incumbent upon them with regard to the maintenance of law and order and the safeguarding of internal security, a national unit shall not in any particular case be obliged to supply information or intelligence if that would entail:

(a) harming essential national security interests;

(b) jeopardising the success of a current investigation or the safety of individuals; or

(c) disclosing information relating to organisations or specific intelligence activities in the field of State security.

6. The costs incurred by the national units in communications with Europol shall be borne by the Member States and, apart from the costs of connection, shall not be charged to Europol.

7. The heads of the national units shall meet on a regular basis to assist Europol on operational matters, on their own initiative or at the request of the Management Board or the Director, in particular to:

(a) consider and develop proposals that will improve Europol's operational effectiveness and encourage commitment from Member States;

(b) evaluate the reports and analyses drafted by Europol in accordance with Article 5(1)(f) and develop measures in order to help to implement their findings;

(c) provide support in the establishment of joint investigation teams involving Europol in accordance with Article 5(1)(d) and Article 6.

*Article 9*

**Liaison officers**

1. Each national unit shall second at least one liaison officer to Europol. Except as otherwise stipulated in specific provisions of this Decision, liaison officers shall be subject to the national law of the seconding Member State.

2. Liaison officers shall constitute the national liaison bureaux at Europol and shall be instructed by their national units to represent the interests of the latter within Europol in accordance with the national law of the seconding Member State and the provisions applicable to the administration of Europol.

3. Without prejudice to Article 8(4) and (5), liaison officers shall:

(a) provide Europol with information from the seconding national unit;

(b) forward information from Europol to the seconding national unit;

(c) cooperate with Europol staff by providing information and giving advice; and

(d) assist in the exchange of information from their national units with the liaison officers of other Member States under their responsibility in accordance with national law. Such bilateral exchanges may also cover crimes outwith the competence of Europol, as far as allowed by national law.

4. Article 35 shall apply *mutatis mutandis* to the activities of liaison officers.

5. The rights and obligations of liaison officers in relation to Europol shall be determined by the Management Board.

6. Liaison officers shall enjoy the privileges and immunities necessary for the performance of their tasks in accordance with Article 51(2).

7. Europol shall ensure that liaison officers are fully informed of and associated with all of its activities, as far as that is compatible with their position.

8. Europol shall provide Member States free of charge with the necessary premises in the Europol building and adequate support for the performance of the activities of their liaison officers. All other costs which arise in connection with the secondment of liaison officers shall be borne by the seconding Member State, including the costs of equipment for liaison officers, unless the Management Board recommends otherwise in specific cases when drawing up Europol's budget.

CHAPTER II

**INFORMATION PROCESSING SYSTEMS**

*Article 10*

**Information processing**

1. In so far as it is necessary for the achievement of its objectives, Europol shall process information and intelligence, including personal data, in accordance with this Decision. Europol shall establish and maintain the Europol Information System referred to in Article 11 and the analysis work files referred to in Article 14. Europol may also establish and maintain other systems processing personal data set up in accordance with paragraphs 2 and 3 of this Article.

2. The Management Board, acting on a proposal from the Director after having taken into account the possibilities offered by existing Europol information processing systems and after consulting the Joint Supervisory Body, shall decide on the establishment of a new system processing personal data. That Management Board decision shall be submitted to the Council for approval.

3. The Management Board decision referred to in paragraph 2 shall determine the conditions and limitations under which Europol may establish the new system processing personal data. The Management Board decision may allow processing of personal data relating to the categories of persons referred to in Article 14(1), but not the processing of personal data revealing racial or ethnic origin, political opinions, religious or philosophical beliefs or trade-union membership and the processing of data concerning health or sex life. The Management Board decision shall ensure that the measures and principles referred to in Articles 18, 19, 20, 27, 29 and 35 are properly implemented. In particular, the Management Board decision shall define the purpose of the new system, access to and the use of the data, as well as time limits for the storage and deletion of the data.

4. Europol may process data for the purpose of determining whether such data are relevant to its tasks and can be included in the Europol Information System referred to in Article 11, in the analysis work files referred to in Article 14 or in other systems processing personal data established in accordance with paragraphs 2 and 3 of this Article. The Management Board, acting on a proposal from the Director and after consulting the Joint Supervisory Body, shall determine the conditions relating to the processing of such data, in particular with respect to access to and the use of the data, as well as time limits for the storage and deletion of the data that may not exceed six months, having due regard to the principles referred to in Article 27. That Management Board decision shall be submitted to the Council for approval.

*Article 11*

**Europol Information System**

1. Europol shall maintain the Europol Information System.

2. Europol shall ensure compliance with the provisions of this Decision governing operation of the Europol Information System. It shall be responsible for the proper working of the Europol Information System in technical and operational respects and shall, in particular, take all measures necessary to ensure that the measures referred to in Articles 20, 29, 31 and 35 regarding the Europol Information System are properly implemented.

3. The national unit in each Member State shall be responsible for communication with the Europol Information System. It shall, in particular, be responsible for the security measures referred to in Article 35 in respect of the data-processing equipment used within the territory of the Member State in question, for the review provided for in Article 20 and, in so far as required under the laws, regulations, administrative provisions and procedures of that Member State, for the proper implementation of this Decision in other respects.

*Article 12*

**Content of the Europol Information System**

1. The Europol Information System may be used to process only such data as are necessary for the performance of Europol's tasks. The data input shall relate to:

(a) persons who, in accordance with the national law of the Member State concerned, are suspected of having committed or having taken part in a criminal offence in respect of which Europol is competent or who have been convicted of such an offence;

(b) persons regarding whom there are factual indications or reasonable grounds under the national law of the Member State concerned to believe that they will commit criminal offences in respect of which Europol is competent.

2. Data relating to the persons referred to in paragraph 1 may include only the following particulars:

(a) surname, maiden name, given names and any alias or assumed name;

(b) date and place of birth;

(c) nationality;

(d) sex;

(e) place of residence, profession and whereabouts of the person concerned;

(f) social security numbers, driving licences, identification documents and passport data; and

(g) where necessary, other characteristics likely to assist in identification, including any specific objective physical characteristics not subject to change such as dactyloscopic data and DNA profile (established from the non-coding part of DNA).

3. In addition to the data referred to in paragraph 2, the Europol Information System may also be used to process the following particulars concerning the persons referred to in paragraph 1:

(a) criminal offences, alleged criminal offences and when, where and how they were (allegedly) committed;

(b) means which were or may be used to commit those criminal offences including information concerning legal persons;

(c) departments handling the case and their filing references;

(d) suspected membership of a criminal organisation;

(e) convictions, where they relate to criminal offences in respect of which Europol is competent;

(f) inputting party.

These data may also be input when they do not yet contain any references to persons. Where Europol inputs the data itself, as well as when it gives its filing reference, it shall also indicate the source of the data.

4. Additional information held by Europol or national units concerning the persons referred to in paragraph 1 may be communicated to any national unit or Europol should either so request. National units shall do so in compliance with their national law.

Where the additional information concerns one or more related criminal offences as defined in Article 4(3), the data stored in the Europol Information System shall be marked accordingly to enable national units and Europol to exchange information concerning the related criminal offences.

5. If proceedings against the person concerned are definitively dropped or if that person is definitively acquitted, the data relating to the case in respect of which either decision has been taken shall be deleted.

*Article 13*

**Use of the Europol Information System**

1. National units, liaison officers, the Director, Deputy Directors and duly empowered Europol staff shall have the right to input data directly into the Europol Information System and retrieve them from it. Data may be retrieved by Europol where that is necessary for the performance of its tasks in a particular case. Retrieval by the national units and liaison officers shall be effected in accordance with the laws, regulations, administrative provisions and procedures of the accessing party, subject to any additional provisions laid down in this Decision.

2. Only the party which has input data may modify, correct or delete such data. Where another party has reason to believe that data as referred to in Article 12(2) are incorrect or wishes to supplement them, it shall immediately inform the inputting party. The inputting party shall examine such information without delay and if necessary modify, supplement, correct or delete the data immediately.

3. Where the system contains data as referred to in Article 12(3) concerning a person, any party may input additional data as referred to in that provision. Where there is an obvious contradiction between the data input, the parties concerned shall consult each other and reach agreement.

4. Where a party intends to delete altogether data as referred to in Article 12(2) which it has input concerning a person and data as referred to in Article 12(3) in respect of the same person have been input by other parties, responsibility in terms of data-protection legislation pursuant to Article 29(1) and the right to modify, supplement, correct and delete such data pursuant to Article 12(2) shall be transferred to the next party to have input data as referred to in Article 12(3) on that person. The party intending to delete shall inform the party to which responsibility in terms of data protection is transferred of its intention.

5. Responsibility for the permissibility of retrieval from, input into and modifications within the Europol Information System shall lie with the retrieving, inputting or modifying party. It must be possible to identify that party. The communication of information between national units and the competent authorities of the Member States shall be governed by national law.

6. In addition to the national units and persons referred to in paragraph 1, competent authorities designated to that effect by the Member States may also query the Europol Information System. However, the result of the query shall indicate only whether the data requested are available in the Europol Information System. Further information may then be obtained via the national unit.

7. Information concerning the competent authorities designated in accordance with paragraph 6, including subsequent modifications, shall be transmitted to the General Secretariat of the Council, which shall publish the information in the *Official Journal of the European Union*.

*Article 14*

**Analysis work files**

1. Where this is necessary for the performance of its tasks, Europol may store, modify, and use data concerning criminal offences in respect of which it is competent, including data on the related criminal offences referred to in Article 4(3), in analysis work files. The analysis work files may contain data on the following categories of persons:

(a) persons as referred to in Article 12(1);

(b) persons who might be called on to testify in investigations in connection with the offences under consideration or in subsequent criminal proceedings;

(c) persons who have been the victims of one of the offences under consideration or with regard to whom certain facts give reason to believe that they could be the victims of such an offence;

(d) contacts and associates; and

(e) persons who can provide information on the criminal offences under consideration.

The processing of personal data revealing racial or ethnic origin, political opinions, religious or philosophical beliefs or trade-union membership and the processing of data concerning health or sex life shall not be permitted unless strictly necessary for the purposes of the file concerned and unless such data supplement other personal data already input in that file. The selection of a particular group of persons solely on the basis of the abovementioned sensitive data, in breach of the aforementioned rules with regard to purpose, shall be prohibited.

The Council, acting by qualified majority after consulting the European Parliament, shall adopt implementing rules for analysis work files prepared by the Management Board, which shall previously have obtained the opinion of the Joint Supervisory Body, containing additional details, in particular with regard to the categories of personal data referred to in this Article, to the security of the data concerned and to the internal supervision of their use.

2. Analysis work files shall be opened for the purposes of analysis defined as the assembly, processing or use of data with the aim of assisting criminal investigations. Each analysis project shall entail the establishment of an analysis group closely associating the following participants:

(a) analysts and other Europol staff designated by the Director;

(b) liaison officers and/or experts from the Member States supplying the information or concerned by the analysis within the meaning of paragraph 4.

Only analysts shall be authorised to input data into the file concerned and modify such data. All participants in the analysis group may retrieve data from the file.

3. At the request of Europol or on their own initiative, national units shall, subject to Article 8(5), communicate to Europol all the information which it may require for the purpose of a particular analysis work file. Member States shall communicate such data only where processing thereof for the purposes of preventing, analysing or combating offences is also authorised by their national law. Depending on their degree of urgency, data from designated competent authorities may be routed directly to the analysis work file in accordance with Article 8(2).

4. If an analysis is of a general nature and of a strategic type, all Member States, through liaison officers and/or experts, shall be fully associated in the findings thereof, in particular through the communication of reports drawn up by Europol.

If the analysis bears on specific cases not concerning all Member States and has a direct operational aim, representatives of the following Member States shall participate therein:

(a) Member States which were the source of the information giving rise to the decision to open the analysis work file, or those which are directly concerned by that information, and Member States subsequently invited by the analysis group to take part in the analysis because they are also becoming concerned;

(b) Member States which learn from consulting the index function referred to in Article 15 that they need to be informed and assert that need to know under the conditions laid down in paragraph 5 of this Article.

5. The need to be informed may be claimed by authorised liaison officers. Each Member State shall nominate and authorise a limited number of such liaison officers.

A liaison officer shall claim the need to be informed as provided for in point (b) of the second subparagraph of paragraph 4 by means of a written reasoned statement approved by the authority to which he is subordinate in his Member State and forwarded to all the participants in the analysis. He shall then be associated automatically in the analysis in progress.

If an objection is raised in the analysis group, automatic association shall be deferred until the completion of a conciliation procedure, which shall comprise three stages as follows:

(a) the participants in the analysis shall endeavour to reach agreement with the liaison officer claiming the need to be informed. They shall have no more than eight days for that purpose;

(b) if no agreement is reached, the heads of the national units concerned and the Director shall meet within three days and try to reach agreement;

L 121/46 EN Official Journal of the European Union 15.5.2009

(c) if the disagreement persists, the representatives of the parties concerned on the Management Board shall meet within eight days. If the Member State concerned does not waive its need to be informed, association of that Member State shall be decided on by consensus.

6. The Member State communicating an item of data to Europol shall be the sole judge of the degree of its sensitivity and variations thereof and shall be entitled to determine the conditions for the handling of the data. Any dissemination or operational use of data communicated shall be decided on by the Member State that communicated the data to Europol. If it cannot be determined which Member State communicated the data to Europol, the decision on dissemination or operational use of data shall be taken by the participants in the analysis. A Member State or an associated expert joining an analysis in progress may not, in particular, disseminate or use the data without the prior agreement of the Member States initially concerned.

7. By way of derogation from paragraph 6, in cases in which Europol finds, after the time of inclusion of data in an analysis work file, that those data relate to a person or object on which data submitted by another Member State or third party were already input in the file, the Member State or third party concerned shall be informed immediately of the link identified, in accordance with Article 17.

8. Europol may invite experts from the entities referred to in Articles 22(1) or 23(1) to be associated with the activities of an analysis group, where:

(a) an agreement or working arrangement such as referred to in Articles 22(2) and 23(2) which contains appropriate provisions on the exchange of information, including the transmission of personal data, and on the confidentiality of exchanged information, is in force between Europol and the entity concerned;

(b) the association of the experts from the entity is in the interest of the Member States;

(c) the entity is directly concerned by the analysis work; and

(d) all participants agree on the association of the experts from the entity with the activities of the analysis group.

Under the conditions laid down in points (b), (c) and (d) of the first subparagraph, Europol shall invite experts of the European Anti-Fraud Office to be associated with the activities of the analysis group if the analysis project concerns fraud or any other illegal activities affecting the financial interests of the European Communities.

The association of experts from an entity with the activities of an analysis group shall be subject to an arrangement between Europol and the entity. The rules governing such arrangements shall be determined by the Management Board.

Details of the arrangements between Europol and entities shall be sent to the Joint Supervisory Body, which may address any comments it deems necessary to the Management Board.

*Article 15*

**Index function**

1. An index function shall be created by Europol for the data stored in the analysis work files.

2. The Director, the Deputy Directors, duly empowered Europol staff, liaison officers and duly empowered members of national units shall have the right to access the index function. The index function shall be such that it is clear to the person using it, from the data being consulted, whether an analysis work file contains data which are of interest for the performance of the tasks of the person using the index function.

3. Access to the index function shall be defined in such a way that it is possible to determine whether or not an item of information is stored in an analysis work file, but not to establish connections or further conclusions regarding the content of the file.

4. The Management Board shall define the detailed procedures for the design of the index function, including the conditions of access to the index function, after obtaining the advice of the Joint Supervisory Body.

*Article 16*

**Order opening an analysis work file**

1. For every analysis work file, the Director shall specify in an order opening the file:

(a) the file name;

(b) the purpose of the file;

(c) the groups of persons concerning whom data are stored;

(d) the nature of the data to be stored and personal data revealing racial or ethnic origin, political opinions, religious or philosophical beliefs or trade-union membership and data concerning health or sex life which are strictly necessary;

(e) the general context leading to the decision to open the file;

(f) the participants in the analysis group at the time of opening the file;

(g) the conditions under which the personal data stored in the file may be communicated, to which recipients and under what procedure;

(h) the time limits for examination of the data and the duration of storage;

(i) the method of establishment of the audit log.

2. The Management Board and the Joint Supervisory Body shall immediately be informed by the Director of the order opening the file or any subsequent change in the particulars referred to in paragraph 1 and shall receive the dossier. The Joint Supervisory Body may address any comments it deems necessary to the Management Board. The Director may request the Joint Supervisory Body to do that within a specified period of time.

3. The analysis work file shall be retained for a maximum period of three years. Before the expiry of that three-year period, Europol shall review the need for the continuation of the file. When it is strictly necessary for the purpose of the file, the Director may order the continuation of the file for a further period of three years. The Management Board and the Joint Supervisory Body shall immediately be informed by the Director of the elements in the file justifying the strict need for its continuation. The Joint Supervisory Body shall address any comments it deems necessary to the Management Board. The Director may request the Joint Supervisory Body to do that within a specified period of time.

4. At any time the Management Board may instruct the Director to amend an opening order or to close an analysis work file. The Management Board shall decide on what date any such amendment or closure will take effect.

CHAPTER III

## COMMON PROVISIONS ON INFORMATION PROCESSING

*Article 17*

### Duty to notify

Without prejudice to Article 14(6) and (7), Europol shall promptly notify the national units and, if the national units so request, their liaison officers of any information concerning their Member State and of connections identified between criminal offences in respect of which Europol is competent under Article 4. Information and intelligence concerning other serious crime of which Europol becomes aware in the course of its duties may also be communicated.

*Article 18*

### Provisions on control of retrievals

Europol shall establish, in cooperation with the Member States, appropriate control mechanisms to allow the verification of the legality of retrievals from any of its automated data files used to process personal data and to allow Member States access to the audit logs on request. The data thus collected shall be used only for the purpose of such verification by Europol and the supervisory bodies referred to in Articles 33 and 34 and shall be deleted after 18 months, unless the data are further required for ongoing control. The Management Board shall decide on the details of such control mechanisms after consulting the Joint Supervisory Body.

*Article 19*

### Rules on the use of data

1. Personal data retrieved from any of Europol's data processing files or communicated by any other appropriate means shall be transmitted or used only by the competent authorities of the Member States in order to prevent and combat crimes in respect of which Europol is competent, and to prevent and combat other serious forms of crime. Europol shall use the data only for the performance of its tasks.

2. If, in the case of certain data, the communicating Member State or the communicating third State or third body stipulates particular restrictions on use to which such data is subject in that Member State, third State or third body, such restrictions shall also be complied with by the user of the data except in the specific case where national law lays down that the restrictions on use be waived for judicial authorities, legislative bodies or any other independent body set up under the law and made responsible for supervising the national competent authorities. In such cases, the data shall be used only after consultation of the communicating Member State the interests and views of which shall be taken into account as far as possible.

3. Use of the data for other purposes or by authorities other than the national competent authorities shall be possible only after consultation of the Member State which transmitted the data in so far as the national law of that Member State permits.

*Article 20*

**Time limits for the storage and deletion of data**

1. Europol shall hold data in data files only for as long as is necessary for the performance of its tasks. The need for continued storage shall be reviewed no later than three years after the input of data. Review of data stored in the Europol Information System and their deletion shall be carried out by the inputting unit. Review of data stored in other Europol data files and their deletion shall be carried out by Europol. Europol shall automatically inform the Member States three months in advance of the expiry of the time limits for reviewing the storage of data.

2. During the review, the units referred to in the third and fourth sentences of paragraph 1 may decide on the continued storage of data until the following review which shall take place after another period of three years if that is still necessary for the performance of Europol's tasks. If no decision is taken on the continued storage of data, those data shall be deleted automatically.

3. Where a Member State deletes from its national data files data communicated to Europol which are stored in other Europol data files, it shall inform Europol accordingly. In such cases, Europol shall delete the data unless it has further interest in them, based on intelligence that is more extensive than that possessed by the communicating Member State. Europol shall inform the Member State concerned of the continued storage of such data.

4. Such data shall not be deleted if this would damage the interests of a data subject who requires protection. In such cases, the data shall be used only with the consent of the data subject.

*Article 21*

**Access to data from other information systems**

In so far as Europol is entitled under Union, international or national legal instruments to gain computerised access to data from other information systems, of national or international nature, Europol may retrieve personal data by such means if that is necessary for the performance of its tasks. The applicable provisions of such Union, international or national legal instruments shall govern access to and the use of this data by Europol, in so far as they provide for stricter rules on access and use than those of this Decision.

CHAPTER IV

**RELATIONS WITH PARTNERS**

*Article 22*

**Relations with Union or Community institutions, bodies, offices and agencies**

1. In so far as it is relevant to the performance of its tasks, Europol may establish and maintain cooperative relations with the institutions, bodies, offices and agencies set up by, or on the basis of, the Treaty on European Union and the Treaties establishing the European Communities, in particular:

(a) Eurojust;

(b) the European Anti-Fraud Office (OLAF) [1];

(c) the European Agency for the Management of Operational Cooperation at the External Borders of the Member States of the European Union (Frontex) [2];

(d) the European Police College (CEPOL);

(e) the European Central Bank;

(f) the European Monitoring Centre for Drugs and Drug Addiction (EMCDDA) [3].

2. Europol shall conclude agreements or working arrangements with the entities referred to in paragraph 1. Such agreements or working arrangements may concern the exchange of operational, strategic or technical information, including personal data and classified information. Any such agreement or working arrangement may be concluded only after approval by the Management Board which shall previously have obtained, as far as it concerns the exchange of personal data, the opinion of the Joint Supervisory Body.

3. Before the entry into force of the agreement or working arrangement referred to in paragraph 2, Europol may directly receive and use information, including personal data, from the entities referred to in paragraph 1, in so far as that is necessary for the legitimate performance of its tasks, and it may, under the conditions laid down in Article 24(1), directly transmit information, including personal data, to such entities, in so far as that is necessary for the legitimate performance of the recipient's tasks.

(1) Commission Decision 1999/352/EC, ECSC, Euratom of 28 April 1999 establishing the European Anti-fraud Office (OLAF) (OJ L 136, 31.5.1999, p. 20).

(2) Council Regulation (EC) No 2007/2004 of 26 October 2004 establishing a European Agency for the Management of Operational Co-operation at the External Borders of the Member States of the European Union (OJ L 349, 25.11.2004, p. 1).

(3) Regulation (EC) No 1920/2006 of the European Parliament and of the Council of 12 December 2006 on the European Monitoring Centre for Drugs and Drug Addiction (OJ L 376, 27.12.2006, p. 1).

15.5.2009 EN Official Journal of the European Union L 121/49

4. Transmission by Europol of classified information to the entities referred to in paragraph 1 shall be permissible only in so far as agreement on confidentiality exists between Europol and the recipient.

*Article 23*

**Relations with third States and organisations**

1. In so far as it is necessary for the performance of its tasks, Europol may also establish and maintain cooperative relations with:

(a) third States;

(b) organisations such as:

(i) international organisations and their subordinate bodies governed by public law;

(ii) other bodies governed by public law which are set up by, or on the basis of, an agreement between two or more States; and

(iii) the International Criminal Police Organisation (Interpol).

2. Europol shall conclude agreements with the entities referred to in paragraph 1 which have been put on the list referred to in Article 26(1)(a). Such agreements may concern the exchange of operational, strategic or technical information, including personal data and classified information, if transmitted via a designated contact point identified by the agreement referred to in paragraph 6(b) of this Article. Such agreements may be concluded only after the approval by the Council, which shall previously have consulted the Management Board and, as far as it concerns the exchange of personal data, obtained the opinion of the Joint Supervisory Body via the Management Board.

3. Before the entry into force of the agreements referred to in paragraph 2, Europol may directly receive and use information, including personal data and classified information, in so far as that is necessary for the legitimate performance of its tasks.

4. Before the entry into force of the agreements referred to in paragraph 2, Europol may, under the conditions laid down in Article 24(1), directly transmit information other than personal data and classified information to the entities referred to in paragraph 1 of this Article, in so far as that is necessary for the legitimate performance of the recipient's tasks.

5. Europol may, under the conditions laid down in Article 24(1), directly transmit information other than personal data and classified information to the entities referred to in paragraph 1 of this Article which are not on the list referred to in Article 26(1)(a), in so far as that is absolutely necessary in individual cases for the purposes of preventing or combating criminal offences in respect of which Europol is competent.

6. Europol may, under the conditions laid down in Article 24(1), transmit to the entities referred to in paragraph 1 of this Article:

(a) personal data and classified information, where that is necessary in individual cases for the purposes of preventing or combating criminal offences in respect of which Europol is competent; and

(b) personal data, where Europol has concluded with the entity concerned an agreement as referred to in paragraph 2 of this Article which permits the transmission of such data on the basis of an assessment of the existence of an adequate level of data protection ensured by that entity.

7. Transmission by Europol of classified information to the entities referred to in paragraph 1 shall be permissible only in so far as agreement on confidentiality exists between Europol and the recipient.

8. By way of derogation from paragraphs 6 and 7 and without prejudice to Article 24(1), Europol may transmit personal data and classified information which it holds to the entities referred to in paragraph 1 of this Article where the Director considers the transmission of the data to be absolutely necessary to safeguard the essential interests of the Member States concerned within the scope of Europol's objectives or in the interests of preventing imminent danger associated with crime or terrorist offences. The Director shall in all circumstances consider the data-protection level applicable to the body in question with a view to balancing that data-protection level and those interests. The Director shall inform the Management Board and the Joint Supervisory Body as soon as possible of his or her decision and of the basis of the assessment of the adequacy of the level of data protection afforded by the entities concerned.

9. Before the transmission of personal data in accordance with paragraph 8, the Director shall assess the adequacy of the level of data protection afforded by the entities concerned, taking into account all the circumstances relevant to the transmission of personal data, in particular:

(a) the nature of the data;

(b) the purpose for which the data is intended;

(c) the duration of the intended processing;

(d) the general or specific data-protection provisions applying to the entity;

(e) whether or not the entity has agreed to specific conditions required by Europol concerning the data.

L 121/50 EN Official Journal of the European Union 15.5.2009

*Article 24*

**Transmission of data**

1. If the data concerned were transmitted to Europol by a Member State, Europol shall transmit them to the entities referred to in Article 22(1) and Article 23(1) only with that Member State's consent. The Member State concerned may give its prior consent, in general terms or subject to specific conditions, to such transmission. Such consent may be withdrawn at any time.

If the data were not transmitted by a Member State, Europol shall satisfy itself that transmission of those data is not liable to:

(a) obstruct the proper performance of the tasks in respect of which a Member State is competent;

(b) jeopardise the security or public order of a Member State or otherwise prejudice its general welfare.

2. Europol shall be responsible for the legality of the transmission of data. Europol shall keep a record of all transmissions of data under this Article and of the grounds for such transmissions. Data shall be transmitted only if the recipient gives an undertaking that the data will be used only for the purpose for which they were transmitted.

*Article 25*

**Information from private parties and private persons**

1. For the purpose of this Decision:

(a) 'private parties' shall mean entities and bodies established under the law of a Member State or a third State, especially companies and firms, business associations, non-profit organisations and other legal persons governed by private law, which do not fall under Article 23(1);

(b) 'private persons' shall mean all natural persons.

2. In so far as it is necessary for the legitimate performance of its tasks, Europol may process information, including personal data, from private parties under the conditions laid down in paragraph 3.

3. Personal data from private parties may be processed by Europol under the following conditions:

(a) Personal data from private parties which are established under the law of a Member State may be processed by Europol only if they are transmitted via the national unit of that Member State in accordance with its national law. Europol may not contact private parties in the Member States directly in order to retrieve information.

(b) Personal data from private parties which are established under the law of a third State with which Europol has, in accordance with Article 23, concluded a cooperation agreement allowing for the exchange of personal data may be transmitted to Europol only via the contact point of that State as identified by, and in accordance with, the cooperation agreement in force.

(c) Personal data from private parties which are established under the law of a third State with which Europol has no cooperation agreement allowing for the exchange of personal data may be processed by Europol only if:

(i) the private party concerned is on the list referred to in Article 26(2); and

(ii) Europol and the private party concerned have concluded a memorandum of understanding on the transmission of information, including personal data, confirming the legality of the collection and transmission of the personal data by that private party and specifying that the personal data transmitted may be used only for the legitimate performance of Europol's tasks. Such a memorandum of understanding may be concluded only after approval by the Management Board which shall previously have obtained the opinion of the Joint Supervisory Body.

If the transmitted data affect interests of a Member State, Europol shall immediately inform the national unit of the Member State concerned.

4. In addition to the processing of data from private parties in accordance with paragraph 3, Europol may directly retrieve and process data, including personal data, from publicly available sources, such as media and public data and commercial intelligence providers, in accordance with the data-protection provisions of this Decision. In accordance with Article 17, Europol shall forward all relevant information to the national units.

5. Information, including personal data, from private persons may be processed by Europol if it is received via a national unit in accordance with national law or via the contact point of a third State with which Europol has concluded a cooperation agreement in accordance with Article 23. If Europol receives information, including personal data, from a private person residing in a third State with which Europol has no cooperation agreement, Europol may forward it only to the Member State or the third State concerned with which Europol has concluded a cooperation agreement in accordance with Article 23. Europol may not contact private persons directly in order to retrieve information.

15.5.2009 EN Official Journal of the European Union L 121/51

6. Personal data transmitted to or retrieved by Europol under paragraph 3(c) of this Article may only be processed for the purpose of their inclusion in the Europol Information System referred to in Article 11 and the analysis work files referred to in Article 14 or other systems processing personal data established in accordance with Article 10(2) and (3) if those data are related to other data already entered in one of the aforementioned systems or if they are related to a previous query by a national unit within one of the aforementioned systems.

The responsibility for data processed by Europol, which have been transmitted under the conditions laid down in paragraph 3(b) and (c) and paragraph 4 of this Article, and for the information transmitted via the contact point of a third State with which Europol has concluded a cooperation agreement in accordance with Article 23, shall lie with Europol in accordance with Article 29(1)(b).

7. The Director shall submit a comprehensive report to the Management Board on the application of this Article two years after the date of application of this Decision. On the advice of the Joint Supervisory Body or on its own initiative, the Management Board may take any measure deemed appropriate in accordance with Article 37(9)(b).

*Article 26*

**Implementing rules governing Europol's relations**

1. The Council, acting by qualified majority after consulting the European Parliament, shall:

(a) determine, in a list, the third States and organisations referred to in Article 23(1) with which Europol shall conclude agreements. The list shall be prepared by the Management Board and reviewed when necessary; and

(b) adopt implementing rules governing the relations of Europol with the entities referred to in Articles 22(1) and 23(1), including the exchange of personal data and classified information. The implementing rules shall be prepared by the Management Board which shall previously have obtained the opinion of the Joint Supervisory Body.

2. The Management Board shall draw up and review, when necessary, a list determining the private parties with which Europol may conclude memoranda of understanding in accordance with Article 25(3)(c)(ii) and adopt rules governing the content of and the procedure for the conclusion of such memoranda of understanding after obtaining the opinion of the Joint Supervisory Body.

CHAPTER V

## DATA PROTECTION AND DATA SECURITY

*Article 27*

**Standard of data protection**

Without prejudice to specific provisions of this Decision, Europol shall take account of the principles of the Council of Europe Convention for the Protection of Individuals with regard to Automatic Processing of Personal Data of 28 January 1981 and of Recommendation No R (87) 15 of the Committee of Ministers of the Council of Europe of 17 September 1987. Europol shall observe those principles in the processing of personal data, inter alia, in respect of automated and non-automated data held in the form of data files, especially any structured set of personal data accessible in accordance with specific criteria.

*Article 28*

**Data Protection Officer**

1. The Management Board shall appoint, on the proposal of the Director, a Data Protection Officer who shall be a member of the staff. In the performance of his or her duties, he or she shall act independently.

2. The Data Protection Officer shall in particular have the following tasks:

(a) ensuring, in an independent manner, lawfulness and compliance with the provisions of this Decision concerning the processing of personal data, including the processing of personal data relating to Europol staff;

(b) ensuring that a written record of the transmission and receipt of personal data is kept in accordance with this Decision;

(c) ensuring that data subjects are informed of their rights under this Decision at their request;

(d) cooperating with Europol staff responsible for procedures, training and advice on data processing;

(e) cooperating with the Joint Supervisory Body;

(f) preparing an annual report and communicating that report to the Management Board and to the Joint Supervisory Body.

3. In the performance of his or her tasks, the Data Protection Officer shall have access to all the data processed by Europol and to all Europol premises.

4. If the Data Protection Officer considers that the provisions of this Decision concerning the processing of personal data have not been complied with, he or she shall inform the Director, requiring him or her to resolve the non-compliance within a specified time.

If the Director does not resolve the non-compliance of the processing within the specified time, the Data Protection Officer shall inform the Management Board and shall agree with the Management Board a specified time for a response.

If the Management Board does not resolve the non-compliance of the processing within the specified time, the Data Protection Officer shall refer the matter to the Joint Supervisory Body.

5. The Management Board shall adopt further implementing rules concerning the Data Protection Officer. Those implementing rules shall in particular concern selection and dismissal, tasks, duties and powers and safeguards for the independence of the Data Protection Officer.

*Article 29*

**Responsibility in data protection matters**

1. The responsibility for data processed at Europol, in particular as regards the legality of the collection, the transmission to Europol and the input of data, as well as their accuracy, their up-to-date nature and verification of the storage time limits, shall lie with:

(a) the Member State which input or otherwise communicated the data;

(b) Europol in respect of data communicated to Europol by third parties, including data communicated by private parties in accordance with Article 25(3)(b) and (c) and Article 25(4) as well as data communicated via the contact point of a third State with which Europol has concluded a cooperation agreement in accordance with Article 23 or which result from analyses conducted by Europol.

2. Data which have been transmitted to Europol but have not yet been input in one of Europol's data files shall remain under the data-protection responsibility of the party transmitting the data. Europol shall, however, be responsible for ensuring the security of the data in accordance with Article 35(2) in that until such data have been input in a data file, they may be accessed only by authorised Europol staff for the purpose of determining whether they can be processed at Europol, or by authorised officials of the party which supplied the data. If Europol, after appraising them, has reason to assume that data supplied are inaccurate or no longer up-to-date, it shall inform the party which supplied the data.

3. In addition, subject to other provisions in this Decision, Europol shall be responsible for all data processed by it.

4. If Europol has evidence that data input into one of its systems referred to in Chapter II are factually incorrect or have been unlawfully stored, it shall inform the Member State or other party involved accordingly.

5. Europol shall store data in such a way that it can be established by which Member State or third party they were transmitted or whether they are the result of an analysis by Europol.

*Article 30*

**Individual's right of access**

1. Any person shall be entitled, at reasonable intervals, to obtain information on whether personal data relating to him or her are processed by Europol and to have such data communicated to him or her in an intelligible form, or checked, in all cases under the conditions laid down in this Article.

2. Any person wishing to exercise his or her rights under this Article may make a request to that effect without excessive costs in the Member State of his or her choice to the authority appointed for that purpose in that Member State. That authority shall refer the request to Europol without delay, and in any case within one month of receipt.

3. The request shall be answered by Europol without undue delay and in any case within three months of its receipt by Europol in accordance with this Article.

4. Europol shall consult the competent authorities of the Member States concerned before deciding on its response to a request under paragraph 1. A decision on access to data shall be conditional upon close cooperation between Europol and the Member States directly concerned by the communication of such data. In any case in which a Member State objects to Europol's proposed response, it shall notify Europol of the reasons for its objection.

5. The provision of information in response to a request under paragraph 1 shall be refused to the extent that such refusal is necessary to:

(a) enable Europol to fulfil its tasks properly;

(b) protect security and public order in the Member States or to prevent crime;

(c) guarantee that any national investigation will not be jeopardised;

(d) protect the rights and freedoms of third parties.

When the applicability of an exemption is assessed, the interests of the person concerned shall be taken into account.

6. If the provision of information in response to a request under paragraph 1 is refused, Europol shall notify the person concerned that it has carried out checks, without giving any information which might reveal to him or her whether or not personal data concerning him or her are processed by Europol.

7. Any person shall have the right to request the Joint Supervisory Body, at reasonable intervals, to check whether the manner in which his or her personal data have been collected, stored, processed and used by Europol is in compliance with the provisions of this Decision concerning the processing of personal data. The Joint Supervisory Body shall notify the person concerned that it has carried out checks, without giving any information which might reveal to him or her whether or not personal data concerning him or her are processed by Europol.

*Article 31*

**Data subject's right to correctionand deletion of data**

1. Any person shall have the right to ask Europol to correct or delete incorrect data concerning him or her. If it emerges, either on the basis of the exercise of this right or otherwise, that data held by Europol which have been communicated to it by third parties or which are the result of its own analyses are incorrect or that their input or storage is in breach of this Decision, Europol shall correct or delete such data.

2. If data that are incorrect or processed in breach of this Decision were transmitted directly to Europol by Member States, the Member States concerned shall correct or delete such data in collaboration with Europol.

3. If incorrect data were transmitted by another appropriate means or if the errors in the data supplied by Member States are due to faulty transmission or were transmitted in breach of this Decision or if they result from their being input, taken over or stored in an incorrect manner or in breach of this Decision by Europol, Europol shall correct or delete the data in collaboration with the Member States concerned.

4. In the cases referred to in paragraphs 1, 2 and 3, the Member States or third parties which have received the data shall be notified forthwith. The recipient Member States and the third parties shall also correct or delete those data. Where deletion is not possible, the data shall be blocked to prevent any future processing.

5. The data subject making the request shall be informed by Europol in writing without undue delay and in any case within three months that data concerning him or her have been corrected or deleted.

*Article 32*

**Appeals**

1. In its reply to a request for a check, for access to data, or for correction and deletion of data, Europol shall inform the person making the request that if he or she is not satisfied with the decision, he or she may appeal to the Joint Supervisory Body. Such person may also refer the matter to the Joint Supervisory Body if there has been no response to his or her request within the time limit laid down in Article 30 or 31.

2. If the person making the request lodges an appeal to the Joint Supervisory Body, the appeal shall be examined by that body.

3. Where an appeal relates to a decision as referred to in Article 30 or 31, the Joint Supervisory Body shall consult the national supervisory bodies or the competent judicial body in the Member State which was the source of the data or the Member State directly concerned. The decision of the Joint Supervisory Body, which may extend to a refusal to communicate any information, shall be taken in close cooperation with the national supervisory body or competent judicial body.

4. Where an appeal relates to access to data input by Europol in the Europol Information System or data stored in the analysis work files or in any other system established by Europol for the processing of personal data pursuant to Article 10 and where objections from Europol persist, the Joint Supervisory Body shall be able to overrule such objections only by a majority of two thirds of its members after having heard Europol and the Member State or Member States referred to in Article 30(4). If there is no such majority, the Joint Supervisory Body shall notify the person making the request of the refusal, without giving any information which might reveal the existence of any personal data concerning that person.

5. Where an appeal relates to the checking of data input by a Member State in the Europol Information System or of data stored in the analysis work files or in any other system established by Europol for the processing of personal data pursuant to Article 10, the Joint Supervisory Body shall ensure that the necessary checks have been carried out correctly in close co-operation with the national supervisory body of the Member State which has input the data. The Joint Supervisory Body shall notify the person making the request that it has carried out the checks, without giving any information which might reveal the existence of any personal data concerning that person.

6. Where an appeal relates to the checking of data input by Europol in the Europol Information System or of data stored in the analysis work files or in any other system established by Europol for the processing of personal data pursuant to Article 10, the Joint Supervisory Body shall ensure that the necessary checks have been carried out by Europol. The Joint Supervisory Body shall notify the person making the request that it has carried out the checks, without giving any information which might reveal the existence of any personal data concerning that person.

*Article 33*

**National supervisory body**

1. Each Member State shall designate a national supervisory body with the task to monitor independently, in accordance with its national law, the permissibility of the input, the retrieval and any communication to Europol of personal data by the Member State concerned and to examine whether such input, retrieval or communication violates the rights of the data subject. For that purpose, the national supervisory body shall have access, at the national unit or at liaison officers' premises, to the data input by the Member State in the Europol Information System or in any other system established by Europol for the processing of personal data pursuant to Article 10 in accordance with the relevant national procedures.

For the purpose of exercising their supervisory function, national supervisory bodies shall have access to the offices and documents of their respective liaison officers at Europol.

In addition, in accordance with the relevant national procedures, the national supervisory bodies shall supervise the activities of national units and the activities of liaison officers, in so far as such activities are of relevance to the protection of personal data. They shall also keep the Joint Supervisory Body informed of any actions they take with respect to Europol.

2. Any person shall have the right to request the national supervisory body to ensure that the input or communication to Europol of data concerning him or her in any form and the consultation of the data by the Member State concerned are lawful.

This right shall be exercised in accordance with the national law of the Member State in which the request is made.

*Article 34*

**Joint Supervisory Body**

1. An independent Joint Supervisory Body shall be set up to review, in accordance with this Decision, the activities of Europol in order to ensure that the rights of the individual are not violated by the storage, processing and use of the data held by Europol. In addition, the Joint Supervisory Body shall monitor the permissibility of the transmission of data originating from Europol. The Joint Supervisory Body shall be composed of a maximum of two members or representatives, where appropriate assisted by alternates, of each of the independent national supervisory bodies, having the necessary abilities and appointed for five years by each Member State. Each delegation shall be entitled to one vote.

The Joint Supervisory Body shall choose a chairman from among its members.

In the performance of their duties, the members of the Joint Supervisory Body shall not receive instructions from any other body.

2. Europol shall assist the Joint Supervisory Body in the performance of the latter's tasks. In doing so, it shall in particular:

(a) supply the information the Joint Supervisory Body requests and give it access to all documents and paper files as well as to the data stored in its data files;

(b) allow the Joint Supervisory Body free access at all times to all its premises;

(c) implement the Joint Supervisory Body's decisions on appeals.

3. The Joint Supervisory Body shall be competent to examine questions relating to implementation and interpretation in connection with Europol's activities as regards the processing and use of personal data, to examine questions relating to checks carried out independently by the national supervisory bodies of the Member States or relating to the exercise of the right of access, and to draw up harmonised proposals for common solutions to existing problems.

4. If the Joint Supervisory Body identifies any violations of the provisions of this Decision in the storage, processing or use of personal data, it shall make any complaints it deems necessary to the Director and shall request him to reply within a specified time limit. The Director shall keep the Management Board informed of the entire procedure. If it is not satisfied with the response given by the Director to its request, the Joint Supervisory Body shall refer the matter to the Management Board.

5. For the fulfilment of its tasks and to contribute to the improvement of consistency in the application of the rules and procedures for data processing, the Joint Supervisory Body shall cooperate as necessary with other supervisory authorities.

6. The Joint Supervisory Body shall draw up activity reports at regular intervals. Such reports shall be forwarded to the European Parliament and to the Council. The Management Board shall have the opportunity to make comments, which shall be attached to the reports.

The Joint Supervisory Body shall decide whether or not to publish its activity report, and, if it decides to do so, shall determine how it should be published.

7. The Joint Supervisory Body shall adopt its rules of procedure by a majority of two thirds of its members and shall submit them to the Council for approval. The Council shall act by qualified majority.

8. The Joint Supervisory Body shall set up an internal committee comprising one qualified representative from each Member State with the right to vote. The committee shall have the task of examining the appeals provided for in Article 32 by all appropriate means. Should they so request, the parties, assisted by their advisers if they so wish, shall be heard by the committee. The decisions taken in this context shall be final as regards all the parties concerned.

9. The Joint Supervisory Body may set up one or more other committees in addition to the one referred to in paragraph 8.

10. The Joint Supervisory Body shall be consulted on that part of Europol's budget which concerns it. Its opinion shall be annexed to the draft budget in question.

11. The Joint Supervisory Body shall be assisted by a secretariat, the tasks of which shall be defined in the rules of procedure.

*Article 35*

**Data security**

1. Europol shall take the necessary technical and organisational measures to ensure the implementation of this Decision. Measures shall be considered necessary where the effort they involve is proportionate to the objective they are designed to achieve in terms of protection.

2. In respect of automated data processing at Europol, each Member State and Europol shall implement measures designed to:

(a) deny unauthorised persons access to data-processing equipment used for processing personal data (equipment access control);

(b) prevent the unauthorised reading, copying, modification or removal of data media (data media control);

(c) prevent the unauthorised input of data and the unauthorised inspection, modification or deletion of stored personal data (storage control);

(d) prevent the use of automated data-processing systems by unauthorised persons using data-communication equipment (user control);

(e) ensure that persons authorised to use an automated data-processing system have access only to the data covered by their access authorisation (data access control);

(f) ensure that it is possible to verify and establish to which bodies personal data may be or have been transmitted using data communication equipment (communication control);

(g) ensure that it is possible to verify and establish which personal data have been input into automated data-processing systems and when and by whom the data were input (input control);

(h) prevent the unauthorised reading, copying, modification or deletion of personal data during transfers of personal data or during the transportation of data media (transport control);

(i) ensure that installed systems may, in the event of interruption, be restored immediately (recovery);

(j) ensure that the functions of the system perform without fault, that the appearance of faults in the functions is immediately reported (reliability) and that stored data cannot be corrupted by system malfunctions (integrity).

CHAPTER VI

**ORGANISATION**

*Article 36*

**Organs of Europol**

The organs of Europol shall be:

(a) the Management Board;

(b) the Director.

*Article 37*

**Management Board**

1. The Management Board shall be composed of one representative of each Member State and one representative of the Commission. Each member of the Management Board shall have one vote. Each member of the Management Board may be represented by an alternate member; in the absence of the full member, the alternate member may exercise his right to vote.

2. The Chairperson and the Deputy Chairperson of the Management Board shall be selected by and from within the group of three Member States who have jointly prepared the Council's eighteen-month programme. They shall serve for the eighteen-month period corresponding to that Council programme. During that period the Chairperson shall no longer act as a representative of his or her respective Member State in the Management Board. The Deputy shall *ex officio* replace the Chairperson in the event of his or her being prevented from attending to his or her duties.

3. The Chairperson shall be responsible for the efficient operation of the Management Board in the performance of its tasks set out in paragraph 9 while ensuring a specific focus on strategic issues and Europol's principal tasks as set out in Article 5(1).

4. The Chairperson shall be supported by the Secretariat of the Management Board. The Secretariat shall in particular:

(a) be closely and continuously involved in organising, coordinating and ensuring the coherence of the Management Board's work. Under the responsibility and guidance of the Chairperson, it shall assist the latter in seeking solutions;

(b) provide the Management Board with the administrative support necessary for it to carry out its duties.

5. The Director shall participate in the meetings of the Management Board, without the right to vote.

6. Members of the Management Board or their alternates and the Director may be accompanied by experts.

7. The Management Board shall meet at least twice a year.

8. The Management Board shall act by a majority of two thirds of its members unless otherwise stipulated in this Decision.

9. The Management Board shall:

(a) adopt a strategy for Europol, which shall include benchmarks to measure whether the objectives set have been reached;

(b) oversee the Director's performance including the implementation of Management Board decisions;

(c) take any decision or implementing measures in accordance with this Decision;

(d) adopt the implementing rules applicable to Europol staff, on a proposal from the Director and after seeking agreement from the Commission;

(e) adopt the financial regulation and appoint the accounting officer in conformity with Commission Regulation (EC, Euratom) No 2343/2002 of 19 November 2002 on the framework Financial Regulation for the bodies referred to in Article 185 of Council Regulation (EC, Euratom) No 1605/2002 on the Financial Regulation applicable to the general budget of the European Communities (1), after consulting the Commission;

(f) establish the internal audit function and appoint its auditing staff, who shall be members of Europol staff. The Management Board shall adopt further implementing rules concerning the internal audit function. Those implementing rules should, in particular, cover selection, dismissal, tasks, duties, powers and safeguards for the independence of the function. The internal audit function shall be accountable solely to the Management Board and shall have access to all documentation necessary to the performance of its duties;

(g) adopt a list of at least three candidates for the post of Director and the Deputy Directors for submission to the Council;

(h) be responsible for the performance of any other tasks assigned to it by the Council, in particular in provisions implementing this Decision;

(i) establish its rules of procedure, including provisions providing for the independence of the Secretariat.

10. Each year the Management Board shall adopt:

(a) the draft estimate of revenue and expenditure, including the draft establishment plan, to be submitted to the Commission; and the final budget;

(b) a work programme for Europol's future activities taking into account Member States' operational requirements and budgetary and staffing implications for Europol, after the Commission has delivered an opinion;

(1) OJ L 357, 31.12.2002, p. 72.

15.5.2009 EN Official Journal of the European Union L 121/57

(c) a general report on Europol's activities during the previous year including the results achieved on the priorities set by the Council.

Those documents shall be submitted to the Council for endorsement. The Council shall forward them to the European Parliament for information.

11. Within four years of the date of application of this Decision and every four years thereafter, the Management Board shall commission an independent external evaluation of the implementation of this Decision and of the activities carried out by Europol.

The Management Board shall issue specific terms of reference to that effect.

The report of the evaluation shall be forwarded to the European Parliament, the Council and the Commission.

12. The Management Board may decide to establish working groups. The rules governing the creation and functioning of such working groups shall be laid down in its rules of procedure.

13. The Management Board shall exercise the powers laid down in Article 39(3) in respect of the Director, without prejudice to Article 38(1) and (7).

*Article 38*

**Director**

1. Europol shall be headed by a Director appointed by the Council, acting by qualified majority, from a list of at least three candidates presented by the Management Board, for a four-year period. The Council, acting on a proposal from the Management Board, which shall have evaluated the Director's performance, may extend the term of office of the Director once for not more than four years.

2. The Director shall be assisted by three Deputy Directors appointed for a four-year period extendable once in accordance with the procedure laid down in paragraph 1. Their tasks shall be defined in greater detail by the Director.

3. The Management Board shall establish rules concerning the selection of candidates for the position of Director or Deputy Director, including the extension of their terms of office. Such rules shall be approved by the Council, acting by qualified majority, before their entry into force.

4. The Director shall be responsible for:

(a) performance of the tasks assigned to Europol;

(b) day-to-day administration;

(c) exercising, in respect of the staff and Deputy Directors without prejudice to paragraphs 2 and 7 of this Article, the powers laid down in Article 39(3);

(d) preparing and implementing the Management Board's decisions and responding to requests from the Management Board;

(e) supporting the Chairperson of the Management Board in the preparation of the Management Board meetings;

(f) drawing up the draft estimate of revenue and expenditure, including the draft establishment plan; and the preliminary work programme;

(g) elaborating the report referred to in Article 37(10)(c);

(h) implementing Europol's budget;

(i) informing the Management Board on a regular basis regarding the implementation of the priorities defined by the Council and Europol's external relations;

(j) establishing and implementing, in cooperation with the Management Board, an effective and efficient monitoring and evaluation procedure relating to Europol's performance in terms of the achievement of its objectives. The Director shall report regularly to the Management Board on the results of that monitoring;

(k) performance of all other tasks assigned to the Director in this Decision.

5. The Director shall be accountable to the Management Board in respect of the performance of his duties.

6. The Director shall be Europol's legal representative.

7. The Director and the Deputy Directors may be dismissed by decision of the Council, acting by qualified majority after obtaining the opinion of the Management Board. The Management Board shall establish the rules to be applied in such cases. Such rules shall be approved by the Council, acting by qualified majority, before their entry into force.

*Article 39*

**Staff**

1. The Staff Regulations of officials of the European Communities and the Conditions of employment of other servants of the European Communities (hereinafter referred to as the Staff Regulations and the Conditions of employment respectively) laid down in Regulation (EEC, Euratom, ECSC) No 259/68 of the Council [1] and the rules adopted jointly by the institutions of the European Communities for the purpose of applying the Staff Regulations and the Conditions of employment shall apply to the Director, the Deputy Directors and to the Europol staff engaged after the date of application of this Decision.

2. For the purpose of implementing the Staff Regulations and the Conditions of employment, Europol shall be considered as an agency within the meaning of Article 1a(2) of the Staff Regulations.

3. The powers conferred on the appointing authority by the Staff Regulations and on the authority authorised to conclude contracts by the Conditions of employment shall be exercised by Europol in respect of its staff and of the Director in accordance with Articles 37(13) and 38(4)(c) of this Decision.

4. Europol staff shall consist of temporary staff and/or contract staff. The Management Board shall give its consent on a yearly basis in so far as the Director intends to grant contracts of indefinite duration. The Management Board shall decide which temporary posts provided for in the establishment plan can be filled only by staff engaged from the competent authorities of the Member States. Staff recruited to occupy such posts shall be temporary agents under Article 2(a) of the Conditions of employment and may be awarded only fixed-term contracts renewable once for a fixed period.

5. Member States may second national experts to Europol. The Management Board shall adopt the necessary implementing arrangements for that purpose.

6. Europol shall apply the principles of Regulation (EC) No 45/2001 to the processing of personal data relating to Europol staff.

CHAPTER VII

**CONFIDENTIALITY ISSUES**

*Article 40*

**Confidentiality**

1. Europol and the Member States shall take appropriate measures to protect information subject to the requirement of confidentiality which is obtained by or exchanged with Europol pursuant to this Decision. To that end the Council, acting by qualified majority after consulting the European Parliament, shall adopt appropriate rules on confidentiality prepared by the Management Board. Those rules shall include provisions concerning the cases in which Europol may exchange information subject to the requirement of confidentiality with third parties.

2. Where Europol intends to entrust persons with a sensitive activity, Member States shall undertake to arrange, at the request of the Director, for security screening of their own nationals to be carried out in accordance with their national provisions and to provide each other with mutual assistance for that purpose. The relevant authority under national provisions shall inform Europol only of the results of the security screening. Those results shall be binding on Europol.

3. Each Member State and Europol may entrust the processing of data at Europol only to those persons who have had special training and undergone security screening. The Management Board shall adopt rules for the security clearance of Europol staff. The Director shall regularly inform the Management Board on the state of security screening of Europol staff.

*Article 41*

**Obligation of discretion and confidentiality**

1. The members of the Management Board, the Director, the Deputy Directors, employees of Europol and liaison officers shall refrain from any action and any expression of opinion which might be harmful to Europol or prejudice its activities.

2. The members of the Management Board, the Director, the Deputy Directors, employees of Europol and liaison officers, as well as any other person under a particular obligation of discretion or confidentiality, shall be bound not to disclose any facts or information which come to their knowledge in the performance of their duties or the exercise of their activities to any unauthorised person or to the public. This shall not apply to facts or information too insignificant to require confidentiality. The obligation of discretion and confidentiality shall apply even after the termination of office or employment, or after the termination of activities. Notification of the particular obligation referred to in the first sentence shall be given by Europol together with a warning of the legal consequences of any infringement. A written record shall be drawn up of such notification.

3. The members of the Management Board, the Director, the Deputy Directors, employees of Europol and liaison officers, as well as other persons under the obligation provided for in paragraph 2, shall not give evidence in or outside a court or make any statements on any facts or information which come to their knowledge in the performance of their duties or the exercise of their activities without reference to the Director or, in the case of the Director himself, to the Management Board.

[1] OJ L 56, 4.3.1968, p. 1.

The Management Board or the Director, depending on the case, shall approach the judicial body or any other competent body with a view to ensuring that the necessary measures under the national law applicable to the body approached are taken.

Such measures may either be to adjust the procedures for giving evidence in order to ensure the confidentiality of the information or, provided that the national law concerned so permits, to refuse to make any communication concerning data in so far as it is vital for the protection of the interests of Europol or of a Member State.

Where a Member State's legislation provides for the right to refuse to give evidence, persons referred to in paragraph 2 asked to give evidence shall be required to obtain permission to do so. Permission shall be granted by the Director or, in the case of evidence to be given by the Director, by the Management Board. Where a liaison officer is asked to give evidence concerning information he receives from Europol, such permission shall be given after the agreement of the Member State responsible for the officer concerned has been obtained. The obligation to seek permission to give evidence shall apply even after the termination of office or employment or after the termination of activities.

Furthermore, if the possibility exists that the evidence may extend to information and knowledge which a Member State has communicated to Europol or which clearly involves a Member State, the position of that Member State concerning the evidence shall be sought before permission is granted.

Permission to give evidence may be refused only in so far as that is necessary to protect the overriding interests of Europol or of a Member State or Member States that need protection.

4. Each Member State shall treat any infringement of the obligation of discretion or confidentiality laid down in paragraphs 2 and 3 as a breach of the obligations imposed by its law on official or professional secrets or its provisions for the protection of classified material.

It shall ensure that the rules and provisions concerned also apply to its own employees who have contact with Europol in the course of their work.

## CHAPTER VIII

## BUDGET PROVISIONS

### *Article 42*

### Budget

1. The revenues of Europol shall consist, without prejudice to other types of income, of a subsidy from the Community entered in the general budget of the European Union (Commission section) as from the date of application of this Decision. The financing of Europol shall be subject to an agreement by the European Parliament and the Council (hereinafter referred to as the budgetary authority) as provided for in the Interinstitutional Agreement of 17 May 2006 between the European Parliament, the Council and the Commission on budgetary discipline and sound financial management [1].

2. Europol's expenditure shall include its staff, administrative, infrastructure and operational expenses.

3. The Director shall draw up the draft estimate of revenue and expenditure of Europol for the following financial year, including a draft establishment plan, and shall forward it to the Management Board. The draft establishment plan shall consist of posts of a permanent or temporary nature and a reference to national experts seconded, and shall state the number, grade and category of staff employed by Europol for the financial year in question.

4. Revenue and expenditure shall be in balance.

5. The Management Board shall adopt the draft estimate of revenue and expenditure, including the draft establishment plan and accompanied by the preliminary work programme, and forward them by 31 March of each year to the Commission. If the Commission has objections to the draft estimate, it shall inform the Management Board accordingly within 30 days of receiving it.

6. The Commission shall forward the estimate to the budgetary authority together with the preliminary draft general budget of the European Union.

7. On the basis of the estimate, the Commission shall enter in the preliminary draft general budget of the European Union, which it shall place before the budgetary authority, in accordance with Article 272 of the Treaty establishing the European Community, the estimates it deems necessary for the establishment plan and the amount of the subsidy to be charged to that budget.

8. The budgetary authority shall authorise the appropriations for the subsidy to Europol and the establishment plan when adopting the general budget of the European Union.

9. The Management Board shall adopt Europol's budget and the establishment plan. They shall become definitive following the final adoption of the general budget of the European Union. Where appropriate, they shall be adjusted accordingly by means of the adoption of a revised budget.

10. Any amendment of the budget, including the establishment plan, shall be effected in accordance with the procedure laid down in paragraphs 5 to 9.

[1] OJ C 139, 14.6.2006, p. 1.

11. The Management Board shall, as soon as possible, notify the budgetary authority of its intention of implementing any project that may have significant financial implications for the funding of its budget, in particular any projects relating to property such as the rental or purchase of buildings. It shall inform the Commission thereof. Where a branch of the budgetary authority notifies its intention of delivering an opinion, it shall forward its opinion to the Management Board within six weeks of the date on which it notified the budgetary authority of the project.

*Article 43*

**Implementation and control of the budget**

1. The Director shall implement Europol's budget.

2. By 28 February at the latest following each financial year, Europol's accounting officer shall communicate the provisional accounts to the Commission's accounting officer together with a report on the budgetary and financial management for that financial year. The Commission's accounting officer shall consolidate the provisional accounts of the institutions and decentralised bodies in accordance with Article 128 of Council Regulation (EC, Euratom) No 1605/2002 of 25 June 2002 on the Financial Regulation applicable to the general budget of the European Communities ([1]).

3. By 31 March at the latest following each financial year, the Commission's accounting officer shall forward Europol's provisional accounts to the Court of Auditors, together with a report on the budgetary and financial management for that financial year. The report on the budgetary and financial management for that financial year shall also be forwarded to the European Parliament and the Council.

4. On receipt of the Court of Auditors' observations on Europol's provisional accounts pursuant to Article 129 of Regulation (EC, Euratom) No 1605/2002, the Director shall draw up Europol's final accounts under his own responsibility and forward them to the Management Board for an opinion.

5. The Management Board shall deliver an opinion on Europol's final accounts.

6. By 1 July at the latest following each financial year, the Director shall send the final accounts, together with the opinion of the Management Board, to the European Parliament, the Council, the Commission and the Court of Auditors.

7. The final accounts shall be published.

8. The Director shall send the Court of Auditors a reply to its observations by 30 September at the latest. He shall also send a copy of that reply to the Management Board.

9. The Director shall submit to the European Parliament, at the latter's request, any information required for the smooth application of the discharge procedure for the financial year in question, as laid down in Article 146(3) of Regulation (EC, Euratom) No 1605/2002.

10. The European Parliament, taking into account a recommendation from the Council acting by qualified majority, shall, before 30 April of year n + 2, give a discharge to the Director in respect of the implementation of the budget for year n.

*Article 44*

**Financial regulation**

The Management Board shall adopt the financial regulation applicable to Europol after consulting the Commission. It may not depart from Regulation (EC, Euratom) No 2343/2002 unless that is specifically required for Europol's operation. The prior consent of the Commission shall be required for the adoption of any rules which derogate from Regulation (EC, Euratom) No 2343/2002. The budgetary authority shall be informed of any such derogations.

CHAPTER IX

**MISCELLANEOUS PROVISIONS**

*Article 45*

**Rules concerning access to Europol documents**

On the basis of a proposal by the Director, and not later than six months after the date of application of this Decision, the Management Board shall adopt rules concerning access to Europol documents, taking into account the principles and limits set out in Regulation (EC) No 1049/2001 of the European Parliament and of the Council of 30 May 2001 regarding public access to European Parliament, Council and Commission documents ([2]).

*Article 46*

**EU classified information**

Europol shall apply the security principles and minimum standards set out in Council Decision 2001/264/EC of 19 March 2001 adopting the Council's security regulations ([3]) regarding EU classified information.

*Article 47*

**Languages**

1. Regulation No 1 of 15 April 1958 determining the languages to be used in the European Economic Community ([4]) shall apply to Europol.

2. The Management Board shall decide by unanimity on the internal language arrangements of Europol.

([1]) OJ L 248, 16.9.2002, p. 1.

([2]) OJ L 145, 31.5.2001, p. 43.

([3]) OJ L 101, 11.4.2001, p. 1.

([4]) OJ 17, 6.10.1958, p. 385/58.

3. The translations required for Europol's work shall be provided by the Translation Centre for bodies of the European Union (1).

*Article 48*

**Informing the European Parliament**

The Presidency of the Council, the Chairperson of the Management Board and the Director shall appear before the European Parliament at its request to discuss matters relating to Europol taking into account the obligations of discretion and confidentiality.

*Article 49*

**Combating fraud**

The rules laid down by Regulation (EC) No 1073/1999 of the European Parliament and of the Council of 25 May 1999 concerning investigations conducted by the European Anti-Fraud Office (OLAF) (2) shall apply to Europol. On the basis of the proposal by the Director, and not later than six months after the date of application of this Decision, the Management Board shall adopt the implementing measures necessary, which may exclude operational data from the scope of OLAF's investigations.

*Article 50*

**Headquarters Agreement**

The necessary arrangements concerning the accommodation to be provided for Europol in the headquarters State and the facilities to be made available by that State as well as the particular rules applicable in the Europol headquarters State to the Director, the members of the Management Board, the Deputy Directors, employees of Europol and members of their families shall be laid down in a Headquarters Agreement between Europol and the Kingdom of the Netherlands to be concluded once the approval of the Management Board has been obtained.

*Article 51*

**Privileges and immunities**

1. The Protocol on the Privileges and Immunities of the European Communities and a specific Regulation to be adopted on the basis of Article 16 of the Protocol on the Privileges and Immunities of the European Communities shall apply to the Director and Deputy Directors of Europol and to Europol staff.

2. The Protocol on the Privileges and Immunities of the European Communities shall apply to Europol.

3. The Kingdom of the Netherlands and the other Member States shall agree that liaison officers seconded from the other Member States and members of their families shall enjoy such privileges and immunities as are necessary for the proper performance of the tasks of liaison officers at Europol.

*Article 52*

**Liability for unauthorised or incorrect data processing**

1. Each Member State shall be liable, in accordance with its national law, for any damage caused to an individual as a result of legal or factual errors in data stored or processed at Europol. Only the Member State in which the event which gave rise to the damage occurred shall be the subject of an action for compensation on the part of the injured party, who shall apply to the courts having jurisdiction under the national law of the Member State concerned. A Member State may not plead that another Member State or Europol had transmitted inaccurate data in order to avoid its liability under its national legislation vis-à-vis an injured party.

2. If the legal or factual errors referred to in paragraph 1 occurred as a result of the erroneous communication of data or of failure to comply with the obligations laid down in this Decision on the part of one or more Member States or as a result of unauthorised or incorrect storage or processing by Europol, Europol or the other Member State in question shall be bound to reimburse, on request, for the amounts paid as compensation pursuant to paragraph 1 unless the data were used in breach of this Decision by the Member State in the territory of which the damage was caused.

3. Any dispute between the Member State that has paid the compensation pursuant to paragraph 1 and Europol or another Member State over the principle or the amount of the reimbursement shall be referred to the Management Board, which shall settle the matter by a majority of two thirds of its members.

*Article 53*

**Other liability**

1. Europol's contractual liability shall be governed by the law applicable to the contract in question.

2. In the case of non-contractual liability, Europol shall be obliged, independently of any liability under Article 52, to make good any damage caused by the fault of its organs, or of its staff in the performance of their duties, in so far as it may be imputed to them and regardless of the different procedures for claiming damages which exist under the law of the Member States.

3. The injured party shall have the right to demand that Europol refrain from or cease any action.

(1) Council Regulation (EC) No 2965/94 of 28 November 1994 setting up a Translation Centre for bodies of the European Union (OJ L 314, 7.12.1994, p. 1).
(2) OJ L 136, 31.5.1999, p. 1.

4. The national courts of the Member States competent to deal with disputes involving Europol's liability as referred to in this Article shall be determined by reference to Council Regulation (EC) No 44/2001 of 22 December 2000 on jurisdiction and the recognition and enforcement of judgments in civil and commercial matters (1).

*Article 54*

**Liability with regard to Europol's participationin joint investigation teams**

1. The Member State in the territory of which damage is caused by Europol staff operating in accordance with Article 6 in that Member State during their assistance in operational measures shall make good such damage under the conditions applicable to damage caused by its own officials.

2. Unless otherwise agreed by the Member State concerned, Europol shall reimburse in full any sums that that Member State has paid to the victims or persons entitled on their behalf for damage referred to in paragraph 1. Any dispute between that Member State and Europol over the principle or the amount of the reimbursement shall be referred to the Management Board, which shall settle the matter.

CHAPTER X

**TRANSITIONAL PROVISIONS**

*Article 55*

**General legal succession**

1. This Decision shall not affect the legal force of agreements concluded by Europol as established by the Europol Convention before the date of application of this Decision.

2. Paragraph 1 shall apply in particular to the Headquarters Agreement concluded on the basis of Article 37 of the Europol Convention, as well as the agreements between the Kingdom of the Netherlands and the other Member States established on the basis of Article 41(2) of the Europol Convention and to all international agreements, including their provisions on the exchange of information, and to contracts concluded by, liabilities incumbent on and properties acquired by Europol, as established by the Europol Convention.

*Article 56*

**Director and Deputy Directors**

1. The Director and Deputy Directors appointed on the basis of Article 29 of the Europol Convention shall, for the remaining periods of their terms of office, be the Director and Deputy Directors within the meaning of Article 38 of this Decision. If their terms of office end one year or less after the date of application of this Decision, they shall be extended automatically until one year after the date of application of this Decision.

2. Should the Director or one or more of the Deputy Directors be unwilling or unable to act in accordance with paragraph 1, the Management Board shall appoint an interim Director or interim Deputy Director(s) as required for a maximum period of 18 months, pending the appointments provided for in Article 38(1) and (2).

*Article 57*

**Staff**

1. By way of derogation from Article 39, all employment contracts concluded by Europol as established by the Europol Convention and in force on the date of application of this Decision shall be honoured until their expiry date and may not be renewed on the basis of the Europol Staff Regulations (2) after the date of application of this Decision.

2. All members of staff under contracts as referred to in paragraph 1 shall be offered the possibility of concluding temporary agent contracts under Article 2(a) of the Conditions of employment at the various grades as set out in the establishment plan or contract agent contracts under Article 3a of the Conditions of employment.

To that end, an internal selection process limited to staff who have contracts with Europol on the date of application of this Decision shall be carried out after the entry into force and within two years of the date of application of this Decision by the authority authorised to conclude contracts in order to check the ability, efficiency and integrity of those to be engaged.

Depending on the type and level of the functions performed, a successful candidate shall be offered either a temporary agent contract or a contract agent contract for a period corresponding at least to the time remaining under the contract concluded before the date of application of this Decision.

3. If a second fixed-term contract was concluded by Europol before the date of application of this Decision and the staff member accepted a temporary agent contract or contract agent contract under the conditions laid down in the third subparagraph of paragraph 2, any subsequent renewal may be concluded only for an indefinite period, in accordance with Article 39(4).

4. If a contract of an indefinite duration was concluded by Europol before the date of application of this Decision and the staff member accepted a temporary agent or contract agent contract under the conditions laid down in the third subparagraph of paragraph 2, that contract shall be concluded for an indefinite period in accordance with the first paragraph of Article 8 and Article 85(1) of the Conditions of employment.

(1) OJ L 12, 16.1.2001, p. 1.

(2) Council Act of 3 December 1998 laying down the staff regulations applicable to Europol employees (OJ C 26, 30.1.1999, p. 23).

5. The Europol Staff Regulations and other relevant instruments shall continue to apply to staff members who are not recruited in accordance with paragraph 2. By way of derogation from Chapter 5 of the Europol Staff Regulations, the percentage rate of the annual adjustment of remuneration decided by the Council in accordance with Article 65 of the Staff Regulations shall apply to Europol staff.

*Article 58*

**Budget**

1. The discharge procedure in respect of the budgets approved on the basis of Article 35(5) of the Europol Convention shall be carried out in accordance with the rules established by Article 36(5) of the Europol Convention and the financial regulation adopted on the basis of Article 35(9) of the Europol Convention.

2. In carrying out the discharge procedure described in paragraph 1, the following shall apply:

(a) for the purpose of carrying out the discharge procedure in respect of the annual accounts for the year preceding the date of application of this Decision, the Joint Audit Committee shall continue to operate in accordance with the procedures established by Article 36 of the Europol Convention. The discharge procedures established by the Europol Convention shall apply to the extent required for this purpose;

(b) the Management Board referred to in Article 36 of this Decision shall have the right to decide upon the substitution of the functions previously performed by the financial controller and the Financial Committee on the basis of the Europol Convention.

3. All expenditure resulting from commitments made by Europol in accordance with the financial regulation adopted on the basis of Article 35(9) of the Europol Convention before the date of application of this Decision which has not yet been paid at that time shall be paid in the manner described in paragraph 4 of this Article.

4. Before the expiry of a period of twelve months after the date of application of this Decision, the Management Board shall establish the amount covering the expenditure referred to in paragraph 3. A corresponding amount, financed from the accumulated surplus of the budgets approved on the basis of Article 35(5) of the Europol Convention, shall be transferred into the first budget established under this Decision and shall constitute an assigned revenue to cover that expenditure.

If the surpluses are not sufficient to cover the expenditure referred to in paragraph 3, Member States shall provide the financing necessary in accordance with the procedures established by the Europol Convention.

5. The remainder of the surpluses of the budgets approved on the basis of Article 35(5) of the Europol Convention shall be paid back to the Member States. The amount to be paid to each of the Member States shall be calculated on the basis of the annual contributions from the Member States to Europol's budgets established on the basis of Article 35(2) of the Europol Convention.

The payment shall be made within three months of the establishment of the amount covering the expenditure referred to in paragraph 3 and the completion of discharge procedures regarding the budgets approved on the basis of Article 35(5) of the Europol Convention.

*Article 59*

**Measures to be prepared and adoptedbefore the date of application of this Decision**

1. The Management Board set up on the basis of the Europol Convention, the Director appointed on the basis of that Convention and the Joint Supervisory Body set up on the basis of that Convention shall prepare the adoption of the following instruments:

(a) the rules regarding the rights and obligations of liaison officers referred to in Article 9(5);

(b) the rules applicable to the analysis work files referred to in the third subparagraph of Article 14(1);

(c) the rules regarding the relations of Europol referred to in Article 26(1)(b);

(d) the implementing rules applicable to Europol staff referred to in Article 37(9)(d);

(e) the rules on the selection and dismissal of the Director and Deputy Directors referred to in Article 38(3) and (7);

(f) the rules on confidentiality referred to in Article 40(1);

(g) the financial regulation referred to in Article 44;

(h) any other instrument necessary for the preparation of the application of this Decision.

2. For the purpose of adopting the measures referred to in paragraph 1(a), (d), (e), (g) and (h), the composition of the Management Board shall be as laid down in Article 37(1). The Management Board shall adopt those measures in accordance with the procedure laid down in the provisions referred to in paragraph 1(a), (d), (e) and (g) of this Article.

The Council shall adopt the measures referred to in paragraph 1(b), (c) and (f) in accordance with the procedure laid down in the provisions referred to in paragraph 1(b), (c) and (f).

*Article 60*

**Financial actions and decisions to be takenbefore the date of application of this Decision**

1. The Management Board, in its composition as laid down in Article 37(1), shall take all financial actions and decisions necessary for the application of the new financial framework.

2. The actions and decisions referred to in paragraph 1 shall be taken in accordance with Regulation (EC, Euratom) No 2343/2002 and shall include, inter alia, the following:

(a) the preparation and adoption of all actions and decisions referred to in Article 42 in relation to the first budgetary year after the date of application of this Decision;

(b) the appointment of the accounting officer as provided for in Article 37(9)(e) by 15 November in the year preceding the first budgetary year after the date of application of this Decision;

(c) the establishment of the internal audit function as provided for in Article 37(9)(f).

3. The authorisation of operations which accrue to the first budgetary year after the date of application of this Decision shall be performed by the Director appointed under Article 29 of the Europol Convention from 15 November in the year preceding the first budgetary year after the date of application of this Decision. From that date onwards, the Director shall also be entitled to delegate the function of authorising officer as necessary. In the performance of the role of authorising officer, the requirements of Regulation (EC, Euratom) No 2343/2002 shall be observed.

4. The *ex-ante* verification of operations that accrue to the first budgetary year following the date of application of this Decision shall be taken by the financial controller established under Article 27(3) of the Europol Convention during the period 15 November to 31 December in the year preceding the first budgetary year following the date of application of this Decision. The financial controller shall perform that function in accordance with Regulation (EC, Euratom) No 2343/2002.

5. A proportion of the transition costs incurred by Europol to prepare for the new financial framework from the year preceding the first budgetary year following the date of application of this Decision shall be borne by the general budget of the European Union. The financing of those costs may take the form of a Community grant.

CHAPTER XI

**FINAL PROVISIONS**

*Article 61*

**Transposition**

The Member States shall ensure that their national law conforms to this Decision by the date of application of this Decision.

*Article 62*

**Replacement**

This Decision replaces the Europol Convention and the Protocol on the privileges and immunities of Europol, the members of its organs, the Deputy Directors and employees of Europol as of the date of application of this Decision.

*Article 63*

**Repeal**

Unless otherwise provided in this Decision, all measures implementing the Europol Convention shall be repealed with effect from the date of application of this Decision.

*Article 64*

**Entry into force and application**

1. This Decision shall enter into force on the 20th day following its publication in the *Official Journal of the European Union*.

2. It shall apply from 1 January 2010 or the date of application of the Regulation referred to in Article 51(1), whichever is the later.

However, the second subparagraph of Article 57(2) and Articles 59, 60 and 61 shall apply from the date of entry into force of this Decision.

Done at Luxembourg, 6 April 2009.

*For the Council*

*The President*

J. POSPÍŠIL

*ANNEX*

List of other forms of serious crime which Europol is competent to deal with in accordance with Article 4(1):

— unlawful drug trafficking,

— illegal money-laundering activities,

— crime connected with nuclear and radioactive substances,

— illegal immigrant smuggling,

— trafficking in human beings,

— motor vehicle crime,

— murder, grievous bodily injury,

— illicit trade in human organs and tissue,

— kidnapping, illegal restraint and hostage taking,

— racism and xenophobia,

— organised robbery,

— illicit trafficking in cultural goods, including antiquities and works of art,

— swindling and fraud,

— racketeering and extortion,

— counterfeiting and product piracy,

— forgery of administrative documents and trafficking therein,

— forgery of money and means of payment,

— computer crime,

— corruption,

— illicit trafficking in arms, ammunition and explosives,

— illicit trafficking in endangered animal species,

— illicit trafficking in endangered plant species and varieties,

— environmental crime,

— illicit trafficking in hormonal substances and other growth promoters.

With regard to the forms of crime listed in Article 4(1) for the purposes of this Decision:

(a) 'crime connected with nuclear and radioactive substances' means the criminal offences listed in Article 7(1) of the Convention on the Physical Protection of Nuclear Material, signed at Vienna and New York on 3 March 1980, and relating to the nuclear and/or radioactive materials defined in Article 197 of the Treaty establishing the European Atomic Community and in Council Directive 96/29/Euratom of 13 May 1996 laying down basic safety standards for the protection of the health of workers and the general public against the dangers arising from ionizing radiation [1];

(b) 'illegal immigrant smuggling' means activities intended deliberately to facilitate, for financial gain, the entry into, residence or employment in the territory of the Member States, contrary to the rules and conditions applicable in the Member States;

[1] OJ L 159, 29.6.1996, p. 1.

(c) 'trafficking in human beings' means the recruitment, transportation, transfer, harbouring or receipt of persons, by means of the threat or use of force or other forms of coercion, of abduction, of fraud, of deception, of the abuse of power or of a position of vulnerability or of the giving or receiving of payments or benefits to achieve the consent of a person having control over another person, for the purpose of exploitation. Exploitation shall include, as a minimum, the exploitation of the prostitution of others or other forms of sexual exploitation, the production, sale or distribution of child-pornography material, forced labour or services, slavery or practices similar to slavery, servitude or the removal of organs;

(d) 'motor vehicle crime' means the theft or misappropriation of motor vehicles, lorries, semi-trailers, the loads of lorries or semi-trailers, buses, motorcycles, caravans and agricultural vehicles, works vehicles and the spare parts for such vehicles, and the receiving and concealing of such objects;

(e) 'illegal money-laundering activities' means the criminal offences listed in Article 6(1) to (3) of the Council of Europe Convention on Laundering, Search, Seizure and Confiscation of the Proceeds from Crime, signed in Strasbourg on 8 November 1990;

(f) 'unlawful drug trafficking' means the criminal offences listed in Article 3(1) of the United Nations Convention of 20 December 1988 against Illicit Traffic in Narcotic Drugs and Psychotropic Substances and in the provisions amending or replacing that Convention.

The forms of crime referred to in Article 4 and in this Annex shall be assessed by the competent authorities of the Member States in accordance with the law of the Member States to which they belong.

# Decision 2009/1010 on the conditions related to the processing of data on the basis of Article 10(4) of the Europol Decision, 4 June 2009

[OJ 2009, L 348/1–2]

29.12.2009 EN Official Journal of the European Union L 348/1

III

*(Acts adopted under the EU Treaty)*

# ACTS ADOPTED UNDER TITLE VI OF THE EU TREATY

## DECISION OF THE MANAGEMENT BOARD OF EUROPOL

**of 4 June 2009**

**on the conditions related to the processing of data on the basis of Article 10(4) of the Europol Decision**

(2009/1010/JHA)

THE MANAGEMENT BOARD OF EUROPOL,

Having regard to the Council Decision 2009/371/JHA of 6 April 2009 establishing the European Police Office (Europol) ([1]) (hereinafter the Europol Decision) and in particular Article 10(4) thereof,

Whereas:

(1) It is for the Management Board, acting on a proposal from the Director and after consulting the Joint Supervisory Body, to determine the conditions relating to the processing of data for the purpose of determining whether such data are relevant to Europol's tasks and can be included in one of its information processing systems, in particular with respect to access to and the use of the data, as well as time limits for the storage and deletion of the data.

(2) The Management Board, by adopting this Decision, shall take account of the principles of the Council of Europe Convention for the Protection of Individuals with regard to Automatic Processing of Personal Data of 28 January 1981 and of Recommendation No R(87)15 of the Committee of Ministers of the Council of Europe of 17 September 1987 regulating the use of personal data in the police sector.

(3) The Management Board Decision shall be submitted to the Council for approval,

HAS ADOPTED THE FOLLOWING DECISION:

*Article 1*

**Definitions**

For the purpose of this Decision:

(a) 'personal data' means any information relating to an identified or identifiable natural person: an identifiable person is one who can be identified, directly or indirectly, in particular by reference to an identification number or to one or more factors specific to his physical, physiological, mental, economic, cultural or social identity;

(b) 'processing of personal data' means any operation or set of operations which is performed upon personal data, whether or not by automatic means, such as collection, recording, organisation, storage, adaptation or alteration, retrieval, consultation, use, disclosure by transmission, dissemination or otherwise making available, alignment or combination, blocking, erasure or destruction;

(c) 'information processing systems' means the Europol Information System, the analysis work files and other systems processing personal data, as referred to in Article 10(1) of the Europol Decision;

(d) 'Europol Information System' means the system referred to in Article 11(1) of the Europol Decision;

(e) 'analysis work file' means a file opened for the purpose of analysis, as referred to in Article 14 of the Europol Decision;

(f) 'EU bodies' means institutions, bodies, offices and agencies set up by, or on the basis of, the Treaty on European Union and the Treaties establishing the European Communities, as referred to in Article 22(1) of the Europol Decision;

(g) 'third parties' means third States and organisations as referred to in Article 23(1) of the Europol Decision;

(h) 'duly authorised Europol staff' means Europol staff designated by the Director to process personal data in accordance with this Decision.

([1]) OJ L 121, 15.5.2009, p. 37.

*Article 2*

**Scope**

This Decision shall apply to personal data communicated to Europol for the purpose of determining whether such data are relevant to its tasks and can be included in its information processing systems, with the exception of:

(a) personal data entered into the Europol Information System pursuant to Article 13(1) of the Europol Decision;

(b) personal data offered by a Member State, an EU body or a third party for inclusion in a specific analysis work file as well as personal data entered into an analysis work file pursuant to Article 14 of the Europol Decision;

(c) personal data provided to Europol for inclusion in another specific system processing personal data as referred to in Article 10(1) last sentence of the Europol Decision.

*Article 3*

**Access and use**

1. Access to personal data processed by Europol under this Decision shall be limited to duly authorised Europol staff.

2. Without prejudice to Article 17 of the Europol Decision, personal data processed by Europol under this Decision shall only be used for the purposes of determining whether such data are relevant for Europol's tasks and can be included in its information processing systems.

3. Where Europol determines that the data are relevant to its tasks and can be included in the Europol Information System, Europol shall suggest that the providing Member State should input the data in the Europol Information System, in accordance with Article 13(1) of the Europol Decision. If the Member State does not follow Europol's suggestion, Article 5 of this Decision shall apply.

*Article 4*

**Rules on personal data protection and on data security**

1. Europol shall, when processing personal data under this Decision, comply with the rules on personal data protection and on data security laid down in the Europol Decision, in particular Articles 18, 27, and 35 and the rules adopted in the implementation thereof.

2. In case Europol decides to include such data in the information processing systems or to delete or destroy it, it shall inform the providing Member State, EU body or third party thereof.

*Article 5*

**Time limit for the storage of data**

1. A decision on the use of personal data in accordance with Article 3(2) shall be taken as soon as possible and in any case not later than six months after such data was received by Europol.

2. In the absence of such a decision upon expiry of the six-month period, the personal data in question shall be deleted or destroyed and the providing Member State, EU body or third party shall be informed thereof.

*Article 6*

**Responsibility**

Europol shall be responsible for ensuring compliance with Articles 3, 4 and 5 of this Decision.

*Article 7*

**Entry into force**

This Decision shall enter into force on the same day as the date of application of the Europol Decision.

The Hague, 4 June 2009.

Approved by the Council on 30 November 2009

*The President*

S. CLERTON

# Directive 2009/52 providing for minimum standards on sanctions and measures against employers of illegally staying third-country nationals, 18 June 2009

**[Consolidated version. Original version OJ 2009, L 168/24–32 corrected by OJ 2012, L 208/22]**

**►B DIRECTIVE 2009/52/EC OF THE EUROPEAN PARLIAMENT AND OF THE COUNCIL**

**of 18 June 2009**

**providing for minimum standards on sanctions and measures against employers of illegally staying third-country nationals**

(OJ L 168, 30.6.2009, p. 24)

Corrected by:

►C1 Corrigendum, OJ L 208, 3.8.2012, p. 22 (2009/52/EC)

▼B

**DIRECTIVE 2009/52/EC OF THE EUROPEAN PARLIAMENT AND OF THE COUNCIL**

**of 18 June 2009**

**providing for minimum standards on sanctions and measures against employers of illegally staying third-country nationals**

THE EUROPEAN PARLIAMENT AND THE COUNCIL OF THE EUROPEAN UNION,

Having regard to the Treaty establishing the European Community, and in particular Article 63(3)(b) thereof,

Having regard to the proposal from the Commission,

Having regard to the opinion of the European Economic and Social Committee [1],

Having regard to the opinion of the Committee of the Regions [2],

Acting in accordance with the procedure laid down in Article 251 of the Treaty [3],

Whereas:

(1) The European Council meeting of 14 and 15 December 2006 agreed that cooperation among Member States should be strengthened in the fight against illegal immigration and in particular that measures against illegal employment should be intensified at Member State and EU level.

(2) A key pull factor for illegal immigration into the EU is the possibility of obtaining work in the EU without the required legal status. Action against illegal immigration and illegal stay should therefore include measures to counter that pull factor.

(3) The centrepiece of such measures should be a general prohibition on the employment of third-country nationals who do not have the right to be resident in the EU, accompanied by sanctions against employers who infringe that prohibition.

(4) As this Directive provides for minimum standards, Member States should remain free to adopt or maintain stricter sanctions and measures and impose stricter obligations on employers.

(1) OJ C 204, 9.8.2008, p. 70.
(2) OJ C 257, 9.10.2008, p. 20.
(3) ►C1 Opinion of the European Parliament of 19 February 2009 ◄ (not yet published in the Official Journal) and Council Decision of 25 May 2009.

▼B

(5) This Directive should not apply to third-country nationals staying legally in a Member State regardless of whether they are allowed to work in its territory. Furthermore, it should not apply to persons enjoying the Community right of free movement, as defined in Article 2(5) of Regulation (EC) No 562/2006 of the European Parliament and of the Council of 15 March 2006 establishing a Community Code on the rules governing the movement of persons across borders (Schengen Borders Code) ([1]). Moreover it should not apply to third-country nationals who are in a situation covered by Community law, such as those who are lawfully employed in a Member State and who are posted by a service provider to another Member State in the context of the provision of services. This Directive should apply without prejudice to national law prohibiting the employment of legally staying third-country nationals who work in breach of their residence status.

(6) For the specific purposes of this Directive, certain terms should be defined and such definitions should be used only for the purposes of this Directive.

(7) The definition of employment should encompass its constituent elements, namely activities that are or ought to be remunerated, undertaken for or under the direction and/or supervision of an employer, irrespective of the legal relationship.

(8) The definition of employer may include an association of persons recognised as having the capacity to perform legal acts without having legal personality.

(9) To prevent the employment of illegally staying third-country nationals, employers should be required, before recruiting a third-country national, including in cases where the third-country national is being recruited for the purpose of posting to another Member State in the context of the provision of services, to check that the third-country national has a valid residence permit or another authorisation for stay showing that he or she is legally staying on the territory of the Member State of recruitment.

(10) To enable Member States in particular to check for forged documents, employers should also be required to notify the competent authorities of the employment of a third-country national. In order to minimise the administrative burden, Member States should be free to provide for such notifications to be undertaken within the framework of other notification schemes. Member States should be free to decide a simplified procedure for notification by employers who are natural persons where the employment is for their private purposes.

(11) Employers that have fulfilled the obligations set out in this Directive should not be held liable for having employed illegally staying third-country nationals, in particular if the competent authority later finds that the document presented by an employee had in fact been forged or misused, unless the employer knew that the document was a forgery.

([1]) OJ L 105, 13.4.2006, p. 1.

▼B

(12) To facilitate the fulfilment by employers of their obligations, Member States should use their best endeavours to handle requests for renewal of residence permits in a timely manner.

(13) To enforce the general prohibition and to deter infringements, Member States should provide for appropriate sanctions. These should include financial sanctions and contributions to the costs of returning illegally staying third-country nationals, together with the possibility of reduced financial sanctions on employers who are natural persons where the employment is for their private purposes.

(14) The employer should in any event be required to pay to the third-country nationals any outstanding remuneration for the work which they have undertaken and any outstanding taxes and social security contributions. If the level of remuneration cannot be determined, it should be presumed to be at least as high as the wage provided for by the applicable laws on minimum wages, by collective agreements or in accordance with established practice in the relevant occupational branches. The employer should also be required to pay, where appropriate, any costs arising from the sending of outstanding remuneration to the country to which the illegally employed third-country national has, or has been, returned. In those cases where back payments are not made by the employer, Member States should not be obliged to fulfil that obligation in place of the employer.

(15) An illegally employed third-country national should not derive a right to entry, stay and access to the labour market from the illegal employment relationship or from the payment or back payment of remuneration, social security contributions or taxes by the employer or by a legal entity which has to pay instead of the employer.

(16) Member States should ensure that claims are or may be lodged and that mechanisms are in place to ensure that recovered amounts of outstanding remuneration are able to be received by the third-country nationals to whom they are due. Member States should not be obliged to involve their missions or representations in third countries in those mechanisms. Member States should, in the context of establishing effective mechanisms to facilitate complaints and if not already provided for by national legislation, consider the possibility and added value of enabling a competent authority to bring proceedings against an employer for the purpose of recovering outstanding remuneration.

(17) Member States should further provide for a presumption of an employment relationship of at least three months' duration so that the burden of proof is on the employer in respect of at least a certain period. Among others, the employee should also have the opportunity of proving the existence and duration of an employment relationship.

▼B

(18) Member States should provide for the possibility of further sanctions against employers, inter alia, exclusions from entitlement to some or all public benefits, aids or subsidies, including agricultural subsidies, exclusions from public procurement procedures and recovery of some or all public benefits, aids or subsidies, including EU funding managed by Member States, that have already been granted. Member States should be free to decide not to apply those further sanctions against employers who are natural persons where the employment is for their private purposes.

(19) This Directive, and in particular its Articles 7, 10 and 12, should be without prejudice to Council Regulation (EC, Euratom) No 1605/2002 of 25 June 2002 on the Financial Regulation applicable to the general budget of the European Communities ([1]).

(20) In view of the prevalence of subcontracting in certain affected sectors, it is necessary to ensure that at least the contractor of which the employer is a direct subcontractor may be liable to pay financial sanctions in addition to or in place of the employer. In specific cases, other contractors may be liable to pay financial sanctions in addition to or in place of an employer of illegally staying third-country nationals. Back payments which are to be covered by the liability provisions of this Directive should also include contributions to national holiday pay funds and social funds regulated by law or collective agreements.

(21) Experience has shown that the existing systems of sanctions have not been sufficient to achieve complete compliance with prohibitions against the employment of illegally staying third-country nationals. One of the reasons is that administrative sanctions alone are likely not to be enough to deter certain unscrupulous employers. Compliance can and should be strengthened by the application of criminal penalties.

(22) To guarantee the full effectiveness of the general prohibition, there is therefore a particular need for more dissuasive sanctions in serious cases, such as persistently repeated infringements, the illegal employment of a significant number of third-country nationals, particularly exploitative working conditions, the employer knowing that the worker is a victim of trafficking in human beings and the illegal employment of a minor. This Directive obliges Member States to provide for criminal penalties in their national legislation in respect of those serious infringements. It creates no obligations regarding the application of such penalties, or any other available system of law enforcement, in individual cases.

(23) In all cases deemed to be serious according to this Directive the infringement should be considered a criminal offence throughout the Community when committed intentionally. The provisions of this Directive regarding criminal offences should be without prejudice to the application of Council Framework Decision 2002/629/JHA of 19 July 2002 on combating trafficking in human beings ([2]).

([1]) OJ L 248, 16.9.2002, p. 1.
([2]) OJ L 203, 1.8.2002, p. 1.

▼B

(24) The criminal offence should be punishable by effective, proportionate and dissuasive criminal penalties. The obligation to ensure effective, proportionate and dissuasive criminal penalties under this Directive is without prejudice to the internal organisation of criminal law and criminal justice in the Member States.

(25) Legal persons may also be held liable for the criminal offences referred to in this Directive, because many employers are legal persons. The provisions of this Directive do not entail an obligation for Member States to introduce criminal liability of legal persons.

(26) To facilitate the enforcement of this Directive, there should be effective complaint mechanisms by which relevant third-country nationals may lodge complaints directly or through designated third parties such as trade unions or other associations. The designated third parties should be protected, when providing assistance to lodge complaints, against possible sanctions under rules prohibiting the facilitation of unauthorised residence.

(27) To supplement the complaint mechanisms, Member States should be free to grant residence permits of limited duration, linked to the length of the relevant national proceedings, to third-country nationals who have been subjected to particularly exploitative working conditions or who were illegally employed minors and who cooperate in criminal proceedings against the employer. Such permits should be granted under arrangements comparable to those applicable to third-country nationals who fall within the scope of Council Directive 2004/81/EC of 29 April 2004 on the residence permit issued to third-country nationals who are victims of trafficking in human beings or who have been the subject of an action to facilitate illegal immigration, who cooperate with the competent authorities [1].

(28) To ensure a satisfactory level of enforcement of this Directive and to reduce, as far as possible, differences in the level of enforcement in the Member States, Member States should ensure that effective and adequate inspections are carried out on their territory and should communicate data on the inspections they carry out to the Commission.

(29) Member States should be encouraged to determine every year a national target for the number of inspections in respect of the sectors of activity in which the employment of illegally staying third-country nationals is concentrated on their territory.

(30) With a view to increasing the effectiveness of inspections for the purposes of applying this Directive, Member States should ensure that national legislation gives adequate powers to competent authorities to carry out inspections; that information about illegal employment, including the results of previous inspections, is collected and processed for the effective implementation of this Directive; and that sufficient staff are available with the skills and qualifications needed to carry out inspections effectively.

---
(1) OJ L 261, 6.8.2004, p. 19.

▼B

(31) Member States should ensure that inspections for the purposes of applying this Directive do not affect, from a quantitative or qualitative point of view, inspections carried out to assess employment and working conditions.

(32) In the case of posted workers who are third-country nationals, Member States' inspection authorities may avail themselves of the cooperation and exchange of information provided for in Directive 96/71/EC of the European Parliament and of the Council of 16 December 1996 concerning the posting of workers in the framework of the provision of services [1], in order to verify that the third-country nationals concerned are lawfully employed in the Member State of origin.

(33) This Directive should be seen as complementary to measures to counter undeclared work and exploitation.

(34) In accordance with point 34 of the Interinstitutional Agreement on better law-making [2], Member States are encouraged to draw up, for themselves and in the interests of the Community, their own tables, which will, as far as possible, illustrate the correlation between this Directive and the transposition measures and to make them public.

(35) Any processing of personal data undertaken in the implementation of this Directive should be in compliance with Directive 95/46/EC of the European Parliament and of the Council of 24 October 1995 on the protection of individuals with regard to the processing of personal data and on the free movement of such data [3].

(36) Since the objective of this Directive, namely to counteract illegal immigration by acting against the employment pull factor, cannot be sufficiently achieved by the Member States and can therefore, by reason of the scale and effects of this Directive, be better achieved at Community level, the Community may adopt measures, in accordance with the principle of subsidiarity as set out in Article 5 of the Treaty. In accordance with the principle of proportionality, as set out in that Article, this Directive does not go beyond what is necessary to achieve that objective.

(37) This Directive respects the fundamental rights and observes the principles recognised in particular by the European Convention for the Protection of Human Rights and Fundamental Freedoms and the Charter of Fundamental Rights of the European Union. Specifically, it should be applied with due respect for the freedom to conduct a business, equality before the law and the principle of non-discrimination, the right to an effective remedy and to a fair trial and the principles of legality and proportionality of criminal offences and penalties, in accordance with Articles 16, 20, 21, 47 and 49 of the Charter.

(1) OJ L 18, 21.1.1997, p. 1.
(2) OJ C 321, 31.12.2003, p. 1.
(3) OJ L 281, 23.11.1995, p. 31.

▼B

(38) In accordance with Articles 1 and 2 of the Protocol on the position of the United Kingdom and Ireland, annexed to the Treaty on European Union and to the Treaty establishing the European Community, and without prejudice to Article 4 of that Protocol, those Member States are not taking part in the adoption of this Directive and are therefore not bound by it or subject to its application.

(39) In accordance with Articles 1 and 2 of the Protocol on the position of Denmark annexed to the Treaty on European Union and to the Treaty establishing the European Community, Denmark is not taking part in the adoption of this Directive and is therefore not bound by it or subject to its application,

HAVE ADOPTED THIS DIRECTIVE:

*Article 1*

**Subject matter and scope**

This Directive prohibits the employment of illegally staying third-country nationals in order to fight illegal immigration. To this end, it lays down minimum common standards on sanctions and measures to be applied in the Member States against employers who infringe that prohibition.

*Article 2*

**Definitions**

For the specific purposes of this Directive, the following definitions shall apply:

(a) 'third-country national' means any person who is not a citizen of the Union within the meaning of Article 17(1) of the Treaty and who is not a person enjoying the Community right of free movement, as defined in Article 2(5) of the Schengen Borders Code;

(b) 'illegally staying third-country national' means a third-country national present on the territory of a Member State, who does not fulfil, or no longer fulfils, the conditions for stay or residence in that Member State;

(c) 'employment' means the exercise of activities covering whatever form of labour or work regulated under national law or in accordance with established practice for or under the direction and/or supervision of an employer;

(d) 'illegal employment' means the employment of an illegally staying third-country national;

(e) 'employer' means any natural person or any legal entity, including temporary work agencies, for or under the direction and/or supervision of whom the employment is undertaken;

(f) 'subcontractor' means any natural person or any legal entity, to whom the execution of all or part of the obligations of a prior contract is assigned;

▼B

(g) 'legal person' means any legal entity having such status under applicable national law, except for States or public bodies exercising State authority and for public international organisations;

(h) 'temporary work agency' means any natural or legal person who, in compliance with national law, concludes contracts of employment or employment relationships with temporary agency workers in order to assign them to user undertakings to work there temporarily under their supervision and direction;

(i) 'particularly exploitative working conditions' means working conditions, including those resulting from gender based or other discrimination, where there is a striking disproportion compared with the terms of employment of legally employed workers which, for example, affects workers' health and safety, and which offends against human dignity;

(j) 'remuneration of illegally staying third-country national' means the wage or salary and any other consideration, whether in cash or in kind, which a worker receives directly or indirectly in respect of his employment from his employer and which is equivalent to that which would have been enjoyed by comparable workers in a legal employment relationship.

*Article 3*

**Prohibition of illegal employment**

1. Member States shall prohibit the employment of illegally staying third-country nationals.

2. Infringements of this prohibition shall be subject to the sanctions and measures laid down in this Directive.

3. A Member State may decide not to apply the prohibition referred to in paragraph 1 to illegally staying third-country nationals whose removal has been postponed and who are allowed to work in accordance with national law.

*Article 4*

**Obligations on employers**

1. Member States shall oblige employers to:

(a) require that a third-country national before taking up the employment holds and presents to the employer a valid residence permit or other authorisation for his or her stay;

(b) keep for at least the duration of the employment a copy or record of the residence permit or other authorisation for stay available for possible inspection by the competent authorities of the Member States;

(c) notify the competent authorities designated by Member States of the start of employment of third-country nationals within a period laid down by each Member State.

2. Member States may provide for a simplified procedure for notification under paragraph 1(c) where the employers are natural persons and the employment is for their private purposes.

▼B

Member States may provide that notification under paragraph 1(c) is not required where the employee has been granted long-term residence status under Council Directive 2003/109/EC of 25 November 2003 concerning the status of third-country nationals who are long-term residents ([1]).

3. Member States shall ensure that employers who have fulfilled their obligations set out in paragraph 1 shall not be held liable for an infringement of the prohibition referred to in Article 3 unless the employers knew that the document presented as a valid residence permit or another authorisation for stay was a forgery.

*Article 5*

**Financial sanctions**

1. Member States shall take the necessary measures to ensure that infringements of the prohibition referred to in Article 3 are subject to effective, proportionate and dissuasive sanctions against the employer.

2. Sanctions in respect of infringements of the prohibition referred to in Article 3 shall include:

(a) financial sanctions which shall increase in amount according to the number of illegally employed third-country nationals; and

(b) payments of the costs of return of illegally employed third-country nationals in those cases where return procedures are carried out. Member States may instead decide to reflect at least the average costs of return in the financial sanctions under point (a).

3. Member States may provide for reduced financial sanctions where the employer is a natural person who employs an illegally staying third-country national for his or her private purposes and where no particularly exploitative working conditions are involved.

*Article 6*

**Back payments to be made by employers**

1. In respect of each infringement of the prohibition referred to in Article 3, Member States shall ensure that the employer shall be liable to pay:

(a) any outstanding remuneration to the illegally employed third-country national. The agreed level of remuneration shall be presumed to have been at least as high as the wage provided for by the applicable laws on minimum wages, by collective agreements or in accordance with established practice in the relevant occupational branches, unless either the employer or the employee can prove otherwise, while respecting, where appropriate, the mandatory national provisions on wages;

(b) an amount equal to any taxes and social security contributions that the employer would have paid had the third-country national been legally employed, including penalty payments for delays and relevant administrative fines;

([1]) OJ L 16, 23.1.2004, p. 44.

▼B

(c) where appropriate, any cost arising from sending back payments to the country to which the third-country national has returned or has been returned.

2. In order to ensure the availability of effective procedures to apply paragraph 1(a) and (c), and having due regard to Article 13, Member States shall enact mechanisms to ensure that illegally employed third-country nationals:

(a) may introduce a claim, subject to a limitation period defined in national law, against their employer and eventually enforce a judgment against the employer for any outstanding remuneration, including in cases in which they have, or have been, returned; or

(b) when provided for by national legislation, may call on the competent authority of the Member State to start procedures to recover outstanding remuneration without the need for them to introduce a claim in that case.

Illegally employed third-country nationals shall be systematically and objectively informed about their rights under this paragraph and under Article 13 before the enforcement of any return decision.

3. In order to apply paragraph 1(a) and (b), Member States shall provide that an employment relationship of at least three months duration be presumed unless, among others, the employer or the employee can prove otherwise.

4. Member States shall ensure that the necessary mechanisms are in place to ensure that illegally employed third-country nationals are able to receive any back payment of remuneration referred to in paragraph 1(a) which is recovered as part of the claims referred to in paragraph 2, including in cases in which they have, or have been, returned.

5. In respect of cases where residence permits of limited duration have been granted under Article 13(4), Member States shall define under national law the conditions under which the duration of these permits may be extended until the third-country national has received any back payment of his or her remuneration recovered under paragraph 1 of this Article.

*Article 7*

**Other measures**

1. Member States shall take the necessary measures to ensure that employers shall also, if appropriate, be subject to the following measures:

(a) exclusion from entitlement to some or all public benefits, aid or subsidies, including EU funding managed by Member States, for up to five years;

▼B

(b) exclusion from participation in a public contract as defined in Directive 2004/18/EC of the European Parliament and of the Council of 31 March 2004 on the coordination of procedures for the award of public works contracts, public supply contracts and public service contracts (1) for up to five years;

(c) recovery of some or all public benefits, aid, or subsidies, including EU funding managed by Member States, granted to the employer for up to 12 months preceding the detection of illegal employment;

(d) temporary or permanent closure of the establishments that have been used to commit the infringement, or temporary or permanent withdrawal of a licence to conduct the business activity in question, if justified by the gravity of the infringement.

2. Member States may decide not to apply paragraph 1 where the employers are natural persons and the employment is for their private purposes.

*Article 8*

**Subcontracting**

1. Where the employer is a subcontractor and without prejudice to the provisions of national law concerning the rights of contribution or recourse or to the provisions of national law in the field of social security, Member States shall ensure that the contractor of which the employer is a direct subcontractor may, in addition to or in place of the employer, be liable to pay:

(a) any financial sanction imposed under Article 5; and

(b) any back payments due under Article 6(1)(a) and (c) and Article 6(2) and(3).

2. Where the employer is a subcontractor, Member States shall ensure that the main contractor and any intermediate subcontractor, where they knew that the employing subcontractor employed illegally staying third-country nationals, may be liable to make the payments referred to in paragraph 1 in addition to or in place of the employing subcontractor or the contractor of which the employer is a direct subcontractor.

3. A contractor that has undertaken due diligence obligations as defined by national law shall not be liable under paragraphs 1 and 2.

4. Member States may provide for more stringent liability rules under national law.

*Article 9*

**Criminal offence**

1. Member States shall ensure that the infringement of the prohibition referred to in Article 3 constitutes a criminal offence when committed intentionally, in each of the following circumstances as defined by national law:

(a) the infringement continues or is persistently repeated;

(1) OJ L 134, 30.4.2004, p. 114.

▼B

(b) the infringement is in respect of the simultaneous employment of a significant number of illegally staying third-country nationals;

(c) the infringement is accompanied by particularly exploitative working conditions;

(d) the infringement is committed by an employer who, while not having been charged with or convicted of an offence established pursuant to Framework Decision 2002/629/JHA, uses work or services exacted from an illegally staying third-country national with the knowledge that he or she is a victim of trafficking in human beings;

(e) the infringement relates to the illegal employment of a minor.

2. Member States shall ensure that inciting, aiding and abetting the intentional conduct referred to in paragraph 1 is punishable as a criminal offence.

*Article 10*

**Criminal penalties**

1. Member States shall take the necessary measures to ensure that natural persons who commit the criminal offence referred to in Article 9 are punishable by effective, proportionate and dissuasive criminal penalties.

2. Unless prohibited by general principles of law, the criminal penalties provided for in this Article may be applied under national law without prejudice to other sanctions or measures of a non-criminal nature, and they may be accompanied by the publication of the judicial decision relevant to the case.

*Article 11*

**Liability of legal persons**

1. Member States shall ensure that legal persons may be held liable for the offence referred to in Article 9 where such an offence has been committed for their benefit by any person who has a leading position within the legal person, acting either individually or as part of an organ of the legal person, on the basis of:

(a) a power of representation of the legal person;

(b) an authority to take decisions on behalf of the legal person; or

(c) an authority to exercise control within the legal person.

2. Member States shall also ensure that a legal person may be held liable where the lack of supervision or control, by a person referred to in paragraph 1, has made possible the commission of the criminal offence referred to in Article 9 for the benefit of that legal person by a person under its authority.

3. Liability of a legal person under paragraphs 1 and 2 shall not exclude criminal proceedings against natural persons who are perpetrators, inciters or accessories in the offence referred to in Article 9.

▼B

*Article 12*

**Penalties for legal persons**

Member States shall take the necessary measures to ensure that a legal person held liable pursuant to Article 11 is punishable by effective, proportionate and dissuasive penalties, which may include measures such as those referred to in Article 7.

Member States may decide that a list of employers who are legal persons and who have been held liable for the criminal offence referred to in Article 9 is made public.

*Article 13*

**Facilitation of complaints**

1. Member States shall ensure that there are effective mechanisms through which third-country nationals in illegal employment may lodge complaints against their employers, directly or through third parties designated by Member States such as trade unions or other associations or a competent authority of the Member State when provided for by national legislation.

2. Member States shall ensure that third parties which have, in accordance with the criteria laid down in their national law, a legitimate interest in ensuring compliance with this Directive, may engage either on behalf of or in support of an illegally employed third-country national, with his or her approval, in any administrative or civil proceedings provided for with the objective of implementing this Directive.

3. Providing assistance to third-country nationals to lodge complaints shall not be considered as facilitation of unauthorised residence under Council Directive 2002/90/EC of 28 November 2002 defining the facilitation of unauthorised entry, transit and residence (1).

4. In respect of criminal offences covered by Article 9(1)(c) or (e), Member States shall define in national law the conditions under which they may grant, on a case-by-case basis, permits of limited duration, linked to the length of the relevant national proceedings, to the third-country nationals involved, under arrangements comparable to those applicable to third-country nationals who fall within the scope of Directive 2004/81/EC.

*Article 14*

**Inspections**

1. Member States shall ensure that effective and adequate inspections are carried out on their territory to control employment of illegally staying third-country nationals. Such inspections shall be based primarily on a risk assessment to be drawn up by the competent authorities in the Member States.

(1) OJ L 328, 5.12.2002, p. 17.

▼B

2. With a view to increasing the effectiveness of inspections, Member States shall, on the basis of a risk assessment, regularly identify the sectors of activity in which the employment of illegally staying third-country nationals is concentrated on their territory.

In respect of each of those sectors, Member States shall, before 1 July of each year, communicate to the Commission the inspections, both in absolute numbers and as a percentage of the employers for each sector, carried out in the previous year as well as their results.

*Article 15*

**More favourable provisions**

This Directive shall be without prejudice to the right of Member States to adopt or maintain provisions that are more favourable to third-country nationals to whom it applies in relation with Articles 6 and 13, provided that such provisions are compatible with this Directive.

*Article 16*

**Reporting**

1. By 20 July 2014, and every three years thereafter, the Commission shall submit a report to the European Parliament and the Council including, where appropriate, proposals for amending Articles 6, 7, 8, 13 and 14. The Commission shall in particular examine in its report the implementation by Member States of Article 6(2) and (5).

2. Member States shall send the Commission all the information that is appropriate for drawing up the report referred to in paragraph 1. The information shall include the number and results of inspections carried out pursuant to Article 14(1), measures applied under Article 13 and, as far as possible, measures applied under Articles 6 and 7.

*Article 17*

**Transposition**

1. Member States shall bring into force the laws, regulations and administrative provisions necessary to comply with this Directive by 20 July 2011. They shall forthwith inform the Commission thereof.

When they are adopted by Member States, those measures shall contain a reference to this Directive or shall be accompanied by such reference on the occasion of their official publication. The methods of making such reference shall be laid down by Member States.

2. Member States shall communicate to the Commission the text of the main provisions of national law which they adopt in the field covered by this Directive.

▼B

*Article 18*

**Entry into force**

This Directive shall enter into force on the 20th day following its publication in the *Official Journal of the European Union*.

*Article 19*

**Addressees**

This Directive is addressed to the Member States in accordance with the Treaty establishing the European Community.

# Framework Decision 2009/829 on the application, between Member States of the European Union, of the principle of mutual recognition to decisions on supervision measures as an alternative to provisional detention, 23 October 2009

[OJ 2009, L 294/20–40]

L 294/20 EN Official Journal of the European Union 11.11.2009

III

*(Acts adopted under the EU Treaty)*

# ACTS ADOPTED UNDER TITLE VI OF THE EU TREATY

## COUNCIL FRAMEWORK DECISION 2009/829/JHA

### of 23 October 2009

### on the application, between Member States of the European Union, of the principle of mutual recognition to decisions on supervision measures as an alternative to provisional detention

THE COUNCIL OF THE EUROPEAN UNION,

Having regard to the Treaty on European Union, and in particular Article 31(1)(a) and (c) and Article 34(2)(b) thereof,

Having regard to the proposal from the Commission,

Having regard to the opinion of the European Parliament [1],

Whereas:

(1) The European Union has set itself the objective of maintaining and developing an area of freedom, security and justice.

(2) According to the Conclusions of the European Council meeting in Tampere on 15 and 16 October 1999, and in particular point 36 thereof, the principle of mutual recognition should apply to pre-trial orders. The programme of measures to implement the principle of mutual recognition in criminal matters addresses mutual recognition of supervision measures in its measure 10.

(3) The measures provided for in this Framework Decision should aim at enhancing the protection of the general public through enabling a person resident in one Member State, but subject to criminal proceedings in a second Member State, to be supervised by the authorities in the State in which he or she is resident whilst awaiting trial. As a consequence, the present Framework Decision has as its objective the monitoring of a defendants' movements in the light of the overriding objective of protecting the general public and the risk posed to the public by the existing regime, which provides only two alternatives: provisional detention or unsupervised movement. The measures will therefore give further effect to the right of law-abiding citizens to live in safety and security.

(4) The measures provided for in this Framework Decision should also aim at enhancing the right to liberty and the presumption of innocence in the European Union and at ensuring cooperation between Member States when a person is subject to obligations or supervision pending a court decision. As a consequence, the present Framework Decision has as its objective the promotion, where appropriate, of the use of non-custodial measures as an alternative to provisional detention, even where, according to the law of the Member State concerned, a provisional detention could not be imposed *ab initio*.

(5) As regards the detention of persons subject to criminal proceedings, there is a risk of different treatment between those who are resident in the trial state and those who are not: a non-resident risks being remanded in custody pending trial even where, in similar circumstances, a resident would not. In a common European area of justice without internal borders, it is necessary to take action to ensure that a person subject to criminal proceedings who is not resident in the trial state is not treated any differently from a person subject to criminal proceedings who is so resident.

(6) The certificate, which should be forwarded together with the decision on supervision measures to the competent authority of the executing State, should specify the address where the person concerned will stay in the executing State, as well as any other relevant information which might facilitate the monitoring of the supervision measures in the executing State.

[1] Opinion not yet published in the Official Journal.

(7) The competent authority in the executing State should inform the competent authority in the issuing State of the maximum length of time, if any, during which the supervision measures could be monitored in the executing State. In Member States in which the supervision measures have to be periodically renewed, this maximum length of time has to be understood as the total length of time after which it is legally not possible anymore to renew the supervision measures.

(8) Any request by the competent authority in the executing State for confirmation of the necessity to prolong the monitoring of supervision measures should be without prejudice to the law of the issuing State, which applies to the decision on renewal, review and withdrawal of the decision on supervision measures. Such a request for confirmation should not oblige the competent authority in the issuing State to take a new decision to prolong the monitoring of supervision measures.

(9) The competent authority in the issuing State should have jurisdiction to take all subsequent decisions relating to a decision on supervision measures, including ordering a provisional detention. Such provisional detention might, in particular, be ordered following a breach of the supervision measures or a failure to comply with a summons to attend any hearing or trial in the course of criminal proceedings.

(10) In order to avoid unnecessary costs and difficulties in relation to the transfer of a person subject to criminal proceedings for the purposes of a hearing or a trial, Member States should be allowed to use telephone- and videoconferences.

(11) Where appropriate, electronic monitoring could be used for monitoring supervision measures in accordance with national law and procedures.

(12) This Framework Decision should make it possible that supervision measures imposed on the person concerned are monitored in the executing State, while ensuring the due course of justice and, in particular, that the person concerned will be available to stand trial. In case the person concerned does not return to the issuing State voluntarily, he or she may be surrendered to the issuing State in accordance with Council Framework Decision 2002/584/JHA of 13 June 2002 on the European Arrest Warrant and the surrender procedures between Member States [1] (hereinafter referred to as the 'Framework Decision on the European Arrest Warrant').

(13) While this Framework Decision covers all crimes and is not restricted to particular types or levels of crime, supervision measures should generally be applied in case of less serious offences. Therefore all the provisions of the Framework Decision on the European Arrest Warrant, except Article 2(1) thereof, should apply in the situation when the competent authority in the executing State has to decide on the surrender of the person concerned. As a consequence, also Article 5(2) and (3) of the Framework Decision on the European Arrest Warrant should apply in that situation.

(14) Costs relating to the travel of the person concerned between the executing and issuing States in connection with the monitoring of supervision measures or for the purpose of attending any hearing are not regulated by this Framework Decision. The possibility, in particular for the issuing State, to bear all or part of such costs is a matter governed by national law.

(15) Since the objective of this Framework Decision, namely the mutual recognition of decisions on supervision measures in the course of criminal proceedings, cannot be sufficiently achieved by the Member States acting unilaterally and can therefore, by reason of its scale and effects, be better achieved at Union level, the Union may adopt measures, in accordance with the principle of subsidiarity as set out in Article 2 of the Treaty on European Union and Article 5 of the Treaty establishing the European Community. In accordance with the principle of proportionality, as set out in that Article, this Framework Decision does not go beyond what is necessary in order to achieve that objective.

(16) This Framework Decision respects fundamental rights and observes the principles recognised, in particular, by Article 6 of the Treaty on European Union and reflected by the Charter of Fundamental Rights of the European Union. Nothing in this Framework Decision should be interpreted as prohibiting refusal to recognise a decision on supervision measures if there are objective indications that it was imposed to punish a person because of his or her sex, race, religion, ethnic origin, nationality, language, political convictions or sexual orientation or that this person might be disadvantaged for one of these reasons.

(17) This Framework Decision should not prevent any Member State from applying its constitutional rules relating to entitlement to due process, freedom of association, freedom of the press, freedom of expression in other media and freedom of religion.

(18) The provisions of this Framework Decision should be applied in conformity with the right of the Union's citizens to move and reside freely within the territory of the Member States, pursuant to Article 18 of the Treaty establishing the European Community.

[1] OJ L 190, 18.7.2002, p. 1.

(19) Personal data processed when implementing this Framework Decision should be protected in accordance with Council Framework Decision 2008/977/JHA of 27 November 2008 on the protection of personal data processed in the framework of police and judicial cooperation in criminal matters ([1]) and in accordance with the principles laid down in the Council of Europe Convention of 28 January 1981 for the Protection of Individuals with regard to Automatic Processing of Personal Data, which all Member States have ratified,

HAS ADOPTED THIS FRAMEWORK DECISION:

*Article 1*

**Subject matter**

This Framework Decision lays down rules according to which one Member State recognises a decision on supervision measures issued in another Member State as an alternative to provisional detention, monitors the supervision measures imposed on a natural person and surrenders the person concerned to the issuing State in case of breach of these measures.

*Article 2*

**Objectives**

1. The objectives of this Framework Decision are:

(a) to ensure the due course of justice and, in particular, that the person concerned will be available to stand trial;

(b) to promote, where appropriate, the use, in the course of criminal proceedings, of non-custodial measures for persons who are not resident in the Member State where the proceedings are taking place;

(c) to improve the protection of victims and of the general public.

2. This Framework Decision does not confer any right on a person to the use, in the course of criminal proceedings, of a non-custodial measure as an alternative to custody. This is a matter governed by the law and procedures of the Member State where the criminal proceedings are taking place.

*Article 3*

**Protection of law and order and the safeguarding of internal security**

This Framework Decision is without prejudice to the exercise of the responsibilities incumbent upon Member States with regard to the protection of victims, the general public and the safeguarding of internal security, in accordance with Article 33 of the Treaty on European Union.

([1]) OJ L 350, 30.12.2008, p. 60.

*Article 4*

**Definitions**

For the purposes of this Framework Decision:

(a) 'decision on supervision measures' means an enforceable decision taken in the course of criminal proceedings by a competent authority of the issuing State in accordance with its national law and procedures and imposing on a natural person, as an alternative to provisional detention, one or more supervision measures;

(b) 'supervision measures' means obligations and instructions imposed on a natural person, in accordance with the national law and procedures of the issuing State;

(c) 'issuing State' means the Member State in which a decision on supervision measures has been issued;

(d) 'executing State' means the Member State in which the supervision measures are monitored.

*Article 5*

**Fundamental rights**

This Framework Decision shall not have the effect of modifying the obligation to respect fundamental rights and fundamental legal principles as enshrined in Article 6 of the Treaty on European Union.

*Article 6*

**Designation of competent authorities**

1. Each Member State shall inform the General Secretariat of the Council which judicial authority or authorities under its national law are competent to act according to this Framework Decision in the situation where that Member State is the issuing State or the executing State.

2. As an exception to paragraph 1 and without prejudice to paragraph 3, Member States may designate non-judicial authorities as the competent authorities for taking decisions under this Framework Decision, provided that such authorities have competence for taking decisions of a similar nature under their national law and procedures.

3. Decisions referred to under Article 18(1)(c) shall be taken by a competent judicial authority.

4. The General Secretariat of the Council shall make the information received available to all Member States and to the Commission.

*Article 7*

**Recourse to a central authority**

1. Each Member State may designate a central authority or, where its legal system so provides, more than one central authority to assist its competent authorities.

2. A Member State may, if it is necessary as a result of the organisation of its internal judicial system, make its central authority(ies) responsible for the administrative transmission and reception of decisions on supervision measures, together with the certificates referred to in Article 10, as well as for all other official correspondence relating thereto. As a consequence, all communications, consultations, exchanges of information, enquiries and notifications between competent authorities may be dealt with, where appropriate, with the assistance of the central authority(ies) of the Member State concerned.

3. Member States wishing to make use of the possibilities referred to in this Article shall communicate to the General Secretariat of the Council information relating to the designated central authority or central authorities. These indications shall be binding upon all the authorities of the issuing Member State.

*Article 8*

**Types of supervision measures**

1. This Framework Decision shall apply to the following supervision measures:

(a) an obligation for the person to inform the competent authority in the executing State of any change of residence, in particular for the purpose of receiving a summons to attend a hearing or a trial in the course of criminal proceedings;

(b) an obligation not to enter certain localities, places or defined areas in the issuing or executing State;

(c) an obligation to remain at a specified place, where applicable during specified times;

(d) an obligation containing limitations on leaving the territory of the executing State;

(e) an obligation to report at specified times to a specific authority;

(f) an obligation to avoid contact with specific persons in relation with the offence(s) allegedly committed.

2. Each Member State shall notify the General Secretariat of the Council, when transposing this Framework Decision or at a later stage, which supervision measures, apart from those referred to in paragraph 1, it is prepared to monitor. These measures may include in particular:

(a) an obligation not to engage in specified activities in relation with the offence(s) allegedly committed, which may include involvement in a specified profession or field of employment;

(b) an obligation not to drive a vehicle;

(c) an obligation to deposit a certain sum of money or to give another type of guarantee, which may either be provided through a specified number of instalments or entirely at once;

(d) an obligation to undergo therapeutic treatment or treatment for addiction;

(e) an obligation to avoid contact with specific objects in relation with the offence(s) allegedly committed.

3. The General Secretariat of the Council shall make the information received under this Article available to all Member States and to the Commission.

*Article 9*

**Criteria relating to the Member State to which the decision on supervision measures may be forwarded**

1. A decision on supervision measures may be forwarded to the competent authority of the Member State in which the person is lawfully and ordinarily residing, in cases where the person, having been informed about the measures concerned, consents to return to that State.

2. The competent authority in the issuing State may, upon request of the person, forward the decision on supervision measures to the competent authority of a Member State other than the Member State in which the person is lawfully and ordinarily residing, on condition that the latter authority has consented to such forwarding.

3. When implementing this Framework Decision, Member States shall determine under which conditions their competent authorities may consent to the forwarding of a decision on supervision measures in cases pursuant to paragraph 2.

4. Each Member State shall make a statement to the General Secretariat of the Council of the determination made under paragraph 3. Member States may modify such a statement at any time. The General Secretariat shall make the information received available to all Member States and to the Commission.

*Article 10*

**Procedure for forwarding a decision on supervision measures together with the certificate**

1. When, in application of Article 9(1) or (2), the competent authority of the issuing State forwards a decision on supervision measures to another Member State, it shall ensure that it is accompanied by a certificate, the standard form of which is set out in Annex I.

2. The decision on supervision measures or a certified copy of it, together with the certificate, shall be forwarded by the competent authority in the issuing State directly to the competent authority in the executing State by any means which leaves a written record under conditions allowing the executing State to establish their authenticity. The original of the decision on supervision measures, or a certified copy of it, and the original of the certificate, shall be sent to the executing State if it so requires. All official communications shall also be made directly between the said competent authorities.

3. The certificate shall be signed, and its content certified as accurate, by the competent authority in the issuing State.

4. The certificate referred to in paragraph 1 of this Article shall include, apart from the measures referred to in Article 8(1), only such measures as notified by the executing State in accordance with Article 8(2).

5. The competent authority in the issuing State shall specify:

(a) where applicable, the length of time to which the decision on supervision measures applies and whether a renewal of this decision is possible;

and

(b) on an indicative basis, the provisional length of time for which the monitoring of the supervision measures is likely to be needed, taking into account all the circumstances of the case that are known when the decision on supervision measures is forwarded.

6. The competent authority in the issuing State shall forward the decision on supervision measures together with the certificate only to one executing State at any one time.

7. If the competent authority in the executing State is not known to the competent authority in the issuing State, the latter shall make all necessary inquiries, including via the contact points of the European Judicial Network set up by Council Joint Action 98/428/JHA of 29 June 1998 on the creation of a European Judicial Network [1], in order to obtain the information from the executing State.

8. When an authority in the executing State which receives a decision on supervision measures together with a certificate has no competence to recognise that decision, this authority shall, ex officio, forward the decision together with the certificate to the competent authority.

*Article 11*

**Competence over the monitoring of the supervision measures**

1. As long as the competent authority of the executing State has not recognised the decision on supervision measures forwarded to it and has not informed the competent authority of the issuing State of such recognition, the competent authority of the issuing State shall remain competent in relation to the monitoring of the supervision measures imposed.

2. If competence for monitoring the supervision measures has been transferred to the competent authority of the executing State, such competence shall revert back to the competent authority of the issuing State:

(a) where the person concerned has established his/her lawful and ordinary residence in a State other than the executing State;

(b) as soon as the competent authority in the issuing State has notified withdrawal of the certificate referred to in Article 10(1), pursuant to Article 13(3), to the competent authority of the executing State;

(c) where the competent authority in the issuing State has modified the supervision measures and the competent authority in the executing State, in application of Article 18(4)(b), has refused to monitor the modified supervision measures because they do not fall within the types of supervision measures referred to in Article 8(1) and/or within those notified by the executing State concerned in accordance with Article 8(2);

(d) when the period of time referred to in Article 20(2)(b) has elapsed;

(e) where the competent authority in the executing State has decided to stop monitoring the supervision measures and has informed the competent authority in the issuing State thereof, in application of Article 23.

3. In cases referred to in paragraph 2, the competent authorities of the issuing and executing States shall consult each other so as to avoid, as far as possible, any discontinuance in the monitoring of the supervision measures.

[1] OJ L 191, 7.7.1998, p. 4.

*Article 12*

**Decision in the executing State**

1. The competent authority in the executing State shall, as soon as possible and in any case within 20 working days of receipt of the decision on supervision measures and certificate, recognise the decision on supervision measures forwarded in accordance with Article 9 and following the procedure laid down in Article 10 and without delay take all necessary measures for monitoring the supervision measures, unless it decides to invoke one of the grounds for non-recognition referred to in Article 15.

2. If a legal remedy has been introduced against the decision referred to in paragraph 1, the time limit for recognition of the decision on supervision measures shall be extended by another 20 working days.

3. If it is not possible, in exceptional circumstances, for the competent authority in the executing State to comply with the time limits laid down in paragraphs 1 and 2, it shall immediately inform the competent authority in the issuing State, by any means of its choosing, giving reasons for the delay and indicating how long it expects to take to issue a final decision.

4. The competent authority may postpone the decision on recognition of the decision on supervision measures where the certificate provided for in Article 10 is incomplete or obviously does not correspond to the decision on supervision measures, until such reasonable time limit set for the certificate to be completed or corrected.

*Article 13*

**Adaptation of the supervision measures**

1. If the nature of the supervision measures is incompatible with the law of the executing State, the competent authority in that Member State may adapt them in line with the types of supervision measures which apply, under the law of the executing State, to equivalent offences. The adapted supervision measure shall correspond as far as possible to that imposed in the issuing State.

2. The adapted supervision measure shall not be more severe than the supervision measure which was originally imposed.

3. Following receipt of information referred to in Article 20(2)(b) or (f), the competent authority in the issuing State may decide to withdraw the certificate as long as monitoring in the executing State has not yet begun. In any case, such a decision shall be taken and communicated as soon as possible and within ten days of the receipt of the relevant notification at the latest.

*Article 14*

**Double criminality**

1. The following offences, if they are punishable in the issuing State by a custodial sentence or a measure involving deprivation of liberty for a maximum period of at least three years, and as they are defined by the law of the issuing State, shall, under the terms of this Framework Decision and without verification of the double criminality of the act, give rise to recognition of the decision on supervision measures:

— participation in a criminal organisation,

— terrorism,

— trafficking in human beings,

— sexual exploitation of children and child pornography,

— illicit trafficking in narcotic drugs and psychotropic substances,

— illicit trafficking in weapons, munitions and explosives,

— corruption,

— fraud, including that affecting the financial interests of the European Communities within the meaning of the Convention of 26 July 1995 on the protection of the European Communities' financial interests [1],

— laundering of the proceeds of crime,

— counterfeiting currency, including of the euro,

— computer-related crime,

— environmental crime, including illicit trafficking in endangered animal species and in endangered plant species and varieties,

— facilitation of unauthorised entry and residence,

— murder, grievous bodily injury,

— illicit trade in human organs and tissue,

— kidnapping, illegal restraint and hostage-taking,

— racism and xenophobia,

[1] OJ C 316, 27.11.1995, p. 49.

— organised or armed robbery,

— illicit trafficking in cultural goods, including antiques and works of art,

— swindling,

— racketeering and extortion,

— counterfeiting and piracy of products,

— forgery of administrative documents and trafficking therein,

— forgery of means of payment,

— illicit trafficking in hormonal substances and other growth promoters,

— illicit trafficking in nuclear or radioactive materials,

— trafficking in stolen vehicles,

— rape,

— arson,

— crimes within the jurisdiction of the International Criminal Court,

— unlawful seizure of aircraft/ships,

— sabotage.

2. The Council may decide to add other categories of offences to the list in paragraph 1 at any time, acting unanimously after consultation of the European Parliament under the conditions laid down in Article 39(1) of the Treaty on European Union. The Council shall examine, in the light of the report submitted to it pursuant to Article 27 of this Framework Decision, whether the list should be extended or amended.

3. For offences other than those covered by paragraph 1, the executing State may make the recognition of the decision on supervision measures subject to the condition that the decision relates to acts which also constitute an offence under the law of the executing State, whatever the constituent elements or however it is described.

4. Member States may, for constitutional reasons, on the adoption of this Framework Decision, by a declaration notified to the General Secretariat of the Council, declare that they will not apply paragraph 1 in respect of some or all of the offences referred to in that paragraph. Any such declaration may be withdrawn at any time. Such declarations or withdrawals of declarations shall be published in the *Official Journal of the European Union.*

*Article 15*

**Grounds for non-recognition**

1. The competent authority in the executing State may refuse to recognise the decision on supervision measures if:

(a) the certificate referred to in Article 10 is incomplete or obviously does not correspond to the decision on supervision measures and is not completed or corrected within a reasonable period set by the competent authority in the executing State;

(b) the criteria laid down in Article 9(1), 9(2) or 10(4) are not met;

(c) recognition of the decision on supervision measures would contravene the *ne bis in idem* principle;

(d) the decision on supervision measures relates, in the cases referred to in Article 14(3) and, where the executing State has made a declaration under Article 14(4), in the cases referred to in Article 14(1), to an act which would not constitute an offence under the law of the executing State; in tax, customs and currency matters, however, execution of the decision may not be refused on the grounds that the law of the executing State does not prescribe any taxes of the same kind or does not contain any tax, customs or currency provisions of the same kind as the law of the issuing State;

(e) the criminal prosecution is statute-barred under the law of the executing State and relates to an act which falls within the competence of the executing State under its national law;

(f) there is immunity under the law of the executing State, which makes it impossible to monitor supervision measures;

(g) under the law of the executing State, the person cannot, because of his age, be held criminally responsible for the act on which the decision on supervision measures is based;

(h) it would, in case of breach of the supervision measures, have to refuse to surrender the person concerned in accordance with Council Framework Decision 2002/584/JHA of 13 June 2002 on the European arrest warrant and the surrender procedures between Member States [1] (hereinafter referred to as the 'Framework Decision on the European Arrest Warrant').

[1] OJ L 190, 18.7.2002, p. 1.

11.11.2009 EN Official Journal of the European Union L 294/27

2. In the cases referred to in paragraph 1(a), (b) and (c), before deciding not to recognise the decision on supervision measures, the competent authority in the executing State shall communicate, by appropriate means, with the competent authority in the issuing State and, as necessary, request the latter to supply without delay all additional information required.

3. Where the competent authority in the executing State is of the opinion that the recognition of a decision on supervision measures could be refused on the basis of paragraph 1 under (h), but it is nevertheless willing to recognise the decision on supervision measures and monitor the supervision measures contained therein, it shall inform the competent authority in the issuing State thereof providing the reasons for the possible refusal. In such a case, the competent authority in the issuing State may decide to withdraw the certificate in accordance with the second sentence of Article 13(3). If the competent authority in the issuing State does not withdraw the certificate, the competent authority in the executing State may recognise the decision on supervision measures and monitor the supervision measures contained therein, it being understood that the person concerned might not be surrendered on the basis of a European Arrest Warrant.

*Article 16*

**Law governing supervision**

The monitoring of supervision measures shall be governed by the law of the executing State.

*Article 17*

**Continuation of the monitoring of supervision measures**

Where the time period referred to in Article 20(2)(b) is due to expire and the supervision measures are still needed, the competent authority in the issuing State may request the competent authority in the executing State to extend the monitoring of the supervision measures, in view of the circumstances of the case at hand and the foreseeable consequences for the person if Article 11(2)(d) would apply. The competent authority in the issuing State shall indicate the period of time for which such an extension is likely to be needed.

The competent authority in the executing State shall decide on this request in accordance with its national law, indicating, where appropriate, the maximum duration of the extension. In these cases, Article 18(3) may apply.

*Article 18*

**Competence to take all subsequent decisions and governing law**

1. Without prejudice to Article 3, the competent authority in the issuing State shall have jurisdiction to take all subsequent decisions relating to a decision on supervision measures. Such subsequent decisions include notably:

(a) renewal, review and withdrawal of the decision on supervision measures;

(b) modification of the supervision measures;

(c) issuing an arrest warrant or any other enforceable judicial decision having the same effect.

2. The law of the issuing State shall apply to decisions taken pursuant to paragraph 1.

3. Where required by its national law, a competent authority in the executing State may decide to use the procedure of recognition set out in this Framework Decision in order to give effect to decisions referred to in paragraph 1(a) and (b) in its national legal system. Such a recognition shall not lead to a new examination of the grounds of non-recognition.

4. If the competent authority in the issuing State has modified the supervision measures in accordance with paragraph 1(b), the competent authority in the executing State may:

(a) adapt these modified measures in application of Article 13, in case the nature of the modified supervision measures is incompatible with the law of the executing State;

or

(b) refuse to monitor the modified supervision measures if these measures do not fall within the types of supervision measures referred to in Article 8(1) and/or within those notified by the executing State concerned in accordance with Article 8(2).

5. The jurisdiction of the competent authority in the issuing State pursuant to paragraph 1 is without prejudice to proceedings that may be initiated in the executing State against the person concerned in relation with criminal offences committed by him/her other than those on which the decision on supervision measures is based.

*Article 19*

**Obligations of the authorities involved**

1. At any time during the monitoring of the supervision measures, the competent authority in the executing State may invite the competent authority in the issuing State to provide information as to whether the monitoring of the measures is still needed in the circumstances of the particular case at hand. The competent authority in the issuing State shall, without delay, reply to such an invitation, where appropriate by taking a subsequent decision referred to in Article 18(1).

2. Before the expiry of the period referred to in Article 10(5), the competent authority in the issuing State shall specify, ex officio or at the request of the competent authority in the executing State, for which additional period, if any, it expects that the monitoring of the measures is still needed.

3. The competent authority in the executing State shall immediately notify the competent authority in the issuing State of any breach of a supervision measure, and any other finding which could result in taking any subsequent decision referred to in Article 18(1). Notice shall be given using the standard form set out in Annex II.

4. With a view to hearing the person concerned, the procedure and conditions contained in instruments of international and European Union law that provide for the possibility of using telephone- and videoconferences for hearing persons may be used *mutatis mutandis*, in particular where the legislation of the issuing State provides that a judicial hearing must be held before a decision referred to in Article 18(1) is taken.

5. The competent authority in the issuing State shall immediately inform the competent authority in the executing State of any decision referred to in Article 18(1) and of the fact that a legal remedy has been introduced against a decision on supervision measures.

6. If the certificate relating to the decision on supervision measures has been withdrawn, the competent authority of the executing State shall end the measures ordered as soon as it has been duly notified by the competent authority of the issuing State.

*Article 20*

**Information from the executing State**

1. The authority in the executing State which has received a decision on supervision measures, which it has no competence to recognise, together with a certificate, shall inform the competent authority in the issuing State to which authority it has forwarded this decision, together with the certificate, in accordance with Article 10(8).

2. The competent authority in the executing State shall, without delay, inform the competent authority in the issuing State by any means which leaves a written record:

(a) of any change of residence of the person concerned;

(b) of the maximum length of time during which the supervision measures can be monitored in the executing State, in case the law of the executing State provides such a maximum;

(c) of the fact that it is in practice impossible to monitor the supervision measures for the reason that, after transmission of the decision on supervision measures and the certificate to the executing State, the person cannot be found in the territory of the executing State, in which case there shall be no obligation of the executing State to monitor the supervision measures;

(d) of the fact that a legal remedy has been introduced against a decision to recognise a decision on supervision measures;

(e) of the final decision to recognise the decision on supervision measures and take all necessary measures for the monitoring of the supervision measures;

(f) of any decision to adapt the supervision measures in accordance with Article 13;

(g) of any decision not to recognise the decision on supervision measures and to assume responsibility for monitoring of the supervision measures in accordance with Article 15, together with the reasons for the decision.

*Article 21*

**Surrender of the person**

1. If the competent authority of the issuing State has issued an arrest warrant or any other enforceable judicial decision having the same effect, the person shall be surrendered in accordance with the Framework Decision on the European Arrest Warrant.

2. In this context, Article 2(1) of the Framework Decision on the European Arrest Warrant may not be invoked by the competent authority of the executing State to refuse to surrender the person.

3. Each Member State may notify the General Secretariat of the Council, when transposing this Framework Decision or at a later stage, that it will also apply Article 2(1) of the Framework Decision on the European Arrest Warrant in deciding on the surrender of the person concerned to the issuing State.

4. The General Secretariat of the Council shall make the information received under paragraph 3 available to all Member States and to the Commission.

*Article 22*

**Consultations**

1. Unless impracticable, the competent authorities of the issuing State and of the executing State shall consult each other:

(a) during the preparation, or, at least, before forwarding a decision on supervision measures together with the certificate referred to in Article 10;

(b) to facilitate the smooth and efficient monitoring of the supervision measures;

(c) where the person has committed a serious breach of the supervision measures imposed.

2. The competent authority in the issuing State shall take due account of any indications communicated by the competent authority of the executing State on the risk that the person concerned might pose to victims and to the general public.

3. In application of paragraph 1, the competent authorities of the issuing State and of the executing State shall exchange all useful information, including:

(a) information allowing verification of the identity and place of residence of the person concerned;

(b) relevant information extracted from criminal records in accordance with applicable legislative instruments.

*Article 23*

**Unanswered notices**

1. Where the competent authority in the executing State has transmitted several notices referred to in Article 19(3) in respect of the same person to the competent authority in the issuing State, without this latter authority having taken any subsequent decision referred to in Article 18(1), the competent authority in the executing State may invite the competent authority in the issuing State to take such a decision, giving it a reasonable time limit to do so.

2. If the competent authority in the issuing State does not act within the time limit indicated by the competent authority in the executing State, the latter authority may decide to stop monitoring the supervision measures. In such case, it shall inform the competent authority in the issuing State of its decision, and the competence for the monitoring of the supervision measures shall revert back to the competent authority in the issuing State in application of Article 11(2).

3. Where the law of the executing State requires a periodic confirmation of the necessity to prolong the monitoring of the supervision measures, the competent authority in the executing State may request the competent authority in the issuing State to provide such confirmation, giving it a reasonable time limit to reply to such a request. In case the competent authority in the issuing State does not answer within the time limit concerned, the competent authority in the executing State may send a new request to the competent authority in the issuing State, giving it a reasonable time limit to reply to such a request and indicating that it may decide to stop monitoring the supervision measures if no reply is received within that time limit. Where the competent authority in the executing State does not receive a reply to such a new request within the time limit set, it may act in accordance with paragraph 2.

*Article 24*

**Languages**

Certificates shall be translated into the official language or one of the official languages of the executing State. Any Member State may, either when this Framework Decision is adopted or at a later date, state in a declaration deposited with the General Secretariat of the Council that it will accept a translation in one or more other official languages of the Institutions of the European Union.

*Article 25*

**Costs**

Costs resulting from the application of this Framework Decision shall be borne by the executing State, except for costs arising exclusively within the territory of the issuing State.

*Article 26*

**Relation to other agreements and arrangements**

1. In so far as such agreements or arrangements allow the objectives of this Framework Decision to be extended or enlarged and help to simplify or facilitate further the mutual recognition of decisions on supervision measures, Member States may:

(a) continue to apply bilateral or multilateral agreements or arrangements in force when this Framework Decision enters into force;

(b) conclude bilateral or multilateral agreements or arrangements after this Framework Decision has entered into force.

2. The agreements and arrangements referred to in paragraph 1 shall in no case affect relations with Member States which are not parties to them.

3. Member States shall, by 1 March 2010, notify the Commission and the Council of the existing agreements and arrangements referred to in paragraph 1(a) which they wish to continue applying.

4. Member States shall also notify the Commission and the Council of any new agreement or arrangement as referred to in paragraph 1(b), within three months of signing any such arrangement or agreement.

*Article 27*

**Implementation**

1. Member States shall take the necessary measures to comply with the provisions of this Framework Decision by 1 December 2012.

2. By the same date Member States shall transmit to the Council and to the Commission the text of the provisions transposing into their national law the obligations imposed on them under this Framework Decision.

*Article 28*

**Report**

1. By 1 December 2013 the Commission shall draw up a report on the basis of the information received from Member States under Article 27(2).

2. On the basis of this report, the Council shall assess:

(a) the extent to which the Member States have taken the necessary measures in order to comply with this Framework Decision; and

(b) the application of this Framework Decision.

3. The report shall be accompanied, if necessary, by legislative proposals.

*Article 29*

**Entry into force**

This Framework Decision shall enter into force on the 20th day following its publication in the *Official Journal of the European Union*.

Done at Luxembourg, 23 October 2009.

*For the Council*

*The President*

T. BILLSTRÖM

*ANNEX I*

**CERTIFICATE**

referred to in Article 10 of Council Framework Decision 2009/829/JHA of 23 October 2009 on the application, between Member States of the European Union, of the principle of mutual recognition to decisions on supervision measures as an alternative to provisional detention (1)

(a) Issuing State:

Executing State:

(b) Authority which issued the decision on supervision measures:

Official name:

Please indicate whether any additional information concerning the decision on supervision measures is to be obtained from:

☐ the authority specified above

☐ the central authority; if you ticked this box, please provide the official name of this central authority:

☐ another competent authority; if you ticked this box, please provide the official name of this authority:

Contact details of the issuing authority/central authority/other competent authority

Address:

Tel. No: (country code) (area/city code)

Fax No: (country code) (area/city code)

Details of the person(s) to be contacted

Surname:

Forename(s):

Position (title/grade):

Tel. No: (country code) (area/city code)

Fax No: (country code) (area/city code)

E-mail (if any):

Languages that may be used for communication:

(1) This certificate must be written in, or translated into, the official language or one of the official languages of the executing Member State, or any other official language of the Institutions of the European Union that is accepted by that State.

(c) Please indicate which authority is to be contacted if any additional information is to be obtained for the purposes of monitoring the supervision measures:

☐ the authority referred to in point (b)

☐ another authority; if you ticked this box, please provide the official name of this authority:

Contact details of the authority, if this information has not yet been provided under point (b)

Address:

Tel. No: (country code) (area/city code)

Fax No: (country code) (area/city code)

Details of the person(s) to be contacted

Surname:

Forename(s):

Position (title/grade):

Tel. No: (country code) (area/city code)

Fax No: (country code) (area/city code)

E-mail (if any):

Languages that may be used for communication:

(d) Information regarding the natural person in respect of whom the decision on supervision measures has been issued:

Surname:

Forename(s):

Maiden name, where applicable:

Aliases, where applicable:

Sex:

Nationality:

Identity number or social security number (if any):

Date of birth:

Place of birth:

Addresses/residences:

— in the issuing State:

— in the executing State:

— elsewhere:

Language(s) understood (if known):

If available, please provide the following information:

— Type and number of the identity document(s) of the person (ID card, passport):

— Type and number of the residence permit of the person in the executing State:

(e) Information regarding the Member State to which the decision on supervision measures, together with the certificate are being forwarded

The decision on supervision measures, together with the certificate are being forwarded to the executing State indicated in point (a) for the following reason:

☐ the person concerned has his/her lawful and ordinary residence in the executing State and, having been informed about the measures concerned, consents to return to that State

☐ the person concerned has requested to forward the decision on supervision measures to the Member State other than that in which the person is lawfully and ordinarily residing, for the following reason(s):

(f) Indications regarding the decision on supervision measures:

The decision was issued on (date: DD-MM-YYYY):

The decision became enforceable on (date: DD-MM-YYYY):

If, at the time of transmission of this certificate, a legal remedy has been introduced against the decision on supervision measures, please tick this box ........................................... ☐

File reference of the decision (if available):

The person concerned was in provisional detention during the following period (where applicable):

1. The decision covers in total: ........................................... alleged offences.

   Summary of the facts and description of the circumstances in which the alleged offence(s) was (were) committed, including the time and place, and the nature of the involvement of the person concerned:

   Nature and legal classification of the alleged offence(s) and applicable statutory provisions on the basis of which the decision was issued:

2. If the alleged offence(s) referred to in point 1 constitute(s) one or more of the following offences, as defined in the law of the issuing State which are punishable in the issuing State by a custodial sentence or measure involving deprivation of liberty of a maximum of at least three years, please confirm by ticking the relevant box(es):

   ☐ participation in a criminal organisation

   ☐ terrorism

   ☐ trafficking in human beings

   ☐ sexual exploitation of children and child pornography

- ☐ illicit trafficking in narcotic drugs and psychotropic substances
- ☐ illicit trafficking in weapons, munitions and explosives
- ☐ corruption
- ☐ fraud, including that affecting the financial interests of the European Communities within the meaning of the Convention of 26 July 1995 on the protection of the European Communities' financial interests
- ☐ laundering of the proceeds of crime
- ☐ counterfeiting of currency, including the euro
- ☐ computer-related crime
- ☐ environmental crime, including illicit trafficking in endangered animal species and in endangered plant species and varieties
- ☐ facilitation of unauthorised entry and residence
- ☐ murder, grievous bodily injury
- ☐ illicit trade in human organs and tissue
- ☐ kidnapping, illegal restraint and hostage-taking
- ☐ racism and xenophobia
- ☐ organised or armed robbery
- ☐ illicit trafficking in cultural goods, including antiques and works of art
- ☐ swindling
- ☐ racketeering and extortion
- ☐ counterfeiting and piracy of products
- ☐ forgery of administrative documents and trafficking therein
- ☐ forgery of means of payment
- ☐ illicit trafficking in hormonal substances and other growth promoters
- ☐ illicit trafficking in nuclear or radioactive materials
- ☐ trafficking in stolen vehicles
- ☐ rape
- ☐ arson
- ☐ crimes within the jurisdiction of the International Criminal Court
- ☐ unlawful seizure of aircraft/ships
- ☐ sabotage

3. To the extent that the alleged offence(s) identified under point 1 is (are) not covered by point 2 or if the decision, as well as the certificate are forwarded to a Member State, which has declared that it will verify the double criminality (Article 14(4) of the Framework Decision), please give a full description of the alleged offence(s) concerned:

(g) Indications regarding the duration and nature of the supervision measure(s)

1. Length of time to which the decision on supervision measures applies and whether a renewal of this decision is possible (where applicable):

2. Provisional length of time for which the monitoring of the supervision measures is likely to be needed, taking into account all the circumstances of the case that are known when the decision on supervision measures is forwarded (indicative information)

3. Nature of the supervision measure(s)(it is possible to tick multiple boxes):

☐ an obligation for the person to inform the competent authority in the executing State of any change of residence, in particular for the purpose of receiving a summons to attend a hearing or a trial in the course of criminal proceedings;

☐ an obligation not to enter certain localities, places or defined areas in the issuing or executing State;

☐ an obligation to remain at a specified place, where applicable during specified times;

☐ an obligation containing limitations on leaving the territory of the executing State;

☐ an obligation to report at specified times to a specific authority;

☐ an obligation to avoid contact with specific persons in relation with the offence(s) allegedly committed;

☐ other measures that the executing State is prepared to supervise in accordance with a notification under Article 8(2) of the Framework Decision:

If you ticked the box regarding 'other measures', please specify which measure is concerned by ticking the appropriate box(es):

☐ an obligation not to engage in specified activities in relation with the offence(s) allegedly committed, which may include involvement in a specified profession or field of employment;

☐ an obligation not to drive a vehicle;

☐ an obligation to deposit a certain sum of money or to give another type of guarantee, which may either be provided through a specified number of instalments or entirely at once;

☐ an obligation to undergo therapeutic treatment or treatment for addiction;

☐ an obligation to avoid contact with specific objects in relation with the offence(s) allegedly committed;

☐ other measure (please specify):

4. Please provide a detailed description of the supervision measure(s) indicated under 3:

(h) Other circumstances relevant to the case, including specific reasons for the imposition of the supervision measure(s) (optional information):

The text of the decision is attached to the certificate.

Signature of the authority issuing the certificate and/or of its representative to confirm the accuracy of the content of the certificate:

Name:

Position (title/grade):

Date:

File reference (if any):

(Where appropriate) Official stamp:

11.11.2009 EN Official Journal of the European Union L 294/37

*ANNEX II*

**FORM**

referred to in Article 19 of Council Framework Decision 2009/829/JHA of 23 October 2009 on the application, between Member States of the European Union, of the principle of mutual recognition to decisions on supervision measures as an alternative to provisional detention

REPORT OF A BREACH OF A SUPERVISION MEASURE AND/OR ANY OTHER FINDINGS WHICH COULD RESULT IN TAKING ANY SUBSEQUENT DECISION

(a) Details of the identity of the person subject to supervision:

Surname:

Forename(s):

Maiden name, where applicable:

Aliases, where applicable:

Sex:

Nationality:

Identity number or social security number (if any):

Date of birth:

Place of birth:

Address:

Language(s) understood (if known):

(b) Details of the decision on supervision measure(s):

Decision issued on:

File reference (if any):

Authority which issued the decision

Official name:

Address:

Certificate issued on:

Authority which issued the certificate:

File reference (if any):

(c) Details of the authority responsible for monitoring the supervision measure(s):

Official name of the authority:

Name of the person to be contacted:

Position (title/grade):

Address:

Tel. (country code) (area code)

Fax (country code) (area code)

E-mail:

Languages that may be used for communication:

(d) Breach of supervision measure(s) and/or other findings which could result in taking any subsequent decision:

The person referred to in (a) is in breach of the following supervision measure(s):

☐ an obligation for the person to inform the competent authority in the executing State of any change of residence, in particular for the purpose of receiving a summons to attend a hearing or a trial in the course of criminal proceedings;

☐ an obligation not to enter certain localities, places or defined areas in the issuing or executing State;

☐ an obligation to remain at a specified place, where applicable during specified times;

☐ an obligation containing limitations on leaving the territory of the executing State;

☐ an obligation to report at specified times to a specific authority;

☐ an obligation to avoid contact with specific persons in relation with the offence(s) allegedly committed.

☐ other measures (please specify):

Description of the breach(es) (place, date and specific circumstances):

— other findings which could result in taking any subsequent decision

Description of the findings:

(e) Details of the person to be contacted if additional information is to be obtained concerning the breach:

Surname:

Forename(s):

Address:

Tel. No: (country code) (area/city code)

Fax No: (country code) (area/city code)

E-mail:

Languages that may be used for communication:

Signature of the authority issuing the form and/or its representative, to confirm that the contents of the form are correct:

Name:

Position (title/grade):

Date:

Official stamp (where applicable):

**DECLARATION BY GERMANY**

*'The Federal Republic of Germany hereby gives notification, pursuant to Article 14(4) of the Council Framework Decision on the application of the principle of mutual recognition to decisions on supervision measures as an alternative to provisional detention, that it will not apply Article 14(1) in respect of all of the offences referred to in that paragraph.'*

This declaration will be published in the *Official Journal of the European Union*.

---

**DECLARATION BY POLAND**

*'Pursuant to Article 14(4) of the EU Council Framework Decision on the application, between Member States of the European Union, of the principle of mutual recognition to decisions on supervision measures as an alternative to provisional detention, the Republic of Poland declares that it will not apply paragraph (1) of the aforementioned Article 14 in respect of all of the offences referred to in that paragraph.'*

This declaration will be published in the *Official Journal of the European Union*.

---

**DECLARATION BY HUNGARY**

*'Pursuant to Article 14(4) of the EU Council Framework Decision on the application, between Member States of the European Union, of the principle of mutual recognition to decisions on supervision measures as an alternative to provisional detention, the Republic of Hungary declares that it will not apply paragraph (1) of Article 14 of the above Framework Decision in respect of the offences referred to in that paragraph.'*

This declaration will be published in the *Official Journal of the European Union*.

Referring to the 'constitutional reasons' mentioned in Article 14(4), Hungary provided the following explanation:

'Following the ratification of the Lisbon Treaty, Hungary amended its Constitution in order to comply with the obligations referred to therein, including the necessity not to apply the double criminality condition in criminal matters. This constitutional provision will enter into force at the same time as the Lisbon Treaty. Nevertheless, until the entry into force of the Treaty, double criminality remains an important constitutional issue and — as a constitutional principle enshrined by Article 57 of the Constitution — cannot be, shall not be disregarded. Therefore, Article 14(1) of the Framework Decision shall not be applied to any of the offences listed (or as formulated by the relevant article: shall not be applied "in respect of all of the offences").'

---

**DECLARATION BY LITHUANIA**

*'Pursuant to Article 14(4) of the Council Framework Decision on the application, between Member States of the European Union, of the principle of mutual recognition to decisions on supervision measures as an alternative to provisional detention, the Republic of Lithuania declares that for constitutional reasons it will not apply Article 14(1) in respect of any of the offences referred to therein.'*

This declaration will be published in the *Official Journal of the European Union*.

---

# Exchange of Letters between the European Union and the Republic of Seychelles on the Conditions and Modalities for the Transfer of Suspected Pirates and Armed Robbers from EUNAVFOR to the Republic of Seychelles and for their Treatment after such Transfer, 23 October 2009

[OJ 2009, L 315/37–43]

2.12.2009 EN Official Journal of the European Union L 315/37

**Exchange of Letters between the European Union and the Republic of Seychelles on the Conditions and Modalities for the Transfer of Suspected Pirates and Armed Robbers from EUNAVFOR to the Republic of Seychelles and for their Treatment after such Transfer**

A. *Letter from the Republic of Seychelles*

Your Excellency,

Reference is made to the working session held in Seychelles on the 18th and 19th August 2009 to discuss the EU Agreements on Piracy and Armed Robbery which involved the participation of representatives of the EU, the members of the Seychelles High Level Committee and other related institutions and to our subsequent letter of August 21, 2009.

In the course of the working session, the concerns of the different related institutions on the transfer of suspected pirates and armed robbers were tabled. The *'Guidance for the Transfer of Suspected pirates, armed robbers and seized property to Seychelles'* prepared by the Attorney General of the Republic of Seychelles, which is intended to ensure that any transfer of persons suspected of acts of piracy and armed robbery is done in accordance with the laws of Seychelles was approved in principle. It was also agreed that the Implementing Arrangements (which clarifies Article 10 of the proposed Transfer Agreement) could be agreed upon after the proposed Transfer Agreement has been finalised and that a common Guidance on the handover of suspected pirates, armed robbers and seized property is prepared. Furthermore, that the Republic of Seychelles will be provided with the necessary assistance for the detention, maintenance, investigation, prosecution trial and repatriation of the suspected pirates and armed robbers.

Following the working session and our letter, further discussions have taken place within the High Level Committee on the transfer of suspected pirates and armed robbers to the territory of the Republic of Seychelles.

The Government of the Republic of Seychelles would like to take this opportunity to renew its reassurance to the EU of its commitment to cooperate to its fullest possible extent, having regard to its available resources and infrastructure capacities, in the repression of piracy to accept the transfer of captured suspected pirates and armed robbers.

At the same time, the Government of the Republic of Seychelles would like to express its desire that the EU SOFA be signed as discussions continue on the proposed EU Transfer Agreement.

In view of ongoing negotiations and pending conclusion of a mutually acceptable arrangement between the EU and the Government of the Republic of Seychelles on the transfer of pirates and armed robbers to its territory, the Government of the Republic of Seychelles may authorize the EUNAVFOR to transfer suspected pirates and armed robbers captured in the course of its operations in the exclusive economic zone, territorial sea, archipelagic waters and internal waters of the Republic of Seychelles. This authorization is extended to the protection of Seychelles flagged vessels and Seychellois Citizens on a non-Seychelles flagged vessel beyond the limit aforementioned and in other circumstances on the high seas at the discretion of the Republic of the Seychelles.

Provided always that:

— The EU, aware of the limited capacities of the Republic of Seychelles to accept, try, detain and incarcerate suspected pirates and armed robbers and in consideration of the acceptance by the Republic of Seychelles of the transfer of any suspected pirates and armed robbers to its territory, shall provide the Republic of Seychelles with such full financial, human resource, material, logistical and infrastructural assistance for the detention, incarceration maintenance, investigation, prosecution, trial and repatriation of the suspected or convicted pirates and armed robbers;

— The Attorney General shall have at least 10 days from the date of transfer of the suspected pirates or armed robbers to decide on the sufficiency of the available evidence in view of prosecution,

— In the event that the Attorney General decides that there is insufficient evidence to prosecute, the EUNAVFOR shall take the full responsibility, including the financial costs, of transferring the suspected pirates and armed robbers back to their country of origin within 10 days of EUNAVFOR having been notified of such a decision;

— Any transfer of suspected pirates and armed robbers shall as far as possible be in accordance with the *'Guidance for the Transfer of Suspected pirates, armed robbers and seized property to Seychelles'*,

— The Government of the Republic of the Seychelles also confirms that:

— Any transferred person will be treated humanely and will not be subjected to torture or cruel, inhuman or degrading treatment or punishment, will receive adequate accommodation and nourishment, access to medical treatment and will be able to carry out religious observance.

— Any transferred person will be brought promptly before a judge or other officer authorised by law to exercise judicial power, who will decide without delay on the lawfulness of his detention and will order his release if the detention is not lawful,

— Any transferred person will be entitled to trial within a reasonable time or to release,

— In the determination of any criminal charge against him, any transferred person will be entitled to a fair and public hearing by a competent, independent and impartial tribunal established by law,

— Any transferred person charged with a criminal offence will be presumed innocent until proved guilty according to law,

— In the determination of any criminal charge against him, every transferred person will be entitled to the following minimum guarantees, in full equality:

(1) to be informed promptly and in detail in a language which he understands of the nature of the charge against him;

(2) to have adequate time and facilities for the preparation of his defence and to communicate with counsel of his own choice,

(3) to defend himself in person or through legal assistance of his own choice; to be informed, if he does not have legal assistance, of this right; and to have legal assistance assigned to him, in any case where the interests of justice so require, and without payment by him in any such case if he does not have sufficient means to pay for it;

(4) to examine, or have examined, all evidence against him, including affidavits of witnesses who conducted the arrest, and to obtain the attendance and examination of witnesses on his behalf under the same conditions as witnesses against him;

(5) to have the free assistance of an interpreter if he cannot understand or speak the language used in court;

(6) not to be compelled to testify against himself or to confess guilt.

— Any transferred person convicted of a crime will be permitted to have the right to have its conviction and sentence reviewed by or appealed to a higher tribunal in accordance with the law of the Seychelles,

— The Seychelles will not transfer any transferred person to any other State without prior written consent from EUNAVFOR,

This arrangement has been discussed and agreed by the Seychelles authorities. The arrangements proposed herewith may come into force when the European Union indicates its agreement in writing.

Yours Sincerely,

Mr J. Morgan

THE MINISTER

Chairman of the High Level Committee of Piracy

B. *Letter from the European Union*

Your Excellency,

I have the honour to acknowledge receipt of your letter dated 29 September 2009 regarding the conditions and modalities for the transfer of suspected pirates and armed robbers from EUNAVFOR to the Republic of Seychelles and for their treatment after such transfer, which reads as follows:

'Reference is made to the working session held in Seychelles on August 18 and 19, 2009 to discuss the EU Agreements on Piracy and Armed Robbery which involved the participation of representatives of the EU, the members of the Seychelles High Level Committee and other related institutions and to our subsequent letter of August 21, 2009.

In the course of the working session, the concerns of the different related institutions on the transfer of suspected pirates and armed robbers were tabled. The *"Guidance for the Transfer of Suspected pirates, armed robbers and seized property to Seychelles"* prepared by the Attorney General of the Republic of Seychelles, which is intended to ensure that any transfer of persons suspected of acts of piracy and armed robbery is done in accordance with the laws of Seychelles was approved in principle. It was also agreed that the Implementing Arrangements (which clarifies Article 10 of the proposed Transfer Agreement) could be agreed upon after the proposed Transfer Agreement has been finalised and that a common Guidance on the handover of suspected pirates, armed robbers and seized property is prepared. Furthermore, that the Republic of Seychelles will be provided with the necessary assistance for the detention, maintenance, investigation, prosecution trial and repatriation of the suspected pirates and armed robbers.

Following the working session and our letter, further discussions have taken place within the High Level Committee on the transfer of suspected pirates and armed robbers to the territory of the Republic of Seychelles.

The Government of the Republic of Seychelles would like to take this opportunity to renew its reassurance to the EU of its commitment to cooperate to its fullest possible extent, having regard to its available resources and infrastructure capacities, in the repression of piracy to accept the transfer of captured suspected pirates and armed robbers.

At the same time, the Government of the Republic of Seychelles would like to express its desire that the EU SOFA be signed as discussions continue on the proposed EU Transfer Agreement.

In view of ongoing negotiations and pending conclusion of a mutually acceptable arrangement between the EU and the Government of the Republic of Seychelles on the transfer of pirates and armed robbers to its territory, the Government of the Republic of Seychelles may authorize the EUNAVFOR to transfer suspected pirates and armed robbers captured in the course of its operations in the exclusive economic zone, territorial sea, archipelagic waters and internal waters of the Republic of Seychelles. This authorization is extended to the protection of Seychelles flagged vessels and Seychellois Citizens on a non-Seychelles flagged vessel beyond the limit aforementioned and in other circumstances on the high seas at the discretion of the Republic of the Seychelles.

Provided always that:

— The EU, aware of the limited capacities of the Republic of Seychelles to accept, try, detain and incarcerate suspected pirates and armed robbers and in consideration of the acceptance by the Republic of Seychelles of the transfer of any suspected pirates and armed robbers to its territory, shall provide the Republic of Seychelles with such full financial, human resource, material, logistical and infrastructural assistance for the detention, incarceration maintenance, investigation, prosecution, trial and repatriation of the suspected or convicted pirates and armed robbers;

— The Attorney General shall have at least 10 days from the date of transfer of the suspected pirates or armed robbers to decide on the sufficiency of the available evidence in view of prosecution,

— In the event that the Attorney General decides that there is insufficient evidence to prosecute, the EUNAVFOR shall take the full responsibility, including the financial costs, of transferring the suspected pirates and armed robbers back to their country of origin within 10 days of EUNAVFOR having been notified of such a decision;

— Any transfer of suspected pirates and armed robbers shall as far as possible be in accordance with the "*Guidance for the Transfer of Suspected pirates, armed robbers and seized property to Seychelles*",

— The Government of the Republic of the Seychelles also confirms that:

— Any transferred person will be treated humanely and will not be subjected to torture or cruel, inhuman or degrading treatment or punishment, will receive adequate accommodation and nourishment, access to medical treatment and will be able to carry out religious observance.

— Any transferred person will be brought promptly before a judge or other officer authorised by law to exercise judicial power, who will decide without delay on the lawfulness of his detention and will order his release if the detention is not lawful,

— Any transferred person will be entitled to trial within a reasonable time or to release,

— In the determination of any criminal charge against him, any transferred person will be entitled to a fair and public hearing by a competent, independent and impartial tribunal established by law,

— Any transferred person charged with a criminal offence will be presumed innocent until proved guilty according to law,

— In the determination of any criminal charge against him, every transferred person will be entitled to the following minimum guarantees, in full equality:

(1) to be informed promptly and in detail in a language which he understands of the nature of the charge against him;

(2) to have adequate time and facilities for the preparation of his defence and to communicate with counsel of his own choice;

(3) to defend himself in person or through legal assistance of his own choice; to be informed, if he does not have legal assistance, of this right; and to have legal assistance assigned to him, in any case where the interests of justice so require, and without payment by him in any such case if he does not have sufficient means to pay for it;

(4) to examine, or have examined, all evidence against him, including affidavits of witnesses who conducted the arrest, and to obtain the attendance and examination of witnesses on his behalf under the same conditions as witnesses against him;

(5) to have the free assistance of an interpreter if he cannot understand or speak the language used in court;

(6) not to be compelled to testify against himself or to confess guilt.

— Any transferred person convicted of a crime will be permitted to have the right to have its conviction and sentence reviewed by or appealed to a higher tribunal in accordance with the law of the Seychelles,

— The Seychelles will not transfer any transferred person to any other State without prior written consent from EUNAVFOR,

This arrangement has been discussed and agreed by the Seychelles authorities. The arrangements proposed herewith may come into force when the European Union indicates its agreement in writing. This is without prejudice to the legal or policy positions taken by the delegations of both parties in the ongoing negotiations.'.

I have the honour to confirm, on behalf of the European Union, that the content of your letter is acceptable to the European Union. This Instrument will be applied provisionally by the European Union from the date of signature of this letter and will enter into force definitively once the European Union has completed its internal procedures for conclusion.

With regard to the reference in your letter to the consideration by the Seychelles Attorney General of the sufficiency of the available evidence in view of prosecution, the European Union understands that you have agreed that, since EUNAVFOR will communicate in each case all the evidence available to it at the time, such as logbooks, pictures and videos, this will allow the Seychelles Attorney General to take a decision on the sufficiency of such evidence before accepting the transfer of suspected pirates and armed robbers.

I also recall that, as mentioned in your letter, this Instrument will apply on a transitional basis, pending the conclusion of a mutually acceptable transfer agreement between the EU and the Republic of Seychelles on the transfer of pirates and armed robbers to the territory of the Republic of Seychelles.

Please, accept Sir, the assurance of my highest consideration.

*For the European Union*

J. SOLANA MADARIAGA

2.12.2009 EN Official Journal of the European Union L 315/43

**DECLARATION BY THE EUROPEAN UNION ON THE OCCASION OF THE SIGNATURE OF THE EXCHANGE OF LETTERS BETWEEN THE EUROPEAN UNION AND THE REPUBLIC OF SEYCHELLES ON THE CONDITIONS AND MODALITIES FOR THE TRANSFER OF SUSPECTED PIRATES AND ARMED ROBBERS FROM EUNAVFOR TO THE REPUBLIC OF SEYCHELLES AND FOR THEIR TREATMENT AFTER SUCH TRANSFER**

1. The European Union (EU) notes that nothing in the Exchange of letters between the European Union and the Republic of Seychelles on the conditions and modalities for the transfer of suspected pirates and armed robbers is intended to derogate, or may be construed as derogating, from any rights that a transferred person may have under applicable domestic or international law.

2. The EU notes that representatives of the EU and of EUNAVFOR will be granted access to any persons transferred to the Republic of Seychelles (Seychelles) pursuant to the Exchange of Letters as long as such persons are held in custody there, and that representatives of the EU and of EUNAVFOR will be entitled to question them.

   For this purpose, the EU notes that an accurate account will be made available to representatives of the EU and of EUNAVFOR of all transferred persons, including records of any seized property, the persons' physical condition, their place of detention, any charges against them and any significant decisions taken in the course of their prosecution and trial.

   EUNAVFOR is willing to provide timely assistance to Seychelles through the attendance of witnesses from EUNAVFOR and the provision of relevant evidence. For this purpose, Seychelles should notify EUNAVFOR of its intention to initiate criminal proceedings against any transferred person and the timetable for the provision and hearing of evidence.

   The EU notes that national and international humanitarian agencies will also be allowed, at their request, to visit persons transferred under the Exchange of Letters.

# Decision 2009/1023 on the signing, on behalf of the European Union, and on the provisional application of certain provisions of the Agreement between the European Union and Iceland and Norway on the application of certain provisions of Council Decision 2008/615/JHA on the stepping up of cross-border cooperation, particularly in combating terrorism and cross-border crime and Council Decision 2008/616/JHA on the implementation of Decision 2008/615/JHA on the stepping up of cross-border cooperation, particularly in combating terrorism and cross-border crime, and the Annex thereto, 26 and 30 November 2009

**[OJ 2009, L 353/3–6, 8]**

**[Editor's note: signatures omitted]**

31.12.2009 EN Official Journal of the European Union L 353/3

## AGREEMENT

### between the European Union and Iceland and Norway on the application of certain provisions of Council Decision 2008/615/JHA on the stepping up of cross-border cooperation, particularly in combating terrorism and cross-border crime and Council Decision 2008/616/JHA on the implementation of Decision 2008/615/JHA on the stepping up of cross-border cooperation, particularly in combating terrorism and cross-border crime, and the Annex thereto

THE EUROPEAN UNION,

on the one hand, and

ICELAND,

and

NORWAY,

on the other hand,

hereinafter referred to as 'the Contracting Parties',

WISHING to improve police and judicial cooperation between the Member States of the European Union and Iceland and Norway, without prejudice to the rules protecting individual freedom,

CONSIDERING that current relationships between the Contracting Parties, in particular the Agreement concluded by the Council of the European Union and the Republic of Iceland and the Kingdom of Norway concerning the latters' association with the implementation, application and development of the Schengen acquis, demonstrate close cooperation in the fight against crime,

POINTING OUT the Contracting Parties' common interest in ensuring that police cooperation between the Member States of the European Union and Iceland and Norway is carried out in a fast and efficient manner compatible with the basic principles of their national legal systems, and in compliance with the individual rights and principles of the European Convention for the Protection of Human Rights and Fundamental Freedoms, signed at Rome on 4 November 1950,

RECOGNISING that Council Framework Decision 2006/960/JHA of 18 December 2006 on simplifying the exchange of information and intelligence between law enforcement authorities of the Member States of the European Union [1] already lays down rules whereby the law enforcement authorities of the Member States of the European Union and Iceland and Norway may exchange existing information and intelligence expeditiously and effectively for the purpose of carrying out criminal investigations or criminal intelligence operations,

RECOGNISING that, in order to stimulate international cooperation in this area, it is of fundamental importance that precise information can be exchanged swiftly and efficiently. The aim is to introduce procedures for promoting fast, efficient and inexpensive means of data exchange. For the joint use of data these procedures should be subject to accountability and incorporate appropriate guarantees as to the accuracy and security of the data during transmission and storage as well as procedures for recording data exchange and restrictions on the use of information exchanged,

CONSIDERING that Iceland and Norway have expressed their wish to enter into an agreement enabling them to apply certain provisions of Council Decision 2008/615/JHA on the stepping up of cross-border cooperation, particularly in combating terrorism and cross-border crime, and Council Decision 2008/616/JHA on the implementation of Decision 2008/615/JHA on the stepping up of cross-border cooperation, particularly in combating terrorism and cross-border crime, and the Annex thereto, in relations with each other and with the Member States of the European Union,

CONSIDERING that the European Union also considers it necessary to enter into such an agreement,

---

[1] OJ L 386, 29.12.2006, p. 89.

POINTING OUT that this Agreement therefore contains provisions which are based on the main provisions of Decision 2008/615/JHA and Decision 2008/616/JHA, and the Annex thereto, and are designed to improve the exchange of information whereby Member States of the European Union and Iceland and Norway grant one another access rights to their automated DNA analysis files, automated dactyloscopic identification systems and vehicle registration data. In the case of data from national DNA analysis files and automated dactyloscopic identification systems, a hit/no hit system should enable the searching State, in a second step, to request specific related personal data from the State administering the file and, where necessary, to request further information through mutual assistance procedures, including those adopted pursuant to Framework Decision 2006/960/JHA,

CONSIDERING that these provisions would considerably speed up existing procedures enabling Member States, Iceland and Norway to find out whether another State, and if so, which, has the information it needs,

CONSIDERING that cross-border data comparison will open up a new dimension in crime fighting. The information obtained by comparing data will open up new investigative approaches and thus play a crucial role in assisting States' law enforcement and judicial authorities,

CONSIDERING that the rules are based on networking States' national databases,

CONSIDERING that subject to certain conditions, States should be able to supply personal and non-personal data in order to improve the exchange of information with a view to preventing criminal offences and maintaining public order and security in connection with major events with a cross-border dimension,

RECOGNISING that in addition to improving the exchange of information, there is a need to regulate other forms of closer cooperation between police authorities, in particular by means of joint security operations (e.g. joint patrols),

CONSIDERING that closer police and judicial cooperation in criminal matters must go hand in hand with respect for fundamental rights, in particular the right to respect for privacy and to protection of personal data, to be guaranteed by special data protection arrangements, which should be tailored to the specific nature of different forms of data exchange. Such data protection provisions should take particular account of the specific nature of cross-border on-line access to databases. Since, with on-line access, it is not possible for the State administering the file to make any prior checks, a system ensuring post hoc monitoring should be in place,

CONSIDERING that the hit/no hit system provides for a structure of comparing anonymous profiles, where additional personal data is exchanged only after a hit, the supply and receipt of which is governed by national law, including the legal assistance rules. This set-up guarantees an adequate system of data protection, it being understood that the supply of personal data to another State requires an adequate level of data protection on the part of the receiving State,

AWARE OF the comprehensive exchange of information and data resulting from closer police and judicial cooperation, this Agreement seeks to warrant an appropriate level of data protection. It observes the level of protection designed for the processing of personal data in the Council of Europe Convention of 28 January 1981 for the Protection of Individuals with regard to Automatic Processing of Personal Data, the Additional Protocol of 8 November 2001 to the Convention and the principles of Recommendation No R (87) 15 of the Council of Europe Regulating the Use of Personal Data in the Police Sector,

TAKING AS A BASIS the mutual confidence of the Member States of the European Union and Iceland and Norway in the structure and operation of their legal systems,

RECOGNISING that the provisions of bilateral and multilateral agreements remain applicable for all matters not covered by this Agreement,

HAVE DECIDED TO CONCLUDE THIS AGREEMENT:

*Article 1*

**Object and purpose**

1. Subject to the provisions of this Agreement, the content of Articles 1-24, 25(1), 26-32 and 34 of Council Decision 2008/615/JHA on the stepping up of cross-border cooperation, particularly in combating terrorism and cross-border crime, shall be applicable in bilateral relations between Iceland or Norway and each of the Member States of the European Union and in relations between Iceland and Norway.

2. Subject to the provisions of this Agreement, the content of Articles 1-19 and 21 of Council Decision 2008/616/JHA on the implementation of Decision 2008/615/JHA on the stepping up of cross-border cooperation, particularly in combating terrorism and cross-border crime, and the Annex thereto except its chapter 4, point 1, shall be applicable in the relations referred to in paragraph 1.

3. The declarations made by Member States in accordance with Decisions 2008/616/JHA and 2008/615/JHA shall also be applicable in their relations with Iceland and Norway.

*Article 2*

**Definitions**

1. 'Contracting Parties' shall mean the European Union and Iceland and Norway.

2. 'Member State' shall mean a Member State of the European Union.

3. 'State' shall mean a Member State, Iceland or Norway.

*Article 3*

**Uniform application and interpretation**

1. The Contracting Parties, in order to achieve the objective of arriving at as uniform an application and interpretation as possible of the provisions referred to in Article 1, shall keep under constant review the development of the case-law of the Court of Justice of the European Communities, as well as the development of the case-law of the competent courts of Iceland and Norway relating to such provisions. To this end a mechanism shall be set up to ensure regular mutual exchange of such case-law.

2. Iceland and Norway shall be entitled to submit statements of case or written observations to the Court of Justice in cases where a question has been referred to it by a court or tribunal of a Member State for a preliminary ruling concerning the interpretation of any provisions referred to in Article 1.

*Article 4*

**Dispute settlement**

Any dispute between either Iceland or Norway and a Member State regarding the interpretation or the application of this Agreement or of any of the provisions referred to in Article 1 and amendments thereto may be referred by a Party to the dispute to a meeting of representatives of the governments of the Member States and of Iceland and Norway, with a view to its speedy settlement.

*Article 5*

**Amendments**

1. Where it is necessary to amend the provisions of Decision 2008/615/JHA referred to in Article 1(1), and/or the provisions of Decision 2008/616/JHA including the Annex thereto, referred to in Article 1(2), the European Union shall inform Iceland and Norway at the earliest possible occasion and collect any comments they may have.

2. Iceland and Norway shall be notified of any amendment of the provisions of Decision 2008/615/JHA referred to in Article 1(1), and any amendment of the provisions of Decision 2008/616/JHA including the Annex thereto, referred to in Article 1(2) by the depository as soon as the amendment is adopted.

Iceland and Norway shall decide independently whether to accept the content of the amendment and to implement it into their internal legal order. These decisions shall be notified to the depository within three months of the date of notification.

3. If the content of the amendment can be binding on Iceland or Norway only after fulfilment of constitutional requirements, Iceland or Norway shall inform the depository of this at the time of its notification. Iceland or Norway shall promptly, and at the latest six months from the notification by the depository, inform the depository in writing upon fulfilment of all constitutional requirements. From the date laid down for the entry into force of the amendment for Iceland or Norway and until the information upon fulfilment of constitutional requirements, Iceland or Norway shall provisionally apply, where possible, the content of such act or measure.

4. If either Iceland or Norway, or both, do not accept the amendment, this Agreement shall be suspended from the date on which the amendment is to be implemented in relation to the State or States which have not accepted the amendment. A meeting of the Contracting Parties shall be convened to examine all further possibilities with a view to continue the good functioning of this Agreement, including the possibility to take notice of equivalence of legislation. Suspension shall be terminated as soon as the State or States concerned notifies its/their acceptance of the amendment or if the Contracting Parties agree to reinstate the Agreement with respect to the State or States concerned.

5. If, after a period of six months of suspension, the Contracting Parties have not agreed to reinstate the Agreement, it shall cease to apply to the State which has not accepted the amendment.

6. Paragraphs 4 and 5 do not apply to amendments relating to Chapters 3, 4 or 5 of Decision 2008/615/JHA or Article 17 of Decision 2008/616/JHA, in respect of which Iceland or Norway, or both, have notified the depositary that they do not accept the amendment stating the reasons thereof. In that case, and without prejudice to Article 10, the content of the relevant provisions in their version prior to amendment shall continue to be applicable in the relations with the State or States having made the notification.

*Article 6*

**Review**

The Contracting Parties agree to carry out a common review of this Agreement no later than five years after its entry into force. The review shall in particular address the practical implementation, interpretation and development of the Agreement and shall also include issues such as the consequences of development of the European Union relating to the subject-matter of this Agreement.

*Article 7*

**Relationship with other instruments**

1. Iceland and Norway may continue to apply bilateral or multilateral agreements or arrangements on cross-border cooperation with Member States that are in force on the date this Agreement is adopted in so far as such agreements or arrangements are not incompatible with the objectives of this Agreement. Iceland and Norway shall notify the depository of any such agreements or arrangements which will continue to apply.

2. Iceland and Norway may conclude or bring into force additional bilateral or multilateral agreements or arrangements on cross-border cooperation with Member States after this Agreement has entered into force insofar as such agreements or arrangements provide for the objectives of this Agreement to be extended or enlarged. Iceland and Norway shall notify the depository of any such new agreement or arrangement within three months of signing or, in the case of instruments that were signed before the entry into force of the Agreement, within three months of their entry into force.

3. The agreements and arrangements referred to in paragraphs 1 and 2 may not affect relations with States that are not parties thereto.

4. This Agreement shall be without prejudice to existing agreements on legal assistance or mutual recognition of court decisions.

*Article 8*

**Notifications, declarations and entry into force**

1. The Contracting Parties shall notify each other of the completion of the procedures required to express their consent to be bound by this Agreement.

2. The European Union may express its consent to be bound by this Agreement even if the decisions referred to in Article 25(2) of Decision 2008/615/JHA have not yet been taken in respect of all the Member States to which that provision applies.

3. Article 5(1) and (2) shall apply provisionally as from the time of signature of this Agreement.

4. With respect to amendments adopted after the signature of this Agreement but before its entry into force, the period of three months referred to in the last sentence of Article 5(2) shall start to run from the day of entry into force of this Agreement.

5. When giving their notification under paragraph 1 or, if so provided, at any time thereafter, Iceland and Norway shall make the declarations provided for in this Agreement.

6. This Agreement shall enter into force between the European Union and Iceland on the first day of the third month following the day on which the Secretary-General of the Council of the European Union establishes that all formal requirements concerning the expression of consent by or on behalf of the European Union and Iceland to be bound by the Agreement have been fulfilled.

7. This Agreement shall enter into force between the European Union and Norway on the first day of the third month following the day on which the Secretary-General of the Council of the European Union establishes that all formal requirements concerning the expression of consent by or on behalf of the European Union and Norway to be bound by the Agreement have been fulfilled.

8. As soon as this Agreement is in force between the European Union and Iceland and the European Union and Norway, it shall also be in force between Iceland and Norway.

9. The supply by Member States of personal data under this Agreement may not take place until the provisions of Chapter 6 of Decision 2008/615/JHA have been implemented in the national law of the States involved in such supply.

10. In order to verify whether this is the case for Iceland and Norway, an evaluation visit and a pilot run shall be carried out in respect of and under conditions and arrangements acceptable to those States, similar to those concluded in respect of Member States pursuant to Chapter 4 of the Annex to Decision 2008/616/JHA.

On the basis of an overall evaluation report the Council, acting unanimously, shall determine the date or dates as from which personal data may be supplied by Member States to Iceland and Norway pursuant to this Agreement.

*Article 9*

**Accession**

Accession by new Member States to the European Union shall create rights and obligations under this Agreement between those new Member States and Iceland and Norway.

*Article 10*

**Termination**

1. This Agreement may be terminated at any time by one of the Contracting Parties. In the event of termination by either Iceland or Norway, this Agreement shall remain in force between the European Union and the State for which it has not been terminated. In the event of termination by the European Union, the Agreement shall lapse.

2. Termination of this Agreement pursuant to paragraph 1 shall take effect six months after the deposit of the notification of termination.

*Article 11*

**Depository**

1. The Secretary-General of the Council of the European Union shall act as the depository of this Agreement.

2. The depository shall make public information on any notification made concerning this Agreement.

Done at Stockholm on 26 November 2009 and at Brussels on 30 November 2009 in a single original in the Bulgarian, Czech, Danish, Dutch, English, Estonian, Finnish, French, German, Greek, Hungarian, Italian, Latvian, Lithuanian, Maltese, Polish, Portuguese, Romanian, Slovak, Slovenian, Spanish, Swedish, Icelandic and Norwegian languages, each text being equally authentic.

DECLARATION TO BE ADOPTED AT THE OCCASION OF THE SIGNATURE OF THE AGREEMENT

The European Union and Iceland and Norway, signatories to the Agreement on the application of certain provisions of Council Decision 2008/615/JHA on the stepping up of cross-border cooperation, particularly in combating terrorism and cross-border crime and Council Decision 2008/616/JHA on the implementation of Council Decision 2008/615/JHA on the stepping up of cross-border cooperation, particularly in combating terrorism and cross-border crime, and the Annex thereto, ('the Agreement'),

declare:

The implementation of the DNA, dactyloscopic and vehicle registration data exchange pursuant to the Agreement will require that Iceland and Norway set up bilateral connections for each of these data categories with each of the Member States.

To enable and facilitate this work, Iceland and Norway will be provided with all the available documentation, software products and contact lists.

Iceland and Norway will have the opportunity to set up an informal partnership with Member States that have already implemented such data exchange, with a view to sharing experiences and getting practical and technical support. The details of such partnerships are to be arranged in direct contacts with the Member States concerned.

The Icelandic and Norwegian experts can contact at any time the Presidency of the Council, the Commission and/or leading experts in these matters to obtain information, clarification or any other support. Similarly the Commission will, whenever in preparation of proposals or communications it contacts representatives of the Member States, avail itself of the opportunity to contact also representatives of Iceland and Norway.

Icelandic and Norwegian experts may be invited to attend on an ad hoc basis meetings where Member States' experts discuss within the Council technical aspects of the DNA, dactyloscopic or vehicle registration data exchange which are directly relevant to the proper application of the content of the aforementioned Council Decisions by Iceland and/or Norway.

# Decision 2009/902 setting up a European Crime Prevention Network (EUCPN) and repealing Decision 2001/427, 30 November 2009

**[OJ 2009, L 321/44–46]**

L 321/44 EN Official Journal of the European Union 8.12.2009

III

*(Acts adopted under the EU Treaty)*

# ACTS ADOPTED UNDER TITLE VI OF THE EU TREATY

## COUNCIL DECISION 2009/902/JHA

**of 30 November 2009**

**setting up a European Crime Prevention Network (EUCPN) and repealing Decision 2001/427/JHA**

THE COUNCIL OF THE EUROPEAN UNION,

Having regard to the Treaty on European Union and in particular Articles 30(1), 31 and 34(2)(c) thereof,

Having regard to the initiative of the Kingdom of Belgium, the Czech Republic, the Federal Republic of Germany, the Kingdom of Spain, the French Republic, the Republic of Hungary, the Kingdom of the Netherlands, the Slovak Republic, the Republic of Finland, the Kingdom of Sweden, the United Kingdom of Great Britain and Northern Ireland (1),

Having regard to the Opinion of the European Parliament,

Whereas:

(1) The Tampere European Council of 15 and 16 October 1999 concluded that there was a need to develop crime prevention measures, to exchange best practices and to strengthen the network of competent national authorities for crime prevention, as well as cooperation between national organisations specialising in this field, specifying that this cooperation could have as its chief priorities juvenile, urban and drug-related crime. To this end, a study of the possibility of a programme financed by the Community was called for.

(2) Recommendation 6 of the European Union strategy for the beginning of the new millennium on the prevention and control of organised crime (2) calls for the Council to be assisted by suitably qualified experts on crime prevention, such as the national focal points, or by establishing a network of experts from national crime prevention organisations.

(3) Council Decision 2001/427/JHA established a European Crime Prevention Network (3).

(4) An external evaluation of the European Crime Prevention Network which was conducted in 2008-2009 identified opportunities for strengthening the Network which were accepted by the EUCPN Board and which make it necessary to repeal Decision 2001/427/JHA and to replace it by a new Council Decision concerning the Network.

(5) The evaluation identified the need for more engagement in the activities of the Network by the national representatives.

(6) A number of changes are required to strengthen the Network which include amendments to the provisions dealing with contact points, the Secretariat, the structure of the Board and its tasks, including the appointment of the Chair.

(7) Changes in the composition of the Network should be efficient and cost-effective, drawing on previous experiences of Member States in funding and carrying out the secretarial and other Network tasks. The Board should increase efforts in cooperating to investigate and exploit to their full potential, the possibilities for funding through the general budget of the European Union. This could be done on the basis of either framework partnerships or that the Network is included in the list of recognised monopoly bodies in the relevant financing programme.

(8) Other provisions should be based on Decision 2001/427/JHA,

(1) OJ C 222, 15.9.2009, p. 2.
(2) OJ C 124, 3.5.2000, p. 1.
(3) OJ L 153, 8.6.2001, p. 1.

8.12.2009 EN Official Journal of the European Union L 321/45

HAS DECIDED AS FOLLOWS:

*Article 1*

**Setting-up**

A European Crime Prevention Network, hereinafter referred to as 'the Network', is hereby set up. It shall be regarded as the successor to the European Crime Prevention Network established by Decision 2001/427/JHA.

*Article 2*

**Objective**

1. The Network shall contribute to developing the various aspects of crime prevention at the Union level, taking account of the European Union crime preventive strategy, and shall support crime prevention activities at the national and local level.

2. Crime prevention shall cover all measures that are intended to reduce or otherwise contribute to reducing crime and citizens' feeling of insecurity, both quantitatively and qualitatively, either through directly deterring criminal activities or through policies and actions designed to reduce the potential for crime and the causes of crime. It includes work of government, competent authorities, criminal justice agencies, local authorities and the specialist associations they have set up in Europe, the private and voluntary sectors, researchers and the public, supported by the media.

*Article 3*

**Structure and composition**

1. The Network shall consist of a Board and a Secretariat as well as contact points which may be designated by each Member State.

2. The Board shall be made up of national representatives, with a Chair and an Executive Committee.

3. Each Member State shall appoint a national representative and may appoint a substitute.

4. The Chair shall be appointed from within the body of the national representatives.

5. The Executive Committee shall be led by the Chair and shall be composed of up to six further members of the Board and a representative designated by the Commission.

*Article 4*

**Tasks of the Network**

The Network shall, in particular:

(a) facilitate cooperation, contacts and exchanges of information and experience between actors in the field of crime prevention;

(b) collect, assess and communicate evaluated information including good practice on existing crime prevention activities;

(c) organise conferences, in particular an annual Best Practice Conference, and other activities, including the annual European Crime Prevention Award, designed to achieve the objectives of the Network and to share widely the results thereof;

(d) provide its expertise to the Council and the Commission as required;

(e) report to the Council on its activities each year through the Board and the competent working bodies. The Council shall be invited to endorse the report and forward it to the European Parliament;

(f) develop and implement a work programme based on a clearly defined strategy that takes account of identifying and responding to relevant crime threats.

*Article 5*

**Information exchange**

To accomplish its tasks, the Network shall:

(a) favour a multidisciplinary approach;

(b) be in close contact, through the national representatives and the contact points, with crime prevention bodies, local authorities, local partnerships and civil society as well as with research institutions and nongovernmental organisations in the Member States;

(c) set up and maintain its own website, containing its regular reports and any other useful information, in particular a compendium of best practices;

(d) endeavour to use and promote the results of projects, relevant for crime prevention, funded through Union programmes.

*Article 6*

**Responsibilities**

1. The Executive Committee shall provide support to the Chair to ensure, inter alia:

(a) the development of the Network's strategy for approval by the Board;

(b) the effective running of the Board, and

(c) the development and carrying-out of the work programme.

2. The tasks of the Board shall include:

(a) to ensure the proper functioning of the Network in accordance with this Decision, including deciding on the practical organisation of the Secretariat functions;

(b) to develop and adopt a financial regulation;

(c) to approve the Network's strategy, which contributes to developing crime prevention at the Union level;

(d) to adopt and ensure delivery of the Network's work programme;

(e) to adopt an annual report of the Network's activities.

3. The Board shall adopt its Rules of Procedure by unanimous decision containing, *inter alia*, the provisions on the appointment and term of office of the Chair and of the members of the Executive Committee, the decision-making arrangements of the Board, the language arrangements, the tasks, organisation and resources of the Secretariat, and administrative arrangements for the cooperation with other entities as referred to in Article 8.

4. The Secretariat shall support the Board. It shall function on a permanent basis, for the full benefit of the Network, while respecting confidentiality as required. It shall have the following tasks:

(a) to provide administrative and general support in the preparation of meetings, seminars and conferences; to draft the annual report and the work programme, to support implementation of the work programme and to provide a focal point for communication with the Network members;

(b) to provide an analytical and support function to identify ongoing research activity in the field of crime prevention and related information that would be of use to the Network;

(c) to take overall responsibility for hosting, developing and maintaining the Network website.

5. Each national representative shall promote the Network's activities at the national and local level and facilitate the provision, maintenance and exchange of crime prevention material between his Member State and the Network.

6. Contact points shall support national representatives in exchanging national crime prevention information and expertise within the Network.

7. The Secretariat shall report to and its performance shall be overseen by the Chair and the Executive Committee.

8. Member States are responsible for the financing of the Network and its activities. Member States shall, through the Board, cooperate to ensure cost-effective financing of the Network and its activities.

9. Paragraph 8 is without prejudice to the possibilities to seek and obtain financial support from the general budget of the European Union.

*Article 7*

**Board meetings**

The Board shall meet at least once during each half year on the invitation of the Chair.

*Article 8*

**Cooperation with other entities**

The Network may cooperate with other entities competent in the field of crime prevention where it is relevant to meeting its objectives.

*Article 9*

**Evaluation**

The Commission shall present an evaluation report to the Council on the activities of the Network with a special focus on the efficiency of the work of the Network and its Secretariat, taking due account of the interaction between the Network and other relevant stakeholders, by 30 November 2012. Based on the results of this evaluation, an assessment shall be carried out to identify possible opportunities that could be achieved by for example transferring the Secretariat to an existing Agency.

*Article 10*

**Repeal**

Decision 2001/427/JHA is hereby repealed.

*Article 11*

**Taking of effect**

This Decision shall take effect on the day of its adoption.

Done at Brussels, 30 November 2009.

*For the Council*
*The President*
B. ASK

# Framework Decision 2009/905 on accreditation of forensic service providers carrying out laboratory activities, 30 November 2009

[OJ 2009, L 322/14–16]

L 322/14 EN Official Journal of the European Union 9.12.2009

III

*(Acts adopted under the EU Treaty)*

# ACTS ADOPTED UNDER TITLE VI OF THE EU TREATY

## COUNCIL FRAMEWORK DECISION 2009/905/JHA

**of 30 November 2009**

**on Accreditation of forensic service providers carrying out laboratory activities**

THE COUNCIL OF THE EUROPEAN UNION,

Having regard to the Treaty on European Union, and in particular Article 30(1)(a) and (c) and Article 34(2)(b) thereof,

Having regard to the initiative of the Kingdom of Sweden and the Kingdom of Spain (1),

Having regard to the opinion of the European Parliament,

Whereas:

(1) The European Union has set itself the objective of maintaining and developing the Union as an area of freedom, security and justice; a high level of safety is to be provided by common action among the Member States in the field of police and judicial cooperation in criminal matters.

(2) That objective is to be achieved by preventing and combating crime through closer cooperation between law enforcement authorities in the Member States, while respecting the principles and rules relating to human rights, fundamental freedoms and the rule of law on which the Union is founded and which are common to the Member States.

(3) Exchange of information and intelligence on crime and criminal activities is crucial for the possibility for law enforcement authorities to successfully prevent, detect and investigate crime or criminal activities. Common action in the field of police cooperation under Article 30(1)(a) of the Treaty entails the need to process relevant information which should be subject to appropriate provisions on the protection of personal data.

(1) OJ C 174, 28.7.2009, p. 7.

(4) The intensified exchange of information regarding forensic evidence and the increased use of evidence from one Member State in the judicial processes of another, highlights the need to establish common standards for forensic service providers.

(5) Information originating from forensic processes in one Member State may currently be associated with a level of uncertainty in another Member State regarding the way in which an item has been handled, what methods have been used and how the results have been interpreted.

(6) In point 3.4 (h) of the Council and Commission Action Plan implementing The Hague Programme on strengthening freedom, security and justice in the European Union (2) Member States stressed the need for a definition of the quality standards of forensic laboratories by 2008.

(7) It is particularly important to introduce common standards for forensic service providers relating to such sensitive personal data as DNA profiles and dactyloscopic data.

(8) Pursuant to Article 7(4) of Council Decision 2008/616/JHA of 23 June 2008 on the implementation of Decision 2008/615/JHA on the stepping up of cross-border cooperation, particularly in combating terrorism and cross-border crime (3), Member States shall take the necessary measures to guarantee the integrity of DNA profiles made available or sent for comparison to other Member States and to ensure that these measures comply with international standards, such as EN ISO/IEC 17025 'General requirements for the competence of testing and calibration laboratories' (hereinafter 'EN ISO/IEC 17025').

(2) OJ C 198, 12.8.2005, p. 1.
(3) OJ L 210, 6.8.2008, p. 12.

9.12.2009 EN Official Journal of the European Union L 322/15

(9) DNA profiles and dactyloscopic data are not only used in criminal proceedings but are also crucial for the identification of victims, particularly after disasters.

(10) The accreditation of forensic service providers carrying out laboratory activities is an important step towards a safer and more effective exchange of forensic information within the Union.

(11) Accreditation is granted by the national accreditation body which has exclusive competence to assess if a laboratory meets the requirements set by harmonised standards. An accreditation body derives its authority from the State. Regulation (EC) No 765/2008 of the European Parliament and of the Council of 9 July 2008 setting out the requirements for accreditation and market surveillance relating to the marketing of products [1] contains detailed provisions on the competence of such national accreditation bodies. Inter alia, Article 7 of that Regulation regulates cross-border accreditation in cases where accreditation may be requested from another national accreditation body.

(12) The absence of an agreement to apply a common accreditation standard for the analysis of scientific evidence is a deficiency that should be remedied; it is, therefore, necessary to adopt a legally binding instrument on the accreditation of all forensic service providers carrying out laboratory activities. Accreditation offers the necessary guarantees that laboratory activities are performed in accordance with relevant international standards, in particular EN ISO/IEC 17025, as well as relevant applicable guidelines.

(13) An accreditation standard allows any Member State to require, if it wishes, complementary standards in laboratory activities within its national jurisdiction.

(14) Accreditation will help establish mutual trust in the validity of the basic analytic methods used. However, accreditation does not state which method to use, only that the method used has to be suitable for its purpose.

(15) Any measure taken outside a laboratory is beyond the scope of this Framework Decision. For example, the taking of dactyloscopic data or measures taken at the scene of incident, the scene of crime or forensic analyses carried out outside laboratories are not included in its scope.

(16) This Framework Decision does not aim to harmonise national rules regarding the judicial assessment of forensic evidence.

(17) This Decision does not affect the validity, established in accordance with national applicable rules, of the results of laboratory activities carried out prior to its implementation, even if the forensic service provider was not accredited to comply with EN ISO/IEC 17025,

HAS ADOPTED THIS FRAMEWORK DECISION:

*Article 1*

**Objective**

1. The purpose of this Framework Decision is to ensure that the results of laboratory activities carried out by accredited forensic service providers in one Member State are recognised by the authorities responsible for the prevention, detection and investigation of criminal offences as being equally reliable as the results of laboratory activities carried out by forensic service providers accredited to EN ISO/IEC 17025 within any other Member State.

2. This purpose is achieved by ensuring that forensic service providers carrying out laboratory activities are accredited by a national accreditation body as complying with EN ISO/IEC 17025.

*Article 2*

**Scope**

This Framework Decision shall apply to laboratory activities resulting in:

(a) DNA-profile; and

(b) dactyloscopic data.

*Article 3*

**Definitions**

For the purposes of this Framework Decision:

(a) 'laboratory activity' means any measure taken in a laboratory when locating and recovering traces on items, as well as developing, analysing and interpreting forensic evidence, with a view to providing expert opinions or exchanging forensic evidence;

(b) 'results of laboratory activities' means any analytical outputs and directly associated interpretation;

(c) 'forensic service provider' means any organisation, public or private, that carries out forensic laboratory activities at the request of competent law enforcement or judicial authorities;

[1] OJ L 218, 13.8.2008, p. 30.

(d) 'national accreditation body' means the sole body in a Member State that performs accreditation with authority derived from the State as referred to in Regulation (EC) No 765/2008;

(e) 'DNA-profile' means a letter or number code which represents a set of identification characteristics of the non-coding part of an analysed human DNA sample, i.e. the particular molecular structure at the various DNA locations (loci);

(f) 'dactyloscopic data' means fingerprint images, images of fingerprint latents, palm prints, palm print latents and templates of such images (coded minutiae).

*Article 4*

**Accreditation**

Member States shall ensure that their forensic service providers carrying out laboratory activities are accredited by a national accreditation body as complying with EN ISO/IEC 17025.

*Article 5*

**Recognition of results**

1. Each Member State shall ensure that the results of accredited forensic service providers carrying out laboratory activities in other Member States are recognised by its authorities responsible for the prevention, detection, and investigation of criminal offences as being equally reliable as the results of domestic forensic service providers carrying out laboratory activities accredited to EN ISO/IEC 17025.

2. This Framework Decision does not affect national rules on the judicial assessment of evidence.

*Article 6*

**Costs**

1. Each Member State shall bear any public costs resulting from this Framework Decision in accordance with national arrangements.

2. The Commission shall examine the means to provide financial support from the general budget of the European Union for national and transnational projects intended to contribute to the implementation of this Framework Decision, inter alia for the exchange of experience, dissemination of know-how and proficiency testing.

*Article 7*

**Implementation**

1. Member States shall take the necessary steps to comply with the provisions of this Framework Decision in relation to DNA-profiles by 30 November 2013.

2. Member States shall take the necessary steps to comply with the provisions of this Framework Decision in relation to dactyloscopic data by 30 November 2015.

3. Member States shall forward to the General Secretariat of the Council and to the Commission the text of the provisions transposing into their national laws the obligations imposed on them under this Framework Decision by 30 May 2016 at the latest.

4. On the basis of the information referred to in paragraph 3 and other information provided by the Member States on request, the Commission shall, before 1 July 2018, submit a report to the Council on the implementation and application of this Framework Decision.

5. The Council shall, by the end of 2018, assess the extent to which Member States have complied with this Framework Decision.

*Article 8*

**Entry into force**

This Framework Decision shall enter into force on the twentieth day following its publication in the *Official Journal of the European Union*.

Done at Brussels, 30 November 2009.

*For the Council*
*The President*
B. ASK

# Decision 2009/917 on the use of information technology for customs purposes, 30 November 2009

[OJ 2009, L 323/20–30]

L 323/20 EN Official Journal of the European Union 10.12.2009

# ACTS ADOPTED UNDER TITLE VI OF THE EU TREATY

## COUNCIL DECISION 2009/917/JHA
## of 30 November 2009
## on the use of information technology for customs purposes

THE COUNCIL OF THE EUROPEAN UNION,

Having regard to the Treaty on European Union, and in particular Article 30(1)(a) and Article 34(2)(c) thereof,

Having regard to the initiative of the French Republic,

Having regard to the Opinion of the European Parliament ([1]),

Whereas:

(1) At the external borders of the Community and within its territory, customs administrations are responsible, together with other competent authorities, for the prevention, investigation and prosecution of offences not only against Community rules, but also against national laws.

(2) The developing trend towards illicit trafficking of all kinds constitutes a serious threat to public health, morality and security.

(3) It is necessary to reinforce cooperation between customs administrations, by laying down procedures under which customs administrations may act jointly and exchange personal and other data concerned with illicit trafficking activities, using new technology for the management and transmission of such information, taking into account Council Framework Decision 2008/977/JHA of 27 November 2008 on the protection of personal data processed in the framework of police and judicial cooperation in criminal matters ([2]) and the principles contained in Recommendation No R (87) 15 of the Committee of Ministers of the Council of Europe of 17 September 1987 regulating the use of personal data in the police sector (hereinafter referred to as Recommendation No R (87) 15).

(4) It is also necessary to enhance complementarity with actions in the context of cooperation with the European Police Office (Europol) and the European Judicial Cooperation Unit (Eurojust), by granting those bodies access to the Customs Information System, including the customs files identification database, to fulfil their tasks within their mandate.

(5) Reading access to the Customs Information System should allow Europol to cross-check information obtained through other means with the information available in those databases, to identify new links that were so far not detectable and thus to produce a more comprehensive analysis. Reading access to the customs files identification database should allow Europol to uncover connections between cases of criminal investigations, so far unknown to Europol that have a dimension in and outside the European Union.

(6) Reading access to the Customs Information System should allow Eurojust to obtain immediate information required for an accurate initial overview enabling to identify and overcome legal obstacles and to achieve better prosecution results. Reading access to the customs files identification database should allow Eurojust to receive information of ongoing and closed investigations in different Members States and thus to enhance the support of judicial authorities in the Member States.

(7) Since customs administrations have to implement both Community and non-Community provisions in their day-to-day work, it is necessary to ensure that the provisions on mutual assistance and administrative cooperation evolve in parallel. Account should therefore be taken of the provisions on the Customs Information System and the customs files identification database in Regulation (EC) No 766/2008 ([3]).

([1]) Opinion of 24 November 2009 (not yet published in the Official Journal).
([2]) OJ L 350, 30.12.2008, p. 60.
([3]) Regulation (EC) No 766/2008 of the European Parliament and of the Council of 9 July 2008 amending Council Regulation (EC) No 515/97 on mutual assistance between the administrative authorities of the Member States and cooperation between the latter and the Commission to ensure the correct application of the law on customs and agricultural matters (OJ L 218, 13.8.2008, p. 48).

(8) Member States recognise the advantage which the full use of the customs files identification database will provide for coordinating and strengthening the fight against cross-border criminality and therefore commit themselves to enter data into that database to the greatest extent possible.

(9) Experience gained since the Convention of 26 July 1995 on the use of information technology for customs purposes (hereinafter the CIS Convention) (1) entered into force has shown that the use of the Customs Information System for the sole purposes of sighting and reporting, discreet surveillance or specific checks does not make it possible to achieve fully the system's objective, which is to assist in preventing, investigating and prosecuting serious contraventions of national laws.

(10) A strategic analysis should help those responsible at the highest level to determine projects, objectives and policies for combating fraud, to plan activities and to deploy the resources needed to achieve the operational objectives.

(11) An operational analysis of the activities, resources and intentions of certain persons or businesses that do not comply or appear not to comply with national laws should help the customs authorities to take the appropriate measures in specific cases to achieve the objectives as regards the fight against fraud.

(12) The CIS Convention should therefore be replaced.

(13) This Decision respects the fundamental rights and observes the principles recognised in particular by the Charter of Fundamental Rights of the European Union.

(14) This Decision does not prevent the Member States from applying their constitutional rules relating to public access to official documents,

HAS DECIDED AS FOLLOWS:

CHAPTER I

**ESTABLISHMENT OF A CUSTOMS INFORMATION SYSTEM**

*Article 1*

1. A joint automated information system for customs purposes (hereinafter referred to as the 'Customs Information System' or the 'System') is hereby established.

2. The aim of the Customs Information System, in accordance with this Decision, shall be to assist in preventing, investigating and prosecuting serious contraventions of national laws by making information available more rapidly, thereby increasing the effectiveness of the cooperation and control procedures of the customs administrations of the Member States.

(1) OJ C 316, 27.11.1995, p. 33.

CHAPTER II

**DEFINITIONS**

*Article 2*

For the purposes of this Decision:

1. 'national laws' mean laws or regulations of a Member State, in the application of which the customs administration of that Member State has total or partial competence, concerning:

(a) the movement of goods subject to measures of prohibition, restriction or control, in particular those measures covered by Articles 30 and 296 of the Treaty establishing the European Community (the EC Treaty);

(b) measures to control cash movements within the Community, where such measures are taken in accordance with Article 58 of the EC Treaty;

(c) the transfer, conversion, concealment, or disguise of property or proceeds acquired or obtained directly or indirectly through illicit international drug trafficking or by infringement of:

(i) the laws, regulations or administrative provisions of a Member State in the application of which the customs administration of that Member State has partial or total competence, concerning the cross-border movement of goods subject to measures of prohibition, restriction or control, in particular those measures referred to in Articles 30 and 296 of the EC Treaty, and non-harmonised excise duties;

(ii) the body of Community provisions and associated implementing provisions governing the import, export, transit and presence of goods traded between Member States and third countries, and between Member States in the case of goods that do not have Community status within the meaning of Article 23 of the EC Treaty or goods subject to additional controls or investigations for the purposes of establishing their Community status;

(iii) the body of provisions adopted at Community level under the common agricultural policy and the specific provisions adopted with regard to goods resulting from the processing of agricultural products; or

(iv) the body of provisions adopted at Community level for harmonised excise duties and for value-added tax on importation together with the national provisions implementing them, or those which have been used in that context;

2. 'personal data' mean any information relating to an identified or identifiable natural person (data subject), whereby an identifiable person is one who can be identified, directly or indirectly, in particular by reference to an identification number or to one or more factors specific to his physical, physiological, mental, economic, cultural or social identity;

3. 'supplying Member State' means a Member State which enters an item of data into the Customs Information System;

4. 'operational analysis' means analysis of operations which constitute, or appear to constitute, breaches of national laws, involving the following stages:

(a) the collection of information, including personal data;

(b) evaluation of the reliability of the information source and the information itself;

(c) research, methodical presentation and interpretation of links between these items of information or between them and other significant data;

(d) the formulation of observations, hypotheses or recommendations directly usable as risk information by the competent authorities to prevent and detect other operations in breach of national laws and/or to identify with precision the person or businesses implicated in such operations;

5. 'strategic analysis' means research and presentation of the general trends in breaches of national laws through an evaluation of the threat, scale and impact of certain types of operation in breach of national laws, with a view to setting priorities, gaining a better picture of the phenomenon or threat, reorienting action to prevent and detect fraud and reviewing departmental organisation. Only data from which identifying factors have been removed may be used for strategic analysis.

CHAPTER III

## OPERATION AND USE OF THE CUSTOMS INFORMATION SYSTEM

*Article 3*

1. The Customs Information System shall consist of a central database facility, accessible through terminals in each Member State. It shall comprise exclusively data necessary to achieve its aim as stated in Article 1(2), including personal data, in the following categories:

(a) commodities;

(b) means of transport;

(c) businesses;

(d) persons;

(e) fraud trends;

(f) availability of expertise;

(g) items detained, seized or confiscated;

(h) cash detained, seized or confiscated.

2. The Commission shall ensure the technical management of the infrastructure of the Customs Information System in accordance with the rules provided for by the implementing measures adopted by the Council.

The Commission shall report on management to the Committee referred to in Article 27.

3. The Commission shall communicate to that Committee the practical arrangements adopted for technical management.

*Article 4*

1. Member States shall determine the items to be entered into the Customs Information System relating to each of the categories referred to in Article 3(1), to the extent that this is necessary to achieve the aim of the System. No items of personal data shall be entered in any event within the category set out in Article 3(1)(e).

2. With regard to the categories set out in Article 3(1)(a) to (d), the items of information entered in respect of persons shall comprise no more than:

(a) name, maiden name, forenames, former surnames and aliases;

(b) date and place of birth;

(c) nationality;

(d) sex;

(e) number and place and date of issue of the identity papers (passports, identity cards, driving licences);

(f) address;

(g) any particular objective and permanent physical characteristics;

(h) reason for entering data;

(i) suggested action;

(j) a warning code indicating any history of being armed, violent or of escaping;

(k) registration number of the means of transport.

3. With regard to the category set out in Article 3(1)(f), the items of information entered in respect of persons shall comprise no more than the experts surnames and forenames.

4. With regard to the categories set out in Article 3(1)(g) and (h), the items of information entered in respect of persons shall comprise no more than:

(a) name, maiden name, forenames, former surnames and aliases;

(b) date and place of birth;

(c) nationality;

(d) sex;

(e) address.

5. In no case shall personal data listed in Article 6 of the Framework Decision 2008/977/JHA be entered into the Customs Information System.

*Article 5*

1. Data in the categories referred to in Article 3(1)(a) to (g) shall be entered into the Customs Information System only for the purpose of sighting and reporting, discreet surveillance, specific checks and strategic or operational analysis.

Data in the category referred to in Article 3(1)(h) shall be entered into the Customs Information System only for the purpose of strategic or operational analysis.

2. For the purpose of the actions referred to in paragraph 1, personal data in any of the categories referred to in Article 3(1) may be entered into the Customs Information System only if there are real indications, in particular on the basis of prior illegal activities, to suggest that the person concerned has committed, is in the act of committing or will commit serious contraventions of national laws.

*Article 6*

1. If the actions referred to in Article 5(1) are carried out, the following information may in whole or in part be collected and transferred to the supplying Member State:

(i) the fact that the commodity, means of transport, business or person reported has been found;

(ii) the place, time and reason for the check;

(iii) the route and destination of the journey;

(iv) persons accompanying the person concerned or occupants of the means of transport;

(v) the means of transport used;

(vi) objects carried;

(vii) the circumstances under which the commodity, means of transport, business or person was found.

When such information is collected in the course of discreet surveillance, steps have to be taken to ensure that the discreet nature of the surveillance is not jeopardised.

2. In the context of a specific check referred to in Article 5(1), persons, means of transport and objects may be searched to the extent permissible and in accordance with the laws, regulations and procedures of the Member State in which the search takes place. If the specific check is not permitted by the law of a Member State, it shall automatically be converted by that Member State into sighting and reporting or discreet surveillance.

*Article 7*

1. Direct access to data entered into the Customs Information System shall be reserved to the national authorities designated by each Member State. Those national authorities shall be customs administrations, but may also include other authorities competent, according to the laws, regulations and procedures of the Member State in question, to act in order to achieve the aim stated in Article 1(2).

2. Each Member State shall send the other Member States and the Committee referred to in Article 27 a list of its competent authorities which have been designated in accordance with paragraph 1 of this Article to have direct access to the Customs Information System stating, for each authority, to which data it may have access and for what purposes.

3. Notwithstanding paragraphs 1 and 2, the Council may, by a unanimous decision, permit access to the Customs Information System by international or regional organisations. In making this decision the Council shall take account of any reciprocal arrangements and any opinion on the adequacy of data protection measures by the Joint Supervisory Authority referred to in Article 25.

*Article 8*

1. Member States, Europol and Eurojust may use data obtained from the Customs Information System only in order to achieve the aim stated in Article 1(2). However, they may use it for administrative or other purposes with the prior authorisation of, and subject to any conditions imposed by, the Member State which entered the data in the System. Such other use shall be in accordance with the laws, regulations and procedures of the Member State which seeks to use it in accordance with Article 3(2) of Framework Decision 2008/977/JHA, and should take into account Principle 5.2.i of the Recommendation No R (87) 15.

2. Without prejudice to paragraphs 1 and 4 of this Article, Article 7(3) and Articles 11 and 12, data obtained from the Customs Information System shall only be used by national authorities in each Member State designated by the Member State in question, which are competent, in accordance with the laws, regulations and procedures of that Member State, to act in order to achieve the aim stated in Article 1(2).

3. Each Member State shall send the other Member States and the Committee referred to in Article 27 a list of the competent authorities it has designated in accordance with paragraph 2 of this Article.

4. Data obtained from the Customs Information System may, with the prior authorisation of, and subject to any conditions imposed by, the Member State which entered them into the System, be transferred for use by national authorities other than those designated under paragraph 2 of this Article, third countries, and international or regional organisations wishing to make use of them. Each Member State shall take special measures to ensure the security of such data when they are being transferred to services located outside its territory. Details of such measures have to be communicated to the Joint Supervisory Authority referred to in Article 25.

*Article 9*

1. The entry of data into the Customs Information System shall be governed by the laws, regulations and procedures of the supplying Member State unless this Decision lays down more stringent provisions.

2. The use of data obtained from the Customs Information System, including performance of any action under Article 5(1) suggested by the supplying Member State, shall be governed by the laws, regulations and procedures of the Member State using such data, unless this Decision lays down more stringent provisions.

*Article 10*

1. Each Member State shall designate a competent customs administration which shall have national responsibility for the Customs Information System.

2. The administration referred to in paragraph 1 shall be responsible for the correct operation of the Customs Information System within the Member State and shall take the measures necessary to ensure compliance with this Decision.

3. Member States shall inform one another of the administration referred to in paragraph 1.

*Article 11*

1. Europol shall, within its mandate and for the fulfilment of its tasks, have the right to have access to the data entered into the Customs Information System in accordance with Articles 1, 3 to 6 and 15 to 19 and to search those data.

2. Where a search by Europol reveals the existence of a match between information processed by Europol and an entry in the Customs Information System, Europol shall, through the channels defined in Council Decision 2009/371/JHA of 6 April 2009 establishing a European Police Office (Europol) ([1]), inform the Member State which made the entry.

3. Use of information obtained from a search in the Customs Information System is subject to the consent of the Member State which entered the data into the System. If that Member State allows the use of such information, the handling thereof shall be governed by the Decision 2009/371/JHA. Europol may transfer such information to third countries and third bodies only with the consent of the Member State which entered the data into the System.

4. Europol may request further information from the Member States concerned, in accordance with the Decision 2009/371/JHA.

5. Without prejudice to paragraphs 3 and 4, Europol shall not connect the parts of the Customs Information System to which it has access to any computer system for data collection and processing operated by or at Europol, nor transfer the data contained therein to any such system, nor download or otherwise copy any part of the Customs Information System.

Europol shall limit access to data entered into the Customs Information System to duly authorised staff of Europol.

([1]) OJ L 121, 15.5.2009, p. 37.

Europol shall allow the Joint Supervisory Body, set up under Article 34 of the Decision 2009/371/JHA, to review the activities of Europol in the exercise of its right to accede to and to search data entered into the Customs Information System.

6. Nothing in this Article shall be interpreted as affecting the provisions of the Decision 2009/371/JHA concerning data protection and the liability for any unauthorised or incorrect processing of such data by Europol staff, or as affecting the powers of the Joint Supervisory Body set up pursuant to that Decision.

*Article 12*

1. The national members of Eurojust, their deputies, assistants and specifically authorised staff shall, within their mandate and for the fulfilment of Eurojust's tasks, have the right to have access to the data entered into the Customs Information System in accordance with Articles 1, 3 to 6 and 15 to 19 and to search those data.

2. Where a search by a national member of Eurojust, their deputies, assistants or specifically authorised staff reveals the existence of a match between information processed by Eurojust and an entry in the Customs Information System, he or she shall inform the Member State which made the entry. Any communication of information obtained from such a search may be communicated to third countries and third bodies only with the consent of the Member State which made the entry.

3. Nothing in this Article shall be interpreted as affecting the provisions of Council Decision 2009/426/JHA of 16 December 2008 on the strengthening of Eurojust and amending Decision 2002/187/JHA setting up Eurojust with a view to reinforcing the fight against serious crime [1] which concern data protection and the liability for any unauthorised or incorrect processing of such data by national members of Eurojust, their deputies, assistants and specifically authorised staff, or as affecting the powers of the Joint Supervisory Body set up pursuant to that Decision.

4. No parts of the Customs Information System to which the national members of Eurojust, their deputies, assistants and specifically authorised staff have access shall be connected to any computer system for data collection and processing in operation by or at Eurojust, nor shall any data contained in the former be transferred to the latter, nor shall any part of the Customs Information System be downloaded.

5. Access to data entered in the Customs Information System shall be limited to the national members of Eurojust, their deputies, assistants and specifically authorised staff and shall not be extended to other Eurojust staff.

(1) OJ L 138, 4.6.2009, p. 14.

CHAPTER IV

**AMENDMENT OF DATA**

*Article 13*

1. Only the supplying Member State shall have the right to amend, supplement, rectify or erase data which it has entered in the Customs Information System.

2. Should a supplying Member State note, or have drawn to its attention, that the data it entered are factually inaccurate or were entered, or are stored contrary to this Decision, it shall amend, supplement, rectify or erase the data, as appropriate, and shall inform the other Member States, Europol and Eurojust accordingly.

3. If a Member State, Europol or Eurojust has evidence to suggest that an item of data is factually inaccurate, or was entered or is stored in the Customs Information System, contrary to this Decision, it shall inform thereof the supplying Member State as soon as possible. The latter shall check the data concerned and, if necessary, rectify or erase the item without delay. The supplying Member State shall inform the other Member States, Europol and Eurojust of any rectification or erasure effected.

4. If, when entering data in the Customs Information System, a Member State notes that its report conflicts with a previous report as to content or suggested action, it shall immediately inform thereof the Member State which made the previous report. The two Member States shall then attempt to resolve the matter. In the event of disagreement, the first report shall stand, but those parts of the new report which do not conflict with the first report shall be entered in the System.

5. Subject to this Decision, where in any Member State a court, or other competent authority within that Member State, makes a final decision as to amendment, supplementation, rectification or erasure of data in the Customs Information System, the Member States undertake mutually to enforce such a decision. In the event of conflict between such decisions of courts or other competent authorities in different Member States, including those referred to in Article 23(1), concerning rectification or erasure, the Member State which entered the data in question shall erase them from the System.

CHAPTER V

**RETENTION OF DATA**

*Article 14*

1. Data entered into the Customs Information System shall be kept only for the time necessary to achieve the purpose for which they were entered. The need for their retention shall be reviewed at least annually by the supplying Member State.

2. The supplying Member State may, within the review period, decide to retain data until the next review if their retention is necessary for the purposes for which they were entered. Without prejudice to Articles 22 and 23, if there is no decision to retain data, they shall automatically be transferred to that part of the Customs Information System to which access shall be limited in accordance with paragraph 4 of this Article.

3. The Customs Information System shall automatically inform the supplying Member State of a scheduled transfer of data from the Customs Information System under paragraph 2, giving one month's notice.

4. Data transferred under paragraph 2 of this Article shall continue to be retained for one year within the Customs Information System but, without prejudice to Articles 22 and 23, shall be accessible only to a representative of the Committee referred to in Article 27 or to the supervisory authorities referred to in Articles 24 and 25(1). During that period they may consult the data only for the purposes of checking their accuracy and lawfulness, after which the data have to be erased.

CHAPTER VI

**CREATION OF A CUSTOMS FILES IDENTIFICATION DATABASE**

*Article 15*

1. The Customs Information System shall contain data in accordance with this Chapter, in addition to data contained in accordance with Article 3, in a special database (hereinafter referred to as the customs files identification database). Without prejudice to the provisions of this Chapter and of Chapters VII and VIII, all the provisions of this Decision shall also apply to the customs files identification database. However, the exception in Article 21(2) shall not apply.

2. The aim of the customs files identification database shall be to enable the national authorities responsible for carrying out customs investigations designated pursuant to Article 7, when opening a file on or investigating one or more persons or businesses, and for Europol and Eurojust, to identify competent authorities of other Member States which are investigating or have investigated those persons or businesses, in order, through information on the existence of investigation files, to achieve the aim referred to in Article 1(2).

3. For the purposes of the customs files identification database, each Member State shall send the other Member States, Europol, Eurojust and the Committee referred to in Article 27 a list of serious contraventions of its national laws.

This list shall comprise only contraventions that are punishable:

(a) by deprivation of liberty or a detention order for a maximum period of not less than 12 months; or

(b) by a fine of at least EUR 15 000.

4. If the Member State retrieving data from the customs files identification database requires further information on the stored investigation file on a person or a business, it shall request the assistance of the supplying Member State on the basis of the instruments in force relating to mutual assistance.

CHAPTER VII

**OPERATION AND USE OF THE CUSTOMS FILES IDENTIFICATION DATABASE**

*Article 16*

1. Data from investigation files will be entered into the customs files identification database only for the purposes set out in Article 15(2). The data shall only cover the following categories:

(a) a person or a business which is or has been the subject of an investigation file opened by a competent authority of a Member State, and which:

(i) in accordance with the national law of the Member State concerned, is suspected of committing or having committed, or participating or having participated in the commission of, a serious infringement of national laws;

(ii) has been the subject of a report establishing that such an infringement has taken place; or

(iii) has been the subject of an administrative or judicial sanction for such an infringement;

(b) the field covered by the investigation file;

(c) the name, nationality and contact information of the Member State's authority handling the case, together with the file number.

Data referred to in points (a) to (c) shall be entered in a data record separately for each person or business. Links between data records shall not be permitted.

2. The personal data referred to in paragraph 1(a) shall consist of only the following:

(a) for persons: name, maiden name, forenames, former surnames and aliases, date and place of birth, nationality and sex;

(b) for businesses: business name, name under which trade is conducted, address, VAT identifier and excise duties identification number.

3. Data shall be entered for a limited period in accordance with Article 19.

*Article 17*

A Member State shall not be obliged to make entries pursuant to Article 16 in any particular case if, and for such time as, this would harm public policy or other essential interests, especially as this would present an immediate and serious threat to its public security or to the public security of another Member State or a third country; or where other essential interests of equal importance are at stake; or where such entries could pose serious harm to the rights of individuals or would prejudice an ongoing investigation.

*Article 18*

1. Entry of data in the customs files identification database and consultation thereof shall be reserved to the authorities referred to in Article 15(2).

2. Any consultation concerning the customs files identification database shall cover the following personal data:

(a) for persons: forename, and/or name, and/or maiden name, and/or former surnames, and/or aliases, and/or date of birth;

(b) for businesses: business name, and/or name under which trade is conducted, and/or address, and/or VAT identifier, and/or excise duties identification number.

CHAPTER VIII

**PERIOD OF RETENTION OF DATA IN THE CUSTOMS FILES IDENTIFICATION DATABASE**

*Article 19*

1. Storage periods shall be determined in accordance with the laws, regulations and procedures of the Member State entering the data. However, the following time limits, starting on the date on which the data were entered in the file, shall not be exceeded:

(a) data relating to current investigation files shall not be retained beyond a period of three years if it has not been established that an infringement has taken place within that time period. The data shall be erased before the expiry of the three-year period if 12 months have passed since the last investigative act;

(b) data relating to investigation files which have established that an infringement has taken place but which have not yet led to a conviction or to imposition of a fine shall not be retained beyond a period of six years;

(c) data relating to investigation files which have led to a conviction or a fine shall not be retained beyond a period of 10 years.

2. At all stages of an investigation as referred to in points (a) to (c) of paragraph 1, as soon as a person or business within the scope of Article 16 is eliminated from an investigation pursuant to the laws and administrative regulations of the supplying Member State, all data relating to that person or business shall be erased immediately.

3. Data shall automatically be erased from the customs files identification database as from the date on which the data retention periods laid down in paragraph 1 are exceeded.

CHAPTER IX

**PERSONAL DATA PROTECTION**

*Article 20*

Framework Decision 2008/977/JHA shall apply to the protection of the data exchange in accordance with this Decision unless otherwise provided in this Decision.

*Article 21*

1. Data may be duplicated only for technical purposes, provided that such duplication is necessary for direct searching by the authorities referred to in Article 7.

2. Subject to Article 8(1), personal data entered by other Member States may not be copied from the Customs Information System into other national data files, except those copies held in systems of risk management used to direct national customs controls or copies held in an operational analysis system used to coordinate actions. Such copies may be made to the extent necessary for specific cases or investigations.

3. In the two exceptional cases provided for in paragraph 2, only the analysts authorised by the national authorities of each Member State shall be empowered to process personal data obtained from the Customs Information System within the framework of a risk management system used to direct customs controls by national authorities or of an operational analysis system used to coordinate actions.

4. Each Member State shall send other Member States and the Committee referred to in Article 27 a list of the risk-management departments whose analysts are authorised to copy and process personal data entered in the Customs Information System.

5. Personal data copied from the Customs Information System shall be kept only for the time necessary to achieve the purpose for which they were copied. The need for their retention shall be reviewed at least annually by the Member State which carried out the copying. The storage period shall not exceed ten years. Personal data which are not necessary for the continuation of the operational analysis shall be erased immediately or have any identifying factors removed.

*Article 22*

The rights of persons with regard to personal data in the Customs Information System, in particular their right of access, to rectification, erasure or blocking shall be exercised in accordance with the laws, regulations and procedures of the Member State implementing Framework Decision 2008/977/JHA in which such rights are invoked. Access shall be refused to the extent that such refusal is necessary and proportionate in order not to jeopardise any ongoing national investigations, or during the period of discreet surveillance or sighting and reporting. When the applicability of such an exemption is assessed, the legitimate interests of the person concerned shall be taken into account.

*Article 23*

1. In the territory of each Member State, any person may, in accordance with the laws, regulations and procedures of the Member State in question, bring an action or, if appropriate, a complaint before the courts or the authority competent under the laws, regulations and procedures of that Member State concerning personal data relating to himself on the Customs Information System, in order to:

(a) rectify or erase factually inaccurate personal data;

(b) rectify or erase personal data entered or stored in the Customs Information System contrary to this Decision;

(c) obtain access to personal data;

(d) block personal data;

(e) obtain compensation pursuant to Article 30(2).

2. Without prejudice to the provisions of Article 31, the Member States concerned undertake mutually to enforce the final decisions taken by a court, or other competent authority, pursuant to points (a) to (c) of paragraph 1 of this Article.

*Article 24*

Each Member State shall designate a national supervisory authority or authorities responsible for personal data protection to carry out independent supervision of such data included in the Customs Information System in accordance with Framework Decision 2008/977/JHA.

*Article 25*

1. A Joint Supervisory Authority shall be set up, consisting of two representatives from each Member State's respective independent national supervisory authority or authorities.

2. The Joint Supervisory Authority shall monitor and ensure the application of the provisions of this Decision and Framework Decision 2008/977/JHA as concerns the protection of natural persons with respect to the processing of personal data through the Customs Information System.

3. To that end, the Joint Supervisory Authority shall be competent to supervise operation of the Customs Information System, to examine any difficulties of application or interpretation which may arise during its operation, to study problems which may arise with regard to the exercise of independent supervision by the national supervisory authorities of the Member States, or in the exercise of rights of access by individuals to the System, and to draw up proposals for the purpose of finding joint solutions to problems.

4. For the purpose of fulfilling its responsibilities, the Joint Supervisory Authority shall have access to the Customs Information System.

5. Reports drawn up by the Joint Supervisory Authority shall be forwarded to the authorities to which the national supervisory authorities submit their reports, to the European Parliament and the Council.

*Article 26*

1. The European Data Protection Supervisor shall supervise the activities of the Commission regarding the Customs Information System. The duties and powers referred to in Articles 46 and 47 of Regulation (EC) No 45/2001 of the European Parliament and of the Council of 18 December 2000 on the protection of individuals with regard to the processing of personal data by the Community institutions and bodies and on the free movement of such data [1] shall apply accordingly.

2. The Joint Supervisory Authority and the European Data Protection Supervisor, each acting within the scope of their respective competences, shall cooperate in the framework of their responsibilities and shall ensure coordinated supervision of the Customs Information System, including for issuing relevant recommendations.

3. The Joint Supervisory Authority and the European Data Protection Supervisor shall meet for that purpose at least once a year. The costs and servicing of these meetings shall be for the account of the European Data Protection Supervisor.

(1) OJ L 8, 12.1.2001, p. 1.

10.12.2009 EN Official Journal of the European Union L 323/29

CHAPTER X

**INSTITUTIONAL FRAMEWORK**

*Article 27*

1. A Committee consisting of representatives from the customs administrations of the Member States shall be set up. The Committee shall take its decisions unanimously where the provisions of paragraph 2(a) are concerned and by a two-thirds majority where the provisions of paragraph 2(b) are concerned. It shall adopt its rules of procedure by unanimity.

2. The Committee shall be responsible:

(a) for the implementation and correct application of the provisions of this Decision, without prejudice to the powers of the authorities referred to in Articles 24, 25(1) and 26(1);

(b) for the proper functioning of the Customs Information System with regard to technical and operational aspects. The Committee shall take all necessary steps to ensure that the measures set out in Articles 14 and 28 are properly implemented with regard to the Customs Information System.

For the purpose of applying this paragraph, the Committee may have direct access to, and use of, data from the Customs Information System.

3. The Committee shall report annually to the Council, in accordance with Title VI of the Treaty on European Union, regarding the efficiency and effectiveness of the Customs Information System, making recommendations as necessary. That report shall be sent to the European Parliament for information.

4. The Commission shall take part in the Committee's proceedings.

CHAPTER XI

**SECURITY OF THE CUSTOMS INFORMATION SYSTEM**

*Article 28*

1. All necessary administrative measures to maintain security shall be taken:

(a) by the competent authorities of the Member States in respect of the terminals of the Customs Information System in their respective Member States and by Europol and Eurojust;

(b) by the Committee referred to in Article 27 in respect of the Customs Information System and the terminals located on the same premises as the System and used for technical purposes and the checks required by paragraph 3 of this Article.

2. In particular the competent authorities, Europol, Eurojust and the Committee referred to in Article 27 shall take measures:

(a) to prevent any unauthorised person from having access to installations used for the processing of data;

(b) to prevent data and data media from being read, copied, modified or removed by unauthorised persons;

(c) to prevent the unauthorised entry of data and any unauthorised consultation, modification or erasure of data;

(d) to prevent data in the Customs Information System from being accessed by unauthorised persons by means of data transmission equipment;

(e) to guarantee that, with respect to the use of the Customs Information System, authorised persons have right of access only to data for which they have competence;

(f) to guarantee that it is possible to check and establish to which authorities data may be transmitted by data-transmission equipment;

(g) to guarantee that it is possible to check and establish *a posteriori* what data have been entered in the Customs Information System, when and by whom, and to monitor searches;

(h) to prevent the unauthorised reading, copying, modification or erasure of data during the transmission of data and the transport of data media.

3. The Committee referred to in Article 27 shall monitor queries of the Customs Information System for the purpose of checking that searches made were admissible and were made by authorised users. At least 1 % of all searches made shall be checked. A record of such searches and checks shall be maintained in the System and shall be used only for the above-mentioned purpose by that Committee and the supervisory authorities referred to in Articles 24 and 25. It shall be erased after six months.

*Article 29*

The competent customs administration referred to in Article 10(1) shall be responsible for the security measures set out in Article 28, in relation to the terminals located in the territory of the Member State concerned, the review functions set out in Article 14(1) and (2) and Article 19, and otherwise for the proper implementation of this Decision so far as is necessary under the laws, regulations and procedures of that Member State.

CHAPTER XII

**RESPONSIBILITIES AND LIABILITIES**

*Article 30*

1. Each Member State shall ensure that the data it has entered into the Customs Information System in accordance with Articles 3, 4(1) and 8 of Framework Decision 2008/977/JHA are accurate, up to date, complete, reliable and entered lawfully.

2. Each Member State shall be liable in accordance with its national law for any damage caused to a person through the use of the Customs Information System. This shall also apply to damage caused by a Member State entering inaccurate data or entering or storing data unlawfully.

3. If a recipient Member State pays compensation for damage caused by the use of inaccurate data entered into the Customs Information System by another Member State, the latter Member States shall refund to the recipient Member State the amount paid in damages, taking into account any fault that may lie with the recipient Member State.

4. Europol and Eurojust shall be liable in accordance with the acts which established them.

*Article 31*

1. Costs relating to the acquisition, study, development and maintenance of central computer infrastructure (hardware), software and dedicated network connections, and to related production, support and training services, which cannot be kept separate from the operation of the Customs Information System for the purpose of applying the customs and agricultural rules of the Community, and costs relating to the use of the Customs Information System by the Member States in their territories, including communication costs, shall be borne by the general budget of the European Communities.

2. Costs relating to the maintenance of the national work stations/terminals incurred in the implementation of this Decision shall be borne by the Member States.

CHAPTER XIII

**IMPLEMENTATION AND FINAL PROVISIONS**

*Article 32*

The information provided for under this Decision shall be exchanged directly between the authorities of the Member States.

*Article 33*

The Member States shall ensure that their national law conforms to this Decision by 27 May 2011.

*Article 34*

1. This Decision replaces the CIS Convention, as well as the Protocol of 12 March 1999 drawn up on the basis of Article K.3 of the Treaty on European Union, on the scope of the laundering of proceeds in the Convention on the use of information technology for customs purposes and the inclusion of the registration number of the means of transport in the Convention [1] and the Protocol of 8 May 2003 established in accordance with Article 34 of the Treaty on European Union, amending, as regards the creation of a customs files identification database, the Convention on the use of information technology for customs purposes [2] with effect from 27 May 2011.

2. Consequently, the CIS Convention and the Protocols referred to in paragraph 1 shall be repealed with effect from the date of application of this Decision.

*Article 35*

Unless otherwise provided in this Decision, measures implementing the CIS Convention and Protocols referred to in Article 34(1) shall be repealed with effect from 27 May 2011.

*Article 36*

1. This Decision shall enter into force on the 20th day following its publication in the *Official Journal of the European Union*.

2. It shall apply from 27 May 2011.

Done at Brussels, 30 November 2009.

*For the Council*
*The President*
B. ASK

(1) OJ C 91, 31.3.1999, p. 2.
(2) OJ C 139, 13.6.2003, p. 2.

# Decision 2009/934 adopting the implementing rules governing Europol's relations with partners, including the exchange of personal data and classified information, 30 November 2009

**[OJ 2009, L 325/6–11]**

L 325/6 EN Official Journal of the European Union 11.12.2009

# ACTS ADOPTED UNDER TITLE VI OF THE EU TREATY

## COUNCIL DECISION 2009/934/JHA

## of 30 November 2009

## adopting the implementing rules governing Europol's relations with partners, including the exchange of personal data and classified information

THE COUNCIL OF THE EUROPEAN UNION,

Having regard to Council Decision 2009/371/JHA of 6 April 2009 establishing the European Police Office (Europol) (1) (the Europol Decision) and in particular Articles 26(1)(b) and 59(1)(c) thereof,

Having regard to the draft rules submitted by the Management Board, on which the Joint Supervisory Body has issued an opinion,

Having regard to the Opinion of the European Parliament,

Whereas in accordance with the Europol Decision, it is for the Council, acting by qualified majority after having consulted the European Parliament, to adopt implementing rules governing Europol's relations with partners, including the exchange of personal data and classified information (hereinafter the rules),

HAS DECIDED AS FOLLOWS:

TITLE I

**GENERAL PROVISIONS**

*Article 1*

**Definitions**

For the purposes of these rules,

(a) 'third States' as referred to in Article 23(1)(a) of the Europol Decision means States not being Member States of the European Union;

(b) 'organisations', as referred to in Article 23(1)(b) of the Europol Decision means organisations such as international organisations and their subordinate bodies governed by public law or other bodies governed by public law which are set up by, or on the basis of, an agreement between two or more States;

(c) 'third parties' means third States and organisations;

(d) 'EU bodies' means institutions, bodies, offices and agencies set up by, or on the basis of, the Treaty on European Union and the Treaties establishing the European Communities, as referred to in Article 22(1) of the Europol Decision;

(e) 'personal data' means any information relating to an identified or identifiable natural person; an identifiable person is one who can be identified, directly or indirectly, in particular by reference to an identification number or to one or more factors specific to his physical, physiological, mental, economic, cultural or social identity;

(f) 'classified information' means any information and material in any form, an unauthorised disclosure of which could cause varying degrees of prejudice to the essential interests of Europol, of one or more Member States or of Europol's cooperation partners, and that requires the application of appropriate security measures;

(g) 'strategic agreement' means an agreement allowing for the exchange of information, excluding personal data;

(h) 'operational agreement' means an agreement allowing for the exchange of information, including personal data;

(i) 'cooperation agreement' means either a strategic or an operational agreement;

(1) OJ L 121, 15.5.2009, p. 37.

(j) 'working arrangement' means an arrangement between Europol and an EU body on their cooperation, allowing for the exchange of information including personal data;

(k) 'processing of personal data' or 'processing' means any operation or set of operations performed upon personal data, whether or not by automatic means, such as collection, recording, organisation, storage, adaptation or alteration, retrieval, consultation, use, disclosure by transmission, dissemination or otherwise making available, alignment or combination, blocking, erasure or destruction;

(l) 'competent authorities' means all public bodies existing in the Member States or in third States which are responsible under national law for preventing and combating criminal offences.

*Article 2*

**Scope**

These rules govern the relations of Europol with EU bodies and third parties, including the exchange of personal data and classified information and set out the procedures applicable to the negotiation and conclusion of cooperation agreements and working arrangements.

TITLE II

**CONCLUSION OF COOPERATION AGREEMENTS AND WORKING ARRANGEMENTS**

*Article 3*

**Establishment of relations with EU bodies**

In accordance with Article 22(1) of the Europol Decision, Europol may establish and maintain cooperative relations with EU bodies in so far as it is relevant to the performance of its tasks.

Europol shall seek the opinion of the Management Board if it intends to enter into negotiations on a cooperation agreement or working arrangement with an EU body not explicitly referred to in Article 22(1)(a) to (f) of the Europol Decision.

*Article 4*

**Procedure for the conclusion of cooperation agreements or working arrangements with EU bodies**

1. In accordance with Article 22(2) of the Europol Decision, Europol shall conclude cooperation agreements or working arrangements with EU bodies for the purposes of establishing cooperative relations. Such agreements or working arrangements may concern the exchange of operational, strategic or technical information, including personal data and classified information.

2. The transmission of classified information shall be permissible only in so far as agreement on confidentiality exists between Europol and the EU body. The Security Committee shall be informed of such agreement, which shall subsequently be formalised in the cooperation agreement or working arrangement.

3. Any such cooperation agreement or working arrangement shall only be concluded after approval by the Management Board.

4. If the cooperation agreement or working arrangement concerns the exchange of personal data, the Management Board shall obtain the opinion of the Joint Supervisory Body prior to the approval referred to in paragraph 3.

*Article 5*

**Establishment of relations with third parties**

1. In accordance with Article 23(1) of the Europol Decision, Europol may establish and maintain cooperative relations with third parties in so far as it is necessary for the performance of its tasks.

2. In accordance with Article 23(2) of the Europol Decision, Europol shall conclude agreements with the third parties which have been placed on the list of third States and organisations referred to in Article 26(1)(a) of the Europol Decision. Such agreements may concern the exchange of operational, strategic or technical information, including personal data and classified information. In the case of agreement with a third State, such information shall be transmitted via a designated contact point identified in the agreement.

3. Europol may initiate the procedure for the conclusion of an agreement with a third party as soon as that third party has been placed on the list referred to in paragraph 2.

4. Where the conclusion of an operational agreement with a third party is envisaged, Europol shall carry out an assessment of the existence of an adequate level of data protection ensured by that third party. That assessment shall be forwarded to the Management Board, which shall have obtained the prior opinion of the Joint Supervisory Body. For the purposes of this assessment, account shall be taken of the regulatory framework and the administrative practice of the third party concerned in the field of data protection, including any existing independent authority responsible for the supervision of data protection matters.

*Article 6*

**Procedure for the conclusion of cooperation agreements with third parties**

1. The Management Board shall decide, based on the assessment referred to in Article 5(4) and taking into account the opinion of the Joint Supervisory Body, whether or not the Director shall enter into negotiations with the third party on the conclusion of an operational agreement. Having obtained a prior positive decision of the Management Board, the Director shall enter into negotiations with the third party on the conclusion of such an agreement. In case of a negative decision, the Management Board may consider the conclusion of a strategic agreement with the third party concerned.

2. The transmission of classified information by Europol shall be permissible only in so far as agreement on confidentiality exists between Europol and the third party. The Security Committee shall be informed of such agreement, which shall subsequently be formalised in the cooperation agreement.

3. After finalising the negotiations to an agreement, the Director shall submit the draft agreement to the Management Board. In the case of the conclusion of an operational agreement, the Management Board shall obtain the opinion of the Joint Supervisory Body. The Management Board shall endorse the draft agreement before submitting it to the Council for approval.

In case of endorsement of an operational agreement, that draft agreement and the opinion of the Joint Supervisory Body shall be submitted to the Council.

4. In accordance with Article 23(2) of the Europol Decision, such agreements shall only be concluded after the approval by the Council, which shall previously have consulted the Management Board and, as far as such agreements concern the exchange of personal data, obtained the opinion of the Joint Supervisory Body via the Management Board.

*Article 7*

**Information for the Management Board**

The Director shall inform the Management Board on a regular basis on the state of play of ongoing negotiations with EU bodies and third parties.

TITLE III

**EXCHANGE OF INFORMATION**

*CHAPTER I*

***Receipt of information***

*Article 8*

**Receipt of information prior to the entry into force of an agreement**

Before the entry into force of an agreement or working arrangement with an EU body or third party, Europol may, in accordance with Articles 22(3) and Article 23(3) of the Europol Decision, directly receive and use information, including personal data and classified information, in so far as it is necessary for the legitimate performance of its tasks, listed in Article 5 of the Europol Decision.

*CHAPTER II*

***Transmission of information***

*Article 9*

**Conditions for the transmission of information to EU bodies and third parties**

Europol may only transmit information to an EU body or third party under the following conditions:

1. Notwithstanding Articles 11 to 14, information may be transmitted only after an agreement or working arrangement has been concluded with the EU body or third party in accordance with the provisions of Title II.

2. Where the data concerned were transmitted to Europol by a Member State, Europol shall transmit them to EU bodies or third parties only with that Member State's consent. The Member State concerned may give its prior consent to such transmission, either in general terms or subject to specific conditions. Such consent may be withdrawn at any time.

3. If the data were not transmitted by a Member State, Europol shall satisfy itself that transmission of those data is not liable to:

(a) obstruct the proper performance of the tasks in respect of which a Member State is competent;

(b) jeopardise the security or public order of a Member State or otherwise prejudice its general welfare.

4. The transmission of personal data to third parties shall only be permissible where:

(a) it is necessary in individual cases for the purposes of preventing or combating criminal offences in respect of which Europol is competent; and

(b) Europol has concluded an operational agreement with the third parties concerned which permits the transmission of such data on the basis of an assessment confirming an adequate level of data protection ensured by those third parties in accordance with Article 5(4).

5. The transmission of classified information by Europol shall only be permissible where:

(a) agreement on confidentiality exists between Europol and the EU body or the third party, in accordance with Articles 4(2) and 6(2); and

(b) in the case of transmission of data to third parties, it is necessary in individual cases for the purposes of preventing or combating criminal offences in respect of which Europol is competent.

11.12.2009 EN Official Journal of the European Union L 325/9

*Article 10*

**Responsibility for the transmission of data**

Europol shall be responsible for the legality of the transmission of data. Europol shall keep a record of all transmissions of data under these rules and of the grounds for such transmissions. Data shall be transmitted only if the recipient gives an undertaking that the data will be used only for the purposes for which they were transmitted.

*Article 11*

**Transmission of information to EU bodies prior to the entry into force of a cooperation agreement or working arrangement**

1. Before the entry into force of an operational agreement or working arrangement with an EU body, Europol may, in accordance with Article 22(3) of the Europol Decision and under the conditions laid down in Article 9(2) and 9(3) of these rules, directly transmit information, including personal data, to such EU body in so far as it is necessary for the legitimate performance of the recipient's tasks.

2. The transmission by Europol of classified information shall be permissible only in so far as agreement on confidentiality exists between Europol and the EU body, in accordance with Article 4(2).

*Article 12*

**Transmission of information to third parties prior to the entry into force of an agreement**

Before the entry into force of an agreement with a third party, Europol may, in accordance with Article 23(4) of the Europol Decision and under the conditions laid down in Article 9(2) and 9(3) of these rules, directly transmit information, with the exception of personal data and classified information, to that third party, in so far as this is necessary for the legitimate performance of the recipient's tasks.

*Article 13*

**Transmission of information to third parties which are not included in the Council list**

In accordance with Article 23(5) of the Europol Decision and under the conditions laid down in Article 9(2) and 9(3) of these rules, Europol may directly transmit information, with the exception of personal data and classified information, to third parties which are not included in the list referred to in Article 26(1)(a) of the Europol Decision, in so far as it is absolutely necessary in individual cases for the purposes of preventing or combating criminal offences in respect of which Europol is competent.

*CHAPTER III*

***Transmission of information in exceptional cases***

*Article 14*

**Transmission of personal data and classified information in exceptional cases**

1. In accordance with Article 23(8) and 23(9) of the Europol Decision, and under the conditions laid down in Article 9(2) and 9(3) of these rules, Europol may transmit personal data and classified information which it holds to third parties in so far as the Director considers their transmission to be absolutely necessary to safeguard the essential interests of the Member States concerned, which are within the scope of Europol's objectives, or in the interests of preventing imminent danger associated with crime or terrorist offences.

2. In case of transmission of classified information, the Director shall inform the Management Board and the Security Committee as soon as possible of his decision.

3. In case of transmission of personal data, the Director shall in all circumstances consider the data protection level applicable to the third party in question with a view to balancing that data protection level and those interests. In doing so, the Director shall take into account all relevant elements, such as the danger that might occur if Europol does not transmit the personal data concerned. The Director shall inform the Management Board and the Joint Supervisory Body as soon as possible of his decision and of the basis of the assessment of the adequacy of the level of data protection afforded by the third party concerned.

4. Before the transmission of personal data in accordance with paragraph 1, the Director shall asses the adequacy of the level of data protection afforded by the third parties concerned, taking into account all the circumstances relevant to the transmission of personal data, in particular:

(a) the nature of the data;

(b) the purpose for which the data is intended;

(c) the duration of the intended processing;

(d) the general or specific data protection provisions applying to the third parties;

(e) whether the third parties have agreed to specific conditions required by Europol concerning such data.

CHAPTER IV

***Specific conditions for the transmission of personal data***

*Article 15*

**Purposes for which personal data are transmitted**

1. Personal data requested without any indication as to the purpose of, and reason for, the request shall not be transmitted.

2. The transmission of personal data revealing racial or ethnic origin, political opinions, religious or philosophical beliefs or trade union membership and the transmission of data concerning a person's health or sex life shall not be permitted unless strictly necessary.

*Article 16*

**Correction and deletion of personal data**

1. When Europol transmits personal data to an EU body or third party, it shall ensure that the recipient EU body or third party give an undertaking that the personal data shall be corrected or deleted if it emerges that they are incorrect, inaccurate, no longer up to date or should not have been transmitted. Where Europol notes that the personal data are incorrect, inaccurate, no longer up to date, or should not have been transmitted, the recipient EU body or third party shall forthwith be informed thereof and requested to notify Europol that the data will be corrected or deleted. The Director shall inform the Management Board and the Joint Supervisory Body of Europol's activities in this field.

2. Any agreement concluded shall stipulate the obligation to correct or delete data in accordance with the procedure referred to in paragraph 1.

3. When Europol transmits personal data, it shall ensure that the recipient EU body or third party give an undertaking that the data will be deleted where they are no longer necessary for the purposes for which they were transmitted.

CHAPTER V

***Onward transmission of data to EU bodies and third parties***

*Article 17*

**Competent authorities and onward transmission**

1. The transmission of personal data by Europol to a third State and transmission within that State shall be restricted to competent authorities, which shall be explicitly mentioned in any agreement concluded.

2. In negotiating agreements, Europol shall make every effort to ensure that, where possible, a third State designates one competent authority to act as the national contact point between Europol and the other competent authorities of that third State.

3. When transmitting personal data, Europol shall ensure that the recipient EU body or third party give an undertaking that onward transmission of such data will be limited to competent authorities and will take place under the same conditions as those applying to the original transmission.

4. Where it is not possible for a third State to designate one competent authority to act as national contact point, agreements may, exceptionally, provide for the direct transmission of information by Europol to one or more competent authorities within the third State concerned.

*Article 18*

**Conditions for onward transmission**

1. Europol shall only transmit personal data to a competent authority of a third State or transmit personal data to an organisation or EU body if that authority, organisation or body agrees that it will not communicate those personal data to other EU bodies or third parties, except under the conditions laid down in paragraph 2.

2. The onward transmission of personal data by a competent authority of a third State, an organisation or an EU body with which Europol has concluded an operational agreement may only take place:

(a) with the prior consent of Europol, in cases where the EU body or third party receiving the personal data has concluded an operational agreement with Europol; or

(b) exceptionally, after authorisation by the Director, taking account of the data protection level applicable to the EU body or third party, if he considers onward transmission of the personal data by the EU body or third party to be absolutely necessary:

   (i) to safeguard the essential interests of the Member States concerned which are within the scope of Europol's objectives; or

   (ii) in the interests of preventing imminent danger associated with crime or terrorist offences.

3. No onward transmission of data communicated to Europol by a Member State shall be allowed without the prior consent of the Member State concerned. The Director shall inform the Member State concerned of the reasons for transmission via an EU body or third party as opposed to the direct transmission of such data.

*CHAPTER VI*

***Specific conditions for the receipt of information by Europol from third parties***

*Article 19*

**Assessment of the source and of the information**

1. In order to determine the reliability of information received by Europol, as well as its source, Europol shall ask the EU body or third party to assess, as far as possible, the information and its source in accordance with the criteria laid down in Article 12 of Council Decision 2009/936/JHA of 30 November 2009 adopting the implementing rules for Europol analysis work files (1) (the rules for Europol analysis work files).

2. If this assessment is not provided, Europol shall attempt, as far as possible, to assess the reliability of the source or of the information on the basis of information already in its possession, in accordance with the criteria laid down in Article 12 of the rules for Europol analysis work files.

3. In an agreement, Europol and an EU body or third party may agree in general terms on the assessment of specified types of information and specified sources in accordance with the criteria laid down in Article 12 of the rules for Europol analysis work files.

*Article 20*

**Correction and deletion of information received by Europol**

1. Agreements shall stipulate that the EU body or third party shall inform Europol when it corrects or deletes information transmitted to Europol.

2. When an EU body or third party informs Europol that it has corrected or deleted information transmitted to Europol, Europol shall correct or delete that information accordingly. Europol shall not delete the information if it still needs processing for the purposes of the analysis work file concerned or, where the information is stored in another Europol data file, Europol has a further interest in it, based on intelligence that is more extensive than that possessed by the transmitting EU body or third party. Europol shall inform the EU body or third party concerned of the continued storage of such information.

3. If Europol has reason to believe that information supplied is inaccurate or no longer up to date, it shall inform the EU body or third party which supplied the information and request that the EU body or third party inform Europol of its position on the matter. Where information is corrected or deleted by Europol in conformity with Article 31(1) of the Europol Decision, Europol shall inform the supplying EU body or third party of the correction or deletion.

4. Without prejudice to Article 31 of the Europol Decision, information which has clearly been obtained by a third State in obvious violation of human rights shall not be processed.

5. Agreements shall stipulate that the EU body or third party shall inform Europol as far as possible in cases where that EU body or third party has reason to believe that the information supplied is inaccurate or no longer up to date.

TITLE IV

**FINAL PROVISIONS**

*Article 21*

**Entry into force**

These rules shall enter into force on 1 January 2010.

Done at Brussels, 30 November 2009.

*For the Council*

*The President*

B. ASK

(1) See page 14 of this Official Journal.

# Decision 2009/935 as regards the list of third States and organisations with which Europol shall conclude agreements, 30 November 2009

**[Original version OJ 2009, L 325/12–13 amended by OJ 2014, L 138/104–105]**

Effective 1 July 2013, the electronic edition of the *Official Journal* (e-OJ) is authentic and produces legal effects.

**COUNCIL DECISION 2009/935/JHA**

**of 30 November 2009**

**determining the list of third States and organisations with which Europol shall conclude agreements**

THE COUNCIL OF THE EUROPEAN UNION,

Having regard to Council Decision 2009/371/JHA of 6 April 2009 establishing the European Police Office (Europol) ([1]) (the Europol Decision) and in particular Article 26(1)(a) thereof,

Having regard to Council Decision 2009/934/JHA of 30 November 2009 adopting the implementing rules governing Europol's relations with partners, including the exchange of personal data and classified information ([2]) and in particular Articles 5 and 6 thereof,

Having regard to the Opinion of the European Parliament,

Whereas:

(1) It is for the Council, acting by qualified majority after consulting the European Parliament, to determine, in a list, the third States and organisations referred to in Article 23(1) of the Europol Decision with which Europol shall conclude agreements.

(2) It is for the Management Board to prepare such list.

(3) It is desirable to provide for a procedure establishing how additional third States and organisations may be added to the list of third States and organisations with which Europol shall conclude agreements,

HAS DECIDED AS FOLLOWS:

*Article 1*

1. In accordance with Article 23(2) of the Europol Decision, Europol shall conclude agreements with the third States and organisations placed on the list in the Annex to this Decision. Europol may initiate the procedure for the conclusion of an agreement as soon as the third State or organisation has been placed on that list. Europol shall strive for the conclusion of a cooperation agreement with those third States and organisations which allows for the exchange of personal data, unless decided otherwise by the Management Board.

2. Europol shall prioritise the conclusion of cooperation agreements with third States and organisations placed on the list, taking account of its operational needs and the human and financial resources available. The Management Board may provide the Director with any further instructions concerning the negotiation of a specific agreement as it considers necessary.

3. The Director shall inform the Management Board on a regular basis of the state of play of ongoing negotiations with third parties and shall submit a progress report every six months.

*Article 2*

1. A Member of the Management Board or Europol may propose to add a new third State or organisation to the list. In doing so, they shall outline the operational need to conclude a cooperation agreement with that third State or organisation.

2. The Management Board shall decide whether or not to propose to the Council the addition of that third State or organisation to the list.

3. The Council shall decide on the addition of the third State or organisation to the list by amending the Annex to this Decision.

*Article 3*

This Decision shall enter into force on 1 January 2010.

*Article 4*

This Decision shall be published in the *Official Journal of the European Union.*

Done at Brussels, 30 November 2009.

*For the Council*

*The President*

B. ASK

([1]) OJ L 121, 15.5.2009, p. 37.

([2]) See page 6 of this Official Journal.

*ANNEX*

List of third States and organisations with which Europol shall conclude agreements:

1. Third States (in alphabetical order):

— Albania

— Australia

— Bolivia

— Bosnia and Herzegovina

— Brazil

— Canada

— China

— Colombia

— Croatia

— former Yugoslav Republic of Macedonia

— Georgia

— Iceland

— India

— Israel

— Liechtenstein

— Mexico

— Moldova

— Monaco

— Montenegro

— Morocco

— Norway

— Peru

— Russia

— Serbia

— Switzerland

— Turkey

— Ukraine

— United Arab Emirates

— United States of America

2. Organisations (in alphabetical order):

— ICPO-Interpol

— United Nations Office on Drugs and Crime (UNODC)

— World Customs Organisation

# Decision 2009/936 adopting the implementing rules for Europol analysis work files, 30 November 2009

[OJ 2009, L 325/14–22]

L 325/14 EN Official Journal of the European Union 11.12.2009

**COUNCIL DECISION 2009/936/JHA**

**of 30 November 2009**

**adopting the implementing rules for Europol analysis work files**

THE COUNCIL OF THE EUROPEAN UNION,

Having regard to Council Decision 2009/371/JHA of 6 April 2009 establishing the European Police Office (EUROPOL) [1] (the 'Europol Decision') and in particular Articles 14(1) and 59(1)(b) thereof,

Taking account of the Convention for the Protection of Individuals with regard to Automatic Processing of Personal Data, adopted by the Council of Europe on 28 January 1981,

Taking account of Recommendation No R(87)15 of the Committee of Ministers regulating the use of personal data in the police sector, adopted by the Council of Europe on 17 September 1987,

Having regard to the draft rules for Europol analysis work files submitted by the Management Board,

Having regard to the Opinion of the European Parliament,

Whereas it is for the Council, acting by qualified majority after consulting the European Parliament, to adopt implementing rules for analysis work files (hereinafter the 'rules'),

HAS DECIDED AS FOLLOWS:

CHAPTER I

**GENERAL PRINCIPLES**

*Article 1*

**Definitions**

For the purposes of these rules:

(a) 'personal data' means any information relating to an identified or identifiable natural person; an 'identifiable person' is one who can be identified, directly or indirectly, in particular by reference to an identification number or to one or more factors specific to his physical, physiological, mental, economic, cultural or social identity;

(b) 'analysis work file' means a file opened for the purpose of analysis, as referred to in Article 14(1) of the Europol Decision;

(c) 'analysis' means the assembly, processing or use of data with the aim of assisting criminal investigations, in accordance with Article 14(2) of the Europol Decision;

(d) 'participants in an analysis group' means analysts and other Europol staff designated by the Director, as well as liaison officers and/or experts from the Member States supplying the information or concerned by the analysis within the meaning of Article 14(4) of the Europol Decision;

(e) 'processing of personal data' or 'processing' means any operation or set of operations which is performed upon personal data, whether or not by automatic means, such as collection, recording, organisation, storage, adaptation or alteration, retrieval, consultation, use, disclosure by transmission, dissemination or otherwise making available, alignment or combination, blocking, erasure or destruction.

*Article 2*

**Scope**

The rules laid down in this Decision shall apply to the processing of data for the purpose of analysis, as referred to in Article 14(1) of the Europol Decision.

*Article 3*

**Data supplied for the purpose of analysis**

1. In accordance with Articles 8(2) and 14(3) of the Europol Decision, data supplied for the purpose of analysis shall be communicated either in a structured or unstructured form by national units or, depending on their degree of urgency, may be routed directly from the designated competent authorities to Europol, in order to be included in an analysis work file. The Member State supplying the data shall notify Europol of the purpose for which they are supplied and of any restriction on their use, deletion or destruction, including possible access restrictions in general or specific terms. That Member State may also inform Europol of any such restrictions at a later stage.

Europol shall ensure that third parties supplying such data notify Europol of the purpose for which they are supplied and of any restriction on their use.

After receipt of such data, it shall be determined as soon as possible to what extent they shall be included in a specific file.

(1) OJ L 121, 15.5.2009, p. 37.

11.12.2009 EN Official Journal of the European Union L 325/15

2. In accordance with Article 29(1) of the Europol Decision, the data referred to in paragraph 1 shall remain under the responsibility of the Member State which supplied them, and shall be subject to the national legislation of that Member State until such data are included in an analysis work file. This shall be without prejudice to Europol's responsibilities for the data as outlined in the second and third subparagraphs.

Europol shall be responsible for ensuring that such data may be accessed only by the Member States which supplied them, or analysts and other Europol staff designated by the Director in accordance with Article 14(2)(a) of the Europol Decision, for the purpose of determining whether or not the data may be included in an analysis work file.

If Europol, after appraising the data supplied, has reason to assume that they are inaccurate or no longer up-to-date, it shall inform the Member State which supplied them.

3. Data which, after appraisal, have not been selected for inclusion in an analysis work file, as well as paper files and documents containing data which have been included in such a file, shall remain under the responsibility of the Member State which supplied the data in accordance with Article 29(1) of the Europol Decision, and shall be subject to its national legislation. This shall be without prejudice to Europol's responsibilities as outlined in the Europol Decision.

Europol shall be responsible for ensuring that the data, paper files and documents referred to in the first subparagraph are stored separately from analysis work files, and may be accessed only by the Member States which supplied the data, or by analysts and other Europol staff designated by the Director in accordance with Article 14(2)(a) of the Europol Decision, for the purposes of:

(a) their later inclusion in an analysis work file;

(b) verifying whether the data which have already been included in an analysis file are accurate and relevant; or

(c) verifying whether the requirements contained in these rules or the Europol Decision have been met.

Such data, may also be accessed in the interests of the data subject who requires protection. In this case, the data may only be used with the consent of the individual concerned.

Such data, paper files and documents shall be returned to the Member State which supplied them, or be deleted or destroyed, where they are no longer necessary for the purposes set out in this Article. They must in any case be deleted or destroyed after the analysis work file is closed.

4. Where the data referred to in paragraph 1 have been supplied by a third party, Europol shall be responsible for ensuring that the principles laid down in this Article are applied to such data by following the rules laid down in accordance with Article 26 of the Europol Decision.

*Article 4*

**Processing of data**

1. Where necessary in order to achieve the objective laid down in Article 3 of the Europol Decision, personal data referred to in Articles 5 and 6 of these rules may be processed by Europol to the extent that they are adequate, accurate, relevant, and not excessive in relation to the purpose of the analysis work file in which they are included, and provided that they are stored for no longer than necessary for this purpose. The need for continued data storage for the purpose of the analysis work file shall be reviewed regularly in accordance with Article 7 of these rules and Article 20 of the Europol Decision.

2. Each Member State involved in an analysis project shall decide, in accordance with its national legislation, on the extent to which it can supply such data, as specified in Article 14(3) of the Europol Decision.

*Article 5*

**Orders opening analysis work files**

1. In each order opening an analysis work file, as referred to in Article 16 of the Europol Decision, the Director shall specify which of the categories of personal data listed in Article 6 of these rules are considered to be necessary for the purpose of the analysis work file concerned.

2. The Director shall also specify in the order referred to in paragraph 1 whether data revealing racial or ethnic origin, political opinions, religious or philosophical beliefs or trade-union membership and data concerning health or sex life are to be included in the analysis work file under the categories listed in Article 6, and why such data are considered to be strictly necessary for the purposes of the analysis work file concerned. Such data may only be processed when supplementing other personal data which have already been included in that file.

Where the data referred to in the first subparagraph relate to the categories of persons mentioned in Article 6(3) to 6(6), the specific grounds for requiring such data must be included in the order opening the file, and such data shall be processed only at the explicit request of two or more Member States participating in the analysis project. The data concerned shall be deleted when they are no longer necessary for the purposes for which they were stored.

3. Orders opening an analysis work file, including later amendments thereto, shall be established in accordance with the procedure set out in Article 16 of the Europol Decision.

*Article 6*

**Personal data in analysis work files**

1. Whenever personal data are stored in analysis work files, a note shall be added which refers to the category of persons on which the data are stored.

2. The following categories of personal data, including associated administrative data, may be processed on the categories of persons referred to in Article 14(1)(a) of the Europol Decision:

(a) Personal details:

1. Present and former surnames
2. Present and former forenames
3. Maiden name
4. Father's name (where necessary for the purpose of identification)
5. Mother's name (where necessary for the purpose of identification)
6. Sex
7. Date of birth
8. Place of birth
9. Nationality
10. Marital status
11. Alias
12. Nickname
13. Assumed or false name
14. Present and former residence and/or domicile

(b) Physical description:

1. Physical description
2. Distinguishing features (marks/scars/tattoos etc.)

(c) Identification means:

1. Identity documents/driving licence
2. National identity card/passport numbers
3. National identification number/social security number, if applicable
4. Visual images and other information on appearance
5. Forensic identification information such as fingerprints, DNA profile (established from the non-coding part of DNA), voice profile, blood group, dental information

(d) Occupation and skills:

1. Present employment and occupation
2. Former employment and occupation
3. Education (school/university/professional)
4. Qualifications
5. Skills and other fields of knowledge (language/other)

(e) Economic and financial information:

1. Financial data (bank accounts and codes, credit cards etc.)
2. Cash assets
3. Share holdings/other assets
4. Property data
5. Links with companies
6. Bank and credit contacts
7. Tax position
8. Other information revealing a person's management of their financial affairs

(f) Behavioural data:

1. Lifestyle (such as living above means) and routine
2. Movements
3. Places frequented
4. Weapons and other dangerous instruments
5. Danger rating
6. Specific risks such as escape probability, use of double agents, connections with law enforcement personnel
7. Criminal-related traits and profiles
8. Drug abuse

(g) Contacts and associates, including type and nature of the contact or association

(h) Means of communication used, such as telephone (static/mobile), fax, pager, electronic mail, postal addresses, Internet connection(s)

(i) Means of transport used, such as vehicles, boats, aircraft, including information identifying these means of transport (registration numbers)

(j) Information relating to criminal activities for which Europol has competence under Article 4 of the Europol Decision:

1. Previous convictions

2. Suspected involvement in criminal activities

3. *Modi operandi*

4. Means which were or may be used to prepare and/or commit crimes

5. Membership of criminal groups/organisations and position in the group/organisation

6. Role in the criminal organisation

7. Geographical range of criminal activities

8. Material gathered in the course of an investigation, such as video and photographic images

(k) References to other databases in which information on the person is stored:

1. Europol

2. Police/customs agencies

3. Other enforcement agencies

4. International organisations

5. Public entities

6. Private entities

(l) Information on legal persons associated with the data referred to in points (e) and (j):

1. Designation of the legal person

2. Location

3. Date and place of establishment

4. Administrative registration number

5. Legal form

6. Capital

7. Area of activity

8. National and international subsidiaries

9. Directors

10. Links with banks.

3. 'Contacts and associates', as referred to in Article 14(1)(d) of the Europol Decision, are persons through whom there is sufficient reason to believe that information, which relates to the persons referred to in paragraph 2 of this Article and which is relevant for the analysis, can be gained, provided they are not included in one of the categories of persons referred to in paragraphs 2, 4, 5 or 6. 'Contacts' are those persons who have sporadic contact with the persons referred to in paragraph 2. 'Associates' are those persons who have regular contact with the persons referred to in paragraph 2.

In relation to contacts and associates, the data pursuant to paragraph 2 may be stored as necessary, provided there is reason to assume that such data are required for the analysis of the role of such persons as contacts or associates.

In this context, the following shall be observed:

(a) the relationship of these persons with the persons referred to in Article 14(1)(a) of the Europol Decision shall be clarified as soon as possible;

(b) if the assumption that a relationship exists between these persons and the persons referred to in Article 14(1)(a) of the Europol Decision turns out to be unfounded, the data shall be deleted without delay;

(c) if such persons are suspected of committing an offence for which Europol has competence under Article 4 of the Europol Decision, or have been convicted for such an offence, or if there are factual indications or reasonable grounds under the national law of the Member State concerned to believe that they will commit such an offence, all data pursuant to paragraph 2 may be stored;

(d) data on contacts and associates of contacts as well as data on contacts and associates of associates shall not be stored, with the exception of data on the type and nature of their contacts or associations with the persons referred to in paragraph 2;

L 325/18 EN Official Journal of the European Union 11.12.2009

(e) if a clarification pursuant to the previous points is not possible, this shall be taken into account when deciding on the need and the extent of storage for further analysis.

4. With regard to persons who, as referred to in Article 14(1)(c) of the Europol Decision, have been the victims of one of the offences under consideration or who, certain facts give reason to believe, could be the victims of such an offence, data referred to in paragraph 2(a)(1) to 2(c)(3) of this Article, as well as the following categories of data, may be stored:

(a) Victim identification data;

(b) Reason for victimisation;

(c) Damage (physical/financial/psychological/other);

(d) Whether anonymity is to be guaranteed;

(e) Whether participation in a court hearing is possible;

(f) Crime-related information provided by or through persons referred to in Article 14(1)(c) of the Europol Decision, including information on their relationship with other persons, where necessary, to identify the persons referred to in Article 12(1) of the Europol Decision.

Other data pursuant to paragraph 2 may be stored as necessary, provided there is reason to assume that they are required for the analysis of a person's role as victim or potential victim.

Data not required for any further analysis shall be deleted.

5. With regard to persons who, as referred to in Article 14(1)(b) of the Europol Decision, might be called on to testify in investigations in connection with the offences under consideration or in subsequent criminal proceedings, data referred to in paragraph 2(a)(1) to 2(c)(3) of this Article as well as categories of data complying with the following criteria, may be stored:

(a) crime-related information provided by such persons, including information on their relationship with other persons included in the analysis work file;

(b) whether anonymity is to be guaranteed;

(c) whether protection is to be guaranteed and by whom;

(d) new identity;

(e) whether participation in a court hearing is possible.

Other data pursuant to paragraph 2 may be stored as necessary, provided there is reason to assume that they are required for the analysis of such persons' role as witnesses.

Data not required for any further analysis shall be deleted.

6. With regard to persons who, as referred to in Article 14(1)(e) of the Europol Decision, can provide information on the criminal offences under consideration, data referred to in paragraph 2(a)(1) to 2(c)(3) of this Article may be stored, as well as categories of data complying with the following criteria:

(a) coded personal details;

(b) type of information supplied;

(c) whether anonymity is to be guaranteed;

(d) whether protection is to be guaranteed and by whom;

(e) new identity;

(f) whether participation in court hearing is possible;

(g) negative experiences;

(h) rewards (financial/favours).

Other data pursuant to paragraph 2 may be stored as necessary, provided there is reason to assume that they are required for the analysis of such persons' role as informants.

Data not required for any further analysis shall be deleted.

7. If, at any moment during the course of an analysis, it becomes clear on the basis of serious and corroborating indications that a person included in an analysis work file should be placed under a different category of persons, as defined in this Article, from the category in which that person was initially placed, Europol may process only the data on that person which is permitted under that new category, and all other data shall be deleted.

If, on the basis of such indications, it becomes clear that a person should be included in two or more different categories as defined in this Article, all data allowed under such categories may be processed by Europol.

*Article 7*

**Time-limits for examination and the duration of storage**

1. When a decision is taken on whether personal data should continue to be stored under Article 6 of these rules, in accordance with Article 20 of the Europol Decision, the interests of Europol in performing its tasks shall be weighed against the legitimate data protection interests of the data subject concerning whom data are stored.

The need for continued storage of all personal data included in an analysis work file shall be reviewed, in accordance with Article 20 of the Europol Decision, no later than three years after the input or latest review of the data. Notwithstanding this review, the need for continued storage shall be reviewed if circumstances arise which suggest that the data have to be deleted or corrected.

The review shall take account of the need to retain data in the light of the conclusion of an enquiry into a particular case; a final judicial decision – in particular an acquittal, a rehabilitation order, a spent conviction, and an amnesty – the age of the data subject and the particular categories of data.

2. In accordance with Article 16(3) of the Europol Decision, Europol shall review the need for the continuation of an analysis work file. On the basis of that review, a decision shall be taken by the Director on the continuation or closure of the file. The Management Board and the Joint Supervisory Body shall immediately be informed by the Director of the elements in the file justifying the strict need for its continuation.

3. Where criminal proceedings against persons referred to in Article 6(2) are concluded, without the possibility of appeal, either by a court decision or otherwise, and that decision is notified to Europol by the Member State or third party concerned, Europol shall verify whether the data affected by such decision may still be stored, modified or used. If it can be assumed from the reasons for the decision or from other intelligence that the person concerned has not, or not unlawfully, committed the offence, or if the reasons for the decision leave this question open, the data affected by this decision shall be deleted, unless there are substantial grounds for assuming that they are still relevant for the purpose of the analysis work file. In that case, information concerning the court decision shall be added to the data already included in the file. Furthermore, these data may be processed and kept only with due respect for the context and the pronouncement of the aforementioned decision and to the rights it gives to the person concerned.

4. Personal data may not be retained for a period which is longer than that referred to in Article 20(1) of the Europol Decision. Where, as a consequence of the continuation of the analysis file, data concerning persons referred to in Article 6(3) to 6(6) are stored in a file for a period exceeding five years, the Joint Supervisory Body referred to in Article 34(1) of the Europol Decision shall be informed accordingly.

5. If, during the course of a review of Europol's activities by the Joint Supervisory Body it is discovered that personal data are being kept in violation of these rules, the Joint Supervisory Body shall inform the Director of this as it deems necessary, in accordance with Article 34(4) of the Europol Decision.

When the Joint Supervisory Body, in accordance with Article 34(4) of the Europol Decision, has referred a matter concerning the storage, processing or use of personal data to the Management Board, the transmission of the data concerned shall be prohibited without prior authorisation of the Management Board. In exceptional cases, the Director may authorise the transmission of that data prior to approval by the Management Board, where this is considered to be absolutely necessary to safeguard the essential interests of the Member States concerned which are within the scope of Europol's objectives, or in the interest of preventing imminent danger associated with crime or terrorist offences. In such cases, the authorisation by the Director shall be set out in a document, which shall be forwarded to the Management Board and the Joint Supervisory Body.

*Article 8*

**Association of third parties**

Europol may associate experts of institutions, bodies, offices and agencies, as referred to in Article 22(1) of the Europol Decision, and experts of third States and organisations, as referred to in Article 23(1) of that Decision, with the activities of an analysis group under the conditions laid down in Article 14(8) of that Decision.

The Director shall conclude an arrangement with any of the entities referred to in the first subparagraph in accordance with the rules governing such arrangements, as determined by the Management Board. Details of these arrangements shall be sent to the Management Board and the Joint Supervisory Board. The Joint Supervisory Board may address any comments it deems necessary to the Management Board.

*Article 9*

**Collection and recording of data**

Data stored in files for analysis purposes shall be distinguished according to the assessment grading of the source and the degree of accuracy or reliability of the information, in accordance with Article 11. Data based on facts shall be distinguished from data based on opinions or personal assessments.

*Article 10*

**Internal data protection**

The Director shall take the measures needed to ensure compliance with these rules and with other data protection provisions. To this end, the Director shall seek the advice of the Data Protection Officer, as referred to in Article 28 of the Europol Decision.

CHAPTER II

**CLASSIFICATION**

*Article 11*

**Classes of analysis work files**

Analysis work files may be:

(a) general or strategic, where the aim is to process relevant information concerning a particular problem or to develop or improve initiatives by the competent authorities, as defined in Article 3 of the Europol Decision;

(b) operational, where the aim is to obtain information on one or more of the criminal activities referred to in Article 3 of the Europol Decision, which relates to a case, person or organisation, in order to commence, assist or conclude, in accordance with Article 14(2) of the Europol Decision, bilateral or multilateral investigations of an international nature, provided that two or more Member States are among the parties concerned.

*Article 12*

**Assessment of the source and of the information**

1. The source of information originating from a Member State shall be assessed as far as possible by the Member State supplying the information using the following source evaluation codes:

(A): where there is no doubt as to the authenticity, trustworthiness and competence of the source, or if the information is supplied by a source which has proved to be reliable in all instances;

(B): where the information is supplied by a source which has in most instances proved to be reliable;

(C): where the information is supplied by a source which has in most instances proved to be unreliable;

(X): where the reliability of the source cannot be assessed.

2. Information originating from a Member State shall be assessed as far as possible by the Member State supplying the information on the basis of its reliability using the following information evaluation codes:

(1): information the accuracy of which is not in doubt;

(2): information known personally to the source but not known personally to the official passing it on;

(3): information not known personally to the source but corroborated by other information already recorded;

(4): information which is not known personally to the source and cannot be corroborated.

3. If Europol, on the basis of information already in its possession, comes to the conclusion that the assessment needs to be corrected, it shall inform the Member State concerned and seek to agree on an amendment to the assessment. Europol shall not change the assessment without such agreement.

4. If Europol receives data or information from a Member State without an assessment, Europol shall attempt as far as possible to assess the reliability of the source or the information on the basis of information already in its possession. The assessment of specific data and information must take place in agreement with the supplying Member State. A Member State and Europol may also agree in general terms on the assessment of specified types of data and specified sources. The Management Board shall be informed of such general agreements. If data have been supplied to Europol on the basis of such general agreements, this shall be noted with the data.

If no agreement is reached in a specific case, or no agreement in general terms exists, Europol shall evaluate the information or data and shall attribute to such information or data the evaluation codes (X) and (4), referred to in paragraphs 1 and 2 respectively.

5. If Europol receives data or information from a third party, this Article shall apply accordingly.

6. Where information included in an analysis work file is the result of an analysis, Europol shall assess such information in accordance with this Article, and in agreement with the Member States participating in the analysis.

CHAPTER III

**RULES FOR THE USE OF ANALYSIS WORK FILES AND ANALYSIS DATA**

*Article 13*

**Opening analysis work files**

1. Analysis work files shall be opened at Europol's initiative or at the request of the Member States supplying the data, in accordance with the procedure established in Article 16 of the Europol Decision.

2. The Management Board may invite representatives of the Joint Supervisory Body to take part in its discussions on the orders opening analysis work files.

3. In accordance with Article 16(2) of the Europol Decision, analysis activities and the dissemination of analysis results may begin immediately after the analysis file has been opened. Should the Management Board instruct the Director to amend an opening order or close the file in accordance with Article 16(4) of the Europol Decision, data which may not be included in the file or, if the file is to be closed, all data contained in that file, shall be deleted immediately.

4. If, during the course of an analysis, it becomes necessary to amend the order opening the analysis work file, the procedures outlined in Article 16 of the Europol Decision and this Article shall apply accordingly.

*Article 14*

**Retrieval of data**

1. In accordance with Article 14(2)(b) of the Europol Decision, the retrieval of data by participants of the analysis project shall only be granted after they have been accredited by Europol and following a training on their specific obligations under the Europol legal framework.

2. In accordance with the second subparagraph of Article 14(2) of the Europol Decision, all participants of the analysis group may retrieve data from the file. The analysis group shall decide unanimously on the extent to which such retrieval may take place and any conditions and restrictions that apply.

*Article 15*

**Transmission of data or information held in analysis work files**

1. The transmission of personal data contained in analysis work files to any Member State or third party shall be recorded in the file concerned.

In collaboration with the Member State or third party which has provided the data, Europol shall, where necessary and no later than at the time of transmission, check that the data are accurate and consistent with the Europol Decision.

As far as possible, all communications shall indicate judicial decisions, as well as decisions not to prosecute. Before data based on opinions or personal assessments are transmitted and their degree of accuracy or reliability indicated, such data shall be checked in cooperation with the Member State or third party which supplied them.

The recipient Member State shall inform the Member State transmitting the data, at the latter's request, of the use made of the data transmitted and the results subsequently obtained, where the national legislation of the recipient Member State so allows.

Should there be any restrictions on the use of data under Article 19 of the Europol Decision, such restrictions shall be recorded with the data, and the recipients of analysis results shall be informed thereof.

2. In accordance with Article 14(7) of the Europol Decision, in cases in which Europol finds, after the time of inclusion of data in an analysis work file, that those data relate to a person or object on which data submitted by another Member State or third party was already input in the file, each Member State or third party concerned shall be informed immediately of the link identified.

*Article 16*

**Control procedures**

In order to meet the data security requirements laid down in Article 35 of the Europol Decision and to provide assurance over the secure processing of data within the meaning of these rules, the Management Board shall accredit the analysis system, in accordance with Article 8 of the Rules on the Confidentiality of Europol Information adopted by Council Decision 2009/…/JHA of 30 November 2009 (1) after prior consultation of the Security Committee, as foreseen in Article 4(2) of those rules. The accreditation shall be granted on the basis of System Specific Security Requirements and other security documentation deemed necessary by the Management Board.

*Article 17*

**Use and storage of analysis data and analysis results**

1. All personal data and analysis results transmitted from an analysis work file may only be used in accordance with the purpose of the file or for the purposes of preventing and combating other serious forms of crime, and shall be in accordance with any restrictions on use as specified by a Member State on the basis of Article 19(2) of the Europol Decision. The data referred to in Article 5(2) of these rules may be transmitted only by agreement with the Member State which supplied such data.

2. After an analysis work file is closed, all data contained in that file shall be stored by Europol in a separate file, which shall only be accessible for the purposes of internal or external control. Without prejudice to Article 20(4) of the Europol Decision, such data shall not be kept for longer than 18 months after the analysis work file is closed.

3. The results of an analysis work file may be stored by Europol in electronic form for a maximum period of three years from the date the relevant file is closed, provided they are stored in a separate file, and no new data are added to them. After this period, the results may be stored only in the form of a paper document.

(1) Not yet published in the Official Journal.

*Article 18*

**Combination of files and communication between files**

1. Where it becomes apparent that information contained in an analysis work file may also be relevant for different analysis work files, the following procedures shall be followed:

(a) where a complete combination of the information in two files is proposed, a new file containing all the information in both files shall be established in accordance with Article 16 of the Europol Decision. The decision to combine the two files shall be reached by all the participants in both the original files. In that case, the original files shall be closed;

(b) where some of the information in one file is relevant to another file, the providers of that information shall decide whether or not this information may be communicated to the latter file.

2. In the circumstances referred to in paragraph 1, the time-limits for the review of data communicated from one analysis work file to another shall not be affected by such transfer.

*Article 19*

**New technical means**

New technical means for processing data for analysis purposes may be introduced only if all reasonable measures for ensuring that their use is consistent with the rules on the protection of personal data applicable to Europol have been adopted. The Director shall consult the Joint Supervisory Body in advance in all cases where the introduction of such technical means raises problems for the application of these data protection rules.

CHAPTER IV

**FINAL PROVISIONS**

*Article 20*

**Review of the rules**

By 1 January 2013, these rules shall be evaluated under the supervision of the Management Board.

Any proposals for amendments to these rules shall be considered by the Management Board with a view to their adoption by the Council in accordance with the procedure provided for in the third subparagraph of Article 14(1) of the Europol Decision.

*Article 21*

**Entry into force**

These rules shall enter into force on 1 January 2010.

Done at Brussels, 30 November 2009.

*For the Council*

*The President*

B. ASK

# Framework Decision 2009/948 on prevention and settlement of conflicts of exercise of jurisdiction in criminal proceedings, 30 November 2009

[OJ 2009, L 328/42–47]

L 328/42 EN Official Journal of the European Union 15.12.2009

III

*(Acts adopted under the EU Treaty)*

## ACTS ADOPTED UNDER TITLE VI OF THE EU TREATY

### COUNCIL FRAMEWORK DECISION 2009/948/JHA

### of 30 November 2009

### on prevention and settlement of conflicts of exercise of jurisdiction in criminal proceedings

THE COUNCIL OF THE EUROPEAN UNION,

Having regard to the Treaty on European Union, and in particular Article 31(1)(c) and (d) and Article 34(2)(b) thereof,

Having regard to the initiative of the Czech Republic, the Republic of Poland, the Republic of Slovenia, the Slovak Republic and of the Kingdom of Sweden,

Having regard to the Opinion of the European Parliament,

Whereas:

(1) The European Union has set itself the objective of maintaining and developing an area of freedom, security and justice.

(2) The Hague Programme [1] on strengthening freedom, security and justice in the European Union, which was approved by the European Council at its meeting on 4 and 5 November 2004, requires Member States to consider legislation on conflicts of jurisdiction, with a view to increasing the efficiency of prosecutions while guaranteeing the proper administration of justice, so as to complete the comprehensive programme of measures to implement the principle of mutual recognition of judicial decisions in criminal matters.

(3) The measures provided for in this Framework Decision should aim to prevent situations where the same person is subject to parallel criminal proceedings in different Member States in respect of the same facts, which might lead to the final disposal of those proceedings in two or more Member States. The Framework Decision therefore seeks to prevent an infringement of the principle of '*ne bis in idem*', as set out in Article 54 of the Convention implementing the Schengen Agreement of 14 June 1985 between the Governments of the States of the Benelux Economic Union, the Federal Republic of Germany and the French Republic on the gradual abolition of checks at their common borders [2] as interpreted by the Court of Justice of the European Communities.

(4) There should be direct consultations between competent authorities of the Member States with the aim of achieving a consensus on any effective solution aimed at avoiding the adverse consequences arising from parallel proceedings and avoiding waste of time and resources of the competent authorities concerned. Such effective solution could notably consist in the concentration of the criminal proceedings in one Member State, for example through the transfer of criminal proceedings. It could also consist in any other step allowing efficient and reasonable handling of those proceedings, including concerning the allocation in time, for example through a referral of the case to Eurojust when the competent authorities are not able to reach consensus. In this respect, specific attention should be paid to the issue of gathering the evidence which can be influenced by the parallel proceedings being conducted.

(5) When a competent authority in a Member State has reasonable grounds to believe that parallel criminal proceedings are being conducted in another Member State in respect of the same facts involving the same person, which could lead to the final disposal of those proceedings in two or more Member States, it should contact the competent authority of that other Member State. The question whether or not reasonable grounds exist should be examined solely by the contacting authority. Reasonable grounds could, inter alia, include cases where a suspected or accused person invokes, while giving details, that he is subject to parallel criminal proceedings in respect of the same facts in another Member State, or in case a relevant request for mutual legal assistance by a competent authority in another Member State reveals the possible existence of such parallel criminal proceedings, or in case a police authority provides information to this effect.

---

[1] OJ C 53, 3.3.2005, p. 1.

[2] OJ L 239, 22.9.2000, p. 19.

15.12.2009 EN Official Journal of the European Union L 328/43

(6) The process of exchange of information between competent authorities should be based upon the obligatory exchange of a specific minimum set of information, which should always be provided. The information concerned should notably facilitate the process of ensuring the proper identification of the person concerned and the nature and stage of the respective parallel proceedings.

(7) A competent authority which has been contacted by a competent authority of another Member State should have a general obligation to reply to the request submitted. The contacting authority is encouraged to set a deadline within which the contacted authority should respond, if possible. The specific situation of a person deprived of liberty should be fully taken into account by the competent authorities throughout the procedure of taking contact.

(8) Direct contact between competent authorities should be the leading principle of cooperation established under this Framework Decision. Member States should have discretion to decide which authorities are competent to act in accordance with this Framework Decision, in compliance with the principle of national procedural autonomy, provided that such authorities have competence to intervene and decide accordingly with its provisions.

(9) When striving to reach consensus on any effective solution aimed at avoiding the adverse consequences arising from parallel proceedings being conducted in two or more Member States, the competent authorities should take into account that each case is specific and give consideration to all its facts and merits. In order to reach consensus, the competent authorities should consider relevant criteria, which may include those set out in the Guidelines which were published in the Eurojust Annual Report 2003 and which were drawn up for the needs of practitioners, and take into account for example the place where the major part of the criminality occurred, the place where the majority of the loss was sustained, the location of the suspected or accused person and possibilities for securing its surrender or extradition to other jurisdictions, the nationality or residence of the suspected or accused person, significant interests of the suspected or accused person, significant interests of victims and witnesses, the admissibility of evidence or any delays that may occur.

(10) The obligation for competent authorities to enter into direct consultations in order to reach consensus in the context of this Framework Decision should not exclude the possibility that such direct consultations be conducted with the assistance of Eurojust.

(11) No Member State should be obliged to waive or to exercise jurisdiction unless it wishes to do so. As long as consensus on the concentration of criminal proceedings has not been reached, the competent authorities of the Member States should be able to continue criminal proceedings for any criminal offence which falls within their national jurisdiction.

(12) Since the very aim of this Framework Decision is to prevent unnecessary parallel criminal proceedings which could result in an infringement of the principle of *ne bis in idem*, its application should not give rise to a conflict of exercise of jurisdiction which would not occur otherwise. In the common area of freedom, security and justice, the principle of mandatory prosecution, governing the law of procedure in several Member States, should be understood and applied in a way that it is deemed to be fulfilled when any Member State ensures the criminal prosecution of a particular criminal offence.

(13) Where consensus has been reached on the concentration of criminal proceedings in one Member State, the competent authorities in the other Member State should act in a way that is compatible with that consensus.

(14) As Eurojust is particularly well suited to provide assistance in resolving conflicts of jurisdiction, the referral of a case to Eurojust should be a usual step, when it has not been possible to reach consensus. It should be noted that, in accordance with Article 13(7)(a) of Council Decision 2002/187/JHA of 28 February 2002 setting up Eurojust with a view to reinforcing the fight against serious crime [1] (the 'Eurojust Decision'), as modified, most recently by Council Decision 2009/426/JHA of 16 December 2008 on the strengthening of Eurojust [2], Eurojust has to be informed of any case where conflicts of jurisdiction have arisen or are likely to arise and that a case can be referred to Eurojust at any moment if at least one competent authority involved in the direct consultations deems it appropriate.

(15) This Framework Decision is without prejudice to proceedings under the European Convention on the Transfer of Proceedings in Criminal Matters, signed in Strasbourg on 15 May 1972, as well as any other arrangements concerning the transfer of proceedings in criminal matters between the Member States.

(16) This Framework Decision should not lead to an undue administrative burden in cases where for the problems addressed more suitable options are readily available. Thus in situations where more flexible instruments or arrangements are in place between Member States, those should prevail over this Framework Decision.

(1) OJ L 63, 6.3.2002, p. 1.
(2) OJ L 138, 4.6.2009, p. 14.

(17) This Framework Decision is limited to establishing provisions on the exchange of information and direct consultations between the competent authorities of the Member States and therefore does not affect any right of individuals to argue that they should be prosecuted in their own or in another jurisdiction, if such right exists under national law.

(18) Council Framework Decision 2008/977/JHA of 27 November 2008 on the protection of personal data processed in the framework of police and judicial cooperation in criminal matters [1] should apply to the processing of personal data exchanged under this Framework Decision.

(19) When making a declaration concerning the language regime, Member States are encouraged to include at least one language which is commonly used in the European Union other than their official language.

(20) This Framework Decision respects the fundamental rights and observes the principles recognised by Article 6 of the Treaty on European Union and reflected by the Charter of Fundamental Rights of the European Union,

HAS ADOPTED THIS FRAMEWORK DECISION:

*CHAPTER 1*

**GENERAL PRINCIPLES**

*Article 1*

**Objective**

1. The objective of this Framework Decision is to promote a closer cooperation between the competent authorities of two or more Member States conducting criminal proceedings, with a view to improving the efficient and proper administration of justice.

2. Such closer cooperation aims to:

(a) prevent situations where the same person is subject to parallel criminal proceedings in different Member States in respect of the same facts, which might lead to the final disposal of the proceedings in two or more Member States thereby constituting an infringement of the principle of '*ne bis in idem*'; and

(b) reach consensus on any effective solution aimed at avoiding the adverse consequences arising from such parallel proceedings.

(1) OJ L 350, 30.12.2008, p. 60.

*Article 2*

**Subject matter and scope**

1. With a view to achieving the objective set out in Article 1, this Framework Decision establishes a framework on:

(a) a procedure for establishing contact between the competent authorities of Member States, with a view to confirming the existence of parallel criminal proceedings in respect of the same facts involving the same person;

(b) the exchange of information, through direct consultations, between the competent authorities of two or more Member States conducting parallel criminal proceedings in respect of the same facts involving the same person, in case they already have knowledge of the existence of parallel criminal proceedings, with a view to reaching consensus on any effective solution aimed at avoiding the adverse consequences arising from such parallel proceedings.

2. This Framework Decision shall not apply to proceedings which are covered by the terms of Articles 5 and 13 of Council Regulation (EC) No 1/2003 of 16 December 2002 on the implementation of the rules on competition laid down in Articles 81 and 82 of the Treaty [2].

*Article 3*

**Definitions**

For the purposes of this Framework Decision:

(a) 'parallel proceedings' means criminal proceedings, including both the pre-trial and the trial phases, which are conducted in two or more Member States concerning the same facts involving the same person;

(b) 'competent authority' means a judicial authority or another authority, which is competent, under the law of its Member State, to carry out the acts envisaged by Article 2(1) of this Framework Decision;

(c) 'contacting authority' means a competent authority of a Member State, which contacts a competent authority of another Member State to confirm the existence of parallel proceedings;

(d) 'contacted authority' means the competent authority which is asked by a contacting authority to confirm the existence of parallel criminal proceedings.

(2) OJ L 1, 4.1.2003, p. 1.

*Article 4*

**Determination of competent authorities**

1. Member States shall determine the competent authorities in a way that promotes the principle of direct contact between authorities.

2. In accordance with paragraph 1, each Member State shall inform the General Secretariat of the Council which authorities under its national law are competent to act in accordance with this Framework Decision.

3. Notwithstanding paragraphs 1 and 2, each Member State may designate, if it is necessary as a result of the organisation of its internal system, one or more central authorities responsible for the administrative transmission and reception of requests for information according to Article 5 and/or for the purpose of assisting the competent authorities in the consultation process. Member States wishing to make use of the possibility to designate a central authority or authorities shall communicate this information to the General Secretariat of the Council.

4. The General Secretariat of the Council shall make the information received under paragraphs 2 and 3 available to all Member States and to the Commission.

*CHAPTER 2*

**EXCHANGE OF INFORMATION**

*Article 5*

**Obligation to contact**

1. When a competent authority of a Member State has reasonable grounds to believe that parallel proceedings are being conducted in another Member State, it shall contact the competent authority of that other Member State to confirm the existence of such parallel proceedings, with a view to initiating direct consultations as provided for in Article 10.

2. If the contacting authority does not know the identity of the competent authority to be contacted, it shall make all necessary inquiries, including via the contact points of the European Judicial Network, in order to obtain the details of that competent authority.

3. The procedure of contacting shall not apply when the competent authorities conducting parallel proceedings have already been informed of the existence of these proceedings by any other means.

*Article 6*

**Obligation to reply**

1. The contacted authority shall reply to a request submitted in accordance with Article 5(1) within any reasonable deadline indicated by the contacting authority, or, if no deadline has been indicated, without undue delay, and inform the contacting authority whether parallel proceedings are taking place in its Member State. In cases where the contacting authority has informed the contacted authority that the suspected or accused person is held in provisional detention or custody, the latter authority shall treat the request as a matter of urgency.

2. If the contacted authority cannot provide a reply within any deadline set by the contacting authority, it shall promptly inform the contacting authority of the reasons thereof and indicate the deadline within which it shall provide the requested information.

3. If the authority which has been contacted by a contacting authority is not the competent authority under Article 4, it shall without undue delay transmit the request for information to the competent authority and shall inform the contacting authority accordingly.

*Article 7*

**Means of communication**

The contacting and contacted authorities shall communicate by any means whereby a written record can be produced.

*Article 8*

**Minimum information to be provided in the request**

1. When submitting a request in accordance with Article 5, the contacting authority shall provide the following information:

(a) the contact details of the competent authority;

(b) a description of the facts and circumstances that are the subject of the criminal proceedings concerned;

(c) all relevant details about the identity of the suspected or accused person and about the victims, if applicable;

(d) the stage that has been reached in the criminal proceedings; and

(e) information about provisional detention or custody of the suspected or accused person, if applicable.

2. The contacting authority may provide relevant additional information relating to the criminal proceedings that are being conducted in its Member State, for example relating to any difficulties which are being encountered in that State.

*Article 9*

**Minimum information to be provided in the response**

1. The response by the contacted authority in accordance with Article 6 shall contain the following information:

(a) whether criminal proceedings are being or were conducted in respect of some or all of the same facts as those which are subject of the criminal proceedings referred to in the request for information submitted by the contacting authority, and whether the same persons are involved;

in case of a positive answer under (a):

(b) the contact details of the competent authority; and

(c) the stage of these proceedings, or, where a final decision has been reached, the nature of that final decision.

2. The contacted authority may provide relevant additional information relating to the criminal proceedings that are being or were conducted in its Member State, in particular concerning any related facts which are the subject of the criminal proceedings in that State.

*CHAPTER 3*

**DIRECT CONSULTATIONS**

*Article 10*

**Obligation to enter into direct consultations**

1. When it is established that parallel proceedings exist, the competent authorities of the Member States concerned shall enter into direct consultations in order to reach consensus on any effective solution aimed at avoiding the adverse consequences arising from such parallel proceedings, which may, where appropriate, lead to the concentration of the criminal proceedings in one Member State.

2. As long as the direct consultations are being conducted, the competent authorities concerned shall inform each other of any important procedural measures which they have taken in the proceedings.

3. In the course of the direct consultations, competent authorities involved in those consultations shall whenever reasonably possible reply to requests for information emanating from other competent authorities that are involved in those consultations. However, when a competent authority is requested by another competent authority to provide specific information which could harm essential national security interests or could jeopardise the safety of individuals, it shall not be required to provide that information.

*Article 11*

**Procedure of reaching consensus**

When the competent authorities of Member States enter into direct consultations on a case in order to reach consensus in accordance with Article 10, they shall consider the facts and merits of the case and all the factors which they consider to be relevant.

*Article 12*

**Cooperation with Eurojust**

1. This Framework Decision shall be complementary and without prejudice to the Eurojust Decision.

2. Where it has not been possible to reach consensus in accordance with Article 10, the matter shall, where appropriate, be referred to Eurojust by any competent authority of the Member States involved, if Eurojust is competent to act under Article 4(1) of the Eurojust Decision.

*Article 13*

**Providing information about the outcome of the proceedings**

If during the course of the direct consultations in accordance with Article 10 consensus has been reached on the concentration of the criminal proceedings in one Member State, the competent authority of that Member State shall inform the respective competent authority (authorities) of the other Member State(s) about the outcome of the proceedings.

*CHAPTER 4*

**GENERAL AND FINAL PROVISIONS**

*Article 14*

**Languages**

1. Each Member State shall state in a declaration to be deposited with the General Secretariat of the Council which languages, among the official languages of the institutions of the Union, may be used in the procedure of taking contact in accordance with Chapter 2.

2. The competent authorities may agree to use any language in the course of their direct consultations in accordance with Article 10.

15.12.2009 EN Official Journal of the European Union L 328/47

*Article 15*

**Relation to other legal instruments and other arrangements**

1. In so far as other legal instruments or arrangements allow the objectives of this Framework Decision to be extended or help to simplify or facilitate the procedure under which national authorities exchange information about their criminal proceedings, enter into direct consultations and try to reach consensus on any effective solution aimed at avoiding adverse consequences arising from the parallel proceedings, the Member States may:

(a) continue to apply bilateral or multilateral agreements or arrangements in force when this Framework Decision comes into force;

(b) conclude bilateral or multilateral agreements or arrangements after this Framework Decision has come into force.

2. The agreements and arrangements referred to in paragraph 1 shall in no case affect relations with Member States which are not parties to them.

*Article 16*

**Implementation**

Member States shall take the necessary measures to comply with the provisions of this Framework Decision by 15 June 2012.

By 15 June 2012 Member States shall transmit to the General Secretariat of Council and to the Commission the text of the provisions transposing into their national law the obligations imposed on them under this Framework Decision.

*Article 17*

**Report**

The Commission shall, by 15 December 2012, submit a report to the European Parliament and to the Council, assessing the extent to which the Member States have complied with this Framework Decision, accompanied, if necessary, by legislative proposals.

*Article 18*

**Entry into force**

This Framework Decision shall enter into force on the day of its publication in the *Official Journal of the European Union.*

Done at Brussels, 30 November 2009.

*For the Council*

*The President*

B. ASK

# Decision 2009/968 adopting the rules on the confidentiality of Europol information, 30 November 2009

**[OJ 2009, L 332/17–22]**

17.12.2009 EN Official Journal of the European Union L 332/17

III

*(Acts adopted under the EU Treaty)*

# ACTS ADOPTED UNDER TITLE VI OF THE EU TREATY

## COUNCIL DECISION 2009/968/JHA

**of 30 November 2009**

**adopting the rules on the confidentiality of Europol information**

THE COUNCIL OF THE EUROPEAN UNION,

Having regard to Council Decision 2009/371/JHA of 6 April 2009 establishing the European Police Office (Europol) [1] (the Europol Decision) and in particular Article 40 thereof,

Having regard to the draft rules submitted by the Management Board,

Having regard to the Opinion of the European Parliament,

Whereas in accordance with the Europol Decision, it is for the Council, acting by qualified majority after consulting the European Parliament, to adopt implementing rules on the confidentiality of information which is obtained by, or exchanged with, Europol (hereinafter the rules),

HAS DECIDED AS FOLLOWS:

*CHAPTER I*

**DEFINITIONS AND SCOPE**

*Article 1*

**Definitions**

For the purposes of these rules,

(a) 'processing of information' or 'processing' means any operation or set of operations which is performed on personal or non-personal data, whether or not by automatic means, such as collection, recording, organisation, storage, adaptation or alteration, retrieval, consultation, use, disclosure by transmission, dissemination or otherwise making available, alignment or combination, blocking, erasure or destruction;

(b) 'third party' means an entity referred to in Articles 22(1) and 23(1) of the Europol Decision;

(c) 'Security Committee' means the Committee consisting of representatives of the Member States and Europol, as described in Article 4;

(d) 'Security Coordinator' means the Deputy Director to whom the Director — in pursuance of Article 38(2) of the Europol Decision — assigns, alongside his other tasks, the function of coordination and control in matters of security;

(e) 'Security Officers' means the Europol staff, appointed by the Director, responsible for security issues in accordance with Article 6;

(f) 'Security Manual' means the manual implementing these rules, to be established in accordance with Article 7;

(g) 'classification level' means a security marking assigned to a document processed by or through Europol, as referred to in Article 10;

(h) 'security package' means a specified combination of security measures to be applied to information subject to a Europol classification level as referred to in Article 10;

(i) 'basic protection level' means the level of protection which shall be applied to all information processed by or through Europol, except information which is expressly marked or is clearly recognisable as being public information, as referred to in Article 10(1);

(j) 'staff' means temporary staff and contract staff as defined in Article 39(4) of the Europol Decision;

(k) 'Europol classified information' means any information and material in any form, an unauthorised disclosure of which could cause varying degrees of prejudice to the essential interests of Europol or of one or more Member States, and that requires the application of appropriate security measures as defined in Article 7(2)(b).

*Article 2*

**Scope**

1. These rules establish the security measures to be applied to all information which is processed by or through Europol.

[1] OJ L 121, 15.5.2009, p. 37.

2. Communication channels between Europol and the national units of the Member States, referred to in Article 8 of the Europol Decision, shall provide a level of protection which is equivalent to the level offered by these measures. A common standard for these communication channels shall be approved by the Security Committee.

3. The Annex sets out an overview of the Europol classification levels, as referred to in Article 10, and the equivalent markings currently applied by the Member States to information subject to those classification levels. When a Member State informs the other Member States and Europol of any changes in its national provisions on classification levels or in the equivalent markings, Europol shall elaborate a revised version of the overview reproduced in the Annex. At least once a year the Security Committee shall ascertain whether the overview is up to date.

*CHAPTER II*

**SECURITY RESPONSIBILITIES**

*Article 3*

**Member States' Responsibilities**

1. Member States shall undertake to ensure that, within their territory, Europol information receive a level of protection which is equivalent to the level of protection offered by the security measures established under these rules.

2. Member States shall undertake to inform the Security Coordinator of all security breaches that may compromise the interests of Europol or of a Member State. In the latter case, the Member State concerned shall also be informed directly through the national unit.

*Article 4*

**Security Committee**

1. A Security Committee shall be set up, consisting of representatives of the Member States and of Europol, which shall meet at least twice a year.

2. The Security Committee shall have as its task to advise the Management Board and Director of Europol on issues relating to security policy, including the application of the Security Manual.

3. The Security Committee shall establish its rules of procedure. The meetings of the Security Committee shall be chaired by the Security Coordinator.

*Article 5*

**Security Coordinator**

1. The Security Coordinator shall have general responsibility for all issues relating to security, including the security measures laid down in these rules and in the Security Manual. The Security Coordinator shall monitor the enforcement of security provisions and inform the Director of all breaches of security. In serious cases, the Director shall inform the Management Board. If such breaches risk compromising the interests of a Member State, that Member State shall also be informed.

2. The Security Coordinator shall be directly answerable to the Director of Europol.

3. The Security Coordinator shall be security cleared to the highest level in accordance with the laws and regulations applicable in the Member State of which the Security Coordinator is a national.

*Article 6*

**Security Officers**

1. Security Officers shall support the Director in the implementation of the security measures laid down in these rules and in the Security Manual. Security Officers shall be directly answerable to the Security Coordinator. The specific tasks of the Security Officers shall be:

(a) to instruct, assist and advise all persons at Europol — as well as any other person involved in Europol-related activities who is under a particular obligation of discretion or confidentiality — as to their duties under these rules and under the Security Manual;

(b) to enforce security provisions, investigate breaches thereof and report on them immediately to the Security Coordinator;

(c) to regularly review the adequacy of security measures on the basis of risk assessments; to that end, they shall report to the Security Coordinator as a rule at least once a month and, in exceptional cases, whenever it is deemed necessary and shall provide appropriate recommendations and advice;

(d) to perform the tasks assigned to them under these rules or under the Security Manual; and

(e) to perform any other tasks assigned to them by the Security Coordinator.

2. Security Officers shall be security cleared to the appropriate level required by their duties and in accordance with the laws and regulations applicable in the Member States of which they are a national.

*Article 7*

**Security Manual, procedure and content**

1. The Security Manual shall be adopted by the Management Board after having consulted the Security Committee.

2. The Security Manual shall provide management direction and support for security in accordance with business requirements and shall set out Europol's approach to managing security. The Security Manual shall contain:

(a) detailed rules on the security measures to be applied within Europol in order to provide for the basic protection level referred to in Article 10(1) of these rules, such measures being based on Articles 35 and 41(2) of the Europol Decision and taking account of Article 40(3) thereof; and

(b) detailed rules on the security measures associated with the different Europol classification levels and the corresponding security packages referred to in Article 10(2) and 10(3); the Security Manual shall also take account of Article 46 of the Europol Decision.

3. The Security Manual shall be reviewed at regular intervals, or when significant changes occur, in order to ensure its continuing suitability, adequacy, and effectiveness.

4. Amendments to the Security Manual shall be adopted in accordance with the procedure set out in paragraph 1.

*Article 8*

**Security accreditation of systems**

1. All Europol systems used to process Europol classified information shall be accredited by the Management Board after having consulted the Security Committee and after having obtained assurance of the effective implementation of the required security measures deriving from the system specific security requirements (SSSR), Information Risk Register and any other relevant documentation. Subsystems and remote terminals or workstations shall be accredited as part of all the systems to which they are connected.

2. The SSSR shall be adopted and amended by the Management Board after having consulted the Security Committee. This SSSR shall comply with the relevant provisions of the Security Manual.

*Article 9*

**Observance**

1. The security measures laid down in these rules and in the Security Manual shall be observed by all persons at Europol, as well as by any other person involved in Europol-related activities who is under a particular obligation of discretion or confidentiality.

2. The Director, the liaison bureaus and Europol national units shall be responsible for ensuring observance of these rules and of the Security Manual in accordance with paragraph 1.

*CHAPTER III*

**GENERAL PRINCIPLES**

*Article 10*

**Basic protection level, classification levels and security packages**

1. All information processed by or through Europol, with the exception of information which is expressly marked or is clearly recognisable as being public information, shall be subject to a basic protection level within Europol and in Member States.

2. In accordance with Article 3, Member States shall ensure the application of the basic protection level referred to in paragraph 1, by a variety of measures in accordance with national legislation and regulations, including the obligation of discretion and confidentiality, limiting access to information to authorised personnel, data protection requirements as far as personal data are concerned and general technical and procedural measures to safeguard the security of the information, taking into account Article 41(2) of the Europol Decision.

3. Information requiring additional security measures shall be subject to a Europol classification level, which shall be indicated by a specific marking. Information shall be subject to a security level only where strictly necessary and only for the time necessary.

4. The following Europol classification levels shall be used:

(a) 'RESTREINT UE/EU RESTRICTED': this classification shall be applied to information and material the unauthorised disclosure of which could be disadvantageous to the interests of Europol, the EU or one or more Member States;

(b) 'CONFIDENTIEL UE/EU CONFIDENTIAL': this classification shall be applied to information and material the unauthorised disclosure of which could harm the essential interests of Europol, the EU or one or more Member States;

(c) 'SECRET UE/EU SECRET': this classification shall be applied to information and material the unauthorised disclosure of which could seriously harm the essential interests of Europol, the EU or one or more Member States;

(d) 'TRÈS SECRET UE/EU TOP SECRET': this classification shall be applied to information and material the unauthorised disclosure of which could cause exceptionally grave prejudice to the essential interests of Europol, the EU or one or more Member States.

Such classified information and material shall bear an additional marking ('EUROPOL') under the classification marking to indicate that it originates in Europol.

Each Europol classification level shall relate to a specific security package, to be applied within Europol. The security packages shall offer different levels of protection, depending on the content of the information, and taking account of the detrimental effect which unauthorised access, dissemination or use of the information might have on the interests of Europol or the Member States.

When information classified at different levels is gathered, the classification level to be applied shall be at least as high as that applicable to the information protected at the highest level. In any event, a group of information may be given a higher protection level than that of each of its parts.

The translation of a classified document shall be given the same classification level, and shall be subject to the same protection, as the original document.

5. A caveat marking may be used for specifying additional conditions such as distribution of the information is limited to specific information exchange channels, embargo and a particular distribution on a need-to-know basis. Such caveat markings shall be defined in the Security Manual.

6. The security packages shall consist of various measures of a physical, technical, organisational or administrative nature, as laid down in the Security Manual.

*Article 11*

**Choice of classification level**

1. The Member State supplying information to Europol shall be responsible for the choice of any appropriate classification level for such information in accordance with Article 10. Where applicable, when supplying information to Europol, the Member State shall mark it with a Europol classification level as referred to in Article 10(4).

2. In choosing a classification level, Member States shall take account of the classification of the information under their national regulations, the need for the operational flexibility required for Europol to function adequately and the requirement that classification of law enforcement information should be the exception and that, if such information has to be classified, the lowest possible level should be assigned.

3. If Europol, on the basis of information already in its possession, comes to the conclusion that the choice of a classification level needs changing (for instance removing or adding a classification level, or adding a classification level to a document previously subject to the basic protection level), it shall inform the Member State concerned and seek to agree on an appropriate classification level. Europol shall not specify, change, add or remove a classification level without such agreement.

4. Where information generated by Europol is based upon, or contains, information supplied by a Member State, Europol shall determine, in agreement with the Member State concerned, whether the basic protection level is sufficient or whether the application of a Europol classification level is required.

5. Where information is generated by Europol itself, and such information is not based upon, nor contains, information supplied by a Member State, Europol shall determine any appropriate classification level for such information, using criteria laid down by the Security Committee. Where necessary, Europol shall mark the information accordingly.

6. Member States and Europol shall, where information also concerns the essential interests of another Member State, consult that Member State on whether any classification level should be applied to that information and, if so, which classification level should be applied.

*Article 12*

**Changing the classification level**

1. A Member State which has supplied information to Europol may, at any time, require that the selected classification level be changed, including by removing or adding a classification level. Europol shall be obliged to remove, amend or add a classification level in accordance with the wishes of the Member State concerned.

2. The Member State concerned shall, as soon as circumstances allow, request that the classification level in question be downgraded or removed altogether.

3. A Member State supplying information to Europol may specify the time period for which the choice of classification level will apply, and any possible amendments to the classification level thereafter.

4 Where the basic protection level or classification level has been determined by Europol in accordance with Article 11(4), Europol shall only change the basic protection or classification level in agreement with the Member States concerned.

5. Where the classification level has been determined by Europol in accordance with Article 11(5), Europol may change or remove the classification level at any time it is deemed necessary.

6. Where information, the classification level of which is changed in accordance with this Article, has already been supplied to other Member States, Europol shall inform the recipients of the change to the classification level.

17.12.2009 EN Official Journal of the European Union L 332/21

*Article 13*

**Processing, access and security clearance**

1. Access to, and possession of, information shall be restricted within the Europol organisation to those persons who, by reason of their duties or obligations, need to be acquainted with such information or need to handle it. Persons entrusted with the processing of information shall have obtained an appropriate security clearance and shall further receive special training.

2. All persons who may have access to information subject to a classification level processed by Europol shall undergo security clearance in accordance with Article 40(2) of the Europol Decision and the Security Manual. The Security Coordinator shall, on the basis of the result of the security clearance procedure, subject to the provisions of the Security Manual, grant authorisation to those persons cleared at the appropriate national level, who by reason of their duties or obligations, need to be acquainted with information subject to a Europol classification level. The authorisation is subject to regular review by the Security Coordinator. Authorisation may be withdrawn immediately by the Security Coordinator on justifiable grounds. The Security Coordinator shall also be responsible for ensuring the implementation of paragraph 3.

3. No person shall have access to information subject to a classification level without having been granted security clearance at the appropriate level. Exceptionally, however, the Security Coordinator may, after consultation of a Security Officer,

(a) give a specific and limited authorisation to persons cleared at 'CONFIDENTIEL UE/EU CONFIDENTIAL' level to have access to specific information classified up to 'SECRET UE/EU SECRET' level, if, by reason of their duties or obligations in a specific case, they need to be acquainted with information subject to a higher Europol classification level; or

(b) grant temporary authorisation to access classified information for a period not exceeding six months, pending the outcome of the security clearance referred to in paragraph 2, if it is in the interest of Europol, and after giving the national competent authorities notification and provided there is no reaction from them within three months; the Security Coordinator shall inform the national competent authorities concerned of the granting of such temporary authorisation. The granting of this temporary authorisation shall not give access to information classified as 'SECRET UE/EU SECRET' and above.

4. Such authorisation shall not be granted where a Member State, when supplying the information concerned, has specified that the discretion afforded to the Security Coordinator under paragraph 3 shall not be exercised in relation to that information.

*Article 14*

**Third parties**

When concluding confidentiality agreements with third parties, or when concluding agreements in accordance with Articles 22(4) and 23(7) of the Europol Decision, Europol shall take account of the principles laid down in these rules and in the Security Manual, which should be applied accordingly to information exchanged with such third parties.

*CHAPTER IV*

**FINAL PROVISIONS**

*Article 15*

**Review of the rules**

Any proposals for amendments to these rules shall be considered by the Management Board with a view to their adoption by the Council in accordance with the procedure provided for in Article 40(1) of the Europol Decision.

*Article 16*

**Entry into force**

These rules shall enter into force on 1 January 2010.

Done at Brussels, 30 November 2009.

*For the Council*

*The President*

B. ASK

*ANNEX*

**TABLE OF EQUIVALENCE OF CLASSIFICATION LEVELS**

| | Equivalence of classification levels | | | |
|---|---|---|---|---|
| Europol (1) | TRÈS SECRET UE/EU TOP SECRET | SECRET UE/EU SECRET | CONFIDENTIEL UE/EU CONFIDENTIAL | RESTREINT UE/EU RESTRICTED |
| Belgium | Très Secret<br>Zeer Geheim | Secret<br>Geheim | Confidentiel<br>Vertrouwelijk | Diffusion restreinte<br>Beperkte verspreiding |
| Bulgaria | СТРОГО СЕКРЕТНО | СЕКРЕТНО | ПОВЕРИТЕЛНО | ЗА СЛУЖЕБНО ПОЛЗВАНЕ |
| Czech Republic | Přísně tajné | Tajné | Důvěrné | Vyhrazené |
| Denmark | Yderst hemmeligt | Hemmeligt | Fortroligt | Til tjenestebrug |
| Germany | Streng geheim | Geheim | VS — Vertraulich | VS — Nur für den Dienstgebrauch |
| Estonia | Täiesti Salajane | Salajane | Konfidentsiaalne | Piiratud |
| Ireland | Top Secret | Secret | Confidential | Confidential |
| Greece | Άκρως Απόρρητο | Απόρρητο | Εμπιστευτικό | Περιορισμένης Χρήσης |
| Spain | Secreto | Reservado | Confidencial | Difusión Limitada |
| France | Très Secret Défense | Secret Défense | Confidentiel Défense | |
| Italy | Segretissimo | Segreto | Riservatissimo | Riservato |
| Cyprus | Άκρως Απόρρητο | Απόρρητο | Εμπιστευτικό | Περιορισμένης Χρήσης |
| Latvia | Sevišķi slepeni | Slepeni | Konfidenciāli | Dienesta vajadzībām |
| Lithuania | Visiškai slaptai | Slaptai | Konfidencialiai | Riboto naudojimo |
| Luxembourg | Très secret | Secret | Confidentiel | Diffusion restreinte |
| Hungary | Szigorúan titkos! | Titkos! | Bizalmas! | Korlátozott terjesztésű! |
| Malta | L-Għola Segretezza | Sigriet | Kunfidenzjali | Ristrett |
| Netherlands | BE Zeer geheim | STG Zeer geheim | STG Confidentieel | Vertrouwelijk |
| Austria | Streng geheim | Geheim | Vertraulich | Eingeschränkt |
| Poland | Ściśle Tajne | Tajne | Poufne | Zastrzeżone |
| Portugal | Muito Secreto | Secreto | Confidencial | Reservado |
| Romania | Strict secret de importanţă deosebită | Strict secret | Secret | Secret de serviciu |
| Slovenia | Strogo tajno | Tajno | Zaupno | Interno |
| Slovakia | Prísne tajné | Tajné | Dôverné | Vyhradené |
| Finland | Erittäin salainen | Salainen | Luottamuksellinen | Viranomaiskäyttö |
| Sweden | Kvalificerat hemlig | Hemlig | Hemlig | Hemlig |
| United Kingdom | Top Secret | Secret | Confidential | Restricted |

(1) The marking 'Europol' shall be inserted under the classification marking.

# Agreement between the European Union and Japan on mutual legal assistance in criminal matters, 30 November 2009

**[OJ 2010, L 39/20–35]**

L 39/20 EN Official Journal of the European Union 12.2.2010

**AGREEMENT**

**between the European Union and Japan on mutual legal assistance in criminal matters**

THE EUROPEAN UNION,

and

JAPAN,

DESIRING to establish more effective cooperation between the European Union Member States and Japan in the area of mutual legal assistance in criminal matters,

DESIRING that such cooperation will contribute to combating crime,

REAFFIRMING their commitment to respect for justice, principles of the rule of law and democracy, and judicial independence,

HAVE AGREED AS FOLLOWS:

*Article 1*

**Object and purpose**

1. The requested State shall, upon request by the requesting State, provide mutual legal assistance (hereinafter referred to as 'assistance') in connection with investigations, prosecutions and other proceedings, including judicial proceedings, in criminal matters in accordance with the provisions of this Agreement.

2. This Agreement does not apply to extradition, transfer of proceedings in criminal matters and enforcement of sentences other than confiscation provided for under Article 25.

*Article 2*

**Definitions**

For the purpose of this Agreement:

(a) the term 'Contracting Parties' means the European Union and Japan;

(b) the term 'Member State' means a Member State of the European Union;

(c) the term 'State' means a Member State or Japan;

(d) the term 'items' means documents, records and other articles of evidence;

(e) the term 'property' means assets of every kind, whether corporeal or incorporeal, movable or immovable, tangible or intangible, and legal documents or instruments evidencing title to or interest in such assets;

(f) the term 'instrumentalities' means any property used or intended to be used, in any manner, wholly or in part, to commit a criminal offence;

(g) the term 'proceeds' means any property derived from or obtained, directly or indirectly, through the commission of a criminal offence;

(h) the term 'freezing or seizure' means temporarily prohibiting the transfer, conversion, disposition or movement of property or temporarily assuming custody or control of property on the basis of an order issued by a court or other competent authority; and

(i) the term 'confiscation', which includes forfeiture where applicable, means a penalty or a measure, ordered by a court or other judicial authority following proceedings in relation to a criminal offence or criminal offences resulting in the final deprivation of property.

*Article 3*

**Scope of assistance**

Assistance shall include the following:

(a) taking testimony or statements;

(b) enabling the hearing by videoconference;

(c) obtaining items, including through the execution of search and seizure;

(d) obtaining records, documents or reports of bank accounts;

(e) examining persons, items or places;

(f) locating or identifying persons, items or places;

(g) providing items in the possession of the legislative, administrative or judicial authorities of the requested State as well as the local authorities thereof;

(h) serving documents and informing a person of an invitation to appear in the requesting State;

(i) temporary transfer of a person in custody for testimony or other evidentiary purposes;

(j) assisting in proceedings related to freezing or seizure and confiscation of proceeds or instrumentalities; and

(k) any other assistance permitted under the laws of the requested State and agreed upon between a Member State and Japan.

*Article 4*

**Designation and responsibilities of Central Authorities**

Each State shall designate the Central Authority that is the authority responsible for sending, receiving and responding to requests for assistance, the execution of such requests or their transmission to the authorities having jurisdiction to execute such requests under the laws of the State. The Central Authorities shall be the authorities listed in Annex I to this Agreement.

*Article 5*

**Communication between Central Authorities**

1. Requests for assistance under this Agreement shall be sent by the Central Authority of the requesting State to the Central Authority of the requested State.

2. The Central Authorities of the Member States and Japan shall communicate directly with one another for the purpose of this Agreement.

*Article 6*

**Authorities competent to originate requests**

The authorities which are competent under the laws of the States to originate requests for assistance pursuant to this Agreement are set out in Annex II to this Agreement.

*Article 7*

**Authentication**

Documents transmitted by a State pursuant to this Agreement which are attested by the signature or seal of a competent authority or the Central Authority of the State need not be authenticated.

*Article 8*

**Requests for assistance**

1. The requesting State shall make a request in writing.

2. The requesting State may, in urgent cases, after having been in contact with the requested State, make a request by any other reliable means of communication, including fax or e-mail. In such cases, the requesting State shall provide supplementary confirmation of the request in writing promptly thereafter, if the requested State so requires.

3. A request shall include the following:

(a) the name of the competent authority conducting the investigation, prosecution or other proceeding, including judicial proceeding;

(b) the facts pertaining to the subject of the investigation, prosecution or other proceeding, including judicial proceeding;

(c) the nature and stage of the investigation, prosecution or other proceeding, including judicial proceeding;

(d) the text or a statement of the relevant laws, including applicable penalties, of the requesting State;

(e) a description of the assistance requested; and

(f) a description of the purpose of the assistance requested.

4. A request shall, to the extent possible and relevant to the assistance requested, include the following:

(a) information on the identity and location of any person from whom testimony, statements or items are sought;

(b) a list of questions to be asked to the person from whom testimony or statements are sought;

(c) a precise description of persons or places to be searched and of items to be sought;

(d) a description of why the requesting State considers that the requested records, documents or reports of bank accounts are relevant and necessary for the purpose of the investigation into the offence, and other information that may facilitate the execution of the request;

(e) information regarding persons, items or places to be examined;

(f) information regarding persons, items or places to be located or identified;

(g) information on the identity and location of a person to be served with a document or informed of an invitation, that person's relationship to the proceeding, and the manner in which service is to be made;

(h) information on the allowances and expenses to which a person whose appearance is sought before the competent authority of the requesting State will be entitled; and

(i) a precise description of proceeds or instrumentalities, the location thereof, and the identity of the owner thereof.

5. A request shall, to the extent necessary, also include the following:

(a) a description of any particular manner or procedure to be followed in executing the request;

(b) a description of the reasons for confidentiality concerning the request; and

(c) any other information that should be brought to the attention of the requested State to facilitate the execution of the request.

6. If the requested State considers that the information contained in a request for assistance is not sufficient to meet the requirements under this Agreement to enable the execution of the request, the requested State may request that additional information be provided.

*Article 9*

**Language**

A request and any documents attached thereto shall be accompanied by a translation into an official language of the requested State or, in all or, in urgent cases, into a language specified in Annex III to this Agreement.

*Article 10*

**Execution of requests**

1. The requested State shall promptly execute a request in accordance with the relevant provisions of this Agreement. The competent authorities of the requested State shall take every possible measure in their power to ensure the execution of a request.

2. A request shall be executed by using measures that are in accordance with the laws of the requested State. The particular manner or procedure described in the request referred to in paragraph 4(g) or paragraph 5(a) of Article 8 shall be followed to the extent that it is not contrary to the laws of the requested State, and where it is practically possible. In case the execution of the request in the manner or procedure described in the request poses a practical problem for the requested State, the requested State shall consult with the requesting State in order to solve the practical problem.

3. If the execution of a request is deemed to interfere with an ongoing investigation, prosecution or other proceeding, including judicial proceeding, in the requested State, the requested State may postpone the execution. The requested State shall inform the requesting State of the reasons for the postponement and consult the further procedure. Instead of postponing the execution, the requested State may make the execution subject to conditions deemed necessary after consultations with the requesting State. If the requesting State accepts such conditions, the requesting State shall comply with them.

4. The requested State shall make its best efforts to keep confidential the fact that a request has been made, the contents of the request, the outcome of the execution of the request and other relevant information concerning the execution of the request if such confidentiality is requested by the requesting State. If a request cannot be executed without disclosure of such information, the requested State shall so inform the requesting State, which shall then determine whether the request should nevertheless be executed.

5. The requested State shall respond to reasonable inquiries by the requesting State concerning the status of the execution of a request.

6. The requested State shall promptly inform the requesting State of the result of the execution of a request, and shall provide the requesting State with the testimony, statements or items, obtained as a result of the execution, including any claim from a person from whom testimony, statements or items are sought regarding immunity, incapacity or privilege under the laws of the requesting State. The requested State shall provide originals or, if there are reasonable grounds, certified copies of records or documents. If a request cannot be executed in whole or in part, the requested State shall inform the requesting State of the reasons therefore.

*Article 11*

**Grounds for refusal of assistance**

1. Assistance may be refused if the requested State considers that:

(a) a request concerns a political offence or an offence connected with a political offence;

(b) the execution of a request is likely to prejudice its sovereignty, security, ordre public or other essential interests. For the purpose of this subparagraph, the requested State may consider that the execution of a request concerning an offence punishable by death under the laws of the requesting State or, in the relations between one Member State, set out in Annex IV to this Agreement, and Japan, an offence punishable by life imprisonment under the laws of the requesting State, could prejudice essential interests of the requested State, unless the requested State and the requesting State agree on the conditions under which the request can be executed;

(c) there are well-founded reasons to suppose that the request for assistance has been made with a view to prosecuting or punishing a person by reason of race, religion, nationality, ethnic origin, political opinions or sex, or that such person's position may be prejudiced for any of those reasons;

(d) the person, who is subject to criminal investigations, prosecutions or other proceedings, including judicial proceedings, for which the assistance is requested, in the requesting State, has already been finally convicted or acquitted for the same facts in a Member State or Japan; or

(e) a request does not conform to the requirements of this Agreement.

2. The requested State may refuse assistance which would necessitate coercive measures under its laws if it considers that the conduct that is the subject of the investigation, prosecution or other proceeding, including judicial proceeding, in the requesting State would not constitute a criminal offence under the laws of the requested State. In the relations between Japan and two Member States, set out in Annex IV to this Agreement, assistance may be refused if the requested State considers that the conduct that is the subject of the investigation, prosecution or other proceeding, including judicial proceeding, in the requesting State would not constitute a criminal offence under the laws of the requested State.

3. Assistance shall not be refused on the ground of bank secrecy.

4. Before refusing assistance pursuant to this Article, the requested State shall consult with the requesting State when the requested State considers that assistance may be provided subject to certain conditions. If the requesting State accepts such conditions, the requesting State shall comply with them.

5. If assistance is refused, the requested State shall inform the requesting State of the reasons for the refusal.

*Article 12*

**Costs**

1. The requested State shall bear all costs related to the execution of a request, unless otherwise agreed between the requesting State and the requested State.

2. Notwithstanding the provisions of paragraph 1, the requesting State shall bear:

(a) the fees of an expert witness;

(b) the costs of translation, interpretation and transcription;

(c) the allowances and expenses related to travel of persons pursuant to Articles 22 and 24;

(d) the costs of establishing a video link and costs related to the servicing of a video link in the requested State; and

(e) the costs of an extraordinary nature;

unless otherwise agreed between the requesting State and the requested State.

3. If the execution of a request would impose costs of an extraordinary nature, the requesting State and the requested State shall consult in order to determine the conditions under which the request will be executed.

*Article 13*

**Limitations on use of testimony, statements, items or information**

1. The requesting State shall not use testimony, statements, items or any information, including personal data, provided or otherwise obtained under this Agreement other than in the investigation, prosecution or other proceeding, including judicial proceeding, described in the request without prior consent of the requested State. In giving such prior consent, the requested State may impose such conditions as it deems appropriate.

2. The requested State may request that testimony, statements, items or any information, including personal data, provided or otherwise obtained under this Agreement be kept confidential or be used only subject to other conditions it may specify. If the requesting State agrees to such confidentiality or accepts such conditions, it shall comply with them.

3. In exceptional circumstances a State may, at the time it is providing testimony, statements, items or any information, including personal data, request that the receiving State will give information on the use made of them.

*Article 14*

**Transport, maintenance and return of items**

1. The requested State may request that the requesting State transport and maintain items provided under this Agreement in accordance with the conditions specified by the requested State, including the conditions deemed necessary to protect third-party interests in the items to be transferred.

2. The requested State may request that the requesting State return any items provided under this Agreement in accordance with the conditions specified by the requested State, after such items have been used for the purpose described in a request.

3. The requesting State shall comply with a request made pursuant to paragraph 1 or 2. When such a request has been made, the requesting State shall not examine the items without the prior consent of the requested State if the examination impairs or could impair the item.

*Article 15*

**Taking of testimony or statements**

1. The requested State shall take testimony or statements. The requested State shall employ coercive measures in order to do so, if such measures are necessary and the requesting State provides the requested State with information justifying those measures under the laws of the requested State.

2. The requested State shall make its best efforts to make possible the presence of such persons as specified in a request for taking testimony or statements during the execution of the request, and to allow such persons to question the person from whom testimony or statements are sought. In the case that such direct questioning is not permitted, such persons shall be allowed to submit questions to be posed to the person from whom testimony or statements are sought.

3. If a person, from whom testimony or statements are sought pursuant to this Article, asserts a claim of immunity, incapacity or privilege under the laws of the requesting State, testimony or statements may nevertheless be taken, unless the request includes a statement from the requesting State that when such immunity, incapacity or privilege is claimed, the testimony or statements cannot be taken.

*Article 16*

**Hearing by videoconference**

1. If a person is in the requested State and has to be heard as a witness or an expert witness by the competent authorities of the requesting State, the requested State may enable testimony or a statement to be taken from that person by those competent authorities by videoconference, if such hearing is necessary for the proceedings of the requesting State. The requesting and the requested States shall consult, if necessary, in order to facilitate resolution of legal, technical or logistical issues that may arise in the execution of the request.

2. The following rules shall apply to the hearing by videoconference unless otherwise agreed between the requesting State and the requested State:

(a) the authority of the requested State will identify the person to be heard specified in the request, and invite the person to facilitate his or her appearance;

(b) the hearing will be conducted directly by, or under the direction of, the competent authority of the requesting State in accordance with its own laws and the fundamental principles of the law of the requested State;

(c) the authority of the requested State will be present during the hearing, where necessary assisted by an interpreter, and will observe the hearing. If the authority of the requested State is of the view that during the hearing the fundamental principles of the law of the requested State are being infringed, it will immediately take the necessary measures to ensure that the hearing continues in accordance with the said principles;

(d) at the request of the requesting State or the person to be heard, the requested State will ensure, if necessary, that the person is assisted by an interpreter; and

(e) the person to be heard may claim the right not to testify which would accrue to him or her under the laws of either the requesting or the requested State. Other measures necessary for the protection of the person as agreed upon between the authorities of the requesting and the requested States will also be taken.

*Article 17*

**Obtaining of items**

1. The requested State shall obtain items. The requested State shall employ coercive measures, including search and seizure in order to do so, if such measures are necessary and the requesting State provides the requested State with information justifying those measures under the laws of the requested State.

2. The requested State shall make its best efforts to make possible the presence of such persons as specified in a request for obtaining items during the execution of the request.

*Article 18*

**Bank accounts**

1. The requested State shall confirm whether a natural or legal person that is the subject of a criminal investigation holds or controls one or more accounts in the banks specified in the request.

2. The requested State shall provide the specified records, documents or reports of the specified accounts, the records of banking operations which have been carried out during a specified period through the accounts specified in the request, or identified in accordance with paragraph 1 and the specified records, documents or reports of any sending or recipient account.

3. The obligations set out in this Article shall apply only to the extent that the information is in the possession of the bank keeping the account.

4. The requested State may make an execution of a request in paragraphs 1 and 2 dependent on the conditions it applies in respect of requests for obtaining items.

*Article 19*

**Examination of persons, items or places**

1. The requested State shall examine persons, items or places. The requested State shall employ coercive measures in order to do so, if such measures are necessary and the requesting State provides the requested State with information justifying those measures under the laws of the requested State.

2. The requested State shall make its best efforts to make possible the presence of such persons as specified in a request for examining persons, items or places during the execution of the request.

*Article 20*

**Locating or identifying persons, items or places**

The requested State shall make its best efforts to locate or identify persons, items or places.

*Article 21*

**Providing items in possession of the legislative, administrative, judicial or local authorities**

1. The requested State shall provide the requesting State with items that are in the possession of the legislative, administrative or judicial authorities of the requested State as well as the local authorities thereof and are available to the general public.

2. The requested State shall make its best efforts to provide the requesting State with items, including criminal records, that are in the possession of the legislative, administrative or judicial authorities of the requested State as well as the local authorities thereof and are not available to the general public, to the same extent and under the same conditions as such items would be available to its investigative and prosecuting authorities.

*Article 22*

**Service of documents and informing a person of an invitation**

1. The requested State shall effect service of documents, including service of summons or other documents requiring the appearance of a person before the competent authority of the requesting State, on persons in the requested State. The requested State shall inform a person in that State of an invitation to appear before the competent authority of the requesting State.

2. Where a request concerns service of a document requiring the appearance of a person before the competent authority of the requesting State, the request shall be received by the Central Authority of the requested State not less than 50 days before the scheduled appearance date. In urgent cases, the requested State may waive this requirement.

3. Where the requesting State knows that the addressee does not understand the language which the documents, served or sent pursuant to paragraph 1, are drawn up in or translated into, the requesting State shall endeavour to translate the documents, or shall, at least, translate the important passages thereof, also into the language the addressee understands.

4. Documents served pursuant to paragraph 1 shall include a statement that the addressee may obtain information from the competent authority by which the document was issued or from other authorities of the requesting State regarding his or her essential rights and obligations concerning the documents, if any.

5. In informing the result of the service of documents in accordance with paragraph 6 of Article 10, the requested State shall give proof of service by means of a receipt dated and signed by the person served or by means of a statement made by the requested State that service has been effected, as well as on the date, place and manner of service. The requested State shall, upon request by the requesting State, promptly inform the requesting State, where possible, of the response of the person who is invited or required to appear before the competent authority of the requesting State under paragraph 1.

6. A person who has been invited or required to appear before the competent authority of the requesting State under paragraph 1, but does not appear before that authority shall not, by reason thereof, be liable to any penalty or be subjected to any coercive measure in the requesting State, notwithstanding any contrary statement in the request or documents served or sent.

*Article 23*

**Safe conduct**

1. A person who is invited or required to appear before the competent authority of the requesting State under paragraph 1 of Article 22 shall not:

(a) be subject to detention or any restriction of personal liberty in that State by reason of any conduct or conviction that precedes the departure of the person from the requested State; or

(b) be obliged to give evidence or to assist in any investigation, prosecution or other proceeding, including judicial proceeding, other than the proceeding specified in the request.

2. If the safe conduct provided for in paragraph 1 cannot be provided, the requesting State shall be able to make a decision whether to appear before the competent authority of the requesting State.

3. The safe conduct provided for in paragraph 1 shall cease when:

(a) the person, having had, for a period of 15 consecutive days from the date when his or her presence is no longer required by the competent authority or from the day when he or she failed to appear before that authority on the scheduled appearance date, an opportunity of leaving, has nevertheless remained voluntarily in the requesting State; or

(b) the person, having left the requesting State, voluntarily returns to it.

4. When the requesting State knows that the safe conduct provided for in paragraph 1 has ceased pursuant to paragraphs 3(a) and 3(b), the requesting State shall so inform the requested State without delay, if such information is requested by the requested State and considered necessary by the requesting State.

*Article 24*

**Temporary transfer of persons in custody**

1. A person in custody of the requested State whose presence in the requesting State is necessary for testimony or other evidentiary purposes shall be temporarily transferred for those purposes to the requesting State, if the person consents and if the requesting State and the requested State agree, when permitted under the laws of the requested State.

2. The requesting State shall keep the person transferred pursuant to paragraph 1 in the custody of the requesting State, unless permitted by the requested State to do otherwise.

3. The requesting State shall immediately return the person transferred to the requested State, as agreed beforehand, or as otherwise agreed between the requesting State and the requested State.

4. The person transferred shall receive credit for service of the sentence being served in the requested State for the time spent in the custody of the requesting State.

5. The person transferred to the requesting State pursuant to this Article shall enjoy the safe conduct provided for in paragraph 1 of Article 23 in the requesting State until the return to the requested State, unless the person consents to give evidence or assist in any investigation, prosecution or other proceeding, including judicial proceeding, other than the proceeding specified in the request and the requesting State and the requested State agree thereto.

6. A person who does not consent to be transferred pursuant to this Article shall not, by reason thereof, be liable to any penalty or be subjected to any coercive measure in the requesting State, notwithstanding any contrary statement in the request.

*Article 25*

**Freezing or seizure and confiscation of proceeds or instrumentalities**

1. The requested State shall assist, to the extent permitted by its laws, in proceedings related to freezing or seizure and confiscation of the proceeds or instrumentalities.

2. A request for the confiscation described in paragraph 1 shall be accompanied by a decision of a court or other judicial authority imposing the confiscation.

3. The requested State that has custody over proceeds or instrumentalities may transfer such proceeds or instrumentalities, in whole or in part, to the requesting State, to the extent permitted by the laws of the requested State and upon such conditions as it deems appropriate.

4. In applying this Article, the legitimate rights and interests of *bona fide* third parties shall be respected under the laws of the requested State.

*Article 26*

**Spontaneous exchange of information**

1. Member States and Japan may, without prior request, provide information relating to criminal matters to each other to the extent permitted by the laws of the providing State.

2. The providing State may impose conditions on the use of such information by the receiving State. In such a case, the providing State shall give prior notice to the receiving State of the nature of the information to be provided and of the conditions to be imposed. The receiving State shall be bound by those conditions if it agrees to them.

*Article 27*

**Relation to other instruments**

1. Nothing in this Agreement shall prevent any State from requesting assistance or providing assistance in accordance with other applicable international agreements, or pursuant to its laws that may be applicable.

2. Nothing in this Agreement shall prevent a Member State and Japan from concluding international agreements confirming, supplementing, extending or amplifying the provisions thereof.

*Article 28*

**Consultations**

1. The Central Authorities of the Member States and Japan shall, if necessary, hold consultations for the purpose of resolving any difficulties with regard to the execution of a request, and facilitating speedy and effective assistance under this Agreement, and may decide on such measures as may be necessary for this purpose.

2. The Contracting Parties shall, as appropriate, hold consultations on any matter that may arise in the interpretation or application of this Agreement.

*Article 29*

**Territorial application**

1. This Agreement shall apply to the territory of Japan and, in relation to the European Union, to:

(a) the territories of the Member States; and

(b) territories for whose external relations a Member State has responsibility, or countries that are not Member States for whom a Member State has other duties with respect to external relations, where agreed upon by an exchange of diplomatic notes between the Contracting Parties, duly confirmed by the relevant Member State.

2. The application of this Agreement to any territory or country in respect of which extension has been made in accordance with paragraph 1(b) may be terminated by either Contracting Party giving six months' written notice to the other Contracting Party through the diplomatic channel, where duly confirmed between the relevant Member State and Japan.

*Article 30*

**Status of annexes**

Annexes to this Agreement form an integral part of this Agreement. Annexes I, II and III may be modified by mutual consent in writing of the Contracting Parties without amendment of this Agreement.

*Article 31*

**Entry into force and termination**

1. This Agreement shall enter into force on the 30th day after the date on which the Contracting Parties exchange diplomatic notes informing each other that their respective internal procedures necessary to give effect to this Agreement have been completed.

2. This Agreement shall apply to any request for assistance presented on or after the date upon which this Agreement enters into force, whether the acts relevant to the request were committed before, on or after that date.

3. Either Contracting Party may terminate this Agreement at any time by giving written notice to the other Contracting Party, and such termination shall be effective six months after the date of such notice.

IN WITNESS WHEREOF, the undersigned Plenipotentiaries have signed this Agreement.

DONE in duplicate, in the English and Japanese languages, both texts being equally authentic, and signed at Brussels on the thirtieth day of November 2009, and at Tokyo on the fifteenth day of December 2009. This Agreement shall also be drawn up in the Bulgarian, Czech, Danish, Dutch, Estonian, Finnish, French, German, Greek, Hungarian, Italian, Latvian, Lithuanian, Maltese, Polish, Portuguese, Romanian, Slovak, Slovenian, Spanish and Swedish languages, and the Contracting Parties shall authenticate those language versions by an exchange of diplomatic notes.

| *For the European Union* | *For Japan* |
| --- | --- |

L 39/28 EN Official Journal of the European Union 12.2.2010

*ANNEX I*

**THE CENTRAL AUTHORITIES**

The Central Authorities of the Contracting Parties are the following authorities:

the Kingdom of Belgium: the Federal Public Service Justice, International Criminal Cooperation Department;

the Republic of Bulgaria: the Ministry of Justice;

the Czech Republic:

— before the case is brought before a court (i.e. in pre-trial proceedings): the Supreme Public Prosecutor's Office of the Czech Republic, and

— after the case has been brought before a court (i.e. in trial stage of criminal proceedings): the Ministry of Justice of the Czech Republic;

the Kingdom of Denmark: the Ministry of Justice;

the Federal Republic of Germany: the Federal Office of Justice;

the Republic of Estonia: the Ministry of Justice;

Ireland: the Minister for Justice, Equality and Law Reform or a person designated by the Minister;

the Hellenic Republic: the Ministry of Justice, Transparency and Human Rights;

the Kingdom of Spain: the Ministry of Justice, the Subdirectorate General for international legal cooperation;

the French Republic: the Ministry of Justice, the Office for International Mutual Assistance in Criminal Matters, Directorate for Criminal Matters and Pardons;

the Italian Republic: the Ministry of Justice, Department of Judicial Affairs – Directorate General of Criminal Matters;

the Republic of Cyprus: the Ministry of Justice and Public Order;

the Republic of Latvia:

— during pre-trial investigation until prosecution: State Police,

— during pre-trial investigation until submitting the case to the court: the General Prosecutor's Office, and

— during the trial: the Ministry of Justice;

the Republic of Lithuania:

— the Ministry of Justice of the Republic of Lithuania, and

— the General Prosecutor's Office of the Republic of Lithuania;

the Grand Duchy of Luxembourg: the Prosecutor General;

the Republic of Hungary:

— the Ministry of Justice and Law Enforcement, and

— the Office of the Prosecutor General;

the Republic of Malta: the Office of the Attorney General;

the Kingdom of the Netherlands: the Ministry of Justice in The Hague;

the Republic of Austria: the Ministry of Justice;

the Republic of Poland:

— during pre-trial stage: the National Public Prosecutor's Office,

— during the trial: the Ministry of Justice,

the Portuguese Republic: the Prosecutor General's Office;

Romania: the Ministry of Justice and Civil Liberties, the General Directorate for Cooperation, Directorate for International Law and Treaties, Division for International Judicial Cooperation in Criminal Matters;

the Republic of Slovenia: the Ministry of Justice, the Directorate for international cooperation and international legal assistance;

the Slovak Republic:

— in pre-trial proceedings: the General Prosecutor's Office,

— in trial stage: the Ministry of Justice, and,

— for receiving: the Ministry of Justice,

the Republic of Finland: the Ministry of Justice;

the Kingdom of Sweden: the Ministry of Justice;

the United Kingdom of Great Britain and Northern Ireland:the Home Office (United Kingdom Central Authority), Her Majesty's Revenue and Customs, Crown Office and Procurator Fiscal Service;

Japan: the Minister of Justice and the National Public Safety Commission or persons designated by them.

*ANNEX II*

With regard to Article 6 of this Agreement, the authorities which are competent under the laws of the States to originate requests for assistance pursuant to this Agreement are set out below:

the Kingdom of Belgium: the judicial authorities: to be understood as meaning members of the judiciary responsible for administering the law, examining magistrates and members of the Department of Public Prosecution;

the Republic of Bulgaria: the Supreme Cassation Prosecutor's Office of the Republic of Bulgaria for pre-trial cases of criminal proceedings and the courts of the Republic of Bulgaria for pending cases in trial phase of criminal proceedings;

the Czech Republic: public prosecutors and courts of the Czech Republic;

the Kingdom of Denmark:

— the District Courts, the High Courts and the Supreme Court,

— the Department of Public Prosecutions, which includes:

  — the Ministry of Justice,

  — the director of Public Prosecutions,

  — the Prosecutor, and

  — the Police Commissioners;

the Federal Republic of Germany:

— the Federal Ministry of Justice;

— Federal Court of Justice, Karlsruhe;

— the Public Prosecutor General of the Federal Court of Justice, Karlsruhe;

— the Federal Office of Justice;

— the Ministry of Justice of Baden-Württemberg, Stuttgart;

— the Bavarian State Ministry of Justice and Consumer Protection, Munich;

— the Senate Department for Justice, Berlin;

— the Ministry of Justice of Land Brandenburg, Potsdam;

— the Senator for Justice and Constitution of the Free Hanseatic City of Bremen, Bremen;

— the Justice Authority of the Free and Hanseatic City of Hamburg, Hamburg;

— the Hessian Ministry of Justice, Integration and Europe, Wiesbaden;

— the Ministry of Justice of Mecklenburg-Vorpommern, Schwerin;

— the Ministry of Justice of Lower-Saxony, Hanover;

— the Ministry of Justice of Land North-Rhine/Westphalia, Düsseldorf;

— the Ministry of Justice of Land Rhineland-Palatinate, Mainz;

— the Ministry of Justice of the Saarland, Saarbrücken;

— the Saxonian State Ministry of Justice, Dresden;

— the Ministry of Justice of Land Saxony-Anhalt, Magdeburg;

— the Ministry of Justice, Equality and Integration of Schleswig-Holstein, Kiel;

— the Thuringian Ministry of Justice, Erfurt;

— the Higher Regional Courts;

— the Regional Courts;

— the Local Courts;

— the Chief Public Prosecutor at the Higher Regional Courts;

— the Directors of Public Prosecutions at the Regional Courts;

— the Central Office of the Land Judicial Administrations for the Investigation of National Socialist Crimes, Ludwigsburg;

— the Federal Criminal Police Office;

— the Central Office of the German Customs Investigations Service;

the Republic of Estonia: judges and prosecutors;

Ireland: the Director for Public Prosecutions;

the Hellenic Republic: the Public Prosecutor's Office at the Court of Appeal;

the Kingdom of Spain: criminal court magistrates and judges, and public prosecutors;

the French Republic:

— first presidents, presidents, judges and magistrates at criminal courts,

— examining magistrates at such courts,

— members of the public prosecution service at such courts, namely:

  — principal public prosecutors,

  — deputy principal public prosecutors,

  — assistant principal public prosecutors,

  — public prosecutors and assistant public prosecutors,

  — representatives of police court public prosecutors, and

  — military court public prosecutors;

the Italian Republic

Prosecutors:

— Director of Public Prosecution

— Assistant Public Prosecutor

— Director of Military Public Prosecution

— Assistant Military Public Prosecutor

— General Public Prosecutor

— Assistant General Public Prosecutor

— General Military Public Prosecutor

— Assistant General Military Public Prosecutor

Judges:

— Judge of Peace

— Investigation Judge

— Preliminary hearing Judge

— Ordinary Court

— Military Court

— Court of Assizes

— Court of Appeal

— Court of Assizes of Appeal

— Military Court of Appeal

— Court of Cassation;

the Republic of Cyprus:

— the Attorney General of the Republic,

— the Chief of Police,

— the Director of Customs & Excise,

— members of the Unit for Combating Money Laundering (MOKAS), and,

— any other authority or person who is entitled to make inquiries and prosecutions in the Republic of Cyprus,

the Republic of Latvia: investigators, prosecutors and judges;

the Republic of Lithuania: judges and prosecutors;

the Grand Duchy of Luxembourg: the judicial authorities: to be understood as meaning members of the judiciary responsible for administering the law, examining magistrates and members of the Department of Public Prosecution;

the Republic of Hungary: prosecutor's offices and courts;

the Republic of Malta:

— the Magistrates Court,

— the Juvenile Court,

— the Criminal Court and the Court of Criminal Appeal,

— the Attorney General,

— the Deputy Attorney General,

— the Legal Officers within the Attorney General's office; and

— the Magistrates;

the Kingdom of the Netherlands: members of the judiciary responsible for administering the law, examining magistrates and members of the Department of Public Prosecutions;

the Republic of Austria: courts and prosecutors;

the Republic of Poland: prosecutors and courts;

the Portuguese Republic: prosecution services in the investigation phase, investigation judges and trial judges;

Romania: courts and the prosecutor's offices of the courts;

the Republic of Slovenia:

— local court judges,

— investigative judges,

— district court judges,

— higher court judges,

— supreme court judges,

— constitutional court judges,

— district state prosecutors,

— higher state prosecutors,

— supreme state prosecutors;

the Slovak Republic: judges and prosecutors;

the Republic of Finland:

— the Ministry of Justice,

— the Courts of First Instance, the Courts of Appeal, and the Supreme Court,

— the public prosecutors,

— the police authorities, the custom authorities, and the frontier guard officers in their capacity of preliminary criminal investigations authorities in criminal proceedings under the Preliminary Criminal Investigations Act,

the Kingdom of Sweden: courts and prosecutors;

the United Kingdom of Great Britain and Northern Ireland: courts and prosecutors;

Japan: Courts, Presiding Judges, Judges, Public Prosecutors, Public Prosecutor's Assistant Officers, and Judicial Police Officials.

L 39/34 EN Official Journal of the European Union 12.2.2010

*ANNEX III*

With regard to Article 9 of this Agreement, the Member States and Japan accept the following languages:

the Kingdom of Belgium: Dutch, French and German in all cases and English in urgent cases;

the Republic of Bulgaria: Bulgarian in all cases and English in urgent cases;

the Czech Republic: Czech in all cases and English in urgent cases;

the Kingdom of Denmark: Danish in all cases and English in urgent cases;

the Federal Republic of Germany: German in all cases and English in urgent cases;

the Republic of Estonia: Estonian and English in all cases;

Ireland: English and Irish in all cases;

the Hellenic Republic: Greek in all cases and English in urgent cases;

the Kingdom of Spain: Spanish in all cases;

the French Republic: French in all cases;

the Italian Republic: Italian in all cases and English in urgent cases;

the Republic of Cyprus: Greek and English in all cases;

the Republic of Latvia: Latvian in all cases and English in urgent cases;

the Republic of Lithuania: Lithuanian in all cases and English in urgent cases;

the Grand Duchy of Luxembourg: French and German in all cases and English in urgent cases;

the Republic of Hungary: Hungarian in all cases and English in urgent cases;

the Republic of Malta: Maltese in all cases;

the Kingdom of the Netherlands: Dutch in all cases and English in urgent cases;

the Republic of Austria: German in all cases and English in urgent cases;

the Republic of Poland: Polish in all cases;

the Portuguese Republic: Portuguese in all cases and English or French in urgent cases;

Romania: Romanian, English or French in all cases. With regard to longer documents, Romania reserves the right, in any specific case, to require a Romanian translation or to have one made at the expense of the requesting State;

the Republic of Slovenia: Slovenian and English in all cases;

the Slovak Republic: Slovak in all cases;

the Republic of Finland: Finnish, Swedish and English in all cases;

the Kingdom of Sweden: Swedish, Danish or Norwegian in all cases, unless the authority dealing with the application otherwise allows in the individual case;

the United Kingdom of Great Britain and Northern Ireland: English in all cases;

Japan: Japanese in all cases and English in urgent cases. However, Japan reserves the right, in any specific urgent case, to require translation into Japanese with regard to the request from the requesting State which does not accept translation into English under this Annex.

ANNEX IV

With regard to paragraph 1(b) of Article 11 of this Agreement, 'one Member State' referred to in this paragraph is the Portuguese Republic.

With regard to paragraph 2 of Article 11 of this Agreement, 'two Member States' referred to in this paragraph are the Republic of Austria and the Republic of Hungary.

# Agreement between the European Union and the United States of America on the processing and transfer of Financial Messaging Data from the European Union to the United States for the purposes of the Terrorist Finance Tracking Program, 28 June 2010

**[OJ 2010, L 195/5–14]**

27.7.2010 EN Official Journal of the European Union L 195/5

# AGREEMENT

## between the European Union and the United States of America on the processing and transfer of Financial Messaging Data from the European Union to the United States for the purposes of the Terrorist Finance Tracking Program

THE EUROPEAN UNION,

of the one part, and

THE UNITED STATES OF AMERICA,

of the other part,

Together hereinafter referred to as 'the Parties',

DESIRING to prevent and combat terrorism and its financing, in particular by mutual sharing of information, as a means of protecting their respective democratic societies and common values, rights, and freedoms;

SEEKING to enhance and encourage cooperation between the Parties in the spirit of transatlantic partnership;

RECALLING the United Nations conventions for combating terrorism and its financing, and relevant resolutions of the United Nations Security Council in the field of fighting terrorism, in particular United Nations Security Council Resolution 1373 (2001) and its directives that all States shall take the necessary steps to prevent the commission of terrorist acts, including by provision of early warning to other States by exchange of information; that States shall afford one another the greatest measure of assistance in connection with criminal investigations or criminal proceedings relating to the financing or support of terrorist acts; that States should find ways of intensifying and accelerating the exchange of operational information; that States should exchange information in accordance with international and domestic law; and that States should cooperate, particularly through bilateral and multilateral arrangements and agreements, to prevent and suppress terrorist attacks and to take action against perpetrators of such attacks;

RECOGNISING that the United States Department of the Treasury's (U.S. Treasury Department) Terrorist Finance Tracking Program (TFTP) has been instrumental in identifying and capturing terrorists and their financiers and has generated many leads that have been disseminated for counter terrorism purposes to competent authorities around the world, with particular value for European Union Member States (Member States);

NOTING the importance of the TFTP in preventing and combating terrorism and its financing in the European Union and elsewhere, and the important role of the European Union in ensuring that designated providers of international financial payment messaging services provide financial payment messaging data stored in the territory of the European Union which are necessary for preventing and combating terrorism and its financing, subject to strict compliance with safeguards on privacy and the protection of personal data;

MINDFUL of Article 6(2) of the Treaty on European Union on respect for fundamental rights, the right to privacy with regard to the processing of personal data as stipulated in Article 16 of the Treaty on the Functioning of the European Union, the principles of proportionality and necessity concerning the right to private and family life, the respect for privacy, and the protection of personal data under Article 8(2) of the European Convention on the Protection of Human Rights and Fundamental Freedoms, Council of Europe Convention No 108 for the Protection of Individuals with regard to Automatic Processing of Personal Data, and Articles 7 and 8 of the Charter of Fundamental Rights of the European Union;

MINDFUL of the breadth of privacy protections in the United States of America (United States), as reflected in the United States Constitution, and in its criminal and civil legislation, regulations, and long-standing policies, which are enforced and maintained by checks and balances applied by the three branches of government;

STRESSING the common values governing privacy and the protection of personal data in the European Union and the United States, including the importance which both Parties assign to due process and the right to seek effective remedies for improper government action;

MINDFUL of the mutual interest in the expeditious conclusion of a binding agreement between the European Union and the United States based on common principles regarding the protection of personal data when transferred for the general purposes of law enforcement, bearing in mind the importance of carefully considering its effect on prior agreements and the principle of effective administrative and judicial redress on a non-discriminatory basis;

NOTING the rigorous controls and safeguards utilised by the U.S. Treasury Department for the handling, use, and dissemination of financial payment messaging data pursuant to the TFTP, as described in the representations of the U.S. Treasury Department published in the *Official Journal of the European Union* on 20 July 2007 and the Federal Register of the United States on 23 October 2007, which reflect the ongoing cooperation between the United States and the European Union in the fight against global terrorism;

RECOGNISING the two comprehensive reviews and reports of the independent person appointed by the European Commission to verify compliance with the data protection safeguards of the TFTP, concluding that the United States was complying with the data privacy protection practices outlined in its Representations and further that the TFTP has generated significant security benefits for the European Union and has been extremely valuable not only in investigating terrorist attacks but also in preventing a number of terrorist attacks in Europe and elsewhere;

MINDFUL of the European Parliament's resolution of 5 May 2010 on the Recommendation from the Commission to the Council to authorise the opening of negotiations for an agreement between the European Union and the United States to make available to the U.S. Treasury Department financial messaging data to prevent and combat terrorism and terrorist financing;

RECALLING that, to guarantee effective exercise of their rights, any person irrespective of nationality is able to lodge a complaint before an independent data protection authority, other similar authority, or independent and impartial court or tribunal, to seek effective remedies;

MINDFUL that non-discriminatory administrative and judicial redress is available under U.S. law for the mishandling of personal data, including under the Administrative Procedure Act of 1946, the Inspector General Act of 1978, the Implementing Recommendations of the 9/11 Commission Act of 2007, the Computer Fraud and Abuse Act, and the Freedom of Information Act;

RECALLING that by law within the European Union customers of financial institutions and of providers of financial payment messaging services are informed in writing that personal data contained in financial transaction records may be transferred to Member States' or third countries' public authorities for law enforcement purposes and that this notice may include information with respect to the TFTP;

RECOGNISING the principle of proportionality guiding this Agreement and implemented by both the European Union and the United States; in the European Union as derived from the European Convention on Human Rights and Fundamental Freedoms, its applicable jurisprudence, and EU and Member State legislation; and in the United States through reasonableness requirements derived from the United States Constitution and federal and state laws, and their interpretive jurisprudence, as well as through prohibitions on overbreadth of production orders and on arbitrary action by government officials;

AFFIRMING that this Agreement does not constitute a precedent for any future arrangements between the United States and the European Union, or between either of the Parties and any State, regarding the processing and transfer of financial payment messaging data or any other form of data, or regarding data protection;

RECOGNISING that Designated Providers are bound by generally applicable EU or national data protection rules, intended to protect individuals with regard to the processing of their personal data, under the supervision of competent Data Protection Authorities in a manner consistent with the specific provisions of this Agreement; and

FURTHER AFFIRMING that this Agreement is without prejudice to other law enforcement or information sharing agreements or arrangements between the Parties or between the United States and Member States,

HAVE AGREED AS FOLLOWS:

*Article 1*

**Purpose of Agreement**

1. The purpose of this Agreement is to ensure, with full respect for the privacy, protection of personal data, and other conditions set out in this Agreement, that:

(a) financial payment messages referring to financial transfers and related data stored in the territory of the European Union by providers of international financial payment messaging services, that are jointly designated pursuant to this Agreement, are provided to the U.S. Treasury Department for the exclusive purpose of the prevention, investigation, detection, or prosecution of terrorism or terrorist financing; and

(b) relevant information obtained through the TFTP is provided to law enforcement, public security, or counter terrorism authorities of Member States, or Europol or Eurojust, for the purpose of the prevention, investigation, detection, or prosecution of terrorism or terrorist financing.

2. The United States, the European Union, and its Member States shall take all necessary and appropriate measures within their authority to carry out the provisions and achieve the purpose of this Agreement.

*Article 2*

**Scope of application**

**Conduct pertaining to terrorism or terrorist financing**

This Agreement applies to the obtaining and use of financial payment messaging and related data with a view to the prevention, investigation, detection, or prosecution of:

(a) acts of a person or entity that involve violence, or are otherwise dangerous to human life or create a risk of damage to property or infrastructure, and which, given their nature and context, are reasonably believed to be committed with the aim of:

(i) intimidating or coercing a population;

(ii) intimidating, compelling, or coercing a government or international organisation to act or abstain from acting; or

(iii) seriously destabilising or destroying the fundamental political, constitutional, economic, or social structures of a country or an international organisation;

(b) a person or entity assisting, sponsoring, or providing financial, material, or technological support for, or financial or other services to or in support of, acts described in subparagraph (a);

(c) a person or entity providing or collecting funds, by any means, directly or indirectly, with the intention that they should be used or in the knowledge that they are to be used, in full or in part, in order to carry out any of the acts described in subparagraphs (a) or (b); or

(d) a person or entity aiding, abetting, or attempting acts described in subparagraphs (a), (b), or (c).

*Article 3*

**Ensuring provision of data by Designated Providers**

The Parties, jointly and individually, shall ensure, in accordance with this Agreement and in particular Article 4, that entities jointly designated by the Parties under this Agreement as providers of international financial payment messaging services (Designated Providers) provide to the U.S. Treasury Department requested financial payment messaging and related data which are necessary for the purpose of the prevention, investigation, detection, or prosecution of terrorism or terrorist financing (Provided Data). The Designated Providers shall be identified in the Annex to this Agreement and may be updated, as necessary, by exchange of diplomatic notes. Any amendments to the Annex shall be duly published in the *Official Journal of the European Union*.

*Article 4*

**U.S. Requests to obtain data from Designated Providers**

1. For the purposes of this Agreement, the U.S. Treasury Department shall serve production orders (Requests), under authority of U.S. law, upon a Designated Provider present in the territory of the United States in order to obtain data necessary for the purpose of the prevention, investigation, detection, or prosecution of terrorism or terrorist financing that are stored in the territory of the European Union.

L 195/8 EN Official Journal of the European Union 27.7.2010

2. The Request (together with any supplemental documents) shall:

(a) identify as clearly as possible the data, including the specific categories of data requested, that are necessary for the purpose of the prevention, investigation, detection, or prosecution of terrorism or terrorist financing;

(b) clearly substantiate the necessity of the data;

(c) be tailored as narrowly as possible in order to minimise the amount of data requested, taking due account of past and current terrorism risk analyses focused on message types and geography as well as perceived terrorism threats and vulnerabilities, geographic, threat, and vulnerability analyses; and

(d) not seek any data relating to the Single Euro Payments Area.

3. Upon service of the Request on the Designated Provider, the U.S. Treasury Department shall simultaneously provide a copy of the Request, with any supplemental documents, to Europol.

4. Upon receipt of the copy, Europol shall verify as a matter of urgency whether the Request complies with the requirements of paragraph 2. Europol shall notify the Designated Provider that it has verified that the Request complies with the requirements of paragraph 2.

5. For the purposes of this Agreement, once Europol has confirmed that the Request complies with the requirements of paragraph 2, the Request shall have binding legal effect as provided under U.S. law, within the European Union as well as the United States. The Designated Provider is thereby authorised and required to provide the data to the U.S. Treasury Department.

6. The Designated Provider shall thereupon provide the data (i.e., on a 'push basis') directly to the U.S. Treasury Department. The Designated Provider shall keep a detailed log of all data transmitted to the U.S. Treasury Department for the purposes of this Agreement.

7. Once the data have been provided pursuant to these procedures, the Designated Provider shall be deemed to have complied with this Agreement and with all other applicable legal requirements in the European Union related to the transfer of such data from the European Union to the United States.

8. Designated Providers shall have all administrative and judicial redress available under U.S. law to recipients of U.S. Treasury Department Requests.

9. The Parties shall jointly coordinate with regard to the technical modalities necessary to support the Europol verification process.

*Article 5*

**Safeguards applicable to the processing of Provided Data**

**General obligations**

1. The U.S. Treasury Department shall ensure that Provided Data are processed in accordance with the provisions of this Agreement. The U.S. Treasury Department shall ensure the protection of personal data by means of the following safeguards, which shall be applied without discrimination, in particular on the basis of nationality or country of residence.

2. Provided Data shall be processed exclusively for the prevention, investigation, detection, or prosecution of terrorism or its financing.

3. The TFTP does not and shall not involve data mining or any other type of algorithmic or automated profiling or computer filtering.

**Data security and integrity**

4. To prevent unauthorised access to or disclosure or loss of the data or any unauthorised form of processing:

(a) Provided Data shall be held in a secure physical environment, stored separately from any other data, and maintained with high-level systems and physical intrusion controls;

(b) Provided Data shall not be interconnected with any other database;

(c) access to Provided Data shall be limited to analysts investigating terrorism or its financing and to persons involved in the technical support, management, and oversight of the TFTP;

(d) Provided Data shall not be subject to any manipulation, alteration, or addition; and

(e) no copies of Provided Data shall be made, other than for disaster recovery back-up purposes.

**Necessary and proportionate processing of data**

5. All searches of Provided Data shall be based upon pre-existing information or evidence which demonstrates a reason to believe that the subject of the search has a nexus to terrorism or its financing.

6. Each individual TFTP search of Provided Data shall be narrowly tailored, shall demonstrate a reason to believe that the subject of the search has a nexus to terrorism or its financing, and shall be logged, including such nexus to terrorism or its financing required to initiate the search.

7. Provided Data may include identifying information about the originator and/or recipient of a transaction, including name, account number, address, and national identification number. The Parties recognise the special sensitivity of personal data revealing racial or ethnic origin, political opinions, or religious or other beliefs, trade union membership, or health and sexual life (sensitive data). In the exceptional circumstance that extracted data were to include sensitive data, the U.S. Treasury Department shall protect such data in accordance with the safeguards and security measures set forth in this Agreement and with full respect and taking due account of their special sensitivity.

*Article 6*

**Retention and deletion of data**

1. During the term of this Agreement, the U.S. Treasury Department shall undertake an ongoing and at least annual evaluation to identify non-extracted data that are no longer necessary to combat terrorism or its financing. Where such data are identified, the U.S. Treasury Department shall permanently delete them as soon as technologically feasible.

2. If it transpires that financial payment messaging data were transmitted which were not requested, the U.S. Treasury Department shall promptly and permanently delete such data and shall inform the relevant Designated Provider.

3. Subject to any earlier deletion of data resulting from paragraphs 1, 2, or 5, all non-extracted data received prior to 20 July 2007 shall be deleted not later than 20 July 2012.

4. Subject to any earlier deletion of data resulting from paragraphs 1, 2, or 5, all non-extracted data received on or after 20 July 2007 shall be deleted not later than five (5) years from receipt.

5. During the term of this Agreement, the U.S. Treasury Department shall undertake an ongoing and at least annual evaluation to assess the data retention periods specified in paragraphs 3 and 4 to ensure that they continue to be no longer than necessary to combat terrorism or its financing. Where any such retention periods are determined to be longer than necessary to combat terrorism or its financing, the U.S. Treasury Department shall reduce such retention periods, as appropriate.

6. Not later than three years from the date of entry into force of this Agreement, the European Commission and the U.S. Treasury Department shall prepare a joint report regarding the value of TFTP Provided Data, with particular emphasis on the value of data retained for multiple years and relevant information obtained from the joint review conducted pursuant to Article 13. The Parties shall jointly determine the modalities of this report.

7. Information extracted from Provided Data, including information shared under Article 7, shall be retained for no longer than necessary for specific investigations or prosecutions for which they are used.

*Article 7*

**Onward transfer**

Onward transfer of information extracted from the Provided Data shall be limited pursuant to the following safeguards:

(a) only information extracted as a result of an individualised search as described in this Agreement, in particular Article 5, shall be shared;

(b) such information shall be shared only with law enforcement, public security, or counter terrorism authorities in the United States, Member States, or third countries, or with Europol or Eurojust, or other appropriate international bodies, within the remit of their respective mandates;

(c) such information shall be shared for lead purposes only and for the exclusive purpose of the investigation, detection, prevention, or prosecution of terrorism or its financing;

(d) where the U.S. Treasury Department is aware that such information involves a citizen or resident of a Member State, any sharing of the information with the authorities of a third country shall be subject to the prior consent of competent authorities of the concerned Member State or pursuant to existing protocols on such information sharing between the U.S. Treasury Department and that Member State, except where the sharing of the data is essential for the prevention of an immediate and serious threat to public security of a Party to this Agreement, a Member State, or a third country. In the latter case the competent authorities of the concerned Member State shall be informed of the matter at the earliest opportunity;

(e) in sharing such information, the U.S. Treasury Department shall request that the information shall be deleted by the recipient authority as soon as it is no longer necessary for the purpose for which it was shared; and

(f) each onward transfer shall be duly logged.

*Article 8*

**Adequacy**

Subject to ongoing compliance with the commitments on privacy and protection of personal data set out in this Agreement, the U.S. Treasury Department is deemed to ensure an adequate level of data protection for the processing of financial payment messaging and related data transferred from the European Union to the United States for the purposes of this Agreement.

*Article 9*

**Spontaneous provision of information**

1. The U.S. Treasury Department shall ensure the availability, as soon as practicable and in the most expedient manner, to law enforcement, public security, or counter terrorism authorities of concerned Member States, and, as appropriate, to Europol and Eurojust, within the remit of their respective mandates, of information obtained through the TFTP that may contribute to the investigation, prevention, detection, or prosecution by the European Union of terrorism or its financing. Any follow-on information that may contribute to the investigation, prevention, detection, or prosecution by the United States of terrorism or its financing shall be conveyed back to the United States on a reciprocal basis and in a reciprocal manner.

2. In order to facilitate the efficient exchange of information, Europol may designate a liaison officer to the U.S. Treasury Department. The modalities of the liaison officer's status and tasks shall be decided jointly by the Parties.

*Article 10*

**EU requests for TFTP searches**

Where a law enforcement, public security, or counter terrorism authority of a Member State, or Europol or Eurojust, determines that there is reason to believe that a person or entity has a nexus to terrorism or its financing as defined in Articles 1 to 4 of Council Framework Decision 2002/475/JHA, as amended by Council Framework Decision 2008/919/JHA and Directive 2005/60/EC, such authority may request a search for relevant information obtained through the TFTP. The U.S. Treasury Department shall promptly conduct a search in accordance with Article 5 and provide relevant information in response to such requests.

*Article 11*

**Cooperation with future equivalent EU system**

1. During the course of this Agreement, the European Commission will carry out a study into the possible introduction of an equivalent EU system allowing for a more targeted transfer of data.

2. If, following this study, the European Union decides to establish an EU system, the United States shall cooperate and provide assistance and advice to contribute to the effective establishment of such a system.

3. Since the establishment of an EU system could substantially change the context of this Agreement, if the European Union decides to establish such a system, the Parties should consult to determine whether this Agreement would need to be adjusted accordingly. In that regard, U.S. and EU authorities shall cooperate to ensure the complementariness and efficiencies of the U.S. and EU systems in a manner that further enhances the security of citizens of the United States, the European Union, and elsewhere. In the spirit of this cooperation, the Parties shall actively pursue, on the basis of reciprocity and appropriate safeguards, the cooperation of any relevant international financial payment messaging service providers which are based in their respective territories for the purposes of ensuring the continued and effective viability of the U.S. and EU systems.

*Article 12*

**Monitoring of safeguards and controls**

1. Compliance with the strict counter terrorism purpose limitation and the other safeguards set out in Articles 5 and 6 shall be subject to monitoring and oversight by independent overseers, including by a person appointed by the European Commission, with the agreement of and subject to appropriate security clearances by the United States. Such oversight shall include the authority to review in real time and retrospectively all searches made of the Provided Data, the authority to query such searches and, as appropriate, to request additional justification of the terrorism nexus. In particular, independent overseers shall have the authority to block any or all searches that appear to be in breach of Article 5.

2. The oversight described in paragraph 1 shall be subject to regular monitoring, including of the independence of the oversight described in paragraph 1, in the framework of the review foreseen in Article 13. The Inspector General of the U.S. Treasury Department will ensure that the independent oversight described in paragraph 1 is undertaken pursuant to applicable audit standards.

*Article 13*

**Joint review**

1. At the request of one of the Parties and at any event after a period of six (6) months from the date of entry into force of this Agreement, the Parties shall jointly review the safeguards, controls, and reciprocity provisions set out in this Agreement. The review shall be conducted thereafter on a regular basis, with additional reviews scheduled as necessary.

2. The review shall have particular regard to (a) the number of financial payment messages accessed, (b) the number of occasions on which leads have been shared with Member States, third countries, and Europol and Eurojust, (c) the implementation and effectiveness of this Agreement, including the suitability of the mechanism for the transfer of information, (d) cases in which the information has been used for the prevention, investigation, detection, or prosecution of terrorism or its financing, and (e) compliance with data protection obligations specified in this Agreement. The review shall include a representative and random sample of searches in order to verify compliance with the safeguards and controls set out in this Agreement, as well as a proportionality assessment of the Provided Data, based on the value of such data for the investigation, prevention, detection, or prosecution of terrorism or its financing. Following the review, the European Commission will present a report to the European Parliament and the Council on the functioning of this Agreement, including the areas mentioned in this paragraph.

3. For the purposes of the review, the European Union shall be represented by the European Commission, and the United States shall be represented by the U.S. Treasury Department. Each Party may include in its delegation for the review experts in security and data protection, as well as a person with judicial experience. The European Union review delegation shall include representatives of two data protection authorities, at least one of which shall be from a Member State where a Designated Provider is based.

4. For the purposes of the review, the U.S. Treasury Department shall ensure access to relevant documentation, systems, and personnel. The Parties shall jointly determine the modalities of the review.

*Article 14*

**Transparency — providing information to the data subjects**

The U.S. Treasury Department shall post on its public website detailed information concerning the TFTP and its purposes, including contact information for persons with questions. In addition, it shall post information about the procedures available for the exercise of the rights described in Articles 15 and 16, including the availability of administrative and judicial redress as appropriate in the United States regarding the processing of personal data received pursuant to this Agreement.

*Article 15*

**Right of access**

1. Any person has the right to obtain, following requests made at reasonable intervals, without constraint and without excessive delay, at least a confirmation transmitted through his or her data protection authority in the European Union as to whether that person's data protection rights have been respected in compliance with this Agreement, after all necessary verifications have taken place, and, in particular, whether any processing of that person's personal data has taken place in breach of this Agreement.

2. Disclosure to a person of his or her personal data processed under this Agreement may be subject to reasonable legal limitations applicable under national law to safeguard the prevention, detection, investigation, or prosecution of criminal offences, and to protect public or national security, with due regard for the legitimate interest of the person concerned.

3. Pursuant to paragraph 1, a person shall send a request to his or her European national supervisory authority, which shall transmit the request to the Privacy Officer of the U.S. Treasury Department, who shall make all necessary verifications pursuant to the request. The Privacy Officer of the U.S. Treasury Department shall without undue delay inform the relevant European national supervisory authority whether personal data may be disclosed to the data subject and whether the data subject's rights have been duly respected. In the case that access to personal data is refused or restricted pursuant to the limitations referred to in paragraph 2, such refusal or restriction shall be explained in writing and provide information on the means available for seeking administrative and judicial redress in the United States.

*Article 16*

**Right to rectification, erasure, or blocking**

1. Any person has the right to seek the rectification, erasure, or blocking of his or her personal data processed by the U.S. Treasury Department pursuant to this Agreement where the data are inaccurate or the processing contravenes this Agreement.

2. Any person exercising the right expressed in paragraph 1 shall send a request to his or her relevant European national supervisory authority, which shall transmit the request to the Privacy Officer of the U.S. Treasury Department. Any request to obtain rectification, erasure, or blocking shall be duly substantiated. The Privacy Officer of the U.S. Treasury Department shall make all necessary verifications pursuant to the request and shall without undue delay inform the relevant European national supervisory authority whether personal data have been rectified, erased, or blocked, and whether the data subject's rights have been duly respected. Such notification shall be explained in writing and provide information on the means available for seeking administrative and judicial redress in the United States.

*Article 17*

**Maintaining the accuracy of information**

1. Where a Party becomes aware that data received or transmitted pursuant to this Agreement are not accurate, it shall take all appropriate measures to prevent and discontinue erroneous reliance on such data, which may include supplementation, deletion, or correction of such data.

2. Each Party shall, where feasible, notify the other if it becomes aware that material information it has transmitted to or received from the other Party under this Agreement is inaccurate or unreliable.

*Article 18*

**Redress**

1. The Parties shall take all reasonable steps to ensure that the U.S. Treasury Department and any relevant Member State promptly inform one another, and consult with one another and the Parties, if necessary, where they consider that personal data have been processed in breach of this Agreement.

2. Any person who considers his or her personal data to have been processed in breach of this Agreement is entitled to seek effective administrative and judicial redress in accordance with the laws of the European Union, its Member States, and the United States, respectively. For this purpose and as regards data transferred to the United States pursuant to this Agreement, the U.S. Treasury Department shall treat all persons equally in the application of its administrative process, regardless of nationality or country of residence. All persons, regardless of nationality or country of residence, shall have available under U.S. law a process for seeking judicial redress from an adverse administrative action.

*Article 19*

**Consultation**

1. The Parties shall, as appropriate, consult each other to enable the most effective use to be made of this Agreement, including to facilitate the resolution of any dispute regarding the interpretation or application of this Agreement.

2. The Parties shall take measures to avoid the imposition of extraordinary burdens on one another through application of this Agreement. Where extraordinary burdens nonetheless result, the Parties shall immediately consult with a view to facilitating the application of this Agreement, including the taking of such measures as may be required to reduce pending and future burdens.

3. The Parties shall immediately consult in the event that any third party, including an authority of another country, challenges or asserts a legal claim with respect to any aspect of the effect or implementation of this Agreement.

*Article 20*

**Implementation and non-derogation**

1. This Agreement shall not create or confer any right or benefit on any person or entity, private or public. Each Party shall ensure that the provisions of this Agreement are properly implemented.

2. Nothing in this Agreement shall derogate from existing obligations of the United States and Member States under the Agreement on Mutual Legal Assistance between the European Union and the United States of America of 25 June 2003 and the related bilateral mutual legal assistance instruments between the United States and Member States.

*Article 21*

**Suspension or termination**

1. Either Party may suspend the application of this Agreement with immediate effect, in the event of breach of the other Party's obligations under this Agreement, by notification through diplomatic channels.

2. Either Party may terminate this Agreement at any time by notification through diplomatic channels. Termination shall take effect six (6) months from the date of receipt of such notification.

3. The Parties shall consult prior to any possible suspension or termination in a manner which allows a sufficient time for reaching a mutually agreeable resolution.

4. Notwithstanding any suspension or termination of this Agreement, all data obtained by the U.S. Treasury Department under the terms of this Agreement shall continue to be processed in accordance with the safeguards of this Agreement, including the provisions on deletion of data.

*Article 22*

**Territorial application**

1. Subject to paragraphs 2 to 4, this Agreement shall apply to the territory in which the Treaty on European Union and the Treaty on the Functioning of the European Union are applicable and to the territory of the United States.

2. This Agreement will only apply to Denmark, the United Kingdom, or Ireland if the European Commission notifies the United States in writing that Denmark, the United Kingdom, or Ireland has chosen to be bound by this Agreement.

3. If the European Commission notifies the United States before the entry into force of this Agreement that it will apply to Denmark, the United Kingdom, or Ireland, this Agreement shall apply to the territory of such State on the same day as for the other EU Member States bound by this Agreement.

4. If the European Commission notifies the United States after the entry into force of this Agreement that it applies to Denmark, the United Kingdom, or Ireland, this Agreement shall apply to the territory of such State on the first day of the month following receipt of the notification by the United States.

*Article 23*

**Final provisions**

1. This Agreement shall enter into force on the first day of the month after the date on which the Parties have exchanged notifications indicating that they have completed their internal procedures for this purpose.

2. Subject to Article 21, paragraph 2, this Agreement shall remain in force for a period of five (5) years from the date of its entry into force and shall automatically extend for subsequent periods of one (1) year unless one of the Parties notifies the other in writing through diplomatic channels, at least six (6) months in advance, of its intention not to extend this Agreement.

Done at Brussels, on 28 June 2010, in two originals, in the English language. This Agreement shall also be drawn up in the Bulgarian, Czech, Danish, Dutch, Estonian, Finnish, French, German, Greek, Hungarian, Italian, Latvian, Lithuanian, Maltese, Polish, Portuguese, Romanian, Slovak, Slovenian, Spanish, and Swedish languages. Upon approval by both Parties, these language versions shall be considered equally authentic.

За Европейския съюз
Por la Unión Europea
Za Evropskou unii
For Den Europæiske Union
Für die Europäische Union
Euroopa Liidu nimel
Για την Ευρωπαϊκή Ένωση
For the European Union
Pour l'Union européenne
Per l'Unione europea
Eiropas Savienības vārdā
Europos Sajungos vardu
Az Európai Unió részéről
Għall-Unjoni Ewropea
Voor de Europese Unie
W imieniu Unii Europejskiej
Pela União Europeia
Peuntu Uniunea Europeană
Za Európsku úniu
Za Evropsko unijo
Euroopan unionin puolesta
För Europeiska unionen

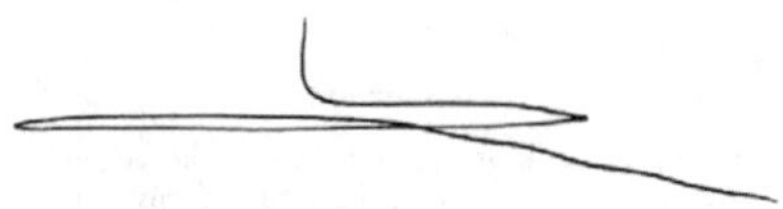

За Съединените американски щати
Por los Estados Unidos de América
Za Spojené státy americké
For Amerikas Forenede Stater
Für die Vereinigten Staaten von Amerika
Ameerika Ühendriikide nimel
Για τις Ηνωμένες Πολιτείες της Αμερικής
For the United States of America
Pour les États-Unis d'Amérique
Per gli Stati Uniti d'America
Amerikas Savienoto Valstu vārdā
Jungtinių Amerikos Valstijų vardu
az Amerikai Egyesült Államok részéről
Għall-Istati Uniti ta'l-Amerika
Voor de Verenigde Staten van Amerika
W imieniu Stanów Zjednoczonych Ameryki
Pelos Estados Unidos da América
Pentru Statele Unite ale Americii
Za Spojené štáty americké
Za Združene države Amerike
Amerikan yhdysvaltojen puolesta
För Amerikas förenta stater

L 195/14 EN Official Journal of the European Union 27.7.2010

*ANNEX*

Society for Worldwide Interbank Financial Telecommunication (SWIFT).

# Regulation 904/2010 on administrative cooperation and combating fraud in the field of value added tax, 7 October 2010

**[Consolidated version. Original version OJ 2010, L 268/1–15 amended by OJ 2013, L 158/1–71]**

**[Editor's note: annexes omitted]**

►B

**COUNCIL REGULATION (EU) No 904/2010**

**of 7 October 2010**

**on administrative cooperation and combating fraud in the field of value added tax**

**(recast)**

(OJ L 268, 12.10.2010, p. 1)

Amended by:

| | | Official Journal | | |
|---|---|---|---|---|
| | | No | page | date |
| ►M1 | Council Regulation (EU) No 517/2013 of 13 May 2013 | L 158 | 1 | 10.6.2013 |

▼B

**COUNCIL REGULATION (EU) No 904/2010**

**of 7 October 2010**

**on administrative cooperation and combating fraud in the field of value added tax**

**(recast)**

THE COUNCIL OF THE EUROPEAN UNION,

Having regard to the Treaty on the Functioning of the European Union, and in particular Article 113 thereof,

Having regard to the proposal from the European Commission,

Having regard to the opinion of the European Parliament [1],

Having regard to the opinion of the European Economic and Social Committee [2],

Acting in accordance with a special legislative procedure,

Whereas:

(1) Council Regulation (EC) No 1798/2003 of 7 October 2003 on administrative cooperation in the field of value added tax [3] has been substantially amended several times. Since further amendments are to be made, it should be recast in the interests of clarity.

(2) The instruments to combat fraud in the field of value added tax (hereinafter 'VAT') in Regulation (EC) No 1798/2003 should be improved and supplemented subsequent to the Council Conclusions of 7 October 2008; the Communication from the Commission to the Council, the European Parliament and the European Economic and Social Committee on a coordinated strategy to improve the fight against VAT fraud in the European Union; and the Report from the Commission to the Council and the European Parliament on the application of Council Regulation (EC) No 1798/2003 concerning administrative cooperation in the field of VAT (hereinafter the 'Commission's report'). Editorial and practical clarifications of the provisions of Regulation (EC) No 1798/2003 are also required.

(3) Tax evasion and tax avoidance extending across the frontiers of Member States lead to budget losses and violations of the principle of fair taxation. They are also liable to bring about distortions of capital movements and of the conditions of competition. They thus affect the operation of the internal market.

[1] Opinion of 5 May 2010 (not yet published in the Official Journal).
[2] Opinion of 17 February 2010 (not yet published in the Official Journal).
[3] OJ L 264, 15.10.2003, p. 1.

▼B

(4) Combating VAT evasion calls for close cooperation between the competent authorities in each Member State responsible for the application of the provisions in that field.

(5) The tax harmonisation measures taken to complete the internal market should include the establishment of a common system for cooperation between the Member States, in particular as concerns exchange of information, whereby the Member States' competent authorities are to assist each other and to cooperate with the Commission in order to ensure the proper application of VAT on supplies of goods and services, intra-Community acquisition of goods and importation of goods.

(6) Administrative cooperation should not lead to an undue shift of administrative burdens between Member States.

(7) For the purposes of collecting the tax owed, Member States should cooperate to help ensure that VAT is correctly assessed. They must therefore not only monitor the correct application of tax owed in their own territory, but should also provide assistance to other Member States for ensuring the correct application of tax relating to activity carried out on their own territory but owed in another Member State.

(8) Monitoring the correct application of VAT on cross-border transactions taxable in a Member State other than that where the supplier is established depends in many cases on information which is held by the Member State of establishment or which can be much more easily obtained by that Member State. Effective supervision of such transactions is therefore dependent on the Member State of establishment collecting, or being in a position to collect, that information.

(9) In order to establish the one-stop shop scheme provided for by Council Directive 2006/112/EC of 28 November 2006 on the common system of value added tax [1], and to apply the refund procedure for taxable persons not established in the Member State of refund provided for in Council Directive 2008/9/EC of 12 February 2008 laying down detailed rules for the refund of value added tax, provided for in Directive 2006/112/EC, to taxable persons not established in the Member State of refund but established in another Member State [2], rules on the exchange and storage of information by Member States are required.

(10) In cross-border situations, it is important to specify the obligations of each Member State so that the tax can be effectively monitored in the Member State in which it is owed.

(1) OJ L 347, 11.12.2006, p. 1.
(2) OJ L 44, 20.2.2008, p. 23.

▼B

(11) Electronic storage and transmission of certain data for VAT control purposes are indispensable for the proper functioning of the VAT system. They allow for rapid information exchange and automated access to information, which strengthen the fight against fraud. That can be achieved by enhancing the databases on VAT-taxable persons and their intra-Community transactions through the inclusion in those databases of a range of information on the taxable persons and their transactions.

(12) The Member States should implement proper verification procedures to ensure that the information is up-to-date, comparable and of good quality, thereby increasing its reliability. The conditions for the exchange of, and the automated access of Member States to, electronically stored data should be clearly defined.

(13) In order to fight fraud effectively, it is necessary to provide for information exchange without prior request. To facilitate the exchange of information, the categories for which an automatic exchange needs to be established should be specified.

(14) As indicated in the Commission's report, feedback is an appropriate means to ensure continual improvement of the quality of the information exchanged. A framework for the provision of feedback should therefore be put in place.

(15) For the effective monitoring of VAT on cross-border transactions, it is necessary to provide for the possibility of simultaneous controls by Member States and of the presence of officials of one Member State in the territory of another Member State, within the framework of administrative cooperation.

(16) Online confirmation of the validity of VAT identification numbers is a tool which is increasingly used by operators. The system for confirming the validity of VAT identification numbers should provide automated confirmation of the relevant information to operators.

(17) Some taxable persons are subject to specific obligations which are different from those in force in the Member State in which they are established, particularly as regards invoicing, when they supply goods or services to customers established on the territory of another Member State. A mechanism should be established to make information on such obligations readily available for those taxable persons.

▼B

(18) Recent practical experience of the application of Regulation (EC) No 1798/2003 in the fight against carrousel fraud has shown that in some cases it is essential to establish a much faster mechanism for the exchange of information, covering much more, and better targeted, information in order to combat fraud effectively. In accordance with the Council Conclusions of 7 October 2008, a decentralised network without legal personality, to be called Eurofisc, should be established within the framework of this Regulation for all the Member States, to promote and facilitate multilateral and decentralised cooperation permitting targeted and swift action to combat specific types of fraud.

(19) The Member State of consumption has primary responsibility for assuring that non-established suppliers comply with their obligations. To this end, the application of the temporary special scheme for electronically supplied services that is provided for in Chapter 6 of Title XII of Directive 2006/112/EC requires the definition of rules concerning the provision of information and transfer of money between the Member State of identification and the Member State of consumption.

(20) Information obtained by a Member State from third countries may be very useful to other Member States. Likewise information obtained by a Member State from other Member States may be very useful to third countries. The conditions for the exchange of such information should therefore be specified.

(21) National rules on banking secrecy should not stand in the way of the application of this Regulation.

(22) This Regulation should not affect other measures adopted at Union level which contribute to combating VAT fraud.

(23) In the interests of effectiveness and speed and on grounds of cost, it is essential that the information communicated under this Regulation should be provided by electronic means wherever possible.

(24) In view of the repetitive nature of certain requests and the linguistic diversity within the Union, it is important to enhance the use of standard forms in the exchange of information so that information requests can be more rapidly processed.

(25) The time limits laid down in this Regulation for the provision of information are to be understood as maximum periods not to be exceeded, the principle being that, in order for cooperation to be effective, information already available to the requested Member State should be provided without further delay.

▼B

(26) For the purposes of this Regulation, it is appropriate to consider limitations of certain rights and obligations laid down by Directive 95/46/EC of the European Parliament and of the Council of 24 October 1995 on the protection of individuals with regard to the processing of personal data and on the free movement of such data (1) in order to safeguard the interests referred to in Article 13(1)(e) of that Directive. Such limitations are necessary and proportionate in view of the potential loss of revenue for Member States and the crucial importance of information covered by this Regulation for the effectiveness of the fight against fraud.

(27) As the measures necessary to implement this Regulation are measures of general scope within the meaning of Article 2 of Council Decision 1999/468/EC of 28 June 1999 laying down the procedures for the exercise of implementing powers conferred on the Commission (2), they must be adopted in conformity with the regulatory procedure provided for in Article 5 of that Decision,

HAS ADOPTED THIS REGULATION:

## CHAPTER I

## GENERAL PROVISIONS

### *Article 1*

1. This Regulation lays down the conditions under which the competent authorities in the Member States responsible for the application of the laws on VAT are to cooperate with each other and with the Commission to ensure compliance with those laws.

To that end, it lays down rules and procedures to enable the competent authorities of the Member States to cooperate and to exchange with each other any information that may help to effect a correct assessment of VAT, monitor the correct application of VAT, particularly on intra-Community transactions, and combat VAT fraud. In particular, it lays down rules and procedures for Member States to collect and exchange such information by electronic means.

2. This Regulation lays down the conditions under which the authorities referred to in paragraph 1 are to assist in the protection of VAT revenue in all the Member States.

3. This Regulation shall not affect the application in the Member States of the rules on mutual assistance in criminal matters.

(1) OJ L 281, 23.11.1995, p. 31.
(2) OJ L 184, 17.7.1999, p. 23.

▼B

4. This Regulation also lays down rules and procedures for the exchange by electronic means of VAT information on services supplied electronically in accordance with the special scheme provided for in Chapter 6 of Title XII of Directive 2006/112/EC and also for any subsequent exchange of information and, as far as services covered by that special scheme are concerned, for the transfer of money between Member States' competent authorities.

*Article 2*

1. For the purposes of this Regulation, the following definitions shall apply:

(a) 'central liaison office' means the office which has been designated pursuant to Article 4(1) with principal responsibility for contacts with other Member States in the field of administrative cooperation;

(b) 'liaison department' means any office other than the central liaison office which has been designated as such by the competent authority pursuant to Article 4(2) to exchange directly information on the basis of this Regulation;

(c) 'competent official' means any official who can directly exchange information on the basis of this Regulation for which he has been authorised pursuant to Article 4(3);

(d) 'requesting authority' means the central liaison office, a liaison department or any competent official of a Member State who makes a request for assistance on behalf of the competent authority;

(e) 'requested authority' means the central liaison office, a liaison department or any competent official of Member State who receives a request for assistance on behalf of the competent authority;

(f) 'intra-Community transactions' means the intra-Community supply of goods or services;

(g) 'intra-Community supply of goods' means any supply of goods which must be declared in the recapitulative statement provided for in Article 262 of Directive 2006/112/EC;

(h) 'intra-Community supply of services' means any supply of services which must be declared in the recapitulative statement provided for in Article 262 of Directive 2006/112/EC;

(i) 'intra-Community acquisition of goods' means the acquisition of the right pursuant to Article 20 of Directive 2006/112/EC to dispose as owner of moveable tangible property;

(j) 'VAT identification number' means the number provided for in Articles 214, 215 and 216 of Directive 2006/112/EC;

(k) 'administrative enquiry' means all the controls, checks and other action taken by Member States in the performance of their duties with a view to ensuring proper application of VAT legislation;

▼B

(l) 'automatic exchange' means the systematic communication of predefined information to another Member State, without prior request;

(m) 'spontaneous exchange' means the non-systematic communication, at any moment and without prior request, of information to another Member State;

(n) 'person' means:

(i) a natural person;

(ii) a legal person;

(iii) where the legislation in force so provides, an association of persons recognised as having the capacity to perform legal acts but lacking the legal status of a legal person; or

(iv) any other legal arrangement of whatever nature and form, which has legal personality or not, and conducts transactions which are subject to VAT;

(o) 'automated access' means the possibility of access without delay to an electronic system in order to consult certain information contained therein;

(p) 'by electronic means' means using electronic equipment for the processing (including digital compression) and storage of data, and employing wires, radio transmission, optical technologies or other electromagnetic means;

(q) 'CCN/CSI network' means the common platform based on the common communication network (hereinafter the 'CCN') and common system interface (hereinafter the 'CSI'), developed by the Union to ensure all transmissions by electronic means between competent authorities in the area of customs and taxation;

(r) 'simultaneous control' means coordinated checks on the tax situation of a taxable person or related taxable persons, organised by two or more participating Member States with common or complementary interests.

2. From 1 January 2015, the definitions contained in Articles 358, 358a and 369a of Directive 2006/112/EC shall also apply for the purposes of this Regulation.

*Article 3*

The competent authorities are the authorities in whose name this Regulation is to be applied, whether directly or by delegation.

Each Member State shall inform the Commission by 1 December 2010 of its competent authority for the purposes of this Regulation and shall subsequently inform the Commission without delay about any change thereof.

▼M1

Croatia shall inform the Commission by 1 July 2013 of its competent authority for the purposes of this Regulation and of the subsequent changes as mentioned in the second paragraph.

▼B

The Commission shall make available to the Member States a list of all competent authorities and publish this information in the *Official Journal of the European Union*.

*Article 4*

1. Each Member State shall designate a single central liaison office to which principal responsibility shall be delegated for contacts with other Member States in the field of administrative cooperation. It shall inform the Commission and the other Member States thereof. The central liaison office may also be designated as responsible for contacts with the Commission.

2. The competent authority of each Member State may designate liaison departments. The central liaison office shall be responsible for keeping the list of those departments up-to-date and making it available to the central liaison offices of the other Member States concerned.

3. The competent authority of each Member State may in addition designate, under the conditions laid down by it, competent officials who can directly exchange information on the basis of this Regulation. When it does so, it may limit the scope of such designation. The central liaison office shall be responsible for keeping the list of those officials up-to-date and making it available to the central liaison offices of the other Member States concerned.

4. The officials exchanging information pursuant to Articles 28, 29 and 30 shall in any case be deemed to be competent officials for this purpose, in accordance with conditions laid down by the competent authorities.

*Article 5*

Where a liaison department or a competent official sends or receives a request or a reply to a request for assistance, it shall inform the central liaison office of its Member State under the conditions laid down by the latter.

*Article 6*

Where a liaison department or a competent official receives a request for assistance requiring action outside its territorial or operational area, it shall forward such request without delay to the central liaison office of its Member State and inform the requesting authority thereof. In such a case, the period laid down in Article 10 shall start the day after the request for assistance has been forwarded to the central liaison office.

▼B

CHAPTER II

**EXCHANGE OF INFORMATION ON REQUEST**

*SECTION 1*

***Request for information and for administrative enquiries***

*Article 7*

1. At the request of the requesting authority, the requested authority shall communicate the information referred to in Article 1, including any information relating to a specific case or cases.

2. For the purpose of forwarding the information referred to in paragraph 1, the requested authority shall arrange for the conduct of any administrative enquiries necessary to obtain such information.

3. Until 31 December 2014, the request referred to in paragraph 1 may contain a reasoned request for an administrative enquiry. If the requested authority takes the view that the administrative enquiry is not necessary, it shall immediately inform the requesting authority of the reasons thereof.

4. As from 1 January 2015, the request referred to in paragraph 1 may contain a reasoned request for a specific administrative enquiry. If the requested authority takes the view that no administrative enquiry is necessary, it shall immediately inform the requesting authority of the reasons thereof.

Notwithstanding the first subparagraph, an enquiry into the amounts declared by a taxable person in connection with the supplies of goods or services listed in Annex I, which are made by a taxable person established in the Member State of the requested authority and are taxable in the Member State of the requesting authority, may be refused solely:

(a) on the grounds provided for in Article 54(1), assessed by the requested authority in conformity with a statement of best practices concerning the interaction of this paragraph and Article 54(1), to be adopted in accordance with the procedure provided for in Article 58(2);

(b) on the grounds provided for in paragraphs 2, 3 and 4 of Article 54; or

(c) on the grounds that the requested authority had already supplied the requesting authority with information on the same taxable person as a result of an administrative enquiry held less than two years previously.

Where the requested authority refuses an administrative enquiry referred to in the second subparagraph on the grounds set out in points (a) or (b), it shall nevertheless provide to the requesting authority the dates and values of any relevant supplies made by the taxable person in the Member State of the requesting authority over the previous two years.

▼B

5. In order to obtain the information sought or to conduct the administrative enquiry requested, the requested authority or the administrative authority to which it has recourse shall proceed as though acting on its own account or at the request of another authority in its own Member State.

*Article 8*

Requests for information and for administrative enquiries pursuant to Article 7 shall be sent using a standard form adopted in accordance with the procedure provided for in Article 58(2), except in the cases referred to in Article 50 or in exceptional cases where the request includes the reasons for which the requesting authority considers the standard form not to be appropriate.

*Article 9*

1. At the request of the requesting authority, the requested authority shall communicate to it any pertinent information it obtains or has in its possession as well as the results of administrative enquiries, in the form of reports, statements and any other documents, or certified true copies or extracts thereof.

2. Original documents shall be provided only where this is not contrary to the provisions in force in the Member State in which the requested authority is established.

*SECTION 2*

***Time limit for providing information***

*Article 10*

The requested authority shall provide the information referred to in Articles 7 and 9 as quickly as possible and no later than three months following the date of receipt of the request.

However, where the requested authority is already in possession of that information, the time limit shall be reduced to a maximum period of one month.

*Article 11*

In certain special categories of cases, time limits which are different from those provided for in Article 10 may be agreed between the requested and the requesting authorities.

*Article 12*

Where the requested authority is unable to respond to the request by the deadline, it shall inform the requesting authority in writing forthwith of the reasons for its failure to do so, and when it considers it would be likely to be able to respond.

▼B

## CHAPTER III

## EXCHANGE OF INFORMATION WITHOUT PRIOR REQUEST

### *Article 13*

1. The competent authority of each Member State shall, without prior request, forward the information referred to in Article 1 to the competent authority of any other Member State concerned, in the following cases:

(a) where taxation is deemed to take place in the Member State of destination and the information provided by the Member State of origin is necessary for the effectiveness of the control system of the Member State of destination;

(b) where a Member State has grounds to believe that a breach of VAT legislation has been committed or is likely to have been committed in the other Member State;

(c) where there is a risk of tax loss in the other Member State.

2. The exchange of information without prior request shall either be automatic, in accordance with Article 14, or spontaneous, in accordance with Article 15.

3. The information shall be forwarded by means of standard forms adopted in accordance with the procedure provided for in Article 58(2).

### *Article 14*

1. The following shall be determined in accordance with the procedure provided for in Article 58(2):

(a) the exact categories of information subject to automatic exchange;

(b) the frequency of the automatic exchange for each category of information; and

(c) the practical arrangements for the automatic exchange of information.

A Member State may abstain from taking part in the automatic exchange of information with respect to one or more categories where the collection of information for such exchange would require the imposition of new obligations on persons liable for VAT or would impose a disproportionate administrative burden on the Member State.

The results of the automatic exchange of information for each category shall be reviewed once a year by the Committee referred to in Article 58(1), so as to ensure that this type of exchange takes places only where it is the most efficient means for the exchange of information.

▼B

2. As from 1 January 2015, the competent authority of each Member State shall, in particular, exchange information automatically in order to enable Member States of consumption to ascertain whether taxable persons not established in their territory declare and correctly pay the VAT due with regard to telecommunication services, broadcasting services and electronically supplied services, regardless of whether those taxable persons make use of the special scheme provided for in Section 3 of Chapter 6 of Title XII of Directive 2006/112/EC. The Member State of establishment shall inform the Member State of consumption of any discrepancies of which it becomes aware.

*Article 15*

The competent authorities of the Member States shall, by spontaneous exchange, forward to the competent authorities of the other Member States any information referred to in Article 13(1) which has not been forwarded under the automatic exchange referred to in Article 14 of which they are aware and which they consider may be useful to those competent authorities.

## CHAPTER IV

## FEEDBACK

*Article 16*

Where a competent authority provides information pursuant to Article 7 or 15, it may request the competent authority which receives the information to give feedback thereon. If such request is made, the competent authority which receives the information shall, without prejudice to the rules on tax secrecy and data protection applicable in its Member State, send feedback as soon as possible, provided that this does not impose a disproportionate administrative burden on it. Practical arrangements shall be determined in accordance with the procedure provided for in Article 58(2).

## CHAPTER V

## STORAGE AND EXCHANGE OF SPECIFIC INFORMATION

*Article 17*

1. Each Member State shall store in an electronic system the following information:

(a) information which it collects pursuant to Chapter 6 of Title XI of Directive 2006/112/EC;

(b) data on the identity, activity, legal form and address of persons to whom it has issued a VAT identification number, collected pursuant to Article 213 of Directive 2006/112/EC, as well as the date on which that number was issued;

(c) data on VAT identification numbers it has issued which have become invalid, and the dates on which those numbers became invalid; and

▼B

(d) information which it collects pursuant to Articles 360, 361, 364 and 365 of Directive 2006/112/EC as well as, from 1 January 2015, information which it collects pursuant to Articles 369c, 369f and 369g of that Directive.

2. The technical details concerning the automated enquiry of the information referred to in points (b), (c) and (d) of paragraph 1 shall be adopted in accordance with the procedure provided for in Article 58(2).

*Article 18*

To enable the information referred to in Article 17 to be used in the procedures provided for in this Regulation, that information shall be available for at least five years from the end of the first calendar year in which access to the information is to be granted.

*Article 19*

Member States shall ensure that the information available in the electronic system referred to in Article 17 is kept up-to-date, and is complete and accurate.

Criteria shall be defined, in accordance with the procedure provided for in Article 58(2), to determine which changes are not pertinent, essential or useful and therefore need not be made.

*Article 20*

1. The information referred to in Article 17 shall be entered into the electronic system without delay.

2. By way of derogation from paragraph 1, the information referred to in Article 17(1)(a) shall be entered into the electronic system no later than one month after the end of the period to which that information relates.

3. By way of derogation from paragraphs 1 and 2, where information is to be corrected in, or added to, the electronic system pursuant to Article 19, the information must be entered no later than one month after the period in which it was collected.

*Article 21*

1. Every Member State shall grant the competent authority of any other Member State automated access to the information stored pursuant to Article 17.

2. With respect to the information referred to in Article 17(1)(a), at least the following details shall be accessible:

(a) VAT identification numbers issued by the Member State receiving the information;

▼B

(b) the total value of all intra-Community supplies of goods and the total value of all intra-Community supplies of services to persons holding a VAT identification number referred to in point (a) by all operators identified for the purposes of VAT in the Member State providing the information;

(c) the VAT identification numbers of the persons who carried out the supplies of goods and services referred to in point (b);

(d) the total value of the supplies of goods and services referred to in point (b) from each person referred to in point (c) to each person holding a VAT identification number referred to in point (a);

(e) the total value of the supplies of goods and services referred to in point (b) from each person referred to in point (c) to each person holding a VAT identification number issued by another Member State under the following conditions:

(i) access is in connection with an investigation into suspected fraud;

(ii) access is through a Eurofisc liaison official, as referred to in Article 36(1), who holds a personal user identification for the electronic systems allowing access to this information; and

(iii) access is only granted during general working hours.

The values referred to in points (b), (d) and (e) shall be expressed in the currency of the Member State providing the information and shall relate to the periods for submission of the recapitulative statements specific to each taxable person which are established in accordance with Article 263 of Directive 2006/112/EC.

*Article 22*

1. In order to provide a reasonable level of assurance to tax administrations with regard to the quality and reliability of the information available through the electronic system referred to in Article 17, Member States shall adopt the measures necessary to ensure that the data provided by taxable persons and non-taxable legal persons for their identification for VAT purposes in accordance with Article 214 of Directive 2006/112/EC, are, in their assessment, complete and accurate.

Member States shall implement procedures for checking these data as determined by the results of their risk assessment. The checks shall be carried out, in principle, prior to identification for VAT purposes or, where only preliminary checks are conducted before such identification, no later than six months from such identification.

▼B

2. The Member States shall inform the Committee referred to in Article 58(1) of the measures implemented at national level to ensure the quality and reliability of the information in accordance with paragraph 1.

*Article 23*

Member States shall ensure that the VAT identification number, referred to in Article 214 of Directive 2006/112/EC, is shown as invalid in the electronic system referred to in Article 17 of this Regulation at least in the following situations:

(a) where persons identified for VAT purposes have stated that their economic activity, as defined in Article 9 of Directive 2006/112/EC, has ceased or where the competent tax administration considers that they have ceased such activity. A tax administration may presume in particular that a person has ceased economic activity when, despite being required to do so, that person has failed to submit VAT returns and recapitulative statements for a year after expiry of the deadline for submission of the first return or statement missed. The person shall have the right to prove the existence of an economic activity by other means;

(b) where persons have declared false data in order to obtain VAT identification or have failed to communicate changes to their data and, had the tax administration known, the latter would have refused identification for VAT purposes or withdrawn the VAT identification number.

*Article 24*

Where, for the purposes of Articles 17 to 21, the competent authorities of the Member States exchange information by electronic means, they shall take all measures necessary to ensure compliance with Article 55.

Member States shall be responsible for all necessary developments to their systems to permit the exchange of that information using the CCN/CSI network.

CHAPTER VI

**REQUEST FOR ADMINISTRATIVE NOTIFICATION**

*Article 25*

The requested authority shall, at the request of the requesting authority and in accordance with the rules governing the notification of similar instruments in the Member State in which the requested authority is established, notify the addressee of all instruments and decisions which emanate from the competent authorities and concern the application of VAT legislation in the territory of the Member State in which the requesting authority is established.

▼B

*Article 26*

Requests for notification, mentioning the subject of the instrument or decision to be notified, shall indicate the name, address and any other relevant information for identifying the addressee.

*Article 27*

The requested authority shall inform the requesting authority immediately of its response to the request for notification and notify it, in particular, of the date of notification of the decision or instrument to the addressee.

CHAPTER VII

**PRESENCE IN ADMINISTRATIVE OFFICES AND PARTICIPATION IN ADMINISTRATIVE ENQUIRIES**

*Article 28*

1. By agreement between the requesting authority and the requested authority, and in accordance with the arrangements laid down by the latter, officials authorised by the requesting authority may, with a view to exchanging the information referred to in Article 1, be present in the offices of the administrative authorities of the requested Member State, or any other place where those authorities carry out their duties. Where the requested information is contained in documentation to which the officials of the requested authority have access, the officials of the requesting authority shall be given copies thereof.

2. By agreement between the requesting authority and the requested authority, and in accordance with the arrangements laid down by the latter, officials authorised by the requesting authority may, with a view to exchanging the information referred to in Article 1, be present during the administrative enquiries carried out in the territory of the requested Member State. Such administrative enquiries shall be carried out exclusively by the officials of the requested authority. The officials of the requesting authority shall not exercise the powers of inspection conferred on officials of the requested authority. They may, however, have access to the same premises and documents as the latter, through the intermediation of the officials of the requested authority and for the sole purpose of carrying out the administrative enquiry.

3. The officials of the requesting authority present in another Member State in accordance with paragraphs 1 and 2 must at all times be able to produce written authority stating their identity and their official capacity.

CHAPTER VIII

**SIMULTANEOUS CONTROLS**

*Article 29*

Member States may agree to conduct simultaneous controls whenever they consider such controls to be more effective than controls carried out by only one Member State.

▼B

*Article 30*

1. A Member State shall identify independently the taxable persons which it intends to propose for a simultaneous control. The competent authority of that Member State shall notify the competent authority of the other Member States concerned of the cases proposed for a simultaneous control. It shall give reasons for its choice, as far as possible, by providing the information which led to its decision. It shall specify the period of time during which such controls should be conducted.

2. The competent authority of the Member State that receives the proposal for a simultaneous control shall confirm its agreement or communicate its reasoned refusal to its counterpart authority, in principle within two weeks of receipt of the proposal, but within a month at the latest.

3. Each competent authority of the Member States concerned shall appoint a representative to be responsible for supervising and coordinating the control operation.

CHAPTER IX

**PROVIDING INFORMATION TO TAXABLE PERSONS**

*Article 31*

1. The competent authorities of each Member State shall ensure that persons involved in the intra-Community supply of goods or of services and non-established taxable persons supplying telecommunication services, broadcasting services and electronically supplied services, in particular those referred to in Annex II to Directive 2006/112/EC, are allowed to obtain, for the purposes of such transactions, confirmation by electronic means of the validity of the VAT identification number of any specified person as well as the associated name and address. This information shall correspond to the data referred to in Article 17.

2. Each Member State shall provide confirmation by electronic means of the name and address of the person to whom the VAT identification number has been issued in accordance with its national data protection rules.

3. During the period provided for in Article 357 of Directive 2006/112/EC, paragraph 1 of this Article shall not apply to non-established taxable persons supplying telecommunication services and radio and television broadcasting services.

*Article 32*

1. The Commission shall, on the basis of the information provided by the Member States, publish on its website the details of the provisions approved by each Member State which transpose Chapter 3 of Title XI of Directive 2006/112/EC.

2. The details and format of the information to be submitted shall be decided in accordance with the procedure provided for in Article 58(2).

▼B

CHAPTER X

**EUROFISC**

*Article 33*

1. In order to promote and facilitate multilateral cooperation in the fight against VAT fraud, this Chapter establishes a network for the swift exchange of targeted information between Member States hereinafter called 'Eurofisc'.

2. Within the framework of Eurofisc, Member States shall:

(a) establish a multilateral early warning mechanism for combating VAT fraud;

(b) coordinate the swift multilateral exchange of targeted information in the subject areas in which Eurofisc will operate (hereinafter 'Eurofisc working fields');

(c) coordinate the work of the Eurofisc liaison officials of the participating Member States in acting on warnings received.

*Article 34*

1. Member States shall participate in the Eurofisc working fields of their choice and may also decide to terminate their participation therein.

2. Member States having chosen to take part in a Eurofisc working field shall actively participate in the multilateral exchange of targeted information between all participating Member States.

3. Information exchanged shall be confidential, as provided for in Article 55.

*Article 35*

The Commission shall provide Eurofisc with technical and logistical support. The Commission shall not have access to the information referred to in Article 1, which may be exchanged over Eurofisc.

*Article 36*

1. The competent authorities of each Member State shall designate at least one Eurofisc liaison official. Eurofisc liaison officials shall be competent officials within the meaning of Article 2(1)(c) and shall carry out the activities referred to in Article 33(2). They shall remain answerable only to their national administrations.

2. The liaison officials of the Member States participating in a particular Eurofisc working field (hereinafter 'participating Eurofisc liaison officials') shall designate a coordinator (hereinafter 'Eurofisc working field coordinator'), among the participating Eurofisc liaison officials, for a limited period of time. Eurofisc working field coordinators shall:

▼B

(a) collate the information received from the participating Eurofisc liaison officials and make all information available to the other participating Eurofisc liaison officials. The information shall be exchanged by electronic means;

(b) ensure that the information received from the participating Eurofisc liaison officials is processed, as agreed by the participants in the working field, and make the result available to the participating Eurofisc liaison officials;

(c) provide feedback to the participating Eurofisc liaison officials.

*Article 37*

Eurofisc working field coordinators shall submit an annual report of the activities of all working fields to the Committee referred to in Article 58(1).

CHAPTER XI

**PROVISIONS CONCERNING THE SPECIAL SCHEMES IN CHAPTER 6 OF TITLE XII OF DIRECTIVE 2006/112/EC**

*SECTION 1*

***Provisions applicable until 31 December 2014***

*Article 38*

The following provisions shall apply concerning the special scheme provided for in Chapter 6 of Title XII of Directive 2006/112/EC. The definitions contained in Article 358 of that Directive shall also apply for the purpose of this Chapter.

*Article 39*

1. The information provided by the taxable person not established in the Community to the Member State of identification, when his activities commence pursuant to Article 361 of Directive 2006/112/EC, shall be submitted by electronic means. The technical details, including a common electronic message, shall be determined in accordance with the procedure provided for in Article 58(2) of this Regulation.

2. The Member State of identification shall transmit this information by electronic means to the competent authorities of the other Member States within 10 days from the end of the month during which the information was received from the non-established taxable person. In the same manner the competent authorities of the other Member States shall be informed of the allocated identification number. The technical details, including a common electronic message, by which this information is to be transmitted, shall be determined in accordance with the procedure provided for in Article 58(2).

▼B

3. The Member State of identification shall without delay inform by electronic means the competent authorities of the other Members States if a non-established taxable person is excluded from the identification register.

*Article 40*

1. The return with the details set out in Article 365 of Directive 2006/112/EC is to be submitted by electronic means. The technical details, including a common electronic message, shall be determined in accordance with the procedure provided for in Article 58(2) of this Regulation.

2. The Member State of identification shall transmit this information by electronic means to the competent authority of the Member State concerned at the latest 10 days after the end of the month during which the return was received. Member States which have required the tax return to be made in a national currency other than euro, shall convert the amounts into euro using the exchange rate valid for the last date of the reporting period. The exchange shall be done following the exchange rates published by the European Central Bank for that day, or, if there is no publication on that day, on the next day of publication. The technical details by which this information is to be transmitted shall be determined in accordance with the procedure provided for in Article 58(2).

3. The Member State of identification shall transmit by electronic means to the Member State of consumption the information needed to link each payment with a relevant quarterly tax return.

*Article 41*

1. The Member State of identification shall ensure that the amount the non-established taxable person has paid is transferred to the bank account denominated in euro which has been designated by the Member State of consumption to which the payment is due. Member States which required the payments in a national currency other than euro shall convert the amounts into euro using the exchange rate valid for the last date of the reporting period. The exchange shall be done following the exchange rates published by the European Central Bank for that day, or, if there is no publication on that day, on the next day of publication. The transfer shall take place at the latest 10 days after the end of the month during which the payment was received.

2. If the non-established taxable person does not pay the total tax due, the Member State of identification shall ensure that the payment is transferred to the Member States of consumption in proportion to the tax due in each Member State. The Member State of identification shall inform by electronic means the competent authorities of the Member States of consumption thereof.

*Article 42*

Member States shall notify by electronic means the competent authorities of the other Member States of the relevant bank account numbers for receiving payments according to Article 41.

▼B

Member States shall without delay notify by electronic means the competent authorities of the other Member States and the Commission of changes in the standard tax rate.

*SECTION 2*

***Provisions applicable from 1 January 2015***

*Article 43*

The following provisions shall apply concerning the special schemes provided for in Chapter 6 of Title XII of Directive 2006/112/EC.

*Article 44*

1. The information provided by the taxable person not established in the Community to the Member State of identification when his activities commence pursuant to Article 361 of Directive 2006/112/EC shall be submitted by electronic means. The technical details, including a common electronic message, shall be determined in accordance with the procedure provided for in Article 58(2) of this Regulation.

2. The Member State of identification shall transmit the information referred to in paragraph 1 by electronic means to the competent authorities of the other Member States within 10 days from the end of the month during which the information was received from the taxable person not established within the Community. Similar details for the identification of the taxable person applying the special scheme pursuant to Article 369b of Directive 2006/112/EC shall be transmitted within 10 days from the end of the month during which the taxable person stated that his taxable activities under that scheme commenced. In the same manner the competent authorities of the other Member States shall be informed of the allocated identification number.

The technical details, including a common electronic message, by which this information is to be transmitted, shall be determined in accordance with the procedure provided for in Article 58(2) of this Regulation.

3. The Member State of identification shall without delay inform by electronic means the competent authorities of the other Member States if a taxable person not established in the Community or a taxable person not established in the Member State of consumption is excluded from the special scheme.

*Article 45*

1. The return with the details set out in Articles 365 and 369g of Directive 2006/112/EC is to be submitted by electronic means. The technical details, including a common electronic message, shall be determined in accordance with the procedure provided for in Article 58(2) of this Regulation.

2. The Member State of identification shall transmit this information by electronic means to the competent authority of the Member State of consumption concerned at the latest 10 days after the end of the month during which the return was received. The information provided for in the second paragraph of Article 369g of Directive 2006/112/EC shall also be transmitted to the competent authority of the Member State of

▼B

establishment concerned. Member States which have required the tax return to be made in a national currency other that euro, shall convert the amounts into euro using the exchange rate valid for the last date of the reporting period. The exchange shall be done following the exchange rates published by the European Central Bank for that day, or, if there is no publication on that day, on the next day of publication. The technical details by which this information is to be transmitted shall be determined in accordance with the procedure provided for in Article 58(2) of this Regulation.

3. The Member State of identification shall transmit by electronic means to the Member State of consumption the information needed to link each payment with a relevant quarterly tax return.

*Article 46*

1. The Member State of identification shall ensure that the amount the non-established taxable person has paid is transferred to the bank account denominated in euro which has been designated by the Member State of consumption to which the payment is due. Member States which required the payments in a national currency other than euro shall convert the amounts into euro using the exchange rate valid for the last date of the reporting period. The exchange shall be done following the exchange rates published by the European Central Bank for that day, or, if there is no publication on that day, on the next day of publication. The transfer shall take place at the latest 10 days after the end of the month during which the payment was received.

2. If the non-established taxable person does not pay the total tax due, the Member State of identification shall ensure that the payment is transferred to the Member States of consumption in proportion to the tax due in each Member State. The Member State of identification shall inform by electronic means the competent authorities of the Member States of consumption thereof.

3. Concerning the payments to be transferred to the Member State of consumption in accordance with the special scheme provided for in Section 3 of Chapter 6 of Title XII of Directive 2006/112/EC, the Member State of identification shall, of the amounts referred to in paragraphs 1 and 2 of this Article, be entitled to retain:

(a) from 1 January 2015 until 31 December 2016 — 30 %;

(b) from 1 January 2017 until 31 December 2018 — 15 %;

(c) from 1 January 2019 — 0 %.

*Article 47*

Member States shall notify by electronic means the competent authorities of the other Member States of the relevant bank account numbers for receiving payments in accordance with Article 46.

Member States shall without delay notify by electronic means the competent authorities of the other Member States and the Commission of changes in the tax rate applicable for supplies of telecommunication services, broadcasting services and electronically supplied services.

▼B

CHAPTER XII

**EXCHANGE AND CONSERVATION OF INFORMATION IN THE CONTEXT OF THE PROCEDURE FOR THE REFUND OF VAT TO TAXABLE PERSONS NOT ESTABLISHED IN THE MEMBER STATE OF REFUND BUT ESTABLISHED IN ANOTHER MEMBER STATE**

*Article 48*

1. Where the competent authority of the Member State of establishment receives an application for refund of VAT pursuant to Article 5 of Directive 2008/9/EC, and Article 18 of that Directive is not applicable, it shall, within 15 calendar days of its receipt and by electronic means, forward the application to the competent authorities of each Member State of refund concerned with confirmation that the applicant as defined in Article 2(5) of Directive 2008/9/EC is a taxable person for the purposes of VAT and that the identification or registration number given by this person is valid for the refund period.

2. The competent authorities of each Member State of refund shall notify by electronic means the competent authorities of the other Member States of any information required by them pursuant to Article 9(2) of Directive 2008/9/EC. The technical details, including a common electronic message by which this information is to be transmitted, shall be determined in accordance with the procedure provided for in Article 58(2) of this Regulation.

3. The competent authorities of each Member State of refund shall notify by electronic means the competent authorities of the other Member States if they want to make use of the option to require the applicant to provide the description of business activity by harmonised codes as referred to in Article 11 of Directive 2008/9/EC.

The harmonised codes referred to in the first subparagraph shall be determined in accordance with the procedure provided for in Article 58(2) of this Regulation on the basis of the NACE classification established by Regulation (EC) No 1893/2006 of the European Parliament and of the Council of 20 December 2006 establishing the statistical classification of economic activities NACE Revision 2 ([1]).

CHAPTER XIII

**RELATIONS WITH THE COMMISSION**

*Article 49*

1. The Member States and the Commission shall examine and evaluate how the arrangements for administrative cooperation provided for in this Regulation are working. The Commission shall pool the Member States' experience with the aim of improving the operation of those arrangements.

2. The Member States shall communicate to the Commission any available information relevant to their application of this Regulation.

([1]) OJ L 393, 30.12.2006, p. 1.

▼B

3. A list of statistical data needed for evaluation of this Regulation shall be determined in accordance with the procedure provided for in Article 58(2). The Member States shall communicate these data to the Commission in so far as they are available and the communication is not likely to involve administrative burdens which would be unjustified.

4. With a view to evaluating the effectiveness of this system of administrative cooperation in combating tax evasion and tax avoidance, Member States may communicate to the Commission any other information referred to in Article 1.

5. The Commission shall forward the information referred to in paragraphs 2, 3 and 4 to the other Member States concerned.

6. Where necessary, in addition to what is required by other provisions in this Regulation, the Commission shall send to the competent authorities of each Member State any information that might enable them to combat fraud in the field of VAT as soon as it obtains such information.

7. The Commission may, at the request of a Member State, provide its expert opinions, technical or logistical assistance, or any other support with a view to attaining the objectives of this Regulation.

## CHAPTER XIV

## RELATIONS WITH THIRD COUNTRIES

### *Article 50*

1. When the competent authority of a Member State receives information from a third country, that authority may pass the information on to the competent authorities of Member States which might be interested in it and, in any event, to all those which request it, in so far as permitted by assistance arrangements with that particular third country.

2. Competent authorities may communicate, in accordance with their domestic provisions on the communication of personal data to third countries, information obtained in accordance with this Regulation to a third country, provided that the following conditions are met:

(a) the competent authority of the Member State from which the information originates has consented to that communication; and

(b) the third country concerned has given an undertaking to provide the cooperation required to gather evidence of the irregular nature of transactions which appear to contravene VAT legislation.

## CHAPTER XV

## CONDITIONS GOVERNING THE EXCHANGE OF INFORMATION

### *Article 51*

1. Information communicated pursuant to this Regulation shall, as far as possible, be provided by electronic means under arrangements to be adopted in accordance with the procedure provided for in Article 58(2).

▼B

2. Where the request has not been lodged completely through the electronic system referred to in paragraph 1, the requested authority shall confirm receipt of the request by electronic means without delay and, in any event, no later than five working days after receipt.

Where an authority has received a request or information of which it is not the intended recipient, it shall send a message by electronic means to the sender without delay and, in any event, no later than five working days after receipt.

*Article 52*

Requests for assistance, including requests for notification, and attached documents may be made in any language agreed between the requested and requesting authority. The said requests shall be accompanied by a translation into the official language or one of the official languages of the Member State in which the requested authority is established only in special cases when the requested authority gives a reason for asking for such a translation.

*Article 53*

The Commission and the Member States shall ensure that such existing or new communication and information exchange systems which are necessary to provide for the exchanges of information described in this Regulation are operational. A service level agreement ensuring the technical quality and quantity of the services to be delivered by the Commission and the Member States for the functioning of those communication and information exchange systems shall be decided in accordance with the procedure provided for in Article 58(2). The Commission shall be responsible for whatever development of the CCN/CSI network is necessary to permit the exchange of this information between Member States. Member States shall be responsible for whatever development of their systems is necessary to permit this information to be exchanged using the CCN/CSI network.

Member States shall waive all claims for the reimbursement of expenses incurred in applying this Regulation except, where appropriate, in respect of fees paid to experts.

*Article 54*

1. The requested authority in one Member State shall provide a requesting authority in another Member State with the information referred to in Article 1 provided that:

(a) the number and the nature of the requests for information made by the requesting authority within a specific period do not impose a disproportionate administrative burden on that requested authority;

(b) that requesting authority has exhausted the usual sources of information which it could have used in the circumstances to obtain the information requested, without running the risk of jeopardising the achievement of the desired end.

▼B

2. This Regulation shall impose no obligation to have enquiries carried out or to provide information on a particular case if the laws or administrative practices of the Member State which would have to supply the information do not authorise the Member State to carry out those enquiries or collect or use that information for that Member State's own purposes.

3. The competent authority of a requested Member State may refuse to provide information where the requesting Member State is unable, for legal reasons, to provide similar information. The Commission shall be informed of the grounds of the refusal by the requested Member State.

4. The provision of information may be refused where it would lead to the disclosure of a commercial, industrial or professional secret or of a commercial process, or of information whose disclosure would be contrary to public policy.

5. Paragraphs 2, 3 and 4 should on no account be interpreted as authorising the requested authority of a Member State to refuse to supply information on a taxable person identified for VAT purposes in the Member State of the requesting authority on the sole grounds that this information is held by a bank, other financial institution, nominee or person acting in an agency or fiduciary capacity or because it relates to ownership interests in a legal person.

6. The requested authority shall inform the requesting authority of the grounds for refusing a request for assistance.

7. A minimum threshold triggering a request for assistance may be adopted in accordance with the procedure provided for in Article 58(2).

*Article 55*

1. Information communicated or collected in any form pursuant to this Regulation, including any information to which an official has had access in the circumstances set out in Chapters VII, VIII and X, and in the cases referred to in paragraph 2 of this Article, shall be covered by the obligation of official secrecy and enjoy the protection extended to similar information under both the national law of the Member State which received it and the corresponding provisions applicable to Union authorities. Such information shall be used only in the circumstances provided for in this Regulation.

Such information may be used for the purpose of establishing the assessment base or the collection or administrative control of tax for the purpose of establishing the assessment base.

▼B

The information may also be used for the assessment of other levies, duties, and taxes covered by Article 2 of Council Directive 2008/55/EC of 26 May 2008 on mutual assistance for the recovery of claims relating to certain levies, duties, taxes and other measures (1).

In addition, it may be used in connection with judicial proceedings that may involve penalties, initiated as a result of infringements of tax law without prejudice to the general rules and legal provisions governing the rights of defendants and witnesses in such proceedings.

2. Persons duly accredited by the Security Accreditation Authority of the Commission may have access to this information only in so far as it is necessary for care, maintenance and development of the CCN/CSI network.

3. By way of derogation from paragraph 1, the competent authority of the Member State providing the information shall permit its use for other purposes in the Member State of the requesting authority, if, under the legislation of the Member State of the requested authority, the information can be used for similar purposes.

4. Where the requesting authority considers that information it has received from the requested authority is likely to be useful to the competent authority of a third Member State, it may transmit it to the latter authority. It shall inform the requested authority thereof in advance. The requested authority may require that the transmission of the information to a third party be subject to its prior agreement.

5. All storage or exchange of information referred to in this Regulation is subject to the provisions implementing Directive 95/46/EC. However, Member States shall, for the purpose of the correct application of this Regulation, restrict the scope of the obligations and rights provided for in Article 10, Article 11(1) and Articles 12 and 21 of Directive 95/46/EC to the extent required in order to safeguard the interests referred to in Article 13(1)(e) of that Directive.

*Article 56*

Reports, statements and any other documents, or certified true copies or extracts thereof, obtained by the staff of the requested authority and communicated to the requesting authority under the assistance provided for by this Regulation may be invoked as evidence by the competent bodies of the Member State of the requesting authority on the same basis as similar documents provided by another authority of that country.

(1) OJ L 150, 10.6.2008, p. 28.

▼B

*Article 57*

1. For the purpose of applying this Regulation, Member States shall take all necessary measures to:

(a) ensure effective internal coordination between the competent authorities;

(b) establish direct cooperation between the authorities authorised for the purposes of such coordination;

(c) ensure the smooth operation of the information exchange arrangements provided for in this Regulation.

2. The Commission shall communicate to each Member State, as quickly as possible, any information which it receives and which it is able to provide.

CHAPTER XVI

**FINAL PROVISIONS**

*Article 58*

1. The Commission shall be assisted by the Standing Committee on Administrative Cooperation.

2. Where reference is made to this paragraph, Articles 5 and 7 of Decision 1999/468/EC shall apply, having regard to the provisions of Article 8 thereof.

The period laid down in Article 5(6) of Decision 1999/468/EC shall be set at three months.

*Article 59*

1. By 1 November 2013 and thereafter every five years, the Commission shall report to the European Parliament and the Council on the application of this Regulation.

2. Member States shall communicate to the Commission the text of any provisions of national law which they adopt in the field covered by this Regulation.

*Article 60*

1. This Regulation shall be without prejudice to the fulfilment of any wider obligations in relation to mutual assistance ensuing from other legal acts, including bilateral or multilateral agreements.

2. Where the Member States conclude bilateral arrangements on matters covered by this Regulation, in particular pursuant to Article 11, other than to deal with individual cases, they shall inform the Commission without delay. The Commission shall in turn inform the other Member States.

▼B

*Article 61*

Regulation (EC) No 1798/2003 shall be repealed with effect from 1 January 2012. However, the effects of Article 2(1) of that Regulation shall be maintained until the date of publication by the Commission of the list of competent authorities referred to in Article 3 of this Regulation.

Chapter V, with the exception of Article 27(4), of that Regulation shall remain applicable until 31 December 2012.

References made to the repealed Regulation shall be construed as references to this Regulation.

*Article 62*

This Regulation shall enter into force on the 20th day following its publication in the *Official Journal of the European Union*.

It shall apply from 1 January 2012.

However, Articles 33 to 37 shall apply from 1 November 2010;

Chapter V, with the exception of Articles 22 and 23, shall apply from 1 January 2013;

— Articles 38 to 42 shall apply from 1 January 2012 until 31 December 2014; and

— Articles 43 to 47 shall apply from 1 January 2015.

This Regulation shall be binding in its entirety and directly applicable in all Member States.

# Directive 2010/64 on the right to interpretation and translation in criminal proceedings, 20 October 2010

[OJ 2010, L 280/1–7]

26.10.2010 EN Official Journal of the European Union L 280/1

I

*(Legislative acts)*

# DIRECTIVES

## DIRECTIVE 2010/64/EU OF THE EUROPEAN PARLIAMENT AND OF THE COUNCIL

**of 20 October 2010**

**on the right to interpretation and translation in criminal proceedings**

THE EUROPEAN PARLIAMENT AND THE COUNCIL OF THE EUROPEAN UNION,

Having regard to the Treaty on the Functioning of the European Union, and in particular point (b) of the second subparagraph of Article 82(2) thereof,

Having regard to the initiative of the Kingdom of Belgium, the Federal Republic of Germany, the Republic of Estonia, the Kingdom of Spain, the French Republic, the Italian Republic, the Grand-Duchy of Luxembourg, the Republic of Hungary, the Republic of Austria, the Portuguese Republic, Romania, the Republic of Finland and the Kingdom of Sweden [1],

After transmission of the draft legislative act to the national parliaments,

Acting in accordance with the ordinary legislative procedure [2],

Whereas:

(1) The Union has set itself the objective of maintaining and developing an area of freedom, security and justice. According to the Presidency Conclusions of the European Council in Tampere of 15 and 16 October 1999, and in particular point 33 thereof, the principle of mutual recognition of judgments and other decisions of judicial authorities should become the cornerstone of judicial cooperation in civil and criminal matters within the Union because enhanced mutual recognition and the necessary approximation of legislation would facilitate cooperation between competent authorities and the judicial protection of individual rights.

(2) On 29 November 2000, the Council, in accordance with the Tampere Conclusions, adopted a programme of measures to implement the principle of mutual recognition of decisions in criminal matters [3]. The introduction to the programme states that mutual recognition is 'designed to strengthen cooperation between Member States but also to enhance the protection of individual rights'.

(3) The implementation of the principle of mutual recognition of decisions in criminal matters presupposes that Member States have trust in each other's criminal justice systems. The extent of mutual recognition is very much dependent on a number of parameters, which include mechanisms for safeguarding the rights of suspected or accused persons and common minimum standards necessary to facilitate the application of the principle of mutual recognition.

(4) Mutual recognition of decisions in criminal matters can operate effectively only in a spirit of trust in which not only judicial authorities but all actors in the criminal process consider decisions of the judicial authorities of other Member States as equivalent to their own, implying not only trust in the adequacy of other Member States' rules, but also trust that those rules are correctly applied.

(5) Article 6 of the European Convention for the Protection of Human Rights and Fundamental Freedoms (hereinafter the ECHR) and Article 47 of the Charter of Fundamental Rights of the European Union (hereinafter the Charter) enshrine the right to a fair trial. Article 48(2) of the Charter guarantees respect for the right of defence. This Directive respects those rights and should be implemented accordingly.

---

(1) OJ C 69, 18.3.2010, p. 1.
(2) Position of the European Parliament of 16 June 2010 (not yet published in the Official Journal) and decision of the Council of 7 October 2010.
(3) OJ C 12, 15.1.2001, p. 10.

(6) Although all the Member States are party to the ECHR, experience has shown that that alone does not always provide a sufficient degree of trust in the criminal justice systems of other Member States.

(7) Strengthening mutual trust requires a more consistent implementation of the rights and guarantees set out in Article 6 of the ECHR. It also requires, by means of this Directive and other measures, further development within the Union of the minimum standards set out in the ECHR and the Charter.

(8) Article 82(2) of the Treaty on the Functioning of the European Union provides for the establishment of minimum rules applicable in the Member States so as to facilitate mutual recognition of judgments and judicial decisions and police and judicial cooperation in criminal matters having a cross-border dimension. Point (b) of the second subparagraph of Article 82(2) refers to 'the rights of individuals in criminal procedure' as one of the areas in which minimum rules may be established.

(9) Common minimum rules should lead to increased confidence in the criminal justice systems of all Member States, which, in turn, should lead to more efficient judicial cooperation in a climate of mutual trust. Such common minimum rules should be established in the fields of interpretation and translation in criminal proceedings.

(10) On 30 November 2009, the Council adopted a resolution on a Roadmap for strengthening procedural rights of suspected or accused persons in criminal proceedings ([1]). Taking a step-by-step approach, the Roadmap called for the adoption of measures regarding the right to translation and interpretation (measure A), the right to information on rights and information about the charges (measure B), the right to legal advice and legal aid (measure C), the right to communication with relatives, employers and consular authorities (measure D), and special safeguards for suspected or accused persons who are vulnerable (measure E).

(11) In the Stockholm programme, adopted on 10 December 2009, the European Council welcomed the Roadmap and made it part of the Stockholm programme (point 2.4). The European Council underlined the non-exhaustive character of the Roadmap, by inviting the Commission to examine further elements of minimum procedural rights for suspected and accused persons, and to assess whether other issues, for instance the presumption of innocence, need to be addressed, in order to promote better cooperation in that area.

(12) This Directive relates to measure A of the Roadmap. It lays down common minimum rules to be applied in the fields of interpretation and translation in criminal proceedings with a view to enhancing mutual trust among Member States.

(13) This Directive draws on the Commission proposal for a Council Framework Decision on the right to interpretation and to translation in criminal proceedings of 8 July 2009, and on the Commission proposal for a Directive of the European Parliament and of the Council on the right to interpretation and translation in criminal proceedings of 9 March 2010.

(14) The right to interpretation and translation for those who do not speak or understand the language of the proceedings is enshrined in Article 6 of the ECHR, as interpreted in the case-law of the European Court of Human Rights. This Directive facilitates the application of that right in practice. To that end, the aim of this Directive is to ensure the right of suspected or accused persons to interpretation and translation in criminal proceedings with a view to ensuring their right to a fair trial.

(15) The rights provided for in this Directive should also apply, as necessary accompanying measures, to the execution of a European arrest warrant ([2]) within the limits provided for by this Directive. Executing Members States should provide, and bear the costs of, interpretation and translation for the benefit of the requested persons who do not speak or understand the language of the proceedings.

(16) In some Member States an authority other than a court having jurisdiction in criminal matters has competence for imposing sanctions in relation to relatively minor offences. That may be the case, for example, in relation to traffic offences which are committed on a large scale and which might be established following a traffic control. In such situations, it would be unreasonable to require that the competent authority ensure all the rights under this Directive. Where the law of a Member State provides for the imposition of a sanction regarding minor offences by such an authority and there is a right of appeal to a court having jurisdiction in criminal matters, this Directive should therefore apply only to the proceedings before that court following such an appeal.

([1]) OJ C 295, 4.12.2009, p. 1.

([2]) Council Framework Decision 2002/584/JHA of 13 June 2002 on the European arrest warrant and the surrender procedures between Member States (OJ L 190, 18.7.2002, p. 1).

(17) This Directive should ensure that there is free and adequate linguistic assistance, allowing suspected or accused persons who do not speak or understand the language of the criminal proceedings fully to exercise their right of defence and safeguarding the fairness of the proceedings.

(18) Interpretation for the benefit of the suspected or accused persons should be provided without delay. However, where a certain period of time elapses before interpretation is provided, that should not constitute an infringement of the requirement that interpretation be provided without delay, as long as that period of time is reasonable in the circumstances.

(19) Communication between suspected or accused persons and their legal counsel should be interpreted in accordance with this Directive. Suspected or accused persons should be able, inter alia, to explain their version of the events to their legal counsel, point out any statements with which they disagree and make their legal counsel aware of any facts that should be put forward in their defence.

(20) For the purposes of the preparation of the defence, communication between suspected or accused persons and their legal counsel in direct connection with any questioning or hearing during the proceedings, or with the lodging of an appeal or other procedural applications, such as an application for bail, should be interpreted where necessary in order to safeguard the fairness of the proceedings.

(21) Member States should ensure that there is a procedure or mechanism in place to ascertain whether suspected or accused persons speak and understand the language of the criminal proceedings and whether they need the assistance of an interpreter. Such procedure or mechanism implies that competent authorities verify in any appropriate manner, including by consulting the suspected or accused persons concerned, whether they speak and understand the language of the criminal proceedings and whether they need the assistance of an interpreter.

(22) Interpretation and translation under this Directive should be provided in the native language of the suspected or accused persons or in any other language that they speak or understand in order to allow them fully to exercise their right of defence, and in order to safeguard the fairness of the proceedings.

(23) The respect for the right to interpretation and translation contained in this Directive should not compromise any other procedural right provided under national law.

(24) Member States should ensure that control can be exercised over the adequacy of the interpretation and translation provided when the competent authorities have been put on notice in a given case.

(25) The suspected or accused persons or the persons subject to proceedings for the execution of a European arrest warrant should have the right to challenge the finding that there is no need for interpretation, in accordance with procedures in national law. That right does not entail the obligation for Member States to provide for a separate mechanism or complaint procedure in which such finding may be challenged and should not prejudice the time limits applicable to the execution of a European arrest warrant.

(26) When the quality of the interpretation is considered insufficient to ensure the right to a fair trial, the competent authorities should be able to replace the appointed interpreter.

(27) The duty of care towards suspected or accused persons who are in a potentially weak position, in particular because of any physical impairments which affect their ability to communicate effectively, underpins a fair administration of justice. The prosecution, law enforcement and judicial authorities should therefore ensure that such persons are able to exercise effectively the rights provided for in this Directive, for example by taking into account any potential vulnerability that affects their ability to follow the proceedings and to make themselves understood, and by taking appropriate steps to ensure those rights are guaranteed.

(28) When using videoconferencing for the purpose of remote interpretation, the competent authorities should be able to rely on the tools that are being developed in the context of European e-Justice (e.g. information on courts with videoconferencing equipment or manuals).

(29) This Directive should be evaluated in the light of the practical experience gained. If appropriate, it should be amended so as to improve the safeguards which it lays down.

(30) Safeguarding the fairness of the proceedings requires that essential documents, or at least the relevant passages of such documents, be translated for the benefit of suspected or accused persons in accordance with this Directive. Certain documents should always be considered essential for that purpose and should therefore be translated, such as any decision depriving a person of his liberty, any charge or indictment, and any judgment. It is for the competent authorities of the Member States to decide, on their own motion or upon a request of suspected or accused persons or of their legal counsel, which other documents are essential to safeguard the fairness of the proceedings and should therefore be translated as well.

(31) Member States should facilitate access to national databases of legal translators and interpreters where such databases exist. In that context, particular attention should be paid to the aim of providing access to existing databases through the e-Justice portal, as planned in the multiannual European e-Justice action plan 2009-2013 of 27 November 2008 (1).

(32) This Directive should set minimum rules. Member States should be able to extend the rights set out in this Directive in order to provide a higher level of protection also in situations not explicitly dealt with in this Directive. The level of protection should never fall below the standards provided by the ECHR or the Charter as interpreted in the case-law of the European Court of Human Rights or the Court of Justice of the European Union.

(33) The provisions of this Directive that correspond to rights guaranteed by the ECHR or the Charter should be interpreted and implemented consistently with those rights, as interpreted in the relevant case-law of the European Court of Human Rights and the Court of Justice of the European Union.

(34) Since the objective of this Directive, namely establishing common minimum rules, cannot be sufficiently achieved by the Member States and can therefore, by reason of its scale and effects, be better achieved at Union level, the Union may adopt measures in accordance with the principle of subsidiarity as set out in Article 5 of the Treaty on European Union. In accordance with the principle of proportionality, as set out in that Article, this Directive does not go beyond what is necessary in order to achieve that objective.

(35) In accordance with Article 3 of the Protocol (No 21) on the position of the United Kingdom and Ireland in respect of the Area of Freedom, Security and Justice, annexed to the Treaty on European Union and to the Treaty on the Functioning of the European Union, those Member States have notified their wish to take part in the adoption and application of this Directive.

(36) In accordance with Articles 1 and 2 of the Protocol (No 22) on the position of Denmark, annexed to the Treaty on European Union and to the Treaty on the Functioning of the European Union, Denmark is not taking part in the adoption of this Directive and is not bound by it or subject to its application,

HAVE ADOPTED THIS DIRECTIVE:

*Article 1*

**Subject matter and scope**

1. This Directive lays down rules concerning the right to interpretation and translation in criminal proceedings and proceedings for the execution of a European arrest warrant.

2. The right referred to in paragraph 1 shall apply to persons from the time that they are made aware by the competent authorities of a Member State, by official notification or otherwise, that they are suspected or accused of having committed a criminal offence until the conclusion of the proceedings, which is understood to mean the final determination of the question whether they have committed the offence, including, where applicable, sentencing and the resolution of any appeal.

3. Where the law of a Member State provides for the imposition of a sanction regarding minor offences by an authority other than a court having jurisdiction in criminal matters, and the imposition of such a sanction may be appealed to such a court, this Directive shall apply only to the proceedings before that court following such an appeal.

(1) OJ C 75, 31.3.2009, p. 1.

4. This Directive does not affect national law concerning the presence of legal counsel during any stage of the criminal proceedings, nor does it affect national law concerning the right of access of a suspected or accused person to documents in criminal proceedings.

*Article 2*

**Right to interpretation**

1. Member States shall ensure that suspected or accused persons who do not speak or understand the language of the criminal proceedings concerned are provided, without delay, with interpretation during criminal proceedings before investigative and judicial authorities, including during police questioning, all court hearings and any necessary interim hearings.

2. Member States shall ensure that, where necessary for the purpose of safeguarding the fairness of the proceedings, interpretation is available for communication between suspected or accused persons and their legal counsel in direct connection with any questioning or hearing during the proceedings or with the lodging of an appeal or other procedural applications.

3. The right to interpretation under paragraphs 1 and 2 includes appropriate assistance for persons with hearing or speech impediments.

4. Member States shall ensure that a procedure or mechanism is in place to ascertain whether suspected or accused persons speak and understand the language of the criminal proceedings and whether they need the assistance of an interpreter.

5. Member States shall ensure that, in accordance with procedures in national law, suspected or accused persons have the right to challenge a decision finding that there is no need for interpretation and, when interpretation has been provided, the possibility to complain that the quality of the interpretation is not sufficient to safeguard the fairness of the proceedings.

6. Where appropriate, communication technology such as videoconferencing, telephone or the Internet may be used, unless the physical presence of the interpreter is required in order to safeguard the fairness of the proceedings.

7. In proceedings for the execution of a European arrest warrant, the executing Member State shall ensure that its competent authorities provide persons subject to such proceedings who do not speak or understand the language of the proceedings with interpretation in accordance with this Article.

8. Interpretation provided under this Article shall be of a quality sufficient to safeguard the fairness of the proceedings, in particular by ensuring that suspected or accused persons have knowledge of the case against them and are able to exercise their right of defence.

*Article 3*

**Right to translation of essential documents**

1. Member States shall ensure that suspected or accused persons who do not understand the language of the criminal proceedings concerned are, within a reasonable period of time, provided with a written translation of all documents which are essential to ensure that they are able to exercise their right of defence and to safeguard the fairness of the proceedings.

2. Essential documents shall include any decision depriving a person of his liberty, any charge or indictment, and any judgment.

3. The competent authorities shall, in any given case, decide whether any other document is essential. Suspected or accused persons or their legal counsel may submit a reasoned request to that effect.

4. There shall be no requirement to translate passages of essential documents which are not relevant for the purposes of enabling suspected or accused persons to have knowledge of the case against them.

5. Member States shall ensure that, in accordance with procedures in national law, suspected or accused persons have the right to challenge a decision finding that there is no need for the translation of documents or passages thereof and, when a translation has been provided, the possibility to complain that the quality of the translation is not sufficient to safeguard the fairness of the proceedings.

6. In proceedings for the execution of a European arrest warrant, the executing Member State shall ensure that its competent authorities provide any person subject to such proceedings who does not understand the language in which the European arrest warrant is drawn up, or into which it has been translated by the issuing Member State, with a written translation of that document.

7. As an exception to the general rules established in paragraphs 1, 2, 3 and 6, an oral translation or oral summary of essential documents may be provided instead of a written translation on condition that such oral translation or oral summary does not prejudice the fairness of the proceedings.

8. Any waiver of the right to translation of documents referred to in this Article shall be subject to the requirements that suspected or accused persons have received prior legal advice or have otherwise obtained full knowledge of the consequences of such a waiver, and that the waiver was unequivocal and given voluntarily.

9. Translation provided under this Article shall be of a quality sufficient to safeguard the fairness of the proceedings, in particular by ensuring that suspected or accused persons have knowledge of the case against them and are able to exercise their right of defence.

*Article 4*

**Costs of interpretation and translation**

Member States shall meet the costs of interpretation and translation resulting from the application of Articles 2 and 3, irrespective of the outcome of the proceedings.

*Article 5*

**Quality of the interpretation and translation**

1. Member States shall take concrete measures to ensure that the interpretation and translation provided meets the quality required under Article 2(8) and Article 3(9).

2. In order to promote the adequacy of interpretation and translation and efficient access thereto, Member States shall endeavour to establish a register or registers of independent translators and interpreters who are appropriately qualified. Once established, such register or registers shall, where appropriate, be made available to legal counsel and relevant authorities.

3. Member States shall ensure that interpreters and translators be required to observe confidentiality regarding interpretation and translation provided under this Directive.

*Article 6*

**Training**

Without prejudice to judicial independence and differences in the organisation of the judiciary across the Union, Member States shall request those responsible for the training of judges, prosecutors and judicial staff involved in criminal proceedings to pay special attention to the particularities of communicating with the assistance of an interpreter so as to ensure efficient and effective communication.

*Article 7*

**Record-keeping**

Member States shall ensure that when a suspected or accused person has been subject to questioning or hearings by an investigative or judicial authority with the assistance of an interpreter pursuant to Article 2, when an oral translation or oral summary of essential documents has been provided in the presence of such an authority pursuant to Article 3(7), or when a person has waived the right to translation pursuant to Article 3(8), it will be noted that these events have occurred, using the recording procedure in accordance with the law of the Member State concerned.

*Article 8*

**Non-regression**

Nothing in this Directive shall be construed as limiting or derogating from any of the rights and procedural safeguards that are ensured under the European Convention for the Protection of Human Rights and Fundamental Freedoms, the Charter of Fundamental Rights of the European Union, other relevant provisions of international law or the law of any Member State which provides a higher level of protection.

*Article 9*

**Transposition**

1. Member States shall bring into force the laws, regulations and administrative provisions necessary to comply with this Directive by 27 October 2013.

2. Member States shall transmit the text of those measures to the Commission.

3. When Member States adopt those measures, they shall contain a reference to this Directive or be accompanied by such a reference on the occasion of their official publication. The methods of making such reference shall be laid down by the Member States.

*Article 10*

**Report**

The Commission shall, by 27 October 2014, submit a report to the European Parliament and to the Council, assessing the extent to which the Member States have taken the necessary measures in order to comply with this Directive, accompanied, if necessary, by legislative proposals.

*Article 11*

**Entry into force**

This Directive shall enter into force on the 20th day following its publication in the *Official Journal of the European Union*.

*Article 12*

**Addressees**

This Directive is addressed to the Member States in accordance with the Treaties.

Done at Strasbourg, 20 October 2010.

| | |
|---|---|
| *For the European Parliament* | *For the Council* |
| *The President* | *The President* |
| J. BUZEK | O. CHASTEL |

# Directive 2011/16 on administrative cooperation in the field of taxation and repealing Directive 77/799/EEC, 15 February 2011

[OJ 2011, L 64/1–12]

11.3.2011 EN Official Journal of the European Union L 64/1

I

*(Legislative acts)*

# DIRECTIVES

## COUNCIL DIRECTIVE 2011/16/EU
**of 15 February 2011**
**on administrative cooperation in the field of taxation and repealing Directive 77/799/EEC**

THE COUNCIL OF THE EUROPEAN UNION,

Having regard to the Treaty on the Functioning of the European Union, and in particular Articles 113 and 115 thereof,

Having regard to the proposal from the European Commission,

Having regard to the opinion of the European Parliament ([1]),

Having regard to the opinion of the European Economic and Social Committee ([2]),

Acting in accordance with a special legislative procedure,

Whereas:

(1) The Member States' need for mutual assistance in the field of taxation is growing rapidly in a globalised era. There is a tremendous development of the mobility of taxpayers, of the number of cross-border transactions and of the internationalisation of financial instruments, which makes it difficult for Member States to assess taxes due properly. This increasing difficulty affects the functioning of taxation systems and entails double taxation, which itself incites tax fraud and tax evasion, while the powers of controls remain at national level. It thus jeopardises the functioning of the internal market.

(2) Therefore, a single Member State cannot manage its internal taxation system, especially as regards direct taxation, without receiving information from other Member States. In order to overcome the negative effects of this phenomenon, it is indispensable to develop new administrative cooperation between the Member States' tax administrations. There is a need for instruments likely to create confidence between Member States, by setting up the same rules, obligations and rights for all Member States.

(3) Therefore, a completely new approach should be taken by creating a new text to give Member States the power to efficiently cooperate at international level to overcome the negative effects of an ever-increasing globalisation on the internal market.

(4) In such a context, the existing Council Directive 77/799/EEC of 19 December 1977 concerning mutual assistance by the competent authorities of the Member States in the field of direct taxation and taxation of insurance premiums ([3]) no longer provides for appropriate measures. Its deep weaknesses have been looked into by the Ad hoc Council Working Party on Tax Fraud in its report of 22 May 2000 and more recently by the Commission Communication on Preventing and Combating Corporate and Financial Malpractice of 27 September 2004 and the Commission Communication concerning the need to develop a coordinated strategy to improve the fight against fiscal fraud of 31 May 2006.

(5) Directive 77/799/EEC, even with its later amendments, was designed in a different context to current internal market requirements and is no longer able to meet the new requirements of administrative cooperation.

(6) Due to the number and the importance of adaptations to be made to Directive 77/799/EEC, a mere amendment thereof would not be sufficient to fulfil the objectives described above. Directive 77/799/EEC should therefore be repealed and replaced by a new legal instrument. That instrument should apply to direct taxes and indirect taxes that are not yet covered by other Union legislation. To this end, this new Directive is considered to be the proper instrument in terms of effective administrative cooperation.

([1]) Opinion of 10 February 2010 (not yet published in the Official Journal).
([2]) Opinion of 16 July 2009 (not yet published in the Official Journal).
([3]) OJ L 336, 27.12.1977, p. 15.

(7) This Directive builds on the achievements of Directive 77/799/EEC but provides for clearer and more precise rules governing administrative cooperation between Member States where necessary, in order to establish, especially as regards the exchange of information, a wider scope of administrative cooperation between Member States. Clearer rules should also make it possible in particular to cover all legal and natural persons in the Union, taking into account the ever-increasing range of legal arrangements, including not only traditional arrangements such as trusts, foundations and investment funds, but any new instrument which may be set up by taxpayers in the Member States.

(8) There should be more direct contact between Member States' local or national offices in charge of administrative cooperation, with communication between central liaison offices being the rule. The lack of direct contacts leads to inefficiency, under-use of the arrangements for administrative cooperation and delays in communication. Provision should therefore be made to bring about more direct contacts between services with a view to making cooperation more efficient and faster. The assignment of competences to the liaison departments should be deferred to the national provisions of each Member State.

(9) Member States should exchange information concerning particular cases where requested by another Member State and should make the necessary enquiries to obtain such information. The standard of 'foreseeable relevance' is intended to provide for exchange of information in tax matters to the widest possible extent and, at the same time, to clarify that Member States are not at liberty to engage in 'fishing expeditions' or to request information that is unlikely to be relevant to the tax affairs of a given taxpayer. While Article 20 of this Directive contains procedural requirements, those provisions need to be interpreted liberally in order not to frustrate the effective exchange of information.

(10) It is recognised that the mandatory automatic exchange of information without preconditions is the most effective means of enhancing the correct assessment of taxes in cross-border situations and of fighting fraud. To that end, a step-by-step approach should therefore be followed starting with the automatic exchange of available information on five categories and reviewing the relevant provisions after a report by the Commission.

(11) The spontaneous exchange of information between Member States should also be strengthened and encouraged.

(12) Time limits for the provision of information under this Directive should be laid down in order to ensure that the information exchange is timely and thus effective.

(13) It is important that officials of the tax administration of one Member State are allowed to be present in the territory of another Member State.

(14) Since the tax situation of one or more persons liable to tax established in several Member States is often of common or complementary interest, it should be made possible for simultaneous controls to be carried out on such persons by two or more Member States, by mutual agreement and on a voluntary basis.

(15) In view of the legal requirement in certain Member States that a taxpayer be notified of decisions and instruments concerning his tax liability and of the ensuing difficulties for the tax authorities, including cases where the taxpayer has relocated to another Member State, it is desirable that, in such circumstances, the tax authorities should be able to call upon the cooperation of the competent authorities of the Member State to which the taxpayer has relocated.

(16) Feedback on information sent will encourage administrative cooperation between Member States.

(17) Collaboration between the Member States and the Commission is necessary for the permanent study of cooperation procedures and the sharing of experience and best practices in the fields considered.

(18) It is important for the efficiency of administrative cooperation that information and documents obtained under this Directive could, subject to the restrictions laid down in this Directive, be used by the Member State that received them also for other purposes. It is also important that Member States could transmit that information to a third country, under certain conditions.

(19) The situations in which a requested Member State may refuse to provide information should be clearly defined and limited, taking into account certain private interests which should be protected as well as the public interest.

(20) However, a Member State should not refuse to transmit information because it has no domestic interest or because the information is held by a bank, other financial institution, nominee or person acting in an agency or fiduciary capacity or because it relates to ownership interests in a person.

(21) This Directive contains minimum rules and should therefore not affect Member States' right to enter into wider cooperation with other Member States under their national legislation or in the framework of bilateral or multilateral agreements concluded with other Member States.

(22) It should also be made clear that where a Member State provides a wider cooperation to a third country than is provided for under this Directive, it should not refuse to provide such wider cooperation to other Member States wishing to enter into such mutual wider cooperation.

(23) The exchange of information should be made through standardised forms, formats and channels of communication.

(24) An evaluation of the effectiveness of administrative cooperation should be made, especially on the basis of statistics.

(25) The measures necessary for the implementation of this Directive should be adopted in accordance with Council Decision 1999/468/EC of 28 June 1999 laying down the procedures for the exercise of implementing powers conferred on the Commission (1).

(26) In accordance with point 34 of the Interinstitutional Agreement on better law-making, Member States are encouraged to draw up, for themselves and in the interests of the Union, their own tables illustrating, as far as possible, the correlation between this Directive and the transposition measures, and to make them public.

(27) All exchange of information referred to in this Directive is subject to the provisions implementing Directive 95/46/EC of the European Parliament and of the Council of 24 October 1995 on the protection of individuals with regard to the processing of personal data and on the free movement of such data (2) and to Regulation (EC) No 45/2001 of the European Parliament and of the Council of 18 December 2000 on the protection of individuals with regard to the processing of personal data by the Community institutions and bodies and on the free movement of such data (3). However, it is appropriate to consider limitations of certain rights and obligations laid down by Directive 95/46/EC in order to safeguard the interests referred to in Article 13(1)(e) of that Directive. Such limitations are necessary and proportionate in view of the potential loss of revenue for Member States and the crucial importance of information covered by this Directive for the effectiveness of the fight against fraud.

(28) This Directive respects the fundamental rights and observes the principles which are recognised in particular by the Charter of Fundamental Rights of the European Union.

(29) Since the objective of this Directive, namely the efficient administrative cooperation between Member States to overcome the negative effects of the increasing globalisation on the internal market, cannot be sufficiently achieved by the Member States and can therefore, by reason of the uniformity and effectiveness required, be better achieved at the level of the Union, the Union may adopt measures, in accordance with the principle of subsidiarity as set out in Article 5 of the Treaty on the European Union. In accordance with the principle of proportionality, as set out in that Article, this Directive does not go beyond what is necessary in order to achieve that objective,

HAS ADOPTED THIS DIRECTIVE:

CHAPTER I

**GENERAL PROVISIONS**

*Article 1*

**Subject matter**

1. This Directive lays down the rules and procedures under which the Member States shall cooperate with each other with a view to exchanging information that is foreseeably relevant to the administration and enforcement of the domestic laws of the Member States concerning the taxes referred to in Article 2.

2. This Directive also lays down provisions for the exchange of information referred to in paragraph 1 by electronic means, as well as rules and procedures under which the Member States and the Commission are to cooperate on matters concerning coordination and evaluation.

3. This Directive shall not affect the application in the Member States of the rules on mutual assistance in criminal matters. It shall also be without prejudice to the fulfilment of any obligations of the Member States in relation to wider administrative cooperation ensuing from other legal instruments, including bilateral or multilateral agreements.

*Article 2*

**Scope**

1. This Directive shall apply to all taxes of any kind levied by, or on behalf of, a Member State or the Member State's territorial or administrative subdivisions, including the local authorities.

2. Notwithstanding paragraph 1, this Directive shall not apply to value added tax and customs duties, or to excise duties covered by other Union legislation on administrative cooperation between Member States. This Directive shall also not apply to compulsory social security contributions payable to the Member State or a subdivision of the Member State or to social security institutions established under public law.

(1) OJ L 184, 17.7.1999, p. 23.
(2) OJ L 281, 23.11.1995, p. 31.
(3) OJ L 8, 12.1.2001, p. 1.

3. In no case shall the taxes referred to in paragraph 1 be construed as including:

(a) fees, such as for certificates and other documents issued by public authorities; or

(b) dues of a contractual nature, such as consideration for public utilities.

4. This Directive shall apply to the taxes referred to in paragraph 1 levied within the territory to which the Treaties apply by virtue of Article 52 of the Treaty on the European Union.

*Article 3*

**Definitions**

For the purposes of this Directive the following definitions shall apply:

1. 'competent authority' of a Member State means the authority which has been designated as such by that Member State. When acting pursuant to this Directive, the central liaison office, a liaison department or a competent official shall also be deemed to be competent authorities by delegation according to Article 4;

2. 'central liaison office' means the office which has been designated as such with principal responsibility for contacts with other Member States in the field of administrative cooperation;

3. 'liaison department' means any office other than the central liaison office which has been designated as such to directly exchange information pursuant to this Directive;

4. 'competent official' means any official who is authorised to directly exchange information pursuant to this Directive;

5. 'requesting authority' means the central liaison office, a liaison department or any competent official of a Member State who makes a request for assistance on behalf of the competent authority;

6. 'requested authority' means the central liaison office, a liaison department or any competent official of a Member State who receives a request for assistance on behalf of the competent authority;

7. 'administrative enquiry' means all controls, checks and other action taken by Member States in the performance of their duties with a view to ensuring the proper application of tax legislation;

8. 'exchange of information on request' means the exchange of information based on a request made by the requesting Member State to the requested Member State in a specific case;

9. 'automatic exchange' means the systematic communication of predefined information to another Member State, without prior request, at pre-established regular intervals. In the context of Article 8, available information refers to information in the tax files of the Member State communicating the information, which is retrievable in accordance with the procedures for gathering and processing information in that Member State;

10. 'spontaneous exchange' means the non-systematic communication, at any moment and without prior request, of information to another Member State;

11. 'person' means:

(a) a natural person;

(b) a legal person;

(c) where the legislation in force so provides, an association of persons recognised as having the capacity to perform legal acts but lacking the status of a legal person; or

(d) any other legal arrangement of whatever nature and form, regardless of whether it has legal personality, owning or managing assets, which, including income derived therefrom, are subject to any of the taxes covered by this Directive;

12. 'by electronic means' means using electronic equipment for the processing, including digital compression, and storage of data, and employing wires, radio transmission, optical technologies or other electromagnetic means;

13. 'CCN network' means the common platform based on the common communication network (CCN), developed by the Union for all transmissions by electronic means between competent authorities in the area of customs and taxation.

*Article 4*

**Organisation**

1. Each Member State shall inform the Commission, within one month from 11 March 2011, of its competent authority for the purposes of this Directive and shall inform the Commission without delay of any change thereto.

The Commission shall make the information available to the other Member States and publish a list of the authorities of the Member States in the *Official Journal of the European Union*.

2. The competent authority shall designate a single central liaison office. The competent authority shall be responsible for informing the Commission and the other Member States thereof.

The central liaison office may also be designated as responsible for contacts with the Commission. The competent authority shall be responsible for informing the Commission thereof.

3. The competent authority of each Member State may designate liaison departments with the competence assigned according to its national legislation or policy. The central liaison office shall be responsible for keeping the list of liaison departments up to date and making it available to the central liaison offices of the other Member States concerned and to the Commission.

4. The competent authority of each Member State may designate competent officials. The central liaison office shall be responsible for keeping the list of competent officials up to date and making it available to the central liaison offices of the other Member States concerned and to the Commission.

5. The officials engaged in administrative cooperation pursuant to this Directive shall in any case be deemed to be competent officials for that purpose, in accordance with arrangements laid down by the competent authorities.

6. Where a liaison department or a competent official sends or receives a request or a reply to a request for cooperation, it shall inform the central liaison office of its Member State under the procedures laid down by that Member State.

7. Where a liaison department or a competent official receives a request for cooperation requiring action which falls outside the competence it is assigned according to the national legislation or policy of its Member State, it shall forward such request without delay to the central liaison office of its Member State and inform the requesting authority thereof. In such a case, the period laid down in Article 7 shall start the day after the request for cooperation is forwarded to the central liaison office.

## CHAPTER II

## EXCHANGE OF INFORMATION

### *SECTION I*

### *Exchange of information on request*

*Article 5*

**Procedure for the exchange of information on request**

At the request of the requesting authority, the requested authority shall communicate to the requesting authority any information referred to in Article 1(1) that it has in its possession or that it obtains as a result of administrative enquiries.

*Article 6*

**Administrative enquiries**

1. The requested authority shall arrange for the carrying out of any administrative enquiries necessary to obtain the information referred to in Article 5.

2. The request referred to in Article 5 may contain a reasoned request for a specific administrative enquiry. If the requested authority takes the view that no administrative enquiry is necessary, it shall immediately inform the requesting authority of the reasons thereof.

3. In order to obtain the requested information or to conduct the administrative enquiry requested, the requested authority shall follow the same procedures as it would when acting on its own initiative or at the request of another authority in its own Member State.

4. When specifically requested by the requesting authority, the requested authority shall communicate original documents provided that this is not contrary to the provisions in force in the Member State of the requested authority.

*Article 7*

**Time limits**

1. The requested authority shall provide the information referred to in Article 5 as quickly as possible, and no later than six months from the date of receipt of the request.

However, where the requested authority is already in possession of that information, the information shall be transmitted within two months of that date.

2. In certain special cases, time limits other than those provided for in paragraph 1 may be agreed upon between the requested and the requesting authorities.

3. The requested authority shall confirm immediately and in any event no later than seven working days from receipt, if possible by electronic means, receipt of a request to the requesting authority.

4. Within one month of receipt of the request, the requested authority shall notify the requesting authority of any deficiencies in the request and of the need for any additional background information. In such a case, the time limits provided for in paragraph 1 shall start the day after the requested authority has received the additional information needed.

5. Where the requested authority is unable to respond to the request by the relevant time limit, it shall inform the requesting authority immediately and in any event within three months of the receipt of the request, of the reasons for its failure to do so, and the date by which it considers it might be able to respond.

6. Where the requested authority is not in possession of the requested information and is unable to respond to the request for information or refuses to do so on the grounds provided for in Article 17, it shall inform the requesting authority of the reasons thereof immediately and in any event within one month of receipt of the request.

*SECTION II*

***Mandatory automatic exchange of information***

*Article 8*

**Scope and conditions of mandatory automatic exchange of information**

1. The competent authority of each Member State shall, by automatic exchange, communicate to the competent authority of any other Member State, information regarding taxable periods as from 1 January 2014 that is available concerning residents in that other Member State, on the following specific categories of income and capital as they are to be understood under the national legislation of the Member State which communicates the information:

(a) income from employment;

(b) director's fees;

(c) life insurance products not covered by other Union legal instruments on exchange of information and other similar measures;

(d) pensions;

(e) ownership of and income from immovable property.

2. Before 1 January 2014, Member States shall inform the Commission of the categories listed in paragraph 1 in respect of which they have information available. They shall inform the Commission of any subsequent changes thereto.

3. The competent authority of a Member State may indicate to the competent authority of any other Member State that it does not wish to receive information on the categories of income and capital referred to in paragraph 1, or that it does not wish to receive information on income or capital not exceeding a threshold amount. It shall also inform the Commission thereof. A Member State may be considered as not wishing to receive information in accordance with paragraph 1, if it does not inform the Commission of any single category in respect of which it has information available.

4. Before 1 July 2016, Member States shall provide the Commission on an annual basis with statistics on the volume of automatic exchanges and, to the extent possible, with information on the administrative and other relevant costs and benefits relating to exchanges that have taken place and any potential changes, for both tax administrations and third parties.

5. Before 1 July 2017, the Commission shall submit a report that provides an overview and an assessment of the statistics and information received, on issues such as the administrative and other relevant costs and benefits of the automatic exchange of information, as well as practical aspects linked thereto. If appropriate, the Commission shall present a proposal to the Council regarding the categories of income and capital and/or the conditions laid down in paragraph 1, including the condition that information concerning residents in other Member States has to be available.

When examining a proposal put forward by the Commission, the Council shall assess further strengthening of the efficiency and functioning of the automatic exchange of information and raising the standard thereof, with the aim of providing that:

(a) the competent authority of each Member State shall, by automatic exchange, communicate to the competent authority of any other Member State, information regarding taxable periods as from 1 January 2017 concerning residents in that other Member State, on at least three of the specific categories of income and capital listed in paragraph 1, as they are to be understood under the national legislation of the Member State communicating the information; and

(b) the list of categories in paragraph 1 be extended to include dividends, capital gains and royalties.

6. The communication of information shall take place at least once a year, within six months following the end of the tax year of the Member State during which the information became available.

7. The Commission shall adopt the practical arrangements for the automatic exchange of information, in accordance with the procedure referred to in Article 26(2), before the dates referred to in Article 29(1).

8. Where Member States agree on the automatic exchange of information for additional categories of income and capital in bilateral or multilateral agreements which they conclude with other Member States, they shall communicate those agreements to the Commission which shall make those agreements available to all the other Member States

*SECTION III*

***Spontaneous exchange of information***

*Article 9*

**Scope and conditions of spontaneous exchange of information**

1. The competent authority of each Member State shall communicate the information referred to in Article 1(1) to the competent authority of any other Member State concerned, in any of the following circumstances:

(a) the competent authority of one Member State has grounds for supposing that there may be a loss of tax in the other Member State;

(b) a person liable to tax obtains a reduction in, or an exemption from, tax in one Member State which would give rise to an increase in tax or to liability to tax in the other Member State;

(c) business dealings between a person liable to tax in one Member State and a person liable to tax in the other Member State are conducted through one or more countries in such a way that a saving in tax may result in one or the other Member State or in both;

(d) the competent authority of a Member State has grounds for supposing that a saving of tax may result from artificial transfers of profits within groups of enterprises;

(e) information forwarded to one Member State by the competent authority of the other Member State has enabled information to be obtained which may be relevant in assessing liability to tax in the latter Member State.

2. The competent authorities of each Member State may communicate, by spontaneous exchange, to the competent authorities of the other Member States any information of which they are aware and which may be useful to the competent authorities of the other Member States.

*Article 10*

**Time limits**

1. The competent authority to which information referred to in Article 9(1) becomes available, shall forward that information to the competent authority of any other Member State concerned as quickly as possible, and no later than one month after it becomes available.

2. The competent authority to which information is communicated pursuant to Article 9 shall confirm, if possible by electronic means, the receipt of the information to the competent authority which provided the information immediately and in any event no later than seven working days.

CHAPTER III

**OTHER FORMS OF ADMINISTRATIVE COOPERATION**

*SECTION I*

***Presence in administrative offices and participation in administrative enquiries***

*Article 11*

**Scope and conditions**

1. By agreement between the requesting authority and the requested authority and in accordance with the arrangements laid down by the latter, officials authorised by the requesting authority may, with a view to exchanging the information referred to in Article 1(1):

(a) be present in the offices where the administrative authorities of the requested Member State carry out their duties;

(b) be present during administrative enquiries carried out in the territory of the requested Member State.

Where the requested information is contained in documentation to which the officials of the requested authority have access, the officials of the requesting authority shall be given copies thereof.

2. In so far as this is permitted under the legislation of the requested Member State, the agreement referred to in paragraph 1 may provide that, where officials of the requesting authority are present during administrative enquiries, they may interview individuals and examine records.

Any refusal by the person under investigation to respect the inspection measures of the officials of the requesting authority shall be treated by the requested authority as if that refusal was committed against officials of the latter authority.

3. Officials authorised by the requesting Member State present in another Member State in accordance with paragraph 1 shall at all times be able to produce written authority stating their identity and their official capacity.

*SECTION II*

***Simultaneous controls***

*Article 12*

**Simultaneous controls**

1. Where two or more Member States agree to conduct simultaneous controls, in their own territory, of one or more persons of common or complementary interest to them, with a view to exchanging the information thus obtained, paragraphs 2, 3 and 4 shall apply.

2. The competent authority in each Member State shall identify independently the persons for whom it intends to propose a simultaneous control. It shall notify the competent authority of the other Member States concerned of any cases for which it proposes a simultaneous control, giving reasons for its choice.

It shall specify the period of time during which those controls are to be conducted.

3. The competent authority of each Member State concerned shall decide whether it wishes to take part in simultaneous controls. It shall confirm its agreement or communicate its reasoned refusal to the authority that proposed a simultaneous control.

4. The competent authority of each Member State concerned shall appoint a representative with responsibility for supervising and coordinating the control operation.

*SECTION III*

***Administrative notification***

*Article 13*

**Request for notification**

1. At the request of the competent authority of a Member State, the competent authority of another Member State shall, in accordance with the rules governing the notification of similar instruments in the requested Member State, notify the addressee of any instruments and decisions which emanate from the administrative authorities of the requesting Member State and concern the application in its territory of legislation on taxes covered by this Directive.

2. Requests for notification shall indicate the subject of the instrument or decision to be notified and shall specify the name and address of the addressee, together with any other information which may facilitate identification of the addressee.

3. The requested authority shall inform the requesting authority immediately of its response and, in particular, of the date of notification of the instrument or decision to the addressee.

4. The requesting authority shall only make a request for notification pursuant to this Article when it is unable to notify in accordance with the rules governing the notification of the instruments concerned in the requesting Member State, or where such notification would give rise to disproportionate difficulties. The competent authority of a Member State may notify any document by registered mail or electronically directly to a person within the territory of another Member State.

*SECTION IV*

***Feedback***

*Article 14*

**Conditions**

1. Where a competent authority provides information pursuant to Articles 5 or 9, it may request the competent authority which receives the information to send feedback thereon. If feedback is requested, the competent authority which received the information shall, without prejudice to the rules on tax secrecy and data protection applicable in its Member State, send feedback to the competent authority which provided the information as soon as possible and no later than three months after the outcome of the use of the requested information is known. The Commission shall determine the practical arrangements in accordance with the procedure referred to in Article 26(2).

2. Member States' competent authorities shall send feedback on the automatic exchange of information to the other Member States concerned once a year, in accordance with practical arrangements agreed upon bilaterally.

*SECTION V*

***Sharing of best practices and experience***

*Article 15*

**Scope and conditions**

1. Member States shall, together with the Commission, examine and evaluate administrative cooperation pursuant to this Directive and shall share their experience, with a view to improving such cooperation and, where appropriate, drawing up rules in the fields concerned.

2. Member States may, together with the Commission, produce guidelines on any aspect deemed necessary for sharing best practices and sharing experience.

CHAPTER IV

## CONDITIONS GOVERNING ADMINISTRATIVE COOPERATION

*Article 16*

### Disclosure of information and documents

1. Information communicated between Member States in any form pursuant to this Directive shall be covered by the obligation of official secrecy and enjoy the protection extended to similar information under the national law of the Member State which received it. Such information may be used for the administration and enforcement of the domestic laws of the Member States concerning the taxes referred to in Article 2.

Such information may also be used for the assessment and enforcement of other taxes and duties covered by Article 2 of Council Directive 2010/24/EU of 16 March 2010 concerning mutual assistance for the recovery of claims relating to taxes, duties and other measures [1], or for the assessment and enforcement of compulsory social security contributions.

In addition, it may be used in connection with judicial and administrative proceedings that may involve penalties, initiated as a result of infringements of tax law, without prejudice to the general rules and provisions governing the rights of defendants and witnesses in such proceedings.

2. With the permission of the competent authority of the Member State communicating information pursuant to this Directive, and only in so far as this is allowed under the legislation of the Member State of the competent authority receiving the information, information and documents received pursuant to this Directive may be used for other purposes than those referred to in paragraph 1. Such permission shall be granted if the information can be used for similar purposes in the Member State of the competent authority communicating the information.

3. Where a competent authority of a Member State considers that information which it has received from the competent authority of another Member State is likely to be useful for the purposes referred to in paragraph 1 to the competent authority of a third Member State, it may transmit that information to the latter competent authority, provided that transmission is in accordance with the rules and procedures laid down in this Directive. It shall inform the competent authority of the Member State from which the information originates about its intention to share that information with a third Member State. The Member State of origin of the information may oppose such a sharing of information within 10 working days of receipt of the communication from the Member State wishing to share the information.

4. Permission to use information pursuant to paragraph 2, which has been transmitted pursuant to paragraph 3, may be granted only by the competent authority of the Member State from which the information originates.

5. Information, reports, statements and any other documents, or certified true copies or extracts thereof, obtained by the requested authority and communicated to the requesting authority in accordance with this Directive may be invoked as evidence by the competent bodies of the requesting Member State on the same basis as similar information, reports, statements and any other documents provided by an authority of that Member State.

*Article 17*

### Limits

1. A requested authority in one Member State shall provide a requesting authority in another Member State with the information referred to in Article 5 provided that the requesting authority has exhausted the usual sources of information which it could have used in the circumstances for obtaining the information requested, without running the risk of jeopardising the achievement of its objectives.

2. This Directive shall impose no obligation upon a requested Member State to carry out enquiries or to communicate information, if it would be contrary to its legislation to conduct such inquiries or to collect the information requested for its own purposes.

3. The competent authority of a requested Member State may decline to provide information where the requesting Member State is unable, for legal reasons, to provide similar information.

4. The provision of information may be refused where it would lead to the disclosure of a commercial, industrial or professional secret or of a commercial process, or of information whose disclosure would be contrary to public policy.

5. The requested authority shall inform the requesting authority of the grounds for refusing a request for information.

*Article 18*

### Obligations

1. If information is requested by a Member State in accordance with this Directive, the requested Member State shall use its measures aimed at gathering information to obtain the requested information, even though that Member State may not need such information for its own tax purposes. That obligation is without prejudice to paragraphs 2, 3 and 4 of Article 17, the invocation of which shall in no case be construed as permitting a requested Member State to decline to supply information solely because it has no domestic interest in such information.

[1] OJ L 84, 31.3.2010, p. 1.

2. In no case shall Article 17(2) and (4) be construed as permitting a requested authority of a Member State to decline to supply information solely because this information is held by a bank, other financial institution, nominee or person acting in an agency or a fiduciary capacity or because it relates to ownership interests in a person.

3. Notwithstanding paragraph 2, a Member State may refuse the transmission of requested information where such information concerns taxable periods prior to 1 January 2011 and where the transmission of such information could have been refused on the basis of Article 8(1) of Directive 77/799/EEC if it had been requested before 11 March 2011.

*Article 19*

**Extension of wider cooperation provided to a third country**

Where a Member State provides a wider cooperation to a third country than that provided for under this Directive, that Member State may not refuse to provide such wider cooperation to any other Member State wishing to enter into such mutual wider cooperation with that Member State.

*Article 20*

**Standard forms and computerised formats**

1. Requests for information and for administrative enquiries pursuant to Article 5 and their replies, acknowledgements, requests for additional background information, inability or refusal pursuant to Article 7 shall, as far as possible, be sent using a standard form adopted by the Commission in accordance with the procedure referred to in Article 26(2).

The standard forms may be accompanied by reports, statements and any other documents, or certified true copies or extracts thereof.

2. The standard form referred to in paragraph 1 shall include at least the following information to be provided by the requesting authority:

(a) the identity of the person under examination or investigation;

(b) the tax purpose for which the information is sought.

The requesting authority may, to the extent known and in line with international developments, provide the name and address of any person believed to be in possession of the requested information as well as any element that may facilitate the collection of information by the requested authority.

3. Spontaneous information and its acknowledgement pursuant to Articles 9 and 10 respectively, requests for administrative notifications pursuant to Article 13 and feedback information pursuant to Article 14 shall be sent using the standard form adopted by the Commission in accordance with the procedure referred to in Article 26(2).

4. The automatic exchange of information pursuant to Article 8 shall be sent using a standard computerised format aimed at facilitating such automatic exchange and based on the existing computerised format pursuant to Article 9 of Council Directive 2003/48/EC of 3 June 2003 on taxation of savings income in the form of interest payments [1], to be used for all types of automatic exchange of information, adopted by the Commission in accordance with the procedure referred to in Article 26(2).

*Article 21*

**Practical arrangements**

1. Information communicated pursuant to this Directive shall, as far as possible, be provided by electronic means using the CCN network.

Where necessary, the Commission shall adopt practical arrangements necessary for the implementation of the first subparagraph in accordance with the procedure referred to in Article 26(2).

2. The Commission shall be responsible for whatever development of the CCN network is necessary to permit the exchange of that information between Member States.

Member States shall be responsible for whatever development of their systems is necessary to enable that information to be exchanged using the CCN network.

Member States shall waive all claims for the reimbursement of expenses incurred in applying this Directive except, where appropriate, in respect of fees paid to experts.

3. Persons duly accredited by the Security Accreditation Authority of the Commission may have access to that information only in so far as it is necessary for the care, maintenance and development of the CCN network.

4. Requests for cooperation, including requests for notification, and attached documents may be made in any language agreed between the requested and requesting authority.

Those requests shall be accompanied by a translation into the official language or one of the official languages of the Member State of the requested authority only in special cases when the requested authority states its reason for requesting a translation.

[1] OJ L 157, 26.6.2003, p. 38.

*Article 22*

**Specific obligations**

1. Member States shall take all necessary measures to:

(a) ensure effective internal coordination within the organisation referred to in Article 4;

(b) establish direct cooperation with the authorities of the other Member States referred to in Article 4;

(c) ensure the smooth operation of the administrative cooperation arrangements provided for in this Directive.

2. The Commission shall communicate to each Member State any general information concerning the implementation and application of this Directive which it receives and which it is able to provide.

CHAPTER V

**RELATIONS WITH THE COMMISSION**

*Article 23*

**Evaluation**

1. Member States and the Commission shall examine and evaluate the functioning of the administrative cooperation provided for in this Directive.

2. Member States shall communicate to the Commission any relevant information necessary for the evaluation of the effectiveness of administrative cooperation in accordance with this Directive in combating tax evasion and tax avoidance.

3. Member States shall communicate to the Commission a yearly assessment of the effectiveness of the automatic exchange of information referred to in Article 8 as well as the practical results achieved. The form and the conditions of communication of that yearly assessment shall be adopted by the Commission in accordance with the procedure referred to in Article 26(2).

4. The Commission shall, in accordance with the procedure referred to in Article 26(2), determine a list of statistical data which shall be provided by the Member States for the purposes of evaluation of this Directive.

5. Information communicated to the Commission under paragraphs 2, 3 and 4 shall be kept confidential by the Commission in accordance with the provisions applicable to Union authorities.

6. Information communicated to the Commission by a Member State under paragraphs 2, 3 and 4, as well as any report or document produced by the Commission using such information, may be transmitted to other Member States. Such transmitted information shall be covered by the obligation of official secrecy and enjoy the protection extended to similar information under the national law of the Member State which received it.

Reports and documents produced by the Commission referred to in this paragraph may only be used by the Member States for analytical purposes but shall not be published or made available to any other person or body without express agreement of the Commission.

CHAPTER VI

**RELATIONS WITH THIRD COUNTRIES**

*Article 24*

**Exchange of information with third countries**

1. Where the competent authority of a Member State receives from a third country information that is foreseeably relevant to the administration and enforcement of the domestic laws of that Member State concerning the taxes referred to in Article 2, that authority may, in so far as this is allowed pursuant to an agreement with that third country, provide that information to the competent authorities of Member States for which that information might be useful and to any requesting authorities.

2. Competent authorities may communicate, in accordance with their domestic provisions on the communication of personal data to third countries, information obtained in accordance with this Directive to a third country, provided that all of the following conditions are met:

(a) the competent authority of the Member State from which the information originates have consented to that communication;

(b) the third country concerned has given an undertaking to provide the cooperation required to gather evidence of the irregular or illegal nature of transactions which appear to contravene or constitute an abuse of tax legislation.

CHAPTER VII

**GENERAL AND FINAL PROVISIONS**

*Article 25*

**Data protection**

All exchange of information pursuant to this Directive shall be subject to the provisions implementing Directive 95/46/EC. However, Member States shall, for the purpose of the correct application of this Directive, restrict the scope of the obligations and rights provided for in Article 10, Article 11(1), Articles 12 and 21 of Directive 95/46/EC to the extent required in order to safeguard the interests referred to in Article 13(1)(e) of that Directive.

*Article 26*

**Committee**

1. The Commission shall be assisted by a committee referred to as the 'Committee on Administrative Cooperation for Taxation'.

2. Where reference is made to this paragraph, Articles 5 and 7 of Decision 1999/468/EC shall apply.

The period laid down in Article 5(6) of Decision 1999/468/EC shall be set at three months.

*Article 27*

**Reporting**

Every five years after 1 January 2013, the Commission shall submit a report on the application of this Directive to the European Parliament and to the Council.

*Article 28*

**Repeal of Directive 77/799/EEC**

Directive 77/799/EEC is repealed with effect from 1 January 2013.

References made to the repealed Directive shall be construed as references to this Directive.

*Article 29*

**Transposition**

1. Member States shall bring into force the laws, regulations and administrative provisions necessary to comply with this Directive with effect from 1 January 2013.

However, they shall bring into force the laws, regulations and administrative provisions necessary to comply with Article 8 of this Directive with effect from 1 January 2015.

They shall forthwith inform the Commission thereof.

When Member States adopt those measures, they shall contain a reference to this Directive or shall be accompanied by such a reference on the occasion of their official publication. The methods of making such reference shall be laid down by the Member States.

2. Member States shall communicate to the Commission the text of the main provisions of national law which they adopt in the field covered by this Directive.

*Article 30*

**Entry into force**

This Directive shall enter into force on the day of its publication in the *Official Journal of the European Union*.

*Article 31*

**Addressees**

This Directive is addressed to the Member States.

Done at Brussels, 15 February 2011.

*For the Council*

*The President*

MATOLCSY Gy.

# Directive 2011/36 on preventing and combating trafficking in human beings and protecting its victims, and replacing Council Framework Decision 2002/629, 5 April 2011

**[OJ 2011, L 101/1–11]**

15.4.2011 EN Official Journal of the European Union L 101/1

I

*(Legislative acts)*

# DIRECTIVES

## DIRECTIVE 2011/36/EU OF THE EUROPEAN PARLIAMENT AND OF THE COUNCIL

**of 5 April 2011**

**on preventing and combating trafficking in human beings and protecting its victims, and replacing Council Framework Decision 2002/629/JHA**

THE EUROPEAN PARLIAMENT AND THE COUNCIL OF THE EUROPEAN UNION,

Having regard to the Treaty on the Functioning of the European Union, and in particular Article 82(2) and Article 83(1) thereof,

Having regard to the proposal from the European Commission,

Having regard to the opinion of the European Economic and Social Committee [1],

After consulting the Committee of the Regions,

After transmission of the draft legislative act to the national parliaments,

Acting in accordance with the ordinary legislative procedure [2],

Whereas:

(1) Trafficking in human beings is a serious crime, often committed within the framework of organised crime, a gross violation of fundamental rights and explicitly prohibited by the Charter of Fundamental Rights of the European Union. Preventing and combating trafficking in human beings is a priority for the Union and the Member States.

(2) This Directive is part of global action against trafficking in human beings, which includes action involving third countries as stated in the 'Action-oriented Paper on strengthening the Union external dimension on action against trafficking in human beings; Towards global EU action against trafficking in human beings' approved by the Council on 30 November 2009. In this context, action should be pursued in third countries of origin and transfer of victims, with a view to raising awareness, reducing vulnerability, supporting and assisting victims, fighting the root causes of trafficking and supporting those third countries in developing appropriate anti-trafficking legislation.

(3) This Directive recognises the gender-specific phenomenon of trafficking and that women and men are often trafficked for different purposes. For this reason, assistance and support measures should also be gender-specific where appropriate. The 'push' and 'pull' factors may be different depending on the sectors concerned, such as trafficking in human beings into the sex industry or for labour exploitation in, for example, construction work, the agricultural sector or domestic servitude.

(4) The Union is committed to the prevention of and fight against trafficking in human beings, and to the protection of the rights of trafficked persons. For this purpose, Council Framework Decision 2002/629/JHA of 19 July 2002 on combating trafficking in human beings [3], and an EU Plan on best practices, standards and procedures for combating and preventing trafficking in human beings [4] were adopted. Moreover, the Stockholm Programme — An open and secure Europe serving and protecting citizens [5], adopted by the European Council, gives a clear priority to the fight against trafficking in human beings. Other measures should be envisaged, such as support for the development of general common indicators of the Union for the identification of victims of trafficking, through the exchange of best practices between all the relevant actors, particularly public and private social services.

[1] Opinion of 21 October 2010 (not yet published in the Official Journal).
[2] Position of the European Parliament of 14 December 2010 (not yet published in the Official Journal) and decision of the Council of 21 March 2011.

[3] OJ L 203, 1.8.2002, p. 1.
[4] OJ C 311, 9.12.2005, p. 1.
[5] OJ C 115, 4.5.2010, p. 1.

(5) The law enforcement authorities of the Member States should continue to cooperate in order to strengthen the fight against trafficking in human beings. In this regard, close cross-border cooperation, including the sharing of information and the sharing of best practices, as well as a continued open dialogue between the police, judicial and financial authorities of the Member States, is essential. The coordination of investigations and prosecutions of cases of trafficking in human beings should be facilitated by enhanced cooperation with Europol and Eurojust, the setting-up of joint investigation teams, as well as by the implementation of Council Framework Decision 2009/948/JHA of 30 November 2009 on prevention and settlement of conflict of jurisdiction in criminal proceedings (1).

(6) Member States should encourage and work closely with civil society organisations, including recognised and active non-governmental organisations in this field working with trafficked persons, in particular in policy-making initiatives, information and awareness-raising campaigns, research and education programmes and in training, as well as in monitoring and evaluating the impact of anti-trafficking measures.

(7) This Directive adopts an integrated, holistic, and human rights approach to the fight against trafficking in human beings and when implementing it, Council Directive 2004/81/EC of 29 April 2004 on the residence permit issued to third-country nationals who are victims of trafficking in human beings or who have been the subject of an action to facilitate illegal immigration, who cooperate with the competent authorities (2) and Directive 2009/52/EC of the European Parliament and of the Council of 18 June 2009 providing for minimum standards on sanctions and measures against employers of illegally staying third-country nationals (3) should be taken into consideration. More rigorous prevention, prosecution and protection of victims' rights, are major objectives of this Directive. This Directive also adopts contextual understandings of the different forms of trafficking and aims at ensuring that each form is tackled by means of the most efficient measures.

(8) Children are more vulnerable than adults and therefore at greater risk of becoming victims of trafficking in human beings. In the application of this Directive, the child's best interests must be a primary consideration, in accordance with the Charter of Fundamental Rights of the European Union and the 1989 United Nations Convention on the Rights of the Child.

(9) The 2000 United Nations Protocol to Prevent, Suppress and Punish Trafficking in Persons, Especially Women and Children, supplementing the United Nations Convention against Transnational Organised Crime and the 2005 Council of Europe Convention on Action against Trafficking in Human Beings are crucial steps in the process of enhancing international cooperation against trafficking in human beings. It should be noted that the Council of Europe Convention contains an evaluation mechanism, composed of the Group of experts on action against trafficking in human beings (GRETA) and the Committee of the Parties. Coordination between international organisations with competence with regard to action against trafficking in human beings should be supported in order to avoid duplication of effort.

(10) This Directive is without prejudice to the principle of non-refoulement in accordance with the 1951 Convention relating to the Status of Refugees (Geneva Convention), and is in accordance with Article 4 and Article 19(2) of the Charter of Fundamental Rights of the European Union.

(11) In order to tackle recent developments in the phenomenon of trafficking in human beings, this Directive adopts a broader concept of what should be considered trafficking in human beings than under Framework Decision 2002/629/JHA and therefore includes additional forms of exploitation. Within the context of this Directive, forced begging should be understood as a form of forced labour or services as defined in the 1930 ILO Convention No 29 concerning Forced or Compulsory Labour. Therefore, the exploitation of begging, including the use of a trafficked dependent person for begging, falls within the scope of the definition of trafficking in human beings only when all the elements of forced labour or services occur. In the light of the relevant case-law, the validity of any possible consent to perform such labour or services should be evaluated on a case-by-case basis. However, when a child is concerned, no possible consent should ever be considered valid. The expression 'exploitation of criminal activities' should be understood as the exploitation of a person to commit, inter alia, pick-pocketing, shop-lifting, drug trafficking and other similar activities which are subject to penalties and imply financial gain. The definition also covers trafficking in human beings for the purpose of the removal of organs, which constitutes a serious violation of human dignity and physical integrity, as well as, for instance, other behaviour such as illegal adoption or forced marriage in so far as they fulfil the constitutive elements of trafficking in human beings.

(12) The levels of penalties in this Directive reflect the growing concern among Member States regarding the development of the phenomenon of trafficking in human beings. For this reason this Directive uses as a basis levels 3 and 4 of the Council conclusions of 24-25 April 2002 on the approach to apply regarding

(1) OJ L 328, 15.12.2009, p. 42.
(2) OJ L 261, 6.8.2004, p. 19.
(3) OJ L 168, 30.6.2009, p. 24.

approximation of penalties. When the offence is committed in certain circumstances, for example against a particularly vulnerable victim, the penalty should be more severe. In the context of this Directive, particularly vulnerable persons should include at least all children. Other factors that could be taken into account when assessing the vulnerability of a victim include, for example, gender, pregnancy, state of health and disability. When the offence is particularly grave, for example when the life of the victim has been endangered or the offence has involved serious violence such as torture, forced drug/medication usage, rape or other serious forms of psychological, physical or sexual violence, or has otherwise caused particularly serious harm to the victim, this should also be reflected in a more severe penalty. When, under this Directive, a reference is made to surrender, such reference should be interpreted in accordance with Council Framework Decision 2002/584/JHA of 13 June 2002 on the European arrest warrant and the surrender procedures between Member States [1]. The gravity of the offence committed could be taken into account within the framework of the execution of the sentence.

(13) In combating trafficking in human beings, full use should be made of existing instruments on the seizure and confiscation of the proceeds of crime, such as the United Nations Convention against Transnational Organised Crime and the Protocols thereto, the 1990 Council of Europe Convention on Laundering, Search, Seizure and Confiscation of the Proceeds from Crime, Council Framework Decision 2001/500/JHA of 26 June 2001 on money laundering, the identification, tracing, freezing, seizing and confiscation of instrumentalities and the proceeds of crime [2], and Council Framework Decision 2005/212/JHA of 24 February 2005 on Confiscation of Crime-Related Proceeds, Instrumentalities and Property [3]. The use of seized and confiscated instrumentalities and the proceeds from the offences referred to in this Directive to support victims' assistance and protection, including compensation of victims and Union trans-border law enforcement counter-trafficking activities, should be encouraged.

(14) Victims of trafficking in human beings should, in accordance with the basic principles of the legal systems of the relevant Member States, be protected from prosecution or punishment for criminal activities such as the use of false documents, or offences under legislation on prostitution or immigration, that they have been compelled to commit as a direct consequence of being subject to trafficking. The aim of such protection is to safeguard the human rights of victims, to avoid further victimisation and to encourage them to act as witnesses in criminal proceedings against the perpetrators. This safeguard should not exclude prosecution or punishment for offences that a person has voluntarily committed or participated in.

(1) OJ L 190, 18.7.2002, p. 1.
(2) OJ L 182, 5.7.2001, p. 1.
(3) OJ L 68, 15.3.2005, p. 49.

(15) To ensure the success of investigations and prosecutions of human trafficking offences, their initiation should not depend, in principle, on reporting or accusation by the victim. Where the nature of the act calls for it, prosecution should be allowed for a sufficient period of time after the victim has reached the age of majority. The length of the sufficient period of time for prosecution should be determined in accordance with respective national law. Law enforcement officials and prosecutors should be adequately trained, in particular with a view to enhancing international law enforcement and judicial cooperation. Those responsible for investigating and prosecuting such offences should also have access to the investigative tools used in organised crime or other serious crime cases. Such tools could include the interception of communications, covert surveillance including electronic surveillance, the monitoring of bank accounts and other financial investigations.

(16) In order to ensure effective prosecution of international criminal groups whose centre of activity is in a Member State and which carry out trafficking in human beings in third countries, jurisdiction should be established over the offence of trafficking in human beings where the offender is a national of that Member State, and the offence is committed outside the territory of that Member State. Similarly, jurisdiction could also be established where the offender is an habitual resident of a Member State, the victim is a national or an habitual resident of a Member State, or the offence is committed for the benefit of a legal person established in the territory of a Member State, and the offence is committed outside the territory of that Member State.

(17) While Directive 2004/81/EC provides for the issue of a residence permit to victims of trafficking in human beings who are third-country nationals, and Directive 2004/38/EC of the European Parliament and of the Council of 29 April 2004 on the rights of the citizens of the Union and their family members to move and reside freely within the territory of the Member States [4] regulates the exercise of the right to move and reside freely in the territory of the Member States by citizens of the Union and their families, including protection from expulsion, this Directive establishes specific protective measures for any victim of trafficking in human beings. Consequently, this Directive does not deal with the conditions of the residence of the victims of trafficking in human beings in the territory of the Member States.

(18) It is necessary for victims of trafficking in human beings to be able to exercise their rights effectively. Therefore assistance and support should be available to them before, during and for an appropriate time after criminal proceedings. Member States should provide for resources to support victim assistance, support and protection. The assistance and support provided should

(4) OJ L 158, 30.4.2004, p. 77.

include at least a minimum set of measures that are necessary to enable the victim to recover and escape from their traffickers. The practical implementation of such measures should, on the basis of an individual assessment carried out in accordance with national procedures, take into account the circumstances, cultural context and needs of the person concerned. A person should be provided with assistance and support as soon as there is a reasonable-grounds indication for believing that he or she might have been trafficked and irrespective of his or her willingness to act as a witness. In cases where the victim does not reside lawfully in the Member State concerned, assistance and support should be provided unconditionally at least during the reflection period. If, after completion of the identification process or expiry of the reflection period, the victim is not considered eligible for a residence permit or does not otherwise have lawful residence in that Member State, or if the victim has left the territory of that Member State, the Member State concerned is not obliged to continue providing assistance and support to that person on the basis of this Directive. Where necessary, assistance and support should continue for an appropriate period after the criminal proceedings have ended, for example if medical treatment is ongoing due to the severe physical or psychological consequences of the crime, or if the victim's safety is at risk due to the victim' s statements in those criminal proceedings.

(19) Council Framework Decision 2001/220/JHA of 15 March 2001 on the standing of victims in criminal proceedings ([1]) establishes a set of victims' rights in criminal proceedings, including the right to protection and compensation. In addition, victims of trafficking in human beings should be given access without delay to legal counselling and, in accordance with the role of victims in the relevant justice systems, to legal representation, including for the purpose of claiming compensation. Such legal counselling and representation could also be provided by the competent authorities for the purpose of claiming compensation from the State. The purpose of legal counselling is to enable victims to be informed and receive advice about the various possibilities open to them. Legal counselling should be provided by a person having received appropriate legal training without necessarily being a lawyer. Legal counselling and, in accordance with the role of victims in the relevant justice systems, legal representation should be provided free of charge, at least when the victim does not have sufficient financial resources, in a manner consistent with the internal procedures of Member States. As child victims in particular are unlikely to have such resources, legal counselling and legal representation would in practice be free of charge for them. Furthermore, on the basis of an individual risk assessment carried out in accordance with national procedures, victims should be protected from retaliation, from intimidation, and from the risk of being re-trafficked.

(20) Victims of trafficking who have already suffered the abuse and degrading treatment which trafficking commonly entails, such as sexual exploitation, sexual abuse, rape, slavery-like practices or the removal of organs, should be protected from secondary victimisation and further trauma during the criminal proceedings. Unnecessary repetition of interviews during investigation, prosecution and trial should be avoided, for instance, where appropriate, through the production, as soon as possible in the proceedings, of video recordings of those interviews. To this end victims of trafficking should during criminal investigations and proceedings receive treatment that is appropriate to their individual needs. The assessment of their individual needs should take into consideration circumstances such as their age, whether they are pregnant, their health, a disability they may have and other personal circumstances, as well as the physical and psychological consequences of the criminal activity to which the victim was subjected. Whether and how the treatment is applied is to be decided in accordance with grounds defined by national law, rules of judicial discretion, practice and guidance, on a case-by-case basis.

(21) Assistance and support measures should be provided to victims on a consensual and informed basis. Victims should therefore be informed of the important aspects of those measures and they should not be imposed on the victims. A victim's refusal of assistance or support measures should not entail obligations for the competent authorities of the Member State concerned to provide the victim with alternative measures.

(22) In addition to measures available to all victims of trafficking in human beings, Member States should ensure that specific assistance, support and protective measures are available to child victims. Those measures should be provided in the best interests of the child and in accordance with the 1989 United Nations Convention on the Rights of the Child. Where the age of a person subject to trafficking is uncertain, and there are reasons to believe it is less than 18 years, that person should be presumed to be a child and receive immediate assistance, support and protection. Assistance and support measures for child victims should focus on their physical and psycho-social recovery and on a durable solution for the person in question. Access to education would help children to be reintegrated into society. Given that child victims of trafficking are particularly vulnerable, additional protective measures should be available to protect them during interviews forming part of criminal investigations and proceedings.

(23) Particular attention should be paid to unaccompanied child victims of trafficking in human beings, as they need specific assistance and support due to their situation of particular vulnerability. From the moment an unaccompanied child victim of trafficking in human beings is identified and until a durable solution is found, Member States should apply reception measures appropriate to the needs of the child and should ensure that relevant procedural safeguards apply. The necessary measures should be taken to ensure that, where appropriate, a guardian and/or a representative are appointed

([1]) OJ L 82, 22.3.2001, p. 1.

in order to safeguard the minor's best interests. A decision on the future of each unaccompanied child victim should be taken within the shortest possible period of time with a view to finding durable solutions based on an individual assessment of the best interests of the child, which should be a primary consideration. A durable solution could be return and reintegration into the country of origin or the country of return, integration into the host society, granting of international protection status or granting of other status in accordance with national law of the Member States.

(24) When, in accordance with this Directive, a guardian and/or a representative are to be appointed for a child, those roles may be performed by the same person or by a legal person, an institution or an authority.

(25) Member States should establish and/or strengthen policies to prevent trafficking in human beings, including measures to discourage and reduce the demand that fosters all forms of exploitation, and measures to reduce the risk of people becoming victims of trafficking in human beings, by means of research, including research into new forms of trafficking in human beings, information, awareness-raising, and education. In such initiatives, Member States should adopt a gender perspective and a child-rights approach. Officials likely to come into contact with victims or potential victims of trafficking in human beings should be adequately trained to identify and deal with such victims. That training obligation should be promoted for members of the following categories when they are likely to come into contact with victims: police officers, border guards, immigration officials, public prosecutors, lawyers, members of the judiciary and court officials, labour inspectors, social, child and health care personnel and consular staff, but could, depending on local circumstances, also involve other groups of public officials who are likely to encounter trafficking victims in their work.

(26) Directive 2009/52/EC provides for sanctions for employers of illegally staying third-country nationals who, while not having been charged with or convicted of trafficking in human beings, use work or services exacted from a person with the knowledge that that person is a victim of such trafficking. In addition, Member States should take into consideration the possibility of imposing sanctions on the users of any service exacted from a victim, with the knowledge that the person has been trafficked. Such further criminalisation could cover the behaviour of employers of legally staying third-country nationals and Union citizens, as well as buyers of sexual services from any trafficked person, irrespective of their nationality.

(27) National monitoring systems such as national rapporteurs or equivalent mechanisms should be established by Member States, in the way in which they consider appropriate according to their internal organisation, and taking into account the need for a minimum structure with identified tasks, in order to carry out assessments of trends in trafficking in human beings, gather statistics, measure the results of anti-trafficking actions, and regularly report. Such national rapporteurs or equivalent mechanisms are already constituted in an informal Union Network established by the Council Conclusions on establishing an informal EU Network of National Rapporteurs or Equivalent Mechanisms on Trafficking in Human Beings of 4 June 2009. An anti-trafficking coordinator would take part in the work of that Network, which provides the Union and the Member States with objective, reliable, comparable and up-to-date strategic information in the field of trafficking in human beings and exchanges experience and best practices in the field of preventing and combating trafficking in human beings at Union level. The European Parliament should be entitled to participate in the joint activities of the national rapporteurs or equivalent mechanisms.

(28) In order to evaluate the results of anti-trafficking action, the Union should continue to develop its work on methodologies and data collection methods to produce comparable statistics.

(29) In the light of the Stockholm Programme and with a view to developing a consolidated Union strategy against trafficking in human beings aimed at further strengthening the commitment of, and efforts made, by the Union and the Member States to prevent and combat such trafficking, Member States should facilitate the tasks of an anti-trafficking coordinator, which may include for example improving coordination and coherence, avoiding duplication of effort, between Union institutions and agencies as well as between Member States and international actors, contributing to the development of existing or new Union policies and strategies relevant to the fight against trafficking in human beings or reporting to the Union institutions.

(30) This Directive aims to amend and expand the provisions of Framework Decision 2002/629/JHA. Since the amendments to be made are of substantial number and nature, the Framework Decision should in the interests of clarity be replaced in its entirety in relation to Member States participating in the adoption of this Directive.

(31) In accordance with point 34 of the Interinstitutional Agreement on better law-making ([1]), Member States are encouraged to draw up, for themselves and in the interest of the Union, their own tables which will, as far as possible, illustrate the correlation between this Directive and the transposition measures, and to make them public.

([1]) OJ C 321, 31.12.2003, p. 1.

(32) Since the objective of this Directive, namely to fight against trafficking in human beings, cannot be sufficiently achieved by the Member States and can therefore, by reason of the scale and effects of the action be better achieved at Union level, the Union may adopt measures in accordance with the principle of subsidiarity as set out in Article 5 of the Treaty on European Union. In accordance with the principle of proportionality, as set out in that Article, this Directive does not go beyond what is necessary to achieve that objective.

(33) This Directive respects fundamental rights and observes the principles recognised in particular by the Charter of Fundamental Rights of the European Union and notably human dignity, the prohibition of slavery, forced labour and trafficking in human beings, the prohibition of torture and inhuman or degrading treatment or punishment, the rights of the child, the right to liberty and security, freedom of expression and information, the protection of personal data, the right to an effective remedy and to a fair trial and the principles of the legality and proportionality of criminal offences and penalties. In particular, this Directive seeks to ensure full respect for those rights and principles and must be implemented accordingly.

(34) In accordance with Article 3 of the Protocol on the position of the United Kingdom and Ireland in respect of the area of freedom, security and justice, annexed to the Treaty on European Union and the Treaty on the Functioning of the European Union, Ireland has notified its wish to take part in the adoption and application of this Directive.

(35) In accordance with Articles 1 and 2 of the Protocol on the position of the United Kingdom and Ireland in respect of the area of freedom, security and justice, annexed to the Treaty on European Union and to the Treaty on the Functioning of the European Union, and without prejudice to Article 4 of that Protocol, the United Kingdom is not taking part in the adoption of this Directive and is not bound by it or subject to its application.

(36) In accordance with Articles 1 and 2 of the Protocol on the position of Denmark annexed to the Treaty on European Union and to the Treaty on the Functioning of the European Union, Denmark is not taking part in the adoption of this Directive and is not bound by it or subject to its application,

HAVE ADOPTED THIS DIRECTIVE:

*Article 1*

**Subject matter**

This Directive establishes minimum rules concerning the definition of criminal offences and sanctions in the area of trafficking in human beings. It also introduces common provisions, taking into account the gender perspective, to strengthen the prevention of this crime and the protection of the victims thereof.

*Article 2*

**Offences concerning trafficking in human beings**

1. Member States shall take the necessary measures to ensure that the following intentional acts are punishable:

The recruitment, transportation, transfer, harbouring or reception of persons, including the exchange or transfer of control over those persons, by means of the threat or use of force or other forms of coercion, of abduction, of fraud, of deception, of the abuse of power or of a position of vulnerability or of the giving or receiving of payments or benefits to achieve the consent of a person having control over another person, for the purpose of exploitation.

2. A position of vulnerability means a situation in which the person concerned has no real or acceptable alternative but to submit to the abuse involved.

3. Exploitation shall include, as a minimum, the exploitation of the prostitution of others or other forms of sexual exploitation, forced labour or services, including begging, slavery or practices similar to slavery, servitude, or the exploitation of criminal activities, or the removal of organs.

4. The consent of a victim of trafficking in human beings to the exploitation, whether intended or actual, shall be irrelevant where any of the means set forth in paragraph 1 has been used.

5. When the conduct referred to in paragraph 1 involves a child, it shall be a punishable offence of trafficking in human beings even if none of the means set forth in paragraph 1 has been used.

6. For the purpose of this Directive, 'child' shall mean any person below 18 years of age.

*Article 3*

**Incitement, aiding and abetting, and attempt**

Member States shall take the necessary measures to ensure that inciting, aiding and abetting or attempting to commit an offence referred to in Article 2 is punishable.

*Article 4*

**Penalties**

1. Member States shall take the necessary measures to ensure that an offence referred to in Article 2 is punishable by a maximum penalty of at least five years of imprisonment.

2. Member States shall take the necessary measures to ensure that an offence referred to in Article 2 is punishable by a maximum penalty of at least 10 years of imprisonment where that offence:

(a) was committed against a victim who was particularly vulnerable, which, in the context of this Directive, shall include at least child victims;

(b) was committed within the framework of a criminal organisation within the meaning of Council Framework Decision 2008/841/JHA of 24 October 2008 on the fight against organised crime ([1]);

(c) deliberately or by gross negligence endangered the life of the victim; or

(d) was committed by use of serious violence or has caused particularly serious harm to the victim.

3. Member States shall take the necessary measures to ensure that the fact that an offence referred to in Article 2 was committed by public officials in the performance of their duties is regarded as an aggravating circumstance.

4. Member States shall take the necessary measures to ensure that an offence referred to in Article 3 is punishable by effective, proportionate and dissuasive penalties, which may entail surrender.

*Article 5*

**Liability of legal persons**

1. Member States shall take the necessary measures to ensure that legal persons can be held liable for the offences referred to in Articles 2 and 3 committed for their benefit by any person, acting either individually or as part of an organ of the legal person, who has a leading position within the legal person, based on:

(a) a power of representation of the legal person;

(b) an authority to take decisions on behalf of the legal person; or

(c) an authority to exercise control within the legal person.

2. Member States shall also ensure that a legal person can be held liable where the lack of supervision or control, by a person referred to in paragraph 1, has made possible the commission of the offences referred to in Articles 2 and 3 for the benefit of that legal person by a person under its authority.

3. Liability of a legal person under paragraphs 1 and 2 shall not exclude criminal proceedings against natural persons who are perpetrators, inciters or accessories in the offences referred to in Articles 2 and 3.

4. For the purpose of this Directive, 'legal person' shall mean any entity having legal personality under the applicable law, except for States or public bodies in the exercise of State authority and for public international organisations.

*Article 6*

**Sanctions on legal persons**

Member States shall take the necessary measures to ensure that a legal person held liable pursuant to Article 5(1) or (2) is subject to effective, proportionate and dissuasive sanctions, which shall include criminal or non-criminal fines and may include other sanctions, such as:

(a) exclusion from entitlement to public benefits or aid;

(b) temporary or permanent disqualification from the practice of commercial activities;

(c) placing under judicial supervision;

(d) judicial winding-up;

(e) temporary or permanent closure of establishments which have been used for committing the offence.

*Article 7*

**Seizure and confiscation**

Member States shall take the necessary measures to ensure that their competent authorities are entitled to seize and confiscate instrumentalities and proceeds from the offences referred to in Articles 2 and 3.

*Article 8*

**Non-prosecution or non-application of penalties to the victim**

Member States shall, in accordance with the basic principles of their legal systems, take the necessary measures to ensure that competent national authorities are entitled not to prosecute or impose penalties on victims of trafficking in human beings for their involvement in criminal activities which they have been compelled to commit as a direct consequence of being subjected to any of the acts referred to in Article 2.

*Article 9*

**Investigation and prosecution**

1. Member States shall ensure that investigation into or prosecution of offences referred to in Articles 2 and 3 is not dependent on reporting or accusation by a victim and that criminal proceedings may continue even if the victim has withdrawn his or her statement.

2. Member States shall take the necessary measures to enable, where the nature of the act calls for it, the prosecution of an offence referred to in Articles 2 and 3 for a sufficient period of time after the victim has reached the age of majority.

3. Member States shall take the necessary measures to ensure that persons, units or services responsible for investigating or prosecuting the offences referred to in Articles 2 and 3 are trained accordingly.

4. Member States shall take the necessary measures to ensure that effective investigative tools, such as those which are used in organised crime or other serious crime cases are available to persons, units or services responsible for investigating or prosecuting the offences referred to in Articles 2 and 3.

([1]) OJ L 300, 11.11.2008, p. 42.

*Article 10*

**Jurisdiction**

1. Member States shall take the necessary measures to establish their jurisdiction over the offences referred to in Articles 2 and 3 where:

(a) the offence is committed in whole or in part within their territory; or

(b) the offender is one of their nationals.

2. A Member State shall inform the Commission where it decides to establish further jurisdiction over the offences referred to in Articles 2 and 3 committed outside its territory, inter alia, where:

(a) the offence is committed against one of its nationals or a person who is an habitual resident in its territory;

(b) the offence is committed for the benefit of a legal person established in its territory; or

(c) the offender is an habitual resident in its territory.

3. For the prosecution of the offences referred to in Articles 2 and 3 committed outside the territory of the Member State concerned, each Member State shall, in those cases referred to in point (b) of paragraph 1, and may, in those cases referred to in paragraph 2, take the necessary measures to ensure that its jurisdiction is not subject to either of the following conditions:

(a) the acts are a criminal offence at the place where they were performed; or

(b) the prosecution can be initiated only following a report made by the victim in the place where the offence was committed, or a denunciation from the State of the place where the offence was committed.

*Article 11*

**Assistance and support for victims of trafficking in human beings**

1. Member States shall take the necessary measures to ensure that assistance and support are provided to victims before, during and for an appropriate period of time after the conclusion of criminal proceedings in order to enable them to exercise the rights set out in Framework Decision 2001/220/JHA, and in this Directive.

2. Member States shall take the necessary measures to ensure that a person is provided with assistance and support as soon as the competent authorities have a reasonable-grounds indication for believing that the person might have been subjected to any of the offences referred to in Articles 2 and 3.

3. Member States shall take the necessary measures to ensure that assistance and support for a victim are not made conditional on the victim's willingness to cooperate in the criminal investigation, prosecution or trial, without prejudice to Directive 2004/81/EC or similar national rules.

4. Member States shall take the necessary measures to establish appropriate mechanisms aimed at the early identification of, assistance to and support for victims, in cooperation with relevant support organisations.

5. The assistance and support measures referred to in paragraphs 1 and 2 shall be provided on a consensual and informed basis, and shall include at least standards of living capable of ensuring victims' subsistence through measures such as the provision of appropriate and safe accommodation and material assistance, as well as necessary medical treatment including psychological assistance, counselling and information, and translation and interpretation services where appropriate.

6. The information referred to in paragraph 5 shall cover, where relevant, information on a reflection and recovery period pursuant to Directive 2004/81/EC, and information on the possibility of granting international protection pursuant to Council Directive 2004/83/EC of 29 April 2004 on minimum standards for the qualification and status of third country nationals or stateless persons as refugees or as persons who otherwise need international protection and the content of the protection granted [1] and Council Directive 2005/85/EC of 1 December 2005 on minimum standards on procedures in Member States for granting and withdrawing refugee status [2] or pursuant to other international instruments or other similar national rules.

7. Member States shall attend to victims with special needs, where those needs derive, in particular, from whether they are pregnant, their health, a disability, a mental or psychological disorder they have, or a serious form of psychological, physical or sexual violence they have suffered.

*Article 12*

**Protection of victims of trafficking in human beings in criminal investigation and proceedings**

1. The protection measures referred to in this Article shall apply in addition to the rights set out in Framework Decision 2001/220/JHA.

2. Member States shall ensure that victims of trafficking in human beings have access without delay to legal counselling, and, in accordance with the role of victims in the relevant justice system, to legal representation, including for the purpose of claiming compensation. Legal counselling and legal representation shall be free of charge where the victim does not have sufficient financial resources.

(1) OJ L 304, 30.9.2004, p. 12.
(2) OJ L 326, 13.12.2005, p. 13.

15.4.2011 EN Official Journal of the European Union L 101/9

3. Member States shall ensure that victims of trafficking in human beings receive appropriate protection on the basis of an individual risk assessment, inter alia, by having access to witness protection programmes or other similar measures, if appropriate and in accordance with the grounds defined by national law or procedures.

4. Without prejudice to the rights of the defence, and according to an individual assessment by the competent authorities of the personal circumstances of the victim, Member States shall ensure that victims of trafficking in human beings receive specific treatment aimed at preventing secondary victimisation by avoiding, as far as possible and in accordance with the grounds defined by national law as well as with rules of judicial discretion, practice or guidance, the following:

(a) unnecessary repetition of interviews during investigation, prosecution or trial;

(b) visual contact between victims and defendants including during the giving of evidence such as interviews and cross-examination, by appropriate means including the use of appropriate communication technologies;

(c) the giving of evidence in open court; and

(d) unnecessary questioning concerning the victim's private life.

*Article 13*

**General provisions on assistance, support and protection measures for child victims of trafficking in human beings**

1. Child victims of trafficking in human beings shall be provided with assistance, support and protection. In the application of this Directive the child's best interests shall be a primary consideration.

2. Member States shall ensure that, where the age of a person subject to trafficking in human beings is uncertain and there are reasons to believe that the person is a child, that person is presumed to be a child in order to receive immediate access to assistance, support and protection in accordance with Articles 14 and 15.

*Article 14*

**Assistance and support to child victims**

1. Member States shall take the necessary measures to ensure that the specific actions to assist and support child victims of trafficking in human beings, in the short and long term, in their physical and psycho-social recovery, are undertaken following an individual assessment of the special circumstances of each particular child victim, taking due account of the child's views, needs and concerns with a view to finding a durable solution for the child. Within a reasonable time, Member States shall provide access to education for child victims and the children of victims who are given assistance and support in accordance with Article 11, in accordance with their national law.

2. Members States shall appoint a guardian or a representative for a child victim of trafficking in human beings from the moment the child is identified by the authorities where, by national law, the holders of parental responsibility are, as a result of a conflict of interest between them and the child victim, precluded from ensuring the child's best interest and/or from representing the child.

3. Member States shall take measures, where appropriate and possible, to provide assistance and support to the family of a child victim of trafficking in human beings when the family is in the territory of the Member States. In particular, Member States shall, where appropriate and possible, apply Article 4 of Framework Decision 2001/220/JHA to the family.

4. This Article shall apply without prejudice to Article 11.

*Article 15*

**Protection of child victims of trafficking in human beings in criminal investigations and proceedings**

1. Member States shall take the necessary measures to ensure that in criminal investigations and proceedings, in accordance with the role of victims in the relevant justice system, competent authorities appoint a representative for a child victim of trafficking in human beings where, by national law, the holders of parental responsibility are precluded from representing the child as a result of a conflict of interest between them and the child victim.

2. Member States shall, in accordance with the role of victims in the relevant justice system, ensure that child victims have access without delay to free legal counselling and to free legal representation, including for the purpose of claiming compensation, unless they have sufficient financial resources.

3. Without prejudice to the rights of the defence, Member States shall take the necessary measures to ensure that in criminal investigations and proceedings in respect of any of the offences referred to in Articles 2 and 3:

(a) interviews with the child victim take place without unjustified delay after the facts have been reported to the competent authorities;

(b) interviews with the child victim take place, where necessary, in premises designed or adapted for that purpose;

(c) interviews with the child victim are carried out, where necessary, by or through professionals trained for that purpose;

(d) the same persons, if possible and where appropriate, conduct all the interviews with the child victim;

(e) the number of interviews is as limited as possible and interviews are carried out only where strictly necessary for the purposes of criminal investigations and proceedings;

(f) the child victim may be accompanied by a representative or, where appropriate, an adult of the child's choice, unless a reasoned decision has been made to the contrary in respect of that person.

4. Member States shall take the necessary measures to ensure that in criminal investigations of any of the offences referred to in Articles 2 and 3 all interviews with a child victim or, where appropriate, with a child witness, may be video recorded and that such video recorded interviews may be used as evidence in criminal court proceedings, in accordance with the rules under their national law.

5. Member States shall take the necessary measures to ensure that in criminal court proceedings relating to any of the offences referred to in Articles 2 and 3, it may be ordered that:

(a) the hearing take place without the presence of the public; and

(b) the child victim be heard in the courtroom without being present, in particular, through the use of appropriate communication technologies.

6. This Article shall apply without prejudice to Article 12.

*Article 16*

**Assistance, support and protection for unaccompanied child victims of trafficking in human beings**

1. Member States shall take the necessary measures to ensure that the specific actions to assist and support child victims of trafficking in human beings, as referred to in Article 14(1), take due account of the personal and special circumstances of the unaccompanied child victim.

2. Member States shall take the necessary measures with a view to finding a durable solution based on an individual assessment of the best interests of the child.

3. Member States shall take the necessary measures to ensure that, where appropriate, a guardian is appointed to unaccompanied child victims of trafficking in human beings.

4. Member States shall take the necessary measures to ensure that, in criminal investigations and proceedings, in accordance with the role of victims in the relevant justice system, competent authorities appoint a representative where the child is unaccompanied or separated from its family.

5. This Article shall apply without prejudice to Articles 14 and 15.

*Article 17*

**Compensation to victims**

Member States shall ensure that victims of trafficking in human beings have access to existing schemes of compensation to victims of violent crimes of intent.

*Article 18*

**Prevention**

1. Member States shall take appropriate measures, such as education and training, to discourage and reduce the demand that fosters all forms of exploitation related to trafficking in human beings.

2. Member States shall take appropriate action, including through the Internet, such as information and awareness-raising campaigns, research and education programmes, where appropriate in cooperation with relevant civil society organisations and other stakeholders, aimed at raising awareness and reducing the risk of people, especially children, becoming victims of trafficking in human beings.

3. Member States shall promote regular training for officials likely to come into contact with victims or potential victims of trafficking in human beings, including front-line police officers, aimed at enabling them to identify and deal with victims and potential victims of trafficking in human beings.

4. In order to make the preventing and combating of trafficking in human beings more effective by discouraging demand, Member States shall consider taking measures to establish as a criminal offence the use of services which are the objects of exploitation as referred to in Article 2, with the knowledge that the person is a victim of an offence referred to in Article 2.

*Article 19*

**National rapporteurs or equivalent mechanisms**

Member States shall take the necessary measures to establish national rapporteurs or equivalent mechanisms. The tasks of such mechanisms shall include the carrying out of assessments of trends in trafficking in human beings, the measuring of results of anti-trafficking actions, including the gathering of statistics in close cooperation with relevant civil society organisations active in this field, and reporting.

*Article 20*

**Coordination of the Union strategy against trafficking in human beings**

In order to contribute to a coordinated and consolidated Union strategy against trafficking in human beings, Member States shall facilitate the tasks of an anti-trafficking coordinator (ATC). In particular, Member States shall transmit to the ATC the information referred to in Article 19, on the basis of which the ATC shall contribute to reporting carried out by the Commission every two years on the progress made in the fight against trafficking in human beings.

*Article 21*

**Replacement of Framework Decision 2002/629/JHA**

Framework Decision 2002/629/JHA on combating trafficking in human beings is hereby replaced in relation to Member States participating in the adoption of this Directive, without prejudice to the obligations of the Member States relating to the time limit for transposition of the Framework Decision into national law.

In relation to Member States participating in the adoption of this Directive, references to the Framework Decision 2002/629/JHA shall be construed as references to this Directive.

*Article 22*

**Transposition**

1. Member States shall bring into force the laws, regulations and administrative provisions necessary to comply with this Directive by 6 April 2013.

2. Member States shall transmit to the Commission the text of the provisions transposing into their national law the obligations imposed on them under this Directive.

3. When Member States adopt these measures, they shall contain a reference to this Directive or shall be accompanied by such a reference on the occasion of their official publication. The methods of making such reference shall be laid down by the Member States.

*Article 23*

**Reporting**

1. The Commission shall, by 6 April 2015, submit a report to the European Parliament and the Council, assessing the extent to which the Member States have taken the necessary measures in order to comply with this Directive, including a description of action taken under Article 18(4), accompanied, if necessary, by legislative proposals.

2. The Commission shall, by 6 April 2016, submit a report to the European Parliament and the Council, assessing the impact of existing national law, establishing as a criminal offence the use of services which are the objects of exploitation of trafficking in human beings, on the prevention of trafficking in human beings, accompanied, if necessary, by adequate proposals.

*Article 24*

**Entry into force**

This Directive shall enter into force on the day of its publication in the *Official Journal of the European Union*.

*Article 25*

**Addressees**

This Directive is addressed to the Member States in accordance with the Treaties.

Done at Strasbourg, 5 April 2011.

| *For the European Parliament* | *For the Council* |
|---|---|
| *The President* | *The President* |
| J. BUZEK | GYŐRI E. |

18.10.2011 EN Official Journal of the European Union L 271/49

**COMMISSION DECISION**

**of 14 October 2011**

**on the request by the United Kingdom to accept Directive 2011/36/EU of the European Parliament and of the Council on preventing and combating trafficking in human beings and protecting its victims, and replacing Council Framework Decision 2002/629/JHA**

*(notified under document C(2011) 7228)*

**(Only the English text is authentic)**

(2011/692/EU)

THE EUROPEAN COMMISSION,

Having regard to the Treaty on the Functioning of the European Union, and in particular Article 331(1) thereof,

Whereas:

(1) The European Parliament and the Council adopted on 5 April 2011 Directive 2011/36/EU on preventing and combating trafficking in human beings and protecting its victims, and replacing Council Framework Decision 2002/629/JHA [1].

(2) Pursuant to Articles 1 and 2 of the Protocol on the position of the United Kingdom and Ireland in respect of the Area of Freedom, Security and Justice, annexed to the Treaty on European Union and to the Treaty on the Functioning of the European Union, the United Kingdom did not take part in the adoption of the Directive and is not bound by it or subject to its application.

(3) In accordance with Article 4 of the said Protocol, the United Kingdom notified the Commission by letter of 14 July 2011 of its intention to accept the Directive,

HAS ADOPTED THIS DECISION:

*Article 1*

Directive 2011/36/EU shall apply to the United Kingdom.

*Article 2*

Directive 2011/36/EU shall come into force for the United Kingdom from the date of notification of this Decision.

*Article 3*

This Decision is addressed to the United Kingdom of Great Britain and Northern Ireland.

Done at Brussels, 14 October 2011.

*For the Commission*

Cecilia MALMSTRÖM

*Member of the Commission*

[1] OJ L 101, 15.4.2011, p. 1.

# Agreement between the European Union and the Republic of Mauritius on the conditions of transfer of suspected pirates and associated seized property from the European Union-led naval force to the Republic of Mauritius and on the conditions of suspected pirates after transfer, 14 July 2011

**[OJ 2011, L 254/3–6]**

30.9.2011 EN Official Journal of the European Union L 254/3

# AGREEMENT

## between the European Union and the Republic of Mauritius on the conditions of transfer of suspected pirates and associated seized property from the European Union-led naval force to the Republic of Mauritius and on the conditions of suspected pirates after transfer

THE EUROPEAN UNION (EU),

of the one part, and

THE REPUBLIC OF MAURITIUS,

hereinafter referred to as 'Mauritius',

of the other part,

together hereinafter referred to as the 'Parties',

TAKING INTO ACCOUNT:

— United Nations (UN) Security Council Resolutions (UNSCR) 1814 (2008), 1838 (2008), 1846 (2008), 1851 (2008) and successor UNSCRs,

— the 1982 UN Convention on the Law of the Sea (UNCLOS), in particular Articles 100 to 107 and Article 110 thereof,

— EU Council Joint Action 2008/851/CFSP of 10 November 2008 on a European Union military operation to contribute to the deterrence, prevention and repression of acts of piracy and armed robbery off the Somali coast ([1]) (Operation EUNAVFOR Atalanta), as amended by Council Decision 2009/907/CFSP of 8 December 2009 ([2]),

— International Human Rights Law, including the 1966 International Covenant on Civil and Political Rights, and the 1984 Convention against Torture and Other Cruel, Inhuman or Degrading Treatment or Punishment,

— that this Agreement will not affect the Parties' rights and obligations under international agreements and other instruments establishing international courts and tribunals, including the Statute of the International Criminal Court,

HAVE AGREED AS FOLLOWS:

*Article 1*

**Aim**

This Agreement defines the conditions and modalities for

(a) the transfer of persons suspected of attempting to commit, committing or having committed acts of piracy within the area of operation of EUNAVFOR, on the high seas off the territorial seas of Mauritius, Madagascar, the Comoros Islands, Seychelles and Réunion Island, and detained by EUNAVFOR;

(b) the transfer of associated property seized by EUNAVFOR from EUNAVFOR to Mauritius; and

(c) the treatment of transferred persons.

([1]) OJ L 301, 12.11.2008, p. 33, as corrected in OJ L 253, 25.9.2009, p. 18.
([2]) OJ L 322, 9.12.2009, p. 27.

*Article 2*

**Definitions**

For the purposes of this Agreement:

(a) '*European Union-led naval force (EUNAVFOR)*' shall mean EU military headquarters and national contingents contributing to the EU operation 'Atalanta', their ships, aircrafts and assets;

(b) '*Operation*' shall mean the preparation, establishment, execution and support of the military mission established by EU Council Joint Action 2008/851/CFSP and/or its successors;

(c) '*national contingents*' shall mean units and ships belonging to the Member States of the European Union and, as indicated by the EU, to other States participating in the operation;

(d) '*Sending State*' shall mean a State providing a national contingent for EUNAVFOR;

L 254/4 EN Official Journal of the European Union 30.9.2011

(e) '*piracy*' shall mean piracy as defined in Article 101 of UNCLOS;

(f) '*transferred person*' shall mean any person suspected of attempting to commit, committing or having committed acts of piracy, transferred by EUNAVFOR to Mauritius under this Agreement.

*Article 3*

**General principles**

1. Mauritius may accept, upon request by EUNAVFOR, the transfer of persons detained by EUNAVFOR in connection with piracy and associated property seized by EUNAVFOR and submit such persons and property to its competent authorities for the purpose of investigation and prosecution. Agreement on acceptance of a proposed handover will be made on a case to case basis by Mauritius, taking into account all relevant circumstances including the location of the incident.

2. EUNAVFOR shall only transfer persons to the competent law enforcement authorities of Mauritius.

3. Transfer shall not be carried out before the competent law enforcement authorities of Mauritius decide within 5 working days as of the date of receipt of evidence as forwarded by EUNAVFOR that there are reasonable prospects of securing a conviction of persons detained by EUNAVFOR.

4. The decision as to whether there are reasonable prospects of securing a conviction shall be taken by the competent law enforcement authorities of Mauritius on the basis of evidence forwarded by EUNAVFOR through relevant communication channels.

5. Any transferred person shall be treated humanely and in accordance with international human rights obligations, embodied in the Constitution of Mauritius, including the prohibition of torture and cruel, inhumane and degrading treatment or punishment, the prohibition of arbitrary detention and in accordance with the requirement to have a fair trial.

*Article 4*

**Treatment, prosecution and trial of transferred persons**

1. In accordance with international human rights obligations, embodied in the Constitution of Mauritius, any transferred person shall be treated humanely and shall not be subjected to torture or cruel, inhuman or degrading treatment or punishment, shall receive adequate accommodation, nourishment and access to medical treatment and shall be able to carry out religious observance.

2. Any transferred person shall be brought promptly before a judge or other officer authorised by law to exercise judicial power, who shall decide without delay on the lawfulness of his detention and shall order his release if the detention is not justified.

3. Any transferred person shall be entitled to trial within a reasonable time or to release.

4. In the determination of any criminal charge against him, any transferred person shall be entitled to a fair and public hearing by a competent, independent and impartial tribunal established by law.

5. Any transferred person charged with a criminal offence shall be presumed innocent until proved guilty according to law.

6. In the determination of any criminal charge against him, every transferred person shall be entitled to the following minimum guarantees, in full equality:

(a) to be informed promptly and in detail in a language which he understands of the nature and cause of the charge against him;

(b) to have adequate time and facilities for the preparation of his defence and to communicate with counsel of his own choice;

(c) to be tried without undue delay;

(d) to be tried in his presence, and to defend himself in person or through legal assistance of his own choice; to be informed, if he does not have legal assistance, of this right; and to have legal assistance assigned to him, in any case where the interests of justice so require, and without payment by him in any such case if he does not have sufficient means to pay for it;

(e) to examine, or have examined, all evidence against him, including affidavits of witnesses who conducted the arrest, and to obtain the attendance and examination of witnesses on his behalf under the same conditions as witnesses against him;

(f) to have the free assistance of an interpreter if he cannot understand or speak the language used in court;

(g) not to be compelled to testify against himself or to confess guilt.

7. Any transferred person convicted of a crime shall be permitted to have the right to his conviction and sentence reviewed by, or appealed to, a higher tribunal in accordance with the law of Mauritius.

8. Mauritius may, after consultation with the EU, transfer such persons convicted and serving sentence in Mauritius to another State guaranteeing the respect of the above mentioned human rights standards, with a view to serving the remainder of the sentence in that other State. In case of serious

concerns about the human rights situation in that other State, no transfer shall take place before a satisfactory solution will have been found through consultations between the Parties to address the concerns expressed.

*Article 5*

**Death penalty**

No transferred person shall, in accordance with Mauritius Abolition of Death Penalty Act, be charged with an offence that carries the death penalty, be sentenced to death or be the subject of an application of the death penalty.

*Article 6*

**Records and notifications**

1. Any transfer shall be the subject of an appropriate document signed by a representative of EUNAVFOR and a representative of the competent Mauritius law enforcement authorities.

2. EUNAVFOR shall provide detention records to Mauritius with regard to any transferred person. These records shall include, so far as possible, the physical condition of the transferred person while in detention, the time of transfer to Mauritius authorities, the reason for his detention, the time and place of the commencement of his detention, and any decisions taken with regard to his detention.

3. Mauritius shall be responsible for keeping an accurate account of all transferred persons, including but not limited to keeping records of any seized property, the persons' physical condition, the location of their places of detention, any charges against them and any significant decisions taken in the course of their prosecution and trial.

4. These records shall be available to representatives of the EU and EUNAVFOR upon request in writing to the Mauritius Ministry of Foreign Affairs.

5. In addition, Mauritius shall notify the EU and EUNAVFOR of the place of detention of any person transferred under this Agreement, of any deterioration of his physical condition and of any allegations of alleged improper treatment. Representatives of the EU and EUNAVFOR shall have access to any persons transferred under this Agreement as long as such persons are in custody and shall be entitled to question them.

6. National and international humanitarian agencies shall, at their request, be allowed to visit persons transferred under this Agreement.

7. For the purposes of ensuring that EUNAVFOR is able to provide timely assistance to Mauritius with attendance of witnesses from EUNAVFOR and the provision of relevant evidence, Mauritius shall notify EUNAVFOR of its intention to initiate criminal trial proceedings against any transferred person and the timetable for provision of evidence, and the hearing of evidence.

*Article 7*

**EU and EUNAVFOR assistance**

1. EUNAVFOR, within its means and capabilities, shall provide all assistance to Mauritius with a view to the investigation and prosecution of transferred persons.

2. In particular, EUNAVFOR shall:

(a) hand over detention records drawn up pursuant to Article 6(2) of this Agreement;

(b) process any evidence in accordance with the requirements of the competent authorities of Mauritius as agreed in the implementing arrangements described in Article 10;

(c) produce statements or affidavits by witnesses belonging to EUNAVFOR involved in any incident in relation to which persons have been transferred under this Agreement;

(d) endeavour to produce statements of witnesses or affidavits by other witnesses who are not in Mauritius;

(e) preserve or hand over all relevant seized property, exhibits, photographs and any article of evidential value in the possession of EUNAVFOR;

(f) secure the attendance of witnesses belonging to EUNAVFOR, where necessary, for the purpose of giving evidence in Court (or by live TV link or any other approved technological means) during the trial;

(g) facilitate the attendance of other witnesses, where necessary, for the purpose of giving evidence in Court (or by live TV link or any other approved technological means) during the trial;

(h) facilitate the attendance of such interpreters as may be required by the Mauritius competent authorities for the purpose of assisting in investigations and trials involving transferred persons.

3. As far as such resources are not provided through other financial donors, the Parties shall develop, subject to the applicable procedures, implementing arrangements on financial, technical and other assistance to enable the transfer, detention, investigation, prosecution and trial of transferred persons. These implementing arrangements shall also aim at covering technical and logistical assistance to Mauritius in the fields of revision of legislation, training of investigators and prosecutors, investigative and judicial procedures, and particularly, arrangements for storage and handing-over of evidence and appeal procedures. In addition, these implementing arrangements shall aim at providing for the repatriation of transferred persons in case of acquittal or non-prosecution, their transfer for completion of sentence in another State or their repatriation after serving their prison sentence in Mauritius.

L 254/6 EN Official Journal of the European Union 30.9.2011

*Article 8*

**Relationship to other rights of transferred persons**

Nothing in this Agreement is intended to derogate, or may be construed as derogating, from any rights that a transferred person may have under applicable domestic or international law.

*Article 9*

**Liaison and disputes**

1. All issues arising in connection with the application of this Agreement shall be examined jointly by Mauritius and EU competent authorities.

2. Failing any prior settlement, disputes concerning the interpretation or application of this Agreement shall be settled exclusively by diplomatic means between Mauritius and EU representatives.

*Article 10*

**Implementing arrangements**

1. For the purposes of the application of this Agreement, operational, administrative and technical matters may be the subject of implementing arrangements to be concluded between competent Mauritius authorities on the one hand and the competent EU authorities, as well as the competent authorities of the Sending States, on the other hand.

2. Implementing arrangements may cover, inter alia:

(a) the identification of competent law enforcement authorities of Mauritius to whom EUNAVFOR may transfer persons;

(b) the detention facilities where transferred persons will be held;

(c) the handling of documents, including those related to the gathering of evidence, which will be handed over to the competent law enforcement authorities of Mauritius upon transfer of a person;

(d) points of contact for notifications;

(e) forms to be used for transfers;

(f) the provision of technical support, expertise, training and other assistance referred to in Article 7 upon request by Mauritius in order to achieve the objectives of this Agreement.

*Article 11*

**Entry into force and termination**

1. This Agreement shall be applied provisionally as from the date on which it is signed and it shall enter into force when each of the Parties has notified the other that it has completed its internal procedure for the ratification of the Agreement.

2. This Agreement shall remain in force until termination of the Operation as notified by EUNAVFOR. Nevertheless, either Party may, by written notification, denounce this Agreement. The denunciation shall take effect 6 months after the date of receipt of the notification. In the event that the EU consider that the immediate denunciation of this Agreement is justified on grounds of a modification of Mauritius' substantive criminal legislation as mentioned in this Agreement, the EU shall be entitled to denounce the Agreement with effect from the date of sending of the notification. Any change in Mauritius' substantive criminal legislation shall not adversely affect persons already transferred pursuant to this Agreement.

3. This Agreement may be amended by written agreement between the Parties.

4. Termination of this Agreement shall not affect any rights or obligations arising out of the execution of this Agreement before such termination, including the rights of any transferred persons as long as they are held in custody or are prosecuted by Mauritius.

5. After the termination of the Operation, all rights of EUNAVFOR under this Agreement may be exercised by any person or entity designated by the EU High Representative for Foreign Affairs and Security Policy. This designated person or entity may, inter alia, be the Head or staff member of the EU delegation to Mauritius or a diplomatic agent or consular official of an EU Member State accredited to Mauritius. After the termination of the Operation, all notifications that were to be made to EUNAVFOR under this Agreement shall be made to the EU High Representative for Foreign Affairs and Security Policy.

Done at Port Louis on 14 July 2011 in two originals, each in the English language.

*For the European Union* *For Mauritius*

# Agreement between the European Union and Australia on the processing and transfer of Passenger Name Record (PNR) data by air carriers to the Australian Customs and Border Protection Service, 29 September 2011

**[OJ 2012, L 186/4–16]**

L 186/4 EN Official Journal of the European Union 14.7.2012

**AGREEMENT**

**between the European Union and Australia on the processing and transfer of Passenger Name Record (PNR) data by air carriers to the Australian Customs and Border Protection Service**

THE EUROPEAN UNION, hereafter also referred to as the EU,

of the one part, and

AUSTRALIA,

of the other part,

Together hereinafter referred to as 'the Parties',

DESIRING to prevent and combat terrorism and serious transnational crime effectively as a means of protecting their respective democratic societies and common values;

SEEKING to enhance and encourage cooperation between the Parties in the spirit of the EU-Australian partnership;

RECOGNISING that information sharing is a fundamental component of the fight against terrorism and serious transnational crime, and that in this context the use of Passenger Name Record (PNR) data is an essential tool;

RECOGNISING the importance of preventing and combating terrorism and serious transnational crime, while respecting fundamental rights and freedoms, in particular, privacy and the protection of personal data;

MINDFUL of Article 6 of the Treaty on European Union on respect for fundamental rights, the right to privacy with regard to the processing of personal data as stipulated in Article 16 of the Treaty on the Functioning of the European Union, the principles of proportionality and necessity concerning the right to private and family life, the respect for privacy, and the protection of personal data under Article 8 of the European Convention on the Protection of Human Rights and Fundamental Freedoms, Council of Europe Convention No 108 for the Protection of Individuals with regard to Automatic Processing of Personal Data and its additional Protocol 181, Articles 7 and 8 of the Charter of Fundamental Rights of the European Union and Article 17 of the International Covenant on Civil and Political Rights on the right to privacy;

RECOGNISING that, in 2008, Australia and the EU signed the Agreement Between the European Union and Australia on the Processing and Transfer of European Union – Sourced Passenger Name Record (PNR) Data by Air Carriers to the Australian Customs Service which is applied provisionally from the time of signature but has not entered into force;

NOTING that the European Parliament decided on 5 May 2010 to postpone the vote on the request for consent to that Agreement and by its Resolution of 11 November 2010 welcomed the recommendation from the European Commission to the Council of the European Union to negotiate a new agreement;

RECOGNISING the relevant provisions of the Australian *Customs Act 1901* (Cth) (the Customs Act), and in particular section 64AF thereof whereby, if requested, all international passenger air service operators, flying to, from or through Australia, are required to provide the Australian Customs and Border Protection Service with PNR data, to the extent that they are collected and contained in the air carrier's reservations and departure control systems, in a particular manner and form;

RECOGNISING that the Australian *Customs Administration Act 1985* (Cth), *Migration Act 1958* (Cth), *Crimes Act 1914* (Cth), *Privacy Act 1988* (Cth), *Freedom of Information Act 1982* (Cth), *Auditor-General Act 1997* (Cth), *Ombudsman Act 1976* (Cth) and *Public Service Act 1999* (Cth) provide for data protection, rights of access and redress, rectification and annotation and remedies and sanctions for misuse of personal data;

NOTING the commitment of Australia that the Australian Customs and Border Protection Service processes PNR data strictly for the purpose of preventing, detecting, investigating and prosecuting terrorist offences and serious transnational crime in strict compliance with safeguards on privacy and the protection of personal data, as set out in this Agreement;

14.7.2012 EN Official Journal of the European Union L 186/5

STRESSING the importance of sharing of analytical data obtained from PNR by Australia with police and judicial authorities of Member States of the European Union, and Europol or Eurojust, as a means to foster international police and judicial cooperation;

AFFIRMING that this Agreement does not constitute a precedent for any future arrangements between Australia and the European Union, or between either of the Parties and any State, regarding the processing and transfer of PNR data or any other form of data and noting that the necessity and feasibility of similar arrangements for sea passengers may be examined,

HAVE AGREED AS FOLLOWS:

CHAPTER I

## GENERAL PROVISIONS

*Article 1*

### Purpose of Agreement

To ensure the security and safety of the public this Agreement provides for the transfer of EU-sourced PNR data to the Australian Customs and Border Protection Service. This Agreement stipulates the conditions under which such data may be transferred and used, and the manner in which the data shall be protected.

*Article 2*

### Definitions

For the purposes of this Agreement:

(a) 'Agreement' shall mean this Agreement and its Annexes, and any amendments thereto;

(b) 'personal data' shall mean any information relating to an identified or identifiable natural person: an identifiable person is one who can be identified, directly or indirectly, in particular by reference to an identification number or to one or more factors specific to his physical, physiological, mental, economic, cultural or social identity;

(c) 'processing' shall mean any operation or set of operations which is performed upon PNR data, whether or not by automatic means, such as collection, recording, organisation, retention, adaptation or alteration, retrieval, consultation, use, disclosure by transmission or transfer, dissemination or otherwise making available, alignment or combination, blocking, erasure or destruction;

(d) 'air carriers' shall mean air carriers that have reservation systems and/or PNR data processed in the territory of the European Union and operate passenger flights in international air transportation to, from or through Australia;

(e) 'reservation systems' shall mean an air carrier's reservation system, departure control system or equivalent systems providing the same functionalities;

(f) 'Passenger Name Record data' or 'PNR data' shall mean the information processed in the EU by air carriers on each passenger's travel requirements as listed in Annex 1 which contains the information necessary for processing and control of reservations by the booking and participating air carriers;

(g) 'passenger' shall mean passenger or crew member including the captain;

(h) 'sensitive data' shall mean any personal data revealing racial or ethnic origin, political opinions, religious or philosophical beliefs, trade union membership, or health or sex life.

*Article 3*

### Scope of application

1. Australia shall ensure that the Australian Customs and Border Protection Service processes PNR data received pursuant to this Agreement strictly for the purpose of preventing, detecting, investigating and prosecuting terrorist offences or serious transnational crime:

2. Terrorist offences shall include:

(a) acts of a person that involve violence, or are otherwise dangerous to human life or create a risk of damage to property or infrastructure, and which, given their nature and context, are reasonably believed to be committed with the aim of:

(i) intimidating or coercing a population;

(ii) intimidating, compelling, or coercing a government or international organisation to act or abstain from acting;

(iii) seriously destabilising or destroying the fundamental political, constitutional, economic, or social structures of a country or an international organisation;

(b) assisting, sponsoring or providing financial, material or technological support for, or financial or other services to or in support of, acts described in subparagraph (a);

(c) providing or collecting funds, by any means, directly or indirectly, with the intention that they should be used or in the knowledge that they are to be used, in full or in part, in order to carry out any of the acts described in subparagraphs (a) or (b); or

(d) aiding, abetting, or attempting acts described in subparagraphs (a), (b) or (c).

3. Serious transnational crime shall mean any offence punishable in Australia by a custodial sentence or a detention order for a maximum period of at least four years or a more serious penalty and as it is defined by the Australian law, if the crime is transnational in nature. A crime is considered as transnational in nature in particular if:

(a) it is committed in more than one country;

(b) it is committed in one country but a substantial part of its preparation, planning, direction or control takes place in another country;

(c) it is committed in one country but involves an organised criminal group that engages in criminal activities in more than one country; or

(d) it is committed in one country but has substantial effects in another country.

4. In exceptional cases, PNR data may be processed by Australia where necessary for the protection of the vital interests of any individual, such as risk of death, serious injury or threat to health.

5. In addition, for the purpose of supervision and accountability of public administration and the facilitation of redress and sanctions for the misuse of data, PNR data may be processed on a case-by-case basis where such processing is specifically required by Australian law.

*Article 4*

**Ensuring provision of PNR data**

1. Air carriers shall provide PNR data contained in their reservation systems to the Australian Customs and Border Protection Service. They shall not be prevented by any provision of the law of either Party from complying with relevant Australian law which obliges them to so provide the data.

2. Australia shall not require air carriers to provide PNR data elements which are not already collected or held in their reservation systems.

3. Should PNR data transferred by air carriers include data beyond those listed in Annex 1, the Australian Customs and Border Protection Service shall delete it.

*Article 5*

**Adequacy**

Compliance with this Agreement by the Australian Customs and Border Protection Service shall, within the meaning of relevant EU data-protection law, constitute an adequate level of protection for PNR data transferred to the Australian Customs and Border Protection Service for the purpose of this Agreement.

*Article 6*

**Police and judicial cooperation**

1. The Australian Customs and Border Protection Service shall ensure the availability, as soon as practicable, of relevant and appropriate analytical information obtained from PNR data to police or judicial authorities of the Member State of the European Union concerned, or to Europol or Eurojust within the remit of their respective mandates, and in accordance with law enforcement or other information sharing agreements or arrangements between Australia and any Member State of the European Union, Europol or Eurojust, as applicable.

2. A police or judicial authority of a Member State of the European Union, or Europol or Eurojust within the remit of their respective mandates, may request access to PNR data or relevant and appropriate analytical information obtained from PNR data which is necessary in a specific case to prevent, detect, investigate, or prosecute within the European Union a terrorist offence or serious transnational crime. The Australian Customs and Border Protection Service shall, in accordance with the agreements or arrangements referred to in paragraph 1, make such information available.

CHAPTER II

**SAFEGUARDS APPLICABLE TO THE PROCESSING OF PNR DATA**

*Article 7*

**Data protection and non-discrimination**

1. PNR data shall be subject to the provisions of the Australian *Privacy Act 1988* (Cth) (Privacy Act) which governs the collection, use, storage and disclosure, security and access and alteration of personal information held by most Australian Government departments and agencies.

2. Australia shall ensure that the safeguards applicable to the processing of PNR data under this Agreement and relevant national laws apply to all passengers without discrimination, in particular on the basis of nationality or country of residence or physical presence in Australia.

*Article 8*

**Sensitive data**

Any processing by the Australian Customs and Border Protection Service of sensitive PNR data shall be prohibited. To the extent that the PNR data of a passenger which is transferred to the Australian Customs and Border Protection Service include sensitive data, the Australian Customs and Border Protection Service shall delete such sensitive data.

*Article 9*

**Data security and integrity**

1. To prevent accidental or unlawful destruction or accidental loss, alteration, unauthorised disclosure or access or any unlawful forms of processing:

(a) PNR data-processing equipment shall be held in a secure physical environment, and maintained with high-level systems and physical intrusion controls;

(b) PNR data shall be stored separately from any other data. For the purpose of matching, data may flow to the PNR system, but not from the PNR system to other databases. Access to the PNR system shall be limited to a restricted number of officials within the Australian Customs and Border Protection Service who are specifically authorised by the Chief Executive Officer of the Australian Customs and Border Protection Service to process PNR data for the purpose of this Agreement. These officials shall access the PNR system in secure work locations that are inaccessible to unauthorised individuals;

(c) access to the PNR system, by the officials described in subparagraph (b) shall be controlled by security access systems such as layered logins using a user ID and password;

(d) access to the network of the Australian Customs and Border Protection Service and any data contained in the PNR system shall be audited. The audit record generated shall contain the user name, the work location of the user, the date and time of access, the content of the query and the number of records returned;

(e) all PNR data shall be transferred from the Australian Customs and Border Protection Service to other authorities in a secure manner;

(f) the PNR system shall ensure fault detection and reporting;

(g) PNR data shall be protected against any manipulation, alteration or addition or corruption by means of malfunctioning of the system;

(h) no copies of the PNR database shall be made, other than for disaster recovery back-up purposes.

2. Any breach of data security, in particular leading to accidental or unlawful destruction or accidental loss, alteration, unauthorised disclosure or access, or any unlawful forms of processing shall be subject to effective and dissuasive sanctions.

3. The Australian Customs and Border Protection Service shall report any breach of data security to the Office of the Australian Information Commissioner, and notify the European Commission that such a breach has been reported.

*Article 10*

**Oversight and accountability**

1. Compliance with data protection rules by the Australian government authorities processing PNR data shall be subject to the oversight by the Australian Information Commissioner who, under the provisions of the Privacy Act, has effective powers to investigate compliance by agencies with the Privacy Act, and monitor and investigate the extent to which the Australian Customs and Border Protection Service complies with the Privacy Act.

2. The Australian Customs and Border Protection Service has arrangements in place under the Privacy Act for the Australian Information Commissioner to undertake regular formal audits of all aspects of Australian Customs and Border Protection Service's EU-sourced PNR data use, handling and access policies and procedures.

3. The Australian Information Commissioner will, in particular, hear claims lodged by an individual regardless of his or her nationality or country of residence, concerning the protection of his or her rights and freedoms with regard to the processing of personal data. The individual concerned will be informed of the outcome of the claim. The Australian Information Commissioner will further assist individuals concerned in the exercise of their rights under this Agreement, in particular rights of access, rectification and redress.

4. Individuals also have the right to lodge a complaint with the Commonwealth Ombudsman regarding their treatment by the Australian Customs and Border Protection Service.

*Article 11*

**Transparency**

1. Australia shall request air carriers to provide passengers with clear and meaningful information in relation to the collection, processing and purpose of the use of PNR data. Preferably this information will be provided at the time of booking.

2. Australia shall make available to the public, in particular on relevant government websites, information on the purpose of collection and use of PNR by the Australian Customs and Border Protection Service. This shall include information on how to request access, correction and redress.

*Article 12*

**Right of access**

1. Any individual shall have the right to access his or her PNR data, following a request made to the Australian Customs and Border Protection Service. Such access shall be provided without undue constraint or delay. This right is conferred by the Australian *Freedom of Information Act 1982* (Cth) (Freedom of Information Act) and the Privacy Act. The right of access shall further extend to the ability to request and to obtain documents held by the Australian Customs and Border Protection Service as to whether or not data relating to him or her have been transferred or made available and information on the recipients or categories of recipients to whom the data have been disclosed.

2. Disclosure of information pursuant to paragraph 1 may be subject to reasonable legal limitations applicable under Australian law to safeguard the prevention, detection, investigation, or prosecution of criminal offences, and to protect public or national security, with due regard for the legitimate interest of the individual concerned.

3. Any refusal or restriction of access shall be set out in writing to the individual within thirty (30) days or any statutory extension of time. At the same time, the factual or legal reasons on which the decision is based shall also be communicated to him or her. The latter communication may be omitted where a reason under paragraph 2 exists. In all of these cases, individuals shall be informed of their right to lodge a complaint against the decision of the Australian Customs and Border Protection Service. This complaint will be lodged with the Australian Information Commissioner. The individual shall be further informed of the means available under Australian law for seeking administrative and judicial redress.

4. Where an individual submits a complaint to the Australian Information Commissioner as referred to in paragraph 3, he or she shall be formally advised of the outcome of the investigation of the complaint. He or she shall at least receive a confirmation whether his or her data protection rights have been respected in compliance with this Agreement.

5. The Australian Customs and Border Protection Service shall not disclose PNR data to the public, except to the individuals whose PNR data have been processed or their representatives.

*Article 13*

**Right of rectification and erasure**

1. Any individual shall have the right to seek the rectification of his or her PNR data processed by the Australian Customs and Border Protection Service where the data is inaccurate. Rectification may require erasure.

2. Requests for the rectification of PNR data held by the Australian Customs and Border Protection Service may be made directly to the Australian Customs and Border Protection Service pursuant to the Freedom of Information Act or the Privacy Act.

3. The Australian Customs and Border Protection Service shall make all necessary verifications pursuant to the request and without undue delay inform the individual whether his or her PNR data have been rectified or erased. Such notification shall be set out to the individual in writing within thirty (30) days or any statutory extension of time and provide information on a possibility of a complaint against the decision of the Australian Customs and Border Protection Service to the Australian Information Commissioner and otherwise on the means available under Australian law for seeking administrative and judicial redress.

4. Where an individual lodges a complaint to the Australian Information Commissioner as referred to in paragraph 3, the individual shall be formally advised of the outcome of the investigation.

*Article 14*

**Right of redress**

1. Any individual shall have the right to effective administrative and judicial redress in case any of his or her rights referred to in this Agreement have been violated.

2. Any individual who has suffered damage as a result of an unlawful processing operation or of any act incompatible with rights referred to in this Agreement shall have the right to apply for effective remedies, which may include compensation from Australia.

3. The rights referred to in paragraphs 1 and 2 shall be afforded to individuals regardless of their nationality or country of origin, place of residence or physical presence in Australia.

*Article 15*

**Automated processing of PNR data**

1. The Australian Customs and Border Protection Service or other government authorities listed in Annex 2 shall not take any decision which significantly affects or produces an adverse legal effect on a passenger solely on the basis of the automated processing of PNR data.

2. The Australian Customs and Border Protection Service shall not carry out the automated processing of data on the basis of sensitive data.

*Article 16*

**Retention of data**

1. PNR data shall be retained not longer than five and a half years from the date of the initial receipt of PNR data by the Australian Customs and Border Protection Service. During this period PNR data shall be retained in the PNR system only for the purpose of preventing, detecting, investigating and prosecuting terrorist offences or serious transnational crime, and in the following manner:

(a) from the initial receipt to three years, all PNR data shall be accessible to a limited number of the Australian Customs and Border Protection Service's officials specifically authorised by the Chief Executive Officer of the Australian Customs and Border Protection Service to identify passengers who may be potential persons of interest;

(b) from three years after initial receipt to the end of the five and a half year period, PNR data shall be retained in the PNR system but all data elements which could serve to identify the passenger to whom PNR data relate shall be masked out. Such depersonalised PNR data shall be accessible only to a limited number of Australian Customs and Border Protection Service officials specifically authorised by the Chief Executive Officer of the Australian Customs and Border Protection Service to carry out analyses related to terrorist offences or serious transnational crime. Full access to PNR data shall be permitted only by a member of the Senior Executive Service of the Australian Customs and Border Protection Service if it is necessary to carry out investigations for the purpose of preventing, detecting, investigating and prosecuting terrorist offences and serious transnational crimes.

2. To achieve depersonalisation, the following PNR elements shall be masked out:

(a) name(s);

(b) other names on PNR, including number of travellers on PNR;

(c) all available contact information (including originator information);

(d) general remarks including other supplementary information (OSI), special service information (SSI) and special service request (SSR) information, to the extent that it contains any information capable of identifying a natural person; and

(e) any collected advance passenger processing (APP) or advance passenger information (API) data to the extent that it contains any information capable of identifying a natural person.

3. Notwithstanding paragraph 1, PNR data required for a specific investigation, prosecution or enforcement of penalties for terrorist offences or serious transnational crime may be processed for the purpose of that investigation, prosecution or enforcement of penalties. PNR data may be retained until the relevant investigation or prosecution is concluded or the penalty enforced.

4. Upon the expiry of the data retention period specified in paragraphs 1 and 3, PNR data shall be permanently deleted.

*Article 17*

**Logging and documentation of PNR data**

1. All processing, including accessing and consulting or transfer of PNR data as well as requests for PNR data by the authorities of Australia or third countries, even if refused, shall be logged or documented by the Australian Customs and Border Protection Service for the purpose of verification of lawfulness of the data processing, self-monitoring and ensuring appropriate data integrity and security of data processing.

2. Logs or documentation prepared under paragraph 1 shall be used only for oversight and auditing purposes including investigation and resolution of matters pertaining to unauthorised access.

3. Logs or documentation prepared under paragraph 1 shall be communicated on request to the Australian Information Commissioner. The Australian Information Commissioner shall use this information only for the oversight of data protection and for ensuring proper data processing as well as data integrity and security.

*Article 18*

**Sharing PNR data with other government authorities of Australia**

1. Subject to the following safeguards, the Australian Customs and Border Protection Service may share PNR data only with those government authorities of Australia which are listed in Annex 2:

(a) receiving government authorities shall afford to PNR data the safeguards as set out in this Agreement;

(b) data shall be shared strictly for the purposes stated in Article 3;

(c) data shall be shared only on a case-by-case basis unless the data has been depersonalised;

(d) prior to the sharing, the Australian Customs and Border Protection Service shall carefully assess the relevance of data to be shared. Only those particular PNR data elements which are clearly demonstrated as necessary in particular circumstances shall be shared. In any case, the minimum amount of data possible shall be shared;

(e) receiving government authorities shall ensure that the data is not further disclosed without the permission of the Australian Customs and Border Protection Service, which permission shall not be granted by the Australian Customs and Border Protection Service except for the purposes stated in Article 3 of the Agreement.

2. The list of authorities set forth in Annex 2 may be amended by exchange of diplomatic notes between the Parties, to include:

(a) any successor departments or agencies of those which are listed in Annex 2; and

(b) any new departments and agencies established after the entry into force of this Agreement whose functions are directly related to preventing, detecting, investigating or prosecuting terrorist offences or serious transnational crime; and

(c) any existing departments and agencies whose functions become directly related to preventing, detecting, investigating or prosecuting terrorist offences or serious transnational crime.

3. When transferring analytical information containing PNR data obtained under this Agreement, the safeguards applying to PNR data in this Article shall be respected.

L 186/10 EN Official Journal of the European Union 14.7.2012

4. Nothing in this Article prevents the disclosure of PNR data where necessary for the purposes of Article 3(4) and (5) and Article 10.

*Article 19*

**Transfers to authorities of third countries**

1. Subject to the following safeguards, the Australian Customs and Border Protection Service may transfer PNR data only to specific third country authorities:

(a) the Australian Customs and Border Protection Service is satisfied that the receiving third country authority has agreed to afford to the data transferred the same safeguards as set out in this Agreement;

(b) only a third country authority whose functions are directly related to preventing, detecting, investigating and prosecuting terrorist offences or serious transnational crime may receive PNR data;

(c) data shall be transferred for the exclusive purpose of preventing, detecting, investigating and prosecuting terrorist offences or serious transnational crime as defined in Article 3;

(d) data shall be transferred only on a case-by-case basis;

(e) prior to the transfer, the Australian Customs and Border Protection Service shall carefully assess the relevance of data to be transferred. Only those particular PNR data elements which are clearly demonstrated as necessary in particular circumstances shall be transferred. In any case, the minimum amount of data possible shall be transferred;

(f) where the Australian Customs and Border Protection Service is aware that data of a national or a resident of a Member State is transferred, the competent authorities of the Member State concerned shall be informed of the matter at the earliest appropriate opportunity;

(g) the Australian Customs and Border Protection Service is satisfied that the receiving third country authority has agreed to retain PNR data only until the relevant investigation or prosecution is concluded or the penalty enforced or are no longer required for the purposes set out in Article 3(4), and in any case no longer than necessary;

(h) the Australian Customs and Border Protection Service is satisfied that the receiving third country authority has agreed not to further transfer PNR data;

(i) the Australian Customs and Border Protection Service shall ensure, where appropriate, that the passenger is informed of a transfer of his or her PNR data.

2. When transferring analytical information containing PNR data obtained under this Agreement, the safeguards applying to PNR data in this Article shall be respected.

3. Nothing in this Article prevents the disclosure of PNR data where necessary for the purposes of Article 3(4).

CHAPTER III

**MODALITIES OF TRANSFERS**

*Article 20*

**The method of transfer**

For the purpose of this Agreement, the Parties shall ensure that air carriers transfer to the Australian Customs and Border Protection Service PNR data exclusively on the basis of the push method and in accordance with the following procedures:

(a) Air carriers shall transfer PNR data by electronic means in compliance with technical requirements of the Australian Customs and Border Protection Service or, in case of technical failure, by any other appropriate means ensuring an appropriate level of data security.

(b) Air carriers shall transfer PNR data using an agreed messaging format.

(c) Air carriers shall transfer PNR data in a secure manner using common protocols required by the Australian Customs and Border Protection Service.

*Article 21*

**The frequency of transfer**

1. The Parties shall ensure that air carriers transfer to the Australian Customs and Border Protection Service all requested PNR data of passengers as described in Article 20 at a maximum of five scheduled points in time per flight, with the first point being up to 72 hours before scheduled departure. The Australian Customs and Border Protection Service shall communicate to air carriers the specified times for the transfers.

2. In specific cases where there is an indication that early access is necessary to respond to a specific threat related to terrorist offences or serious transnational crime, the Australian Customs and Border Protection Service may require an air carrier to provide PNR data prior to the first scheduled transfer. In exercising this discretion, the Australian Customs and Border Protection Service shall act judiciously and proportionately and use exclusively the push method.

3. In specific cases where there is an indication that access is necessary to respond to a specific threat related to terrorist offences or serious transnational crime, the Australian Customs and Border Protection Service may require an air carrier to transfer PNR data in between or after regular transfers referred to in paragraph 1. In exercising this discretion, the Australian Customs and Border Protection Service shall act judiciously and proportionately and use exclusively the push method.

CHAPTER IV

## IMPLEMENTING AND FINAL PROVISIONS

*Article 22*

### Non-derogation/Relationship to other instruments

1. This Agreement shall not create or confer any right or benefit on any person or entity, private or public. Each Party shall ensure that the provisions of this Agreement are properly implemented.

2. Nothing in this Agreement shall limit rights or safeguards contained in the laws of Australia.

3. Nothing in this Agreement shall derogate from existing obligations under any bilateral mutual legal assistance instruments between Australia and Member States of the European Union to assist with a request to obtain data for evidence in criminal proceedings concerning terrorism or serious transnational crime.

*Article 23*

### Dispute resolution and suspension of the Agreement

1. Any dispute arising from the interpretation, application or implementation of this Agreement and any matters related thereto shall give rise to consultation between the Parties with a view to reaching a mutually agreeable resolution, including providing an opportunity for either Party to comply within a reasonable time.

2. In the event that consultations do not result in a resolution of the dispute, either Party may suspend the application of this Agreement by written notification through diplomatic channels, with any such suspension to take effect 120 days from the date of such notification, unless otherwise agreed.

3. Any suspension shall cease as soon as the dispute is resolved to the satisfaction of Australia and the EU.

4. Notwithstanding any suspension of this Agreement, all data obtained by the Australian Customs and Border Protection Service under the terms of this Agreement shall continue to be processed in accordance with the safeguards of this Agreement, including the provisions on retention and deletion of data.

*Article 24*

### Consultation and review

1. The Parties shall notify each other, where appropriate before adoption, of any legislative or regulatory changes which may materially affect the implementation of this Agreement. References in this Agreement to Australian legislation shall be deemed to include any successor legislation.

2. The Parties shall jointly review the implementation of this Agreement and any matters related thereto one year after the entry into force of this Agreement and regularly thereafter within the duration of this Agreement and additionally as requested by either Party. The Parties agree that the review should in particular look into the mechanism of masking out data according to Article 16(1)(b), any difficulties related to the operational efficiency or cost effectiveness of the mechanism, and experience acquired with similar mechanisms in other mature PNR schemes, including the EU scheme. In the event that an operationally efficient and cost effective mechanism is not available, access to the data will instead be restricted by archiving, and may be accessed only in the way that depersonalised data is accessed under Article 16.

3. The Parties shall agree in advance of the joint review its modalities and shall communicate to each other the composition of their respective teams. For the purpose of the joint review, the European Union shall be represented by the European Commission and Australia shall be represented by the Australian Customs and Border Protection Service. The teams may include experts on data protection and law enforcement. Subject to applicable laws, any participants to the joint review shall be required to respect confidentiality of the discussions and have appropriate security clearances. For the purpose of the joint review, the Australian Customs and Border Protection Service shall ensure access to relevant documentation, systems and personnel.

4. The Parties shall evaluate the Agreement, in particular its operational effectiveness no later than four years after its entry into force.

5. Following the joint review, the European Commission shall present a report to the European Parliament and to the Council of the European Union. Australia shall be given an opportunity to provide written comments which shall be attached to the report.

6. Since the establishment of an EU PNR system could change the context of this Agreement, if and when an EU PNR system is adopted, the Parties shall consult to determine whether this Agreement would need to be adjusted accordingly.

*Article 25*

### Termination

1. Either Party may terminate this Agreement at any time by written notification through diplomatic channels. Termination shall take effect 120 days from the date of receipt of such notification, or as otherwise agreed.

2. Notwithstanding any termination of this Agreement, all data obtained by the Australian Customs and Border Protection Service under the terms of this Agreement shall continue to be processed in accordance with the safeguards of this Agreement, including the provisions on retention and deletion of data.

*Article 26*

**Duration**

1. Subject to Article 25, this Agreement shall remain in force for a period of seven years from the date of its entry into force.

2. Upon the expiry of the period set forth in paragraph 1, as well as any subsequent period of renewal under this paragraph, the Agreement shall be renewed for a subsequent period of seven years unless one of the Parties notifies the other in writing through diplomatic channels, at least 12 months in advance, of its intention not to renew the Agreement.

3. Notwithstanding the expiration of this Agreement, all data obtained by the Australian Customs and Border Protection Service under the terms of this Agreement shall continue to be processed in accordance with the safeguards of this Agreement, including the provisions on retention and deletion of data.

*Article 27*

**PNR data received prior to the entry into force of this Agreement**

Australia shall treat any PNR data held by the Australian Customs and Border Protection Service at the time of the entry into force of this Agreement in accordance with the provisions of this Agreement. However, no data shall be required to be masked out before 1 January 2015.

*Article 28*

**Territorial application**

1. Subject to paragraphs 2 to 4, this Agreement shall apply to the territory in which the Treaty on European Union and the Treaty on the Functioning of the European Union are applicable and to the territory of Australia.

2. This Agreement will only apply to Denmark, the United Kingdom or Ireland, if the European Commission notifies Australia in writing that Denmark, the United Kingdom, or Ireland has chosen to be bound by this Agreement.

3. If the European Commission notifies Australia before the entry into force of this Agreement that it will apply to Denmark, the United Kingdom or Ireland, this Agreement shall apply to the territory of such State on the same day as for the other Member States of the European Union bound by this Agreement.

4. If the European Commission notifies Australia after the entry into force of this Agreement that it applies to Denmark, the United Kingdom, or Ireland, this Agreement shall apply to the territory of such State on the first day following receipt of the notification by Australia.

*Article 29*

**Final Provisions**

1. This Agreement shall enter into force on the first day of the month after the date on which the Parties have exchanged notifications indicating that they have completed their internal procedures for this purpose.

2. This Agreement replaces the Agreement between the European Union and Australia on the Processing and Transfer of European Union – Sourced Passenger Name Record (PNR) Data by Air Carriers to the Australian Customs Service done at Brussels on 30 June 2008, which will cease to apply upon the entry into force of this Agreement.

Done at Brussels, on 29 September 2011, in two originals, in the English language. This Agreement shall be also drawn up in the Bulgarian, Czech, Danish, Dutch, Estonian, Finnish, French, German, Greek, Hungarian, Italian, Latvian, Lithuanian, Maltese, Polish, Portuguese, Romanian, Slovak, Slovenian, Spanish and Swedish languages, each version being equally authentic. In case of divergence between the language versions, the English version shall prevail.

For the European Union

For Australia

*ANNEX 1*

PNR data elements referred to in Article 2(f) which air carriers are required to provide to the Australian Customs and Border Protection Service but only to the extent they already collect them:

1. PNR record locator code
2. Date of reservation/issue of ticket
3. Date(s) of intended travel
4. Name(s)
5. Available frequent flier and benefit information (i.e. free tickets, upgrades, etc.)
6. Other names on PNR, including number of travellers on PNR
7. All available contact information (including originator information)
8. All available payment/billing information (not including other transaction details linked to a credit card or account and not connected to the travel transaction)
9. Travel itinerary for specific PNR
10. Travel agency/travel agent
11. Code share information
12. Split/divided information
13. Travel status of passenger (including confirmations and check-in status)
14. Ticketing information, including ticket number, one-way tickets and Automated Ticket Fare Quote
15. All baggage information
16. Seat information, including seat number
17. General remarks including OSI, SSI and SSR information
18. Any collected APIS information
19. All historical changes to the PNR listed in numbers 1 to 18

*ANNEX 2*

List of other government authorities of Australia with whom the Australian Customs and Border Protection Service is authorised to share PNR data:

1. Australian Crime Commission;

2. Australian Federal Police;

3. Australian Security Intelligence Organisation;

4. Commonwealth Director of Public Prosecutions;

5. Department of Immigration and Citizenship;

6. Office of Transport Security, Department of Infrastructure and Transport.

14.7.2012 EN Official Journal of the European Union L 186/15

**FINAL ACT**

The representatives of:

THE EUROPEAN UNION,

of the one part, and

AUSTRALIA,

of the other part,

meeting at Brussels, on 29 September 2011, for the signature of the Agreement between the European Union and Australia on the processing and transfer of Passenger Name Record (PNR) data by air carriers to the Australian Customs and Border Protection Service, have at the time of signature of this Agreement:

— adopted the Joint Declaration attached to this Final Act.

IN WITNESS WHEREOF, the undersigned Plenipotentiaries have signed this Final Act.

Done at Brussels, on 29 September 2011.

For the European Union

For Australia

**JOINT DECLARATION OF THE EUROPEAN UNION AND AUSTRALIA ON THE AGREEMENT ON THE PROCESSING AND TRANSFER OF PASSENGER NAME RECORD (PNR) DATA BY AIR CARRIERS TO THE AUSTRALIAN CUSTOMS AND BORDER PROTECTION SERVICE**

When implementing the Agreement on the processing and transfer of Passenger Name Record (PNR) data by air carriers to the Australian Customs and Border Protection Service ('the Agreement'), the European Union and Australia have reached the following understandings in respect of their obligations under Articles 19 and 24 of the Agreement:

1. in the context of the joint consultation and review mechanism set out in Article 24 of the Agreement, Australia and the European Union will exchange information where appropriate, regarding the transfers of European Union citizens' and residents' PNR data to the authorities of third countries as laid down in Article 19 of the Agreement;
2. provide that, in the context of the consultation and review mechanism set out in Article 24 of the Agreement, all appropriate information will be supplied on the conditions governing those transfers on a case-by-case basis in accordance with the provisions of Article 19;
3. pay particular attention to providing all the safeguards for the implementation of the provisions of Article 19(1)(a), so as to be satisfied that third countries receiving such data have agreed to afford to the data the legal and practical safeguards provided by the Agreement;
4. set up specific reporting mechanisms between the authorities of Member States and of Australia, where the data of a European Union citizen or resident is transferred under Article 19(1)(f).

# Directive 2011/82 facilitating the cross-border exchange of information on road safety related traffic offences, 25 October 2011

**[OJ 2011, L 288/1–15]**

5.11.2011 EN Official Journal of the European Union L 288/1

I

*(Legislative acts)*

# DIRECTIVES

## DIRECTIVE 2011/82/EU OF THE EUROPEAN PARLIAMENT AND OF THE COUNCIL

**of 25 October 2011**

**facilitating the cross-border exchange of information on road safety related traffic offences**

THE EUROPEAN PARLIAMENT AND THE COUNCIL OF THE EUROPEAN UNION,

Having regard to the Treaty on the Functioning of the European Union, and in particular Article 87(2) thereof,

Having regard to the proposal from the European Commission,

Acting in accordance with the ordinary legislative procedure ([1]),

Whereas:

(1) Improving road safety is a prime objective of the Union's transport policy. The Union is pursuing a policy to improve road safety with the objective of reducing fatalities, injuries and material damage. An important element of that policy is the consistent enforcement of sanctions for road traffic offences committed in the Union which considerably jeopardise road safety.

(2) However, due to a lack of appropriate procedures and notwithstanding existing possibilities under Council Decision 2008/615/JHA of 23 June 2008 on the stepping up of cross-border cooperation, particularly in combating terrorism and cross-border crime ([2]) and Council Decision 2008/616/JHA of 23 June 2008 on the implementation of Decision 2008/615/JHA ([3]) (the 'Prüm Decisions'), sanctions in the form of financial penalties for certain road traffic offences are often not enforced if those offences are committed with a vehicle which is registered in a Member State other than the Member State where the offence took place. This Directive aims to ensure that even in such cases, the effectiveness of the investigation of road safety related traffic offences should be ensured.

(3) The Commission, in its Communication of 20 July 2010 entitled 'Towards a European road safety area: policy orientations on road safety 2011-2020', emphasised that enforcement remains a key factor in creating the conditions for a considerable reduction in the number of deaths and injuries. The Council, in its conclusions of 2 December 2010 on road safety, called also for consideration of the need for further strengthening of enforcement of road traffic rules by Member States and, where appropriate, at Union level. It invited the Commission to examine the possibilities of harmonising traffic rules at Union level where appropriate. The Commission should therefore assess the need to propose in the future further measures on facilitating cross-border enforcement with regard to road traffic offences, in particular those related to serious traffic accidents.

(4) Greater convergence of control measures between Member States should also be encouraged and the Commission should examine in this respect the need for developing common standards for automatic checking equipment for road safety controls.

(5) The awareness of Union citizens should be raised as regards the road safety traffic rules in force in different Member States and as regards the implementation of this Directive, in particular through appropriate measures guaranteeing the provision of sufficient information on the consequences of not respecting the road safety traffic rules when travelling in a Member State other than the Member State of registration.

(6) In order to improve road safety throughout the Union and to ensure equal treatment of drivers, namely resident and non-resident offenders, enforcement should be facilitated irrespective of the Member State of registration

([1]) Position of the European Parliament of 17 December 2008 (OJ C 45 E, 23.2.2010, p. 149) and position of the Council at first reading of 17 March 2011 (OJ C 136 E, 6.5.2011, p. 1). Position of the European Parliament of 6 July 2011 (not yet published in the Official Journal) and decision of the Council of 29 September 2011.
([2]) OJ L 210, 6.8.2008, p. 1.
([3]) OJ L 210, 6.8.2008, p. 12.

of the vehicle. To this end, a system of cross-border exchange of information should be put in place for certain identified road safety related traffic offences, regardless of their administrative or criminal nature under the law of the Member State concerned, granting the Member State of the offence access to vehicle registration data (VRD) of the Member State of registration.

(7) A more efficient cross-border exchange of VRD, which should facilitate the identification of persons suspected of committing a road safety related traffic offence, may increase the deterrent effect and induce more cautious behaviour by the driver of a vehicle that is registered in a Member State other than the Member State of the offence, thereby preventing casualties due to road traffic accidents.

(8) The road safety related traffic offences covered by this Directive are not subject to homogeneous treatment in the Member States. Some Member States qualify such offences under national law as 'administrative' offences while others qualify them as 'criminal' offences. This Directive should apply regardless of how those offences are qualified under national law.

(9) In the framework of the Prüm Decisions, Member States grant each other the right of access to their VRD in order to improve the exchange of information and to speed up the procedures in force. The provisions concerning the technical specifications and the availability of automated data exchange set out in the Prüm Decisions should, as far as possible, be included in this Directive.

(10) Existing software applications should be the basis for the data exchange under this Directive and should, at the same time, also facilitate the reporting by Member States to the Commission. Such applications should provide for the expeditious, secure and confidential exchange of specific VRD between Member States. Advantage should be taken of the European Vehicle and Driving Licence Information System (Eucaris) software application, which is mandatory for Member States under the Prüm Decisions as regards VRD. The Commission should report on an assessment of the functioning of the software applications used for the purposes of this Directive.

(11) The scope of the above-mentioned software applications should be limited to the processes used in the exchange of information between the national contact points in the Member States. Procedures and automated processes in which the information is to be used are outside the scope of such applications.

(12) The Information Management Strategy for EU internal security aims at finding the simplest and most easily traceable and cost-effective solutions for data exchange.

(13) Member States should be able to contact the owner, the holder of the vehicle or the otherwise identified person suspected of committing the road safety related traffic offence in order to keep the person concerned informed of the applicable procedures and the legal consequences under the law of the Member State of the offence. In doing so, Member States should consider sending the information concerning road safety related traffic offences in the language of the registration documents or the language most likely to be understood by the person concerned, to ensure that that person has a clear understanding of the information which is being shared with the person concerned. Member States should apply the appropriate procedures to ensure that only the person concerned is informed and not a third party. To that effect, Member States should use detailed arrangements similar to those adopted for following up such offences including means such as, where appropriate, registered delivery. This will allow that person to respond to the information in an appropriate way, in particular by asking for more information, settling the fine or by exercising his/her rights of defence, in particular in the case of mistaken identity. Further proceedings are covered by applicable legal instruments, including instruments on mutual assistance and on mutual recognition, for example Council Framework Decision 2005/214/JHA of 24 February 2005 on the application of the principle of mutual recognition to financial penalties (1).

(14) Member States should consider providing equivalent translation with respect to the information letter sent by the Member State of the offence, as provided for in Directive 2010/64/EU of the European Parliament and of the Council of 20 October 2010 on the right to interpretation and translation in criminal proceedings (2).

(15) With a view to pursuing a road safety policy aiming for a high level of protection for all road users in the Union and taking into account the widely differing circumstances pertaining within the Union, Member States should act, without prejudice to more restrictive policies and laws, in order to ensure greater convergence of road traffic rules and of their enforcement between Member States. In the framework of its report to the European Parliament and to the Council on the application of this Directive, the Commission should examine the need to develop common standards in order to establish comparable methods, practices and minimum standards at Union level taking into account

(1) OJ L 76, 22.3.2005, p. 16.
(2) OJ L 280, 26.10.2010, p. 1.

international cooperation and existing agreements in the field of road safety, in particular the Vienna Convention on Road Traffic of 8 November 1968.

(16) In the framework of its report to the European Parliament and to the Council on the application of this Directive by the Member States, the Commission should examine the need for common criteria for follow-up procedures by the Member States in the event of non-payment of a financial penalty, in accordance with Member States' laws and procedures. In this report, the Commission should address issues such as the procedures between the competent authorities of the Member States for the transmission of the final decision to impose a sanction and/or financial penalty as well as the recognition and enforcement of the final decision.

(17) In preparing the review of this Directive, the Commission should consult the relevant stakeholders, such as road safety and law enforcement authorities or bodies, victims' associations and other non-governmental organisations active in the field of road safety.

(18) Closer cooperation between law enforcement authorities should go hand in hand with respect for fundamental rights, in particular the right to respect for privacy and to protection of personal data, guaranteed by special data protection arrangements which should take particular account of the specific nature of cross-border online access to databases. It is necessary that the software applications to be set up enable the exchange of information to be carried out in secure conditions and ensure the confidentiality of the data transmitted. The data gathered under this Directive should not be used for purposes other than those of this Directive. Member States should comply with the obligations on the conditions of use and of temporary storage of the data.

(19) Since the data relating to the identification of an offender are personal data, Member States should take the measures necessary to ensure that the relevant provisions of Council Framework Decision 2008/977/JHA of 27 November 2008 on the protection of personal data processed in the framework of police and judicial cooperation in criminal matters [1] are applied. Without prejudice to the observance of the procedural requirements for appeal and the redress mechanisms of the Member State concerned, the data subject should be informed accordingly, when notified of the offence, of the right to access, the right to rectification and deletion of personal data as well as of the maximum legal storage period of the data and should have the right to obtain the correction of any inaccurate personal data or the immediate deletion of any data recorded unlawfully.

(20) It should be possible for third countries to participate in the exchange of VRD provided that they have concluded an agreement with the Union to this effect. Such an agreement would have to include necessary provisions on data protection.

(21) This Directive respects the fundamental rights and observes the principles recognised in particular by the Charter of Fundamental Rights of the European Union, as referred to in Article 6 of the Treaty on European Union.

(22) In accordance with Articles 1 and 2 of the Protocol (No 21) on the Position of the United Kingdom and Ireland in respect of the Area of Freedom, Security and Justice, annexed to the Treaty on European Union and to the Treaty on the Functioning of the European Union, and without prejudice to Article 4 of that Protocol, those Member States are not taking part in the adoption of this Directive and are not bound by it or subject to its application.

(23) In accordance with Articles 1 and 2 of the Protocol (No 22) on the position of Denmark, annexed to the Treaty on European Union and the Treaty on the Functioning of the European Union, Denmark is not taking part in the adoption of this Directive and is not bound by it or subject to its application.

(24) In order to achieve the objective of exchange of information between Member States through interoperable means, the power to adopt acts in accordance with Article 290 of the Treaty on the Functioning of the European Union should be delegated to the Commission in respect of taking into account relevant changes to Decision 2008/615/JHA and Decision 2008/616/JHA or where required by legal acts of the Union directly relevant for the update of Annex I. It is of particular importance that the Commission carry out appropriate consultations during its preparatory work, including at expert level. The Commission, when preparing and drawing up delegated acts, should ensure a simultaneous, timely and appropriate transmission of relevant documents to the European Parliament and Council.

(25) In accordance with point 34 of the Interinstitutional Agreement on better law-making [2], Member States are encouraged to draw up, for themselves and in the interest of the Union, their own tables, which will, as far as possible, illustrate the correlation between this Directive and the transposition measures, and to make them public.

(26) Since the objective of this Directive, namely to ensure a high level of protection for all road users in the Union by facilitating the cross-border exchange of information on road safety related traffic offences, where they are committed with a vehicle registered in a Member State other than the Member State where the offence took place, cannot be sufficiently achieved by the Member States and can therefore by reason of the scale and effects of the action be better achieved at Union level, the Union may adopt measures, in accordance with the principle of subsidiarity as set out in Article 5 of the Treaty on European Union. In accordance with the

[1] OJ L 350, 30.12.2008, p. 60.

[2] OJ C 321, 31.12.2003, p. 1.

principle of proportionality as set out in that Article, this Directive does not go beyond what is necessary in order to achieve that objective.

(27) The European Data Protection Supervisor was consulted and adopted an opinion [1],

HAVE ADOPTED THIS DIRECTIVE:

*Article 1*

**Objective**

This Directive aims to ensure a high level of protection for all road users in the Union by facilitating the cross-border exchange of information on road safety related traffic offences and thereby the enforcement of sanctions, where those offences are committed with a vehicle registered in a Member State other than the Member State where the offence took place.

*Article 2*

**Scope**

This Directive shall apply to the following road safety related traffic offences:

(a) speeding;

(b) non-use of a seat-belt;

(c) failing to stop at a red traffic light;

(d) drink-driving;

(e) driving under the influence of drugs;

(f) failing to wear a safety helmet;

(g) use of a forbidden lane;

(h) illegally using a mobile telephone or any other communication devices while driving.

*Article 3*

**Definitions**

For the purposes of this Directive, the following definitions shall apply:

(a) 'vehicle' means any power-driven vehicle including motorcycles, which is normally used for carrying persons or goods by road;

(b) 'Member State of the offence' means the Member State where the offence has been committed;

(c) 'Member State of registration' means the Member State where the vehicle with which the offence has been committed is registered;

(d) 'speeding' means exceeding the speed limits in force in the Member State of the offence for the road and the type of vehicle concerned;

(e) 'non-use of a seat-belt' means failing to comply with the requirement to wear a seat-belt or use a child restraint in accordance with Council Directive 91/671/EEC of 16 December 1991 relating to the compulsory use of safety belts and child-restraint systems in vehicles [2] and the law of the Member State of the offence;

(f) 'failing to stop at a red traffic light' means driving through a red traffic light or any other relevant stop signal, as defined in the law of the Member State of the offence;

(g) 'drink-driving' means driving while impaired by alcohol, as defined in the law of the Member State of the offence;

(h) 'driving under the influence of drugs' means driving while impaired by drugs or other substances having a similar effect, as defined in the law of the Member State of the offence;

(i) 'failing to wear a safety helmet' means not wearing a safety helmet, as defined in the law of the Member State of the offence;

(j) 'use of a forbidden lane' means illegally using part of a road section, such as an emergency lane, public transport lane or temporary closed lane for reasons of congestion or road works, as defined in the law of the Member State of the offence;

(k) 'illegally using a mobile telephone or any other communication devices while driving' means illegally using a mobile telephone or any other communication devices while driving, as defined in the law of the Member State of the offence;

(l) 'national contact point' means a designated competent authority for the exchange of VRD;

(m) 'automated search' means an online access procedure for consulting the databases of one, several, or all of the Member States or of the participating countries;

(1) OJ C 310, 5.12.2008, p. 9.

(2) OJ L 373, 31.12.1991, p. 26.

(n) 'holder of the vehicle' means the person in whose name the vehicle is registered, as defined in the law of the Member State of registration.

*Article 4*

**Procedure for the exchange of information between Member States**

1. For the investigation of the road safety related traffic offences referred to in Article 2, the Member States shall allow other Member States' national contact points, as referred to in paragraph 3 of this Article, access to the following national VRD, with the power to conduct automated searches on:

(a) data relating to vehicles; and

(b) data relating to owners or holders of the vehicle.

The data elements referred to in points (a) and (b) which are necessary to conduct the search shall be in compliance with Annex I.

2. Any searches in the form of outgoing requests shall be conducted by the national contact point of the Member State of the offence using a full registration number.

Those searches shall be conducted in compliance with the procedures as described in Chapter 3 of the Annex to Decision 2008/616/JHA, except for point 1 of Chapter 3 of the Annex to Decision 2008/616/JHA, for which Annex I to this Directive shall apply.

The Member State of the offence shall, under this Directive, use the data obtained in order to establish who is personally liable for road safety related traffic offences referred to in Articles 2 and 3.

3. For the purposes of the exchange of data as referred to in paragraph 1, each Member State shall designate a national contact point. The powers of the national contact points shall be governed by the applicable law of the Member State concerned.

4. Member States shall take all necessary measures to ensure that the exchange of information is carried out by interoperable electronic means without exchange of data involving other databases. Member States shall ensure that this exchange of information is conducted in a cost efficient and secure manner and ensure the security and protection of the data transmitted, as far as possible using existing software applications such as the one especially designed for the purposes of Article 12 of Decision 2008/615/JHA, and amended versions of those software applications, in compliance with Annex I to this Directive and with points 2 and 3 of Chapter 3 of the Annex to Decision 2008/616/JHA. The amended versions of the software applications shall provide for both online real-time exchange mode and batch exchange mode, the latter allowing for the exchange of multiple requests or responses within one message.

5. Each Member State shall bear its costs arising from the administration, use and maintenance of the software applications referred to in paragraph 4.

*Article 5*

**Information letter on the road safety related traffic offence**

1. The Member State of the offence shall decide whether to initiate follow-up proceedings in relation to the road safety related traffic offences referred to in Article 2 or not.

In the event that the Member State of the offence decides to initiate such proceedings, that Member State shall, in conformity with its national law, inform the owner, the holder of the vehicle or the otherwise identified person suspected of committing the road safety related traffic offence accordingly.

This information shall, as applicable under national law, include the legal consequences thereof within the territory of the Member State of the offence under the law of that Member State.

2. When sending the information letter to the owner, the holder of the vehicle or the otherwise identified person suspected of committing the road safety related traffic offence, the Member State of the offence shall, in accordance with its law, include any relevant information, notably the nature of the road safety related traffic offence referred to in Article 2, the place, date and time of the offence, the title of the texts of the national law infringed and the sanction and, where appropriate, data concerning the device used for detecting the offence. For that purpose, the Member State of the offence may use the template as set out in Annex II.

3. Where the Member State of the offence decides to initiate follow-up proceedings in relation to the road safety related traffic offences referred to in Article 2, the Member State of the offence, for the purpose of ensuring the respect of fundamental rights, sends the information letter in the language of the registration document, if available, or in one of the official languages of the Member State of registration.

*Article 6*

**Reporting by Member States to the Commission**

Member States shall send a preliminary report to the Commission by 7 November 2014. They shall also send a comprehensive report to the Commission by 6 May 2016 and every two years thereafter.

The comprehensive report shall indicate the number of automated searches conducted by the Member State of the offence addressed to the national contact point of the Member State of registration following offences committed on its territory, together with the type of offences for which requests were addressed and the number of failed requests.

The comprehensive report shall also include a description of the situation at national level in relation to the follow-up given to the road safety related traffic offences, based on the proportion of such offences which have been followed up by information letters.

*Article 7*

**Data protection**

1. The provisions on data protection set out in Framework Decision 2008/977/JHA shall apply to personal data processed under this Directive.

2. In particular, each Member State shall ensure that personal data processed under this Directive are, within an appropriate time period, rectified if inaccurate, or erased or blocked when they are no longer required, in accordance with Articles 4 and 5 of Framework Decision 2008/977/JHA, and that a time limit for the storage of data is established in accordance with Article 9 of that Framework Decision.

Member States shall ensure that all personal data processed under this Directive are only used for the objective set out in Article 1, and that the data subjects have the same rights to information to access, to rectification, erasure and blocking, to compensation and to judicial redress as those adopted under national law in implementation of relevant provisions of Framework Decision 2008/977/JHA.

All relevant provisions on data protection set out in the Prüm Decisions shall also apply to personal data processed under this Directive.

3. Any person concerned shall have the right to obtain information on which personal data recorded in the Member State of registration were transmitted to the Member State of the offence, including the date of the request and the competent authority of the Member State of the offence.

*Article 8*

**Information for road users in the Union**

1. The Commission shall make available on its website a summary in all official languages of the institutions of the Union of the rules in force in Member States in the field covered by this Directive. Member States shall provide information on these rules to the Commission.

2. Member States shall provide road users with the necessary information about the rules applicable in their territory and the measures implementing this Directive in association with, among other organisations, road safety bodies, non-governmental organisations active in the field of road safety and automobile clubs.

*Article 9*

**Delegated acts**

The Commission shall be empowered to adopt delegated acts in accordance with Article 10 concerning the update of Annex I in the light of technical progress to take into account relevant changes to Decision 2008/615/JHA and Decision 2008/616/JHA or where required by legal acts of the Union directly relevant for the update of Annex I.

*Article 10*

**Exercise of the delegation**

1. The power to adopt delegated acts is conferred on the Commission subject to the conditions laid down in this Article.

2. The delegation of power referred to in Article 9 shall be conferred on the Commission for a period of five years from 6 November 2011. The Commission shall draw up a report in respect of the delegation of power not later than nine months before the end of the five-year period. The delegation of power shall be tacitly extended for periods of an identical duration, unless the European Parliament or the Council opposes such extension not later than three months before the end of each period.

3. The delegation of power referred to in Article 9 may be revoked at any time by the European Parliament or by the Council. A decision to revoke shall put an end to the delegation of the power specified in that decision. It shall take effect on the day following the publication of the decision in the Official Journal of the European Union or at a later date specified therein. It shall not affect the validity of any delegated acts already in force.

4. As soon as it adopts a delegated act, the Commission shall notify it simultaneously to the European Parliament and to the Council.

5. A delegated act adopted pursuant to Article 9 shall enter into force only if no objection has been expressed either by the European Parliament or the Council within a period of two months of notification of that act to the European Parliament and the Council or if, before the expiry of that period, the European Parliament and the Council have both informed the Commission that they will not object. That period shall be extended by two months at the initiative of the European Parliament or of the Council.

*Article 11*

**Revision of the Directive**

By 7 November 2016, the Commission shall submit a report to the European Parliament and the Council on the application of this Directive by the Member States. In its report, the Commission shall focus in particular on the following aspects and shall, as appropriate, make proposals to cover those aspects:

— an assessment of whether other road safety related traffic offences should be added to the scope of this Directive,

— an assessment of the effectiveness of this Directive on the reduction in the number of fatalities on Union roads, in particular whether the effectiveness of this Directive is affected by its territorial scope,

— an assessment of the need for developing common standards for automatic checking equipment and for procedures. In this context, the Commission is invited to develop at Union level road safety guidelines within the framework of the common transport policy in order to ensure greater convergence of the enforcement of road traffic rules by Member States through comparable methods and practices. These guidelines may cover at least the non-respect of speed limits, drink-driving, non-use of seat belts and failure to stop at a traffic red light,

— an assessment of the need to strengthen the enforcement of sanctions with regard to road safety related traffic offences and to propose common criteria concerning the follow-up procedures in the case of non-payment of a financial penalty, within the framework of all relevant EU policies, including the common transport policy,

— possibilities to harmonise traffic rules where appropriate,

— an assessment of the software applications as referred to in Article 4(4), with a view to ensuring proper implementation of this Directive as well as guaranteeing an effective, expeditious, secure and confidential exchange of specific VRD.

*Article 12*

**Transposition**

1. Member States shall bring into force the laws, regulations and administrative provisions necessary to comply with this Directive by 7 November 2013. They shall forthwith communicate to the Commission the text of those provisions.

When Member States adopt those provisions, they shall contain a reference to this Directive or be accompanied by such a reference on the occasion of their official publication. Member States shall determine how such reference is to be made.

2. Member States shall communicate to the Commission the text of the main provisions of national law which they adopt in the field covered by this Directive.

*Article 13*

**Entry into force**

This Directive shall enter into force on the day following its publication in the *Official Journal of the European Union*.

*Article 14*

**Addressees**

This Directive is addressed to the Member States in accordance with the Treaties.

Done at Strasbourg, 25 October 2011.

*For the European Parliament*
*The President*
J. BUZEK

*For the Council*
*The President*
M. DOWGIELEWICZ

L 288/8 EN Official Journal of the European Union 5.11.2011

*ANNEX I*

**DATA ELEMENTS RELATED TO THE SEARCH REFERRED TO IN ARTICLE 4**

| Item | M/O ([1]) | Remarks |
|---|---|---|
| Data relating to the vehicle | M | |
| Member State of registration | M | |
| Licence number | M | (A ([2])) |
| Data relating to the offence | M | |
| Member State of the offence | M | |
| Reference date of the offence | M | |
| Reference time of the offence | M | |
| Purpose of the search | M | Code indicating the type of offence as listed in Article 2<br>1 = Speeding<br>2 = Drink-driving<br>3 = Non-use of seat belt<br>4 = Failing to stop at red traffic light<br>5 = Use of forbidden lane<br>10 = Driving under the influence of drugs<br>11 = Failing to wear a safety helmet<br>12 = Illegally using a mobile phone or any other communication devices while driving |

([1]) M = mandatory when available in national register, O = optional.
([2]) Harmonised document abbreviation, see Council Directive 1999/37/EC of 29 April 1999 on the registration documents for vehicles (OJ L 138, 1.6.1999, p. 57).

**DATA ELEMENTS PROVIDED REFERRED TO IN ARTICLE 4**

Part I. Data relating to vehicles

| Item | M/O ([1]) | Remarks |
|---|---|---|
| Licence number | M | |
| Chassis number/VIN | M | |
| Country of registration | M | |
| Make | M | (D.1 ([2])) e.g. Ford, Opel, Renault |
| Commercial type of the vehicle | M | (D.3) e.g. Focus, Astra, Megane |
| EU Category Code | M | (J) e.g. mopeds, motorbikes, cars |

([1]) M = mandatory when available in national register, O = optional.
([2]) Harmonised document abbreviation, see Directive 1999/37/EC.

Part II. Data relating to holders or owners of the vehicle

| Item | M/O (1) | Remarks |
|---|---|---|
| Data relating to holders of the vehicle | | (C.1 (2))<br>The data refer to the holder of the specific registration certificate. |
| Registration holders' (company) name | M | (C.1.1)<br>Separate fields shall be used for surname, infixes, titles, etc.,<br>and<br>the name in printable format shall be communicated. |
| First name | M | (C.1.2)<br>Separate fields for first name(s) and initials shall be used,<br>and<br>the name in printable format shall be communicated. |
| Address | M | (C.1.3)<br>Separate fields shall be used for Street, House number and Annex, Post code, Place of residence, Country of residence, etc.,<br>and<br>the Address in printable format shall be communicated. |
| Gender | O | Male, female |
| Date of birth | M | |
| Legal entity | M | Individual, association, company, firm, etc. |
| Place of Birth | O | |
| ID Number | O | An identifier that uniquely identifies the person or the company. |
| Data relating to owners of the vehicle | | (C.2) The data refer to the owner of the vehicle. |
| Owners' (company) name | M | (C.2.1) |
| First name | M | (C.2.2) |
| Address | M | (C.2.3) |
| Gender | O | Male, female |
| Date of birth | M | |
| Legal entity | M | Individual, association, company, firm, etc. |
| Place of Birth | O | |
| ID Number | O | An identifier that uniquely identifies the person or the company. |
| | | In case of scrap vehicles, stolen vehicles or number plates, or outdated vehicle registration no owner/holder information shall be provided. Instead, the message 'Information not disclosed' shall be returned. |

(1) M = mandatory when available in national register, O = optional.
(2) Harmonised document abbreviation, see Directive 1999/37/EC.

*ANNEX II*

**TEMPLATE FOR THE INFORMATION LETTER**

**referred to in Article 5**

**[Coverpage]**

................................................................................................................................................

***[Name, address and telephone number of sender]***

................................................................................................................................................

***[Name and address of addressee]***

**INFORMATION LETTER**

regarding a road safety related traffic offence committed in ..........................................................................................
***[name of Member State where the offence has been committed]***

**Page 2**

On ...................................... a road safety related traffic offence committed with the vehicle with registration
*[date]*
number ..................................................., make ..................................................., model ...................................................

was detected by ...................................................................................................................................................................
***[name of the responsible body]***

[Option 1] (1)

You are registered as the holder of the registration certificate of the abovementioned vehicle.

[Option 2] (1)

The holder of the registration certificate of the abovementioned vehicle indicated that you were driving that vehicle when the road safety related traffic offence was committed.

The relevant details of the offence are described on page 3 below.

The amount of the financial penalty due for this offence is ............................................................. EUR/national currency.

Deadline for the payment is ....................................................................................................................................................

You are advised to complete the attached reply form (page 4) and send it to the address shown, if you do not pay this financial penalty.

This letter shall be processed in accordance with the national law of ..................................................................................
***[name of the Member State of the offence].***

(1) Delete if not applicable.

**Page 3**

**Relevant details concerning the offence**

(a) *Data concerning the vehicle with which the offence has been committed:*

Registration number: ..........

Country of registration: ..........

Make and model: ..........

(b) *Data concerning the offence:*

Place, date and time where the offence has been committed:

..........

..........

Nature and legal classification of the offence:

..........

..........

speeding, non-use of seatbelt, failing to stop at a red traffic light, drink-driving, driving under the influence of drugs, failing to wear a safety helmet, use of a forbidden lane, illegally using a mobile telephone or any other communication device while driving (1)

Detailed description of the offence:

..........

..........

Reference to the relevant legal provision(s):

..........

..........

Description of or reference to the evidence for the offence:

..........

..........

(c) *Data concerning the device that has been used for detecting the offence* (2):

Type of device for detection of speeding, non-use of seatbelt, failing to stop at a red traffic light, drink-driving, driving under the influence of drugs, failing to wear a safety helmet, use of a forbidden lane, illegally using a mobile telephone or any other communication devices while driving (1):

Specification of the device:

..........

Identification number of the device:

..........

Expiry date for the last gauging:

..........

(d) *The result of the application of the device:*

..........

***[example for speeding; other offences to be added:]***

The maximum speed:

..........

The measured speed:

..........

The measured speed corrected for margin of error:

..........

(1) Delete if not applicable.
(2) Not applicable if no device has been used.

**Page 4**

**Reply form**

***(please complete using block capitals)***

A. **Identity of the driver:**

— Full name: ..................................................................................

..................................................................................

— Place and date of birth: ..................................................................................

..................................................................................

— Number of driving licence: ........................... delivered (date): ........................... and at (place): ...........................

..................................................................................

— Address: ..................................................................................

..................................................................................

B. **List of questions:**

1. Is the vehicle, make ............... registration number ............... registered in your name? yes/no [1]

   If not, the holder of the registration certificate is: ..................................................................................

   ..................................................................................
   ***(name, first name, address)***

2. Do you acknowledge that you committed the offence? yes/no [1]

3. If you do not acknowledge this, please explain why:

   ..................................................................................

   ..................................................................................

   ..................................................................................

   ..................................................................................

Please send the completed form within 60 days from the date of this information letter to the following authority: ...........

..................................................................................

at the following address: ..................................................................................

..................................................................................

**INFORMATION**

This case will be examined by the competent authority of ..................................................................................
***[name of the Member State of the offence]***

If this case is not pursued, you will be informed within 60 days after receipt of the reply form.

[1] Delete if not applicable.

If this case is pursued, the following procedure applies:

..........................................................................................................................................

..........................................................................................................................................

..........................................................................................................................................

..........................................................................................................................................

..........................................................................................................................................

..........................................................................................................................................

..........................................................................................................................................

..........................................................................................................................................

..........................................................................................................................................

..........................................................................................................................................

*[to be filled in by the Member State of the offence — what the further procedure will be, including details of the possibility and procedure of appeal against the decision to pursue the case. These details shall in any event include: name and address of the authority in charge of pursuing the case; deadline for payment; name and address of the body of appeal concerned; deadline for appeal].*

This letter as such does not lead to legal consequences.

**COMMISSION STATEMENT ON THE LEGAL BASIS**

"The Commission notes that both Council and European Parliament agree on the replacement of the legal basis proposed by the Commission, namely Article 91, paragraph 1c, TFEU by Article 87, paragraph 2, TFEU. While the Commission shares the view of both co-legislators about the importance of pursuing the aims of the proposed Directive to improve road safety, it considers however from a legal and institutional perspective that Article 87, paragraph 2, TFEU does not constitute the appropriate legal basis and therefore reserves its right to use all legal means at its disposal."

# Directive 2011/92 on combating the sexual abuse and sexual exploitation of children and child pornography, and replacing Council Framework Decision 2004/68, 13 December 2011

[OJ 2011, L 335/1–14]

17.12.2011 EN Official Journal of the European Union L 335/1

I

*(Legislative acts)*

# DIRECTIVES

## DIRECTIVE 2011/92/EU OF THE EUROPEAN PARLIAMENT AND OF THE COUNCIL

**of 13 December 2011**

**on combating the sexual abuse and sexual exploitation of children and child pornography, and replacing Council Framework Decision 2004/68/JHA**

THE EUROPEAN PARLIAMENT AND THE COUNCIL OF THE EUROPEAN UNION,

Having regard to the Treaty on the Functioning of the European Union, and in particular Article 82(2) and Article 83(1) thereof,

Having regard to the proposal from the European Commission,

After transmission of the draft legislative act to the national parliaments,

Having regard to the opinion of the European Economic and Social Committee [1],

After consulting the Committee of the Regions,

Acting in accordance with the ordinary legislative procedure [2],

Whereas:

(1) Sexual abuse and sexual exploitation of children, including child pornography, constitute serious violations of fundamental rights, in particular of the rights of children to the protection and care necessary for their well-being, as provided for by the 1989 United Nations Convention on the Rights of the Child and by the Charter of Fundamental Rights of the European Union [3].

(2) In accordance with Article 6(1) of the Treaty on European Union, the Union recognises the rights, freedoms and principles set out in the Charter of Fundamental Rights of the European Union, in which Article 24(2) provides that in all actions relating to children, whether taken by public authorities or private institutions, the child's best interests must be a primary consideration. Moreover, the Stockholm Programme — An Open and Secure Europe Serving and Protecting Citizens [4] gives a clear priority to combating the sexual abuse and sexual exploitation of children and child pornography.

(3) Child pornography, which consists of images of child sexual abuse, and other particularly serious forms of sexual abuse and sexual exploitation of children are increasing and spreading through the use of new technologies and the Internet.

(4) Council Framework Decision 2004/68/JHA of 22 December 2003 on combating the sexual exploitation of children and child pornography [5] approximates Member States' legislation to criminalise the most serious forms of child sexual abuse and sexual exploitation, to extend domestic jurisdiction, and to provide for a minimum level of assistance for victims. Council Framework Decision 2001/220/JHA of 15 March 2001 on the standing of victims in criminal proceedings [6] establishes a set of victims' rights in criminal proceedings, including the right to protection and compensation. Moreover, the coordination of prosecution of cases of sexual abuse, sexual exploitation of children and child pornography will be facilitated by the implementation of Council Framework Decision 2009/948/JHA of 30 November 2009 on prevention and settlement of conflicts of exercise of jurisdiction in criminal proceedings [7].

(5) In accordance with Article 34 of the United Nations Convention on the Rights of the Child, States Parties undertake to protect the child from all forms of sexual exploitation and sexual abuse. The 2000 United Nations Optional Protocol to the Convention on the Rights of the Child on the sale of children, child prostitution and child pornography and, in particular, the 2007 Council

(1) OJ C 48, 15.2.2011, p. 138.
(2) Position of the European Parliament of 27 October 2011 (not yet published in the Official Journal) and decision of the Council of 15 November 2011.
(3) OJ C 364, 18.12.2000, p. 1.
(4) OJ C 115, 4.5.2010, p. 1.
(5) OJ L 13, 20.1.2004, p. 44.
(6) OJ L 82, 22.3.2001, p. 1.
(7) OJ L 328, 15.12.2009, p. 42.

of Europe Convention on the Protection of Children against Sexual Exploitation and Sexual Abuse are crucial steps in the process of enhancing international cooperation in this field.

(6) Serious criminal offences such as the sexual exploitation of children and child pornography require a comprehensive approach covering the prosecution of offenders, the protection of child victims, and prevention of the phenomenon. The child's best interests must be a primary consideration when carrying out any measures to combat these offences in accordance with the Charter of Fundamental Rights of the European Union and the United Nations Convention on the Rights of the Child. Framework Decision 2004/68/JHA should be replaced by a new instrument providing such comprehensive legal framework to achieve that purpose.

(7) This Directive should be fully complementary with Directive 2011/36/EU of the European Parliament and of the Council of 5 April 2011 on preventing and combating trafficking in human beings and protecting its victims, and replacing Council Framework Decision 2002/629/JHA ([1]), as some victims of human trafficking have also been child victims of sexual abuse or sexual exploitation.

(8) In the context of criminalising acts related to pornographic performance, this Directive refers to such acts which consist of an organised live exhibition, aimed at an audience, thereby excluding personal face-to-face communication between consenting peers, as well as children over the age of sexual consent and their partners from the definition.

(9) Child pornography frequently includes images recording the sexual abuse of children by adults. It may also include images of children involved in sexually explicit conduct, or of their sexual organs, where such images are produced or used for primarily sexual purposes and exploited with or without the child's knowledge. Furthermore, the concept of child pornography also covers realistic images of a child, where a child is engaged or depicted as being engaged in sexually explicit conduct for primarily sexual purposes.

(10) Disability, by itself, does not automatically constitute an impossibility to consent to sexual relations. However, the abuse of the existence of such a disability in order to engage in sexual activities with a child should be criminalised.

(11) In adopting legislation on substantive criminal law, the Union should ensure consistency of such legislation in particular with regard to the level of penalties. The Council conclusions of 24 and 25 April 2002 on the approach to apply regarding approximation of penalties, which indicate four levels of penalties, should be kept in mind in the light of the Lisbon Treaty. This Directive, because it contains an exceptionally high number of different offences, requires, in order to reflect the various degrees of seriousness, a differentiation in the level of penalties which goes further than what should usually be provided in Union legal instruments.

(12) Serious forms of sexual abuse and sexual exploitation of children should be subject to effective, proportionate and dissuasive penalties. This includes, in particular, various forms of sexual abuse and sexual exploitation of children which are facilitated by the use of information and communication technology, such as the online solicitation of children for sexual purposes via social networking websites and chat rooms. The definition of child pornography should also be clarified and brought closer to that contained in international instruments.

(13) The maximum term of imprisonment provided for in this Directive for the offences referred to therein should apply at least to the most serious forms of such offences.

(14) In order to reach the maximum term of imprisonment provided for in this Directive for offences concerning sexual abuse and sexual exploitation of children and child pornography, Member States may combine, taking into account their national law, the imprisonment terms provided for in national legislation in respect of those offences.

(15) This Directive obliges Member States to provide for criminal penalties in their national legislation in respect of the provisions of Union law on combating sexual abuse, sexual exploitation of children and child pornography. This Directive creates no obligations regarding the application of such penalties, or any other available system of law enforcement, in individual cases.

(16) Especially for those cases where the offences referred to in this Directive are committed with the purpose of financial gain, Member States are invited to consider providing for the possibility to impose financial penalties in addition to imprisonment.

(17) In the context of child pornography, the term 'without right' allows Member States to provide a defence in respect of conduct relating to pornographic material having for example, a medical, scientific or similar purpose. It also allows activities carried out under domestic legal powers, such as the legitimate possession of child pornography by the authorities in order to conduct criminal proceedings or to prevent, detect or investigate crime. Furthermore, it does not exclude legal defences or similar relevant principles that relieve a person of responsibility under specific circumstances, for example where telephone or Internet hotlines carry out activities to report those cases.

([1]) OJ L 101, 15.4.2011, p. 1.

(18) Knowingly obtaining access, by means of information and communication technology, to child pornography should be criminalised. To be liable, the person should both intend to enter a site where child pornography is available and know that such images can be found there. Penalties should not be applied to persons inadvertently accessing sites containing child pornography. The intentional nature of the offence may notably be deduced from the fact that it is recurrent or that the offence was committed via a service in return for payment.

(19) Solicitation of children for sexual purposes is a threat with specific characteristics in the context of the Internet, as the latter provides unprecedented anonymity to users because they are able to conceal their real identity and personal characteristics, such as their age. At the same time, Member States acknowledge the importance of also combating the solicitation of a child outside the context of the Internet, in particular where such solicitation is not carried out by using information and communication technology. Member States are encouraged to criminalise the conduct where the solicitation of a child to meet the offender for sexual purposes takes place in the presence or proximity of the child, for instance in the form of a particular preparatory offence, attempt to commit the offences referred to in this Directive or as a particular form of sexual abuse. Whichever legal solution is chosen to criminalise 'off-line grooming', Member States should ensure that they prosecute the perpetrators of such offences one way or another.

(20) This Directive does not govern Member States' policies with regard to consensual sexual activities in which children may be involved and which can be regarded as the normal discovery of sexuality in the course of human development, taking account of the different cultural and legal traditions and of new forms of establishing and maintaining relations among children and adolescents, including through information and communication technologies. These issues fall outside of the scope of this Directive. Member States which avail themselves of the possibilities referred to in this Directive do so in the exercise of their competences.

(21) Member States should provide for aggravating circumstances in their national law in accordance with the applicable rules established by their legal systems on aggravating circumstances. They should ensure that those aggravating circumstances are available for judges to consider when sentencing offenders, although there is no obligation on judges to apply those aggravating circumstances. The aggravating circumstances should not be provided for in Member States' law when irrelevant taking into account the nature of the specific offence. The relevance of the various aggravating circumstances provided for in this Directive should be evaluated at national level for each of the offences referred to in this Directive.

(22) Physical or mental incapacity under this Directive should be understood as also including the state of physical or mental incapacity caused by the influence of drugs and alcohol.

(23) In combating sexual exploitation of children, full use should be made of existing instruments on the seizure and confiscation of the proceeds of crime, such as the United Nations Convention against Transnational Organized Crime and the Protocols thereto, the 1990 Council of Europe Convention on Laundering, Search, Seizure and Confiscation of the Proceeds from Crime, Council Framework Decision 2001/500/JHA of 26 June 2001 on money laundering, the identification, tracing, freezing, seizing and confiscation of instrumentalities and the proceeds of crime [1], and Council Framework Decision 2005/212/JHA of 24 February 2005 on Confiscation of Crime Related Proceeds, Instrumentalities and Property [2]. The use of seized and confiscated instrumentalities and the proceeds from the offences referred to in this Directive to support victims' assistance and protection should be encouraged.

(24) Secondary victimisation should be avoided for victims of offences referred to in this Directive. In Member States where prostitution or the appearance in pornography is punishable under national criminal law, it should be possible not to prosecute or impose penalties under those laws where the child concerned has committed those acts as a result of being victim of sexual exploitation or where the child was compelled to participate in child pornography.

(25) As an instrument of approximation of criminal law, this Directive provides for levels of penalties which should apply without prejudice to the specific criminal policies of the Member States concerning child offenders.

(26) Investigating offences and bringing charges in criminal proceedings should be facilitated, to take into account the difficulty for child victims of denouncing sexual abuse and the anonymity of offenders in cyberspace. To ensure successful investigations and prosecutions of the offences referred to in this Directive, their initiation should not depend, in principle, on a report or accusation made by the victim or by his or her representative. The length of the sufficient period of time for prosecution should be determined in accordance with national law.

(27) Effective investigatory tools should be made available to those responsible for the investigation and prosecutions

(1) OJ L 182, 5.7.2001, p. 1.
(2) OJ L 68, 15.3.2005, p. 49.

of the offences referred to in this Directive. Those tools could include interception of communications, covert surveillance including electronic surveillance, monitoring of bank accounts or other financial investigations, taking into account, inter alia, the principle of proportionality and the nature and seriousness of the offences under investigation. Where appropriate, and in accordance with national law, such tools should also include the possibility for law enforcement authorities to use a concealed identity on the Internet.

(28) Member States should encourage any person who has knowledge or suspicion of the sexual abuse or sexual exploitation of a child to report to the competent services. It is the responsibility of each Member State to determine the competent authorities to which such suspicions may be reported. Those competent authorities should not be limited to child protection services or relevant social services. The requirement of suspicion 'in good faith' should be aimed at preventing the provision being invoked to authorise the denunciation of purely imaginary or untrue facts carried out with malicious intent.

(29) Rules on jurisdiction should be amended to ensure that sexual abusers or sexual exploiters of children from the Union face prosecution even if they commit their crimes outside the Union, in particular via so-called sex tourism. Child sex tourism should be understood as the sexual exploitation of children by a person or persons who travel from their usual environment to a destination abroad where they have sexual contact with children. Where child sex tourism takes place outside the Union, Member States are encouraged to seek to increase, through the available national and international instruments including bilateral or multilateral treaties on extradition, mutual assistance or a transfer of the proceedings, cooperation with third countries and international organisations with a view to combating sex tourism. Member States should foster open dialogue and communication with countries outside the Union in order to be able to prosecute perpetrators, under the relevant national legislation, who travel outside the Union borders for the purposes of child sex tourism.

(30) Measures to protect child victims should be adopted in their best interest, taking into account an assessment of their needs. Child victims should have easy access to legal remedies and measures to address conflicts of interest where sexual abuse or sexual exploitation of a child occurs within the family. When a special representative should be appointed for a child during a criminal investigation or proceeding, this role may be also carried out by a legal person, an institution or an authority. Moreover, child victims should be protected from penalties, for example under national legislation on prostitution, if they bring their case to the attention of competent authorities. Furthermore, participation in criminal proceedings by child victims should not cause additional trauma to the extent possible, as a result of interviews or visual contact with offenders. A good understanding of children and how they behave when faced with traumatic experiences will help to ensure a high quality of evidence-taking and also reduce the stress placed on children when carrying out the necessary measures.

(31) Member States should consider giving short and long term assistance to child victims. Any harm caused by the sexual abuse and sexual exploitation of a child is significant and should be addressed. Because of the nature of the harm caused by sexual abuse and sexual exploitation, such assistance should continue for as long as necessary for the child's physical and psychological recovery and may last into adulthood if necessary. Assistance and advice should be considered to be extended to parents or guardians of the child victims where they are not involved as suspects in relation to the offence concerned, in order to help them to assist child victims throughout the proceedings.

(32) Framework Decision 2001/220/JHA establishes a set of victims' rights in criminal proceedings, including the right to protection and compensation. In addition child victims of sexual abuse, sexual exploitation and child pornography should be given access to legal counselling and, in accordance with the role of victims in the relevant justice systems, to legal representation, including for the purpose of claiming compensation. Such legal counselling and legal representation could also be provided by the competent authorities for the purpose of claiming compensation from the State. The purpose of legal counselling is to enable victims to be informed and receive advice about the various possibilities open to them. Legal counselling should be provided by a person having received appropriate legal training without necessarily being a lawyer. Legal counselling and, in accordance with the role of victims in the relevant justice systems, legal representation should be provided free of charge, at least when the victim does not have sufficient financial resources, in a manner consistent with the internal procedures of Member States.

(33) Member States should undertake action to prevent or prohibit acts related to the promotion of sexual abuse of children and child sex tourism. Different preventative measures could be considered, such as the drawing up and reinforcement of a code of conduct and self-regulatory mechanisms in the tourism industry, the setting-up of a code of ethics or 'quality labels' for tourist organisations combating child sex tourism, or establishing an explicit policy to tackle child sex tourism.

(34) Member States should establish and/or strengthen policies to prevent sexual abuse and sexual exploitation of children, including measures to discourage and reduce the demand that fosters all forms of sexual exploitation of children, and measures to reduce the risk of children becoming victims, by means of, information and awareness-raising campaigns, and research and education programmes. In such initiatives, Member States should adopt a child-rights based approach. Particular care should be taken to ensure that awareness-raising campaigns aimed at children are appropriate and sufficiently easy to understand. The establishment of help-lines or hotlines should be considered.

(35) Regarding the system of reporting sexual abuse and sexual exploitation of children and helping children in need, hotlines under the number 116 000 for missing children, 116 006 for victims of crime and 116 111 for children, as introduced by Commission Decision 2007/116/EC of 15 February 2007 on reserving the national numbering beginning with 116 for harmonised numbers for harmonised services of social value [1], should be promoted and experience regarding their functioning should be taken into account.

(36) Professionals likely to come into contact with child victims of sexual abuse and sexual exploitation should be adequately trained to identify and deal with such victims. That training should be promoted for members of the following categories when they are likely to come into contact with child victims: police officers, public prosecutors, lawyers, members of the judiciary and court officials, child and health care personnel, but could also involve other groups of persons who are likely to encounter child victims of sexual abuse and sexual exploitation in their work.

(37) In order to prevent the sexual abuse and sexual exploitation of children, intervention programmes or measures targeting sex offenders should be proposed to them. Those intervention programmes or measures should meet a broad, flexible approach focusing on the medical and psycho-social aspects and have a non-obligatory character. Those intervention programmes or measures are without prejudice to intervention programmes or measures imposed by the competent judicial authorities.

(38) Intervention programmes or measures are not provided as an automatic right. It is for the Member State to decide which intervention programmes or measures are appropriate.

(39) To prevent and minimise recidivism, offenders should be subject to an assessment of the danger posed by the offenders and the possible risks of repetition of sexual offences against children. Arrangements for such assessment, such as the type of authority competent to order and carry out the assessment or the moment in or after the criminal proceedings when that assessment should take place as well as arrangements for effective intervention programmes or measures offered following that assessment should be consistent with the internal procedures of Member States. For the same objective of preventing and minimising recidivism, offenders should also have access to effective intervention programmes or measures on a voluntary basis. Those intervention programmes or measures should not interfere with national schemes set up to deal with the treatment of persons suffering from mental disorders.

(40) Where the danger posed by the offenders and the possible risks of repetition of the offences make it appropriate, convicted offenders should be temporarily or permanently prevented from exercising at least professional activities involving direct and regular contacts with children. Employers when recruiting for a post involving direct and regular contact with children are entitled to be informed of existing convictions for sexual offences against children entered in the criminal record, or of existing disqualifications. For the purposes of this Directive, the term 'employers' should also cover persons running an organisation that is active in volunteer work related to the supervision and/or care of children involving direct and regular contact with children. The manner in which such information is delivered, such as for example access via the person concerned, and the precise content of the information, the meaning of organised voluntary activities and direct and regular contact with children should be laid down in accordance with national law.

(41) With due regard to the different legal traditions of the Member States, this Directive takes into account the fact that access to criminal records is allowed only either by the competent authorities or by the person concerned. This Directive does not establish an obligation to modify the national systems governing criminal records or the means of access to those records.

(42) The aim of this Directive is not to harmonise rules concerning consent of the person concerned when exchanging information from the criminal registers, i.e. whether or not to require such consent. Whether the consent is required or not under national law, this Directive does not establish any new obligation to change the national law and national procedures in this respect.

[1] OJ L 49, 17.2.2007, p. 30.

(43) Member States may consider adopting additional administrative measures in relation to perpetrators, such as the registration in sex offender registers of persons convicted of offences referred to in this Directive. Access to those registers should be subject to limitation in accordance with national constitutional principles and applicable data protection standards, for instance by limiting access to the judiciary and/or law enforcement authorities.

(44) Member States are encouraged to create mechanisms for data collection or focal points, at the national or local levels and in collaboration with civil society, for the purpose of observing and evaluating the phenomenon of sexual abuse and sexual exploitation of children. In order to be able to properly evaluate the results of actions to combat sexual abuse and sexual exploitation of children and child pornography, the Union should continue to develop its work on methodologies and data collection methods to produce comparable statistics.

(45) Member States should take appropriate action for setting up information services to provide information on how to recognise the signs of sexual abuse and sexual exploitation.

(46) Child pornography, which constitutes child sexual abuse images, is a specific type of content which cannot be construed as the expression of an opinion. To combat it, it is necessary to reduce the circulation of child sexual abuse material by making it more difficult for offenders to upload such content onto the publicly accessible web. Action is therefore necessary to remove the content and apprehend those guilty of making, distributing or downloading child sexual abuse images. With a view to supporting the Union's efforts to combat child pornography, Member States should use their best endeavours to cooperate with third countries in seeking to secure the removal of such content from servers within their territory.

(47) However, despite such efforts, the removal of child pornography content at its source is often not possible when the original materials are not located within the Union, either because the State where the servers are hosted is not willing to cooperate or because obtaining removal of the material from the State concerned proves to be particularly long. Mechanisms may also be put in place to block access from the Union's territory to Internet pages identified as containing or disseminating child pornography. The measures undertaken by Member States in accordance with this Directive in order to remove or, where appropriate, block websites containing child pornography could be based on various types of public action, such as legislative, non-legislative, judicial or other. In that context, this Directive is without prejudice to voluntary action taken by the Internet industry to prevent the misuse of its services or to any support for such action by Member States. Whichever basis for action or method is chosen, Member States should ensure that it provides an adequate level of legal certainty and predictability to users and service providers. Both with a view to the removal and the blocking of child abuse content, cooperation between public authorities should be established and strengthened, particularly in the interests of ensuring that national lists of websites containing child pornography material are as complete as possible and of avoiding duplication of work. Any such developments must take account of the rights of the end users and comply with existing legal and judicial procedures and the European Convention for the Protection of Human Rights and Fundamental Freedoms and the Charter of Fundamental Rights of the European Union. The Safer Internet Programme has set up a network of hotlines the goal of which is to collect information and to ensure coverage and exchange of reports on the major types of illegal content online.

(48) This Directive aims to amend and expand the provisions of Framework Decision 2004/68/JHA. Since the amendments to be made are of substantial number and nature, the Framework Decision should, in the interests of clarity, be replaced in its entirety in relation to Member States participating in the adoption of this Directive.

(49) Since the objective of this Directive, namely to combat sexual abuse, sexual exploitation of children and child pornography, cannot be sufficiently achieved by the Member States alone and can therefore, by reasons of the scale and effects, be better achieved at Union level, the Union may adopt measures, in accordance with the principle of subsidiarity as set out in Article 5 of the Treaty on European Union. In accordance with the principle of proportionality, as set out in that Article, this Directive does not go beyond what is necessary to achieve that objective.

(50) This Directive respects fundamental rights and observes the principles recognised in particular by the Charter of Fundamental Rights of the European Union and in particular the right to the protection of human dignity, the prohibition of torture and inhuman or degrading treatment or punishment, the rights of the child, the right to liberty and security, the right to freedom of expression and information, the right to the protection of personal data, the right to an effective remedy and to a fair trial and the principles of legality and proportionality of criminal offences and penalties. This Directive seeks to ensure full respect for those rights and principles and must be implemented accordingly.

17.12.2011 EN Official Journal of the European Union L 335/7

(51) In accordance with Article 3 of the Protocol (No 21) on the position of United Kingdom and Ireland in respect of the area of freedom, security and justice, annexed to the Treaty on European Union and the Treaty on the Functioning of the European Union, the United Kingdom and Ireland have notified their wish to take part in the adoption and application of this Directive.

(52) In accordance with Articles 1 and 2 of the Protocol (No 22) on the position of Denmark annexed to the Treaty on European Union and to the Treaty on the Functioning of the European Union, Denmark is not taking part in the adoption of this Directive and is not bound by it or subject to its application,

HAVE ADOPTED THIS DIRECTIVE:

*Article 1*

**Subject matter**

This Directive establishes minimum rules concerning the definition of criminal offences and sanctions in the area of sexual abuse and sexual exploitation of children, child pornography and solicitation of children for sexual purposes. It also introduces provisions to strengthen the prevention of those crimes and the protection of the victims thereof.

*Article 2*

**Definitions**

For the purposes of this Directive, the following definitions apply:

(a) 'child' means any person below the age of 18 years;

(b) 'age of sexual consent' means the age below which, in accordance with national law, it is prohibited to engage in sexual activities with a child;

(c) 'child pornography' means:

(i) any material that visually depicts a child engaged in real or simulated sexually explicit conduct;

(ii) any depiction of the sexual organs of a child for primarily sexual purposes;

(iii) any material that visually depicts any person appearing to be a child engaged in real or simulated sexually explicit conduct or any depiction of the sexual organs of any person appearing to be a child, for primarily sexual purposes; or

(iv) realistic images of a child engaged in sexually explicit conduct or realistic images of the sexual organs of a child, for primarily sexual purposes;

(d) 'child prostitution' means the use of a child for sexual activities where money or any other form of remuneration or consideration is given or promised as payment in exchange for the child engaging in sexual activities, regardless of whether that payment, promise or consideration is made to the child or to a third party;

(e) 'pornographic performance' means a live exhibition aimed at an audience, including by means of information and communication technology, of:

(i) a child engaged in real or simulated sexually explicit conduct; or

(ii) the sexual organs of a child for primarily sexual purposes;

(f) 'legal person' means an entity having legal personality under the applicable law, except for States or public bodies in the exercise of State authority and for public international organisations.

*Article 3*

**Offences concerning sexual abuse**

1. Member States shall take the necessary measures to ensure that the intentional conduct referred to in paragraphs 2 to 6 is punishable.

2. Causing, for sexual purposes, a child who has not reached the age of sexual consent to witness sexual activities, even without having to participate, shall be punishable by a maximum term of imprisonment of at least 1 year.

3. Causing, for sexual purposes, a child who has not reached the age of sexual consent to witness sexual abuse, even without having to participate, shall be punishable by a maximum term of imprisonment of at least 2 years.

4. Engaging in sexual activities with a child who has not reached the age of sexual consent shall be punishable by a maximum term of imprisonment of at least 5 years.

5. Engaging in sexual activities with a child, where:

(i) abuse is made of a recognised position of trust, authority or influence over the child, shall be punishable by a maximum term of imprisonment of at least 8 years if the child has not reached the age of sexual consent, and of at least 3 years of imprisonment, if the child is over that age; or

(ii) abuse is made of a particularly vulnerable situation of the child, in particular because of a mental or physical disability or a situation of dependence, shall be punishable by a maximum term of imprisonment of at least 8 years if the child has not reached the age of sexual consent, and of at least 3 years of imprisonment if the child is over that age; or

(iii) use is made of coercion, force or threats shall be punishable by a maximum term of imprisonment of at least 10 years if the child has not reached the age of sexual consent, and of at least 5 years of imprisonment if the child is over that age.

6. Coercing, forcing or threatening a child into sexual activities with a third party shall be punishable by a maximum term of imprisonment of at least 10 years if the child has not reached the age of sexual consent, and of at least 5 years of imprisonment if the child is over that age.

*Article 4*

**Offences concerning sexual exploitation**

1. Member States shall take the necessary measures to ensure that the intentional conduct referred to in paragraphs 2 to 7 is punishable.

2. Causing or recruiting a child to participate in pornographic performances, or profiting from or otherwise exploiting a child for such purposes shall be punishable by a maximum term of imprisonment of at least 5 years if the child has not reached the age of sexual consent and of at least 2 years of imprisonment if the child is over that age.

3. Coercing or forcing a child to participate in pornographic performances, or threatening a child for such purposes shall be punishable by a maximum term of imprisonment of at least 8 years if the child has not reached the age of sexual consent, and of at least 5 years of imprisonment if the child is over that age.

4. Knowingly attending pornographic performances involving the participation of a child shall be punishable by a maximum term of imprisonment of at least 2 years if the child has not reached the age of sexual consent, and of at least 1 year of imprisonment if the child is over that age.

5. Causing or recruiting a child to participate in child prostitution, or profiting from or otherwise exploiting a child for such purposes shall be punishable by a maximum term of imprisonment of at least 8 years if the child has not reached the age of sexual consent, and of at least 5 years of imprisonment if the child is over that age.

6. Coercing or forcing a child into child prostitution, or threatening a child for such purposes shall be punishable by a maximum term of imprisonment of at least 10 years if the child has not reached the age of sexual consent, and of at least 5 years of imprisonment if the child is over that age.

7. Engaging in sexual activities with a child, where recourse is made to child prostitution shall be punishable by a maximum term of imprisonment of at least 5 years if the child has not reached the age of sexual consent, and of at least 2 years of imprisonment if the child is over that age.

*Article 5*

**Offences concerning child pornography**

1. Member States shall take the necessary measures to ensure that the intentional conduct, when committed without right, referred to in paragraphs 2 to 6 is punishable.

2. Acquisition or possession of child pornography shall be punishable by a maximum term of imprisonment of at least 1 year.

3. Knowingly obtaining access, by means of information and communication technology, to child pornography shall be punishable by a maximum term of imprisonment of at least 1 year.

4. Distribution, dissemination or transmission of child pornography shall be punishable by a maximum term of imprisonment of at least 2 years.

5. Offering, supplying or making available child pornography shall be punishable by a maximum term of imprisonment of at least 2 years.

6. Production of child pornography shall be punishable by a maximum term of imprisonment of at least 3 years.

7. It shall be within the discretion of Member States to decide whether this Article applies to cases involving child pornography as referred to in Article 2(c)(iii), where the person appearing to be a child was in fact 18 years of age or older at the time of depiction.

8. It shall be within the discretion of Member States to decide whether paragraphs 2 and 6 of this Article apply to cases where it is established that pornographic material as referred to in Article 2(c)(iv) is produced and possessed by the producer solely for his or her private use in so far as no pornographic material as referred to in Article 2(c)(i), (ii) or (iii) has been used for the purpose of its production and provided that the act involves no risk of dissemination of the material.

*Article 6*

**Solicitation of children for sexual purposes**

1. Member States shall take the necessary measures to ensure that the following intentional conduct is punishable:

the proposal, by means of information and communication technology, by an adult to meet a child who has not reached the age of sexual consent, for the purpose of committing any of the offences referred to in Article 3(4) and Article 5(6), where that proposal was followed by material acts leading to such a meeting, shall be punishable by a maximum term of imprisonment of at least 1 year.

2. Member States shall take the necessary measures to ensure that an attempt, by means of information and communication technology, to commit the offences provided for in Article 5(2) and (3) by an adult soliciting a child who has not reached the age of sexual consent to provide child pornography depicting that child is punishable.

*Article 7*

**Incitement, aiding and abetting, and attempt**

1. Member States shall take the necessary measures to ensure that inciting or aiding and abetting to commit any of the offences referred to in Articles 3 to 6 is punishable.

2. Member States shall take the necessary measures to ensure that an attempt to commit any of the offences referred to in Article 3(4), (5) and (6), Article 4(2), (3), (5), (6) and (7), and Article 5(4), (5) and (6) is punishable.

*Article 8*

**Consensual sexual activities**

1. It shall be within the discretion of Member States to decide whether Article 3(2) and (4) apply to consensual sexual activities between peers, who are close in age and degree of psychological and physical development or maturity, in so far as the acts did not involve any abuse.

2. It shall be within the discretion of Member States to decide whether Article 4(4) applies to a pornographic performance that takes place in the context of a consensual relationship where the child has reached the age of sexual consent or between peers who are close in age and degree of psychological and physical development or maturity, in so far as the acts did not involve any abuse or exploitation and no money or other form of remuneration or consideration is given as payment in exchange for the pornographic performance.

3. It shall be within the discretion of Member States to decide whether Article 5(2) and (6) apply to the production, acquisition or possession of material involving children who have reached the age of sexual consent where that material is produced and possessed with the consent of those children and only for the private use of the persons involved, in so far as the acts did not involve any abuse.

*Article 9*

**Aggravating circumstances**

In so far as the following circumstances do not already form part of the constituent elements of the offences referred to in Articles 3 to 7, Member States shall take the necessary measures to ensure that the following circumstances may, in accordance with the relevant provisions of national law, be regarded as aggravating circumstances, in relation to the relevant offences referred to in Articles 3 to 7:

(a) the offence was committed against a child in a particularly vulnerable situation, such as a child with a mental or physical disability, in a situation of dependence or in a state of physical or mental incapacity;

(b) the offence was committed by a member of the child's family, a person cohabiting with the child or a person who has abused a recognised position of trust or authority;

(c) the offence was committed by several persons acting together;

(d) the offence was committed within the framework of a criminal organisation within the meaning of Council Framework Decision 2008/841/JHA of 24 October 2008 on the fight against organised crime [1];

(e) the offender has previously been convicted of offences of the same nature;

(f) the offender has deliberately or recklessly endangered the life of the child; or

(g) the offence involved serious violence or caused serious harm to the child.

*Article 10*

**Disqualification arising from convictions**

1. In order to avoid the risk of repetition of offences, Member States shall take the necessary measures to ensure that a natural person who has been convicted of any of the offences referred to in Articles 3 to 7 may be temporarily or permanently prevented from exercising at least professional activities involving direct and regular contacts with children.

2. Member States shall take the necessary measures to ensure that employers, when recruiting a person for professional or organised voluntary activities involving direct and regular contacts with children, are entitled to request information in accordance with national law by way of any appropriate means, such as access upon request or via the person concerned, of the existence of criminal convictions for any of the offences referred to in Articles 3 to 7 entered in the criminal record or of the existence of any disqualification from exercising activities involving direct and regular contacts with children arising from those criminal convictions.

3. Member States shall take the necessary measures to ensure that, for the application of paragraphs 1 and 2 of this Article, information concerning the existence of criminal convictions for any of the offences referred to in Articles 3 to 7, or of any disqualification from exercising activities involving direct and regular contacts with children arising from those criminal convictions, is transmitted in accordance with the procedures set out in Council Framework Decision 2009/315/JHA of 26 February 2009 on the organisation and content of the exchange of information extracted from the criminal record between Member States [2] when requested under Article 6 of that Framework Decision with the consent of the person concerned.

[1] OJ L 300, 11.11.2008, p. 42.
[2] OJ L 93, 7.4.2009, p. 23.

L 335/10 EN Official Journal of the European Union 17.12.2011

*Article 11*

**Seizure and confiscation**

Member States shall take the necessary measures to ensure that their competent authorities are entitled to seize and confiscate instrumentalities and proceeds from the offences referred to in Articles 3, 4 and 5.

*Article 12*

**Liability of legal persons**

1. Member States shall take the necessary measures to ensure that legal persons may be held liable for any of the offences referred to in Articles 3 to 7 committed for their benefit by any person, acting either individually or as part of an organ of the legal person, and having a leading position within the legal person, based on:

(a) a power of representation of the legal person;

(b) an authority to take decisions on behalf of the legal person; or

(c) an authority to exercise control within the legal person.

2. Member States shall also take the necessary measures to ensure that legal persons may be held liable where the lack of supervision or control by a person referred to in paragraph 1 has made possible the commission, by a person under its authority, of any of the offences referred to in Articles 3 to 7 for the benefit of that legal person.

3. Liability of legal persons under paragraphs 1 and 2 shall be without prejudice to criminal proceedings against natural persons who are perpetrators, inciters or accessories to the offences referred to in Articles 3 to 7.

*Article 13*

**Sanctions on legal persons**

1. Member States shall take the necessary measures to ensure that a legal person held liable pursuant to Article 12(1) is punishable by effective, proportionate and dissuasive sanctions, which shall include criminal or non-criminal fines and may include other sanctions, such as:

(a) exclusion from entitlement to public benefits or aid;

(b) temporary or permanent disqualification from the practice of commercial activities;

(c) placing under judicial supervision;

(d) judicial winding-up; or

(e) temporary or permanent closure of establishments which have been used for committing the offence.

2. Member States shall take the necessary measures to ensure that a legal person held liable pursuant to Article 12(2) is punishable by sanctions or measures which are effective, proportionate and dissuasive.

*Article 14*

**Non-prosecution or non-application of penalties to the victim**

Member States shall, in accordance with the basic principles of their legal systems take the necessary measures to ensure that competent national authorities are entitled not to prosecute or impose penalties on child victims of sexual abuse and sexual exploitation for their involvement in criminal activities, which they have been compelled to commit as a direct consequence of being subjected to any of the acts referred to in Article 4(2), (3), (5) and (6), and in Article 5(6).

*Article 15*

**Investigation and prosecution**

1. Member States shall take the necessary measures to ensure that investigations into or the prosecution of the offences referred to in Articles 3 to 7 are not dependent on a report or accusation being made by the victim or by his or her representative, and that criminal proceedings may continue even if that person has withdrawn his or her statements.

2. Member States shall take the necessary measures to enable the prosecution of any of the offences referred to in Article 3, Article 4(2), (3), (5), (6) and (7) and of any serious offences referred to in Article 5(6) when child pornography as referred to in Article 2(c)(i) and (ii) has been used, for a sufficient period of time after the victim has reached the age of majority and which is commensurate with the gravity of the offence concerned.

3. Member States shall take the necessary measures to ensure that effective investigative tools, such as those which are used in organised crime or other serious crime cases are available to persons, units or services responsible for investigating or prosecuting offences referred to in Articles 3 to 7.

4. Member States shall take the necessary measures to enable investigative units or services to attempt to identify the victims of the offences referred to in Articles 3 to 7, in particular by analysing child pornography material, such as photographs and audiovisual recordings transmitted or made available by means of information and communication technology.

*Article 16*

**Reporting suspicion of sexual abuse or sexual exploitation**

1. Member States shall take the necessary measures to ensure that the confidentiality rules imposed by national law on certain professionals whose main duty is to work with children do not constitute an obstacle to the possibility, for those professionals, of their reporting to the services responsible for child protection any situation where they have reasonable grounds for believing that a child is the victim of offences referred to in Articles 3 to 7.

2. Member States shall take the necessary measures to encourage any person who knows about or suspects, in good faith that any of the offences referred to in Articles 3 to 7 have been committed, to report this to the competent services.

*Article 17*

**Jurisdiction and coordination of prosecution**

1. Member States shall take the necessary measures to establish their jurisdiction over the offences referred to in Articles 3 to 7 where:

(a) the offence is committed in whole or in part within their territory; or

(b) the offender is one of their nationals.

2. A Member State shall inform the Commission where it decides to establish further jurisdiction over an offence referred to in Articles 3 to 7 committed outside its territory, inter alia, where:

(a) the offence is committed against one of its nationals or a person who is an habitual resident in its territory;

(b) the offence is committed for the benefit of a legal person established in its territory; or

(c) the offender is an habitual resident in its territory.

3. Member States shall ensure that their jurisdiction includes situations where an offence referred to in Articles 5 and 6, and in so far as is relevant, in Articles 3 and 7, is committed by means of information and communication technology accessed from their territory, whether or not it is based on their territory.

4. For the prosecution of any of the offences referred to in Article 3(4), (5) and (6), Article 4(2), (3), (5), (6) and (7) and Article 5(6) committed outside the territory of the Member State concerned, as regards paragraph 1(b) of this Article, each Member State shall take the necessary measures to ensure that its jurisdiction is not subordinated to the condition that the acts are a criminal offence at the place where they were performed.

5. For the prosecution of any of the offences referred to in Articles 3 to 7 committed outside the territory of the Member State concerned, as regards paragraph 1(b) of this Article, each Member State shall take the necessary measures to ensure that its jurisdiction is not subordinated to the condition that the prosecution can only be initiated following a report made by the victim in the place where the offence was committed, or a denunciation from the State of the place where the offence was committed.

*Article 18*

**General provisions on assistance, support and protection measures for child victims**

1. Child victims of the offences referred to in Articles 3 to 7 shall be provided assistance, support and protection in accordance with Articles 19 and 20, taking into account the best interests of the child.

2. Member States shall take the necessary measures to ensure that a child is provided with assistance and support as soon as the competent authorities have a reasonable-grounds indication for believing that a child might have been subject to any of the offences referred to in Articles 3 to 7.

3. Member States shall ensure that, where the age of a person subject to any of the offences referred to in Articles 3 to 7 is uncertain and there are reasons to believe that the person is a child, that person is presumed to be a child in order to receive immediate access to assistance, support and protection in accordance with Articles 19 and 20.

*Article 19*

**Assistance and support to victims**

1. Member States shall take the necessary measures to ensure that assistance and support are provided to victims before, during and for an appropriate period of time after the conclusion of criminal proceedings in order to enable them to exercise the rights set out in Framework Decision 2001/220/JHA, and in this Directive. Member States shall, in particular, take the necessary steps to ensure protection for children who report cases of abuse within their family.

2. Member States shall take the necessary measures to ensure that assistance and support for a child victim are not made conditional on the child victim's willingness to cooperate in the criminal investigation, prosecution or trial.

3. Member States shall take the necessary measures to ensure that the specific actions to assist and support child victims in enjoying their rights under this Directive, are undertaken following an individual assessment of the special circumstances of each particular child victim, taking due account of the child's views, needs and concerns.

4. Child victims of any of the offences referred to in Articles 3 to 7 shall be considered as particularly vulnerable victims pursuant to Article 2(2), Article 8(4) and Article 14(1) of Framework Decision 2001/220/JHA.

5. Member States shall take measures, where appropriate and possible, to provide assistance and support to the family of the child victim in enjoying the rights under this Directive when the family is in the territory of the Member States. In particular, Member States shall, where appropriate and possible, apply Article 4 of Framework Decision 2001/220/JHA to the family of the child victim.

*Article 20*

**Protection of child victims in criminal investigations and proceedings**

1. Member States shall take the necessary measures to ensure that in criminal investigations and proceedings, in accordance with the role of victims in the relevant justice system, competent authorities appoint a special representative for the child victim where, under national law, the holders of parental responsibility are precluded from representing the child as a result of a conflict of interest between them and the child victim, or where the child is unaccompanied or separated from the family.

2. Member States shall ensure that child victims have, without delay, access to legal counselling and, in accordance with the role of victims in the relevant justice system, to legal representation, including for the purpose of claiming compensation. Legal counselling and legal representation shall be free of charge where the victim does not have sufficient financial resources.

3. Without prejudice to the rights of the defence, Member States shall take the necessary measures to ensure that in criminal investigations relating to any of the offences referred to in Articles 3 to 7:

(a) interviews with the child victim take place without unjustified delay after the facts have been reported to the competent authorities;

(b) interviews with the child victim take place, where necessary, in premises designed or adapted for this purpose;

(c) interviews with the child victim are carried out by or through professionals trained for this purpose;

(d) the same persons, if possible and where appropriate, conduct all interviews with the child victim;

(e) the number of interviews is as limited as possible and interviews are carried out only where strictly necessary for the purpose of criminal investigations and proceedings;

(f) the child victim may be accompanied by his or her legal representative or, where appropriate, by an adult of his or her choice, unless a reasoned decision has been made to the contrary in respect of that person.

4. Member States shall take the necessary measures to ensure that in criminal investigations of any of the offences referred to in Articles 3 to 7 all interviews with the child victim or, where appropriate, with a child witness, may be audio-visually recorded and that such audio-visually recorded interviews may be used as evidence in criminal court proceedings, in accordance with the rules under their national law.

5. Member States shall take the necessary measures to ensure that in criminal court proceedings relating to any of the offences referred to in Articles 3 to 7, that it may be ordered that:

(a) the hearing take place without the presence of the public;

(b) the child victim be heard in the courtroom without being present, in particular through the use of appropriate communication technologies.

6. Member States shall take the necessary measures, where in the interest of child victims and taking into account other overriding interests, to protect the privacy, identity and image of child victims, and to prevent the public dissemination of any information that could lead to their identification.

*Article 21*

**Measures against advertising abuse opportunities and child sex tourism**

Member States shall take appropriate measures to prevent or prohibit:

(a) the dissemination of material advertising the opportunity to commit any of the offences referred to in Articles 3 to 6; and

(b) the organisation for others, whether or not for commercial purposes, of travel arrangements with the purpose of committing any of the offences referred to in Articles 3 to 5.

*Article 22*

**Preventive intervention programmes or measures**

Member States shall take the necessary measures to ensure that persons who fear that they might commit any of the offences referred to in Articles 3 to 7 may have access, where appropriate, to effective intervention programmes or measures designed to evaluate and prevent the risk of such offences being committed.

*Article 23*

**Prevention**

1. Member States shall take appropriate measures, such as education and training, to discourage and reduce the demand that fosters all forms of sexual exploitation of children.

2. Member States shall take appropriate action, including through the Internet, such as information and awareness-raising campaigns, research and education programmes, where appropriate in cooperation with relevant civil society organisations and other stakeholders, aimed at raising awareness and reducing the risk of children, becoming victims of sexual abuse or exploitation.

3. Member States shall promote regular training for officials likely to come into contact with child victims of sexual abuse or exploitation, including front-line police officers, aimed at enabling them to identify and deal with child victims and potential child victims of sexual abuse or exploitation.

*Article 24*

**Intervention programmes or measures on a voluntary basis in the course of or after criminal proceedings**

1. Without prejudice to intervention programmes or measures imposed by the competent judicial authorities under national law, Member States shall take the necessary measures to ensure that effective intervention programmes or measures are made available to prevent and minimise the risks of repeated offences of a sexual nature against children. Such programmes or measures shall be accessible at any time during the criminal proceedings, inside and outside prison, in accordance with national law.

2. The intervention programmes or measures, referred to in paragraph 1 shall meet the specific developmental needs of children who sexually offend.

3. Member States shall take the necessary measures to ensure that the following persons may have access to the intervention programmes or measures referred to in paragraph 1:

(a) persons subject to criminal proceedings for any of the offences referred to in Articles 3 to 7, under conditions which are neither detrimental nor contrary to the rights of the defence or to the requirements of a fair and impartial trial, and, in particular, in compliance with the principle of the presumption of innocence; and

(b) persons convicted of any of the offences referred to in Articles 3 to 7.

4. Member States shall take the necessary measures to ensure that the persons referred to in paragraph 3 are subject to an assessment of the danger that they present and the possible risks of repetition of any of the offences referred to in Articles 3 to 7, with the aim of identifying appropriate intervention programmes or measures.

5. Member States shall take the necessary measures to ensure that the persons referred to in paragraph 3 to whom intervention programmes or measures in accordance with paragraph 4 have been proposed:

(a) are fully informed of the reasons for the proposal;

(b) consent to their participation in the programmes or measures with full knowledge of the facts;

(c) may refuse and, in the case of convicted persons, are made aware of the possible consequences of such a refusal.

*Article 25*

**Measures against websites containing or disseminating child pornography**

1. Member States shall take the necessary measures to ensure the prompt removal of web pages containing or disseminating child pornography hosted in their territory and to endeavour to obtain the removal of such pages hosted outside of their territory.

2. Member States may take measures to block access to web pages containing or disseminating child pornography towards the Internet users within their territory. These measures must be set by transparent procedures and provide adequate safeguards, in particular to ensure that the restriction is limited to what is necessary and proportionate, and that users are informed of the reason for the restriction. Those safeguards shall also include the possibility of judicial redress.

*Article 26*

**Replacement of Framework Decision 2004/68/JHA**

Framework Decision 2004/68/JHA is hereby replaced in relation to Member States participating in the adoption of this Directive without prejudice to the obligations of those Member States relating to the time limits for transposition of the Framework Decision into national law.

In relation to Member States participating in the adoption of this Directive, references to Framework Decision 2004/68/JHA shall be construed as references to this Directive.

*Article 27*

**Transposition**

1. Member States shall bring into force the laws, regulations and administrative provisions necessary to comply with this Directive by 18 December 2013.

2. Member States shall transmit to the Commission the text of the provisions transposing into their national law the obligations imposed on them under this Directive.

3. When Member States adopt those measures, they shall contain a reference to this Directive or be accompanied by such a reference on the occasion of their official publication. The methods of making such reference shall be laid down by the Member States.

*Article 28*

**Reporting**

1. The Commission shall, by 18 December 2015, submit a report to the European Parliament and the Council assessing the extent to which the Member States have taken the necessary measures in order to comply with this Directive, accompanied, if necessary, by a legislative proposal.

2. The Commission shall, by 18 December 2015, submit a report to the European Parliament and the Council assessing the implementation of the measures referred to in Article 25.

*Article 29*

**Entry into force**

This Directive shall enter into force on the day of its publication in the *Official Journal of the European Union*.

*Article 30*

**Addressees**

This Directive is addressed to the Member States in accordance with the Treaties.

Done at Strasbourg, 13 December 2011.

*For the European Parliament*
*The President*
J. BUZEK

*For the Council*
*The President*
M. SZPUNAR

# Directive 2011/99 on the European protection order, 13 December 2011

[OJ 2011, L 338/2–18]

L 338/2 EN Official Journal of the European Union 21.12.2011

# DIRECTIVES

## DIRECTIVE 2011/99/EU OF THE EUROPEAN PARLIAMENT AND OF THE COUNCIL

**of 13 December 2011**

**on the European protection order**

THE EUROPEAN PARLIAMENT AND THE COUNCIL OF THE EUROPEAN UNION,

Having regard to the Treaty on the Functioning of the European Union, and in particular Article 82(1)(a) and (d) thereof,

Having regard to the initiative of the Kingdom of Belgium, the Republic of Bulgaria, the Republic of Estonia, the Kingdom of Spain, the French Republic, the Italian Republic, the Republic of Hungary, the Republic of Poland, the Portuguese Republic, Romania, the Republic of Finland and the Kingdom of Sweden,

After transmission of the draft legislative act to the national parliaments,

Acting in accordance with the ordinary legislative procedure ([1]),

Whereas:

(1) The European Union has set itself the objective of maintaining and developing an area of freedom, security and justice.

(2) Article 82(1) of the Treaty on the Functioning of the European Union (TFEU) provides that judicial cooperation in criminal matters in the Union shall be based on the principle of mutual recognition of judgments and judicial decisions.

(3) According to the Stockholm Programme — An open and secure Europe serving and protecting citizens ([2]), mutual recognition should extend to all types of judgments and decisions of a judicial nature, which may, depending on the legal system, be either criminal or administrative. It also calls on the Commission and the Member States to examine how to improve legislation and practical support measures for the protection of victims. The programme also points out that victims of crime can be offered special protection measures which should be effective within the Union. This Directive forms part of a coherent and comprehensive set of measures on victims' rights.

(4) The resolution of the European Parliament of 26 November 2009 on the elimination of violence against women calls on Member States to improve their national laws and policies to combat all forms of violence against women and to act in order to tackle the causes of violence against women, not least by employing preventive measures and calls on the Union to guarantee the right to assistance and support for all victims of violence. The resolution of the European Parliament of 10 February 2010 on equality between women and men in the European Union 2009 endorses the proposal to introduce the European protection order for victims.

(5) In its Resolution of 10 June 2011 on a Roadmap for strengthening the rights and protection of victims, in particular in criminal proceedings, the Council stated that action should be taken at the level of the Union in order to strengthen the rights and protection of victims of crime and called on the Commission to present appropriate proposals to that end. In this framework, a mechanism should be created to ensure mutual recognition among Member States of decisions concerning protection measures for victims of crime. According to that Resolution, this Directive, which concerns the mutual recognition of protection measures taken in criminal matters, should be complemented by an appropriate mechanism concerning measures taken in civil matters.

(6) In a common area of justice without internal borders, it is necessary to ensure that the protection provided to a natural person in one Member State is maintained and

([1]) Position of the European Parliament of 14 December 2010 (not yet published in the Official Journal) and position of the Council at first reading of 24 November 2011 (not yet published in the Official Journal). Position of the European Parliament of 13 December 2011 (not yet published in the Official Journal).

([2]) OJ C 115, 4.5.2010, p. 1.

continued in any other Member State to which the person moves or has moved. It should also be ensured that the legitimate exercise by citizens of the Union of their right to move and reside freely within the territory of Member States, in accordance with Article 3(2) of the Treaty on European Union (TEU) and Article 21 TFEU, does not result in a loss of their protection.

(7) In order to attain these objectives, this Directive should set out rules whereby the protection stemming from certain protection measures adopted according to the law of one Member State ('the issuing State') can be extended to another Member State in which the protected person decides to reside or stay ('the executing State').

(8) This Directive takes account of the different legal traditions of the Member States as well as the fact that effective protection can be provided by means of protection orders issued by an authority other than a criminal court. This Directive does not create obligations to modify national systems for adopting protection measures nor does it create obligations to introduce or amend a criminal law system for executing a European protection order.

(9) This Directive applies to protection measures which aim specifically to protect a person against a criminal act of another person which may, in any way, endanger that person's life or physical, psychological and sexual integrity, for example by preventing any form of harassment, as well as that person's dignity or personal liberty, for example by preventing abductions, stalking and other forms of indirect coercion, and which aim to prevent new criminal acts or to reduce the consequences of previous criminal acts. These personal rights of the protected person correspond to fundamental values recognised and upheld in all Member States. However, a Member State is not obliged to issue a European protection order on the basis of a criminal measure which does not serve specifically to protect a person, but primarily serves other aims, for example the social rehabilitation of the offender. It is important to underline that this Directive applies to protection measures which aim to protect all victims and not only the victims of gender violence, taking into account the specificities of each type of crime concerned.

(10) This Directive applies to protection measures adopted in criminal matters, and does not therefore cover protection measures adopted in civil matters. For a protection measure to be executable in accordance with this Directive, it is not necessary for a criminal offence to have been established by a final decision. Nor is the criminal, administrative or civil nature of the authority adopting a protection measure relevant. This Directive does not oblige Member States to amend their national law to enable them to adopt protection measures in the context of criminal proceedings.

(11) This Directive is intended to apply to protection measures adopted in favour of victims, or possible victims, of crimes. This Directive should not therefore apply to measures adopted with a view to witness protection.

(12) If a protection measure, as defined in this Directive, is adopted for the protection of a relative of the main protected person, a European protection order may also be requested by and issued in respect of that relative, subject to the conditions laid down in this Directive.

(13) Any request for the issuing of a European protection order should be treated with appropriate speed, taking into account the specific circumstances of the case, including the urgency of the matter, the date foreseen for the arrival of the protected person on the territory of the executing State and, where possible, the degree of risk for the protected person.

(14) Where information is to be provided under this Directive to the protected person or to the person causing danger, this information should also, where relevant, be provided to the guardian or the representative of the person concerned. Due attention should also be paid to the need for the protected person, the person causing danger or the guardian or representative in the proceedings, to receive the information provided for by this Directive, in a language that that person understands.

(15) In the procedures for the issuing and recognition of a European protection order, competent authorities should give appropriate consideration to the needs of victims, including particularly vulnerable persons, such as minors or persons with disabilities.

(16) For the application of this Directive, a protection measure may have been imposed following a judgment within the meaning of Council Framework Decision 2008/947/JHA of 27 November 2008 on the application of the principle of mutual recognition to judgments and probation decisions with a view to the supervision of probation measures and alternative sanctions [1], or following a decision on supervision measures within the meaning of Council Framework Decision 2009/829/JHA of 23 October 2009 on the application, between Member States of the European Union, of the

[1] OJ L 337, 16.12.2008, p. 102.

principle of mutual recognition to decisions on supervision measures as an alternative to provisional detention [1]. If a decision was adopted in the issuing State on the basis of one of those Framework Decisions, the recognition procedure should be followed accordingly in the executing State. This, however, should not exclude the possibility to transfer a European protection order to a Member State other than the State executing decisions based on those Framework Decisions.

(17) In accordance with Article 6 of the European Convention for the Protection of Human Rights and Fundamental Freedoms and with the second paragraph of Article 47 of the Charter of Fundamental Rights of the European Union, the person causing danger should be provided, either during the procedure leading to the adoption of a protection measure or before issuing a European protection order, with the possibility of being heard and challenging the protection measure.

(18) In order to prevent a crime being committed against the victim in the executing State, that State should have the legal means for recognising the decision previously adopted in the issuing State in favour of the victim, while also avoiding the need for the victim to start new proceedings or to produce evidence in the executing State again, as if the issuing State had not adopted the decision. The recognition of the European protection order by the executing State implies, inter alia, that the competent authority of that State, subject to the limitations set out in this Directive, accepts the existence and validity of the protection measure adopted in the issuing State, acknowledges the factual situation described in the European protection order, and agrees that protection should be provided and should continue to be provided in accordance with its national law.

(19) This Directive contains an exhaustive list of prohibitions and restrictions which, when imposed in the issuing State and included in the European protection order, should be recognised and enforced in the executing State, subject to the limitations set out in this Directive. Other types of protection measures may exist at national level, such as, if provided by national law, the obligation on the person causing danger to remain in a specified place. Such measures may be imposed in the issuing State in the framework of the procedure leading to the adoption of one of the protection measures which, according to this Directive, may be the basis for a European protection order.

(20) Since, in the Member States, different kinds of authorities (civil, criminal or administrative) are competent to adopt and enforce protection measures, it is appropriate to provide a high degree of flexibility in the cooperation mechanism between the Member States under this Directive. Therefore, the competent authority in the executing State is not required in all cases to take the same protection measure as those which were adopted in the issuing State, and has a degree of discretion to adopt any measure which it deems adequate and appropriate under its national law in a similar case in order to provide continued protection to the protected person in the light of the protection measure adopted in the issuing State as described in the European protection order.

(21) The prohibitions or restrictions to which this Directive applies include, among others, measures aimed at limiting personal or remote contacts between the protected person and the person causing danger, for example by imposing certain conditions on such contacts or imposing restrictions on the contents of communications.

(22) The competent authority of the executing State should inform the person causing danger, the competent authority of the issuing State and the protected person of any measure adopted on the basis of the European protection order. In the notification to the person causing danger, due regard should be taken of the interest of the protected person in not having that person's address or other contact details disclosed. Such details should be excluded from the notification, provided that the address or other contact details are not included in the prohibition or restriction imposed as an enforcement measure on the person causing danger.

(23) When the competent authority in the issuing State withdraws the European protection order, the competent authority in the executing State should discontinue the measures which it has adopted in order to enforce the European protection order, it being understood that the competent authority in the executing State may — autonomously, and in accordance with its national law — adopt any protection measure under its national law in order to protect the person concerned.

(24) Given that this Directive deals with situations in which the protected person moves to another Member State, issuing or executing a European protection order should not imply any transfer to the executing State of powers relating to principal, suspended, alternative, conditional or secondary penalties, or relating to security measures imposed on the person causing danger, if the latter continues to reside in the State that adopted the protection measure.

(25) Where appropriate, it should be possible to use electronic means with a view to putting into practice the measures adopted in application of this Directive, in accordance with national laws and procedures.

[1] OJ L 294, 11.11.2009, p. 20.

(26) In the context of cooperation among the authorities involved in ensuring the protection of the protected person, the competent authority of the executing State should communicate to the competent authority of the issuing State any breach of the measures adopted in the executing State with a view to executing the European protection order. This communication should enable the competent authority of the issuing State to promptly decide on any appropriate response with respect to the protection measure imposed in its State on the person causing danger. Such a response may comprise, where appropriate, the imposition of a custodial measure in substitution of the non-custodial measure that was originally adopted, for example, as an alternative to preventive detention or as a consequence of the conditional suspension of a penalty. It is understood that such a decision, since it does not impose *ex novo* a penalty in relation to a new criminal offence, does not interfere with the possibility that the executing State may, where applicable, impose penalties in the event of a breach of the measures adopted in order to execute the European protection order.

(27) In view of the different legal traditions of the Member States, where no protection measure would be available in the executing State in a case similar to the factual situation described in the European protection order, the competent authority of the executing State should report any breach of the protection measure described in the European protection order of which it is aware to the competent authority of the issuing State.

(28) In order to ensure the smooth application of this Directive in each particular case, the competent authorities of the issuing and the executing States should exercise their competencies in accordance with the provisions of this Directive, taking into account the principle of *ne bis in idem*.

(29) The protected person should not be required to sustain costs related to the recognition of the European protection order which are disproportionate to a similar national case. When implementing this Directive, Member States should ensure that, after recognition of the European protection order, the protected person is not required to initiate further national proceedings to obtain from the competent authority of the executing State, as a direct consequence of the recognition of the European protection order, a decision adopting any measure that would be available under its national law in a similar case in order to ensure the protection of the protected person.

(30) Bearing in mind the principle of mutual recognition upon which this Directive is based, Member States should promote, to the widest extent possible, direct contact between the competent authorities when they apply this Directive.

(31) Without prejudice to judicial independence and differences in the organisation of the judiciary across the Union, Member States should consider requesting those responsible for the training of judges, prosecutors, police and judicial staff involved in the procedures aimed at issuing or recognising a European protection order to provide appropriate training with respect to the objectives of this Directive.

(32) In order to facilitate the evaluation of the application of this Directive, Member States should communicate to the Commission relevant data related to the application of national procedures on the European protection order, at least with regard to the number of European protection orders requested, issued and/or recognised. In this respect, other types of data, such as, for example, the types of crimes concerned, would also be useful.

(33) This Directive should contribute to the protection of persons who are in danger, thereby complementing, but not affecting, the instruments already in place in this field, such as Framework Decision 2008/947/JHA and Framework Decision 2009/829/JHA.

(34) When a decision relating to a protection measure falls within the scope of Council Regulation (EC) No 44/2001 of 22 December 2000 on jurisdiction and the recognition and enforcement of judgments in civil and commercial matters [1], Council Regulation (EC) No 2201/2003 of 27 November 2003 concerning jurisdiction and the recognition and enforcement of judgments in matrimonial matters and the matters of parental responsibility [2], or the 1996 Hague Convention on Jurisdiction, Applicable Law, Recognition, Enforcement and Cooperation in respect of Parental Responsibility and Measures for the Protection of Children [3], the recognition and enforcement of that decision should be carried out in accordance with the provisions of the relevant legal instrument.

(35) Member States and the Commission should include information about the European protection order, where it is appropriate, in existing education and awareness-raising campaigns on the protection of victims of crime.

(36) Personal data processed when implementing this Directive should be protected in accordance with Council Framework Decision 2008/977/JHA of 27 November 2008 on the protection of personal data processed in the framework of police and judicial cooperation in criminal matters [4] and with the principles laid down in the 1981 Council of Europe Convention for the Protection of Individuals with regard to Automatic Processing of Personal Data.

(1) OJ L 12, 16.1.2001, p. 1.
(2) OJ L 338, 23.12.2003, p. 1.
(3) OJ L 48, 21.2.2003, p. 3.
(4) OJ L 350, 30.12.2008, p. 60.

(37) This Directive should respect the fundamental rights guaranteed by the Charter of Fundamental Rights of the European Union and by the European Convention for the Protection of Human Rights and Fundamental Freedoms, in accordance with Article 6 TEU.

(38) When implementing this Directive, Member States are encouraged to take into account the rights and principles enshrined in the 1979 United Nations Convention on the elimination of all forms of discrimination against women.

(39) Since the objective of this Directive, namely to protect persons who are in danger, cannot be sufficiently achieved by the Member States and can therefore, by reason of its scale and effects, be better achieved at Union level, the Union may adopt measures, in accordance with the principle of subsidiarity as set out in Article 5 TEU. In accordance with the principle of proportionality, as set out in that Article, this Directive does not go beyond what is necessary in order to achieve that objective.

(40) In accordance with Article 3 of the Protocol (No 21) on the position of the United Kingdom and Ireland in respect of the Area of Freedom, Security and Justice annexed to the Treaty on European Union and to the Treaty on the Functioning of the European Union, the United Kingdom has notified its wish to take part in the adoption and application of this Directive.

(41) In accordance with Articles 1 and 2 of the Protocol (No 21) on the position of the United Kingdom and Ireland in respect of the Area of Freedom, Security and Justice annexed to the Treaty on European Union and to the Treaty on the Functioning of the European Union, and without prejudice to Article 4 of that Protocol, Ireland is not taking part in the adoption of this Directive and is not bound by it or subject to its application.

(42) In accordance with Articles 1 and 2 of the Protocol (No 22) on the position of Denmark annexed to the Treaty on European Union and to the Treaty on the Functioning of the European Union, Denmark is not taking part in the adoption of this Directive and is not bound by it or subject to its application,

HAVE ADOPTED THIS DIRECTIVE:

*Article 1*

**Objective**

This Directive sets out rules allowing a judicial or equivalent authority in a Member State, in which a protection measure has been adopted with a view to protecting a person against a criminal act by another person which may endanger his life, physical or psychological integrity, dignity, personal liberty or sexual integrity, to issue a European protection order enabling a competent authority in another Member State to continue the protection of the person in the territory of that other Member State, following criminal conduct, or alleged criminal conduct, in accordance with the national law of the issuing State.

*Article 2*

**Definitions**

For the purposes of this Directive the following definitions shall apply:

(1) 'European protection order' means a decision, taken by a judicial or equivalent authority of a Member State in relation to a protection measure, on the basis of which a judicial or equivalent authority of another Member State takes any appropriate measure or measures under its own national law with a view to continuing the protection of the protected person;

(2) 'protection measure' means a decision in criminal matters adopted in the issuing State in accordance with its national law and procedures by which one or more of the prohibitions or restrictions referred to in Article 5 are imposed on a person causing danger in order to protect a protected person against a criminal act which may endanger his life, physical or psychological integrity, dignity, personal liberty or sexual integrity;

(3) 'protected person' means a natural person who is the object of the protection resulting from a protection measure adopted by the issuing State;

(4) 'person causing danger' means the natural person on whom one or more of the prohibitions or restrictions referred to in Article 5 have been imposed;

(5) 'issuing State' means the Member State in which a protection measure has been adopted that constitutes the basis for issuing a European protection order;

(6) 'executing State' means the Member State to which a European protection order has been forwarded with a view to its recognition;

(7) 'State of supervision' means the Member State to which a judgment within the meaning of Article 2 of Framework Decision 2008/947/JHA, or a decision on supervision measures within the meaning of Article 4 of Framework Decision 2009/829/JHA, has been transferred.

*Article 3*

**Designation of competent authorities**

1. Each Member State shall inform the Commission which judicial or equivalent authority or authorities are competent under its national law to issue a European protection order and to recognise such an order, in accordance with this Directive, when that Member State is the issuing State or the executing State.

2. The Commission shall make the information received available to all Member States. Member States shall inform the Commission of any change to the information referred to in paragraph 1.

*Article 4*

**Recourse to a central authority**

1. Each Member State may designate a central authority or, where its legal system so provides, more than one central authority, to assist its competent authorities.

2. A Member State may, if it is necessary as a result of the organisation of its internal judicial system, make its central authority or authorities responsible for the administrative transmission and reception of any European protection order, as well as for all other official correspondence relating thereto. As a consequence, all communications, consultations, exchanges of information, enquiries and notifications between competent authorities may be dealt with, where appropriate, with the assistance of the designated central authority or authorities of the Member State concerned.

3. Member States wishing to make use of the possibilities referred to in this Article shall communicate to the Commission information relating to the designated central authority or authorities. These indications shall be binding upon all the authorities of the issuing State.

*Article 5*

**Need for an existing protection measure under national law**

A European protection order may only be issued when a protection measure has been previously adopted in the issuing State, imposing on the person causing danger one or more of the following prohibitions or restrictions:

(a) a prohibition from entering certain localities, places or defined areas where the protected person resides or visits;

(b) a prohibition or regulation of contact, in any form, with the protected person, including by phone, electronic or ordinary mail, fax or any other means; or

(c) a prohibition or regulation on approaching the protected person closer than a prescribed distance.

*Article 6*

**Issuing of a European protection order**

1. A European protection order may be issued when the protected person decides to reside or already resides in another Member State, or when the protected person decides to stay or already stays in another Member State. When deciding upon the issuing of a European protection order, the competent authority in the issuing State shall take into account, inter alia, the length of the period or periods that the protected person intends to stay in the executing State and the seriousness of the need for protection.

2. A judicial or equivalent authority of the issuing State may issue a European protection order only at the request of the protected person and after verifying that the protection measure meets the requirements set out in Article 5.

3. The protected person may submit a request for the issuing of a European protection order either to the competent authority of the issuing State or to the competent authority of the executing State. If such a request is submitted in the executing State, its competent authority shall transfer this request as soon as possible to the competent authority of the issuing State.

4. Before issuing a European protection order, the person causing danger shall be given the right to be heard and the right to challenge the protection measure, if that person has not been granted these rights in the procedure leading to the adoption of the protection measure.

5. When a competent authority adopts a protection measure containing one or more of the prohibitions or restrictions referred to in Article 5, it shall inform the protected person in an appropriate way, in accordance with the procedures under its national law, about the possibility of requesting a European protection order in the case that that person decides to leave for another Member State, as well as of the basic conditions for such a request. The authority shall advise the protected person to submit an application before leaving the territory of the issuing State.

6. If the protected person has a guardian or representative, that guardian or representative may introduce the request referred to in paragraphs 2 and 3, on behalf of the protected person.

7. If the request to issue a European protection order is rejected, the competent authority of the issuing State shall inform the protected person of any applicable legal remedies that are available, under its national law, against such a decision.

*Article 7*

**Form and content of the European protection order**

The European protection order shall be issued in accordance with the form set out in Annex I to this Directive. It shall, in particular, contain the following information:

(a) the identity and nationality of the protected person, as well as the identity and nationality of the guardian or representative if the protected person is a minor or is legally incapacitated;

(b) the date from which the protected person intends to reside or stay in the executing State, and the period or periods of stay, if known;

(c) the name, address, telephone and fax numbers and e-mail address of the competent authority of the issuing State;

(d) identification (for example, through a number and date) of the legal act containing the protection measure on the basis of which the European protection order is issued;

(e) a summary of the facts and circumstances which have led to the adoption of the protection measure in the issuing State;

(f) the prohibitions or restrictions imposed, in the protection measure underlying the European protection order, on the person causing danger, their duration and the indication of the penalty, if any, in the event of the breach of any of the prohibitions or restrictions;

(g) the use of a technical device, if any, that has been provided to the protected person or to the person causing danger as a means of enforcing the protection measure;

(h) the identity and nationality of the person causing danger, as well as that person's contact details;

(i) where such information is known by the competent authority of the issuing State without requiring further inquiry, whether the protected person and/or the person causing danger has been granted free legal aid in the issuing State;

(j) a description, where appropriate, of other circumstances that could have an influence on the assessment of the danger that confronts the protected person;

(k) an express indication, where applicable, that a judgment within the meaning of Article 2 of Framework Decision 2008/947/JHA, or a decision on supervision measures within the meaning of Article 4 of Framework Decision 2009/829/JHA, has already been transferred to the State of supervision, when this is different from the State of execution of the European protection order, and the identification of the competent authority of that State for the enforcement of such a judgment or decision.

*Article 8*

**Transmission procedure**

1. Where the competent authority of the issuing State transmits the European protection order to the competent authority of the executing State, it shall do so by any means which leaves a written record so as to allow the competent authority of the executing State to establish its authenticity. All official communication shall also be made directly between those competent authorities.

2. If the competent authority of either the executing State or the issuing State is not known to the competent authority of the other State, the latter authority shall make all the relevant enquiries, including via the contact points of the European Judicial Network referred to in Council Decision 2008/976/JHA of 16 December 2008 on the European Judicial Network ([1]), the National Member of Eurojust or the National System for the coordination of Eurojust of its State, in order to obtain the necessary information.

3. When an authority of the executing State which receives a European protection order has no competence to recognise it, that authority shall, *ex officio*, forward the European protection order to the competent authority and shall, without delay, inform the competent authority of the issuing State accordingly by any means which leaves a written record.

*Article 9*

**Measures in the executing State**

1. Upon receipt of a European protection order transmitted in accordance with Article 8, the competent authority of the executing State shall, without undue delay, recognise that order and take a decision adopting any measure that would be available under its national law in a similar case in order to ensure the protection of the protected person, unless it decides to invoke one of the grounds for non-recognition referred to in Article 10. The executing State may apply, in accordance with its national law, criminal, administrative or civil measures.

([1]) OJ L 348, 24.12.2008, p. 130.

2. The measure adopted by the competent authority of the executing State in accordance with paragraph 1, as well as any other measure taken on the basis of a subsequent decision as referred to in Article 11, shall, to the highest degree possible, correspond to the protection measure adopted in the issuing State.

3. The competent authority of the executing State shall inform the person causing danger, the competent authority of the issuing State and the protected person of any measures adopted in accordance with paragraph 1, as well as of the possible legal consequence of a breach of such measure provided for under national law and in accordance with Article 11(2). The address or other contact details of the protected person shall not be disclosed to the person causing danger unless such details are necessary in view of the enforcement of the measure adopted in accordance with paragraph 1.

4. If the competent authority in the executing State considers that the information transmitted with the European protection order in accordance with Article 7 is incomplete, it shall without delay inform the competent authority of the issuing State by any means which leaves a written record, assigning a reasonable period for it to provide the missing information.

*Article 10*

**Grounds for non-recognition of a European protection order**

1. The competent authority of the executing State may refuse to recognise a European protection order in the following circumstances:

(a) the European protection order is not complete or has not been completed within the time limit set by the competent authority of the executing State;

(b) the requirements set out in Article 5 have not been met;

(c) the protection measure relates to an act that does not constitute a criminal offence under the law of the executing State;

(d) the protection derives from the execution of a penalty or measure that, according to the law of the executing State, is covered by an amnesty and relates to an act or conduct which falls within its competence according to that law;

(e) there is immunity conferred under the law of the executing State on the person causing danger, which makes it impossible to adopt measures on the basis of a European protection order;

(f) criminal prosecution, against the person causing danger, for the act or the conduct in relation to which the protection measure has been adopted is statute-barred under the law of the executing State, when the act or the conduct falls within its competence under its national law;

(g) recognition of the European protection order would contravene the *ne bis in idem* principle;

(h) under the law of the executing State, the person causing danger cannot, because of that person's age, be held criminally responsible for the act or the conduct in relation to which the protection measure has been adopted;

(i) the protection measure relates to a criminal offence which, under the law of the executing State, is regarded as having been committed, wholly or for a major or essential part, within its territory.

2. Where the competent authority of the executing State refuses to recognise a European protection order in application of one of the grounds referred to in paragraph 1, it shall:

(a) without undue delay, inform the issuing State and the protected person of this refusal and of the grounds relating thereto;

(b) where appropriate, inform the protected person about the possibility of requesting the adoption of a protection measure in accordance with its national law;

(c) inform the protected person of any applicable legal remedies that are available under its national law against such a decision.

*Article 11*

**Governing law and competence in the executing State**

1. The executing State shall be competent to adopt and to enforce measures in that State following the recognition of a European protection order. The law of the executing State shall apply to the adoption and enforcement of the decision provided for in Article 9(1), including rules on legal remedies against decisions adopted in the executing State relating to the European protection order.

2. In the event of a breach of one or more of the measures taken by the executing State following the recognition of a European protection order, the competent authority of the executing State shall, in accordance with paragraph 1, be competent to:

(a) impose criminal penalties and take any other measure as a consequence of the breach, if that breach amounts to a criminal offence under the law of the executing State;

(b) take any non-criminal decisions related to the breach;

(c) take any urgent and provisional measure in order to put an end to the breach, pending, where appropriate, a subsequent decision by the issuing State.

3. If there is no available measure at national level in a similar case that could be taken in the executing State, the competent authority of the executing State shall report to the competent authority of the issuing State any breach of the protection measure described in the European protection order of which it is aware.

*Article 12*

**Notification in the event of breach**

The competent authority of the executing State shall notify the competent authority of the issuing State or of the State of supervision of any breach of the measure or measures taken on the basis of the European protection order. Notice shall be given using the standard form set out in Annex II.

*Article 13*

**Competence in the issuing State**

1. The competent authority of the issuing State shall have exclusive competence to take decisions relating to:

(a) the renewal, review, modification, revocation and withdrawal of the protection measure and, consequently, of the European protection order;

(b) the imposition of a custodial measure as a consequence of revocation of the protection measure, provided that the protection measure has been applied on the basis of a judgment within the meaning of Article 2 of Framework Decision 2008/947/JHA, or on the basis of a decision on supervision measures within the meaning of Article 4 of Framework Decision 2009/829/JHA;

2. The law of the issuing State shall apply to decisions adopted in accordance with paragraph 1.

3. Where a judgment within the meaning of Article 2 of Framework Decision 2008/947/JHA, or a decision on supervision measures within the meaning of Article 4 of Framework Decision 2009/829/JHA, has already been transferred, or is transferred after the issuing of the European protection order, to another Member State, subsequent decisions, as provided for by those Framework Decisions, shall be taken in accordance with the relevant provisions of those Framework Decisions.

4. When the protection measure is contained in a judgment within the meaning of Article 2 of Framework Decision 2008/947/JHA which has been transferred or is transferred after the issuing of the European protection order to another Member State, and the competent authority of the State of supervision has made subsequent decisions affecting the obligations or instructions contained in the protection measure in accordance with Article 14 of that Framework Decision, the competent authority of the issuing State shall renew, review, modify, revoke or withdraw without delay the European protection order accordingly.

5. The competent authority of the issuing State shall inform the competent authority of the executing State without delay of any decision taken in accordance with paragraph 1 or 4.

6. If the competent authority in the issuing State has revoked or withdrawn the European protection order in accordance with point (a) of paragraph 1 or with paragraph 4, the competent authority in the executing State shall discontinue the measures adopted in accordance with Article 9(1) as soon as it has been duly notified by the competent authority of the issuing State.

7. If the competent authority in the issuing State has modified the European protection order in accordance with point (a) of paragraph 1 or with paragraph 4, the competent authority in the executing State shall, as appropriate:

(a) modify the measures adopted on the basis of the European protection order, acting in accordance with Article 9; or

(b) refuse to enforce the modified prohibition or restriction when it does not fall within the types of prohibitions or restrictions referred to in Article 5, or if the information transmitted with the European protection order in accordance with Article 7 is incomplete or has not been completed within the time limit set by the competent authority of the executing State in accordance with Article 9(4).

*Article 14*

**Grounds for discontinuation of measures taken on the basis of a European protection order**

1. The competent authority of the executing State may discontinue the measures taken in execution of a European protection order:

(a) where there is clear indication that the protected person does not reside or stay in the territory of the executing State, or has definitively left that territory;

(b) where, according to its national law, the maximum term of duration of the measures adopted in execution of the European protection order has expired;

(c) in the case referred to in Article 13(7)(b); or

(d) where a judgment within the meaning of Article 2 of Framework Decision 2008/947/JHA, or a decision on supervision measures within the meaning of Article 4 of Framework Decision 2009/829/JHA, is transferred to the executing State after the recognition of the European protection order.

2. The competent authority of the executing State shall immediately inform the competent authority of the issuing State and, where possible, the protected person of such decision.

3. Before discontinuing measures in accordance with point (b) of paragraph 1 the competent authority of the executing State may invite the competent authority of the issuing State to provide information as to whether the protection provided for by the European protection order is still needed in the circumstances of the case in question. The competent authority of the issuing State shall, without delay, reply to such an invitation.

*Article 15*

**Priority in recognition of a European protection order**

A European protection order shall be recognised with the same priority which would be applicable in a similar national case, taking into consideration any specific circumstances of the case, including the urgency of the matter, the date foreseen for the arrival of the protected person on the territory of the executing State and, where possible, the degree of risk for the protected person.

*Article 16*

**Consultations between competent authorities**

Where appropriate, the competent authorities of the issuing State and of the executing State may consult each other in order to facilitate the smooth and efficient application of this Directive.

*Article 17*

**Languages**

1. A European protection order shall be translated by the competent authority of the issuing State into the official language or one of the official languages of the executing State.

2. The form referred to in Article 12 shall be translated by the competent authority of the executing State into the official language or one of the official languages of the issuing State.

3. Any Member State may, either when this Directive is adopted or at a later date, state in a declaration that it shall deposit with the Commission that it will accept a translation in one or more other official languages of the Union.

*Article 18*

**Costs**

Costs resulting from the application of this Directive shall be borne by the executing State, in accordance with its national law, except for costs arising exclusively within the territory of the issuing State.

*Article 19*

**Relationship with other agreements and arrangements**

1. Member States may continue to apply bilateral or multilateral agreements or arrangements which are in force upon the entry into force of this Directive, in so far as they allow the objectives of this Directive to be extended or enlarged and help to simplify or facilitate further the procedures for taking protection measures.

2. Member States may conclude bilateral or multilateral agreements or arrangements after the entry into force of this Directive, in so far as they allow the objectives of this Directive to be extended or enlarged and help to simplify or facilitate the procedures for taking protection measures.

3. By 11 April 2012, Member States shall notify the Commission of the existing agreements and arrangements referred to in paragraph 1 which they wish to continue applying. Member States shall also notify the Commission of any new agreements or arrangements referred to in paragraph 2 within three months of the signing thereof.

*Article 20*

**Relationship with other instruments**

1. This Directive shall not affect the application of Regulation (EC) No 44/2001, Regulation (EC) No 2201/2003, the 1996 Hague Convention on Jurisdiction, Applicable Law, Recognition, Enforcement and Cooperation in respect of Parental Responsibility and Measures for the Protection of Children, or the 1980 Hague Convention on the Civil Aspects of International Child Abduction.

2. This Directive shall not affect the application of Framework Decision 2008/947/JHA or Framework Decision 2009/829/JHA.

*Article 21*

**Implementation**

1. Member States shall bring into force the laws, regulations and administrative provisions to comply with this Directive by 11 January 2015. They shall forthwith inform the Commission thereof.

When Member States adopt those measures, they shall contain a reference to this Directive or shall be accompanied by such reference on the occasion of their official publication. The methods of making such reference shall be laid down by the Member States.

2. Member States shall communicate to the Commission the text of the main provisions of national law which they adopt in the field covered by this Directive.

*Article 22*

**Data collection**

Member States shall, in order to facilitate the evaluation of the application of this Directive, communicate to the Commission relevant data related to the application of national procedures on the European protection order, at least on the number of European protection orders requested, issued and/or recognised.

*Article 23*

**Review**

By 11 January 2016, the Commission shall submit a report to the European Parliament and to the Council on the application of this Directive. That report shall be accompanied, if necessary, by legislative proposals.

*Article 24*

**Entry into force**

This Directive shall enter into force on the 20th day following its publication in the *Official Journal of the European Union*.

*Article 25*

**Addressees**

This Directive is addressed to the Member States in accordance with the Treaties.

Done at Strasbourg, 13 December 2011.

| *For the European Parliament* | *For the Council* |
| --- | --- |
| *The President* | *The President* |
| J. BUZEK | M. SZPUNAR |

21.12.2011 EN Official Journal of the European Union L 338/13

*ANNEX I*

**EUROPEAN PROTECTION ORDER**

referred to in Article 7 of

**DIRECTIVE 2011/99/EU OF THE EUROPEAN PARLIAMENT AND OF THE COUNCIL OF 13 DECEMBER 2011 ON THE EUROPEAN PROTECTION ORDER**

**The information contained in this form is to be treated with appropriate confidentiality**

Issuing State:

Executing State:

---

(a) Information regarding the protected person:

Surname:

Forename(s):

Maiden or previous name, where applicable:

Sex:

Nationality:

Identity number or social security number (if any):

Date of birth:

Place of birth:

Addresses/residences:

— in the issuing State:

— in the executing State:

— elsewhere:

Language(s) understood (if known):

---

Has the protected person been granted free legal aid in the issuing State (if information is available without further enquiry)?

☐ Yes.

☐ No.

☐ Unknown.

Where the protected person is a minor or is legally incapacitated, information regarding the person's guardian or representative:

Surname:

Forename(s):

Maiden name or previous name, where applicable:

Sex:

Nationality:

Office/Address:

(b) The protected person has decided to reside or already resides in the executing State, or has decided to stay or already stays in the executing State.

Date from which the protected person intends to reside or stay in the executing State (if known):

Period(s) of stay (if known):

(c) Have any technical devices been provided to the protected person or to the person causing danger to enforce the protection measure:

☐ Yes; please give a short summary of the devices used:

☐ No.

(d) Competent authority which issued the European protection order:

Official name:

Full address:

Tel. No (country code) (area/city code) (number):

Fax No (country code) (area/city code) (number):

Details of the person(s) to be contacted

Surname:

Forename(s):

Position (title/grade):

Tel. No (country code) (area/city code) (number):

Fax No (country code) (area/city code) (number):

E-mail (if any):

Languages that may be used for communication:

(e) Identification of the protection measure on the basis of which the European protection order has been issued:

The protection measure was adopted on (date: DD-MM-YYYY):

The protection measure became enforceable on (date: DD-MM-YYYY):

File reference of the protection measure (if available):

Authority that adopted the protection measure:

(f) Summary of the facts and description of the circumstances — including, where applicable, the classification of the offence — which have led to the imposition of the protection measure mentioned under (e) above:

(g) Indications regarding the prohibition(s) or restriction(s) that have been imposed by the protection measure on the person causing danger:

— Nature of the prohibition(s) or restriction(s): (more than one box may be ticked):

☐ a prohibition from entering certain localities, places or defined areas where the protected person resides or visits;

— if you ticked this box, please indicate precisely which localities, places or defined areas the person causing danger is prohibited from entering:

☐ a prohibition or regulation of contact, in any form, with the protected person, including by phone, electronic or ordinary mail, fax or any other means;

— if you ticked this box, please provide any relevant details:

☐ a prohibition or regulation on approaching the protected person closer than a prescribed distance;

— if you ticked this box, please indicate precisely the distance which the person causing danger has to observe in respect of the protected person:

— Please indicate the length of time during which the abovementioned prohibition(s) or restriction(s) are imposed on the person causing danger:

— Indication of the penalty (if any) in the event of the breach of the prohibition or restriction:

(h) Information regarding the person causing danger on whom the prohibition(s) or restriction(s) mentioned under (g) have been imposed:

Surname:

Forename(s):

Maiden or previous name, where applicable:

Aliases, where applicable:

Sex:

Nationality:

Identity number or social security number (if any):

Date of birth:

Place of birth:

Addresses/residences:

— in the issuing State:

— in the executing State:

— elsewhere:

Language(s) understood (if known):

If available, please provide the following information:

— Type and number of the identity document(s) of the person (ID card, passport):

Has the person causing danger been granted free legal aid in the issuing State (if information is available without further enquiry)?

☐ Yes.

☐ No.

☐ Unknown.

(i) Other circumstances that could have an influence on the assessment of the danger that could affect the protected person (optional information):

(j) Other useful information (such as, where available and necessary, information on other States where protection measures have been previously adopted with respect to the same protected person):

(k) Please complete:

☐ a judgment within the meaning of Article 2 of Framework Decision 2008/947/JHA, has already been transmitted to another Member State

— If you ticked this box, please provide the contact details of the competent authority to whom the judgment has been forwarded:

☐ a decision on supervision measures within the meaning of Article 4 of Framework Decision 2009/829/JHA has already been transmitted to another Member State

— If you ticked this box, please provide the contact details of the competent authority to whom the decision on supervision measures has been forwarded:

Signature of the authority issuing the European protection order and/or of its representative to confirm the accuracy of the content of the order:

Name:

Position (title/grade):

Date:

File reference (if any):

(Where appropriate) Official stamp:

21.12.2011 EN Official Journal of the European Union L 338/17

*ANNEX II*

**FORM**

referred to in Article 12 of

**DIRECTIVE 2011/99/EU OF THE EUROPEAN PARLIAMENT AND OF THE COUNCIL OF 13 DECEMBER 2011 ON THE EUROPEAN PROTECTION ORDER**

**NOTIFICATION OF A BREACH OF THE MEASURE TAKEN ON THE BASIS OF THE EUROPEAN PROTECTION ORDER**

**The information contained in this form is to be treated with appropriate confidentiality**

(a) Details of the identity of the person causing danger:

Surname:

Forename(s):

Maiden or previous name, where applicable:

Aliases, where applicable:

Sex:

Nationality:

Identity number or social security number (if any):

Date of birth:

Place of birth:

Address:

Language(s) understood (if known):

(b) Details of the identity of the protected person:

Surname:

Forename(s):

Maiden or previous name, where applicable:

Sex:

Nationality:

Date of birth:

Place of birth:

Address:

Language(s) understood (if known):

(c) Details of the European protection order:

Order issued on:

File reference (if any):

Authority which issued the order:

Official name:

Address:

(d) Details of the authority responsible for the execution of the protection measure, if any, which was taken in the executing State in line with the European protection order:

Official name of the authority:

Name of the person to be contacted:

Position (title/grade):

Address:

Tel. No (country code) (area code) (number):

Fax No (country code) (area code) (number):

E-mail:

Languages that may be used for communication:

(e) Breach of the prohibition(s) or restriction(s) imposed by the competent authorities of the executing State following recognition of the European protection order and/or other findings which could result in taking any subsequent decision:

The breach concerns the following prohibition(s) or restriction(s) (more than one box may be ticked):

☐ a prohibition from entering certain localities, places or defined areas where the protected person resides or visits;

☐ a prohibition or regulation of contact, in any form, with the protected person, including by phone, electronic or ordinary mail, fax or any other means;

☐ a prohibition or regulation on approaching the protected person closer than a prescribed distance;

☐ any other measure, corresponding to the protection measure at the basis of the European protection order, taken by the competent authorities of the executing State following recognition of the European protection order

Description of the breach(es) (place, date and specific circumstances):

In accordance with Article 11(2):

— measures taken in the executing State as a consequence of the breach:

— possible legal consequence of the breach in the executing State:

Other findings which could result in taking any subsequent decision

Description of the findings:

(f) Details of the person to be contacted if additional information is to be obtained concerning the breach:

Surname:

Forename(s):

Address:

Tel. No (country code) (area/city code) (number):

Fax No (country code) (area/city code) (number):

E-mail:

Languages that may be used for communication:

Signature of the authority issuing the form and/or its representative, to confirm that the contents of the form are correct:

Name:

Position (title/grade):

Date:

Official stamp (where applicable):

# Agreement between the United States of America and the European Union on the use and transfer of passenger name records to the United States Department of Homeland Security, 14 December 2011

[OJ 2012, L 215/5–14]

11.8.2012 EN Official Journal of the European Union L 215/5

**AGREEMENT**

**between the United States of America and the European Union on the use and transfer of passenger name records to the United States Department of Homeland Security**

THE UNITED STATES OF AMERICA,

hereinafter referred to also as 'the United States', and

THE EUROPEAN UNION,

hereinafter referred to also as 'the EU',

together hereinafter referred to as 'the Parties',

DESIRING to prevent and combat terrorism and serious transnational crime effectively as a means of protecting their respective democratic societies and common values;

SEEKING to enhance and encourage cooperation between the Parties in the spirit of transatlantic partnership;

RECOGNISING the right and responsibility of States to ensure the security of their citizens and protect their borders and mindful of the responsibility of all nations to protect the life and safety of the public including those using international transportation systems;

CONVINCED that information sharing is an essential component in the fight against terrorism and serious transnational crime and that in this context, the processing and use of passenger name records (PNR) is a necessary tool that gives information that cannot be obtained by other means;

DETERMINED to prevent and combat terrorist offences and transnational crime, while respecting fundamental rights and freedoms and recognising the importance of privacy and the protection of personal data and information;

HAVING REGARD for international instruments, US statutes and regulations requiring each air carrier operating passenger flights in foreign air transportation to or from the United States to make PNR available to the Department of Homeland Security (DHS) to the extent they are collected and contained in the air carrier's automated reservation/departure control systems, and comparable requirements that are or may be implemented in the EU;

NOTING that DHS processes and uses PNR for the purpose of preventing, detecting, investigating and prosecuting terrorist offences and transnational crime in compliance with safeguards on privacy and the protection of personal data and information, as set out in this Agreement;

STRESSING the importance of sharing PNR and relevant and appropriate analytical information obtained from PNR by the United States with competent police and judicial authorities of Member States of the European Union, hereinafter 'EU Member States', and Europol or Eurojust as a means to foster international police and judicial cooperation;

ACKNOWLEDGING both Parties' longstanding traditions of respect for individual privacy, as reflected in their laws and founding documents;

MINDFUL of the EU's commitments pursuant to Article 6 of the Treaty on European Union on respect for fundamental rights, the right to privacy with regard to the processing of personal data as stipulated in Article 16 of the Treaty on the Functioning of the European Union, the principles of proportionality and necessity concerning the right to private and family life, the respect for privacy, and the protection of personal data under Article 8 of the European Convention on the Protection of Human Rights and Fundamental Freedoms, Council of Europe Convention No 108 for the Protection of Individuals with regard to Automatic Processing of Personal Data and its additional Protocol 181, and Articles 7 and 8 of the Charter of Fundamental Rights of the European Union;

MINDFUL that DHS currently employs robust processes to protect personal privacy and ensure data integrity, including physical security, access controls, data separation and encryption, audit capabilities and effective accountability measures;

RECOGNISING the importance of ensuring data quality, accuracy, integrity, and security, and instituting appropriate accountability to ensure these principles are observed;

NOTING in particular the principle of transparency and the various means by which the United States ensures that passengers whose PNR is collected by DHS are made aware of the need for and use of their PNR;

FURTHER RECOGNISING that the collection and analysis of PNR is necessary for DHS to carry out its border security mission, while ensuring that collection and use of PNR remains relevant and necessary for the purposes for which it is collected;

RECOGNISING that, in consideration of this Agreement and its implementation, DHS shall be deemed to ensure an adequate level of data protection for the processing and use of PNR transferred to DHS;

MINDFUL that the United States and the European Union are committed to ensuring a high level of protection of personal information while fighting crime and terrorism, and are determined to reach, without delay, an agreement to protect personal information exchanged in the context of fighting crime and terrorism in a comprehensive manner that will advance our mutual goals;

ACKNOWLEDGING the successful Joint Reviews in 2005 and 2010 of the 2004 and 2007 Agreements between the Parties on the transfer of PNR;

NOTING the interest of the Parties, as well as EU Member States, in exchanging information regarding the method of transmission of PNR as well as the onward transfer of PNR as set forth in the relevant articles of this Agreement, and further noting the EU's interest in having this addressed in the context of the consultation and review mechanism set forth in this Agreement;

AFFIRMING that this Agreement does not constitute a precedent for any future arrangements between the Parties, or between either of the Parties and any other party, regarding the processing, use, or transfer of PNR or any other form of data, or regarding data protection;

RECOGNISING the related principles of proportionality as well as relevance and necessity that guide this Agreement and its implementation by the European Union and the United States; and

HAVING REGARD to the possibility of the Parties to further discuss the transfer of PNR data in the maritime mode;

HEREBY AGREE:

## CHAPTER I

## GENERAL PROVISIONS

*Article 1*

### Purpose

1. The purpose of this Agreement is to ensure security and to protect the life and safety of the public.

2. For this purpose, this Agreement sets forth the responsibilities of the Parties with respect to the conditions under which PNR may be transferred, processed and used, and protected.

*Article 2*

### Scope

1. PNR, as set forth in the Guidelines of the International Civil Aviation Organisation, shall mean the record created by air carriers or their authorised agents for each journey booked by or on behalf of any passenger and contained in carriers' reservation systems, departure control systems, or equivalent systems providing similar functionality (collectively referred to in this Agreement as 'reservation systems'). Specifically, as used in this Agreement, PNR consists of the data types set forth in the Annex to this Agreement ('Annex').

2. This Agreement shall apply to carriers operating passenger flights between the European Union and the United States.

3. This Agreement shall also apply to carriers incorporated or storing data in the European Union and operating passenger flights to or from the United States.

*Article 3*

### Provision of PNR

The Parties agree that carriers shall provide PNR contained in their reservation systems to DHS as required by and in accordance with DHS standards and consistent with this Agreement. Should PNR transferred by carriers include data beyond those listed in the Annex, DHS shall delete such data upon receipt.

*Article 4*

### Use of PNR

1. The United States collects, uses and processes PNR for the purposes of preventing, detecting, investigating, and prosecuting:

(a) Terrorist offences and related crimes, including:

(i) Conduct that —

1. involves a violent act or an act dangerous to human life, property, or infrastructure; and

2. appears to be intended to —

a. intimidate or coerce a civilian population;

b. influence the policy of a government by intimidation or coercion; or

c. affect the conduct of a government by mass destruction, assassination, kidnapping, or hostage-taking;

(ii) Activities constituting an offence within the scope of and as defined in applicable international conventions and protocols relating to terrorism;

(iii) Providing or collecting funds, by any means, directly or indirectly, with the intention that they should be used or in the knowledge that they are to be used, in full or in part, in order to carry out any of the acts described in subparagraphs (i) or (ii);

(iv) Attempting to commit any of the acts described in subparagraphs (i), (ii), or (iii);

(v) Participating as an accomplice in the commission of any of the acts described in subparagraphs (i), (ii), or (iii);

(vi) Organising or directing others to commit any of the acts described in subparagraphs (i), (ii), or (iii);

(vii) Contributing in any other way to the commission of any of the acts described in subparagraphs (i), (ii), or (iii);

(viii) Threatening to commit an act described in subparagraph (i) under circumstances which indicate that the threat is credible;

(b) Other crimes that are punishable by a sentence of imprisonment of three years or more and that are transnational in nature.

A crime is considered as transnational in nature in particular if:

(i) it is committed in more than one country;

(ii) it is committed in one country but a substantial part of its preparation, planning, direction or control takes place in another country;

(iii) it is committed in one country but involves an organised criminal group that engages in criminal activities in more than one country;

(iv) it is committed in one country but has substantial effects in another country; or

(v) it is committed in one country and the offender is in or intends to travel to another country.

2. PNR may be used and processed on a case-by-case basis where necessary in view of a serious threat and for the protection of vital interests of any individual or if ordered by a court.

3. PNR may be used and processed by DHS to identify persons who would be subject to closer questioning or examination upon arrival to or departure from the United States or who may require further examination.

4. Paragraphs 1, 2, and 3 shall be without prejudice to domestic law enforcement, judicial powers, or proceedings, where other violations of law or indications thereof are detected in the course of the use and processing of PNR.

CHAPTER II

**SAFEGUARDS APPLICABLE TO THE USE OF PNR**

*Article 5*

**Data security**

1. DHS shall ensure that appropriate technical measures and organisational arrangements are implemented to protect personal data and personal information contained in PNR against accidental, unlawful or unauthorised destruction, loss, disclosure, alteration, access, processing or use.

2. DHS shall make appropriate use of technology to ensure data protection, security, confidentiality and integrity. In particular, DHS shall ensure that:

(a) encryption, authorisation and documentation procedures recognised by competent authorities are applied. In particular, access to PNR shall be secured and limited to specifically authorised officials;

(b) PNR shall be held in a secure physical environment and protected with physical intrusion controls; and

(c) a mechanism exists to ensure that PNR queries are conducted consistent with Article 4.

3. In the event of a privacy incident (including unauthorised access or disclosure), DHS shall take reasonable measures to notify affected individuals as appropriate, to mitigate the risk of harm of unauthorised disclosures of personal data and information, and to institute remedial measures as may be technically practicable.

4. Within the scope of this Agreement, DHS shall inform without undue delay the relevant European authorities about cases of significant privacy incidents involving PNR of EU citizens or residents resulting from accidental or unlawful destruction or accidental loss, alteration, unauthorised disclosure or access, or any unlawful forms of processing or use.

5. The United States confirms that effective administrative, civil, and criminal enforcement measures are available under US law for privacy incidents. DHS may take disciplinary action against persons responsible for any such privacy incident, as appropriate, to include denial of system access, formal reprimands, suspension, demotion, or removal from duty.

6. All access to PNR, as well as its processing and use, shall be logged or documented by DHS. Logs or documentation shall be used only for oversight, auditing, and system maintenance purposes or as otherwise required by law.

*Article 6*

**Sensitive data**

1. To the extent that PNR of a passenger as collected includes sensitive data (i.e. personal data and information revealing racial or ethnic origin, political opinions, religious or philosophical beliefs, trade union membership, or data concerning the health or sex life of the individual), DHS shall employ automated systems to filter and mask out sensitive data from PNR. In addition, DHS shall not further process or use such data, except in accordance with paragraphs 3 and 4.

2. DHS shall provide to the European Commission within 90 days of the entry into force of this Agreement a list of codes and terms identifying sensitive data that shall be filtered out.

3. Access to, as well as processing and use of, sensitive data shall be permitted in exceptional circumstances where the life of an individual could be imperilled or seriously impaired. Such data may be exclusively accessed using restrictive processes on a case-by-case basis with the approval of a DHS senior manager.

4. Sensitive data shall be permanently deleted not later than 30 days from the last receipt of PNR containing such data by DHS. However, sensitive data may be retained for the time specified in US law for the purpose of a specific investigation, prosecution or enforcement action.

*Article 7*

**Automated individual decisions**

The United States shall not make decisions that produce significant adverse actions affecting the legal interests of individuals based solely on automated processing and use of PNR.

*Article 8*

**Retention of data**

1. DHS retains PNR in an active database for up to five years. After the initial six months of this period, PNR shall be depersonalised and masked in accordance with paragraph 2 of this Article. Access to this active database shall, unless otherwise permitted by this Agreement, be restricted to a limited number of specifically authorised officials.

2. To achieve depersonalisation, personally identifiable information contained in the following PNR data types shall be masked out:

(a) name(s);

(b) other names on PNR;

(c) all available contact information (including originator information);

(d) general remarks, including other supplementary information (OSI), special service information (SSI), and special service request (SSR); and

(e) any collected Advance Passenger Information System (APIS) information.

3. After this active period, PNR shall be transferred to a dormant database for a period of up to ten years. This dormant database shall be subject to additional controls, including a more restricted number of authorised personnel, as well as a higher level of supervisory approval required before access. In this dormant database, PNR shall not be repersonalised except in connection with law enforcement operations and then only in connection with an identifiable case, threat or risk. As regards the purposes as set out in Article 4(1)(b), PNR in this dormant database may only be repersonalised for a period of up to five years.

4. Following the dormant period, data retained must be rendered fully anonymised by deleting all data types which could serve to identify the passenger to whom PNR relate without the possibility of repersonalisation.

5. Data that are related to a specific case or investigation may be retained in an active PNR database until the case or investigation is archived. This paragraph is without prejudice to data retention requirements for individual investigation or prosecution files.

6. The Parties agree that, within the framework of the evaluation as provided for in Article 23(1), the necessity of a 10-year dormant period of retention will be considered.

*Article 9*

**Non-discrimination**

The United States shall ensure that the safeguards applicable to processing and use of PNR under this Agreement apply to all passengers on an equal basis without unlawful discrimination.

*Article 10*

**Transparency**

1. DHS shall provide information to the travelling public regarding its use and processing of PNR through:

(a) publications in the Federal Register;

(b) publications on its website;

(c) notices that may be incorporated by the carriers into contracts of carriage;

(d) statutorily required reporting to Congress; and

(e) other appropriate measures as may be developed.

2. DHS shall publish and provide to the EU for possible publication its procedures and modalities regarding access, correction or rectification, and redress procedures.

3. The Parties shall work with the aviation industry to encourage greater visibility to passengers at the time of booking on the purpose of the collection, processing and use of PNR by DHS, and on how to request access, correction and redress.

*Article 11*

**Access for individuals**

1. In accordance with the provisions of the Freedom of Information Act, any individual, regardless of nationality, country of origin, or place of residence is entitled to request his or her PNR from DHS. DHS shall timely provide such PNR subject to the provisions of paragraphs 2 and 3 of this Article.

2. Disclosure of information contained in PNR may be subject to reasonable legal limitations, applicable under US law, including any such limitations as may be necessary to safeguard privacy-protected, national security, and law enforcement sensitive information.

3. Any refusal or restriction of access shall be set forth in writing and provided to the requesting individual on a timely basis. Such notification shall include the legal basis on which information was withheld and shall inform the individual of the options available under US law for seeking redress.

4. DHS shall not disclose PNR to the public, except to the individual whose PNR has been processed and used or his or her representative, or as required by US law.

*Article 12*

**Correction or rectification for individuals**

1. Any individual regardless of nationality, country of origin, or place of residence may seek the correction or rectification, including the possibility of erasure or blocking, of his or her PNR by DHS pursuant to the processes described in this Agreement.

2. DHS shall inform, without undue delay, the requesting individual in writing of its decision whether to correct or rectify the PNR at issue.

3. Any refusal or restriction of correction or rectification shall be set forth in writing and provided to the requesting individual on a timely basis. Such notification shall include the legal basis of such refusal or restriction and shall inform the individual of the options available under US law for seeking redress.

*Article 13*

**Redress for individuals**

1. Any individual regardless of nationality, country of origin, or place of residence whose personal data and personal information has been processed and used in a manner inconsistent with this Agreement may seek effective administrative and judicial redress in accordance with US law.

2. Any individual is entitled to seek to administratively challenge DHS decisions related to the use and processing of PNR.

3. Under the provisions of the Administrative Procedure Act and other applicable law, any individual is entitled to petition for judicial review in US federal court of any final agency action by DHS. Further, any individual is entitled to petition for judicial review in accordance with applicable law and relevant provisions of:

(a) the Freedom of Information Act;

(b) the Computer Fraud and Abuse Act;

(c) the Electronic Communications Privacy Act; and

(d) other applicable provisions of US law.

4. In particular, DHS provides all individuals an administrative means (currently the DHS Traveller Redress Inquiry Program (DHS TRIP)) to resolve travel-related inquiries including those related to the use of PNR. DHS TRIP provides

a redress process for individuals who believe they have been delayed or prohibited from boarding a commercial aircraft because they were wrongly identified as a threat. Pursuant to the Administrative Procedure Act and Title 49, United States Code, Section 46110, any such aggrieved individual is entitled to petition for judicial review in US federal court from any final agency action by DHS relating to such concerns.

*Article 14*

**Oversight**

1. Compliance with the privacy safeguards in this Agreement shall be subject to independent review and oversight by Department Privacy Officers, such as the DHS Chief Privacy Officer, who:

(a) have a proven record of autonomy;

(b) exercise effective powers of oversight, investigation, intervention, and review; and

(c) have the power to refer violations of law related to this Agreement for prosecution or disciplinary action, when appropriate.

They shall, in particular, ensure that complaints relating to non-compliance with this Agreement are received, investigated, responded to, and appropriately redressed. These complaints may be brought by any individual, regardless of nationality, country of origin, or place of residence.

2. In addition, application of this Agreement by the United States shall be subject to independent review and oversight by one or more of the following entities:

(a) the DHS Office of Inspector General;

(b) the Government Accountability Office as established by Congress; and

(c) the US Congress.

Such oversight may be manifested in the findings and recommendations of public reports, public hearings, and analyses.

CHAPTER III

**MODALITIES OF TRANSFERS**

*Article 15*

**Method of PNR transmission**

1. For the purposes of this Agreement, carriers shall be required to transfer PNR to DHS using the 'push' method, in furtherance of the need for accuracy, timeliness and completeness of PNR.

2. Carriers shall be required to transfer PNR to DHS by secure electronic means in compliance with the technical requirements of DHS.

3. Carriers shall be required to transfer PNR to DHS in accordance with paragraphs 1 and 2, initially at 96 hours before the scheduled flight departure and additionally either in real time or for a fixed number of routine and scheduled transfers as specified by DHS.

4. In any case, the Parties agree that all carriers shall be required to acquire the technical ability to use the 'push' method not later than 24 months following entry into force of this Agreement.

5. DHS may, where necessary, on a case-by-case basis, require a carrier to provide PNR between or after the regular transfers described in paragraph 3. Wherever carriers are unable, for technical reasons, to respond timely to requests under this Article in accordance with DHS standards, or, in exceptional circumstances in order to respond to a specific, urgent, and serious threat, DHS may require carriers to otherwise provide access.

*Article 16*

**Domestic sharing**

1. DHS may share PNR only pursuant to a careful assessment of the following safeguards:

(a) Exclusively as consistent with Article 4;

(b) Only with domestic government authorities when acting in furtherance of the uses outlined in Article 4;

(c) Receiving authorities shall afford to PNR equivalent or comparable safeguards as set out in this Agreement; and

(d) PNR shall be shared only in support of those cases under examination or investigation and pursuant to written understandings and US law on the exchange of information between domestic government authorities.

2. When transferring analytical information obtained from PNR under this Agreement, the safeguards set forth in paragraph 1 of this Article shall be respected.

*Article 17*

**Onward transfer**

1. The United States may transfer PNR to competent government authorities of third countries only under terms consistent with this Agreement and only upon ascertaining that the recipient's intended use is consistent with those terms.

11.8.2012 EN Official Journal of the European Union L 215/11

2. Apart from emergency circumstances, any such transfer of data shall occur pursuant to express understandings that incorporate data privacy protections comparable to those applied to PNR by DHS as set out in this Agreement.

3. PNR shall be shared only in support of those cases under examination or investigation.

4. Where DHS is aware that PNR of a citizen or a resident of an EU Member State is transferred, the competent authorities of the concerned Member State shall be informed of the matter at the earliest appropriate opportunity.

5. When transferring analytical information obtained from PNR under this Agreement, the safeguards set forth in paragraphs 1 to 4 shall be respected.

*Article 18*

**Police, law enforcement and judicial cooperation**

1. Consistent with existing law enforcement or other information-sharing agreements or arrangements between the United States and any EU Member State or Europol and Eurojust, DHS shall provide to competent police, other specialised law enforcement or judicial authorities of the EU Member States and Europol and Eurojust within the remit of their respective mandates, as soon as practicable, relevant, and appropriate, analytical information obtained from PNR in those cases under examination or investigation to prevent, detect, investigate, or prosecute within the European Union terrorist offences and related crimes or transnational crime as described in Article 4(1)(b).

2. A police or judicial authority of an EU Member State, or Europol or Eurojust, may request, within its mandate, access to PNR or relevant analytical information obtained from PNR that are necessary in a specific case to prevent, detect, investigate, or prosecute within the European Union terrorist offences and related crimes or transnational crime as described in Article 4(1)(b). DHS shall, subject to the agreements and arrangements noted in paragraph 1 of this Article, provide such information.

3. Pursuant to paragraphs 1 and 2 of this Article, DHS shall share PNR only following a careful assessment of the following safeguards:

(a) Exclusively as consistent with Article 4;

(b) Only when acting in furtherance of the uses outlined in Article 4; and

(c) Receiving authorities shall afford to PNR equivalent or comparable safeguards as set out in this Agreement.

4. When transferring analytical information obtained from PNR under this Agreement, the safeguards set forth in paragraphs 1 to 3 of this Article shall be respected.

CHAPTER IV

**IMPLEMENTING AND FINAL PROVISIONS**

*Article 19*

**Adequacy**

In consideration of this Agreement and its implementation, DHS shall be deemed to provide, within the meaning of relevant EU data protection law, an adequate level of protection for PNR processing and use. In this respect, carriers which have provided PNR to DHS in compliance with this Agreement shall be deemed to have complied with applicable legal requirements in the EU related to the transfer of such data from the EU to the United States.

*Article 20*

**Reciprocity**

1. The Parties shall actively promote the cooperation of carriers within their respective jurisdictions with any PNR system operating or as may be adopted in the other's jurisdiction, consistent with this Agreement.

2. Given that the establishment of an EU PNR system could have a material effect on the Parties' obligations under this Agreement, if and when an EU PNR system is adopted, the Parties shall consult to determine whether this Agreement would need to be adjusted accordingly to ensure full reciprocity. Such consultations shall in particular examine whether any future EU PNR system would apply less stringent data protection standards than those provided for in this Agreement, and whether, therefore, this Agreement should be amended.

*Article 21*

**Implementation and non-derogation**

1. This Agreement shall not create or confer, under US law, any right or benefit on any person or entity, private or public. Each Party shall ensure that the provisions of this Agreement are properly implemented.

2. Nothing in this Agreement shall derogate from existing obligations of the United States and EU Member States, including under the Agreement on Mutual Legal Assistance between the European Union and the United States of 25 June 2003 and the related bilateral mutual legal assistance instruments between the United States and EU Member States.

*Article 22*

**Notification of changes in domestic law**

The Parties shall advise each other regarding the enactment of any legislation that materially affects the implementation of this Agreement.

*Article 23*

**Review and evaluation**

1. The Parties shall jointly review the implementation of this Agreement one year after its entry into force and regularly thereafter as jointly agreed. Further, the Parties shall jointly evaluate this Agreement four years after its entry into force.

2. The Parties shall jointly determine in advance the modalities and terms of the joint review and shall communicate to each other the composition of their respective teams. For the purpose of the joint review, the European Union shall be represented by the European Commission, and the United States shall be represented by DHS. The teams may include appropriate experts on data protection and law enforcement. Subject to applicable laws, participants in the joint review shall be required to have appropriate security clearances and to respect the confidentiality of the discussions. For the purpose of the joint review, DHS shall ensure appropriate access to relevant documentation, systems, and personnel.

3. Following the joint review, the European Commission shall present a report to the European Parliament and the Council of the European Union. The United States shall be given an opportunity to provide written comments which shall be attached to the report.

*Article 24*

**Resolution of disputes and suspension of agreement**

1. Any dispute arising from the implementation of this Agreement, and any matters related thereto, shall give rise to consultations between the Parties, with a view to reaching a mutually agreeable resolution, including providing an opportunity for either Party to cure within a reasonable time.

2. In the event that consultations do not result in a resolution of the dispute, either Party may suspend the application of this Agreement by written notification through diplomatic channels, with any such suspension to take effect 90 days from the date of such notification, unless the Parties otherwise agree to a different effective date.

3. Notwithstanding any suspension of this Agreement, all PNR obtained by DHS pursuant to this Agreement prior to its suspension shall continue to be processed and used in accordance with the safeguards of this Agreement.

*Article 25*

**Termination**

1. Either Party may terminate this Agreement at any time by written notification through diplomatic channels.

2. Termination shall take effect 120 days from the date of such notification, unless the Parties otherwise agree to a different effective date.

3. Prior to any termination of this Agreement, the Parties shall consult each other in a manner which allows sufficient time for reaching a mutually agreeable resolution.

4. Notwithstanding any termination of this Agreement, all PNR obtained by DHS pursuant to this Agreement prior to its termination shall continue to be processed and used in accordance with the safeguards of this Agreement.

*Article 26*

**Duration**

1. Subject to Article 25, this Agreement shall remain in force for a period of seven years from the date of its entry into force.

2. Upon the expiry of the period set forth in paragraph 1 of this Article, as well as any subsequent period of renewal under this paragraph, the Agreement shall be renewed for a subsequent period of seven years unless one of the Parties notifies the other in writing through diplomatic channels, at least twelve months in advance, of its intention not to renew the Agreement.

3. Notwithstanding the expiration of this Agreement, all PNR obtained by DHS under the terms of this Agreement shall continue to be processed and used in accordance with the safeguards of this Agreement. Similarly, all PNR obtained by DHS under the terms of the Agreement between the United States of America and the European Union on the processing and transfer of passenger name record (PNR) data by air carriers to the United States Department of Homeland Security (DHS), signed at Brussels and Washington, 23 and 26 July 2007, shall continue to be processed and used in accordance with the safeguards of that Agreement.

*Article 27*

**Final provisions**

1. This Agreement shall enter into force on the first day of the month after the date on which the Parties have exchanged notifications indicating that they have completed their internal procedures for this purpose.

2. This Agreement, as of the date of its entry into force, shall supersede the 23 and 26 July 2007 Agreement.

3. This Agreement will only apply to the territory of Denmark, the United Kingdom or Ireland, if the European Commission notifies the United States in writing that Denmark, the United Kingdom or Ireland has chosen to be bound by this Agreement.

4. If the European Commission notifies the United States before the entry into force of this Agreement that it will apply to the territory of Denmark, the United Kingdom or Ireland, this Agreement shall apply to the territory of the relevant State on the same day as for the other EU Member States bound by this Agreement.

11.8.2012 EN Official Journal of the European Union L 215/13

5. If the European Commission notifies the United States before the entry into force of this Agreement that it will apply to the territory of Denmark, the United Kingdom or Ireland, this Agreement shall apply to the territory of the relevant State on the first day following receipt of the notification by the United States.

Done at Brussels this fourteenth day of December in the year two thousand and eleven, in two originals.

Pursuant to EU law, this Agreement shall also be drawn up by the EU in the Bulgarian, Czech, Danish, Dutch, Estonian, Finnish, French, German, Greek, Hungarian, Italian, Latvian, Lithuanian, Maltese, Polish, Portuguese, Romanian, Slovak, Slovenian, Spanish and Swedish languages.

For the European Union

For the United States of America

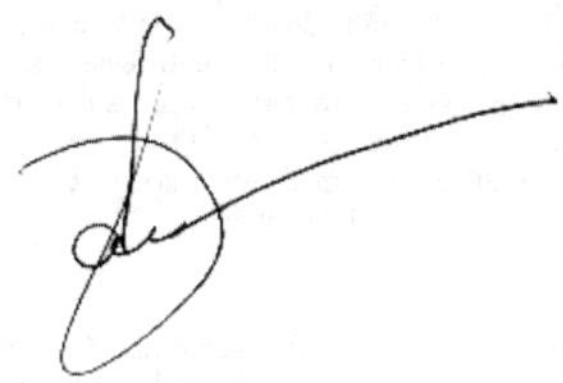

*ANNEX*

**PNR DATA TYPES**

1. PNR record locator code
2. Date of reservation/issue of ticket
3. Date(s) of intended travel
4. Name(s)
5. Available frequent flier and benefit information (i.e. free tickets, upgrades, etc.)
6. Other names on PNR, including number of travellers on PNR
7. All available contact information (including originator information)
8. All available payment/billing information (not including other transaction details linked to a credit card or account and not connected to the travel transaction)
9. Travel itinerary for specific PNR
10. Travel agency/travel agent
11. Code share information
12. Split/divided information
13. Travel status of passenger (including confirmations and check-in status)
14. Ticketing information, including ticket number, one-way tickets and automated ticket fare quote
15. All baggage information
16. Seat information, including seat number
17. General remarks including OSI, SSI and SSR information
18. Any collected APIS information
19. All historical changes to the PNR listed under points 1 to 18

# Directive 2012/13 on the right to information in criminal proceedings, 22 May 2012

**[OJ 2012, L 142/1–10]**

1.6.2012 EN Official Journal of the European Union L 142/1

I

*(Legislative acts)*

# DIRECTIVES

## DIRECTIVE 2012/13/EU OF THE EUROPEAN PARLIAMENT AND OF THE COUNCIL

### of 22 May 2012

### on the right to information in criminal proceedings

THE EUROPEAN PARLIAMENT AND THE COUNCIL OF THE EUROPEAN UNION,

Having regard to the Treaty on the Functioning of the European Union, and in particular Article 82(2) thereof,

Having regard to the proposal from the European Commission,

After transmission of the draft legislative act to the national parliaments,

Having regard to the opinion of the European Economic and Social Committee [1],

After consulting the Committee of the Regions,

Acting in accordance with the ordinary legislative procedure [2],

Whereas:

(1) The Union has set itself the objective of maintaining and developing an area of freedom, security and justice. According to the Presidency Conclusions of the European Council in Tampere of 15 and 16 October 1999, and in particular point 33 thereof, the principle of mutual recognition of judgments and other decisions of judicial authorities should become the cornerstone of judicial cooperation in both civil and criminal matters within the Union because enhanced mutual recognition and the necessary approximation of legislation would facilitate cooperation between competent authorities and the judicial protection of individual rights.

(2) On 29 November 2000, the Council, in accordance with the Tampere conclusions, adopted a programme of measures to implement the principle of mutual recognition of decisions in criminal matters [3]. The introduction to the programme states that mutual recognition is 'designed to strengthen cooperation between Member States but also to enhance the protection of individual rights'.

(3) The implementation of the principle of mutual recognition of decisions in criminal matters presupposes that Member States trust in each other's criminal justice systems. The extent of mutual recognition is very much dependent on a number of parameters, which include mechanisms for safeguarding the rights of suspects or accused persons and common minimum standards necessary to facilitate the application of the principle of mutual recognition.

(4) Mutual recognition of decisions in criminal matters can operate effectively only in a spirit of trust in which not only judicial authorities but all actors in the criminal process consider decisions of the judicial authorities of other Member States as equivalent to their own, implying not only trust in the adequacy of other Member States' rules, but also trust that those rules are correctly applied.

(5) Article 47 of the Charter of Fundamental Rights of the European Union (hereinafter 'the Charter') and Article 6 of the European Convention for the Protection of Human Rights and Fundamental Freedoms (hereinafter 'the ECHR') enshrine the right to a fair trial. Article 48(2) of the Charter guarantees respect for the rights of the defence.

(6) Article 6 of the Charter and Article 5 ECHR enshrine the right to liberty and security of person. Any restrictions on that right must not exceed those permitted in accordance with Article 5 ECHR and inferred from the case-law of the European Court of Human Rights.

(7) Although all the Member States are party to the ECHR, experience has shown that that alone does not always provide a sufficient degree of trust in the criminal justice systems of other Member States.

(8) Strengthening mutual trust requires detailed rules on the protection of the procedural rights and guarantees arising from the Charter and from the ECHR.

[1] OJ C 54, 19.2.2011, p. 48.
[2] Position of the European Parliament of 13 December 2011 (not yet published in the Official Journal) and decision of the Council of 26 April 2012.
[3] OJ C 12, 15.1.2001, p. 10.

(9) Article 82(2) of the Treaty on the Functioning of the European Union provides for the establishment of minimum rules applicable in the Member States so as to facilitate mutual recognition of judgments and judicial decisions and police and judicial cooperation in criminal matters having a cross-border dimension. That Article refers to 'the rights of individuals in criminal procedure' as one of the areas in which minimum rules may be established.

(10) Common minimum rules should lead to increased confidence in the criminal justice systems of all Member States, which, in turn, should lead to more efficient judicial cooperation in a climate of mutual trust. Such common minimum rules should be established in the field of information in criminal proceedings.

(11) On 30 November 2009, the Council adopted a resolution on a Roadmap for strengthening procedural rights of suspected or accused persons in criminal proceedings ([1]) (hereinafter 'the Roadmap'). Taking a step-by-step approach, the Roadmap called for the adoption of measures regarding the right to translation and interpretation (measure A), the right to information on rights and information about the charges (measure B), the right to legal advice and legal aid (measure C), the right to communication with relatives, employers and consular authorities (measure D), and special safeguards for suspects or accused persons who are vulnerable (measure E). The Roadmap emphasises that the order of the rights is only indicative and thus implies that it may be changed in accordance with priorities. The Roadmap is designed to operate as a whole; only when all its component parts have been implemented will its benefits be felt in full.

(12) On 11 December 2009, the European Council welcomed the Roadmap and made it part of the Stockholm Programme — An open and secure Europe serving and protecting citizens ([2]) (point 2.4). The European Council underlined the non-exhaustive character of the Roadmap, by inviting the Commission to examine further elements of minimum procedural rights for suspects and accused persons, and to assess whether other issues, for instance the presumption of innocence, need to be addressed, in order to promote better cooperation in that area.

(13) The first measure adopted pursuant to the Roadmap, measure A, was Directive 2010/64/EU of the European Parliament and of the Council of 20 October 2010 on the right to interpretation and translation in criminal proceedings ([3]).

(14) This Directive relates to measure B of the Roadmap. It lays down common minimum standards to be applied in the field of information about rights and about the accusation to be given to persons suspected or accused of having committed a criminal offence, with a view to enhancing mutual trust among Member States. This Directive builds on the rights laid down in the Charter, and in particular Articles 6, 47 and 48 thereof, by building upon Articles 5 and 6 ECHR as interpreted by the European Court of Human Rights. In this Directive, the term 'accusation' is used to describe the same concept as the term 'charge' used in Article 6(1) ECHR.

(15) In its Communication of 20 April 2010 entitled 'Delivering an area of freedom, security and justice for Europe's citizens — Action Plan Implementing the Stockholm Programme', the Commission announced that it would present a proposal on the right to information on rights and information about charges in 2010.

(16) This Directive should apply to suspects and accused persons regardless of their legal status, citizenship or nationality.

(17) In some Member States an authority other than a court having jurisdiction in criminal matters has competence for imposing sanctions in relation to relatively minor offences. That may be the case, for example, in relation to traffic offences which are committed on a large scale and which might be established following a traffic control. In such situations, it would be unreasonable to require that the competent authority ensure all the rights under this Directive. Where the law of a Member State provides for the imposition of a sanction regarding minor offences by such an authority and there is either a right of appeal or the possibility for the case to be otherwise referred to a court having jurisdiction in criminal matters, this Directive should therefore apply only to the proceedings before that court following such an appeal or referral.

(18) The right to information about procedural rights, which is inferred from the case-law of the European Court of Human Rights, should be explicitly established by this Directive.

(19) The competent authorities should inform suspects or accused persons promptly of those rights, as they apply under national law, which are essential to safeguarding the fairness of the proceedings, either orally or in writing, as provided for by this Directive. In order to allow the practical and effective exercise of those rights, the information should be provided promptly in the course of the proceedings and at the latest before the first official interview of the suspect or accused person by the police or by another competent authority.

(20) This Directive lays down minimum rules with respect to the information on rights of suspects or accused persons. This is without prejudice to information to be given on other procedural rights arising out of the Charter, the ECHR, national law and applicable Union law as interpreted by the relevant courts and tribunals. Once the information about a particular right has been provided, the competent authorities should not be required to

([1]) OJ C 295, 4.12.2009, p. 1.
([2]) OJ C 115, 4.5.2010, p. 1.
([3]) OJ L 280, 26.10.2010, p. 1.

reiterate it, unless the specific circumstances of the case or the specific rules laid down in national law so require.

(21) References in this Directive to suspects or accused persons who are arrested or detained should be understood to refer to any situation where, in the course of criminal proceedings, suspects or accused persons are deprived of liberty within the meaning of Article 5(1)(c) ECHR, as interpreted by the case-law of the European Court of Human Rights.

(22) Where suspects or accused persons are arrested or detained, information about applicable procedural rights should be given by means of a written Letter of Rights drafted in an easily comprehensible manner so as to assist those persons in understanding their rights. Such a Letter of Rights should be provided promptly to each arrested person when deprived of liberty by the intervention of law enforcement authorities in the context of criminal proceedings. It should include basic information concerning any possibility to challenge the lawfulness of the arrest, obtaining a review of the detention, or requesting provisional release where, and to the extent that, such a right exists in national law. To help Member States draw up such a Letter of Rights, a model is provided in Annex I. That model is indicative and may be subject to review in the context of the Commission's report on the implementation of this Directive and also once all the Roadmap measures have entered into force. The Letter of Rights may include other relevant procedural rights that apply in Member States.

(23) Specific conditions and rules relating to the right of suspects or accused persons to have another person informed about their arrest or detention are to be determined by the Member States in their national law. As set out in the Roadmap, the exercise of that right should not prejudice the due course of the criminal proceedings.

(24) This Directive is without prejudice to the provisions of national law concerning safety of persons remaining in detention facilities.

(25) Member States should ensure that, when providing information in accordance with this Directive, suspects or accused persons are provided, where necessary, with translations or interpretation into a language that they understand, in accordance with the standards set out in Directive 2010/64/EU.

(26) When providing suspects or accused persons with information in accordance with this Directive, competent authorities should pay particular attention to persons who cannot understand the content or meaning of the information, for example because of their youth or their mental or physical condition.

(27) Persons accused of having committed a criminal offence should be given all the information on the accusation necessary to enable them to prepare their defence and to safeguard the fairness of the proceedings.

(28) The information provided to suspects or accused persons about the criminal act they are suspected or accused of having committed should be given promptly, and at the latest before their first official interview by the police or another competent authority, and without prejudicing the course of ongoing investigations. A description of the facts, including, where known, time and place, relating to the criminal act that the persons are suspected or accused of having committed and the possible legal classification of the alleged offence should be given in sufficient detail, taking into account the stage of the criminal proceedings when such a description is given, to safeguard the fairness of the proceedings and allow for an effective exercise of the rights of the defence.

(29) Where, in the course of the criminal proceedings, the details of the accusation change to the extent that the position of suspects or accused persons is substantially affected, this should be communicated to them where necessary to safeguard the fairness of the proceedings and in due time to allow for an effective exercise of the rights of the defence.

(30) Documents and, where appropriate, photographs, audio and video recordings, which are essential to challenging effectively the lawfulness of an arrest or detention of suspects or accused persons in accordance with national law, should be made available to suspects or accused persons or to their lawyers at the latest before a competent judicial authority is called to decide upon the lawfulness of the arrest or detention in accordance with Article 5(4) ECHR, and in due time to allow the effective exercise of the right to challenge the lawfulness of the arrest or detention.

(31) For the purpose of this Directive, access to the material evidence, as defined in national law, whether for or against the suspect or accused person, which is in the possession of the competent authorities in relation to the specific criminal case, should include access to materials such as documents, and where appropriate photographs and audio and video recordings. Such materials may be contained in a case file or otherwise held by competent authorities in any appropriate way in accordance with national law.

(32) Access to the material evidence in the possession of the competent authorities, whether for or against the suspect or accused person, as provided for under this Directive, may be refused, in accordance with national law, where such access may lead to a serious threat to the life or fundamental rights of another person or where refusal of such access is strictly necessary to safeguard an important public interest. Any refusal of such access must be weighed against the rights of the defence of the suspect or accused person, taking into account the different stages of the criminal proceedings. Restrictions on such access should be interpreted strictly and in accordance

with the principle of the right to a fair trial under the ECHR and as interpreted by the case-law of the European Court of Human Rights.

(33) The right of access to the materials of a case should be without prejudice to the provisions of national law on the protection of personal data and the whereabouts of protected witnesses.

(34) Access to the materials of the case, as provided for by this Directive, should be provided free of charge, without prejudice to provisions of national law providing for fees to be paid for documents to be copied from the case file or for sending materials to the persons concerned or to their lawyer.

(35) Where information is provided in accordance with this Directive, the competent authorities should take note of this in accordance with existing recording procedures under national law and should not be subject to any additional obligation to introduce new mechanisms or to any additional administrative burden.

(36) Suspects or accused persons or their lawyers should have the right to challenge, in accordance with national law, the possible failure or refusal of the competent authorities to provide information or to disclose certain materials of the case in accordance with this Directive. That right does not entail the obligation for Member States to provide for a specific appeal procedure, a separate mechanism, or a complaint procedure in which such failure or refusal may be challenged.

(37) Without prejudice to judicial independence and to differences in the organisation of the judiciary across the Union, Member States should provide or encourage the provision of adequate training with respect to the objectives of this Directive to the relevant officials in Member States.

(38) Member States should undertake all the necessary action to comply with this Directive. A practical and effective implementation of some of the provisions such as the obligation to provide suspects or accused persons with information about their rights in simple and accessible language could be achieved by different means including non-legislative measures such as appropriate training for the competent authorities or by a Letter of Rights drafted in simple and non-technical language so as to be easily understood by a lay person without any knowledge of criminal procedural law.

(39) The right to written information about rights on arrest provided for in this Directive should also apply, *mutatis mutandis*, to persons arrested for the purpose of the execution of a European Arrest Warrant under Council Framework Decision 2002/584/JHA of 13 June 2002 on the European arrest warrant and the surrender procedures between Member States (1). To help Member States draw up a Letter of Rights for such persons, a model is provided in Annex II. That model is indicative and may be subject to review in the context of the Commission's report on implementation of this Directive and also once all the Roadmap measures have come into force.

(40) This Directive sets minimum rules. Member States may extend the rights set out in this Directive in order to provide a higher level of protection also in situations not explicitly dealt with in this Directive. The level of protection should never fall below the standards provided by the ECHR as interpreted in the case-law of the European Court of Human Rights.

(41) This Directive respects fundamental rights and observes the principles recognised by the Charter. In particular, this Directive seeks to promote the right to liberty, the right to a fair trial and the rights of the defence. It should be implemented accordingly.

(42) The provisions of this Directive that correspond to rights guaranteed by the ECHR should be interpreted and implemented consistently with those rights, as interpreted in the case-law of the European Court of Human Rights.

(43) Since the objective of this Directive, namely establishing common minimum standards relating to the right to information in criminal proceedings, cannot be achieved by Member States acting unilaterally, at national, regional or local level, and can therefore, by reason of its scale and effects, be better achieved at Union level, the Union may adopt measures in accordance with the principle of subsidiarity as set out in Article 5 of the Treaty on European Union. In accordance with the principle of proportionality, as set out in that Article, this Directive does not go beyond what is necessary in order to achieve that objective.

(44) In accordance with Article 3 of the Protocol (No 21) on the position of the United Kingdom and Ireland in respect of the Area of Freedom, Security and Justice, annexed to the Treaty on European Union and to the Treaty on the Functioning of the European Union, those Member States have notified their wish to take part in the adoption and application of this Directive.

(45) In accordance with Articles 1 and 2 of the Protocol (No 22) on the position of Denmark, annexed to the Treaty on European Union and to the Treaty on the Functioning of the European Union, Denmark is not taking part in the adoption of this Directive and is not bound by it or subject to its application,

(1) OJ L 190, 18.7.2002, p. 1.

1.6.2012 EN Official Journal of the European Union L 142/5

HAVE ADOPTED THIS DIRECTIVE:

*Article 1*

**Subject matter**

This Directive lays down rules concerning the right to information of suspects or accused persons, relating to their rights in criminal proceedings and to the accusation against them. It also lays down rules concerning the right to information of persons subject to a European Arrest Warrant relating to their rights.

*Article 2*

**Scope**

1. This Directive applies from the time persons are made aware by the competent authorities of a Member State that they are suspected or accused of having committed a criminal offence until the conclusion of the proceedings, which is understood to mean the final determination of the question whether the suspect or accused person has committed the criminal offence, including, where applicable, sentencing and the resolution of any appeal.

2. Where the law of a Member State provides for the imposition of a sanction regarding minor offences by an authority other than a court having jurisdiction in criminal matters, and the imposition of such a sanction may be appealed to such a court, this Directive shall apply only to the proceedings before that court, following such an appeal.

*Article 3*

**Right to information about rights**

1. Member States shall ensure that suspects or accused persons are provided promptly with information concerning at least the following procedural rights, as they apply under national law, in order to allow for those rights to be exercised effectively:

(a) the right of access to a lawyer;

(b) any entitlement to free legal advice and the conditions for obtaining such advice;

(c) the right to be informed of the accusation, in accordance with Article 6;

(d) the right to interpretation and translation;

(e) the right to remain silent.

2. Member States shall ensure that the information provided for under paragraph 1 shall be given orally or in writing, in simple and accessible language, taking into account any particular needs of vulnerable suspects or vulnerable accused persons.

*Article 4*

**Letter of Rights on arrest**

1. Member States shall ensure that suspects or accused persons who are arrested or detained are provided promptly with a written Letter of Rights. They shall be given an opportunity to read the Letter of Rights and shall be allowed to keep it in their possession throughout the time that they are deprived of liberty.

2. In addition to the information set out in Article 3, the Letter of Rights referred to in paragraph 1 of this Article shall contain information about the following rights as they apply under national law:

(a) the right of access to the materials of the case;

(b) the right to have consular authorities and one person informed;

(c) the right of access to urgent medical assistance; and

(d) the maximum number of hours or days suspects or accused persons may be deprived of liberty before being brought before a judicial authority.

3. The Letter of Rights shall also contain basic information about any possibility, under national law, of challenging the lawfulness of the arrest; obtaining a review of the detention; or making a request for provisional release.

4. The Letter of Rights shall be drafted in simple and accessible language. An indicative model Letter of Rights is set out in Annex I.

5. Member States shall ensure that suspects or accused persons receive the Letter of Rights written in a language that they understand. Where a Letter of Rights is not available in the appropriate language, suspects or accused persons shall be informed of their rights orally in a language that they understand. A Letter of Rights in a language that they understand shall then be given to them without undue delay.

*Article 5*

**Letter of Rights in European Arrest Warrant proceedings**

1. Member States shall ensure that persons who are arrested for the purpose of the execution of a European Arrest Warrant are provided promptly with an appropriate Letter of Rights containing information on their rights according to the law implementing Framework Decision 2002/584/JHA in the executing Member State.

2. The Letter of Rights shall be drafted in simple and accessible language. An indicative model Letter of Rights is set out in Annex II.

*Article 6*

**Right to information about the accusation**

1. Member States shall ensure that suspects or accused persons are provided with information about the criminal act they are suspected or accused of having committed. That information shall be provided promptly and in such detail as is necessary to safeguard the fairness of the proceedings and the effective exercise of the rights of the defence.

2. Member States shall ensure that suspects or accused persons who are arrested or detained are informed of the reasons for their arrest or detention, including the criminal act they are suspected or accused of having committed.

3. Member States shall ensure that, at the latest on submission of the merits of the accusation to a court, detailed information is provided on the accusation, including the nature and legal classification of the criminal offence, as well as the nature of participation by the accused person.

4. Member States shall ensure that suspects or accused persons are informed promptly of any changes in the information given in accordance with this Article where this is necessary to safeguard the fairness of the proceedings.

*Article 7*

**Right of access to the materials of the case**

1. Where a person is arrested and detained at any stage of the criminal proceedings, Member States shall ensure that documents related to the specific case in the possession of the competent authorities which are essential to challenging effectively, in accordance with national law, the lawfulness of the arrest or detention, are made available to arrested persons or to their lawyers.

2. Member States shall ensure that access is granted at least to all material evidence in the possession of the competent authorities, whether for or against suspects or accused persons, to those persons or their lawyers in order to safeguard the fairness of the proceedings and to prepare the defence.

3. Without prejudice to paragraph 1, access to the materials referred to in paragraph 2 shall be granted in due time to allow the effective exercise of the rights of the defence and at the latest upon submission of the merits of the accusation to the judgment of a court. Where further material evidence comes into the possession of the competent authorities, access shall be granted to it in due time to allow for it to be considered.

4. By way of derogation from paragraphs 2 and 3, provided that this does not prejudice the right to a fair trial, access to certain materials may be refused if such access may lead to a serious threat to the life or the fundamental rights of another person or if such refusal is strictly necessary to safeguard an important public interest, such as in cases where access could prejudice an ongoing investigation or seriously harm the national security of the Member State in which the criminal proceedings are instituted. Member States shall ensure that, in accordance with procedures in national law, a decision to refuse access to certain materials in accordance with this paragraph is taken by a judicial authority or is at least subject to judicial review.

5. Access, as referred to in this Article, shall be provided free of charge.

*Article 8*

**Verification and remedies**

1. Member States shall ensure that when information is provided to suspects or accused persons in accordance with Articles 3 to 6 this is noted using the recording procedure specified in the law of the Member State concerned.

2. Member States shall ensure that suspects or accused persons or their lawyers have the right to challenge, in accordance with procedures in national law, the possible failure or refusal of the competent authorities to provide information in accordance with this Directive.

*Article 9*

**Training**

Without prejudice to judicial independence and differences in the organisation of the judiciary across the Union, Member States shall request those responsible for the training of judges, prosecutors, police and judicial staff involved in criminal proceedings to provide appropriate training with respect to the objectives of this Directive.

*Article 10*

**Non-regression**

Nothing in this Directive shall be construed as limiting or derogating from any of the rights or procedural safeguards that are ensured under the Charter, the ECHR, other relevant provisions of international law or the law of any Member State which provides a higher level of protection.

*Article 11*

**Transposition**

1. Member States shall bring into force the laws, regulations and administrative provisions necessary to comply with this Directive by 2 June 2014.

2. Member States shall transmit the text of those measures to the Commission.

3. When Member States adopt those measures they shall contain a reference to this Directive or be accompanied by such a reference on the occasion of their official publication. The methods of making such reference shall be laid down by the Member States.

*Article 12*

**Report**

The Commission shall, by 2 June 2015, submit a report to the European Parliament and to the Council, assessing the extent to which the Member States have taken the necessary measures in order to comply with this Directive, accompanied, if necessary, by legislative proposals.

*Article 13*

**Entry into force**

This Directive shall enter into force on the twentieth day following that of its publication in the *Official Journal of the European Union*.

*Article 14*

**Addressees**

This Directive is addressed to the Member States in accordance with the Treaties.

Done at Strasbourg, 22 May 2012.

| | |
|---|---|
| *For the European Parliament* | *For the Council* |
| *The President* | *The President* |
| M. SCHULZ | N. WAMMEN |

*ANNEX I*

**Indicative model Letter of Rights**

The sole purpose of this model is to assist national authorities in drawing up their Letter of Rights at national level. Member States are not bound to use this model. When preparing their Letter of Rights, Member States may amend this model in order to align it with their national rules and add further useful information. The Member State's Letter of Rights must be given upon arrest or detention. This however does not prevent Member States from providing suspects or accused persons with written information in other situations during criminal proceedings.

You have the following rights when you are arrested or detained:

A. ASSISTANCE OF A LAWYER/ENTITLEMENT TO LEGAL AID

You have the right to speak confidentially to a lawyer. A lawyer is independent from the police. Ask the police if you need help to get in contact with a lawyer, the police shall help you. In certain cases the assistance may be free of charge. Ask the police for more information.

B. INFORMATION ABOUT THE ACCUSATION

You have the right to know why you have been arrested or detained and what you are suspected or accused of having done.

C. INTERPRETATION AND TRANSLATION

If you do not speak or understand the language spoken by the police or other competent authorities, you have the right to be assisted by an interpreter, free of charge. The interpreter may help you to talk to your lawyer and must keep the content of that communication confidential. You have the right to translation of at least the relevant passages of essential documents, including any order by a judge allowing your arrest or keeping you in custody, any charge or indictment and any judgment. You may in some circumstances be provided with an oral translation or summary.

D. RIGHT TO REMAIN SILENT

While questioned by the police or other competent authorities, you do not have to answer questions about the alleged offence. Your lawyer can help you to decide on that.

E. ACCESS TO DOCUMENTS

When you are arrested and detained, you (or your lawyer) have the right to access essential documents you need to challenge the arrest or detention. If your case goes to court, you (or your lawyer) have the right to access the material evidence for or against you.

F. INFORMING SOMEONE ELSE ABOUT YOUR ARREST OR DETENTION/INFORMING YOUR CONSULATE OR EMBASSY

When you are arrested or detained, you should tell the police if you want someone to be informed of your detention, for example a family member or your employer. In certain cases the right to inform another person of your detention may be temporarily restricted. In such cases the police will inform you of this.

If you are a foreigner, tell the police if you want your consular authority or embassy to be informed of your detention. Please also tell the police if you want to contact an official of your consular authority or embassy.

G. URGENT MEDICAL ASSISTANCE

When you are arrested or detained, you have the right to urgent medical assistance. Please let the police know if you are in need of such assistance.

H. PERIOD OF DEPRIVATION OF LIBERTY

After your arrest you may be deprived of liberty or detained for a maximum period of … [fill in applicable number of hours/days]. At the end of that period you must either be released or be heard by a judge who will decide on your further detention. Ask your lawyer or the judge for information about the possibility to challenge your arrest, to review the detention or to ask for provisional release.

*ANNEX II*

**Indicative model Letter of Rights for persons arrested on the basis of a European Arrest Warrant**

The sole purpose of this model is to assist national authorities in drawing up their Letter of Rights at national level. Member States are not bound to use this model. When preparing their Letter of Rights, Member States may amend this model in order to align it with their national rules and add further useful information.

You have been arrested on the basis of a European Arrest Warrant. You have the following rights:

A. INFORMATION ABOUT THE EUROPEAN ARREST WARRANT

You have the right to be informed about the content of the European Arrest Warrant on the basis of which you have been arrested.

B. ASSISTANCE OF A LAWYER

You have the right to speak confidentially to a lawyer. A lawyer is independent from the police. Ask the police if you need help to get in contact with a lawyer, the police shall help you. In certain cases the assistance may be free of charge. Ask the police for more information.

C. INTERPRETATION AND TRANSLATION

If you do not speak or understand the language spoken by the police or other competent authorities, you have the right to be assisted by an interpreter, free of charge. The interpreter may help you to talk to your lawyer and must keep the content of that communication confidential. You have the right to a translation of the European Arrest Warrant in a language you understand. You may in some circumstances be provided with an oral translation or summary.

D. POSSIBILITY TO CONSENT

You may consent or not consent to being surrendered to the State seeking you. Your consent would speed up the proceedings. [Possible addition of certain Member States: It may be difficult or even impossible to change this decision at a later stage.] Ask the authorities or your lawyer for more information.

E. HEARING

If you do not consent to your surrender, you have the right to be heard by a judicial authority.

# Directive 2012/29 establishing minimum standards on the rights, support and protection of victims of crime, and replacing Council Framework Decision 2001/220, 25 October 2012

**[OJ 2012, L 315/57–73]**

14.11.2012 EN Official Journal of the European Union L 315/57

# DIRECTIVE 2012/29/EU OF THE EUROPEAN PARLIAMENT AND OF THE COUNCIL

## of 25 October 2012

## establishing minimum standards on the rights, support and protection of victims of crime, and replacing Council Framework Decision 2001/220/JHA

THE EUROPEAN PARLIAMENT AND THE COUNCIL OF THE EUROPEAN UNION,

Having regard to the Treaty on the Functioning of the European Union, and in particular Article 82(2) thereof,

Having regard to the proposal from the European Commission,

After transmission of the draft legislative act to the national parliaments,

Having regard to the opinion of the European Economic and Social Committee [1],

Having regard to the opinion of the Committee of the Regions [2],

Acting in accordance with the ordinary legislative procedure [3],

Whereas:

(1) The Union has set itself the objective of maintaining and developing an area of freedom, security and justice, the cornerstone of which is the mutual recognition of judicial decisions in civil and criminal matters.

(2) The Union is committed to the protection of, and to the establishment of minimum standards in regard to, victims of crime and the Council has adopted Framework Decision 2001/220/JHA of 15 March 2001 on the standing of victims in criminal proceedings [4]. Under the Stockholm Programme – An open and secure Europe serving and protecting citizens [5], adopted by the European Council at its meeting on 10 and 11 December 2009, the Commission and the Member States were asked to examine how to improve legislation and practical support measures for the protection of victims, with particular attention paid to, support for and recognition of, all victims, including for victims of terrorism, as a priority.

(3) Article 82(2) of the Treaty on the Functioning of the European Union (TFEU) provides for the establishment of minimum rules applicable in the Member States to facilitate mutual recognition of judgments and judicial decisions and police and judicial cooperation in criminal matters having a cross-border dimension, in particular with regard to the rights of victims of crime.

(4) In its resolution of 10 June 2011 on a roadmap for strengthening the rights and protection of victims, in particular in criminal proceedings [6] ('the Budapest roadmap'), the Council stated that action should be taken at Union level in order to strengthen the rights of, support for, and protection of victims of crime. To that end and in accordance with that resolution, this Directive aims to revise and supplement the principles set out in Framework Decision 2001/220/JHA and to take significant steps forward in the level of protection of victims throughout the Union, in particular within the framework of criminal proceedings.

(5) The resolution of the European Parliament of 26 November 2009 on the elimination of violence against women [7] called on the Member States to improve their national laws and policies to combat all forms of violence against women and to act in order to tackle the causes of violence against women, not least by employing preventive measures, and called on the Union to guarantee the right to assistance and support for all victims of violence.

(6) In its resolution of 5 April 2011 on priorities and outline of a new EU policy framework to fight violence against women [8] the European Parliament proposed a strategy to combat violence against women, domestic violence and female genital mutilation as a basis for future legislative criminal-law instruments against gender-based violence including a framework to fight violence against women (policy, prevention, protection, prosecution, provision and partnership) to be followed up by a Union action plan. International regulation within this area includes the United Nations Convention on the Elimination of All Forms of Discrimination against Women (CEDAW) adopted on 18 December 1979, the CEDAW Committee's recommendations and decisions, and the Council of Europe Convention on preventing and combating violence against women and domestic violence adopted on 7 April 2011.

(1) OJ C 43, 15.2.2012, p. 39.
(2) OJ C 113, 18.4.2012, p. 56.
(3) Position of the European Parliament of 12 September 2012 (not yet published in the Official Journal) and decision of the Council of 4 October 2012.
(4) OJ L 82, 22.3.2001, p. 1.
(5) OJ C 115, 4.5.2010, p. 1.
(6) OJ C 187, 28.6.2011, p. 1.
(7) OJ C 285 E, 21.10.2010, p. 53.
(8) OJ C 296 E, 2.10.2012, p. 26.

(7) Directive 2011/99/EU of the European Parliament and of the Council of 13 December 2011 on the European protection order [1] establishes a mechanism for the mutual recognition of protection measures in criminal matters between Member States. Directive 2011/36/EU of the European Parliament and of the Council of 5 April 2011 on preventing and combating trafficking in human beings and protecting its victims [2] and Directive 2011/93/EU of the European Parliament and of the Council of 13 December 2011 on combating the sexual abuse and sexual exploitation of children and child pornography [3] address, inter alia, the specific needs of the particular categories of victims of human trafficking, child sexual abuse, sexual exploitation and child pornography.

(8) Council Framework Decision 2002/475/JHA of 13 June 2002 on combating terrorism [4] recognises that terrorism constitutes one of the most serious violations of the principles on which the Union is based, including the principle of democracy, and confirms that it constitutes, inter alia, a threat to the free exercise of human rights.

(9) Crime is a wrong against society as well as a violation of the individual rights of victims. As such, victims of crime should be recognised and treated in a respectful, sensitive and professional manner without discrimination of any kind based on any ground such as race, colour, ethnic or social origin, genetic features, language, religion or belief, political or any other opinion, membership of a national minority, property, birth, disability, age, gender, gender expression, gender identity, sexual orientation, residence status or health. In all contacts with a competent authority operating within the context of criminal proceedings, and any service coming into contact with victims, such as victim support or restorative justice services, the personal situation and immediate needs, age, gender, possible disability and maturity of victims of crime should be taken into account while fully respecting their physical, mental and moral integrity. Victims of crime should be protected from secondary and repeat victimisation, from intimidation and from retaliation, should receive appropriate support to facilitate their recovery and should be provided with sufficient access to justice.

(10) This Directive does not address the conditions of the residence of victims of crime in the territory of the Member States. Member States should take the necessary measures to ensure that the rights set out in this Directive are not made conditional on the victim's residence status in their territory or on the victim's citizenship or nationality. Reporting a crime and participating in criminal proceedings do not create any rights regarding the residence status of the victim.

(11) This Directive lays down minimum rules. Member States may extend the rights set out in this Directive in order to provide a higher level of protection.

(12) The rights set out in this Directive are without prejudice to the rights of the offender. The term 'offender' refers to a person who has been convicted of a crime. However, for the purposes of this Directive, it also refers to a suspected or accused person before any acknowledgement of guilt or conviction, and it is without prejudice to the presumption of innocence.

(13) This Directive applies in relation to criminal offences committed in the Union and to criminal proceedings that take place in the Union. It confers rights on victims of extra-territorial offences only in relation to criminal proceedings that take place in the Union. Complaints made to competent authorities outside the Union, such as embassies, do not trigger the obligations set out in this Directive.

(14) In applying this Directive, children's best interests must be a primary consideration, in accordance with the Charter of Fundamental Rights of the European Union and the United Nations Convention on the Rights of the Child adopted on 20 November 1989. Child victims should be considered and treated as the full bearers of rights set out in this Directive and should be entitled to exercise those rights in a manner that takes into account their capacity to form their own views.

(15) In applying this Directive, Member States should ensure that victims with disabilities are able to benefit fully from the rights set out in this Directive, on an equal basis with others, including by facilitating the accessibility to premises where criminal proceedings are conducted and access to information.

(16) Victims of terrorism have suffered attacks that are intended ultimately to harm society. They may therefore need special attention, support and protection due to the particular nature of the crime that has been committed against them. Victims of terrorism can be under significant public scrutiny and often need social recognition and respectful treatment by society. Member States should therefore take particular account of the needs of victims of terrorism, and should seek to protect their dignity and security.

[1] OJ L 338, 21.12.2011, p. 2.
[2] OJ L 101, 15.4.2011, p. 1.
[3] OJ L 335, 17.12.2011, p. 1.
[4] OJ L 164, 22.6.2002, p. 3.

(17) Violence that is directed against a person because of that person's gender, gender identity or gender expression or that affects persons of a particular gender disproportionately, is understood as gender-based violence. It may result in physical, sexual, emotional or psychological harm, or economic loss, to the victim. Gender-based violence is understood to be a form of discrimination and a violation of the fundamental freedoms of the victim and includes violence in close relationships, sexual violence (including rape, sexual assault and harassment), trafficking in human beings, slavery, and different forms of harmful practices, such as forced marriages, female genital mutilation and so-called 'honour crimes'. Women victims of gender-based violence and their children often require special support and protection because of the high risk of secondary and repeat victimisation, of intimidation and of retaliation connected with such violence.

(18) Where violence is committed in a close relationship, it is committed by a person who is a current or former spouse, or partner or other family member of the victim, whether or not the offender shares or has shared the same household with the victim. Such violence could cover physical, sexual, psychological or economic violence and could result in physical, mental or emotional harm or economic loss. Violence in close relationships is a serious and often hidden social problem which could cause systematic psychological and physical trauma with severe consequences because the offender is a person whom the victim should be able to trust. Victims of violence in close relationships may therefore be in need of special protection measures. Women are affected disproportionately by this type of violence and the situation can be worse if the woman is dependent on the offender economically, socially or as regards her right to residence.

(19) A person should be considered to be a victim regardless of whether an offender is identified, apprehended, prosecuted or convicted and regardless of the familial relationship between them. It is possible that family members of victims are also harmed as a result of the crime. In particular, family members of a person whose death has been directly caused by a criminal offence could be harmed as a result of the crime. Such family members, who are indirect victims of the crime, should therefore also benefit from protection under this Directive. However, Member States should be able to establish procedures to limit the number of family members who can benefit from the rights set out in this Directive. In the case of a child, the child or, unless this is not in the best interests of the child, the holder of parental responsibilty on behalf of the child, should be entitled to exercise the rights set out in this Directive. This Directive is without prejudice to any national administrative procedures required to establish that a person is a victim.

(20) The role of victims in the criminal justice system and whether they can participate actively in criminal proceedings vary across Member States, depending on the national system, and is determined by one or more of the following criteria: whether the national system provides for a legal status as a party to criminal proceedings; whether the victim is under a legal requirement or is requested to participate actively in criminal proceedings, for example as a witness; and/or whether the victim has a legal entitlement under national law to participate actively in criminal proceedings and is seeking to do so, where the national system does not provide that victims have the legal status of a party to the criminal proceedings. Member States should determine which of those criteria apply to determine the scope of rights set out in this Directive where there are references to the role of the victim in the relevant criminal justice system.

(21) Information and advice provided by competent authorities, victim support services and restorative justice services should, as far as possible, be given by means of a range of media and in a manner which can be understood by the victim. Such information and advice should be provided in simple and accessible language. It should also be ensured that the victim can be understood during proceedings. In this respect, the victim's knowledge of the language used to provide information, age, maturity, intellectual and emotional capacity, literacy and any mental or physical impairment should be taken into account. Particular account should be taken of difficulties in understanding or communicating which may be due to a disability of some kind, such as hearing or speech impediments. Equally, limitations on a victim's ability to communicate information should be taken into account during criminal proceedings.

(22) The moment when a complaint is made should, for the purposes of this Directive, be considered as falling within the context of the criminal proceedings. This should also include situations where authorities initiate criminal proceedings *ex officio* as a result of a criminal offence suffered by a victim.

(23) Information about reimbursement of expenses should be provided, from the time of the first contact with a competent authority, for example in a leaflet stating the basic conditions for such reimbursement of expenses. Member States should not be required, at this early stage of the criminal proceedings, to decide on whether the victim concerned fulfils the conditions for reimbursement of expenses.

(24) When reporting a crime, victims should receive a written acknowledgement of their complaint from the police, stating the basic elements of the crime, such as the type of crime, the time and place, and any damage or harm caused by the crime. This acknowledgement should include a file number and the time and place for reporting of the crime in order to serve as evidence that the crime has been reported, for example in relation to insurance claims.

(25) Without prejudice to rules relating to limitation periods, the delayed reporting of a criminal offence due to fear of retaliation, humiliation or stigmatisation should not result in refusing acknowledgement of the victim's complaint.

(26) When providing information, sufficient detail should be given to ensure that victims are treated in a respectful manner and to enable them to make informed decisions about their participation in proceedings. In this respect, information allowing the victim to know about the current status of any proceedings is particularly important. This is equally relevant for information to enable a victim to decide whether to request a review of a decision not to prosecute. Unless otherwise required, it should be possible to provide the information communicated to the victim orally or in writing, including through electronic means.

(27) Information to a victim should be provided to the last known correspondence address or electronic contact details given to the competent authority by the victim. In exceptional cases, for example due to the high number of victims involved in a case, it should be possible to provide information through the press, through an official website of the competent authority or through a similar communication channel.

(28) Member States should not be obliged to provide information where disclosure of that information could affect the proper handling of a case or harm a given case or person, or if they consider it contrary to the essential interests of their security.

(29) Competent authorities should ensure that victims receive updated contact details for communication about their case unless the victim has expressed a wish not to receive such information.

(30) A reference to a 'decision' in the context of the right to information, interpretation and translation, should be understood only as a reference to the finding of guilt or otherwise ending criminal proceedings. The reasons for that decision should be provided to the victim through a copy of the document which contains that decision or through a brief summary of them.

(31) The right to information about the time and place of a trial resulting from the complaint with regard to a criminal offence suffered by the victim should also apply to information about the time and place of a hearing related to an appeal of a judgment in the case.

(32) Specific information about the release or the escape of the offender should be given to victims, upon request, at least in cases where there might be a danger or an identified risk of harm to the victims, unless there is an identified risk of harm to the offender which would result from the notification. Where there is an identified risk of harm to the offender which would result from the notification, the competent authority should take into account all other risks when determining an appropriate action. The reference to 'identified risk of harm to the victims' should cover such factors as the nature and severity of the crime and the risk of retaliation. Therefore, it should not be applied to those situations where minor offences were committed and thus where there is only a slight risk of harm to the victim.

(33) Victims should receive information about any right to appeal of a decision to release the offender, if such a right exists in national law.

(34) Justice cannot be effectively achieved unless victims can properly explain the circumstances of the crime and provide their evidence in a manner understandable to the competent authorities. It is equally important to ensure that victims are treated in a respectful manner and that they are able to access their rights. Interpretation should therefore be made available, free of charge, during questioning of the victim and in order to enable them to participate actively in court hearings, in accordance with the role of the victim in the relevant criminal justice system. For other aspects of criminal proceedings, the need for interpretation and translation can vary depending on specific issues, the role of the victim in the relevant criminal justice system and his or her involvement in proceedings and any specific rights they have. As such, interpretation and translation for these other cases need only be provided to the extent necessary for victims to exercise their rights.

(35) The victim should have the right to challenge a decision finding that there is no need for interpretation or translation, in accordance with procedures in national law. That right does not entail the obligation for Member States to provide for a separate mechanism or complaint procedure in which such decision may be challenged and should not unreasonably prolong the criminal proceedings. An internal review of the decision in accordance with existing national procedures would suffice.

(36) The fact that a victim speaks a language which is not widely spoken should not, in itself, be grounds to decide that interpretation or translation would unreasonably prolong the criminal proceedings.

(37) Support should be available from the moment the competent authorities are aware of the victim and throughout criminal proceedings and for an appropriate time after such proceedings in accordance with the needs of the victim and the rights set out in this Directive. Support should be provided through a variety of means, without excessive formalities and through a sufficient geographical distribution across the Member State to allow all victims the opportunity to access such services. Victims who have suffered considerable harm due to the severity of the crime could require specialist support services.

(38) Persons who are particularly vulnerable or who find themselves in situations that expose them to a particularly high risk of harm, such as persons subjected to repeat violence in close relationships, victims of gender-based violence, or persons who fall victim to other types of crime in a Member State of which they are not nationals or residents, should be provided with specialist support and legal protection. Specialist support services should be based on an integrated and targeted approach which should, in particular, take into account the specific needs of victims, the severity of the harm suffered as a result of a criminal offence, as well as the relationship between victims, offenders, children and their wider social environment. A main task of these services and their staff, which play an important role in supporting the victim to recover from and overcome potential harm or trauma as a result of a criminal offence, should be to inform victims about the rights set out in this Directive so that they can take decisions in a supportive environment that treats them with dignity, respect and sensitivity. The types of support that such specialist support services should offer could include providing shelter and safe accommodation, immediate medical support, referral to medical and forensic examination for evidence in cases of rape or sexual assault, short and long-term psychological counselling, trauma care, legal advice, advocacy and specific services for children as direct or indirect victims.

(39) Victim support services are not required to provide extensive specialist and professional expertise themselves. If necessary, victim support services should assist victims in calling on existing professional support, such as psychologists.

(40) Although the provision of support should not be dependent on victims making a complaint with regard to a criminal offence to a competent authority such as the police, such authorities are often best placed to inform victims of the possibility of support. Member States are therefore encouraged to establish appropriate conditions to enable the referral of victims to victim support services, including by ensuring that data protection requirements can be and are adhered to. Repeat referrals should be avoided.

(41) The right of victims to be heard should be considered to have been fulfilled where victims are permitted to make statements or explanations in writing.

(42) The right of child victims to be heard in criminal proceedings should not be precluded solely on the basis that the victim is a child or on the basis of that victim's age.

(43) The right to a review of a decision not to prosecute should be understood as referring to decisions taken by prosecutors and investigative judges or law enforcement authorities such as police officers, but not to the decisions taken by courts. Any review of a decision not to prosecute should be carried out by a different person or authority to that which made the original decision, unless the initial decision not to prosecute was taken by the highest prosecuting authority, against whose decision no review can be made, in which case the review may be carried out by that same authority. The right to a review of a decision not to prosecute does not concern special procedures, such as proceedings against members of parliament or government, in relation to the exercise of their official position.

(44) A decision ending criminal proceedings should include situations where a prosecutor decides to withdraw charges or discontinue proceedings.

(45) A decision of the prosecutor resulting in an out-of-court settlement and thus ending criminal proceedings, excludes victims from the right to a review of a decision of the prosecutor not to prosecute, only if the settlement imposes a warning or an obligation.

(46) Restorative justice services, including for example victim-offender mediation, family group conferencing and sentencing circles, can be of great benefit to the victim, but require safeguards to prevent secondary and repeat victimisation, intimidation and retaliation. Such services should therefore have as a primary consideration the interests and needs of the victim, repairing the harm done to the victim and avoiding further harm. Factors such as the nature and severity of the crime, the ensuing degree of trauma, the repeat violation of a victim's physical, sexual, or psychological integrity, power imbalances, and the age, maturity or intellectual capacity of the victim, which could limit or reduce the victim's ability to make an informed choice or could prejudice a positive outcome for the victim, should be taken into consideration in referring a case to the restorative justice services and in conducting a restorative justice process. Restorative justice processes should, in principle, be confidential, unless agreed otherwise by the parties, or as required by national law due to an overriding public interest. Factors such as threats made or any forms of violence committed during the process may be considered as requiring disclosure in the public interest.

(47) Victims should not be expected to incur expenses in relation to their participation in criminal proceedings. Member States should be required to reimburse only necessary expenses of victims in relation to their participation in criminal proceedings and should not be required to reimburse victims' legal fees. Member States should be able to impose conditions in regard to the reimbursement of expenses in national law, such as time limits for claiming reimbursement, standard rates for subsistence and travel costs and maximum daily amounts for loss of earnings. The right to reimbursement of expenses in criminal proceedings should not arise in a situation where a victim makes a statement on a criminal offence. Expenses should only be covered to the extent that the victim is obliged or requested by the competent authorities to be present and actively participate in the criminal proceedings.

(48) Recoverable property which is seized in criminal proceedings should be returned as soon as possible to the victim of the crime, subject to exceptional circumstances, such as in a dispute concerning the ownership or where the possession of the property or the property itself is illegal. The right to have property returned should be without prejudice to its legitimate retention for the purposes of other legal proceedings.

(49) The right to a decision on compensation from the offender and the relevant applicable procedure should also apply to victims resident in a Member State other than the Member State where the criminal offence was committed.

(50) The obligation set out in this Directive to transmit complaints should not affect Member States' competence to institute proceedings and is without prejudice to the rules of conflict relating to the exercise of jurisdiction, as laid down in Council Framework Decision 2009/948/JHA of 30 November 2009 on prevention and settlement of conflicts of exercise of jurisdiction in criminal proceedings ([1]).

(51) If the victim has left the territory of the Member State where the criminal offence was committed, that Member State should no longer be obliged to provide assistance, support and protection except for what is directly related to any criminal proceedings it is conducting regarding the criminal offence concerned, such as special protection measures during court proceedings. The Member State of the victim's residence should provide assistance, support and protection required for the victim's need to recover.

(52) Measures should be available to protect the safety and dignity of victims and their family members from secondary and repeat victimisation, from intimidation and from retaliation, such as interim injunctions or protection or restraining orders.

([1]) OJ L 328, 15.12.2009, p. 42.

(53) The risk of secondary and repeat victimisation, of intimidation and of retaliation by the offender or as a result of participation in criminal proceedings should be limited by carrying out proceedings in a coordinated and respectful manner, enabling victims to establish trust in authorities. Interaction with competent authorities should be as easy as possible whilst limiting the number of unnecessary interactions the victim has with them through, for example, video recording of interviews and allowing its use in court proceedings. As wide a range of measures as possible should be made available to practitioners to prevent distress to the victim during court proceedings in particular as a result of visual contact with the offender, his or her family, associates or members of the public. To that end, Member States should be encouraged to introduce, especially in relation to court buildings and police stations, feasible and practical measures enabling the facilities to include amenities such as separate entrances and waiting areas for victims. In addition, Member States should, to the extent possible, plan the criminal proceedings so that contacts between victims and their family members and offenders are avoided, such as by summoning victims and offenders to hearings at different times.

(54) Protecting the privacy of the victim can be an important means of preventing secondary and repeat victimisation, intimidation and retaliation and can be achieved through a range of measures including non-disclosure or limitations on the disclosure of information concerning the identity and whereabouts of the victim. Such protection is particularly important for child victims, and includes non-disclosure of the name of the child. However, there might be cases where, exceptionally, the child can benefit from the disclosure or even widespread publication of information, for example where a child has been abducted. Measures to protect the privacy and images of victims and of their family members should always be consistent with the right to a fair trial and freedom of expression, as recognised in Articles 6 and 10, respectively, of the European Convention for the Protection of Human Rights and Fundamental Freedoms.

(55) Some victims are particularly at risk of secondary and repeat victimisation, of intimidation and of retaliation by the offender during criminal proceedings. It is possible that such a risk derives from the personal characteristics of the victim or the type, nature or circumstances of the crime. Only through individual assessments, carried out at the earliest opportunity, can such a risk be effectively identified. Such assessments should be carried out for all victims to determine whether they are at risk of secondary and repeat victimisation, of intimidation and of retaliation and what special protection measures they require.

(56) Individual assessments should take into account the personal characteristics of the victim such as his or her age, gender and gender identity or expression, ethnicity, race, religion, sexual orientation, health, disability, residence status, communication difficulties, relationship to or dependence on the offender and previous experience of crime. They should also take into account the type or nature and the circumstances of the crime such as whether it is a hate crime, a bias crime or a crime committed with a discriminatory motive, sexual violence, violence in a close relationship, whether the offender was in a position of control, whether the victim's residence is in a high crime or gang dominated area, or whether the victim's country of origin is not the Member State where the crime was committed.

(57) Victims of human trafficking, terrorism, organised crime, violence in close relationships, sexual violence or exploitation, gender-based violence, hate crime, and victims with disabilities and child victims tend to experience a high rate of secondary and repeat victimisation, of intimidation and of retaliation. Particular care should be taken when assessing whether such victims are at risk of such victimisation, intimidation and of retaliation and there should be a strong presumption that those victims will benefit from special protection measures.

(58) Victims who have been identified as vulnerable to secondary and repeat victimisation, to intimidation and to retaliation should be offered appropriate measures to protect them during criminal proceedings. The exact nature of such measures should be determined through the individual assessment, taking into account the wish of the victim. The extent of any such measure should be determined without prejudice to the rights of the defence and in accordance with rules of judicial discretion. The victims' concerns and fears in relation to proceedings should be a key factor in determining whether they need any particular measure.

(59) Immediate operational needs and constraints may make it impossible to ensure, for example, that the same police officer consistently interview the victim; illness, maternity or parental leave are examples of such constraints. Furthermore, premises specially designed for interviews with victims may not be available due, for example, to renovation. In the event of such operational or practical constraints, a special measure envisaged following an individual assessment may not be possible to provide on a case-by-case basis.

(60) Where, in accordance with this Directive, a guardian or a representative is to be appointed for a child, those roles could be performed by the same person or by a legal person, an institution or an authority.

(61) Any officials involved in criminal proceedings who are likely to come into personal contact with victims should be able to access and receive appropriate initial and ongoing training, to a level appropriate to their contact with victims, so that they are able to identify victims and their needs and deal with them in a respectful, sensitive, professional and non-discriminatory manner. Persons who are likely to be involved in the individual assessment to identify victims' specific protection needs and to determine their need for special protection measures should receive specific training on how to carry out such an assessment. Member States should ensure such training for police services and court staff. Equally, training should be promoted for lawyers, prosecutors and judges and for practitioners who provide victim support or restorative justice services. This requirement should include training on the specific support services to which victims should be referred or specialist training where their work focuses on victims with specific needs and specific psychological training, as appropriate. Where relevant, such training should be gender sensitive. Member States' actions on training should be complemented by guidelines, recommendations and exchange of best practices in accordance with the Budapest roadmap.

(62) Member States should encourage and work closely with civil society organisations, including recognised and active non-governmental organisations working with victims of crime, in particular in policymaking initiatives, information and awareness-raising campaigns, research and education programmes and in training, as well as in monitoring and evaluating the impact of measures to support and protect victims of crime. For victims of crime to receive the proper degree of assistance, support and protection, public services should work in a coordinated manner and should be involved at all administrative levels — at Union level, and at national, regional and local level. Victims should be assisted in finding and addressing the competent authorities in order to avoid repeat referrals. Member States should consider developing 'sole points of access' or 'one-stop shops', that address victims' multiple needs when involved in criminal proceedings, including the need to receive information, assistance, support, protection and compensation.

(63) In order to encourage and facilitate reporting of crimes and to allow victims to break the cycle of repeat victimisation, it is essential that reliable support services are available to victims and that competent authorities are prepared to respond to victims' reports in a respectful, sensitive, professional and non-discriminatory manner. This could increase victims' confidence in the criminal justice systems of Member States and reduce the number of unreported crimes. Practitioners who are likely to receive complaints from victims with regard to criminal offences should be appropriately trained to facilitate reporting of crimes, and measures should be put in place to enable third-party reporting, including by civil society organisations. It should be possible to make use of communication technology, such as e-mail, video recordings or online electronic forms for making complaints.

(64) Systematic and adequate statistical data collection is recognised as an essential component of effective policymaking in the field of rights set out in this Directive. In order to facilitate evaluation of the application of this Directive, Member States should communicate to the Commission relevant statistical data related to the application of national procedures on victims of crime, including at least the number and type of the reported crimes and, as far as such data are known and are available, the number and age and gender of the victims. Relevant statistical data can include data recorded by the judicial authorities and by law enforcement agencies and, as far as possible, administrative data compiled by healthcare and social welfare services and by public and non-governmental victim support or restorative justice services and other organisations working with victims of crime. Judicial data can include information about reported crime, the number of cases that are investigated and persons prosecuted and sentenced. Service-based administrative data can include, as far as possible, data on how victims are using services provided by government agencies and public and private support organisations, such as the number of referrals by police to victim support services, the number of victims that request, receive or do not receive support or restorative justice.

(65) This Directive aims to amend and expand the provisions of Framework Decision 2001/220/JHA. Since the amendments to be made are substantial in number and nature, that Framework Decision should, in the interests of clarity, be replaced in its entirety in relation to Member States participating in the adoption of this Directive.

(66) This Directive respects fundamental rights and observes the principles recognised by the Charter of Fundamental Rights of the European Union. In particular, it seeks to promote the right to dignity, life, physical and mental integrity, liberty and security, respect for private and family life, the right to property, the principle of non-discrimination, the principle of equality between women and men, the rights of the child, the elderly and persons with disabilities, and the right to a fair trial.

(67) Since the objective of this Directive, namely to establish minimum standards on the rights, support and protection of victims of crime, cannot be sufficiently achieved by the Member States, and can therefore, by reason of its scale and potential effects, be better achieved at Union level, the Union may adopt measures in accordance with the principle of subsidiarity as set out in Article 5 of the Treaty on European Union (TEU). In accordance with the principle of proportionality, as set out in that Article, this Directive does not go beyond what is necessary in order to achieve that objective.

(68) Personal data processed when implementing this Directive should be protected in accordance with Council Framework Decision 2008/977/JHA of 27 November 2008 on the protection of personal data processed in the framework of police and judicial cooperation in criminal matters [1] and in accordance with the principles laid down in the Council of Europe Convention of 28 January 1981 for the Protection of Individuals with regard to Automatic Processing of Personal Data, which all Member States have ratified.

(69) This Directive does not affect more far reaching provisions contained in other Union acts which address the specific needs of particular categories of victims, such as victims of human trafficking and victims of child sexual abuse, sexual exploitation and child pornography, in a more targeted manner.

(70) In accordance with Article 3 of Protocol No 21 on the position of the United Kingdom and Ireland in respect of the Area of Freedom, Security and Justice, annexed to the TEU and to the TFEU, those Member States have notified their wish to take part in the adoption and application of this Directive.

(71) In accordance with Articles 1 and 2 of Protocol No 22 on the position of Denmark, annexed to the TEU and to the TFEU, Denmark is not taking part in the adoption of this Directive and is not bound by it or subject to its application.

(72) The European Data Protection Supervisor delivered an opinion on 17 October 2011 [2] based on Article 41(2) of Regulation (EC) No 45/2001 of the European Parliament and of the Council of 18 December 2000 on the protection of individuals with regard to the processing of personal data by the Community institutions and bodies and on the free movement of such data [3],

HAVE ADOPTED THIS DIRECTIVE:

CHAPTER 1

## GENERAL PROVISIONS

*Article 1*

### Objectives

1. The purpose of this Directive is to ensure that victims of crime receive appropriate information, support and protection and are able to participate in criminal proceedings.

Member States shall ensure that victims are recognised and treated in a respectful, sensitive, tailored, professional and non-discriminatory manner, in all contacts with victim support or restorative justice services or a competent authority, operating within the context of criminal proceedings. The rights set out in this Directive shall apply to victims in a non-discriminatory manner, including with respect to their residence status.

2. Member States shall ensure that in the application of this Directive, where the victim is a child, the child's best interests shall be a primary consideration and shall be assessed on an individual basis. A child-sensitive approach, taking due account of the child's age, maturity, views, needs and concerns, shall prevail. The child and the holder of parental responsibility or other legal representative, if any, shall be informed of any measures or rights specifically focused on the child.

*Article 2*

### Definitions

1. For the purposes of this Directive the following definitions shall apply:

(a) 'victim' means:

(i) a natural person who has suffered harm, including physical, mental or emotional harm or economic loss which was directly caused by a criminal offence;

(ii) family members of a person whose death was directly caused by a criminal offence and who have suffered harm as a result of that person's death;

[1] OJ L 350, 30.12.2008, p. 60.

[2] OJ C 35, 9.2.2012, p. 10.

[3] OJ L 8, 12.1.2001, p. 1.

(b) 'family members' means the spouse, the person who is living with the victim in a committed intimate relationship, in a joint household and on a stable and continuous basis, the relatives in direct line, the siblings and the dependants of the victim;

(c) 'child' means any person below 18 years of age;

(d) 'restorative justice' means any process whereby the victim and the offender are enabled, if they freely consent, to participate actively in the resolution of matters arising from the criminal offence through the help of an impartial third party.

2. Member States may establish procedures:

(a) to limit the number of family members who may benefit from the rights set out in this Directive taking into account the individual circumstances of each case; and

(b) in relation to paragraph (1)(a)(ii), to determine which family members have priority in relation to the exercise of the rights set out in this Directive.

CHAPTER 2

## PROVISION OF INFORMATION AND SUPPORT

*Article 3*

### Right to understand and to be understood

1. Member States shall take appropriate measures to assist victims to understand and to be understood from the first contact and during any further necessary interaction they have with a competent authority in the context of criminal proceedings, including where information is provided by that authority.

2. Member States shall ensure that communications with victims are given in simple and accessible language, orally or in writing. Such communications shall take into account the personal characteristics of the victim including any disability which may affect the ability to understand or to be understood.

3. Unless contrary to the interests of the victim or unless the course of proceedings would be prejudiced, Member States shall allow victims to be accompanied by a person of their choice in the first contact with a competent authority where, due to the impact of the crime, the victim requires assistance to understand or to be understood.

*Article 4*

### Right to receive information from the first contact with a competent authority

1. Member States shall ensure that victims are offered the following information, without unnecessary delay, from their first contact with a competent authority in order to enable them to access the rights set out in this Directive:

(a) the type of support they can obtain and from whom, including, where relevant, basic information about access to medical support, any specialist support, including psychological support, and alternative accommodation;

(b) the procedures for making complaints with regard to a criminal offence and their role in connection with such procedures;

(c) how and under what conditions they can obtain protection, including protection measures;

(d) how and under what conditions they can access legal advice, legal aid and any other sort of advice;

(e) how and under what conditions they can access compensation;

(f) how and under what conditions they are entitled to interpretation and translation;

(g) if they are resident in a Member State other than that where the criminal offence was committed, any special measures, procedures or arrangements, which are available to protect their interests in the Member State where the first contact with the competent authority is made;

(h) the available procedures for making complaints where their rights are not respected by the competent authority operating within the context of criminal proceedings;

(i) the contact details for communications about their case;

(j) the available restorative justice services;

(k) how and under what conditions expenses incurred as a result of their participation in the criminal proceedings can be reimbursed.

2. The extent or detail of information referred to in paragraph 1 may vary depending on the specific needs and personal circumstances of the victim and the type or nature of the crime. Additional details may also be provided at later stages depending on the needs of the victim and the relevance, at each stage of proceedings, of such details.

14.11.2012 EN Official Journal of the European Union L 315/67

*Article 5*

**Right of victims when making a complaint**

1. Member States shall ensure that victims receive written acknowledgement of their formal complaint made by them to the competent authority of a Member State, stating the basic elements of the criminal offence concerned.

2. Member States shall ensure that victims who wish to make a complaint with regard to a criminal offence and who do not understand or speak the language of the competent authority be enabled to make the complaint in a language that they understand or by receiving the necessary linguistic assistance.

3. Member States shall ensure that victims who do not understand or speak the language of the competent authority, receive translation, free of charge, of the written acknowledgement of their complaint provided for in paragraph 1, if they so request, in a language that they understand.

*Article 6*

**Right to receive information about their case**

1. Member States shall ensure that victims are notified without unnecessary delay of their right to receive the following information about the criminal proceedings instituted as a result of the complaint with regard to a criminal offence suffered by the victim and that, upon request, they receive such information:

(a) any decision not to proceed with or to end an investigation or not to prosecute the offender;

(b) the time and place of the trial, and the nature of the charges against the offender.

2. Member States shall ensure that, in accordance with their role in the relevant criminal justice system, victims are notified without unnecessary delay of their right to receive the following information about the criminal proceedings instituted as a result of the complaint with regard to a criminal offence suffered by them and that, upon request, they receive such information:

(a) any final judgment in a trial;

(b) information enabling the victim to know about the state of the criminal proceedings, unless in exceptional cases the proper handling of the case may be adversely affected by such notification.

3. Information provided for under paragraph 1(a) and paragraph 2(a) shall include reasons or a brief summary of reasons for the decision concerned, except in the case of a jury decision or a decision where the reasons are confidential in which cases the reasons are not provided as a matter of national law.

4. The wish of victims as to whether or not to receive information shall bind the competent authority, unless that information must be provided due to the entitlement of the victim to active participation in the criminal proceedings. Member States shall allow victims to modify their wish at any moment, and shall take such modification into account.

5. Member States shall ensure that victims are offered the opportunity to be notified, without unnecessary delay, when the person remanded in custody, prosecuted or sentenced for criminal offences concerning them is released from or has escaped detention. Furthermore, Member States shall ensure that victims are informed of any relevant measures issued for their protection in case of release or escape of the offender.

6. Victims shall, upon request, receive the information provided for in paragraph 5 at least in cases where there is a danger or an identified risk of harm to them, unless there is an identified risk of harm to the offender which would result from the notification.

*Article 7*

**Right to interpretation and translation**

1. Member States shall ensure that victims who do not understand or speak the language of the criminal proceedings concerned are provided, upon request, with interpretation in accordance with their role in the relevant criminal justice system in criminal proceedings, free of charge, at least during any interviews or questioning of the victim during criminal proceedings before investigative and judicial authorities, including during police questioning, and interpretation for their active participation in court hearings and any necessary interim hearings.

2. Without prejudice to the rights of the defence and in accordance with rules of judicial discretion, communication technology such as videoconferencing, telephone or internet may be used, unless the physical presence of the interpreter is required in order for the victims to properly exercise their rights or to understand the proceedings.

3. Member States shall ensure that victims who do not understand or speak the language of the criminal proceedings concerned are provided, in accordance with their role in the relevant criminal justice system in criminal proceedings, upon request, with translations of information essential to the exercise of their rights in criminal proceedings in a language that they understand, free of charge, to the extent that such information is made available to the victims. Translations of such information shall include at least any decision ending the criminal proceedings related to the criminal offence suffered by the victim, and upon the victim's request, reasons or a brief summary of reasons for such decision, except in the case of a jury decision or a decision where the reasons are confidential in which cases the reasons are not provided as a matter of national law.

4. Member States shall ensure that victims who are entitled to information about the time and place of the trial in accordance with Article 6(1)(b) and who do not understand the language of the competent authority, are provided with a translation of the information to which they are entitled, upon request.

5. Victims may submit a reasoned request to consider a document as essential. There shall be no requirement to translate passages of essential documents which are not relevant for the purpose of enabling victims to actively participate in the criminal proceedings.

6. Notwithstanding paragraphs 1 and 3, an oral translation or oral summary of essential documents may be provided instead of a written translation on condition that such oral translation or oral summary does not prejudice the fairness of the proceedings.

7. Member States shall ensure that the competent authority assesses whether victims need interpretation or translation as provided for under paragraphs 1 and 3. Victims may challenge a decision not to provide interpretation or translation. The procedural rules for such a challenge shall be determined by national law.

8. Interpretation and translation and any consideration of a challenge of a decision not to provide interpretation or translation under this Article shall not unreasonably prolong the criminal proceedings.

*Article 8*

**Right to access victim support services**

1. Member States shall ensure that victims, in accordance with their needs, have access to confidential victim support services, free of charge, acting in the interests of the victims before, during and for an appropriate time after criminal proceedings. Family members shall have access to victim support services in accordance with their needs and the degree of harm suffered as a result of the criminal offence committed against the victim.

2. Member States shall facilitate the referral of victims, by the competent authority that received the complaint and by other relevant entities, to victim support services.

3. Member States shall take measures to establish free of charge and confidential specialist support services in addition to, or as an integrated part of, general victim support services, or to enable victim support organisations to call on existing specialised entities providing such specialist support. Victims, in accordance with their specific needs, shall have access to such services and family members shall have access in accordance with their specific needs and the degree of harm suffered as a result of the criminal offence committed against the victim.

4. Victim support services and any specialist support services may be set up as public or non-governmental organisations and may be organised on a professional or voluntary basis.

5. Member States shall ensure that access to any victim support services is not dependent on a victim making a formal complaint with regard to a criminal offence to a competent authority.

*Article 9*

**Support from victim support services**

1. Victim support services, as referred to in Article 8(1), shall, as a minimum, provide:

(a) information, advice and support relevant to the rights of victims including on accessing national compensation schemes for criminal injuries, and on their role in criminal proceedings including preparation for attendance at the trial;

(b) information about or direct referral to any relevant specialist support services in place;

(c) emotional and, where available, psychological support;

(d) advice relating to financial and practical issues arising from the crime;

(e) unless otherwise provided by other public or private services, advice relating to the risk and prevention of secondary and repeat victimisation, of intimidation and of retaliation.

2. Member States shall encourage victim support services to pay particular attention to the specific needs of victims who have suffered considerable harm due to the severity of the crime.

3. Unless otherwise provided by other public or private services, specialist support services referred to in Article 8(3), shall, as a minimum, develop and provide:

(a) shelters or any other appropriate interim accommodation for victims in need of a safe place due to an imminent risk of secondary and repeat victimisation, of intimidation and of retaliation;

(b) targeted and integrated support for victims with specific needs, such as victims of sexual violence, victims of gender-based violence and victims of violence in close relationships, including trauma support and counselling.

CHAPTER 3

## PARTICIPATION IN CRIMINAL PROCEEDINGS

*Article 10*

### Right to be heard

1. Member States shall ensure that victims may be heard during criminal proceedings and may provide evidence. Where a child victim is to be heard, due account shall be taken of the child's age and maturity.

2. The procedural rules under which victims may be heard during criminal proceedings and may provide evidence shall be determined by national law.

*Article 11*

### Rights in the event of a decision not to prosecute

1. Member States shall ensure that victims, in accordance with their role in the relevant criminal justice system, have the right to a review of a decision not to prosecute. The procedural rules for such a review shall be determined by national law.

2. Where, in accordance with national law, the role of the victim in the relevant criminal justice system will be established only after a decision to prosecute the offender has been taken, Member States shall ensure that at least the victims of serious crimes have the right to a review of a decision not to prosecute. The procedural rules for such a review shall be determined by national law.

3. Member States shall ensure that victims are notified without unnecessary delay of their right to receive, and that they receive sufficient information to decide whether to request a review of any decision not to prosecute upon request.

4. Where the decision not to prosecute is taken by the highest prosecuting authority against whose decision no review may be carried out under national law, the review may be carried out by the same authority.

5. Paragraphs 1, 3 and 4 shall not apply to a decision of the prosecutor not to prosecute, if such a decision results in an out-of-court settlement, in so far as national law makes such provision.

*Article 12*

### Right to safeguards in the context of restorative justice services

1. Member States shall take measures to safeguard the victim from secondary and repeat victimisation, from intimidation and from retaliation, to be applied when providing any restorative justice services. Such measures shall ensure that victims who choose to participate in restorative justice processes have access to safe and competent restorative justice services, subject to at least the following conditions:

(a) the restorative justice services are used only if they are in the interest of the victim, subject to any safety considerations, and are based on the victim's free and informed consent, which may be withdrawn at any time;

(b) before agreeing to participate in the restorative justice process, the victim is provided with full and unbiased information about that process and the potential outcomes as well as information about the procedures for supervising the implementation of any agreement;

(c) the offender has acknowledged the basic facts of the case;

(d) any agreement is arrived at voluntarily and may be taken into account in any further criminal proceedings;

(e) discussions in restorative justice processes that are not conducted in public are confidential and are not subsequently disclosed, except with the agreement of the parties or as required by national law due to an overriding public interest.

2. Member States shall facilitate the referral of cases, as appropriate to restorative justice services, including through the establishment of procedures or guidelines on the conditions for such referral.

*Article 13*

### Right to legal aid

Member States shall ensure that victims have access to legal aid, where they have the status of parties to criminal proceedings. The conditions or procedural rules under which victims have access to legal aid shall be determined by national law.

L 315/70 EN Official Journal of the European Union 14.11.2012

*Article 14*

**Right to reimbursement of expenses**

Member States shall afford victims who participate in criminal proceedings, the possibility of reimbursement of expenses incurred as a result of their active participation in criminal proceedings, in accordance with their role in the relevant criminal justice system. The conditions or procedural rules under which victims may be reimbursed shall be determined by national law.

*Article 15*

**Right to the return of property**

Member States shall ensure that, following a decision by a competent authority, recoverable property which is seized in the course of criminal proceedings is returned to victims without delay, unless required for the purposes of criminal proceedings. The conditions or procedural rules under which such property is returned to the victims shall be determined by national law.

*Article 16*

**Right to decision on compensation from the offender in the course of criminal proceedings**

1. Member States shall ensure that, in the course of criminal proceedings, victims are entitled to obtain a decision on compensation by the offender, within a reasonable time, except where national law provides for such a decision to be made in other legal proceedings.

2. Member States shall promote measures to encourage offenders to provide adequate compensation to victims.

*Article 17*

**Rights of victims resident in another Member State**

1. Member States shall ensure that their competent authorities can take appropriate measures to minimise the difficulties faced where the victim is a resident of a Member State other than that where the criminal offence was committed, particularly with regard to the organisation of the proceedings. For this purpose, the authorities of the Member State where the criminal offence was committed shall, in particular, be in a position:

(a) to take a statement from the victim immediately after the complaint with regard to the criminal offence is made to the competent authority;

(b) to have recourse to the extent possible to the provisions on video conferencing and telephone conference calls laid down in the Convention on Mutual Assistance in Criminal Matters between the Member States of the European Union of 29 May 2000 [1] for the purpose of hearing victims who are resident abroad.

2. Member States shall ensure that victims of a criminal offence committed in Member States other than that where they reside may make a complaint to the competent authorities of the Member State of residence, if they are unable to do so in the Member State where the criminal offence was committed or, in the event of a serious offence, as determined by national law of that Member State, if they do not wish to do so.

3. Member States shall ensure that the competent authority to which the victim makes a complaint transmits it without delay to the competent authority of the Member State in which the criminal offence was committed, if the competence to institute the proceedings has not been exercised by the Member State in which the complaint was made.

CHAPTER 4

**PROTECTION OF VICTIMS AND RECOGNITION OF VICTIMS WITH SPECIFIC PROTECTION NEEDS**

*Article 18*

**Right to protection**

Without prejudice to the rights of the defence, Member States shall ensure that measures are available to protect victims and their family members from secondary and repeat victimisation, from intimidation and from retaliation, including against the risk of emotional or psychological harm, and to protect the dignity of victims during questioning and when testifying. When necessary, such measures shall also include procedures established under national law for the physical protection of victims and their family members.

*Article 19*

**Right to avoid contact between victim and offender**

1. Member States shall establish the necessary conditions to enable avoidance of contact between victims and their family members, where necessary, and the offender within premises where criminal proceedings are conducted, unless the criminal proceedings require such contact.

2. Member States shall ensure that new court premises have separate waiting areas for victims.

*Article 20*

**Right to protection of victims during criminal investigations**

Without prejudice to the rights of the defence and in accordance with rules of judicial discretion, Member States shall ensure that during criminal investigations:

(a) interviews of victims are conducted without unjustified delay after the complaint with regard to a criminal offence has been made to the competent authority;

(b) the number of interviews of victims is kept to a minimum and interviews are carried out only where strictly necessary for the purposes of the criminal investigation;

[1] OJ C 197, 12.7.2000, p. 3.

(c) victims may be accompanied by their legal representative and a person of their choice, unless a reasoned decision has been made to the contrary;

(d) medical examinations are kept to a minimum and are carried out only where strictly necessary for the purposes of the criminal proceedings.

*Article 21*

**Right to protection of privacy**

1. Member States shall ensure that competent authorities may take during the criminal proceedings appropriate measures to protect the privacy, including personal characteristics of the victim taken into account in the individual assessment provided for under Article 22, and images of victims and of their family members. Furthermore, Member States shall ensure that competent authorities may take all lawful measures to prevent public dissemination of any information that could lead to the identification of a child victim.

2. In order to protect the privacy, personal integrity and personal data of victims, Member States shall, with respect for freedom of expression and information and freedom and pluralism of the media, encourage the media to take self-regulatory measures.

*Article 22*

**Individual assessment of victims to identify specific protection needs**

1. Member States shall ensure that victims receive a timely and individual assessment, in accordance with national procedures, to identify specific protection needs and to determine whether and to what extent they would benefit from special measures in the course of criminal proceedings, as provided for under Articles 23 and 24, due to their particular vulnerability to secondary and repeat victimisation, to intimidation and to retaliation.

2. The individual assessment shall, in particular, take into account:

(a) the personal characteristics of the victim;

(b) the type or nature of the crime; and

(c) the circumstances of the crime.

3. In the context of the individual assessment, particular attention shall be paid to victims who have suffered considerable harm due to the severity of the crime; victims who have suffered a crime committed with a bias or discriminatory motive which could, in particular, be related to their personal characteristics; victims whose relationship to and dependence on the offender make them particularly vulnerable. In this regard, victims of terrorism, organised crime, human trafficking, gender-based violence, violence in a close relationship, sexual violence, exploitation or hate crime, and victims with disabilities shall be duly considered.

4. For the purposes of this Directive, child victims shall be presumed to have specific protection needs due to their vulnerability to secondary and repeat victimisation, to intimidation and to retaliation. To determine whether and to what extent they would benefit from special measures as provided for under Articles 23 and 24, child victims shall be subject to an individual assessment as provided for in paragraph 1 of this Article.

5. The extent of the individual assessment may be adapted according to the severity of the crime and the degree of apparent harm suffered by the victim.

6. Individual assessments shall be carried out with the close involvement of the victim and shall take into account their wishes including where they do not wish to benefit from special measures as provided for in Articles 23 and 24.

7. If the elements that form the basis of the individual assessment have changed significantly, Member States shall ensure that it is updated throughout the criminal proceedings.

*Article 23*

**Right to protection of victims with specific protection needs during criminal proceedings**

1. Without prejudice to the rights of the defence and in accordance with rules of judicial discretion, Member States shall ensure that victims with specific protection needs who benefit from special measures identified as a result of an individual assessment provided for in Article 22(1), may benefit from the measures provided for in paragraphs 2 and 3 of this Article. A special measure envisaged following the individual assessment shall not be made available if operational or practical constraints make this impossible, or where there is a an urgent need to interview the victim and failure to do so could harm the victim or another person or could prejudice the course of the proceedings.

2. The following measures shall be available during criminal investigations to victims with specific protection needs identified in accordance with Article 22(1):

(a) interviews with the victim being carried out in premises designed or adapted for that purpose;

(b) interviews with the victim being carried out by or through professionals trained for that purpose;

(c) all interviews with the victim being conducted by the same persons unless this is contrary to the good administration of justice;

(d) all interviews with victims of sexual violence, gender-based violence or violence in close relationships, unless conducted by a prosecutor or a judge, being conducted by a person of the same sex as the victim, if the victim so wishes, provided that the course of the criminal proceedings will not be prejudiced.

3. The following measures shall be available for victims with specific protection needs identified in accordance with Article 22(1) during court proceedings:

(a) measures to avoid visual contact between victims and offenders including during the giving of evidence, by appropriate means including the use of communication technology;

(b) measures to ensure that the victim may be heard in the courtroom without being present, in particular through the use of appropriate communication technology;

(c) measures to avoid unnecessary questioning concerning the victim's private life not related to the criminal offence; and

(d) measures allowing a hearing to take place without the presence of the public.

*Article 24*

**Right to protection of child victims during criminal proceedings**

1. In addition to the measures provided for in Article 23, Member States shall ensure that where the victim is a child:

(a) in criminal investigations, all interviews with the child victim may be audiovisually recorded and such recorded interviews may be used as evidence in criminal proceedings;

(b) in criminal investigations and proceedings, in accordance with the role of victims in the relevant criminal justice system, competent authorities appoint a special representative for child victims where, according to national law, the holders of parental responsibility are precluded from representing the child victim as a result of a conflict of interest between them and the child victim, or where the child victim is unaccompanied or separated from the family;

(c) where the child victim has the right to a lawyer, he or she has the right to legal advice and representation, in his or her own name, in proceedings where there is, or there could be, a conflict of interest between the child victim and the holders of parental responsibility.

The procedural rules for the audiovisual recordings referred to in point (a) of the first subparagraph and the use thereof shall be determined by national law.

2. Where the age of a victim is uncertain and there are reasons to believe that the victim is a child, the victim shall, for the purposes of this Directive, be presumed to be a child.

CHAPTER 5

**OTHER PROVISIONS**

*Article 25*

**Training of practitioners**

1. Member States shall ensure that officials likely to come into contact with victims, such as police officers and court staff, receive both general and specialist training to a level appropriate to their contact with victims to increase their awareness of the needs of victims and to enable them to deal with victims in an impartial, respectful and professional manner.

2. Without prejudice to judicial independence and differences in the organisation of the judiciary across the Union, Member States shall request that those responsible for the training of judges and prosecutors involved in criminal proceedings make available both general and specialist training to increase the awareness of judges and prosecutors of the needs of victims.

3. With due respect for the independence of the legal profession, Member States shall recommend that those responsible for the training of lawyers make available both general and specialist training to increase the awareness of lawyers of the needs of victims.

4. Through their public services or by funding victim support organisations, Member States shall encourage initiatives enabling those providing victim support and restorative justice services to receive adequate training to a level appropriate to their contact with victims and observe professional standards to ensure such services are provided in an impartial, respectful and professional manner.

5. In accordance with the duties involved, and the nature and level of contact the practitioner has with victims, training shall aim to enable the practitioner to recognise victims and to treat them in a respectful, professional and non-discriminatory manner.

14.11.2012 EN Official Journal of the European Union L 315/73

*Article 26*

**Cooperation and coordination of services**

1. Member States shall take appropriate action to facilitate cooperation between Member States to improve the access of victims to the rights set out in this Directive and under national law. Such cooperation shall be aimed at least at:

(a) the exchange of best practices;

(b) consultation in individual cases; and

(c) assistance to European networks working on matters directly relevant to victims' rights.

2. Member States shall take appropriate action, including through the internet, aimed at raising awareness of the rights set out in this Directive, reducing the risk of victimisation, and minimising the negative impact of crime and the risks of secondary and repeat victimisation, of intimidation and of retaliation, in particular by targeting groups at risk such as children, victims of gender-based violence and violence in close relationships. Such action may include information and awareness raising campaigns and research and education programmes, where appropriate in cooperation with relevant civil society organisations and other stakeholders.

CHAPTER 6

**FINAL PROVISIONS**

*Article 27*

**Transposition**

1. Member States shall bring into force the laws, regulations and administrative provisions necessary to comply with this Directive by 16 November 2015.

2. When Member States adopt those provisions they shall contain a reference to this Directive or be accompanied by such a reference on the occasion of their official publication. Member States shall determine how such a reference is to be made.

*Article 28*

**Provision of data and statistics**

Member States shall, by 16 November 2017 and every three years thereafter, communicate to the Commission available data showing how victims have accessed the rights set out in this Directive.

*Article 29*

**Report**

The Commission shall, by 16 November 2017, submit a report to the European Parliament and to the Council, assessing the extent to which the Member States have taken the necessary measures in order to comply with this Directive, including a description of action taken under Articles 8, 9 and 23, accompanied, if necessary, by legislative proposals.

*Article 30*

**Replacement of Framework Decision 2001/220/JHA**

Framework Decision 2001/220/JHA is hereby replaced in relation to Member States participating in the adoption of this Directive, without prejudice to the obligations of the Member States relating to the time limits for transposition into national law.

In relation to Member States participating in the adoption of this Directive, references to that Framework Decision shall be construed as references to this Directive.

*Article 31*

**Entry into force**

This Directive shall enter into force on the day following that of its publication in the *Official Journal of the European Union*.

*Article 32*

**Addressees**

This Directive is addressed to the Member States in accordance with the Treaties.

Done at Strasbourg, 25 October 2012.

| *For the European Parliament* | *For the Council* |
|---|---|
| *The President* | *The President* |
| M. SCHULZ | A. D. MAVROYIANNIS |

# Recommendations to national courts and tribunals in relation to the initiation of preliminary ruling proceedings, 5 November 2012

**[OJ 2012, C 338/1–6]**

6.11.2012 EN Official Journal of the European Union C 338/1

I

*(Resolutions, recommendations and opinions)*

RECOMMENDATIONS

# COURT OF JUSTICE OF THE EUROPEAN UNION

These recommendations follow on from the adoption on 25 September 2012 in Luxembourg of the new Rules of Procedure of the Court of Justice (OJ L 265, 29.9.2012, p. 1). They replace the information note on references from national courts for a preliminary ruling (OJ C 160, 28.5.2011, p. 1) and reflect innovations introduced by those Rules which may affect both the principle of a reference for a preliminary ruling to the Court of Justice and the procedure for making such a reference.

## RECOMMENDATIONS

**to national courts and tribunals in relation to the initiation of preliminary ruling proceedings**

(2012/C 338/01)

I — **GENERAL PROVISIONS**

### The Court's jurisdiction in preliminary rulings

1. The reference for a preliminary ruling is a fundamental mechanism of European Union law aimed at enabling the courts and tribunals of the Member States to ensure uniform interpretation and application of that law within the European Union.

2. Under Article 19(3)(b) of the Treaty on European Union ('TEU') and Article 267 of the Treaty on the Functioning of the European Union ('TFEU'), the Court of Justice of the European Union has jurisdiction to give preliminary rulings on the interpretation of Union law and on the validity of acts adopted by the institutions, bodies, offices or agencies of the Union.

3. Article 256(3) TFEU provides that the General Court is to have jurisdiction to hear and determine questions referred for a preliminary ruling under Article 267 TFEU, in specific areas laid down by the Statute. However, since no provisions have been introduced into the Statute in that regard, the Court of Justice alone currently has jurisdiction to give preliminary rulings.

4. While Article 267 TFEU confers on the Court of Justice a general jurisdiction in that regard, a number of primary law provisions exist which lay down exceptions to or temporary restrictions on that jurisdiction. This is true, in particular, of Articles 275 TFEU and 276 TFEU and Article 10 of Protocol (No 36) on Transitional Provisions of the Treaty of Lisbon (OJEU 2010 C 83, p. 1) (1).

(1) Article 10(1) to (3) of Protocol No 36 provides that the powers of the Court of Justice in relation to acts of the Union adopted in the field of police cooperation and judicial cooperation in criminal matters before the entry into force of the Treaty of Lisbon, and which have not since been amended, are to remain the same for a maximum period of five years from the date of entry into force of the Treaty of Lisbon (1 December 2009). During that period, such acts may, therefore, form the subject-matter of a reference for a preliminary ruling only where the order for reference is made by a court or tribunal of a Member State which has accepted the jurisdiction of the Court of Justice, it being a matter for each of those States to determine whether the right to refer a question to the Court is to be available to all of its national courts and tribunals or is to be reserved to the courts or tribunals of last instance.

5. Since the preliminary ruling procedure is based on cooperation between the Court of Justice and the courts and tribunals of the Member States, it may be helpful, in order to ensure that that procedure is fully effective, to provide those courts and tribunals with the following recommendations.

6. While in no way binding, these recommendations are intended to supplement Title III of the Rules of Procedure of the Court of Justice (Articles 93 to 118) and to provide guidance to the courts and tribunals of the Member States as to whether it is appropriate to make a reference for a preliminary ruling, as well as practical information concerning the form and effect of such a reference.

**The role of the Court of Justice in the preliminary ruling procedure**

7. As stated above, under the preliminary ruling procedure the Court's role is to give an interpretation of European Union law or to rule on its validity, not to apply that law to the factual situation underlying the main proceedings. That is the task of the national court or tribunal and it is not, therefore, for the Court either to decide issues of fact raised in the main proceedings or to resolve any differences of opinion on the interpretation or application of rules of national law.

8. When ruling on the interpretation or validity of European Union law, the Court makes every effort to give a reply which will be of assistance in resolving the dispute in the main proceedings, but it is for the referring court or tribunal to draw specific conclusions from that reply, if necessary by disapplying the rule of national law in question.

**The decision to make a reference for a preliminary ruling**

*The originator of the request for a preliminary ruling*

9. Under Article 267 TFEU, any court or tribunal of a Member State, in so far as it is called upon to give a ruling in proceedings intended to arrive at a decision of a judicial nature, may as a rule submit a request for a preliminary ruling to the Court of Justice. Status as a court or tribunal is interpreted by the Court of Justice as a self-standing concept of European Union law, the Court taking account of a number of factors such as whether the body making the reference is established by law, whether it is permanent, whether its jurisdiction is compulsory, whether its procedure is *inter partes*, whether it applies rules of law and whether it is independent.

10. Whether or not the parties to the main proceedings have expressed the wish that it do so, it is for the national court or tribunal alone to decide whether to refer a question to the Court of Justice for a preliminary ruling.

*References on interpretation*

11. Article 267 TFEU provides that any court or tribunal may submit a request for a preliminary ruling to the Court of Justice on the interpretation of a rule of European Union law if it considers it necessary to do so in order to resolve the dispute brought before it.

12. However, courts or tribunals against whose decisions there is no judicial remedy under national law must bring such a request before the Court, unless the Court has already ruled on the point (and there is no new context that raises any serious doubt as to whether that case-law may be applied in that instance), or unless the correct interpretation of the rule of law in question is obvious.

13. Thus, a national court or tribunal may, in particular when it considers that sufficient guidance is given by the case-law of the Court of Justice, itself decide on the correct interpretation of European Union law and its application to the factual situation before it. However, a reference for a preliminary ruling may prove particularly useful when there is a new question of interpretation of general interest for the uniform application of European Union law, or where the existing case-law does not appear to be applicable to a new set of facts.

14. In order to enable the Court of Justice properly to identify the subject-matter of the main proceedings and the questions that arise, it is helpful if, in respect of each question referred, the national court or tribunal explains why the interpretation sought is necessary to enable it to give judgment.

*References on determination of validity*

15. Although the courts and tribunals of the Member States may reject pleas raised before them challenging the validity of acts of an institution, body, office or agency of the Union, the Court of Justice has exclusive jurisdiction to declare such an act invalid.

16. All national courts or tribunals **must** therefore submit a request for a preliminary ruling to the Court when they have doubts about the validity of such an act, stating the reasons for which they consider that the act may be invalid.

17. However, if a national court or tribunal has serious doubts about the validity of an act of an institution, body, office or agency of the Union on which a national measure is based, it may exceptionally suspend application of that measure temporarily or grant other interim relief with respect to it. It must then refer the question of validity to the Court of Justice, stating the reasons for which it considers the act to be invalid.

**The appropriate stage at which to make a reference for a preliminary ruling**

18. A national court or tribunal may submit a request for a preliminary ruling to the Court as soon as it finds that a ruling on the interpretation or validity of European Union law is necessary to enable it to give judgment. It is that court or tribunal which is in fact in the best position to decide at what stage of the proceedings such a request should be made.

19. It is, however, desirable that a decision to make a reference for a preliminary ruling should be taken when the national proceedings have reached a stage at which the referring court or tribunal is able to define the legal and factual context of the case, so that the Court of Justice has available to it all the information necessary to check, where appropriate, that European Union law applies to the main proceedings. In the interests of the proper administration of justice, it may also be desirable for the reference to be made only after both sides have been heard.

**The form and content of the request for a preliminary ruling**

20. The decision by which a court or tribunal of a Member State refers one or more questions to the Court of Justice for a preliminary ruling may be in any form allowed by national law as regards procedural steps. However, it must be borne in mind that it is that document which will serve as the basis of the proceedings before the Court and that it must therefore contain such information as will enable the Court to give a reply which is of assistance to the referring court or tribunal. Moreover, it is only the request for a preliminary ruling which is notified to the parties to the main proceedings and to the other interested persons referred to in Article 23 of the Statute, including the Member States, in order to obtain any written observations.

21. Owing to the need to translate it into all the official languages of the European Union, the request for a preliminary ruling should therefore be drafted simply, clearly and precisely, avoiding superfluous detail.

22. About 10 pages is often sufficient to set out in a proper manner the context of a request for a preliminary ruling. That request must be succinct but sufficiently complete and must contain all the relevant information to give the Court and the interested persons entitled to submit observations a clear understanding of the factual and legal context of the main proceedings. In accordance with Article 94 of the Rules of Procedure, the request for a preliminary ruling must contain, in addition to the text of the questions referred to the Court for a preliminary ruling:

— a summary of the subject-matter of the dispute and the relevant findings of fact as determined by the referring court or tribunal, or, at least, an account of the facts on which the questions referred are based;

— the tenor of any national provisions applicable in the case and, where appropriate, the relevant national case-law (1);

(1) The referring court or tribunal is requested to provide precise references for those texts and their publication, such as a page of an official journal or a specific law report, or a reference to an internet site.

— a statement of the reasons which prompted the referring court or tribunal to inquire about the interpretation or validity of certain provisions of European Union law, and the relationship between those provisions and the national legislation applicable to the main proceedings.

23. The European Union law provisions relevant to the case should be identified as accurately as possible in the request for a preliminary ruling, which should include, if need be, a brief summary of the relevant arguments of the parties to the main proceedings.

24. If it considers itself able to do so, the referring court or tribunal may, finally, briefly state its view on the answer to be given to the questions referred for a preliminary ruling. That information may be useful to the Court, particularly where it is called upon to give a preliminary ruling in an expedited or urgent procedure.

25. In order to make the request for a preliminary ruling easier to read, it is essential that the Court receive it in typewritten form. To enable the Court to refer to the request it is also very helpful if the pages and paragraphs of the order for reference – which must be dated and signed – are numbered.

26. The questions themselves should appear in a separate and clearly identified section of the order for reference, preferably at the beginning or the end. It must be possible to understand them on their own terms, without referring to the statement of the grounds for the request, which will however provide the necessary background for a proper understanding of the implications of the case.

27. Under the preliminary ruling procedure, the Court will, as a rule, use the information contained in the order for reference, including nominative or personal data. It is therefore for the referring court or tribunal itself, if it considers it necessary, to delete certain details in its request for a preliminary ruling or to render anonymous one or more persons or entities concerned by the dispute in the main proceedings.

28. After the request for a preliminary ruling has been lodged, the Court may also render such persons or entities anonymous of its own motion, or at the request of the referring court or tribunal or of a party to the main proceedings. In order to maintain its effectiveness, such a request for anonymity must, however, be made at the earliest possible stage of the proceedings, and in any event prior to publication in the *Official Journal of the European Union* of the notice relating to the case concerned, and to service of the request for a preliminary ruling on the interested persons referred to in Article 23 of the Statute.

**The effects of the reference for a preliminary ruling on the national proceedings**

29. Although the national court or tribunal may still order protective measures, particularly in connection with a reference on determination of validity (see point 17 above), the lodging of a request for a preliminary ruling nevertheless calls for the national proceedings to be stayed until the Court of Justice has given its ruling.

30. In the interests of the proper conduct of the preliminary ruling proceedings before the Court and in order to maintain their effectiveness, it is incumbent on the referring court or tribunal to inform the Court of Justice of any procedural step that may affect the referral and, in particular, if any new parties are admitted to the national proceedings.

**Costs and legal aid**

31. Preliminary ruling proceedings before the Court of Justice are free of charge and the Court does not rule on the costs of the parties to the proceedings pending before the referring court or tribunal; it is for the referring court or tribunal to rule on those costs.

32. If a party to the main proceedings has insufficient means and where it is possible under national rules, the referring court or tribunal may grant that party legal aid to cover the costs, including those of lawyers' fees, which it incurs before the Court. The Court itself may also grant legal aid where the party in question is not already in receipt of aid under national rules or to the extent to which that aid does not cover, or covers only partly, costs incurred before the Court.

**Communication between the Court of Justice and the national courts and tribunals**

33. The request for a preliminary ruling and the relevant documents (including, where applicable, the case file or a copy of it) are to be sent by the national court or tribunal making the reference directly to the Court of Justice. They must be sent by registered post to the Registry of the Court of Justice (Rue du Fort Niedergrünewald, L-2925 Luxembourg).

34. Until the decision containing the Court's ruling on the referring court's or tribunal's request for a preliminary ruling is served on that court or tribunal, the Court Registry will stay in contact with the referring court or tribunal, and will send it copies of the procedural documents.

35. The Court of Justice will send its ruling to the referring court or tribunal. It would welcome information from that court or tribunal on the action taken upon its ruling in the main proceedings, and communication of the referring court's or tribunal's final decision.

II — SPECIAL PROVISIONS IN RELATION TO URGENT REFERENCES FOR A PRELIMINARY RULING

36. As provided in Article 23a of the Statute and Articles 105 to 114 of the Rules of Procedure, a reference for a preliminary ruling may, in certain circumstances, be determined pursuant to an expedited procedure or an urgent procedure.

**Conditions for the application of the expedited and urgent procedures**

37. The Court of Justice decides whether these procedures are to be applied. Such a decision is generally taken only on a reasoned request from the referring court or tribunal. Exceptionally, the Court may, however, decide of its own motion to determine a reference for a preliminary ruling under an expedited procedure or an urgent procedure where that appears to be required by the nature or the particular circumstances of the case.

38. Article 105 of the Rules of Procedure provides that a reference for a preliminary ruling may be determined pursuant to an **expedited procedure** derogating from the provisions of those Rules, where the nature of the case requires that it be dealt with within a short time. Since that procedure imposes significant constraints on all those involved in it, and, in particular, on all the Member States called upon to lodge their observations, whether written or oral, within much shorter time-limits than would ordinarily apply, its application should be sought only in particular circumstances that warrant the Court giving its ruling quickly on the questions referred. The large number of persons or legal situations potentially affected by the decision that the referring court or tribunal has to deliver after bringing a matter before the Court for a preliminary ruling does not, in itself, constitute an exceptional circumstance that would justify the use of the expedited procedure [1].

39. The same applies *a fortiori* to the **urgent preliminary ruling procedure**, provided for in Article 107 of the Rules of Procedure. That procedure, which applies only in the areas covered by Title V of Part Three of the TFEU, relating to the area of freedom, security and justice, imposes even greater constraints on those concerned, since it limits in particular the number of parties authorised to lodge written observations and, in cases of extreme urgency, allows the written part of the procedure before the Court to be omitted altogether. The application of the urgent procedure should therefore be requested only where it is absolutely necessary for the Court to give its ruling very quickly on the questions submitted by the referring court or tribunal.

40. Although it is not possible to provide an exhaustive list of such circumstances, particularly because of the varied and evolving nature of the rules of European Union law governing the area of freedom, security and justice, a national court or tribunal might, for example, consider submitting a request for the urgent preliminary ruling procedure to be applied in the case, referred to in the fourth paragraph of Article 267 TFEU, of a person in custody or deprived of his liberty, where the answer to the question raised is decisive as to the assessment of that person's legal situation, or in proceedings concerning parental authority or custody of children, where the identity of the court having jurisdiction under European Union law depends on the answer to the question referred for a preliminary ruling.

(1) For an insight into circumstances that have resulted in the approval or refusal of requests for the application of the accelerated procedure, made on the basis of Article 104a of the Rules of Procedure of the Court of Justice of 19 June 1991, as amended, see the orders made by the President of the Court of Justice, available at www.curia.europa.eu (the orders can be found under 'Case-law', by selecting each of the following in turn in the search form: Documents – Documents not published in the ECR – Orders – Expedited procedure).

**The request for application of the expedited procedure or the urgent procedure**

41. To enable the Court to decide quickly whether the expedited procedure or the urgent preliminary ruling procedure should be applied, the request must set out precisely the matters of fact and law which establish the urgency and, in particular, the risks involved in following the ordinary procedure.

42. In so far as it is able to do so, the referring court should briefly state its view on the answer to be given to the questions referred. Such a statement makes it easier for the parties to the main proceedings and the other interested persons participating in the procedure to define their positions and facilitates the Court's decision, thereby contributing to the rapidity of the procedure.

43. The request for the application of the expedited procedure or the urgent procedure must be submitted in an unambiguous form that enables the Court Registry to establish immediately that the file has to be dealt with in a particular way. Accordingly, the referring court or tribunal is asked to specify which of the two procedures is required in that particular case, and to mention in its request the relevant article of the Rules of Procedure (Article 105 for the expedited procedure or Article 107 for the urgent procedure). That mention must be included in a clearly identifiable place in its order for reference (for example, at the head of the page or in a separate judicial document). Where appropriate, a covering letter from the referring court or tribunal can usefully refer to that request.

44. As regards the order for reference itself, it is particularly important that it should be succinct where the matter is urgent, as this will help to ensure the rapidity of the procedure.

**Communication between the Court of Justice, the referring court or tribunal and the parties to the main proceedings**

45. In order to expedite and facilitate communication with the referring court or tribunal and the parties before it, a court or tribunal submitting a request for the expedited procedure or the urgent procedure to be applied is asked to state the e-mail address and any fax number which may be used by the Court of Justice, together with the e-mail addresses and any fax numbers of the representatives of the parties to the proceedings.

46. A copy of the signed order for reference together with a request for the expedited procedure or the urgent procedure to be applied can initially be sent to the Court by e-mail (ECJ-Registry@curia.europa.eu) or by fax (+352 43 37 66). Processing of the reference and of the request can then begin upon receipt of the e-mailed or faxed copy. The originals of those documents must, however, be sent to the Court Registry as soon as possible.

# Agreement between the European Union and the Russian Federation on drug precursors, 4 June 2013

**[OJ 2014, L 165/7–14]**

4.6.2014 EN Official Journal of the European Union L 165/7

## AGREEMENT

## between the European Union and the Russian Federation on drug precursors

THE EUROPEAN UNION

on the one part, and

THE RUSSIAN FEDERATION,

on the other part,

hereinafter referred to as the 'The Parties',

WITHIN THE FRAMEWORK of the United Nations Convention of 1988 against Illicit Traffic in Narcotic Drugs and Psychotropic Substances, hereinafter referred to as the '1988 Convention';

DETERMINED to prevent and to combat the illicit manufacture of narcotic drugs and psychotropic substances by preventing the diversion from the legitimate trade of substances frequently used in the illicit manufacture of narcotic drugs and psychotropic substances (hereinafter referred to as the 'precursors');

TAKING into account the overall legal framework between the Russian Federation and the European Union;

NOTING that international trade may be used for the diversion of such precursors;

CONVINCED of the necessity to conclude and to implement agreements between the Parties concerned, with the purpose of establishing wide cooperation, in particular pertaining to export and import controls;

RECOGNISING that precursors are also mainly and widely used for legitimate purposes and that international trade must not be hindered by excessive monitoring procedures.

HAVE AGREED AS FOLLOWS:

*Article 1*

### Scope of the Agreement

1. This Agreement sets out measures to strengthen cooperation between the Parties to prevent the diversion from the legitimate trade of precursors, without prejudice to the legitimate trade in these precursors.

2. The Parties shall assist each other, as set out in this Agreement, in particular by:

— monitoring the trade between the Parties in the precursors with the aim of preventing their use for illicit purposes;

— providing mutual assistance for the purpose of prevention of diversion of such precursors.

3. The measures referred to in paragraph 2 of this Article shall apply to the precursors listed in Annex I of this Agreement (hereinafter referred to as 'scheduled precursors').

*Article 2*

### Implementation measures

1. The Parties shall inform each other in writing about their respective competent authorities. These authorities shall communicate directly with one another for the purposes of this Agreement.

2. The Parties shall inform each other about their respective legal provisions and other measures applied to implement this Agreement.

*Article 3*

### Trade monitoring

1. The competent authorities of the Parties shall inform each other on their own initiative whenever they have reasonable grounds to believe that scheduled precursors in legitimate trade between the Parties may be diverted to the illicit manufacture of narcotic drugs or psychotropic substances.

L 165/8 EN Official Journal of the European Union 4.6.2014

2. With regard to the scheduled precursors the competent authorities of the exporting Party shall forward a pre-export notification containing the information referred to in Article 12 (10) point a) of the 1988 Convention to the competent authorities of the importing Party.

The reply in writing by the competent authorities of the importing Party shall be provided through technical means of communication within 21 days after the receipt of the message from the competent authorities of the exporting Party. The absence of a reply within this period shall be considered as non-objection to sending the shipment. Any objection shall be notified in writing through technical means of communication to the competent authorities of the exporting Party within this period after the receiptof the pre-export notification giving the reasons for refusal.

*Article 4*

**Mutual assistance**

1. The Parties shall within the scope of this agreement provide each other mutual assistance through exchange of information referred to in Article 12 (10) point a) of the 1988 Convention to prevent the diversion of scheduled precursors to the illicit manufacture of narcotic drugs or psychotropic substances. They shall, in accordance with the legislation of the Parties, take appropriate steps to prevent diversion.

2. The Parties shall also provide each other upon written request or at their own initiative with mutual assistance if there are reasons to believe that other relevant information is of interest to the other Party.

3. The request shall contain information about the following:

— aim and foundation of the request;

— time of the expected execution of the request;

— other information that may be used for the execution of the request.

4. The request directed in writing on the official letter head of the competent authorities of the requesting Party shall be accompanied by a translation in one of the official languages of the requested Party and shall be signed by duly authorised persons of the competent authorities of the requesting Party.

5. The competent authorities of the requested Party shall take all necessary measures for the complete execution of the request as promptly as possible.

6. Requests for assistance shall be executed in accordance with the legislation of the requested Party.

7. The competent authorities of the requested Party should as promptly as possible inform the competent authorities of the requesting Party about the circumstances that prevent or delay the execution of the request.

If the competent authorities of the requesting Party state that there is no more necessity to complete the request, they shall as promptly as possible inform the competent authorities of the requested Party accordingly.

8. The Parties may cooperate with each other to minimise the risk of illicit shipments of scheduled precursors brought into or out of the territory of the Russian Federation and the customs territory of the European Union.

9. Assistance provided under this Article shall not prejudice the rules governing mutual assistance in criminal matters and extradition, nor shall it apply to information obtained under powers exercised at the request of a judicial authority, except where communication of such information is authorised by that authority.

*Article 5*

**Confidentiality and data protection**

1. The Parties shall take all measures to ensure confidentiality of the received information. If it is impossible to ensure confidentiality of the requested information, the Party requesting the information shall inform the other Party accordingly which shall decide whether to provide the information upon these conditions.

2. Information obtained under this Agreement, including personal data, shall be used solely for the purposes of this Agreement and must not be kept longer than necessary for the purposes for which it is transferred pursuant to this Agreement.

4.6.2014 EN Official Journal of the European Union L 165/9

3. By derogation to paragraph 2, the use of information, including personal data, for further purposes by the Authorities or public bodies of the Party which received the information shall only be authorized after prior express and written approval of the authority of the Party which transmitted the information in accordance with the legislation of that Party. Such use shall then be subject to any conditions established by that authority.

4. The Parties may in proceedings instituted for failure to comply with legislation on scheduled precursors use as evidence information obtained and documents consulted in accordance with the provisions of this Agreement following prior written consent of the competent authorities of the requested Party which provided the data.

5. In case personal data are exchanged, their processing shall comply with the principles set out in Annex II which are mandatory for the Parties to the Agreement.

*Article 6*

**Exceptions to the obligation to provide mutual assistance**

1. Provision of assistance may be refused or may be made subject to certain conditions or requirements, in cases where a Party is of the opinion that assistance under this Agreement would be likely to prejudice the sovereignty, the security, the public policy or other essential interests of the Russian Federation or that of a Member State of the European Union which has been requested to provide assistance under this Agreement.

2. For the cases referred to in this Article, the decision of the competent authorities of the requested Party and the reasons therefore must be communicated to the competent authorities of the requesting Party as promptly as possible.

*Article 7*

**Cooperation regarding precursors not listed in Annex I**

1. The Parties may, on a voluntary basis, exchange information about precursors not listed in Annex I of this Agreement (hereinafter referred to as 'non-scheduled precursors').

2. In the case of paragraph 1 of this Article, the provisions of Article 4 (2) — (9) shall apply.

3. The Parties may exchange their available lists of non-scheduled precursors.

*Article 8*

**Technical and scientific cooperation**

The Parties shall cooperate in the identification of new diversion methods as well as appropriate countermeasures, including technical cooperation and in particular, training and exchange programmes for the officials concerned, to strengthen administrative and enforcement structures in this field and to promote cooperation with trade and industry.

*Article 9*

**Joint Follow-Up Expert Group**

1. According to this Agreement, a Joint Follow-Up Expert Group is hereby established which consists of the representatives of competent authorities of the Parties (hereinafter referred to as 'the Joint Follow-Up Expert Group'.)

2. The Joint Follow-Up Expert Group shall make recommendations by consensus.

3. The Joint Follow-Up Expert Group shall meet, with the date, place and programme being fixed by consensus.

4. The Joint Follow-Up Expert Group shall administer this Agreement and ensure its proper implementation. For this purpose:

— It shall address questions relating to the implementation of the Agreement;

— It shall study and recommend technical cooperation measures referred to in Article 8;

— It shall study and recommend other possible forms of cooperation;

— It shall consider other issues of the Parties about the implementation of this Agreement.

5. The Joint Follow-Up Expert Group may recommend amendments to this Agreement to the Parties.

*Article 10*

**Obligations under other international agreements**

1. Unless otherwise provided by this Agreement, its provisions shall not affect the obligations of the Parties under any other international agreement.

2. The exchange of secret information is regulated by the Agreement between the Government of the Russian Federation and the European Union on the protection of classified information [1].

3. The provisions of this Agreement shall take precedence over the provisions of any bilateral or multilateral international agreement covering drug precursors between the Russian Federation and the EU Member States.

4. The Parties shall inform each other about the conclusion of international agreements on the aforementioned issues with other countries.

5. This Agreement is to be seen and interpreted in the context of the overall legal framework in force between the EU and the Russian Federation, including in respect of any obligation contained therein.

*Article 11*

**Entry into force**

This Agreement shall enter into force on the first day of the second month following the date of the reception of the last written notification of the Parties about completion of their internal procedures required for its entry into force.

*Article 12*

**Duration, denunciation and amendments**

1. This Agreement shall be concluded for five years at the end of which it is automatically/tacitly renewed for further successive five year periods until one of the Parties, no later than 6 months prior to the termination of the relevant 5 year period notifies the other Party in writing of its intention to terminate this present agreement.

2. This Agreement may be amended by mutual consent of the Parties.

*Article 13*

**Costs**

Each Party shall bear the costs it incurs arising from the measures to implement this Agreement.

Done at Yekaterinburg on 4 June 2013 in duplicate in the Bulgarian, Czech, Danish, Dutch, Estonian, English, Finnish, French, German, Greek, Hungarian, Italian, Latvian, Lithuanian, Maltese, Polish, Portuguese, Romanian, Slovak, Slovenian, Spanish, Swedish and Russian languages, all these texts being equally authentic.

[1] OJ L 155, 22.6.2010, p. 57.

За Европейския съюз
Por la Unión Europea
Za Evropskou unii
For Den Europæiske Union
Für die Europäische Union
Euroopa Liidu nimel
Για την Ευρωπαϊκή Ένωση
For the European Union
Pour l'Union européenne
Per l'Unione europea
Eiropas Savienības vārdā –
Europos Sąjungos vardu
Az Európai Unió részéről
Għall-Unjoni Ewropea
Voor de Europese Unie
W imieniu Unii Europejskiej
Pela União Europeia
Pentru Uniunea Europeană
Za Európsku úniu
Za Evropsko unijo
Euroopan unionin puolesta
För Europeiska unionen
За Европейский союз

За Руската Федерация
Por la Federación de Rusia
Za Ruskou Federaci
For Den Russiske Føderation
Für die Russische Föderation
Venemaa Föderatsiooni nimel
Για τη Ρωσική Ομοσπονδία
For the Russian Federation
Pour la Fédération de Russie
Per la Federazione Russa
Krievijas Federācijas vārdā –
Rusijos Federacijos vardu
Az Oroszországi Föderáció részéről
Għall-Federazzjoni Russa
Voor de Russische Federatie
W imieniu Federacji Rosyjskiej
Pela Federação da Rússia
Pentru Federația Rusă
Za Ruskú Federáciu
Za Rusko Federacijo
Venäjän Federaation puolesta
För Ryska Federationen
За Российскую Федерацию

*ANNEX I*

Acetic Anhydride

Acetone

Anthranilic Acid

Ephedrine

Ergometrine

Ergotamine

Ethyl Ether

Hydrochloric Acid

Isosafrol

Lysergic Acid

3,4-Methylenedioxyphenyl-2-propanone

Methyl Ethyl Ketone

N-Acetylanthranilic Acid

Norephedrine

Phenylacetic Acid

1-Phenyl-2-propanone

Piperidine

Piperonal

Potassium Permanganate

Pseudoephedrine

Safrole

Sulphuric Acid

Toluene

The salts of the substances listed in this Annex are included whenever the existence of such salts is possible. (With the exception of the salts of Hydrochloric Acid and Sulphuric Acid.)

4.6.2014 EN Official Journal of the European Union L 165/13

*ANNEX II*

**DATA PROTECTION DEFINITIONS AND PRINCIPLES**

**Definitions**

For the purpose of this Agreement,

'personal data' shall mean any information relating to an identified or identifiable natural person;

'Processing of personal data' shall mean any operation or set of operations which is performed upon personal data, whether or not by automatic means, such as collection, recording, organisation, storage, adaptation or alteration, retrieval, consultation, use, disclosure by transmission, dissemination or otherwise making available, alignment or combination, blocking, erasure or destruction.

**Principles**

'Data quality and proportionality': Data shall be adequate, accurate relevant and not excessive in relation to the purposes for which they are transferred and, where necessary, kept up to date. The Parties shall in particular ensure that the accuracy of data exchanged is regularly reviewed.

'Transparency': A data subject shall be provided with information as to the purposes of the processing and the identity of the data controller, the recipients and categories of recipients of the personal data, the existence of the right of access and the right to rectify, erasure or blocking data concerning him/her, the right to administrative and judicial recourses and other information insofar as this is necessary to ensure fair processing, unless such information has already been provided by the Parties to the Agreement.

'Rights of access, rectification, erasure and blocking of data': A data subject shall have a right of direct access without constraint to all data relating to him/her that are processed and, as appropriate, the right to the rectification, erasure or blocking of data the processing of which does not comply with this Agreement because the data are incomplete or inaccurate.

'Redress': The Parties shall provide that a data subject who considers that his/her right to privacy or that personal data concerning him/her have been processed in breach of this Agreement, shall have the right in accordance with their legislation to an effective administrative remedy before a competent authority and a judicial remedy before an independent and impartial tribunal accessible by individuals regardless of their nationality or country of residence.

Any such infringements or violation shall be subject to appropriate, proportionate and effective sanctions including compensation for damages suffered as a result of an infringement of data protection rules. Where data protection provisions are found to have been breached sanctions including compensation are to be imposed in accordance with applicable domestic rules.

Onward transfers:

Onward transfers of personal data to other authorities and public bodies of a third country shall be allowed only with the prior written consent of the authority which has transmitted the data and for the purposes for which the data have been transmitted and if this country provides an adequate level of data protection. Subject to reasonable legal limitations provided by national law, the Parties shall inform the data subject on such onward transfer.

'Supervision of data processing': Compliance with data protection rules by each Party shall be subject to control by one or more independent public authorities that have effective powers of investigation, intervention and to engage in legal proceedings or to bring to the attention of the competent judicial authorities any violation of the data protection principles of this agreement. Each independent public authority shall, in particular, hear claims lodged by any person concerning protection of his or her rights and freedoms with regard to the processing of personal data pursuant to this Agreement. The person concerned shall be informed of the outcome of the claim.

'Exemptions from transparency and right of access': The Parties may restrict the right of access and transparency principles in accordance with their legislation when necessary in order not to:

— jeopardise an official investigation,

— violate the human rights of other persons.

# Regulation 603/2013 on the establishment of 'Eurodac' for the comparison of fingerprints for the effective application of Regulation (EU) No 604/2013 establishing the criteria and mechanisms for determining the Member State responsible for examining an application for international protection lodged in one of the Member States by a third-country national or a stateless person and on requests for the comparison with Eurodac data by Member States' law enforcement authorities and Europol for law enforcement purposes, and amending Regulation (EU) No 1077/2011 establishing a European Agency for the operational management of large-scale IT systems in the area of freedom, security and justice, 26 June 2013

**[OJ 2013, L 180/1–30]**

29.6.2013 EN Official Journal of the European Union L 180/1

I

*(Legislative acts)*

# REGULATIONS

## REGULATION (EU) No 603/2013 OF THE EUROPEAN PARLIAMENT AND OF THE COUNCIL

**of 26 June 2013**

**on the establishment of 'Eurodac' for the comparison of fingerprints for the effective application of Regulation (EU) No 604/2013 establishing the criteria and mechanisms for determining the Member State responsible for examining an application for international protection lodged in one of the Member States by a third-country national or a stateless person and on requests for the comparison with Eurodac data by Member States' law enforcement authorities and Europol for law enforcement purposes, and amending Regulation (EU) No 1077/2011 establishing a European Agency for the operational management of large-scale IT systems in the area of freedom, security and justice (recast)**

THE EUROPEAN PARLIAMENT AND THE COUNCIL OF THE EUROPEAN UNION,

Having regard to the Treaty on the Functioning of the European Union, and in particular Articles 78 (2)(e), 87(2)(a) and 88(2)(a) thereof,

Having regard to the proposal from the European Commission

Having regard to the opinion of the European Data Protection Supervisor [1],

Acting in accordance with the ordinary legislative procedure [2],

Whereas:

(1) A number of substantive changes are to be made to Council Regulation (EC) No 2725/2000 of 11 December 2000 concerning the establishment of 'Eurodac' for the comparison of fingerprints for the effective application of the Dublin Convention [3] and to Council Regulation (EC) No 407/2002 of 28 February 2002 laying down certain rules to implement Regulation (EC) No 2725/2000 concerning the establishment of "Eurodac" for the comparison of fingerprints for the effective application of the Dublin Convention [4]. In the interest of clarity, those Regulations should be recast.

(2) A common policy on asylum, including a Common European Asylum System, is a constituent part of the European Union's objective of progressively establishing an area of freedom, security and justice open to those who, forced by circumstances, seek international protection in the Union.

(3) The European Council of 4 November 2004 adopted The Hague Programme which set the objectives to be implemented in the area of freedom, security and justice in the period 2005-2010. The European Pact on Immigration and Asylum endorsed by the European Council of 15-16 October 2008 called for the completion of the establishment of a Common European Asylum System by creating a single procedure comprising common guarantees and a uniform status for refugees and for persons eligible for subsidiary protection.

(4) For the purposes of applying Regulation (EU) No 604/2013 of the European Parliament and of the Council of 26 June 2013 establishing the criteria and mechanisms for determining the Member State responsible for examining an application for international protection lodged in one of the Member States by a third-country national or a stateless person [5], it is necessary to establish the identity of applicants for international protection and of persons apprehended in

---

[1] OJ C 92 10.4.2010, p. 1.
[2] Position of the European Parliament of 12 June 2013 (not yet published in the Official Journal) and decision of the Council of 20 June 2013.
[3] OJ L 316, 15.12.2000, p. 1.
[4] OJ L 62, 5.3.2002, p. 1.
[5] See page 31 of this Official Journal.

connection with the unlawful crossing of the external borders of the Union. It is also desirable, in order effectively to apply Regulation (EU) No 604/2013, and in particular Article 18(1)(b) and (d) thereof, to allow each Member State to check whether a third-country national or stateless person found illegally staying on its territory has applied for international protection in another Member State.

(5) Fingerprints constitute an important element in establishing the exact identity of such persons. It is necessary to set up a system for the comparison of their fingerprint data.

(6) To that end, it is necessary to set up a system known as 'Eurodac', consisting of a Central System, which will operate a computerised central database of fingerprint data, as well as of the electronic means of transmission between the Member States and the Central System, hereinafter the "Communication Infrastructure".

(7) The Hague Programme called for the improvement of access to existing data filing systems in the Union. In addition, The Stockholm Programme called for well targeted data collection and a development of information exchange and its tools that is driven by law enforcement needs.

(8) It is essential in the fight against terrorist offences and other serious criminal offences for the law enforcement authorities to have the fullest and most up-to-date information if they are to perform their tasks. The information contained in Eurodac is necessary for the purposes of the prevention, detection or investigation of terrorist offences as referred to in Council Framework Decision 2002/475/JHA of 13 June 2002 on combating terrorism (1) or of other serious criminal offences as referred to in Council Framework Decision 2002/584/JHA of 13 June 2002 on the European arrest warrant and the surrender procedures between Member States (2). Therefore, the data in Eurodac should be available, subject to the conditions set out in this Regulation, for comparison by the designated authorities of Member States and the European Police Office (Europol).

(9) The powers granted to law enforcement authorities to access Eurodac should be without prejudice to the right of an applicant for international protection to have his or her application processed in due course in accordance with the relevant law. Furthermore, any subsequent follow-up after obtaining a 'hit' from Eurodac should also be without prejudice to that right.

(1) OJ L 164, 22.6.2002, p. 3.
(2) OJ L 190, 18.7.2002, p. 1.

(10) The Commission outlines in its Communication to the Council and the European Parliament of 24 November 2005 on improved effectiveness, enhanced interoperability and synergies among European databases in the area of Justice and Home Affairs that authorities responsible for internal security could have access to Eurodac in well defined cases, when there is a substantiated suspicion that the perpetrator of a terrorist or other serious criminal offence has applied for international protection. In that Communication the Commission also found that the proportionality principle requires that Eurodac be queried for such purposes only if there is an overriding public security concern, that is, if the act committed by the criminal or terrorist to be identified is so reprehensible that it justifies querying a database that registers persons with a clean criminal record, and it concluded that the threshold for authorities responsible for internal security to query Eurodac must therefore always be significantly higher than the threshold for querying criminal databases.

(11) Moreover, Europol plays a key role with respect to cooperation between Member States' authorities in the field of cross-border crime investigation in supporting Union-wide crime prevention, analyses and investigation. Consequently, Europol should also have access to Eurodac within the framework of its tasks and in accordance with Council Decision 2009/371/JHA of 6 April 2009 establishing the European Police Office (Europol) (3).

(12) Requests for comparison of Eurodac data by Europol should be allowed only in specific cases, under specific circumstances and under strict conditions.

(13) Since Eurodac was originally established to facilitate the application of the Dublin Convention, access to Eurodac for the purposes of preventing, detecting or investigating terrorist offences or other serious criminal offences constitutes a change of the original purpose of Eurodac, which interferes with the fundamental right to respect for the private life of individuals whose personal data are processed in Eurodac. Any such interference must be in accordance with the law, which must be formulated with sufficient precision to allow individuals to adjust their conduct and it must protect individuals against arbitrariness and indicate with sufficient clarity the scope of discretion conferred on the competent authorities and the manner of its exercise. Any interference must be necessary in a democratic society to protect a legitimate and proportionate interest and proportionate to the legitimate objective it aims to achieve.

(14) Even though the original purpose of the establishment of Eurodac did not require the facility of requesting comparisons of data with the database on the basis of

(3) OJ L 121, 15.5.2009, p. 37.

a latent fingerprint, which is the dactyloscopic trace which may be found at a crime scene, such a facility is fundamental in the field of police cooperation. The possibility to compare a latent fingerprint with the fingerprint data which is stored in Eurodac in cases where there are reasonable grounds for believing that the perpetrator or victim may fall under one of the categories covered by this Regulation will provide the designated authorities of the Member States with a very valuable tool in preventing, detecting or investigating terrorist offences or other serious criminal offences, when for example the only evidence available at a crime scene are latent fingerprints.

(15) This Regulation also lays down the conditions under which requests for comparison of fingerprint data with Eurodac data for the purposes of preventing, detecting or investigating terrorist offences or other serious criminal offences should be allowed and the necessary safeguards to ensure the protection of the fundamental right to respect for the private life of individuals whose personal data are processed in Eurodac. The strictness of those conditions reflects the fact that the Eurodac database registers fingerprint data of persons who are not presumed to have committed a terrorist offence or other serious criminal offence.

(16) With a view to ensuring equal treatment for all applicants and beneficiaries of international protection, as well as in order to ensure consistency with the current Union asylum acquis, in particular with Directive 2011/95/EU of the European Parliament and of the Council of 13 December 2011 on standards for the qualification of third-country nationals or stateless persons as beneficiaries of international protection, for a uniform status for refugees or for persons eligible for subsidiary protection, and for the content of the protection granted [1] and Regulation (EU) No 604/2013, it is appropriate to extend the scope of this Regulation in order to include applicants for subsidiary protection and persons eligible for subsidiary protection.

(17) It is also necessary to require the Member States promptly to take and transmit the fingerprint data of every applicant for international protection and of every third-country national or stateless person who is apprehended in connection with the irregular crossing of an external border of a Member State, if they are at least 14 years of age.

(18) It is necessary to lay down precise rules for the transmission of such fingerprint data to the Central System, the recording of such fingerprint data and of other relevant data in the Central System, their storage, their comparison with other fingerprint data, the transmission of the results of such comparison and the marking and erasure of the recorded data. Such rules may be different for, and should be specifically adapted to, the situation of different categories of third-country nationals or stateless persons.

(19) Member States should ensure the transmission of fingerprint data of an appropriate quality for the purpose of comparison by means of the computerised fingerprint recognition system. All authorities with a right of access to Eurodac should invest in adequate training and in the necessary technological equipment. The authorities with a right of access to Eurodac should inform the European Agency for the operational management of large-scale IT systems in the area of freedom, security and justice established by Regulation (EU) No 1077/2011 of the European Parliament and of the Council [2] (the "Agency") of specific difficulties encountered with regard to the quality of data, in order to resolve them.

(20) The fact that it is temporarily or permanently impossible to take and/or to transmit fingerprint data, due to reasons such as insufficient quality of the data for appropriate comparison, technical problems, reasons linked to the protection of health or due to the data subject being unfit or unable to have his or her fingerprints taken owing to circumstances beyond his or her control, should not adversely affect the examination of or the decision on the application for international protection lodged by that person.

(21) Hits obtained from Eurodac should be verified by a trained fingerprint expert in order to ensure the accurate determination of responsibility under Regulation (EU) No 604/2013 and the exact identification of the criminal suspect or victim of crime whose data might be stored in Eurodac.

(22) Third-country nationals or stateless persons who have requested international protection in one Member State may have the option of requesting international protection in another Member State for many years to come. Therefore, the maximum period during which fingerprint data should be kept by the Central System should be of considerable length. Given that most third-country nationals or stateless persons who have stayed in the Union for several years will have obtained a settled status or even citizenship of a Member State after that period, a period of ten years should be considered a reasonable period for the storage of fingerprint data.

(23) The storage period should be shorter in certain special situations where there is no need to keep fingerprint data for that length of time. Fingerprint data should be erased immediately once third-country nationals or stateless persons obtain citizenship of a Member State.

[1] OJ L 337, 20.12.2011, p. 9.

[2] OJ L 286, 1.11.2011, p. 1.

(24) It is appropriate to store data relating to those data subjects whose fingerprints were initially recorded in Eurodac upon lodging their applications for international protection and who have been granted international protection in a Member State in order to allow data recorded upon lodging an application for international protection to be compared against them.

(25) The Agency has been entrusted with the Commission's tasks relating to the operational management of Eurodac in accordance with this Regulation and with certain tasks relating to the Communication Infrastructure as from the date on which the Agency took up its responsibilities on 1 December 2012. The Agency should take up the tasks entrusted to it under this Regulation, and the relevant provisions of Regulation (EU) No 1077/2011 should be amended accordingly. In addition, Europol should have observer status at the meetings of the Management Board of the Agency when a question in relation to the application of this Regulation concerning access for consultation of Eurodac by designated authorities of Member States and by Europol for the purposes of the prevention, detection or investigation of terrorist offences or of other serious criminal offences is on the agenda. Europol should be able to appoint a representative to the Eurodac Advisory Group of the Agency.

(26) The Staff Regulations of Officials of the European Union (Staff Regulations of Officials) and the Conditions of Employment of Other Servants of the European Union ('Conditions of Employment'), laid down in Regulation (EEC, Euratom, ECSC) No 259/68 of the Council ([1]) (together referred to as the 'Staff Regulations') should apply to all staff working in the Agency on matters pertaining to this Regulation.

(27) It is necessary to lay down clearly the respective responsibilities of the Commission and the Agency, in respect of the Central System and the Communication Infrastructure, and of the Member States, as regards data processing, data security, access to, and correction of, recorded data.

(28) It is necessary to designate the competent authorities of the Member States as well as the National Access Point through which the requests for comparison with Eurodac data are made and to keep a list of the operating units within the designated authorities that are authorised to request such comparison for the specific purposes of the prevention, detection or investigation of terrorist offences or of other serious criminal offences.

(29) Requests for comparison with data stored in the Central System should be made by the operating units within the designated authorities to the National Access Point, through the verifying authority and should be reasoned. The operating units within the designated authorities that are authorised to request comparisons with Eurodac data should not act as a verifying authority. The verifying authorities should act independently of the designated authorities and should be responsible for ensuring, in an independent manner, strict compliance with the conditions for access as established in this Regulation. The verifying authorities should then forward the request, without forwarding the reasons for it, for comparison through the National Access Point to the Central System following verification that all conditions for access are fulfilled. In exceptional cases of urgency where early access is necessary to respond to a specific and actual threat related to terrorist offences or other serious criminal offences, the verifying authority should process the request immediately and only carry out the verification afterwards.

(30) The designated authority and the verifying authority may be part of the same organisation, if permitted under national law, but the verifying authority should act independently when performing its tasks under this Regulation.

(31) For the purposes of protection of personal data, and to exclude systematic comparisons which should be forbidden, the processing of Eurodac data should only take place in specific cases and when it is necessary for the purposes of preventing, detecting or investigating terrorist offences or other serious criminal offences. A specific case exists in particular when the request for comparison is connected to a specific and concrete situation or to a specific and concrete danger associated with a terrorist offence or other serious criminal offence, or to specific persons in respect of whom there are serious grounds for believing that they will commit or have committed any such offence. A specific case also exists when the request for comparison is connected to a person who is the victim of a terrorist offence or other serious criminal offence. The designated authorities and Europol should thus only request a comparison with Eurodac when they have reasonable grounds to believe that such a comparison will provide information that will substantially assist them in preventing, detecting or investigating a terrorist offence or other serious criminal offence.

(32) In addition, access should be allowed only on condition that comparisons with the national fingerprint databases of the Member State and with the automated fingerprinting identification systems of all other Member States under Council Decision 2008/615/JHA of 23 June 2008 on the stepping up of cross-border cooperation, particularly in combating terrorism and cross-border crime ([2]) did not lead to the establishment of the identity of the data subject. That condition requires the requesting Member State to conduct comparisons with the automated fingerprinting identification systems of all other Member States under Decision 2008/615/JHA which are technically available, unless that Member State can justify that there are reasonable

([1]) OJ L 56, 4.3.1968, p. 1.

([2]) OJ L 210, 6.8.2008, p. 1.

grounds to believe that it would not lead to the establishment of the identity of the data subject. Such reasonable grounds exist in particular where the specific case does not present any operational or investigative link to a given Member State. That condition requires prior legal and technical implementation of Decision 2008/615/JHA by the requesting Member State in the area of fingerprint data, as it should not be permitted to conduct a Eurodac check for law enforcement purposes where those above steps have not been first taken.

(33) Prior to searching Eurodac, designated authorities should also, provided that the conditions for a comparison are met, consult the Visa Information System under Council Decision 2008/633/JHA of 23 June 2008 concerning access for consultation of the Visa Information System (VIS) by designated authorities of Member States and by Europol for the purposes of the prevention, detection and investigation of terrorist offences and of other serious criminal offences ([1]).

(34) For the purpose of efficient comparison and exchange of personal data, Member States should fully implement and make use of the existing international agreements as well as of Union law concerning the exchange of personal data already in force, in particular of Decision 2008/615/JHA.

(35) The best interests of the child should be a primary consideration for Member States when applying this Regulation. Where the requesting Member State establishes that Eurodac data pertain to a minor, these data may only be used for law enforcement purposes by the requesting Member State in accordance with that State's laws applicable to minors and in accordance with the obligation to give primary consideration to the best interests of the child.

(36) While the non-contractual liability of the Union in connection with the operation of the Eurodac system will be governed by the relevant provisions of the Treaty on the Functioning of the European Union (TFEU), it is necessary to lay down specific rules for the non-contractual liability of the Member States in connection with the operation of the system.

(37) Since the objective of this Regulation, namely the creation of a system for the comparison of fingerprint data to assist the implementation of Union asylum policy, cannot, by its very nature, be sufficiently achieved by the Member States and can therefore be better achieved at Union level, the Union may adopt measures in accordance with the principle of subsidiarity as set out in Article 5 of the Treaty on European Union (TEU). In accordance with the principle of proportionality, as set out in that Article, this Regulation does not go beyond what is necessary in order to achieve that objective.

(38) Directive 95/46/EC of the European Parliament and of the Council of 24 October 1995 on the protection of individuals with regard to the processing of personal data and on the free movement of such data ([2]) applies to the processing of personal data by the Member States carried out in application of this Regulation unless such processing is carried out by the designated or verifying authorities of the Member States for the purposes of the prevention, detection or investigation of terrorist offences or of other serious criminal offences.

(39) The processing of personal data by the authorities of the Member States for the purposes of the prevention, detection or investigation of terrorist offences or of other serious criminal offences pursuant to this Regulation should be subject to a standard of protection of personal data under their national law which complies with Council Framework Decision 2008/977/JHA of 27 November 2008 on the protection of personal data processed in the framework of police and judicial cooperation in criminal matters ([3]).

(40) The principles set out in Directive 95/46/EC regarding the protection of the rights and freedoms of individuals, notably their right to privacy, with regard to the processing of personal data should be supplemented or clarified, in particular as far as certain sectors are concerned.

(41) Transfers of personal data obtained by a Member State or Europol pursuant to this Regulation from the Central System to any third country or international organisation or private entity established in or outside the Union should be prohibited, in order to ensure the right to asylum and to safeguard applicants for international protection from having their data disclosed to a third country. This implies that Member States should not transfer information obtained from the Central System concerning: the Member State(s) of origin; the place and date of application for international protection; the reference number used by the Member State of origin; the date on which the fingerprints were taken as well as the date on which the Member State(s) transmitted the data to Eurodac; the operator user ID; and any information relating to any transfer of the data subject under Regulation (EU) No 604/2013. That prohibition should be without prejudice to the right of Member States to transfer such data to third countries to which Regulation (EU) No 604/2013 applies, in order to ensure that Member States have the possibility of cooperating with such third countries for the purposes of this Regulation.

([1]) OJ L 218, 13.8.2008, p. 129.

([2]) OJ L 281, 23.11.1995, p. 31.

([3]) OJ L 350, 30.12.2008, p. 60.

(42) National supervisory authorities should monitor the lawfulness of the processing of personal data by the Member States, and the supervisory authority set up by Decision 2009/371/JHA should monitor the lawfulness of data processing activities performed by Europol.

(43) Regulation (EC) No 45/2001 of the European Parliament and of the Council of 18 December 2000 on the protection of individuals with regard to the processing of personal data by the Community institutions and bodies and on the free movement of such data (1), and in particular Articles 21 and 22 thereof concerning confidentiality and security of processing, applies to the processing of personal data by Union institutions, bodies, offices and agencies carried out in application of this Regulation. However, certain points should be clarified in respect of the responsibility for the processing of data and of the supervision of data protection, bearing in mind that data protection is a key factor in the successful operation of Eurodac and that data security, high technical quality and lawfulness of consultations are essential to ensure the smooth and proper functioning of Eurodac as well as to facilitate the application of Regulation (EU) No 604/2013.

(44) The data subject should be informed of the purpose for which his or her data will be processed within Eurodac, including a description of the aims of Regulation (EU) No 604/2013, and of the use to which law enforcement authorities may put his or her data.

(45) It is appropriate that national supervisory authorities monitor the lawfulness of the processing of personal data by the Member States, whilst the European Data Protection Supervisor, as referred to in Regulation (EC) No 45/2001, should monitor the activities of the Union institutions, bodies, offices and agencies in relation to the processing of personal data carried out in application of this Regulation.

(46) Member States, the European Parliament, the Council and the Commission should ensure that the national and European supervisory authorities are able to supervise the use of and access to Eurodac data adequately.

(47) It is appropriate to monitor and evaluate the performance of Eurodac at regular intervals, including in terms of whether law enforcement access has led to indirect discrimination against applicants for international protection, as raised in the Commission's evaluation of the compliance of this Regulation with the Charter of Fundamental Rights of the European Union ('the Charter'). The Agency should submit an annual report on the activities of the Central System to the European Parliament and to the Council.

(48) Member States should provide for a system of effective, proportionate and dissuasive penalties to sanction the processing of data entered in the Central System contrary to the purpose of Eurodac.

(49) It is necessary that Member States be informed of the status of particular asylum procedures, with a view to facilitating the adequate application of Regulation (EU) No 604/2013.

(50) This Regulation respects the fundamental rights and observes the principles recognised in particular by the Charter. In particular, this Regulation seeks to ensure full respect for the protection of personal data and for the right to seek international protection, and to promote the application of Articles 8 and 18 of the Charter. This Regulation should therefore be applied accordingly.

(51) In accordance with Articles 1 and 2 of Protocol No 22 on the position of Denmark, annexed to the TEU and to the TFEU, Denmark is not taking part in the adoption of this Regulation and is not bound by it or subject to its application.

(52) In accordance with Article 3 of Protocol No 21 on the position of the United Kingdom and Ireland in respect of the Area of Freedom, Security and Justice, annexed to the TEU and to the TFEU, the United Kingdom has notified its wish to take part in the adoption and application of this Regulation.

(53) In accordance with Article 1 and 2 of Protocol No 21 on the position of the United Kingdom and Ireland in respect of the Area of Freedom, Security and Justice, annexed to the TEU and to the TFEU, and without prejudice to Article 4 of that Protocol, Ireland is not taking part in the adoption of this Regulation and is not bound by it or subject to its application.

(54) It is appropriate to restrict the territorial scope of this Regulation so as to align it on the territorial scope of Regulation (EU) No 604/2013,

(1) OJ L 8, 12.1.2001, p. 1.

29.6.2013 EN Official Journal of the European Union L 180/7

HAVE ADOPTED THIS REGULATION:

CHAPTER I

**GENERAL PROVISIONS**

*Article 1*

**Purpose of "Eurodac"**

1. A system known as "Eurodac" is hereby established, the purpose of which shall be to assist in determining which Member State is to be responsible pursuant to Regulation (EU) No 604/2013 for examining an application for international protection lodged in a Member State by a third-country national or a stateless person, and otherwise to facilitate the application of Regulation (EU) No 604/2013 under the conditions set out in this Regulation.

2. This Regulation also lays down the conditions under which Member States' designated authorities and the European Police Office (Europol) may request the comparison of fingerprint data with those stored in the Central System for law enforcement purposes.

3. Without prejudice to the processing of data intended for Eurodac by the Member State of origin in databases set up under the latter's national law, fingerprint data and other personal data may be processed in Eurodac only for the purposes set out in this Regulation and Article 34(1) of Regulation (EU) No 604/2013.

*Article 2*

**Definitions**

1. For the purposes of this Regulation:

(a) 'applicant for international protection' means a third-country national or a stateless person who has made an application for international protection as defined in Article 2(h) of Directive 2011/95/EU in respect of which a final decision has not yet been taken;

(b) 'Member State of origin' means:

(i) in relation to a person covered by Article 9(1), the Member State which transmits the personal data to the Central System and receives the results of the comparison;

(ii) in relation to a person covered by Article 14(1), the Member State which transmits the personal data to the Central System;

(iii) in relation to a person covered by Article 17(1), the Member State which transmits the personal data to the Central System and receives the results of the comparison;

(c) 'beneficiary of international protection' means a third-country national or a stateless person who has been granted international protection as defined in Article 2(a) of Directive 2011/95/EU;

(d) 'hit' means the existence of a match or matches established by the Central System by comparison between fingerprint data recorded in the computerised central database and those transmitted by a Member State with regard to a person, without prejudice to the requirement that Member States shall immediately check the results of the comparison pursuant to Article 25(4);

(e) 'National Access Point' means the designated national system which communicates with the Central System;

(f) 'Agency' means the Agency established by Regulation (EU) No 1077/2011;

(g) 'Europol' means the European Police Office established by Decision 2009/371/JHA;

(h) 'Eurodac data' means all data stored in the Central System in accordance with Article 11 and Article 14(2);

(i) 'law enforcement' means the prevention, detection or investigation of terrorist offences or of other serious criminal offences;

(j) 'terrorist offences' means the offences under national law which correspond or are equivalent to those referred to in Articles 1 to 4 of Framework Decision 2002/475/JHA;

(k) 'serious criminal offences' means the forms of crime which correspond or are equivalent to those referred to in Article 2(2) of Framework Decision 2002/584/JHA, if they are punishable under national law by a custodial sentence or a detention order for a maximum period of at least three years;

(l) 'fingerprint data' means the data relating to fingerprints of all or at least the index fingers, and if those are missing, the prints of all other fingers of a person, or a latent fingerprint.

2. The terms defined in Article 2 of Directive 95/46/EC shall have the same meaning in this Regulation in so far as personal data are processed by the authorities of the Member States for the purposes laid down in Article 1(1) of this Regulation.

3. Unless stated otherwise, the terms defined in Article 2 of Regulation (EU) No 604/2013 shall have the same meaning in this Regulation.

4. The terms defined in Article 2 of Framework Decision 2008/977/JHA shall have the same meaning in this Regulation in so far as personal data are processed by the authorities of the Member States for the purposes laid down in Article 1(2) of this Regulation.

*Article 3*

**System architecture and basic principles**

1. Eurodac shall consist of:

(a) a computerised central fingerprint database ("Central System") composed of:

(i) a Central Unit,

(ii) a Business Continuity Plan and System;

(b) a communication infrastructure between the Central System and Member States that provides an encrypted virtual network dedicated to Eurodac data ("Communication Infrastructure").

2. Each Member State shall have a single National Access Point.

3. Data on persons covered by Articles 9(1), 14(1) and 17(1) which are processed in the Central System shall be processed on behalf of the Member State of origin under the conditions set out in this Regulation and separated by appropriate technical means.

4. The rules governing Eurodac shall also apply to operations carried out by the Member States as from the transmission of data to the Central System until use is made of the results of the comparison.

5. The procedure for taking fingerprints shall be determined and applied in accordance with the national practice of the Member State concerned and in accordance with the safeguards laid down in the Charter of Fundamental Rights of the European Union, in the Convention for the Protection of Human Rights and Fundamental Freedoms and in the United Nations Convention on the Rights of the Child.

*Article 4*

**Operational management**

1. The Agency shall be responsible for the operational management of Eurodac.

The operational management of Eurodac shall consist of all the tasks necessary to keep Eurodac functioning 24 hours a day, 7 days a week in accordance with this Regulation, in particular the maintenance work and technical developments necessary to ensure that the system functions at a satisfactory level of operational quality, in particular as regards the time required for interrogation of the Central System. A Business Continuity Plan and System shall be developed taking into account maintenance needs and unforeseen downtime of the system, including the impact of business continuity measures on data protection and security.

The Agency shall ensure, in cooperation with the Member States, that at all times the best available and most secure technology and techniques, subject to a cost-benefit analysis, are used for the Central System.

2. The Agency shall be responsible for the following tasks relating to the Communication Infrastructure:

(a) supervision;

(b) security;

(c) the coordination of relations between the Member States and the provider.

3. The Commission shall be responsible for all tasks relating to the Communication Infrastructure other than those referred to in paragraph 2, in particular:

(a) the implementation of the budget;

(b) acquisition and renewal;

(c) contractual matters.

4. Without prejudice to Article 17 of the Staff Regulations, the Agency shall apply appropriate rules of professional secrecy or other equivalent duties of confidentiality to all its staff required to work with Eurodac data. This obligation shall also apply after such staff leave office or employment or after the termination of their duties.

*Article 5*

**Member States' designated authorities for law enforcement purposes**

1. For the purposes laid down in Article 1(2), Member States shall designate the authorities that are authorised to request comparisons with Eurodac data pursuant to this Regulation. Designated authorities shall be authorities of the Member States which are responsible for the prevention, detection or investigation of terrorist offences or of other serious criminal offences. Designated authorities shall not include agencies or units exclusively responsible for intelligence relating to national security.

2. Each Member State shall keep a list of the designated authorities.

3. Each Member State shall keep a list of the operating units within the designated authorities that are authorised to request comparisons with Eurodac data through the National Access Point.

*Article 6*

**Member States' verifying authorities for law enforcement purposes**

1. For the purposes laid down in Article 1(2), each Member State shall designate a single national authority or a unit of such an authority to act as its verifying authority. The verifying authority shall be an authority of the Member State which is responsible for the prevention, detection or investigation of terrorist offences or of other serious criminal offences.

The designated authority and the verifying authority may be part of the same organisation, if permitted under national law, but the verifying authority shall act independently when performing its tasks under this Regulation. The verifying authority shall be separate from the operating units referred to in Article 5(3) and shall not receive instructions from them as regards the outcome of the verification.

Member States may designate more than one verifying authority to reflect their organisational and administrative structures, in accordance with their constitutional or legal requirements.

2. The verifying authority shall ensure that the conditions for requesting comparisons of fingerprints with Eurodac data are fulfilled.

Only duly empowered staff of the verifying authority shall be authorised to receive and transmit a request for access to Eurodac in accordance with Article 19.

Only the verifying authority shall be authorised to forward requests for comparison of fingerprints to the National Access Point.

*Article 7*

**Europol**

1. For the purposes laid down in Article 1(2), Europol shall designate a specialised unit with duly empowered Europol officials to act as its verifying authority, which shall act independently of the designated authority referred to in paragraph 2 of this Article when performing its tasks under this Regulation and shall not receive instructions from the designated authority as regards the outcome of the verification. The unit shall ensure that the conditions for requesting comparisons of fingerprints with Eurodac data are fulfilled. Europol shall designate in agreement with any Member State the National Access Point of that Member State which shall communicate its requests for comparison of fingerprint data to the Central System.

2. For the purposes laid down in Article 1(2), Europol shall designate an operating unit that is authorised to request comparisons with Eurodac data through its designated National Access Point. The designated authority shall be an operating unit of Europol which is competent to collect, store, process, analyse and exchange information to support and strengthen action by Member States in preventing, detecting or investigating terrorist offences or other serious criminal offences falling within Europol's mandate.

*Article 8*

**Statistics**

1. The Agency shall draw up statistics on the work of the Central System every quarter, indicating in particular:

(a) the number of data sets transmitted on persons referred to in Articles 9(1), 14(1) and 17(1);

(b) the number of hits for applicants for international protection who have lodged an application for international protection in another Member State;

(c) the number of hits for persons referred to in Article 14(1) who have subsequently lodged an application for international protection;

(d) the number of hits for persons referred to in Article 17(1) who had previously lodged an application for international protection in another Member State;

(e) the number of fingerprint data which the Central System had to request more than once from the Member States of origin because the fingerprint data originally transmitted did not lend themselves to comparison using the computerised fingerprint recognition system;

(f) the number of data sets marked, unmarked, blocked and unblocked in accordance with Article 18(1) and (3);

(g) the number of hits for persons referred to in Article 18(1) for whom hits have been recorded under points (b) and (d) of this Article;

(h) the number of requests and hits referred to in Article 20(1);

(i) the number of requests and hits referred to in Article 21(1).

2. At the end of each year, statistical data shall be established in the form of a compilation of the quarterly statistics for that year, including an indication of the number of persons for whom hits have been recorded under paragraph 1(b), (c) and (d). The statistics shall contain a breakdown of data for each Member State. The results shall be made public.

CHAPTER II

## APPLICANTS FOR INTERNATIONAL PROTECTION

*Article 9*

### Collection, transmission and comparison of fingerprints

1. Each Member State shall promptly take the fingerprints of all fingers of every applicant for international protection of at least 14 years of age and shall, as soon as possible and no later than 72 hours after the lodging of his or her application for international protection, as defined by Article 20(2) of Regulation (EU) No 604/2013, transmit them together with the data referred to in Article 11(b) to (g) of this Regulation to the Central System.

Non-compliance with the 72-hour time-limit shall not relieve Member States of the obligation to take and transmit the fingerprints to the Central System. Where the condition of the fingertips does not allow the taking of the fingerprints of a quality ensuring appropriate comparison under Article 25, the Member State of origin shall retake the fingerprints of the applicant and resend them as soon as possible and no later than 48 hours after they have been successfully retaken.

2. By way of derogation from paragraph 1, where it is not possible to take the fingerprints of an applicant for international protection on account of measures taken to ensure his or her health or the protection of public health, Member States shall take and send such fingerprints as soon as possible and no later than 48 hours after those health grounds no longer prevail.

In the event of serious technical problems, Member States may extend the 72-hour time-limit in paragraph 1 by a maximum of a further 48 hours in order to carry out their national continuity plans.

3. Fingerprint data within the meaning of Article 11(a) transmitted by any Member State, with the exception of those transmitted in accordance with Article 10(b), shall be compared automatically with the fingerprint data transmitted by other Member States and already stored in the Central System.

4. The Central System shall ensure, at the request of a Member State, that the comparison referred to in paragraph 3 covers the fingerprint data previously transmitted by that Member State, in addition to the data from other Member States.

5. The Central System shall automatically transmit the hit or the negative result of the comparison to the Member State of origin. Where there is a hit, it shall transmit for all data sets corresponding to the hit the data referred to in Article 11(a) to (k) along with, where appropriate, the mark referred to in Article 18(1).

*Article 10*

### Information on the status of the data subject

The following information shall be sent to the Central System in order to be stored in accordance with Article 12 for the purpose of transmission under Article 9(5):

(a) when an applicant for international protection or another person as referred to in Article 18(1)(d) of Regulation (EU) No 604/2013 arrives in the Member State responsible following a transfer pursuant to a decision acceding to a take back request as referred to in Article 25 thereof, the Member State responsible shall update its data set recorded in conformity with Article 11 of this Regulation relating to the person concerned by adding his or her date of arrival;

(b) when an applicant for international protection arrives in the Member State responsible following a transfer pursuant to a decision acceding to a take charge request according to Article 22 of Regulation (EU) No 604/2013, the Member State responsible shall send a data set recorded in conformity with Article 11 of this Regulation relating to the person concerned and shall include his or her date of arrival;

(c) as soon as the Member State of origin establishes that the person concerned whose data was recorded in Eurodac in accordance with Article 11 of this Regulation has left the territory of the Member States, it shall update its data set recorded in conformity with Article 11 of this Regulation relating to the person concerned by adding the date when that person left the territory, in order to facilitate the application of Articles 19(2) and 20(5) of Regulation (EU) No 604/2013;

(d) as soon as the Member State of origin ensures that the person concerned whose data was recorded in Eurodac in accordance with Article 11 of this Regulation has left the territory of the Member States in compliance with a return decision or removal order issued following the withdrawal or rejection of the application for international protection as provided for in Article 19(3) of Regulation (EU) No 604/2013, it shall update its data set recorded in conformity with Article 11 of this Regulation relating to the person concerned by adding the date of his or her removal or when he or she left the territory;

(e) the Member State which becomes responsible in accordance with Article 17(1) of Regulation (EU) No 604/2013 shall update its data set recorded in conformity with Article 11 of this Regulation relating to the applicant for international protection by adding the date when the decision to examine the application was taken.

*Article 11*

**Recording of data**

Only the following data shall be recorded in the Central System:

(a) fingerprint data;

(b) Member State of origin, place and date of the application for international protection; in the cases referred to in Article 10(b), the date of application shall be the one entered by the Member State who transferred the applicant;

(c) sex;

(d) reference number used by the Member State of origin;

(e) date on which the fingerprints were taken;

(f) date on which the data were transmitted to the Central System;

(g) operator user ID;

(h) where applicable in accordance with Article 10(a) or (b), the date of the arrival of the person concerned after a successful transfer;

(i) where applicable in accordance with Article 10(c), the date when the person concerned left the territory of the Member States;

(j) where applicable in accordance with Article 10(d), the date when the person concerned left or was removed from the territory of the Member States;

(k) where applicable in accordance with Article 10(e), the date when the decision to examine the application was taken.

*Article 12*

**Data storage**

1. Each set of data, as referred to in Article 11, shall be stored in the Central System for ten years from the date on which the fingerprints were taken.

2. Upon expiry of the period referred to in paragraph 1, the Central System shall automatically erase the data from the Central System.

*Article 13*

**Advance data erasure**

1. Data relating to a person who has acquired citizenship of any Member State before expiry of the period referred to in Article 12(1) shall be erased from the Central System in accordance with Article 27(4) as soon as the Member State of origin becomes aware that the person concerned has acquired such citizenship.

2. The Central System shall, as soon as possible and no later than after 72 hours, inform all Member States of origin of the erasure of data in accordance with paragraph 1 by another Member State of origin having produced a hit with data which they transmitted relating to persons referred to in Article 9(1) or 14(1).

CHAPTER III

**THIRD-COUNTRY NATIONALS OR STATELESS PERSONS APPREHENDED IN CONNECTION WITH THE IRREGULAR CROSSING OF AN EXTERNAL BORDER**

*Article 14*

**Collection and transmission of fingerprint data**

1. Each Member State shall promptly take the fingerprints of all fingers of every third-country national or stateless person of at least 14 years of age who is apprehended by the competent control authorities in connection with the irregular crossing by land, sea or air of the border of that Member State having come from a third country and who is not turned back or who remains physically on the territory of the Member States and who is not kept in custody, confinement or detention during the entirety of the period between apprehension and removal on the basis of the decision to turn him or her back.

2. The Member State concerned shall, as soon as possible and no later than 72 hours after the date of apprehension, transmit to the Central System the following data in relation to any third-country national or stateless person, as referred to in paragraph 1, who is not turned back:

(a) fingerprint data;

(b) Member State of origin, place and date of the apprehension;

(c) sex;

(d) reference number used by the Member State of origin;

(e) date on which the fingerprints were taken;

(f) date on which the data were transmitted to the Central System;

(g) operator user ID.

3. By way of derogation from paragraph 2, the data specified in paragraph 2 relating to persons apprehended as described in paragraph 1 who remain physically on the territory of the Member States but are kept in custody, confinement or detention upon their apprehension for a period exceeding 72 hours shall be transmitted before their release from custody, confinement or detention.

4. Non-compliance with the 72-hour time-limit referred to in paragraph 2 of this Article shall not relieve Member States of the obligation to take and transmit the fingerprints to the Central System. Where the condition of the fingertips does not allow the taking of fingerprints of a quality ensuring appropriate comparison under Article 25, the Member State of origin shall retake the fingerprints of persons apprehended as described in paragraph 1 of this Article, and resend them as soon as possible and no later than 48 hours after they have been successfully retaken.

5. By way of derogation from paragraph 1, where it is not possible to take the fingerprints of the apprehended person on account of measures taken to ensure his or her health or the protection of public health, the Member State concerned shall take and send such fingerprints as soon as possible and no later than 48 hours after those health grounds no longer prevail.

In the event of serious technical problems, Member States may extend the 72-hour time-limit in paragraph 2 by a maximum of a further 48 hours in order to carry out their national continuity plans.

*Article 15*

**Recording of data**

1. The data referred to in Article 14(2) shall be recorded in the Central System.

Without prejudice to Article 8, data transmitted to the Central System pursuant to Article 14(2) shall be recorded solely for the purposes of comparison with data on applicants for international protection subsequently transmitted to the Central System and for the purposes laid down in Article 1(2).

The Central System shall not compare data transmitted to it pursuant to Article 14(2) with any data previously recorded in the Central System, or with data subsequently transmitted to the Central System pursuant to Article 14(2).

2. As regards the comparison of data on applicants for international protection subsequently transmitted to the Central System with the data referred to in paragraph 1, the procedures provided for in Article 9(3) and (5) and in Article 25(4) shall apply.

*Article 16*

**Storage of data**

1. Each set of data relating to a third-country national or stateless person as referred to in Article 14(1) shall be stored in the Central System for 18 months from the date on which his or her fingerprints were taken. Upon expiry of that period, the Central System shall automatically erase such data.

2. The data relating to a third-country national or stateless person as referred to in Article 14(1) shall be erased from the Central System in accordance with Article 28(3) as soon as the Member State of origin becomes aware of one of the following circumstances before the 18 month period referred to in paragraph 1 of this Article has expired:

(a) the third-country national or stateless person has been issued with a residence document;

(b) the third-country national or stateless person has left the territory of the Member States;

29.6.2013 EN Official Journal of the European Union L 180/13

(c) the third-country national or stateless person has acquired the citizenship of any Member State.

3. The Central System shall, as soon as possible and no later than after 72 hours, inform all Member States of origin of the erasure of data for the reason specified in paragraph 2(a) or (b) of this Article by another Member State of origin having produced a hit with data which they transmitted relating to persons referred to in Article 14(1).

4. The Central System shall, as soon as possible and no later than after 72 hours, inform all Member States of origin of the erasure of data for the reason specified in paragraph 2(c) of this Article by another Member State of origin having produced a hit with data which they transmitted relating to persons referred to in Article 9(1) or 14(1).

## CHAPTER IV

## THIRD-COUNTRY NATIONALS OR STATELESS PERSONS FOUND ILLEGALLY STAYING IN A MEMBER STATE

*Article 17*

### Comparison of fingerprint data

1. With a view to checking whether a third-country national or a stateless person found illegally staying within its territory has previously lodged an application for international protection in another Member State, a Member State may transmit to the Central System any fingerprint data relating to fingerprints which it may have taken of any such third-country national or stateless person of at least 14 years of age together with the reference number used by that Member State.

As a general rule there are grounds for checking whether the third-country national or stateless person has previously lodged an application for international protection in another Member State where:

(a) the third-country national or stateless person declares that he or she has lodged an application for international protection but without indicating the Member State in which he or she lodged the application;

(b) the third-country national or stateless person does not request international protection but objects to being returned to his or her country of origin by claiming that he or she would be in danger, or

(c) the third-country national or stateless person otherwise seeks to prevent his or her removal by refusing to cooperate in establishing his or her identity, in particular by showing no, or false, identity papers.

2. Where Member States take part in the procedure referred to in paragraph 1, they shall transmit to the Central System the fingerprint data relating to all or at least the index fingers and, if those are missing, the prints of all the other fingers, of third-country nationals or stateless persons referred to in paragraph 1.

3. The fingerprint data of a third-country national or a stateless person as referred to in paragraph 1 shall be transmitted to the Central System solely for the purpose of comparison with the fingerprint data of applicants for international protection transmitted by other Member States and already recorded in the Central System.

The fingerprint data of such a third-country national or a stateless person shall not be recorded in the Central System, nor shall they be compared with the data transmitted to the Central System pursuant to Article 14(2).

4. Once the results of the comparison of fingerprint data have been transmitted to the Member State of origin, the record of the search shall be kept by the Central System only for the purposes of Article 28. Other than for those purposes, no other record of the search may be stored either by Member States or by the Central System.

5. As regards the comparison of fingerprint data transmitted under this Article with the fingerprint data of applicants for international protection transmitted by other Member States which have already been stored in the Central System, the procedures provided for in Article 9(3) and (5) and in Article 25(4) shall apply.

## CHAPTER V

## BENEFICIARIES OF INTERNATIONAL PROTECTION

*Article 18*

### Marking of data

1. For the purposes laid down in Article 1(1), the Member State of origin which granted international protection to an applicant for international protection whose data were previously recorded in the Central System pursuant to Article 11 shall mark the relevant data in conformity with the requirements for electronic communication with the Central System established by the Agency. That mark shall be stored in the Central System in accordance with Article 12 for the purpose of transmission under Article 9(5). The Central System shall inform all Member States of origin of the marking of data by another Member State of origin having produced a hit with data which they transmitted relating to persons referred to in Article 9(1) or 14(1). Those Member States of origin shall also mark the corresponding data sets.

2. The data of beneficiaries of international protection stored in the Central System and marked pursuant to paragraph 1 of this Article shall be made available for comparison for the purposes laid down in Article 1(2) for a period of three years after the date on which the data subject was granted international protection.

Where there is a hit, the Central System shall transmit the data referred to in Article 11(a) to (k) for all the data sets corresponding to the hit. The Central System shall not transmit the mark referred to in paragraph 1 of this Article. Upon the expiry of the period of three years, the Central System shall automatically block such data from being transmitted in the event of a request for comparison for the purposes laid down in Article 1(2), whilst leaving those data available for comparison for the purposes laid down in Article 1(1) until the point of their erasure. Blocked data shall not be transmitted, and the Central System shall return a negative result to the requesting Member State in the event of a hit.

3. The Member State of origin shall unmark or unblock data concerning a third-country national or stateless person whose data were previously marked or blocked in accordance with paragraphs 1 or 2 of this Article if his or her status is revoked or ended or the renewal of his or her status is refused under Articles 14 or 19 of Directive 2011/95/EU.

CHAPTER VI

## PROCEDURE FOR COMPARISON AND DATA TRANSMISSION FOR LAW ENFORCEMENT PURPOSES

*Article 19*

### Procedure for comparison of fingerprint data with Eurodac data

1. For the purposes laid down in Article 1(2), the designated authorities referred to in Articles 5(1) and 7(2) may submit a reasoned electronic request as provided for in Article 20(1) together with the reference number used by them, to the verifying authority for the transmission for comparison of fingerprint data to the Central System via the National Access Point. Upon receipt of such a request, the verifying authority shall verify whether all the conditions for requesting a comparison referred to in Articles 20 or 21, as appropriate, are fulfilled.

2. Where all the conditions for requesting a comparison referred to in Articles 20 or 21 are fulfilled, the verifying authority shall transmit the request for comparison to the National Access Point which will process it to the Central System in accordance with Article 9(3) and (5) for the purpose of comparison with the data transmitted to the Central System pursuant to Articles 9(1) and 14(2).

3. In exceptional cases of urgency where there is a need to prevent an imminent danger associated with a terrorist offence or other serious criminal offence, the verifying authority may transmit the fingerprint data to the National Access Point for comparison immediately upon receipt of a request by a designated authority and only verify ex-post whether all the conditions for requesting a comparison referred to in Article 20 or Article 21 are fulfilled, including whether an exceptional case of urgency actually existed. The ex-post verification shall take place without undue delay after the processing of the request.

4. Where an ex-post verification determines that the access to Eurodac data was not justified, all the authorities that have accessed such data shall erase the information communicated from Eurodac and shall inform the verifying authority of such erasure.

*Article 20*

### Conditions for access to Eurodac by designated authorities

1. For the purposes laid down in Article 1(2), designated authorities may submit a reasoned electronic request for the comparison of fingerprint data with the data stored in the Central System within the scope of their powers only if comparisons with the following databases did not lead to the establishment of the identity of the data subject:

— national fingerprint databases;

— the automated fingerprinting identification systems of all other Member States under Decision 2008/615/JHA where comparisons are technically available, unless there are reasonable grounds to believe that a comparison with such systems would not lead to the establishment of the identity of the data subject. Such reasonable grounds shall be included in the reasoned electronic request for comparison with Eurodac data sent by the designated authority to the verifying authority; and

— the Visa Information System provided that the conditions for such a comparison laid down in Decision 2008/633/JHA are met;

and where the following cumulative conditions are met:

(a) the comparison is necessary for the purpose of the prevention, detection or investigation of terrorist offences or of other serious criminal offences, which means that there is an overriding public security concern which makes the searching of the database proportionate;

(b) the comparison is necessary in a specific case (i.e. systematic comparisons shall not be carried out); and

29.6.2013 EN Official Journal of the European Union L 180/15

(c) there are reasonable grounds to consider that the comparison will substantially contribute to the prevention, detection or investigation of any of the criminal offences in question. Such reasonable grounds exist in particular where there is a substantiated suspicion that the suspect, perpetrator or victim of a terrorist offence or other serious criminal offence falls in a category covered by this Regulation.

2. Requests for comparison with Eurodac data shall be limited to searching with fingerprint data.

*Article 21*

**Conditions for access to Eurodac by Europol**

1. For the purposes laid down in Article 1(2), Europol's designated authority may submit a reasoned electronic request for the comparison of fingerprint data with the data stored in the Central System within the limits of Europol's mandate and where necessary for the performance of Europol's tasks only if comparisons with fingerprint data stored in any information processing systems that are technically and legally accessible by Europol did not lead to the establishment of the identity of the data subject and where the following cumulative conditions are met:

(a) the comparison is necessary to support and strengthen action by Member States in preventing, detecting or investigating terrorist offences or other serious criminal offences falling under Europol's mandate, which means that there is an overriding public security concern which makes the searching of the database proportionate;

(b) the comparison is necessary in a specific case (i.e. systematic comparisons shall not be carried out); and

(c) there are reasonable grounds to consider that the comparison will substantially contribute to the prevention, detection or investigation of any of the criminal offences in question. Such reasonable grounds exist in particular where there is a substantiated suspicion that the suspect, perpetrator or victim of a terrorist offence or other serious criminal offence falls in a category covered by this Regulation.

2. Requests for comparison with Eurodac data shall be limited to comparisons of fingerprint data.

3. Processing of information obtained by Europol from comparison with Eurodac data shall be subject to the authorisation of the Member State of origin. Such authorisation shall be obtained via the Europol national unit of that Member State.

*Article 22*

**Communication between the designated authorities, the verifying authorities and the National Access Points**

1. Without prejudice to Article 26, all communication between the designated authorities, the verifying authorities and the National Access Points shall be secure and take place electronically.

2. For the purposes laid down in Article 1(2), fingerprints shall be digitally processed by the Member States and transmitted in the data format referred to in Annex I, in order to ensure that the comparison can be carried out by means of the computerised fingerprint recognition system.

CHAPTER VII

**DATA PROCESSING, DATA PROTECTION AND LIABILITY**

*Article 23*

**Responsibility for data processing**

1. The Member State of origin shall be responsible for ensuring that:

(a) fingerprints are taken lawfully;

(b) fingerprint data and the other data referred to in Article 11, Article 14(2) and Article 17(2) are lawfully transmitted to the Central System;

(c) data are accurate and up-to-date when they are transmitted to the Central System;

(d) without prejudice to the responsibilities of the Agency, data in the Central System are lawfully recorded, stored, corrected and erased;

(e) the results of fingerprint data comparisons transmitted by the Central System are lawfully processed.

2. In accordance with Article 34, the Member State of origin shall ensure the security of the data referred to in paragraph 1 before and during transmission to the Central System as well as the security of the data it receives from the Central System.

3. The Member State of origin shall be responsible for the final identification of the data pursuant to Article 25(4).

4. The Agency shall ensure that the Central System is operated in accordance with the provisions of this Regulation. In particular, the Agency shall:

(a) adopt measures ensuring that persons working with the Central System process the data recorded therein only in accordance with the purposes of Eurodac as laid down in Article 1;

(b) take the necessary measures to ensure the security of the Central System in accordance with Article 34;

(c) ensure that only persons authorised to work with the Central System have access thereto, without prejudice to the competences of the European Data Protection Supervisor.

The Agency shall inform the European Parliament and the Council as well as the European Data Protection Supervisor of the measures it takes pursuant to the first subparagraph.

*Article 24*

**Transmission**

1. Fingerprints shall be digitally processed and transmitted in the data format referred to in Annex I. As far as necessary for the efficient operation of the Central System, the Agency shall establish the technical requirements for transmission of the data format by Member States to the Central System and vice versa. The Agency shall ensure that the fingerprint data transmitted by the Member States can be compared by the computerised fingerprint recognition system.

2. Member States shall transmit the data referred to in Article 11, Article 14(2) and Article 17(2) electronically. The data referred to in Article 11 and Article 14(2) shall be automatically recorded in the Central System. As far as necessary for the efficient operation of the Central System, the Agency shall establish the technical requirements to ensure that data can be properly electronically transmitted from the Member States to the Central System and vice versa.

3. The reference number referred to in Articles 11(d), 14(2)(d), 17(1) and 19(1) shall make it possible to relate data unambiguously to one particular person and to the Member State which is transmitting the data. In addition, it shall make it possible to tell whether such data relate to a person referred to in Article 9(1), 14(1) or 17(1).

4. The reference number shall begin with the identification letter or letters by which, in accordance with the norm referred to in Annex I, the Member State transmitting the data is identified. The identification letter or letters shall be followed by the identification of the category of person or request. "1" refers to data relating to persons referred to in Article 9(1), "2" to persons referred to in Article 14(1), "3" to persons referred to in Article 17(1), "4" to requests referred to in Article 20, "5" to requests referred to in Article 21 and "9" to requests referred to in Article 29.

5. The Agency shall establish the technical procedures necessary for Member States to ensure receipt of unambiguous data by the Central System.

6 The Central System shall confirm receipt of the transmitted data as soon as possible. To that end, the Agency shall establish the necessary technical requirements to ensure that Member States receive the confirmation receipt if requested.

*Article 25*

**Carrying out comparisons and transmitting results**

1. Member States shall ensure the transmission of fingerprint data of an appropriate quality for the purpose of comparison by means of the computerised fingerprint recognition system. As far as necessary to ensure that the results of the comparison by the Central System reach a very high level of accuracy, the Agency shall define the appropriate quality of transmitted fingerprint data. The Central System shall, as soon as possible, check the quality of the fingerprint data transmitted. If fingerprint data do not lend themselves to comparison using the computerised fingerprint recognition system, the Central System shall inform the Member State concerned. That Member State shall then transmit fingerprint data of the appropriate quality using the same reference number as the previous set of fingerprint data.

2. The Central System shall carry out comparisons in the order of arrival of requests. Each request shall be dealt with within 24 hours. A Member State may for reasons connected with national law require particularly urgent comparisons to be carried out within one hour. Where such time-limits cannot be respected owing to circumstances which are outside the Agency's responsibility, the Central System shall process the request as a matter of priority as soon as those circumstances no longer prevail. In such cases, as far as is necessary for the efficient operation of the Central System, the Agency shall establish criteria to ensure the priority handling of requests.

3. As far as necessary for the efficient operation of the Central System, the Agency shall establish the operational procedures for the processing of the data received and for transmitting the result of the comparison.

4. The result of the comparison shall be immediately checked in the receiving Member State by a fingerprint expert as defined in accordance with its national rules, specifically trained in the types of fingerprint comparisons provided for in this Regulation. For the purposes laid down in Article 1(1) of this Regulation, final identification shall be made by the Member State of origin in cooperation with the other Member States concerned, pursuant to Article 34 of Regulation (EU) No 604/2013.

Information received from the Central System relating to other data found to be unreliable shall be erased as soon as the unreliability of the data is established.

5. Where final identification in accordance with paragraph 4 reveals that the result of the comparison received from the Central System does not correspond to the fingerprint data sent for comparison, Member States shall immediately erase the result of the comparison and communicate this fact as soon as possible and no later than after three working days to the Commission and to the Agency.

*Article 26*

**Communication between Member States and the Central System**

Data transmitted from the Member States to the Central System and vice versa shall use the Communication Infrastructure. As far as is necessary for the efficient operation of the Central System, the Agency shall establish the technical procedures necessary for the use of the Communication Infrastructure.

*Article 27*

**Access to, and correction or erasure of, data recorded in Eurodac**

1. The Member State of origin shall have access to data which it has transmitted and which are recorded in the Central System in accordance with this Regulation.

No Member State may conduct searches of the data transmitted by another Member State, nor may it receive such data apart from data resulting from the comparison referred to in Article 9(5).

2. The authorities of Member States which, pursuant to paragraph 1 of this Article, have access to data recorded in the Central System shall be those designated by each Member State for the purposes laid down in Article 1(1). That designation shall specify the exact unit responsible for carrying out tasks related to the application of this Regulation. Each Member State shall without delay communicate to the Commission and the Agency a list of those units and any amendments thereto. The Agency shall publish the consolidated list in the *Official Journal of the European Union*. Where there are amendments thereto, the Agency shall publish once a year an updated consolidated list online.

3. Only the Member State of origin shall have the right to amend the data which it has transmitted to the Central System by correcting or supplementing such data, or to erase them, without prejudice to erasure carried out in pursuance of Article 12(2) or 16(1).

4. If a Member State or the Agency has evidence to suggest that data recorded in the Central System are factually inaccurate, it shall advise the Member State of origin as soon as possible.

If a Member State has evidence to suggest that data were recorded in the Central System in breach of this Regulation, it shall advise the Agency, the Commission and the Member State of origin as soon as possible. The Member State of origin shall check the data concerned and, if necessary, amend or erase them without delay.

5. The Agency shall not transfer or make available to the authorities of any third country data recorded in the Central System. This prohibition shall not apply to transfers of such data to third countries to which Regulation (EU) No 604/2013 applies.

*Article 28*

**Keeping of records**

1. The Agency shall keep records of all data processing operations within the Central System. These records shall show the purpose, date and time of access, the data transmitted, the data used for interrogation and the name of both the unit entering or retrieving the data and the persons responsible.

2. The records referred to in paragraph 1 of this Article may be used only for the data protection monitoring of the admissibility of data processing as well as to ensure data security pursuant to Article 34. The records must be protected by appropriate measures against unauthorised access and erased after a period of one year after the storage period referred to in Article 12(1) and in Article 16(1) has expired, unless they are required for monitoring procedures which have already begun.

3. For the purposes laid down in Article 1(1), each Member State shall take the necessary measures in order to achieve the objectives set out in paragraphs 1 and 2 of this Article in relation to its national system. In addition, each Member State shall keep records of the staff duly authorised to enter or retrieve the data.

*Article 29*

**Rights of the data subject**

1. A person covered by Article 9(1), Article 14(1) or Article 17(1) shall be informed by the Member State of origin in writing, and where necessary, orally, in a language that he or she understands or is reasonably supposed to understand, of the following:

(a) the identity of the controller within the meaning of Article 2(d) of Directive 95/46/EC and of his or her representative, if any;

(b) the purpose for which his or her data will be processed in Eurodac, including a description of the aims of Regulation (EU) No 604/2013, in accordance with Article 4 thereof and an explanation in intelligible form, using clear and plain language, of the fact that Eurodac may be accessed by the Member States and Europol for law enforcement purposes;

(c) the recipients of the data;

(d) in relation to a person covered by Article 9(1) or 14(1), the obligation to have his or her fingerprints taken;

(e) the right of access to data relating to him or her, and the right to request that inaccurate data relating to him or her be corrected or that unlawfully processed data relating to him or her be erased, as well as the right to receive information on the procedures for exercising those rights including the contact details of the controller and the national supervisory authorities referred to in Article 30(1).

2. In relation to a person covered by Article 9(1) or 14(1), the information referred to in paragraph 1 of this Article shall be provided at the time when his or her fingerprints are taken.

In relation to a person covered by Article 17(1), the information referred to in paragraph 1 of this Article shall be provided no later than at the time when the data relating to that person are transmitted to the Central System. That obligation shall not apply where the provision of such information proves impossible or would involve a disproportionate effort.

Where a person covered by Article 9(1), Article 14(1) and Article 17(1) is a minor, Member States shall provide the information in an age-appropriate manner.

3. A common leaflet, containing at least the information referred to in paragraph 1 of this Article and the information referred to in Article 4(1) of Regulation (EU) No 604/2013 shall be drawn up in accordance with the procedure referred to in Article 44(2) of that Regulation.

The leaflet shall be clear and simple, drafted in a language that the person concerned understands or is reasonably supposed to understand.

The leaflet shall be established in such a manner as to enable Member States to complete it with additional Member State-specific information. This Member State-specific information shall include at least the rights of the data subject, the possibility of assistance by the national supervisory authorities, as well as the contact details of the office of the controller and the national supervisory authorities.

4. For the purposes laid down in Article 1(1) of this Regulation, in each Member State any data subject may, in accordance with the laws, regulations and procedures of that State, exercise the rights provided for in Article 12 of Directive 95/46/EC.

Without prejudice to the obligation to provide other information in accordance with Article 12(a) of Directive 95/46/EC, the data subject shall have the right to obtain communication of the data relating to him or her recorded in the Central System and of the Member State which transmitted them to the Central System. Such access to data may be granted only by a Member State.

5. For the purposes laid down in Article 1(1), in each Member State, any person may request that data which are factually inaccurate be corrected or that data recorded unlawfully be erased. The correction and erasure shall be carried out without excessive delay by the Member State which transmitted the data, in accordance with its laws, regulations and procedures.

6. For the purposes laid down in Article 1(1), if the rights of correction and erasure are exercised in a Member State other than that, or those, which transmitted the data, the authorities of that Member State shall contact the authorities of the Member State or States which transmitted the data so that the latter may check the accuracy of the data and the lawfulness of their transmission and recording in the Central System.

7. For the purposes laid down in Article 1(1), if it emerges that data recorded in the Central System are factually inaccurate or have been recorded unlawfully, the Member State which transmitted them shall correct or erase the data in accordance with Article 27(3). That Member State shall confirm in writing to the data subject without excessive delay that it has taken action to correct or erase data relating to him or her.

8. For the purposes laid down in Article 1(1), if the Member State which transmitted the data does not agree that data recorded in the Central System are factually inaccurate or have been recorded unlawfully, it shall explain in writing to the data subject without excessive delay why it is not prepared to correct or erase the data.

That Member State shall also provide the data subject with information explaining the steps which he or she can take if he or she does not accept the explanation provided. This shall include information on how to bring an action or, if appropriate, a complaint before the competent authorities or courts of that Member State and any financial or other assistance that is available in accordance with the laws, regulations and procedures of that Member State.

9. Any request under paragraphs 4 and 5 shall contain all the necessary particulars to identify the data subject, including fingerprints. Such data shall be used exclusively to permit the exercise of the rights referred to in paragraphs 4 and 5 and shall be erased immediately afterwards.

10. The competent authorities of the Member States shall cooperate actively to enforce promptly the rights laid down in paragraphs 5, 6 and 7.

11. Whenever a person requests data relating to him or her in accordance with paragraph 4, the competent authority shall keep a record in the form of a written document that such a request was made and how it was addressed, and shall make that document available to the national supervisory authorities without delay.

12. For the purposes laid down in Article 1(1) of this Regulation, in each Member State, the national supervisory authority shall, on the basis of his or her request, assist the data subject in accordance with Article 28(4) of Directive 95/46/EC in exercising his or her rights.

13. For the purposes laid down in Article 1(1) of this Regulation, the national supervisory authority of the Member State which transmitted the data and the national supervisory authority of the Member State in which the data subject is present shall assist and, where requested, advise him or her in exercising his or her right to correct or erase data. Both national supervisory authorities shall cooperate to this end. Requests for such assistance may be made to the national supervisory authority of the Member State in which the data subject is present, which shall transmit the requests to the authority of the Member State which transmitted the data.

14. In each Member State any person may, in accordance with the laws, regulations and procedures of that State, bring an action or, if appropriate, a complaint before the competent authorities or courts of the State if he or she is refused the right of access provided for in paragraph 4.

15. Any person may, in accordance with the laws, regulations and procedures of the Member State which transmitted the data, bring an action or, if appropriate, a complaint before the competent authorities or courts of that State concerning the data relating to him or her recorded in the Central System, in order to exercise his or her rights under paragraph 5. The obligation of the national supervisory authorities to assist and, where requested, advise the data subject in accordance with paragraph 13 shall subsist throughout the proceedings.

*Article 30*

**Supervision by the national supervisory authorities**

1. For the purposes laid down in Article 1(1) of this Regulation, each Member State shall provide that the national supervisory authority or authorities designated pursuant to Article 28(1) of Directive 95/46/EC shall monitor independently, in accordance with its respective national law, the lawfulness of the processing, in accordance with this Regulation, of personal data by the Member State in question, including their transmission to the Central System.

2. Each Member State shall ensure that its national supervisory authority has access to advice from persons with sufficient knowledge of fingerprint data.

*Article 31*

**Supervision by the European Data Protection Supervisor**

1. The European Data Protection Supervisor shall ensure that all the personal data processing activities concerning Eurodac, in particular by the Agency, are carried out in accordance with Regulation (EC) No 45/2001 and with this Regulation.

2. The European Data Protection Supervisor shall ensure that an audit of the Agency's personal data processing activities is carried out in accordance with international auditing standards at least every three years. A report of such audit shall be sent to the European Parliament, the Council, the Commission, the Agency, and the national supervisory authorities. The Agency shall be given an opportunity to make comments before the report is adopted.

*Article 32*

**Cooperation between national supervisory authorities and the European Data Protection Supervisor**

1. The national supervisory authorities and the European Data Protection Supervisor shall, each acting within the scope of their respective competences, cooperate actively in the framework of their responsibilities and shall ensure coordinated supervision of Eurodac.

2. Member States shall ensure that every year an audit of the processing of personal data for the purposes laid down in Article 1(2) is carried out by an independent body, in accordance with Article 33(2), including an analysis of a sample of reasoned electronic requests.

The audit shall be attached to the annual report of the Member States referred to in Article 40(7).

3. The national supervisory authorities and the European Data Protection Supervisor shall, each acting within the scope of their respective competences, exchange relevant information, assist each other in carrying out audits and inspections, examine difficulties of interpretation or application of this Regulation, study problems with the exercise of independent supervision or in the exercise of the rights of data subjects, draw up harmonised proposals for joint solutions to any problems and promote awareness of data protection rights, as necessary.

4. For the purpose laid down in paragraph 3, the national supervisory authorities and the European Data Protection Supervisor shall meet at least twice a year. The costs and servicing of these meetings shall be for the account of the European Data Protection Supervisor. Rules of procedure shall be adopted at the first meeting. Further working methods shall be developed jointly as necessary. A joint report of activities shall be sent to the European Parliament, the Council, the Commission and the Agency every two years.

*Article 33*

**Protection of personal data for law enforcement purposes**

1. Each Member State shall provide that the provisions adopted under national law implementing Framework Decision 2008/977/JHA are also applicable to the processing of personal data by its national authorities for the purposes laid down in Article 1(2) of this Regulation.

2. The monitoring of the lawfulness of the processing of personal data under this Regulation by the Member States for the purposes laid down in Article 1(2) of this Regulation, including their transmission to and from Eurodac, shall be carried out by the national supervisory authorities designated pursuant to Framework Decision 2008/977/JHA.

3. The processing of personal data by Europol pursuant to this Regulation shall be in accordance with Decision 2009/371/JHA and shall be supervised by an independent external data protection supervisor. Articles 30, 31 and 32 of that Decision shall be applicable to the processing of personal data by Europol pursuant to this Regulation. The independent external data protection supervisor shall ensure that the rights of the individual are not violated.

4. Personal data obtained pursuant to this Regulation from Eurodac for the purposes laid down in Article 1(2) shall only be processed for the purposes of the prevention, detection or investigation of the specific case for which the data have been requested by a Member State or by Europol.

5. The Central System, the designated and verifying authorities and Europol shall keep records of the searches for the purpose of permitting the national data protection authorities and the European Data Protection Supervisor to monitor the compliance of data processing with Union data protection rules, including for the purpose of maintaining records in order to prepare the annual reports referred to in Article 40(7). Other than for such purposes, personal data, as well as the records of the searches, shall be erased in all national and Europol files after a period of one month, unless the data are required for the purposes of the specific ongoing criminal investigation for which they were requested by a Member State or by Europol.

*Article 34*

**Data security**

1. The Member State of origin shall ensure the security of the data before and during transmission to the Central System.

2. Each Member State shall, in relation to all data processed by its competent authorities pursuant to this Regulation, adopt the necessary measures, including a security plan, in order to:

(a) physically protect the data, including by making contingency plans for the protection of critical infrastructure;

(b) deny unauthorised persons access to national installations in which the Member State carries out operations in accordance with the purposes of Eurodac (checks at entrance to the installation);

(c) prevent the unauthorised reading, copying, modification or removal of data media (data media control);

(d) prevent the unauthorised input of data and the unauthorised inspection, modification or erasure of stored personal data (storage control);

(e) prevent the unauthorised processing of data in Eurodac and any unauthorised modification or erasure of data processed in Eurodac (control of data entry);

(f) ensure that persons authorised to access Eurodac have access only to the data covered by their access authorisation, by means of individual and unique user IDs and confidential access modes only (data access control);

(g) ensure that all authorities with a right of access to Eurodac create profiles describing the functions and responsibilities of persons who are authorised to access, enter, update, erase and search the data, and make those profiles and any other relevant information which those authorities may require for supervisory purposes available to the national supervisory authorities referred to in Article 28 of Directive 95/46/EC and in Article 25 of Framework Decision 2008/977/JHA without delay at their request (personnel profiles);

(h) ensure that it is possible to verify and establish to which bodies personal data may be transmitted using data communication equipment (communication control);

(i) ensure that it is possible to verify and establish what data have been processed in Eurodac, when, by whom and for what purpose (control of data recording);

(j) prevent the unauthorised reading, copying, modification or erasure of personal data during the transmission of personal data to or from Eurodac or during the transport of data media, in particular by means of appropriate encryption techniques (transport control);

(k) monitor the effectiveness of the security measures referred to in this paragraph and take the necessary organisational measures related to internal monitoring in order to ensure compliance with this Regulation (self-auditing) and to automatically detect within 24 hours any relevant events arising from the application of measures listed in points (b) to (j) that might indicate the occurrence of a security incident.

3. Member States shall inform the Agency of security incidents detected on their systems. The Agency shall inform the Member States, Europol and the European Data Protection Supervisor in case of security incidents. The Member States concerned, the Agency and Europol shall collaborate during a security incident.

4. The Agency shall take the necessary measures in order to achieve the objectives set out in paragraph 2 as regards the operation of Eurodac, including the adoption of a security plan.

*Article 35*

**Prohibition of transfers of data to third countries, international organisations or private entities**

1. Personal data obtained by a Member State or Europol pursuant to this Regulation from the Central System shall not be transferred or made available to any third country, international organisation or private entity established in or outside the Union. This prohibition shall also apply if those data are further processed at national level or between Member States within the meaning of Article 2(b) of Framework Decision 2008/977/JHA.

2. Personal data which originated in a Member State and are exchanged between Member States following a hit obtained for the purposes laid down in Article 1(2) shall not be transferred to third countries if there is a serious risk that as a result of such transfer the data subject may be subjected to torture, inhuman and degrading treatment or punishment or any other violation of his or her fundamental rights.

3. The prohibitions referred to in paragraphs 1 and 2 shall be without prejudice to the right of Member States to transfer such data to third countries to which Regulation (EU) No 604/2013 applies.

*Article 36*

**Logging and documentation**

1. Each Member State and Europol shall ensure that all data processing operations resulting from requests for comparison with Eurodac data for the purposes laid down in Article 1(2) are logged or documented for the purposes of checking the admissibility of the request, monitoring the lawfulness of the data processing and data integrity and security, and self-monitoring.

2. The log or documentation shall show in all cases:

(a) the exact purpose of the request for comparison, including the concerned form of a terrorist offence or other serious criminal offence and, for Europol, the exact purpose of the request for comparison;

(b) the reasonable grounds given not to conduct comparisons with other Member States under Decision 2008/615/JHA, in accordance with Article 20(1) of this Regulation;

(c) the national file reference;

(d) the date and exact time of the request for comparison by the National Access Point to the Central System;

(e) the name of the authority having requested access for comparison, and the person responsible who made the request and processed the data;

(f) where applicable, the use of the urgent procedure referred to in Article 19(3) and the decision taken with regard to the ex-post verification;

(g) the data used for comparison;

(h) in accordance with national rules or with Decision 2009/371/JHA, the identifying mark of the official who carried out the search and of the official who ordered the search or supply.

3. Logs and documentation shall be used only for monitoring the lawfulness of data processing and for ensuring data integrity and security. Only logs containing non-personal data may be used for the monitoring and evaluation referred to in Article 40. The competent national supervisory authorities responsible for checking the admissibility of the request and monitoring the lawfulness of the data processing and data integrity and security shall have access to these logs at their request for the purpose of fulfilling their duties.

*Article 37*

**Liability**

1. Any person who, or Member State which, has suffered damage as a result of an unlawful processing operation or any act incompatible with this Regulation shall be entitled to receive compensation from the Member State responsible for the damage suffered. That State shall be exempted from its liability, in whole or in part, if it proves that it is not responsible for the event giving rise to the damage.

2. If the failure of a Member State to comply with its obligations under this Regulation causes damage to the Central System, that Member State shall be liable for such damage, unless and insofar as the Agency or another Member State failed to take reasonable steps to prevent the damage from occurring or to minimise its impact.

3. Claims for compensation against a Member State for the damage referred to in paragraphs 1 and 2 shall be governed by the provisions of national law of the defendant Member State.

CHAPTER VIII

**AMENDMENTS TO REGULATION (EU) NO 1077/2011**

*Article 38*

**Amendments to Regulation (EU) No 1077/2011**

Regulation (EU) No 1077/2011 is amended as follows:

(1) Article 5 is replaced by the following:

"*Article 5*

*Tasks relating to Eurodac*

In relation to Eurodac, the Agency shall perform:

(a) the tasks conferred on it by Regulation (EU) No 603/2013 of the European Parliament and of the Council of 26 June 2013 on the establishment of 'Eurodac' for the comparison of fingerprints for the effective application of Regulation (EU) No 604/2013 establishing the criteria and mechanisms for determining the Member State responsible for examining an application for international protection lodged in one of the Member States by a third-country national or a stateless person), and on requests for the comparison with Eurodac data by Member States' law enforcement authorities and Europol for law enforcement purposes (*); and

(b) tasks relating to training on the technical use of Eurodac.

(*) OJ L 180, 29.6.2013, p. 1.";

(2) Article 12(1) is amended as follows:

(a) points (u) and (v) are replaced by the following:

"(u) adopt the annual report on the activities of the Central System of Eurodac pursuant to Article 40(1) of Regulation (EU) No 603/2013;

(v) make comments on the European Data Protection Supervisor's reports on the audits pursuant to Article 45(2) of Regulation (EC) No 1987/2006, Article 42(2) of Regulation (EC) No 767/2008 and Article 31(2) of Regulation (EU) No 603/2013 and ensure appropriate follow-up of those audits;";

(b) point (x) is replaced by the following:

"(x) compile statistics on the work of the Central System of Eurodac pursuant to Article 8(2) of Regulation (EU) No 603/2013;";

(c) point (z) is replaced by the following:

"(z) ensure annual publication of the list of units pursuant to Article 27(2) of Regulation (EU) No 603/2013;";

(3) Article 15(4) is replaced by the following:

"4. Europol and Eurojust may attend the meetings of the Management Board as observers when a question concerning SIS II, in relation to the application of Decision 2007/533/JHA, is on the agenda. Europol may also attend the meetings of the Management Board as observer when a question concerning VIS, in relation to the application of Decision 2008/633/JHA, or a question concerning Eurodac, in relation to the application of Regulation (EU) No 603/2013, is on the agenda.";

(4) Article 17 is amended as follows:

(a) in paragraph 5, point (g) is replaced by the following:

"(g) without prejudice to Article 17 of the Staff Regulations, establish confidentiality requirements in order to comply with Article 17 of Regulation (EC) No 1987/2006, Article 17 of Decision 2007/533/JHA, Article 26(9) of Regulation (EC) No 767/2008 and Article 4(4) of Regulation (EU) No 603/2013;";

(b) in paragraph 6, point (i) is replaced by the following:

"(i) reports on the technical functioning of each large-scale IT system referred to in Article 12(1)(t) and the annual report on the activities of the Central System of Eurodac referred to in Article 12(1)(u), on the basis of the results of monitoring and evaluation.";

(5) Article 19(3) is replaced by the following:

"3. Europol and Eurojust may each appoint a representative to the SIS II Advisory Group. Europol may also appoint a representative to the VIS and Eurodac Advisory Groups.".

## CHAPTER IX

## FINAL PROVISIONS

*Article 39*

### Costs

1. The costs incurred in connection with the establishment and operation of the Central System and the Communication Infrastructure shall be borne by the general budget of the European Union.

2. The costs incurred by national access points and the costs for connection to the Central System shall be borne by each Member State.

3. Each Member State and Europol shall set up and maintain at their expense the technical infrastructure necessary to implement this Regulation, and shall be responsible for bearing its costs resulting from requests for comparison with Eurodac data for the purposes laid down in Article 1(2)

*Article 40*

### Annual report: monitoring and evaluation

1. The Agency shall submit to the European Parliament, the Council, the Commission and the European Data Protection Supervisor an annual report on the activities of the Central System, including on its technical functioning and security. The annual report shall include information on the management and performance of Eurodac against pre-defined quantitative indicators for the objectives referred to in paragraph 2.

2. The Agency shall ensure that procedures are in place to monitor the functioning of the Central System against objectives relating to output, cost-effectiveness and quality of service.

3. For the purposes of technical maintenance, reporting and statistics, the Agency shall have access to the necessary information relating to the processing operations performed in the Central System.

4. By 20 July 2018 and every four years thereafter, the Commission shall produce an overall evaluation of Eurodac, examining the results achieved against objectives and the impact on fundamental rights, including whether law enforcement access has led to indirect discrimination against persons covered by this Regulation, and assessing the continuing validity of the underlying rationale and any implications for future operations, and shall make any necessary recommendations. The Commission shall transmit the evaluation to the European Parliament and the Council.

5. Member States shall provide the Agency and the Commission with the information necessary to draft the annual report referred to in paragraph 1.

6. The Agency, Member States and Europol shall provide the Commission with the information necessary to draft the overall evaluation provided for in paragraph 4. This information shall not jeopardise working methods or include information that reveals sources, staff members or investigations of the designated authorities.

7. While respecting the provisions of national law on the publication of sensitive information, each Member State and Europol shall prepare annual reports on the effectiveness of the comparison of fingerprint data with Eurodac data for law enforcement purposes, containing information and statistics on:

— the exact purpose of the comparison, including the type of terrorist offence or serious criminal offence,

— grounds given for reasonable suspicion,

— the reasonable grounds given not to conduct comparison with other Member States under Decision 2008/615/JHA, in accordance with Article 20(1) of this Regulation,

— number of requests for comparison,

— the number and type of cases which have ended in successful identifications, and

— the need and use made of the exceptional case of urgency, including those cases where that urgency was not accepted by the ex post verification carried out by the verifying authority.

Member States' and Europol annual reports shall be transmitted to the Commission by 30 June of the subsequent year.

8. On the basis of Member States and Europol annual reports provided for in paragraph 7 and in addition to the overall evaluation provided for in paragraph 4, the Commission shall compile an annual report on law enforcement access to Eurodac and shall transmit it to the European Parliament, the Council and the European Data Protection Supervisor.

*Article 41*

**Penalties**

Member States shall take the necessary measures to ensure that any processing of data entered in the Central System contrary to the purposes of Eurodac as laid down in Article 1 is punishable by penalties, including administrative and/or criminal penalties in accordance with national law, that are effective, proportionate and dissuasive.

*Article 42*

**Territorial scope**

The provisions of this Regulation shall not be applicable to any territory to which Regulation (EU) No 604/2013 does not apply.

*Article 43*

**Notification of designated authorities and verifying authorities**

1. By 20 October 2013, each Member State shall notify the Commission of its designated authorities, of the operating units referred to in Article 5(3) and of its verifying authority, and shall notify without delay any amendment thereto.

2. By 20 October 2013, Europol shall notify the Commission of its designated authority, of its verifying authority and of the National Access Point which it has designated, and shall notify without delay any amendment thereto.

3. The Commission shall publish the information referred to in paragraphs 1 and 2 in the *Official Journal of the European Union* on an annual basis and via an electronic publication that shall be available online and updated without delay.

*Article 44*

**Transitional provision**

Data blocked in the Central System in accordance with Article 12 of Regulation (EC) No 2725/2000 shall be unblocked and marked in accordance with Article 18(1) of this Regulation on 20 July 2015.

*Article 45*

**Repeal**

Regulation (EC) No 2725/2000 and Regulation (EC) No 407/2002 are repealed with effect from 20 July 2015.

References to the repealed Regulations shall be construed as references to this Regulation and shall be read in accordance with the correlation table in Annex III.

29.6.2013 EN Official Journal of the European Union L 180/25

*Article 46*

**Entry into force and applicability**

This Regulation shall enter into force on the twentieth day following that of its publication in the *Official Journal of the European Union*.

This Regulation shall apply from 20 July 2015.

Member States shall notify the Commission and the Agency as soon as they have made the technical arrangements to transmit data to the Central System, and in any event no later than 20 July 2015.

This Regulation shall be binding in its entirety and directly applicable in the Member States in accordance with the Treaties.

Done at Brussels, 26 June 2013.

*For the European Parliament*
*The President*
M. SCHULZ

*For the Council*
*The President*
A. SHATTER

*ANNEX I*

**Data format and fingerprint form**

Data format for the exchange of fingerprint data

The following format is prescribed for the exchange of fingerprint data:

ANSI/NIST-ITL 1a-1997, Ver.3, June 2001 (INT-1) and any future further developments of this standard.

Norm for Member State identification letters

The following ISO norm will apply: ISO 3166 - 2 letters code.

# Eurodac – Fingerprint form

105 mm from top of form

155 mm from top of form

205 mm from top of form

| | | |
|---|---|---|
| 1. | Reference number | |
| 2. | Place of the application for international protection or place where the third country national or stateless person was apprehended | |
| 3. | Date of the application for international protection or date on which the third country national or stateless person was apprehended | |
| 4. | Sex | |
| 5. | Date on which the fingerprints were taken | |
| 6. | Date on which the data where transmitted to the Central System | |

## ROLLED IMPRESSIONS

| 1. Right thumb | 2. Right forefinger | 3. Right middle finger | 4. Right ring finger | 5. Right little finger |
|---|---|---|---|---|
| 50 mm<br>40 mm | 40 mm | 40 mm | 40 mm | 40 mm |
| 6. Left thumb | 7. Left forefinger | 8. Left middle finger | 9. Left ring finger | 10. Left little finger |
| 40 mm | | | | |

## PLAIN IMPRESSIONS

| LEFT HAND Four fingers taken simultaneously | TWO THUMBS Impressions taken simultaneously | | RIGHT HAND Four fingers taken simultaneously |
|---|---|---|---|
| | LEFT | RIGHT | |
| 75 mm<br>65 mm | 30 mm<br>55 mm | 30 mm | 75 mm |

*ANNEX II*

**Repealed Regulations (referred to in Article 45)**

| | |
|---|---|
| Council Regulation (EC) No 2725/2000 | (OJ L 316, 15.12.2000, p. 1.) |
| Council Regulation (EC) No 407/2002 | (OJ L 62, 5.3.2002 p. 1.) |

*ANNEX III*

**Correlation table**

| Regulation (EC) No 2725/2000 | This Regulation |
|---|---|
| Article 1(1) | Article 1(1) |
| Article 1(2), first subparagraph, points (a) and (b) | Article 3(1)(a) |
| Article 1(2), first subparagraph, point (c) | — |
| Article 1(2), second subparagraph | Article 3(4) |
| Article 1(3) | Article 1(3) |
| Article 2(1)(a) | — |
| Article 2(1)(b) to (e) | Article 2(1)(a) to (d) |
| — | Article 2(1)(e) to (j) |
| Article 3(1) | — |
| Article 3(2) | Article 3(3) |
| Article 3(3)(a) to (e) | Article 8(1)(a) to (e) |
| — | Article 8(1)(f) to (i) |
| Article 3(4) | — |
| Article 4(1) | Article 9(1) and Article 3(5) |
| Article 4(2) | — |
| Article 4(3) | Article 9(3) |
| Article 4(4) | Article 9(4) |
| Article 4(5) | Article 9(5) |
| Article 4(6) | Article 25(4) |
| Article 5(1), points (a) to (f) | Article 11, points (a) to (f) |
| — | Article 11, points (g) to (k) |
| Article 5(1), points (g) and (h) | — |
| Article 6 | Article 12 |
| Article 7 | Article 13 |
| Article 8 | Article 14 |
| Article 9 | Article 15 |
| Article 10 | Article 16 |
| Article 11(1) to (3) | Article 17(1) to (3) |
| Article 11(4) | Article 17(5) |
| Article 11(5) | Article 17(4) |
| Article 12 | Article 18 |
| Article 13 | Article 23 |
| Article 14 | — |

| Regulation (EC) No 2725/2000 | This Regulation |
|---|---|
| Article 15 | Article 27 |
| Article 16 | Article 28(1) and (2) |
| — | Article 28(3) |
| Article 17 | Article 37 |
| Article 18 | Article 29(1), (2), (4) to (10) and (12) to (15) |
| — | Article 29(3) and (11) |
| Article 19 | Article 30 |
| — | Articles 31 to 36 |
| Article 20 | — |
| Article 21 | Article 39(1) and (2) |
| Article 22 | — |
| Article 23 | — |
| Article 24(1) and (2) | Article 40(1) and (2) |
| — | Article 40(3) to (8) |
| Article 25 | Article 41 |
| Article 26 | Article 42 |
| — | Articles 43 to 45 |
| Article 27 | Article 46 |

| Regulation 407/2002/EC | This Regulation |
|---|---|
| Article 2 | Article 24 |
| Article 3 | Article 25(1) to (3) |
| — | Article 25(4) and (5) |
| Article 4 | Article 26 |
| Article 5(1) | Article 3(3) |
| Annex I | Annex I |
| Annex II | — |

# Directive 2013/40 on attacks against information systems and replacing Framework Decision 2005/222, 12 August 2013

[OJ 2013, L 218/8–14]

Effective 1 July 2013, the electronic version of the *Official Journal* (e-OJ) is authentic and produces legal effects.

L 218/8 EN Official Journal of the European Union 14.8.2013

# DIRECTIVE 2013/40/EU OF THE EUROPEAN PARLIAMENT AND OF THE COUNCIL

## of 12 August 2013

## on attacks against information systems and replacing Council Framework Decision 2005/222/JHA

THE EUROPEAN PARLIAMENT AND THE COUNCIL OF THE EUROPEAN UNION,

Having regard to the Treaty on the Functioning of the European Union, and in particular Article 83(1) thereof,

Having regard to the proposal from the European Commission,

After transmission of the draft legislative act to the national parliaments,

Having regard to the opinion of the European Economic and Social Committee [1],

Acting in accordance with the ordinary legislative procedure [2],

Whereas:

(1) The objectives of this Directive are to approximate the criminal law of the Member States in the area of attacks against information systems by establishing minimum rules concerning the definition of criminal offences and the relevant sanctions and to improve cooperation between competent authorities, including the police and other specialised law enforcement services of the Member States, as well as the competent specialised Union agencies and bodies, such as Eurojust, Europol and its European Cyber Crime Centre, and the European Network and Information Security Agency (ENISA).

(2) Information systems are a key element of political, social and economic interaction in the Union. Society is highly and increasingly dependent on such systems. The smooth operation and security of those systems in the Union is vital for the development of the internal market and of a competitive and innovative economy. Ensuring an appropriate level of protection of information systems should form part of an effective comprehensive framework of prevention measures accompanying criminal law responses to cybercrime.

(3) Attacks against information systems, and, in particular, attacks linked to organised crime, are a growing menace in the Union and globally, and there is increasing concern about the potential for terrorist or politically motivated attacks against information systems which form part of the critical infrastructure of Member States and of the Union. This constitutes a threat to the achievement of a safer information society and of an area of freedom, security, and justice, and therefore requires a response at Union level and improved cooperation and coordination at international level.

(4) There are a number of critical infrastructures in the Union, the disruption or destruction of which would have a significant cross-border impact. It has become apparent from the need to increase the critical infrastructure protection capability in the Union that the measures against cyber attacks should be complemented by stringent criminal penalties reflecting the gravity of such attacks. Critical infrastructure could be understood to be an asset, system or part thereof located in Member States, which is essential for the maintenance of vital societal functions, health, safety, security, economic or social well-being of people, such as power plants, transport networks or government networks, and the disruption or destruction of which would have a significant impact in a Member State as a result of the failure to maintain those functions.

(5) There is evidence of a tendency towards increasingly dangerous and recurrent large-scale attacks conducted against information systems which can often be critical to Member States or to particular functions in the public or private sector. This tendency is accompanied by the development of increasingly sophisticated methods, such as the creation and use of so-called 'botnets', which involves several stages of a criminal act, where each stage alone could pose a serious risk to public interests. This Directive aims, inter alia, to introduce criminal penalties for the creation of botnets, namely, the act of establishing remote control over a significant number of computers by infecting them with malicious software through targeted cyber attacks. Once created, the infected network of computers that constitute the botnet can be activated without the computer users' knowledge in order to launch a large-scale cyber attack, which usually has the capacity to cause serious damage, as referred to in this Directive. Member States may determine what constitutes serious damage according to their national law and practice, such as disrupting system services of significant public importance, or causing major financial cost or loss of personal data or sensitive information.

(6) Large-scale cyber attacks can cause substantial economic damage both through the interruption of information systems and communication and through the loss or alteration of commercially important confidential information or other data. Particular attention should be paid to raising the awareness of innovative small and medium-sized enterprises to threats relating to such attacks and their vulnerability to such attacks, due to their increased dependence on the proper functioning and availability of information systems and often limited resources for information security.

[1] OJ C 218, 23.7.2011, p. 130.
[2] Position of the European Parliament of 4 July 2013 (not yet published in the Official Journal) and decision of the Council of 22 July 2013.

(7) Common definitions in this area are important in order to ensure a consistent approach in the Member States to the application of this Directive.

(8) There is a need to achieve a common approach to the constituent elements of criminal offences by introducing common offences of illegal access to an information system, illegal system interference, illegal data interference, and illegal interception.

(9) Interception includes, but is not necessarily limited to, the listening to, monitoring or surveillance of the content of communications and the procuring of the content of data either directly, through access and use of the information systems, or indirectly through the use of electronic eavesdropping or tapping devices by technical means.

(10) Member States should provide for penalties in respect of attacks against information systems. Those penalties should be effective, proportionate and dissuasive and should include imprisonment and/or fines.

(11) This Directive provides for criminal penalties at least for cases which are not minor. Member States may determine what constitutes a minor case according to their national law and practice. A case may be considered minor, for example, where the damage caused by the offence and/or the risk to public or private interests, such as to the integrity of a computer system or to computer data, or to the integrity, rights or other interests of a person, is insignificant or is of such a nature that the imposition of a criminal penalty within the legal threshold or the imposition of criminal liability is not necessary.

(12) The identification and reporting of threats and risks posed by cyber attacks and the related vulnerability of information systems is a pertinent element of effective prevention of, and response to, cyber attacks and to improving the security of information systems. Providing incentives to report security gaps could add to that effect. Member States should endeavour to provide possibilities for the legal detection and reporting of security gaps.

(13) It is appropriate to provide for more severe penalties where an attack against an information system is committed by a criminal organisation, as defined in Council Framework Decision 2008/841/JHA of 24 October 2008 on the fight against organised crime ([1]), where a cyber attack is conducted on a large scale, thus affecting a significant number of information systems, including where it is intended to create a botnet, or where a cyber attack causes serious damage, including where it is carried out through a botnet. It is also appropriate to provide for more severe penalties where an attack is conducted against a critical infrastructure of the Member States or of the Union.

(14) Setting up effective measures against identity theft and other identity-related offences constitutes another important element of an integrated approach against cybercrime. Any need for Union action against this type of criminal behaviour could also be considered in the context of evaluating the need for a comprehensive horizontal Union instrument.

(15) The Council Conclusions of 27 to 28 November 2008 indicated that a new strategy should be developed with the Member States and the Commission, taking into account the content of the 2001 Council of Europe Convention on Cybercrime. That Convention is the legal framework of reference for combating cybercrime, including attacks against information systems. This Directive builds on that Convention. Completing the process of ratification of that Convention by all Member States as soon as possible should be considered to be a priority.

(16) Given the different ways in which attacks can be conducted, and given the rapid developments in hardware and software, this Directive refers to tools that can be used in order to commit the offences laid down in this Directive. Such tools could include malicious software, including those able to create botnets, used to commit cyber attacks. Even where such a tool is suitable or particularly suitable for carrying out one of the offences laid down in this Directive, it is possible that it was produced for a legitimate purpose Motivated by the need to avoid criminalisation where such tools are produced and put on the market for legitimate purposes, such as to test the reliability of information technology products or the security of information systems, apart from the general intent requirement, a direct intent requirement that those tools be used to commit one or more of the offences laid down in this Directive must be also fulfilled.

(17) This Directive does not impose criminal liability where the objective criteria of the offences laid down in this Directive are met but the acts are committed without criminal intent, for instance where a person does not know that access was unauthorised or in the case of mandated testing or protection of information systems, such as where a person is assigned by a company or vendor to test the strength of its security system. In the context of this Directive, contractual obligations or agreements to restrict access to information systems by way of a user policy or terms of service, as well as labour disputes as regards the access to and use of information systems of an employer for private purposes, should not incur criminal liability where the access under such circumstances would be deemed unauthorised and thus would constitute the sole basis for criminal proceedings. This Directive is without prejudice to the right of access to information as laid down in national and Union law, while at the same time it may not serve as a justification for unlawful or arbitrary access to information.

([1]) OJ L 300, 11.11.2008, p. 42.

(18) Cyber attacks could be facilitated by various circumstances, such as where the offender has access to security systems inherent in the affected information systems within the scope of his or her employment. In the context of national law, such circumstances should be taken into account in the course of criminal proceedings as appropriate.

(19) Member States should provide for aggravating circumstances in their national law in accordance with the applicable rules established by their legal systems on aggravating circumstances. They should ensure that those aggravating circumstances are available for judges to consider when sentencing offenders. It remains within the discretion of the judge to assess those circumstances together with the other facts of the particular case.

(20) This Directive does not govern conditions for exercising jurisdiction over any of the offences referred to herein, such as a report by the victim in the place where the offence was committed, a denunciation from the State of the place where the offence was committed, or the non-prosecution of the offender in the place where the offence was committed.

(21) In the context of this Directive, States and public bodies remain fully bound to guarantee respect for human rights and fundamental freedoms, in accordance with existing international obligations.

(22) This Directive strengthens the importance of networks, such as the G8 or the Council of Europe's network of points of contact available on a 24 hour, seven-day-a-week basis. Those points of contact should be able to deliver effective assistance thus, for example, facilitating the exchange of relevant information available and the provision of technical advice or legal information for the purpose of investigations or proceedings concerning criminal offences relating to information systems and associated data involving the requesting Member State. In order to ensure the smooth operation of the networks, each contact point should have the capacity to communicate with the point of contact of another Member State on an expedited basis with the support, inter alia, of trained and equipped personnel. Given the speed with which large-scale cyber attacks can be carried out, Member States should be able to respond promptly to urgent requests from this network of contact points. In such cases, it may be expedient that the request for information be accompanied by telephone contact in order to ensure that the request is processed swiftly by the requested Member State and that feedback is provided within eight hours.

(23) Cooperation between public authorities on the one hand, and the private sector and civil society on the other, is of great importance in preventing and combating attacks against information systems. It is necessary to foster and improve cooperation between service providers, producers, law enforcement bodies and judicial authorities, while fully respecting the rule of law. Such cooperation could include support by service providers in helping to preserve potential evidence, in providing elements helping to identify offenders and, as a last resort, in shutting down, completely or partially, in accordance with national law and practice, information systems or functions that have been compromised or used for illegal purposes. Member States should also consider setting up cooperation and partnership networks with service providers and producers for the exchange of information in relation to the offences within the scope of this Directive.

(24) There is a need to collect comparable data on the offences laid down in this Directive. Relevant data should be made available to the competent specialised Union agencies and bodies, such as Europol and ENISA, in line with their tasks and information needs, in order to gain a more complete picture of the problem of cybercrime and network and information security at Union level and thereby to contribute to formulating a more effective response. Member States should submit information on the modus operandi of the offenders to Europol and its European Cybercrime Centre for the purpose of conducting threat assessments and strategic analyses of cybercrime in accordance with Council Decision 2009/371/JHA of 6 April 2009 establishing the European Police Office (Europol) ([1]). Providing information can facilitate a better understanding of present and future threats and thus contribute to more appropriate and targeted decision-making on combating and preventing attacks against information systems.

(25) The Commission should submit a report on the application of this Directive and make necessary legislative proposals which could lead to broadening its scope, taking into account developments in the field of cybercrime. Such developments could include technological developments, for example those enabling more effective enforcement in the area of attacks against information systems or facilitating prevention or minimising the impact of such attacks. For that purpose, the Commission should take into account the available analyses and reports produced by relevant actors and, in particular, Europol and ENISA.

(26) In order to fight cybercrime effectively, it is necessary to increase the resilience of information systems by taking appropriate measures to protect them more effectively against cyber attacks. Member States should take the necessary measures to protect their critical infrastructure from cyber attacks, as part of which they should consider the protection of their information systems and associated data. Ensuring an adequate level of protection

([1]) OJ L 121, 15.5.2009, p. 37.

and security of information systems by legal persons, for example in connection with the provision of publicly available electronic communications services in accordance with existing Union legislation on privacy and electronic communication and data protection, forms an essential part of a comprehensive approach to effectively counteracting cybercrime. Appropriate levels of protection should be provided against reasonably identifiable threats and vulnerabilities in accordance with the state of the art for specific sectors and the specific data processing situations. The cost and burden of such protection should be proportionate to the likely damage a cyber attack would cause to those affected. Member States are encouraged to provide for relevant measures incurring liabilities in the context of their national law in cases where a legal person has clearly not provided an appropriate level of protection against cyber attacks.

(27) Significant gaps and differences in Member States' laws and criminal procedures in the area of attacks against information systems may hamper the fight against organised crime and terrorism, and may complicate effective police and judicial cooperation in this area. The transnational and borderless nature of modern information systems means that attacks against such systems have a cross-border dimension, thus underlining the urgent need for further action to approximate criminal law in this area. In addition, the coordination of prosecution of cases of attacks against information systems should be facilitated by the adequate implementation and application of Council Framework Decision 2009/948/JHA of 30 November 2009 on prevention and settlement of conflict of jurisdiction in criminal proceedings [1]. Member States, in cooperation with the Union, should also seek to improve international cooperation relating to the security of information systems, computer networks and computer data. Proper consideration of the security of data transfer and storage should be given in any international agreement involving data exchange.

(28) Improved cooperation between the competent law enforcement bodies and judicial authorities across the Union is essential in an effective fight against cybercrime. In this context, stepping up the efforts to provide adequate training to the relevant authorities in order to raise the understanding of cybercrime and its impact, and to foster cooperation and the exchange of best practices, for example via the competent specialised Union agencies and bodies, should be encouraged. Such training should, inter alia, aim at raising awareness about the different national legal systems, the possible legal and technical challenges of criminal investigations, and the distribution of competences between the relevant national authorities.

(29) This Directive respects human rights and fundamental freedoms and observes the principles recognised in particular by the Charter of Fundamental Rights of the European Union and the European Convention for the Protection of Human Rights and Fundamental Freedoms, including the protection of personal data, the right to privacy, freedom of expression and information, the right to a fair trial, the presumption of innocence and the rights of the defence, as well as the principles of legality and proportionality of criminal offences and penalties. In particular, this Directive seeks to ensure full respect for those rights and principles and must be implemented accordingly.

(30) The protection of personal data is a fundamental right in accordance with Article 16(1) TFEU and Article 8 of the Charter on Fundamental Rights of the European Union. Therefore, any processing of personal data in the context of the implementation of this Directive should fully comply with the relevant Union law on data protection.

(31) In accordance with Article 3 of the Protocol on the position of the United Kingdom and Ireland in respect of the Area of Freedom, Security and Justice, annexed to the Treaty on European Union and to the Treaty on the Functioning of the European Union, those Member States have notified their wish to take part in the adoption and application of this Directive.

(32) In accordance with Articles 1 and 2 of the Protocol on the position of Denmark annexed to the Treaty on European Union and to the Treaty on the Functioning of the European Union, Denmark is not taking part in the adoption of this Directive and is not bound by it or subject to its application.

(33) Since the objectives of this Directive, namely to subject attacks against information systems in all Member States to effective, proportionate and dissuasive criminal penalties and to improve and encourage cooperation between judicial and other competent authorities, cannot be sufficiently achieved by the Member States, and can therefore, by reason of their scale or effects, be better achieved at Union level, the Union may adopt measures in accordance with the principle of subsidiarity as set out in Article 5 of the Treaty on European Union. In accordance with the principle of proportionality, as set out in that Article, this Directive does not go beyond what is necessary in order to achieve those objectives.

(34) This Directive aims to amend and expand the provisions of Council Framework Decision 2005/222/JHA of 24 February 2005 on attacks against information systems [2]. Since the amendments to be made are of substantial number and nature, Framework Decision 2005/222/JHA should, in the interests of clarity, be replaced in its entirety in relation to Member States participating in the adoption of this Directive,

(1) OJ L 328, 15.12.2009, p. 42.

(2) OJ L 69, 16.3.2005, p. 67.

L 218/12 EN Official Journal of the European Union 14.8.2013

HAVE ADOPTED THIS DIRECTIVE:

*Article 1*

**Subject matter**

This Directive establishes minimum rules concerning the definition of criminal offences and sanctions in the area of attacks against information systems. It also aims to facilitate the prevention of such offences and to improve cooperation between judicial and other competent authorities.

*Article 2*

**Definitions**

For the purposes of this Directive, the following definitions shall apply:

(a) 'information system' means a device or group of inter-connected or related devices, one or more of which, pursuant to a programme, automatically processes computer data, as well as computer data stored, processed, retrieved or transmitted by that device or group of devices for the purposes of its or their operation, use, protection and maintenance;

(b) 'computer data' means a representation of facts, information or concepts in a form suitable for processing in an information system, including a programme suitable for causing an information system to perform a function;

(c) 'legal person' means an entity having the status of legal person under the applicable law, but does not include States or public bodies acting in the exercise of State authority, or public international organisations;

(d) 'without right' means conduct referred to in this Directive, including access, interference, or interception, which is not authorised by the owner or by another right holder of the system or of part of it, or not permitted under national law.

*Article 3*

**Illegal access to information systems**

Member States shall take the necessary measures to ensure that, when committed intentionally, the access without right, to the whole or to any part of an information system, is punishable as a criminal offence where committed by infringing a security measure, at least for cases which are not minor.

*Article 4*

**Illegal system interference**

Member States shall take the necessary measures to ensure that seriously hindering or interrupting the functioning of an information system by inputting computer data, by transmitting, damaging, deleting, deteriorating, altering or suppressing such data, or by rendering such data inaccessible, intentionally and without right, is punishable as a criminal offence, at least for cases which are not minor.

*Article 5*

**Illegal data interference**

Member States shall take the necessary measures to ensure that deleting, damaging, deteriorating, altering or suppressing computer data on an information system, or rendering such data inaccessible, intentionally and without right, is punishable as a criminal offence, at least for cases which are not minor.

*Article 6*

**Illegal interception**

Member States shall take the necessary measures to ensure that intercepting, by technical means, non-public transmissions of computer data to, from or within an information system, including electromagnetic emissions from an information system carrying such computer data, intentionally and without right, is punishable as a criminal offence, at least for cases which are not minor.

*Article 7*

**Tools used for committing offences**

Member States shall take the necessary measures to ensure that the intentional production, sale, procurement for use, import, distribution or otherwise making available, of one of the following tools, without right and with the intention that it be used to commit any of the offences referred to in Articles 3 to 6, is punishable as a criminal offence, at least for cases which are not minor:

(a) a computer programme, designed or adapted primarily for the purpose of committing any of the offences referred to in Articles 3 to 6;

(b) a computer password, access code, or similar data by which the whole or any part of an information system is capable of being accessed.

*Article 8*

**Incitement, aiding and abetting and attempt**

1. Member States shall ensure that the incitement, or aiding and abetting, to commit an offence referred to in Articles 3 to 7 is punishable as a criminal offence.

2. Member States shall ensure that the attempt to commit an offence referred to in Articles 4 and 5 is punishable as a criminal offence.

*Article 9*

**Penalties**

1. Member States shall take the necessary measures to ensure that the offences referred to in Articles 3 to 8 are punishable by effective, proportionate and dissuasive criminal penalties.

2. Member States shall take the necessary measures to ensure that the offences referred to in Articles 3 to 7 are punishable by a maximum term of imprisonment of at least two years, at least for cases which are not minor.

3. Member States shall take the necessary measures to ensure that the offences referred to in Articles 4 and 5, when committed intentionally, are punishable by a maximum term of imprisonment of at least three years where a significant

number of information systems have been affected through the use of a tool, referred to in Article 7, designed or adapted primarily for that purpose.

4. Member States shall take the necessary measures to ensure that offences referred to in Articles 4 and 5 are punishable by a maximum term of imprisonment of at least five years where:

(a) they are committed within the framework of a criminal organisation, as defined in Framework Decision 2008/841/JHA, irrespective of the penalty provided for therein;

(b) they cause serious damage; or

(c) they are committed against a critical infrastructure information system.

5. Member States shall take the necessary measures to ensure that when the offences referred to in Articles 4 and 5 are committed by misusing the personal data of another person, with the aim of gaining the trust of a third party, thereby causing prejudice to the rightful identity owner, this may, in accordance with national law, be regarded as aggravating circumstances, unless those circumstances are already covered by another offence, punishable under national law.

*Article 10*

**Liability of legal persons**

1. Member States shall take the necessary measures to ensure that legal persons can be held liable for offences referred to in Articles 3 to 8, committed for their benefit by any person, acting either individually or as part of a body of the legal person, and having a leading position within the legal person, based on one of the following:

(a) a power of representation of the legal person;

(b) an authority to take decisions on behalf of the legal person;

(c) an authority to exercise control within the legal person.

2. Member States shall take the necessary measures to ensure that legal persons can be held liable where the lack of supervision or control by a person referred to in paragraph 1 has allowed the commission, by a person under its authority, of any of the offences referred to in Articles 3 to 8 for the benefit of that legal person.

3. The liability of legal persons under paragraphs 1 and 2 shall not exclude criminal proceedings against natural persons who are perpetrators or inciters of, or accessories to, any of the offences referred to in Articles 3 to 8.

*Article 11*

**Sanctions against legal persons**

1. Member States shall take the necessary measures to ensure that a legal person held liable pursuant to Article 10(1) is punishable by effective, proportionate and dissuasive sanctions, which shall include criminal or non-criminal fines and which may include other sanctions, such as:

(a) exclusion from entitlement to public benefits or aid;

(b) temporary or permanent disqualification from the practice of commercial activities;

(c) placing under judicial supervision;

(d) judicial winding-up;

(e) temporary or permanent closure of establishments which have been used for committing the offence.

2. Member States shall take the necessary measures to ensure that a legal person held liable pursuant to Article 10(2) is punishable by effective, proportionate and dissuasive sanctions or other measures.

*Article 12*

**Jurisdiction**

1. Member States shall establish their jurisdiction with regard to the offences referred to in Articles 3 to 8 where the offence has been committed:

(a) in whole or in part within their territory; or

(b) by one of their nationals, at least in cases where the act is an offence where it was committed.

2. When establishing jurisdiction in accordance with point (a) of paragraph 1, a Member State shall ensure that it has jurisdiction where:

(a) the offender commits the offence when physically present on its territory, whether or not the offence is against an information system on its territory; or

(b) the offence is against an information system on its territory, whether or not the offender commits the offence when physically present on its territory.

3. A Member State shall inform the Commission where it decides to establish jurisdiction over an offence referred to in Articles 3 to 8 committed outside its territory, including where:

(a) the offender has his or her habitual residence in its territory; or

(b) the offence is committed for the benefit of a legal person established in its territory.

*Article 13*

**Exchange of information**

1. For the purpose of exchanging information relating to the offences referred to in Articles 3 to 8, Member States shall ensure that they have an operational national point of contact and that they make use of the existing network of operational points of contact available 24 hours a day and seven days a week. Member States shall also ensure that they have procedures in place so that for urgent requests for assistance, the competent authority can indicate, within eight hours of receipt, at least whether the request will be answered, and the form and estimated time of such an answer.

L 218/14 EN Official Journal of the European Union 14.8.2013

2. Member States shall inform the Commission of their appointed point of contact referred to in paragraph 1. The Commission shall forward that information to the other Member States and competent specialised Union agencies and bodies.

3. Member States shall take the necessary measures to ensure that appropriate reporting channels are made available in order to facilitate the reporting of the offences referred to in Article 3 to 6 to the competent national authorities without undue delay.

*Article 14*

**Monitoring and statistics**

1. Member States shall ensure that a system is in place for the recording, production and provision of statistical data on the offences referred to in Articles 3 to 7.

2. The statistical data referred to in paragraph 1 shall, as a minimum, cover existing data on the number of offences referred to in Articles 3 to 7 registered by the Member States, and the number of persons prosecuted for and convicted of the offences referred to in Articles 3 to 7.

3. Member States shall transmit the data collected pursuant to this Article to the Commission. The Commission shall ensure that a consolidated review of the statistical reports is published and submitted to the competent specialised Union agencies and bodies.

*Article 15*

**Replacement of Framework Decision 2005/222/JHA**

Framework Decision 2005/222/JHA is hereby replaced in relation to Member States participating in the adoption of this Directive, without prejudice to the obligations of the Member States relating to the time limit for transposition of the Framework Decision into national law.

In relation to Member States participating in the adoption of this Directive, references to the Framework Decision 2005/222/JHA shall be construed as references to this Directive.

*Article 16*

**Transposition**

1. Member States shall bring into force the laws, regulations and administrative provisions necessary to comply with this Directive by 4 September 2015.

2. Member States shall transmit to the Commission the text of the measures transposing into their national law the obligations imposed on them under this Directive.

3. When Member States adopt those measures, they shall contain a reference to this Directive or shall be accompanied by such a reference on the occasion of their official publication. The methods of making such a reference shall be laid down by the Member States.

*Article 17*

**Reporting**

The Commission shall, by 4 September 2017, submit a report to the European Parliament and the Council, assessing the extent to which the Member States have taken the necessary measures in order to comply with this Directive, accompanied, if necessary, by legislative proposals. The Commission shall also take into account the technical and legal developments in the field of cybercrime, particularly with regard to the scope of this Directive.

*Article 18*

**Entry into force**

This Directive shall enter into force on the twentieth day following that of its publication in the *Official Journal of the European Union*.

*Article 19*

**Addressees**

This Directive is addressed to the Member States in accordance with the Treaties.

Done at Brussels, 12 August 2013.

| *For the European Parliament* | *For the Council* |
|---|---|
| *The President* | *The President* |
| M. SCHULZ | L. LINKEVIČIUS |

# Regulation 883/2013 concerning investigations conducted by the European Anti-Fraud Office (OLAF) and repealing Regulation (EC) No 1073/1999 of the European Parliament and of the Council and Council Regulation (Euratom) No 1074/1999, 11 September 2013

[OJ 2013, L 248/1–22]

Effective 1 July 2013, the electronic version of the *Official Journal* (e-OJ) is authentic and produces legal effects.

18.9.2013 EN Official Journal of the European Union L 248/1

I

*(Legislative acts)*

# REGULATIONS

## REGULATION (EU, EURATOM) No 883/2013 OF THE EUROPEAN PARLIAMENT AND OF THE COUNCIL

**of 11 September 2013**

**concerning investigations conducted by the European Anti-Fraud Office (OLAF) and repealing Regulation (EC) No 1073/1999 of the European Parliament and of the Council and Council Regulation (Euratom) No 1074/1999**

THE EUROPEAN PARLIAMENT AND THE COUNCIL OF THE EUROPEAN UNION,

Having regard to the Treaty on the Functioning of the European Union, and in particular Article 325 thereof, in conjunction with the Treaty establishing the European Atomic Energy Community, and in particular Article 106a thereof,

Having regard to the proposal from the European Commission,

After transmission of the draft legislative act to the national parliaments,

Having regard to the opinion of the Court of Auditors ([1]),

Acting in accordance with the ordinary legislative procedure ([2]),

Whereas:

(1) The Union institutions and the Member States attach great importance to the protection of the financial interests of the Union and to the fight against fraud, corruption and any other illegal activity affecting those interests. The Commission's responsibility in that connection is closely bound up with its duty to implement the budget pursuant to Article 317 of the Treaty on the Functioning of the European Union (TFEU) and the importance of action to that end is confirmed by Article 325 TFEU.

(2) All available means should be deployed fully to attain that objective, notably in the context of investigative duties devolving upon the Union, while the current distribution and balance of responsibilities between the Union and the Member States should be maintained.

(3) To reinforce the means available for combating fraud, while respecting the principle of each institution's internal organisational autonomy, the Commission, by Decision 1999/352/EC, ECSC, Euratom ([3]), has established the European Anti-Fraud Office ('the Office') among its own services with responsibility for conducting administrative fraud investigations. The Commission has given the Office full independence to exercise its investigative function. Decision 1999/352/EC, ECSC, Euratom provides that for the purposes of investigations the Office is to exercise the powers conferred by Union law.

(4) Regulation (EC) No 1073/1999 of the European Parliament and of the Council ([4]) was adopted to regulate investigations conducted by the Office. In order to make the Office's investigative activities more effective, and in the light of the evaluations of its activities made by the Union institutions, in particular the Commission's evaluation report of April 2003 and the Special Reports No 1/2005 ([5]) and No 2/2011 ([6]) of the Court of Auditors concerning the management of the Office, there is a need to revise the current legal framework.

---

([1]) OJ C 254, 30.8.2011, p. 1.

([2]) Position of the European Parliament of 20 November 2008 (OJ C 16 E, 22.1.2010, p. 201) and position of the Council at first reading of 25 February 2013 (OJ C 89 E, 27.3.2013, p. 1). Position of the European Parliament of 3 July 2013 (not yet published in the Official Journal).

([3]) Commission Decision 1999/352/EC, ECSC, Euratom of 28 April 1999 establishing the European Anti-fraud Office (OLAF) (OJ L 136, 31.5.1999, p. 20).

([4]) Regulation (EC) No 1073/1999 of the European Parliament and of the Council of 25 May 1999 concerning investigations conducted by the European Anti-Fraud Office (OLAF) (OJ L 136, 31.5.1999, p. 1).

([5]) OJ C 202, 18.8.2005, p. 1.

([6]) OJ C 124, 27.4.2011, p. 9.

(5) The Office's mandate should comprise the conduct of investigations within the institutions, bodies, offices and agencies established by, or on the basis of, the Treaties ('institutions, bodies, offices and agencies') and the exercise of the power of investigation conferred on the Commission by the relevant Union acts, as well as providing the Member States with assistance from the Commission in organising close and regular cooperation between their competent authorities. The Office should also contribute to the design and development of methods for preventing and combating fraud, corruption and any other illegal activity affecting the financial interests of the Union, based on its operational practice in this field.

(6) The responsibility of the Office as set up by the Commission also extends beyond the protection of financial interests to include all activities relating to safeguarding Union interests against irregular conduct liable to result in administrative or criminal proceedings.

(7) This Regulation should apply without prejudice to more extensive protection which may derive from the provisions of the Treaties.

(8) Given the need to step up the fight against fraud, corruption and any other illegal activity affecting the financial interests of the Union, the Office should be able to conduct internal investigations in all the institutions, bodies, offices and agencies.

(9) In the context of external investigations, the Office should be entrusted with the exercise of the powers conferred on the Commission by Council Regulation (Euratom, EC) No 2185/96 of 11 November 1996 concerning on-the-spot checks and inspections carried out by the Commission in order to protect the European Communities' financial interests against fraud and other irregularities [1]. The Office should also be allowed to exercise the other powers conferred on the Commission to conduct on-the-spot checks and inspections in the Member States, notably for the purpose of detecting irregularities as required by Article 9 of Council Regulation (EC, Euratom) No 2988/95 of 18 December 1995 on the protection of the European Communities' financial interests [2].

(10) The operational efficiency of the Office depends greatly on cooperation with the Member States. There is a need for the Member States to identify their competent authorities which are able to provide the Office with the assistance needed in the performance of its duties. In cases where a Member State has not set up a specialist department at national level with the task of coordinating the protection of the financial interests of the Union and the fight against fraud, a service (the anti-fraud coordination service) should be designated to facilitate effective cooperation and exchange of information with the Office.

(11) The Office should have access to any relevant information held by the institutions, bodies, offices and agencies of the Union in connection with external investigations.

(12) Investigations should be conducted in accordance with the Treaties and in particular with Protocol No 7 on the privileges and immunities of the European Union, while respecting the Staff Regulations of Officials and the Conditions of Employment of Other Servants of the European Union laid down in Council Regulation (EEC, Euratom, ECSC) No 259/68 [3] ('the Staff Regulations') and the Statute for Members of the European Parliament, and with full respect for human rights and fundamental freedoms, in particular the principle of fairness, for the right of persons involved to express their views on the facts concerning them and for the principle that the conclusions of an investigation may be based solely on elements which have evidential value. To that end, the institutions, bodies, offices and agencies should lay down the terms and conditions under which internal investigations are to be conducted.

(13) Internal investigations can be conducted only if the Office is guaranteed access to all premises of the institutions, bodies, offices and agencies and to all information and documents held by them.

(14) The accuracy of the information sent to the Office in connection with its mandate should be assessed promptly. To that end, the Office, prior to the opening of an investigation, should have access to any relevant information in databases held by the institutions, bodies, offices or agencies, when this is indispensable for assessing the basis in fact of allegations.

(15) The Office should be placed under precise obligations to inform the institutions, bodies, offices and agencies of investigations in progress where an official, other servant, member of an institution or body, head of office or agency, or staff member is concerned by the matter under investigation or where precautionary measures may be required in order to protect the financial interests of the Union.

(1) OJ L 292, 15.11.1996, p. 2.
(2) OJ L 312, 23.12.1995, p. 1.
(3) OJ L 56, 4.3.1968, p. 1.

(16) Clear rules should be laid down which, while confirming the priority enjoyed by the Office for conducting internal investigations on matters affecting the financial interests of the Union, enable the institutions, bodies, offices and agencies quickly to conduct such investigations in cases where the Office decides not to intervene.

(17) To ensure the independence of the Office in carrying out the tasks conferred on it by this Regulation, its Director-General should be able to open an investigation on his own initiative. Where the Office is conducting an investigation, the relevant institutions, bodies, offices or agencies should not conduct an investigation into the same facts in parallel, unless agreed otherwise with the Office.

(18) Investigations should be conducted under the authority of the Director-General, in full independence from the institutions, bodies, offices and agencies and from the Supervisory Committee. To that end, the Director-General should be able to adopt guidelines on investigation procedures for the staff of the Office. Those guidelines should provide practical guidance to the staff of the Office on the conduct of investigations and the procedural guarantees and rights of persons concerned or witnesses, and details on the internal advisory and control procedures to be followed, including a legality check. In order to provide greater transparency with regard to the conduct of investigations, those guidelines should be available to the public on the Office's website. Those guidelines should not create or alter any rights or obligations arising under this Regulation.

(19) In accordance with Article 21 of the Staff Regulations, the staff of the Office should conduct the investigations in accordance with the guidelines on investigation procedures and on the basis of individual instructions given by the Director-General in specific cases.

(20) In accordance with the Staff Regulations, the staff of the Office should carry out their investigative tasks in full independence and should avoid conflicts of interest. Members of the staff of the Office should immediately inform the Director-General if an investigation concerns a matter in which they have any personal interest such as to impair, or to be seen as impairing, their independence, in particular if they are or have been involved in another capacity in the matter under investigation.

(21) External and internal investigations by the Office follow, in part, distinct rules. However, the Office should be allowed, whenever necessary, to combine in one single investigation the aspects of an external and an internal investigation, without having to open two separate investigations.

(22) It is necessary, in the interests of legal certainty, to specify the procedural guarantees applicable to investigations conducted by the Office, taking into account the administrative nature of those investigations.

(23) The procedural guarantees and fundamental rights of persons concerned and of witnesses should be respected without discrimination at all times and at all stages of both external and internal investigations, in particular when information about ongoing investigations is provided. Provision of any information concerning investigations conducted by the Office to the European Parliament, the Council, the Commission or the Court of Auditors, whether bilaterally or as part of an exchange of views, should respect the confidentiality of investigations, the legitimate rights of the persons concerned and, where applicable, the national provisions governing judicial proceedings. Information transmitted or obtained during investigations should be treated in accordance with Union law on data protection. Exchanges of information should be governed by the principle of proportionality and by the need-to-know principle.

(24) In order to strengthen the protection of the individual rights of persons under investigation, conclusions referring by name to a person concerned should not be drawn, at the final stage of an investigation, without that person being given the opportunity to comment on facts concerning him.

(25) The Director-General should ensure that any information supplied to the public respects the legitimate rights of the persons concerned.

(26) The Office and the institutions, bodies, offices and agencies involved in the investigation should protect freedom of expression, in accordance with the Charter of Fundamental Rights of the European Union, and journalistic sources.

(27) It should be incumbent on the Director-General to ensure the protection of personal data and respect for confidentiality of information gathered in the course of investigations. Officials and other servants of the Union should be assured of legal protection equivalent to that provided for by the Staff Regulations.

(28) To ensure that the findings of investigations conducted by the Office are taken into account and that the requisite follow-up action is taken, the reports should have the status of admissible evidence in administrative or judicial proceedings. To that end, those reports should be drawn up in a manner compatible with the rules governing administrative reports in the Member States.

(29) Where it is found that facts brought to light by the final report on an internal investigation could give rise to criminal proceedings, the information to that effect should be transmitted to the national judicial authorities of the Member State concerned. In the recommendations accompanying the final investigation report, the Director-General should indicate whether, in the light of the nature of the facts and the scale of their financial impact, internal measures by the institution, body, office or agency concerned would allow for a more effective follow-up.

(30) In cases where the Director-General transmits to the judicial authorities of the Member State concerned information obtained by the Office in the course of internal investigations, that transmission of information should be without prejudice to subsequent classification in law by the national judicial authority as to whether investigative proceedings are required.

(31) It is for the competent authorities of the Member States or the institutions, bodies, offices or agencies, as the case may be, to decide what action should be taken on completed investigations on the basis of the final investigation reports drawn up by the Office.

(32) In order to improve its efficiency, the Office should know how the results of its investigations have been followed up. Hence, the institutions, bodies, offices and agencies of the Union and, where appropriate, the competent authorities of the Member States should report to the Office, at its request, on the action taken, if any, on the basis of the information transmitted to them by the Office.

(33) In view of the major benefits of strengthening cooperation between the Office, Eurojust, Europol and the competent authorities of the Member States, the Office should be able to conclude with them administrative arrangements which may, in particular, aim at facilitating practical cooperation and exchange of information on technical and operational matters, without creating any additional legal obligations.

(34) In order to strengthen the cooperation between the Office, Eurojust and the competent authorities of the Member States in respect of deeds which may be the subject of a criminal investigation, the Office should inform Eurojust of, in particular, those cases of suspected fraud, corruption or any other illegal activity affecting the financial interests of the Union and involving serious forms of criminality. The transmission of information to the competent authorities of the Member States concerned should occur, as appropriate, before the information provided by them is transmitted by the Office to Eurojust or Europol, where such information is accompanied by an invitation to take specific criminal investigative action.

(35) For the sake of successful cooperation between the Office, the relevant institutions, bodies, offices and agencies of the Union, the competent authorities of the Member States, the competent authorities in third countries, and international organisations, a mutual exchange of information should be organised. Such exchange of information should respect the principles of confidentiality and the rules on data protection laid down in Regulation (EC) No 45/2001 of the European Parliament and of the Council of 18 December 2000 on the protection of individuals with regard to the processing of personal data by the Community institutions and bodies and on the free movement of such data [1]. In particular, the Office should verify that the recipient has the appropriate competence and that the transmission of information is necessary. Exchanges of information with Eurojust should be covered by Eurojust's mandate, which extends to coordination in transnational cases of serious crime.

(36) Given the scale of the Union funds allocated to the external-aid sector, the number of investigations carried out by the Office in that sector and the existence of international cooperation for investigation purposes, the Office should be able, where appropriate in coordination with other competent services, to seek in the performance of its tasks, by means of administrative arrangements, practical assistance from the competent authorities in third countries and from international organisations, without creating any additional legal obligations.

(37) The Office should enjoy independence in the discharge of its functions. To reinforce that independence, the Office should be subject to regular monitoring of its investigative functions by a Supervisory Committee, composed of outside independent persons who are highly qualified in the Office's areas of activity. The Supervisory Committee should not interfere with the conduct of ongoing investigations. Its duties should also include assisting the Director-General in discharging his responsibilities.

(38) It is appropriate to specify the criteria and procedure for appointing the members of the Supervisory Committee and to further specify the tasks of the Supervisory Committee arising from its mandate.

(39) A reserve list should be drawn up designating candidates who may replace members of the Supervisory Committee for the remainder of their term of office in the event that one or more of those members resigns, dies or becomes otherwise unable to perform his duties.

[1] OJ L 8, 12.1.2001, p. 1.

(40) In order to ensure that the Supervisory Committee can carry out its mission efficiently, the independent functioning of its secretariat should be guaranteed by the Office.

(41) An exchange of views should take place once a year between the European Parliament, the Council and the Commission. Such exchange of views should cover, inter alia, the strategic priorities for investigation policies and the effectiveness of the work of the Office with regard to the performance of its mandate, without in any way interfering with the independence of the Office in the conduct of its investigations. Preparation for the exchange of views should take place at technical level and should include, in so far as may be necessary, a preparatory meeting between the relevant services of the institutions concerned. When discussing the effectiveness of the work of the Office with regard to the performance of its mandate, the institutions participating in the exchange of views should be able to address statistical information concerning the follow-up given to the Office's investigations and to the information transmitted by the Office.

(42) In order to ensure complete independence in the running of the Office, its Director-General should be appointed for a non-renewable term of seven years.

(43) The function of the Director-General of the Office is particularly important also for the European Parliament and the Council. The person appointed as Director-General should enjoy the widest possible support and recognition from the European Parliament, the Council and the Commission. The Commission should therefore seek to achieve a common accord with the European Parliament and the Council in the framework of the consultation procedure.

(44) A call for applications for the post of Director-General should be published in the *Official Journal of the European Union* at the latest six months before the end of the term of office of the Director-General in office. The call for applications should be prepared by the Commission on the basis of the outcome of close consultations with the European Parliament and the Council. It should specify the selection criteria, including the requirements which candidates should meet in order to be eligible for the post.

(45) The Director-General should inform the Supervisory Committee periodically of those cases in which information has been transmitted to the judicial authorities of the Member States and of the total number of the Office's cases dealt with by the same judicial authorities of the Member States in question, by way of follow-up to an investigation conducted by the Office.

(46) Experience from operational practice has shown that it would be useful to allow the Director-General to delegate the exercise of certain of his functions to one or more members of the staff of the Office.

(47) The Director-General should put in place an internal advisory and control mechanism, including a legality check, with particular reference to the obligation to respect the procedural guarantees and fundamental rights of the persons concerned and the national law of the Member States concerned.

(48) In order to ensure the Office's independence, the Commission should decide on appropriate delegations of the powers of the appointing authority to the Director-General.

(49) This Regulation in no way diminishes the powers and responsibilities of the Member States to take measures to combat fraud, corruption and any other illegal activity affecting the financial interests of the Union. Entrusting to an independent Office the task of conducting external administrative investigations in this area is accordingly in full compliance with the principle of subsidiarity as set out in Article 5 of the Treaty on European Union. In accordance with the principle of proportionality, as set out in that Article, this Regulation does not go beyond what is necessary in order to step up the fight against fraud, corruption and any other illegal activity affecting the financial interests of the Union.

(50) The Commission should assess the need for revision of this Regulation in the event that a European Public Prosecutor's Office is established.

(51) This Regulation respects fundamental rights and complies, in particular, with the principles recognised in the Charter of Fundamental Rights of the European Union.

(52) The European Data Protection Supervisor has been consulted in accordance with Article 28(2) of Regulation (EC) No 45/2001 and delivered an opinion on 1 June 2011 ([1]).

(53) Given the substantial number of amendments necessary, Regulation (EC) No 1073/1999 should be repealed and replaced by this Regulation.

([1]) OJ C 279, 23.9.2011, p. 11.

(54) Pursuant to Article 106a(1) of the Treaty establishing the European Atomic Energy Community (TEAEC), which extends the application of Article 325 TFEU to the European Atomic Energy Community (Euratom), the rules governing investigations conducted by the Office as regards the Union should also apply as regards Euratom. Pursuant to Article 106a(2) TEAEC, references to the Union in Article 325 TFEU must be taken as references to Euratom and references to the Union in this Regulation therefore include, when the context so requires, references to Euratom. Council Regulation (Euratom) No 1074/1999 of 25 May 1999 concerning investigations conducted by the European Anti-Fraud Office (OLAF) [1] should therefore be repealed,

HAVE ADOPTED THIS REGULATION:

*Article 1*

**Objectives and tasks**

1. In order to step up the fight against fraud, corruption and any other illegal activity affecting the financial interests of the European Union and of the European Atomic Energy Community (hereinafter referred to collectively, when the context so requires, as 'the Union'), the European Anti-Fraud Office established by Decision 1999/352/EC, ECSC, Euratom ('the Office') shall exercise the powers of investigation conferred on the Commission by:

(a) the relevant Union acts; and

(b) the relevant cooperation and mutual assistance agreements concluded by the Union with third countries and international organisations.

2. The Office shall provide the Member States with assistance from the Commission in organising close and regular cooperation between their competent authorities in order to coordinate their action aimed at protecting the financial interests of the Union against fraud. The Office shall contribute to the design and development of methods of preventing and combating fraud, corruption and any other illegal activity affecting the financial interests of the Union. The Office shall promote and coordinate, with and among the Member States, the sharing of operational experience and best procedural practices in the field of the protection of the financial interests of the Union, and shall support joint anti-fraud actions undertaken by Member States on a voluntary basis.

3. This Regulation shall apply without prejudice to:

(a) Protocol No 7 on the privileges and immunities of the European Union attached to the Treaty on European Union and to the Treaty on the Functioning of the European Union;

(b) the Statute for Members of the European Parliament;

(c) the Staff Regulations;

(d) Regulation (EC) No 45/2001.

4. Within the institutions, bodies, offices and agencies established by, or on the basis of, the Treaties ('institutions, bodies, offices and agencies'), the Office shall conduct administrative investigations for the purpose of fighting fraud, corruption and any other illegal activity affecting the financial interests of the Union. To that end, it shall investigate serious matters relating to the discharge of professional duties constituting a dereliction of the obligations of officials and other servants of the Union liable to result in disciplinary or, as the case may be, criminal proceedings, or an equivalent failure to discharge obligations on the part of members of institutions and bodies, heads of offices and agencies or staff members of institutions, bodies, offices or agencies not subject to the Staff Regulations (hereinafter collectively referred to as 'officials, other servants, members of institutions or bodies, heads of offices or agencies, or staff members').

5. For the application of this Regulation, competent authorities of the Member States and institutions, bodies, offices or agencies may establish administrative arrangements with the Office. Those administrative arrangements may concern, in particular, the transmission of information and the conduct of investigations.

*Article 2*

**Definitions**

For the purposes of this Regulation:

(1) 'financial interests of the Union' shall include revenues, expenditures and assets covered by the budget of the European Union and those covered by the budgets of the institutions, bodies, offices and agencies and the budgets managed and monitored by them;

(2) 'irregularity' shall mean 'irregularity' as defined in Article 1(2) of Regulation (EC, Euratom) No 2988/95;

(3) 'fraud, corruption and any other illegal activity affecting the financial interests of the Union' shall have the meaning applied to those words in the relevant Union acts;

(4) 'administrative investigations' ('investigations') shall mean any inspection, check or other measure undertaken by the Office in accordance with Articles 3 and 4, with a view to achieving the objectives set out in Article 1 and to establishing, where necessary, the irregular nature of the activities under investigation; those investigations shall not affect the powers of the competent authorities of the Member States to initiate criminal proceedings;

[1] OJ L 136, 31.5.1999, p. 8.

(5) 'person concerned' shall mean any person or economic operator suspected of having committed fraud, corruption or any other illegal activity affecting the financial interests of the Union and who is therefore subject to investigation by the Office;

(6) 'economic operator' shall have the meaning applied to that term by Regulation (EC, Euratom) No 2988/95 and Regulation (Euratom, EC) No 2185/96;

(7) 'administrative arrangements' shall mean arrangements of a technical and/or operational nature concluded by the Office, which may in particular aim at facilitating the cooperation and the exchange of information between the parties thereto, and which do not create additional legal obligations.

*Article 3*

**External investigations**

1. The Office shall exercise the power conferred on the Commission by Regulation (Euratom, EC) No 2185/96 to carry out on-the-spot checks and inspections in the Member States and, in accordance with the cooperation and mutual assistance agreements and any other legal instrument in force, in third countries and on the premises of international organisations.

As part of its investigative function, the Office shall carry out the checks and inspections provided for in Article 9(1) of Regulation (EC, Euratom) No 2988/95 and in the sectoral rules referred to in Article 9(2) of that Regulation in the Member States and, in accordance with the cooperation and mutual assistance agreements and any other legal instrument in force, in third countries and on the premises of international organisations.

2. With a view to establishing whether there has been fraud, corruption or any other illegal activity affecting the financial interests of the Union in connection with a grant agreement or decision or a contract concerning Union funding, the Office may, in accordance with the provisions and procedures laid down by Regulation (Euratom, EC) No 2185/96, conduct on-the-spot checks and inspections on economic operators.

3. During on-the-spot checks and inspections, the staff of the Office shall act, subject to the Union law applicable, in compliance with the rules and practices of the Member State concerned and with the procedural guarantees provided for in this Regulation.

At the request of the Office, the competent authority of the Member State concerned shall provide the staff of the Office with the assistance needed in order to carry out their tasks effectively, as specified in the written authorisation referred to in Article 7(2). If that assistance requires authorisation from a judicial authority in accordance with national rules, such authorisation shall be applied for.

The Member State concerned shall ensure, in accordance with Regulation (Euratom, EC) No 2185/96, that the staff of the Office are allowed access, under the same terms and conditions as its competent authorities and in compliance with its national law, to all information and documents relating to the matter under investigation which prove necessary in order for the on-the-spot checks and inspections to be carried out effectively and efficiently.

4. Member States shall, for the purposes of this Regulation, designate a service ('the anti-fraud coordination service') to facilitate effective cooperation and exchange of information, including information of an operational nature, with the Office. Where appropriate, in accordance with national law, the anti-fraud coordination service may be regarded as a competent authority for the purposes of this Regulation.

5. During an external investigation, the Office may have access to any relevant information, including information in databases, held by the institutions, bodies, offices and agencies, connected with the matter under investigation, where necessary in order to establish whether there has been fraud, corruption or any other illegal activity affecting the financial interests of the Union. For that purpose Article 4(2) and (4) shall apply.

6. Where, before a decision has been taken whether or not to open an external investigation, the Office handles information which suggests that there has been fraud, corruption or any other illegal activity affecting the financial interests of the Union, it may inform the competent authorities of the Member States concerned and, where necessary, the competent Commission services.

Without prejudice to the sectoral rules referred to in Article 9(2) of Regulation (EC, Euratom) No 2988/95, the competent authorities of the Member States concerned shall ensure that appropriate action is taken, in which the Office may take part, in compliance with national law. Upon request, the competent authorities of the Member States concerned shall inform the Office of the action taken and of their findings on the basis of information as referred to in the first subparagraph of this paragraph.

*Article 4*

**Internal investigations**

1. In the areas referred to in Article 1, the Office shall carry out administrative investigations within the institutions, bodies, offices and agencies ('internal investigations').

Those internal investigations shall be conducted in accordance with the conditions set out in this Regulation and in the decisions adopted by the respective institution, body, office or agency.

2. Provided that the provisions referred to in paragraph 1 are complied with:

(a) the Office shall have the right of immediate and unannounced access to any relevant information, including information in databases, held by the institutions, bodies, offices and agencies, and to their premises. The Office shall be empowered to inspect the accounts of the institutions, bodies, offices and agencies. The Office may take a copy of, and obtain extracts from, any document or the contents of any data medium held by the institutions, bodies, offices and agencies and, if necessary, assume custody of such documents or data to ensure that there is no danger of their disappearance;

(b) the Office may request oral information, including through interviews, and written information from officials, other servants, members of institutions or bodies, heads of offices or agencies, or staff members.

3. In accordance with the provisions and procedures laid down by Regulation (Euratom, EC) No 2185/96, the Office may carry out on-the-spot checks and inspections at the premises of economic operators in order to obtain access to information relevant to the matter under internal investigation.

4. The institutions, bodies, offices and agencies shall be informed whenever the staff of the Office conduct an internal investigation on their premises or consult a document or request information held by them. Without prejudice to Articles 10 and 11, the Office may at any time forward to the institution, body, office or agency concerned the information obtained in the course of internal investigations.

5. The institutions, bodies, offices and agencies shall put in place appropriate procedures and take necessary measures to ensure at all stages the confidentiality of internal investigations.

6. Where internal investigations reveal that an official, other servant, member of an institution or body, head of office or agency, or staff member may be a person concerned, the institution, body, office or agency to which that person belongs shall be informed.

In cases where the confidentiality of the internal investigation cannot be ensured using the usual channels of communication, the Office shall use appropriate alternative channels for transmitting information.

In exceptional cases, the provision of such information may be deferred on the basis of a reasoned decision by the Director-General, which shall be transmitted to the Supervisory Committee after the closure of the investigation.

7. The decision to be adopted by each institution, body, office or agency as provided for in paragraph 1 shall include, in particular, a rule concerning a duty on the part of officials, other servants, members of institutions or bodies, heads of offices or agencies, or staff members to cooperate with and supply information to the Office, while ensuring the confidentiality of the internal investigation.

8. Where, before a decision has been taken whether or not to open an internal investigation, the Office handles information which suggests that there has been fraud, corruption or any other illegal activity affecting the financial interests of the Union, it may inform the institution, body, office or agency concerned. Upon request, the institution, body, office or agency concerned shall inform the Office of any action taken and of its findings on the basis of such information.

Where necessary, the Office shall also inform the competent authorities of the Member State concerned. In this case, the procedural requirements laid down in the second and third subparagraphs of Article 9(4) shall apply. If the competent authorities decide to take any action on the basis of the information transmitted to them, in accordance with national law, they shall, upon request, inform the Office thereof.

*Article 5*

**Opening of investigations**

1. The Director-General may open an investigation when there is a sufficient suspicion, which may also be based on information provided by any third party or anonymous information, that there has been fraud, corruption or any other illegal activity affecting the financial interests of the Union. The decision by the Director-General whether or not to open an investigation shall take into account the investigation policy priorities and the annual management plan of the Office established in accordance with Article 17(5). That decision shall also take into account the need for efficient use of the Office's resources and for proportionality of the means employed. With regard to internal investigations, specific account shall be taken of the institution, body, office or agency best placed to conduct them, based, in particular, on the nature of the facts, the actual or potential financial impact of the case, and the likelihood of any judicial follow-up.

2. The decision to open an external investigation shall be taken by the Director-General, acting on his own initiative or following a request from a Member State concerned or any institution, body, office or agency of the Union.

18.9.2013 EN Official Journal of the European Union L 248/9

The decision to open an internal investigation shall be taken by the Director-General, acting on his own initiative or following a request from the institution, body, office or agency within which the investigation is to be conducted or from a Member State.

3. While the Director-General is considering whether or not to open an internal investigation following a request as referred to in paragraph 2, and/or while the Office is conducting an internal investigation, the institutions, bodies, offices or agencies concerned shall not open a parallel investigation into the same facts, unless agreed otherwise with the Office.

4. Within two months of receipt by the Office of a request as referred to in paragraph 2, a decision whether or not to open an investigation shall be taken. It shall be communicated without delay to the Member State, institution, body, office or agency which made the request. Reasons shall be given for a decision not to open an investigation. If, on the expiry of that period of two months, the Office has not taken any decision, the Office shall be deemed to have decided not to open an investigation.

Where an official, other servant, member of an institution or body, head of office or agency, or staff member, acting in accordance with Article 22a of the Staff Regulations, provides information to the Office relating to a suspected fraud or irregularity, the Office shall inform that person of the decision whether or not to open an investigation in relation to the facts in question.

5. If the Director-General decides not to open an internal investigation, he may without delay send any relevant information to the institution, body, office or agency concerned for appropriate action to be taken in accordance with the rules applicable to that institution, body, office or agency. The Office shall agree with that institution, body, office or agency, if appropriate, on suitable measures to protect the confidentiality of the source of that information and shall, if necessary, ask to be informed of the action taken.

6. If the Director-General decides not to open an external investigation, he may without delay send any relevant information to the competent authorities of the Member State concerned for action to be taken where appropriate, in accordance with its national rules. Where necessary, the Office shall also inform the institution, body, office or agency concerned.

*Article 6*

**Access to information in databases prior to the opening of an investigation**

1. Prior to the opening of an investigation, the Office shall have the right of access to any relevant information in databases held by the institutions, bodies, offices or agencies when this is indispensable in order to assess the basis in fact of allegations. That right of access shall be exercised within the time-limit, to be set by the Office, required for a prompt assessment of the allegations. In exercising that right of access, the Office shall respect the principles of necessity and proportionality.

2. The institution, body, office or agency concerned shall sincerely cooperate by allowing the Office to obtain any relevant information under conditions to be specified in the decisions adopted under Article 4(1).

*Article 7*

**Investigations procedure**

1. The Director-General shall direct the conduct of investigations on the basis, where appropriate, of written instructions. Investigations shall be conducted under his direction by the staff of the Office designated by him.

2. The staff of the Office shall carry out their tasks on production of a written authorisation showing their identity and their capacity. The Director-General shall issue such authorisation indicating the subject matter and the purpose of the investigation, the legal bases for conducting the investigation and the investigative powers stemming from those bases.

3. The competent authorities of the Member States shall, in conformity with national rules, give the necessary assistance to enable the staff of the Office to fulfil their tasks effectively.

The institutions, bodies, offices and agencies shall ensure that their officials, other servants, members, heads and staff members provide the necessary assistance to enable the staff of the Office to fulfil their tasks effectively.

4. Where an investigation combines external and internal elements, Articles 3 and 4 shall apply respectively.

5. Investigations shall be conducted continuously over a period which must be proportionate to the circumstances and complexity of the case.

6. Where investigations show that it might be appropriate to take precautionary administrative measures to protect the financial interests of the Union, the Office shall without delay inform the institution, body, office or agency concerned of the investigation in progress. The information supplied shall include the following:

(a) the identity of the official, other servant, member of an institution or body, head of office or agency, or staff member concerned and a summary of the facts in question;

(b) any information that could assist the institution, body, office or agency concerned in deciding whether it is appropriate to take precautionary administrative measures in order to protect the financial interests of the Union;

(c) any special measures of confidentiality recommended, in particular in cases entailing the use of investigative measures falling within the competence of a national judicial authority or, in the case of an external investigation, within the competence of a national authority, in accordance with the national rules applicable to investigations.

The institution, body, office or agency concerned may at any time decide to take, in close cooperation with the Office, any appropriate precautionary measures, including measures for the safeguarding of evidence, and shall inform the Office without delay of such decision.

7. Where necessary, it shall be for the competent authorities of the Member States, at the Office's request, to take the appropriate precautionary measures under their national law, in particular measures for the safeguarding of evidence.

8. If an investigation cannot be closed within 12 months after it has been opened, the Director-General shall, at the expiry of that 12-month period and every six months thereafter, report to the Supervisory Committee, indicating the reasons and the remedial measures envisaged with a view to speeding up the investigation.

*Article 8*

**Duty to inform the Office**

1. The institutions, bodies, offices and agencies shall transmit to the Office without delay any information relating to possible cases of fraud, corruption or any other illegal activity affecting the financial interests of the Union.

2. The institutions, bodies, offices and agencies and, in so far as their national law allows, the competent authorities of the Member States shall, at the request of the Office or on their own initiative, transmit to the Office any document or information they hold which relates to an ongoing investigation by the Office.

3. The institutions, bodies, offices and agencies and, in so far as their national law allows, the competent authorities of the Member States shall transmit to the Office any other document or information considered pertinent which they hold relating to the fight against fraud, corruption and any other illegal activity affecting the financial interests of the Union.

*Article 9*

**Procedural guarantees**

1. In its investigations the Office shall seek evidence for and against the person concerned. Investigations shall be conducted objectively and impartially and in accordance with the principle of the presumption of innocence and with the procedural guarantees set out in this Article.

2. The Office may interview a person concerned or a witness at any time during an investigation. Any person interviewed shall have the right to avoid self-incrimination.

The invitation to an interview shall be sent to a person concerned with at least 10 working days' notice. That notice period may be shortened with the express consent of the person concerned or on duly reasoned grounds of urgency of the investigation. In the latter case, the notice period shall not be less than 24 hours. The invitation shall include a list of the rights of the person concerned, in particular the right to be assisted by a person of his choice.

The invitation to an interview shall be sent to a witness with at least 24 hours' notice. That notice period may be shortened with the express consent of the witness or on duly reasoned grounds of urgency of the investigation.

The requirements referred to in the second and third subparagraphs shall not apply to the taking of statements in the context of on-the-spot checks and inspections.

Where, in the course of an interview, evidence emerges that a witness may be a person concerned, the interview shall be ended. The procedural rules provided for in this paragraph and in paragraphs 3 and 4 shall immediately apply. That witness shall be informed forthwith of his rights as a person concerned and shall receive, upon request, a copy of the records of any statements made by him in the past. The Office may not use that person's past statements against him without giving him first the opportunity to comment on those statements.

The Office shall draw up a record of the interview and give the person interviewed access to it so that the person interviewed may either approve the record or add observations. The Office shall give the person concerned a copy of the record of the interview.

3. As soon as an investigation reveals that an official, other servant, member of an institution or body, head of office or agency, or staff member may be a person concerned, that official, other servant, member of an institution or body, head of office or agency, or staff member shall be informed to that effect, provided that this does not prejudice the conduct of the investigation or of any investigative proceedings falling within the remit of a national judicial authority.

18.9.2013 EN Official Journal of the European Union L 248/11

4. Without prejudice to Articles 4(6) and 7(6), once the investigation has been completed and before conclusions referring by name to a person concerned are drawn up, that person shall be given the opportunity to comment on facts concerning him.

To that end, the Office shall send the person concerned an invitation to comment either in writing or at an interview with staff designated by the Office. That invitation shall include a summary of the facts concerning the person concerned and the information required by Articles 11 and 12 of Regulation (EC) No 45/2001, and shall indicate the time-limit for submitting comments, which shall not be less than 10 working days from receipt of the invitation to comment. That notice period may be shortened with the express consent of the person concerned or on duly reasoned grounds of urgency of the investigation. The final investigation report shall make reference to any such comments.

In duly justified cases where it is necessary to preserve the confidentiality of the investigation and/or entailing the use of investigative proceedings falling within the remit of a national judicial authority, the Director-General may decide to defer the fulfilment of the obligation to invite the person concerned to comment.

In cases referred to in Article 1(2) of Annex IX to the Staff Regulations, failure on the part of the institution, body, office or agency to respond within one month to the request of the Director-General for deferral of the fulfilment of the obligation to invite the person concerned to comment shall be deemed to constitute a reply in the affirmative.

5. Any person interviewed shall be entitled to use any of the official languages of the institutions of the Union. However, officials or other servants of the Union may be required to use an official language of the institutions of the Union of which they have a thorough knowledge.

*Article 10*

**Confidentiality and data protection**

1. Information transmitted or obtained in the course of external investigations, in whatever form, shall be protected by the relevant provisions.

2. Information transmitted or obtained in the course of internal investigations, in whatever form, shall be subject to professional secrecy and shall enjoy the protection afforded by the rules applicable to the Union institutions.

3. The institutions, bodies, offices or agencies concerned shall ensure that the confidentiality of the investigations conducted by the Office is respected, together with the legitimate rights of the persons concerned, and, where judicial proceedings have been initiated, that all national rules applicable to such proceedings have been adhered to.

4. The Office may designate a Data Protection Officer in accordance with Article 24 of Regulation (EC) No 45/2001.

5. The Director-General shall ensure that any information provided to the public is given neutrally and impartially, and that its disclosure respects the confidentiality of investigations and complies with the principles set out in this Article and in Article 9(1).

In accordance with the Staff Regulations, the staff of the Office shall refrain from any unauthorised disclosure of information received in the line of duty, unless that information has already been made public or is accessible to the public, and shall continue to be bound by that obligation after leaving the service.

*Article 11*

**Investigation report and action to be taken following investigations**

1. On completion of an investigation by the Office, a report shall be drawn up, under the authority of the Director-General. That report shall give an account of the legal basis for the investigation, the procedural steps followed, the facts established and their preliminary classification in law, the estimated financial impact of the facts established, the respect of the procedural guarantees in accordance with Article 9 and the conclusions of the investigation.

The report shall be accompanied by recommendations of the Director-General on whether or not action should be taken. Those recommendations shall, where appropriate, indicate any disciplinary, administrative, financial and/or judicial action by the institutions, bodies, offices and agencies and by the competent authorities of the Member States concerned, and shall specify in particular the estimated amounts to be recovered, as well as the preliminary classification in law of the facts established.

2. In drawing up such reports and recommendations, account shall be taken of the national law of the Member State concerned. Reports drawn up on that basis shall constitute admissible evidence in administrative or judicial proceedings of the Member State in which their use proves necessary, in the same way and under the same conditions as administrative reports drawn up by national administrative inspectors. They shall be subject to the same evaluation rules as those applicable to administrative reports drawn up by national administrative inspectors and shall have the same evidentiary value as such reports.

3. Reports and recommendations drawn up following an external investigation and any relevant related documents shall be sent to the competent authorities of the Member States concerned in accordance with the rules relating to external investigations and, if necessary, to the competent Commission services.

4. Reports and recommendations drawn up following an internal investigation and any relevant related documents shall be sent to the institution, body, office or agency concerned. That institution, body, office or agency shall take such action, in particular of a disciplinary or legal nature, as the results of the internal investigation warrant, and shall report thereon to the Office, within a time-limit laid down in the recommendations accompanying the report, and, in addition, at the request of the Office.

5. Where the report drawn up following an internal investigation reveals the existence of facts which could give rise to criminal proceedings, that information shall be transmitted to the judicial authorities of the Member State concerned.

6. At the request of the Office, the competent authorities of the Member States concerned shall, in due time, send to the Office information on action taken, if any, following the transmission by the Director-General of his recommendations in accordance with paragraph 3, and following the transmission by the Office of any information in accordance with paragraph 5.

7. Without prejudice to paragraph 4, if, on completion of an investigation, no evidence has been found against the person concerned, the Director-General shall close the investigation regarding that person and inform that person within 10 working days.

8. Where an informant who has provided the Office with information leading or relating to an investigation so requests, the Office may notify that informant that the investigation has been closed. The Office may, however, refuse any such request if it considers that it is such as to prejudice the legitimate interests of the person concerned, the effectiveness of the investigation and of the action to be taken subsequent thereto, or any confidentiality requirements.

*Article 12*

**Exchange of information between the Office and the competent authorities of the Member States**

1. Without prejudice to Articles 10 and 11 of this Regulation and to the provisions of Regulation (Euratom, EC) No 2185/96, the Office may transmit to the competent authorities of the Member States concerned information obtained in the course of external investigations in due time to enable them to take appropriate action in accordance with their national law.

2. Without prejudice to Articles 10 and 11, the Director-General shall transmit to the judicial authorities of the Member State concerned information obtained by the Office, in the course of internal investigations, concerning facts which fall within the jurisdiction of a national judicial authority.

In accordance with Article 4 and without prejudice to Article 10, the Director-General shall also transmit to the institution, body, office or agency concerned the information referred to in the first subparagraph of this paragraph, including the identity of the person concerned, a summary of the facts established, their preliminary classification in law and the estimated impact on the financial interests of the Union.

Article 9(4) shall apply.

3. The competent authorities of the Member State concerned shall, without prejudice to their national law, inform the Office in due time, on their own initiative or at the request of the Office, of the action taken on the basis of the information transmitted to them under this Article.

4. The Office may provide evidence in proceedings before national courts and tribunals in conformity with national law and the Staff Regulations.

*Article 13*

**Cooperation of the Office with Eurojust and Europol**

1. Within its mandate to protect the financial interests of the Union, the Office shall cooperate, as appropriate, with Eurojust and with the European Police Office (Europol). Where necessary in order to facilitate that cooperation, the Office shall agree with Eurojust and Europol on administrative arrangements. Such working arrangements may concern exchange of operational, strategic or technical information, including personal data and classified information and, on request, progress reports.

Where this may support and strengthen coordination and cooperation between national investigating and prosecuting authorities, or where the Office has forwarded to the competent authorities of the Member States information giving grounds for suspecting the existence of fraud, corruption or any other illegal activity affecting the financial interests of the Union in the form of serious crime, it shall transmit relevant information to Eurojust, within the mandate of Eurojust.

2. The competent authorities of the Member States concerned shall be informed, in a timely manner, by the Office in cases where information provided by them is transmitted by the Office to Eurojust or Europol.

*Article 14*

**Cooperation with third countries and international organisations**

1. Administrative arrangements may be agreed, as appropriate, by the Office with competent authorities in third countries and with international organisations. The Office shall coordinate its action, as appropriate, with the competent Commission services and with the European External Action Service, in particular before agreeing on such arrangements. Such arrangements may concern exchange of operational, strategic or technical information, including, on request, progress reports.

2. The Office shall inform the competent authorities of the Member States concerned before information provided by them is transmitted by the Office to competent authorities in third countries or to international organisations.

The Office shall keep a record of all transmissions of personal data, including the grounds for such transmissions, in accordance with Regulation (EC) No 45/2001.

*Article 15*

**Supervisory Committee**

1. The Supervisory Committee shall regularly monitor the implementation by the Office of its investigative function, in order to reinforce the Office's independence in the proper exercise of the competences conferred upon it by this Regulation.

The Supervisory Committee shall in particular monitor developments concerning the application of procedural guarantees and the duration of investigations in the light of the information supplied by the Director-General in accordance with Article 7(8).

The Supervisory Committee shall address to the Director-General opinions, including where appropriate, recommendations on, inter alia, the resources needed to carry out the investigative function of the Office, on the investigative priorities of the Office and on the duration of investigations. Those opinions may be delivered on its own initiative, at the request of the Director-General or at the request of an institution, body, office or agency, without however interfering with the conduct of investigations in progress.

The institutions, bodies, offices or agencies shall be provided with a copy of opinions delivered pursuant to the third subparagraph.

In duly justified situations, the Supervisory Committee may ask the Office for additional information on investigations, including reports and recommendations on closed investigations, without however interfering with the conduct of investigations in progress.

2. The Supervisory Committee shall be composed of five independent members having experience in senior judicial or investigative functions or comparable functions relating to the areas of activity of the Office. They shall be appointed by common accord of the European Parliament, the Council and the Commission.

The decision appointing the members of the Supervisory Committee shall also include a reserve list of potential members to replace members of the Supervisory Committee for the remainder of their term of office in the event of the resignation, death or permanent incapacity of one or more of those members.

3. The term of office of members of the Supervisory Committee shall be five years and shall not be renewable. Three and two members shall be replaced alternately in order to preserve the Supervisory Committee's expertise.

4. On expiry of their term of office, members of the Supervisory Committee shall remain in office until they are replaced.

5. If a member of the Supervisory Committee ceases to fulfil the conditions governing the performance of his duties, or if he has been found guilty of serious misconduct, the European Parliament, the Council and the Commission may, by common accord, relieve him of his duties.

6. In accordance with the applicable Commission rules, members of the Supervisory Committee shall receive a daily allowance and shall be reimbursed for expenses incurred by them in the course of their duties.

7. In carrying out their duties, the members of the Supervisory Committee shall neither seek nor take instructions from any government or any institution, body, office or agency.

8. The Supervisory Committee shall appoint its chair. It shall adopt its own rules of procedure, which shall, before adoption, be submitted to the European Parliament, the Council, the Commission and the European Data Protection Supervisor for information. Meetings of the Supervisory Committee shall be convened on the initiative of its chair or the Director-General. It shall hold at least 10 meetings per year. The Supervisory Committee shall take its decisions by a majority of its component members. Its secretariat shall be provided by the Office, in close consultation with the Supervisory Committee.

9. The Supervisory Committee shall adopt at least one report on its activities per year, covering in particular the assessment of the Office's independence, the application of procedural guarantees and the duration of investigations. Those reports shall be sent to the European Parliament, the Council, the Commission and the Court of Auditors.

The Supervisory Committee may submit reports to the European Parliament, the Council, the Commission and the Court of Auditors on the results of the Office's investigations and the action taken on the basis of those results.

*Article 16*

**Exchange of views with the institutions**

1. The European Parliament, the Council and the Commission shall once a year meet the Director-General for an exchange of views at political level to discuss the Office's policy relating to methods of preventing and combating fraud, corruption or any other illegal activity affecting the financial interests of the Union. The Supervisory Committee shall participate in the exchange of views. Representatives of the Court of Auditors, Eurojust and/or Europol may be invited to attend on an ad hoc basis upon request of the European Parliament, the Council, the Commission, the Director-General or the Supervisory Committee.

2. The exchange of views may relate to:

(a) the strategic priorities for the Office's investigation policies;

(b) the opinions and activity reports of the Supervisory Committee provided for under Article 15;

(c) the reports of the Director-General under Article 17(4) and, as appropriate, any other reports by the institutions relating to the mandate of the Office;

(d) the framework of the relations between the Office and the institutions, bodies, offices and agencies;

(e) the framework of the relations between the Office and the competent authorities of the Member States;

(f) the relations between the Office and the competent authorities in third countries as well as international organisations in the framework of the arrangements referred to in this Regulation;

(g) the effectiveness of the work of the Office with regard to the performance of its mandate.

3. All institutions participating in the exchange of views shall ensure that the exchange of views does not interfere with the conduct of investigations in progress.

4. The institutions participating in the exchange of views shall take into account in their actions the opinions expressed in that exchange. The Director-General shall provide, in the reports referred to in Article 17(4), information on the actions, if any, taken by the Office.

*Article 17*

**Director-General**

1. The Office shall be headed by a Director-General. The Director-General shall be appointed by the Commission, in accordance with the procedure specified in paragraph 2. The term of office of the Director-General shall be seven years and shall not be renewable.

2. In order to appoint a new Director-General, the Commission shall publish a call for applications in the *Official Journal of the European Union*. Such publication shall take place at the latest six months before the end of the term of office of the Director-General in office. After a favourable opinion has been given by the Supervisory Committee on the selection procedure applied by the Commission, the Commission shall draw up a list of suitably qualified candidates. After consultation with the European Parliament and the Council, the Commission shall appoint the Director-General.

3. The Director-General shall neither seek nor take instructions from any government or any institution, body, office or agency in the performance of his duties with regard to the opening and carrying-out of external and internal investigations or to the drafting of reports following such investigations. If the Director-General considers that a measure taken by the Commission calls his independence into question, he shall immediately inform the Supervisory Committee, and shall decide whether to bring an action against the Commission before the Court of Justice.

4. The Director-General shall report regularly to the European Parliament, the Council, the Commission and the Court of Auditors on the findings of investigations carried out by the Office, the action taken and the problems encountered, whilst respecting the confidentiality of the investigations, the legitimate rights of the persons concerned and of informants, and, where appropriate, national law applicable to judicial proceedings.

5. The Director-General shall each year determine, within the context of the annual management plan, the investigation policy priorities of the Office and shall, prior to their publication, forward them to the Supervisory Committee.

The Director-General shall keep the Supervisory Committee periodically informed of the Office's activities, the implementation of its investigative function and the action taken by way of follow-up to investigations.

The Director-General shall inform the Supervisory Committee periodically:

(a) of cases in which the recommendations made by the Director-General have not been followed;

(b) of cases in which information has been transmitted to judicial authorities of the Member States;

(c) on the duration of investigations in accordance with Article 7(8).

6. The Director-General may delegate in writing the exercise of certain of his functions under Article 5, Article 7(2), Article 11(7) and Article 12(2) to one or more members of the staff of the Office, specifying the conditions and limits governing such delegation.

7. The Director-General shall put in place an internal advisory and control procedure, including a legality check, relating, inter alia, to the respect of procedural guarantees and fundamental rights of the persons concerned and of the national law of the Member States concerned, with particular reference to Article 11(2).

8. The Director-General shall adopt guidelines on investigation procedures for the staff of the Office. Those guidelines shall be in accordance with this Regulation and shall cover, inter alia:

(a) the conduct of investigations;

(b) the procedural guarantees;

(c) details on the internal advisory and control procedures, including the legality check;

(d) data protection.

Those guidelines, and any modification thereto, shall be adopted after the Supervisory Committee has been given the opportunity to submit its observations thereon and shall then be transmitted for information to the European Parliament, the Council and the Commission, and published for information purposes on the Office's website in the official languages of the institutions of the Union.

9. Before imposing any disciplinary penalty on the Director-General, the Commission shall consult the Supervisory Committee.

The imposition of any disciplinary penalty on the Director-General shall be the subject of a reasoned decision, which shall be forwarded for information to the European Parliament, the Council and the Supervisory Committee.

10. Any reference to the 'Director' of the Office in any legal text shall be read as a reference to the Director-General.

*Article 18*

**Financing**

The total appropriations for the Office, including for the Supervisory Committee and its secretariat, shall be entered under a specific budget line within the section of the general budget of the European Union relating to the Commission and shall be set out in detail in an Annex to that section.

The establishment plan of the Office, including the secretariat of the Supervisory Committee, shall be annexed to the establishment plan of the Commission.

*Article 19*

**Evaluation report**

By 2 October 2017, the Commission shall submit to the European Parliament and the Council an evaluation report on the application of this Regulation. That report shall be accompanied by an opinion of the Supervisory Committee and shall state whether there is a need to amend this Regulation.

*Article 20*

**Repeal**

Regulation (EC) No 1073/1999 and Regulation (Euratom) No 1074/1999 are hereby repealed.

References to the repealed Regulations shall be construed as references to this Regulation and shall be read in accordance with the correlation table set out in Annex II.

*Article 21*

**Entry into force and transitional provisions**

1. This Regulation shall enter into force on the first day of the month following its publication in the *Official Journal of the European Union*.

2. Article 15(3) shall apply to the duration of the term of office of the members of the Supervisory Committee in office at the date of entry into force of this Regulation. Immediately after the entry into force of this Regulation, the President of the European Parliament shall choose by lot, from amongst the members of the Supervisory Committee, two members whose duties are to end, by way of derogation from the first sentence of Article 15(3), upon expiry of the first 36 months of their term of office. Two new members shall be appointed automatically for a term of office of five years to replace the outgoing members, on the basis and in the order of the list set out in Article 1(2) of Decision 2012/45/EU, Euratom of the European Parliament, the Council and the Commission of 23 January 2012 appointing the members of the Supervisory Committee of the European Anti-Fraud Office (OLAF) (1). Those new members shall be the first two persons whose names appear in that list.

3. The third sentence of Article 17(1) shall apply to the duration of the term of office of the Director-General in office at the date of entry into force of this Regulation.

This Regulation shall be binding in its entirety and directly applicable in all Member States.

Done at Strasbourg, 11 September 2013.

*For the European Parliament*
*The President*
M. SCHULZ

*For the Council*
*The President*
V. LEŠKEVIČIUS

---

(1) OJ L 26, 28.1.2012, p. 30.

*ANNEX I*

**REPEALED REGULATIONS (REFERRED TO IN ARTICLE 20)**

Regulation (EC) No 1073/1999 of the European Parliament and of the Council

(OJ L 136, 31.5.1999, p. 1).

Council Regulation (Euratom) No 1074/1999

(OJ L 136, 31.5.1999, p. 8)

*ANNEX II*

**CORRELATION TABLE**

| Regulation (EC) No 1073/1999 and Regulation (Euratom) No 1074/1999 | This Regulation |
|---|---|
| Article 1(1) | Article 1(1) |
| Article 1(2) | Article 1(2) |
| — | Article 1(3) |
| Article 1(3) | Article 1(4) |
| — | Article 1(5) |
| — | Article 2, point 1 |
| — | Article 2, point 2 |
| — | Article 2, point 3 |
| Article 2 | Article 2, point 4 |
| — | Article 2, point 5 |
| — | Article 2, point 6 |
| — | Article 2, point 7 |
| Article 3, first paragraph | Article 3(1), first subparagraph |
| Article 3, second paragraph | Article 3(1), second subparagraph |
| — | Article 3(2) |
| — | Article 3(3), second subparagraph |
| — | Article 3(3), third subparagraph |
| — | Article 3(4) |
| — | Article 3(5) |
| — | Article 3(6) |
| Article 4(1), first subparagraph | Article 4(1), first subparagraph |
| Article 4(1), second subparagraph | Article 4(1), second subparagraph |
| Article 4(2) | Article 4(2) |
| Article 4(3), first subparagraph | Article 4(3) |
| Article 4(3), second subparagraph | — |
| Article 4(4) | Article 4(4), first sentence |
| — | Article 4(5) |
| Article 4(5), first subparagraph | Article 4(6), first subparagraph |
| — | Article 4(6), second subparagraph |
| Article 4(5), second subparagraph | Article 4(6), third subparagraph |
| Article 4(6), point (a) | Article 4(7) |
| Article 4(6), point (b) | — |

| Regulation (EC) No 1073/1999 and Regulation (Euratom) No 1074/1999 | This Regulation |
|---|---|
| — | Article 4(8) |
| — | Article 5(1) |
| Article 5, first paragraph | Article 5(2), first subparagraph |
| Article 5, second paragraph | Article 5(2), second subparagraph |
| — | Article 5(3) |
| — | Article 5(4) |
| — | Article 5(5) |
| — | Article 5(6) |
| — | Article 6 |
| Article 6(1) | Article 7(1) |
| Article 6(2) | Article 7(2), first sentence |
| Article 6(3) | Article 7(2), second sentence |
| Article 6(4) | Article 3(3), first subparagraph |
| — | Article 7(4) |
| Article 6(5) | Article 7(5) |
| Article 6(6) | Article 7(3) |
| — | Article 7(6) |
| — | Article 7(7) |
| — | Article 7(8) |
| Article 7(1) | Article 8(1) |
| Article 7(2) | Article 8(2) |
| Article 7(3) | Article 8(3) |
| — | Article 9 |
| Article 8(1) | Article 10(1) |
| Article 8(2), first subparagraph | Article 10(2) |
| Article 8(2), second subparagraph | — |
| Article 8(3) | — |
| Article 8(4) | — |
| — | Article 10(4) |
| — | Article 10(5) |
| Article 9(1) | Article 11(1), first subparagraph |
| — | Article 11(1), second subparagraph |
| Article 9(2) | Article 11(2) |
| Article 9(3) | Article 11(3) |
| Article 9(4) | Article 11(4) |

| Regulation (EC) No 1073/1999 and Regulation (Euratom) No 1074/1999 | This Regulation |
|---|---|
| — | Article 11(5) |
| — | Article 11(6) |
| — | Article 11(7) |
| — | Article 11(8) |
| Article 10(1) | Article 12(1) |
| Article 10(2) | Article 12(2), first subparagraph |
| — | Article 12(2), second subparagraph |
| — | Article 12(2), third subparagraph |
| Article 10(3) | Article 4(4), second sentence |
| — | Article 12(3) |
| — | Article 12(4) |
| — | Article 13 |
| — | Article 14 |
| Article 11(1), first subparagraph | Article 15(1), first subparagraph |
| — | Article 15(1), second subparagraph |
| Article 11(1), second subparagraph | Article 15(1), third subparagraph |
| — | Article 15(1), fourth subparagraph |
| — | Article 15(1), fifth subparagraph |
| Article 11(2) | Article 15(2), first subparagraph |
| — | Article 15(2), second subparagraph |
| Article 11(3) | Article 15(3) |
| Article 11(4) | Article 15(4) |
| — | Article 15(5) |
| — | Article 15(6) |
| Article 11(5) | Article 15(7) |
| Article 11(6) | Article 15(8) |
| Article 11(7) | Article 17(5), third subparagraph |
| Article 11(8) | Article 15(9) |
| — | Article 16 |
| Article 12(1) | Article 17(1) |
| Article 12(2) | Article 17(2) |
| Article 12(3), first subparagraph | Article 17(3) |
| Article 12(3), second subparagraph | Article 17(4) |
| Article 12(3), third subparagraph | Article 10(3) |
| — | Article 17(5), first subparagraph |

| Regulation (EC) No 1073/1999 and Regulation (Euratom) No 1074/1999 | This Regulation |
|---|---|
| — | Article 17(5), second subparagraph |
| — | Article 17(6) |
| — | Article 17(7) |
| — | Article 17(8) |
| Article 12(4), first sentence | Article 17(9), first subparagraph |
| Article 12(4), second sentence | Article 17(9), second subparagraph |
| — | Article 17(10) |
| Article 13 | Article 18 |
| Article 14 | — |
| Article 15 | Article 19 |
| — | Article 20 |
| Article 16 | Article 21(1) |
| — | Article 21(2) |
| — | Article 21(3) |
| — | Annex I |
| — | Annex II |

L 248/22 EN Official Journal of the European Union 18.9.2013

**Commission statement**

The Commission confirms that the Office has declared that it will at all times act in compliance with the Protocol No 7 on the Privileges and Immunities of the European Union and the Statute for Members of the European Parliament, fully respecting the freedom and independence of Members as provided for in Article 2 of the Statute.

**Commission statement**

The Commission intends to maintain the current powers of the Director-General of the European Anti-fraud Office to lay down the conditions and detailed arrangements for recruiting at the Office, in particular as to the length of contracts and their renewals.

**Statement by the European Parliament, the Council and the Commission**

Each time the European Parliament, the Council and the Commission appoint new members of the new Supervisory Committee they should also appoint those members to take office at the next partial replacement.

# Directive 2013/48 on the right of access to a lawyer in criminal proceedings and in European arrest warrant proceedings, and on the right to have a third party informed upon deprivation of liberty and to communicate with third persons and with consular authorities while deprived of liberty, 22 October 2013

**[OJ 2013, L 294/1–12]**

Effective 1 July 2013, the electronic version of the *Official Journal* (e-OJ) is authentic and produces legal effects.

6.11.2013 EN Official Journal of the European Union L 294/1

I

*(Legislative acts)*

# DIRECTIVES

## DIRECTIVE 2013/48/EU OF THE EUROPEAN PARLIAMENT AND OF THE COUNCIL

**of 22 October 2013**

**on the right of access to a lawyer in criminal proceedings and in European arrest warrant proceedings, and on the right to have a third party informed upon deprivation of liberty and to communicate with third persons and with consular authorities while deprived of liberty**

THE EUROPEAN PARLIAMENT AND THE COUNCIL OF THE EUROPEAN UNION,

Having regard to the Treaty on the Functioning of the European Union, and in particular point (b) of Article 82(2) thereof,

Having regard to the proposal from the European Commission,

After transmission of the draft legislative act to the national parliaments,

Having regard to the opinion of the European Economic and Social Committee [1],

After consulting the Committee of the Regions,

Acting in accordance with the ordinary legislative procedure [2],

Whereas:

(1) Article 47 of the Charter of Fundamental Rights of the European Union (the Charter), Article 6 of the European Convention for the Protection of Human Rights and Fundamental Freedoms (the ECHR) and Article 14 of the International Covenant on Civil and Political Rights (the ICCPR) enshrine the right to a fair trial. Article 48(2) of the Charter guarantees respect for the rights of the defence.

(2) The Union has set itself the objective of maintaining and developing an area of freedom, security and justice. According to the Presidency conclusions of the European Council in Tampere of 15 and 16 October 1999, and in particular point (33) thereof, the principle of mutual recognition of judgments and other decisions of judicial authorities should become the cornerstone of judicial cooperation in civil and criminal matters within the Union because enhanced mutual recognition and the necessary approximation of legislation would facilitate cooperation between competent authorities and the judicial protection of individual rights.

(3) Pursuant to Article 82(1) of the Treaty on the Functioning of the European Union (TFEU), 'judicial cooperation in criminal matters in the Union shall be based on the principle of mutual recognition of judgments and judicial decisions…'.

(4) The implementation of the principle of mutual recognition of decisions in criminal matters presupposes that Member States trust in each other's criminal justice systems. The extent of the mutual recognition is very much dependent on a number of parameters, which include mechanisms for safeguarding the rights of suspects or accused persons and common minimum standards necessary to facilitate the application of the principle of mutual recognition.

(5) Although the Member States are party to the ECHR and to the ICCPR, experience has shown that that alone does not always provide a sufficient degree of trust in the criminal justice systems of other Member States.

(6) Mutual recognition of decisions in criminal matters can operate effectively only in a spirit of trust in which not only judicial authorities, but all actors in the criminal process consider decisions of the judicial authorities of other Member States as equivalent to their own, implying not only trust in the adequacy of other Member States' rules, but also trust that those rules are correctly applied. Strengthening mutual trust requires detailed rules on the protection of the procedural rights and guarantees arising from the Charter, the ECHR and the ICCPR. It also requires, by means of this Directive and by means of other measures, further development within the Union of the minimum standards set out in the Charter and in the ECHR.

[1] OJ C 43, 15.2.2012, p. 51.
[2] Position of the European Parliament of 10 September 2013 (not yet published in the Official Journal) and decision of the Council of 7 October 2013.

(7) Article 82(2) TFEU provides for the establishment of minimum rules applicable in the Member States so as to facilitate mutual recognition of judgments and judicial decisions and police and judicial cooperation in criminal matters having a cross-border dimension. That Article refers to 'the rights of individuals in criminal procedure' as one of the areas in which minimum rules may be established.

(8) Common minimum rules should lead to increased confidence in the criminal justice systems of all Member States, which, in turn, should lead to more efficient judicial cooperation in a climate of mutual trust and to the promotion of a fundamental rights culture in the Union. Such common minimum rules should also remove obstacles to the free movement of citizens throughout the territory of the Member States. Such common minimum rules should be established in relation to the right of access to a lawyer in criminal proceedings, the right to have a third party informed upon deprivation of liberty and the right to communicate with third persons and with consular authorities while deprived of liberty.

(9) On 30 November 2009, the Council adopted a Resolution on a Roadmap for strengthening the procedural rights of suspected or accused persons in criminal proceedings ('the Roadmap') ([1]). Taking a step-by-step approach, the Roadmap calls for the adoption of measures regarding the right to translation and interpretation (measure A), the right to information on rights and information about the charges (measure B), the right to legal advice and legal aid (measure C), the right to communicate with relatives, employers and consular authorities (measure D), and special safeguards for suspects or accused persons who are vulnerable (measure E). The Roadmap emphasises that the order of the rights is only indicative and thus implies that it may be changed in accordance with priorities. The Roadmap is designed to operate as a whole; only when all its components are implemented will its benefits be felt in full.

(10) On 11 December 2009, the European Council welcomed the Roadmap and made it part of the Stockholm programme — An open and secure Europe serving and protecting citizens ([2]) (point 2.4). The European Council underlined the non-exhaustive character of the Roadmap, by inviting the Commission to examine further elements of minimum procedural rights for suspects and accused persons, and to assess whether other issues, for instance the presumption of innocence, need to be addressed, in order to promote better cooperation in that area.

(11) Two measures have been adopted pursuant to the Roadmap to date, namely Directive 2010/64/EU of the European Parliament and of the Council of 20 October 2010 on the right to interpretation and translation in criminal proceedings ([3]) and Directive 2012/13/EU of the European Parliament and of the Council of 22 May 2012 on the right to information in criminal proceedings ([4]).

(12) This Directive lays down minimum rules concerning the right of access to a lawyer in criminal proceedings and in proceedings for the execution of a European arrest warrant pursuant to Council Framework Decision 2002/584/JHA of 13 June 2002 on the European arrest warrant and the surrender procedures between Member States ([5]) (European arrest warrant proceedings) and the right to have a third party informed upon deprivation of liberty and to communicate with third persons and with consular authorities while deprived of liberty. In doing so, it promotes the application of the Charter, in particular Articles 4, 6, 7, 47 and 48 thereof, by building upon Articles 3, 5, 6 and 8 ECHR, as interpreted by the European Court of Human Rights, which, in its case-law, on an ongoing basis, sets standards on the right of access to a lawyer. That case-law provides, inter alia, that the fairness of proceedings requires that a suspect or accused person be able to obtain the whole range of services specifically associated with legal assistance. In that regard, the lawyers of suspects or accused persons should be able to secure without restriction, the fundamental aspects of the defence.

(13) Without prejudice to the obligations of Member States under the ECHR to ensure the right to a fair trial, proceedings in relation to minor offending which take place within a prison and proceedings in relation to offences committed in a military context which are dealt with by a commanding officer should not be considered to be criminal proceedings for the purposes of this Directive.

(14) This Directive should be implemented taking into account the provisions of Directive 2012/13/EU, which provide that suspects or accused persons are provided promptly with information concerning the right of access to a lawyer, and that suspects or accused persons who are arrested or detained are provided promptly with a written Letter of Rights containing information about the right of access to a lawyer.

(15) The term 'lawyer' in this Directive refers to any person who, in accordance with national law, is qualified and entitled, including by means of accreditation by an authorised body, to provide legal advice and assistance to suspects or accused persons.

(16) In some Member States an authority other than a court having jurisdiction in criminal matters has competence for imposing sanctions other than deprivation of liberty in relation to relatively minor offences. That may be the case, for example, in relation to traffic offences which are committed on a large scale and which might be established following a traffic control. In such situations, it would be unreasonable to require that the competent

([1]) OJ C 295, 4.12.2009, p. 1.
([2]) OJ C 115, 4.5.2010, p. 1.
([3]) OJ L 280, 26.10.2010, p. 1.
([4]) OJ L 142, 1.6.2012, p. 1.
([5]) OJ L 190, 18.7.2002, p. 1.

authorities ensure all the rights under this Directive. Where the law of a Member State provides for the imposition of a sanction regarding minor offences by such an authority and there is either a right of appeal or the possibility for the case to be otherwise referred to a court having jurisdiction in criminal matters, this Directive should therefore apply only to the proceedings before that court following such an appeal or referral.

(17) In some Member States certain minor offences, in particular minor traffic offences, minor offences in relation to general municipal regulations and minor public order offences, are considered to be criminal offences. In such situations, it would be unreasonable to require that the competent authorities ensure all the rights under this Directive. Where the law of a Member State provides in respect of minor offences that deprivation of liberty cannot be imposed as a sanction, this Directive should therefore apply only to the proceedings before a court having jurisdiction in criminal matters.

(18) The scope of application of this Directive in respect of certain minor offences should not affect the obligations of Member States under the ECHR to ensure the right to a fair trial including obtaining legal assistance from a lawyer.

(19) Member States should ensure that suspects or accused persons have the right of access to a lawyer without undue delay in accordance with this Directive. In any event, suspects or accused persons should be granted access to a lawyer during criminal proceedings before a court, if they have not waived that right.

(20) For the purposes of this Directive, questioning does not include preliminary questioning by the police or by another law enforcement authority the purpose of which is to identify the person concerned, to verify the possession of weapons or other similar safety issues or to determine whether an investigation should be started, for example in the course of a road-side check, or during regular random checks when a suspect or accused person has not yet been identified.

(21) Where a person other than a suspect or accused person, such as a witness, becomes a suspect or accused person, that person should be protected against self-incrimination and has the right to remain silent, as confirmed by the case-law of the European Court of Human Rights. This Directive therefore makes express reference to the practical situation where such a person becomes a suspect or accused person during questioning by the police or by another law enforcement authority in the context of criminal proceedings. Where, in the course of such questioning, a person other than a suspect or accused person becomes a suspect or accused person, questioning should be suspended immediately. However, questioning may be continued if the person concerned has been made aware that he or she is a suspect or accused person and is able to fully exercise the rights provided for in this Directive.

(22) Suspects or accused persons should have the right to meet in private with the lawyer representing them. Member States may make practical arrangements concerning the duration and frequency of such meetings, taking into account the circumstances of the proceedings, in particular the complexity of the case and the procedural steps applicable. Member States may also make practical arrangements to ensure safety and security, in particular of the lawyer and of the suspect or accused person, in the place where such a meeting is conducted. Such practical arrangements should not prejudice the effective exercise or essence of the right of suspects or accused persons to meet their lawyer.

(23) Suspects or accused persons should have the right to communicate with the lawyer representing them. Such communication may take place at any stage, including before any exercise of the right to meet that lawyer. Member States may make practical arrangements concerning the duration, frequency and means of such communication, including concerning the use of video-conferencing and other communication technology in order to allow such communications to take place. Such practical arrangements should not prejudice the effective exercise or essence of the right of suspects or accused persons to communicate with their lawyer.

(24) In respect of certain minor offences, this Directive should not prevent Member States from organising the right of suspects or accused persons to have access to a lawyer by telephone. However, limiting the right in this way should be restricted to cases where a suspect or accused person will not be questioned by the police or by another law enforcement authority.

(25) Member States should ensure that suspects or accused persons have the right for their lawyer to be present and participate effectively when they are questioned by the police or by another law enforcement or judicial authority, including during court hearings. Such participation should be in accordance with any procedures under national law which may regulate the participation of a lawyer during questioning of the suspect or accused person by the police or by another law enforcement or judicial authority, including during court hearings, provided that such procedures do not prejudice the effective exercise and essence of the right concerned. During questioning by the police or by another law

enforcement or judicial authority of the suspect or accused person or in a court hearing, the lawyer may, inter alia, in accordance with such procedures, ask questions, request clarification and make statements, which should be recorded in accordance with national law.

(26) Suspects or accused persons have the right for their lawyer to attend investigative or evidence-gathering acts, insofar as they are provided for in the national law concerned and in so far as the suspects or accused persons are required or permitted to attend. Such acts should at least include identity parades, at which the suspect or accused person figures among other persons in order to be identified by a victim or witness; confrontations, where a suspect or accused person is brought together with one or more witnesses or victims where there is disagreement between them on important facts or issues; and reconstructions of the scene of a crime in the presence of the suspect or accused person, in order to better understand the manner and circumstances under which a crime was committed and to be able to ask specific questions to the suspect or accused person. Member States may make practical arrangements concerning the presence of a lawyer during investigative or evidence-gathering acts. Such practical arrangements should not prejudice the effective exercise and essence of the rights concerned. Where the lawyer is present during an investigative or evidence-gathering act, this should be noted using the recording procedure in accordance with the law of the Member State concerned.

(27) Member States should endeavour to make general information available, for instance on a website or by means of a leaflet that is available at police stations, to facilitate the obtaining of a lawyer by suspects or accused persons. However, Member States would not need to take active steps to ensure that suspects or accused persons who are not deprived of liberty will be assisted by a lawyer if they have not themselves arranged to be assisted by a lawyer. The suspect or accused person concerned should be able freely to contact, consult and be assisted by a lawyer.

(28) Where suspects or accused persons are deprived of liberty, Member States should make the necessary arrangements to ensure that such persons are in a position to exercise effectively the right of access to a lawyer, including by arranging for the assistance of a lawyer when the person concerned does not have one, unless they have waived that right. Such arrangements could imply, inter alia, that the competent authorities arrange for the assistance of a lawyer on the basis of a list of available lawyers from which the suspect or accused person could choose. Such arrangements could include those on legal aid if applicable.

(29) The conditions in which suspects or accused persons are deprived of liberty should fully respect the standards set out in the ECHR, in the Charter, and in the case-law of the Court of Justice of the European Union (the Court of Justice) and of the European Court of Human Rights. When providing assistance under this Directive to a suspect or to an accused person who is deprived of liberty, the lawyer concerned should be able to raise a question with the competent authorities regarding the conditions in which that person is deprived of liberty.

(30) In cases of geographical remoteness of the suspect or accused person, such as in overseas territories or where the Member State undertakes or participates in military operations outside its territory, Member States are permitted to derogate temporarily from the right of the suspect or accused person to have access to a lawyer without undue delay after deprivation of liberty. During such a temporary derogation, the competent authorities should not question the person concerned or carry out any of the investigative or evidence-gathering acts provided for in this Directive. Where immediate access to a lawyer is not possible because of the geographical remoteness of the suspect or accused person, Member States should arrange for communication via telephone or video conference unless this is impossible.

(31) Member States should be permitted to derogate temporarily from the right of access to a lawyer in the pre-trial phase when there is a need, in cases of urgency, to avert serious adverse consequences for the life, liberty or physical integrity of a person. During a temporary derogation on that ground, the competent authorities may question suspects or accused persons without the lawyer being present, provided that they have been informed of their right to remain silent and can exercise that right, and provided that such questioning does not prejudice the rights of the defence, including the privilege against self-incrimination. Questioning may be carried out for the sole purpose and to the extent necessary to obtain information that is essential to avert serious adverse consequences for the life, liberty or physical integrity of a person. Any abuse of this derogation would in principle irretrievably prejudice the rights of the defence.

(32) Member States should also be permitted to derogate temporarily from the right of access to a lawyer in the pre-trial phase where immediate action by the investigating authorities is imperative to prevent substantial jeopardy to criminal proceedings, in particular to prevent destruction or alteration of essential evidence, or to prevent interference with witnesses. During a temporary derogation on that ground, the competent authorities may question suspects or accused persons without a lawyer being present, provided that they have been informed of their right to remain silent and can exercise that right, and provided that such questioning does not prejudice the rights of the defence, including the privilege against self-incrimination. Questioning may be carried out for the sole purpose and to the extent necessary to obtain information that is essential to prevent substantial jeopardy to criminal proceedings. Any abuse of this derogation would in principle irretrievably prejudice the rights of the defence.

(33) Confidentiality of communication between suspects or accused persons and their lawyer is key to ensuring the effective exercise of the rights of the defence and is an essential part of the right to a fair trial. Member States should therefore respect the confidentiality of meetings and other forms of communication between the lawyer and the suspect or accused person in the exercise of the right of access to a lawyer provided for in this Directive, without derogation. This Directive is without prejudice to procedures that address the situation where there are objective and factual circumstances giving rise to the suspicion that the lawyer is involved with the suspect or accused person in a criminal offence. Any criminal activity on the part of a lawyer should not be considered to be legitimate assistance to suspects or accused persons within the framework of this Directive. The obligation to respect confidentiality not only implies that Member States should refrain from interfering with or accessing such communication but also that, where suspects or accused persons are deprived of liberty or otherwise find themselves in a place under the control of the State, Member States should ensure that arrangements for communication uphold and protect confidentiality. This is without prejudice to any mechanisms that are in place in detention facilities with the purpose of avoiding illicit enclosures being sent to detainees, such as screening correspondence, provided that such mechanisms do not allow the competent authorities to read the communication between suspects or accused persons and their lawyer. This Directive is also without prejudice to procedures under national law according to which forwarding correspondence may be rejected if the sender does not agree to the correspondence first being submitted to a competent court.

(34) This Directive should be without prejudice to a breach of confidentiality which is incidental to a lawful surveillance operation by competent authorities. This Directive should also be without prejudice to the work that is carried out, for example, by national intelligence services to safeguard national security in accordance with Article 4(2) of the Treaty on European Union (TEU) or that falls within the scope of Article 72 TFEU, pursuant to which Title V on an area of Freedom, Security and Justice must not affect the exercise of the responsibilities incumbent upon Member States with regard to the maintenance of law and order and the safeguarding of internal security.

(35) Suspects or accused persons who are deprived of liberty should have the right to have at least one person, such as a relative or an employer, nominated by them, informed of their deprivation of liberty without undue delay, provided that this does not prejudice the due course of the criminal proceedings against the person concerned or any other criminal proceedings. Member States may make practical arrangements in relation to the application of that right. Such practical arrangements should not prejudice the effective exercise and essence of the right. In limited, exceptional circumstances, however, it should be possible to derogate temporarily from that right when this is justified, in the light of the particular circumstances of the case, by a compelling reason as specified in this Directive. When the competent authorities envisage making such a temporary derogation in respect of a specific third person, they should firstly consider whether another third person, nominated by the suspect or accused person, could be informed of the deprivation of liberty.

(36) Suspects or accused persons should, while deprived of liberty, have the right to communicate without undue delay with at least one third person, such as a relative, nominated by them. Member States may limit or defer the exercise of that right in view of imperative requirements or proportionate operational requirements. Such requirements could include, inter alia, the need to avert serious adverse consequences for the life, liberty or physical integrity of a person, the need to prevent prejudice to criminal proceedings, the need to prevent a criminal offence, the need to await a court hearing, and the need to protect victims of crime. When the competent authorities envisage limiting or deferring the exercise of the right to communicate in respect of a specific third person, they should first consider whether the suspects or accused persons could communicate with another third person nominated by them. Member States may make practical arrangements concerning the timing, means, duration and frequency of communication with third persons, taking account of the need to maintain good order, safety and security in the place where the person is being deprived of liberty.

(37) The right of suspects and accused persons who are deprived of liberty to consular assistance is enshrined in Article 36 of the 1963 Vienna Convention on Consular Relations where it is a right conferred on States to have access to their nationals. This Directive confers a corresponding right on suspects or accused persons who are deprived of liberty, subject to their wishes. Consular protection may be exercised by diplomatic authorities where such authorities act as consular authorities.

(38) Member States should clearly set out in their national law the grounds and criteria for any temporary derogations from the rights granted under this Directive, and they should make restricted use of those temporary derogations. Any such temporary derogations should be proportional, should be strictly limited in time, should not be based exclusively on the type or the seriousness of the alleged offence, and should not prejudice the overall fairness of the proceedings. Member States should ensure that where a temporary derogation has been authorised under this Directive by a judicial authority which is not a judge or a court, the decision on authorising the temporary derogation can be assessed by a court, at least during the trial stage.

(39) Suspects or accused persons should be able to waive a right granted under this Directive provided that they have been given information about the content of the right concerned and the possible consequences of waiving that right. When providing such information, the specific conditions of the suspects or accused persons concerned should be taken into account, including their age and their mental and physical condition.

(40) A waiver and the circumstances in which it was given should be noted using the recording procedure in accordance with the law of the Member State concerned. This should not lead to any additional obligation for Member States to introduce new mechanisms or to any additional administrative burden.

(41) Where a suspect or accused person revokes a waiver in accordance with this Directive, it should not be necessary to proceed again with questioning or any procedural acts that have been carried out during the period when the right concerned was waived.

(42) Persons subject to a European arrest warrant ('requested persons') should have the right of access to a lawyer in the executing Member State in order to allow them to exercise their rights effectively under Framework Decision 2002/584/JHA. Where a lawyer participates in a hearing of a requested person by an executing judicial authority, that lawyer may, inter alia, in accordance with procedures provided for under national law, ask questions, request clarification and make statements. The fact that the lawyer has participated in such a hearing should be noted using the recording procedure in accordance with the law of the Member State concerned.

(43) Requested persons should have the right to meet in private with the lawyer representing them in the executing Member State. Member States may make practical arrangements concerning the duration and frequency of such meetings, taking into account the particular circumstances of the case. Member States may also make practical arrangements to ensure safety and security, in particular of the lawyer and of the requested person, in the place where the meeting between the lawyer and the requested person is conducted. Such practical arrangements should not prejudice the effective exercise and essence of the right of requested persons to meet with their lawyer.

(44) Requested persons should have the right to communicate with the lawyer representing them in the executing Member State. It should be possible for such communication to take place at any stage, including before any exercise of the right to meet with the lawyer. Member States may make practical arrangements concerning the duration, frequency and means of communication between requested persons and their lawyer, including concerning the use of videoconferencing and other communication technology in order to allow such communications to take place. Such practical arrangements should not prejudice the effective exercise and essence of the right of requested persons to communicate with their lawyer.

(45) Executing Member States should make the necessary arrangements to ensure that requested persons are in a position to exercise effectively their right of access to a lawyer in the executing Member State, including by arranging for the assistance of a lawyer when requested persons do not have one, unless they have waived that right. Such arrangements, including those on legal aid if applicable, should be governed by national law. They could imply, inter alia, that the competent authorities arrange for the assistance of a lawyer on the basis of a list of available lawyers from which requested persons could choose.

(46) Without undue delay after being informed that a requested person wishes to appoint a lawyer in the issuing Member State, the competent authority of that Member State should provide the requested person with

information to facilitate the appointment of a lawyer in that Member State. Such information could, for example, include a current list of lawyers, or the name of a lawyer on duty in the issuing State, who can provide information and advice in European arrest warrant cases. Member States could request that the appropriate bar association draw up such a list.

(47) The surrender procedure is crucial for cooperation in criminal matters between the Member States. Observance of the time-limits contained in Framework Decision 2002/584/JHA is essential for such cooperation. Therefore, while requested persons should be able to exercise fully their rights under this Directive in European arrest warrant proceedings, those time-limits should be respected.

(48) Pending a legislative act of the Union on legal aid, Member States should apply their national law in relation to legal aid, which should be in line with the Charter, the ECHR and the case-law of the European Court of Human Rights.

(49) In accordance with the principle of effectiveness of Union law, Member States should put in place adequate and effective remedies to protect the rights that are conferred upon individuals by this Directive.

(50) Member States should ensure that in the assessment of statements made by suspects or accused persons or of evidence obtained in breach of their right to a lawyer, or in cases where a derogation from that right was authorised in accordance with this Directive, the rights of the defence and the fairness of the proceedings are respected. In this context, regard should be had to the case-law of the European Court of Human Rights, which has established that the rights of the defence will, in principle, be irretrievably prejudiced when incriminating statements made during police interrogation without access to a lawyer are used for a conviction. This should be without prejudice to the use of statements for other purposes permitted under national law, such as the need to execute urgent investigative acts to avoid the perpetration of other offences or serious adverse consequences for any person or related to an urgent need to prevent substantial jeopardy to criminal proceedings where access to a lawyer or delaying the investigation would irretrievably prejudice the ongoing investigations regarding a serious crime. Further, this should be without prejudice to national rules or systems regarding admissibility of evidence, and should not prevent Member States from maintaining a system whereby all existing evidence can be adduced before a court or a judge, without there being any separate or prior assessment as to admissibility of such evidence.

(51) The duty of care towards suspects or accused persons who are in a potentially weak position underpins a fair administration of justice. The prosecution, law enforcement and judicial authorities should therefore facilitate the effective exercise by such persons of the rights provided for in this Directive, for example by taking into account any potential vulnerability that affects their ability to exercise the right of access to a lawyer and to have a third party informed upon deprivation of liberty, and by taking appropriate steps to ensure those rights are guaranteed.

(52) This Directive upholds the fundamental rights and principles recognised by the Charter, including the prohibition of torture and inhuman and degrading treatment, the right to liberty and security, respect for private and family life, the right to the integrity of the person, the rights of the child, integration of persons with disabilities, the right to an effective remedy and the right to a fair trial, the presumption of innocence and the rights of the defence. This Directive should be implemented in accordance with those rights and principles.

(53) Member States should ensure that the provisions of this Directive, where they correspond to rights guaranteed by the ECHR, are implemented consistently with those of the ECHR and as developed by case-law of the European Court of Human Rights.

(54) This Directive sets minimum rules. Member States may extend the rights set out in this Directive in order to provide a higher level of protection. Such higher level of protection should not constitute an obstacle to the mutual recognition of judicial decisions that those minimum rules are designed to facilitate. The level of protection should never fall below the standards provided by the Charter or by the ECHR, as interpreted by the case-law of the Court of Justice and of the European Court of Human Rights.

(55) This Directive promotes the rights of children and takes into account the Guidelines of the Council of Europe on child friendly justice, in particular its provisions on information and advice to be given to children. This Directive ensures that suspects and accused persons, including children, are provided with adequate information to understand the consequences of waiving a right under this Directive and that any such waiver is made voluntarily and unequivocally. Where the suspect or accused person is a child, the holder of parental responsibility should be notified as soon as possible after the child's deprivation of liberty and should be provided with the reasons therefor. If providing such information to the holder of parental responsibility is contrary to the best interests of the child, another suitable adult such as a relative should be informed instead. This should be without prejudice to provisions

of national law which require that any specified authorities, institutions or individuals, in particular those that are responsible for the protection or welfare of children, should be informed of the deprivation of liberty of a child. Member States should refrain from limiting or deferring the exercise of the right to communicate with a third party in respect of suspects or accused persons who are children and who are deprived of liberty, save in the most exceptional circumstances. Where a deferral is applied the child should, however, not be held incommunicado and should be permitted to communicate, for example with an institution or an individual responsible for the protection or welfare of children.

(56) In accordance with the Joint Political Declaration of 28 September 2011 of Member States and the Commission on explanatory documents [1], Member States have undertaken to accompany, in justified cases, the notification of their transposition measures with one or more documents explaining the relationship between the components of a directive and the corresponding parts of national transposition instruments. With regard to this Directive, the legislator considers the transmission of such documents to be justified.

(57) Since the objectives of this Directive, namely setting common minimum rules for the right of access to a lawyer in criminal proceedings and in European arrest warrant proceedings and the right to have a third person informed of the deprivation of liberty and to communicate with third persons and with consular authorities while deprived of liberty, cannot be sufficiently achieved by the Member States, but can rather, by reason of the scale of the measure, be better achieved at Union level, the Union may adopt measures, in accordance with the principle of subsidiarity as set out in Article 5 TEU. In accordance with the principle of proportionality, as set out in that Article, this Directive does not go beyond what is necessary in order to achieve those objectives.

(58) In accordance with Articles 1 and 2 of Protocol No 21 on the position of the United Kingdom and Ireland in respect of the Area of Freedom, Security and Justice, annexed to the TEU and to the TFEU and without prejudice to Article 4 of that Protocol, those Member States are not taking part in the adoption of this Directive and are not bound by it or subject to its application.

(59) In accordance with Articles 1 and 2 of Protocol No 22 on the position of Denmark, annexed to the TEU and to the TFEU, Denmark is not taking part in the adoption of this Directive, and is not bound by it or subject to its application,

(1) OJ C 369, 17.12.2011, p. 14.

HAVE ADOPTED THIS DIRECTIVE:

*Article 1*

**Subject matter**

This Directive lays down minimum rules concerning the rights of suspects and accused persons in criminal proceedings and of persons subject to proceedings pursuant to Framework Decision 2002/584/JHA ('European arrest warrant proceedings') to have access to a lawyer, to have a third party informed of the deprivation of liberty and to communicate with third persons and with consular authorities while deprived of liberty.

*Article 2*

**Scope**

1. This Directive applies to suspects or accused persons in criminal proceedings from the time when they are made aware by the competent authorities of a Member State, by official notification or otherwise, that they are suspected or accused of having committed a criminal offence, and irrespective of whether they are deprived of liberty. It applies until the conclusion of the proceedings, which is understood to mean the final determination of the question whether the suspect or accused person has committed the offence, including, where applicable, sentencing and the resolution of any appeal.

2. This Directive applies to persons subject to European arrest warrant proceedings (requested persons) from the time of their arrest in the executing Member State in accordance with Article 10.

3. This Directive also applies, under the same conditions as provided for in paragraph 1, to persons other than suspects or accused persons who, in the course of questioning by the police or by another law enforcement authority, become suspects or accused persons.

4. Without prejudice to the right to a fair trial, in respect of minor offences:

(a) where the law of a Member State provides for the imposition of a sanction by an authority other than a court having jurisdiction in criminal matters, and the imposition of such a sanction may be appealed or referred to such a court; or

(b) where deprivation of liberty cannot be imposed as a sanction;

this Directive shall only apply to the proceedings before a court having jurisdiction in criminal matters.

In any event, this Directive shall fully apply where the suspect or accused person is deprived of liberty, irrespective of the stage of the criminal proceedings.

*Article 3*

**The right of access to a lawyer in criminal proceedings**

1. Member States shall ensure that suspects and accused persons have the right of access to a lawyer in such time and in such a manner so as to allow the persons concerned to exercise their rights of defence practically and effectively.

2. Suspects or accused persons shall have access to a lawyer without undue delay. In any event, suspects or accused persons shall have access to a lawyer from whichever of the following points in time is the earliest:

(a) before they are questioned by the police or by another law enforcement or judicial authority;

(b) upon the carrying out by investigating or other competent authorities of an investigative or other evidence-gathering act in accordance with point (c) of paragraph 3;

(c) without undue delay after deprivation of liberty;

(d) where they have been summoned to appear before a court having jurisdiction in criminal matters, in due time before they appear before that court.

3. The right of access to a lawyer shall entail the following:

(a) Member States shall ensure that suspects or accused persons have the right to meet in private and communicate with the lawyer representing them, including prior to questioning by the police or by another law enforcement or judicial authority;

(b) Member States shall ensure that suspects or accused persons have the right for their lawyer to be present and participate effectively when questioned. Such participation shall be in accordance with procedures under national law, provided that such procedures do not prejudice the effective exercise and essence of the right concerned. Where a lawyer participates during questioning, the fact that such participation has taken place shall be noted using the recording procedure in accordance with the law of the Member State concerned;

(c) Member States shall ensure that suspects or accused persons shall have, as a minimum, the right for their lawyer to attend the following investigative or evidence-gathering acts where those acts are provided for under national law and if the suspect or accused person is required or permitted to attend the act concerned:

(i) identity parades;

(ii) confrontations;

(iii) reconstructions of the scene of a crime.

4. Member States shall endeavour to make general information available to facilitate the obtaining of a lawyer by suspects or accused persons.

Notwithstanding provisions of national law concerning the mandatory presence of a lawyer, Member States shall make the necessary arrangements to ensure that suspects or accused persons who are deprived of liberty are in a position to exercise effectively their right of access to a lawyer, unless they have waived that right in accordance with Article 9.

5. In exceptional circumstances and only at the pre-trial stage, Member States may temporarily derogate from the application of point (c) of paragraph 2 where the geographical remoteness of a suspect or accused person makes it impossible to ensure the right of access to a lawyer without undue delay after deprivation of liberty.

6. In exceptional circumstances and only at the pre-trial stage, Member States may temporarily derogate from the application of the rights provided for in paragraph 3 to the extent justified in the light of the particular circumstances of the case, on the basis of one of the following compelling reasons:

(a) where there is an urgent need to avert serious adverse consequences for the life, liberty or physical integrity of a person;

(b) where immediate action by the investigating authorities is imperative to prevent substantial jeopardy to criminal proceedings.

*Article 4*

**Confidentiality**

Member States shall respect the confidentiality of communication between suspects or accused persons and their lawyer in the exercise of the right of access to a lawyer provided for under this Directive. Such communication shall include meetings, correspondence, telephone conversations and other forms of communication permitted under national law.

*Article 5*

**The right to have a third person informed of the deprivation of liberty**

1. Member States shall ensure that suspects or accused persons who are deprived of liberty have the right to have at least one person, such as a relative or an employer, nominated by them, informed of their deprivation of liberty without undue delay if they so wish.

2. If the suspect or accused person is a child, Member States shall ensure that the holder of parental responsibility of the child is informed as soon as possible of the deprivation of liberty and of the reasons pertaining thereto, unless it would be contrary to the best interests of the child, in which case another appropriate adult shall be informed. For the purposes of this paragraph, a person below the age of 18 years shall be considered to be a child.

3. Member States may temporarily derogate from the application of the rights set out in paragraphs 1 and 2 where justified in the light of the particular circumstances of the case on the basis of one of the following compelling reasons:

(a) where there is an urgent need to avert serious adverse consequences for the life, liberty or physical integrity of a person;

(b) where there is an urgent need to prevent a situation where criminal proceedings could be substantially jeopardised.

4. Where Member States temporarily derogate from the application of the right set out in paragraph 2, they shall ensure that an authority responsible for the protection or welfare of children is informed without undue delay of the deprivation of liberty of the child.

*Article 6*

**The right to communicate, while deprived of liberty, with third persons**

1. Member States shall ensure that suspects or accused persons who are deprived of liberty have the right to communicate without undue delay with at least one third person, such as a relative, nominated by them.

2. Member States may limit or defer the exercise of the right referred to in paragraph 1 in view of imperative requirements or proportionate operational requirements.

*Article 7*

**The right to communicate with consular authorities**

1. Member States shall ensure that suspects or accused persons who are non-nationals and who are deprived of liberty have the right to have the consular authorities of their State of nationality informed of the deprivation of liberty without undue delay and to communicate with those authorities, if they so wish. However, where suspects or accused persons have two or more nationalities, they may choose which consular authorities, if any, are to be informed of the deprivation of liberty and with whom they wish to communicate.

2. Suspects or accused persons also have the right to be visited by their consular authorities, the right to converse and correspond with them and the right to have legal representation arranged for by their consular authorities, subject to the agreement of those authorities and the wishes of the suspects or accused persons concerned.

3. The exercise of the rights laid down in this Article may be regulated by national law or procedures, provided that such law or procedures enable full effect to be given to the purposes for which these rights are intended.

*Article 8*

**General conditions for applying temporary derogations**

1. Any temporary derogation under Article 3(5) or (6) or under Article 5(3) shall

(a) be proportionate and not go beyond what is necessary;

(b) be strictly limited in time;

(c) not be based exclusively on the type or the seriousness of the alleged offence; and

(d) not prejudice the overall fairness of the proceedings.

2. Temporary derogations under Article 3(5) or (6) may be authorised only by a duly reasoned decision taken on a case-by-case basis, either by a judicial authority, or by another competent authority on condition that the decision can be submitted to judicial review. The duly reasoned decision shall be recorded using the recording procedure in accordance with the law of the Member State concerned.

3. Temporary derogations under Article 5(3) may be authorised only on a case-by-case basis, either by a judicial authority, or by another competent authority on condition that the decision can be submitted to judicial review.

*Article 9*

**Waiver**

1. Without prejudice to national law requiring the mandatory presence or assistance of a lawyer, Member States shall ensure that, in relation to any waiver of a right referred to in Articles 3 and 10:

(a) the suspect or accused person has been provided, orally or in writing, with clear and sufficient information in simple and understandable language about the content of the right concerned and the possible consequences of waiving it; and

(b) the waiver is given voluntarily and unequivocally.

2. The waiver, which can be made in writing or orally, shall be noted, as well as the circumstances under which the waiver was given, using the recording procedure in accordance with the law of the Member State concerned.

3. Member States shall ensure that suspects or accused persons may revoke a waiver subsequently at any point during the criminal proceedings and that they are informed about that possibility. Such a revocation shall have effect from the moment it is made.

*Article 10*

**The right of access to a lawyer in European arrest warrant proceedings**

1. Member States shall ensure that a requested person has the right of access to a lawyer in the executing Member State upon arrest pursuant to the European arrest warrant.

2. With regard to the content of the right of access to a lawyer in the executing Member State, requested persons shall have the following rights in that Member State:

(a) the right of access to a lawyer in such time and in such a manner as to allow the requested persons to exercise their rights effectively and in any event without undue delay from deprivation of liberty;

(b) the right to meet and communicate with the lawyer representing them;

(c) the right for their lawyer to be present and, in accordance with procedures in national law, participate during a hearing of a requested person by the executing judicial authority. Where a lawyer participates during the hearing this shall be noted using the recording procedure in accordance with the law of the Member State concerned.

3. The rights provided for in Articles 4, 5, 6, 7, 9, and, where a temporary derogation under Article 5(3) is applied, in Article 8, shall apply, *mutatis mutandis*, to European arrest warrant proceedings in the executing Member State.

4. The competent authority in the executing Member State shall, without undue delay after deprivation of liberty, inform requested persons that they have the right to appoint a lawyer in the issuing Member State. The role of that lawyer in the issuing Member State is to assist the lawyer in the executing Member State by providing that lawyer with information and advice with a view to the effective exercise of the rights of requested persons under Framework Decision 2002/584/JHA.

5. Where requested persons wish to exercise the right to appoint a lawyer in the issuing Member State and do not already have such a lawyer, the competent authority in the executing Member State shall promptly inform the competent authority in the issuing Member State. The competent authority of that Member State shall, without undue delay, provide the requested persons with information to facilitate them in appointing a lawyer there.

6. The right of a requested person to appoint a lawyer in the issuing Member State is without prejudice to the time-limits set out in Framework Decision 2002/584/JHA or the obligation on the executing judicial authority to decide, within those time-limits and the conditions defined under that Framework Decision, whether the person is to be surrendered.

*Article 11*

**Legal aid**

This Directive is without prejudice to national law in relation to legal aid, which shall apply in accordance with the Charter and the ECHR.

*Article 12*

**Remedies**

1. Member States shall ensure that suspects or accused persons in criminal proceedings, as well as requested persons in European arrest warrant proceedings, have an effective remedy under national law in the event of a breach of the rights under this Directive.

2. Without prejudice to national rules and systems on the admissibility of evidence, Member States shall ensure that, in criminal proceedings, in the assessment of statements made by suspects or accused persons or of evidence obtained in breach of their right to a lawyer or in cases where a derogation to this right was authorised in accordance with Article 3(6), the rights of the defence and the fairness of the proceedings are respected.

*Article 13*

**Vulnerable persons**

Member States shall ensure that the particular needs of vulnerable suspects and vulnerable accused persons are taken into account in the application of this Directive.

*Article 14*

**Non-regression clause**

Nothing in this Directive shall be construed as limiting or derogating from any of the rights and procedural safeguards that are ensured under the Charter, the ECHR, or other relevant provisions of international law or the law of any Member State which provides a higher level of protection.

*Article 15*

**Transposition**

1. Member States shall bring into force the laws, regulations and administrative provisions necessary to comply with this Directive by 27 November 2016. They shall immediately inform the Commission thereof.

L 294/12 EN Official Journal of the European Union 6.11.2013

2. When Member States adopt those measures, they shall contain a reference to this Directive or shall be accompanied by such a reference on the occasion of their official publication. The methods of making such a reference shall be laid down by the Member States.

3. Member States shall communicate to the Commission the text of the measures of national law which they adopt in the field covered by this Directive.

*Article 16*

**Report**

The Commission shall, by 28 November 2019, submit a report to the European Parliament and to the Council, assessing the extent to which the Member States have taken the necessary measures in order to comply with this Directive, including an evaluation of the application of Article 3(6) in conjunction with Article 8(1) and (2), accompanied, if necessary, by legislative proposals.

*Article 17*

**Entry into force**

This Directive shall enter into force on the twentieth day following that of its publication in the *Official Journal of the European Union*.

*Article 18*

**Addressees**

This Directive is addressed to the Member States in accordance with the Treaties.

Done at Strasbourg, 22 October 2013.

*For the European Parliament*
*The President*
M. SCHULZ

*For the Council*
*The President*
V. LEŠKEVIČIUS

# Practice directions to parties concerning cases brought before the Court, 25 November 2013

[OJ 2014, L 31/1–13]

31.1.2014 EN Official Journal of the European Union L 31/1

II

*(Non-legislative acts)*

# RULES OF PROCEDURE

## PRACTICE DIRECTIONS TO PARTIES CONCERNING CASES BROUGHT BEFORE THE COURT

*Table of Contents*

THE COURT OF JUSTICE,

Having regard to the Rules of Procedure of 25 September 2012 [1] and, in particular, Article 208 thereof,

Whereas:

(1) On 25 September 2012, the Court of Justice, with the approval of the Council, adopted new Rules of Procedure repealing the Rules of Procedure of 19 June 1991, as last amended on 24 May 2011. The new Rules entered into force on 1 November 2012 and are intended, inter alia, to ensure that the structure and content of the Rules of Procedure of the Court are adapted to changes in its caseload and, in particular, to the increasing number of references for a preliminary ruling made by the courts and tribunals of the Member States of the European Union, while at the same time supplementing and clarifying, in several important respects, the rules applicable to the conduct of proceedings before the Court.

[1] OJ L 265, 29.9.2012, p. 1, as amended on 18 June 2013 (OJ L 173, 26.6.2013, p. 65).

(2) In the interests of the proper administration of justice and of making the Rules easier to understand, it is appropriate, therefore, to replace the practice directions relating to direct actions and appeals, adopted on the basis of the earlier Rules of Procedure, and to give the parties and their representatives practice directions based on the new Rules of Procedure that take into account, in particular, the experience gained in the course of their implementation.

(3) These new directions, which apply to all categories of cases brought before the Court, are not intended to replace the relevant provisions of the Statute and of the Rules of Procedure. Their purpose is to afford the parties and their representatives a better understanding of the implications of those provisions and to outline in greater detail the conduct of proceedings before the Court and, in particular, the constraints on the Court, particularly those associated with the processing and translation of procedural documents or the simultaneous interpretation of the observations submitted in the course of a hearing. In a context notable, on the one hand, for a constant increase in the number of cases brought before the Court and, on the other hand, for the growing complexity of their subject-matter, observing and taking into account these directions constitutes, both for the parties and for the Court, the best guarantee that the latter will be able to deal with cases with the greatest efficiency.

(4) In the interests of clarification, it is also necessary to incorporate into these new directions certain provisions of a rather more practical nature — which have until now been included in the Notes for the guidance of Counsel, the Instructions to the Registrar of the Court or letters of notice to attend a hearing — relating to the lodging and service of procedural documents and to the actual conduct of the oral part of the procedure,

HEREBY ADOPTS THE FOLLOWING PRACTICE DIRECTIONS:

## I. GENERAL PROVISIONS

### The stages in the procedure before the Court and their essential characteristics

1. Subject to special provisions laid down in the Protocol on the Statute of the Court of Justice of the European Union ('the Statute') or in the Rules of Procedure, the procedure before the Court is to consist, as a general rule, of a written part and an oral part. The purpose of the written part of the procedure is to put before the Court the claims, pleas and arguments of the parties to the proceedings or, in preliminary rulings, the observations which the interested persons referred to in Article 23 of the Statute intend to submit concerning the questions put by the courts and tribunals of the Member States of the European Union. The oral part, which follows it, is intended for its part to allow the Court to complete its knowledge of the case by the possible hearing of submissions from those parties or interested persons at a hearing and, if appropriate, by hearing the Opinion of the Advocate General.

### Representation of the parties before the Court

2. In accordance with Article 19 of the Statute, parties to proceedings before the Court must be represented by a person who is duly authorised to represent them. With the exception of the Member States, other States which are parties to the Agreement on the European Economic Area ('the EEA Agreement'), the European Free Trade Association ('EFTA') Surveillance Authority and the institutions of the European Union, which are to be represented by an agent appointed for each case, other parties to the proceedings must be represented by a lawyer authorised to practise before a court of a Member State or of another State which is a party to the EEA Agreement. The evidence of that capacity must be capable of being produced, on request, at any stage of the proceedings. University teachers who are nationals of a Member State whose law accords them a right of audience are treated as lawyers by virtue of the seventh paragraph of Article 19 of the Statute.

3. In preliminary ruling proceedings, the Court is to take account, so far as concerns the representation of the parties to the main proceedings, of the procedural rules applicable in the court or tribunal which made the reference. Any person empowered to represent a party before that court or tribunal may therefore also represent him before the Court of Justice and, if the national procedural rules do not require parties to be represented, the parties to the main proceedings are entitled to submit their own written and oral observations. In the event of uncertainty in this respect, the Court may, at any time, request those parties, their representatives or the court or tribunal which made the reference to provide the relevant information.

4. The persons called upon to present oral argument before the Court, irrespective of their qualifications or the capacity in which they are called upon, are required to wear gowns. Where a hearing is organised, agents and lawyers taking part in that hearing are therefore requested to provide their own gowns; the Court has a number of plain gowns available for parties or representatives who have none.

**Costs of proceedings before the Court and legal aid**

5. Subject to the provisions set out in Article 143 of the Rules of Procedure, proceedings before the Court are to be free of charge, no charge or tax being payable to that latter on account of the initiation of proceedings or the lodging of a procedural document. The costs referred to in Article 137 et seq. of the Rules of Procedure include only 'recoverable' costs, that is, any sums payable to witnesses and experts, and expenses necessarily incurred by the parties for the purpose of the proceedings before the Court, in connection with the remuneration of their representative and the expenses of his travel to and subsistence in Luxembourg, if a hearing is organised. The Court rules on the amount of those costs and the party ordered to pay them in the judgment or order which closes the proceedings, whereas in preliminary rulings it is for the referring court or tribunal to rule on the costs of the proceedings.

6. A party or, in preliminary ruling proceedings, a party to the main proceedings who is wholly or partly unable to meet the costs of the proceedings before the Court may, at any time, apply for legal aid under the conditions provided for, respectively, in Articles 115 to 118 and 185 to 189 of the Rules of Procedure. In order for it to be possible for such applications to be considered, they must however be accompanied by all the information and supporting documents necessary to enable the Court to assess the legal aid applicant's true financial situation. Since, in preliminary rulings, the Court gives its ruling at the request of a court or tribunal of a Member State, the parties to the main proceedings must, first of all, apply for any legal aid from that court or tribunal or the competent authorities of the Member State concerned, the aid granted by the Court being only subsidiary to the aid granted at national level.

7. It is worth noting that, where it grants the application for legal aid, the Court is responsible, where applicable within the limits set by the formation of the Court, solely for costs involved in the assistance and representation before the Court of the applicant for legal aid. In accordance with the rules set out in the Rules of Procedure, those costs can be recovered subsequently by the Court in the decision ending the proceedings and ruling on costs, and the formation of the Court which gave a decision on the application for legal aid may, moreover, withdraw that legal aid at any time if the circumstances which led to its being granted alter during the proceedings.

**Anonymity**

8. Where a party considers it necessary that its identity or certain information concerning it should not be disclosed in a case brought before the Court, it may request that the Court 'anonymise' the relevant case, in whole or in part. To be effective, such an application must, however, be made as early as possible. On account of the increasing use of new information and communication technologies, granting anonymity becomes much more difficult if the notice of the case concerned has already been published in the *Official Journal of the European Union* or, in preliminary ruling proceedings, if the request for a preliminary ruling has already been served on the interested persons referred to in Article 23 of the Statute, about one month after the request has been lodged at the Court.

## II. THE WRITTEN PART OF THE PROCEDURE

**The purpose of the written part of the procedure**

9. The written part of the procedure plays an essential role in the Court's understanding of the case in so far as it must allow the Court, by reading the written pleadings or observations lodged, to acquire a detailed and accurate idea of the subject-matter of the case before it and the issues raised by that case. Although this is the Court's objective when dealing with any case brought before it, the conduct and the pattern of the written part of the procedure differ depending on the nature of the action. Whereas in direct actions or appeals the parties are requested to adopt a position on the written pleadings lodged by the other parties to the proceedings, the written part of the procedure in preliminary rulings is characterised by the absence of adversarial proceedings, the interested persons referred to in Article 23 of the Statute being merely requested to submit any observations they may make on the questions referred by a national court or tribunal, without as a general rule knowing the position adopted by the other interested persons on those questions. This gives rise to different requirements as regards both the form and length of those observations and also the subsequent conduct of the procedure.

**The written part of the procedure in references for a preliminary ruling**

10. On account of the non-adversarial nature of preliminary ruling proceedings, the lodging of written observations by the interested persons referred to in Article 23 of the Statute does not involve any specific formalities. Where a request for a preliminary ruling is served on them by the Court, those persons may thus submit, if they wish, written observations in which they set out their point of view on the request made by the referring court or tribunal. The purpose of those observations — which must be lodged within a time-limit of two months from service of the request for a preliminary ruling (extended on account of distance by a single period of 10 days) that cannot otherwise be extended — is to help clarify for the Court the scope of that request, and above all the answers to be provided to the questions referred by the referring court or tribunal.

11. Although the statement must be complete and include, in particular, the arguments on which the Court may base its answer to the questions referred, it is not necessary, on the other hand, to repeat the factual and legal background of the dispute set out in the order for reference, unless it requires further comment. Subject to special circumstances or specific provisions of the Rules of Procedure providing for a restriction of the length of the documents because of the urgency of the case, written observations lodged in a preliminary ruling should not exceed 20 pages.

**The written part of the procedure in direct actions**

*The application*

12. On account of its adversarial nature, the written part of the procedure in direct actions follows stricter rules. These are set out in Article 119 et seq. (Title IV) of the Rules of Procedure and concern both the obligation for the parties to be represented by an agent or lawyer and the formal requirements linked to the content and the submission of written pleadings. It is apparent, in particular, from Article 120 of the Rules of Procedure, that the application initiating proceedings must, in addition to stating the name and address of the applicant and the name of the party against whom the application is made, state accurately the subject-matter of the proceedings, the pleas in law and arguments relied upon supported, as appropriate, by any evidence produced or offered, and the form of order sought by the applicant. Failure to comply with those requirements renders the application inadmissible. Unless there are special circumstances, the application should not exceed 30 pages.

13. As is apparent from Article 120(c) of the Rules of Procedure, the application must also include a summary of the pleas in law relied upon. That summary — which must not exceed two pages — is intended to facilitate the drafting of the notice, on each case brought before the Court, which must be published in the *Official Journal of the European Union* in accordance with Article 21(4) of the Rules of Procedure.

*The defence*

14. The defence, to which Article 124 of the Rules of Procedure relates, is essentially subject to the same formal requirements as the application and must be lodged within two months of service of that latter. That time-limit — extended on account of distance by a single period of 10 days — may otherwise be extended only exceptionally and where a duly reasoned request setting out the circumstances capable of justifying such an extension has been submitted within the prescribed time-limit.

15. Since the legal framework of the proceedings is fixed by the application, the structure of the legal argument developed in the defence must, so far as is possible, reflect that of the pleas in law or complaints put forward in the application. No new plea in law may be introduced in the course of the proceedings unless it is based on matters of law or of fact which come to light in the course of the procedure. The factual and legal background is to be recapitulated in the defence only in so far as its presentation in the application is disputed or calls for further particulars. As in the case of the application, unless there are special circumstances the defence should not exceed 30 pages.

*The reply and rejoinder*

16. If they consider it necessary, the applicant and the defendant may supplement their arguments, the former by a reply and the latter by a rejoinder. Those written pleadings are subject to the same formal rules as the application and the defence but, since they are optional and supplementary, they are necessarily shorter than those documents. The framework and the pleas in law or claims at the heart of the dispute having been set out (or disputed) in depth in the application and the defence, the only purpose of the reply and the rejoinder is to allow the applicant and the defendant to make clear their position or to refine their arguments on an important issue, the President also being able, pursuant to Article 126 of the Rules of Procedure, to specify himself the matters to which those documents should relate. Except in special circumstances, a reply or a rejoinder should therefore be no more than approximately 10 pages long. Those documents must be lodged with the Registry within the time-limits set by the Court, an extension of those time-limits being granted by the President only in exceptional circumstances and on a duly reasoned request.

*Request for an expedited procedure*

17. Where the nature of the case requires it to be dealt with within a short time, the applicant or defendant may request the Court to deal with the case under an expedited procedure derogating from the provisions of the Rules of Procedure. Provided for in Article 133 of those Rules, that possibility is nevertheless subject to the lodging, by a separate document, of an express request to that effect setting out in detail the circumstances capable of justifying the use of such a procedure and involves, where such a request is granted, an adjustment to the written part of the procedure. The ordinary time-limits for the lodging of written pleadings are reduced, as is the length of those pleadings and, pursuant to Article 134 of the Rules of Procedure, a reply, a rejoinder or a statement in intervention can be submitted only if the President considers this to be necessary.

*Application for suspension of operation or for interim measures (Interim proceedings)*

18. A direct action may also be accompanied by an application for suspension of operation of a measure or by an application for interim measures, as referred to in Articles 278 and 279 respectively of the Treaty on the Functioning of the European Union ('TFEU'). In accordance with the provisions of Article 160 of the Rules of Procedure, such an application is however admissible only if it is made by the applicant having challenged the measure at issue before the Court or another party to the case before the Court and it must be made by a separate document stating the subject-matter of the proceedings and the circumstances giving rise to urgency as well as the pleas of fact and law establishing a prima facie case for the measure applied for. As a general rule, the application is then served on the opposite party, and the President is to prescribe a short period within which that party may submit written or oral observations. In cases of extreme urgency, the President may grant the application provisionally even before such observations have been submitted. In such a case, the decision closing the interim proceedings can, however, be adopted only after that party has been heard.

**The written part of the procedure in appeals**

19. The written part of the procedure in an appeal is similar in many respects to the conduct of that part of the procedure in direct actions. The relevant rules are in Article 167 et seq. (Title V) of the Rules of Procedure, which state both the mandatory content of the appeal and of the response and the scope of the forms of order sought.

*The appeal*

20. As is apparent from Articles 168 and 169 of the Rules of Procedure (which supplement, in this respect, Articles 56 to 58 of the Statute), an appeal is not brought against a measure of an institution, a body or an office or agency of the European Union, but against the decision of the General Court ruling on an action brought at first instance. It is apparent from that information that the form of order sought in the appeal must necessarily seek to have set aside, in whole or in part, the decision of the General Court as set out in the operative part of that decision, and not the annulment of the measure challenged before the General Court. If they are not to be held inadmissible, the pleas in law and legal arguments relied upon in the appeal — which, unless there are special circumstances, should not exceed 25 pages — must moreover identify precisely those points in the grounds of that decision that are contested and set out in detail the reasons for which that decision is alleged to be vitiated by an error of law.

21. In order to facilitate the drawing up of the notice published in the *Official Journal of the European Union*, in accordance with Article 21(4) of the Rules of Procedure, the appellant must also attach to his appeal a summary of those pleas in law, no more than two pages long, and lodge at the Registry the necessary items and documents attesting that the requirements set out in Article 19 of the Statute and reiterated in Article 119 of the Rules of Procedure are met.

*The response*

22. Within a time-limit of two months from the service upon him of the appeal (extended on account of distance by a single period of 10 days), which may not otherwise be extended, any party to the case at issue before the General Court may submit a response. The content of the written pleadings is subject to the requirements fixed in Article 173 of the Rules of Procedure and, in accordance with Article 174 of those Rules, the form of order must seek to have the appeal allowed or dismissed, in whole or in part. The structure of the legal arguments in the response must, so far as is possible, reflect the pleas in law put forward by the appellant but it is not necessary to reiterate in those pleadings the factual and legal background to the proceedings, unless its presentation in the appeal is disputed or calls for further particulars. On the other hand, any challenge to the admissibility, in whole or in part, of that appeal must be included in the actual body of the response, since the possibility — provided for in Article 151 of the Rules of Procedure — of raising a plea of inadmissibility in relation to the proceedings by a separate document is not applicable to appeals. Like the appeal, and subject to special circumstances, the response should not exceed 25 pages.

*The cross-appeal*

23. If, when the appeal has been served on him, one of the parties to the relevant case before the General Court intends to dispute that court's decision on an aspect which was not mentioned in the appeal, that party must bring a cross-appeal against the General Court's decision. That appeal must be introduced by a separate document, within the same time-limit, which may not be extended, as the time-limit for submission of the response and meet the requirements set out in Articles 177 and 178 of the Rules of Procedure. The pleas in law and legal arguments which it contains must be separate from those relied on in the response.

*The response to the cross-appeal*

24. Where such a cross-appeal is brought, the applicant, or any other party to the relevant case before the General Court having an interest in the cross-appeal being allowed or dismissed, may submit a response, which must be limited to the pleas in law relied on in that cross-appeal. In accordance with Article 179 of the Rules of Procedure, those written pleadings must be submitted within a time-limit, which may not be extended, of two months from service of the cross-appeal (extended on account of distance by a single period of 10 days).

*The reply and rejoinder*

25. Whether in the case of a main appeal or a cross-appeal, the appeal and the response may be supplemented by a reply and a rejoinder, in particular in order to allow the parties to adopt a position on a plea of inadmissibility or new matters raised in the response. Unlike the rules applicable to direct actions, that possibility is however made subject to the express authorisation of the President of the Court. To that effect, the appellant (or the party having brought the cross-appeal) is requested to submit, within a time-limit of seven days from service of the response (or of the response to the cross-appeal), extended on account of distance by a single period of 10 days, a duly reasoned application setting out the reasons for which, in that party's opinion, a reply is necessary. That application — which should not exceed three pages — must be intelligible in itself, without necessitating reference to the appeal or to the response.

26. Due to the special nature of appeals, which are restricted to the examination of questions of law, the President may also, if he grants the application to lodge a reply, limit the number of pages and the subject-matter of that reply and of the rejoinder submitted subsequently. The observance of those instructions is an essential condition for the proper conduct of the procedure, and exceeding the number of pages authorised or referring to other questions in the reply or the rejoinder will lead to the pleadings being sent back to their author.

*Appeals brought under Article 57 of the Statute*

27. The rules set out in points 19 to 26 of these directions are nevertheless not applicable in their entirety to appeals brought against decisions of the General Court dismissing an application to intervene or adopted following an application for interim measures submitted under Articles 278 or 279 TFEU. Pursuant to the third paragraph of Article 57 of the Statute, such appeals are subject to the same procedure as an application for interim measures made directly to the Court. The parties are therefore set a short period for the submission of any observations on the appeal and the Court rules on that appeal without any additional written part of the procedure, or even without an oral part of the procedure.

**Intervention in direct actions and appeals**

*The application to intervene*

28. In accordance with Article 40 of the Statute, the Member States and institutions of the European Union, on the one hand, and, in the circumstances provided for in the second and third paragraphs of that article, non-Member States party to the Agreement on the EEA, the EFTA Surveillance Authority, the bodies, offices and agencies of the European Union and any other natural or legal person, on the other hand, may intervene in cases before the Court for the purposes of supporting, in whole or in part, the form of order sought by one of the parties. To be taken into account, the application to intervene must be submitted within the time-limit referred to in Article 130(1) (direct actions), or Article 190(2) (appeals) of the Rules of Procedure and meet the conditions set in Article 130(2) to (4) of those Rules.

*The statement in intervention*

29. If the application to intervene is granted, the intervener receives a copy of every procedural document served on the parties save, where applicable, secret or confidential items or documents, and he has one month from receipt of those documents to submit a statement in intervention. Although that statement must meet the requirements in Article 132(2) of the Rules of Procedure, its content is, however, necessarily more succinct than the written pleadings of the party supported and its length should not exceed 10 pages. Since the intervention is ancillary to the main proceedings, the intervener must refrain from repeating in his statement the pleas in law and arguments in the written pleadings of the party which he is supporting and must set out only additional pleas in law or arguments which bear out that party's submissions. Recapitulation of the factual or legal background to the case is not necessary, except in so far as its presentation in the written pleadings of the main parties is disputed or, exceptionally, calls for further particulars.

*Observations on the statement in intervention*

30. After the statement in intervention has been lodged, the President may, if he considers this necessary, prescribe a time-limit for the submission of brief observations on that statement. The lodging of those observations, the length of which should not exceed five pages, is nevertheless optional. The purpose of such observations is merely to enable the main parties to respond to inaccurate claims or to adopt a position on new pleas in law or arguments raised by the intervener. Where there are no such matters, it is recommended that the parties desist from lodging those observations in order to avoid unnecessarily prolonging the written part of the procedure.

*Applications to intervene made out of time*

31. In so far as it meets the conditions set out in Article 130(2) to (4) of the Rules of Procedure, the Court may also give consideration to an application to intervene made after the passing of the time-limit prescribed in Article 130(1) or 190(2) of the Rules of Procedure, provided, however, that that application reaches it before the decision to open the oral part of the procedure provided for in Article 60(4) of those Rules is adopted. In that case, the intervener will be able to submit his observations, if any, during the hearing, if it takes place.

*Intervention in the context of an application for interim measures or an expedited procedure*

32. The same is true in general in the context of an application for interim measures or where a case is to be dealt with under an expedited procedure. If there are no special circumstances warranting the lodging of written observations, the person or entity authorised to intervene in the context of such a procedure may submit his observations only orally, if a hearing is organised.

*No intervention in preliminary rulings*

33. The above rules on intervention are, in contrast, not applicable to references for a preliminary ruling. Due to the non-adversarial nature of that category of cases and the special function of the Court when it is called upon to give a preliminary ruling on the interpretation or validity of European Union law, only the interested persons referred to in Article 23 of the Statute are authorised to submit observations, written or oral, on the questions submitted to the Court by the courts or tribunals of the Member States.

**The form and structure of procedural documents**

34. Irrespective of the foregoing matters and the prerequisites relating to the content of procedural documents resulting from the provisions of the Statute and the Rules of Procedure, the written pleadings and observations lodged before the Court must meet certain additional requirements intended to facilitate the reading and processing of those documents by the Court, in particular by electronic means. Those requirements concern the form and the presentation of procedural documents as well as their length or structure.

35. As to the formal conditions, first of all, it is essential that the written pleadings or observations lodged by the parties are presented in a form in which they can be processed electronically by the Court and that, in particular, documents can be scanned and character recognition used. To that end, the following requirements must be taken into account:

— the written pleadings or observations are to be drafted on white, unlined and A4-size paper, with text on one side of the page only (recto), and not on both sides of the page (recto-verso),

— the text is to be in a commonly-used font (such as Times New Roman, Courier or Arial), in at least 12 point in the body of the text and at least 10 point in the footnotes, with 1,5 line spacing and horizontal and vertical margins of at least 2,5 cm (above, below, at the left and at the right of the page),

— all the paragraphs of the written pleadings or observations are to be numbered consecutively,

— the same is true for the pages of the written pleadings or observations, including any annexes to them and their schedule, which are to be numbered consecutively, at the top right-hand corner,

— lastly, where they are not sent to the Court by electronic means, pages of written pleadings or observations are to be assembled in such a way as to be easily separable and not permanently attached by means such as glue or staples.

36. In addition to these formal requirements, the procedural documents lodged before the Court must be drafted in a form which allows their structure and scope to be grasped from the first few pages. Besides stating, on the first page of the written pleadings or observations concerned, the title of the document, the case number (if it has already been notified by the Registry) and the parties concerned (parties to the dispute in the main proceedings, the applicant (appellant) and the defendant (respondent) or parties to the case at issue before the General Court), the written pleadings or observations lodged are to begin with a brief summary of the schema adopted by the author or by a table of contents. Those written pleadings or those observations must end with the forms of order sought by the author or, in preliminary ruling proceedings, by the answers which the author proposes to the questions of the referring court or tribunal.

37. Although the documents which are sent to the Court are not subject, as regards their content, to any requirement other than those resulting from the Statute and the Rules of Procedure, it must nevertheless be borne in mind that such documents constitute the basis for the Court's study of the file and that they must, as a general rule, be translated by the Court or the institution which produced them. In the interests of the proper conduct of the procedure as in the interests of the parties themselves, the written pleadings or observations must therefore be drafted in clear, concise language, without use of technical terms specific to a national legal system. Repetition must be avoided and short sentences must, as far as possible, be used in preference to long and complex sentences which include parenthetical and subordinate clauses.

38. When, in their written pleadings or observations, the parties refer to a specific text or piece of legislation, of national or European Union law, references to that text or legislation must be accurately cited, both so far as concerns the date of adoption and, where possible, the date of publication of that document and so far as concerns its temporal applicability. Likewise, when they cite an extract or a passage of a judgment or of an Opinion of an Advocate General, the parties are requested to specify both the name and number of the case concerned and the exact references of the extract or the passage at issue.

39. Lastly, it must be pointed out that legal argument of the parties or the interested persons referred to in Article 23 of the Statute must appear in the written pleadings or observations, and not in any attached annexes, which are not as a general rule translated. Only documents mentioned in the actual body of written pleadings or observations and necessary in order to prove or illustrate its contents may be submitted as annexes. Annexes are furthermore not accepted, pursuant to Article 57(4) of the Rules of Procedure, unless they are accompanied by a schedule of annexes. That schedule is to indicate, for each document annexed, the number of the annex, a short description of the document and the page or paragraph of the written pleadings or observations in which the document is cited and which justifies its production.

**The lodging and transmission of procedural documents**

40. Only the documents expressly provided for by the procedural rules may be lodged at the Registry. Those documents must be lodged within the prescribed time-limits and observing the requirements set out in Article 57 of the Rules of Procedure. Documents may be lodged electronically or by post, or delivered in person to the Court Registry or, outside the opening hours of the Registry, to the reception of the Court buildings (rue du Fort Niedergrünewald) where the janitor will acknowledge receipt of that document by recording on it the date and time of lodgement.

41. The most reliable, quickest way to lodge a procedural document is by using the *e-Curia application*. That application, common to the three constituent courts of the Court of Justice of the European Union, was introduced in 2011. It allows the lodging and service of procedural documents by exclusively electronic means, without it being necessary to provide certified copies of the document transmitted to the Court or to duplicate that transmission by sending the document by post. The procedure for access to the e-Curia application and its conditions of use are described in detail in the Decision of the Court of 13 September 2011 on the lodging and service of procedural documents by means of e-Curia and in the conditions of use to which that decision refers. Those documents are available on the Court's internet site (under 'Court of Justice Procedure').

42. If it is not transmitted to the Court by means of the abovementioned application, a procedural document may also be sent to the Court *by post*. The envelope containing that document must be addressed to the Court Registry at the following address: Rue du Fort Niedergrünewald — L-2925 Luxembourg. In this connection, it is appropriate to mention that pursuant to Article 57(7) of the Rules of Procedure, only the date and time of lodgement of the original at the Registry are taken into consideration in the calculation of procedural time-limits. To prevent any time-barring, it is therefore strongly recommended that it be sent by registered post or by express delivery, several days before the passing of the time-limit prescribed for lodgement of the document.

43. At the present time, a copy of the signed original of a procedural document may also be transmitted to the Registry *by fax* ((+ 352 433766) or as an attachment to an *electronic mail* (ecj.registry@curia.europa.eu). However, a document lodged by either of these methods will be treated as complying with the relevant time-limit only if the signed original itself, together with the annexes and copies referred to in Article 57(2) of the Rules of Procedure, reaches the Registry at the latest 10 days after that electronic mail or telefax was sent. That original must therefore be sent without delay, immediately after the dispatch of the copy, without any corrections or amendments, even of a minor nature. In the event of any discrepancy between the signed original and the copy previously transmitted, only the date on which the signed original was lodged will be taken into consideration.

III. THE ORAL PART OF THE PROCEDURE

44. As is apparent from the fourth paragraph of Article 20 of the Statute, the oral part of the procedure essentially consists of two distinct stages: the hearing of the parties or interested persons referred to in Article 23 of the Statute and the presentation of the Advocate General's Opinion. Under the fifth paragraph of Article 20 of the Statute, the Court may nevertheless decide, where it considers that the case raises no new point of law, that the case is to be determined without hearing the Advocate General's Opinion. A hearing will not automatically be arranged.

**The purpose of the hearing**

45. Having regard to the importance of the written part of the procedure in cases brought before the Court and subject to the application of Article 76(3) of the Rules of Procedure, the decisive criterion for holding a hearing is not so much whether an express request has been made to that effect as the assessment made by the Court itself as to the potential contribution of that hearing to the outcome of the dispute or to determining the answers which it could provide to the questions referred by a court or tribunal of a Member State. A hearing is therefore arranged by the Court whenever it is likely to contribute to a better understanding of the case and the issues raised by it, whether or not a request to that effect has been made by the parties or the interested persons referred to in Article 23 of the Statute.

**The request for a hearing**

46. Where those parties or interested persons consider that a hearing must be arranged in a case, the onus is on them, in any event, as soon as they have received notification of the end of the written part of the procedure, to inform the Court by letter why they wish be heard. That reasoning — which is not to be confused with written pleadings or observations and should not exceed three pages — must be based on a real assessment of the benefit of a hearing to the party in question and must indicate the documentary elements or arguments which that party considers it necessary to develop or disprove more fully at the hearing. It is not in itself sufficient to provide a general statement of reasons referring, for example, to the importance of the case or of the questions to be decided by the Court.

**The notice to attend the hearing and the need for a rapid answer to that notice**

47. When the Court decides to arrange a hearing in a particular case, it fixes the exact date and time and the parties or interested persons referred to in Article 23 of the Statute are immediately sent a letter of notice to attend by the Registry, which also notifies them of the composition of the formation to which the Court has assigned the case, of any measures of organisation of procedure decided on by the Court and, where applicable, that there is to be no Advocate General's Opinion. In order to enable the Court to arrange that hearing in the best possible conditions, the parties or abovementioned interested persons are requested to reply to the Registry's letter within a short period stating, in particular, whether they intend actually to attend the hearing and the name of the lawyer or agent who will represent them at it. A late reply to the Registry's letter of notice to attend is likely to jeopardise the proper organisation of the hearing, both from the point of view of the speaking time allocated by the Court to the party concerned and with regard to the constraints on the operation of the interpretation service.

**The steps to be taken with a view to the hearing**

48. On account both of the sometimes difficult traffic conditions in Luxembourg and of the security measures applicable to access to the Court buildings, it is advisable to take the steps necessary to be present in the room where the hearing will take place on the day of the hearing well before it is due to start. Before the hearing begins, the members of the formation of the Court usually hold a short meeting with the representatives of the parties or interested persons referred to in Article 23 of the Statute about the organisation of the hearing. At that meeting the Judge-Rapporteur and the Advocate General may invite those representatives to provide, at the hearing, further information on certain questions or to develop one or more specific aspects of the case at issue.

**The normal procedure at a hearing**

49. While the procedure at a hearing before the Court may vary depending on the circumstances of each case, in general it consists of three separate parts: the oral submissions proper, questions from the members of the Court and replies.

**The first stage of the hearing: oral submissions**

*The purpose of the oral submissions*

50. Subject to any special circumstances, the hearing usually starts with the *oral submissions* of the parties or the interested persons referred to in Article 23 of the Statute. The aim of those submissions is, firstly, to respond to any requests to concentrate on specified issues in the submissions and to answer the questions that the Court might have put to the parties or interested persons before the hearing, under Articles 61 or 62 of the Rules of Procedure, and, if applicable, then to draw attention to the points which the person presenting oral argument considers to be particularly important for the Court's decision, in particular, in preliminary ruling proceedings, having regard to the written observations submitted by the other participants in the proceedings.

51. In the light of the knowledge which the Court already has of the case following the written part of the procedure, it is not necessary, at the hearing, to recall the content of the written pleadings or observations lodged or, in particular, the factual or legal background to the case. Only the decisive points for the purposes of the Court's decision must be brought to its attention. It must none the less be stated that where, before the hearing, the Court has requested the parties or the abovementioned interested persons to concentrate in their submissions on a question or a particular aspect of the case, in general only that question or that aspect should be addressed during those submissions. As far as possible, participants in the hearing who are advocating the same line of argument or adopting the same position must also liaise before the hearing to avoid repeating arguments which have already been submitted.

*Speaking time and its possible extension*

52. The speaking time is fixed by the President of the formation of the Court, after consulting the Judge-Rapporteur and, if applicable, the Advocate General responsible for the case. As a general rule, the speaking time is fixed at 15 minutes, irrespective of the formation of the Court to which the case has been assigned. However, that duration may be made longer or shorter depending on the nature or the specific complexity of the case, the number and procedural status of the participants in the hearing and any measures of organisation of procedure. An extension of the speaking time allocated may, exceptionally, be granted by the President of the formation of the Court on the duly reasoned application of a party or one of the interested persons referred to in Article 23 of the Statute. To be taken into account, such an application must nevertheless be made by the party or interested person concerned in his reply to the letter of notice to attend and, in any event, reach the Court at least two weeks before the actual date of the hearing.

*The number of persons presenting oral argument*

53. For reasons connected with the proper conduct of the hearing, the oral submissions of the parties or the interested persons present at the hearing must, as regards each of them, be made by a single person. In exceptional circumstances, a second person may nevertheless be authorised to present oral argument where the nature or specific complexity of the case warrants this, provided a duly reasoned application to this effect has been submitted in the reply of the party or interested person concerned to the letter of notice to attend the hearing and, in any event, at least two weeks before the actual date of the hearing. If it is granted, that authorisation does not however include any extension of the speaking time, and the two persons presenting oral argument must share the speaking time allocated to the party concerned.

**The second stage of the hearing: questions from members of the Court**

54. Without prejudice to the questions which may be asked or the clarifications which may be sought by the members of the Court during the oral submissions, the persons presenting oral argument may be requested, at the end of the oral submissions, to answer *additional questions from the members of the Court.* The purpose of those questions is to supplement the members' knowledge of the file and to allow the persons presenting oral argument to explain or elaborate on certain points on which additional information may be required following the written part of the procedure and the oral submissions.

**The third stage of the hearing: replies**

55. After that exchange, the representatives of the parties or the interested persons referred to in Article 23 of the Staff Regulations finally have the opportunity, if they consider it necessary, of replying briefly. Those *replies*, of a maximum duration of five minutes each, do not constitute a second round of oral submissions. They are designed only to enable the persons presenting oral argument to react succinctly to observations made or questions put during the hearing by the other participants or by the members of the Court. If two persons have been authorised to speak for a party, only one of them is authorised to reply.

**The implications and constraints of simultaneous interpretation**

56. Whether in their oral submissions, their replies or their responses to questions from the Court, the persons presenting oral argument must bear in mind that very frequently the members of the formation of the Court will listen to their argument by means of simultaneous interpretation. In the interests of the proper conduct of the hearing and in order to guarantee the quality of the interpretation provided, the representatives of the parties or the interested persons referred to in Article 23 of the Statute are therefore requested, if they have a text available, however short, of notes for the oral submissions or an outline of their argument, to send it in advance to the interpretation directorate, either by fax ((+ 352 43033697), or by electronic mail (interpret@curia.europa.eu). That text or those notes for the oral submissions is intended solely for the interpreters and is neither transmitted to the members of the formation of the Court and the Advocate General responsible for the case nor included in the case file.

57. At the hearing itself, it is however inadvisable to read out a text. To facilitate interpretation, it is recommended to speak freely on the basis of properly structured notes. In any event, it is essential to speak directly into the microphone, at a natural pace and not too quickly, stating in advance the outline of the argument made and using short and simple sentences as a matter of course.

**The procedure following the hearing**

58. The active participation of the parties or interested persons referred to in Article 23 of the Statute comes to an end at the end of the hearing. Subject to the exceptional situation in which the oral part of the procedure is reopened, pursuant to Article 83 of the Rules of Procedure, the parties or abovementioned interested persons are no longer authorised to put forward written or oral observations, in particular in response to the Advocate General's Opinion, once the President of the formation of the Court has declared the hearing closed.

IV. FINAL PROVISIONS

59. The practice directions relating to direct actions and appeals of 15 October 2004 (OJ L 361, p. 15), as amended on 27 January 2009 (OJ L 29, p. 51), are hereby revoked and replaced by these Practice Directions.

60. These Practice Directions shall be published in the *Official Journal of the European Union*. They shall enter into force on the day following their publication.

Adopted at Luxembourg, 25 November 2013.

# Supplementary Rules of the Court of Justice, 14 January 2014

**[OJ 2014, L 32/37–45]**

Effective 1 July 2013, the electronic version of the *Official Journal* (e-OJ) is authentic and produces legal effects.

1.2.2014 EN Official Journal of the European Union L 32/37

# RULES OF PROCEDURE

## SUPPLEMENTARY RULES OF THE COURT OF JUSTICE

*Table of contents*

THE COURT OF JUSTICE,

Having regard to Article 207 of the Rules of Procedure ([1]),

Having regard to Article 46(3) of the act concerning the conditions of accession to the European Union of the Republic of Bulgaria and Romania and the adjustments to the Treaties on which the European Union is founded ([2]),

Having regard to Article 45 of the act concerning the conditions of accession to the European Union of the Republic of Croatia and the adjustments to the Treaty on European Union, the Treaty on the Functioning of the European Union and the Treaty establishing the European Atomic Energy Community ([3]),

Whereas:

(1) On 25 September 2012 the Court adopted new Rules of Procedure containing various amendments, both of substance and of form, in relation to the previous Rules, which they repealed. Those amendments concern, in particular, the terminology used in the new Rules of Procedure and the procedure followed when legal aid is granted. Those alterations must, therefore, be reflected in the wording of the Supplementary Rules.

(2) In consequence of several Member States' designation of new authorities responsible for the handling of the matters referred to in Articles 2, 4 and 6 of the Supplementary Rules and of the accession to the European Union of the Republic of Bulgaria and Romania on 1 January 2007 and of the Republic of Croatia on 1 July 2013, it would furthermore appear necessary to bring up to date the lists in the three annexes to those Rules.

With the Council's approval given on 17 December 2013,

HAS ADOPTED THESE SUPPLEMENTARY RULES:

CHAPTER I

## Letters rogatory

*Article 1*

1. Letters rogatory shall be issued in the form of an order which shall contain the names, forenames, description and address of the witness or expert, set out the facts on which the witness or expert is to be examined, name the parties, their agents, lawyers or advisers, indicate their addresses for service and briefly describe the subject-matter of the proceedings.

2. Notice of the order shall be served on the parties by the Registrar.

*Article 2*

1. The Registrar shall send the order to the competent authority named in Annex I of the Member State in whose territory the witness or expert is to be examined. Where necessary, the order shall be accompanied by a translation into the official languages of the Member State to which it is addressed.

2. The authority named pursuant to paragraph 1 shall pass on the order to the judicial authority which is competent according to its national law.

3. The competent judicial authority shall give effect to the letters rogatory in accordance with its national law. After implementation the competent judicial authority shall transmit to the authority named pursuant to paragraph 1 the order embodying the letters rogatory, any documents arising from the implementation and a detailed statement of costs. These documents shall be sent to the Registrar of the Court.

4. The Registrar shall be responsible for the translation of the documents into the language of the case.

([1]) OJ L 265, 29.9.2012, p. 1, as amended on 18 June 2013 (OJ L 173, 26.6.2013, p. 65).
([2]) OJ L 157, 21.6.2005, p. 203.
([3]) OJ L 112, 24.4.2012, p. 21.

*Article 3*

The Court shall defray the expenses occasioned by the letters rogatory without prejudice to the right to charge them, where appropriate, to the parties.

CHAPTER II

**Legal aid**

*Article 4*

1. The Court, by any order by which it decides that a person is entitled to receive legal aid, shall order that a lawyer be appointed to act for him.

2. If the person does not indicate his choice of lawyer, or if the Court considers that his choice is unacceptable, the Registrar shall send a copy of the order and of the application for legal aid to the authority named in Annex II, being the competent authority of the State concerned.

3. The Court, in the light of the suggestions made by that authority, shall of its own motion appoint a lawyer to act for the person concerned.

*Article 5*

The Court shall adjudicate on the lawyer's expenses and fees; on request, an advance on those expenses and fees may be paid.

CHAPTER III

**Reports of perjury by a witness or expert**

*Article 6*

The Court, after hearing the Advocate General, may decide to report to the competent authority referred to in Annex III of the Member State whose courts have penal jurisdiction any case of perjury on the part of a witness or expert before the Court.

*Article 7*

The Registrar shall be responsible for communicating the decision of the Court. The decision shall set out the facts and circumstances on which the report is based.

**Final provisions**

*Article 8*

These Supplementary Rules replace the Supplementary Rules of 4 December 1974 (OJ L 350, 28.12.1974, p. 29), as most recently amended on 21 February 2006 (OJ L 72, 11.3.2006, p. 1).

*Article 9*

1. These Rules, which shall be authentic in the languages referred to in Article 36 of the Rules of Procedure, shall be published in the *Official Journal of the European Union*.

2. These Rules shall enter into force on the date of their publication.

Done at Luxembourg, 14 January 2014.

*ANNEX I*

**List referred to in Article 2(1)**

**Belgium**

Service public fédéral Justice – Federale Overheidsdienst Justitie

**Bulgaria**

Министър на правосъдието

**Czech Republic**

Ministr spravedlnosti

**Denmark**

Justitsministeriet

**Germany**

Bundesministerium der Justiz

**Estonia**

Justiitsministeerium

**Ireland**

Minister for Justice and Equality

**Greece**

Υπουργείο Δικαιοσύνης, Διαφάνειας και Ανθρωπίνων Δικαιωμάτων

**Spain**

Ministerio de Justicia

**France**

Ministère de la justice

**Croatia**

Ministarstvo pravosuđa

**Italy**

Ministero della Giustizia

**Cyprus**

Υπουργός Δικαιοσύνης και Δημόσιας Τάξεως

**Latvia**

Latvijas Republikas Tieslietu ministrija

**Lithuania**

Lietuvos Respublikos teisingumo ministerija

**Luxembourg**

Parquet général

**Hungary**

Közigazgatási és Igazságügyi Minisztérium

**Malta**

Avukat Ġenerali

**Netherlands**

Minister van Veiligheid en Justitie

**Austria**

Bundesministerium für Justiz

**Poland**

Ministerstwo Sprawiedliwości

**Portugal**

Ministro da Justiça

**Romania**

Ministerul Justiţiei

**Slovenia**

Ministrstvo za pravosodje

**Slovakia**

Minister spravodlivosti

**Finland**

Oikeusministeriö

**Sweden**

Regeringskansliet Justitiedepartementet

**United Kingdom**

Secretary of State for the Home Department

*ANNEX II*

**List referred to in Article 4(2)**

**Belgium**

Service public fédéral Justice – Federale Overheidsdienst Justitie

**Bulgaria**

Министър на правосъдието

**Czech Republic**

Česká advokátní komora

**Denmark**

Justitsministeriet

**Germany**

Bundesrechtsanwaltskammer

**Estonia**

Justiitsministeerium

**Ireland**

Minister for Justice and Equality

**Greece**

Υπουργείο Δικαιοσύνης, Διαφάνειας και Ανθρωπίνων Δικαιωμάτων

**Spain**

Consejo General de la Abogacía Española

**France**

Ministère de la justice

**Croatia**

Ministarstvo pravosuđa

**Italy**

Ministero della Giustizia

**Cyprus**

Υπουργός Δικαιοσύνης και Δημόσιας Τάξεως

**Latvia**

Latvijas Republikas Tieslietu ministrija

**Lithuania**

Lietuvos Respublikos teisingumo ministerija

**Luxembourg**

Ministère de la justice

**Hungary**

Közigazgatási és Igazságügyi Minisztérium

**Malta**

Segretarju Parlamentari għall-Gustizzja

**Netherlands**

Algemene Raad van de Nederlandse Orde van Advocaten

**Austria**

Bundesministerium für Justiz

**Poland**

Ministerstwo Sprawiedliwości

**Portugal**

Ministro da Justiça

**Romania**

Uniunea Națională a Barourilor din România

**Slovenia**

Ministrstvo za pravosodje

**Slovakia**

Slovenská advokátska komora

**Finland**

Oikeusministeriö

**Sweden**

Sveriges advokatsamfund

**United Kingdom**

The Law Society, London (for applicants residing in England or Wales)

The Law Society of Scotland, Edinburgh (for applicants residing in Scotland)

The Law Society of Northern Ireland, Belfast (for applicants residing in Northern Ireland)

L 32/44 EN Official Journal of the European Union 1.2.2014

*ANNEX III*

**List referred to in Article 6**

**Belgium**

Service public fédéral Justice – Federale Overheidsdienst Justitie

**Bulgaria**

Върховна касационна прокуратура на Република България

**Czech Republic**

Nejvyšší státní zastupitelství

**Denmark**

Justitsministeriet

**Germany**

Bundesministerium der Justiz

**Estonia**

Riigiprokuratuur

**Ireland**

The Office of the Attorney General

**Greece**

Υπουργείο Δικαιοσύνης, Διαφάνειας και Ανθρωπίνων Δικαιωμάτων

**Spain**

Consejo General del Poder Judicial

**France**

Ministère de la Justice

**Croatia**

Zamjenik Glavnog državnog odvjetnika

**Italy**

Ministero della Giustizia

**Cyprus**

Γενικός Εισαγγελέας της Δημοκρατίας

**Latvia**

Latvijas Republikas Ģenerālprokuratūra

**Lithuania**

Lietuvos Respublikos generalinė prokuratūra

**Luxembourg**

Parquet général

**Hungary**

Közigazgatási és Igazságügyi Minisztérium

**Malta**

Avukat Ġenerali

**Netherlands**

Minister van Veiligheid en Justitie

**Austria**

Bundesministerium für Justiz

**Poland**

Ministerstwo Sprawiedliwości

**Portugal**

Ministro da Justiça

**Romania**

Parchetul de pe lângă Înalta Curte de Casație și Justiție

**Slovenia**

Ministrstvo za pravosodje

**Slovakia**

Minister spravodlivosti

**Finland**

Keskusrikospoliisi

**Sweden**

Åklagarmyndigheten

**United Kingdom**

Her Majesty's Attorney General (for witnesses or experts residing in England or Wales)

Her Majesty's Advocate General (for witnesses or experts residing in Scotland)

Her Majesty's Attorney General (for witnesses or experts residing in Northern Ireland)

# Agreement between the European Union and the United Republic of Tanzania on the conditions of transfer of suspected pirates and associated seized property from the European Union-led Naval Force to the United Republic of Tanzania, 1 April 2014

**[OJ 2014, L 108/3–8]**

11.4.2014 EN Official Journal of the European Union L 108/3

**AGREEMENT**

**between the European Union and the United Republic of Tanzania on the conditions of transfer of suspected pirates and associated seized property from the European Union-led Naval Force to the United Republic of Tanzania**

THE EUROPEAN UNION, hereinafter also referred to as EU,

of the one part, and

THE UNITED REPUBLIC OF TANZANIA, hereinafter referred to as 'Tanzania',

of the other part,

Together hereinafter referred to as the 'Parties',

TAKING INTO ACCOUNT:

— United Nations (UN) Security Council Resolutions (UNSCR) 1814 (2008), 1838 (2008), 1846 (2008), 1851 (2008) and subsequent UNSCRs,

— The 1982 UN Convention on the Law of the Sea (UNCLOS), in particular Articles 100 to 107 and Article 110 thereof,

— EU Council Joint Action 2008/851/CFSP of 10 November 2008 on a European Union military operation to contribute to the deterrence, prevention and repression of acts of piracy and armed robbery off the Somali coast [1] (Operation EUNAVFOR Atalanta), as subsequently amended,

— International human rights law, including the 1966 International Covenant on Civil and Political Rights, and the 1984 Convention against Torture and Other Cruel, Inhuman or Degrading Treatment or Punishment,

— that this Agreement will not affect the Parties' rights and obligations under international agreements and other instruments establishing international courts and tribunals, including the Statute of the International Criminal Court,

TAKING ALSO INTO ACCOUNT

— the regional initiatives in combating piracy such as initiatives under the African Union (AU), the East African Community (EAC), the Southern Africa Development Community (SADC), the Djibouti Code of Conduct and the Regional Maritime Security and anti-piracy Strategy adopted in Mauritius in 2010,

HAVE AGREED AS FOLLOWS:

*Article 1*

**Aim**

This Agreement defines the conditions and modalities for the transfer from EUNAVFOR to Tanzania of persons suspected of intending to commit, committing or having committed acts of piracy and detained by EUNAVFOR, and associated property seized by EUNAVFOR, and for their treatment after such transfer.

(1) OJ L 301, 12.11.2008, p. 33.

*Article 2*

**Definitions**

For the purposes of this Agreement:

(a) '*European Union-led Naval Force (EUNAVFOR)*' shall mean EU military headquarters and national contingents contributing to the EU operation 'Atalanta', their ships, aircraft and assets;

(b) '*Operation*' shall mean the preparation, establishment, execution and support of the military mission established by EU Council Joint Action 2008/851/CFSP and/or its successors;

(c) '*national contingents*' shall mean units and ships belonging to the Member States of the European Union and to other States participating in the operation;

(d) '*Sending State*' shall mean a State providing a national contingent for EUNAVFOR.

(e) '*Piracy*' shall mean piracy as defined in Article 101 of UNCLOS;

(f) '*Transferred person*' shall mean any person suspected of intending to commit, committing or having committed, acts of piracy and transferred by EUNAVFOR to Tanzania under this Agreement.

*Article 3*

**General principles**

1. Tanzania may accept, upon the request of EUNAVFOR, the transfer by EUNAVFOR of persons detained by EUNAVFOR in connection with piracy and associated seized property and submit such persons and property to its competent authorities for the purpose of investigation and prosecution. Agreement on acceptance of a proposed handover will be made on a case by case basis by Tanzania, taking into account all relevant circumstances including the location of the incident.

2. EUNAVFOR shall transfer persons only to competent law enforcement authorities of Tanzania.

3. The Parties shall treat the persons referred to in Article 1, both prior to and following transfer, humanely and in accordance with international human rights obligations, including the prohibition of torture and cruel, inhuman and degrading treatment or punishment, the prohibition of unlawful detention, and in accordance with the requirement to have a fair trial.

4. Transfers shall not be carried out before the competent law enforcement authorities of Tanzania decide, in accordance with Tanzanian internal procedures, on the basis of evidence forwarded by EUNAVFOR through relevant communication channels, that there are reasonable prospects of securing a conviction of persons detained by EUNAVFOR.

*Article 4*

**Treatment, prosecution and trial of transferred persons**

1. Transferred persons shall be treated humanely and shall not be subjected to torture or cruel, inhuman or degrading treatment or punishment, shall receive reasonable accommodation and nourishment and access to medical treatment, and shall be able to carry out religious observance.

2. Transferred persons shall be brought promptly before a judge or other officer authorised by law to exercise judicial power, who shall decide without delay on the lawfulness of their detention and shall order their release if the detention is not justified.

3. Transferred persons shall be entitled to trial within a reasonable time or to release.

4. In the determination of any criminal charge against them, any transferred persons shall be entitled to a fair and public hearing by a competent, independent and impartial tribunal established by law.

5. Transferred persons charged with a criminal offence shall be presumed innocent until proved guilty according to law.

6. In the determination of any criminal charge against them, transferred persons shall be entitled to the following minimum guarantees, in full equality:

(a) to be informed promptly and in detail in a language which they understand of the nature and cause of the charge against them;

(b) to have adequate time and facilities for the preparation of their defence and to communicate with counsel of their own choice;

(c) to be tried without undue delay;

(d) to be tried in their presence, and to defend themselves in person or through legal assistance of their own choice; to be informed, if they do not have legal assistance, of this right; and to have legal assistance assigned to them, in any case where the interests of justice so require, and without payment by them in any such case if they do not have sufficient means to pay for it;

(e) to examine, or have examined, all evidence against them, including affidavits of witnesses who conducted the arrest, and to obtain the attendance and examination of witnesses on their behalf under the same conditions as witnesses against them;

(f) to have the free assistance of an interpreter if they cannot understand or speak the language used in court;

(g) not to be compelled to testify against themselves or to confess guilt.

7. Transferred persons convicted of a crime shall have the right to their conviction and sentence being reviewed by or appealed to a higher tribunal in accordance with the laws of Tanzania.

8. Tanzania may, after consultation with the EU, transfer such persons convicted and serving their sentences in Tanzania to a third State which complies with human rights standards, with a view to serving their sentences in that third State. In case of serious concerns about the human rights situation in that third Sate, no transfer shall take place before a satisfactory solution is found through consultations between the Parties to address the concerns expressed.

*Article 5*

**Penalty**

No transferred person shall be tried for an offence which has a maximum punishment that is more severe than imprisonment for life.

*Article 6*

**Records and notifications**

1. Any transfer shall be the subject of an appropriate document signed by a representative of EUNAVFOR and a representative of the competent law enforcement authorities of Tanzania.

2. EUNAVFOR shall provide detention records to Tanzania with regard to transferred persons. These records shall include the physical condition of transferred persons while in detention, the time of transfer to Tanzania, the reason for their detention, the time and place of the commencement of their detention, and any decisions taken with regard to their detention.

3. Tanzania shall be responsible for keeping an accurate account of all transferred persons, including but not limited to keeping records of any seized property, the persons' physical condition, the location of their places of detention, any charges against them and any significant decisions taken in the course of their prosecution and trial.

4. Those records shall be available to representatives of the EU and EUNAVFOR in accordance with Tanzanian laws and regulations upon request in writing to the Ministry of Foreign Affairs of Tanzania.

5. In addition, Tanzania shall notify EUNAVFOR of the place of detention of persons transferred under this Agreement, of any deterioration of their physical condition and of any allegations of improper treatment. Representatives of the EU and EUNAVFOR shall have access to persons transferred under this Agreement as long as such persons are in custody, subject to the applicable laws, and shall be entitled to question them.

6. National and international humanitarian agencies shall, at their request, be allowed to visit persons transferred under this Agreement.

7. For the purposes of ensuring that EUNAVFOR is able to provide timely assistance to Tanzania with attendance of witnesses from EUNAVFOR and the provision of relevant evidence, Tanzania shall notify EUNAVFOR of its intention to initiate criminal trial proceedings against transferred persons and the timetable for provision of evidence, and the hearing of evidence.

*Article 7*

**EU and EUNAVFOR obligation to facilitate investigation and prosecution**

1. EU and EUNAVFOR, within their means and capabilities, shall provide all assistance to Tanzania with a view to investigating and prosecuting of transferred persons.

2. In particular, EU and EUNAVFOR shall:

(a) hand over detention records drawn up pursuant to Article 6(2) of this Agreement;

(b) process any evidence in accordance with the requirements of the Tanzanian competent authorities as agreed in the implementing arrangements described in Article 10;

(c) endeavour to produce witness statements or affidavits by EUNAVFOR personnel involved in any incident in relation to which persons have been transferred under this Agreement;

(d) hand over all relevant seized property in the possession of EUNAVFOR;

(e) preserve or hand over all relevant seized property, exhibits, photographs and any article of evidential value in the possession of EUNAVFOR;

(f) secure the attendance of witnesses belonging to EUNAVFOR for the purpose of giving evidence in court (or by TV link or any other approved technological means) during the trial;

(g) facilitate the attendance of such interpreters as may be required by the Tanzanian competent authorities for the purpose of assisting in investigations and trials involving transferred persons.

*Article 8*

**Relationship to other rights of transferred persons**

Nothing in this Agreement is intended to derogate, or may be construed as derogating, from any rights that transferred persons may have under applicable domestic or international law.

*Article 9*

**Liaison and disputes**

1. All issues arising in connection with the application of this Agreement shall be examined jointly by Tanzania and the EU competent authorities.

2. Failing any prior settlement, disputes concerning the interpretation or application of this Agreement shall be settled exclusively by diplomatic means between Tanzania and EU representatives.

*Article 10*

**Implementing arrangements**

1. For the purposes of the application of this Agreement, operational, administrative and technical matters may be the subject of implementing arrangements to be concluded between the competent Tanzanian authorities on the one hand and the competent EU authorities, as well as the competent authorities of the Sending States, on the other hand.

2. Implementing arrangements may cover, inter alia:

(a) the identification of competent law enforcement authorities of Tanzania to whom EUNAVFOR may transfer persons;

(b) the detention facilities where transferred persons will be held;

(c) the handling of documents, including those related to the gathering of evidence, which will be handed over to the competent law enforcement authorities of Tanzania upon transfer of persons;

(d) points of contact for notifications and modalities for alert from EUNAVFOR to the Tanzanian competent authorities;

(e) forms to be used for transfers;

(f) provision of technical support, expertise, training and other assistance in repatriation, custody, determination of nationality, legal representation and issues related to liabilities upon request of Tanzania in order to achieve the objectives of this Agreement.

*Article 11*

**Entry into force and termination**

1. This Agreement shall be provisionally applied as from the date it is signed and shall enter into force after each of the Parties has notified the other Party that it has completed its internal procedure for the ratification of this Agreement.

2. Either Party may, by written notification, terminate this Agreement. In such case, the termination shall take effect three months after the date of receipt of the notification.

3. This Agreement may be amended by written agreement between the Parties.

4. Termination of this Agreement shall not affect any rights or obligations arising out of its execution before such termination, including the rights of transferred persons as long as they are held in custody or are prosecuted in Tanzania.

5. After the termination of this Agreement, all rights of the EU under this Agreement may be exercised by any person designated by the EU High Representative for Foreign Affairs and Security Policy. After the termination of the Agreement, all notifications that were to be made to EUNAVFOR under this Agreement shall be made to the EU High Representative for Foreign Affairs and Security Policy.

Done at Brussels, on the first day of April in the year two thousand and fourteen in two originals, each in the English language.

For the European Union

For the United Republic of Tanzania

# Directive 2014/41 regarding the European Investigation Order in criminal matters, 3 April 2014

[OJ 2014, L 130/1–36]

Effective 1 July 2013, the electronic version of the *Official Journal* (e-OJ) is authentic and produces legal effects.

1.5.2014 EN Official Journal of the European Union L 130/1

I

*(Legislative acts)*

# DIRECTIVES

## DIRECTIVE 2014/41/EU OF THE EUROPEAN PARLIAMENT AND OF THE COUNCIL

**of 3 April 2014**

**regarding the European Investigation Order in criminal matters**

THE EUROPEAN PARLIAMENT AND THE COUNCIL OF THE EUROPEAN UNION,

Having regard to the Treaty on the Functioning of the European Union, and in particular Article 82 (1)(a) thereof,

Having regard to the initiative of the Kingdom of Belgium, the Republic of Bulgaria, the Republic of Estonia, the Kingdom of Spain, the Republic of Austria, the Republic of Slovenia and the Kingdom of Sweden,

After transmission of the draft legislative act to the national parliaments,

Acting in accordance with the ordinary legislative procedure [1],

Whereas:

(1) The European Union has set itself the objective of maintaining and developing an area of freedom, security and justice.

(2) Pursuant to Article 82(1) of the Treaty on the Functioning of the European Union (TFEU), judicial cooperation in criminal matters in the Union is to be based on the principle of mutual recognition of judgments and judicial decisions, which is, since the Tampere European Council of 15 and 16 October 1999, commonly referred to as a cornerstone of judicial cooperation in criminal matters within the Union.

(3) Council Framework Decision 2003/577/JHA [2] addressed the need for immediate mutual recognition of orders to prevent the destruction, transformation, moving, transfer or disposal of evidence. However, since that instrument is restricted to the freezing phase, a freezing order needs to be accompanied by a separate request for the transfer of the evidence to the State issuing the order ('the issuing State') in accordance with the rules applicable to mutual assistance in criminal matters. This results in a two-step procedure detrimental to its efficiency. Moreover, this regime coexists with the traditional instruments of cooperation and is therefore seldom used in practice by the competent authorities.

(4) Council Framework Decision 2008/978/JHA [3] concerning the European evidence warrant (EEW) was adopted to apply the principle of mutual recognition for the purpose of obtaining objects, documents and data for use in proceedings in criminal matters. However, the EEW is only applicable to evidence which already exists and covers therefore a limited spectrum of judicial cooperation in criminal matters with respect to evidence. Because of its limited scope, competent authorities have been free to use the new regime or to use mutual legal assistance procedures which, in any case, remain applicable to evidence falling outside of the scope of the EEW.

---

[1] Position of the European Parliament of 27 February 2014 (not yet published in the Official Journal) and decision of the Council of 14 March 2014.
[2] Council Framework Decision 2003/577/JHA of 22 July 2003 on the execution in the European Union of orders freezing property or evidence (OJ L 196, 2.8.2003, p. 45).
[3] Council Framework Decision 2008/978/JHA of 18 December 2008 on the European evidence warrant for the purpose of obtaining objects, documents and data for use in proceedings in criminal matters (OJ L 350, 30.12.2008, p. 72).

(5) Since the adoption of Framework Decisions 2003/577/JHA and 2008/978/JHA, it has become clear that the existing framework for the gathering of evidence is too fragmented and complicated. A new approach is therefore necessary.

(6) In the Stockholm Programme adopted by the European Council of 10-11 December 2009, the European Council considered that the setting up of a comprehensive system for obtaining evidence in cases with a cross-border dimension, based on the principle of mutual recognition, should be further pursued. The European Council indicated that the existing instruments in this area constituted a fragmentary regime and that a new approach was needed, based on the principle of mutual recognition, but also taking into account the flexibility of the traditional system of mutual legal assistance. The European Council therefore called for a comprehensive system to replace all the existing instruments in this area, including Framework Decision 2008/978/JHA, covering as far as possible all types of evidence, containing time-limits for enforcement and limiting as far as possible the grounds for refusal.

(7) This new approach is based on a single instrument called the European Investigation Order (EIO). An EIO is to be issued for the purpose of having one or several specific investigative measure(s) carried out in the State executing the EIO ('the executing State') with a view to gathering evidence. This includes the obtaining of evidence that is already in the possession of the executing authority.

(8) The EIO should have a horizontal scope and therefore should apply to all investigative measures aimed at gathering evidence. However, the setting up of a joint investigation team and the gathering of evidence within such a team require specific rules which are better dealt with separately. Without prejudice to the application of this Directive, existing instruments should therefore continue to apply to this type of investigative measure.

(9) This Directive should not apply to cross-border surveillance as referred to in the Convention implementing the Schengen Agreement [1].

(10) The EIO should focus on the investigative measure to be carried out. The issuing authority is best placed to decide, on the basis of its knowledge of the details of the investigation concerned, which investigative measure is to be used. However, the executing authority should, wherever possible, use another type of investigative measure if the indicated measure does not exist under its national law or would not be available in a similar domestic case. Availability should refer to occasions where the indicated investigative measure exists under the law of the executing State but is only lawfully available in certain situations, for example where the investigative measure can only be carried out for offences of a certain degree of seriousness, against persons for whom there is already a certain level of suspicion or with the consent of the person concerned. The executing authority may also have recourse to another type of investigative measure where it would achieve the same result as the investigative measure indicated in the EIO by means implying less interference with the fundamental rights of the person concerned.

(11) The EIO should be chosen where the execution of an investigative measure seems proportionate, adequate and applicable to the case in hand. The issuing authority should therefore ascertain whether the evidence sought is necessary and proportionate for the purpose of the proceedings, whether the investigative measure chosen is necessary and proportionate for the gathering of the evidence concerned, and whether, by means of issuing the EIO, another Member State should be involved in the gathering of that evidence. The same assessment should be carried out in the validation procedure, where the validation of an EIO is required under this Directive. The execution of an EIO should not be refused on grounds other than those stated in this Directive. However the executing authority should be entitled to opt for a less intrusive investigative measure than the one indicated in an EIO if it makes it possible to achieve similar results.

(12) When issuing an EIO the issuing authority should pay particular attention to ensuring full respect for the rights as enshrined in Article 48 of the Charter of Fundamental Rights of the European Union (the Charter). The presumption of innocence and the rights of defence in criminal proceedings are a cornerstone of the fundamental rights recognised in the Charter within the area of criminal justice. Any limitation of such rights by an investigative measure ordered in accordance with this Directive should fully conform to the requirements established in Article 52 of the Charter with regard to the necessity, proportionality and objectives that it should pursue, in particular the protection of the rights and freedoms of others.

---

[1] Convention implementing the Schengen Agreement of 14 June 1985 between the Governments of the States of the Benelux Economic Union, the Federal Republic of Germany and the French Republic on the gradual abolition of checks at their common borders (OJ L 239, 22.9.2000, p. 19).

(13) With a view to ensuring the transmission of the EIO to the competent authority of the executing State, the issuing authority may make use of any possible or relevant means of transmission, for example the secure telecommunications system of the European Judicial Network, Eurojust, or other channels used by judicial or law enforcement authorities.

(14) When making a declaration concerning the language regime, Member States are encouraged to include at least one language which is commonly used in the Union other than their official language(s).

(15) This Directive should be implemented taking into account Directives 2010/64/EU ([1]), 2012/13/EU ([2]), and 2013/48/EU ([3]) of the European Parliament and of the Council, which concern procedural rights in criminal proceedings.

(16) Non-coercive measures could be, for example, such measures that do not infringe the right to privacy or the right to property, depending on national law.

(17) The principle of *ne bis in idem* is a fundamental principle of law in the Union, as recognised by the Charter and developed by the case-law of the Court of Justice of the European Union. Therefore the executing authority should be entitled to refuse the execution of an EIO if its execution would be contrary to that principle. Given the preliminary nature of the proceedings underlying an EIO, its execution should not be subject to refusal where it is aimed to establish whether a possible conflict with the *ne bis in idem* principle exists, or where the issuing authority has provided assurances that the evidence transferred as a result of the execution of the EIO would not be used to prosecute or impose a sanction on a person whose case has been finally disposed of in another Member State for the same facts.

(18) As in other mutual recognition instruments, this Directive does not have the effect of modifying the obligation to respect the fundamental rights and fundamental legal principles as enshrined in Article 6 of the Treaty on European Union (TEU) and the Charter. In order to make this clear, a specific provision is inserted in the text.

(19) The creation of an area of freedom, security and justice within the Union is based on mutual confidence and a presumption of compliance by other Member States with Union law and, in particular, with fundamental rights. However, that presumption is rebuttable. Consequently, if there are substantial grounds for believing that the execution of an investigative measure indicated in the EIO would result in a breach of a fundamental right of the person concerned and that the executing State would disregard its obligations concerning the protection of fundamental rights recognised in the Charter, the execution of the EIO should be refused.

(20) It should be possible to refuse an EIO where its recognition or execution in the executing State would involve a breach of an immunity or privilege in that State. There is no common definition of what constitutes an immunity or privilege in Union law,; the precise definition of these terms is therefore left to national law, which may include protections which apply to medical and legal professions, but should not be interpreted in a way to counter the obligation to abolish certain grounds for refusal as set out in the Protocol to the Convention on Mutual Assistance in Criminal Matters between the Member States of the European Union ([4]). This may also include, even though they are not necessarily considered as privilege or immunity, rules relating to freedom of the press and freedom of expression in other media.

(21) Time limits are necessary to ensure quick, effective and consistent cooperation between the Member States in criminal matters. The decision on the recognition or execution, as well as the actual execution of the investigative measure, should be carried out with the same celerity and priority as for a similar domestic case. Time limits should be provided to ensure a decision or execution within reasonable time or to meet procedural constraints in the issuing State.

---

([1]) Directive 2010/64/EU of the European Parliament and of the Council of 20 October 2010 on the right to interpretation and translation in criminal proceedings (OJ L 280, 26.10.2010, p. 1).

([2]) Directive 2012/13/EU of the European Parliament and of the Council of 22 May 2012 on the right to information in criminal proceedings (OJ L 142, 1.6.2012, p. 1).

([3]) Directive 2013/48/EU of the European Parliament and of the Council of 22 October 2013 on the right of access to a lawyer in criminal proceedings and in European arrest warrant proceedings, and on the right to have a third party informed upon deprivation of liberty and to communicate with third persons and with consular authorities while deprived of liberty (OJ L 294, 6.11.2013, p. 1).

([4]) Protocol established by the Council in accordance with Article 34 of the Treaty on European Union to the Convention on Mutual Assistance in Criminal Matters between the Member States of the European Union (OJ C 326, 21.11.2001, p. 2).

(22) Legal remedies available against an EIO should be at least equal to those available in a domestic case against the investigative measure concerned. In accordance with their national law Member States should ensure the applicability of such legal remedies, including by informing in due time any interested party about the possibilities and modalities for seeking those legal remedies. In cases where objections against the EIO are submitted by an interested party in the executing State in respect of the substantive reasons for issuing the EIO, it is advisable that information about such challenge be transmitted to the issuing authority and that the interested party be informed accordingly.

(23) The expenses incurred in the territory of the executing State for the execution of an EIO should be borne exclusively by that State. This arrangement complies with the general principle of mutual recognition. However, the execution of an EIO may incur exceptionally high costs on the executing State. Such exceptionally high costs may, for example, be complex experts' opinions or extensive police operations or surveillance activities over a long period of time. This should not impede the execution of the EIO and the issuing and executing authorities should seek to establish which costs are to be considered as exceptionally high. The issue of costs might become subject to consultations between the issuing State and the executing State and they are recommended to resolve this issue during the consultations stage. As a last resort, the issuing authority may decide to withdraw the EIO or to maintain it, and the part of the costs which are estimated exceptionally high by the executing State and absolutely necessary in the course of the proceedings, should be covered by the issuing State. The given mechanism should not constitute an additional ground for refusal, and in any event should not be abused in a way to delay or impede the execution of the EIO.

(24) The EIO establishes a single regime for obtaining evidence. Additional rules are however necessary for certain types of investigative measures which should be indicated in the EIO, such as the temporary transfer of persons held in custody, hearing by video or telephone conference, obtaining of information related to bank accounts or banking transactions, controlled deliveries or covert investigations. Investigative measures implying a gathering of evidence in real time, continuously and over a certain period of time should be covered by the EIO, but, where necessary, practical arrangements should be agreed between the issuing State and the executing State in order to accommodate the differences existing in the national laws of those States.

(25) This Directive sets out rules on carrying out, at all stages of criminal proceedings, including the trial phase, of an investigative measure, if needed with the participation of the person concerned with a view to collecting evidence. For example an EIO may be issued for the temporary transfer of that person to the issuing State or for the carrying out of a hearing by videoconference. However, where that person is to be transferred to another Member State for the purposes of prosecution, including bringing that person before a court for the purpose of the standing trial, a European Arrest Warrant (EAW) should be issued in accordance with Council Framework Decision 2002/584/JHA ([1]).

(26) With a view to the proportionate use of an EAW, the issuing authority should consider whether an EIO would be an effective and proportionate means of pursuing criminal proceedings. The issuing authority should consider, in particular, whether issuing an EIO for the hearing of a suspected or accused person by videoconference could serve as an effective alternative.

(27) An EIO may be issued in order to obtain evidence concerning the accounts, of whatever nature, held in any bank or any non-banking financial institution by a person subject to criminal proceedings. This possibility is to be understood broadly as comprising not only suspected or accused persons but also any other person in respect of whom such information is found necessary by the competent authorities in the course of criminal proceedings.

(28) Where in this Directive a reference is made to financial institutions, this term should be understood according to the relevant definition of Article 3 of Directive 2005/60/EC of the European Parliament and the Council ([2]).

(29) When an EIO is issued to obtain 'details' of a specified account, 'details' should be understood to include at least the name and address of the account holder, details of any powers of attorney held over the account, and any other details or documents provided by the account holder when the account was opened and that are still held by the bank.

---

([1]) Council Framework Decision 2002/584/JHA of 13 June 2002 on the European arrest warrant and the surrender procedures between Member States (OJ L 190, 18.7.2002, p. 1).

([2]) Directive 2005/60/EC of the European Parliament and of the Council of 26 October 2005 on the prevention of the use of the financial system for the purpose of money laundering and terrorist financing (OJ L 309, 25.11.2005, p. 15).

(30) Possibilities to cooperate under this Directive on the interception of telecommunications should not be limited to the content of the telecommunications, but could also cover collection of traffic and location data associated with such telecommunications, allowing competent authorities to issue an EIO for the purpose of obtaining less intrusive data on telecommunications. An EIO issued to obtain historical traffic and location data related to telecommunications should be dealt with under the general regime related to the execution of the EIO and may be considered, depending on the national law of the executing State, as a coercive investigative measure.

(31) Where several Member States are in a position to provide the necessary technical assistance, an EIO should be sent only to one of them and priority should be given to the Member State where the person concerned is located. Member States where the subject of the interception is located and from which no technical assistance is needed to carry out the interception should be notified thereof in accordance with this Directive. However, where the technical assistance may not be received from merely one Member State, an EIO may be transmitted to more than one executing State.

(32) In an EIO containing the request for interception of telecommunications the issuing authority should provide the executing authority with sufficient information, such as details of the criminal conduct under investigation, in order to allow the executing authority to assess whether that investigative measure, would be authorised in a similar domestic case.

(33) Member States should have regard to the importance of ensuring that technical assistance can be provided by a service provider operating publicly available telecommunications networks and services in the territory of the Member State concerned, in order to facilitate cooperation under this instrument in relation to the lawful interception of telecommunications.

(34) This Directive, by virtue of its scope, deals with provisional measures only with a view to gathering evidence. In this respect, it should be underlined that any item, including financial assets, may be subject to various provisional measures in the course of criminal proceedings, not only with a view to gathering evidence but also with a view to confiscation. The distinction between the two objectives of provisional measures is not always obvious and the objective of the provisional measure may change in the course of the proceedings. For this reason, it is crucial to maintain a smooth relationship between the various instruments applicable in this field. Furthermore, for the same reason, the assessment of whether the item is to be used as evidence and therefore be the object of an EIO should be left to the issuing authority.

(35) Where reference is made to mutual assistance in relevant international instruments, such as in conventions concluded within the Council of Europe, it should be understood that between the Member States bound by this Directive it takes precedence over those conventions.

(36) The categories of offences listed in Annex D should be interpreted consistently with their interpretation under existing legal instruments on mutual recognition.

(37) In accordance with the Joint Political Declaration of 28 September 2011 of Member States and the Commission on explanatory documents ([1]), Member States have undertaken to accompany, in justified cases, the notification of their transposition measures with one or more documents explaining the relationship between the components of a directive and the corresponding parts of national transposition instruments. With regard to this Directive, the European Parliament and the Council consider the transmission of such documents to be justified.

(38) Since the objective of this Directive, namely the mutual recognition of decisions taken to obtain evidence, cannot be sufficiently achieved by the Member States but can rather, by reason of its scale and effects, be better achieved at Union level, the Union may adopt measures in accordance with the principle of subsidiarity as set out in Article 5 of the TEU. In accordance with the principle of proportionality, as set out in that Article, this Directive does not go beyond what is necessary in order to achieve that objective.

(39) This Directive respects the fundamental rights and observes the principles recognised by Article 6 of the TEU and in the Charter, notably Title VI thereof, by international law and international agreements to which the Union or all the Member States are party, including the European Convention for the Protection of Human Rights and Fundamental Freedoms, and in Member States' constitutions in their respective fields of application. Nothing in

([1]) OJ C 369, 17.12.2011, p. 14.

this Directive may be interpreted as prohibiting refusal to execute an EIO when there are reasons to believe, on the basis of objective elements, that the EIO has been issued for the purpose of prosecuting or punishing a person on account of his or her sex, racial or ethnic origin, religion, sexual orientation, nationality, language or political opinions, or that the person's position may be prejudiced for any of these reasons.

(40) The protection of natural persons in relation to the processing of personal data is a fundamental right. In accordance with Article 8(1) of the Charter and Article 16(1) of the TFEU, everyone has the right to the protection of personal data concerning them.

(41) Member States should, in the application of this Directive, provide for transparent policies with regard to the processing of personal data and for the exercise of the rights of data subjects to legal remedies for the protection of their personal data.

(42) Personal data obtained under this Directive should only be processed when necessary and should be proportionate to the purposes compatible with the prevention, investigation, detection and prosecution of crime or enforcement of criminal sanctions and the exercise of the rights of defence. Only authorised persons should have access to information containing personal data which may be obtained through authentication processes.

(43) In accordance with Article 3 of Protocol No 21 on the position of the United Kingdom and Ireland in respect of the area of Freedom, Security and Justice annexed to the TEU and the TFEU, the United Kingdom has notified its wish to take part in the adoption and application of this Directive.

(44) In accordance with Articles 1 and 2 and Article 4a(1) of Protocol No 21 on the position of the United Kingdom and Ireland in respect of the area of Freedom, Security and Justice annexed to the TEU and the TFEU, and without prejudice to Article 4 of that Protocol, Ireland is not taking part in the adoption of this Directive and is not bound by it or subject to its application.

(45) In accordance with Articles 1 and 2 of Protocol No 22 on the Position of Denmark annexed to the TEU and the TFEU, Denmark is not taking part in the adoption of this Directive and is not bound by it or subject to its application.

(46) The European Data Protection Supervisor delivered an opinion on 5 October 2010 [1], based on Article 41(2) of Regulation (EC) No 45/2001 of the European Parliament and of the Council [2],

HAVE ADOPTED THIS DIRECTIVE:

## CHAPTER I

## THE EUROPEAN INVESTIGATION ORDER

*Article 1*

### The European Investigation Order and obligation to execute it

1. A European Investigation Order (EIO) is a judicial decision which has been issued or validated by a judicial authority of a Member State ('OGthe issuing State') to have one or several specific investigative measure(s) carried out in another Member State ('the executing State') to obtain evidence in accordance with this Directive.

The EIO may also be issued for obtaining evidence that is already in the possession of the competent authorities of the executing State.

[1] OJ C 355, 29.12.2010, p. 1.
[2] Regulation (EC) No 45/2001 of the European Parliament and of the Council of 18 December 2000 on the protection of individuals with regard to the processing of personal data by the Community institutions and bodies and on the free movement of such data (OJ L 8, 12.1.2001, p. 1).

2. Member States shall execute an EIO on the basis of the principle of mutual recognition and in accordance with this Directive.

3. The issuing of an EIO may be requested by a suspected or accused person, or by a lawyer on his behalf, within the framework of applicable defence rights in conformity with national criminal procedure.

4. This Directive shall not have the effect of modifying the obligation to respect the fundamental rights and legal principles as enshrined in Article 6 of the TEU, including the rights of defence of persons subject to criminal proceedings, and any obligations incumbent on judicial authorities in this respect shall remain unaffected.

*Article 2*

**Definitions**

For the purposes of this Directive the following definitions apply:

(a) 'issuing State' means the Member State in which the EIO is issued;

(b) 'executing State' means the Member State executing the EIO, in which the investigative measure is to be carried out;

(c) 'issuing authority' means:

(i) a judge, a court, an investigating judge or a public prosecutor competent in the case concerned; or

(ii) any other competent authority as defined by the issuing State which, in the specific case, is acting in its capacity as an investigating authority in criminal proceedings with competence to order the gathering of evidence in accordance with national law. In addition, before it is transmitted to the executing authority the EIO shall be validated, after examination of its conformity with the conditions for issuing an EIO under this Directive, in particular the conditions set out in Article 6.1, by a judge, court, investigating judge or a public prosecutor in the issuing State. Where the EIO has been validated by a judicial authority, that authority may also be regarded as an issuing authority for the purposes of transmission of the EIO;

(d) 'executing authority' means an authority having competence to recognise an EIO and ensure its execution in accordance with this Directive and the procedures applicable in a similar domestic case. Such procedures may require a court authorisation in the executing State where provided by its national law.

*Article 3*

**Scope of the EIO**

The EIO shall cover any investigative measure with the exception of the setting up of a joint investigation team and the gathering of evidence within such a team as provided in Article 13 of the Convention on Mutual Assistance in Criminal Matters between the Member States of the European Union [1] ('the Convention') and in Council Framework Decision 2002/465/JHA [2], other than for the purposes of applying, respectively, Article 13(8) of the Convention and Article 1(8) of the Framework Decision.

*Article 4*

**Types of proceedings for which the EIO can be issued**

An EIO may be issued:

(a) with respect to criminal proceedings that are brought by, or that may be brought before, a judicial authority in respect of a criminal offence under the national law of the issuing State;

(b) in proceedings brought by administrative authorities in respect of acts which are punishable under the national law of the issuing State by virtue of being infringements of the rules of law and where the decision may give rise to proceedings before a court having jurisdiction, in particular, in criminal matters;

(1) Convention established by the Council in accordance with Article 34 of the Treaty on European Union, on Mutual Assistance in Criminal Matters between the Member States of the European Union (OJ C 197, 12.7.2000, p. 3).
(2) Council Framework Decision 2002/465/JHA of 13 June 2002 on joint investigation teams (OJ L 162, 20.6.2002, p. 1).

(c) in proceedings brought by judicial authorities in respect of acts which are punishable under the national law of the issuing State by virtue of being infringements of the rules of law, and where the decision may give rise to proceedings before a court having jurisdiction, in particular, in criminal matters; and

(d) in connection with proceedings referred to in points (a), (b), and (c) which relate to offences or infringements for which a legal person may be held liable or punished in the issuing State.

*Article 5*

**Content and form of the EIO**

1. The EIO in the form set out in Annex A shall be completed, signed, and its content certified as accurate and correct by the issuing authority.

The EIO shall, in particular, contain the following information:

(a) data about the issuing authority and, where applicable, the validating authority;

(b) the object of and reasons for the EIO;

(c) the necessary information available on the person(s) concerned;

(d) a description of the criminal act, which is the subject of the investigation or proceedings, and the applicable provisions of the criminal law of the issuing State;

(e) a description of the investigative measures(s) requested and the evidence to be obtained.

2. Each Member State shall indicate the language(s) which, among the official languages of the institutions of the Union and in addition to the official language(s) of the Member State concerned, may be used for completing or translating the EIO when the Member State concerned is the executing State.

3. The competent authority of the issuing State shall translate the EIO set out in Annex A into an official language of the executing State or any other language indicated by the executing State in accordance with paragraph 2 of this Article.

CHAPTER II

**PROCEDURES AND SAFEGUARDS FOR THE ISSUING STATE**

*Article 6*

**Conditions for issuing and transmitting an EIO**

1. The issuing authority may only issue an EIO where the following conditions have been met:

(a) the issuing of the EIO is necessary and proportionate for the purpose of the proceedings referred to in Article 4 taking into account the rights of the suspected or accused person; and

(b) the investigative measure(s) indicated in the EIO could have been ordered under the same conditions in a similar domestic case.

2. The conditions referred to in paragraph 1 shall be assessed by the issuing authority in each case.

3. Where the executing authority has reason to believe that the conditions referred to in paragraph 1 have not been met, it may consult the issuing authority on the importance of executing the EIO. After that consultation the issuing authority may decide to withdraw the EIO.

*Article 7*

**Transmission of the EIO**

1. The EIO completed in accordance with Article 5 shall be transmitted from the issuing authority to the executing authority by any means capable of producing a written record under conditions allowing the executing State to establish authenticity.

2. Any further official communication shall be made directly between the issuing authority and the executing authority.

3. Without prejudice to Article 2(d), each Member State may designate a central authority or, where its legal system so provides, more than one central authority, to assist the competent authorities. A Member State may, if necessary due to the organisation of its internal judicial system, make its central authority(ies) responsible for the administrative transmission and receipt of EIOs, as well as for other official correspondence relating to EIOs.

4. The issuing authority may transmit EIOs via the telecommunications system of the European Judicial Network (EJN), as set up by Council Joint Action. 98/428/JHA (1).

5. If the identity of the executing authority is unknown, the issuing authority shall make all necessary inquiries, including via the EJN contact points, in order to obtain the information from the executing State.

6. Where the authority in the executing State which receives the EIO has no competence to recognise the EIO or to take the necessary measures for its execution, it shall, *ex officio*, transmit the EIO to the executing authority and so inform the issuing authority.

7. All difficulties concerning the transmission or authenticity of any document needed for the execution of the EIO shall be dealt with by direct contacts between the issuing authority and the executing authority involved or, where appropriate, with the involvement of the central authorities of the Member States.

*Article 8*

**EIO related to an earlier EIO**

1. Where an issuing authority issues an EIO which supplements an earlier EIO, it shall indicate this fact in the EIO in Section D of the form set out in Annex A.

2. If the issuing authority assists in the execution of the EIO in the executing State, in accordance with Article 9(4), it may, without prejudice to notifications made under Article 33(1)(c), address an EIO which supplements an earlier EIO directly to the executing authority, while present in that State.

3. The EIO which supplements an earlier EIO shall be certified in accordance with the first subparagraph of Article 5(1), and, where applicable, be validated in accordance with Article 2(c).

CHAPTER III

**PROCEDURES AND SAFEGUARDS FOR THE EXECUTING STATE**

*Article 9*

**Recognition and execution**

1. The executing authority shall recognise an EIO, transmitted in accordance with this Directive, without any further formality being required, and ensure its execution in the same way and under the same modalities as if the investigative measure concerned had been ordered by an authority of the executing State, unless that authority decides to invoke one of the grounds for non-recognition or non-execution or one of the grounds for postponement provided for in this Directive.

(1) Joint Action 98/428/JHA of 29 June 1998 adopted by the Council on the basis of Article K.3 of the Treaty on European Union, on the creation of a European Judicial Network (OJ L 191, 7.7.1998, p. 4).

2. The executing authority shall comply with the formalities and procedures expressly indicated by the issuing authority unless otherwise provided in this Directive and provided that such formalities and procedures are not contrary to the fundamental principles of law of the executing State.

3. Where an executing authority receives an EIO which has not been issued by an issuing authority as specified in Article 2(c), the executing authority shall return the EIO to the issuing State.

4. The issuing authority may request that one or more authorities of the issuing State assist in the execution of the EIO in support to the competent authorities of the executing State to the extent that the designated authorities of the issuing State would be able to assist in the execution of the investigative measures indicated in the EIO in a similar domestic case. The executing authority shall comply with this request provided that such assistance is not contrary to the fundamental principles of law of the executing State or does not harm its essential national security interests.

5. The authorities of the issuing State present in the executing State shall be bound by the law of the executing State during the execution of the EIO. They shall not have any law enforcement powers in the territory of the executing State, unless the execution of such powers in the territory of the executing State is in accordance with the law of the executing State and to the extent agreed between the issuing authority and the executing authority.

6. The issuing authority and executing authority may consult each other, by any appropriate means, with a view to facilitating the efficient application of this Article.

*Article 10*

**Recourse to a different type of investigative measure**

1. The executing authority shall have, wherever possible, recourse to an investigative measure other than that provided for in the EIO where:

(a) the investigative measure indicated in the EIO does not exist under the law of the executing State; or

(b) the investigative measure indicated in the EIO would not be available in a similar domestic case.

2. Without prejudice to Article 11, paragraph (1) does not apply to the following investigative measures, which always have to be available under the law of the executing State:

(a) the obtaining of information or evidence which is already in the possession of the executing authority and the information or evidence could have been obtained, in accordance with the law of the executing State, in the framework of criminal proceedings or for the purposes of the EIO;

(b) the obtaining of information contained in databases held by police or judicial authorities and directly accessible by the executing authority in the framework of criminal proceedings;

(c) the hearing of a witness, expert, victim, suspected or accused person or third party in the territory of the executing State;

(d) any non coercive investigative measure as defined under the law of the executing State;

(e) the identification of persons holding a subscription of a specified phone number or IP address.

3. The executing authority may also have recourse to an investigative measure other than that indicated in the EIO where the investigative measure selected by the executing authority would achieve the same result by less intrusive means than the investigative measure indicated in the EIO.

4. When the executing authority decides to avail itself of the possibility referred to in paragraphs 1 and 3, it shall first inform the issuing authority, which may decide to withdraw or supplement the EIO.

5. Where, in accordance with paragraph 1, the investigative measure indicated in the EIO does not exist under the law of the executing State or it would not be available in a similar domestic case and where there is no other investigative measure which would have the same result as the investigative measure requested, the executing authority shall notify the issuing authority that it has not been possible to provide the assistance requested.

*Article 11*

**Grounds for non-recognition or non-execution**

1. Without prejudice to Article 1(4), recognition or execution of an EIO may be refused in the executing State where:

(a) there is an immunity or a privilege under the law of the executing State which makes it impossible to execute the EIO or there are rules on determination and limitation of criminal liability relating to freedom of the press and freedom of expression in other media, which make it impossible to execute the EIO;

(b) in a specific case the execution of the EIO would harm essential national security interests, jeopardise the source of the information or involve the use of classified information relating to specific intelligence activities;

(c) the EIO has been issued in proceedings referred to in Article 4(b) and (c) and the investigative measure would not be authorised under the law of the executing State in a similar domestic case;

(d) the execution of the EIO would be contrary to the principle of *ne bis in idem*;

(e) the EIO relates to a criminal offence which is alleged to have been committed outside the territory of the issuing State and wholly or partially on the territory of the executing State, and the conduct in connection with which the EIO is issued is not an offence in the executing State;

(f) there are substantial grounds to believe that the execution of the investigative measure indicated in the EIO would be incompatible with the executing State's obligations in accordance with Article 6 TEU and the Charter;

(g) the conduct for which the EIO has been issued does not constitute an offence under the law of the executing State, unless it concerns an offence listed within the categories of offences set out in Annex D, as indicated by the issuing authority in the EIO, if it is punishable in the issuing State by a custodial sentence or a detention order for a maximum period of at least three years; or

(h) the use of the investigative measure indicated in the EIO is restricted under the law of the executing State to a list or category of offences or to offences punishable by a certain threshold, which does not include the offence covered by the EIO.

2. Paragraphs 1(g) and 1(h) do not apply to investigative measures referred to in Article 10(2).

3. Where the EIO concerns an offence in connection with taxes or duties, customs and exchange, the executing authority shall not refuse recognition or execution on the ground that the law of the executing State does not impose the same kind of tax or duty or does not contain a tax, duty, customs and exchange regulation of the same kind as the law of the issuing State.

4. In the cases referred to in points (a), (b), (d), (e) and (f) of paragraph 1 before deciding not to recognise or not to execute an EIO, either in whole or in part the executing authority shall consult the issuing authority, by any appropriate means, and shall, where appropriate, request the issuing authority to supply any necessary information without delay.

5. In the case referred to in paragraph 1(a) and where power to waive the privilege or immunity lies with an authority of the executing State, the executing authority shall request it to exercise that power forthwith. Where power to waive the privilege or immunity lies with an authority of another State or international organisation, it shall be for the issuing authority to request the authority concerned to exercise that power.

*Article 12*

**Time limits for recognition or execution**

1. The decision on the recognition or execution shall be taken and the investigative measure shall be carried out with the same celerity and priority as for a similar domestic case and, in any case, within the time limits provided in this Article.

2. Where the issuing authority has indicated in the EIO that, due to procedural deadlines, the seriousness of the offence or other particularly urgent circumstances, a shorter deadline than those provided in this Article is necessary, or if the issuing authority has indicated in the EIO that the investigative measure must be carried out on a specific date, the executing authority shall take as full account as possible of this requirement.

3. The executing authority shall take the decision on the recognition or execution of the EIO as soon as possible and, without prejudice to paragraph 5, no later than 30 days after the receipt of the EIO by the competent executing authority.

4. Unless grounds for postponement under Article 15 exist or evidence mentioned in the investigative measure covered by the EIO is already in the possession of the executing State, the executing authority shall carry out the investigative measure without delay and without prejudice to paragraph 5, not later than 90 days following the taking of the decision referred to in paragraph 3.

5. If it is not practicable in a specific case for the competent executing authority to meet the time limit set out in paragraph 3 or the specific date set out in paragraph 2, it shall, without delay, inform the competent authority of the issuing State by any means, giving the reasons for the delay and the estimated time necessary for the decision to be taken. In such a case, the time limit laid down in paragraph 3 may be extended by a maximum of 30 days.

6. If it is not practicable in a specific case for the competent executing authority to meet the time limit set out in paragraph 4, it shall, without delay, inform the competent authority of the issuing State by any means, giving the reasons for the delay and it shall consult with the issuing authority on the appropriate timing to carry out the investigative measure.

*Article 13*

**Transfer of evidence**

1. The executing authority shall, without undue delay, transfer the evidence obtained or already in the possession of the competent authorities of the executing State as a result of the execution of the EIO to the issuing State.

Where requested in the EIO and if possible under the law of the executing State, the evidence shall be immediately transferred to the competent authorities of the issuing State assisting in the execution of the EIO in accordance with Article 9(4).

2. The transfer of the evidence may be suspended, pending a decision regarding a legal remedy, unless sufficient reasons are indicated in the EIO that an immediate transfer is essential for the proper conduct of its investigations or for the preservation of individual rights. However, the transfer of evidence shall be suspended if it would cause serious and irreversible damage to the person concerned.

3. When transferring the evidence obtained, the executing authority shall indicate whether it requires the evidence to be returned to the executing State as soon as it is no longer required in the issuing State.

4. Where the objects, documents, or data concerned are already relevant for other proceedings, the executing authority may, at the explicit request of and after consultations with the issuing authority, temporarily transfer the evidence on the condition that it be returned to the executing State as soon as it is no longer required in the issuing State or at any other time or occasion agreed between the competent authorities.

*Article 14*

**Legal remedies**

1. Member States shall ensure that legal remedies equivalent to those available in a similar domestic case, are applicable to the investigative measures indicated in the EIO.

2. The substantive reasons for issuing the EIO may be challenged only in an action brought in the issuing State, without prejudice to the guarantees of fundamental rights in the executing State.

3. Where it would not undermine the need to ensure confidentiality of an investigation under Article 19(1), the issuing authority and the executing authority shall take the appropriate measures to ensure that information is provided about the possibilities under national law for seeking the legal remedies when these become applicable and in due time to ensure that they can be exercised effectively.

4. Member States shall ensure that the time-limits for seeking a legal remedy shall be the same as those that are provided for in similar domestic cases and are applied in a way that guarantees the possibility of the effective exercise of these legal remedies for the parties concerned.

5. The issuing authority and the executing authority shall inform each other about the legal remedies sought against the issuing, the recognition or the execution of an EIO.

6. A legal challenge shall not suspend the execution of the investigative measure, unless it is provided in similar domestic cases.

7. The issuing State shall take into account a successful challenge against the recognition or execution of an EIO in accordance with its own national law. Without prejudice to national procedural rules Member States shall ensure that in criminal proceedings in the issuing State the rights of the defence and the fairness of the proceedings are respected when assessing evidence obtained through the EIO

*Article 15*

**Grounds for postponement of recognition or execution**

1. The recognition or execution of the EIO may be postponed in the executing State where:

(a) its execution might prejudice an on-going criminal investigation or prosecution, until such time as the executing State deems reasonable;

(b) the objects, documents, or data concerned are already being used in other proceedings, until such time as they are no longer required for that purpose.

2. As soon as the ground for postponement has ceased to exist, the executing authority shall forthwith take the necessary measures for the execution of the EIO and inform the issuing authority by any means capable of producing a written record.

*Article 16*

**Obligation to inform**

1. The competent authority in the executing State which receives the EIO shall, without delay, and in any case within a week of the reception of an EIO, acknowledge reception of the EIO by completing and sending the form set out in Annex B.

Where a central authority has been designated in accordance with Article 7(3), this obligation is applicable both to the central authority and to the executing authority which receives the EIO from the central authority.

In the cases referred to in Article 7(6), this obligation applies both to the competent authority which initially received the EIO and to the executing authority to which the EIO is finally transmitted.

2. Without prejudice to Article 10(4) and (5) the executing authority shall inform the issuing authority immediately by any means:

(a) if it is impossible for the executing authority to take a decision on the recognition or execution due to the fact that the form provided for in Annex A is incomplete or manifestly incorrect;

(b) if the executing authority, in the course of the execution of the EIO, considers without further enquiries that it may be appropriate to carry out investigative measures not initially foreseen, or which could not be specified when the EIO was issued, in order to enable the issuing authority to take further action in the specific case; or

(c) if the executing authority establishes that, in the specific case, it cannot comply with formalities and procedures expressly indicated by the issuing authority in accordance with Article 9.

Upon request by the issuing authority, the information shall be confirmed without delay by any means capable of producing a written record.

3. Without prejudice to Article 10(4) and (5) the executing authority shall inform the issuing authority without delay by any means capable of producing a written record:

(a) of any decision taken pursuant to Articles 10 or 11;

(b) of any decision to postpone the execution or recognition of the EIO, the reasons for the postponement and, if possible, the expected duration of the postponement.

*Article 17*

**Criminal liability regarding officials**

When present in the territory of the executing State in the framework of the application of this Directive, officials from the issuing State shall be regarded as officials of the executing State with respect to offences committed against them or by them.

*Article 18*

**Civil liability regarding officials**

1. Where, in the framework of the application of this Directive, officials of a Member State are present in the territory of another Member State, the former Member State shall be liable for any damage caused by its officials during their operations, in accordance with the law of the Member State in whose territory they are operating.

2. The Member State in whose territory the damage referred to in paragraph 1 was caused shall make good such damage under the conditions applicable to damage caused by its own officials.

3. The Member State whose officials have caused damage to any person in the territory of another Member State shall reimburse in full any sums the latter Member State has paid to the victims or persons entitled on their behalf.

4. Without prejudice to the exercise of its rights vis-à-vis third parties and with the exception of paragraph 3, each Member State shall refrain in cases referred to in paragraph 1 from requesting reimbursement of damages it has sustained from another Member State.

*Article 19*

**Confidentiality**

1. Each Member State shall take the necessary measures to ensure that in the execution of an EIO the issuing authority and the executing authority take due account of the confidentiality of the investigation.

2. The executing authority shall, in accordance with its national law, guarantee the confidentiality of the facts and the substance of the EIO, except to the extent necessary to execute the investigative measure. If the executing authority cannot comply with the requirement of confidentiality, it shall notify the issuing authority without delay.

3. The issuing authority shall, in accordance with its national law and unless otherwise indicated by the executing authority, not disclose any evidence or information provided by the executing authority, except to the extent that its disclosure is necessary for the investigations or proceedings described in the EIO.

4. Each Member State shall take the necessary measures to ensure that banks do not disclose to the bank customer concerned or to other third persons that information has been transmitted to the issuing State in accordance with Articles 26 and 27 or that an investigation is being carried out.

*Article 20*

**Protection of personal data**

When implementing this Directive, Member States shall ensure that personal data are protected and may only be processed in accordance with Council Framework Decision 2008/977/JHA [1] and the principles of the Council of Europe Convention for the protection of Individuals with regard to the Automatic Processing of Personal Data of 28 January 1981 and its Additional Protocol.

Access to such data shall be restricted, without prejudice to the rights of the data subject. Only authorised persons may have access to such data.

*Article 21*

**Costs**

1. Unless otherwise provided in this Directive, the executing State shall bear all costs undertaken on the territory of the executing State which are related to the execution of an EIO.

2. Where the executing authority considers that the costs for the execution of the EIO may be deemed exceptionally high, it may consult with the issuing authority on whether and how the costs could be shared or the EIO modified.

The executing authority shall inform the issuing authority in advance of the detailed specifications of the part of the costs deemed exceptionally high.

3. In exceptional situations where no agreement can be reached with regard to the costs referred to in paragraph 2, the issuing authority may decide to:

(a) withdraw the EIO in whole or in part; or

(b) keep the EIO, and bear the part of the costs deemed exceptionally high.

CHAPTER IV

**SPECIFIC PROVISIONS FOR CERTAIN INVESTIGATIVE MEASURES**

*Article 22*

**Temporary transfer to the issuing State of persons held in custody for the purpose of carrying out an investigative measure**

1. An EIO may be issued for the temporary transfer of a person in custody in the executing State for the purpose of carrying out an investigative measure with a view to gathering evidence for which the presence of that person on the territory of the issuing State is required, provided that he shall be sent back within the period stipulated by the executing State.

2. In addition to the grounds for non-recognition or non-execution referred to in Article 11 the execution of the EIO may also be refused if:

(a) the person in custody does not consent; or

(b) the transfer is liable to prolong the detention of the person in custody.

3. Without prejudice to paragraph 2(a), where the executing State considers it necessary in view of the person's age or physical or mental condition, the opportunity to state the opinion on the temporary transfer shall be given to the legal representative of the person in custody.

---

[1] Council Framework Decision 2008/977/JHA of 27 November 2008 on the protection of personal data processed in the framework of police and judicial cooperation in criminal matters (OJ L 350, 30.12.2008, p. 60).

4. In cases referred to in paragraph 1, transit of the person in custody through the territory of a third Member State ('the Member State of transit') shall be granted on application, accompanied by all necessary documents.

5. The practical arrangements regarding the temporary transfer of the person including the details of his custody conditions in the issuing State, and the dates by which he must be transferred from and returned to the territory of the executing State shall be agreed between the issuing State and the executing State, ensuring that the physical and mental condition of the person concerned, as well as the level of security required in the issuing State, are taken into account.

6. The transferred person shall remain in custody in the territory of the issuing State and, where applicable, in the territory of the Member State of transit, for the acts or convictions for which he has been kept in custody in the executing State, unless the executing State applies for his release.

7. The period of custody in the territory of the issuing State shall be deducted from the period of detention which the person concerned is or will be obliged to undergo in the territory of the executing State.

8. Without prejudice to paragraph 6, a transferred person shall not be prosecuted or detained or subjected to any other restriction of his personal liberty in the issuing State for acts committed or convictions handed down before his departure from the territory of the executing State and which are not specified in the EIO.

9. The immunity referred to in paragraph 8 shall cease to exist if the transferred person, having had an opportunity to leave for a period of 15 consecutive days from the date when his presence is no longer required by the issuing authorities, has either:

(a) nevertheless remained in the territory; or

(b) having left it, has returned.

10. Costs resulting from the application of this Article shall be borne in accordance with Article 21, except for the costs arising from the transfer of the person to and from the issuing State which shall be borne by that State.

*Article 23*

**Temporary transfer to the executing State of persons held in custody for the purpose of carrying out an investigative measure**

1. An EIO may be issued for the temporary transfer of a person held in custody in the issuing State for the purpose of carrying out an investigative measure with a view to gathering evidence for which his presence on the territory of the executing State is required.

2. Paragraph 2(a) and paragraphs 3 to 9 of Article 22 are applicable *mutatis mutandis* to the temporary transfer under this Article.

3. Costs resulting from the application of this Article shall be borne in accordance with Article 21, except for the costs arising from the transfer of the person concerned to and from the executing State which shall be borne by the issuing State.

*Article 24*

**Hearing by videoconference or other audiovisual transmission**

1. Where a person is in the territory of the executing State and has to be heard as a witness or expert by the competent authorities of the issuing State, the issuing authority may issue an EIO in order to hear the witness or expert by videoconference or other audiovisual transmission in accordance with paragraphs 5 to 7.

The issuing authority may also issue an EIO for the purpose of hearing a suspected or accused person by videoconference or other audiovisual transmission.

2. In addition to the grounds for non-recognition or non-execution referred to in Article 11, execution of an EIO may be refused if either:

(a) the suspected or accused person does not consent; or

(b) the execution of such an investigative measure in a particular case would be contrary to the fundamental principles of the law of the executing State.

3. The issuing authority and the executing authority shall agree the practical arrangements. When agreeing such arrangements, the executing authority shall undertake to:

(a) summon the witness or expert concerned, indicating the time and the venue of the hearing;

(b) summon the suspected or accused persons to appear for the hearing in accordance with the detailed rules laid down in the law of the executing State and inform such persons about their rights under the law of the issuing State, in such a time as to allow them to exercise their rights of defence effectively;

(c) ensure the identity of the person to be heard.

4. If in circumstances of a particular case the executing authority has no access to technical means for a hearing held by videoconference, such means may be made available to it by the issuing State by mutual agreement.

5. Where a hearing is held by videoconference or other audiovisual transmission, the following rules shall apply:

(a) the competent authority of the executing State shall be present during the hearing, where necessary assisted by an interpreter, and shall also be responsible for ensuring both the identity of the person to be heard and respect for the fundamental principles of the law of the executing State.

If the executing authority is of the view that during the hearing the fundamental principles of the law of the executing State are being infringed, it shall immediately take the necessary measures to ensure that the hearing continues in accordance with those principles;

(b) measures for the protection of the person to be heard shall be agreed, where necessary, between the competent authorities of the issuing State and the executing State;

(c) the hearing shall be conducted directly by, or under the direction of, the competent authority of the issuing State in accordance with its own laws;

(d) at the request of the issuing State or the person to be heard, the executing State shall ensure that the person to be heard is assisted by an interpreter, if necessary;

(e) suspected or accused persons shall be informed in advance of the hearing of the procedural rights which would accrue to them, including the right not to testify, under the law of the executing State and the issuing State. Witnesses and experts may claim the right not to testify which would accrue to them under the law of either the executing or the issuing State and shall be informed about this right in advance of the hearing.

6. Without prejudice to any measures agreed for the protection of persons, on the conclusion of the hearing, the executing authority shall draw up minutes indicating the date and place of the hearing, the identity of the person heard, the identities and functions of all other persons in the executing State participating in the hearing, any oaths taken and the technical conditions under which the hearing took place. The document shall be forwarded by the executing authority to the issuing authority.

7. Each Member State shall take the necessary measures to ensure that, where the person is being heard within its territory in accordance with this Article and refuses to testify when under an obligation to testify or does not testify the truth, its national law applies in the same way as if the hearing took place in a national procedure.

*Article 25*

**Hearing by telephone conference**

1. If a person is in the territory of one Member State and has to be heard as a witness or expert by competent authorities of another Member State, the issuing authority of the latter Member State may, where it is not appropriate or possible for the person to be heard to appear in its territory in person, and after having examined other suitable means, issue an EIO in order to hear a witness or expert by telephone conference as provided for in paragraph 2.

2. Unless otherwise agreed, Article 24(3), (5), (6) and (7) shall apply *mutatis mutandis* to hearings by telephone conference.

*Article 26*

**Information on bank and other financial accounts**

1. An EIO may be issued in order to determine whether any natural or legal person subject to the criminal proceedings concerned holds or controls one or more accounts, of whatever nature, in any bank located in the territory of the executing State, and if so, to obtain all the details of the identified accounts.

2. Each Member State shall take the measures necessary to enable it to provide the information referred to in paragraph 1 in accordance with the conditions under this Article.

3. The information referred to in paragraph 1 shall also, if requested in the EIO, include accounts for which the person subject to the criminal proceedings concerned has powers of attorney.

4. The obligation set out in this Article shall apply only to the extent that the information is in the possession of the bank keeping the account.

5. In the EIO the issuing authority shall indicate the reasons why it considers that the requested information is likely to be of substantial value for the purpose of the criminal proceedings concerned and on what grounds it presumes that banks in the executing State hold the account and, to the extent available, which banks may be involved. It shall also include in the EIO any information available which may facilitate its execution.

6. An EIO may also be issued to determine whether any natural or legal person subject to the criminal proceedings concerned holds one or more accounts, in any non-bank financial institution located on the territory of the executing State. Paragraphs 3 to 5 shall apply *mutatis mutandis*. In such case and in addition to the grounds for non-recognition and non-execution referred to in Article 11, the execution of the EIO may also be refused if the execution of the investigative measure would not be authorised in a similar domestic case.

*Article 27*

**Information on banking and other financial operations**

1. An EIO may be issued in order to obtain the details of specified bank accounts and of banking operations which have been carried out during a defined period through one or more accounts specified therein, including the details of any sending or recipient account.

2. Each Member State shall take the measures necessary to enable it to provide the information referred to in paragraph 1 in accordance with the conditions under this Article.

3. The obligation set out in this Article shall apply only to the extent that the information is in the possession of the bank in which the account is held.

4. In the EIO the issuing authority shall indicate the reasons why it considers the requested information relevant for the purpose of the criminal proceedings concerned.

5. An EIO may also be issued with regard to the information provided for in paragraph 1 with reference to the financial operations conducted by non-banking financial institutions. Paragraphs 3 to 4 shall apply *mutatis mutandis*. In such case and in addition to the grounds for non-recognition and non-execution referred to in Article 11, the execution of the EIO may also be refused where the execution of the investigative measure would not be authorised in a similar domestic case.

*Article 28*

**Investigative measures implying the gathering of evidence in real time, continuously and over a certain period of time**

1. When the EIO is issued for the purpose of executing an investigative measure requiring the gathering of evidence in real time, continuously and over a certain period of time, such as:

(a) the monitoring of banking or other financial operations that are being carried out through one or more specified accounts;

(b) the controlled deliveries on the territory of the executing State;

its execution may be refused, in addition to the grounds for non-recognition and non-execution referred to in Article 11, if the execution of the investigative measure concerned would not be authorised in a similar domestic case.

2. The practical arrangements regarding the investigative measure referred to in paragraph 1(b) and wherever else necessary shall be agreed between the issuing State and the executing State.

3. The issuing authority shall indicate in the EIO why it considers the information requested relevant for the purpose of the criminal proceedings concerned.

4. The right to act, to direct and to control operations related to the execution of an EIO referred to in paragraph 1 shall lie with the competent authorities of the executing State.

*Article 29*

**Covert investigations**

1. An EIO may be issued for the purpose of requesting the executing State to assist the issuing State in the conduct of investigations into crime by officers acting under covert or false identity ('covert investigations').

2. The issuing authority shall indicate in the EIO why it considers that the covert investigation is likely to be relevant for the purpose of the criminal proceedings. The decision on the recognition and execution of an EIO issued under this Article shall be taken in each individual case by the competent authorities of the executing State with due regard to its national law and procedures.

3. In addition to the grounds for non-recognition and non-execution referred to in Article 11, the executing authority may refuse to execute an EIO referred to in paragraph 1, where:

(a) the execution of the covert investigation would not be authorised in a similar domestic case; or

(b) it was not possible to reach an agreement on the arrangements for the covert investigations under paragraph 4.

4. Covert investigations shall take place in accordance with the national law and procedures of the Member State on the territory of which the covert investigation takes place. The right to act, to direct and to control the operation related to the covert investigation shall lie solely with the competent authorities of the executing State. The duration of the covert investigation, the detailed conditions, and the legal status of the officers concerned during covert investigations shall be agreed between the issuing State and the executing State with due regard to their national laws and procedures.

CHAPTER V

## INTERCEPTION OF TELECOMMUNICATIONS

*Article 30*

### Interception of telecommunications with technical assistance of another Member State

1. An EIO may be issued for the interception of telecommunications in the Member State from which technical assistance is needed.

2. Where more than one Member State is in a position to provide the complete necessary technical assistance for the same interception of telecommunications, the EIO shall be sent only to one of them. Priority shall always be given to the Member State where the subject of the interception is or will be located.

3. An EIO referred to in paragraph 1 shall also contain the following information:

(a) information for the purpose of identifying the subject of the interception;

(b) the desired duration of the interception; and

(c) sufficient technical data, in particular the target identifier, to ensure that the EIO can be executed.

4. The issuing authority shall indicate in the EIO the reasons why it considers the indicated investigative measure relevant for the purpose of the criminal proceedings concerned.

5. In addition to the grounds for non-recognition or non-execution referred to in Article 11, the execution of an EIO referred to in paragraph 1 may also be refused where the investigative measure would not have been authorised in a similar domestic case. The executing State may make its consent subject to any conditions which would be observed in a similar domestic case.

6. An EIO referred to in paragraph 1 may be executed by:

(a) transmitting telecommunications immediately to the issuing State; or

(b) intercepting, recording and subsequently transmitting the outcome of interception of telecommunications to the issuing State.

The issuing authority and the executing authority shall consult each other with a view to agreeing on whether the interception is carried out in accordance with point (a) or (b).

7. When issuing an EIO referred to in paragraph 1 or during the interception, the issuing authority may, where it has a particular reason to do so, also request a transcription, decoding or decrypting of the recording subject to the agreement of the executing authority.

8. Costs resulting from the application of this Article shall be borne in accordance with Article 21, except for the costs arising from the transcription, decoding and decrypting of the intercepted communications which shall be borne by the issuing State.

*Article 31*

### Notification of the Member State where the subject of the interception is located from which no technical assistance is needed

1. Where, for the purpose of carrying out an investigative measure, the interception of telecommunications is authorised by the competent authority of one Member State (the 'intercepting Member State') and the communication address of the subject of the interception specified in the interception order is being used on the territory of another Member State (the 'notified Member State') from which no technical assistance is needed to carry out the interception, the intercepting Member State shall notify the competent authority of the notified Member State of the interception:

(a) prior to the interception in cases where the competent authority of the intercepting Member State knows at the time of ordering the interception that the subject of the interception is or will be on the territory of the notified Member State;

(b) during the interception or after the interception has been carried out, immediately after it becomes aware that the subject of the interception is or has been during the interception, on the territory of the notified Member State.

2. The notification referred to in paragraph 1 shall be made by using the form set out in Annex C.

3. The competent authority of the notified Member States may, in case where the interception would not be authorised in a similar domestic case, notify, without delay and at the latest within 96 hours after the receipt of the notification referred to in paragraph 1, the competent authority of the intercepting Member State:

(a) that the interception may not be carried out or shall be terminated; and

(b) where necessary, that any material already intercepted while the subject of the interception was on its territory may not be used, or may only be used under conditions which it shall specify. The competent authority of the notified Member State shall inform the competent authority of the intercepting Member State of reasons justifying those conditions.

4. Article 5(2) shall be applicable *mutatis mutandis* for the notification referred to in paragraph 2.

CHAPTER VI

**PROVISIONAL MEASURES**

*Article 32*

**Provisional measures**

1. The issuing authority may issue an EIO in order to take any measure with a view to provisionally preventing the destruction, transformation, removal, transfer or disposal of an item that may be used as evidence.

2. The executing authority shall decide and communicate the decision on the provisional measure as soon as possible and, wherever practicable, within 24 hours of receipt of the EIO.

3. Where a provisional measure referred to in paragraph 1 is requested the issuing authority shall indicate in the EIO whether the evidence is to be transferred to the issuing State or is to remain in the executing State. The executing authority shall recognise and execute the EIO and transfer the evidence in accordance with the procedures laid down in this Directive.

4. Where, in accordance with paragraph 3, an EIO is accompanied by an instruction that the evidence shall remain in the executing State, the issuing authority shall indicate the date of lifting the provisional measure referred to in paragraph 1, or the estimated date for the submission of the request for the evidence to be transferred to the issuing State.

5. After consulting the issuing authority, the executing authority may, in accordance with its national law and practice, lay down appropriate conditions in light of the circumstances of the case to limit the period for which the provisional measure referred to in paragraph 1 is to be maintained. If, in accordance with those conditions, it envisages lifting the provisional measure, the executing authority shall inform the issuing authority, which shall be given the opportunity to submit its comments. The issuing authority shall forthwith notify the executing authority that the provisional measure referred to in paragraph 1 has been lifted.

CHAPTER VII

**FINAL PROVISIONS**

*Article 33*

**Notifications**

1. By 22 May 2017 each Member State shall notify the Commission of the following:

(a) the authority or authorities which, in accordance with its national law, are competent according to Article 2(c) and (d) when this Member State is the issuing State or the executing State;

(b) the languages accepted for an EIO, as referred to in Article 5(2);

(c) the information regarding the designated central authority or authorities if the Member State wishes to make use of the possibility under Article 7(3). This information shall be binding upon the authorities of the issuing State.

2. Each Member State may also provide the Commission the list of necessary documents it would require under Article 22(4).

3. Member States shall inform the Commission of any subsequent changes to the information referred to in paragraphs 1 and 2.

4. The Commission shall make the information received under this Article available to all the Member States and to the EJN. The EJN shall make the information available on the website referred to in Article 9 of the Council Decision 2008/976/JHA [1].

*Article 34*

**Relations to other legal instruments, agreements and arrangements**

1. Without prejudice to their application between Member States and third States and their temporary application by virtue of Article 35, this Directive replaces, as from 22 May 2017, the corresponding provisions of the following conventions applicable between the Member States bound by this Directive:

(a) European Convention on Mutual Assistance in Criminal Matters of the Council of Europe of 20 April 1959, as well as its two additional protocols, and the bilateral agreements concluded pursuant to Article 26 thereof;

(b) Convention implementing the Schengen Agreement;

(c) Convention on Mutual Assistance in Criminal Matters between the Member States of the European Union and its protocol.

2. Framework Decision 2008/978/JHA is hereby replaced for the Member States bound by this Directive. Provisions of Framework Decision 2003/577/JHA are replaced for Member States bound by this Directive as regards freezing of evidence.

For the Member States bound by this Directive, references to Framework Decision 2008/978/JHA and, as regards freezing of evidence, to Framework Decision 2003/577/JHA, shall be construed as references to this Directive.

3. In addition to this Directive, Member States may conclude or continue to apply bilateral or multilateral agreements or arrangements with other Member States after 22 May 2017 only insofar as these make it possible to further strengthen the aims of this Directive and contribute to simplifying or further facilitating the procedures for gathering evidence and provided that the level of safeguards set out in this Directive is respected.

4. Member States shall notify to the Commission by 22 May 2017 the existing agreements and arrangements referred to in paragraph 3 which they wish to continue to apply. Member States shall also notify the Commission within three months of the signing of any new agreement or arrangement referred to in paragraph 3.

*Article 35*

**Transitional provisions**

1. Mutual assistance requests received before 22 May 2017 shall continue to be governed by existing instruments relating to mutual assistance in criminal matters. Decisions to freeze evidence by virtue of Framework Decision 2003/577/JHA and received before 22 May 2017 shall also be governed by that Framework Decision.

2. Article 8(1) is applicable *mutatis mutandis* to the EIO following a decision of freezing taken under Framework Decision 2003/577/JHA.

[1] Council Decision 2008/976/JHA of 16 December 2008 on the European Judicial Network (OJ L 348, 24.12.2008, p. 130).

*Article 36*

**Transposition**

1. Member States shall take the necessary measures to comply with this Directive by 22 May 2017.

2. When Member States adopt these measures, they shall contain a reference to this Directive or shall be accompanied by such reference on the occasion of their official publication. The methods of making such reference shall be laid down by Member States.

3. By 22 May 2017, Member States shall transmit to the Commission the text of the provisions transposing into their national law the obligations imposed on them under this Directive.

*Article 37*

**Report on the application**

No later than five years after 21 May 2014, the Commission shall present to the European Parliament and the Council a report on the application of this Directive, on the basis of both qualitative and quantitative information, including in particular, the evaluation of its impact on the cooperation in criminal matters and the protection of individuals, as well as the execution of the provisions on the interception of telecommunications in light of technical developments. The report shall be accompanied, if necessary, by proposals for amendments to this Directive.

*Article 38*

**Entry into force**

This Directive shall enter into force on the twentieth day following its publication in the *Official Journal of the European Union*.

*Article 39*

**Addressees**

This Directive is addressed to the Member States in accordance with the Treaties.

Done at Brussels, 3 April 2014.

| *For the European Parliament* | *For the Council* |
|---|---|
| *The President* | *The President* |
| M. SCHULZ | D. KOURKOULAS |

L 130/24 EN Official Journal of the European Union 1.5.2014

ANNEX A

**EUROPEAN INVESTIGATION ORDER (EIO)**

This EIO has been issued by a competent authority. The issuing authority certifies that the issuing of this EIO is necessary and proportionate for the purpose of the proceedings specified within it taking into account the rights of the suspected or accused person and that the investigative measures requested could have been ordered under the same conditions in a similar domestic case. I request that the investigative measure or measures specified below be carried out taking due account of the confidentiality of the investigation and that the evidence obtained as a result of the execution of the EIO be transferred.

SECTION A

Issuing State: ...........................................................................

Executing State: ...........................................................................

SECTION B: **Urgency**

Please indicate if there is any urgency due to

☐ Evidence being concealed or destroyed

☐ Imminent trial date

☐ Any other reason

Please specify below:

Time limits for execution of the EIO are laid down in Directive 2014/41/EU. However, if a shorter or specific time limit is necessary, please provide the date and explain the reason for this:

...........................................................................

...........................................................................

...........................................................................

SECTION C: Investigative measure(s) to be carried out

1. Describe the assistance/investigative measure(s) required AND indicate, if applicable, if it is one of the following investigative measures:

...........................................................................

...........................................................................

...........................................................................

...........................................................................

...........................................................................

...........................................................................

...........................................................................

...........................................................................

☐ Obtaining information or evidence which is already in the possession of the executing authority

☐ Obtaining information contained in databases held by police or judicial authorities

☐ Hearing

- ☐ witness
- ☐ expert
- ☐ suspected or accused person
- ☐ victim
- ☐ third party

☐ Identification of persons holding a subscription of a specified phone number or IP address

☐ Temporary transfer of a person held in custody to the issuing State

☐ Temporary transfer of a person held in custody to the executing State

☐ Hearing by videoconference or other audiovisual transmission
- ☐ witness
- ☐ expert
- ☐ suspected or accused person

☐ Hearing by telephone conference
- ☐ witness
- ☐ expert

☐ Information on bank and other financial accounts

☐ Information on banking and other financial operations

☐ Investigative measure implying the gathering of evidence in real time, continuously and over a certain period of time
- ☐ monitoring of banking or other financial operations
- ☐ controlled deliveries
- ☐ other

☐ Covert investigation

☐ Interception of telecommunications

☐ Provisional measure(s) to prevent the destruction, transformation, moving, transfer or disposal of an item that may be used as evidence

SECTION D: Relation to an earlier EIO

Indicate whether this EIO supplements an earlier EIO. If applicable, provide information relevant to identify the previous EIO (the date of issue of the EIO, the authority to which it was transmitted and, if available, the date of transmission of the EIO, and reference numbers given by the issuing and executing authorities):

.....................................................................................................................................

.....................................................................................................................................

If relevant please indicate if an EIO has already been addressed to another Member State in the same case:

.....................................................................................................................................

SECTION E: Identity of the person concerned

1. State all information, as far as known, regarding the identity of the (i) natural or (ii) legal person(s) concerned by the investigative measure (if more than one person is concerned, please provide the information for each person):

(i) In the case of natural person(s)

Name: ..........................................................................................................................

First name(s): ................................................................................................................

Other relevant name(s), if applicable: ...........................................................................

Aliases, if applicable: .....................................................................................................

Sex: ...............................................................................................................................

Nationality: ....................................................................................................................

Identity number or social security number: ...................................................................

Type and number of the identity document(s) (ID card, passport), if available:

.....................................................................................................................................

Date of birth: .................................................................................................................

Place of birth: ................................................................................................................

Residence and/or known address; if address not known, state the last known address:

.....................................................................................................................................

Language(s) which the person understands:

.....................................................................................................................................

(ii) In the case of legal person(s)

Name: ...

Form of legal person: ...

Shortened name, commonly used name or trading name, if applicable:

...

Registered seat: ...

Registration number: ...

Address of the legal person: ...

Name of the legal person's representative: ...

Please describe the position the concerned person currently holds in the proceedings:

☐ suspected or accused person

☐ victim

☐ witness

☐ expert

☐ third party

☐ other (please specify) ...

2. If different from the address above, please give the location where investigative measure is to be carried out:

...

...

3. Provide any other information that will assist with the execution of the EIO:

...

...

SECTION F: Type of proceedings for which the EIO is issued:

☐ (a) with respect to criminal proceedings brought by, or that may be brought before, a judicial authority in respect of a criminal offence under the national law of the issuing State; or

☐ (b) proceedings brought by administrative authorities in respect of acts which are punishable under the national law of the issuing State by virtue of being infringements of the rules of law, and where the decision may give rise to proceedings before a court having jurisdiction in particular in criminal matters; or

☐ (c) proceedings brought by judicial authorities in respect of acts which are punishable under the national law of the issuing State by virtue of being infringements of the rules of law, and where the decision may give rise to proceedings before a court having jurisdiction in particular in criminal matters;

☐ (d) in connection with proceedings referred to in points (a), (b), and (c) which relate to offences or infringements for which a legal person may be held liable or punished in the issuing State.

SECTION G: Grounds for issuing the EIO

1. Summary of the facts

Set out the reasons why the EIO is issued, including a summary of the underlying facts, a description of offences charged or under investigation, the stage the investigation has reached, the reasons for any risk factors and any other relevant information.

...

...

...

2. Nature and legal classification of the offence(s) for which the EIO is issued and the applicable statutory provision/code:

..............................................................................................................................................

..............................................................................................................................................

..............................................................................................................................................

3. Is the offence for which the EIO is issued punishable in the issuing State by a custodial sentence or detention order of a maximum of at least three years as defined by the law of the issuing State and included in the list of offences set out below? (please tick the relevant box)

- ☐ participation in a criminal organisation
- ☐ terrorism
- ☐ trafficking in human beings
- ☐ sexual exploitation of children and child pornography
- ☐ illicit trafficking in narcotic drugs and psychotropic substances
- ☐ illicit trafficking in weapons, munitions and explosives
- ☐ corruption
- ☐ fraud, including that affecting the financial interests of the European Union within the meaning of the Convention of 26 July 1995 on the protection of the European Communities' financial interests
- ☐ laundering of the proceeds of crime
- ☐ counterfeiting currency, including of the euro
- ☐ computer-related crime
- ☐ environmental crime, including illicit trafficking in endangered animal species and in endangered plant species and varieties
- ☐ facilitation of unauthorised entry and residence
- ☐ murder, grievous bodily injury
- ☐ illicit trade in human organs and tissue
- ☐ kidnapping, illegal restraint and hostage-taking
- ☐ racism and xenophobia
- ☐ organised or armed robbery
- ☐ illicit trafficking in cultural goods, including antiques and works of art
- ☐ swindling
- ☐ racketeering and extortion
- ☐ counterfeiting and piracy of products
- ☐ forgery of administrative documents and trafficking therein
- ☐ forgery of means of payment
- ☐ illicit trafficking in hormonal substances and other growth promoters
- ☐ illicit trafficking in nuclear or radioactive materials
- ☐ trafficking in stolen vehicles
- ☐ rape
- ☐ arson
- ☐ crimes within the jurisdiction of the International Criminal Court
- ☐ unlawful seizure of aircraft/ships
- ☐ sabotage

L 130/28 EN Official Journal of the European Union 1.5.2014

SECTION H: Additional requirements for certain measures

Fill out the sections relevant to the investigative measure(s) requested:

SECTION H1: Transfer of a person held in custody

(1) If a temporary transfer to the issuing State of a person held in custody for the purpose of the investigation is requested, please indicate whether the person consented to this measure:

☐ Yes ☐ No ☐ I request that the person's consent is sought

(2) If a temporary transfer to the executing State of a person held in custody for the purpose of investigation is requested, please indicate whether the person consented to this measure:

☐ Yes ☐ No

SECTION H2: Video or telephone conference or other audiovisual transmission

If hearing by videoconference or telephone conference or other audiovisual transmission is requested:

Please indicate the name of the authority that will conduct the hearing (contact details/language):

............................................................................................................................................

Please indicate reasons for requesting this measure: ..................................................................................

............................................................................................................................................

☐ (a) hearing by videoconference or other audiovisual transmission:

☐ the suspected or accused person has given his/her consent

☐ (b) hearing by telephone conference

SECTION H3: Provisional measures

If a provisional measure to prevent the destruction, transformation, moving, transfer or disposal of an item that may be used as evidence, is requested, please indicate whether:

☐ the item is to be transferred to the issuing State

☐ the item is to remain in the executing State; please indicate an estimated date:

for lifting of provisional measure: ....................................................................................................

for the submission of a subsequent request concerning the item: .......................................................

SECTION H4: Information on bank and other financial accounts

(1) If information on bank accounts or other financial accounts that the person holds or controls is requested, please indicate, for each of them, the reasons why you consider the measure relevant for the purpose of the criminal proceedings and on what grounds you presume that banks in the executing State hold the account:

☐ information on bank accounts that the person holds or in respect of which he or she has the power of attorney

☐ information on other financial accounts that the person holds or in respect of which he or she has the power of attorney

............................................................................................................................................

............................................................................................................................................

............................................................................................................................................

............................................................................................................................................

(2) If information on banking operations or other financial operations is requested, please indicate, for each of them, the reasons why you consider the measure relevant for the purpose of the criminal proceedings:

☐ information on banking operations

☐ information on other financial operations

..........................................................................................................................................

..........................................................................................................................................

..........................................................................................................................................

..........................................................................................................................................

Indicate the relevant period of time and the related accounts:

..........................................................................................................................................

..........................................................................................................................................

SECTION H5: Investigative measures implying the gathering of evidence in real time, continuously and over a certain period of time

If such investigative measure is requested please indicate the reasons why you consider the requested information relevant for the purpose of the criminal proceedings:

..........................................................................................................................................

..........................................................................................................................................

SECTION H6: Covert investigations

If covert investigation is requested please indicate the reasons why you consider the investigative measure likely to be relevant for the purpose of the criminal proceedings:

..........................................................................................................................................

..........................................................................................................................................

SECTION H7: Interception of telecommunications

(1) If interception of telecommunications is requested please indicate the reasons why you consider the investigative measure relevant for the purpose of the criminal proceedings:

..........................................................................................................................................

..........................................................................................................................................

(2) Please provide following information:

(a) information for the purpose of identifying the subject of the interception:

..........................................................................................................................................

(b) the desired duration of the interception:

..........................................................................................................................................

(c) technical data (in particular the target identifier — such as mobile telephone, landline telephone, email address, internet connection), to ensure that the EIO can be executed:

..........................................................................................................................................

(3) Please indicate your preference concerning the method of execution:

☐ immediate transmission

☐ recording and subsequent transmission

Please indicate if you also require transcription, decoding or decrypting of the intercepted material (*):

..........................................................................................................................................

..........................................................................................................................................

(*) Please be aware that the costs of any transcription, decoding or decrypting must be met by the issuing State.

SECTION I: Formalities and procedures requested for the execution

1. Tick and complete, if applicable

☐ It is requested that the executing authority comply with the following formalities and procedures (…):

……………………………………………………………………………………………………

……………………………………………………………………………………………………

2. Tick and complete, if applicable

☐ It is requested that one or several officials of the issuing State assist in the execution of the EIO in support of the competent authorities of the executing State.

Contact details of the officials:

……………………………………………………………………………………………………

……………………………………………………………………………………………………

Languages that may be used for communication: ……………………………………………

……………………………………………………………………………………………………

SECTION J: Legal remedies

1. Please indicate if a legal remedy has already been sought against the issuing of an EIO, and if so please provide further details (description of the legal remedy, including necessary steps to take and deadlines):

……………………………………………………………………………………………………

……………………………………………………………………………………………………

2. Authority in the issuing State which can supply further information on procedures for seeking legal remedies in the issuing State and on whether legal assistance and interpretation and translation is available:

Name: ………………………………………………………………………………………………

Contact person (if applicable): ……………………………………………………………………

Address: ……………………………………………………………………………………………

Tel. No: (country code) (area/city code) …………………………………………………………

Fax No: (country code) (area/city code) …………………………………………………………

E-mail: ………………………………………………………………………………………………

SECTION K: Details of the authority which issued the EIO

Tick the type of authority which issued the EIO:

☐ judicial authority

☐ (*) any other competent authority as defined by the law of the issuing State

(*) Please also complete section (L)

Name of authority:

……………………………………………………………………………………………………

Name of representative/contact point:

……………………………………………………………………………………………………

File No: ……………………………………………………………………………………………

Address: ……………………………………………………………………………………………

Tel. No: (country code) (area/city code) …………………………………………………………

Fax No: (country code) (area/city code) …………………………………………………………

E-mail: ………………………………………………………………………………………………

Languages in which it is possible to communicate with the issuing authority:

……………………………………………………………………………………………………

If different from above, the contact details of the person(s) to contact for additional information or to make practical arrangements for the transfer of evidence:

Name/Title/Organisation: ..........

Address: ..........

E-mail/Contact Phone No: ..........

Signature of the issuing authority and/or its representative certifying the content of the EIO as accurate and correct:

Name: ..........

Post held (title/grade): ..........

Date: ..........

Official stamp (if available):

SECTION L Details of the judicial authority which validated the EIO

Please indicate the type of judicial authority which has validated this EIO:

- ☐ (a) judge or court
- ☐ (b) investigating judge
- ☐ (c) public prosecutor

Official name of the validating authority:

..........

Name of its representative:

..........

Post held (title/grade):

..........

File no: ..........

Address: ..........

..........

Tel. No: (country code) (area/city code) ..........

Fax No: (country code) (area/city code) ..........

E-mail: ..........

Languages in which it is possible to communicate with the validating authority:

..........

Please indicate if the main contact point for the executing authority should be the:

- ☐ issuing authority
- ☐ validating authority

Signature and details of the validating authority

Name: ..........

Post held (title/grade): ..........

Date: ..........

Official stamp (if available):

L 130/32 EN Official Journal of the European Union 1.5.2014

*ANNEX B*

**CONFIRMATION OF THE RECEIPT OF AN EIO**

This form has to be completed by the authority of the executing State which received the EIO referred to below.

(A) THE EIO CONCERNED
Authority which issued the EIO:
..........
File reference: ..........
Date of issuing: ..........
Date of receipt: ..........

(B) THE AUTHORITY WHICH RECEIVED THE EIO (1)
Official name of the competent authority:
..........
Name of its representative:
..........
Post held (title/grade):
..........
Address:
..........
..........
..........
Tel. No: (country code) (area/city code) ..........
Fax No: (country code) (area/city code) ..........
E-mail: ..........
File reference: ..........
Languages in which it is possible to communicate with the authority:
..........

(C) (WHERE APPLICABLE) THE COMPETENT AUTHORITY TO WHOM THE EIO IS TRANSMITTED BY THE AUTHORITY UNDER (B)
Official name of the authority
..........
Name of its representative:
..........
Post held (title/grade):
..........
Address:
..........
..........
Tel. No: (country code) (area/city code) ..........
Fax No: (country code) (area/city code) ..........
E-mail: ..........
Date of transmission: ..........
File reference: ..........
Language(s) that may be used for communication:
..........

(1) This section is to be completed by each authority which received the EIO. This obligation falls upon the authority competent to recognise and execute the EIO and, where applicable, upon the central authority or the authority which transmitted the EIO to the competent authority.

(D) ANY OTHER INFORMATION WHICH MAY BE RELEVANT FOR THE ISSUING AUTHORITY:

..............................................................................................................................................

..............................................................................................................................................

..............................................................................................................................................

(E) SIGNATURE AND DATE

Signature:

Date: ........................................................................................................................................

Official stamp (if available):

*ANNEX C*

**NOTIFICATION**

This form is used in order to notify a Member State about the interception of telecommunication that will be, is or has been carried out on its territory without its technical assistance. I hereby inform ……… (notified Member State) of the interception.

(A) (1) THE COMPETENT AUTHORITY

Official name of the competent authority of intercepting Member State:

……………………………………………………………………………

Name of its representative:

……………………………………………………………………………

Post held (title/grade):

……………………………………………………………………………

Address:

……………………………………………………………………………

……………………………………………………………………………

……………………………………………………………………………

Tel. No: (country code) (area/city code) ……………………………………

Fax No: (country code) (area/city code) ……………………………………

E-mail:……………………………………………………………………

File reference:……………………………………………………………

Date of issuing:…………………………………………………………

Languages in which it is possible to communicate with the authority:

……………………………………………………………………………

(B) INFORMATION CONCERNING THE INTERCEPTION

(I) Information about state of play: This notification takes place (please tick)

- ☐ prior to the interception
- ☐ during the interception
- ☐ after the interception

(II) The (anticipated) duration of the interception (as known to the issuing authority).

……………………………, starting from ……………………………………

(III) Target of the interception: (telephone number, IP number or e-mail)

……………………………………………………………………………

(IV) Identity of the persons concerned

State all information, as far as they are known, regarding the identity of the (i) natural or (ii) legal person(s) against whom the proceedings are/may be/is taking place:

(i) In the case of natural person(s)

Name: ……………………………………………………………

First name(s):……………………………………………………

Other relevant name(s), if applicable: ……………………………

Aliases, if applicable: ……………………………………………

Sex:………………………………………………………………

Nationality: ………………………………………………………

Identity number or social security number: ………………………

(1) The authority which is referred to here is the one which should be contacted in further correspondence with the issuing State.

Date of birth: ...............................................................................................

Place of birth: ...............................................................................................

Residence and/or known address; if address not known, state the last known address:

...............................................................................................

Language(s) which the person understands:

...............................................................................................

(ii) In the case of legal person(s)

Name: ...............................................................................................

Form of legal person: ...............................................................................................

Shortened name, commonly used name or trading name, if applicable:

...............................................................................................

Registered seat ...............................................................................................

Registration number: ...............................................................................................

Address of the legal person: ...............................................................................................

Name and contact details of the representative of the legal person: ..................................

(V) Information regarding the purpose of this interception:

State all information necessary, including a description of the case, legal classification of the offence(s) and the applicable statutory provision/code, in order to enable the notified authority to assess the following:

☐ whether the interception would be authorised in a similar domestic case; and whether the material obtained can be used in legal proceedings

☐ where the interception has already occurred, whether that material can be used in legal proceedings

...............................................................................................

...............................................................................................

...............................................................................................

...............................................................................................

...............................................................................................

...............................................................................................

Please note that any objection to the interception or the use of already intercepted material must be made no later than 96 hours after the reception of this notification.

(C) SIGNATURE AND DATE

Signature:

Date: ...............................................................................................

Official stamp (if available):

L 130/36 EN Official Journal of the European Union 1.5.2014

*ANNEX D*

**THE CATEGORIES OF OFFENCES REFERRED TO IN ARTICLE 11**

— participation in a criminal organisation,

— terrorism,

— trafficking in human beings,

— sexual exploitation of children and child pornography,

— illicit trafficking in narcotic drugs and psychotropic substances,

— illicit trafficking in weapons, munitions and explosives,

— corruption,

— fraud, including that affecting the financial interests of the European Union within the meaning of the Convention of 26 July 1995 on the protection of the European Communities' financial interests,

— laundering of the proceeds of crime,

— counterfeiting currency, including of the euro,

— computer-related crime,

— environmental crime, including illicit trafficking in endangered animal species and in endangered plant species and varieties,

— facilitation of unauthorised entry and residence,

— murder, grievous bodily injury,

— illicit trade in human organs and tissue,

— kidnapping, illegal restraint and hostage-taking,

— racism and xenophobia,

— organised or armed robbery,

— illicit trafficking in cultural goods, including antiques and works of art,

— swindling,

— racketeering and extortion,

— counterfeiting and piracy of products,

— forgery of administrative documents and trafficking therein,

— forgery of means of payment,

— illicit trafficking in hormonal substances and other growth promoters,

— illicit trafficking in nuclear or radioactive materials,

— trafficking in stolen vehicles,

— rape,

— arson,

— crimes within the jurisdiction of the International Criminal Court,

— unlawful seizure of aircraft/ships,

— sabotage.

# Directive 2014/42 on the freezing and confiscation of instrumentalities and proceeds of crime in the European Union, 3 April 2014

[OJ 2014, L 127/39–50 corrected by OJ 2014, L 138/114]

Effective 1 July 2013, the electronic version of the *Official Journal* (e-OJ) is authentic and produces legal effects.

29.4.2014 EN Official Journal of the European Union L 127/39

**DIRECTIVE 2014/42/EU OF THE EUROPEAN PARLIAMENT AND OF THE COUNCIL**

**of 3 April 2014**

**on the freezing and confiscation of instrumentalities and proceeds of crime in the European Union**

THE EUROPEAN PARLIAMENT AND THE COUNCIL OF THE EUROPEAN UNION,

Having regard to the Treaty on the Functioning of the European Union, and in particular Article 82(2) and Article 83(1) thereof,

Having regard to the proposal from the European Commission,

After transmission of the draft legislative act to the national parliaments,

Having regard to the opinion of the European Economic and Social Committee ([1]),

Having regard to the opinion of the Committee of the Regions ([2]),

Acting in accordance with the ordinary legislative procedure ([3]),

Whereas:

(1) The main motive for cross-border organised crime, including mafia-type criminal organisation, is financial gain. As a consequence, competent authorities should be given the means to trace, freeze, manage and confiscate the proceeds of crime. However, the effective prevention of and fight against organised crime should be achieved by neutralising the proceeds of crime and should be extended, in certain cases, to any property deriving from activities of a criminal nature.

(2) Organised criminal groups operate without borders and increasingly acquire assets in Member States other than those in which they are based and in third countries. There is an increasing need for effective international cooperation on asset recovery and mutual legal assistance.

(3) Among the most effective means of combating organised crime is providing for severe legal consequences for committing such crime, as well as effective detection and the freezing and confiscation of the instrumentalities and proceeds of crime.

(4) Although existing statistics are limited, the amounts recovered from proceeds of crime in the Union seem insufficient compared to the estimated proceeds. Studies have shown that, although regulated by Union and national law, confiscation procedures remain underused.

(5) The adoption of minimum rules will approximate the Member States' freezing and confiscation regimes, thus facilitating mutual trust and effective cross-border cooperation.

([1]) OJ C 299, 4.10.2012, p. 128.
([2]) OJ C 391, 18.12.2012, p. 134.
([3]) Position of the European Parliament of 25 February 2014 (not yet published in the Official Journal) and Council decision of 14 March 2014.

(6) The Stockholm Programme and the Justice and Home Affairs Council Conclusions on confiscation and asset recovery adopted in June 2010 emphasise the importance of a more effective identification, confiscation and re-use of criminal assets.

(7) The current Union legal framework on freezing, seizure and confiscation of assets consists of Joint Action 98/699/JHA ([1]), Council Framework Decision 2001/500/JHA ([2]), Council Framework Decision 2003/577/JHA ([3]), Council Framework Decision 2005/212/JHA ([4]) and Council Framework Decision 2006/783/JHA ([5]).

(8) The Commission implementation reports on Framework Decisions 2003/577/JHA, 2005/212/JHA and 2006/783/JHA show that existing regimes for extended confiscation and for the mutual recognition of freezing and confiscation orders are not fully effective. Confiscation is hindered by differences between Member States' law.

(9) This Directive aims to amend and expand the provisions of Framework Decisions 2001/500/JHA and 2005/212/JHA. Those Framework Decisions should be partially replaced for the Member States bound by this Directive.

(10) Member States are free to bring confiscation proceedings which are linked to a criminal case before any competent court.

(11) There is a need to clarify the existing concept of proceeds of crime to include the direct proceeds from criminal activity and all indirect benefits, including subsequent reinvestment or transformation of direct proceeds. Thus proceeds can include any property including that which has been transformed or converted, fully or in part, into other property, and that which has been intermingled with property acquired from legitimate sources, up to the assessed value of the intermingled proceeds. It can also include the income or other benefits derived from proceeds of crime, or from property into or with which such proceeds have been transformed, converted or intermingled.

(12) This Directive provides for a broad definition of property that can be subject to freezing and confiscation. That definition includes legal documents or instruments evidencing title or interest in such property. Such documents or instruments could include, for example, financial instruments, or documents that may give rise to creditor claims and are normally found in the possession of the person affected by the relevant procedures. This Directive is without prejudice to the existing national procedures for keeping legal documents or instruments evidencing title or interest in property, as they are applied by the competent national authorities or public bodies in accordance with national law.

(13) Freezing and confiscation under this Directive are autonomous concepts, which should not prevent Member States from implementing this Directive using instruments which, in accordance with national law, would be considered as sanctions or other types of measures.

([1]) Joint Action 98/699/JHA of 3 December 1998 adopted by the Council on the basis of Article K.3 of the Treaty on European Union, on money laundering, the identification, tracing, freezing, seizing and confiscation of instrumentalities and the proceeds from crime (OJ L 333, 9.12.1998, p. 1).
([2]) Council Framework Decision 2001/500/JHA of 26 June 2001 on money laundering, the identification, tracing, freezing, seizing and confiscation of instrumentalities and the proceeds of crime (OJ L 182, 5.7.2001, p. 1).
([3]) Council Framework Decision 2003/577/JHA of 22 July 2003 on the execution in the European Union of orders freezing property or evidence (OJ L 196, 2.8.2003, p. 45).
([4]) Council Framework Decision 2005/212/JHA of 24 February 2005 on confiscation of crime-related proceeds, instrumentalities and property (OJ L 68, 15.3.2005, p. 49).
([5]) Council Framework Decision 2006/783/JHA of 6 October 2006 on the application of the principle of mutual recognition to confiscation orders (OJ L 328, 24.11.2006, p. 59).

(14) In the confiscation of instrumentalities and proceeds of crime following a final decision of a court and of property of equivalent value to those instrumentalities and proceeds, the broad concept of criminal offences covered by this Directive should apply. Framework Decision 2001/500/JHA requires Member States to enable the confiscation of instrumentalities and proceeds of crime following a final conviction and to enable the confiscation of property the value of which corresponds to such instrumentalities and proceeds. Such obligations should be maintained for the criminal offences not covered by this Directive, and the concept of proceeds as defined in this Directive should be interpreted in the similar way as regards criminal offences not covered by this Directive. Member States are free to define the confiscation of property of equivalent value as subsidiary or alternative to direct confiscation, as appropriate in accordance with national law.

(15) Subject to a final conviction for a criminal offence, it should be possible to confiscate instrumentalities and proceeds of crime, or property the value of which corresponds to such instrumentalities or proceeds. Such final conviction can also result from proceedings in absentia. When confiscation on the basis of a final conviction is not possible, it should nevertheless under certain circumstances still be possible to confiscate instrumentalities and proceeds, at least in the cases of illness or absconding of the suspected or accused person. However, in such cases of illness and absconding, the existence of proceedings in absentia in Member States would be sufficient to comply with this obligation. When the suspected or accused person has absconded, Member States should take all reasonable steps and may require that the person concerned be summoned to or made aware of the confiscation proceedings.

(16) For the purposes of this Directive, illness should be understood to mean the inability of the suspected or accused person to attend the criminal proceedings for an extended period, as a result of which the proceedings cannot continue under normal conditions. Suspected or accused persons may be requested to prove illness, for example by a medical certificate, which the court should be able to disregard if it finds it unsatisfactory. The right of that person to be represented in the proceedings by a lawyer should not be affected.

(17) When implementing this Directive in respect of confiscation of property the value of which corresponds to instrumentalities, the relevant provisions could be applicable where, in view of the particular circumstances of the case at hand, such a measure is proportionate, having regard in particular to the value of the instrumentalities concerned. Member States may also take into account whether and to what extent the convicted person is responsible for making the confiscation of the instrumentalities impossible.

(18) When implementing this Directive, Member States may provide that, in exceptional circumstances, confiscation should not be ordered, insofar as it would, in accordance with national law, represent undue hardship for the affected person, on the basis of the circumstances of the respective individual case which should be decisive. Member States should make a very restricted use of this possibility, and should only be allowed to provide that confiscation is not to be ordered in cases where it would put the person concerned in a situation in which it would be very difficult for him to survive.

(19) Criminal groups engage in a wide range of criminal activities. In order to effectively tackle organised criminal activities there may be situations where it is appropriate that a criminal conviction be followed by the confiscation not only of property associated with a specific crime, but also of additional property which the court determines constitutes the proceeds of other crimes. This approach is referred to as extended confiscation. Framework Decision 2005/212/JHA provides for three different sets of minimum requirements that Member States can choose from in order to apply extended confiscation. As a result, in the process of transposition of that Framework Decision, Member States have chosen different options which resulted in divergent concepts of extended confiscation in national jurisdictions. That divergence hampers cross-border cooperation in relation to confiscation cases. It is therefore necessary to further harmonise the provisions on extended confiscation by setting a single minimum standard.

(20) When determining whether a criminal offence is liable to give rise to economic benefit, Member States may take into account the modus operandi, for example if a condition of the offence is that it was committed in the context of organised crime or with the intention of generating regular profits from criminal offences. However, this should not, in general, prejudice the possibility to resort to extended confiscation.

(21) Extended confiscation should be possible where a court is satisfied that the property in question is derived from criminal conduct. This does not mean that it must be established that the property in question is derived from criminal conduct. Member States may provide that it could, for example, be sufficient for the court to consider on the balance of probabilities, or to reasonably presume that it is substantially more probable, that the property in question has been obtained from criminal conduct than from other activities. In this context, the court has to consider the specific circumstances of the case, including the facts and available evidence based on which a decision on extended confiscation could be issued. The fact that the property of the person is disproportionate to his lawful income could be among those facts giving rise to a conclusion of the court that the property derives from criminal conduct. Member States could also determine a requirement for a certain period of time during which the property could be deemed to have originated from criminal conduct.

(22) This Directive lays down minimum rules. It does not prevent Member States from providing more extensive powers in their national law, including, for example, in relation to their rules on evidence.

(23) This Directive applies to criminal offences which fall within the scope of the instruments listed herein. Within the scope of those instruments, Member States should apply extended confiscation at least to certain criminal offences as defined in this Directive.

(24) The practice by a suspected or accused person of transferring property to a knowing third party with a view to avoiding confiscation is common and increasingly widespread. The current Union legal framework does not contain binding rules on the confiscation of property transferred to third parties. It is therefore becoming increasingly necessary to allow for the confiscation of property transferred to or acquired by third parties. Acquisition by a third party refers to situations where, for example, property has been acquired, directly or indirectly, for example through an intermediary, by the third party from a suspected or accused person, including when the criminal offence has been committed on their behalf or for their benefit, and when an accused person does not have property that can be confiscated. Such confiscation should be possible at least in cases where third parties knew or ought to have known that the purpose of the transfer or acquisition was to avoid confiscation, on the basis of concrete facts and circumstances, including that the transfer was carried out free of charge or in exchange for an amount significantly lower than the market value. The rules on third party confiscation should extend to both natural and legal persons. In any event the rights of bona fide third parties should not be prejudiced.

(25) Member States are free to define third party confiscation as subsidiary or alternative to direct confiscation, as appropriate in accordance with national law.

(26) Confiscation leads to the final deprivation of property. However, preservation of property can be a prerequisite to confiscation and can be of importance for the enforcement of a confiscation order. Property is preserved by means of freezing. In order to prevent the dissipation of property before a freezing order can be issued, the competent authorities in the Member States should be empowered to take immediate action in order to secure such property.

(27) Since property is often preserved for the purposes of confiscation, freezing and confiscation are closely linked. In some legal systems freezing for the purposes of confiscation is regarded as a separate procedural measure of a provisional nature, which may be followed by a confiscation order. Without prejudice to different national legal systems and to Framework Decision 2003/577/JHA, this Directive should approximate some aspects of the national systems of freezing for the purposes of confiscation.

(28) Freezing measures are without prejudice to the possibility for a specific property to be considered evidence throughout the proceedings, provided that it would ultimately be made available for effective execution of the confiscation order.

29.4.2014 EN Official Journal of the European Union L 127/43

(29) In the context of criminal proceedings, property may also be frozen with a view to its possible subsequent restitution or in order to safeguard compensation for the damage caused by a criminal offence.

(30) Suspected or accused persons often hide property throughout the entire duration of criminal proceedings. As a result confiscation orders cannot be executed, leaving those subject to confiscation orders to benefit from their property once they have served their sentences. It is therefore necessary to enable the determination of the precise extent of the property to be confiscated even after a final conviction for a criminal offence, in order to permit the full execution of confiscation orders when no property or insufficient property was initially identified and the confiscation order remains unexecuted.

(31) Given the limitation of the right to property by freezing orders, such provisional measures should not be maintained longer than necessary to preserve the availability of the property with a view to possible subsequent confiscation. This may require a review by the court in order to ensure that the purpose of preventing the dissipation of property remains valid.

(32) Property frozen with a view to possible subsequent confiscation should be managed adequately in order not to lose its economic value. Member States should take the necessary measures, including the possibility of selling or transferring the property to minimise such losses. Member States should take relevant measures, for example the establishment of national centralised Asset Management Offices, a set of specialised offices or equivalent mechanisms, in order to effectively manage the assets frozen before confiscation and preserve their value, pending judicial determination.

(33) This Directive substantially affects the rights of persons, not only of suspected or accused persons, but also of third parties who are not being prosecuted. It is therefore necessary to provide for specific safeguards and judicial remedies in order to guarantee the preservation of their fundamental rights in the implementation of this Directive. This includes the right to be heard for third parties who claim that they are the owner of the property concerned, or who claim that they have other property rights ('real rights', '*ius in re*'), such as the right of usufruct. The freezing order should be communicated to the affected person as soon as possible after its execution. Nevertheless, the competent authorities may postpone communicating such orders to the affected person due to the needs of the investigation.

(34) The purpose of communicating the freezing order is, inter alia, to allow the affected person to challenge the order. Therefore, such communication should indicate, at least briefly, the reason or reasons for the order concerned, it being understood that such indication can be very succinct.

(35) Member States should consider taking measures allowing confiscated property to be used for public interest or social purposes. Such measures could, inter alia, comprise earmarking property for law enforcement and crime prevention projects, as well as for other projects of public interest and social utility. That obligation to consider taking measures entails a procedural obligation for Member States, such as conducting a legal analysis or discussing the advantages and disadvantages of introducing measures. When managing frozen property and when taking measures concerning the use of confiscated property, Member States should take appropriate action to prevent criminal or illegal infiltration.

(36) Reliable data sources on the freezing and confiscation of the proceeds of crime are scarce. In order to allow for the evaluation of this Directive, it is necessary to collect a comparable minimum set of appropriate statistical data on freezing and confiscation of property, asset tracing, judicial and asset disposal activities.

(37) Member States should endeavour to collect data for certain statistics at a central level, with a view to sending them to the Commission. This means that the Member States should make reasonable efforts to collect the data concerned. It does not mean, however, that the Member States are under an obligation to achieve the result of collecting the data where there is a disproportionate administrative burden or when there are high costs for the Member State concerned.

(38) This Directive respects the fundamental rights and observes the principles recognised by the Charter of Fundamental Rights of the European Union ('the Charter') and the European Convention for the Protection of Human Rights and Fundamental Freedoms ('the ECHR'), as interpreted in the case-law of the European Court of Human Rights. This Directive should be implemented in accordance with those rights and principles. This Directive should be without prejudice to national law in relation to legal aid and does not create any obligations for Member States' legal aid systems, which should apply in accordance with the Charter and the ECHR.

(39) Specific safeguards should be put in place, so as to ensure that as a general rule reasons are given for confiscation orders, unless when, in simplified criminal proceedings in minor cases, the affected person has waived his or her right to be given reasons.

(40) This Directive should be implemented taking account of the provisions of Directive 2010/64/EU of the European Parliament and of the Council [1], Directive 2012/13/EU of the European Parliament and of the Council [2] and Directive 2013/48/EU of the European Parliament and of the Council [3] which concern procedural rights in criminal proceedings.

(41) Since the objective of this Directive, namely facilitating confiscation of property in criminal matters, cannot be sufficiently achieved by the Member States but can rather be better achieved at Union level, the Union may adopt measures, in accordance with the principle of subsidiarity as set out in Article 5 of the Treaty on European Union (TEU). In accordance with the principle of proportionality, as set out in that Article, this Directive does not go beyond what is necessary in order to achieve that objective.

(42) In accordance with Articles 3 and 4a(1) of Protocol (No 21) on the position of the United Kingdom and Ireland in respect of the Area of Freedom, Security and Justice, annexed to the TEU and to the Treaty on the Functioning of the European Union (TFEU), Ireland has notified its wish to take part in the adoption and application of this Directive. In accordance with that Protocol, Ireland is to be bound by this Directive only in respect of the offences covered by the instruments by which it is bound.

(43) In accordance with Articles 1, 2 and 4a(1) of Protocol (No 21) on the position of the United Kingdom and Ireland in respect of the Area of Freedom, Security and Justice, annexed to the TEU and to the TFEU, and without prejudice to Article 4 of that Protocol, the United Kingdom is not taking part in the adoption of this Directive and is not bound by it or subject to its application. Subject to its participation in accordance with Article 4 of that Protocol, the United Kingdom is to be bound by this Directive only in respect of the offences covered by the instruments by which it is bound.

(44) In accordance with Articles 1 and 2 of Protocol (No 22) on the position of Denmark annexed to the TEU and to the TFEU, Denmark is not taking part in the adoption of this Directive and is not bound by it or subject to its application,

[1] Directive 2010/64/EU of the European Parliament and of the Council of 20 October 2010 on the right to interpretation and translation in criminal proceedings (OJ L 280, 26.10.2010, p. 1).
[2] Directive 2012/13/EU of the European Parliament and of the Council of 22 May 2012 on the right to information in criminal proceedings (OJ L 142, 1.6.2012, p. 1).
[3] Directive 2013/48/EU of the European Parliament and of the Council of 22 October 2013 on the right of access to a lawyer in criminal proceedings and in European arrest warrant proceedings, and on the right to have a third party informed upon deprivation of liberty and to communicate with third persons and with consular authorities while deprived of liberty (OJ L 294, 6.11.2013, p. 1).

HAVE ADOPTED THIS DIRECTIVE:

*Article 1*

**Subject matter**

1. This Directive establishes minimum rules on the freezing of property with a view to possible subsequent confiscation and on the confiscation of property in criminal matters.

2. This Directive is without prejudice to the procedures that Member States may use to confiscate the property in question.

*Article 2*

**Definitions**

For the purpose of this Directive, the following definitions apply:

(1) 'proceeds' means any economic advantage derived directly or indirectly from a criminal offence; it may consist of any form of property and includes any subsequent reinvestment or transformation of direct proceeds and any valuable benefits;

(2) 'property' means property of any description, whether corporeal or incorporeal, movable or immovable, and legal documents or instruments evidencing title or interest in such property;

(3) 'instrumentalities' means any property used or intended to be used, in any manner, wholly or in part, to commit a criminal offence or criminal offences;

(4) 'confiscation' means a final deprivation of property ordered by a court in relation to a criminal offence;

(5) 'freezing' means the temporary prohibition of the transfer, destruction, conversion, disposal or movement of property or temporarily assuming custody or control of property;

(6) 'criminal offence' means an offence covered by any of the instruments listed in Article 3.

*Article 3*

**Scope**

This Directive shall apply to criminal offences covered by:

(a) Convention drawn up on the basis of Article K.3(2)(c) of the Treaty on European Union on the fight against corruption involving officials of the European Communities or officials of the Member States of the European Union [1] ('Convention on the fight against corruption involving officials');

(b) Council Framework Decision 2000/383/JHA of 29 May 2000 on increasing protection by criminal penalties and other sanctions against counterfeiting in connection with the introduction of the euro [2];

(c) Council Framework Decision 2001/413/JHA of 28 May 2001 on combating fraud and counterfeiting on non-cash means of payment [3];

---

(1) OJ C 195, 25.6.1997, p. 1.
(2) OJ L 140, 14.6.2000, p. 1.
(3) OJ L 149, 2.6.2001, p. 1.

(d) Council Framework Decision 2001/500/JHA of 26 June 2001 on money laundering, the identification, tracing, freezing, seizing and confiscation of instrumentalities and the proceeds of crime ([1]);

(e) Council Framework Decision 2002/475/JHA of 13 June 2002 on combating terrorism ([2]);

(f) Council Framework Decision 2003/568/JHA of 22 July 2003 on combating corruption in the private sector ([3]);

(g) Council Framework Decision 2004/757/JHA of 25 October 2004 laying down minimum provisions on the constituent elements of criminal acts and penalties in the field of illicit drug trafficking ([4]);

(h) Council Framework Decision 2008/841/JHA of 24 October 2008 on the fight against organised crime ([5]);

(i) Directive 2011/36/EU of the European Parliament and of the Council of 5 April 2011 on preventing and combating trafficking in human beings and protecting its victims, and replacing Council Framework Decision 2002/629/JHA ([6]);

(j) Directive 2011/93/EU of the European Parliament and of the Council of 13 December 2011 on combating the sexual abuse and sexual exploitation of children and child pornography, and replacing Council Framework Decision 2004/68/JHA ([7]);

(k) Directive 2013/40/EU of the European Parliament and of the Council of 12 August 2013 on attacks against information systems and replacing Council Framework Decision 2005/222/JHA ([8]),

as well as other legal instruments if those instruments provide specifically that this Directive applies to the criminal offences harmonised therein.

*Article 4*

**Confiscation**

1. Member States shall take the necessary measures to enable the confiscation, either in whole or in part, of instrumentalities and proceeds or property the value of which corresponds to such instrumentalities or proceeds, subject to a final conviction for a criminal offence, which may also result from proceedings in absentia.

2. Where confiscation on the basis of paragraph 1 is not possible, at least where such impossibility is the result of illness or absconding of the suspected or accused person, Member States shall take the necessary measures to enable the confiscation of instrumentalities and proceeds in cases where criminal proceedings have been initiated regarding a criminal offence which is liable to give rise, directly or indirectly, to economic benefit, and such proceedings could have led to a criminal conviction if the suspected or accused person had been able to stand trial.

*Article 5*

**Extended confiscation**

1. Member States shall adopt the necessary measures to enable the confiscation, either in whole or in part, of property belonging to a person convicted of a criminal offence which is liable to give rise, directly or indirectly, to economic benefit, where a court, on the basis of the circumstances of the case, including the specific facts and available evidence, such as that the value of the property is disproportionate to the lawful income of the convicted person, is satisfied that the property in question is derived from criminal conduct.

([1]) OJ L 182, 5.7.2001, p. 1.
([2]) OJ L 164, 22.6.2002, p. 3.
([3]) OJ L 192, 31.7.2003, p. 54.
([4]) OJ L 335, 11.11.2004, p. 8.
([5]) OJ L 300, 11.11.2008, p. 42.
([6]) OJ L 101, 15.4.2011, p. 1.
([7]) OJ L 335, 17.12.2011, p. 1.
([8]) OJ L 218, 14.8.2013, p. 8.

2. For the purpose of paragraph 1 of this Article, the notion of 'criminal offence' shall include at least the following:

(a) active and passive corruption in the private sector, as provided for in Article 2 of Framework Decision 2003/568/JHA, as well as active and passive corruption involving officials of institutions of the Union or of the Member States, as provided for in Articles 2 and 3 respectively of the Convention on the fight against corruption involving officials;

(b) offences relating to participation in a criminal organisation, as provided for in Article 2 of Framework Decision 2008/841/JHA, at least in cases where the offence has led to economic benefit;

(c) causing or recruiting a child to participate in pornographic performances, or profiting from or otherwise exploiting a child for such purposes if the child is over the age of sexual consent, as provided for in Article 4(2) of Directive 2011/93/EU; distribution, dissemination or transmission of child pornography, as provided for in Article 5(4) of that Directive; offering, supplying or making available child pornography, as provided for in Article 5(5) of that Directive; production of child pornography, as provided for in Article 5(6) of that Directive;

(d) illegal system interference and illegal data interference, as provided for in Articles 4 and 5 respectively of Directive 2013/40/EU, where a significant number of information systems have been affected through the use of a tool, as provided for in Article 7 of that Directive, designed or adapted primarily for that purpose; the intentional production, sale, procurement for use, import, distribution or otherwise making available of tools used for committing offences, at least for cases which are not minor, as provided for in Article 7 of that Directive;

(e) a criminal offence that is punishable, in accordance with the relevant instrument in Article 3 or, in the event that the instrument in question does not contain a penalty threshold, in accordance with the relevant national law, by a custodial sentence of a maximum of at least four years.

*Article 6*

**Confiscation from a third party**

1. Member States shall take the necessary measures to enable the confiscation of proceeds, or other property the value of which corresponds to proceeds, which, directly or indirectly, were transferred by a suspected or accused person to third parties, or which were acquired by third parties from a suspected or accused person, at least if those third parties knew or ought to have known that the purpose of the transfer or acquisition was to avoid confiscation, on the basis of concrete facts and circumstances, including that the transfer or acquisition was carried out free of charge or in exchange for an amount significantly lower than the market value.

2. Paragraph 1 shall not prejudice the rights of bona fide third parties.

*Article 7*

**Freezing**

1. Member States shall take the necessary measures to enable the freezing of property with a view to possible subsequent confiscation. Those measures, which shall be ordered by a competent authority, shall include urgent action to be taken when necessary in order to preserve property.

2. Property in the possession of a third party, as referred to under Article 6, can be subject to freezing measures for the purposes of possible subsequent confiscation.

L 127/48 EN Official Journal of the European Union 29.4.2014

*Article 8*

**Safeguards**

1. Member States shall take the necessary measures to ensure that the persons affected by the measures provided for under this Directive have the right to an effective remedy and a fair trial in order to uphold their rights.

2. Member States shall take the necessary measures to ensure that the freezing order is communicated to the affected person as soon as possible after its execution. Such communication shall indicate, at least briefly, the reason or reasons for the order concerned. When it is necessary to avoid jeopardising a criminal investigation, the competent authorities may postpone communicating the freezing order to the affected person.

3. The freezing order shall remain in force only for as long as it is necessary to preserve the property with a view to possible subsequent confiscation.

4. Member States shall provide for the effective possibility for the person whose property is affected to challenge the freezing order before a court, in accordance with procedures provided for in national law. Such procedures may provide that when the initial freezing order has been taken by a competent authority other than a judicial authority, such order shall first be submitted for validation or review to a judicial authority before it can be challenged before a court.

5. Frozen property which is not subsequently confiscated shall be returned immediately. The conditions or procedural rules under which such property is returned shall be determined by national law.

6. Member States shall take the necessary measures to ensure that reasons are given for any confiscation order and that the order is communicated to the person affected. Member States shall provide for the effective possibility for a person in respect of whom confiscation is ordered to challenge the order before a court.

7. Without prejudice to Directive 2012/13/EU and Directive 2013/48/EU, persons whose property is affected by a confiscation order shall have the right of access to a lawyer throughout the confiscation proceedings relating to the determination of the proceeds and instrumentalities in order to uphold their rights. The persons concerned shall be informed of that right.

8. In proceedings referred to in Article 5, the affected person shall have an effective possibility to challenge the circumstances of the case, including specific facts and available evidence on the basis of which the property concerned is considered to be property that is derived from criminal conduct.

9. Third parties shall be entitled to claim title of ownership or other property rights, including in the cases referred to in Article 6.

10. Where, as a result of a criminal offence, victims have claims against the person who is subject to a confiscation measure provided for under this Directive, Member States shall take the necessary measures to ensure that the confiscation measure does not prevent those victims from seeking compensation for their claims.

29.4.2014 EN Official Journal of the European Union L 127/49

*Article 9*

**Effective confiscation and execution**

Member States shall take the necessary measures to enable the detection and tracing of property to be frozen and confiscated even after a final conviction for a criminal offence or following proceedings in application of Article 4(2) and to ensure the effective execution of a confiscation order, if such an order has already been issued.

*Article 10*

**Management of frozen and confiscated property**

1. Member States shall take the necessary measures, for example by establishing centralised offices, a set of specialised offices or equivalent mechanisms, to ensure the adequate management of property frozen with a view to possible subsequent confiscation.

2. Member States shall ensure that the measures referred to in paragraph 1 include the possibility to sell or transfer property where necessary.

3. Member States shall consider taking measures allowing confiscated property to be used for public interest or social purposes.

*Article 11*

**Statistics**

1. Member States shall regularly collect and maintain comprehensive statistics from the relevant authorities. The statistics collected shall be sent to the Commission each year and shall include:

(a) the number of freezing orders executed;

(b) the number of confiscation orders executed;

(c) the estimated value of property frozen, at least of property frozen with a view to possible subsequent confiscation at the time of freezing;

(d) the estimated value of property recovered at the time of confiscation.

2. Member States shall also send each year the following statistics to the Commission, if they are available at a central level in the Member State concerned:

(a) the number of requests for freezing orders to be executed in another Member State;

(b) the number of requests for confiscation orders to be executed in another Member State;

(c) the value or estimated value of the property recovered following execution in another Member State.

3. Member States shall endeavour to collect data referred to in paragraph 2 at a central level.

L 127/50 EN Official Journal of the European Union 29.4.2014

*Article 12*

**Transposition**

1. Member States shall bring into force the laws, regulations and administrative provisions necessary to comply with this Directive by 4 October 2016. They shall forthwith transmit to the Commission the text of those provisions.

2. When Member States adopt those provisions, they shall contain a reference to this Directive or be accompanied by such a reference on the occasion of their official publication. The methods of making such reference shall be laid down by Member States.

3. Member States shall communicate to the Commission the text of the main provisions of national law which they adopt in the field covered by this Directive.

*Article 13*

**Reporting**

The Commission shall, by 4 October 2019 submit a report to the European Parliament and the Council, assessing the impact of existing national law on confiscation and asset recovery, accompanied, if necessary, by adequate proposals.

In that report, the Commission shall also assess whether there is any need to revise the list of offences in Article 5(2).

*Article 14*

**Replacement of Joint Action 98/699/JHA and of certain provisions of Framework Decisions 2001/500/JHA and 2005/212/JHA**

1. Joint Action 98/699/JHA, point (a) of Article 1 and Articles 3 and 4 of Framework Decision 2001/500/JHA, and the first four indents of Article 1 and Article 3 of Framework Decision 2005/212/JHA, are replaced by this Directive for the Member States bound by this Directive, without prejudice to the obligations of those Member States relating to the time limits for transposition of those Framework Decisions into national law.

2. For the Member States bound by this Directive, references to Joint Action 98/699/JHA and to the provisions of Framework Decisions 2001/500/JHA and 2005/212/JHA referred to in paragraph 1 shall be construed as references to this Directive.

*Article 15*

**Entry into force**

This Directive shall enter into force on the twentieth day following that of its publication in the *Official Journal of the European Union*.

*Article 16*

**Addressees**

This Directive is addressed to Member States in accordance with the Treaties.

Done at Brussels, 3 April 2014.

| *For the European Parliament* | *For the Council* |
|---|---|
| *The President* | *The President* |
| M. SCHULZ | D. KOURKOULAS |

# Directive 2014/57 on criminal sanctions for market abuse (market abuse directive), 16 April 2014

[OJ 2014, L 179–189]

12.6.2014 EN Official Journal of the European Union L 173/179

**DIRECTIVE 2014/57/EU OF THE EUROPEAN PARLIAMENT AND OF THE COUNCIL**

**of 16 April 2014**

**on criminal sanctions for market abuse (market abuse directive)**

THE EUROPEAN PARLIAMENT AND THE COUNCIL OF THE EUROPEAN UNION,

Having regard to the Treaty on the Functioning of the European Union, and in particular Article 83(2) thereof,

Having regard to the proposal from the European Commission,

After transmission of the draft legislative act to the national parliaments,

Having regard to the opinion of the European Central Bank ([1]),

Having regard to the opinion of the European Economic and Social Committee ([2]),

Acting in accordance with the ordinary legislative procedure ([3]),

Whereas:

(1) An integrated and efficient financial market and stronger investor confidence requires market integrity. The smooth functioning of securities markets and public confidence in markets are prerequisites for economic growth and wealth. Market abuse harms the integrity of financial markets and public confidence in securities, derivatives and benchmarks.

(2) Directive 2003/6/EC of the European Parliament and the Council ([4]) completed and updated the Union's legal framework to protect market integrity. It also required Member States to ensure that competent authorities have the power to detect and investigate market abuse. Without prejudice to the right of Member States to impose criminal sanctions, Directive 2003/6/EC also required Member States to ensure that the appropriate administrative measures can be taken or administrative sanctions can be imposed against the persons responsible for violations of the national rules implementing that Directive.

(3) The report of 25 February 2009 by the High-Level Group on Financial Supervision in the EU, chaired by Jacques de Larosière (the 'de Larosière Group'), recommended that a sound prudential and conduct of business framework for the financial sector must rest on strong supervisory and sanctioning regimes. To that end, the de Larosière Group considered that supervisory authorities must be equipped with sufficient powers to act and that there should also be equal, strong and deterrent sanctions regimes against all financial crimes, sanctions which should be enforced effectively, in order to preserve market integrity. The de Larosière Group concluded that Member States' sanctioning regimes are in general weak and heterogeneous.

---

([1]) OJ C 161, 7.6.2012, p. 3.
([2]) OJ C 181, 21.6.2012, p. 64.
([3]) Position of the European Parliament of 4 February 2014 (not yet published in the Official Journal) and decision of the Council of 14 April 2014.
([4]) Directive 2003/6/EC of the European Parliament and the Council of 28 January 2003 on insider dealing and market manipulation (market abuse) (OJ L 96, 12.4.2003, p. 16).

(4) A well-functioning legislative framework in relation to market abuse requires effective enforcement. An evaluation of the national regimes for administrative sanctions under Directive 2003/6/EC showed that not all national competent authorities had a full set of powers at their disposal to ensure that they could respond to market abuse with the appropriate sanction. In particular, not all Member States provided for pecuniary administrative sanctions for insider dealing and market manipulation, and the level of sanctions varied widely among Member States. A new legislative act is therefore needed to ensure common minimum rules across the Union.

(5) The adoption of administrative sanctions by Member States has, to date, proven to be insufficient to ensure compliance with the rules on preventing and fighting market abuse.

(6) It is essential that compliance with the rules on market abuse be strengthened by the availability of criminal sanctions which demonstrate a stronger form of social disapproval compared to administrative penalties. Establishing criminal offences for at least serious forms of market abuse sets clear boundaries for types of behaviour that are considered to be particularly unacceptable and sends a message to the public and to potential offenders that competent authorities take such behaviour very seriously.

(7) Not all Member States have provided for criminal sanctions for some forms of serious breaches of national law implementing Directive 2003/6/EC. Different approaches by Member States undermine the uniformity of conditions of operation in the internal market and may provide an incentive for persons to carry out market abuse in Member States which do not provide for criminal sanctions for those offences. In addition, there has, to date, been no Union-wide understanding of conduct that is considered to constitute a serious breach of the rules on market abuse. Therefore, minimum rules should be established with regard to the definition of criminal offences committed by natural persons, liability of legal persons and the relevant sanctions. Common minimum rules would also make it possible to use more effective methods of investigation and enable more effective cooperation within and between Member States. In the light of the financial crisis, it is evident that market manipulation has a potential for widespread damage on the lives of millions of people. The Libor scandal, which concerned a serious case of benchmark manipulation, demonstrated that relevant problems and loopholes impact gravely on market confidence and may result in significant losses to investors and distortions of the real economy. The absence of common criminal sanction regimes across the Union creates opportunities for perpetrators of market abuse to take advantage of lighter regimes in some Member States. The imposition of criminal sanctions for market abuse will have an increased deterrent effect on potential offenders.

(8) The introduction by all Member States of criminal sanctions for at least serious market abuse offences is therefore essential to ensure the effective implementation of Union policy on fighting market abuse.

(9) In order for the scope of this Directive to be aligned with that of Regulation (EU) No 596/2014 of the European Parliament and of the Council [1], trading in own shares in buy-back programmes and trading in securities or associated instruments for the stabilisation of securities; transactions, orders or behaviour in pursuit of monetary, exchange-rate or public debt management policy; activities concerning emission allowances undertaken in pursuit of the Union's climate policy; and activities undertaken in pursuit of the Union's Common Agricultural Policy and the Union's Common Fisheries Policy, should be exempt from this Directive.

(10) Member States should be required to provide at least for serious cases of insider dealing, market manipulation and unlawful disclosure of inside information to constitute criminal offences when committed with intent.

(11) For the purposes of this Directive, insider dealing and unlawful disclosure of inside information should be deemed to be serious in cases such as those where the impact on the integrity of the market, the actual or potential profit derived or loss avoided, the level of damage caused to the market, or the overall value of the financial instruments traded is high. Other circumstances that might be taken into account are, for instance, where an offence has been committed within the framework of a criminal organisation or where the person has committed such an offence before.

[1] Regulation (EU) No 596/2014 of the European Parliament and of the Council of 16 April 2014 on market abuse (market abuse regulation) and repealing Directive 2003/6/EC of the European Parliament and of the Council and Commission Directives 2003/124/EC, 2003/125/EC and 2004/72/EC (see page 1 of this Official Journal).

(12) For the purposes of this Directive, market manipulation should be deemed to be serious in cases such as those where the impact on the integrity of the market, the actual or potential profit derived or loss avoided, the level of damage caused to the market, the level of alteration of the value of the financial instrument or spot commodity contract, or the amount of funds originally used is high or where the manipulation is committed by a person employed or working in the financial sector or in a supervisory or regulatory authority.

(13) Due to the adverse effects of attempted insider dealing and attempted market manipulation on the integrity of the financial markets and on investor confidence in those markets, those forms of behaviour should also be punishable as a criminal offence.

(14) This Directive should oblige Member States to provide in their national law for criminal penalties in respect of insider dealing, market manipulation and unlawful disclosure of inside information to which this Directive applies. This Directive should not create obligations regarding the application of such penalties or any other available system of law enforcement, to individual cases.

(15) This Directive should also require Member States to ensure that inciting, aiding and abetting the criminal offences are also punishable.

(16) In order for the sanctions for the offences referred to in this Directive to be effective and dissuasive, a minimum level for the maximum term of imprisonment should be set in this Directive.

(17) This Directive should be applied taking into account the legal framework established by Regulation (EU) No 596/2014 and its implementing measures.

(18) In order to ensure effective implementation of the European policy for ensuring the integrity of the financial markets set out in Regulation (EU) No 596/2014, Member States should extend liability for the offences provided for in this Directive to legal persons through the imposition of criminal or non-criminal sanctions or other measures which are effective, proportionate and dissuasive, for example those provided for in Regulation (EU) No 596/2014. Such sanctions or other measures may include the publication of a final decision on a sanction, including the identity of the liable legal person, taking into account fundamental rights, the principle of proportionality and the risks to the stability of financial markets and ongoing investigations. Member States should, where appropriate and where national law provides for criminal liability of legal persons, extend such criminal liability, in accordance with national law, to the offences provided for in this Directive. This Directive should not prevent Member States from publishing final decisions on liability or sanctions.

(19) Member States should take necessary measures to ensure that law enforcement, judicial authorities and other competent authorities responsible for investigating or prosecuting the offences provided for in this Directive have the ability to use effective investigative tools. Taking into account, inter alia, the principle of proportionality, the use of such tools in accordance with national law should be commensurate with the nature and seriousness of the offences under investigation.

(20) As this Directive provides for minimum rules, Member States are free to adopt or maintain more stringent criminal law rules for market abuse.

(21) Member States may, for example, provide that market manipulation committed recklessly or by serious negligence constitutes a criminal offence.

(22) The obligations in this Directive to provide for penalties on natural persons and sanctions on legal persons in their national law do not exempt Member States from the obligation to provide in national law for administrative sanctions and other measures for breaches provided for in Regulation (EU) No 596/2014 unless Member States have decided, in accordance with Regulation (EU) No 596/2014, to provide only for criminal sanctions for such breaches in their national law.

(23) The scope of this Directive is determined in such a way as to complement, and ensure the effective implementation of, Regulation (EU) No 596/2014. Whereas offences should be punishable under this Directive when committed intentionally and at least in serious cases, sanctions for breaches of Regulation (EU) No 596/2014 do not require that intent is proven or that they are qualified as serious. In the application of national law transposing this Directive, Member States should ensure that the imposition of criminal sanctions for offences in accordance with this Directive and of administrative sanctions in accordance with the Regulation (EU) No 596/2014 does not lead to a breach of the principle of ne bis in idem.

(24) Without prejudice to the general rules of national criminal law on the application and execution of sentences in accordance with the concrete circumstances in each individual case, the imposition of sanctions should be proportionate, taking into account the profits made or losses avoided by the persons held liable as well as the damage resulting from the offence to other persons and, where applicable, to the functioning of markets or the wider economy.

(25) Since the objective of this Directive, namely to ensure the availability of criminal sanctions for at least serious market abuse across the Union, cannot be sufficiently achieved by the Member States but can rather, by reason of the scale and effects of this Directive, be better achieved at Union level, the Union may adopt measures, in accordance with the principle of subsidiarity as set out in Article 5 of the Treaty on European Union (TEU). In accordance with the principle of proportionality, as set out in that Article, this Directive does not go beyond what is necessary to achieve that objective.

(26) Increasing cross-border activities require efficient and effective cooperation between national authorities which are competent for the investigation and prosecution of market abuse offences. The organisation and competences of those national authorities in the different Member States should not hinder their cooperation.

(27) This Directive respects the fundamental rights and observes the principles recognised in the Charter of Fundamental Rights of the European Union (the Charter) as recognised in the TEU. Specifically, it should be applied with due respect for the right to protection of personal data (Article 8), the freedom of expression and information (Article 11), the freedom to conduct a business (Article 16), the right to an effective remedy and to a fair trial (Article 47), the presumption of innocence and right of defence (Article 48), the principles of legality and proportionality of criminal offences and penalties (Article 49), and the right not to be tried or punished twice in criminal proceedings for the same offence (Article 50).

(28) In implementing this Directive, Member States should ensure procedural rights of suspected or accused persons in criminal proceedings. Their obligations under this Directive are without prejudice to their obligations under Union law on procedural rights in criminal proceedings. Nothing in this Directive is intended to restrict the freedom of press or the freedom of expression in the media in so far as they are guaranteed in the Union and in the Member States, in particular under Article 11 of the Charter and other relevant provisions. This should be emphasised in particular as regards disclosure of inside information in accordance with the provisions on such disclosure in this Directive.

(29) Without prejudice to Article 4 of Protocol No 21 on the position of the United Kingdom and Ireland in respect of the area of freedom, security and justice, annexed to the TEU and to the Treaty on the Functioning of the European Union (TFEU), the United Kingdom will not participate in the adoption of this Directive and is therefore not bound by or be subject to its application.

(30) In accordance with Articles 1, 2, 3 and 4 of Protocol No 21 on the position of the United Kingdom and Ireland in respect of the area of freedom, security and justice, annexed to the TEU and to the TFEU, Ireland has notified its wish to take part in the adoption and application of this Directive.

(31) In accordance with Articles 1 and 2 of Protocol No 22 on the position of Denmark annexed to the TEU and to the TFEU, Denmark is not taking part in the adoption of this Directive and is therefore not bound by it or subject to its application.

(32) The European Data Protection Supervisor delivered an opinion on 10 February 2012 (1),

HAVE ADOPTED THIS DIRECTIVE:

*Article 1*

**Subject matter and scope**

1. This Directive establishes minimum rules for criminal sanctions for insider dealing, for unlawful disclosure of inside information and for market manipulation to ensure the integrity of financial markets in the Union and to enhance investor protection and confidence in those markets.

2. This Directive applies to the following:

(a) financial instruments admitted to trading on a regulated market or for which a request for admission to trading on a regulated market has been made;

(b) financial instruments traded on a multilateral trading facility (MTF), admitted to trading on an MTF or for which a request for admission to trading on an MTF has been made;

(c) financial instruments traded on an organised trading facility (OTF);

(d) financial instruments not covered by point (a), (b) or (c), the price or value of which depends on, or has an effect on, the price or value of a financial instrument referred to in those points, including, but not limited to, credit default swaps and contracts for difference.

This Directive also applies to behaviour or transactions, including bids, relating to the auctioning on an auction platform authorised as a regulated market of emission allowances or other auctioned products based thereon, including when auctioned products are not financial instruments, pursuant to Commission Regulation (EU) No 1031/2010 (2). Without prejudice to any specific provisions referring to bids submitted in the context of an auction, any provisions in this Directive referring to orders to trade shall apply to such bids.

3. This Directive does not apply to:

(a) trading in own shares in buy-back programmes, where such trading is carried out in accordance with Article 5(1), (2) and (3) of Regulation (EU) No 596/2014;

(b) trading in securities or associated instruments as referred to in points (a) and (b) of Article 3(2) of Regulation (EU) No 596/2014 for the stabilisation of securities, where such trading is carried out in accordance with Article 5(4) and (5) of that Regulation;

(c) transactions, orders or behaviours carried out in pursuit of monetary, exchange rate or public debt management policy in accordance with Article 6(1) of Regulation (EU) No 596/2014, transactions order or behaviours carried out in accordance with Article 6(2) thereof, activities in pursuit of the Union's climate policy in accordance with Article 6(3) thereof, or activities in pursuit of the Union's Common Agricultural Policy or of the Union's Common Fisheries Policy in accordance with Article 6(4) thereof;

4. Article 5 also applies to:

(a) spot commodity contracts that are not wholesale energy products, where the transaction, order or behaviour has an effect on the price or value of a financial instrument referred to in paragraph 2 of this Article;

(1) OJ C 177, 20.6.2012, p. 1.
(2) Commission Regulation (EU) No 1031/2010 of 12 November 2010 on the timing, administration and other aspects of auctioning of greenhouse gas emission allowances pursuant to Directive 2003/87/EC of the European Parliament and of the Council establishing a scheme for greenhouse gas emission allowances trading within the Community (OJ L 302, 18.11.2010, p. 1).

(b) types of financial instruments, including derivative contracts or derivative instruments for the transfer of credit risk, where the transaction, order, bid or behaviour has an effect on the price or value of a spot commodity contract where the price or value depends on the price or value of those financial instruments;

(c) behaviour in relation to benchmarks.

5. This Directive applies to any transaction, order or behaviour concerning any financial instrument as referred to in paragraphs 2 and 4, irrespective of whether or not such transaction, order or behaviour takes place on a trading venue.

*Article 2*

**Definitions**

For the purposes of this Directive, the following definitions apply:

(1) 'financial instrument' means a financial instrument as defined in point (15) of Article 4(1) of Directive 2014/65/EU of the European Parliament and of the Council ([1]);

(2) 'spot commodity contract' means a spot commodity contract as defined in point (15) of Article 3(1) of Regulation (EU) No 596/2014;

(3) 'buy-back programme' means trading in own shares in accordance with Articles 21 to 27 of Directive 2012/30/EU of the European Parliament and of the Council ([2]);

(4) 'inside information' means information within the meaning of Article 7(1) to (4) of Regulation (EU) No 596/2014;

(5) 'emission allowance' means an emission allowance as described in point (11) of Section C of Annex I of Directive 2014/65/EU;

(6) 'benchmark' means a benchmark as defined in point (29) of Article 3(1) of Regulation (EU) No 596/2014;

(7) 'accepted market practice' means a specific market practice that is accepted by the competent authority of a Member State in accordance with Article 13 of Regulation (EU) No 596/2014;

(8) 'stabilisation' means stabilisation as defined in Article 3(2)(d) of Regulation (EU) No 596/2014;

(9) 'regulated market' means a regulated market as defined in point (21) of Article 4(1) of Directive 2014/65/EU;

(10) 'multilateral trading facility' or 'MTF' means a multilateral trading facility as defined in point (22) of Article 4(1) of Directive 2014/65/EU;

(11) 'organised trading facility' or 'OTF' means an organised trading facility as defined in point (23) of Article 4(1) of Directive 2014/65/EU;

(12) 'trading venue' means a trading venue as defined in point (24) of Article 4(1) of Directive 2014/65/EU;

---

([1]) Directive 2014/65/EU of the European Parliament and of the Council of 15 May 2014 on markets in financial instruments and amending Directive 2011/61/EU and Directive 2002/92/EC (see page 349 of this Official Journal).

([2]) Directive 2012/30/EU of the European Parliament and of the Council of 25 October 2012 on coordination of safeguards which, for the protection of the interests of members and others, are required by Member States of companies within the meaning of the second paragraph of Article 54 of the Treaty on the Functioning of the European Union, in respect of the formation of public limited liability companies and the maintenance and alteration of their capital, with a view to making such safeguards equivalent (OJ L 315, 14.11.2012, p. 74).

(13) 'wholesale energy product' means a wholesale energy product as defined in point (4) of Article 2 of Regulation (EU) No 1227/2011 of the European Parliament and of the Council ([1]);

(14) 'issuer' means an issuer as defined in point (21) of Article 3(1) of Regulation (EU) No 596/2014.

*Article 3*

**Insider dealing, recommending or inducing another person to engage in insider dealing**

1. Member States shall take the necessary measures to ensure that insider dealing, recommending or inducing another person to engage in insider dealing as referred to in paragraphs 2 to 8, constitute criminal offences at least in serious cases and when committed intentionally.

2. For the purposes of this Directive, insider dealing arises where a person possesses inside information and uses that information by acquiring or disposing of, for its own account or for the account of a third party, directly or indirectly, financial instruments to which that information relates.

3. This Article applies to any person who possesses inside information as a result of:

(a) being a member of the administrative, management or supervisory bodies of the issuer or emission allowance market participant;

(b) having a holding in the capital of the issuer or emission allowance market participant;

(c) having access to the information through the exercise of an employment, profession or duties; or

(d) being involved in criminal activities.

This Article also applies to any person who has obtained inside information under circumstances other than those referred to in the first subparagraph where that person knows that it is inside information.

4. The use of inside information by cancelling or amending an order concerning a financial instrument to which the information relates where the order was placed before the person concerned possessed the inside information shall also be considered to be insider dealing.

5. In relation to auctions of emission allowances or other auctioned products based thereon that are held pursuant to Regulation (EU) No 1031/2010, the use of inside information referred to in paragraph 4 of this Article shall also comprise submitting, modifying or withdrawing a bid by a person for its own account or for the account of a third party.

6. For the purposes of this Directive, recommending that another person engage in insider dealing, or inducing another person to engage in insider dealing, arises where the person possesses inside information and:

(a) recommends, on the basis of that information, that another person acquire or dispose of financial instruments to which that information relates, or induces that person to make such an acquisition or disposal; or

(b) recommends, on the basis of that information, that another person cancel or amend an order concerning a financial instrument to which that information relates, or induces that person to make such a cancellation or amendment.

([1]) Regulation (EU) No 1227/2011 of the European Parliament and of the Council of 25 October 2011 on wholesale energy market integrity and transparency (OJ L 326, 8.12.2011, p. 1).

7. The use of the recommendations or inducements referred to in paragraph 6 amounts to insider dealing where the person using the recommendation or inducement knows that it is based upon inside information.

8. For the purposes of this Article, it shall not be deemed from the mere fact that a person is or has been in possession of inside information that that person has used that information and has thus engaged in insider dealing on the basis of an acquisition or disposal, where its behaviour qualifies as legitimate behaviour under Article 9 of Regulation (EU) No 596/2014.

*Article 4*

**Unlawful disclosure of inside information**

1. Member States shall take the necessary measures to ensure that unlawful disclosure of inside information as referred to in paragraphs 2 to 5 constitutes a criminal offence at least in serious cases and when committed intentionally.

2. For the purposes of this Directive, unlawful disclosure of inside information arises where a person possesses inside information and discloses that information to any other person, except where the disclosure is made in the normal exercise of an employment, a profession or duties, including where the disclosure qualifies as a market sounding made in compliance with Article 11(1) to (8) of Regulation (EU) No 596/2014.

3. This Article applies to any person in the situations or circumstances referred to in Article 3(3).

4. For the purposes of this Directive, the onward disclosure of recommendations or inducements referred to in Article 3(6) amounts to unlawful disclosure of inside information under this Article where the person disclosing the recommendation or inducement knows that it was based on inside information.

5. This Article shall be applied in accordance with the need to protect the freedom of the press and the freedom of expression.

*Article 5*

**Market manipulation**

1. Member States shall take the necessary measures to ensure that market manipulation as referred to in paragraph 2 constitutes a criminal offence at least in serious cases and when committed intentionally.

2. For the purposes of this Directive, market manipulation shall comprise the following activities:

(a) entering into a transaction, placing an order to trade or any other behaviour which:

(i) gives false or misleading signals as to the supply of, demand for, or price of, a financial instrument or a related spot commodity contract; or

(ii) secures the price of one or several financial instruments or a related spot commodity contract at an abnormal or artificial level;

unless the reasons for so doing of the person who entered into the transactions or issued the orders to trade are legitimate, and those transactions or orders to trade are in conformity with accepted market practices on the trading venue concerned;

(b) entering into a transaction, placing an order to trade or any other activity or behaviour which affects the price of one or several financial instruments or a related spot commodity contract, which employs a fictitious device or any other form of deception or contrivance;

(c) disseminating information through the media, including the internet, or by any other means, which gives false or misleading signals as to the supply of, demand for, or price of a financial instrument, or a related spot commodity contract, or secures the price of one or several financial instruments or a related spot commodity contract at an abnormal or artificial level, where the persons who made the dissemination derive for themselves or for another person an advantage or profit from the dissemination of the information in question; or

(d) transmitting false or misleading information or providing false or misleading inputs or any other behaviour which manipulates the calculation of a benchmark.

*Article 6*

**Inciting, aiding and abetting, and attempt**

1. Member States shall take the necessary measures to ensure that inciting, aiding and abetting the offences referred to in Article 3(2) to (5) and Articles 4 and 5 is punishable as a criminal offence.

2. Member States shall take the necessary measures to ensure that the attempt to commit any of the offences referred to in Article 3(2) to (5) and (7) and Article 5 is punishable as a criminal offence.

3. Article 3(8) applies *mutatis mutandis.*

*Article 7*

**Criminal penalties for natural persons**

1. Member States shall take the necessary measures to ensure that the offences referred to in Articles 3 to 6 are punishable by effective, proportionate and dissuasive criminal penalties.

2. Member States shall take the necessary measures to ensure that the offences referred to in Articles 3 and 5 are punishable by a maximum term of imprisonment of at least four years.

3. Member States shall take the necessary measures to ensure that the offence referred to in Article 4 is punishable by a maximum term of imprisonment of at least two years.

*Article 8*

**Liability of legal persons**

1. Member States shall take the necessary measures to ensure that legal persons can be held liable for offences referred to in Articles 3 to 6 committed for their benefit by any person, acting either individually or as part of an organ of the legal person, and having a leading position within the legal person based on:

(a) a power of representation of the legal person;

(b) an authority to take decisions on behalf of the legal person; or

(c) an authority to exercise control within the legal person.

2. Member States shall also take the necessary measures to ensure that legal persons can be held liable where the lack of supervision or control, by a person referred to in paragraph 1, has made possible the commission of an offence referred to in Articles 3 to 6 for the benefit of the legal person by a person under its authority.

3. Liability of legal persons under paragraphs 1 and 2 shall not exclude criminal proceedings against natural persons who are involved as perpetrators, inciters or accessories in the offences referred to in Articles 3 to 6.

*Article 9*

**Sanctions for legal persons**

Member States shall take the necessary measures to ensure that a legal person held liable pursuant to Article 8 is subject to effective, proportionate and dissuasive sanctions, which shall include criminal or non-criminal fines and may include other sanctions, such as:

(a) exclusion from entitlement to public benefits or aid;

(b) temporary or permanent disqualification from the practice of commercial activities;

(c) placing under judicial supervision;

(d) judicial winding-up;

(e) temporary or permanent closure of establishments which have been used for committing the offence.

*Article 10*

**Jurisdiction**

1. Member States shall take the necessary measures to establish their jurisdiction over the offences referred to in Articles 3 to 6 where the offence has been committed:

(a) in whole or in part within their territory; or

(b) by one of their nationals, at least in cases where the act is an offence where it was committed.

2. A Member State shall inform the Commission where it decides to establish further jurisdiction over the offences referred to in Articles 3 to 6 committed outside its territory where:

(a) the offender is an habitual resident in its territory; or

(b) the offence is committed for the benefit of a legal person established in its territory.

*Article 11*

**Training**

Without prejudice to judicial independence and differences in the organisation of the judiciary across the Union, Member States shall request those responsible for the training of judges, prosecutors, police, judicial and those competent authorities' staff involved in criminal proceedings and investigations to provide appropriate training with respect to the objectives of this Directive.

*Article 12*

**Report**

By 4 July 2018, the Commission shall report to the European Parliament and to the Council on the functioning of this Directive and, if necessary, on the need to amend it, including with regard to the interpretation of serious cases as referred to in Article 3(1), Article 4(1) and Article 5(1), the level of sanctions provided for by Member States and the extent to which the optional elements referred to in this Directive have been adopted.

The Commission's report shall, if appropriate, be accompanied by a legislative proposal.

*Article 13*

**Transposition**

1. Member States shall adopt and publish, by 3 July 2016, the laws, regulations and administrative provisions necessary to comply with this Directive. They shall forthwith communicate to the Commission the text of those measures.

They shall apply those measures from 3 July 2016 subject to the entry into force of Regulation (EU) No 596/2014.

When Member States adopt those measures, they shall contain a reference to this Directive or be accompanied by such a reference on the occasion of their official publication. Member States shall determine how such reference is to be made.

2. Member States shall communicate to the Commission the text of the main provisions of national law which they adopt in the field covered by this Directive.

*Article 14*

**Entry into force**

This Directive shall enter into force on the twentieth day following that of its publication in the *Official Journal of the European Union*.

*Article 15*

**Addressees**

This Directive is addressed to the Member States in accordance with the Treaties.

Done at Strasbourg, 16 April 2014.

*For the European Parliament*
*The President*
M. SCHULZ

*For the Council*
*The President*
D. KOURKOULAS

# Directive 2014/62 on the protection of the euro and other currencies against counterfeiting by criminal law, and replacing Council Framework Decision 2000/383, 15 May 2014

**[OJ 2014, L 151/1–8]**

21.5.2014 EN Official Journal of the European Union L 151/1

I

*(Legislative acts)*

# DIRECTIVES

## DIRECTIVE 2014/62/EU OF THE EUROPEAN PARLIAMENT AND OF THE COUNCIL

**of 15 May 2014**

**on the protection of the euro and other currencies against counterfeiting by criminal law, and replacing Council Framework Decision 2000/383/JHA**

THE EUROPEAN PARLIAMENT AND THE COUNCIL OF THE EUROPEAN UNION,

Having regard to the Treaty on the Functioning of the European Union, and in particular Article 83(1) thereof,

Having regard to the proposal from the European Commission,

After transmission of the draft legislative act to the national parliaments,

Having regard to the opinion of the European Central Bank (1),

Having regard to the opinion of the European Economic and Social Committee (2),

Acting in accordance with the ordinary legislative procedure (3),

Whereas:

(1) As the single currency shared by the Member States of the euro area, the euro has become an important factor in the Union's economy and the everyday life of its citizens. However, since its introduction in 2002, as a currency continuously targeted by organised crime groups active in money counterfeiting, counterfeiting of the euro has caused financial damage of at least EUR 500 million. It is in the interests of the Union as a whole to oppose and pursue any activity that is likely to jeopardise the authenticity of the euro by counterfeiting.

(2) Counterfeit money has a considerable ill-effect on society. It harms citizens and businesses that are not reimbursed for counterfeits even if received in good faith. It could lead to consumer concerns regarding the sufficient protection of cash and to the fear of receiving counterfeit notes and coins. It is therefore of fundamental importance to ensure trust and confidence in the authenticity of notes and coins for citizens, businesses and financial institutions in all Member States as well as in third countries.

(3) It is essential to ensure that effective and efficient criminal law measures protect the euro and any other currency whose circulation is legally authorised in an appropriate way in all Member States.

(4) Council Regulation (EC) No 974/98 (4) obliges the Member States whose currency is the euro to ensure adequate sanctions against counterfeiting and falsification of euro notes and coins.

(1) OJ C 179, 25.6.2013, p. 9.
(2) OJ C 271, 19.9.2013, p. 42.
(3) Position of the European Parliament of 16 April 2014 (not yet published in the Official Journal) and decision of the Council of 6 May 2014.
(4) Council Regulation (EC) No 974/98 of 3 May 1998 on the introduction of the euro (OJ L 139, 11.5.1998, p. 1).

(5) Council Regulations (EC) No 1338/2001 [1] and (EC) No 1339/2001 [2] lay down measures necessary for the protection of the euro against counterfeiting, in particular measures to withdraw counterfeit euro notes and coins from circulation.

(6) The International Convention for the Suppression of Counterfeiting Currency signed at Geneva on 20 April 1929 and its Protocol (the 'Geneva Convention') [3] lays down rules to effectively prevent, prosecute and punish the offence of counterfeiting currency. In particular, it aims at ensuring that severe criminal penalties and other sanctions can be imposed for offences of counterfeiting currency. All contracting parties to the Geneva Convention have to apply the principle of non-discrimination to currencies other than their domestic currency.

(7) This Directive supplements the provisions and facilitates the application of the Geneva Convention by the Member States. To that end, it is important that the Member States are parties to the Geneva Convention.

(8) This Directive builds on and updates Council Framework Decision 2000/383/JHA [4]. It complements that Framework Decision with further provisions on the level of sanctions, on investigative tools and on the analysis, identification and detection of counterfeit euro notes and coins during judicial proceedings.

(9) This Directive should protect any note and coin whose circulation is legally authorised, irrespective of whether it is made of paper, metal or any other material.

(10) The protection of the euro and other currencies calls for a common definition of the criminal offences related to the currency counterfeiting as well as for common, effective, proportionate and dissuasive sanctions both for natural and legal persons. In order to ensure consistency with the Geneva Convention, this Directive should provide for the same offences to be punishable as in the Geneva Convention. Therefore, the production of counterfeit notes and coins and their distribution should be a criminal offence. Important preparatory work to those offences, for example the production of counterfeiting instruments and components, should be punished independently. The common aim of those definitions of offences should be to act as a deterrent to any handling of counterfeit notes and coins, instruments and other means for counterfeiting.

(11) The misuse of legal facilities or material of authorised printers or mints for the production of unauthorised notes and coins for fraudulent use should also be a criminal offence. Such misuse covers the situation where a national central bank or mint or other authorised industry produces notes or coins exceeding the quota authorised by the European Central Bank (ECB). It also covers the situation where an employee of an authorised printer or mint abuses the facilities for his or her own purposes. That conduct should be punishable as a criminal offence even if the authorised quantities have not been exceeded, because the notes and coins produced would, once circulated, not be distinguishable from authorised currency.

(12) Notes and coins which the ECB or the national central banks and mints have not yet formally issued should also fall under the protection of this Directive. Thus, for instance, euro coins with new national sides or new series of euro notes should be protected before they have officially been put into circulation.

(13) Incitement, aiding and abetting and attempt to commit the main counterfeiting offences, including the misuse of legal facilities or material and including the counterfeiting of notes and coins not yet issued but designated for circulation, should also be penalised where appropriate. This Directive does not require Member States to render punishable an attempt to commit an offence relating to an instrument or component for counterfeiting.

(14) Intention should be a part of all the elements constituting the offences laid down in this Directive.

---

[1] Council Regulation (EC) No 1338/2001 of 28 June 2001 laying down measures necessary for the protection of the euro against counterfeiting (OJ L 181, 4.7.2001, p. 6).

[2] Council Regulation (EC) No 1339/2001 of 28 June 2001 extending the effects of Regulation (EC) No 1338/2001 laying down measures necessary for the protection of the euro against counterfeiting to those Member States which have not adopted the euro as their single currency (OJ L 181, 4.7.2001, p. 11).

[3] No 2623, p. 372 League of Nations — Treaty Series 1931.

[4] Council Framework Decision 2000/383/JHA of 29 May 2000 on increasing protection by criminal penalties and other sanctions against counterfeiting in connection with the introduction of the euro (OJ L 140, 14.6.2000, p. 1).

(15) Currency counterfeiting is traditionally a crime subject to a high level of sanctions in the Member States. That is due to the serious nature and the impact of the crime on citizens and businesses, and due to the need to ensure the trust of citizens and businesses in the genuine character of the euro and other currencies. That holds particularly true for the euro, which is the single currency of over 330 million people in the euro area and which is the second most important international currency.

(16) Member States should provide for criminal sanctions in their national law in respect of the provisions of Union law on combating currency counterfeiting. Those sanctions should be effective, proportionate and dissuasive and should include imprisonment. The minimum level of the maximum term of imprisonment provided for in this Directive for the offences laid down herein should apply at least to the most serious forms of those offences.

(17) The levels of the sanctions should be effective and dissuasive but should not go beyond what is proportionate to the offences. Although intentionally passing on counterfeit currency which has been received in good faith could be sanctioned with a different type of criminal sanction, including fines, in the national law of the Member States, those national laws should provide for imprisonment as a maximum sanction. Imprisonment sanctions for natural persons will serve as a strong deterrent for potential criminals, with effect all over the Union.

(18) As this Directive establishes minimum rules, Member States can adopt or maintain more stringent rules for currency counterfeiting offences.

(19) This Directive is without prejudice to the general rules and principles of national criminal law on the application and execution of sentences in accordance with the concrete circumstances in each individual case.

(20) Since confidence in the genuine character of notes and coins can also be harmed or threatened by the conduct of legal persons, legal persons should be liable for the offences committed on their behalf.

(21) To ensure the success of investigations and the prosecution of currency counterfeiting offences, those responsible for investigating and prosecuting such offences should have the possibility to make use of effective investigative tools such as those which are used in combating organised crime or other serious crimes. Such tools could, where appropriate, include, for example, the interception of communications, covert surveillance including electronic surveillance, the monitoring of bank accounts and other financial investigations. Taking into account, inter alia, the principle of proportionality, the use of such tools in accordance with national law should be commensurate with the nature and gravity of the offences under investigation. The right to the protection of personal data should be respected.

(22) Member States should establish their jurisdiction in a manner consistent with the Geneva Convention and the provisions on jurisdiction in other Union criminal law, that is to say, over offences committed on their territory and over offences committed by their nationals, noting that in general offences are best dealt with by the criminal justice system of the country in which they occur.

(23) The pre-eminent role of the euro for the economy and society of the Union, as well as the specific threat to the euro as a currency of worldwide importance as manifested by the existence of a considerable number of print-shops located in third countries, calls for an additional measure to protect it. Therefore, jurisdiction should be established over offences relating to the euro committed outside the territory of a given Member State if either the offender is in the territory of that Member State and is not extradited, or counterfeit euro notes or coins relating to the offence are detected in that Member State.

Given the objectively different situation of the Member States whose currency is the euro, it is appropriate that the obligation to establish such jurisdiction only applies to those Member States. For the purpose of prosecution of the offences laid down in point (a) of Article 3(1), Article 3(2) and (3), where they relate to point (a) of Article 3(1), as well as incitement, aiding and abetting, and attempt to commit those offences, jurisdiction should not be subordinated to the condition that the acts constitute an offence at the place where they were committed. When exercising such jurisdiction, Member States should take into account whether the offences are being dealt with by the criminal justice system of the country where they were committed, and should respect the principle of proportionality, in particular with regard to convictions by a third country for the same conduct.

L 151/4 EN Official Journal of the European Union 21.5.2014

(24) For the euro, the identification of counterfeit euro notes and coins is centralised at the National Analysis Centres and the Coin National Analysis Centres respectively, which are designated or established in accordance with Regulation (EC) No 1338/2001. The analysis, identification and detection of counterfeit euro notes and coins should also be possible during on-going judicial proceedings in order to accelerate the detection of the source of production of counterfeits in a given criminal investigation or prosecution and to avoid and stop such types of counterfeits from further circulation, with due respect for the principle of a fair and effective trial. That would contribute to the efficiency of combating counterfeiting offences and would at the same time increase the number of transmissions of seized counterfeits during on-going criminal proceedings, subject to limited exceptions where only access to counterfeits should be provided. In general, the competent authorities should authorise the physical transmission of the counterfeits to the National Analysis Centres and Coin National Analysis Centres. In certain circumstances, for example where only a few counterfeit notes or coins constitute the evidence for the criminal proceedings, or where physical transmission would result in the risk of destruction of evidence, such as fingerprints, the competent authorities should instead be able to decide to give access to the notes and coins.

(25) There is a need to collect comparable data on the offences laid down in this Directive. In order to gain a more complete picture of the problem of counterfeiting at Union level and thereby contribute to formulating a more effective response, Member States should transmit to the Commission relevant statistical data relating to the number of offences concerning counterfeit notes and coins and the number of persons prosecuted and sentenced.

(26) In order to pursue the objective of fighting the counterfeiting of euro notes and coins, the conclusion of agreements with third countries, in particular those countries that use the euro as a currency, should be pursued in accordance with the relevant Treaty procedures.

(27) This Directive respects fundamental rights and observes the principles recognised in particular by the Charter of Fundamental Rights of the European Union and notably the right to liberty and security, the respect for private and family life, the freedom to choose an occupation and right to engage in work, the freedom to conduct a business, the right to property, the right to an effective remedy and to a fair trial, the presumption of innocence and right of defence, the principles of the legality and proportionality of criminal offences and penalties, as well as the right not to be tried or punished twice in criminal proceedings for the same criminal offence. This Directive seeks to ensure full respect for those rights and principles and should be implemented accordingly.

(28) This Directive aims to amend and expand the provisions of Framework Decision 2000/383/JHA. Since the amendments to be made are of a substantial number and nature, that Framework Decision should in the interests of clarity be replaced in its entirety for the Member States bound by this Directive.

(29) Since the objective of this Directive, namely to protect the euro and other currencies against counterfeiting, cannot be sufficiently achieved by the Member States but can rather, by reasons of its scale and effects, be better achieved at Union level, the Union may adopt the measures, in accordance with the principle of subsidiarity as set out in Article 5 of the Treaty on European Union ('TEU'). In accordance with the principle of proportionality, as set out in that Article, this Directive does not go beyond what is necessary to achieve that objective.

(30) In accordance with Articles 1 and 2 of Protocol No 22 on the position of Denmark annexed to the TEU and to the Treaty on the Functioning of the European Union ('TFEU'), Denmark is not taking part in the adoption of this Directive and is not bound by it or subject to its application.

(31) In accordance with Article 3 of Protocol No 21 on the position of the United Kingdom and Ireland in respect of the Area of Freedom, Security and Justice, annexed to the TEU and to the TFEU, Ireland has notified its wish to take part in the adoption and application of this Directive.

(32) In accordance with Articles 1, 2 and 4a(1) of Protocol No 21 on the position of the United Kingdom and Ireland in respect of the Area of Freedom, Security and Justice, annexed to the TEU and to the TFEU, and without prejudice to Article 4 of that Protocol, the United Kingdom is not taking part in the adoption of this Directive and is not bound by it or subject to its application,

HAVE ADOPTED THIS DIRECTIVE:

*Article 1*

**Subject matter**

This Directive establishes minimum rules concerning the definition of criminal offences and sanctions in the area of counterfeiting of the euro and other currencies. It also introduces common provisions to strengthen the fight against those offences and to improve investigation of them and to ensure better cooperation against counterfeiting.

*Article 2*

**Definitions**

For the purposes of this Directive the following definitions apply:

(a) 'currency' means notes and coins, the circulation of which is legally authorised, including euro notes and coins, the circulation of which is legally authorised pursuant to Regulation (EC) No 974/98;

(b) 'legal person' means any entity having legal personality under the applicable law, except for States or public bodies in the exercise of State authority and for public international organisations.

*Article 3*

**Offences**

1. Member States shall take the necessary measures to ensure that the following conduct is punishable as a criminal offence, when committed intentionally:

(a) any fraudulent making or altering of currency, whatever means are employed;

(b) the fraudulent uttering of counterfeit currency;

(c) the import, export, transport, receiving or obtaining of counterfeit currency with a view to uttering the same and with knowledge that it is counterfeit;

(d) the fraudulent making, receiving, obtaining or possession of

(i) instruments, articles, computer programs and data, and any other means peculiarly adapted for the counterfeiting or altering of currency; or

(ii) security features, such as holograms, watermarks or other components of currency which serve to protect against counterfeiting.

2. Member States shall take the necessary measures to ensure that the conduct referred to in points (a), (b) and (c) of paragraph 1 is punishable also with respect to notes or coins being manufactured or having been manufactured by use of legal facilities or materials in violation of the rights or the conditions under which competent authorities may issue notes or coins.

3. Member States shall take the necessary measures to ensure that the conduct referred to in paragraphs 1 and 2 is punishable also in relation to notes and coins which are not yet issued, but are designated for circulation as legal tender.

*Article 4*

**Incitement, aiding and abetting, and attempt**

1. Member States shall take the necessary measures to ensure that inciting or aiding and abetting an offence referred to in Article 3 is punishable as a criminal offence.

2. Member States shall take the necessary measures to ensure that an attempt to commit an offence referred to in points (a), (b) or (c) of Article 3(1), Article 3(2), or Article 3(3) in relation to conduct referred to in points (a), (b) and (c) of Article 3(1) is punishable as a criminal offence.

*Article 5*

**Sanctions for natural persons**

1. Member States shall take the necessary measures to ensure that the conduct referred to in Articles 3 and 4 is punishable by effective, proportionate and dissuasive criminal sanctions.

2. Member States shall take the necessary measures to ensure that the offences referred to in point (d) of Article 3(1), the offences referred to in Article 3(2), and the offences referred to in Article 3(3) in relation to conduct referred to in point (d) of Article 3(1) shall be punishable by a maximum sanction which provides for imprisonment.

3. Member States shall take the necessary measures to ensure that the offences referred to in point (a) of Article 3(1) and in Article 3(3) in relation to conduct referred to in point (a) of Article 3(1) shall be punishable by a maximum term of imprisonment of at least eight years.

4. Member States shall take the necessary measures to ensure that the offences referred to in points (b) and (c) of Article 3(1) and in Article 3(3) in relation to conduct referred to in points (b) and (c) of Article 3(1) shall be punishable by a maximum term of imprisonment of at least five years.

5. In relation to the offence referred to in point (b) of Article 3(1), Member States may provide for effective, proportionate and dissuasive criminal sanctions other than that referred to in paragraph 4 of this Article, including fines and imprisonment, if the counterfeit currency was received without knowledge but passed on with the knowledge that it is counterfeit.

*Article 6*

**Liability of legal persons**

1. Member States shall take the necessary measures to ensure that legal persons can be held liable for the offences referred to in Articles 3 and 4 committed for their benefit by any person acting either individually or as part of an organ of the legal person who has a leading position within the legal person based on

(a) a power of representation of the legal person;

(b) an authority to take decisions on behalf of the legal person; or

(c) an authority to exercise control within the legal person.

2. Member States shall ensure that a legal person can be held liable where the lack of supervision or control by a person referred to in paragraph 1 of this Article has made possible the commission of an offence referred to in Articles 3 and 4 for the benefit of that legal person by a person under its authority.

3. Liability of a legal person under paragraphs 1 and 2 of this Article shall not exclude criminal proceedings against natural persons who are perpetrators, instigators or accessories in the offences referred to in Articles 3 and 4.

*Article 7*

**Sanctions for legal persons**

Member States shall take the necessary measures to ensure that a legal person held liable pursuant to Article 6 is subject to effective, proportionate and dissuasive sanctions, which shall include criminal or non-criminal fines and may include other sanctions such as

(a) exclusion from entitlement to public benefits or aid;

(b) temporary or permanent disqualification from the practice of commercial activities;

(c) placing under judicial supervision;

(d) judicial winding-up;

(e) temporary or permanent closure of establishments which have been used for committing the offence.

*Article 8*

**Jurisdiction**

1. Each Member State shall take the necessary measures to establish its jurisdiction over the offences referred to in Articles 3 and 4, where

(a) the offence is committed in whole or in part within its territory; or

(b) the offender is one of its nationals.

2. Each Member State whose currency is the euro shall take the necessary measures to establish its jurisdiction over the offences referred to in Articles 3 and 4 committed outside its territory, at least where they relate to the euro and where

(a) the offender is in the territory of that Member State and is not extradited; or

(b) counterfeit euro notes or coins related to the offence have been detected in the territory of that Member State.

For the prosecution of the offences referred to in point (a) of Article 3(1), Article 3(2) and (3), where they relate to point (a) of Article 3(1), as well as incitement, aiding and abetting, and attempt to commit those offences, each Member State shall take the necessary measures to ensure that its jurisdiction is not subordinated to the condition that the acts are a criminal offence at the place where they were committed.

*Article 9*

**Investigative tools**

Member States shall take the necessary measures to ensure that effective investigative tools, such as those which are used in organised crime or other serious crime cases, are available to persons, units or services responsible for investigating or prosecuting the offences referred to in Articles 3 and 4.

*Article 10*

**Obligation to transmit counterfeit euro notes and coins for analysis and detection of counterfeits**

Member States shall ensure that during criminal proceedings the examination by the National Analysis Centre and Coin National Analysis Centre of suspected counterfeit euro notes and coins for analysis, identification and detection of further counterfeits is permitted without delay. The competent authorities shall transmit the necessary samples without any delay, and at the latest once a final decision concerning the criminal proceedings has been reached.

*Article 11*

**Statistics**

Member States shall, at least every two years, transmit data to the Commission on the number of offences laid down in Articles 3 and 4 and the number of persons prosecuted for and convicted of the offences laid down in Articles 3 and 4.

*Article 12*

**Reporting by the Commission and review**

By 23 May 2019, the Commission shall submit a report on the application of this Directive to the European Parliament and to the Council. The report shall assess the extent to which the Member States have taken the necessary measures to comply with this Directive. The report shall be accompanied, if necessary, by a legislative proposal.

*Article 13*

**Replacement of Framework Decision 2000/383/JHA**

Framework Decision 2000/383/JHA is hereby replaced in respect of the Member States bound by this Directive, without prejudice to the obligations of those Member States relating to the time-limit for transposition into national law of Framework Decision 2000/383/JHA.

For the Member States bound by this Directive, references to Framework Decision 2000/383/JHA shall be construed as references to this Directive.

*Article 14*

**Transposition**

1. Member States shall bring into force the laws, regulations and administrative provisions necessary to comply with this Directive by 23 May 2016. They shall immediately inform the Commission thereof.

When Member States adopt those measures, they shall contain a reference to this Directive or shall be accompanied by such reference on the occasion of their official publication. The methods of making such a reference shall be laid down by the Member States.

2. Member States shall communicate to the Commission the text of the main measures of national law which they adopt in the field covered by this Directive.

*Article 15*

**Entry into force**

This Directive shall enter into force on the day following its publication in the *Official Journal of the European Union*.

*Article 16*

**Addressees**

This Directive is addressed to the Member States in accordance with the Treaties.

Done at Brussels, 15 May 2014.

| *For the European Parliament* | *For the Council* |
|---|---|
| *The President* | *The President* |
| M. SCHULZ | D. KOURKOULAS |